CONSUMER
BEHAVIOR

McGRAW-HILL SERIES IN MARKETING

CONSULTING EDITOR
CHARLES D. SCHEWE, University of Massachusetts

ALLEN, SPOHN, and WILSON: Selling Dynamics
BOWERSOX, COOPER, LAMBERT, and TAYLOR: Management in Marketing Channels
BRITT, BOYD, DAVIS, and LARRÉCHÉ: Marketing Management and Administrative Action
BUELL: Marketing Management: A Strategic Planning Approach
BUSKIRK and BUSKIRK: Retailing
COREY, LOVELOCK, and WARD: Problems in Marketing
DeLOZIER: The Marketing Communications Process
DOBLER, LEE, and BURT: Purchasing and Materials Management: Text and Cases
ENGEL: Advertising: The Process and Practice
GUILTINAN and PAUL: Marketing Management: Strategies and Programs
GUILTINAN and PAUL: Readings in Marketing Strategies and Programs
KINNEAR and TAYLOR: Marketing Research: An Applied Approach
LOUDON and DELLA BITTA: Consumer Behavior: Concepts and Applications
MONROE: Pricing: Making Profitable Decisions
REDINBAUGH: Retailing Management: A Planning Approach
REYNOLDS and WELLS: Consumer Behavior
RUSSELL, BEACH, and BUSKIRK: Selling: Principles and Practices
SCHEWE and SMITH: Marketing: Concepts and Applications
SHAPIRO: Sales Program Management: Formulation and Implementation
STANTON: Fundamentals of Marketing
STROH: Managing the Sales Function
WRIGHT, WINTER, and ZEIGLER: Advertising

CONSUMER BEHAVIOR

CONCEPTS
AND
APPLICATIONS

DAVID L. LOUDON
Northeast Louisiana University

ALBERT J. DELLA BITTA
University of Rhode Island

Second Edition

McGRAW-HILL BOOK COMPANY
New York | St. Louis | San Francisco | Auckland | Bogotá
Hamburg | Johannesburg | London | Madrid | Mexico | Montreal | New Delhi
Panama | Paris | São Paulo | Singapore | Sydney | Tokyo | Toronto

CONSUMER BEHAVIOR
CONCEPTS AND APPLICATIONS

Copyright © 1984, 1979 by McGraw-Hill, Inc.
All rights reserved.
Printed in the United States of America.
Except as permitted under the United States Copyright Act of 1976,
no part of this publication may be reproduced or distributed
in any form or by any means, or stored in a data base or retrieval system,
without the prior written permission of the publisher.

4567890 DOCDOC 898765

ISBN 0-07-038758-3

This book was set in ITC Garamond Light by University Graphics, Inc.
The editors were Beth A. Lewis and Peggy Rehberger;
the designer was Nicholas Krenitsky;
the production supervisor was Charles Hess.
New drawings were done by Fine Line Illustrations, Inc.
R. R. Donnelley & Sons Company was printer and binder.

Library of Congress Cataloging in Publication Data

Loudon, David L.
   Consumer behavior.

   (McGraw-Hill series in marketing)
   Includes index.
   1. Consumers. 2. Consumers—Case studies.
I. Della Bitta, Albert J. II. Title. III. Series.
HF5415.3.L68   1984   658.8′34   83-12047
ISBN 0-07-038758-3

TO

**Carol, Bobby, and Susan
Margaret, Michael, and David
Our Parents**

CONTENTS

PREFACE   xvii

PART ONE
STUDYING CONSUMER BEHAVIOR

CHAPTER 1 INTRODUCTION   3

Defining Consumer Behavior   6
  Customers and Consumers / Ultimate Consumer / Individual Buyer / Decision Process / A Subset of Human Behavior
Why Study Consumer Behavior?   9
  A Part of Our Lives / Application to Decision Making
Applying Consumer Behavior Knowledge   10
  Consumer Behavior and Marketing Management / Consumer Behavior, Nonprofit and Social Marketing / Consumer Behavior and Governmental Decision Making / Consumer Behavior and Demarketing / Consumer Behavior and Consumer Education
Summary   21
Discussion Topics   22

CHAPTER 2 A FOUNDATION FOR STUDYING CONSUMER BEHAVIOR   24

Studying Consumer Behavior   24
  Classes of Variables / Dealing with Unobservable Variables
Problems in Studying Consumer Behavior   27
  Difficulty of Inference Process / Behavior Is Subjective / Many Input Variables / Variables Interact with Each Other
Modeling Behavior   29
  Definition of a Model / Types of Models / Uses of Models
Models of Consumer Behavior   31
  Traditional Models of Consumers / Contemporary Consumer Models
A Simplified Framework   39
Summary   44
Discussion Topics   45

CASES FOR PART ONE   47

PART TWO
UNDERSTANDING CONSUMERS AND MARKET SEGMENTS

CHAPTER 3 RESEARCHING CONSUMER BEHAVIOR — 55

The Nature and Significance of Consumer Research — 55
Need for Consumer Research — 56
Consumer Research Strategies — 59
Goals of Consumer Research / Type of Data Used / Research Time Frame
Methods of Gathering Consumer Information — 64
Observation / Experiments / Surveys
Measuring Consumer Characteristics — 68
Demographic Measures / Consumer Activity Measures / Cognitive Measures
Summary — 77
Discussion Topics — 77

CHAPTER 4 MARKET SEGMENTATION: BASIC APPROACHES — 80

Views of the Market and Alternative Marketing Strategies — 80
Market Aggregation / Market Segmentation
Demographic Characteristics and Market Segmentation — 88
United States Population Growth / Changing Age Mix of the Population / Marketing Implications of Population Changes
Geographic Characteristics and Market Segmentation — 94
Regional Distribution of United States Population / Metropolitan Population in the United States / Nonmetropolitan Population in the United States / Geographic Mobility of the Population
Socioeconomic Characteristics and Market Segmentation — 105
Education / Occupation / Income / Expenditures / Willingness to Buy
Limitations of Demographics in Predicting Consumer Behavior — 114
Summary — 115
Discussion Topics — 115

CHAPTER 5 MARKET SEGMENTATION: ADDITIONAL DIMENSIONS — 119

Lifestyle and Psychographic Segmentation — 119
Technique of Lifestyle Segmentation / Applications of Lifestyle Segmentation / Additional Uses of Lifestyle Information / Benefits of Lifestyle Segmentation
Usage Segmentation — 134
Brand-User Segmentation / Product-User Segmentation / Loyalty Segmentation / Volume Segmentation
Benefit Segmentation — 138
Technique of Benefit Segmentation / Applications of Benefit Segmentation / Limitations of Benefit Segmentation

Product Positioning 144
  The Interrelationship of Market Segmentation and Product Positioning / Strategies to Position Products / Repositioning Old Products / Positioning Analysis
The Future of Segmentation and Positioning 154
Summary 155
Discussion Topics 155

CASES FOR PART TWO 158

PART THREE
ENVIRONMENTAL INFLUENCES ON CONSUMER BEHAVIOR

CHAPTER 6 CULTURE 169

Culture Defined 170
Cultural Relevance to Marketing Decisions 171
The Characteristics of Culture 172
  Culture Is Man-made / Culture Is Learned / Culture Is Prescriptive / Culture Is Socially Shared / Cultures Are Similar but Different / Culture Is Gratifying and Persistent / Culture Is Adaptive / Culture Is Organized and Integrated
Cultural Values 173
  United States Cultural Values / Do Values Influence Consumer Behavior?
Cultural Change and Countercultures 183
  Changing Cultural Values in the United States / General Implications of Cultural Change for the Marketer / Specific Implications for Marketing Decisions / Tracking Cultural Change
Cross-Cultural Understanding of Consumer Behavior 192
  Need for Cross-Cultural Understanding / Decision Areas for the International Marketer
Summary 197
Discussion Topics 197

CHAPTER 7 SUBCULTURES 200

The Black Subculture 201
  Demographic Characteristics / Psychographic Characteristics / Consumer Behavior and Marketing Implications
The Hispanic Subculture 208
  Demographic Characteristics / Psychographic Characteristics / Consumer Behavior and Marketing Implications
The Youth Subculture 216
  Demographic Characteristics / Psychographic Characteristics / Consumer Behavior and Marketing Implications

The Older Subculture	230
Demographic Characteristics / Psychographic Characteristics / Consumer Behavior and Marketing Implications	
Summary	236
Discussion Topics	236

CHAPTER 8 SOCIAL CLASS 241

The Process of Social Stratification	241
The Nature of Social Class	241
No Value Judgments / Class and Status / Social Class Indicators / Social Class Categorization / Symbols of Social Standing	
Social Class Lifestyles	248
Upper-Upper Class / Lower-Upper Class / Upper-Middle Class / Lower-Middle Class / Upper-Lower Class / Lower-Lower Class	
The Role of Social Class in Segmenting Markets	252
Social Class and Income Related to Lifestyle Patterns / Social Class and Income Related to Consumer Behavior Patterns	
Social Class and Consumer Behavior	257
Products and Services Consumed / Shopping Behavior / Promotional Response Patterns / Price-Related Behavior	
Are Class Differences Disappearing?	267
Summary	268
Discussion Topics	268

CHAPTER 9 SOCIAL GROUPS 272

What Is a Group?	272
Classification of Groups	272
Content or Function / Degree of Personal Involvement / Degree of Organization	
Group Properties	274
Status / Norms / Role / Socialization / Power	
Reference Groups	279
Types of Reference Groups / Reasons for Accepting Reference-Group Influence	
Research on Reference-Group Influence	282
The Variability of Reference-Group Influence / Identifying Reference Groups	
Summary	291
Discussion Topics	292

CHAPTER 10 FAMILY 295

Families and Households	295
Significance of the Family in Consumer Behavior	296

Family Life Cycle 297
   Traditional Life-Cycle Stages / A Modernized Family Life Cycle /
   Relationship between Life Cycle and Consumer Behavior /
   Life Cycle versus Age in Segmenting Markets
Family Purchasing Decisions 301
   Role Structure / Power Structure / Stage in the Family
   Purchase-Decision Process / Family-Specific Characteristics /
   Marketing Implications of Family Purchasing Decisions
The Changing American Family 316
   Changing Female Roles / Changing Male Roles / Growth of
   the Singles Market
Summary 330
Discussion Topics 330

CHAPTER 11   PERSONAL INFLUENCE AND DIFFUSION OF INNOVATIONS   335

Nature and Significance of Personal Influence 336
Models of Communication and Influence Flow 337
   One-Step Model / Two-Step Flow Model / Multistep Models
Opinion Leadership in Marketing 340
   Who Are Opinion Leaders? / Why Opinion Leaders Attempt to
   Influence Others / Why Followers Accept Personal Influence
Adoption and Diffusion of Innovations 344
   What Is an Innovation? / The Adoption Process /
   The Diffusion Process
Marketing Implications of Personal Influence 353
   Identifying and Using Opinion Leaders Directly / Creating
   Opinion Leaders / Simulating Opinion Leadership /
   Stimulating Opinion Leadership / Stifling Opinion Leadership
Summary 363
Discussion Topics 363

CASES FOR PART THREE 367

PART FOUR
INDIVIDUAL DETERMINANTS OF CONSUMER BEHAVIOR

CHAPTER 12   MOTIVATION AND INVOLVEMENT   383

The Nature and Role of Motives 383
   Role of Motives
Classifying Motives 385
   Simplified Schemes / A Comprehensive Scheme
Motive Arousal 394
   Triggering Arousal / Optimal Stimulation and Arousal /
   Effects of Arousal
Motive Structuring 398
   Motive Hierarchy / Motive Combinations / Self-Concept

Involvement 404
   Dimensions of Involvement / Marketing Implications
Motivation Research 409
Summary 410
Discussion Topics 411

CHAPTER 13 INFORMATION PROCESSING 414

Overview 414
Information Acquisition 418
   Active Search / Passive Reception / Sensation / Attention
Perceptual Encoding 432
   Stages in the Encoding Process / Influences on Encoding / Information Load
Marketing Implications 439
   Product Factors / Price Considerations / Company and Store Image / Advertising Issues
Summary 450
Discussion Topics 451

CHAPTER 14 LEARNING AND MEMORY 458

Characterizing Learning 459
   Learning Defined / Types of Learned Behavior / Principal Elements of Learning
Classifying Learning 462
   Learning Connections / Cognitive Interpretations / Applying Alternative Learning Concepts to Consumer Behavior
Additional Consumer Learning Topics 468
   The Behavior Modification Perspective / Stimulus Generalization / Rate and Degree of Learning / Extinction / Forgetting
Memory 477
   Characteristics of Memory Systems / Retrieval of Information / Advertising Applications
Summary 490
Discussion Topics 490

CHAPTER 15 PERSONALITY AND SELF-CONCEPT 494

Personality Theories and Applications 495
   Measuring Personality / Some Major Personality Theories
Psychographics 505
Personality and Marketing: A Summary 506
Self-Concept 506
   How the Self-Concept Develops / Consistency of the Self / Self-Concept and Consumer Behavior
Summary 516
Discussion Topics 517

CHAPTER 16 ATTITUDES 520

Definitions of Attitude 520
Characteristics of Attitudes 521
  Attitudes Have an Object / Attitudes Have Direction, Degree, and Intensity / Attitudes Have Structure / Attitudes Are Learned
Functions of Attitudes 523
  The Adjustment Function / The Ego-Defensive Function / The Value-Expressive Function / The Knowledge Function
Sources of Attitude Development 524
  Personal Experience / Group Associations / Influential Others
Attitude Theories and Models 526
  Congruity Theory / Balance Theory / Cognitive Dissonance / Multiattribute Models
Summary 539
Discussion Topics 540

CHAPTER 17 CHANGING ATTITUDES 542

Strategies for Changing Attitudes and Intentions 543
  Low-Involvement Strategies / High-Involvement Strategies
The Communication Process 548
Source Factors 549
  Marketing Communication Sources / Influences on Source Effectiveness
Message Factors 557
  Message Structure / Message Appeals / Message Codes
Receiver Factors 569
  Personality Traits / Belief Types
Summary 571
Discussion Topics 572

CASES FOR PART FOUR 575

PART FIVE
CONSUMER DECISION PROCESSES

CHAPTER 18 PROBLEM RECOGNITION 603

Types of Consumer Decisions 603
Introduction to the Consumer Decision-Process Model 604
Problem Recognition 605
  Types of Problem Recognition / Situations Leading to Problem Recognition / Results of Problem Recognition / Problem Recognition under Low-Involvement Conditions
Marketing Implications of Problem Recognition 610
  Measurement of Problem Recognition / Utilizing Problem-Recognition Information

Summary	613
Discussion Topics	613

CHAPTER 19 SEARCH AND EVALUATION — 615

The Information-Seeking Process — 615
Types of Consumer Search Activities / Nature of the Search Process / Amount of Information Seeking by Consumers / Factors That Influence the Search Process / Types of Information Sought / Sources of Information

The Information-Evaluation Process — 628
Evaluative or Choice Criteria / Evaluating Alternatives / Factors Influencing the Amount of Evaluation / Results of Evaluation / Alternative Evaluation in Low-Involvement Situations

Marketing Implications — 634
Researching the Information-Seeking Process / Influencing the Consumer's Evoked Set / Measuring Evaluative Criteria / Influencing Consumers' Evaluation / How Much Information for the Consumer?

Summary — 643
Discussion Topics — 643

CHAPTER 20 PURCHASING PROCESSES — 647

Why Do People Shop? — 647
Personal Motives / Social Motives

Choosing a Store — 649
Factors Determining Store Choice / Attribute Importance Varies by Store / The Effect of Store Image on Purchasing / General Shopper Profiles / Store-Specific Shopper Profiles / Store Loyalty

In-Store Purchasing Behavior — 659
Merchandising Techniques / Personal Selling Effects

The Situational Nature of Consumer Decisions — 670

Nonstore Purchasing Processes — 671
Significance of Nonstore Buying / Characteristics of Purchasers / In-Home Shopping Motivations / Marketing Implications

Purchasing Patterns — 674
Brand Loyalty / Impulse Purchasing

Summary — 680
Discussion Topics — 680

CHAPTER 21 POSTPURCHASE BEHAVIOR — 686

Behavior Related to the Purchase — 686
Decisions on Product Payment / Decisions on Product Set-Up and Use / Decisions on Related Products or Services / Marketing Implications

Postpurchase Evaluation	689
Consumer Satisfaction/Dissatisfaction / Theories of Disconfirmed Expectations / Postpurchase Dissonance	
Product Disposition	700
Disposition Alternatives and Determinants / Marketing Implications	
Summary	705
Discussion Topics	705
CASES FOR PART FIVE	708
INDEX	715

PREFACE

This book is written for the beginning student of consumer behavior, whether he or she is at the undergraduate or the graduate level, with the purpose of blending both concepts and applications from the field of consumer behavior.

No special assumptions have been made regarding student preparation for this text. Although many students will have had previous exposure to some of the behavioral concepts discussed, all can benefit from a review of these topics and from an examination of them from a managerial perspective. Thus, the concepts presented here are regarded as extremely valuable for the career-oriented student in general and indispensable for the marketing major.

Considerable effort has been made to present the material clearly and in a style that is readable, interesting, and motivating to students. Unnecessary jargon has been avoided, and behavioral concepts have been defined in simple language. In addition to topical examples, a large number of graphics and other visuals help to clarify and reinforce text material. Each chapter also has a brief introduction and a summary, the first to prepare the reader and the second to reinforce major points.

As the title indicates, the book not only presents theoretical concepts of consumer behavior, but it also stresses the application of this conceptual material to marketing strategies and decision making in the private, public, and nonprofit sectors. At the conceptual level, it seeks to present an integrated framework around which the major areas of consumer-behavior knowledge can be discussed. The book is thoroughly documented and provides ample opportunity for the reader to pursue a particular area of interest in greater detail. The explosion of consumer research, however, has made it impossible to cite every study relevant to a specific topic. In addition, such an approach tends to confuse the introductory student through information overload and often contradictory findings. Therefore, we have emphasized what is known about consumers, rather than dwell on the present uncertainty and its implications for future research. Nevertheless, controversial areas still exist and will continue to exist for quite some time, and the student is made aware of this fact.

For too long, consumer behavior texts have been crammed with theories and research findings while giving little attention to their pragmatic application in the marketplace. Our teaching experience has been that students, especially at the introductory level, are highly interested in discussions of potential and *actual* applications of these concepts. In addition to its motivating benefit, such an approach also allows students to gain a much greater appreciation of the conceptual material. Rather than just paying token attention to this, the second edition of the text continues to thoroughly incorporate marketing realism in several ways. First, throughout each chapter frequent reference is made to actual or potential applications of the concepts being discussed. Second, questions and exercises following each chapter offer opportunities for experiential learning. Here, research may be conducted, decisions made, or other creative activities undertaken, bringing students closer to the real world of marketing. Third, cases at the end of each part offer opportunities for more extensive discussion and for decision making through application of text material.

The second edition of this book represents a major revision. It has been completely updated to reflect the wealth of new evidence on consumer behavior that has been generated since publication of the first edition. This has been accomplished by rewriting many portions, as well as by adding new sections and by streamlining the discussion in others. In addition, a large number of new examples and applications have been incorporated to keep the book current. Further, many new cases have been added and others have been expanded to allow more meaningful analysis.

The second edition comprises five major sections. Each of these sections is described below along with brief comments about a few of the more significant changes that have been made to the second edition.

Part One, Studying Consumer Behavior, introduces the reader to the discipline of consumer behavior by defining and describing its scope and importance, discussing the marketing function, and providing numerous examples of consumer-behavior relevance in managerial decision making. Traditional and contemporary models of consumer behavior are briefly presented along with the authors' simplified framework, all of which serve as a foundation for studying and understanding the subject of consumer behavior.

Part Two, Understanding Consumers and Market Segments, begins with a brief treatment of some aspects of consumer research. This helps to prepare students for the discussion of specific studies, and it stresses the importance of consumer research as a prerequisite to many marketing decisions. Because of the growing attractiveness of consumer behavior to nonmarketing majors, some students may be unfamiliar with major characteristics of the consumer market and the concept and methods of market segmentation. Consequently, consumer characteristics are discussed with a view toward selecting target markets and developing marketing programs. This edition features greater discussion of the process of segmentation and the topic of product positioning.

Part Three, Environmental Influences on Consumer Behavior, examines the sociocultural influences on consumers and presents them in hierarchical order ranging from the broadest to the most immediate. The roles of culture, subculture, social class, social groups, family, and interpersonal influences are examined. This edition offers greater discussion of significant contemporary cultural values and their lifestyle and marketing implications. The topic of subcultural influence has been condensed into one chapter. Social class and social-group factors have been updated with recent research findings. The chapter on family influences offers more discussion of contemporary life-cycles, family purchasing-decision strategies, and changing male/female roles.

Part Four, Individual Determinants of Consumer Behavior, deals with the consumer's internal variables. Here in the second edition, this section encompasses many changes. The chapter on motivation now includes the concept of involvement to reflect significant attention devoted to this topic. It also incorporates a more-contemporary view of motive classification and a treatment of the relationship between optimal stimulation levels and consumer arousal. The information-processing chapter retains much perceptual material from the first edition, but it also adds many new concepts and research findings to present an organized view of consumer information processing. The chapter on learning and memory reflects inclusion of more-recent evidence on the operation and structuring of consumers' memory systems, including the topic of cognitive response and its implications, and a section on behavior modification. The pragmatic implications of these additions make the chapter quite interesting and applied in nature. The personality and self-concept chapter has been revised and expanded based on the most-recent literature in this area. The attitude chapter has been streamlined as well as updated by an expanded discussion of Fishbein's behavioral intentions model. The chapter on changing attitudes has also been modified by a discussion of strategy options based on Fishbein's model. In addition, the chapter has been updated in a number of topic areas such as fear appeals, distraction, cognitive response, and so forth.

Part Five, Consumer Decision Processes, discusses the way in which consumers make purchase decisions based on their environmental influences and individual determinants. A four-stage model of consumers' decision processes (consisting of problem recognition, information search and evaluation, purchasing processes, and post-purchase behavior) is described. The second edition offers improved treatment of the information-evaluation process by incorporating greater coverage of consumers' evaluative or choice criteria and the decision rules they use. In addition, the treatment of postpurchase behavior is enlarged to include more satisfaction/dissatisfaction material along with theories of disconfirmed expectations and disposition behavior.

Instructors desiring alternative orders in material coverage will find the book very flexible. For example, if students have had an introductory course in marketing and marketing research, Chapters 3 to 5 may be minimized or eliminated. Those who prefer to discuss individual determinants of consumer behavior prior to environmental variables can simply reverse Parts Three and Four. Finally, instructors facing time constraints will find the book quite flexible in regard to topics that can be covered over varying course lengths.

We are indebted to a number of people who helped us during the revision of this text. Dean Van McGraw, Northeast Louisiana University, and Dean Richard Weeks, University of Rhode Island, were highly supportive and offered much administrative assistance. Our reviewers, who offered many helpful suggestions that led to an improved manuscript, included: Chris T. Allen, University of Massachusetts; Mickey Belch, San Diego State University; Robert Eng, Babson College; George B. Glisan, Illinois State University; J. Barry Mason, University of Alabama; James A. Muncy, University of Oklahoma; James P. Neelankavil, New York University; and Bruce E. Texley, Bethany College. Consulting editor Charles D. Schewe, University of Massachusetts, deserves special thanks for his valuable comments and encouragement. Our editors at McGraw-Hill—Beth Lewis, Carol Napier, and Peggy Rehberger—provided outstanding support and assistance with this revision. In addition, Barbara Kener, Marie Garofano, Dorothy Beck, and Jean Gefrich were very helpful in typing the manuscript. Finally, and most importantly, our families deserve special thanks for their patience, understanding and encouragement. As in the first edition, we dedicate this work to them.

David L. Loudon
Albert J. Della Bitta

CONSUMER BEHAVIOR

PART ONE
STUDYING CONSUMER BEHAVIOR

1 Introduction
2 A Foundation for Studying Consumer Behavior
   Cases for Part One

CHAPTER 1
INTRODUCTION

This book deals with fascinating subject matter—the behavior of consumers. Many who have seriously studied consumers find their behavior complex, difficult to influence, and often mystifying. This variety and unpredictability is probably what motivates so many to learn more about the topic.

The present chapter serves as an introduction to this intriguing area of study. A useful way to begin is to examine several actual situations involving various aspects of the nature and scope of consumer behavior.

Foamy Follies To Anheuser-Busch decision makers the potential market for a new product concept looked very attractive. Currently available soft drinks were sweet and designed for consumption by all age groups. The new product idea was to be positioned as an "adult" soft drink which would be a "socially acceptable" substitute for alcoholic beverages. The target market was defined as consumers 25 years of age or older.

Considerable product development and testing yielded a product named Chelsea having numerous attributes designed to appeal to the potential market. It was low in calories, a blend of ginger, apple, lemon, and lime, and it had no saccharin, preservatives, or caffeine. In an effort to appeal to the adult market, the amber-colored drink was designed to form a beerlike head of foam. The bottles were foil wrapped, uniquely packaged, and were higher-priced than all other soft drinks. Promotions introduced Chelsea into five test markets as the "not-so-soft-drink."

That's when the foam really hit the fan. Criticism came from consumers and other groups. One of the many objections was that the term "not-so-soft-drink" implied that Chelsea was an alcoholic beverage. The fact that the product's label clearly stated it contained less than ½ of 1 percent alcohol did not appear to satisfy critics. Neither did the argument that most soft drinks contained traces of alcohol. In fact, some charged that Anheuser-Busch was not even trying to reach the adult market. They argued that with its product design (color, foam, etc.) and packaging characteristics, Chelsea was positioned as beerlike to appeal to children and encourage them to later become beer drinkers!

Criticism and negative publicity became so intense that the company withdrew its advertisements, reduced the product's alcohol content, and dropped its special foamy-head characteristics. It also repackaged Chelsea, and new advertisements stressed natural ingredients instead of the "not-so-soft" theme. This must not have done the trick because in December 1980 Anheuser-Busch took Chelsea off the market.[1]

Melodic Watts To Arne, a college junior, a stereo system was more than something that merely provided music. "Good sounds" enhanced his studies and entertainment, and even provided a type of natural "high." He was therefore understandably disappointed when the system in his dorm room was "ripped off." Because of the risk of future thefts, the small size of his dorm room, and improvements he expected for stereos in the near future, Arne decided that a modestly priced system would best suit his present needs.

While home on vacation, Arne noticed a component system being featured by a Lafayette franchise store. He was impressed with this store's reputation, and his understanding that Lafayette serviced what they sold, instead of returning it to the manufacturer, favorably influenced him.

The system on sale included a LR-100 receiver, a Garrard turntable with a Shure cartridge, and Lafayette HLX speakers. A friend owned a LR-100 receiver, and Arne had always thought highly of it. These feelings were confirmed when he found that *Consumer Reports* had given the model a very favorable rating. His family owned a Garrard turntable with a Shure cartridge, and Arne was impressed with its performance and durability. The HLX speakers were slightly more expensive than another brand he was considering as a substitute. However, after some time spent listening to the two brands in Lafayette's sound room, Arne decided that he preferred the HLX speakers. In addition, he was also persuaded by the knowledge that the HLXs employed an air suspension design like that used on the prestigious KLH brand of speakers.

The entire system carried a regular retail price of $435, but was presently reduced to $365. Arne knew that if he did not act before returning to college he would miss out on the special price. He discussed the purchase with his brother, who offered no negative comments on the system; and the next day, with that funny feeling in his stomach that accompanies big decisions, Arne purchased the system. Returning to school, the set was used for a while before a transistor malfunctioned. It was replaced free of charge in a matter of days. After two years of use, Arne was convinced that his stereo produced sound rivaling that of much higher priced units.[2]

Fly Me On May 25, 1979, a McDonnell Douglas DC-10 crashed at O'Hare International Airport after a wing-mounted engine and its pylon fell off on takeoff. The crash killed 273 people, which made it the worst air disaster to date in U.S. history. An investigation revealed that the engine was lost because its supporting pylon had been severely weakened by a large crack. Early in June 1979, the Federal Aviation Administration suspended the plane's license to fly in the United States when cracks were found in the engine pylons of other DC-10's.

Investigators sought to identify the cause of the cracking pylons. The study was very involved, and it took some time to generate final conclusions. During that time, the press and public speculated about potential causes of the crack and also wondered about the safety of DC-10's. For example, questions were raised about the integrity of the plane's wing slats and hydraulic systems. Unfortunately, two subsequent DC-10 crashes occurred in 1979. Although the plane's design and construction were found to be unrelated to these crashes, air travelers' skepticism regarding the DC-10's safety seemed to grow.

By early 1980, final government reports were released regarding the Chicago disaster and its causes. Conclusions were that improper maintenance, rather than structual or design problems, led to the crash. However, this information, which appeared to confirm the basic integrity of the DC-10, did not seem to restore public confidence in the aircraft. In fact, a study commissioned later in 1980 by McDonnell Douglas found that 5 percent of the people surveyed said they still would not fly on a DC-10. This lack of confidence seemed to be reflected in fewer passengers flying on the plane. To compound problems, some airlines cancelled some of their options to purchase the aircraft. The extent to which these cancellations were due to the public's reaction to the plane is not clear. However, soon after their survey, McDonnell Douglas launched a multimillion-dollar promotional campaign directed at the American public. The thrust of this effort was to restore public confidence in a plane company that officials viewed as the victim of an undeserved lack of trust.[3]

Come on Down In terms of potential students, the 1960s and much of the 1970s were a good time for institutions of higher learning. The post-World War II baby boom generated a large population, and several social factors encouraged youths to obtain a college education. The 1980s and 1990s, however, present a danger of declining enrollments and excess capacity for many ivy towers of learning. This prospect with its financial implications makes academic administrators break out in a cold sweat.

Many colleges have responded to this situation by giving what some would call the "hard sell" of higher education. For example, one admissions office planned to release more than a hundred balloons filled with scholarship offers while another passed out promotional Frisbees to high school students. A different school had also offered existing students $50 tuition rebates for every new prospect they were able to recruit and "sign!"

At the academically respected Carleton College in Minnesota, things are run differently. Detailed market research revealed a number of student desires and perceptions to which college personnel could respond. Among the general findings were that prospective students thought the southeastern Minnesota location was too cold and isolated, that the atmosphere was too academic, and that the library was too small. In addition, it was found that students focused on different aspects of the school depending upon their location. Westerners looked for informality and outdoor activities, southerners especially wondered about the cold weather, easterners were concerned about institutional prestige, and Minnesota residents considered the institution expensive. The college reacted by developing regionalized informational brochures which responded directly to the unique concerns from different geographical areas. For example, brochures sent to southern regions described how the cold and snow could be dealt with and even enjoyed. Westerners were told about nearby hiking trails and canoe trips, while easterners were informed about faculty achievements. The availability of scholarships and other financial aid was stressed to Minnesota residents. In all information, the academic quality of the institution was clearly mentioned so as not to diminish the integrity and high standards that the college had already achieved. An increase of 44 percent in annual applications strongly suggests that these attempts to address student concerns as identified through marketing research have been quite successful.[4]

These diverse examples involve the success and failure of offerings by profit and nonprofit organizations as well as the implementation of public policy. They also involve the decision making of individuals and the impact of group behavior. One theme common to all situations, however, is that they involve the behavior of consumers. Thus, whether we are aware of it or not, consumer behavior is occurring all around us. This might not always be very apparent, because many aspects of consumer behavior are actually quite hard to detect.

The study of consumers usually proves to be highly interesting to students. It is an exciting field, but for two reasons it is also one that requires serious study. First, the behavior of consumers can be quite subtle in nature, making it difficult to understand fully. Second, because consumer behavior is so prevalent, it significantly affects our lives through either our own actions or those of other consumers. Therefore, it has a great deal of practical relevance to our daily living.

To better appreciate the nature and scope of consumer behavior, the remaining sections of this chapter focus on two very basic questions:

1 What is the nature of consumer behavior?
2 Why should we study consumer behavior?

This material will provide a basis that we can build upon in subsequent chapters.

DEFINING CONSUMER BEHAVIOR

Before continuing, it is appropriate to offer a definition in order to clarify the focus of our study. Consumer behavior may be defined as

the decision process and physical activity individuals engage in when evaluating, acquiring, using, or disposing of goods and services.

Several aspects of this statement need emphasis and elaboration so that their meaning can be more fully appreciated.

Customers and Consumers

The term "customer" is typically used to refer to someone who purchases from a particular store or company. Thus, a person who shops at A&P or who uses Getty gasoline is viewed as a customer of these firms. The term "consumer" more generally refers to anyone engaging in any of the activities used in our definition of consumer behavior. Therefore, a customer is defined in terms of a specific firm while a consumer is not.

The traditional viewpoint has been to define consumers strictly in terms of *economic* goods and services. This position holds that consumers are potential *purchasers* of products and services offered for sale. There has been a tendency for this view to broaden over time so that at least some scholars do not consider a monetary exchange essential to the definition of consumers. This implies that potential adopters of free services or even philosophies or ideas can also be encompassed by the definition. Consequently, organizations such as the Red Cross, United Way, or Foster Parents Plan, as well as religious and political groups, can view their various publics as "consumers." The rationale for this position is that many of the activities that people exhibit regarding the adoption of free services, ideas, or philosophies are quite similar to those they engage in for the purchase of products and services. Later sections of this and other chapters will expand on this topic.

Ultimate Consumer

Our primary attention will be directed toward *ultimate consumers*—those individuals who purchase for the purpose of private individual or household consumption. Some have argued that studying ultimate consumers also reveals much about industrial or intermediate buyers and others involved in purchasing for business firms and institutions.[5] While not denying this, we must recognize that much industrial purchasing behavior is unique because it often involves different buying motives and the influence of a large variety of people.[6] For the sake of simplicity we will focus only on ultimate consumer behavior and will not become involved in drawing comparisons with industrial purchasing situations.

Individual Buyer

The most commonly thought of consumer situation is an individual making a purchase with little or no influence from others. However, in some cases a number of people can be jointly involved in a purchase decision. For example, planning a vacation or deciding on a new car can involve an entire family. In other cases the purchaser may just be acquiring a product for someone else who has specified exactly what was wanted. These situations suggest that people can take on different roles in what we have defined as consumer behavior. Table 1-1 presents one way to classify these roles.

Some purchase situations involve at least one person in each of these roles, while in other circumstances a single individual can take on several roles at the same time. For example, in one situation a wife (initiator and influencer) may ask her husband (buyer) to pick up Golden Grahams cereal on his shopping trip because their child (user) said she wanted it. At another time the husband could act as the initiator, buyer, and user by purchasing a health spa membership for himself.

TABLE 1-1 SOME CONSUMER BEHAVIOR ROLES

Role	Description
Initiator	The individual who determines that some need or want is not being met and authorizes a purchase to rectify the situation
Influencer	A person who by some intentional or unintentional word or action influences the purchase decision, the actual purchase, and/or use of the product or service
Buyer	The individual who actually makes the purchase transaction
User	The person most directly indolved in consumption or use of the purchase

Source: Gerald Zaltman and Philip C. Burger, *Marketing Research: Fundamentals and Dynamics,* p. 142. Adapted with permission of the authors.

Any study of consumer behavior would be incomplete if it treated only one consumer role. However, an emphasis on one role, while still devoting adequate treatment to the others, can simplify our study in many cases. When it becomes useful to consider only one role we will tend to choose the *buyer*—the individual who actually makes the purchase. This approach is useful because even when told what to purchase the buyer often makes decisions regarding purchase timing, store choice, package size, and other factors. Therefore, focusing on the buyer, while allowing for the influence of others on the purchase decision, still gives considerable flexibility while concentrating on one consumer role.

Decision Process

The way in which our definition characterizes "behavior" also deserves special attention. That is, consumer behavior is seen to involve a *mental decision process* as well as *physical activity*. The actual act of purchase is just one stage in a series of mental and physical activities that occur during a period of time. Some of these activities precede the actual buying, while others follow it. However, since all are capable of influencing the purchase, they will be considered as part of the behavior in which we are interested.

An example will illustrate the benefits of this viewpoint. Suppose a photographer who regularly purchases one brand of film suddenly switches to a competing brand even though there has been no change in either the films or their prices. What has caused this shift in loyalty? Just noting that the individual's purchase behavior has changed does little to help our understanding of the situation. Perhaps the competing film received a strong recommendation by a friend, or possibly the photographer switched because he believed the competing brand captured the colors of some subject matter of interest. On the other hand, his decision may have been caused either by general dissatisfaction with results from his regular film or from recent exposure to an advertisement for the competing brand.

This example suggests the complexity of decision processes and demonstrates the limitations of viewing consumer behavior as just the act of purchasing. Therefore, to understand consumers adequately we should stress that, in addition to physical activities, their behavior involves a mental decision process that takes place over time.

A Subset of Human Behavior

Viewing consumer behavior in such a broad context suggests it is actually a subset of human behavior. That is, factors affecting individuals in their daily lives also influence their purchase activities. Internal influences, such as learning and motives, as well as external factors, such as social expectations and constraints, affect us in our role as consumers as well as in our other capacities. In fact, it is often difficult to draw a distinct line between consumer-related behavior and other aspects of human behavior. For example, next-door neighbors might find lawn problems a convenient topic for striking up a conversation. However, this can quickly lead to a serious discussion of the merits of Scott fertilizers, Lawn Bird Sprinklers, and Sears riding mowers.

The fact that consumer behavior is a subset of human behavior is to our advantage. The several disciplines collectively referred to as the *behavioral sciences* have studied human behavior for some time, and we can draw upon their contributions for understanding consumer behavior. This borrowing is quite extensive and includes theories used in explaining behavior as well as methods useful in investigating it. In fact, this borrowing is so extensive that consumer behavior is often said to be *multidisciplinary* in nature. The behavior science disciplines that have most contributed to our understanding of consumers are

1. *Psychology*—study of the behavior and mental processes of individuals
2. *Sociology*—study of the collective behavior of people in groups
3. *Social Psychology*—study of how individuals influence and are influenced by groups
4. *Economics*—study of people's production, exchange, and consumption of goods and services
5. *Anthropology*—study of people in relation to their culture

Recently, it has been argued that the multidisciplinary approach to consumer behavior has been based on inadequate means of borrowing from the behavioral sciences.[7] This charge is based on a contention that when people act as consumers certain aspects of their behavior are unique and distinct from other categories of human behavior. These unique aspects, it is argued, have not been adequately recognized by theories and concepts of behavior developed in other disciplines. Therefore, wholesale adoption of such concepts will not provide an adequate understanding of consumers.

This point is well taken. However, it does not mean that those interested in the behavior of consumers should never again borrow from the behavioral sciences. A better approach would involve critical examination of the theories and concepts available from other disciplines that might be useful for understanding consumers. The degree to which they would need modification for the purpose of understanding consumers could then be determined. In this way, the study of consumer behavior would have its own unique aspects and also be in a position to benefit from discoveries about human behavior in other disciplines.

WHY STUDY CONSUMER BEHAVIOR?

Understanding the reasons for studying a discipline enables one to better appreciate the contributions that it has to offer; therefore, this section presents a justification for the time and effort that the reader will expend in learning about consumers.

A Part of Our Lives

In a general sense, the most important reason for studying consumer behavior is the significant role it plays in our lives. Much of our time is spent directly in the marketplace shopping or engaging in other activities. A large amount of additional time is spent thinking about products and services, talking to friends about them, and seeing or hearing advertisements about them. In addition, the goods we purchase and the manner in which we use them significantly influence how we live our daily lives. These general concerns alone are enough to justify our study. However, many seek to understand the behavior of consumers for what are thought to be more immediate and tangible reasons.

Application to Decision Making

Consumers are often studied because certain decisions are significantly affected by their behavior or expected actions. For this reason, consumer behavior is said to be an *applied discipline*. Such applications can exist at two different levels of analysis. The *macro* perspective applies knowledge of consumers to aggregate-level problems faced by large groups or by society as a whole. The *micro* perspective seeks application of this knowledge to problems faced by the individual firm or organization.

Macro Perspective On the macro, or aggregate, level we know that consumers collectively influence economic and social conditions within an entire society. In market systems based on individual choice, consumers strongly influence what will be produced, for whom it will be produced, and what resources will be used to produce it. Consequently, the collective behavior of consumers has a significant influence on the quality and level of our standard of living.[8] For example, consider the overall impact of American consumers' strong desire for private automobile transportation. Vast amounts of resources have been used to produce cars, highway systems, and petroleum products used in their operation. It has also strongly influenced where many of us live (e.g., suburbs) and how we run our daily lives (e.g., what we eat, where we shop, and how we are entertained). Furthermore, this collective desire not only has led to the development of a strong transportation network but also has significantly contributed to our pollution problems and energy needs.

As this illustrates, understanding consumer behavior from a macro perspective can provide insight into aggregate economic and social trends and can perhaps even predict such trends. In addition, this understanding may suggest ways to increase the efficiency of the market system and improve the well-being of people in society.

Micro Perspective The micro perspective involves understanding consumers for the purpose of helping a firm or organization accomplish its objectives. Advertising managers, product designers, and many others in profit-oriented businesses are interested in understanding consumers in order to be more effective at their tasks. In addition, managers of various nonprofit organizations have benefited from the same knowledge. For example, the United Way, the American Red Cross and the American Cancer Society have been effective in applying an understanding of consumer behavior concepts to their activities.

APPLYING CONSUMER BEHAVIOR KNOWLEDGE

The following selections have been made from a variety of practical applications in the field of consumer behavior. Some involve a macro perspective while others illustrate a micro viewpoint. Together they underscore the importance of understanding consumers for solving a variety of contemporary problems.

Consumer Behavior and Marketing Management

Effective business managers realize the importance of marketing to the success of their firm. *Marketing* may be defined as "human activity directed at satisfying needs and wants through exchange processes."[9] Such exchanges may involve products, services, or even social ideas.

A sound understanding of consumer behavior is essential to the long-run success of any marketing program. In fact, it is seen as a cornerstone of the *marketing concept,* an important orientation or philosophy of many marketing managers. The essence of the marketing concept is captured in three interrelated orientations:

Consumers' Wants and Needs This focus is on identifying and satisfying the wants and needs of consumers. The intention of the firm is not seen as merely providing goods and services. Instead, want and need satisfaction is viewed as the purpose, and providing products and services is the means to achieve that end.

Company Objectives Consumers' wants and needs are numerous. Therefore, a firm that concentrates on satisfying a small proportion of all desires will most effectively utilize its resources. Company objectives and any of its special advantages are used as criteria to select the specific wants and needs to be addressed.

Integrated Strategy An integrated effort is most effective in achieving a firm's objective through consumer satisfaction. For maximum impact this requires that marketing efforts be closely coordinated and compatible with each other and with other activities of the firm.

Several limitations of the marketing concept have been noted, especially in regard to the degree to which attempting to satisfy consumers' wants and needs can generate negative consequences for society.[10] For example, convenience packaging has contributed to a solid waste disposal problem for society and the propellant formerly used in aerosol sprays has been linked to depletion of the ozone layer of our atmosphere. Adjustments to the marketing concept which incorporate societal objectives have been suggested to alleviate such shortcomings.[11] However, the basic need to understand consumers is still fundamental to these revised schemes.

Several major activities can be undertaken by an organization that is marketing oriented. These include market-opportunity analysis, target-market selection, and determination of the marketing mix, which includes decisions on the proper combination of marketing variables to offer consumers. Each of these is briefly discussed below with examples to illustrate the relevance of consumer behavior to their accomplishment.

Market-Opportunity Analysis This activity involves examining trends and conditions in the marketplace to identify consumers' needs and wants that are not being fully satisfied. The analysis begins with a study of general market trends, such as consumers' lifestyles and income levels, which may suggest unsatisfied wants and needs. More specific examination involves assessing any unique abilities the company might have in satisfying identified consumer desires.

A variety of recent trends have resulted in many new product offerings for consumer satisfaction. For example, companies attuned to the energy crisis have been quick to offer such new products as triple-paned replacement windows, water-saving shower heads, and energy-efficient hot water heaters. In the health care field, companies sensing consumers' unmet medical needs have offered coin-operated blood pressure testing machines at shopping centers and other convenient locations. Also, low-priced minor surgery centers without meals or overnight accommodations are now available. In addition, a recently introduced device allows consumers to self-administer precisely calibrated medical doses at home, thus eliminating the need for travel to the hospital.

Target-Market Selection The process of reviewing market opportunities often results in identifying distinct groupings of consumers who have unique wants and needs. This can result in a decision to approach each market segment with a unique marketing offering. Consider the soft drink market. Here, major segments of ultimate consumers are distinguished by the type of purchase situation: 1) the food store segment, 2) the "cold bottle" or vending machine segment, and 3) the fountain market which includes fast-food outlets. Unique packaging arrangements (container type and size), point of purchase promotions, and other variations are made for each segment.

In other cases, the marketer may decide to concentrate company efforts on serving only one or a few of the identified target markets. An excellent example of this has occurred in the bath soap market. By segmenting consumers according to their lifestyle patterns and personalities, the Colgate-Palmolive company was able to identify a unique group of consumers in need of a certain type of deodorant soap. Development of Irish Spring for this target group led to the capturing of 15 percent of the deodorant soap market within 3 years of introduction.[12]

Determining the Marketing Mix This stage involves developing and implementing a strategy for delivering an effective combination of want-satisfying features to consumers within target markets. A series of decisions are made on four major ingredients frequently referred to as the marketing mix variables: product, price, place, and promotion. The following characterizes each area and provides a small sampling of how knowledge of consumer behavior is relevant for decision making.

PRODUCT The nature of the physical product and service features are of concern here. Among decisions that are influenced by consumer behavior are

What size, shape, and features should the product have?

How should it be packaged?

How many different models should be included in the product line?

What type of warranties and service programs should be provided?

What type of accessories and associated products should be offered?

Gillette An excellent illustration of how consumer studies can influence product decisions is provided by Gillette—the company that controls about 60 percent of the $450-million-per-year razor blade market. Every day a selected panel of 10,000 men painstakingly record results of their shaves with Gillette products. Five hundred of these men actually shave in company facilities under carefully controlled conditions where they also can be viewed through two-way mirrors and videorecorders. In some cases the shaved whiskers are collected and measured. These and other investigations enable Gillette to learn a great deal about consumers, their beard characteristics, and their shaving habits including the following:

The average man's beard covers an area of one-third of a square foot and grows $\frac{15}{1000}$ of an inch a day.

The average person exerts between one-third of a pound and two pounds of force while shaving.

About 10 to 20 percent of all shavers are "heavy blade damagers" who should change blades after five or so shaves but the rest are "light blade damagers" and could use the same blade for up to three months without significant loss of shave quality. However, habit, sensitivity to pain, and psychological factors (feelings regarding the need for sharpness, and so on) usually result in these shavers discarding blades after nine or ten shaves regardless of their condition.

Most men hold the Trac II razor so that it makes proper contact with the skin approximately 77 percent of the time. This knowledge led Gillette to develop the swivel-head design featured in Atra razors. The Atra model can increase correct razor to skin contact to about 89 percent of shaving time.[13]

Gaines The situation faced by Gaines is considerably different. It illustrates that even when product users are not human their reaction to a product can be the focus of considerable company interest. Gaines produces food for many of the nation's 43 million dogs that most owners treat as family members. Because of this, the bottom line is that if the product isn't devoured by Bowser with apparent relish, it probably won't be purchased again. Since $3 billion of sales are at stake, it is not surprising that Gaines and its competitors spend millions of dollars yearly to maintain dog-food testing laboratories. Here, dogs' reactions to various ingredients (beans, cheese, etc.), food shapes (chunks versus bits), and moisture content are tested under controlled feeding conditions. Side-by-side taste tests comparing Gaines's products with different brands are also made with many dogs. Various measures are used including the amount of each brand eaten, the extent of tail wagging and eye pupil dilation, and heartbeat rates. Results of these tests and nutrition information assist in making decisions on dog-food ingredients and new product ideas.[14]

PRICE   The marketer must make decisions regarding both a price to charge for the company's products or services and any modification to those prices. These decisions will determine the amount of revenues the firm will generate. A few of the factors involving consumer behavior are.

How price-aware are consumers in the relevant product category?

How sensitive are consumers to price differences between brands?

How large a price reduction is needed to encourage purchases during new product introductions and sales promotions?

What size discount should be given to those who pay with cash?

Price Awareness Consumers' price awareness for certain product categories can be surprising. A recent study by *Progressive Grocer* magazine serves to illustrate. The focus was on price awareness of grocery items—goods for which many claim consumers have high price awareness and sensititivy. Results showed that only 22 percent of those interviewed immediately after their grocery store shopping could accurately identify (plus or minus 5 percent) prices of common grocery products. This was true even though they were asked about frequently purchased items. Also, the range of some estimates was staggering. For example, $4.86 separated the low and high estimate for a 6-ounce jar of Maxwell House instant coffee. Those shoppers who rated themselves as "very price aware" were only slightly better than others in their estimating ability.[15]

Watch Prices However, for many products consumers show high concern for prices. As the watch market demonstrates, this certainly is not always directed at saving money. Amazingly, in times of uncertain economic conditions and inflation, Americans have joined many well-heeled Europeans in their interest in expensive watches. In fact, many retailers have noticed that the more a watch costs, the better it seems to sell. This market is not composed of people seeking a highly accurate timepiece because such instruments can be obtained for a mere $500 or less. Instead, the "expensive" market is comprised of those who want to tell the world something about themselves—and their financial situation. Models to satisfy such buyers are priced from $1500 and some are in the $5000 to $8000 range. Top models frequently retail at approximately $15,000, while a special custom order has been known to sell for $4.3 million! For those who believe this expensive watch market is small, it should be noted that one New York dealer sold nearly 50,000 gold Swiss watches in one year alone.[16]

PLACE This variable involves consideration of where and how to offer products and services for sale. It also is concerned with the mechanisms to transfer goods and their ownership to consumers. Decisions influenced by consumer behavior include

What type of retail outlets should sell the firm's offering?

Where should they be located, and how many should there be?

What arrangements are needed to distribute products to retailers?

To what extent is it necessary for the company to own or maintain tight control over activities of firms in the channel of distribution?

What image and clientele should the retailer seek to cultivate?

Retail Outlets Large retailers such as Sears, J.C. Penney, Woolworth, and K mart are located in most of the largest metropolitan centers. Growth requires these corporations to expand with ever-increasing markets. The question then becomes, Where are markets likely to develop and what type of outlets will best serve them? Many people in the industry are being persuaded by an impressive change in U.S. consumer demographics—a move back to smaller cities and towns. The result is that between 1979 and 1990 the ten largest metropolitan areas are projected to have an inflation-adjusted sales growth of only 37 percent, while the ten smallest metropolitan areas are expected to post 54 percent gains. This has led to development of what retailers are calling K30's and K40's. These 30,000 to 40,000 square-foot stores are designed for malls being developed in the smaller markets that were previously ignored because of low consumer density per square mile. They are frequently no more than one-half the size of large city stores and are built to emphasize merchandise that retailers believe will be the most profitable offerings for consumers in smaller markets. Consequently, the stores stress clothing, hardware, appliances, and automotive services but rarely include full furniture, carpet, or candy departments. Consumer reaction has been quite favorable and the major retailers have also been impressed with sales.[17]

Atmospherics Although the location of retail outlets may be critical, it certainly does not guarantee sales. Thus, retailers are continuously searching for the proper product mix and service offerings to satisfy consumers. Sophisticated devices are also used by many to provide an atmosphere that is most pleasing to shoppers. Store background music is employed in this way. The type of songs and their programming are selected on the basis of consumer reactions. For example, the music on some systems increases in rhythm and beat until a climax is reached. This is followed by a period of silence after which the music begins to build again. Studies suggest that such programming gives consumers periodic psychological lifts. Benefits to the retailer are said to include a reduction in consumer complaints and a higher sales volume. In another vein, some psychologists have argued that consumers' sense of space can affect their purchase behavior. Higher-density conditions are said to generate a fairlike atmosphere which consumers perceive in a positive manner. The resulting potential for sales has led some to predict a new trend in "high density" store design. Methods designed to appeal to consumers do not stop there. For example, store colors are often used in ways that research has suggested will foster specific reactions. Artificial odors (pizza, chocolate chips, etc.) are also available in aerosol cans as are special timed-release devices to add to the food retailer's "atmospherics."[18]

PROMOTION   Of concern here are the goals and methods for communicating aspects of the firm and its offerings to target consumers. Consumer-related decisions include:

What methods of promotion are best for each specific situation?

What are the most effective means for gaining consumers' attention?

What methods best convey the intended message?

How often should a given advertisement be repeated?

Cella Wines With over $61 billion spent on advertising alone it is not surprising that marketers try to make effective use of every promotional dollar. In some cases, however, their efforts yield a perplexing kind of success. Consider the experience of Brown-Forman distillers who sought to develop their Cella wines into distinct and well-known brands among consumers. To do this, the plump, amiable character of Aldo Cella, a cuddly kind of Italian Romeo, was created for TV advertisements. Sales of Cella wines seem to have benefited from these advertisements. There may have been a problem, however. Although Aldo, his slogan ("Chill-a-Cella"), and his way with beautiful women were quite memorable to consumers, the consumers didn't seem to know much about his wine! The conclusion was that Aldo actually was stealing consumers' attention away from his product. Consequently, new advertisements featured a considerably more reserved Aldo presenting his wine in a more serious and traditional manner. Unfortunately, immediate consumer reaction was not positive. Many lamented over what had happened to their friend Aldo, and apparently wanted him to return.[19]

Comparative Advertising Another area that often presents marketers with a dilemma is whether to use comparative advertising. This method of promotion is designed to compare the company's brand directly against a competitor. The practice has been encouraged by the U.S. Federal Trade Commission under the belief that the technique is an effective way to present product information on which consumers can base their purchase decisions. It also is said to encourage competition between brands which can lead to lower prices and product improvements. The problem is that evidence is not clear on how consumers react to comparative ads. There certainly seem to be successful aspects to numerous comparative campaigns—Vivitar, a photographic equipment manufacturer, ran an ad naming Kodak products and dramatically boosted their sales; public awareness of Avis and Datril increased significantly when they compared themselves to Hertz and Tylenol, respectively; and Pepsi claims to have increased its market share from its taste-test campaign using Coke as the other brand. However, when responding to surveys about the issue, consumers frequently indicate a dislike of comparative ads because they find them lacking in reliability and usefulness. Studies have also found that such advertisements can confuse consumers and foster negative attitudes toward the promoted brand. As a result, consumers may respond by feeling they should disregard the advertisements and use their own judgment for purchase decisions. Perhaps the worst situation is when the competing brand responds to a comparative ad, as Coke did to the "Pepsi Challenge" taste tests. The fighting that may occur (and did in this situation), can be perceived as childish or immature. This can quickly lead consumers to conclude that both companies lack credibility, and brand images may suffer accordingly.[20]

These examples indicate the relevance of consumer behavior to marketing-management decision making. However, it is useful to also consider other areas where knowledge of consumers has significant practical application.

Consumer Behavior, Nonprofit and Social Marketing

Can crime prevention, charitable contributions, or the concept of family planning be sold to people in much the same way that some business firms sell soap? Recently, a number of writers have suggested that various social and nonprofit organizations can be viewed as having services or ideas which they are attempting to market to target groups of "consumers" or constituents.[21] Such organizations include governmental agencies, religious orders, universities, and charitable institutions. Often these groups must also appeal to the public for support in addition to attempting to satisfy some want or need in society. Clearly, a sound understanding of consumer decision processes can assist their efforts.[22]

Consider, for example, the benefits such knowledge would have to administrators of the American Cancer Society. Two major tasks of this organization are (1) to solicit public contributions for support of cancer research and (2) to encourage regular physical examinations for early detection of the disease. Regarding the first task, fundamental information, such as the characteristics of potential contributors, what motivates their generosity, and how these motives can be most effectively appealed to are highly useful. Similarly, a sound basis for encouraging regular physical examinations would include specific knowledge of reasons why the exams are avoided—the expense, the time involved, the fear of learning about an illness, or some other reason.

Many other examples demonstrate the fundamental role a consumer orientation plays in nonprofit and social-marketing endeavors. The following serve as additional illustrations.

Political Positions Many political groups now base much of their platforms on surveys that reveal public opinion. The 1980 presidential campaign of Ronald Reagan serves as an excellent example. A $1.4 million polling program was employed to determine the public's perception of the candidate, their attitudes on various issues, and other information useful for designing the political campaign. Survey results suggested that the majority of Americans were very interested in reducing government spending, many were mainly concerned with strong national defense, and a significant number thought the most pressing problems were to improve the economy and cut inflation. These issues were strongly addressed by the then-candidate Reagan. Other studies of voter characteristics showed Reagan supporters to obtain high scores on individualism, authoritarianism, and respect for authority. Reagan's leadership and speechmaking style also tended to cater to such individuals.[23]

Red Cross Traditionally the Red Cross has run a passive "good neighbor" theme to foster public awareness and favorable attitudes toward the organization. This approach was thought to gain high public acceptance and encourage financial contributions. However, an opinion survey requested by the organization cast doubt on these hopes. Results indicated that the public had low awareness and significant misperceptions about Red Cross activities. Few associated it with blood collection work, hospital volunteer activities, and water safety programs even though it was quite active in these areas. Although most respondents were aware of its disaster assistance, few felt any personal identification with this work. These findings led to further in-depth testing and subsequent development of specific topics designed to inform the public of the scope of Red Cross activities. They were bound together by the common theme of "Keep Red Cross Ready" to more directly encourage volunteers and financial contributions. Movie and TV personalities who possessed unique characteristics were carefully selected to obtain the greatest degree of message impact.[24]

Many other examples of consumer-oriented social marketing could be mentioned. However, not all of these efforts have met with significant success. For example, not long ago congressional hearings revealed that advertising valued at over $11 million was donated by media to encourage contributions for Radio Free Europe. Unfortunately, the effort was reported to have generated only $100,000 in revenues for the organization![25] This underscores the need for a sound understanding of consumers' decision processes as the basis for more effective social and non-profit marketing.

Consumer Behavior and Governmental Decision Making

In recent years the relevance of consumer-behavior principles to governmental decision making has become quite evident. Two major areas of activity have been affected: (1) government policies that provide services to the public or result in decisions that influence consumer behavior; and (2) the design of legislation to protect consumers or to assist them in evaluating products and services.

Government Services It is increasingly evident that government provision of public services can benefit significantly from an understanding of the consumers or users of these services. Numerous analysts have noted that our frequently failing mass-transportation systems will not be viable alternatives to private automobile travel until government planners fully understand how to appeal to the wants and needs of the public.[26] In other cases, state and municipal planners must make a variety of decisions, including where to locate highways, what areas to consider for future commercial growth, and the type of public services (such as health care and libraries) to offer. The effectiveness of these decisions will be influenced by the extent to which they are based on an adequate understanding of consumers. This requires knowledge of people's attitudes, beliefs, perceptions, and habits as well as their tendencies to behave under a variety of circumstances.

New Currency In 1976, the U.S. government introduced a new two-dollar bill even though there were indications it would meet with some consumer resistance. One reason for developing this bill was to compensate for the dollar which had declined in value due to inflation. However, the market proved more than resistant; it was nearly hostile. Retailers found no space for the two-dollar bills in cash register drawers. Consumers tended to confuse them with twenties and did not like the extra work of keeping track of one more paper denomination. Also, it appears that many people thought the twos would bring bad luck just as they do for dice throwers. Because of this unexpected consumer resistance the deuce failed. Disappointment but not defeatism seemed to characterize Treasury Department attitudes, because in 1979 it introduced the new Susan B. Anthony dollar coin. Apparently, the logic was that if the dollar is here to stay it should be in long-lasting coin form as opposed to nondurable bills. Remembering that in the early 1970s the Eisenhower dollar coin failed because its large size made it heavy, the Treasury Department made the Anthony coin only slightly larger than a quarter. To help distinguish it from the quarter, the Anthony had an eleven-sided design. However, design and considerable promotional efforts were not enough to guarantee success. Consumers rejected the coin in resounding fashion because to them it looked and felt like a quarter. Batting zero for three, reports were that government decisions makers were saying, "Now, if we changed the coin's color to bronze and. . . ."[27]

Locating Parks City planners in Philadelphia decided to build a new recreational park for use by residents living in an impoverished area of the municipality. A central site was selected so that the park would be accessible to the greatest number of neighborhood children. A half-block expanse of swings, monkeybars, and play areas was then developed. Unfortunately, the park went basically unused. Apparently, that city's administrators had unknowingly decided to build the park on an invisible dividing line separating the territories of two rival neighborhood gangs. Even though the area was centrally located, the fact that people perceived it as a "no man's land" virtually guaranteed that the park facilities would go unused.[28]

Consumer Protection Activities Many agencies at all levels of government are involved with regulating business practices for the purpose of protecting consumers' welfare. Some government programs are also designed to directly influence certain consumer actions (such as the use of auto seatbelts) and discourage others (speeding, drug abuse, etc.). In addition, over thirty federal agencies, including the Department of Commerce, the Food and Drug Administration (FDA), and the Federal Trade Commission (FTC) have increased their efforts to provide consumers with information believed useful for making purchase decisions. The following serves to illustrate the nature of some of the issues government agencies confront in their consumer protection efforts:

Regulating Advertisements Government agencies have developed many regulations to protect consumers from potentially misleading and deceptive advertisements. At the federal level, primary responsibility for this activity has been assigned to the FTC. During the past decade, the commission has taken a more active regulatory role. In addition to declaring certain advertisements deceptive, it has been able to require some firms to withdraw their offending promotions. In other cases, firms have also been ordered to sponsor communications designed to correct inappropriate impressions consumers may have formed from exposure to earlier advertisements. In all of these cases the FTC has focused on advertising copy—the words the firms use to make their claims. Recently, however, the commission has shown interest in regulating the nonverbal (picture) content of advertisements. The justification given for this interest is that advertisers can use pictures to convey a considerable amount of meaning to consumers. Therefore, to regulate only verbal portions of ads is only attacking a part of the deception problem. An ad for Belair cigarettes serves as an example. The verbal part telling readers that Belair takes you "all the way to fresh" was evaluated as quite uninformative by a FTC deputy director, but he questioned the meaning consumers might derive from the full-page color picture of a couple frolicking in the ocean. The interpretation might be that Belair cigarettes make people healthy and happy. If such a message were conveyed in verbal form, it would likely draw an FTC deception investigation.

Response from the advertising community has not been positive to such an argument. Many are concerned that the FTC staff is seeking to regulate legitimate attempts at advertising persuasion rather than deceptive practices. Others charge that hardly anything is known about how advertising pictures influence consumers. Therefore, any FTC judgments are bound to be quite arbitrary. FTC staffers tend to agree on this point, but they also believe it is possible to develop methods and standards for judging how such pictures influence consumers. In addition, they believe that a considerable amount of relevant information is presently available from consumer research studies that industry has already conducted for the purpose of developing effective advertising strategies. Industry spokespeople disagree and are quite concerned with an inadequate understanding of how consumers process pictorial stimuli could lead the FTC to develop inappropriate regulations.[29]

Unfortunately, it appears that the effect of many consumer protection efforts has been considerably less than expected, and in some cases they may actually have had negative consequences for consumers.[30] Often this occurs because officials have based their decisions on inadequate understanding of consumers and how they process information.[31]

Consumer Behavior and Demarketing

U.S. history has long been characterized by intensive efforts of private enterprise to stimulate the public to greater levels of consumption. Various government policies have supported such efforts because of their favorable effect on economic development. Recently, however, it has become increasingly clear that we are entering an era of scarcity in terms of some natural resources such as oil, natural gas, and even water. These scarcities have led to promotions stressing conservation rather than consumption. The efforts of electric power companies to encourage reduction of electrical use serves as one illustration. In other circumstances, consumers have been encouraged to decrease or stop their use of particular goods believed to have harmful effects. Programs designed to reduce drug abuse, gambling, and similar types of consumption are examples. These actions have been undertaken by government agencies, nonprofit organizations, and other private groups.

The term "demarketing" refers to all such efforts to encourage consumers to reduce their consumption of a particular product or service. The following examples illustrate two demarketing programs:

> *Anti-Smoking* The U.S. government has expended considerable effort to discourage cigarette smoking. These activities have been supported with other programs mounted by nongovernment agencies such as the American Cancer Society and the Heart Association.
>
> Communications to existing and potential smokers have involved using famous athletes to speak against smoking cigarettes, showing how the habit is socially offensive, and making very liberal uses of fear appeals. Fear campaigns have focused on how smokers increase their risks of developing heart disease, lung cancer, and other health problems. Celebrities who have been heavy smokers and have also been suffering from lung cancer have actually been used in some advertisements. The potential impact of smoking risks on family and loved ones has also served as an appeal in many communications.
>
> Considerable funds have been spent on these programs. For example, in 1967 alone just one agency, the Department of Health, Education, and Welfare, spent $2.1 million in its anti-smoking campaign. Despite all of these efforts, cigarette smoking is still widespread. For example, 1980 sales reached a record 611.7 billion cigarettes. This represented the largest sales increase since 1974.[32]

Drug Abuse Swedish health authorities recently concluded that hashish smoking in Stockholm and other parts of that country had reached epidemic proportions. Concerns about new research evidence suggesting negative medical effects from the drug, and a belief that hash smoking led to using more serious narcotics, prompted Stockholm officials to act. It was decided that the best way to encourage people to reduce or discontinue their use of hash was to really "shake them up." This led to a series of posters and billboards dispersed throughout the city graphically showing potential negative consequences from using the drug. In one poster entitled "One Man's Bread," two men are shown counting money over a dead teenager lying next to a syringe. In another, a former teenage hashish-smoking soccer star is shown lying face down on an operating table. The caption reads: "Mickie: He first smoked hash five years ago. Here he lies today, dead at age 25 of an overdose of heroin."[33]

Some demarketing efforts have met with considerable success while many others have made hardly any impact in changing long-established consumption patterns. An analysis of the success and failures of various efforts strongly suggests that demarketing programs must be based on a sound understanding of consumers' motives, attitudes, and historically established consumption behavior.

Consumer Behavior and Consumer Education

Consumers also stand to benefit directly from orderly investigations of their behavior. This can occur on an individual basis or as part of more formal educational programs. As we study what has been discovered about the behavior of others, we can gain insight into our own interactions with the marketplace. For example, when we learn that a large proportion of the billions spent annually on grocery products is used for impulse purchases, and not spent according to preplanned shopping lists, we may be more willing to plan our purchases in an effort to save money. In general, as we discover the many variables that can influence consumers' purchases, we have the opportunity to better understand how they affect our own behavior.

What is learned about consumer behavior can also directly benefit consumers in a more formal sense. The knowledge can serve as data for educational programs designed to improve their decision-making regarding products and services.[34] Such courses are now available at the high school and college level and are becoming increasingly popular. To be most effective, these educational programs should be based on a clear understanding of the important variables influencing consumers.

SUMMARY

The purpose of this chapter was to serve as a brief introduction to the field of consumer behavior. After several orienting examples, discussion centered on defining consumer behavior and describing the focus we will take in studying it. This approach is to view consumer behavior as the decision process and physical activity of those individuals purchasing for the purpose of individual or household consumption. Therefore, we recognize that in certain situations consumers will purchase products and services for use by other individuals. Also, we must realize that other individuals can have an influence on the consumers's decision process.

Discussion then turned to considering various reasons for studying consumer behavior. Most of our attention focused on the applied nature of the discipline. The relevance of consumer behavior to a variety of practical applications, including marketing management, social marketing, governmental decision making, demarketing, and consumer education was discussed.

With this introduction providing perspective, the next chapter lays additional groundwork for future chapters. It deals with factors influencing how we can best study consumer behavior.

DISCUSSION TOPICS

1 A marketer in the cosmetics industry once remarked: "In the factory, we make cosmetics, in the drugstore we sell hope." How does this relate to the marketing concept and the need for marketers to understand consumer behavior?

2 Review the activities undertaken by marketing-oriented firms and show the relevance of consumer behavior to each activity.

3 What would you recommend to government officials interested in introducing a new type of currency (coin or bill) to the market?

4 Every consumer is unique, and any study that concentrates on the "average" consumer is meaningless. Comment.

5 In terms of understanding consumers, what are the advantages and disadvantages of viewing behavior as both a decision process and a physical activity as opposed to just a physical activity?

6 In what ways is the study of consumer behavior useful to consumer-advocate groups concerned with designing laws to assist and protect consumers?

7 Choose an actual nonprofit organization and suggest areas where knowledge of its "consumers" might improve the services it provides.

8 Refer to the Regulating Advertisements example on page 19. What aspects of consumers' behavior do you think need to be studied in order to resolve the issue raised by the FTC?

NOTES

[1] Based on "Felled by a Head of Foam," *Fortune,* January 15, 1979, p. 96; Keith M. Jones, "Chelsea, The Adult Soft Drink: A Case of Corporate Social Responsibility," *Journal of Contemporary Business,* 7:69–76, 1979; and company information.
[2] Arne H. Sheets, "The Lafayette LR-100," unpublished paper, University of Rhode Island, 1974, 5 pp. Adapted with permission.
[3] See "Fighting the Fears of the DC-10," *Newsweek,* May 18, 1981; and *The DC-10: A Special Report,* McDonnell Douglas Company, 12 pp.
[4] See "Rah! Rah! Sell! Sell!," *Time,* May 4, 1981, p. 52; Lawrence Ingrassia, "College Learns to Use the Fine Art of Marketing," *The Wall Street Journal,* February 23, 1981, p. 21; and Philip Kotler, *Marketing Management: Analysis, Planning, and Control,* Prentice-Hall, Englewood Cliffs, N.J., 1980, pp. 684–685.
[5] John A. Howard and Jagdish N. Sheth, *The Theory of Buyer Behavior,* Wiley, New York, 1969.
[6] Jagdish N. Sheth, "A Model of Industrial Buyer Behavior," *Journal of Marketing,* 37:50–56, October 1973.
[7] See Jagdish N. Sheth, "The Surpluses and Shortages in Consumer Behavior Theory and Research," *Journal of The Academy Of Marketing Science,* 7:414–427, Fall 1979.
[8] W. T. Tucker, *Foundations for a Theory of Consumer Behavior,* Holt, New York, 1967, pp. 1–2.
[9] Philip Kotler, *Marketing Management: Analysis, Planning, and Control,* 3d ed., Prentice-Hall, Englewood Cliffs, N.J., 1976, p. 5.

[10] Martin L. Bell and C. William Emery, "The Faltering Marketing Concept," *Journal of Marketing,* **35**:37–42, October 1971; and Lawrence P. Feldman, "Societal Adaptation: A New Challenge for Marketing," *Journal of Marketing,* **35**:54–60, July 1971.

[11] See James T. Rothe and Lissa Benson, "Intelligent Consumption: An Attractive Alternative to the Marketing Concept," *MSU Business Topics,* **22**:29–34, Winter 1974; George Fisk, "Criteria for a Theory of Responsible Consumption," *Journal of Marketing,* **37**:24–31, April 1973; and Kotler, *Marketing Management,* pp. 16–18.

[12] "How Colgate's Brand Manager Applied Psychos to Market and Media for Irish Spring," *Media Decisions,* December 1976, pp. 70–71, 104–106.

[13] See Chris Welles, "The War of the Razors," *Esquire,* February 1980, pp. 28–30+; Richard Martin, "Lets Face It: There is a Lot of Mystery About a Good Shave," *The Wall Street Journal,* April 23, 1976, p. 1; and Linda Snyder Hayes, "Gillette Takes the Wraps Off," *Fortune,* February 25, 1980, pp. 148–150.

[14] Paul Gigot, "Pet Project: Pursuit of Tastier Dog Food Hounds the Beagles," *The Wall Street Journal,* June 16, 1981, pp. 1, 19.

[15] Jo-Ann Zbytniewski, "Shoppers Cry 'Remember the Price'—But Do They Practice What They Screech?" *Progressive Grocer,* **59**:119–122, November 1980.

[16] Lawrence Minard, "The More It Costs the Better It Sells," *Forbes,* December 22, 1980, pp. 59–62.

[17] Based on Steven Weiner, "With Many Cities Full of Stores, Chains Open Outlets in Small Towns," *The Wall Street Journal,* May 28, 1981, pp. 1, 19.

[18] See Bernard Wysocki, "Sight, Smell, Sound: They're All Arms in Retailers' Arsenal," *The Wall Street Journal,* April 17, 1979, upon which this discussion is based.

[19] See John Curley, "Could Aldo Cella's Image Be Too Good?" *The Wall Street Journal,* January 29, 1981, p. 25.

[20] See Nancy Giges, "Comparative Ads: Better Than . . . ?" *Advertising Age,* September 22, 1980, pp. 59+; Linda L. Golden, "Consumer Reactions to Explicit Brand Comparisons in Advertisements," *Journal of Marketing Research,* **16**:517–32, November 1979; William Wilkie and Paul Farris, "Comparison Advertising: Problems and Potential," *Journal of Marketing,* **39**:7–15, October 1975; Stephen Goodwin and Michael Etgar, "Experimental Investigation of Comparative Advertising: An Impact of Message Appeal, Information Load and Utility of Product Class," *Journal of Marketing Research,* **17**:187–202, May 1980; and William R. Swinyard, "The Interaction Between Comparative Advertising and Copy Claim Variation," *Journal of Marketing Research,* **18**:175–186, May 1981.

[21] Philip Kotler and Gerald Zaltman, "Social Marketing: An Approach to Planned Social Change," *Journal of Marketing,* **35**:3–12, July 1971; and F. Kelly Shuptrine and Frank A. Osmanski, "Marketing's Changing Role: Expanding or Contracting?" *Journal of Marketing,* **39**:58–66, April 1975.

[22] See Karen F. A. Fox and Philip Kotler, "The Marketing of Social Causes: The First Ten Years," *Journal of Marketing,* **44**:24–33, Fall 1980 for a recent evaluation of social marketing programs.

[23] See Jack J. Nonomichl, "The Marketing of a Candidate," *Advertising Age,* December 15, 1980, pp. 64–68.

[24] Based on "Red Cross Drive Result of Research," *Advertising Age,* January 15, 1979, p. 36.

[25] Leo Bogart, "The Marketing of Public Goods," *Conference Board Record,* November 1975, pp. 20–25.

[26] See Arthur Schreiber, Paul Gatons, and Richard Clemmer, *Economics of Urban Problems,* Houghton Mifflin, Boston, 1976, and Rusk Loving, Jr., "Amtrak is About to Miss the Train," *Fortune,* May 1974, pp. 272–275 ff.

[27] See "The Lady Vanishes," *Time,* August 11, 1980, p. 53; and "Numismatic Ms.," *Time,* July 9, 1979, p. 54.

[28] See "Mental Maps," *Time,* March 15, 1976, p. 71.

[29] See "Bell Attacks Measuring Nonverbal Signals in Ads," *Advertising Age,* November 27, 1978, p. 94; and "FTC is Seeking a Way to Decide If Pictures in Advertising Convey False Impressions," *The Wall Street Journal,* August 11, 1978, p. 8.

[30] George S. Day, "Assessing the Effects of Information Disclosure Requirements," *Journal of Marketing,* **40**:42–52, April 1976, and Jacob Jacoby, Donald Speller, and Carol Kohn Berning, "Brand Choice Behavior as a Function of Information Load: Replication and Extension," *Journal of Consumer Research,* **1**:33–42, June 1974.

[31] Jagdish N. Sheth and Nicholas J. Mammana, "Recent Failures in Consumer Protection," *California Management Review,* **16**:64–72, Spring 1974.

[32] See Thomas C. Kinnear and Cynthia J. Frey, "Demarketing of Potentially Hazardous Products: General Framework and Case Studies," *Journal of Contemporary Business,* **17**:57–68, 1979.

[33] Mark Goldsmith, "Swedes Smoke Out Hashish Users," *Advertising Age,* February 23, 1981, p. 62.

[34] Thomas S. Robertson and Scott Ward, "Toward the Development of Consumer Behavior Theory," in Boris W. Becker and Helmut Becker (eds.), *AMA Combined Proceedings,* American Marketing Association, Chicago, 1972, pp. 57–64.

CHAPTER 2
A FOUNDATION FOR STUDYING CONSUMER BEHAVIOR

The study of any subject is made easier by examining it in an organized fashion. This chapter will lay the foundation for such an approach to the topic of consumer behavior. Our first task is to better understand what consumer behavior actually entails. This will lead to a discussion of basic approaches to its study. Attention then will turn to the usefulness of models in describing and understanding consumers. After this review, the chapter ends by offering a simplified framework that will be helpful for integrating the variety of information that will be presented in the text.

STUDYING CONSUMER BEHAVIOR

As suggested in Chapter 1, it is useful to view consumer behavior as part of human behavior because we can then study it by borrowing approaches that have been developed in the behavioral sciences. One such borrowed approach views consumer behavior as entailing a decision process involving considerable mental activity.[1] It treats the three classes of variables discussed below as being essential to understanding behavior.

Classes of Variables

Consumers are continuously confronting and reacting to a great variety of specific situations. Seeing an advertisement, learning of a new product, or experiencing dissatisfaction when using a good or service are examples of such situations. Three classes of variables are involved in understanding consumer behavior in any of these specific situations: stimulus variables, response variables, and intervening variables.

Stimulus variables, such as advertisements, other people, and products, exist in the individual's external environment and are also produced internally. For example, our stomachs produce certain stimuli when we desire food. The role of stimulus variables is to serve as inputs to consumers' behavior.

Response variables are the resulting activities of individuals that are initiated by stimulus variables. These include observable actions such as gesturing, purchasing certain products, and changing the pitch of our voice slightly when we get excited. However, response variables can also include an increase in knowledge about a product, a change in attitudes toward it, or a reduction in an intention to purchase it. The distinction between these two groups of response variables is that some are *overt* or easily observable while others, such as an attitude, are *internal* to the individual and cannot be seen.

The third category of variables that are involved in specific situations consumers confront is referred to as *intervening variables* because they actually intervene between stimuli and responses. This suggests that at least some stimuli do not directly affect responses but that their effects are modified by the influence of intervening variables. These variables are internal to the individual, and can include motives, attitudes toward things and events, and perceptions of the world. Figure 2-1 graphically depicts the central role of intervening variables and how they can modify the influence of stimulus variables.

Intervening variables play a very important role in our study of consumer behavior. Because they exist, we cannot expect a given stimulus to produce the same response among all consumers. Even for the same individual, intervening variables can change during a period of time and have different influences. Consider, for example, how a consumer's reaction toward "old junk" found in trash-and-treasure shops might change upon learning that such items often are antiques of great value.

It should also be noted that the specific situation involved and the goals of any consumer study will strongly influence whether a given variable should be classified as a stimulus, a response, or an intervening variable. For example, attitudes may be thought of as response variables when the goal of some advertisement is to change consumers' attitudes about a particular brand. Alternatively, consumers' existing attitudes toward the same brand can be viewed as intervening variables when a retailer runs a one-day, 50-percent-off sale of the brand to reduce his inventory of it. Here, the response of interest is probably purchase behavior, but attitudes toward the brand may intervene to influence consumers' purchase reactions toward the sale.

Dealing With Unobservable Variables

It is important to realize that intervening variables and many response variables cannot be directly observed. This necessitates the development of methods to determine whether such unobservable variables actually exist and what their characteristics are. One approach to the problem involves devising instruments which we believe will measure or be related to the variables of interest. For example, a variety of methods have been developed to assess consumers' motives, personalities, attitudes, and purchase intentions. These measures, discussed in more detail in subsequent chapters, involve consumers' own verbal assessments of their internal states (for example, attitudes), paper and pencil tests, and technically sophis-

Stimulus variables → Intervening variables → Response variables

FIGURE 2-1

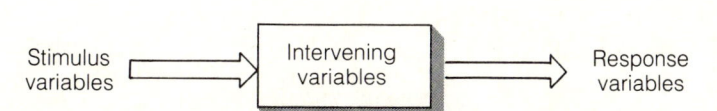

A diagram of the relationship between stimulus, intervening, and response variables.

ticated mechanical devices that record changes in eye pupil diameters and voice characteristics, as well as other potentially useful indicators of consumer reactions.

Another way to view the study of unobservable variables can best be illustrated by the *black-box* concept first originated in electrical engineering.[2] Basically, as depicted in Figure 2-2, we imagine a black box hiding some variable or process from our observation. We can view the stimulus inputs to the box and certain response outputs from it, but we are unable to see the intervening variables which connect these observable inputs and outputs.

Careful observation of inputs and visible responses enables a judgment to be made regarding the contents of the box. This process is referred to as *inference*. For example, in high school chemistry we inferred the existence and nature of invisible oxygen by employing the black-box concept and observing its effect on combustion and life. As another illustration, assume that we show a friend a magazine advertisement using a scantily clad model to attract readers' attention. Upon seeing it, our friend frowns and says, "Disgusting." We might infer that this person has a negative attitude toward sexual exploitation in advertising.

These situations demonstrate that the names used to characterize unobservable variables are actually constructed (invented) by researchers. For this reason, such names are often referred to as *hypothetical constructs*. The constructs are called hypothetical because they are not observable and we cannot directly prove

FIGURE 2-2
A diagram of the black-box approach to inferences about intervening variables.

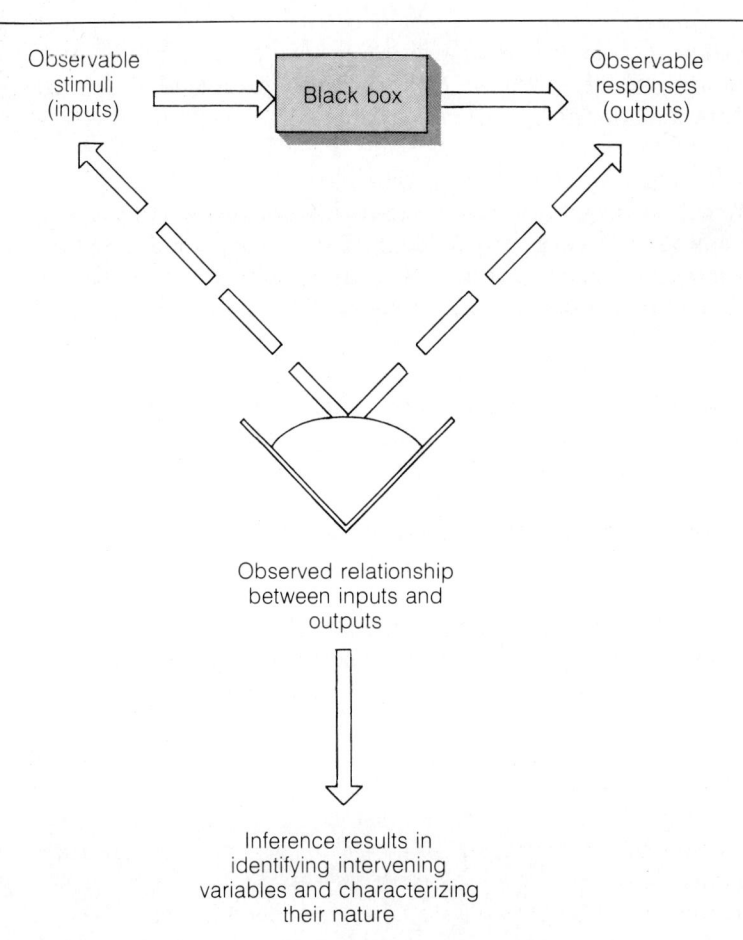

their existence. Instead, special measuring devices and the process of inference provide us with information to speculate about the characteristics of such variables and their role in influencing consumers.

PROBLEMS IN STUDYING CONSUMER BEHAVIOR

As the above discussion suggests, studying consumer behavior is not necessarily an easy undertaking. A number of factors too lengthy to review here contribute to this difficulty. However, it is useful to treat briefly several of the more important constraints.

Difficulty of Inference Process

Unfortunately, even experts frequently disagree about the exact nature of intervening variables. This occurs because the variables are unobservable, because they may have different aspects, and because they can change over time. Thus, if we observe the effect of a variable at two different points in time, and the variable is changing over time, we could easily reach two different inferences regarding its characteristics. The same would hold true if we happened to observe two different aspects of the same variable.

An important implication of this inference problem is that we must be prepared to face some uncertainty regarding the nature of variables that affect consumer behavior. We will even confront some definitions and contradictory research conclusions about the nature of a given variable. Since such ambiguity is to be expected when dealing with complex unobservable behavior, it should be tolerated as we search for ways to minimize it.

Behavior Is Subjective

The experiences of individuals influence how they react to the world. Because the experiences of people differ, any given situation will probably be interpreted at least somewhat differently by each individual. Therefore, we must realize that consumers act on their own perceptions of the world, which are often considerably different from our own.

Unfortunately, there often is a strong tendency to overlook this subjective aspect of behavior. Consequently, many marketing strategies are based on what managers *assume* are consumer motives, attitudes, and preferences rather than on what we actually know about these variables. Researchers and consumer-protection advocates have also been misled by such faulty assumptions. We must therefore be constantly on guard against falling into a similar trap in our studies.

Many Input Variables

The variety of input variables that can potentially influence consumer behavior is astounding. Figure 2-3, which is based on the work of Kurt Lewin, summarizes the major categories of these variables, consisting of internal, external, past, present, and future dimensions.[3]

The individual is shown to exist within the present time frame as represented by the circular portion of the figure. The inner solid circle contains *physiological* variables which are *internal* to the individual and are only minimally influenced by his or her environment. Many basic needs and drives, including nutrition, water, and sleep requirements, exist here.

In addition to their internal physiological needs, individuals are also profoundly influenced by their internal *psychological structure*. This includes processes such as attitude formation, motives, information processing, and learning, as well as the individual's subjective knowledge, values, and beliefs. For this reason, the psychological structure is often said to contain individual determinants of behavior.

As can be seen in the figure, the *external environment* is capable of influencing the individual's psychological condition and therefore his or her behavior. This external environment actually has three different aspects: present, past, and future influences on the individual. Particularly important aspects of the *present* environment are physical, economic, and social factors. Physical variables include distance to stores, weather, and available transportation. Economic variables include the individual's wealth, the cost of various products, and the economic climate of the country. Among others, social variables comprise the individual's social class and social group influences.

Aspects of the *past* environment are also influential. As we know, learning from experience can be useful in understanding and reacting to present situations. However, we also learn from some experiences so well that they often become habitual and we are not aware of their influence on our behavior.

Finally, expectations regarding the *future* can affect consumers' present

FIGURE 2-3

Summary of variable categories influencing the consumer.

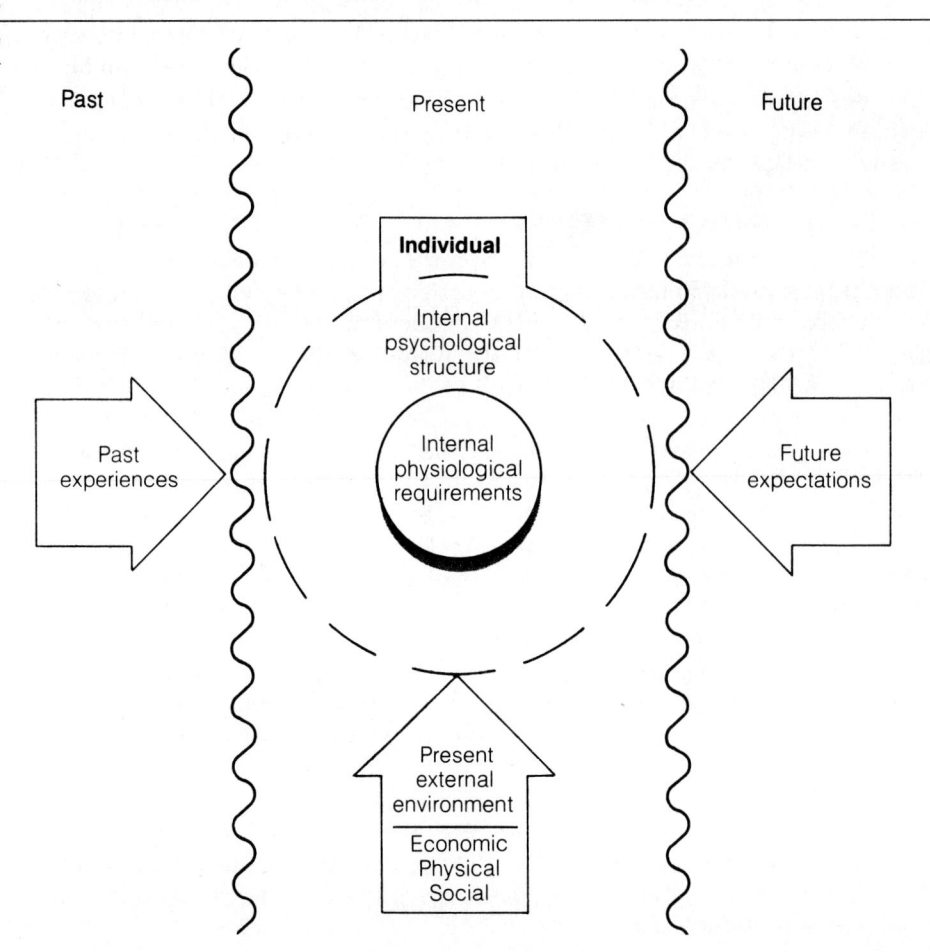

behavior. To illustrate, expectations regarding future income, health, and job security can influence consumers' willingness to purchase capital goods (automobiles and washing machines, for example).[4]

The above paragraphs merely sample the types of specific variables relevant to studying consumer behavior. Many of these variables can go undetected because their influence is so subtle, and this can result in simple but incorrect explanations for complex behavior. Of course, the casual observer of consumers is in more danger of doing this than one who studies it in an organized fashion. We therefore must be constantly vigilant for additional variables influencing the behavior of consumers.

Variables Interact with Each Other

Not only do numerous variables affect consumers but they also frequently interact to magnify, cancel, or redirect each other's influence. For example, it seems that some advertisements may fail to persuade consumers to purchase because the announcer is not perceived as a believable source for the information.[5] In such cases, unfavorable perception of the announcer cancels out the positive effects of the message.

In addition, situations confronted by consumers can interact with other variables to modify their influence.[6] For example, one study found that buyers of tableware were influenced by different sources of information depending on whether the tableware was being purchased as a gift or for personal use.[7] Such findings demonstrate the importance of being alert to the interactive effect of variables and their influence on the behavior of consumers.

While the four factors reviewed above in no way exhaust the list of constraints on studying consumer behavior, they do provide sufficient perspective for the reader. We now direct attention to models developed to facilitate our study.

MODELING BEHAVIOR

As just mentioned, studying consumer behavior can be quite complex, especially because of the many variables involved and their tendency to interact. Models of consumer behavior have been developed in an effort to overcome these difficulties.

Definition of a Model

A *model* can be defined as a simplified representation of reality. It simplifies by incorporating only those aspects of reality that are of interest to the model builder. Other aspects that are not of interest and only add to the complexity of the situation can be ignored. Thus an architect's model of a building may not show furniture arrangements if that is not important to the building's design. Similarly, in modeling consumers we should feel free to exclude any aspects that are not relevant to their behavior. Since we have defined consumer behavior as involving a decision process, models that focus on this process will be of considerable interest to us.

Types of Models

Any given property or process can be modeled in a variety of ways. For example, we could model something by verbally describing it, by representing it with mathematical symbols, or by characterizing it with some physical process such as electrical current. The most common consumer-behavior models are verbal.

Consumer-behavior models can also be classified in terms of scope. Some are designed to represent a very specific aspect of behavior, such as consumers' repetitive purchasing of the same brand over a period of time. Others are much more comprehensive because they attempt to accommodate the great variety of consumer behavior. These comprehensive models are necessarily less detailed in nature so that they may adequately represent diverse situations.

Uses of Models

Models are devised for a variety of reasons, but the two purposes for developing most consumer models are (1) to assist in constructing a theory that guides research on consumer behavior and (2) to facilitate learning what is presently known about consumer behavior. In both cases the model serves to structure systematic and logical thinking about consumers.[8] This entails (1) identifying the relevant variables, (2) indicating their characteristics, and (3) specifying their interrelationships, that is, how they influence each other.

Developing Theory   A *theory* is an interrelated set of concepts, definitions, and propositions that presents a systematic view of some phenomenon.[9] It presents a logical viewpoint that is useful in understanding some process or activity. More specifically, a theory has four major functions: description, prediction, explanation, and control. The *descriptive* function involves characterizing the nature of something such as the steps consumers go through while deciding on a purchase. In its *predictive* role a theory is used to foretell future events, as when learning theory is used to predict which of two brand names will be the easier for consumers to remember. Theory can be used for *explanation* in order to learn the underlying *causes* of some event or activity. This would occur when we want to understand *why* a consumer regularly purchases the same brand of soup. Is it because of habit or loyalty to the brand? Although it is possible to predict events without understanding their causes, knowing why something happens greatly enhances our ability to predict its occurrence. *Control* is the ability to influence or regulate future events. This has been extremely difficult in the behavioral sciences due to the many variables involved and our lack of knowledge about them. Therefore, although marketers and others can sometimes influence consumers, we will find ample evidence that strict control of their behavior is far from reality.

A useful relationship exists between models and theories because models can assist theory development by clearly delineating the relevant variables and their influence on each other. In this way models can present a unified view of what is known about consumer behavior and help identify what remains to be explored. This allows researchers to advance knowledge by selecting the most important aspects of consumer behavior for analysis and testing.

Facilitating Learning   Our primary motivation for using models here is to serve as a learning aid. In this role, models provide a structure helpful for organizing knowledge about consumer behavior into a logical pattern that is easier to comprehend. They also remind us of the interrelationships between relevant variables. Therefore, as we concentrate on one particular variable, reference to the model will remind us to consider how it interacts with other variables to influence behavior.

MODELS OF CONSUMER BEHAVIOR

Comprehensive verbal models will be of most interest to us in our study of consumer behavior. A variety of such models exist, each taking a somewhat different view of consumers. Those chosen for presentation here are well known and represent a broad perspective. The first two represent traditional approaches to the study of consumers while a contemporary viewpoint is presented later in the chapter.

Traditional Models of Consumers

The earliest comprehensive consumer models were actually devised by economists seeking to understand the influence of consumers on economic systems. Economics involves the study of how scarce resources are allocated among unlimited wants and needs.[10] Its two major disciplines—macroeconomics and microeconomics—have each developed alternative views of consumers. Partially because they have undergone some modernization, these models still influence contemporary views of consumers.

Macroeconomic Viewpoints Macroeconomics focuses on aggregate flows in the economy—the monetary value of goods and resources, where they are directed, and how they change over time.[11] From such a focus, the macroeconomist draws conclusions about the behavior of consumers who influence these flows. Although the discipline has not generated a fully unified model of consumers, it does offer a number of insights into their behavior.

One interest centers on how consumers divide their income between consumption and savings. This deals with two economic facts of life: higher-income families spend a smaller proportion of their disposable income than lower-income families, but as economic progress raises all income levels over time these proportions do not seem to change. The *relative-income hypothesis* explains this apparent contradiction by arguing that peoples' consumption standards are mainly influenced by their peers and social groups rather than absolute income levels.[12] Therefore, the proportion of a family's income devoted to consumption is expected to change only when an income change places it in a different social setting. This will not happen when all income levels are rising at the same time.

Another macroeconomic proposition, the *permanent-income hypothesis*, explains why consumers are slow to change their consumption patterns even when their incomes do suddenly change. It proposes that consumers do not use actual income for any period to determine the amount of consumption expenditures but instead are influenced by their estimate of some average, long-term amount that can be consumed without reducing their accumulated wealth.[13] Sudden increases or decreases in income are viewed as transitory, not permanent, income and therefore are expected to have little influence on consumption activity.

A variety of other variables have been suggested by macroeconomists as influencing consumption patterns. Included are consumers' previous income experiences, accumulated liquid assets, and variations in taxes or credits. Although useful, these suggestions represent rather traditional approaches to studying consumers, stressing economic variables while tending to ignore the influence of psychological factors. However, George Katona and the University of Michigan's

Survey Research Center have pioneered studies emphasizing the importance of psychological variables. This research has resulted in two major conclusions:

1 Consumers' sentiment, future expectations, and aspirations have a profound influence on their consumption expenditures.

2 As a result of these factors, consumers strongly influence economic cycles to a greater degree than can be explained by changes in their income alone.[14]

Because of Katona and others, increased emphasis has been given to consumers' motives, expectations, and other psychological factors in explaining aggregate consumption patterns.[15] Although there still is some uncertainty about the usefulness of such variables in predicting aggregate market behavior, few would argue with the need to explore the area further in order to better understand consumers.[16]

The above paragraphs provide only a sampling of macroeconomic consumer studies. Since these efforts focus on aggregate economic activity, they can be useful in predicting total consumption patterns and the broad categories of goods that will be consumed. However, since this aggregate viewpoint can also overlook important details of consumers' behavior, there remains a need to understand how consumers choose between competing *brands*. Thus, microaspects of behavior also need to be explored.

Microeconomic Model The classical microeconomic approach, developed early in the nineteenth century, focused on the behavior of individual consumers. It involved making a series of assumptions about characteristics and goals of the "average" consumer and then developing a theory useful in explaining the workings of an economy made up of many such people. Focus was placed on the *act of purchase* which, of course, is only a portion of what we have defined as consumer behavior. Thus, microeconomists concentrated on explaining *what* consumers would purchase and in *what quantities* these purchases would be made. The tastes and preferences leading to these purchases were assumed to be given—that is, already known. Therefore, microeconomists chose to ignore *why* consumers develop a ranking of certain needs and preferences and *how* such an ordering develops.

The resulting theory was based on a number of assumptions about consumers. Primary among these were the following:

1 Consumers' wants and needs are, in total, *unlimited* and therefore cannot be fully satisfied.

2 Given a limited budget, consumers' goals are to allocate available purchasing dollars in a way that *maximizes* satisfaction of their wants and needs.

3 Consumers *independently* develop their own preferences without the influence of others, and these preferences are consistent over time.

4 Consumers have *perfect knowledge* of the utility of an item; that is, they know exactly how much satisfaction the product can give them.

5 As additional units of a given product or service are acquired, the *marginal* (additional) satisfaction provided by the *next* unit will be less than the marginal

satisfaction provided by previously purchased units. This is referred to as the *law of diminishing marginal utility*.

6 Consumers use the *price* of a good as the sole measure of the sacrifice involved in obtaining it. Price plays no other role in the purchase decision.

7 Consumers are *perfectly rational* in that, given their subjective preferences they will always act in a deliberate manner to maximize their satisfaction.

Given these assumptions, economists argue that perfectly rational consumers will always purchase the good that provides them with the highest ratio of additional benefit to cost. For any given good this benefit/cost ratio can be expressed as a ratio of its marginal utility to price (MU/P). Therefore, it can be shown that the consumer would seek to achieve a situation where the following expression holds for any number (n) of goods:

$$MU_1/P_1 = MU_2/P_2 = MU_3/P_3 = \ldots = MU_n/P_n$$

If any one product's ratio is greater than the others, the consumer can achieve greater satisfaction per dollar from it and will immediately purchase more of it. Assuming a sufficient budget, purchasing will continue until the product's declining marginal utility reduces its MU/P ratio to a position equal to all other ratios. Additional purchasing of that good will then stop.

Although the microeconomic model has had an important influence on our understanding of consumers, it provides a severely limited explanation of consumer behavior, with a major deficiency being its highly unrealistic assumptions. For example, consumers frequently strive for acceptable and not maximum levels of satisfaction.[17] In addition, consumers lack perfect knowledge regarding products, and they often influence each other's preferences.[18] Also, they appear to use many variables in addition to price to assess a product's cost and may frequently use price as a measure of product quality as well as cost.[19] Finally, consumers simply do not appear to be perfectly rational in all their purchase decisions. These unrealistic assumptions may not have hindered the usefulness of this model in explaining the behavior of an entire economic system, but they certainly are not useful in understanding how actual consumers behave in specific purchase situations of concern to marketers and others.

An additional shortcoming of the microeconomic scheme occurs as a result of its focus on the specific act of purchase. We have argued that much consumer behavior occurs before and after this act. Considerable decision making and search for information can precede it, and purchase evaluation as well as additional purchases can follow it. Since the model does not address these activities, we cannot accept it as a comprehensive representation of consumer behavior.

Even with its limitations, the microeconomic model has been useful. It provides a perspective from which to better appreciate contemporary models of consumer behavior. In addition, we should now be more sensitive to the critical way in which the usefulness of a consumer model depends on its assumptions, and we should be ready to evaluate other models in terms of their dependence on stated or implied assumptions. Finally, because economists have modernized certain aspects of the microeconomic model, it still influences contemporary thinking regarding consumer behavior.

Contemporary Consumer Models

As the study of consumers evolved into a distinct discipline, newer approaches were offered to describe and explain their behavior. These contemporary views are quite different from previous models because of their concentration on the *decision process* and other cognitive (mental) activities that consumers engage in. Therefore, contrary to economic models, emphasis is placed on the cognitive aspects of behavior that consumers engage in before, during, and after the purchase.

A second and related distinguishing characteristic of contemporary models is their extensive borrowing from material developed in the behavioral sciences. In fact, many of the variables discussed were originally identified in the fields of psychology and sociology.[20] Explanations of how these variables influence consumer behavior have also been adapted from the behavioral sciences.

Another unique aspect of recent modeling efforts is their format, which generally portrays consumers' decision processes and actions in flowchart fashion as well as verbally. This provides a concrete structure which graphically portrays the sequence of activities involved in purchase decisions.

A large number of contemporary consumer models have been developed, varying considerably in terms of their sophistication, precision, and scope. However, because space limits what can be presented here, only one will be discussed. This model represents the most widely quoted comprehensive view of consumer behavior.

Engel-Blackwell Model The Engel-Blackwell model is graphically presented in Figures 2-4 and 2-5.[21] This is the latest refinement to a highly respected viewpoint of consumer behavior first offered in 1968 by Engel, Kollat, and Blackwell.[22] In its present form, the model contains five components: (1) input stimuli, (2) information processing, (3) a decision process, (4) decision-process variables, and (5) external influences. The form of these components and how they relate to each other varies depending on the degree of involvement that the consumer is experiencing in a given purchase situation.

The term "involvement" describes the personal relevance or importance that a consumer perceives in a given purchase situation. Under conditions of high involvement, as might occur when purchasing a new car, the consumer perceives considerable importance in the purchase situation and is likely to engage in extensive (involved) problem-solving behavior. This is usually characterized by a serious effort at information search and an intensive evaluation of alternatives. Low-involvement situations occur when the consumer perceives little personal relevance or importance to a purchase. In such cases, the purchase is likely to be made on the basis of existing levels of information and with only modest amounts of deliberation. To account for differences due to high- and low-involvement conditions, Engel and Blackwell have offered two versions of their model.

HIGH-INVOLVEMENT VERSION The complete model in its high-involvement version is shown in Figure 2-4. The core of this version is the decision-process component which includes five basic stages: (1) problem recognition, (2) information search, (3) alternative evaluation, (4) choice, and (5) outcomes. These stages are seen as occurring in the order shown in the model. Although the decision-process component serves as a basic core, the model has been termed *mul-*

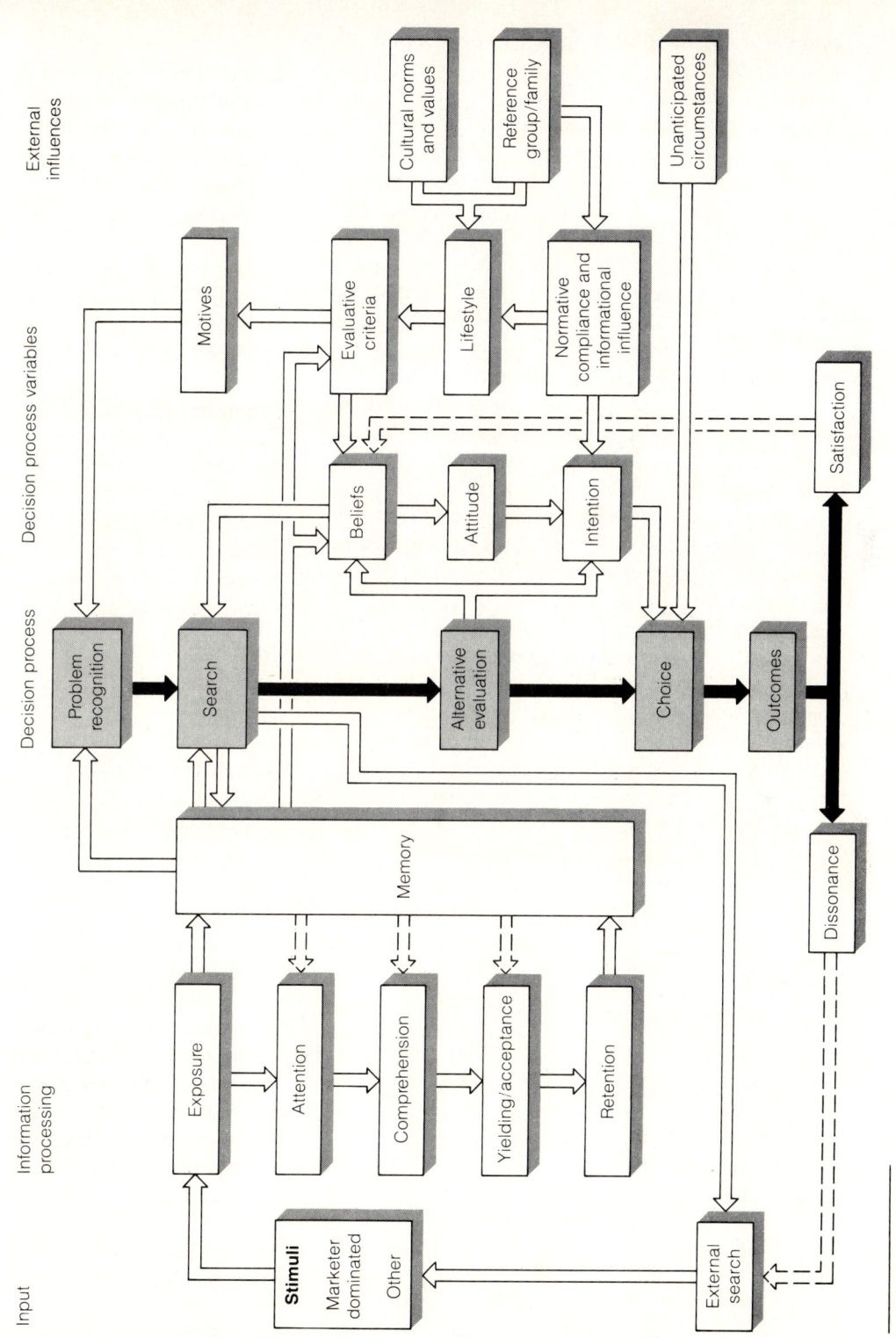

FIGURE 2-4

The complete Engel-Blackwell model for high-involvement situations. (*Source: Consumer Behavior*, 4th ed., by James Engel and Roger Blackwell, p. 500. Copyright © 1982 by CBS College Publishing. Reprinted by permission of CBS College Publishing.)

35

timediational because it focuses considerable attention on the many variables which mediate or influence this decision process. These variables are shown in the four other components of the model. Arrows in the model depict major directions of influence or relationships occurring between variables or processes. For example, in the input component we see that stimuli feed into the exposure step of information processing. The following discussion characterizes the role and nature of these variables.

Problem recognition occurs when the consumer is activated by awareness of a difference between his or her actual state of affairs and his or her concept of the ideal situation. This can occur through internal activation of a motive such as hunger, or by confronting some external stimulus such as an advertisement. In either case, however, action occurs only when the consumer perceives a sufficiently large discrepency between the actual and ideal states.

Given that the consumer is aroused to action, the next stage is to undertake an *information search*. The first step of this activity involves a quick and largely unconscious review of memory for stored information and experiences regarding the problem. This information is in the form of beliefs and attitudes which have influenced the consumer's preferences toward brands. Often such review leads to recognizing a strong brand preference, and *routine purchase action* occurs. That is, many of the model's steps will be passed through quickly because a satisfactory solution to the purchase problem has already been identified. However, if an internal search does not provide sufficient information about products, or how to evaluate them, the consumer will engage in an external information search and more extensive problem-solving behavior. This results in exposure to a variety of informational inputs called *stimuli,* which can arise from personal sources (such as friends and salespeople) as well as from published or mass-media sources. In either case, these sources can be viewed either as being dominated by firms interested in selling goods (marketer dominated) or as being general in nature and not controlled by the marketer (such as government-regulated information tags on products). The extent of external search will be influenced by the consumer's perception of the costs versus benefits of such activity.

Any informational inputs are subjected to *information processing* activities which the consumer uses to derive meaning from stimuli. The first step in processing involves *exposure* to such stimuli. Exposure can happen on an involuntary basis, such as when one sees a billboard next to a highway, or through the active search for information. After exposure, stimuli must capture the consumer's conscious *attention* to significantly influence extensive problem solving. The attention stage is highly selective since it tends to ignore most stimuli and admit only those that the individual believes are important. The *comprehension* stage then involves deriving meaning from information that has been attended to and holding this meaning in what is termed short-term memory where it can be retained briefly to allow further processing.

The final two steps of information processing are related to the third stage of the decision process—alternative evaluation. The *alternative evaluation* stage involves comparing information about alternative brands gained through the search process to *evaluative criteria* which are product-judging standards that have been stored in permanent memory. The first information processing step associated with this evaluation task is termed yielding/acceptance. *Yielding/acceptance* occurs when information is compared to evaluative criteria and, as a result, existing beliefs held in permanent memory are either reinforced or changed. Whether the information tends to reinforce or to change existing beliefs is a function of how consistent it is with the beliefs and the degree to which the consumer generates supportive or negative thoughts about the information being received. In either case, yielding/acceptance results in the *retention* of information in permanent memory, while a lack of yielding/acceptance results in the loss of such information.

Changes in the consumer's beliefs will modify attitudes toward the act of purchasing a brand in question. An *attitude* is viewed as the positive or negative evaluation of the consequences of purchasing and using the brand. Favorable attitudes will, in turn, lead to formation of a *purchase intention*—the consumer's feelings about the likelihood that she or he will purchase the brand. As the model shows, another influence on purchase intention is *normative compliance,* which is the extent that the consumer is influenced to conform to expectations of other important people such as those in a group or family members.

The model shows that although *choice* usually follows strong positive purchase intentions, *unanticipated circumstances,* such as a drop in income, can temporarily or permanently serve as a barrier to purchase. If no barrier is encountered, however, a purchase process is engaged in. This involves a series of selections including the type of retail outlet as well as the specific brand or service to use.

The consumer's choices lead to various *outcomes.* One such outcome is satisfaction (or dissatisfaction) as a result of direct experience in using the brand. The experiences will feed back into beliefs about the brand. A second outcome is *dissonance,* which is post-decision doubt about the merits of a purchase when compared to unchosen alternatives. This can generate a heightened desire for information that supports the choice. As the model demonstrates, such information will be in the form of new inputs which will be processed through external search as previously described.

The model also shows that several external influences and other factors can significantly affect the consumer's decision process. *Cultural norms and values* certainly can affect how the consumer judges the worth of a variety of products. This can occur through their influence on *lifestyle*—the unique pattern of living and methods of behaving that a consumer adopts. As the model shows, a consumer's lifestyle will influence the evaluative criteria used to judge products. A second set of external factors affecting a consumer's behavior work through *reference group* and *family* members. The model shows that these factors affect the consumer through *informational and normative compliance* influence attempts which can affect intentions to purchase. These influences can range from a friend making a subtle, uncomplimentary comment about a shirt to the blatant scolding of a mother about the tattered condition of one's clothes.

LOW-INVOLVEMENT VERSION   The above review provides a very brief description of the rather complicated series of activities a consumer can engage in when using extensive problem-solving behavior under high-involvement conditions. Engel and Blackwell point out, however, that this model is not suited to a second situation which probably describes the majority of purchase cases: low-involvement decision making in which the consumer perceives little personal importance to the purchase, as in the selection of a pair of shoelaces. Significant consequences of low-involvement situations are the changes that they foster in the consumer's decision process. Figure 2-5 focuses on aspects of the Engel-Blackwell model that change when low involvement is operating.

Problem recognition still exists under low-involvement conditions, but its nature has changed significantly. If a consumer is uninterested in a situation, advertisements for brands of the product involved are unlikely to generate problem recognition within her. Instead, she will probably react to an ad by storing some of its facts, such as the brand name, away for future reference. Most probably, problem recognition will not occur until a shopping trip in which the consumer sees the advertised brand on display in a retail store.

A motivated *external search* for information is absent from the situation shown in the low-involvement model. In a situation of such little concern to the consumer, the perceived costs will outweigh the expected benefits of such an activity. In addition, the consumer will employ only a limited number of *evaluative criteria.* These also will probably not be rigorous standards of judgement.

As we saw, in high-involvement situations *choice* is the result of changes (yielding/acceptance) in beliefs, attitudes, and intentions generated from information search and an extensive alternative evaluation process. However, we notice that in the low-involvement model, choice actually occurs *before* alternative evaluation! Without searching for any additional information, the consumer selects a brand on the basis of very limited knowledge, purchases it, and then evaluates it. Yielding/acceptance does not occur because a choice is made before the alternative evaluation. However, an evaluation does occur during use of the brand. Consequently, beliefs, attitudes, and intentions are the *outcomes* of choice, and not its causes. Of course, if a satisfactory evaluation results from the purchase, these outcomes can have a positive influence on future purchases.

We can see from this brief overview that the low-involvement model proposed by Engel and Blackwell is not just a simplification of their high-involvement model. Instead, the way in which consumers operate in low-involvement situations is seen to be quite different from the way they operate in high-involvement situations. In future chapters it will be seen that high-involvement consumer behavior has been studied to a much greater degree than its low-involvement counterpart.

FIGURE 2-5

A portion of the Engel-Blackwell model for low-involvement situations. (*Source: Consumer Behavior,* 4th ed., by James Engel and Roger Blackwell, p. 38. Copyright © 1982 by CBS College Publishing. Reprinted by permission of CBS College Publishing.)

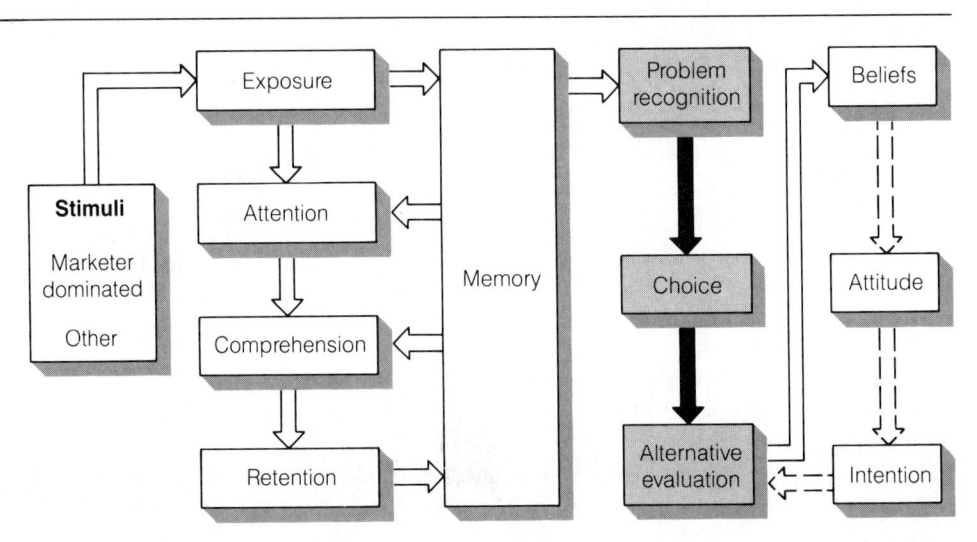

However, because low-involvement situations seem to be so prevalent in the marketplace, much more needs to be understood in this area.

Model Evaluation   Advantages of the Engel-Blackwell model include its consideration of the many variables influencing consumers, its focus on levels of consumer involvement, and its emphasis on the decision-making process regarding purchases. Also, the flow of the model is quite flexible. For example, the authors recognize that in numerous purchase decisions many of the detailed steps are passed through very quickly or are bypassed, as in the case of routine purchase behavior. Factors contributing to the model's clarity and flexibility, however, also generate some of its limitations. The primary drawback appears to be a vagueness regarding the role of some variables. For example, the influence of environmental variables is noted, but their role in affecting behavior is not well specified. The role of motives in influencing behavior is also quite vague. In addition, the model has been criticized as being somewhat mechanistic in its treatment of the decision process. However, despite these limitations, it has been updated regularly to accomodate new evidence about the behavior of consumers. Because of this, the model has withstood the test of time quite well since its first introduction in 1968, and it continues to provide a very comprehensive framework for understanding the many facets of consumer behavior.

A SIMPLIFIED FRAMEWORK

Many insights can be derived from the Engel-Blackwell model as well as from other contemporary views of consumers. These include:

1   Consumer behavior can best be viewed as an ongoing process in which the act of purchase represents only one stage.

2   Other aspects of behavior involve cognitive activity, which includes a decision process, and overt physical actions. All of these aspects of behavior can occur before, during, or after the act of purchase.

3   The decision process can be quite extensive and time-consuming or very automatic and short in duration.

4   The level of consumer involvement is one variable influencing the amount of energy devoted to the decision process and to other activities.

5   Many variables, both internal and external to consumers, can influence consumer behavior. Many of these variables also interact with each other to form new or modified influences.

6   Because many of the variables influencing consumers are unobservable, the process of inference has been used to determine their existence and nature.

7   Because the study of consumers is still young, we should expect to find few concrete laws that explain their behavior. Instead, considerable diversity of opinion exists regarding many consumer behavior aspects.

A strength of most contemporary models is the intricate view they give of consumers. However, for those embarking on an initial study of the topic, these perspectives may present an information overload. That is, their detailed views may be too complex for such an early stage of study. A strategy for handling this problem is to concentrate on the major aspects of behavior and show, on a more general level, how such variables may interact to affect consumers.

We have adopted such a simplified approach to guide our discussion, and a diagram of the result is presented in Figure 2-6. The first important point regarding this framework is that *it is not offered as a model of consumer behavior*. It is merely an organized schematic of the major variables or processes that have been identified as the most important general influences on consumer behavior. It also represents an outline for Parts Three through Five of this text. As the reader's study progresses, the framework may be outgrown because of its simplicity. When this occurs, the detail provided by a more comprehensive model may serve as a useful outline for further analysis.

Reference to Figure 2-6 reveals that it is made up of three major sections: (1) external variables influencing behavior, (2) individual determinants of behavior,

FIGURE 2-6

A simplified framework for studying consumer behavior.

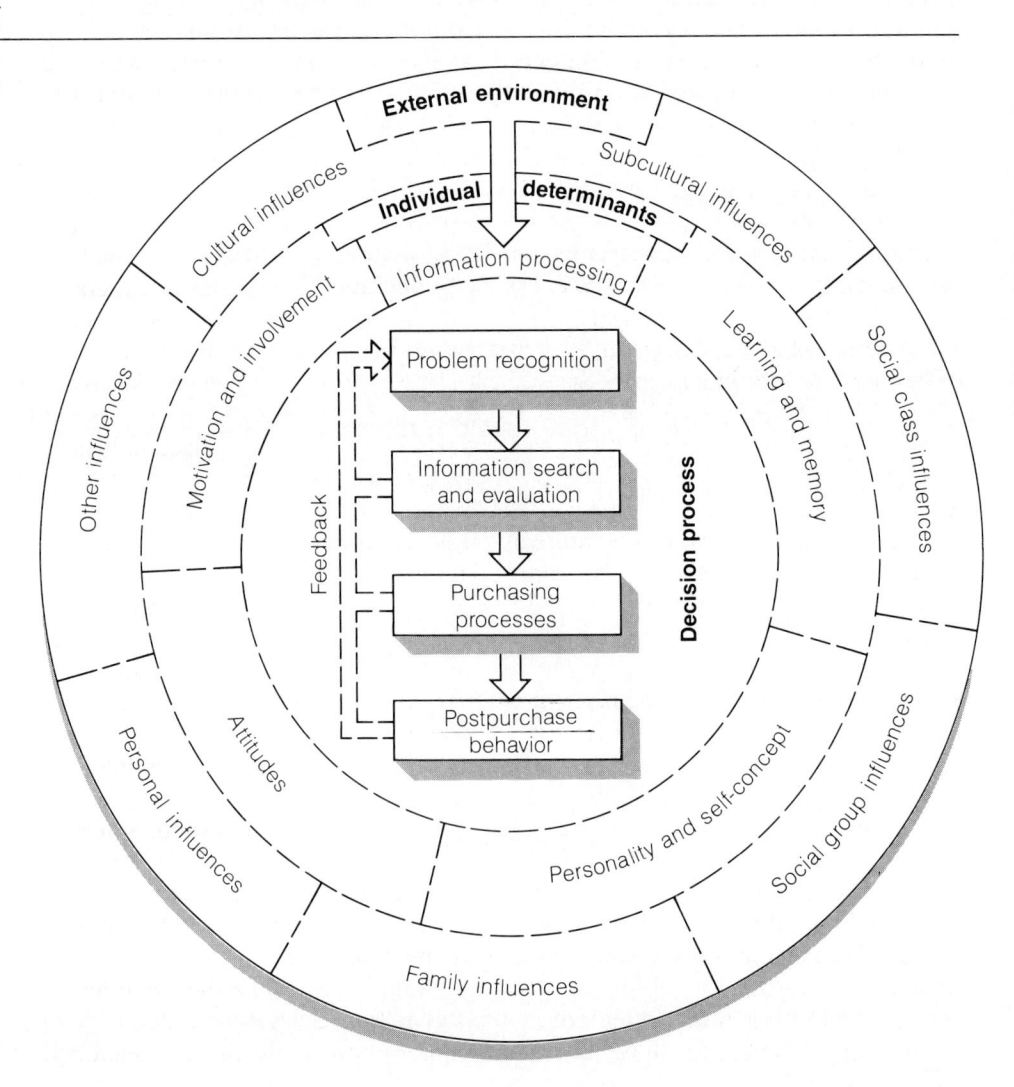

and (3) the consumer's decision process. These major sections are treated in Parts Three through Five, respectively, of the text.

The external environment depicted in the outer circle is made up of six specific influences and one catch-all grouping for all other factors. The six specific influences are culture, subcultures, social class, social groups, the family, and personal influences. The opened partitions denote the influence of these variables on individual determinants and on each other. These environmental influences are discussed in Part Three of the text.

The concept of culture has been characterized as "that complex whole that includes knowledge, belief, art, morals, law, custom, and any other capabilities and habits acquired by man as a member of society."[23] As such, it provides a basis for many of our values, beliefs, and actions as consumers. For example, the emphasis people in our society place on time and punctuality is unique and forms the basis for positive consumer reactions to such market offerings as fast-food franchises, express checkout lanes at supermarkets, and quartz watches. This topic and its influence on consumers is discussed in Chapter 6.

Subcultures are treated in Chapter 7. Here the emphasis is on segments of a given culture that have values, customs, traditions, and other ways of behaving that are unique and that distinguish them from others sharing the same cultural heritage. These aspects of uniqueness can have significant implications for the understanding of consumers and the development of successful marketing strategies. Subcultures distinguished on the basis of age and ethnic dimensions will receive particular attention.

The term "social stratification" refers to the process by which people in a society rank one another into different social positions. The result is a hierarchy often referred to as a set of social classes. People within a given social class tend to share common beliefs, values, and methods of behaving. They also tend to associate more closely with one another than with people from different social classes. The values, wants, and interactions that develop in these distinct groupings tend to have significant influences on consumers. They affect such basic factors as membership in a group, choice of neighborhoods, appreciation of certain styles, and choice of places to shop. Social class and its influence is discussed in Chapter 8.

A social group can be viewed as a collection of people who have a sense of relatedness resulting from some form of interaction with one another.[24] These groups can have many functions. One that is particularly important from a consumer behavior perspective is the influence that group members can have on the individual. That is, the group can serve to persuade and guide the individual's values and behavior. The common interest that college students show in jeans and music serves as an illustration. Another interesting aspect of social groups is their role in providing consumers with various forms of information which can influence subsequent behavior. These topics are treated in Chapter 9.

The family is a special form of social group that is distinguished, at least in part, by numerous and strong face-to-face interactions among its members. The influence of different family members on purchase decisions is one area of interest in the field of consumer behavior. In some cases, decisions are made by one individual with little influence from other family members. In other cases, the interaction is so strong it is said to actually yield a joint decision rather than just an influence of one member on another. Of course, the nature and degree of influence in these decision-making patterns are quite important to marketers attempting to inform and persuade consumers regarding their offerings. Another aspect of family influence on consumer behavior is the way in which the stage of a family's life cycle (newly married, childhood years, and so on) influences the need for products and services. In a similar vein, the changing patterns of family and household structures, including families with working wives and those made up solely of singles, has significant implications for consumer behavior. These and related topics are considered in Chapter 10.

The process of personal influence, which can be described as the effects on an individual resulting from communications with others, has long been of interest to marketers. Interest in this subject is strong because personal influence has an important effect on the amount and type of information that consumers obtain about products. It is also considered to be a significant force acting on a consumer's values, attitudes, brand evaluations, and interest in a product. In fact, personal influence is an important function of opinion leaders. These opinion leaders are people that others look to for advice, opinions, and suggestions regarding purchase decisions. Personal influence also strongly affects the process of diffusion by which new product and service innovations spread in the market place. Personal influence, diffusion of innovations, and other closely related topics are examined in Chapter 11.

The last category of environmental influences portrayed in Figure 2-6 is labeled "other influences." This general category encompasses influences on consumers that are not specifically treated in chapters dealing with the topics just reviewed. An example might be the effects of media that are not incorporated into one of the other categories. Many of these other influences, including physical surroundings, the interpersonal setting, national events, and the consumer's available cash, have been summarized by the term *situational variables*. The influence of these situational variables is treated at a number of points in later chapters.

Major individual determinants of consumer behavior are portrayed in the middle portion of Figure 2-6. These variables influence how the consumer proceeds through a decision process regarding products and services. The decision process itself is shown in the center of the figure. An arrow leading from the external environment into individual determinants demonstrates that environmental stimuli do not directly influence consumers. Instead, the stimuli are modified by internal influences such as learning, attitudes, and motives. The opened circle between the decision process and these variables denotes the great influence they have on the decision process. The opened partitions between the individual determinants themselves represent the influence they have on each other.

Figure 2-6 shows the five major groups of individual determinants to be discussed further in Part Four of the text: motivation and involvement, information processing, learning and memory, personality and self-concept, and attitudes. Motives are internal factors that energize behavior and provide guidance to direct the activated behavior. As we saw in the discussion of the Engel-Blackwell model, involvement describes the personal relevance or importance that the consumer perceives in a given situation. High involvement will lead to a motivated state. Various types of involvement and motive situations, factors that influence them, and their influence on the behavior of consumers are subjects treated in Chapter 12.

The term "information processing" refers to the activities that consumers engage in when acquiring, integrating, and evaluating information. These activities involve actively seeking information or passively receiving it, attending to only certain parts of the information, integrating that which has been attended with information from other sources, and evaluating the information for the purpose of making decisions. These activities are varied and occur at all stages of the decision process. They also strongly involve some individual factors including motivation, learning, and attitudes. Chapter 13 on information processing introduces these issues and also discusses several marketing strategy areas in which an understanding of the process can be of considerable benefit to the marketer. However, because of their importance, treatment of these issues is not reserved to just one chapter or section of this text. Several chapters in Part Four elaborate further on the subject. Additional discussion is also contained in Part Five where the critical role that information processing plays in the consumer's decision process is examined.

The important role of learning and memory is discussed in Chapter 14. What consumers learn, how they learn, and what factors govern the retention of learned material in memory are all issues of considerable importance for understanding consumers. Not only do consumers acquire and remember product names and characteristics, but they also learn standards for judging products, places to shop, problem-solving abilities, behavior patterns, and tastes. Such learned material stored in memory significantly influences how consumers react to each situation that they confront.

Personality and self-concept are forces providing the consumer with a central theme. That is, they provide a structure for the individual so that a consistent pattern of behavior can be developed. Several major personality theories are examined for their usefulness in understanding consumers. Chapter 15 then discusses the importance of self-concept in understanding consumer behavior. How the self-concept develops, its role in influencing purchase decisions, and the practical relevance of the subject to the marketer are reviewed.

The topics of attitude and attitude change are examined in Chapters 16 and 17, respectively. Attitudes guide our basic orientation toward objects, people, and events. As such, attitudes strongly influence how consumers will act and react to products and services, and how they will respond to communications marketers develop to convince them to purchase their products. After reviewing the nature and function of attitudes, attention in Chapter 16 is turned to how attitudes are formed and how they are related to purchase behavior. Chapter 17 then discusses attitude change strategies, marketing communications, and how various aspects of a message, its source, and characteristics of the consumer himself can have a significant effect in modifying the consumer's attitudes.

The inner portion of Figure 2-6 details the consumer decision process regarding products and services. The major steps in this process are shown as problem recognition, information search and evaluation, purchasing processes, and post-purchase behavior.[25] Problem recognition occurs when the consumer recognizes a need and has a desire to achieve a certain state of affairs. Many factors, both internal and external to the consumer, affect this process. Some of these, such as advertisements, are within the control of the marketer, while others are not. However, the need for understanding both sets of factors is equally important.

Once a problem has been recognized and there are no constraints preventing further behavior, the consumer will proceed to search for information relevant to the problem. This can involve the consumer in a memory scan to review his or her existing store of information about the problem. It also can entail a search for additional information in the external environment. The sources of information which are sought or encountered in this stage are of significant interest to marketers and others concerned with the behavior of consumers. After the information is obtained it also must be evaluated. Therefore, the manner in which consumers evaluate or process this information is of considerable interest.

The purchasing process occurs next. Here, factors involved in the final selection of products, services, brands, and retail outlets are considered. Following the purchase, consumers evaluate their choices, consider the appropriateness of their decisions, and try to assess the degree of their satisfaction with the product or service purchased. These aspects of behavior attract our attention because, as Figure 2-6 shows, they provide feedback which can affect problem recognition and subsequent purchase of similar or alternative products and services. The feedback to problem recognition resulting from information search and evaluation and from purchasing processes is also shown in the figure. This suggests that stages of the decision process following problem recognition can have an impact on the consumer's recognition or reassessment of problems. Part Five elaborates on these and other aspects of consumers' decision processes.

The above review provides a very general synopsis of most of the text. However, two topics of special interest have not been mentioned in this review. The first topic is the activity of consumer research and how some specific research approaches and techniques are employed to discover more about consumers. The second topic focuses on the concept of market segmentation, its potential benefits and costs to the marketer, and how some alternatives can be useful in understanding and selecting appropriate target markets from the aggregate consumer market. We will examine these two subjects before discussing environmental influences on consumers.

SUMMARY

The purpose of this chapter is to establish a foundation for an organized study of consumer behavior. First, observable stimulus and response variables were discussed. Unobservable responses and intervening variables were then treated. Both the black-box approach to inference and special measuring techniques were suggested as methods of dealing with these situations.

After addressing some of the problems of studying consumers, the goals and methods of modeling their behavior were discussed. The organizing structure provided by such models was seen as a major benefit. Following this, the traditional macroeconomic and microeconomic views of consumer behavior were critically reviewed.

A model proposed by Engel and Blackwell was then offered as a representative of contemporary behavioral science–oriented models. An overview of this scheme provided many insights into consumer behavior, including consideration of the large number of variables involved and their interactive effects. The flow of consumers' decision making over time was also graphically portrayed.

The level of complexity provided by such contemporary views may result in an overload of information for the beginning student. For this reason, a highly simplified schematic of the major variables influencing consumers was offered as a structure for this book.

DISCUSSION TOPICS

1 What is a model? How can our study of consumer behavior benefit from using models?

2 Characterize the process of inference and indicate its importance to understanding consumer behavior.

3 A hard-nosed marketing manager was heard to remark: "All of this talk about consumers' decision process still just boils down to the same old fact—it's what the consumer buys, and how much of it, that's really important to the practicing marketer." What is your response?

4 Discuss the microeconomic model, indicating its contributions and limitations for the marketer in understanding consumer behavior.

5 What major contributions do contemporary models of consumer behavior make compared to traditional models?

6 How might producers of stereo equipment use the Engel-Blackwell model to understand better the consumers of their products? How might producers of chewing gum do the same?

7 Relate one or your experiences where postpurchase outcomes significantly influenced your future purchase behavior.

NOTES

[1] For a review of other approaches see Robert L. Karen, *An Introduction to Behavior Theory and Its Applications,* Harper & Row, New York, 1974, pp. 8–18.
[2] Van Court Hare, Jr., *Systems Analysis: A Diagnostic Approach,* Harcourt, Brace & World, New York, 1967, p. 30.
[3] Suggested by Kurt Lewin as presented in Calvin S. Hall and Gardner Lindzey, *Theories of Personality,* Wiley, New York, 1957, pp. 206–223.
[4] George Katona, *The Powerful Consumer,* McGraw-Hill, New York, 1960.
[5] See E. Aronson and B. Golden, "The Effect of Relevant and Irrelevant Aspects of Communicator Credibility on Opinion Change," *Journal of Personality,* 30:135–146, for some factors affecting credibility.
[6] See Russell W. Belk, "Situational Variables and Consumer Behavior," *Journal of Consumer Research,* 2:157–164, December 1975.
[7] K. Grønhaug, "Buying Situation and Buyer's Information Behavior," *European Marketing Research Review,* 7:33–48, September 1972.
[8] Rom J. Markin, Jr., *Consumer Behavior: A Cognitive Orientation,* Macmillan, New York, 1974, p. 79.
[9] Fred N. Kerlinger, *Behavioral Research: A Conceptual Approach,* Holt, New York, 1979, p. 64.
[10] Michael J. Brennan, *Theory of Economic Statics,* Prentice-Hall, Englewood Cliffs, N.J., 1965, p. 4.
[11] Richard H. Leftwich, *The Price System and Resource Allocation,* 3d ed., Holt, New York, 1966, p. 8.
[12] J. S. Duesenberry, *Income, Saving, and the Theory of Consumer Behavior,* Harvard, Cambridge, Mass., 1949.
[13] Milton Friedman, *A Theory of the Consumption Function,* Princeton, Princeton, N.J., 1957, and J. William Levedahl, "The Impact of Permanent and Transitory Income on Household Automobile Expenditures," *Journal of Consumer Research,* 7:55–66, June 1980.
[14] George Katona, *Psychological Economics,* Elsevier, New York, 1975, p. 11.
[15] Lee Smith, "The Economist Who Polls Consumers," *Dunn's Review,* 107;68–69+, April 1976.
[16] See John McNeil, "Federal Programs to Measure Consumer Purchase Expectations, 1946–1973: A Post-Mortem," *Journal of Consumer Research,* 1:1–10, December 1974.
[17] See James G. March and Herbert A. Simon, *Organizations,* Wiley, New York, 1958 for evidence of this in executive behavior.
[18] Thomas S. Robertson, *Innovative Behavior and Communication,* Holt, New York, 1971.
[19] Kent B. Monroe and Susan M. Petroshius, "Buyers' Perceptions of Price: An Update of the Evidence," in Harold H. Kassarjian and Thomas S. Robertson (eds.), *Perspectives in Consumer Behavior,* 3d ed., Scott Foresman, Glenview, Ill., 1981, pp. 43–55.
[20] For reviews of a number of consumer behavior models heavily based on behavioral science contribu-

tions see Francesco M. Nicosia and Yoram Wind, *Behavioral Models for Market Analysis: Foundations for Marketing Action,* Dryden, Hinsdale, Ill., 1977; Gerald Zaltman and Melanie Wallendorf, *Consumer Behavior: Basic Findings and Management Implications,* John Wiley & Sons, New York, 1979, pp. 515–542; Charles D. Schewe, "Selected Social Psychological Models for Analyzing Buyers," *Journal of Marketing,* **37**:31–39, July 1973; and Philip Kotler, "Behavioral Models for Analyzing Buyers," *Journal of Marketing,* **29**:37–45, October 1965.

[21] This review is based on James F. Engel and Roger D. Blackwell, *Consumer Behavior,* 4th ed., The Dryden Press, Hinsdale, Ill., 1982, pp. 23–39.

[22] James F. Engel, David T. Kollat, and Roger D. Blackwell, *Consumer Behavior,* Holt, Rinehart and Winston, New York, 1968.

[23] Edward B. Tylor, *Primitive Culture,* Murray, London, 1891, p. 1.

[24] David Dressler and Donald Carns, *Sociology: The Study of Human Interaction,* Knopf, New York, 1973, p. 259.

[25] These steps are based on a more detailed series of activities proposed in Engel and Blackwell, *Consumer Behavior.*

CASES FOR PART ONE

CASE 1-1
THE GREAT ATLANTIC & PACIFIC TEA COMPANY[1]

For decades The Great Atlantic and Pacific Tea Company (A&P) had dominated the U.S. food and grocery market. However, with its size had come increasing managerial inefficiency and an inability to respond to demands of a changing market. A very crucial error was made in the 1950s when A&P failed to follow customers in their move to the suburbs. The result, which plagued the supermarket chain into the 1980s, was a large number of small and inefficient stores serving declining urban neighborhoods.

In 1971, William J. Kane took over as chairman and chief executive officer of A&P. This was a time when company sales had leveled off and profits were declining. In an effort to overcome this slide, Kane ordered the conversion of thousands of regular A&P units to "WEO" (Where Economy Originates) supermarkets, which were described as superduper discount stores.

The average WEO store looked much the same as an old A&P and was about the same size (which was rather small by industry standards). The big difference between WEOs and the company's conventional units was lower prices on 90 percent of the merchandise and a reduction in the variety of products offered from an average of 11,000 items to as few as 8000.

Chairman Kane summed up the company's philosophy regarding this move as a "tonnage recovery program," which emphasized volume business. He hoped to attract many former customers by employing low prices, Unfortunately, food costs began to skyrocket about the same time that WEO was instituted. The pressure caused by price cuts was too much for the company to bear during this period. Therefore, prices were increased and the resulting market response was influential in causing further deterioration of the food giant. In 1973, the chain lost its number 1 market position to Safeway.

Jonathan Scott took over Kane's position in 1975. Recognizing that the chain had too many deteriorating stores in declining urban neighborhoods, Scott embarked on am ambitious program to close more than 1200 unprofitable units. His purge was focused on a store-by-store basis to eliminate the most unprofitable locations. Unfortunately, hindsight revealed that what was also needed was an entire withdrawal from certain geographic areas to achieve efficiencies of operation.

In an effort to regain market position, Scott responded by introducing the ill-fated "Price and Pride" advertising program. This campaign focused on telling A&P employees and consumers that the company had made a rebound and was concentrating on delivering quality products in attractive stores at low prices. It was a spirit-building campaign. Modern stores with pleasing, wide aisles served as a backdrop for the ads. The Price and Pride campaign was quite successful in luring consumers back to A&P. Unfortunately, shoppers' expectations were built on the attractive scenes shown in advertisements, and many were disappointed when they returned because most stores had not really been dramatically changed. As a consequence, consumers again left in substantial numbers to shop at competing stores.

During the mid-1970s, an ambitious program was undertaken to build many new and modern A&P stores and to remodel others. Regrettably, action fell behind plans. For example, in 1977 when seventy new stores were planned, only forty-six were opened due to an inability to manage the program. Remodeling also fell far behind schedule.

The Price and Pride program was finally abandoned in January 1978. Even before this occurred, Scott began to look in earnest for new ways to get the slow-moving giant heading in the right direction again. One result was that a new promotional theme was adopted: "You'll Do Better at A&P." Along with this, three major steps were taken. First, "action prices" were instituted to pass manufacturer's specials directly on to consumers in the form of lower prices. Second, generic products were offered in many stores. These plainly labeled packages were placed in "economy cases" located in special parts of the store. The result was that for some products, customers could choose between national brands, A&P private labels, and generics. Third, trading stamps were instituted in many

---

[1] This case was prepared by Lynelle Reney and the authors based on information in "A&P's Ploy: Cutting Prices to Turn a Profit," *Business Week*, May 20, 1972, p. 76; "Price and Pride," *Forbes*, October 29, 1979, pp. 98–100; Peter W. Bernstein, "A&P Calls in a Reliever," *Fortune*, June 2, 1980, pp. 66–67; and Fran R. Schumer, "Embattled A&P: New Management Fights to Revive the Old Chain," *Barron's*, January 25, 1982, pp. 4–5.

areas. Although some of these measures may have been helpful in slowing the chain's decline, they certainly were not sufficient as a long-run turnaround solution.

In 1979, the diminishing giant fell to third position in the supermarket industry and showed signs of serious economic problems (Table 1 shows financial results from 1971 to 1980). During that year, the Tengelman Group, which owns a large supermarket chain in West Germany, was able to acquire controlling interest in A&P for an attractive price. James Wood was brought in to replace Scott, and one of the first major moves was to stop closing stores. Instead, a number of units were converted into Plus stores which were "limited assortment" units stocking 1000 essential products—far less than the 12,000 products found in a general supermarket. The stores were also "no frill" in design. Goods were kept in their cartons, as opposed to being placed on attractive shelves, and shoppers had to purchase their own papers bags. The emphasis was on offering bare-bone services for low prices. However, perhaps because shoppers could not fulfill all of their shopping needs at Plus stores, and because prices were not really drastically lower than their competitors, the Plus stores proved unsuccessful as A&P entered the 1980s.

Questions

1 Does it seem that A&P has tended to favor any particular model or models of consumer behavior? What appears to be the degree of success that has resulted?

2 Evaluate the relevance of consumer-behavior knowledge to developing a marketing plan for A&P.

3 What additional information about consumers would you like to have before designing such a marketing plan? How might such information be acquired?

4 Trace the development of A&P's operations from 1979 to present based on library research.

CASE 1-2
SPENCER'S TIRE PURCHASE

The Harpins are a two-car family living in a small New England town. Since Spencer uses the old Volvo for his "work car" he rarely drives the family Malibu. However, he did take it on a trip downtown one Saturday morning so that he could listen to the stereo on his drive. It was then that he noticed the steering wheel had a slight "shimmy" to it. On his return home, Spencer mentioned this to his wife Kathy and asked her if she also had noticed it. She said yes, that the car had just started doing it the last couple of weeks. Spencer thought that it probably would be good to have the front end checked out, but since he rarely drives the Malibu, he forgot about doing it.

A few weeks later, Kathy told Spencer that the wheel shimmy had become worse. He took the car for a short trip to assess the situation, and was shocked by the extent of movement in the steering wheel. The following Saturday, Spencer left the car off at a local service station so that they could check out the problem. When he returned for the car, the mechanic on duty, a young man in his late teens or early twenties, told Spencer that his front tires were very bad and his rear tires would also soon need replacement. He said that the steel-belted front tires were so worn on one edge that their belts were actually showing through what little rubber remained. His conclusion was that the car was probably out of alignment and this caused the uneven tire wear. Spencer asked him why that would make the steering wheel shimmy. The mechanic replied that he

TABLE 1

FINANCIAL PERFORMANCE OF A&P

Fiscal Year	Sales in Millions	Net Income (Loss) in Millions
1971	5,509	15
1972	6,369	(51)
1973	6,748	12
1974	6,875	(157)
1975	6,538	4
1976	7,236	24
1977	7,289	3*
1978	7,470	(52)
1979	6,684	(4)
1980	6,990	(43)

*After extraordinary item.
Source: *Moody's Industrial Manual* and *Barron's,* January 25, 1982, p. 5.

didn't know for sure, but he noted that the car had radials and sometimes when radials get really worn down, their steel belts break and that could cause the shimmy.

The mechanic mentioned that the gas station sold new tires, but Spencer told him that he wanted to consider the situation first. Actually, he thought that a tire store would give a better deal, and he wanted to think about what brand to purchase. More than that, he wasn't really sure how much confidence to place in the young mechanic's assessment of the problem.

The next Sunday, Spencer spent some time reading the newspaper, which included ads from tire stores located in and around the state capital that was 30 miles away. He was certain of his desire for steel-belted radial tires, but he had no other strong preferences. After reading a number of ads for sales, he was surprised at the variety of steel-belted radials that were available. It also became apparent that he knew very little about how to evaluate tires. Further, Spencer really didn't know if any of the upstate tire outlets were any cheaper than the two shops in his own town. The logical plan seemed to involve inquiring at these shops first, especially since they were convenient and he liked to keep his business within the local economy.

The next day, Spencer asked some of his lunch buddies if they knew whether bad tires could cause a steering wheel to shimmy. Comments were made by several friends but no one really seemed to know much about the problem. However, his friend Dave, who used to work at a Uniroyal plant, spoke up and Spencer listened to him intently. Dave said some reasons for wheel shimmy could be bad tie-rods, the tires being out of balance, or worn-out tires. He also said that Spencer should get the car checked out because the problem could be dangerous. Conversation then switched to the relative merits of various tire brands. Everett spoke very highly of the good service he had received at the local tire shop named Rite-Tire. Spencer asked what brands they carried, and Everett mentioned Jetson, Michelin, and another brand of which Spencer had never heard. Dave mentioned that Goodyear, Uniroyal, and other major producers made a number of tires that carried different brand names, but one couldn't be sure what the quality level of these brands were. He then mentioned that the Uniroyal Steeler, a steel-belted radial, had been independently tested and was rated as having the top treadwear in the industry. Bob, who had been relatively quiet until then, got quite animated. He spoke of getting more than 55,000 miles on a set of Uniroyal tires and having also owned Goodyear and Michelin tires although they never achieved more than 40,000 miles. Bob also said that he too would soon be looking for tires and was interested in getting the Uniroyal all-weather type. Dave responded that although the all-weather design was somewhat better in snow conditions than a regular radial tire, it was not as good as a radial snow tire. Furthermore, when compared to a regular radial tire, the all-weather tire did not wear as long and its tread design caused higher road friction, which therefore made it less gas economical. He was convinced that the Uniroyal Steeler was the best choice, but because it was February, it was not a good time to be buying tires. When asked why, he said that promotions for winter tires had been over for some time and attractive sales with low prices would start again in the spring.

Spencer left the lunch convinced that, if at all possible, he should wait until spring and at that time buy Uniroyal Steelers. Two more weeks went by before Kathy mentioned that she really didn't feel safe driving the Malibu, especially when the children were in it. She told Spencer that they actually were not sure why the steering sheel had a shimmy, and the car could have a dangerous problem. Spencer agreed that he again should have someone look it over, and 3 days later he drove it into a Midas shop which offered alignment services, brakes, and shocks as well as mufflers. Ten minutes later, the manager brought Spencer over to his car which was up on a lift. The manager said that Spencer had two bad front tires and the rear ones would soon need replacement. It was easy to see the steel belts showing through the front tires. The manager said further that the car must have been drastically out of alignment for some time. He pointed out that the car also seemed to need new shocks, and because of the front tires the car was not safe to drive.

Spencer then was sure that he needed to act right away. He found three Uniroyal dealers listed in the Yellow Pages, and upon calling them he found their price quotes for the proper size Steelers to be identical—$76 per tire, including air valves, mounting, and high-speed balancing. He noticed that this was not much more than a sale price he had recently seen for some Goodyear tires. On the following Friday, Spencer took the Malibu to work, left the office a little early, and arrived at the closest Uniroyal dealer at 4 P.M. He tried to reconfirm the price, and was quoted $335.60 including all taxes. This was quite a shocker, but few options seemed open to him. He was about to say yes when the clerk spoke up. He said that Uniroyal also made the Tiger Paw Plus, which was an all-weather radial, and buying this would only raise the price to $357.80. Given that it had superior traction and that it was rated to last 5000 miles more than the Steeler, the clerk thought it was a better buy. Acting knowledgeable, Spencer said that he found this hard to believe because all-weather tires tended to wear out faster than regular radials. Furthermore, their higher traction would also lead to lower gas economy. The young clerk responded by saying that the Tiger Paw Plus had a new European tread design, firmer rubber than previous all-weather radials, and a heavier sidewall construction which allowed it to carry higher-than-normal air pressure. All of these factors combined to yield longer treadwear and greater fuel efficiency than other all-weather models, even those made by Uniroyal.

The clerk called over a man who looked like the shop manager and asked him to compare the Steeler to the Tiger Paw Plus. The manager provided the same information as the clerk had indicated. He also showed Spencer a brochure on the Tiger Paws that mentioned high treadwear and increased fuel efficiency. The manager then indicated that a testing laboratory had verified these conclusions.

Spencer asked for a minute to "think this over." He considered that the additional price of the Tiger Paws was not much and that they would probably give the Malibu better traction in the snow. Since he was not pleased with how the car performed in snow, this seemed like a good advantage. He also reasoned that if the tires were kept fully inflated, they probably would not be much worse than the Steelers in terms of fuel efficiency.

Spencer bought the Tiger Paw Plus tires and found the ride home to be a pleasing experience. The wheel shimmy was completely gone, and the car handled very well. However, it seemed that the tires made more noise than his old ones. He mentioned this to his wife while they were driving the next day, and he said that this made him wonder about how good the tires were going to be in terms of fuel efficiency. Kathy responded that the noise was not disturbing at all, the extra snow traction would be good, the tires should last a long time, and since they had already been purchased, there was nothing that could be done about fuel efficiency. She also said that he should stop worrying about whether he had made a perfect decision and enjoy the safe feeling of having good tires on the car. Spencer said nothing and decided that he would make a regular effort to keep the tires fully inflated for maximum fuel efficiency.

An appointment was made at Midas the following Wednesday, at which time the front end was aligned and four new Superguard shock absorbers were placed on the car. The total cost was $135.42. After considering that he had spent nearly $500 on the car, Spencer decided to postpone the purchase of that zoom lens he was thinking of for his camera.

Questions

1 Analyze Spencer's experience in terms of the consumer-behavior frameworks presented in Chapter 2. What variables and processes can you identify that appear to be at work in this situation?

2 When did problem recognition occur for Spencer?

3 What information sources did Spencer use? Did they all seem to bear equally on his decision?

4 What were the strongest influences on the decision to buy Uniroyal tires?

CASE 1-3
BURGER BATTLE[1]

Hamburgers, fries and shakes still are served with a smile, but behind the scenes, the burger barons are at war with one another.

The giants of quick-fix meals are scrapping for new customers and hefty sales increases at a time when industry experts warn that the market may be reaching its limits.

"The hamburger end of the fast-food industry is facing the long-awaited problem of saturation," says analyst Michael Culp at the brokerage firm of Bache Halsey Stuart Shields. "It's increasingly difficult to open more restaurants, and it's harder to sell more hamburgers."

Thus, to maintain their growth momentum, the industry's big names are moving aggressively to steal each other's customers, enlarge their menus, and spawn new fast-food concepts. Decors are being spruced up, drive-in windows added and 24-hour operations tested. In the process, these outlets resemble less and less the roadside food stand, and more and more a conventional restaurant—minus the waitresses and tablecloths.

The stakes in the food fight are enormous. Hamburger chains rang up sales of more than 15.5 billion dollars according to industry estimates (see Table 1). Counting fried chicken, pizza and other specialty chains, the take in 1981 was approximately $31 billion. Sales in 1982 climbed to a level four times greater than a decade earlier.

[1] Adapted with permission from Judith Gardner, "A Burger Battle—With Everything," *U.S. News & World Report,* November 8, 1982, p. 76. Copyright © 1982, U.S. News & World Report, Inc.

"This is a highly competitive industry," says Denny Lynch, a spokesman for Wendy's International, the No. 3 burger chain. The reason? "People can change the restaurant they eat in every day of the week. You've got to keep them coming back." Adds John Weir of Burger King, No. 2 behind McDonald's: "You really have to do something special to attract customers."

Burger King did something special by airing television commercials that name names. Its ads tout surveys showing that people prefer Burger King sandwiches to those of McDonald's and Wendy's, and boast that Burger King patties are bigger and better prepared than those of competitors. Wendy's countered with a 25-million dollar suit charging false and misleading advertising. McDonald's sought unsuccessfully to enjoin Burger King from airing the commercials. Burger King's Weir says the ads have had the intended effect—business has increased.

Aggressive promotion is just one weapon in the burger chains' arsenals. In addition, each company is adding new items to menus to lure customers away from the competitors. "The challenge is to keep sales growing, and you can't do it just with hamburgers," says analyst Culp.

McDonald's is testing McRib, a barbecued-pork sandwich, and Chicken McNuggets, deep-fried balls of chicken, as well as biscuits for breakfast. Burger King recently added a bacon double cheeseburger to its lineup and is testing a tacoburger and barbecue sandwich. Burger King also may follow McDonald's into the breakfast market. In some cities, it sells such untraditional fast foods as pancakes, biscuits and gravy and scrambled eggs.

Wendy's is trying out a five-item dinner menu, which includes country-fried beef, beef in mushroom sauce and a chicken Parmesan sandwich. Each one comes with salad and potatoes and sells for $2.99. Part of Wendy's strategy, says a spokesman, is to appeal to families and older people, both important markets as baby-boomers grow up and the elderly increase as a share of U.S. population.

Fast-food restaurants are popping up in places far removed from major highway intersections and shopping centers—preferred locations that are now full. Burger King opened a new outlet at the Pearl Harbor Naval Station in Hawaii—the first, according to the company, inside a military installation. A new McDonald's restaurant recently opened in a public high school. The companies are on the lookout for such locations as bus stations, museums, zoos, college campuses, truck stops and airports, as well as smaller towns that have been skipped over in the past. "We're being more creative in finding the customer," explains Steve Leroy, a McDonald's spokesman.

The firms are moving overseas, too. McDonald's has more than 1200 restaurants in 28 foreign countries, including more than 300 in Japan. Burger King officials see room for growth in Latin America.

As the competition heats up, smaller firms are being gobbled up by companies looking for quick expansion. The Washington, D.C.-based Marriott Corporation, owner of the Roy Rogers hamburger chain, recently acquired Gino's. Hardee's has purchased Burger Chef.

Some, like Wendy's, are branching out into new food lines to bolster the bottom line in the future. The company announced that it will franchise its Sisters Chicken & Biscuits chain nationwide. It expects rapid growth for the new offspring.

The latest fad in quick-fix food is Mexican fare. At least half a dozen chains are being built, under names such as ChiChi's, El Torito, and Cisco's. Rapid growth is possible—thanks to millions whose palates may be jaded from too many sandwiches, burgers, fried chicken and pizzas.

Questions

1 Discuss the various ways in which knowledge of consumer behavior can be useful to these companies.

2 What potential target markets can be identified from information in the case?

TABLE 1 THE BIG CONTENDERS

	McDonald's	Burger King	Wendy's	Hardee's	Arby's	Burger Chef*
Sales in millions	$7,129	$2,356	$1,424	$1,108	$ 527	$333
Number of outlets	6,739	3,115	2,229	1,408	1,146	667

*Acquired by Hardee's.
Note: Figures are from sales of food and beverages in 1981, outlets as of January 1, 1982.
Source: U.S. News & World Report—Basic data: Restaurants & Institutions magazine.

PART TWO
UNDERSTANDING CONSUMERS AND MARKET SEGMENTS

3 Researching Consumer Behavior
4 Market Segmentation: Basic Approaches
5 Market Segmentation: Additional Dimensions
Cases for Part Two

CHAPTER 3

RESEARCHING CONSUMER BEHAVIOR

The following chapters will present a significant amount of evidence about consumers that has been generated by research investigations. Thus, it is useful first to gain an appreciation of the nature of consumer research, its applicability to marketing decision making, and some of the problems and limitations confronting the researcher.

It is impossible to convey the breadth and depth of this subject in a single chapter. Consequently, no attempt is made to train the reader in research methods but merely to give exposure to a sample of important consumer-research concepts.

THE NATURE AND SIGNIFICANCE OF CONSUMER RESEARCH

Consumer research may be defined as the systematic gathering, recording, and analyzing of data about consumers. Such studies are very important to our economy, and particularly to certain companies. An example follows.

> One of the most successful consumer goods companies in the world is Procter & Gamble which produces over eighty brands in the laundry and cleaning, personal care, food, and other product categories. Procter & Gamble owes its success to maintaining close contact with consumers, tuning in to what consumers want, and making products that satisfy those wants. Because the company does business more frequently with consumers than any other U.S. corporation—about 17 million transactions a day—it needs answers to questions about its customers. Edward G. Harness, chairman of Procter & Gamble says, "We study the everchanging consumer and try to identify new trends in tastes, needs, environment, and living habits. We study changes in the marketplace and try to assess the impact of our brands. We study our competition. Competitive brands are continually offering new benefits and new ideas to the consumer, so we must stay ahead of this."[1]
>
> To gather useful information, Procter & Gamble's brands carry a toll-free phone number on their packages or labels so that consumers can call in immediately with their thoughts about the products (more than 500,000 have so far). In addition, Procter & Gamble each year phones or visits approxi-

mately 1.5 million people in connection with approximately 1000 research projects. These people are questioned extensively on their likes and dislikes concerning the company's products, including names, packaging, and other facets. Much continuing "basic" research concerns how people go about washing clothes, preparing meals, doing the dishes, and performing other household chores. Many specialized studies are also conducted on consumers' perceptions of products, reactions to advertisements, and responses in other areas. All of this information is processed and routed to every major segment of the company where it is assessed for implications for Procter & Gamble's sales, advertising, manufacturing, and research-and-development operations.[2]

In addition to such research conducted by many firms in the private sector, consumer research is also conducted by government agencies to solve public-policy issues, and by university researchers seeking to build better consumer-behavior theories. As mentioned in Chapter 1, the researcher may investigate any of several roles played by the consumer, such as user, buyer, initiator, or influencer. Therefore, the unit of analysis must be clearly specified when conducting consumer research.

NEED FOR CONSUMER RESEARCH

Many examples can be cited which emphasize the role and usefulness of consumer research. The following illustrate a variety of applications:

Zales Zales jewelry store chain conducted an intensive 3-year research analysis to understand its position in the jewelry market and to develop a new marketing strategy to assure its leadership in the industry. A study of customer attitudes confirmed Zales' dominant position in the marketplace—not as a luxury jewelry or as a discount operation, but as a jeweler for Middle America. However, the research also revealed that customers have little loyalty to Zales or to any other jeweler. Other research showed jewelers' positions in the marketplace to be ill-defined, undifferentiated, and unfocused, partly as a result of the long purchase cycle. That is, because people don't buy jewelry often, there is a lack of strong allegiance to a particular store. Motivational studies have found loyalty to relate in one way or another to reliability, selection, and sales personnel. In addition, a high level of anxiety has been found to be attached to the jewelry shopping experience. In order to capitalize on its position, Zales developed new advertising to appeal on these bases, and it also developed a guarantee program (Figure 3-1) to address the anxiety and reliability factors. As a result of the research, the company also added new product lines, instituted year-round rather than seasonal bridal advertising programs, started a men's diamond jewelry campaign, and changed to a new catalog sales approach.[3]

Radio Research The use of consumer research has even been extended to radio stations that wish to make better decisions on what will draw more listeners and advertisers. "Radio doctors" try to fix station formats to improve the competitive standing of the stations who hire them. These consultants use surveys, panel discussions, and questionnaires to determine the ages, sexes, and income levels of stations' audiences as well as their buying habits, political beliefs, and leisure activities. (Interestingly, the number 1 leisure activity of people age 18 to 24 has changed from baseball in 1965 to something today called "partying.") The consultants use such information to help program a station, from the music it plays to the vocal patterns of its disc jockeys.

Radio researchers use different techniques. Some try to determine musical taste by doing "call out" research in which hundreds of people are telephoned and their reactions to different songs are tested. Some conduct in-depth discussions with selected audiences. Some send researchers out on the road as hitchhikers to uncover off-the-cuff comments. Others may interview record buyers who fill out questionnaires detailing why they made their purchases. Lists of records played by stations around the country are compiled by researchers and sold to programmers interested in how a successful station operates. Some stations keep track of the ages and sexes of people who call requesting certain songs to be played so that the stations can then determine which songs are popular with which groups. In addition, some firms track how most of their potential and current audience commutes so that billboard space can be bought along the most frequently traveled roads.[4]

FIGURE 3-1

Advertisement for Zales. (Courtesy of Zale Corporation.)

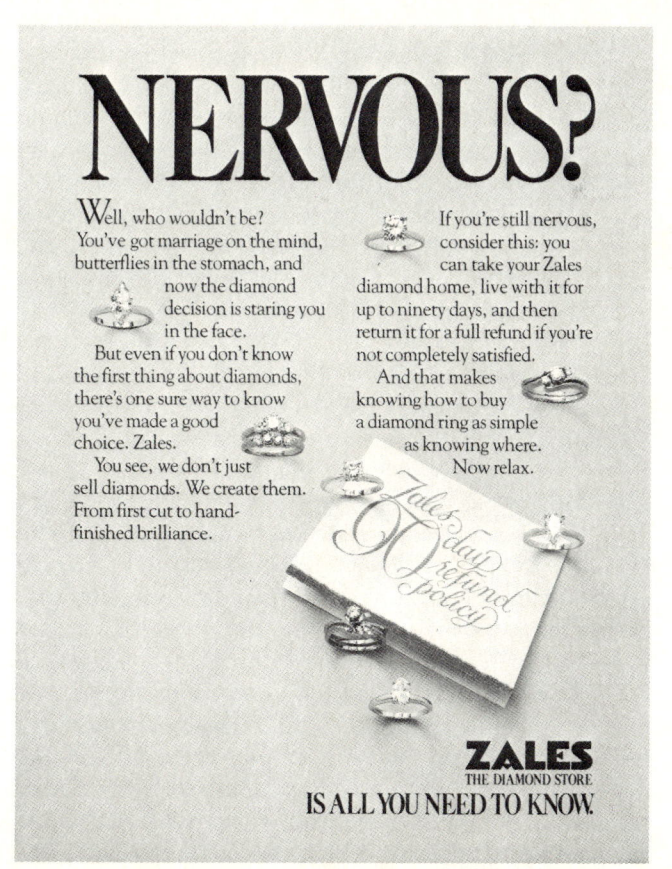

Food Flops The many product failures which have occurred in the marketplace are strong testimony to the need for consumer research. Food products, in particular, have a high failure rate. A. C. Nielsen Company estimates that more than 60 percent of all new grocery products introduced into test markets in 1977 failed (an increase from 50 percent in 1971). And the failure rate is much more than 80 percent when all the food products scrapped in the test kitchens before marketing are counted.[5]

Even though batteries of tests and surveys may be conducted to discern what buyers want, how recipes are to be developed and refined, what brand name to choose, and how packages are to be designed, new products still flop. Sometimes researchers fail to ask the right questions, or they ignore the research evidence gathered. The following example about the development of a new food product illustrates such problems.

Pillsbury Company had what it thought was a sure winner when it came up with a recipe using freeze-dried apples in cinnamon sauce with a crunchy streusel topping. The product idea was inexpensive, easy to fix, and fast. The consumer merely had to add boiling water, stir, wait five minutes, and eat. Consumer panels were interviewed to select a name and "Appleasy" got the nod because it best conveyed the idea of convenience. The product was not market tested, however, because competitors might easily copy it and because Pillsbury executives were certain of their creation's ability to satisfy ravenous after-school kids. After three years of exhaustive research, Appleasy was introduced to the market and flopped. The failure occurred in part because Pillsbury changed the taste formula after successful taste tests had been conducted. Apple prices increased dramatically during this period, therefore less of this ingredient was included in order to maintain what executives thought was an attractive price. Initial sales were very encouraging—twenty-two percent ahead of company projection. However, fate soon showed that success was only skin deep, while failure was to the core. Although many people tried it, few came back for seconds. A Pillsbury executive described the product as a "magnificent flop," and the company lost much more than $1 million on it.[6]

Thus, no matter how good an idea may seem to be, failure to do sufficient research of the correct type and then to follow the recommendations of well-done research are quite likely to result in failure.

Of course, not every product that fails does so because of a lack of research. Unfortunately, research is simply not foolproof. Because of this fact, some companies have launched new products with little or no formal research. Minnetonka, Inc., for example, brought "Softsoap" (Figure 3-2) to the market with no research on the product's package design or color, name, or advertisements. The company credits intuition rather than formalized market research for the fact that the product captured 7 percent of the U.S. soap market in less than a year after its introduction.[7]

Nevertheless, the starting point for developing successful marketing strategy is a proper understanding of the consumer. Whether the marketer's "theory" of how the consumer will respond to a particular marketing mix is based on informal research or on a more formalized understanding, the essential ingredient for success is knowledge of the consumer. This chapter will thus present an overview of research approaches by which the marketer may gain greater insights into consumer behavior.

CONSUMER RESEARCH STRATEGIES

Many strategies are available in the process of researching consumers. For example, studies may differ according to the goal of the research, the type of data used, and the time frame of the investigation. Each of these approaches will be discussed in this section.

Goals of Consumer Research

Two major strategies of consumer research, classified according to their goals, are exploratory and conclusive studies.

Exploratory Research   Exploratory research is used to identify variables influencing consumers and discover how they may tend to react to these factors. This occurs in situations when there is not enough known about consumers to draw conclusions about what variables are influencing their behavior. Two significant methods used in exploratory research are consumer suggestions and focus groups.

CONSUMER SUGGESTIONS   In the business world, many influences and problems encountered by consumers are discovered through the spontaneous suggestions of consumers themselves. For example, Procter & Gamble receives approxi-

FIGURE 3-2

Advertisement for Softsoap. (Courtesy of Minnetonka, Inc.)

mately 4000 ideas for new products each year, but for legal reasons it politely turns almost all of them down.[8] In addition, many retailers conduct an informal type of research similar to the familiar "suggestion box." Printed cards soliciting consumer feedback are placed for easy access, such as on tables in a restaurant or on sales counters in a retail store. Customers with complaints or compliments are able to express themselves instantly. For example, Wendy's restaurants place cards at each table with the headline "At Wendy's you are the chaiman of the board." These cards solicit patrons' comments on the chain's food and service.

FOCUS GROUPS   Another popular technique for exploratory research is the focus-group interview. Focus groups generally bring together in a casual setting six to eight people with similar backgrounds to apply the principles of group dynamics and free association to a marketing problem. A moderator guides the discussion but allows consumers to interact with each other. The sessions, which last about 2 hours, are usually recorded and frequently videotaped. In addition, the group may be observed by other researchers or client representatives through a one-way mirror.

This type of qualitative research gives the marketer a chance to "experience" a "flesh and blood" consumer. That is, the marketer can better understand the framework in which the product is being used by learning about all of the satisfactions, dissatisfactions, rewards, and frustrations experienced by the consumer when buying and using the product.[9]

Specific ways in which focus groups can be helpful are:

- Generate hypotheses about consumers and market situations

- Suggest fresh and revitalized ideas

- Check an advertisement, package, or product concept to determine if anything about it is confusing, misleading, or negative

- Understand the consumer's language and motivations

- Understand consumers' lifestyles and personalities

- Explore a new area as a prelude to a quantitative study

- Do a postmortem on a failed product[10]

An example of a focus group interview is presented in Exhibit 3-1.

EXHIBIT 3-1

A TYPICAL FOCUS GROUP INTERVIEW (Conducted by Tony Wainwright of Wainwright, Spaeth & Wright, Chicago)

WAINWRIGHT   What's going on in the grocery store today?

ALMA   I find myself no longer buying meat in a grocery store. I started this about a month ago. I feel that, for those prices, I might as well go to a butcher, pay a few pennies more, and get premium meat or prime. I find that whereas just going into the store with no meat used to cost me $30 or $40, now it costs me $60 to $75.

LINDA   I bought half a cow a month ago. And I'm still spending the same amount of money in the grocery store every week that I did before I bought the half a cow.

Source: "Focus Group Interview: Consumers Rap About Today's Shopping, Buying," *Advertising Age,* March 3, 1975, p. 37. Reprinted with permission from the March 3, 1975 issue of *Advertising Age.* Copyright © 1975 by Crain Communications, Inc.

WAINWRIGHT   Eileen, how are you making it today? What are you cutting back on, and what are you buying more of?

EILEEN   I have completely done away with Fritos, potato chips, snacks—we were big on that type of stuff. I'm going back to some of the things my grandmother did. I'm baking. We weren't really taught all that much.

WAINWRIGHT   Are you doing anything different, Sandra?

SANDRA   I think so. You know, before I would make a lot of roasts. Now you don't even think about that, except maybe once a week. Now we have more ground meat recipes.

WAINWRIGHT   You add anything to it?

EILEEN   No.

WAINWRIGHT   What's a box mix?

EILEEN   Hamburger Helper!

LINDA   You can do a lot more yourself. You pay 79 cents for noodles.

ALMA   Where I shop, they've been giving us a new cookbook each week. So I've been trying some of the things in there. It's nothing you'd buy a mix for. You make it all yourself.

KATHY   Like a meatloaf.

WAINWRIGHT   How about side dishes? Anybody serving them?

ROSE   Oh, yes.

WAINWRIGHT   More, or about the same?

ROSE   I'm serving less. Of course, they are very expensive, so you don't save much.

WAINWRIGHT   What is there today?

LINDA   Well, the only thing I can say is we're just eating cheaper cuts of meat. I haven't had steak since—I can't remember when. But I have two teenage sons, and it's hard to tell them, "You eat this piece of meat—you don't get any more." You just can't say this to kids.

KATHY   All of a sudden you don't have the cookies and snacks in the house. Buy pop once a week instead of every time it runs out. All these things are changing.

LINDA   I've found what I've done—we get paid twice a month. So my big shopping is twice a month, and I really go in for nothing else but milk and eggs. After they have gone through what I have bought, that's it.

SANDRA   I also find I buy things on sale. If it's something I use, I will buy two, because I know when I run out it's going to be up in price.

MARVELLA   And then, too, don't you shop the specials of the week?

SANDRA   If it's something I use, yes.

WAINWRIGHT   What about private labels?

CHAPTER 3

61

RESEARCHING CONSUMER BEHAVIOR

ALMA A lot of them are a lot better.

LINDA Oh, I got some Del Monte string beans the other day, and they were about half full of string beans and were about the worst tasting stuff, so I just swore off Del Monte right there.

ROSE The only way you can beat it is to do comparison shopping. I would suggest you look at the ads on Thursday nights and go to the A&P, go to the Jewel. You have to hit all the stores.

EILEEN By that time, you've wasted a day.

SANDRA That's the only way you can beat the game. Like, I work. I don't have that kind of time for it. I'm better off sticking to one store.

ALMA They say that dried beans give you the same amount of protein. Supposedly, I've heard that.

ROSE There's no way my husband is going to sit down and eat a plate full of beans—unless he's at a campfire. He's strictly meat. I have to serve him that.

WAINWRIGHT What can you do to meat? If you serve a lot of hamburger, what do you do to vary it?

MARVELLA Make chili, Sloppy Joes. And then the macaroni.

LINDA You can jazz up anything—a meatloaf, even.

EILEEN I think you get tired of it, though.

SANDRA I've been buying ground turkey because that's cheap, but I'm getting tired of that, too. I'd like a good roast.

It is important to appreciate that the primary objective of exploratory research such as focus-group interviewing is hypothesis formulation, that is, forming a conjectural statement about the relationship between two or more variables. For example, assume that the following focus-group interview occurred concerning paper towels. Mrs. Baker says she always buys ScotTowels because they are absorbent. Mrs. Smith claims that a store brand she has tried is not that absorbent, and she always buys Bounty now. She adds that Bounty also comes in a variety of colors. Mrs. Franklin says all paper towels are alike, and she buys whichever brand is on sale. Note that the focus group has revealed three attributes of paper towels: absorbency, color, and price. What does the researcher do with this type of information? He might begin to consider hypotheses regarding the role or these variables in influencing consumers' purchase decisions for the product.

Conclusive Research Exploratory research is not designed to provide conclusive answers to the research questions it generates. More extensive and rigorous studies are needed to determine how the variables that have been identified influence consumers. This is the role of conclusive research. For example, Scripto interviewed students in focus groups conducted for its new erasable disposable ink pen. The company found through these sessions with its most lucrative market prospects that 98 cents would be a reasonable amount for such a pen, and that this price would be preferable to paying 25 cents for a disposable Bic. The hypothesis that this would be a favorable price point was then verified in subsequent placement tests with the actual product.[11] Thus, conclusive research builds upon exploratory research. Specifically, the major goals of conclusive research are to describe fully consumers' behavior and to offer explanations for its causes. In addition, the prediction of consumers' behavior and methods of influencing it can be suggested by conclusive research.

Type of Data Used

Two basic sources of data can be used in consumer research: secondary and primary data. *Primary* data are those the researcher gathers firsthand for the problem being investigated. However, there is a vast amount of information about consumers which is already compiled and readily accessible to the researcher who knows how to find and use it. Such data that have been collected for a purpose other than the research project at hand are termed *secondary data*. Before gathering primary data, the researcher should search through secondary sources to determine if any are applicable to the problem at hand. Because the types of secondary data are too numerous to describe here, an interested reader should refer to other sources for further information.[12] Our focus in this chapter will be on primary data and the methods used to gather them.

Research Time Frame

Generally speaking, in consumer research studies, primary data can be collected either at one time or over a period of time. We refer to these research designs as cross-sectional and longitudinal, respectively. These two approaches have different purposes.

Cross-Sectional Research Sometimes the researcher is interested in assessing the nature of some aspect of consumer behavior at one particular time instead of studying how it changes over time. As its name implies, the cross-sectional design is used to study such a situation by examining a cross section of behavior at any given time. For example, such a study may seek to determine the values and attitudes various consumers have about a particular product at one particular moment.

Longitudinal Research Interest can also focus on how some aspect of consumer behavior occurs or changes over time, as in the case of consumers developing a loyalty for a particular brand of coffee. These situations are best studied by using a longitudinal design, which involves data gathering and analysis over a period of time. One popular type of longitudinal study is the continuous *consumer panel.* Consumers who are deemed representative of a particular group are chosen for inclusion in the panel, where the number of panel members may range from only a few people to several thousand households.

   A continuous consumer panel provides the researcher with a fixed sample that can be repeatedly studied. By asking the same questions of panel members over a period of time, changes in their behavior, as well as reasons for these changes, can be determined. Panel members generally maintain a continuous record or diary of their consumption activities, such as shopping, purchase, use, and product/brand decisions, as well as demographic and attitudinal characteristics. For example, in one major panel, sales are reported by brand for households classified according to such factors as total family income, age of housewife, number and ages of children, occupation and education of family head, and location by region and city size. Sales are also provided according to the types of stores from which purchases are made.

METHODS OF GATHERING CONSUMER INFORMATION

In both cross-sectional and longitudinal designs, there are two general ways of collecting consumer behavior data: observation and communication. These two basic approaches can be further divided, however, into three information-gathering methods: observation, experiments, and surveys.

Observation

One way to study consumers is to observe their overt behavior. In some cases this alternative may be better than asking consumers how they act, because frequently discrepancies exist between how consumers say they behave and what they actually do. Many are not even consciously aware of all their activities or the influences of external purchase stimuli such as point-of-purchase store displays or window exhibits. For example, if a mother were asked why she purchased a particular brand of cereal she might respond, "Because of its nutritional value." Observation of actual shopping behavior, however, might reveal that her child grabbed the box off the shelf, claiming that he wanted the free toy inside. Another benefit of the observation method frequently is that it can be accomplished subtly, so that the consumers do not realize that they are subjects and thus change their behavior. Therefore, this method may be quite successful in obtaining certain types of behavioral information.

There are several illustrations of the observation technique being used in consumer research. Mechanical means of observation are sometimes used by researchers. For example, the A. C. Nielsen Company gathers television viewership data from a selected group of families by means of an electromechanical device that automatically records the times and channels of television viewing. This results in the famous Nielsen Television Ratings, which are issued every two weeks.

In another application of the observation method, a technique has been developed using license plate surveys to help retailers discover where their customers live. Enumerators record a sample of plate numbers from cars in a store or shopping center parking lot. The numbers are fed into a computer and paired with motor vehicle registrations which contain owners' addresses. The result is a map that plots customers' homes by census tracts or zip codes. The resulting picture of the dealer or shopping center's penetration (and gaps) coupled with other demographic data can be very useful in selecting media to reach these customers.[13] Jewel Co. of Chicago conducted a study such as this for one of its supermarkets and found out exactly who shopped at that store, how far they traveled to get there, and in what sort of neighborhood they lived.[14]

Another form of mechanical observation is the use of cameras to observe eye movement and pupil dilation. Eye movement tracking is able to document what actually attracts consumer attention. Also, by observing eye pupil dilation which accompanies the viewing of emotionally charged or interesting visual stimuli, the marketer is able to determine the interest arousing potential of products, packages, and advertisements.[15] For example, a detailed diagnostic eye-tracking study of an advertiser's promotional letter and brochure showed that consumers focused only on certain locations of the brochure pages, exhibited erratic viewing patterns, and frequently failed to read key material. The letter and brochure were revised so that consumers increased their reading of the key copy and obtained greater involvement in the messages.[16]

Cameras (usually hidden) may also be used to observe accurately shoppers' behavior in a store. This information can be very useful in many ways, such as planning or improving a store's layout. For example, the shopping patterns of a supermarket's customers may be observed and recorded. The data can then be used to determine which aisles are most heavily traveled, where "traffic jams" occur, and whether more people pick up meat and dairy items first or last. Because subjects are unaware of being observed, hidden cameras have the potential advantage of being more accurate than personal observation methods. It should be noted, however, that there are critics of this method who believe it is unethical to film shoppers without their permission. Unfortunately, if permission is first obtained, the consumer's behavior may become atypical. Therefore, if this technique is to be used, the consumer researcher should first determine his own view of the ethics involved.

A final observation technique that holds great promise for certain marketers is the use of automatic scanning devices in grocery stores. Scanning is a new measurement technique and a way of gathering data. When a product bearing a universal product code (UPC) containing information related to the brand is passed over an automated scanner at the checkout counter, the scanner translates the UPC. This information is transmitted to the store's computer file where the item's price is found and flashed back to the register. Price is printed on the customer receipt and the transaction is stored in the computer file. Although there are some problems with scanning (for example, not all grocery products are UPC encoded), there is, nevertheless, tremendous potential for this technique as a means of obtaining accurate data.[17] Approximately 3500 supermarkets had such scanners in operation in mid-1981, and some project 10,000 scanner-equipped stores by 1985 accounting for almost 50 percent of the total grocery business.[18]

The output from scanning systems creates the opportunity to expand the marketer's knowledge of the sales effects of advertising, sales promotions, and other marketing stimuli. However, the most important feature to many marketers is that such systems have the ability to electronically segregate the purchases of an individual consumer. Whereas traditional diary panels (such as those referred to in the previous section) have relied on what the consumer said she did, an electronic diary panel offers the opportunity to record what the consumer actually did. Thus, the consumer no longer needs to memorize information about brand, price, coupon usage, and so on, because it is all done electronically.

For stores with such diary capability, panel members can be recruited, asked to fill out a demographic questionnaire, and given a card for each member of the household. Each panel member can shop normally, but she or he should present the panel identification card at the beginning of the checkout process. The checker can then record the card number and each individual transaction for the customer so it can be isolated and stored in the computer for future analysis. Such UPC scanner information can efficiently and economically provide answers to many marketing questions.[19] As scanner stores increase in number, marketers will gain a rich data base to help track and understand purchase behavior.

When scanner technology is used in conjunction with advanced cable television systems, the two offer additional research possibilities. For example, scanner panel members in a city might be used to evaluate advertising effectiveness. If 2500 panel member homes in one city were linked to cable television, half might receive the same commercials being shown to the general public and half could receive a set of test commercials. Purchase response at the store level would then show up via electronic scanning to indicate a measure of that test advertisement's effectiveness.

Experiments

In experimental investigations the researcher selects consumers, stores, and so on (known as test units) and seeks to measure the effect of specific situations or conditions (known as experimental treatments) on a particular dependent variable such as consumers' attitudes or purchase behavior. In this process, an attempt is made to control or hold constant the effects of other so-called extraneous variables so that they will not influence the results. For example, if we wanted to determine whether the size of a magazine advertisement affects readers' attention, then the size of the ad might be varied, while such extraneous variables as the message or appeal used, and the color of the ads were held constant so that they would not influence the results and confuse the issue.

Consumer researchers may conduct experiments in the "field" (that is, the actual setting of the marketplace), or they may test hypotheses under "laboratory" conditions (which include any environment simulating real or actual conditions).

Laboratory Experiments These are useful because they typically allow greater control over extraneous variables than is possible in the real world. Also the investigator may be better able to manipulate experimental treatments in the controlled environment of the laboratory. However, a potential problem with such experiments is that they can sometimes become too artificial, thereby insufficiently representing the real world. An example of a laboratory experiment could be to discover consumer taste preferences regarding Pepsi, Coke, and Royal Crown Cola. Note how the laboratory situation allows control over extraneous variables such as containers, prices, and brand names. For example, rather than using the products' bottles or cans, drinks could be presented to subjects in glasses of the same size and color with no brand name or price information on them.

Field Experiments These provide a natural setting for research in order to overcome the problems of artificiality sometimes found in the laboratory. However, gaining realism from the marketplace environment can come at the cost of losing some control over the experimental situation.

Test marketing is one business equivalent of the scientist's field experiment. In the market test, different marketing variables (such as prices and advertisements) are tried in several market areas to determine which receives the most favorable consumer response. New-product introductions may be tested for approximately 6 months to 2 years or more, during which the product is promoted and treated as if it were on the market in a full-scale way.[20] For example, during 1981 three major fast-food chains were test marketing breakfast menus. Burger King was evaluating a finger-food breakfast for people on the go, Wendy's was testing breakfast entrees, and both were planning for a national launch. Meanwhile,

McDonald's, with several years of experience already offering breakfasts, was testing two items it planned to add to its menu.[21]

In the case of test marketing, experimenters are faced with problems of control much different from those in the laboratory. For instance, competitors who are aware of a market test can interfere with the research by increasing their advertising, offering coupons, cutting prices, or other strategy changes. These changes reduce the experimenter's control over the test and can hide the true effect of the variable or variables under study.

Unfortunately, the expense of many field experiments can be prohibitive, and the length of time involved also makes this type of research inappropriate for some studies. The fact that the field experiment is conducted in the marketplace, however, can enhance the credibility of the results.[22]

Surveys

In the survey method of gathering data, consumers are not only aware of the fact that they are being studied, but they actively participate. There are three survey data-collection techniques: personal interviews, telephone surveys, and mail surveys.

Personal Interviews Direct face-to-face interaction between the interviewer and the respondent is perhaps the personal interview's greatest advantage over other types of surveys. A large amount of information can be obtained with a relatively high degree of accuracy by this approach. Flexibility is a further advantage, since questions can be modified to suit the situation or clarification can be provided if necessary. A major disadvantage of this approach, however, is its high cost.

Telephone Surveys The telephone survey can be a useful alternative to the personal interview because it provides for interviewer-respondent interaction and is quicker and less expensive to conduct than personal interviews. Today, access to Wide Area Telephone Service (WATS) makes it easy for researchers to sample a vast geographic area for a comparatively low price. Telephone surveys work well when the objective is to measure certain behavior at the time of the interview or immediately prior to the interview, such as radio listening or television viewing. It is also easier to reach subjects by telephone, and many people who would not consent to a personal interview are willing to participate over the phone. These surveys generally achieve higher response rates than mail surveys or personal interviews.

Telephone surveys have three basic limitations, however. First, the amount of information that can be obtained is limited because of difficulty in keeping respondents on the phone and interested for any extended period. Second, the type of information obtainable is limited. For example, measuring the intensity of consumers' feelings is difficult, and questions containing numerous response options are cumbersome. Further, the method can produce distorted results because subjects without telephones or those with unlisted numbers often are not reached, and they can differ from other respondents in important ways.

Mail Surveys Mail-questionnaire surveys have long been used by researchers because of their low potential cost per respondent, their ability to reach widely dispersed consumers, and their ability to obtain large amounts of data and allow more sophisticated questioning techniques, such as measuring scales.

In this approach consumers receive a questionnaire in the mail, complete it at their leisure, and return it in a postpaid envelope. Since respondents are seldom asked to identify themselves, a mail survey can reduce their reluctance to reveal sensitive information.

Of course, there are also disadvantages to this type of survey. Mail interviews can result in a small number of responses with many questionnaires ending up in wastebaskets. Another problem concerns the long time it may take for respondents to return the questionnaire. Follow-up letters to remind consumers of their delay can increase response rates, but also boost costs. Also, since there is no interviewer-respondent interaction, questions must be worded carefully to avoid ambiguity, and the questionnaire should be carefully pretested to detect any deficiencies.

MEASURING CONSUMER CHARACTERISTICS

Consumer research may also be classified according to whether demographic, activity, or cognitive information is sought. The following discussion will focus primarily on cognitive research approaches.

Demographic Measures

Demographic research is concerned with gathering vital statistics about consumers—such characteristics as their age, income, sex, occupation, location, race, marital status, and education. Notice that since these characteristics are easily quantifiable they enable the marketer to describe accurately and specifically and to understand certain consumer characteristics. For example, consider the use of demographic information in profiling consumers for the following four situations:

> The motorcycle industry keeps track of current owners of its product to determine how the market may be changing. Trade association data show that the market is approximately 94 percent male, with 60 percent of the men between 18 and 34 years of age, and a median age of 28 and rising. Approximately 45 percent of owners have had some college, 58 percent are married, and 77 percent have previously owned another bike. Information such as this may be very useful in aiming advertisements at potential buyers.[23]

> The average consumer of coffee drinks 2.06 cups per day (down from 3.12 in 1962), is male, in his mid- to late thirties, lives in the western or north-central states, and eats out a lot. However, the target audience for advertising is the housewife in a supermarket who has the major influence on the brands purchased. Consequently, most of the creative thrust of coffee advertising is aimed at her.[24]

> The average buyer of an Oldsmobile diesel car has been profiled by General Motors as follows:
>
> • A male—owners are 93 percent male compared to 85 percent of those who choose the conventional gasoline-powered Oldsmobile models
>
> • Age 55—approximately 5 years older than the conventional engine buyer

- Well-off—the average Olds 98 diesel buyer earns $35,000 per year while the average Olds 88 diesel buyer earns $30,000 per year—approximately $5500 more than conventional buyers for each model

- More mechanically inclined—even though he does not plan to work on the engine

- Intends to keep his car longer—five years compared to three for conventional 98 buyers

- A frequent driver—puts more highway and total miles on his diesel car than conventional owners do on their gasoline-powered cars

- More likely to have a microwave oven in the kitchen and a digital watch on his wrist.[25]

For a retail store or chain, information supplied by customers for their charge-account credit applications may be useful in profiling their shoppers. With such portraits, the retailer may uncover the demographic strengths and weaknesses of the store's primary clientele. For example, a recent study for Sears showed that 48 million U.S. households (57 percent of the total) have a Sears credit card, and 25 million use it actively. This compares with 53 percent for Visa cards, 39 percent for Penney's, 27 percent for Montgomery Ward, and 11 percent for American Express. Sears also found that possession of their cards increases as family incomes rise. Seventy percent of households with more than $36,000 in annual income and 76 percent of households with a net worth of more than $500,000 had Sears cards. In addition, among all brokerage house customers, 62 percent had Sears cards, while 73 percent of stock-market investors making transactions worth $25,000 or more per year carried the card. Such findings have encouraged Sears to aggressively aim at the financial services market sector.[26]

Much of the demographic data on consumer markets is a product of federal, state, and local government sources. One of the best sources of demographic data is the U.S. Census Bureau. Population statistics and other official information are easily obtained and can be useful, even vital, for small businesses that cannot afford to do marketing research. Whether it involves site location, choice of product lines, design of distribution systems, type of advertising, and so on, census information will normally play a part in the business decision.[27] The next chapter will describe in some detail the demographic characteristics of the U.S. consumer market; thus, little treatment of the topic is necessary at this point. However, it should be mentioned here that firms generally desire to obtain a demographic portrait of their customers. Such a profile may be constructed through research.

For those companies large enough to purchase outside research assistance, many research services offer the marketer detailed demographics either by census tracts (that is, statistical subdivisions within metropolitan areas containing an average 4000 population) or postal zip codes (more than 38,000 in the United States). Many marketing applications exist for such demographic data including the following:[28]

- Targeting direct-mail campaigns and analyzing returns
- Evaluating sales territories

- Selecting retail store locations
- Targeting audiences for political campaigns and fund-raising events
- Profiling populations residing in trading areas of retail chain stores
- Targeting consumer promotions
- Evaluating the efficiency of alternative media plans

Consumer Activity Measures

Often the researcher seeks to understand various aspects of consumers' activities. For example, questions such as the following may be of interest: When do customers buy this item? Which stores do they choose? How do they shop in these stores? How often do they shop or buy? How "loyal" are customers to certain brands? Which information sources do they utilize in making a decision on which brand to purchase?

Clearly, many of the above questions have cognitive components to them, but at times interest may focus only on the observable aspects of such situations. To illustrate, brand loyalty has a cognitive dimension to it from the perspective of how psychologically committed the consumer is to the brand. Often, however, concern is directed toward the observable aspects of loyalty, such as measuring how regularly the consumer buys the brand (for example, eight out of ten times).

Many aspects of consumers' activities will be discussed in the last section of the text in which purchasing processes are examined in detail. Therefore, we now turn our attention to cognitive measures in consumer research.

Cognitive Measures

Consumer researchers who desire to know about their market more than just demographic characteristics or activity patterns may attempt to collect cognitive information, that is, information about consumers' knowledge, attitudes, motivations, perceptions and information processing. Merely observing consumers cannot fully explain why they behave as they do, and questioning often does not provide reliable answers because of consumers' inability or reluctance to reveal true feelings to an interviewer. Thus, researchers attempt to explore intervening variables potentially useful in explaining consumer behavior by utilizing other techniques.

This section describes associative and projective techniques that are used in consumer research to help explain the *why* of consumer behavior. Also, the depth interview is discussed because of its primary use in uncovering motives. Next, attitudinal research approaches incorporating rating scales are presented, and finally some approaches to measure how consumers process information are briefly described.

Motivation Research During the 1950s companies became increasingly concerned with *why* consumers bought one product or brand instead of another. With the growth in income levels, particularly discretionary income, and as products became more alike, it grew even more important that marketers determine the attitudes, motives, values, perceptions, and images that might govern consumers' product/brand selections. To provide such answers a group of investigators termed "motivation researchers" came to the forefront of marketing studies using "qualitative" rather than "quantitative" research approaches.[29]

A set of projective techniques that had originally been developed by clinical psychologists was adapted, and began to be used in consumer research along with various notions from the field of psychoanalysis. These techniques and notions became known by the general term of *motivation research,* or in its abbreviated form simply *MR.* It must be emphasized that these techniques are not used exclusively for studying consumers' motivations, nor do they include all the tools available for such study. Actually, motivation research shares many techniques with other areas of consumer research that are seeking to understand consumers. Several of these projective techniques are briefly characterized below.

WORD-ASSOCIATION TESTS   Word association is a relatively old and simple technique used by researchers. Respondents are read a list of words, one at a time, and asked to answer quickly with the first thing that comes into their minds after hearing each one. By answering rapidly, respondents presumably indicate what they associate most closely with the word offered, and they thereby reveal their true inner feelings.

The example in Figure 3-3 illustrates how a retailer might use word associations in determining consumer brand preferences in order to allocate advantageous shelf space and position to favorite brands.

Word-association tests can be used in numerous other ways in consumer research such as to generate brand names, check their meaning, determine the effectiveness of advertising, and compare brand or company images.

The *sentence-completion* test is an adaptation of the word-association test in which the interviewer begins a sentence and the respondent finishes it. In conducting a study for a radio station, the interviewer might use the following statements:

1   WHJY plays music that appeals to . . .

2   The commercials on WHJY are . . .

3   A person who listens to WHJY is . . .

FIGURE 3-3

Word-association questionnaire.

For the following product category list I would like you to respond with the first brand name that comes to mind. For example, if I say "deodorant" you might respond by saying "Sure."

Product category   Brand

1. Hair spray   1. _____

2. Mouthwash   2. _____

3. Perfume   3. _____

4. Lipstick   4. _____

5. Eye makeup   5. _____

Frequently consumers respond to sentence-completion tests without realizing it, such as in contests that say, "Complete the following sentence in ten words or less."

The *story-completion* test is yet another expanded word-association test in which the respondent is told part of a story and is instructed to complete it in his or her own words, as in the following example.

> Mrs. Jones reads in the newspaper that Land O' Lakes butter is on sale at the local supermarket. She decides to take advantage of the sale and goes to the supermarket to buy it. When she gets there, the manager informs her that there is no Land O' Lakes butter left.
>
> How would Mrs. Jones react? Why?

The story technique can be useful in uncovering the images consumers have about stores and products, and this information can be applied in advertising and promotional themes.

The scoring for association tests consists of classifying the responses as either favorable or unfavorable. The numbers of each type of response can then be compared on a demographic basis. For instance, did women or men have more favorable responses, or, did those in upper-income brackets respond more unfavorably?

PROJECTIVE TESTS Projective tests call for the respondent to decide what another person would do in a certain situation. People may be reluctant to admit certain weaknesses or desires, but when they are asked to describe a neighbor or another person, they usually respond without hesitation. Thus projective techniques are based on the assumption that respondents express their own attitudes or motives as they infer the attitudes or motives of someone else.

A classic motivation research study based on this theory was conducted in 1950 by Mason Haire regarding consumer attitudes toward instant coffee.[30] Direct-question interviews revealed a dislike of instant coffee because of the taste, but this was believed to be a stereotyped response rather than the true reason. In an effort to discover other reasons for this negative attitude, an indirect approach was used. Respondents were shown one of two identical grocery shopping lists, varying only in the brand and type of coffee. One list contained "Nescafé Instant Coffee" and the other, "Maxwell House Coffee (drip ground)." They were then asked to characterize the woman who purchased the groceries. Descriptions indicated that compared to the drip-ground buyer, the instant-coffee purchaser was thought to be lazy, a spendthrift, not a good wife, and one who failed to plan household purchases and schedules well. Although these findings are probably not true today, they were initially useful in better understanding consumer motivations. They indicated that respondents were not really dissatisfied with the taste of instant coffee, but rather the idea of using it was unacceptable. Respondents were projecting their own feelings about instant coffee into the descriptions of the woman who purchased it.

Another form of projective test makes use of pictures as stimuli. One example is the *Thematic Appreception Test (TAT)*, in which respondents are shown ambiguous pictures concerning the product or topic under study and asked to describe what is happening in the picture. Because the pictures are so vague, it is believed that the respondents will actually reveal their own personalities, motivations, and inner feelings about the situation.

A modern form of the TAT looks like a comic strip with two characters discussing the topic under study. One character has a statement printed in the "balloon" above him, but above the other character is an empty balloon. Respondents are asked to fill in the balloon as they think the character would reply. Once again, respondents are answering for someone else but are expressing their own ideas. Figure 3-4 illustrates the cartoon technique.

DEPTH INTERVIEWS As described in the focus-group approach, depth interviews are unstructured, informal interviews. General questions are usually asked, followed by more specific questions that probe for needs, desires, motives, and emotions of the consumer. Also, the questioning is sometimes indirect, such as, "Why do you think your friends smoke Marlboros?" as opposed to the direct question, "Why do you prefer Marlboro cigarettes?" Again, this method attempts to circumvent inhibitions the respondent may have about revealing inner feelings. By carefully following cues given by the respondent, an interviewer can ask a series of questions that probe for underlying motivations.

While focus-group research can be a valuable tool for certain types of problems, such as those involved with new products, a useful alternative for many situations is the individual in-depth interview. This technique assumes that one person representing a specific market segment shares similar ideas and experiences with other members of the segment. If so, the hypotheses generated from one in-depth interview will not differ from those arising from a focus-group discussion with eight to ten people. Because the cost of recruiting respondents and obtaining facilities for focus-group research is so substantial, the in-depth interview may find increased use.[31]

The key factor with depth interviewing (as well as focus-group interviewing) is the interviewer's skill, which calls for imagination and thoroughness in probing consumer leads while not influencing the respondent's answers. Because of their very nature, interview results are interpreted subjectively rather than quantitatively. Thus, there is a great possibility for bias. An additional source of error from depth

FIGURE 3-4

Cartoon projective technique.

and focus-group interviews may arise with the use of small samples, which may not be representative of the entire population.

Attitude-Measurement Scales Significant strides have been made in the area of measuring consumers' attitudes. This has resulted in the development of various self-reporting attitude-rating scales. The scales are termed self-reporting because consumers express their own evaluation of their attitudes by responding to the scale in the way they think most appropriate.

The many scales available differ mainly in their structure and in the degree to which they actually measure attitudes. This section presents two of the more widely used scales in consumer research—the Likert scale and the semantic differential.

LIKERT (SUMMATED) SCALES   There are four stages involved in using a Likert scale:

1 A list of statements relevant to the attitudes under investigation is compiled, with each statement identifiable as either favorable or unfavorable.

2 Agreement-disagreement responses are selected. For example, five variations might be used, ranging from "strongly agree" to "strongly disagree."

3 After pretesting identifies the most relevant statements, the scales are administered to consumers who indicate which response most nearly expresses their attitude about the statement.

4 The score for each consumer is computed by summing the weights associated with each response checked.

The following is an example of an individual's response to a Likert scale:

	Strongly Agree 5	Agree 4	Undecided 3	Disagree 2	Strongly Disagree 1
Sears is generally a progressive store.		X			
Sears' stores are generally well stocked.	X				
Sears' merchandise is generally low-priced.		X			

Often the responses are added based on the numerical value assigned to them. This consumer's score of 13 indicates a very favorable attitude toward Sears. A lower total score, such as 6, would be interpreted as an unfavorable attitude.

SEMANTIC DIFFERENTIAL   The semantic differential consists of pairs of bipolar adjectives or antonym phrases as ends of a continuum with response options spaced in between. This technique can be used in marketing to rate the psychological meaning of concepts, products, companies, or people.[32]

Typically, a seven-position scale is utilized between the adjectives with the middle value being neutral. A consumer is asked to mark the position that most closely corresponds to his or her attitude toward the subject being studied. Responses can be tabulated and profiled, a procedure which dramatically illustrates consumer attitudes.

Below is a sample set of semantic differential scales (with only a few adjectives shown) which might be used to have consumers express their attitudes toward three brands of bread. A profile of consumers' responses is also drawn in.

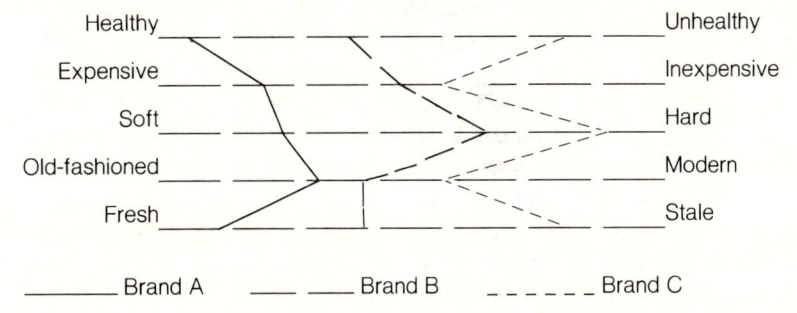

```
Healthy       ___ ___ ___ ___ ___ ___ ___ Unhealthy
Expensive     ___ ___ ___ ___ ___ ___ ___ Inexpensive
Soft          ___ ___ ___ ___ ___ ___ ___ Hard
Old-fashioned ___ ___ ___ ___ ___ ___ ___ Modern
Fresh         ___ ___ ___ ___ ___ ___ ___ Stale
```

_____ Brand A   _ _ _ _ Brand B   - - - - - Brand C

Notice that consumers have a favorable attitude toward Brand A while Brand B is viewed somewhat neutrally, and attitudes toward C are quite negative. Such a finding would be of value to Brand C and could help guide the company in making strategy decisions to overcome this unfavorable image.

As in all of the approaches that have been discussed, the decision to use a specific method or scaling technique must depend on the type of information being sought by the researcher as well as the way in which the data are to be applied.[33]

Information Processing Measures[34] Recently, many researchers have stressed that consumers are active decision makers who can be better understood by examining how they acquire information and manipulate it to arrive at purchase decisions. *Information processing* focuses on such consumer activities as information search, allocation of attention to various information sources, development of product knowledge, and use of strategies to combine information from various sources to arrive at product decisions. Research interest in such topics has fostered the design of new consumer measures to study *processes* (search, attention, and so on) which occur over time. These process measures are different from most previously existing measures which were designed to assess the level or strength of some variable (motivation, attitude, and so on) at a particular point in time.

A number of methods have been developed to study consumer information-processing activities. Among the more frequently used techniques are verbal protocols, eye movement analysis, information monitoring measures, free elicitation, and integration studies.

Verbal protocol methods require the consumer to think "out loud" during or after the performance of some task of interest, such as shopping or choosing among alternatives. In this way subjects verbalize their thoughts; the record of these thoughts is termed a *protocol*. This information allows researchers to gain insight into consumers' thought processes and how information is used in decision making. Since this method focuses on consumers' verbalizations, one of its potential limitations is that it only reveals conscious aspects of information processing that can be communicated.

Eye movement analysis involves use of a sophisticated instrument which is capable of recording the sequence of a consumer's eye movements. In a typical situation, the consumer is presented with some information for viewing, and the recorder is used to track the consumer's pattern of eye movements across the informational display. This can suggest answers to such questions as which aspects of the information appear to draw the most attention and where consumers tend to first look for information in the display. The method has been employed in the advertising field to learn how consumers acquire information from promotions and other types of communications. Since eye movements are not under the conscious control of consumers, the technique represents a potentially useful complement to protocol methods.

Informational monitoring approaches typically present information to consumers on a display board (hence, they are also called information board studies). The display board is essentially a matrix array of available information about various brands. Columns of the matrix may represent the different brands, while the rows represent some product characteristics (such as color and weight). Cards available in all cells of the matrix contain information on specific characteristics for each particular brand. The consumer is requested to select a brand after he reviews whatever information he wishes from the board. The sequence and type of information selected then provides insight into the amount of information acquired and the manner in which the information is chosen and processed. Similar to the protocol method, this technique emphasizes conscious aspects of behavior. However, it more heavily focuses on the information acquisition process. Also, since it directly records information selected from the display board, it is not affected by inaccuracies and omissions occuring in consumers' verbal reports of activities.

The method of *free elicitation* has been used in attempts to discover how consumers organize their product knowledge in their memories. The method involves presenting a consumer subject with a key word or phrase (such as "eating" or "driving") that serves as a probe. The consumer is then asked to quickly relate the "things that came to mind." Recordings are made for later analysis which will focus on determining the knowledge consumers have regarding the probe concept. In addition, the number of responses that consumers make, the associations they draw between various concepts (such as between the probe "eating" and other concepts such as nutrition, a balanced diet, protein, and energy levels) and other relevant measures give insight into consumers' beliefs and how they have organized information in their memory. Results have relevance for many marketing activities, especially those involving the design of advertisements and other communications.

Information integration methods begin in a way similar to the free elicitation technique. That is, subjects are typically provided with some information about a product or situation. However, instead of then asking consumers to relate what comes to their mind, they are asked to make some type of judgment or choice based on the information provided. By varying the type of inputs that are presented, the researcher can begin to understand how consumers integrate or combine information to arrive at decisions. For example, such methods can be designed to reveal whether consumers tend to make judgments by simply averaging various inputs together, by weighing certain information more heavily than others, or by using some other integration method to reach a decision.

Results from an increasing number of information-processing studies are indicating that the consumer's processing ability and the tasks which she confronts will strongly influence how processing occurs. That is, the way the information presentation is organized, the reasons a consumer has for reviewing it, and her ability to process the information will have a significant influence on how she receives and manipulates it.[35] This suggests that researchers must be aware of the information-processing situation in order to appropriately choose among the many combinations of information-processing measurement techniques for studying consumers.

SUMMARY

This chapter has examined the role of consumer research in studying consumer behavior. The goal of consumer research was seen to be either exploratory or conclusive in nature. Sources of consumer information were also discussed, including those already gathered for the marketer (secondary research) and those obtained by the marketer himself (primary research). Consumer information may be gathered at one time (cross-sectional study), or over an extended period (longitudinal research). In addition, data on consumers may be obtained via three basic approaches: observation, survey, or experiment. Finally, the nature of information gathered in consumer studies was discussed under the categories of demographic, activity, and cognitive research.

From the numerous techniques and their applications discussed in this chapter, it becomes clear that consumer research is essential in helping marketers make sound decisions. Yet research should not be used only retrospectively. Sometimes marketers spend so much money finding out what happened in the past that they cannot afford to find out what is about to happen. Therefore, the importance of looking ahead through research needs to be stressed.

In the remaining two chapters of this section, we will explore the use of consumer research in selecting target market segments. Chapter 4 will further discuss demographic research, and Chapter 5 will explain approaches to market selection that are primarily activity and cognitive in orientation.

DISCUSSION TOPICS

1 Define consumer research.

2 Discuss the significance of consumer research to marketers, consumers, and the economy.

3 Discuss the role of focus-group interviewing. Find an example in the literature of its actual use by a company and briefly describe it to the class. Was the technique used properly?

4 Under what conditions should the marketer rely on secondary data? What potential limitations are there in their use?

5 Distinguish between cross-sectional and longitudinal research and illustrate each with an example.

6 Design and conduct a consumer panel for selected purchases among class members.

7   Design and conduct the following types of consumer research on subjects of your choosing:
    a. observation   **b.** survey   **c.** experiment

8   With the objective of determining consumer attitudes toward instant coffee, design and conduct a cognitive research study using the following techniques:
    a. word association   **b.** projective tests   **c.** semantic differential
    What differences are found in the results using these approaches?

NOTES

[1]Kent Larsson, "Retail Management Will Shift Focus from Merchandising to Marketing," *Marketing News,* May 30, 1980, p. 5.

[2]John A. Prestbo, "Good Listener," *The Wall Street Journal,* April 29, 1980, pp. 1, 35.

[3]Tom Bayer, "Zale Sparkles in Strategy Shift," *Advertising Age,* October 5, 1981, pp. 4, 120.

[4]Laurel Leff, "Radio Stations Hire 'Doctors' To Fix Formats," *The Wall Street Journal,* January 7, 1981, p. 21.

[5]Lawrence Ingrassia, "A Matter of Taste," *The Wall Street Journal,* February 26, 1980, p. 1.

[6]Ingrassia, "A Matter of Taste," pp. 1, 23.

[7]"Minnetonka Credits 'Thinking,' Not Research, for Success of Softsoap," *Marketing News,* December 26, 1980, pp. 1, 6.

[8]Prestbo, "Good Listener," p. 35.

[9]Myril D. Axelrod, "Marketers Get an Eyeful When Focus Groups Expose Products, Ideas, Images, Ad Copy, etc. to Consumers," *Marketing News,* February 28, 1975, p. 6.

[10]Roger E. Bengston, "Despite Controversy, Focus Groups are Used to Examine a Wide Range of Marketing Questions," *Marketing News,* September 19, 1980, p. 25; and Yolanda Brugaletta, "Gives Guidelines to Set Up, Use, and Analyze Focus Groups," *Marketing News,* October 24, 1975, p. 1.

[11]"Success of Scripto Erasable Pen Due to Marketing Research: CEO," *Marketing News,* January 23, 1981, p. 8.

[12]See Harper W. Boyd, Jr., Ralph Westfall, and Stanley F. Stasch, *Marketing Research: Text and Cases,* 5th ed., Irwin, Homewood, Ill., 1981; and Gilbert A. Churchill, Jr., *Marketing Research: Methodological Foundations,* 2d ed., The Dryden Press, Hinsdale, Ill., 1979, for a partial list of guides to secondary data.

[13]"Follow That Car!" *Marketing & Media Decisions,* January 1981, pp. 70–71, 103.

[14]David J. Blum, "Census is Eagerly Awaited by Marketers," *The Wall Street Journal,* March 26, 1980, p. 48.

[15]Herbert E. Krugman, "Some Applicagions of Pupil Measurement," *Journal of Marketing Research,* 1:15, November 1964.

[16]Neil Jesuele, "Combined Eye Tracking, Verbal Questioning Technique Now Helps Canadian Advertisers," *Marketing News,* April 18, 1980, p. 22.

[17]See, for example, Jack J. Honomichl, "Turning a Dream Into a Reality," *Advertising Age,* February 9, 1981, pp. S-4–S-9; Carol Poston, "Dear Diary Panel . . ." *Advertising Age,* February 9, 1981, pp. S-10–S-11; Cecelia Lentini, "Research Scans Altered States," *Advertising Age,* April 13, 1981, pp. S-11–S-12; and Polly Summar, "Service Scans the Market," *Advertising Age,* April 27, 1981, pp. S-48–S-49.

[18]"Scanning Data: A Study in Applications," *The Nielsen Researcher,* no. 3, 1981, pp. 13–16.

[19]Edward Tauber, "Purchase Transaction Analysis of UPC Data Identifies Buying Habits," *Marketing News,* January 11, 1980, pp. 10, 14; Jeffrey H. Birnbaum, "Admen Excited over New Marketing Tool, but Critics Contend it Smacks of '1984,'" *Wall Street Journal,* September 25, 1981, p. 35; and Steven E. Scott, "Merchandising in the 80s: How Retailers Will Use Scan Data," *The Nielsen Researcher,* no. 1, 1982, pp. 2–15.

[20]See, for example, Jennifer Alter, "Test Marketing: No Shelving the Future," *Advertising Age,* February 9, 1981, pp. S-1, S-26; Carol Galginaitis, "What's Beneath a Test Market?" *Advertising Age,* February 9, 1981, pp. S-2–S-28; Mary McCabe English, "Marketers: Better Than a Coin Flip," *Advertising Age,* February 9, 1981, pp. S-14–S-16; Dylan Landis, "Durable Goods, Good for a Test?" *Advertising Age,* February 9, 1981, pp. S-18–S-20; and "Testing, Testing, Testing . . ." *Marketing & Media Decisions,* January 1981, pp. 60–61, 112.

[21]*The Wall Street Journal,* March 12, 1981, p. 1.

[22]For a more complete presentation of the experimental approach see Keith Cox and Ben M. Enis, *Experimentation for Marketing Decisions,* International Textbook, Scranton, Pa., 1969; and M. Venkatesan and Robert J. Holloway, *An Introduction to Marketing Experimentation,* Free Press, New York, 1971.

[23]"Open Throttle," *Marketing & Media Decisions,* December 1979, p. 102.

[24] "Brand Report 52: Coffee and Tea," *Marketing & Media Decisions,* April 1980, pp. 129–130.
[25] "Who Buys a G.M. Diesel Car?" *The New York Times,* November 9, 1978, p. D7.
[26] "The New Sears," *Business Week,* November 16, 1981, p. 143.
[27] Sanford L. Jacobs, "Using Official Data Often Helps Avoid Mistakes, Find Customers," *The Wall Street Journal,* January 5, 1981, p. 15; and Manuel D. Plotkin, "What the 1980 Census Can Do for Business," *Business,* 29:2–8, July–August 1979.
[28] "Census Update & ZIProfile Offer Detailed Demographics," *Marketing News,* November 30, 1979, p. 5; and Craig Reiss, "Marketers Target in on Geo-demographics," *Marketing & Media Decisions,* July 1981, pp. 46–47, 193–194.
[29] "Qualitative Research—A Summary of the Concepts Involved," *Journal of the Market Research Society,* 21:107–124, April 1979.
[30] Mason Haire, "Projective Techniques in Marketing Research," *Journal of Marketing,* 14:649–656, April 1950.
[31] Jack H. Grossman, "Individual In-Depth Interviews Are an Economical Alternative to Focus Groups," *Marketing News,* October 3, 1980, p. 4.
[32] William A. Mindak, "Fitting the Semantic Differential to the Marketing Problem," *Journal of Marketing,* 25:28–33, April 1961.
[33] For a more complete presentation of cognitive research techniques see G. David Hughes, *Attitude Measurement for Marketing Strategies,* Scott, Foresman, Glenview, Ill., 1971.
[34] This section is based on James R. Bettman, "Data Collection and Analysis Approaches for Studying Consumer Information Processing," in William D. Perreault, Jr. (ed.), *Advances in Consumer Research, Volume 4,* Association for Consumer Research, Atlanta, 1977, pp. 342–345; Andrew A. Mitchell, "An Information Processing View of Consumer Behavior in Subhash C. Jain (ed.), *Research Frontiers in Marketing: Dialogues and Directions,* American Marketing Association, Chicago, 1978, pp. 188–197; and Jerry C. Olson and Laura Sims, "Consumers' Nutrition Knowledge: An Information Processing Perspective," Pennsylvania State University Working Paper in Marketing Research, no. 83, July 1979.
[35] See Charles M. Schaninger and Donald Sciglimpaglia, "The Influence of Cognitive Personality Traits and Demographics on Consumer Information Acquisition," *Journal of Consumer Research,* 8:208–216, September 1981; Walter A. Henry, "The Effect of Information-Processing Ability on Processing Accuracy," *Journal of Consumer Research,* 7:42–48, June 1980; and Denis A. Lussier and Richard W. Olshavsky, "Task Complexity and Contingent Processing in Brand Choice," *Journal of Consumer Research,* 6:154–164, September 1979, for examples of recent evidence on this point.

CHAPTER 4
MARKET SEGMENTATION: BASIC APPROACHES

One of the most profound realizations to strike any marketer is that there is a great diversity among consumers. Upon closer inspection of the total market, however, it is found that smaller groups of consumers have more homogeneity than the group as a whole in certain characteristics, especially their consumer behavior.

This chapter introduces the concept of identifying and selectively marketing to such homogeneous groups of consumers. The major alternatives in selecting market targets are discussed, stressing the value of market segmentation. Some of the most important bases for segmenting markets are also discussed. In Chapter 5, the topic of segmentation is continued with an examination of additional methods by which markets may be selected. The associated concept of product positioning is also discussed and related to market segmentation.

VIEWS OF THE MARKET AND ALTERNATIVE MARKETING STRATEGIES

Marketers may approach target markets in their aggregate and heterogeneous form or as smaller, more homogeneous segments. The following section will discuss these two alternatives.

Market Aggregation

A market-aggregation strategy means, in effect, that little if any subdivision of the market is applied. With this approach, a firm would produce a single product and offer it to all consumers with a single marketing program. Although the marketer recognizes that not everyone will buy his product, he expects to attract a sufficient number for profitable operations. This approach has also been described as *undifferentiated marketing* or *product differentiation*.

In the past, a number of firms have used market-aggregation strategies including soft drink companies, cigarette manufacturers, gasoline marketers, many packaged food producers, and home appliance manufacturers. For example, Coca-Cola was for many years presented to consumers as a one-flavor soft drink available only in the familiar 6-ounce glass bottle and with the unchanging promotion theme "The Pause That Refreshes." Similarly, in the 1950s all major brands of American cigarettes were 87 millimeters long; without filters; made of nearly identical blends of Kentucky burley tobacco without special flavor additives; packed in soft, paper packets of twenty; and designed to appeal to masculine tastes.

The reasoning behind market aggregation is that although consumers may differ, they are sufficiently alike to approach as a homogeneous grouping for the product under consideration. Market aggregation, therefore, presents a standard product that differs little if any from competition, makes heavy use of mass promotion, and attempts to distinguish the product as being superior.[1] By so doing it seeks to have demand conform to what manufacturers are willing to supply.

The major advantage of pursuing such a strategy is lower costs of doing business. For example, efficiencies are gained from longer production runs with a single product. There may also be greater media discounts from a large-scale, undifferentiated advertising program.

There are dangers in this strategy, however. The marketer exposes himself to competitive attacks by other firms pursuing a strategy of serving unfulfilled consumer needs. Consequently, by attempting to satisfy many consumers *reasonably* well, he becomes vulnerable to other firms seeking to satisfy particular segments of the market *very* well. It is difficult for a product or brand to be all things to all people.[2]

Market Segmentation

In firms employing a strategy of segmentation, the market is viewed as being made up of smaller segments, each more homogeneous than the total in important characteristics. For example, the soft drink and cigarette markets of today are quite different from the situation described earlier. The Coca-Cola Company now offers a variety of soft-drink flavors, calories, and containers. Similarly, today's cigarette market features nonfilters, high-filtration filters, menthol flavors, 100-mm cigarettes, feminine designs, and crush-proof boxes, in addition to the traditional products. Thus, market segmentation is the process of partitioning the heterogeneous market into segments. The goal is to facilitate development of unique marketing programs which will be most effective for these specific segments.

There are ranges of market segmentation alternatives. A firm might pursue *concentrated* marketing, which means that it would seek to serve only one of several market segments. Examples of organizations that have at some point pursued this strategy are Volkswagen, Sony, U.S. Time (Timex), and Gerber. On the other hand, a company may pursue market *atomization* whereby each consumer is treated uniquely. Examples of firms that have adopted this approach abound in the specialty industrial goods field. In addition, those who custom-make cars, homes, and furniture are applying market atomization to consumer goods.

Most companies employing market segmentation, however, select several market segments to appeal to with different products, using different promotional efforts and prices, and perhaps selling through different distribution outlets. Many companies fit this description, such as General Motors with its various car divisions. Similarly, Procter & Gamble produces not only Ivory Snow but Tide, Dash, Duz, Dreft and other detergents to meet different consumers' needs (at least as they are perceived by purchasers of these brands).

Benefits and Costs of Market Segmentation   Clearly, market segmentation conforms supply to what consumers demand. In addition, because the segments contain fewer and more similar consumers, the marketer is able to obtain more detailed knowledge about their characteristics. As one author suggests, potential benefits of this approach lie in its ability to aid the marketing manager to:

- Quickly detect trends in a rapidly changing market
- Design products that truly meet the demands of the market
- Determine the most effective advertising appeals
- Direct the appropriate amounts of promotion in the right media to segments offering the greatest profit potential
- Schedule promotional efforts during time periods when responsiveness is likely to be highest.[3]

Although market segmentation produces benefits for the firm, it also boosts costs. Typically, manufacturing costs are higher because of shorter production runs; research costs are higher because of the need to investigate more segments; promotion costs are higher when quantity media discounts are lost; and, in addition, overlapping market coverage may result in some "cannibalization" as one product steals sales from another in the same company's line. This occurred at General Foods when Maxim freeze-dried instant coffee was introduced. The brand name was selected to trade on the reputation of Maxwell House instant coffee, and as a result, stole millions of dollars in sales from the older product.[4] Ideally, a company would like to achieve what General Foods did when it introduced Cool Whip. Sales were taken away from competing aerosol toppings (which General Foods did not produce) rather than from its other brand of dessert topping, Dream Whip. Thus, market segmentation can result in greater sales for a company, but at higher costs. Of course, the goal is to increase revenue more than costs, thus raising profits.[5]

Market Criteria for Effective Segmentation   A decision to use a market segmentation strategy should rest on consideration of four important criteria that affect its profitability. In order for segmentation to be viable, the market must be: (1) identifiable and measurable, (2) accessible, (3) substantial, and (4) responsive.

IDENTIFIABLE AND MEASURABLE   Segments must be identifiable so that the marketer can determine which consumers belong to a segment and which do not. However, there may be a problem with the segment's measurability (that is, the amount of information available on specific buyer characteristics) because numerous variables are difficult, if not impossible, to measure at the present time. For example, if it is discovered that consumers who perspire profusely favor a particular brand, what can the marketer do with this information? Probably very little since the size of this particular segment will be difficult to estimate through measurement. Consequently, such a variable does not appear to represent an effective means of segmenting the market.

ACCESSIBLE   This criterion refers to the ease of effectively and economically reaching chosen segments with marketing efforts. Some desired segments may be inaccessible because of legal reasons; for example, liquor manufacturers are unable to market directly to young teenagers. It is more likely, however, that segments may be inaccessible because the marketer is unable to reach them via existing promotional media and retail outlets at a reasonable cost and with minimum waste.

There are two ways to reach prospects: (1) controlled coverage of marketing effort and (2) customer self-selection.[6] A controlled-coverage approach involves trying to reach chosen target market segments while avoiding others not in the group. For example, assume a marketer desired to reach advanced skiers with a new product. Suppose that from media studies it can be determined that most of these prospects are regular readers of *Skiing*. With this information the marketer has the ability to largely control the coverage of her advertising so that it reaches mainly the target segment. She may further control her marketing coverage by offering the product only in exclusive ski shops where most advanced skiers might shop. Thus, such an approach is very efficient because it reaches mainly target segments with little "wasted" coverage of segments who are not prime prospects. Controlled coverage is also possible for some products by use of regional editions of such national magazines as *Time, Newsweek, Sports Illustrated,* and *Business Week*.

Customer self-selection, on the other hand, involves reaching a more general audience while relying on the product's and advertisement's special appeal to the intended target segments. For example, a product for skiers may be advertised in national editions of *Time, Newsweek, Sports Illustrated,* or *Business Week*. These general market media will cover many consumers who are not interested in the product, but those who are actually skiers (or perhaps those who may purchase the product as a gift) will be attracted to the ad. These consumers, in effect, select themselves by their attention to the ad. The product can also be sold through mass merchandisers shopped by a wide cross section of people. Yet only those who have an interest in this product category will tend to respond.

Although the approach of customer self-selection results in some wasted effort, such widespread coverage can sometimes reach otherwise inaccessible prospects. A decision must be made on which of these strategies is best for gaining accessibility to the chosen target segment. However, it appears that when a controlled coverage approach can be applied it is economically advantageous.[7]

SUBSTANTIAL   This criterion refers to the degree to which a chosen segment is large enough to support profitably a separate marketing program. As was cited previously, a strategy of market segmentation is costly. Thus, one must carefully consider not only the number of customers available in a segment but also the amount of their purchasing power.

For some product categories the incidence and/or frequency of usage are so low that the entire market can support only one or two brands. Because a brand in this situation must appeal to all segments, segmenting a portion of the market may not be profitable.

Another situation related to the substantiality criterion is when heavy users make up such a large proportion of the sales volume that they are the only relevant target. If only a very few consumers account for most of the sales volume, marketing efforts may have to be directed at this group. If this is so, additional segmentation may be meaningless unless the heavy-user group itself is of sufficient size or volume potential to permit a segmented approach.[8]

RESPONSIVE   There is little to justify the development of a separate and unique marketing program for a target segment unless it responds uniquely to these efforts. Therefore, the problem is to meaningfully define market segments so that they favorably respond to marketing programs designed specifically for them.[9] It is possible for the marketer, using readily available data, to measure differences among market segments in terms of their responsiveness to the marketing decision variables, and these measurements may successfully be used in developing marketing strategy.[10]

Market segmentation is not useful, however, when a brand is the dominant one in the market and is already appealing to the many segments. Targeting the product to only one or two segments of this market is not likely to benefit sales much since these groups are already responding to the marketer's strategy.[11]

If the four criteria above are fulfilled, segmentation will be an attractive marketing strategy. The question remains, however: By which variables or bases may the market be segmented? Before exploring these bases in detail we will first describe the process of performing market-segmentation studies.

Performing Market Segmentation   This section reviews the steps involved in a typical market-segmentation study in order to illustrate a successful approach that may often be taken.[12] The eight steps involved in the process are as follows:

1   Define the problem or determine the usage to be made of the research.

2   Select a segmentation basis.

3   Choose a set of descriptors that defines, characterizes, or relates to the segmentation basis.

4   Select a sample of consumers.

5   Collect data on segment descriptors from the sample of consumers.

6   Form segments based on chosen consumer descriptors.

7   Establish profiles of segments.

8   Translate the results into marketing strategy.

Each of these steps is described below.

The first step in any market segmentation process is to define the problem or determine the usage to be made of the research. For example, market segmentation can be used to answer a wide range of questions about the response of market segments to the firm's marketing strategies (such as price or product changes, new product offerings, and advertising themes) as well as the selection of target market segments for the firm's offerings. Thus, the marketer doing concept testing studies, for instance, may want to know how interested and disinterested respondents for a new product concept differ by demographic, socioeconomic, or attitudinal characteristics. The marketer may also want to know whether the market for new product concepts can be segmented in terms of some benefit sought by the respondents (such as low price) and what the concept evaluations, attitudes, product usage, demographics, and other background characteristics of these benefit-seeking groups may be.

After a decision has been made regarding the purpose of the segmentation research, the marketer must then select a segmentation basis. Segmentation studies are usually conducted by marketing practitioners using one of two general alternatives for choosing a segmentation basis: *a priori* and *clustering* methods. For purposes of illustration, the a priori approach will be described here. The clustering method will also be addressed briefly at the end of this section.

The a priori segmentation approach occurs when management decides *in advance* what basis to use for segmentation. If, for example, concern is with the likely impact of a price increase, consumer income or price sensitivity measures may be chosen as the segmentation basis. When conducting such a market segmentation approach, therefore, the marketer must begin by selecting some basis for it.

A number of bases for segmentation have been suggested as appropriate in certain situations. Some of these are outlined in Table 4-1. Generally, these segmentation bases used by marketers can be categorized as falling into one of two major groupings: general consumer characteristics and situation-specific consumer characteristics. General consumer characteristics to be discussed soon include demographic, geographic, socioeconomic, and lifestyle characteristics. Situation-specific consumer characteristics to be examined include product usage, purchase patterns, and benefits sought in a product. Each of these approaches offers advantages as well as disadvantages depending on the situation faced by the marketer. The relevant considerations for making a selection in the segmentation process are management's specific needs and the state of knowledge about each variable's relevance as a market-segmentation basis.

During selection of a segmentation basis, the criterion of differential responsiveness is a significant concept. It means that different demand elasticities exist for the marketing offerings of product, price, promotion, and distribution. Thus, the marketer is attempting to determine whether different elasticities exist among different groups and what factors cause or, at least, are associated with the differences among the groups. If these factors can be identified, they may then be used

TABLE 4-1

TYPICAL SEGMENTATION BASES

For general understanding of a market:
- Benefits or satisfactions sought in a product
- Product purchase and usage patterns
- Consumer needs
- Brand loyalty and switching patterns
- A hybrid of the variables above

For positioning a product in an existing market:
- Product usage
- Product preferences
- Benefits sought
- A hybrid of the variables above

For new product concepts (and new product introduction):
- Reaction to new concepts (intention to buy, preference over current brand, and so on)
- Benefits sought

For pricing decisions:
- Price sensitivity
- Deal proneness
- Price sensitivity by purchase/usage patterns

For advertising decisions:
- Benefits sought
- Media usage
- Psychographic/lifestyle
- A hybrid of the variables above (and/or purchase/usage patterns)

For distribution decisions:
- Store loyalty and patronage
- Benefits sought in store selection

Source: Adapted from Yoram Wind, "Issues and Advances in Segmentation Research," *Journal of Marketing Research,* **15**:320, August 1978, published by the American Marketing Association.

as bases to divide the market into segments. Notice that some bases may be the real *cause* of different demand elasticities, while others may not explain but simply be *correlates* of the elasticities. For example, demographic characteristics (age, income, and so on) of consumers who use a product such as a video-recorder may be a useful basis for segmentation because these characteristics may correlate with differences in product purchase or usage patterns. However, this basis may not actually serve as an explanation for the differences in purchase or usage patterns. Other factors such as consumers' personalities or lifestyles, which may not be known to the marketer, can be the true cause of the different demand elasticities existing in the marketplace.

Of course, it is usually desirable to discover a basis which not only serves to distinguish market segments, but also causes the formation of such differing groups. However, since this goal is usually difficult to attain, the marketer often must settle for a basis that distinguishes segments but does not explain the existence of these groupings. In either case, the segmentation basis selected should be one that is appropriate to the decision-making needs of management. Although a segmentation basis may theoretically be the best one, if management cannot grasp it easily, it is not likely to be correctly used. Thus, there may be many possible and useful segmentation bases, but those that are easier to measure and understand, and those that suit the marketer's purpose and ability are the ones that will be chosen.

The third step in the process of market segmentation is to choose a set of descriptors that the marketer believes will define, characterize, or somehow be related to the segmentation basis. These descriptors of segments can include virtually any variable (sex, social class, and so on). To illustrate, the degree to which a person may respond to price deals may be linked to such demographic descriptors as age, income, and location. In fact, the enormous number of possible variables from which to select makes it a complex decision process for the marketer. There may be the problem of an often questionable link between the selected basis for segmentation and the segment descriptors. For example, segments with varying elasticities for marketing variables may not be identifiable in terms of standard demographics or other segment descriptors. Conversely, segments defined in terms of demographics may be identifiable, but they may not have varying elasticities for marketing variables. Thus, the marketer may not find a clear link between segment descriptors and a chosen basis for segmentation which could limit strategy implementation. Another problem involves management's ability to use information about those segment descriptors that discriminate between the segments as an input to the design of the firm's marketing strategy. The descriptors must be actionable so that management can relate findings to such decision variables. For example, it would be useful to find that not only do segments differ in age, but media habits also differ by age; thus, each segment can be reached with marketing messages through their own unique media.

The fourth step in market segmentation is to select a sample of consumers; that is, a group that is representative of the larger population of interest. Here, the idea is to research and identify segments on a low-cost basis. Instead of gathering data from the entire population, a less-costly sample of consumers is selected. It is then determined if segments are identifiable within this sample. If this is the case, the next step is to project sample results to the relevant population in order to segment the entire market.

In the fifth step, the market researcher will actually collect data on segment descriptors from the sample of consumers. When obtaining these data, the marketer may rely on primary data collection efforts or on available secondary sources (for example, the Market Research Corporation of America offers clients a variety of measures on a national panel of consumers).

In the sixth stage, the researcher must form segments by sorting the sample group of consumers into categories based on the chosen consumer descriptors.[13] Here the marketer must define and use a dividing line to determine to which segment each sample consumer will be assigned. For example, if the marketer were segmenting consumers into heavy-use and light-use soft-drink users, the decision might be to classify heavy users as those who purchase more than four liters of soft drinks per week.

Once respondents have been classified into segments, the seventh step involves establishing profiles of these segments on the basis of their key discriminating characteristics. For example, a segment of TV viewers who may be frequent watchers of TV movies may be profiled as having the following characteristics: lower income and education; traditional, conservative values; compulsive TV viewing; pride in a clean home; unwillingness to take risks; concern with security; contentment with being homebodies; and price consciousness. Several analytical techniques exist for accomplishing this process; however, discussion of their use is beyond the scope of this text.[14]

Finally, the most difficult aspect of any segmentation project is translating the results into marketing strategy. During this stage the marketer uses findings about the segments' estimated sizes and profiles to select target market groups and design appropriate marketing mixes for the chosen segments. Thus, the key to a successful segmentation study is the ability to interpret results and use them as guidelines for the design, execution, and evaluation of an appropriate marketing strategy. The selection of target segments is a complex "art" in which the marketer considers such factors as the segments' expected responses to marketing variables, their reachability, the nature of competitive activity within each segment, and the company's resources and ability to implement a segmented strategy. Information from the segment profile should help generate diverse ideas and creative strategies for appealing to chosen segments.

The a priori approach has been the traditional method of selecting a basis for segmentation. However, it has the serious potential limitation that the marketer may not have sufficient information in advance to select the best segmentation basis. Unless one is fortunate enough to begin the process by correctly identifying the most useful basis for segmentation, a less-than-optimum segmentation of the market is likely to occur. The *clustering* method presents an alternative which addresses this potential limitation of the a priori method. This approach, rather than selecting a basis for segmentation in advance, first attempts to see how a sample group of consumers may form their own groupings based on a variety of descriptor variables, such as needs, attitudes, benefits sought, and lifestyle characteristics. This procedure typically starts by measuring consumers on a wide variety of descriptors. Then, usually with computer-based grouping methods, the researcher attempts to find how consumers may cluster together on the basis of these measures. Such an approach is said to allow consumers to form "natural" groupings, instead of forming only those preestablished by the researcher when the a priori method is used. If such natural groupings are identified, the next step will be to determine what descriptor or set of descriptors may be associated with or explain these groupings. This information will then be used to form the basis or bases for segmentation.

Although there are newer, hybrid segmentation methods that have been tried by some researchers, the two types just discussed are the most widely practiced approaches.[15]

The remainder of this chapter as well as Chapter 5 will now examine a number of popular segmentation bases in more detail. It should be noted again, however, that no one basis will be appropriate for all marketing decisions; in fact, a combination of approaches may lead to much better information for decision making.

DEMOGRAPHIC CHARACTERISTICS AND MARKET SEGMENTATION

It is essential for us to review the general characteristics of the American consumer market and of some of its major segments. Only with a clear understanding of major consumer characteristics can we begin to appreciate the implications of environmental and individual determinants of their behavior. Hence, the remainder of this chapter will be devoted to isolating the most significant demographic, geographic, and socioeconomic characteristics and trends of American consumers and discussing their relevance for developing segmentation strategies. The following chapter will expand on these approaches by incorporating more-advanced segmentation concepts.

It is often said that a market consists of people with purchasing power and the willingness to buy. That is:

Market = people × purchasing power × willingness to buy

Consequently, if we examine these three elements of the consumer market we will obtain useful insights for segmentation decisions. We will begin by studying the first prerequisite in our definition of a market—people. The U.S. consumer market may be segmented along a number of demographic dimensions. This section discusses the major demographic characteristics with which the reader should be familiar. Figure 4-1 summarizes some important household characteristics to be addressed in this chapter.

United States Population Growth

It is helpful to first examine the overall size of the population in the United States even though it does not represent a "segment" of interest to most firms. In 1980 the population stood at approximately 226 million. Tracing the history of our population growth since World War II, we find that two major distortions have occurred: the "baby boom" and the "baby bust." The baby boom, which began in 1946 and lasted until the early 1960s, generated approximately 4 million births annually. The number of children born to the average woman of childbearing age (age 15 to 44) has varied from 2.1 during the great depression, to 3.8 during the baby boom, to 1.8 at present. This latter statistic gives rise to the characterization of the current period as the baby bust. For our population to level off and reach zero population growth (ZPG), however, the birth rate will have to remain at a rate of 2.1 or less for several decades.[16]

FIGURE 4-1

Distribution of population and income by household characteristics. (*Source:* Fabian Linden, "Per Capitaism," *Across the Board,* June 1980, p. 67.)

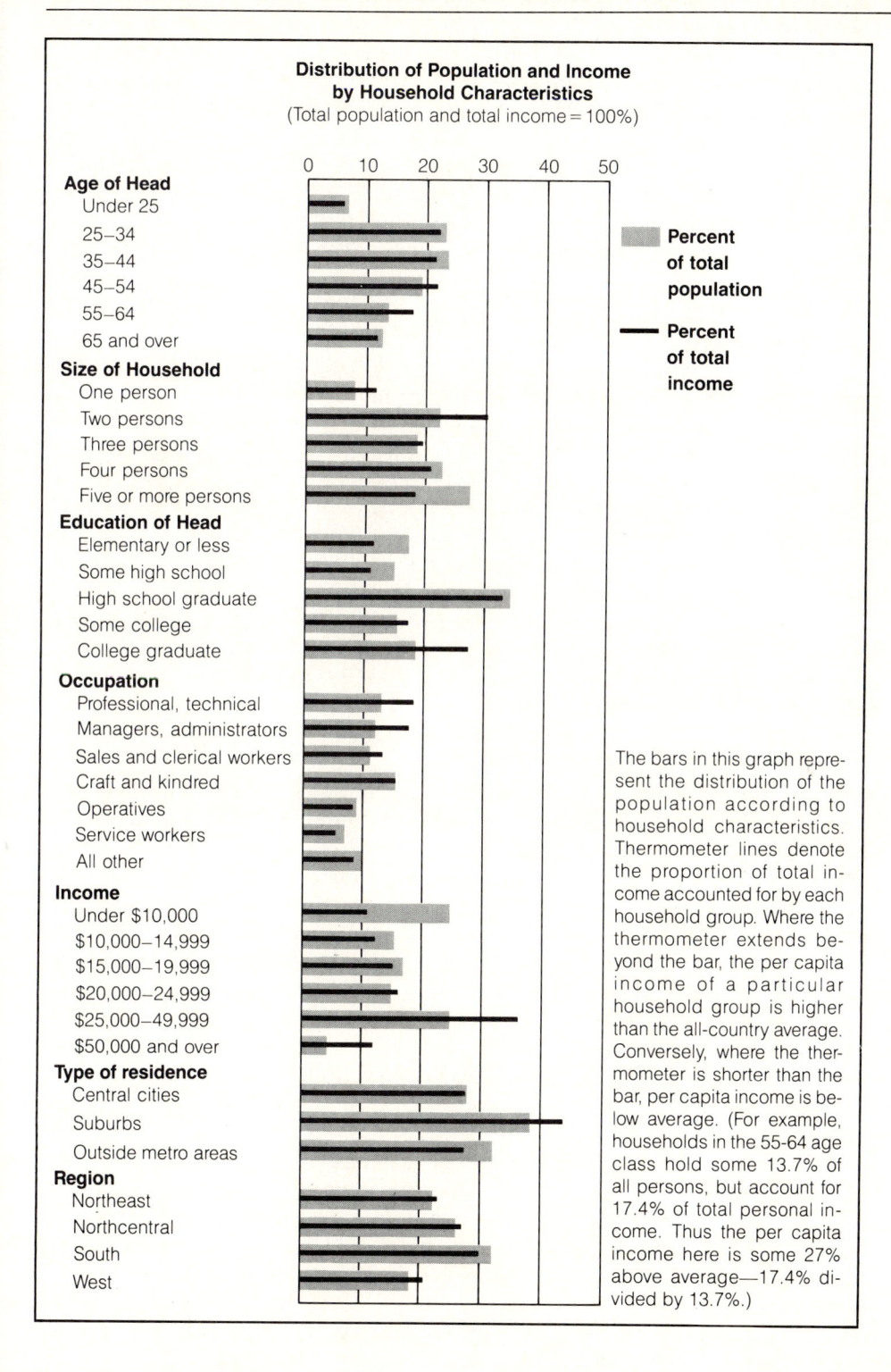

Distribution of Population and Income by Household Characteristics
(Total population and total income = 100%)

■ Percent of total population
— Percent of total income

Age of Head
- Under 25
- 25–34
- 35–44
- 45–54
- 55–64
- 65 and over

Size of Household
- One person
- Two persons
- Three persons
- Four persons
- Five or more persons

Education of Head
- Elementary or less
- Some high school
- High school graduate
- Some college
- College graduate

Occupation
- Professional, technical
- Managers, administrators
- Sales and clerical workers
- Craft and kindred
- Operatives
- Service workers
- All other

Income
- Under $10,000
- $10,000–14,999
- $15,000–19,999
- $20,000–24,999
- $25,000–49,999
- $50,000 and over

Type of residence
- Central cities
- Suburbs
- Outside metro areas

Region
- Northeast
- Northcentral
- South
- West

The bars in this graph represent the distribution of the population according to household characteristics. Thermometer lines denote the proportion of total income accounted for by each household group. Where the thermometer extends beyond the bar, the per capita income of a particular household group is higher than the all-country average. Conversely, where the thermometer is shorter than the bar, per capita income is below average. (For example, households in the 55-64 age class hold some 13.7% of all persons, but account for 17.4% of total personal income. Thus the per capita income here is some 27% above average—17.4% divided by 13.7%.)

The main reasons pointed to for the decline in the United States birthrate include the following:[17]

1. Modernization of our society such that it has become secular, industrialized, educated, and urban, and shifted from a high birth- and death rate to a low birth- and death rate

2. Contraception and the growing availability of abortion

3. The women's liberation movement, which has challenged the traditional roles of motherhood and homemaking among women

4. The growing environmental concern that a large population will use up too much of the world's limited natural resources

5. Economic causes, such as inflation and the high cost of having and supporting children (It now costs the average middle-income family $85,000 in 1980 dollars in direct, out-of-pocket expenditures to raise one child at home through age 18, including providing a public university education for 4 years.)[18]

Although low fertility seems here to stay according to most demographers, marketers can expect to see a new baby boom even with current fertility rates. This will be due to the increased number of annual births from the large pool of baby-boom women who have deferred childbearing. The difference between the next potential baby boom and the one following World War II though, will be that more women will be involved, but each will average fewer children.[19]

Changing Age Mix of the Population

The mix of ages in the United States population can be an important factor to consider. The population age mix of the 1980 to 1990 decade will include more babies, fewer teenagers and young adults, and many more middle-aged and elderly adults than during the 1970s. Evidence of the changing age mix is that the median age in the United States has increased from 27.9 in 1970 to 30 in 1980, and it will rise to an expected 32.8 in 1990.[20] Table 4-2 summarizes trends in age groups to 1990.

Each decade may be characterized according to a "core market thrust"—that market which reflects the largest proportional growth. During the 1950 to 1960 period, the core market focus was babies and young children; in the 1960s, it was

TABLE 4-2

AGE GROUP CHANGES, 1970–1990

Age	Percent of Total Population		
	1970	1980	1990 (projected)
0–5	10.2	8.6	9.2
6–12	14.0	10.6	10.3
13–17	9.8	8.7	6.6
18–24	12.1	13.3	10.4
25–34	12.3	16.3	17.0
35–44	11.3	11.6	15.1
45–54	11.4	10.2	10.5
55–64	9.1	9.5	8.6
65+	9.8	11.2	12.3

Source: U.S. Bureau of the Census.

teenagers and young adults; during the 1970s, it was young marrieds; during the 1980s, it will be early middle agers; and during the 1990s the core market will be middle agers.[21]

Demographers use the term "cohort" to mean the aggregate of persons born in any given year or specified period. Cohort factors, therefore, are the values and attitudes that a population group carries with it throughout life.[22] It will become clear in later chapters (especially Chapters 6 and 7) that values and attitudes differ among age groups within the population. For example, when General Mills asked adults and teens in the same families what expenditures they thought of as luxuries, they found that youngsters were far less likely than their parents to cite a new car each year or hired household help and were far more likely to classify having meat at most meals as a luxury.

Although cohort factors are difficult to predict, the following seem to be realistic trends.[23] First, there will be more working wives in the 1980s. In spite of the fact that the increase will amount to only a percent or two, the growth will be extremely meaningful because it will occur largely among women who have small children. Hence, some suggest there will be demands for more company-sponsored day care, and more paid maternity leave.

Second, there will continue to be few children per family. However, since a very large number of women are entering prime childbearing years, total births can skyrocket to 4 million or more annually, in spite of a low overall birthrate. Also, a large share of these births will be of first children—an estimated 40 percent of births in 1985 versus only 25 percent in 1960. This is significant since it has been estimated that an additional $700 is spent by parents "tooling up" for the first child. In fact, a leading consulting firm estimates that during the first three years, first-born children account for over $2000 in retail sales. Thus, this expected baby boom could account for an incremental $1 billion in retail sales by 1990.[24]

A third cohort factor is the growth in households (which are comprised of those related and unrelated individuals who occupy a housing unit.) Although the total population is an important factor, for many companies it is not nearly so critical as the number of total households. One of the reasons for the rapid growth in households is the high rate of divorce. The divorce rate for all marriages is currently 40 percent, and census experts estimate that approximately half of all children born in 1980 will spend a meaningful part of their childhood with only one parent.[25]

A more important reason for the large growth in households, however, is the increasing tendency for young singles to establish their own accommodations apart from their parents. There is also a growing segment of older adults who live apart from their children. Thus, the dramatic rise in number of households is occurring largely among single adults. Table 4-3 presents data on age cohorts along several important marketing dimensions.

Marketing Implications of Population Changes

There are a number of important marketing changes that have been wrought by shifts in the U.S. population. The baby bust, for instance, has caused some significant marketing reorientations among major entertainment companies:

> Walt Disney World's Experimental Prototype Community of Tomorrow (EPCOT)—a facility designed to display technology from around the world—is seen by Disney as a rich opportunity to tap a new market. The

TABLE 4-3
THE CHARACTERISTICS OF AGE

	Total	Under 25	25–29	30–34	35–39	40–44	45–54	55–64	65+
Consumer Units									
Millions	78.8	7.2	8.3	9.4	6.4	6.0	13.3	12.2	16.0
Distribution	100.0%	9.2	10.6	11.9	8.2	7.6	16.9	15.4	20.3
Growth (1977 to 1985)	16.7	9.2	23.5	29.1	42.2	29.3	−3.1	7.6	18.0
Type of Unit									
Husband/wife	66.1%	50.5	71.8	78.9	79.3	78.9	74.3	65.9	46.0
Other male	10.6	22.3	12.4	7.1	6.7	6.1	8.0	10.0	12.4
Female head	8.5	8.7	9.1	10.0	10.9	11.2	9.7	6.5	6.0
Other female	14.8	18.5	6.7	4.0	3.0	3.7	7.9	17.6	35.6
Number of Persons									
One person	23.8%	39.0	18.2	10.4	8.4	8.4	13.7	25.5	46.6
Two persons	28.4	29.1	24.0	11.8	7.8	11.5	24.7	45.6	43.0
Three	16.1	21.1	25.6	16.4	13.1	14.0	20.4	15.8	7.1
Four	14.6	8.7	21.8	29.9	25.1	22.1	18.3	7.2	1.7
Five or more	17.0	2.1	10.4	31.5	45.6	44.0	22.9	5.9	1.6
Average size (number)	2.8	2.1	2.9	3.8	4.2	4.1	3.3	2.3	1.7
Children: Families Having									
No children	58.1%	65.1	40.1	20.5	16.4	22.1	50.1	86.7	97.9
Children present, total	41.9	34.9	59.9	79.5	83.6	77.9	49.9	13.3	2.1
One	14.6	22.3	25.1	16.2	12.1	17.2	23.2	8.9	1.2
Two	13.8	9.9	23.8	30.8	27.4	25.1	14.6	2.6	0.4
Three or more	13.5	2.7	11.0	32.5	44.2	35.6	12.0	1.7	0.3
Any under 6	19.2%	34.3	54.2	54.4	33.7	17.4	5.0	0.4	0.5
6–17 only	22.6	0.6	5.8	25.0	50.0	60.5	44.8	12.8	1.5
Number of Earners									
None	18.7%	7.6	4.5	4.0	3.7	3.5	5.6	16.0	64.2
One	42.7	56.6	52.1	55.6	48.7	38.4	37.0	47.3	26.8
Two	29.3	35.2	42.8	38.6	37.7	34.7	33.2	27.0	7.6
Three or more	9.3	0.6	0.6	1.9	9.9	23.4	24.1	9.6	1.3
Wife Working (est.)	44.0%	57.0	53.0	50.0	50.0	50.0	50.0	41.0	16.0
Annual income under $ 5,000	19.3%	24.5	9.0	7.6	6.0	6.2	8.8	19.4	47.5
$ 5,000–$ 9,999	19.6	32.3	17.3	12.9	13.8	13.7	13.4	18.7	29.1
$10,000–$14,999	18.6	25.1	27.1	21.2	20.3	16.5	16.4	19.7	11.0
$15,000–$19,999	15.7	11.5	22.6	25.0	20.0	18.1	17.8	15.7	5.0
$20,000–$24,999	10.4	4.4	12.8	15.1	15.1	17.6	13.9	9.2	3.0
$25,000–$29,999	6.9	1.8	6.6	8.4	11.4	12.0	11.6	6.3	1.6
$30,000–$34,999	3.4	0.2	2.3	4.2	5.3	6.0	6.4	3.2	0.9
$35,000 and over	5.7	0.2	2.4	5.6	8.1	10.0	11.3	7.4	1.6
Average income (est.)	$14,900	$9,800	$14,000	$16,200	$17,800	$19,200	$19,700	$16,100	$8,700
Distribution, income	100.0%	6.0	10.0	13.0	9.8	9.9	22.6	16.8	11.9

TABLE 4-3 *(Continued)*

			Consumer Units, Age of Head						
	Total	Under 25	25–29	30–34	35–39	40–44	45–54	55–64	65+
			Education						
Grade school	23.4%	3.8	5.3	7.8	12.5	17.8	21.4	33.7	50.4
Some high school	16.7	15.5	11.8	16.2	16.4	17.9	19.2	18.8	15.7
High school graduate	30.1	40.8	35.8	36.5	35.7	32.8	31.3	26.7	17.3
Some college	14.2	26.3	23.5	16.3	15.6	13.4	12.2	10.0	7.5
College graduate	15.5	13.6	23.7	23.2	19.9	18.2	15.7	10.6	8.8
			Occupation						
All self-employed	10.3%	2.0	4.7	7.7	9.1	10.3	10.9	13.2	30.7
Professional, tech.	14.2	12.9	19.5	19.2	17.4	16.5	12.5	9.2	6.3
Managers, admin.	11.9	6.4	11.3	12.0	13.4	13.9	14.4	11.6	9.0
Clerical, sales	14.6	21.3	15.6	13.3	11.9	10.4	13.8	15.6	14.9
Craft workers	16.5	15.9	16.7	18.2	18.7	18.5	17.9	14.8	8.1
Operatives	16.3	21.4	18.4	16.8	17.2	15.9	14.9	16.1	7.9
Other employed	16.2	20.1	13.8	12.7	12.5	14.4	15.6	19.6	23.1
			Place of Residence						
Metropolitan areas, total	69.8%	71.1	74.8	74.2	71.1	71.9	70.1	68.2	64.1
All central cities	32.8	39.3	35.4	32.2	29.2	29.9	31.0	32.1	33.6
All other	37.0	31.8	39.4	42.0	41.9	42.0	39.1	36.0	30.5
Nonmetropolitan areas	30.1	28.9	25.2	25.8	28.9	28.1	29.8	31.7	35.8
			Homeownership						
Homeowner	62.7%	15.8	39.0	59.8	69.8	75.8	75.1	74.3	67.9
Renter	37.2	84.2	61.0	40.2	30.2	24.2	24.8	25.6	32.0

Note: Data principally based on a survey conducted in 1973. All income figures and working status of wife are for the year 1977.
Source: Fabian Linden, "Marketer's Safari—On the Trail of the American Young," *Across the Board,* September 1978, pp. 52–53.

company, which has long been dependent upon young children (a declining market) and families for its theme parks and movies, is broadening its appeal to adults. In addition to its attempt to gain a larger share than its current 25 percent of the 30 million tourists who visit Florida each year, Disney is now making more sophisticated movies in order to penetrate the older teenage and adult market.[26]

The food and beverage industries have also been strongly affected by these new patterns. For example, companies that have previously catered only to babies have found that during the baby bust it pays to diversify. Thus, Gerber Products Co., the nation's largest producer of baby foods has also gone into life insurance, printing, and prepackaged meals for single diners. However, with the advent of a new baby boom, the company is optimistic about the 1980s.[27] Nevertheless, Gerber is also trying to expand its market by convincing teenagers to think of its baby food as dessert.[28]

The lifeblood of the soft-drink industry has been the 13 to 24 age group who, on the average, consume more than 820 cans per individual per year. By 1985, the decline in this most lucrative age group is expected to cost soft-drink companies more than 3 *billion* in unsold cans annually. Consequently, companies such as Coca-Cola have (1) carefully shifted their advertising and launched numerous new cola products to appeal to their aging market, (2) pushed expansion in foreign markets, and (3) diversified into other products such as wine, orange juice, coffee, and tea.[29]

The changing age mix is causing significant shifts in marketing strategies for those who make and market clothes, cars, appliances, furniture, and hundreds of other products or services.[30] Some companies have been able to benefit from the simultaneous maturing of the baby boom generation and the decline in the birth rate. Johnson & Johnson, for example, still produces its line of baby products (although it has broadened its advertising appeal to stress how good these products are for adults, too). On the other hand, it also owns Ortho Pharmaceutical Corporation, one of the country's largest manufacturers of contraceptives, aimed at those who want to avoid buying its baby products. Thus, Johnson & Johnson has found success by working both sides of the population street.

The changing age mix also brings about changes in consumer expenditures.[31] For example, reports by the Bureau of Labor Statistics show that a family headed by someone between 35 and 44 years of age has an income near that of one headed by someone 45 to 54. However, the younger family spends 16 percent less on personal care services, 21 percent less on over-the-counter drugs, but 10 percent more on meat. Similarly, compared to the under-25 age group, 25 to 34 year olds spend 50 percent more on such household items as major appliances, furniture, curtains, rugs, and housewares.

The increase in the number of working wives means that companies will make greater attempts to attract these busier, more monied women. For example, appliance manufacturers such as Whirlpool are designing their machines to take the burden of operation from the housewife and thus leave her more time for other chores. Convenience foods (particularly more expensive ones) should also grow in demand among this group. In addition, it is expected that working-wife families will make greater use of time-saving, convenience-shopping outlets. Working wives will also represent a positive factor in automobile demand, and offer greater opportunity to life insurance companies to sell two policies to a family.

The combination of two working parents and fewer children may also create a large potential market for selling what are now considered luxury goods. Assuming that inflation does not reach high levels for long periods and reduce the family's purchasing power, the demand is expected to be great for airlines and hotels, automobiles, and such leisure goods as sports equipment, home computers, and videotape recorders.

The advent of smaller families will also affect the housing market, perhaps resulting in smaller units, more multiple-housing units, and locations closer to centers of population. Such a trend has obvious implications for furniture and appliance manufacturers. For example, General Electric is putting its new-product emphasis on compact appliances designed for smaller living quarters.

Market planners across the United States anticipate that the customer of the future will be much more self-confident, discriminating, and independent. This will have important implications for products to be offered this market as well as the nature of retail establishments to be patronized.

GEOGRAPHIC CHARACTERISTICS AND MARKET SEGMENTATION

The American consumer market may also be grouped along geographic dimensions, which is one of the oldest forms of segmentation. It has long been evident that regional differences sometimes result in differences in buyer preferences or variations in product usage; for example, products primarily geared to warm-weather climates, such as swimming pools and air conditioners, have marketing programs built partially on a geographic-segmentation strategy. Other examples of geographic segmentation include gasolines that are "localized" for driving conditions in the area of their sale; magazines that publish regional editions allowing advertisers to tailor their messages and to pinpoint more accurately their audiences; and station wagons, which are primarily a suburban phenomenon and thus sold mainly by dealers in such areas. The technique can also be applied in nonprofit marketing situations. One of the most important roles for geographic segmentation in the nonprofit sector is in connection with charitable organizations which must solicit contributions, particularly those using house-to-house canvasing and direct mail. The American Lung Association, the Epilepsy Foundation, Easter Seals, and the American Heart Association are examples of organizations in which geographic segmentation of the market permits a division of the market according to who the high-dollar contributors are and where they are located. Such a segmentation approach can lead to an improved allocation of programs, publicity, and fund-raising efforts directed toward the most productive target segments.[32]

This section discusses major geographic characteristics potentially useful in segmenting markets.

Regional Distribution of United States Population

Population is not distributed evenly across the United States, but instead is concentrated in certain states and regions, with the states east of the Mississippi River accounting for the great bulk of our population.

Although current population data are important, one should not lose sight of the fact that population shifts are occurring that could dramatically alter the present picture. Examination of Figure 4-2 indicates that between 1970 and 1980 certain areas of the United States have gained population rapidly, while others have gained slowly, and still others have lost population. One of the most important shifts in population evident from this map is the generally southwestward movement toward the *Sunbelt,* the lower arc of warm states. The growing popularity of the Sunbelt is a result of many people's searching for a better quality of life. Escape from the colder weather, higher living expenses, and increasing crime and congestion in northern cities are the key motivations driving industry and individuals alike to relocate in this region.

It is important to understand regional trends in population, since this understanding may be helpful in segmentation and marketing strategy decisions. For example, it has been demonstrated that personality differences exist among geographic regions of the United States, and these may be associated with differences in the demand for many products.[33] Even the design and character of some products varies across the different regions of the country. An obvious example is the differing architecture of housing across the country.[34] Many such differences result from climate, religion, social customs, and other factors. Consequently, gathering demographic data by region can lead to a useful understanding of sales patterns. For example, R. J. Reynolds Tobacco Co., which makes 33 of the approximately 175 cigarette brands on the market, has developed a marketing research program that provides it with the regional demographics of every store where its brands are sold. As a result, the company is able to better target its brands to the correct segments of the market, particularly among ethnic communities.[35]

FIGURE 4-2

Population growth and rank by state. (*Source:* Courtenay M. Slater, "Population Shift to Sunbelt States in Seventies Greater Than Expected," *Business America*, **4**:21, February 23, 1981; and U.S. Department of Commerce.)

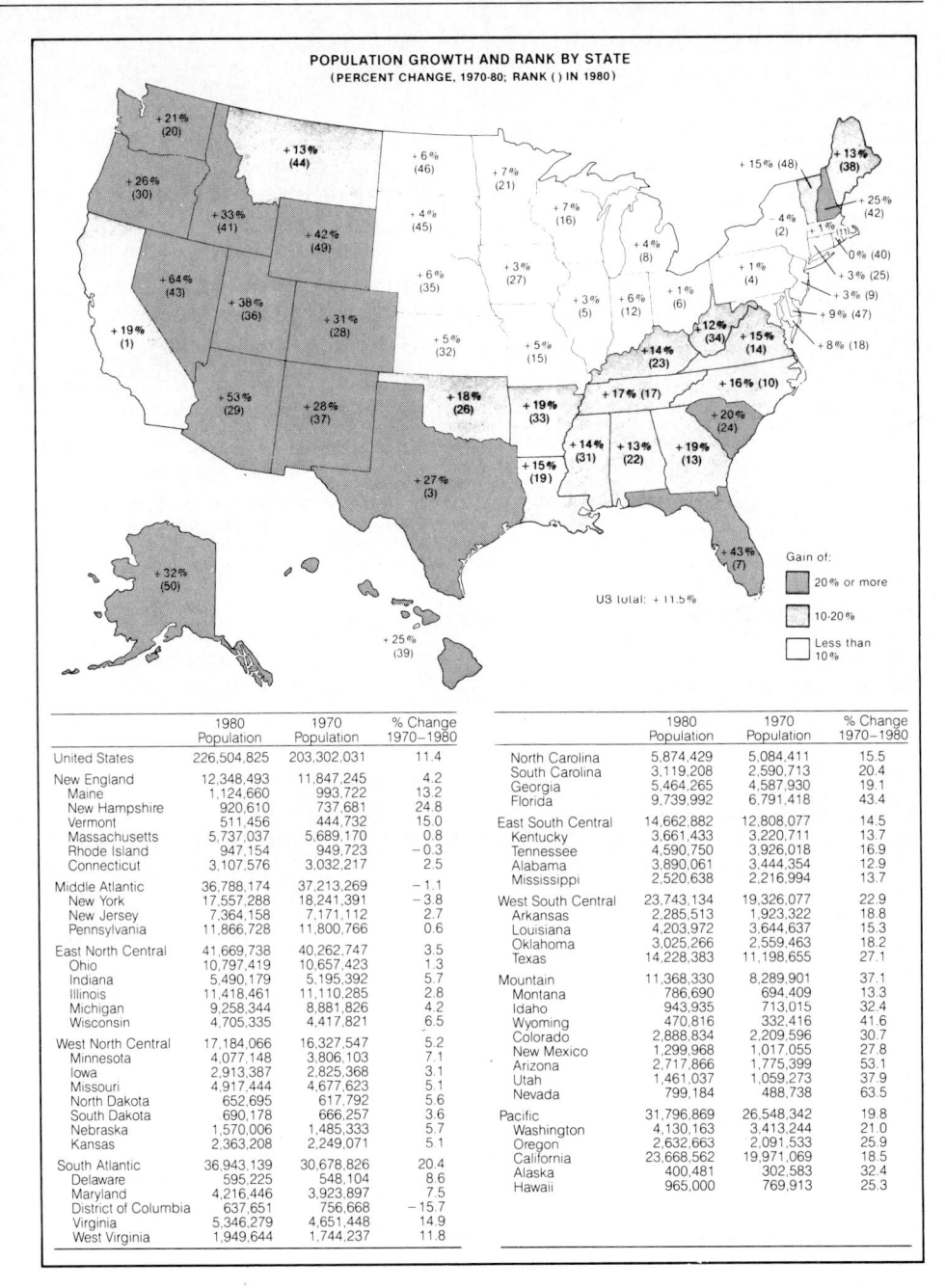

POPULATION GROWTH AND RANK BY STATE
(PERCENT CHANGE, 1970-80; RANK ( ) IN 1980)

US total: +11.5%

Gain of:
- 20% or more
- 10-20%
- Less than 10%

	1980 Population	1970 Population	% Change 1970–1980
United States	226,504,825	203,302,031	11.4
New England	12,348,493	11,847,245	4.2
Maine	1,124,660	993,722	13.2
New Hampshire	920,610	737,681	24.8
Vermont	511,456	444,732	15.0
Massachusetts	5,737,037	5,689,170	0.8
Rhode Island	947,154	949,723	−0.3
Connecticut	3,107,576	3,032,217	2.5
Middle Atlantic	36,788,174	37,213,269	−1.1
New York	17,557,288	18,241,391	−3.8
New Jersey	7,364,158	7,171,112	2.7
Pennsylvania	11,866,728	11,800,766	0.6
East North Central	41,669,738	40,262,747	3.5
Ohio	10,797,419	10,657,423	1.3
Indiana	5,490,179	5,195,392	5.7
Illinois	11,418,461	11,110,285	2.8
Michigan	9,258,344	8,881,826	4.2
Wisconsin	4,705,335	4,417,821	6.5
West North Central	17,184,066	16,327,547	5.2
Minnesota	4,077,148	3,806,103	7.1
Iowa	2,913,387	2,825,368	3.1
Missouri	4,917,444	4,677,623	5.1
North Dakota	652,695	617,792	5.6
South Dakota	690,178	666,257	3.6
Nebraska	1,570,006	1,485,333	5.7
Kansas	2,363,208	2,249,071	5.1
South Atlantic	36,943,139	30,678,826	20.4
Delaware	595,225	548,104	8.6
Maryland	4,216,446	3,923,897	7.5
District of Columbia	637,651	756,668	−15.7
Virginia	5,346,279	4,651,448	14.9
West Virginia	1,949,644	1,744,237	11.8
North Carolina	5,874,429	5,084,411	15.5
South Carolina	3,119,208	2,590,713	20.4
Georgia	5,464,265	4,587,930	19.1
Florida	9,739,992	6,791,418	43.4
East South Central	14,662,882	12,808,077	14.5
Kentucky	3,661,433	3,220,711	13.7
Tennessee	4,590,750	3,926,018	16.9
Alabama	3,890,061	3,444,354	12.9
Mississippi	2,520,638	2,216,994	13.7
West South Central	23,743,134	19,326,077	22.9
Arkansas	2,285,513	1,923,322	18.8
Louisiana	4,203,972	3,644,637	15.3
Oklahoma	3,025,266	2,559,463	18.2
Texas	14,228,383	11,198,655	27.1
Mountain	11,368,330	8,289,901	37.1
Montana	786,690	694,409	13.3
Idaho	943,935	713,015	32.4
Wyoming	470,816	332,416	41.6
Colorado	2,888,834	2,209,596	30.7
New Mexico	1,299,968	1,017,055	27.8
Arizona	2,717,866	1,775,399	53.1
Utah	1,461,037	1,059,273	37.9
Nevada	799,184	488,738	63.5
Pacific	31,796,869	26,548,342	19.8
Washington	4,130,163	3,413,244	21.0
Oregon	2,632,663	2,091,533	25.9
California	23,668,562	19,971,069	18.5
Alaska	400,481	302,583	32.4
Hawaii	965,000	769,913	25.3

Studies have found large variations in consumer behavior among the different geographical regions.[36] For example, Table 4-4 presents selected data on regional differences in consumption, product ownership, and media usage. In addition, Table 4-5 illustrates other differences among consumers in four census regions and for the United States overall. Other research studies have shown that sharp differences exist on social questions among the regions of the United States.[37] For

TABLE 4-4

REGIONAL DIFFERENCES IN CONSUMPTION, PRODUCT OWNERSHIP, AND MEDIA USAGE

Product	\multicolumn{5}{c}{Percentage Reporting Using Once a Week or More}
	Total U.S.	New England	East South Central	West North Central	Pacific
Multiple vitamins	42	38	35	45	48
Chewing gum	37	35	46	39	34
Antiperspirant	75	66	74	76	71
Mouthwash	46	46	56	41	41
Perfume or cologne	77	50	79	79	82
Yogurt	12	17	8	9	16
Domestic wine	16	28	9	11	22
Peanut Butter	60	47	57	51	63
Frozen prepared (TV) dinners	10	31	15	9	7
Potato chips	39	31	50	39	35
Whole milk	52	55	58	40	45
Lowfat (2%) milk	51	37	50	57	58
Regular cereal	60	43	61	58	67

Product	\multicolumn{5}{c}{Percentage Owning}
	Total U.S.	New England	East South Central	West North Central	Pacific
35 mm camera over $150	24	30	17	22	29
Personal or home computer	10	17	10	10	9
Automatic dishwasher	51	42	49	50	62
Digital watch	55	45	60	55	56
Citizens band radio	36	33	42	36	33
Videotape recorder for TV	10	13	12	11	12
Videodisc player	4	9	7	6	1
Color TV set	89	74	90	91	91
Water softener	18	11	18	34	10
Automatic washing machine	83	80	80	86	84
Mutual fund	15	17	17	20	13
Life insurance on your own life	75	67	81	74	67
Freezer	68	51	78	77	69
Microwave oven	47	33	48	54	58
Food processor	31	29	33	25	37
Wallpaper	51	67	54	53	43
Kerosene heater	15	20	22	18	4
Small American car	20	22	19	20	15
Small Japanese car	17	27	17	15	29
Standard size car	35	30	35	38	25
Luxury car	10	11	15	6	11
Electronic TV video game	26	25	23	20	27

Category	\multicolumn{5}{c}{Percentage Exposed}
	Total U.S.	New England	East South Central	West North Central	Pacific
Magazines:					
Newsweek	37	40	33	37	42
People	46	52	43	49	48
TV Guide	50	63	54	45	50
Playboy	27	27	26	29	30
Reader's Digest	66	54	66	71	69
True Story	10	11	14	10	9
TV programs:					
Monday Night Pro Football	52	41	52	51	57
Dallas	48	37	59	55	39

TABLE 4-4
(Continued)

	Percentage Exposed				
Category	Total U.S.	New England	East South Central	West North Central	Pacific
Hill Street Blues	51	51	49	46	48
Public Broadcasting System	55	60	49	62	56
Religious programs	30	21	50	35	18
Radio program types:					
Popular music—Top 40 and/or disco	53	54	57	53	47
Middle-of-the-road music	52	53	53	52	52
Country and western music	56	45	69	59	50

Source: Needham, Harper & Steers Advertising, Inc., *Life Style Survey,* 1983.

example, New England is the most liberal section of the country on many social issues, and the Pacific region is a close second. The south is generally the most conservative.

Metropolitan Population in the United States

Table 4-6 presents a list of the major U.S. cities which shows their 1980 populations and the shifts that have occurred since 1970. Approximately three-fourths of the total population of the United States lives in metropolitan areas, with the ten largest population centers accounting for approximately 25 percent of the total U.S. population. However, thirty-four of the nation's fifty largest central cities lost population during the 1970s, but the rate of loss seems to be decreasing. Thus, Table 4-6 indicates that population has generally moved toward exurbia—out of the central cities and even beyond the larger metropolitan statistical area.

Although traditional U.S. population migration patterns have followed that of people moving from the country to the city, then to the suburbs, and finally to the exurbs, there are some countertrends. For example, approximately half of those people leaving rural areas are going to the suburbs rather than to the cities, and some of those leaving the suburbs are going back to central cities.[38] Many U.S. cities have benefited from this "gentrification" movement in which young professionals are reclaiming deteriorating neighborhoods convenient to downtown. One sign of this movement is the fact that many of the fast-food franchisers have opened new outlets in midtown and central city locations.

How do suburban consumers differ from those in the cities? According to Fabian Linden of the National Industrial Conference Board, the family that moves to the suburbs tends to be younger, to have more children, to have a higher level of educational accomplishments, and to be generally more affluent than the one that remains in the city. The typical city family, by contrast, tends to be older, less well-educated, and less fortunate financially.[39] Thus, there are substantial differences in the demographic characteristics and hence in the consumer-behavior patterns of suburban versus urban consumers.

The marketer needs to be aware of such differences because they may affect the strategy for a product or brand being used. For example, when comparing the percent of urban and rural users of some mature products such as toilet soap, toothpaste, and facial tissues, some significant differences have been found between the

TABLE 4-5

REGIONAL CONSUMER ACTIVITY PROFILE

Item	Total U.S.	New England	East South Central	West North Central	Pacific
Visited an art gallery or museum	41	38	33	43	50
Went bowling	31	33	21	34	32
Rode a bicycle	55	54	61	61	50
Went to an exercise class	24	30	20	25	26
Went to a pop or rock concert	15	18	16	19	12
Went to a classical concert	18	34	13	18	20
Purchased a product at a Tupperware party	38	37	43	43	36
Went to a club meeting	53	49	48	59	55
Attended church	77	76	81	86	66
Cooked outdoors	82	81	81	79	84
Went to the movies	73	74	64	75	74
Read a book	83	77	78	80	89
Gave or attended a dinner party	77	79	66	74	85
Rented a truck or van	11	26	11	9	8
Took an airplane trip for personal reasons	29	40	20	27	31
Played a coin-operated video game	43	44	42	41	44
Went skiing	13	31	13	16	11
Played tennis	15	24	12	14	14
Attended a sporting event	56	53	60	72	54
Played golf	16	26	11	21	13
Used an electronic bank machine to deposit, withdraw or transfer money	27	35	30	22	32
Entertained people in my home	92	86	89	94	94
Returned an unsatisfactory product	56	56	35	56	53
Did volunteer work	52	57	42	60	54
Jogged	31	36	36	33	33
Sent in for a manufacturer's rebate	72	83	72	76	65
Went fishing	47	47	61	57	44
Attended a school	28	34	25	33	28
Went camping	36	38	32	40	48
Went on a weight-reducing diet	48	49	50	45	50
Shopped at a convenience store (7-11, etc.).	87	86	90	84	83
Stayed at a hotel or motel	65	63	62	67	70
Used a "price-off" coupon at a grocery store	84	76	81	83	85
Bought a generic product	80	76	80	82	79
Shopped at Sears	84	85	79	81	83
Purchased from a mail order catalog	70	71	73	71	67
Worked on a do-it-yourself project around the house	77	79	76	83	79

Source: Needham, Harper & Steers Advertising, Inc., *Life Style Survey*, 1983.

TABLE 4-6

1980 POPULATION—TOP MARKETS BY CENTRAL CITY, STANDARD METROPOLITAN STATISTICAL AREA AND AREA OF DOMINANT INFLUENCE

Based on 1980 Preliminary Census Data Compiled by Advertising Age.

	Market (Ranked by ADI)	Central City	% Change vs. '70	SMSA	% Change vs. '70	ADI	% Change vs. '70	ADI minus Central City	% Change vs. '70
1	New York	7,035,348	−10.9	9,080,777	−9	17,920,842	−3.5	10,885,494	1.9
2	Los Angeles	3,309,417	4.4	7,444,521	5.7	11,052,123	13.3	7,742,706	17.6
3	Chicago	2,986,430	−11.4	7,057,853	1.2	8,354,852	1.5	5,368,422	10.4
4	Philadelphia	1,681,175	−13.8	4,700,996	−2.6	6,782,309	0.1	5,101,134	5.6
5	San Francisco/Oakland	1,012,871	−6	3,225,981	3.8	5,237,641	11.4	4,224,770	16.6
6	Boston	562,582	−12.3	2,759,800	−4.8	5,331,309	3.3	4,768,727	5.4
7	Detroit	1,197,325	−20.9	4,339,768	−2.1	4,732,123	−1.2	3,534,798	8
8	Washington	635,233	−16.0	3,041,909	4.5	3,980,570	7.8	3,345,337	14
9	Cleveland	572,657	−23.7	1,895,391	−8.2	3,833,588	3.1	3,260,931	1.7
10	Dallas-Fort Worth	1,284,228	3.7	2,964,342	24.7	3,556,969	23.5	2,272,741	38.3
11	Pittsburgh	424,205	−18.4	2,260,336	−5.9	3,038,415	−2.8	2,614,210	0.3
12	Houston	1,573,847	27.5	2,891,146	44.6	3,364,667	40.9	1,790,820	55.2
13	Minneapolis/St. Paul	638,606	−14.2	2,108,950	7.3	2,881,355	5.5	2,242,749	12.9
14	St. Louis	450,790	−27.6	2,341,351	−2.9	2,926,438	−0.2	2,475,648	7.7
15	Seattle/Everett/Tacoma	704,349[1]	−4.7	2,083,636[1]	−13.4	2,835,995	18.5	2,131,646	28.9
16	Atlanta	422,474	−14.7	2,010,368	26	2,945,848	23	2,485,345	33
17	Miami	335,718	0.3	1,572,842	24.1	2,633,255	35.7	1,060,413	57.6
18	Tampa/St. Petersburg	502,241	1.7	1,550,035	42.4	2,400,203	47.4	850,168	57.5
19	Baltimore	784,554	−13.4	2,164,853	4.5	2,346,359	5.1	1,561,805	17.8
20	Denver	565,554[2]	−2.8	1,613,965[2]	30.2	2,205,939	33.6	1,640,385	53.4
21	Indianapolis	698,753	−5.2	1,161,539	4.5	2,248,241	4.2	1,549,488	9
22	Sacramento/Stockton	274,547	6.8	1,010,989	25.8	2,207,103	30.1	1,932,556	34.3
23	San Diego	874,826	25.4	1,857,492	36.8	1,857,492	36.8	982,666	48.8
24	Portland, Ore.	365,064	−3.9	1,234,007	22.5	2,018,836	23.7	1,653,772	32.2
25	Kansas City	446,865	−11.9	1,322,156	3.9	1,871,873	6.3	1,425,008	13.6

26	Hartford/New Haven	136,320[3]	−13.7	1,963,276	0.6	1,826,956	3.4
27	Cincinnati	383,114	−15.5	1,933,399	−1.7	1,550,285	10
28	Milwaukee	633,845	−11.6	1,878,864	0.8	1,245,016	8.6
29	Buffalo	357,384	−22.8	1,731,184	−8	1,373,800	2.3
30	Nashville	438,888	3	1,753,267	18.5	1,314,379	24.1
31	Phoenix	772,884	32.3	1,899,846	55.6	1,126,962	73.5
32	Columbus	562,462	4.2	1,638,876	6.9	1,076,414	10.8
33	Providence	314,616	−7.4	1,667,476	1.1	1,352,860	4.8
34	Memphis	644,957	3.4	1,699,997	9.1	1,055,040	10.5
35	Charlotte	357,502	23.8	1,684,861	25.7	1,327,359	13.1
36	New Orleans	557,761	−6	1,678,332	13.1	1,120,571	30
37	Greenville/Spartanburg/Asheville	101,692	−4	1,550,507	19.9	1,448,815	17.8
38	Grand Rapids/Kalamazoo/Battle Creek	181,602	−8.1	1,591,203	11.5	1,409,601	13.4
39	Oklahoma City	401,577	9.1	1,383,380	18.7	981,803	20.2
40	Orlando/Daytona Beach	127,811	26	1,470,649	53.3	1,342,838	47.3
41	Raleigh/Durham	248,154	13.7	1,548,095	25.2	1,299,941	18
42	Louisville	298,313	−17.5	1,462,370	4	1,164,057	17.3
43	Charleston/Hungtington/Ashland	152,932[4]	−12.6	1,468,322	4.8	1,315,390	16.6
44	Birmingham	262,081	−6	1,303,505	7.7	1,021,424	15.3
45	Salt Lake City	227,429	−7.4	1,607,597	32.6	1,380,168	5.0
46	Harrisburg/York/Lancaster/Lebanon	152,209[5]	−15.6	1,363,665	12.1	1,211,456	15.9
47	Norfolk/Portsmouth/Newport News/Hampton	894,745	5.3	1,398,292	9.2	503,547	23.7
48	Wilkes-Barre/Scranton	165,538	−13.8	1,308,223	1	1,142,685	−2.5
49	Albany/Troy/Schenectady	226,258	−11.4	1,281,718	2.1	1,055,460	8.9
50	Dayton	193,323	−20.5	1,261,398	3	1,068,075	3.4

[1] Based on Seattle/Everett/Tacoma SMSA data.
[2] Based on Denver/Boulder SMSA data.
[3] Based on Hartford/West Haven SMSA data.
[4] Based on Charleston/Huntington SMSA data.
[5] Based on Harrisburg/York/Lancaster SMSA data.

*Area of Dominant Influence (ADI) refers to the viewing areas defined by Arbitron for television stations. Residents of the ADI constitute a potential market for products being advertised on a particular station.

Source: "Exurban Areas in Decade of Growth," *Advertising Age*, March 9, 1981, p. 36.

PART TWO

102

UNDERSTANDING CONSUMERS AND MARKET SEGMENTS

two groups. In addition, brand-penetration differences exist for some of these product categories, with rural users of a product or brand being followers of the shift rather than leaders.[40] Consequently, different strategies may be called for among urban and rural buyers for some products.

With population migrating to the suburbs and spilling over the relevant political boundaries (such as towns and cities), old descriptions of market areas based on such political entities have become obsolete. Consequently, the federal government now uses the concept of a metropolitan statistical area (MSA) as a geographic unit for measuring market data. An MSA is regarded as a large population nucleus as well as adjacent areas which have a high degree of economic and social integration with that population nucleus. These MSAs are classified into four levels (A, B, C, and D) based on total population size. In addition, areas designated as primary metropolitan statistical areas (PMSAs) are urbanized county clusters linked together economically and socially within MSAs of 1 million or more population. Areas designated consolidated metropolitan statistical areas (CMSAs) are composed of two or more PMSAs within these most populous MSAs. More than 320 metropolitan areas have been identified by the U.S. government.

The combined total of MSAs accounts for more than 70 percent of the nation's population. For the marketer, these areas represent geographically concentrated target segments which hold great market potential. They are the keys to allocation of not only advertising dollars, but also federal funds. Figure 4-3 presents the nation's metropolitan areas. This diagram shows that metropolitan areas have begun to merge as suburbs of one spill over into suburbs of another. Such a development gives rise to the concept of a new type of supercity termed "megalopolis" or "interurbia." This process will continue in the years ahead.

FIGURE 4-3

Metropolitan areas in the United States. (*Source:* U.S. Office of Management and Budget, Statistical Policy Division, *Standard Metropolitan Statistical Areas,* 1981, rev. ed., Washington, D.C., 1981.)

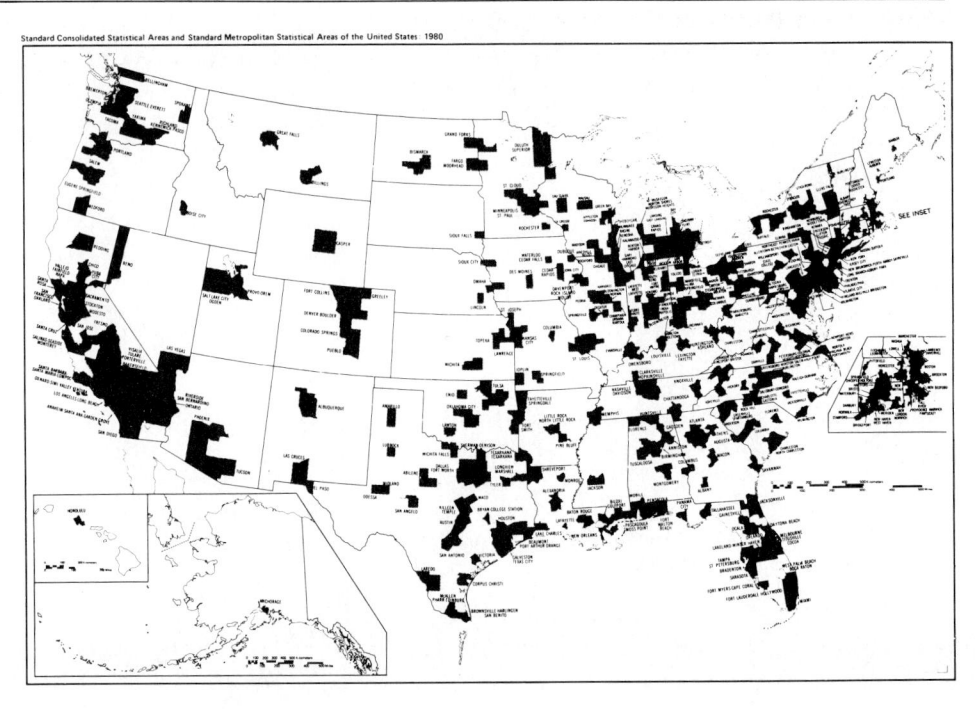

Nonmetropolitan Population in the United States

An almost unnoticed population trend now occurring in the United States is the growth of small towns and rural areas. During the 1970s, rural and small-town America (the nonmetropolitan areas) grew faster than the cities (metropolitan areas) by 15.5 percent, or 8.4 million persons.[41] In fact, recent public opinion polls show that more than half of the American people would prefer to live on a farm or in a small town.[42]

Why the growth in small towns? Authorities include the following among major reasons: (1) a stabilizing farm population, (2) industrial migration to rural areas, and (3) a desire by some for a simpler, safer living environment.[43] Marketers should continue to be aware of this migration pattern and understand the implications it may have for marketing programs. For example, to reach consumers in less-populated areas, major chain retailers such as K mart, Sears, Wal-Mart, and J. C. Penney, are opening approximately 50 percent of their new stores in small towns of 8,000 to 20,000 population outside of metropolitan areas. These stores are typically in the 30,000- to 40,000-square-foot category rather than the 60,000- to 90,000-square-foot variety found in big cities. The rationale for this move is that metropolitan centers are saturated with large retail stores, which contributes to slow sales growth for these companies. Marketing research indicates that the ten largest metropolitan areas are expected to post an inflation-adjusted 37 percent increase in retail sales between 1978 and 1990, while sales in the ten smallest metropolitan areas should grow by 54 percent.[44]

Fast-food franchises are also adapting to the growth of nonmetropolitan areas. For example, McDonald's is assessing the potential of "Mini-Macs," which are smaller establishments designed to serve simple menus to less-populous communities.[45]

Geographic Mobility of the Population

Another characteristic of our population and one that is a potentially useful segmentation dimension is geographic mobility. During a recent five-year period, approximately 82 million Americans changed their place of residence within the United States at least once. Of the families that moved, approximately three out of every five stayed close to home, that is, in the same county; approximately one out of five left the county but stayed in the same state; and another one out of five settled in a different state. Such movement adds up to a significant shift in our demographic geography.[46]

Vance Packard cites some impressive statistics to document our society's mobility:

The average American moves approximately fourteen times in his lifetime, compared with five times for the Japanese.

In many cities, over 35 percent of the population move every year. For example, a school in Great Falls, Montana, annually loses 70 percent of its pupils and 30 percent of its teachers.

The families of many executives have had to move their households as many as twenty times.

Some 6 million Americans now live in mobile homes. Even though these homes are not often moved, their occupants feel little commitment to their home and community.

At any given time, half of the 18- to 22-year-olds in hundreds of towns are living away from home. Many of them come back only to visit.[47]

The largest group of those who move (38 percent) do so to satisfy housing needs such as owning their own home or living in a better neighborhood. Another 27 percent move because of a change in family status such as marriage, divorce, or new children. An additional 22 percent make job-related moves, with the remainder moving for other reasons.[48] It should also be noted that mobility varies from region to region. For example, in the northeast, only slightly over 13 percent of all families moved in 1970, while in the west the percentage was almost twice that.[49]

There are indications, however, that the game of musical houses is slowing down in the United States, particularly due to recent energy and housing financial conditions. There are a number of reasons cited for such a trend:

More people are unwilling to give up the place, climate, and recreational facilities they like, just for more money.

Housewives and working wives are revolting against transfers for executive husbands.

Middle-class Americans are more inward-looking, concerned with the quality of life, and less interested in getting ahead by switching jobs and towns.

Corporate shifts to the Sunbelt have slowed migration to the North.

The trend to smaller families has reduced the need for moving to a larger house.[50]

In spite of the decreases in mobility in the United States, those who do continue to move are seen as a very attractive segment to be cultivated by many marketers because they generally have more income and live in costlier homes.

Studies of mobile consumers have demonstrated that people varying in degree of mobility constitute distinct market segments.[51] One study found the following profiles for low- and high-mobile consumers:[52]

Low Mobiles	High Mobiles
• Infrequently shop outside their community of residence	• Frequently shop outside their community of residence
• Are infrequent convenience store shoppers, purchasing relatively few convenience store products	• Are frequently convenience store shoppers, purchasing relatively more convenience store products
• Are older	• Are younger
• Have lower educational level	• Have higher educational level
• Are most satisfied with life	• Are least satisfied with life
• Have most-traditional family ideology	• Have least-traditional family ideology

The mobile segment has been found to be a potentially superior market for such products as furniture, clothing, drapes, slipcovers, other dry goods, and consumer durables such as automobiles and appliances.

Once relocated, mobiles must rebuild shopping patterns in their new community.[53] They learn about new suppliers primarily from word-of-mouth communication with friends, neighbors, and coworkers. However, mass-media sources such as newspapers and the yellow pages are also important, as is personal observation while driving around. Mobiles tend to rebuild shopping patterns rapidly, in part because of holding charge accounts with national retailers which allow them to transfer their store and brand loyalty to the new community.

Because of the value of this segment, retailers in particular should be cognizant of the efforts necessary to attract the geographically mobile market. For example, a retailer could benefit from setting up a newcomer program to identify new arrivals and make contact with these families before their shopping habits have been rebuilt. Such a program could include: (1) offering to extend check-cashing or credit privileges, (2) delivering a gift to the home, (3) providing coupons redeemable in the store, and (4) offering a price cut or refund on items purchased.[54]

Thus, geographic mobiles are often a worthwhile target segment because they can be identifiable, accessible, and substantial. Concentration of marketing effort on this segment, particularly by retailers, should pay great dividends.

SOCIOECONOMIC CHARACTERISTICS AND MARKET SEGMENTATION

A final dimension for market segmentation to be examined in this chapter involves socioeconomic characteristics. Included within this category are the variables of education, occupation, and income.

Education

The future generation of adults is acquiring considerably more schooling than the present generation.[55] This trend has been occurring as a result of affluence, changing social values, and the shifting employment needs of industry. In 1980, approximately 27 percent of adults age 25 years and older had at least some college training. By 1990, the figure is expected to reach 35 percent. The younger age categories are the key college-educated groups. For example, approximately 45 percent of those age 25 to 34 have some exposure to college, compared to only 15 percent of those older than age 65. A large share of the college-student increase is accounted for by women who now outnumber men on many campuses.

Households headed by those with some college education comprise a lucrative market segment. For example, the college graduate household head tends to be young; approximately half of these are under age 40. Over two-thirds of the households are a husband-wife unit, and in many instances both of them work. Income in households headed by someone who has had at least some exposure to college runs approximately 10 percent above the norm, while college graduate households are 50 percent above the norm. As a group, those who have spent at least some time in college account for approximately 45 percent of the total U.S. spending power.

The relative importance of the educated segment of consumers will continue to expand during the 1980s. Their above-average discretionary income and desire for new products will make them more attractive to many marketers as their size approaches mass-market status.

In addition to the aspects of income associated with increasingly educated consumers, there are also a number of unique characteristics that further differentiate them from the average consumer. They are more sophisticated in their product and store choices, for example. They are also more alert to quality, packaging, and advertising messages. Moreover, they have differing needs from those of the typical consumer, tending to spend somewhat more (after allowing for the income difference) on clothing, home furnishings, medical and personal care, entertainment, travel, and many other items. Thus education does make a difference not only in what the consumer buys but often probably in the brand selected.

Occupation

Just after World War II, the United States labor force contained more blue-collar than white-collar jobs. However, rising industrial productivity and the shifting needs of business have brought about a substantial rise in white-collar workers. In the mid-1960s, approximately 45 percent of the nation's labor force was white-collar workers, whereas today the figure is approximately 51 percent. Blue-collar workers have steadily decreased as a percentage of the workforce, while service occupations have increased during this period.

There are some important differences in households headed by blue- and white-collar workers.[56] First, workweeks typically differ, with 40 hours the standard in blue-collar trades, while 35 hours is usual in white-collar occupations. Second, the household size is smaller for white-collar workers compared with blue-collar workers. Third, substantial income variations exist among the two groups. For example, the average income of the white-collar household is 30 percent larger than the blue-collar household, and although this group accounts for 34 percent of all households, they receive 47 percent of all income. This compares with approximately 27 percent of the nation's households headed by blue-collar workers who receive only 29 percent of all income. Thus, higher average earnings in conjunction with smaller household sizes add up to a much better than average living standard for the white-collar worker's family.

Income

The marketer is highly interested in the second part of our formula concerning what constitutes a market: what people have available to spend. Before we examine income levels, however, we need to understand what is meant by "income" because there are several concepts of this term, not all of which are equally important in evaluating a market.

Personal income is the income from wages, salaries, dividends, rent, interest, business and professions, social security, and farming.

Disposable personal income is the amount available after deducting taxes for personal-consumption expenditures and saving.

Discretionary income is the income available for spending after deducting expenditures for essential or fixed items such as food, clothing, transportation, shelter, and utilities.

Supernumerary (or surplus) income refers to income that accrues to individual families in surplus of $35,000 (in 1980 prices). This represents a general measure of rising consumer affluence.[57]

Since these latter two concepts indicate the extent of the resources available for optional spending after all outlays have been made for the essentials of everyday life, they are better measures of the market potential for luxury goods and services.

One of the most significant developments during the 1980s and beyond is the changing nature of income levels in the United States. Our nation is becoming a more affluent country, with the pattern of income distribution becoming an inverted pyramid as shown in Figure 4-4. In other words, there will be relatively fewer poor families and more wealthy families in future years than there are at present.

The number of families that have moved into the affluent income levels has increased dramatically in recent years. It has been estimated that the top 5 percent of United States families hold over 40 percent of all wealth while the top 20 percent of families have three times the net worth of the lower 80 percent.[58] Table 4-7 presents information on income and household characteristics with projections to 1990. In this table characteristics of the high-income segment may be clearly seen. Less than one-fourth of U.S. households account for almost one-half of all income. A further profile of the affluent is presented in Figure 4-5.

For many business people, this higher-income group is a market of considerable significance. This group is an important audience for a wide array of quality goods and services that appeal to the needs and fancies of the very well-heeled (sometimes referred to as the "carriage trade"). In fact, many industries are heavily dependent on this market's patronage. Such items as boats, second homes, quality photographic and audio equipment, gourmet foods, elegant cars, and top-of-the-line products in general are aimed at this income class.

The supernumerary income market is vast, with approximately 15 million of the nation's households, or 18 percent of the total, in the elite earning brackets in 1980. The dramatic growth and importance of this group, particularly those who are well-educated and in managerial, administrative, professional or technical jobs, is giving rise to descriptions of these consumers as the new American "elite" or "superclass."[59]

CHAPTER 4

107

MARKET SEGMENTATION: BASIC APPROACHES

FIGURE 4-4

The changing income pyramid. (*Source:* Fabian Linden, "The Great Reshuffle of Spending Power—1," *Across the Board,* November 1978, p. 62.)

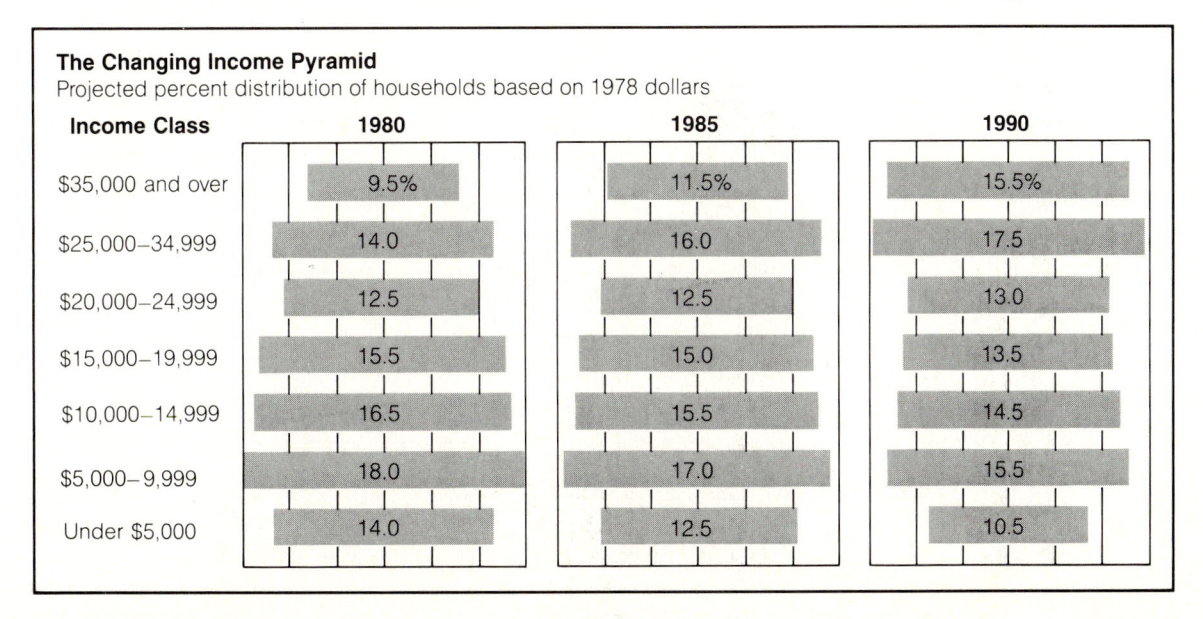

The Changing Income Pyramid
Projected percent distribution of households based on 1978 dollars

Income Class	1980	1985	1990
$35,000 and over	9.5%	11.5%	15.5%
$25,000–34,999	14.0	16.0	17.5
$20,000–24,999	12.5	12.5	13.0
$15,000–19,999	15.5	15.0	13.5
$10,000–14,999	16.5	15.5	14.5
$5,000–9,999	18.0	17.0	15.5
Under $5,000	14.0	12.5	10.5

TABLE 4-7

INCOME AND HOUSEHOLD CHARACTERISTICS

(Dollar Figures in 1978 Prices)

	1980	1985	1990
Gross national product*	$2,298	$2,743	$3,213
Disposable personal income*	$1,569	$1,925	$2,305
Per capita disposable income	$7,062	$8,264	$9,466
U.S. population (millions)	222.2	232.9	243.5
Persons by age	100.0%	100.0%	100.0%
Under 18	27.9	26.7	26.6
18–24	13.3	12.0	10.3
25–34	16.3	17.1	16.9
35–44	11.6	13.5	15.0
45–54	10.2	9.7	10.4
55–64	9.5	9.3	8.5
65 and over	11.2	11.7	12.2
Births (millions)	3.4	3.9	4.0
Families (millions)	58.5	63.1	67.2
Households (millions)	79.7	88.5	96.8
Educational attainment	100.0%	100.0%	100.0%
Elementary or less	18.3	14.4	11.3
Some high school	16.3	15.4	14.5
High school graduate	37.9	38.9	39.3
Some college	12.5	13.7	14.8
College graduate	15.0	17.5	20.1
Labor force participation rates:			
Men	77.2	76.9	76.7
Women	47.8	49.7	51.4
Total employment	100.0%	100.0%	100.0%
White-collar workers	50.3	51.5	52.5
Blue-collar workers	33.6	32.6	32.0
Service workers	13.8	14.1	14.3
Other	2.3	1.8	1.2
Place of residence	100.0%	100.0%	100.0%
Metropolitan areas	67.4	66.7	66.2
Central cities	27.1	25.1	23.2
Outside central cities	40.3	41.6	43.0
Nonmetropolitan areas	32.6	33.3	33.8
Households by income class	100.0%	100.0%	100.0%
Under $5,000	14.1	12.4	10.6
$5,000–$9,999	18.2	17.2	15.8
$10,000–$14,999	16.6	15.6	14.4
$15,000–$24,999	28.1	27.5	26.4
$25,000 and over	22.9	27.4	32.9
Income by household income class	100.0%	100.0%	100.0%
Under $5,000	2.5	2.0	1.6
$5,000–$9,999	7.5	6.5	5.4
$10,000–$14,999	11.4	10.0	8.2
$15,000–$24,999	30.5	27.7	23.9
$25,000 and over	48.1	53.8	60.9

*Billions of dollars

Source: Fabian Linden, "Keys to the '80s–Youth and Affluence," *Across the Board,* December, 1979, pp. 36–37.

FIGURE 4-5

The supernumerary market in profile. (*Source:* Fabian Linden, "Extra! The $150 Billion Market for Luxuries," *Across the Board,* April 1981, p. 48.)

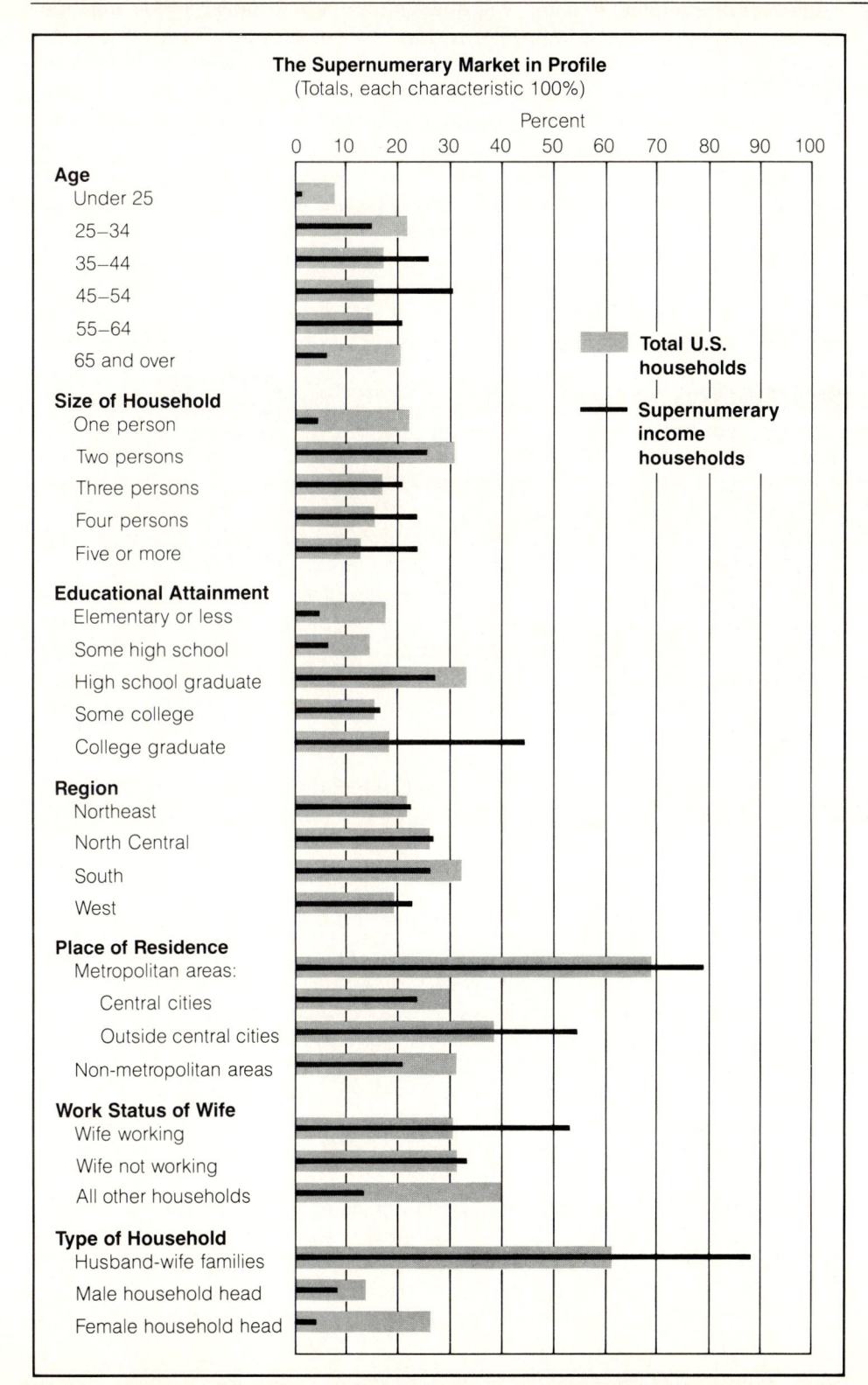

The Supernumerary Market in Profile
(Totals, each characteristic 100%)

Legend: Total U.S. households; Supernumerary income households

Age
- Under 25
- 25–34
- 35–44
- 45–54
- 55–64
- 65 and over

Size of Household
- One person
- Two persons
- Three persons
- Four persons
- Five or more

Educational Attainment
- Elementary or less
- Some high school
- High school graduate
- Some college
- College graduate

Region
- Northeast
- North Central
- South
- West

Place of Residence
- Metropolitan areas:
  - Central cities
  - Outside central cities
- Non-metropolitan areas

Work Status of Wife
- Wife working
- Wife not working
- All other households

Type of Household
- Husband-wife families
- Male household head
- Female household head

109

As these upper-income brackets expand, changes will occur in the pattern of consumer demand and in marketing strategies. Certainly, industries producing for the income elite should find prosperity. Even for everyday merchandise the growing difference will cause consumers to continue to demand more expensive items of better quality.[60]

It is important, therefore, that those in marketing management and marketing research be attentive to changes occurring among this group of comfortable consumers, and to the opportunities they yield for segmentation. However, it appears that many marketers, to describe their markets, are still using traditional income scales, which lump all those with incomes of more than, say, $15,000 or $20,000 into their prime target market. But, as income levels have shifted upward dramatically and swiftly, such a description may no longer be appropriate. Hence, marketers need to constantly examine their automatic assumptions about target-segment income levels and change them when necessary.[61]

Expenditures

The spending patterns of the average American family and how they change over time are matters of great importance to the marketer. Unfortunately, little systematic and reliable information has existed on how the typical family spends its money.

For each of the past 3 decades a consumer expenditure survey has been conducted by the federal government. These studies will now be updated yearly in order to provide answers to many important questions from marketers, government agencies, and consumer agencies.[62] Comparisons among these studies reveal useful insights. For example, during the interval between two recent studies some major expenditure shifts took place. Two reasons account for many of these changes: (1) inflation (some items rose in price much more rapidly than others) and (2) changing demographics (births declined and the number of households increased greatly).

Generally, as can be seen in Table 4-8, expenditures increased markedly for housing, transportation, and recreation (that is, home, car, and fun), and these three areas now account for a larger share of the budget. Food and clothing expenditures increased less dramatically and now account for a smaller share of the household budget.

It is also important to understand how expenditures vary with income level. Figure 4-6 provides data on the differences in spending patterns between lower- and middle-income households and between middle- and upper-income levels.

The 1970s ushered in a period of dramatic change in many consumers' values and expenditure patterns as a result of significant economic upheavals. One of the characteristics of the economy during this period, which may continue to confront marketers in the future, was *stagflation,* a term describing a stagnant economy in a time of inflation, or a combination of inflation, recession, shortages, and high unemployment. The result of this situation is that the middle class feels that they can no longer afford their present lifestyles.[63] This group has probably suffered the most negative *psychological* (as opposed to economic) effects of any class during this period and has made a number of important value and expenditure shifts as a result.[64]

Evidence of the pessimism among consumers is seen in a 1980 survey of American adults that found more than 70 percent saying that their families would

TABLE 4-8

THE HOUSEHOLD BUDGET ALLOCATION OF EXPENDITURES

	1960s	1970s	Increase*
Total current consumption	$5054	$8282	$3228
Percent distribution:	100.0	100.0	100.0
Food	24.4	20.1	13.3
Food at home	19.6	14.0	5.4
Food away from home	4.9	6.0	7.9
Alcoholic beverages	1.5	1.4	1.2
Tobacco	1.8	1.6	1.2
Clothing and upkeep	10.9	7.8	2.9
Men's and boys'	3.9	2.6	0.6
Women's, girls', infants	5.6	4.0	1.5
Materials, services	1.4	1.2	0.9
Housing	28.4	31.4	36.3
Shelter	13.1	16.4	21.6
Renter	5.3	6.9	9.4
Owner	6.9	8.7	11.5
Other	0.9	0.6	0.2
Utilities	4.9	4.9	5.0
Household operations	5.0	5.4	6.0
Housefurnishings, equipment	5.3	4.7	3.7
Transportation	15.2	21.4	30.9
Private	13.7	18.9	27.0
Public and other	1.5	2.4	3.8
Medical and personal care	9.6	8.4	6.4
Medical care	6.7	6.4	5.8
Personal care	2.9	2.0	0.6
Education and reading	1.9	1.8	1.6
Recreation	4.0	4.7	5.8
Miscellaneous	2.2	1.5	0.3

Note: Data are based on surveys conducted by Bureau of Labor Statistics in 1960–1961 and, more recently, in 1972–1973.
*The figures in this column denote the percent distribution of the total *dollar increase* in expenditures by category.
Sources: U.S. Department of Labor; The Conference Board. Adapted from Fabian Linden, "All in the Family Budget," *Across the Board,* August 1977, p. 42.

not return to their once-affluent lifestyles, even after economic improvement occurred. Consumers were found to feel worse-off financially than they had before; they were afraid of increasing inflation; were avoiding debt and credit; were delaying home and car purchases; were staying at home more often; and were taking steps to save money.[65]

Moreover, of all the social, technological, economic, and political factors shaping the nature and direction of marketing, inflation—its permanency and the consumer's preoccupation with it—is expected by some to be the most significant economic force with regard to the future of consumer markets.[66]

These economic shifts have significant impact on consumer buying patterns. For example, a study of supermarket shopping habits found that concern with inflation had led more and more consumers to adopt the following shopping tactics:[67]

- Go to the supermarket without bringing along extra money.
- Put items back at the end of the shopping expedition.
- Buy just the amount needed.

PART TWO

UNDERSTANDING CONSUMERS AND MARKET SEGMENTS

- Buy less meat.
- Stock up on bargains.
- Buy lower-priced brands.
- Buy unplanned products if they are on special.

FIGURE 4-6
The classes of spending. (*Source:* U.S. Department of Labor, The Conference Board, in Fabian Linden, "Downstairs, Upstairs," *Across the Board,* October 1977, p. 59.)

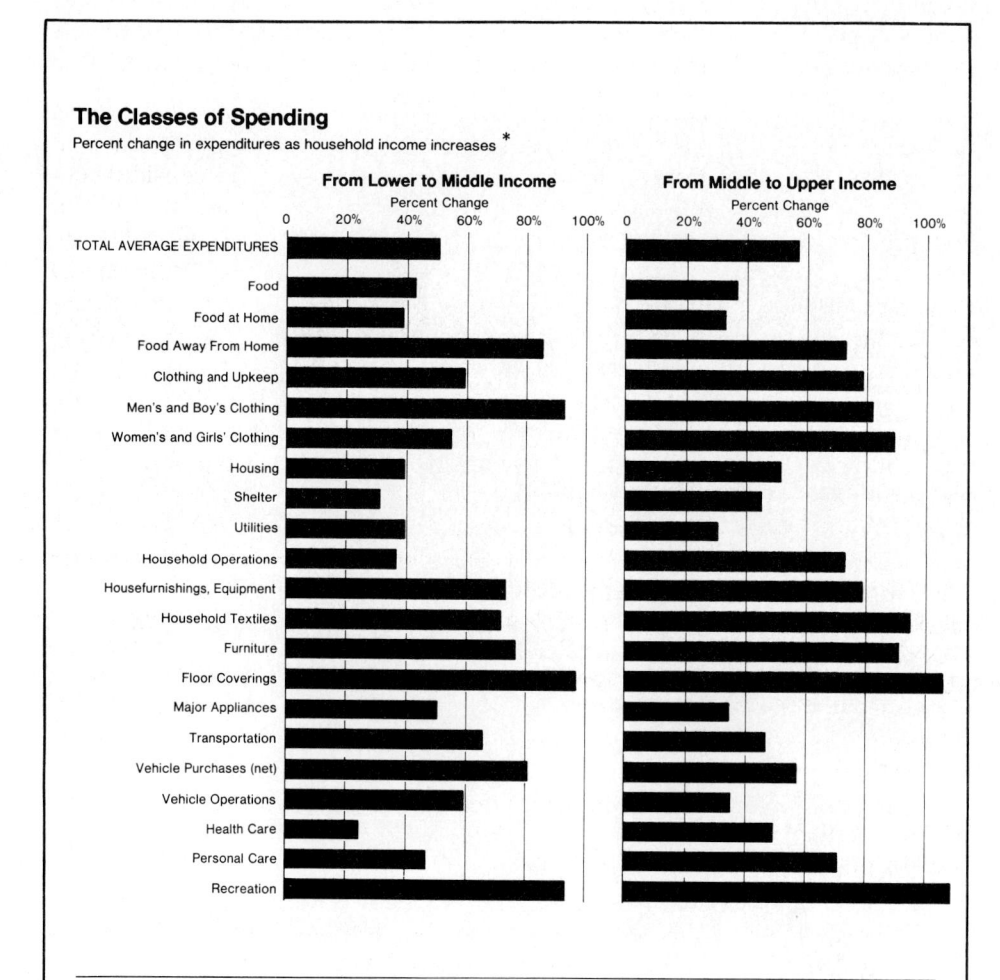

The Classes of Spending
Percent change in expenditures as household income increases *

	From Lower to Middle Income	From Middle to Upper Income
TOTAL AVERAGE EXPENDITURES		
Food		
Food at Home		
Food Away From Home		
Clothing and Upkeep		
Men's and Boy's Clothing		
Women's and Girls' Clothing		
Housing		
Shelter		
Utilities		
Household Operations		
Housefurnishings, Equipment		
Household Textiles		
Furniture		
Floor Coverings		
Major Appliances		
Transportation		
Vehicle Purchases (net)		
Vehicle Operations		
Health Care		
Personal Care		
Recreation		

*This chart shows the percent increase in spending for selected goods and services as household income increases. For example, as we move from the middle to the upper income brackets, total household expenditures for consumption rise by somewhat over 55%. Total spending for food, however, grows by about 35%, while outlays for recreation more than double. As defined in this presentation, "lower income" includes households in the $5,000–$10,000 earning bracket; "middle income," the $10,000–$20,000 bracket; and "upper income," the $20,000-and-over bracket. All data are based on a survey by the Bureau of Labor Statistics on consumer expenditures in the year 1973.

Sources: U.S. Department of Labor; The Conference Board

Such consumer changes have led to numerous retailing experiments as marketers seek to lure frugal food shoppers.[68]

Marketing to the middle class during such an inflationary period may be successful by adopting one or more of the following strategies:[69]

Retarget the product if it is a luxury nonnecessity item whose sales have been affected by the impact of inflation on the middle class. For example, the product may be repackaged and a new promotional campaign developed to appeal to the upper class or other high-income segments. Making the product a so-called status symbol could actually encourage sales in the middle class because its members will want to vicariously experience the prestige associated with the product.

Develop new products. If sales seem affected by inflation, similar yet new products can be developed which can be sold at lower cost. Also, products can be changed to appeal to the middle class. For example, builders may want to consider constructing town houses and condominiums instead of luxury houses. Marketers of high-priced furniture may want to offer the items so they can be assembled or finished by the consumer. Certain products could be made to appeal to the rapidly expanding "Do-it-yourself" market. Changing other policies is another way of combating inflation. For example, extending credit terms can stimulate sales of higher-priced items (such as when auto loans went from three to four years.) Offering "no-frills" or "generic" products is another possibility. Distribution can be simplified by changing to a factory outlet setup. Promotion can be altered to stress economy, durability, and functionalism—attributes deemed valuable by the price-conscious middle class. Of course, the top product in the product line can be eliminated if its suggested retail price is now considered to be too high due to inflation. Companies may want to explore the "financial management" business, which helps consumers budget more effectively. Retailers may repackage their customer-credit departments, expanding their operations so they are full-scale "financial management services."

Discounting is perhaps the quickest technique. Competitive pricing can be emphasized, and companies can take a more realistic look at long-term profits, considering the effects of inflation on real-dollar values.

Willingness to Buy

The last portion of our equation regarding what constitutes a market is the consumer's willingness to buy. As George Katona stated, "Consumers' discretionary demand is a function of both ability to buy—primarily income—and of willingness to buy."[70] Katona maintained it is the combination of these two elements that holds the key to future buying. One indication of willingness to buy is the consumer's plans for future spending.

Probably the most important organization presently active in the quest to determine consumer spending plans is the University of Michigan's Survey Research Center, which polls consumers and attempts to blend psychology and economics to achieve an accurate estimate of consumers' willingness to buy.

Reports provided by such consumer surveys are closely watched by such major companies as General Motors, RCA, and General Electric, and by major banks. The surveys not only help businesses to anticipate trends in the economy, but also provide help in understanding the past.[71] For example, during one year auto sales had an unexpected spurt in the third quarter despite the addition of a 10 percent income-tax surcharge for that period. It was found that consumers expected new car prices to be higher and were trying to beat the increase.[72]

LIMITATIONS OF DEMOGRAPHICS IN PREDICTING CONSUMER BEHAVIOR[73]

There has been much discussion in recent years about the role of demographic factors as determinants or even correlates of consumption behavior of people. A number of researchers have expressed skepticism that such factors can be effectively used.[74] For example, there are some undeniable demographic patterns to purchasing, such as that razor blades are purchased mainly for men. However, except for specific products aimed directly at specific demographic groups, evidence indicates that demographic measures, outside of education, are not an accurate predictor of consumer behavior.[75]

One limitation of demographics in explaining consumer behavior is based on the claim that while demographic factors may have been very relevant in the past (even up until World War II), they are now obsolete because of the narrowing differences in income, education, and occupational status. Nevertheless, there is much evidence showing that group differences among *categories* of income, education, and occupation are large and statistically significant in spite of a large number of within-group differences. It should also be noted that demographic factors include numerous other variables (such as age, sex, race, and religion) which are much less subject to influence from environmental change. For example, older people tend not to listen to rock music, per capita consumption of liquor is three times higher among blacks than whites, and Catholics still tend to use contraceptives much less than the rest of the population.

A second and more basic argument against demographics is that they have generally failed to explain and predict consumption behavior. However, although demographics have failed to explain brand-choice behavior, they seem to succeed in explaining buying behavior at the broad product class level of such items as durable appliances, automobiles, and housing. Thus, before demographics are abandoned because of their lackluster performance, it has been suggested that several past problems with demographic research be subjected to further study. These problems are mainly associated with techniques for measuring demographic variables, assumptions underlying their relationship to consumer behavior, inclusion of a small group of people in such studies who do not have a consistent pattern of behavior, and techniques of statistical analysis that are performed on the data.

Important reasons exist for the continued use of demographics in segmenting markets. First, they are easier to collect, easier to communicate to others, and often more reliable in measurement than many of the competing approaches to segmentation. Moreover, only through demographic factors is the researcher able to project results to the country's population, because the Bureau of the Census collects and updates only demographic profiles.

For these reasons, discarding demographics would seem to be premature. Instead, they should continue to be used as one element along with numerous other variables in the puzzle of explaining consumer behavior. In any event, demographics will continue to be used for projection, identification, and segmentation of markets as long as our census data are limited to a socioeconomic-demographic profile of citizens.

SUMMARY

In this chapter, many consumer characteristics have been presented. All of these consumer attributes were discussed within the framework of market segmentation: that is, an approach to selecting groups of homogeneous consumers as targets for marketing activity. Whereas market segmentation seeks to carve a large heterogeneous market into smaller, more uniform subsets, at the other end of the strategy spectrum—market aggregation—no subdivision of the market is applied. Most firms today follow a market segmentation approach. Furthermore, it was learned that in order for market segmentation to be effective the target group must be identifiable, measurable, accessible, substantial, and responsive.

With these criteria in mind, three alternative bases for segmentation were discussed: demographic, socioeconomic, and geographic. Major characteristics of American consumers were described within each of these categories. In addition, a number of marketing implications were suggested based upon these variables' influence on consumers' behavior.

Although socioeconomic-demographic variables are intuitively appealing and are widely available to marketers, their record as predictors of consumer behavior is not very strong. However, the problems in their use seem to be the result of a state-of-the-art limitation in analysis rather than a fundamental defect in their use. Consequently, they should continue to play an important role in segmentation efforts by marketers.

DISCUSSION TOPICS

1 Cite products (brands) in addition to those mentioned in the text that have followed a policy of market aggregation, concentrated marketing, and market atomization.

2 What are the benefits and costs of market segmentation?

3. Why are the following segmentation approaches or groups not very effective?
   a Segmenting a market on the basis of personality
   b Advertising to skeet shooters in *Time*
   c Developing an insurance plan for all quadruplets born in the United States

4 What are the major population changes taking place in the United States? What implications are there for the marketer of:
   a baby furniture   **d** sporting goods
   b insurance   **e** food
   c electronic products

5 Distinguish between MSA, PMSA, and CMSA.

6 What are the directions of consumer movement? Discuss the implications of these trends to:
   a Allied Van Lines   **c** J. C. Penney
   b Pizza Hut   **d** General Electric

PART TWO

UNDERSTANDING CONSUMERS AND MARKET SEGMENTS

7 What products might effectively segment their market on the basis of education? occupation? income?

8 Find a recent article from *The Wall Street Journal, Business Week,* or *U.S. News & World Report,* and report on the current mood of consumers and their willingness to buy.

NOTES

[1]Theodore Levitt, "Marketing Success through Differentiation—of Anything," *Harvard Business Review,* 58:83–91, January–February 1980.
[2]Burleigh Gardner and Sidney Levy, "The Product and the Brand," *Harvard Business Review,* 33:37, March–April 1955.
[3]Daniel Yankelovich, "New Criteria for Market Segmentation," *Harvard Business Review,* 42:83–84, March–April 1964.
[4]"Name Game," *Time,* August 31, 1981, pp. 41–42.
[5]Frederick W. Winter, "A Cost-Benefit Approach to Market Segmentation," *Journal of Marketing,* 43:103–111, Fall 1979.
[6]Ronald E. Frank, William F. Massy, and Yoram Wind, *Market Segmentation,* Prentice-Hall, Englewood Cliffs, N.J., 1972, pp. 7–11.
[7]Frank, Massy, and Wind, *Market Segmentation,* p. 11.
[8]Shirley Young, Leland Ott, and Barbara Feigin, "Some Practical Considerations in Market Segmentation," *Journal of Marketing Research,* 15:405–412, August 1978.
[9]James F. Engel, Henry F. Fiorillo, and Murray A. Cayley, *Market Segmentation: Concepts and Applications,* Holt, New York, 1972, p. 8.
[10]John M. McCann, "Market Segment Response to the Marketing Decision Variables," *Journal of Marketing Research,* 11:399–412, November 1974; and Arch G. Woodside and William H. Motes, "Sensitivities of Market Segments to Separate Advertising Strategies," *Journal of Marketing,* 45:63–73, Winter 1981.
[11]Young, Ott, and Feigin, "Some Practical Considerations," p. 405.
[12]This section is based on Yoram Wind, "Issues and Advances in Segmentation Research," *Journal of Marketing Research,* 15:321–322, August 1978.
[13]See Douglas MacLachlan and Johny K. Johansson, "Market Segmentation With Multivariate AID," *Journal of Marketing,* 45:74–84, Winter 1981; and Henry Assael and A. Marvin Roscoe, Jr., "Approaches to Market Segmentation Analysis," *Journal of Marketing,* 40:67–76, October 1976.
[14]Wind, "Issues," pp. 330–332.
[15]Wind, "Issues," p. 320.
[16]"Population Changes That Help for a While," *Business Week,* September 3, 1979, pp. 180–187.
[17]"Those Missing Babies," *Time,* September 16, 1974, pp. 56, 61.
[18]James C. Hyatt, "Costs of Being a Parent Keep Going Higher," *The Wall Street Journal,* October 2, 1980, p. 27.
[19]"Baby Boomlet: Its Impact on the '80s," *U.S. News & World Report,* June 15, 1981, pp. 51–52.
[20]"Decade's Boom in Prime-Age Consumers Will Offer Vast Opportunity for Business," *The Wall Street Journal,* June 26, 1980, p. 23.
[21]William Lazer, "The 1980s and Beyond: A Perspective," *M.S.U. Business Topics,* Spring 1977, pp. 21–35.
[22]See Fred D. Reynolds and Joseph D. Rentz, "Cohort Analysis: An Aid to Strategic Planning," *Journal of Marketing,* 45:62–70, Summer 1981, for an illustration of the examination of age–consumer behavior relationships in strategic planning decisions.
[23]"How the Changing Age Mix Changes Markets," *Business Week,* January 12, 1976, pp. 74–75.
[24]Thayer C. Taylor, "We the People: Older, Smarter, Liberated, Richer," *Sales & Marketing Management,* The Marketer's Complete Guide to the 1980s/A Special Report, December 10, 1979.
[25]"Household Growth Could Spurt in '80s, But Much Hinges on Lifestyle Choices," *The Wall Street Journal,* July 1, 1980, p. 23.
[26]Earl C. Gottschalk, Jr., "Disney to Shift Target of Some Parks, Movies, to Teen-Agers, Adults," *The Wall Street Journal,* January 26, 1979, p. 1.
[27]"Gerber: 'Selling More to the Same Mothers Is Our Objective Now,'" *Business Week,* October 16, 1978, pp. 192–194.
[28]Gail Bronson, "Baby Food It Is, But Gerber Wants Teen-Agers to Think of It as Dessert," *The Wall Street Journal,* July 17, 1981, p. 21.
[29]"The Graying of the Soft-Drink Industry," *Business Week,* May 23, 1977, pp. 68–72.
[30]See, for example, Landon Y. Jones, *Great Expectations: America and the Baby Boom Generation,* Coward, McCann & Geoghegan, 1980; "Going After the Mightiest Market," *Time,* September 14, 1981, pp.

56–61; "The Over-the-Thrill Crowd," *Time,* May 28, 1979, p. 39; and "Hart Schaffner & Marx: Expanding Boldly from Class to Mass Markets," *Business Week,* October 20, 1980, pp. 74–77.

[31] This section is drawn largely from "How the Changing Age Mix Changes Markets," pp. 74–75.

[32] Leland L. Beik and Scott M. Smith, "Geographic Segmentation: A Fund-Raising Example," in Neil Beckwith, Michael Houston, Robert Mittlestaedt, Kent B. Monroe, and Scott Ward (eds.), *1979 Educator's Conference Proceedings,* American Marketing Association, Chicago, 1979, pp. 485–488.

[33] Samuel E. Krug and Raymond W. Kulhavy, "Personality Differences Across Regions of the United States," *The Journal of Social Psychology,* 91:73–79, October 1973.

[34] Lawrence Rout, "Regional Architecture Revives, Spurred by Expensive Energy," *The Wall Street Journal,* March 22, 1981, p. 25.

[35] Janet Guyon, "Reynolds Tobacco Is Reversing Decline In Market Share by Aggressive Selling," *The Wall Street Journal,* October 29, 1980, p. 10.

[36] Del I. Hawkins, Don Roupe, and Kenneth A. Coney, "The Influence of Geographic Subcultures in the United States," in Kent B. Monroe (ed.), *Advances in Consumer Research: Volume 8,* Association for Consumer Research, Ann Arbor, Mich., 1981, pp. 713–717.

[37] Sam Allis, "Sharp Differences in Attitudes on Social Questions Divide U.S.," *The Wall Street Journal,* February 25, 1981, p. 25.

[38] "Regions," *The Wall Street Journal,* November 4, 1980, p. 25.

[39] Fabian Linden, "A Decade of Suburban Growth," *The Conference Board Record,* September 1971, pp. 49–50.

[40] Jim L. Grimm and Paul R. Winn, "A Ten-Year Study of Urban-Rural Market Penetration Patterns for Consumer Nondurables," in Robert S. Franz, Robert M. Hopkins, and Alfred G. Toma (eds.), *Proceedings: Southern Marketing Association 1979 Conference,* Southern Marketing Association, Lafayette, Louisiana, 1979, pp. 333–336.

[41] "America's Small Town Boom," *Newsweek,* July 6, 1981, pp. 26–37.

[42] Courtenay Slater, "Population Growth Slows; Shift to Open Spaces Speeds Up in 70's," *Commerce America,* June 5, 1978, p. 19.

[43] "Out of the Cities, Back to the Country," *U.S. News & World Report,* March 31, 1976, p. 46.

[44] Steve Weiner, "Branching Out," *The Wall Street Journal,* May 28, 1981, pp. 1, 20.

[45] Roy Rowan, "Business Triumphs of the Seventies," *Fortune,* December 31, 1979, p. 34.

[46] Fabian Linden, "Geography is Destiny," *Across the Board,* May 1981, pp. 54–57.

[47] "The Nomadic American," *Time,* September 11, 1972, p. 39.

[48] "Mobile Americans: A Moving Target with Sales Potential," *Sales & Marketing Management,* April 7, 1980, p. 40.

[49] Linden, "A Decade of Suburban Growth," p. 52.

[50] "The Immobile Society," *Time,* November 28, 1977, pp. 107–108.

[51] W. Thomas Anderson, Jr. and Linda L. Golden, "Life Trajectory: Population Migrations and Lifestyle Over Time," in Neil Beckwith, Michael Houston, Robert Mittlestaedt, Kent B. Monroe, and Scott Ward (eds.), *1979 Educators' Conference Proceedings,* American Marketing Association, Chicago, 1979, pp. 291–296.

[52] Linda L. Golden, W. Thomas Anderson, Jr., and Nancy M. Ridgway, "Consumer Mobility: A Life History Approach," in Jerry C. Olson (ed.), *Advances in Consumer Research: Volume 7,* Association for Consumer Research, Ann Arbor, Mich., 1980, pp. 460–465.

[53] See Alan R. Andreasen, "Geographic Mobility and Market Seg   .ation," *Journal of Marketing Research,* 3:341–348; and James E. Bell, Jr., "Mobiles—A Neglec⸍   Market Segment," *Journal of Marketing,* 33:37–44, April 1969.

[54] James E. Bell, Jr., "Mobiles—A Possible Segment for Retailer Cultivation," *Journal of Retailing,* 46:13–14, Fall 1970.

[55] Fabian Linden, "Per Capita-ism," *Across the Board,* June 1980, pp. 65–69.

[56] Fabian Linden, "Keys to the '80s—Youth and Affluence," *Across the Board,* December 1979, pp. 33–37; and Linden, "Per Capita-ism," p. 66.

[57] Fabian Linden, "Extra! The 150 Billion Market for Luxuries," *Across the Board,* April 1981, pp. 47–49. The terms "discretionary income" and "supernumerary income" were originated by the National Industrial Conference Board.

[58] "Who Has the Wealth in America" *Business Week,* August 5, 1972, p. 54.

[59] Linden, "Extra! The $150 Billion Market for Luxuries," pp. 47–49; A. F. Ehrbar, "The Upbeat Outlook for Family Incomes," *Fortune,* February 25, 1980, pp. 122–130; Nancy Giges, "Study Follows Baby Boom Spenders," *Advertising Age,* May 11, 1981, p. 45; "Today's Affluent Younger, 'Poorer,' But Still Core Target for Marketers," *Marketing News,* May 15, 1981, section 2, p. 9; "Our New Elite," *U.S. News & World Report,* February 25, 1980, pp. 65–68; and Fabian Linden, "At the End of the Eighties," *Across the Board,* March 1981, pp. 50–52.

[60] Steve Weiner, "Makers Stress Top of the Line in Housewares," *The Wall Street Journal,* January 14, 1981, p. 27; Peter Bohr, "America's Quest for Quality," *Money,* December 1980, pp. 44–66; and "Buyers Swing to Quality, *Business Week,* December 3, 1979, pp. 82–83.

[61] Lynn Upshaw, "Use the New Census to Update 'Upscales,'" *Marketing & Media Decisions,* April 1981, pp. 58–162.

CHAPTER 4

117

MARKET SEGMENTATION: BASIC APPROACHES

[62] Gregory D. Upah and Seymour Sudman, "The Consumer Expenditure Survey: Prospects for Consumer Research," in Kent B. Monroe (ed.), *Advances in Consumer Research: Volume 8,* Association for Consumer Research, Ann Arbor, Mich., 1981, pp. 262–266; and Eva E. Jacobs, "Consumer Expenditure Survey Data: Uses by BLS," in Kent B. Monroe (ed.), *Advances in Consumer Research: Volume 8,* Association for Consumer Research, Ann Arbor, Mich., 1981, pp. 251–253.

[63] "The Shrinking Standard of Living," *Business Week,* January 28, 1980, pp. 72–78; and "Goodbye to Our Good Life?" *U.S. News & World Report,* August 4, 1980, pp. 45–49.

[64] "Middle Class Suffers the Most From 'Stagflation'," *Marketing News,* October 5, 1979, pp. 1, 6.

[65] "Marketing Research Briefs," *Marketing News,* September 19, 1980, p. 28.

[66] "'Permanent Inflation' Is Key Factor in Future of Marketing," *Marketing News,* September 7, 1979, pp. 3–4.

[67] "Inflation Changes Supermart Shopping Habits," *Marketing News,* August 10, 1979, p. 1, 16.

[68] Meg Cox, "Food Stores With Fair Services Spring Up to Lure Increasingly Frugal Customers," *The Wall Street Journal,* January 23, 1981, p. 38.

[69] "Four Ways Marketers Can Cope With Selling to Middle Class During Inflation," *Marketing News,* October 5, 1979, p. 6.

[70] "How Good Are Consumer Pollsters?" *Business Week,* November 8, 1969, p. 108.

[71] Fabian Linden, "The Consumer as Fortune Teller," *Across the Board,* June 1981, p. 62; and Edward Meadows, "The Unhealthy Glow on Retail Sales," *Fortune,* July 3, 1978, pp. 46–48.

[72] "How Good Are Consumer Pollsters?" p. 110.

[73] Much of this section is based on Jagdish N. Sheth, "Demographics in Consumer Behavior," *Journal of Business Research,* 5:129–138, June 1977.

[74] See, for example, Franklin B. Evans, "Psychological and Objective Factors in the Prediction of Brand Choice," *Journal of Business,* 33:340–369, October 1959; and Arthur Koponen, "Personality Characteristics of Purchasers," *Journal of Advertising Research,* 1:6–12, September 1960.

[75] John C. Bieda and Harold W. Kassarjian, "An Overview of Market Segmentation," in Bernard A. Morin (ed.), *Marketing in a Changing World,* American Marketing Association, Chicago, 1969, p. 250.

CHAPTER 5

MARKET SEGMENTATION: ADDITIONAL DIMENSIONS

This chapter will expand on the discussion of the previous chapter by further examining the concept of market segmentation. In addition, the associated concept of product positioning will be explored. As will be seen in this chapter, the marketer has available numerous additional dimensions by which markets may be segmented. Each of these approaches builds on the demographic, socioeconomic, and/or geographic bases described in the previous chapter. As will become clearer in this chapter, the ultimate goal is not merely the definition of market segments and product positions, but the use of this information to develop marketing programs that appeal more strongly to chosen target groups.

LIFESTYLE AND PSYCHOGRAPHIC SEGMENTATION

An advertising executive recently stated: "I've never seen a time when there has been so great a difference between groups in the same demographic limits."[1] As this suggests, one of the major problems of demographic segmentation is its lack of "richness" in describing consumers for market segmentation and strategy development. It lacks color, texture, and dimensionality when describing consumers, and it often needs to be supplemented by something that fills in the bare statistical picture. Consequently, many firms are looking for a better way to define markets. One of the newest, most exciting, and promising approaches to selecting target markets is *lifestyle* and *psychographic segmentation*. Although the concepts of lifestyle and psychographics are often used interchangeably, they are not equivalent but are complementary.

The term "lifestyle" is not new, but its application to marketing has been rather recent. Alfred Adler coined the phrase "style of life" over 50 years ago to refer to the goal a person shapes for himself, and the ways he uses to reach it. From our perspective, lifestyle can be viewed as a unique pattern of living which influences and is reflected by one's consumption behavior.[2] Therefore, the way in which marketers facilitate the expression of an individual's lifestyle is by "providing customers with parts of a potential mosaic from which they, as artists of their own lifestyles, can pick and choose to develop the composition that for the time seems best."[3]

Many products today are "lifestyle" products, that is, they portray a style of life sought by potential users. Revlon's Charlie perfume, for example, is a product that women buy more to live like Charlie (a young, independent, unmarried working woman who enjoys life) than to *look* or *smell* like her.[4] A Charlie advertisement is shown in Figure 5-1.

How does the concept of psychographics relate to lifestyle? Unfortunately, it is not an easy matter to define psychographics because there is no general agreement as to exactly what it is. One of the more precise statements about its nature is the following: *psychographics* is the systematic use of relevant activity, interest, and opinion constructs to quantitatively explore and explain the communicating, purchasing, and consuming behaviors of persons for brands, products, and clusters of products.[5]

Thus, psychographics may be viewed as the method of defining lifestyle in measurable terms. It should be noted, however, that there is some question about the use of psychographic instruments as a precise measure of the lifestyle of the individual consumer.[6] Nevertheless, the basic premise underlying lifestyle research is that the more marketers understand their customers the more effectively they can communicate and market to them.[7] In many cases the primary targets of such marketing efforts are heavy users. Heavy users have traditionally been looked at demographically, but by incorporating lifestyle characteristics the marketer obtains a better, more true-to-life picture of such customers.

Technique of Lifestyle Segmentation

Lifestyle-segmentation research measures (1) how people spend their time engaging in activities, (2) what is of most interest or importance to them in their immediate surroundings, and (3) their opinions and views about themselves and the world around them. Together, these three areas are generally referred to as *Activities, Interests, and Opinions*, or simply *AIOs*. Table 5-1 indicates the lifestyle dimensions (particularly AIOs) that may be investigated among consumers.

In a typical large-scale, lifestyle research project, questionnaires are mailed to members of a nationwide consumer panel. The questionnaires solicit traditional demographic information, average usage rates for as many as 100 different products, media habits, and respondents' activities, interests, and opinions. Approximately 300 AIO statements may be included, to which respondents indicate the extent of their agreement or disagreement on six-point Likert scales ranging from "definitely disagree" to "definitely agree." The following illustrates the nature of typical AIO statements employed:

I like gardening.
I do not get enough sleep.
I enjoy going to concerts.
A news magazine is more interesting than a fiction magazine.
There should be a gun in every home.
Instant coffee is more economical than ground coffee
I stay home most evenings.
There is a lot of love in our family.[8]

FIGURE 5-1

Example of "lifestyle" advertising for Charlie perfume. (Courtesy of Revlon.)

REVLON
Charlie

"AFTER THE PARTY" :30 RVCF 1143

(MUSIC UNDER)
HE: Nice party.

ANNCR: (VO) The best part of the party's when the party's over.

HE: Mmm, Charlie?
SHE: Uh huh.

HE: Would you cancel your trip to the coast if I proposed?

SHE: I wonder how much this lion weighs?

HE: Ciao!
SHE: Great bakery!

HE: Listen, I'm serious about what I said before.
SHE: Eat your breakfast.

HE: Even my mother thinks it's time for you to settle down.

SHE: Your mother's right.

ANNCR: (VO) Charlie. It's a great life.

TABLE 5-1
LIFESTYLE DIMENSIONS

Activities	Interests	Opinions	Demographics
Work	Family	Themselves	Age
Hobbies	Home	Social issues	Education
Social events	Job	Politics	Income
Vacation	Community	Business	Occupation
Entertainment	Recreation	Economics	Family size
Club membership	Fashion	Education	Dwelling
Community	Food	Products	Geography
Shopping	Media	Future	City size
Sports	Achievements	Culture	Stage in life cycle

Source: Reprinted from Joseph T. Plummer, "The Concept and Application of Life Style Segmentation," *Journal of Marketing,* **38**:34, January 1974, published by the American Marketing Association.

Where do AIO items orginate? They may come from intuition, hunches, conversations, research, reading, and group or individual in-depth interviews.[9]

Armed with these three sets of data (AIOs, demographics, and product usage), the marketer constructs user profiles. The analysis involves relating levels of agreement on all AIO items with the levels of usage on a product and with demographic characteristics. Typically, a pattern emerges in which AIO statements cluster together; that is, similar respondents are grouped together from a lifestyle perspective.[10]

Generally, then, the process of lifestyle segmentation involves two steps. First, a determination is made of which lifestyle segments will efficiently produce the greatest number of profitable customers. Often heavy users are sought, but as we have seen, other segments also have potential. The second step involves defining and describing the selected target customers in more depth to understand how they may be attracted and communicated with more efficiently and relevantly.[11]

Applications of Lifestyle Segmentation

Lifestyle may be used as a basis for segmentation in four possible ways. These approaches are discussed below, and examples are provided for each situation.[12]

Segmentation Based on General Lifestyle Characteristics In this approach the marketer seeks to classify the consumer population into groups based on general lifestyle characteristics, so that consumers within the groups have similar lifestyles. Using the research approach described above, a representative sample of consumers respond to a questionnaire containing AIOs, product usage, media consumption, and demographic items. Through statistical routines (clustering and others) the marketer attempts to find out if people can be grouped together into distinct groups. Each group represents a different pattern of needs for and consumption of products and services. Once these groups are identified, the marketer is able to direct his product to appeal to one or several segments.[13]

As an example of this approach, a major study by Needham, Harper & Steers advertising agency categorized almost 3300 respondents into ten different lifestyle types—five female and five male. To help clients understand the lifestyle data, the ten consumer composites were even given names as shown in Table 5-2.

Indexes of product usage for some items of interest can then be developed showing how the groups differ in their consumption. For example, Ben, Scott, Eleanor, and Candice are heavy users of liquor products, while Eleanor, Candice, and Mildred are heavy cosmetics users. Given the varying psychographic profiles, however, quite different strategies will be necessary to reach the different groups. By also understanding the media patterns of these groups, appropriate advertising vehicles can be selected. For example, magazines such as *Glamour, Cosmopolitan,* and *True Story,* and radio stations playing heavy rock are much more likely to

TABLE 5-2 PSYCHOGRAPHIC PROFILES

The Female Segments

Thelma, the old-fashioned traditionalist (25%)
This lady has lived a "good" life—she has been a devoted wife, a doting mother, and a conscientious housewife. She has lived her life by these traditional values and she cherishes them to this day. She does not condone contemporary sexual activities or political liberalism, nor can she sympathize with the women's libbers. Even today, when most of her children have left home, her life is centered around the kitchen. Her one abiding interest outside the household is the church which she attends every week. She lacks higher education and hence has little appreciation for the arts or cultural activities. Her spare time is spent watching TV, which is her prime source of entertainment and information.

Mildred, the militant mother (20%)
Mildred married young and had children before she was quite ready to raise a family. Now she is unhappy. She is having trouble making ends meet on her blue-collar husband's income. She is frustrated and she vents her frustrations by rebelling against the system. She finds escape from her unhappy world in soap operas and movies. Television provides an ideal medium for her to live out her fantasies. She watches TV all through the day and into late night. She likes heavy rock and probably soul music, and she doesn't read much except escapist magazines such as *True Story.*

Candice, the chic suburbanite (20%)
Candice is an urbane woman. She is well educated and genteel. She is a prime mover in her community, active in club affairs and working on community projects. Socializing is an important part of her life. She is a doer, interested in sports and the outdoors, politics and current affairs. Her life is hectic and lived at a fast clip. She is a voracious reader, and there are few magazines she doesn't read. However, TV does relatively poorly in competing for her attention—it is too inane for her.

Cathy, the contented housewife (18%)
Cathy epitomizes simplicity. Her life is untangled. She is married to a worker in the middle of the socioeconomic scale, and they, along with their several preteen children, live in a small town. She is devoted to her family and faithfully serves them as mother, housewife, and cook. There is a certain tranquility in her life. She enjoys a relaxed pace and avoids anything that might disturb her equilibrium. She doesn't like news or news-type programs on TV but enjoys the wholesome family entertainment provided by *Walt Disney, The Waltons,* and *Happy Days.*

Eleanor, the elegant socialite (17%)
Eleanor is a woman with style. She lives in the city because that is where she wants to be. She likes the economic and social aspects of big city living and takes advantage of the city in terms of her career and leisure time activities. She is a self-confident on-the-go woman, not a homebody. She is fashion-conscious and dresses well. She is a woman with panache. She is financially secure; as a result she is not a careful shopper. She shops for quality and style, not price. She is a cosmopolitan woman who has traveled abroad or wants to.

TABLE 5-2
(Continued)   The Male Segments

Herman, the retiring homebody (26%)
Herman is past his prime and is not getting any younger. His attitudes and opinions on life, which are often in conflict with modern trends, have gelled. And he is resistant to change. He is old-fashioned and conservative. He was brought up on "motherhood and apple pie" and cherishes these values. Consequently he finds the attitudes of young people today disturbing. He realizes he cannot affect any change, and has withdrawn into a sheltered existence of his own within the confines of his home and its surroundings. Here he lives a measured life. He goes to church regularly, watches his diet, and lives frugally. He longs for the good old days and regrets that the world around him is changing.

Scott, the successful professional (21%)
Scott is a man who has everything going for him. He is well educated, cosmopolitan, the father of a young family, and is already established in his chosen profession. He lives a fast-paced active life and likes it. He is a man getting ahead in the world. He lives in or near an urban center and seems to like what a big city has to offer—culture, learning opportunities, and people. He also enjoys sports, the out-of-doors, and likes to keep physically fit. He is understandably happy with his life and comfortable in his lifestyle.

Fred, the frustrated factory worker (19%)
Fred is young. He married young and had a family. It is unlikely that he had any plans to get a college degree; if he did, he had to shelve them to find work to support his family. He now is a blue-collar worker having trouble making ends meet. He is discontented, and tends to feel that "they"—big business, government, society—are somehow responsible for his state. He finds escape in movies and in fantasies of foreign lands and cabins by quiet lakes. He likes to appear attractive to women, has an active libido, and likes to think he is a bit of a swinger.

Dale, the devoted family man (17%)
Dale is a wholesome guy with a penchant for country living. He is a blue-collar worker, with a high school education. The father of a relatively large family, he prefers a traditional marriage, with his wife at home taking care of the kids. His home and neighborhood are central in his life. He is an easygoing guy who leads an uncomplicated life. Neither worry nor skepticism are a part of him. He is relaxed and has a casual approach to many things. He is a happy, trusting soul who takes things as they are.

Ben, the self-made businessman (17%)
Ben is the epitome of a self-made man. He was probably not born wealthy, nor had he the benefit of higher education, but through hard work and shrewd risk-taking he has built himself a decent life. He has seen the system work. He believes if you work hard and play by the rules you will get your share (and perhaps some more). Therefore he cannot condone hippies and other fringe groups whom he sees as freeloaders. He embraces conservative ideology and is likely to be a champion of business interests. He is a traditionalist at home, and believes it is a woman's job to look after the home and to raise a family. He is gregarious and enjoys giving and attending parties. And he likes to drink.

Source: Reprinted from Sunil Mehrotra and William D. Wells, "Psychographics and Buyer Behavior: Theory and Recent Empirical Findings," in Arch G. Woodside, Jagdish N. Sheth, and Peter D. Bennett (eds.), *Consumer and Industrial Buying Behavior*, Elsevier North-Holland, New York, 1977, pp. 54–55.

reach Mildred the militant mother, while publications such as *Vogue, Cosmopolitan,* and *Better Homes and Gardens,* and radio stations playing classical music tend to appeal to Eleanor and Candice.[14]

A general segmentation study was successfully used by a manufacturer of intimate apparel for women to diversify its product lines. The maker had been selling a line of old-fashioned, traditional lingerie that appealed to the

Thelmas and Cathys of the United States. As a result of a segmentation study, the company uncovered an opportunity to design and market two new lines of intimate apparel, one to appeal to people resembling Eleanor and Candice, and the other to be aimed at people such as Mildred.[15]

Segmentation Based on Product-Specific Lifestyle Characteristics   In this approach, the marketer seeks to understand consumer behavior related to a particular product or service. That is, in order to obtain more meaningful data the marketer tailors the general AIO questions to make them more product-specific. For example, the general AIO statement "I like to exercise" may be modified to "I like to play tennis." The advantage of this approach is that groups emerge that are more sharply defined in terms of their usage of a particular product or service.

> Such a segmentation study of the leisure travel market led Air Canada to develop new vacation packages to meet the needs of some segments which were identified. For example, the largest segment, a group identified as "cautious homebodies" were found to want safety, security, and a predictable environment on their vacation. Their desire to be led around and made to feel secure was recognized and translated into a vacation package based on a guided coach tour of England. Many other vacation package concepts were designed based on the demographic and vacation-specific lifestyle attributes of the market.[16]

Profiling Based on General Lifestyle Characteristics   The marketer, instead of segmenting to find the most appropriate number of meaningful homogeneous groups into which a heterogeneous population can be divided, may need to profile a homogeneous group of respondents according to the "typical" individual in the group. This use of general AIO items may allow the marketer to more adequately define a segment of interest. For instance, although insurance companies have traditionally relied on demographic characteristics to identify accident-prone drivers, use of general lifestyle characteristics to profile these individuals is also helpful. One study shows that the accident-prone driver is more likely than the safe driver to be a risk taker and an impulse buyer, is restless, feels pressured, has money problems but is optimistic, has a cosmopolitan outlook, is interested in movies (especially X-rated and disaster ones), and is less likely to be socially or politically conservative. Knowledge that such lifestyle characteristics correlate with the propensity to have driving accidents can lead an insurance company to develop more effective communication and other programs as part of its marketing strategy.[17] Even its accident or risk-rating program may be influenced by such data.

Profiling Based on Product-Specific Lifestyle Characteristics   In the previous approach, the marketer developed the psychographic profile for the segment of interest from a large set of general lifestyle items. When a psychographic study is devoted to a single product category, however, the researcher can focus instead on a limited group of relevant, product-related dimensions.

> Introduction of the Ford Pinto illustrates the use of such a psychographic approach.[18] The Pinto was launched with advertising portraying the car as carefree, small, and romantic in order to appeal to prospective small-car buyers, particularly those for imported cars. Advertisements also stressed that the

car was trouble-free, beautifully styled, and economical. However, psychographic research soon showed that potential Pinto buyers did not have such a romantic orientation toward cars and driving. They agreed with such statements as "I wish I could depend on my car more," "I am more practical in car selection," "A car offers me a chance to tinker with machinery," "I like to feel how powerful my car is," and "The only function for a car is transportation." They disagreed with such statements as "The kind of car you have is important as to how people see you," and "Taking care of a car is too much trouble." The research resulted in a change in Pinto's advertising emphasizing the functional nature of the car as basic, economical transportation in the Ford Model A tradition. The Pinto went on to become the largest selling subcompact of its day.

Additional Uses of Lifestyle Information

As stated before, the purpose of using lifestyle or any other variable to segment a market is not as an end in itself, but to help successfully develop and target marketing mixes. To elaborate on some of the marketer's key uses for lifestyle information in this regard, we will examine several areas of application.

Developing New Products Psychographic research can often be used as a springboard to development of new products based on the identification of unserved market segments. The case of Colgate-Palmolive's Irish Spring illustrates such an application.[19]

> Between 1958 and 1970, Colgate introduced eleven bar soaps into test markets, but not one of them was successful enough to reach national distribution. Up to that time, Colgate had been categorizing users into two basic functional segments—a complexion segment and a deodorant segment. There was no real understanding of why persons bought a particular brand of soap, that is, of how consumers perceived that a soap influences their roles in life and their expectations of physical benefits.
>
> Colgate undertook a psychographic segmentation study and uncovered three clearly defined consumer groups—*independents, rejuvenators,* and *compensators*—with the following characteristics:
>
> *Independents*—Forceful leaders concerned about getting ahead, confident, self-assured, calm and unflappable, practical, realistic, rugged, and self-reliant people who don't pamper themselves
>
> *Rejuvenators*—Outward-directed, basically insecure people who need the social reassurance of those around them
>
> *Compensators*—Inward-directed, passive, and withdrawn people
>
> In terms of soap preferences, the independents were on one end of the spectrum, oriented toward cleaning and refreshment in a toilet soap, while compensators were on the other end, desiring luxury and comfort in the bath. Independents were found to have a disproportionate number of men and were shown to be a group ready for something new and fresh in bar-soap benefits. They wanted a long-lasting, hard soap that would keep them clean, fresh, and odor-free and could be used by the whole family.

To fulfill the needs of this vacant market niche, Colgate assessed many possibilities for product name, shape, color, and scent which best fulfilled the concept of a deodorant soap for men yet would be mild enough for the rest of the family. Emerging from this search was the product Irish Spring with an advertising appeal aimed primarily at men. Sean, the ads' rugged-looking, self-assured spokesman, matched the independents' characteristics (see Figure 5-2). However, in order to broaden the appeal to the household

FIGURE 5-2

Lifestyle advertisement for Irish Spring. (Courtesy of Colgate-Palmolive Co.)

IRISH SPRING

COLGATE-PALMOLIVE CO.   CLIS 1100   "ARM WRESTLERS" (:30)

(SFX: GRUNTS, CROWD CHEERING)

SEAN: You're a strong man, John.
GAL: Aye!

JOHN: A mite stronger than I care to be.

SEAN: Then shower up with Irish Spring.

JOHN: Ah, the double deodorant soap.

SEAN: For long lastin' protection.

(MUSIC UNDER) SEAN: (VO) Look. In these green and white stripes...

(SFX: SHOWER) ...are 2 deodorants. That means long lastin' protection.

JOHN: What a fine fresh smell.

GAL: That's why I use it, too.

SEAN: Irish Spring with 2 deodorants.

(VO) For long lastin' deodorant protection.

WILLIAM ESTY COMPANY, INC.

purchasing agent, women were also brought into the commercial with the selling phrase, "Manly, yes, but I like it too." In addition, the Irish setting for the advertisements created a sense of outdoors and freshness. Three years after national introduction Irish Spring was the third leading bar soap on the market.

Developing Promotion Strategy Probably the most extensive use of lifestyle information is in connection with development of advertising campaigns. Here, the marketer can particularly benefit from an understanding of lifestyle as it relates to consumer media usage and as a source of ideas for advertising approaches. Lifestyle, along with other sources of information, can be useful to advertisers in suggesting new or changed advertising characters, settings, moods, and themes.

SELECTING MEDIA Use of lifestyle profiles for different media can suggest appropriate vehicles to use in reaching target markets. For instance, examination of the *Playboy* reader lifestyle profile will reveal a vast difference between that and the lifestyle of readers of many other magazines. To illustrate, Table 5-3 comparing heavy readers of *Playboy* and *Reader's Digest* on only a few lifestyle statements indicates very different orientations regarding optimism, religion, conservatism, and permissiveness.

The *Playboy* reader's full lifestyle profile points to selection of this medium as a good vehicle for such products as liquor, air travel, sports cars, mutual funds, beer, credit cards, moving companies, and new products in general. Their lifestyle profile also suggests a swinging, permissive, light, and rather youth-oriented approach to advertising copy. Such a copy approach and many of the products appropriate for *Playboy* may not be appropriate for *Reader's Digest*. Before including *Playboy* in the media set for a campaign, however, the marketer will need to look at audiences of other relevant media and, particularly, at the cost per thousand of reaching the appropriate audience.

DETERMINING CREATIVE STRATEGY Lifestyle information is frequently used when developing advertising campaigns. A classic case of the use of lifestyle research to develop a national advertising campaign is illustrated by Schlitz beer.[20]

TABLE 5-3 DIFFERENCES IN READERS' LIFESTYLES FOR TWO MEDIA

	Percent Who Definitely Agreed Among	
	Heavy *Playboy* Readers	Heavy *Reader's Digest* Readers
My greatest achievements are still ahead of me	50%	26%
I go to church regularly	18	40
Movies should be censored	14	40
Most men would cheat on their wives if the right opportunity came along	27	12

Source: Douglas J. Tigert, "Life Style Analysis as a Basis for Media Selection," in William D. Wells (ed.), *Life Style and Psychographics,* American Marketing Association, Chicago, 1974, p. 179.

Prior to 1969 Schlitz had been running a successful ad campaign formulated around the copy line of "When you're out of Schlitz, you're out of beer." There was a general feeling that a new, fresh approach was needed. The advertising director visited neighborhood taverns to observe and talk with target customers—heavy beer drinkers. In addition, one element emerged from past Schlitz advertising—the word "gusto." Research showed it to have strong connotations, conveying relevant meanings about beer, taste, and life, and it also turned out to be "owned" by Schlitz. Another element emerging from the review process was that Schlitz is sold almost everywhere in the world—in fact, the world was used as a symbol on the label.

The "tavern tour" of the advertising director yielded the following informal lifestyle portrait of the heavy beer drinker as:

... the man who belongs to the 20 percent of the population that drinks 80 percent of the beer. A man who drinks a case a weekend or even a case a day.... He is a guy who is not making it and probably never will. He is a dreamer, a wisher, a limited edition of Walter Mitty. He is a sports nut because he is a hero worshipper.... He goes to the tavern and has six or seven beers with the boys.... If we are to talk to this man where he lives, in terms he respects and can identify with, we must find for him a believable kind of hero he inwardly admires.[21]

Next, formal research on the lifestyle of the heavy beer drinker was completed as shown in Table 5-4.

It was found that the heavy user

• Had a middle-class income level derived primarily from blue-collar occupations

• Was young with at least a high school education

• Was more hedonistic and pleasure-seeking toward life than the nondrinker

• Had less regard toward family and job responsibilities than nondrinkers

• Had a preference for a physical/male-oriented existence and was inclined to fantasize

• Had a great enjoyment of drinking, particularly beer, which was seen as a real man's drink

Using the lifestyle portrait of the heavy beer drinker, it was decided that the "gusto man, and gusto life" approach would strongly appeal to the heavy user's sense of masculinity, hedonism, and fantasy. From this research Schlitz built a successful ad campaign around imagery of the sea to glamorize the adventure of seamen who lived their lives with gusto and enjoyed a "gusto brew." (See Figure 5-3.) The copy for the ads stated, "You only go around once in life. So grab for all the gusto you can."

Schlitz subsequently sank from its number two position in the industry to fourth place behind Anheuser-Busch, Miller, and Pabst as a result of an unsuccessful product taste modification in which its brewing cycle was accelerated and as a result of numerous substantial changes in the industry, particularly those centering on new products and strong, effective advertising by Busch and Miller.[22]

TABLE 5-4

MALE BEER DRINKERS

	Percentage of Agreement		
	Nonusers	Light Users	Heavy Users
He is self-indulgent, enjoys himself, and likes risks			
I like to play poker	18	37	41
I like to take chances	27	32	44
I would rather spend a quiet evening at home than go out to a party	67	53	44
If I had my way, I would own a convertible	7	11	15
I smoke too much	29	40	42
If I had to choose I would rather have a color TV than a new refrigerator	25	33	38
He rejects responsibility and is a bit impulsive			
I like to work on community projects	24	18	14
I have helped collect money for the Red Cross or United Fund	41	32	24
I'm not very good at saving money	20	29	38
I find myself checking prices, even for small items	51	42	40
He likes sports and a physical orientation			
I would like to be a pro football player	10	15	21
I like bowling	32	36	42
I usually read the sports page	47	48	59
I would do better than average in a fist fight	17	26	32
I like war stories	33	37	45
He rejects old fashioned institutions and moral guidelines			
I go to church regularly	57	37	31
Movies should be censored	67	46	43
I have old-fashioned tastes and habits	69	56	48
There is too much emphasis on sex today	71	59	53
. . . . and has a very masculine view			
Beer is a real man's drink	9	16	44
Playboy is one of my favorite magazines	11	21	28
I am a girl watcher	33	47	54
Men should not do the dishes	18	26	38
Men are smarter than women	22	27	31

Source: Reprinted from Joseph T. Plummer, "Life Style and Advertising: Case Studies," in Fred C. Alvine (ed.), *Combined Proceedings 1971 Spring and Fall Conferences,* American Marketing Association, Chicago, 1971, p. 294, published by the American Marketing Association.

When more than one segment is targeted, different advertising strategies may be needed for each one based on their lifestyle, demographic, and media-usage profiles. For example, the state of South Carolina employed five distinct advertising strategies using different creative approaches, media schedules, and direct-mail literature in order to appeal to five different vacation market segments. The different segments and resulting ad strategies for only two of these segments are illustrated in Table 5-5 and Figure 5-4.

Benefits of Lifestyle Segmentation

Lifestyle segmentation has been the object of increasing research and application in marketing because of its potential benefits. Although the problems involved in

FIGURE 5-3

Lifestyle advertisement for Schlitz beer. (Courtesy of Jos. Schlitz Brewing Co.)

TABLE 5-5

PREIDENTIFIED MARKET SEGMENTS AND ADVERTISING STRATEGIES

Market Segments

	The Beach Vacationer	The Colonial Sightseer	The Fisherman	The Highlands Vacationer	The Second Home Vacationer
Predicted profiles	Married couples with children under 19 living at home. The head of the household is probably a blue-collar worker. They enjoy the ocean along with new exciting activities. Life typically revolves around the family. Travel party size is usually four or more, and summer travel is preferred. Median education, middle socioeconomic status, and young to middle age.	Married couples with no children living at home. Upscale white-collar worker interested in America's historical growth and development. May be retired. Travel party size is usually two, and spring or summer travel is preferred. Enjoy dining out. College educated, middle to upper socioeconomic status, and middle age or older.	Married couples with one or no children living at home, and more likely to be 35 to 55 or older than members of other segments. They enjoy fishing and viewing the scenic beauty of the outdoors. Travel party size is usually less than four. They prefer to travel during the spring and summer. High school education and middle socioeconomic status.	Married couples with children under 19 at home. They enjoy the outdoors, camping, and the scenic breauty of the mountains. Travel party size is usually four or more. Prefer to travel during the spring or summer. High school education, middle socioeconomic status, and young to middle age. Head of household is probably a blue-collar worker.	Married couples with no children living at home and probably in the latter stages of a professional/managerial career or retired. They enjoy the ocean and solitude of their second home. Travel party size is usually small. Prefer to travel during the summer. College educated, upper socioeconomic status, and beyond middle age.

Advertising Strategies

	Myrtle Beach	Charleston	Santee	The Mountains	The Sea Islands
Advertising headlines	"Water slides, roller coasters, arcades, whirling, spinning, playing, winning. And we throw in the Atlantic Ocean . . . free."	"Nearly 300 years ago one of the best ways to see it was by horse and buggy. It still is."	"Here the Stripers, Catfish, Crappie and Largemouth have one thing in common. They're big."	"There's just one way to ride the Chattooga. Downstream. And fast."	"We have 17 sea islands where you can find beaches, sun-drenched resorts, catamaran sailing and horseback riding. Or solitude."
Advertising illustration	A young girl on a waterslide with the beach in the background	A couple and driver in a carriage on a cobblestoned street with a colonial house in the background	Striped Bass, Channel Catfish, Black Crappie, and Largemouth Bass	Four people in a raft on the Chattooga River	Dunes with marshes in the background

TABLE 5-5

(Continued)

	Advertising Strategies				
	Myrtle Beach	Charleston	Santee	The Mountains	The Sea Islands
Advertising copy	"Uninterrupted Beach" "Amusement Park" "Action and Excitement"	"Museum of Colonial America" "Open-air Market" "European Cuisine"	"They come out fighting" "One of the world's top freshwater fishing spots"	"Camp near a waterfall" "Unspoiled South Carolina mountains"	"Vacationers have found a mecca" "Rare wildlife and waterfowl" "Room for the solitary beachcomber"
Magazines	*Better Homes & Gardens, Family Circle, Good Housekeeping, Glamour, Red Book*	*Better Homes & Gardens, Woodall's, Smithsonian, Travel, House Beautiful*	*Fishing World* (Two insertions)	*Camping Journal* and *Popular Science*	*Natural History, New Yorker, Southern Living, Woman's Day, Smithsonian*

Source: Reprinted from Arch G. Woodside and William H. Motes, "Sensitivities of Market Segments to Separate Advertising Strategies," *Journal of Marketing,* **45:**64–65, Winter 1981, published by the American Marketing Association.

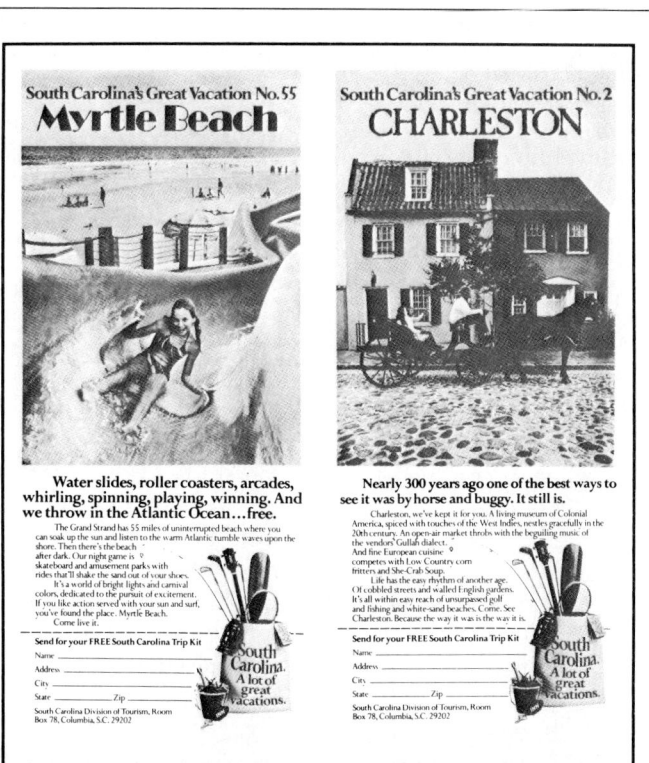

FIGURE 5-4

Advertisements aimed at different vacation market segments. (*Source:* Arch G. Woodside and William H. Motes, "Sensitivities of Market Segments to Separate Advertising Strategies," *Journal of Marketing,* **45:**66–68, Winter 1981, published by the American Marketing Association.)

getting, analyzing, and interpreting lifestyle data are not to be minimized, the examples presented above are good testimony of the technique's ability to assist the development of marketing strategy. Thus, the marketing manager may be able to develop improved multidimensional views of key target segments, uncover new product opportunities, obtain better product position, develop improved advertising communications based on a richer, more lifelike portrait of the target consumer, and generally improve overall marketing strategies.[23]

There are additional benefits of psychographics that are being realized by consumer-behavior researchers who tend to have a more esoteric view than does the practicing marketer. For these researchers, psychographic methods are leading to enhanced general knowledge of consumer behavior in at least three ways. First, they have contributed to a better understanding of numerous consumer behavior facets such as opinion leadership, retail shopping, private-brands buying, consumerist activism, and other attributes. Second, with the repetition of studies, trend data may be accumulated to show how consumers may be changing. Third, general segmentations of consumer groups are creating new typologies for more efficiently describing and understanding consumer behavior.

Thus the result of psychographic research findings such as those presented here may lead marketers to think routinely in terms of segments marked off by common sets of activities, interests, needs, and values and to develop products, services, and media schedules specifically to meet them.[24]

USAGE SEGMENTATION

Another segmentation approach often used by marketers is based on product or brand usage by consumers. Usage segmentation can take a number of directions. For example, the marketer may want to identify various segments of users for a particular product category or users of the company's brand. In other cases, one may want to segment users into those who buy frequently versus those who only buy occasionally (either product or brand), or into those users who purchase the same brand versus those who switch from brand to brand. Any usage segmentation approach needs to specify the relevant dimensions of interest.

Brand-User Segmentation

The marketer is generally most interested in determining whether those who purchase the company's brand are different, either demographically or psychographically, from those buying competitor's brands. If they are able to be distinguished, then marketing programs can perhaps be developed to attract more buyers who resemble the preferred buyer.

> Avon conducted a research study to identify its buyers, and it found them likely to be somewhat older than average, high school but not college graduates, living outside metropolitan areas, having husbands with blue-collar jobs and relatively low incomes, and having large families. Their lifestyles and attitudes tended to be conservative, and they had old-fashioned tastes. They were cost-conscious, centered around their homes and families, and didn't like to buy beauty products in stores because of the lack of privacy and personal attention. The best feature was that they spent 92 percent of their beauty-aid dollars with Avon. Since there was not a strong need to build their acceptance level, the company sought to identify other groups with a high

potential for purchasing Avon products. Close analysis of the data indicated a sizable group of women with a high potential for increased sales. They were like Avon's loyal customers in their attitudes toward in-home buying and personal service and they spent much money on cosmetics. However, they differed in other ways. For example, they were more up-scale, less conservative and family-oriented, more interested in being up-to-the-minute in fashion, and less inclined to believe that Avon products could give them whatever look they wanted. Avon's resulting advertising campaigns designed to attract these high-potential customers featured the themes "You Never Looked So Good," and "We're Going to Make You Feel Beautiful."[25]

A related approach that may be profitable to pursue is to develop new products to appeal to nonusing segments. Such a move may make it difficult for a company to maintain a consistent image, however. If such an image is critical, the marketer may need to work only with buyers similar to present users. Cadillac has faced this problem in the launch of its Cimarron (a lower-priced, small luxury car model) in which it is appealing, not to the traditional Cadillac buyer, but to those who are younger and have been buying expensive, sporty imported cars. The potential result may be a diffused image among customers as to what the brand "Cadillac" means.

Product-User Segmentation

Although buyers of different *brands* may not be found to have different characteristics, the marketer nevertheless will be interested in segmenting *product* users on the basis of any such distinguishing demographic or psychographic characteristics in order to reach them effectively. Within a product category such as soft drinks, for example, it may be found that those who consume low-calorie drinks differ demographically and psychographically from regular soft-drink users, although perhaps Diet Pepsi and Tab drinkers are virtually the same.

Of course, for many products nonusers may represent a significant marketing opportunity. Mercury Outboards, for example, is attempting to expand the boating universe by attracting nonusers—people who like boating but have never owned a boat. Also, public goods and nonprofit-organization specialists are continually confronted with the reality of the need to convert nonusers to users. For example, consider the following marketing problems:

Convincing nonusing men and women to avail themselves of cancer checkups.

Attracting nonriders to mass transportation.

Attracting nonsubscribers to symphonies, lectures, and other cultural events.

Each of these problems represents a marketing opportunity to convert nonusers to users. Obviously, the past rate of success for such projects has not been great, but with increased application of marketing research to understanding the motivations of different market segments, greater success should occur in the future.

Loyalty Segmentation

Marketers are often interested in attracting, not just brand users, but perhaps more importantly, those who consistently purchase the company's brand. When these brand-loyal buyers are able to be identified (assuming they differ on certain characteristics from the nonloyal buyer), appropriate marketing strategies may be developed to attract competitors' buyers who have similar characteristics or to increase the loyalty rate among current less-loyal buyers. Loyalty segmentation can also be successfully applied to retail store customers.[26]

Marketers of new national brands are often advised to target toward those segments that exhibit considerable brand switching. However, one research study of the introduction of a new national brand (Puffs facial tissue) indicated that marketing efforts could actually be successfully targeted toward brand switchers as well as toward households that were loyal to existing national brands and toward purchasers of private-label brands.[27]

Volume Segmentation

Volume segmentation attempts to identify frequent users of a product category or brand. Marketers often refer to the "20–80" thesis, that is, that 20 percent of the market accounts for 80 percent of sales of their product. Although the exact proportions may vary and the rule may not universally apply, it does indicate the importance of a relatively small group of consumers to the health of a firm's product or service.

Technique of Volume Segmentation Research has shown that purchase concentration is not always a simple function of obvious demographic factors such as income or household size. Thus, the marketer must measure consumption and identify the characteristics that are useful in distinguishing the various purchase intensities.

Frequently, this is accomplished by dividing the market into heavy, light, and nonusers of the product and then examining their distinguishing characteristics. At one time this was an extremely difficult process for most companies, but today several marketing research organizations are able to provide such data. For example, Axiom Market Research Bureau, Inc., conducts periodic national studies of product usage, personal characteristics, and media habits of a sample of over 30,000 adults and 8000 teenagers. They regularly analyze 900 product categories and subcategories and publish Target Group Index (TGI) to assist the marketer in identifying potential audiences.

Figure 5-5 is based on analysis of household consumption data from a panel of *Chicago Tribune* newspaper subscribers and indicates the importance of the heavy user. Notice in Figure 5-5 that relatively few households account for the bulk of sales in these products. For instance, 39 percent of the households purchase 90 percent of cola beverages, while an additional 39 percent of the households in the market account for only 10 percent of colas consumed. Also of importance is the finding that 22 percent of the market are nonusers of colas.

Applications of Volume Segmentation Marketers of a broad range of goods and services utilize volume as a fundamental segmentation criterion. The following examples illustrate several areas of application.

Cereal Target markets are often categorized in terms of their lucrativeness. This was the case with Quaker Oats Company when it segmented the market for its breakfast cereal Life, introduced in 1961. The firm determined that family size and age of the housewife were the two characteristics that distinguished intensity of product use. Consequently, Quaker ranked its target segments in the following hierarchy:

Families with above-average consumption ("extremely important" and "important" targets) were characterized by housewives under age 40, families of four or more members, in metropolitan areas of 50,000–500,000 population, with moderate incomes.

FIGURE 5-5

The "heavy user": annual purchase concentration in eighteen product categories. (*Source:* Dik Warren Twedt, "How Important to Marketing Strategy is the 'Heavy User'?" *Journal of Marketing,* **28**:72, January 1964, published by the American Marketing Association.)

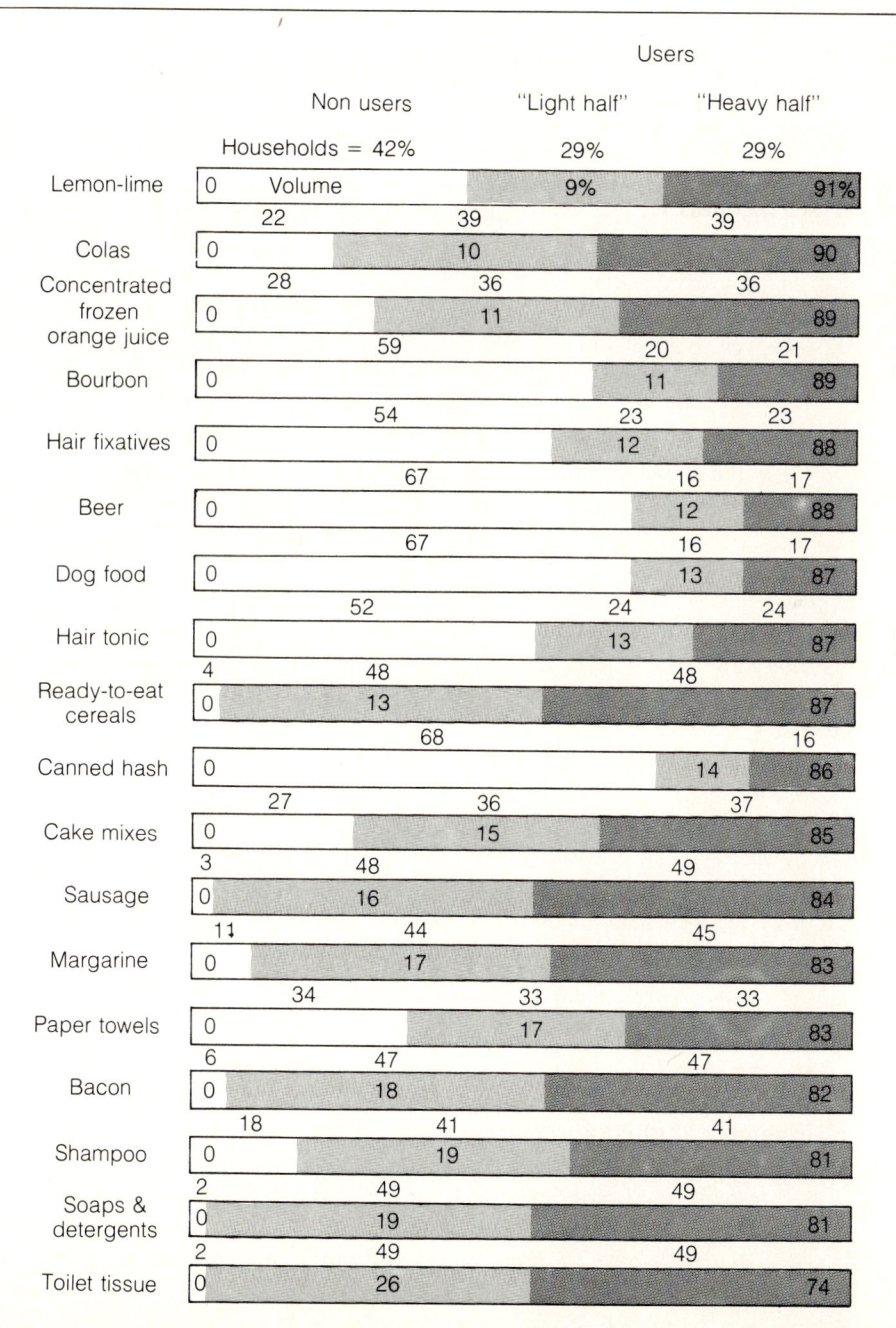

	Non users	Users "Light half"	Users "Heavy half"
	Households = 42%	29%	29%
Lemon-lime	0 Volume	9%	91%
Colas	22 / 0	39 / 10	39 / 90
Concentrated frozen orange juice	28 / 0	36 / 11	36 / 89
Bourbon	59 / 0	20 / 11	21 / 89
Hair fixatives	54 / 0	23 / 12	23 / 88
Beer	67 / 0	16 / 12	17 / 88
Dog food	67 / 0	16 / 13	17 / 87
Hair tonic	52 / 0	24 / 13	24 / 87
Ready-to-eat cereals	4 / 0	48 / 13	48 / 87
Canned hash	68 / 0	14	16 / 86
Cake mixes	27 / 0	36 / 15	37 / 85
Sausage	3 / 0	48 / 16	49 / 84
Margarine	11 / 0	44 / 17	45 / 83
Paper towels	34 / 0	33 / 17	33 / 83
Bacon	6 / 0	47 / 18	47 / 82
Shampoo	18 / 0	41 / 19	41 / 81
Soaps & detergents	2 / 0	49 / 19	49 / 81
Toilet tissue	2 / 0	49 / 26	49 / 74

Families with average consumption ("average" targets) were characterized by housewives 40–49, living in cities of 2 million or more population.

Families with below-average consumption ("unimportant" and "very inferior" targets) were characterized by housewives 50 and over, less than four family members, low and high incomes, and small town or rural areas.[28]

It is probably for this reason that advertising for Life cereal (see Figure 5-6) often shows three children at the breakfast table, thus reflecting the large-family-size characteristics of their most important target segment.

Detergents All detergent manufacturers aim at women age 18 to 49, preferably with two or more children. According to the advertising agency for Sta-Puf brands, "If we can get to the woman with two kids, we know she'll be doing up to nineteen loads of laundry a week. And we also know that as many as 90 percent of the women will use a fabric softener within a 6-month period."[29]

Bank Cards Many banks around the country now charge fees for their credit cards. The banks were determined to turn money-losing credit-card operations into profit makers, even if it meant losing some customers along the way. Research at Citibank indicated, for example, that some customers—typically the "convenience" users (those who carry spare cards and rarely incur monthly interest charges)—would not be happy with the fee. The research allowed estimation of the proportion of credit-card users who would cancel their cards but not result in a significant loss of revenue to the bank.[30]

Research by TGI for packaged consumer goods indicates that the best way to increase sales of a product is to persuade present users to use more of that product, rather than to attract new users. This suggests that marketing efforts should generally be aimed at light- to heavy users rather than at nonusers.[31]

One of the real attractions of the usage approach to market segmentation is the ease with which the technique can be employed by so many firms. Most companies are able to segment consumers by usage rates because of access to marketing research services and data processing systems that can quickly categorize and analyze consumers by purchase activity. Thus, department stores are able to analyze charge account customers' purchases with regularity; banks can assess their customers' banking usage; and as mentioned previously, many packaged-consumer-goods firms can subscribe to syndicated services to provide the same usage information.

BENEFIT SEGMENTATION

The approaches to market segmentation discussed so far are all helpful to the marketer. However, they suffer from an underlying disadvantage—all are based on an ex post facto analysis of the kinds of people who make up specific segments of a market. That is, emphasis is on *describing* the characteristics of different segments rather than on learning what *causes* these segments to develop. However, proponents of benefit segmentation claim that the *benefits* that people are seeking are the basic reason for purchase and therefore the proper basis for market segmentation.[32]

FIGURE 5-6

Example of advertisement for Life cereal aimed at heavy users. (Courtesy of The Quaker Oats Co.)

"What's this stuff?" "Some cereal. Supposed to be good for you." "Did you try it?" "I'm not gonna try it. You try it." "I'm not gonna try it."

"Let's get Mikey!" "He won't eat it. He hates everything."

"He likes it. Hey, Mikey!"

If you have a child like Mikey, you don't have to tell him that Life is good for him. Let him try a bowl. Kids just seem to go for the oatsy, nutsy, crunchy taste of Life. It's the delicious, high-protein cereal. From Quaker.

Kids like Mikey like Life Cereal.

Technique of Benefit Segmentation

The first step in benefit segmentation is to obtain detailed information on consumer value systems. This is typically accomplished by having a representative sample of consumers rate the importance of those benefits or values they seek in the product. Certainly most people would like as many benefits as possible. How-

139

ever, the *relative* importance they attach to individual benefits can differ significantly and thus be used as an effective technique in segmenting markets.[33]

Although the concept appears simple, its implementation is very complex, often requiring computers and sophisticated multivariate attitude-measurement techniques. The statistical methods employed relate the responses of each consumer to those of every other respondent and then develop clusters (typically three to seven segments) of consumers with similar rating patterns. Each of these segments represents a potentially profitable and different opportunity for marketing effort.

Applications of Benefit Segmentation

Two examples of benefit segmentation are discussed below: banking and watches.

Bank Benefit Segments The results of a study of bank benefits is presented in Table 5-6. As can be seen, five benefit segments have been identified in the study. The characteristics of each segment are summarized in the table.

TABLE 5-6 BANK BENEFIT SEGMENTS

	Front Runners	Loan Seekers	Representative Subgroup	Value Seekers	One-Stop Bankers
Principal benefits sought	Large Bank for all Good advertising Modern	Good reputation Loans easily available Low loan interest Encourages financial responsibility Friendly	No difference (about average on all benefits sought)	High savings interest Quick service Low loan interest	Wide variety of services Convenient hours Quick service High savings interest Loans easily available
Banks favored	Commercial Bank A	Commercial B Savings X	Commercial A Commercial B	Savings Y Savings Z	Commercial A
Demographic characteristics	Young Rent home Less time in area	More transient Higher than average income Smaller household		Tend to save more More time in area More blue collar	Fewer minority
Lifestyle characteristics		Liberal about use of credit Positive about bank loans		Conservative overall lifestyle Conservative about use of credit	Conservative about use of credit Low ability to manage money and budget Negative about bank loans
Size of segment	3%	17%	35%	17%	28%

Source: Adapted from Roger J. Calantone and Alan G. Sawyer, "The Stability of Benefit Segments," *Journal of Marketing Research,* **15**:398, August, 1978, published by the American Marketing Association.

It may be noted that one segment—"Representative Subgroup"—has no discernible pattern in terms of benefits sought, with all benefits perceived about equally. Although this segment is the largest, it still leaves 65 percent of the market seeking other benefits which can be attractive segments for other marketing mixes.

One advantage cited for benefit segmentation is its greater potential for directly translating segment descriptions into marketing strategy. Therefore, the following suggestions for banks X and Y might flow from these data:

Savings Bank X (very small) might try to further strengthen, or at least retain, its currently favorable image as an active lender and source of mortgages, and thereby position itself to meet the specific desires of one particular segment. By appealing to the loan-seeker segment, it might seek to advertise directly to high-income smaller households.

Savings Bank Y (much larger) might continue to promote its higher-yield-savings interest rates, might use a serious and conservative tone for interest-rate advertising, and might promote to blue-collar families in older sections of the metropolitan area. Because of the small size of the value-seeker segment the bank might, in addition, attempt to appeal to the one-stop banker segment which also considers high savings interest to be important. To do this, it might add new services (such as checking accounts), publicize its other available services, extend banking hours, and add more tellers to speed service.[34]

Watch Benefit Segments A second illustration of value or benefit segmentation is drawn from the market for watches. Research identified three distinct groups, characterized as the *economy* segment, the *durability and quality* segment, and the *symbolic* segment, which were seeking different benefits as described below:[35]

Economy segment—This group wants to pay the lowest possible price for a watch that works reasonably well. If it fails within a year, they will replace it. (23 percent of buyers)

Durability and quality segment—This group wants a watch with a long life, good material, and styling. They are willing to pay a higher price for these qualities. (46 percent of buyers)

Symbolic segment—This group wants useful product features and meaningful emotional qualities. The watch should suitably symbolize an important occasion. Here, a well-known brand name, fine styling, a gold or diamond case, and a jeweler's recommendation are important. (31 percent of buyers)

At one time, most watch companies were oriented almost exclusively on the third segment, thus leaving the major portion of the market open. Consequently, U.S. Time Company introduced a new low-priced watch, the Timex, and established a very strong position among buyers in the first two segments.

These two examples cite the advantage of benefit segmentation. The greatest difficulty in applying the approach exists in choosing the benefit to be emphasized. For example, the company must be certain that buyers' stated motives are their real motives for purchase, which is not an easy task because of the complexity of human motivation. Consequently, the number of consumers in each benefit segment is difficult to estimate; moreover, the proportions shift over time, presenting further complications. Thus, considerable research is needed to ascertain product benefits and the size of consumer segments for each.

Limitations of Benefit Segmentation

Segmentation based on benefits desired can be a meaningful approach from a marketing standpoint because it directly facilitates product planning, positioning, and marketing communications. This approach is not relevant for all situations, however. Three cases in which it may not be appropriate are the following:[36]

1 Traditional price lines have developed so that all marketing activities are based on price levels. For certain products such as clothing, cosmetics, automobiles, and appliances, traditional price lines have developed to the extent that markets have become segmented into price lines. Because all product offerings and marketing activities are contingent upon the price line offered, marketing considerations dictate that the market be segmented at least initially by price lines. For many product categories, the size of the market for any price line is too low to permit further segmentation.

2 The benefits desired are determined by the situation or purpose for which the product is used. The desires of consumers can vary by the type of occasion for which the product is used. For example, clothes suitable for some occasions will not be suitable for other occasions. For effective marketing, consumer desires must be segmented by usage occasion to determine which products will be most suitable for each occasion. In many complex markets, this type of segmentation is necessary to derive the underlying competitive framework. Conventional segmentation questioning about the product without a specific usage occasion will provide meaningless information.

3 The style or appearance of the product is the overriding criterion of success. If fashion appeal is the major consideration in marketing success, the marketer must segment markets on the basis of styling preference in order to market a successful line of styles to each segment. Some examples of style-oriented lines are silverware, small appliances, fashion accessories, apparel, furniture, and automobiles.

Perhaps the greatest difficulty in applying the approach exists in choosing the correct benefits to be emphasized and making certain that buyers' stated motives are their real motives. Failure to understand the benefits which consumers may be seeking can prevent marketing success. For example,

> When General Foods introduced Shake 'n' Bake—a bread coating for chicken and pork that simulated frying but was prepared untended in the oven rather than using deep fat in a frying pan—its competitor, Best Foods, saw this new product as a threat. Because Best Foods produced Mazola Oil, a product often used in frying chicken and pork, the company decided that it needed to counter Shake 'n' Bake with a similar product that would still entail the use of their oil. The result was Tasti-Fry, a seasoned breading mix used to coat the food which was then fried. The product was taste-tested

against Shake 'n' Bake, and in every instance won, leaving no doubt that food prepared with Tasti-Fry that was fried tasted better than food coated with Shake 'n' Bake that was baked. Based on these tests, Best Foods rushed the product to the test market where, despite heavy marketing expenditures, it was a miserable failure. What Best Foods neglected to research and understand were the other product benefits it was competing against—not just the product's taste, but also the product concept and promise. What General Foods successfully offered the housewife was an easier untended cooking convenience that resulted in an acceptable flavor, which was not placed in a spattering frying pan, and would not be viewed unfavorably as fried food and therefore fattening and possibly harmful to health.[37]

This situation also illustrates the need for a system that can supplement benefit analysis. When marketers ask consumers what benefits or attributes they want in a product, consumers often parrot back to researchers what they have already been told. For example, asking consumers what benefits they want in a toothpaste would likely elicit such benefits as "decay prevention," "whitening," "fresh breath," and so forth—which is what they have heard though advertising. Thus, because consumers are often not highly introspective when asked, they are not likely to provide new information about product benefits which will move the company's brand to the top in market share.

If benefit information is supplemented with information about consumer problems, however, new insights may be developed. One approach to this is problem-inventory analysis in which consumers are provided with a list of problems and for each one are asked what products come to mind as having that problem. Table 5-7 illustrates such a study conducted in the food industry. The findings must be interpreted cautiously, however. Although the table shows that a sizable percentage of respondents mentioned cereal as a package that does not fit well on the cabinet shelf, when General Foods launched a new "compact" cereal box, it failed. Apparently such a "problem" may not be that serious to consumers.

Once general problems are determined, the marketer may proceed to perform more in-depth research for specific new product concepts.[38] For example, one advertising agency uses a research technique known as "problem detection" to identify important problems for a particular product, how frequently those problems occur, and whether the solution to the problem has been preempted by some existing product or service. The "problem score" received by a product is expressed numerically with a larger score indicating a larger opportunity. The contribution of problem analysis to a company is illustrated in the following way:

> Surveys on dog food indicated three most-wanted attributes (1) balanced diet, (2) good nutrition, and (3) containing vitamins. This information was not very helpful to the manufacturer because these benefits were already being served by other dog-food companies. However, when purchasers were asked what their dog-food problems were, the top three mentioned were: (1) it smelled bad, (2) it cost too much, and (3) it did not come in different sizes for different dogs. Three successful new product introductions resulted from these findings: (1) a dog food that smelled good enough to be called stew; (2) mixing chunks used in conjunction with dry food which made it inexpensive; and (3) different size cans for different size dogs.[39]

TABLE 5-7
RESULTS OF A PROBLEM INVENTORY STUDY ABOUT FOOD

Questions Asked and Percent of Respondents Answering

1. The package of _____ doesn't fit well on the shelf.
    - cereal   49%
    - flour   6%

2. My husband/children refuse to eat _____
    - liver   18%
    - vegetables 5%
    - spinach   4%

3. _____ doesn't quench my thirst.
    - soft drinks 58%
    - milk   9%
    - coffee   6%

4. Packaged _____ doesn't dissolve fast enough.
    - jello/gelatin   32%
    - bouillon cubes 8%
    - pudding   5%

5. Everyone always wants different _____.
    - vegetables 23%
    - cereal   11%
    - meat   10%
    - desserts   9%

6. _____ makes a mess in the oven.
    - broiling steaks 19%
    - pie   17%
    - roast/pork/rib   8%

7. Packaged _____ tastes artificial.
    - instant potatoes   12%
    - macaroni and cheese 4%

8. It's difficult to get _____ to pour easily.
    - catsup   16%
    - syrup   13%
    - gallon of milk 11%

9. Packaged _____ looks unappetizing.
    - hamburger helper 6%
    - lunch meat   3%
    - liver   3%

10. I wish my husband/children could take _____ in a carried lunch.
    - hot meal   11%
    - soup   9%
    - ice cream 4%

Source: Reprinted from Edward M. Tauber, "Discovering New Product Opportunities With Problem Inventory Analysis," *Journal of Marketing,* **39:**70, January 1975, published by the American Marketing Association.

PRODUCT POSITIONING

Effective product positioning is a key ingredient of successful marketing today. This section discusses the importance of positioning as it relates to the segmentation process, and discusses several approaches to the process.

The Interrelationship of Market Segmentation and Product Positioning[40]

Segmentation is essentially the accommodation of different consumer groupings in a marketing plan or strategy. Knowing that different consumers respond differently to products, promotions, prices, and channels means that the marketer should not consider just the overall population's reaction to, say, a product, but also the reaction among different market segments. Market segmentation, therefore, is both the process of defining the characteristics of various segments in the marketplace as well as the allocation of marketing resources among these segments. *Product positioning* is closely linked with market segmentation. A product's position is the place that it occupies in a given market as perceived by the relevant group of customers, that is, by the target-market segment. Positioning involves determining how consumers perceive the marketer's product and developing and implementing marketing strategies to achieve the desired position in the market. Product, price, distribution, and promotional ingredients should all be viewed as potential tools for positioning a company and its offerings. Positioning, therefore, has no value in itself, only in its effect on the target-market segment. Marketers must look at segmentation and positioning in tandem. The process may start either by selecting a target-market segment and then trying to develop a suitable position, or by selecting an attractive product position and then identifying an appropriate market segment.

Whether the product is new or old, positioning is a key ingredient for achieving successful market results. For example, even radio stations find that proper positioning can help them carve out a profitable niche in tight competition.

> Radio station KRXV focuses its signals on a narrow audience as competition in radio grows. The average listener to KRXV eats out eighteen times a month, owns a $93,000 house, has a MasterCard credit card, and is about to spend at least $423 in five days—much of it on gambling. The 23 million yearly listeners are almost all southern Californians on their way between Los Angeles and Las Vegas along Interstate 15. The station features programming designed to make its gambling-bound listeners happy—music by entertainers that listeners will see in Las Vegas, advisories on road conditions and gasoline availability, and advertisements for Las Vegas hotels, casinos, and restaurants.[41]

Although business people have long been positioning their products to appeal to target-market segments, these decisions have not always been made consciously or successfully. What is needed is a systematic approach to the decision in order to increase the chances of success. The remainder of this chapter will discuss the various strategies and techniques used in a systematic approach to positioning.

Strategies to Position Products

Many ways exist for positioning a product or service (or even an organization). The following illustrate some of these approaches. It should be noted that combinations of these approaches are also possible.

Position on Product Features   The product may be positioned on the basis of product features. For example, an advertisement may attempt to position the product by reference to its specific features. Although this may be a successful way to indicate product superiority, consumers are generally more interested in what such features mean to them, that is, how they can benefit by the product.

Position on Benefits This approach is closely related to the previous method. Toothpaste advertising often features the benefit approach, as the examples of Crest (decay prevention), Close-Up (sex appeal through white teeth and fresh breath), and Aqua-fresh (a combination of these benefits) illustrate. The difference between this and the former approach is illustrated by the adage, "Don't sell the steak, sell the sizzle." In an untraditional campaign for hair dryers, General Electric has adopted an emotional appeal in ads for its Go Dryer, as opposed to a functional appeal (Figure 5-7). The company's research indicated that the audience for hair dryers was less concerned with the mechanical aspects of the product and more interested in what it could do for the user.[42]

Position on Usage This technique is related to benefit positioning. Many products are sold on the basis of their usage situation by the consumer. For instance, wines may be positioned as being appropriate for various meal or occasion situations. And Michelob has traditionally been positioned as the weekend beer. Such a limited position may actually restrict the marketer, however, by making new usage situations seem inappropriate. Michelob, for instance, has sought to expand

FIGURE 5-7

Advertisement for a product positioned on benefits. (Courtesy of General Electric Company.)

its appropriate usage time beyond just the weekend to any day of the week. Figure 5-8 presents an ad for Sony in which different types of usage situations for the product are shown to consumers.

Position Against Competition   In this approach, the marketer may either directly or indirectly make comparisons with competing products. For example, the famous "Uncola" campaign successfully positioned 7-Up as an alternative to Coke, Pepsi, and other colas (since almost two-thirds of soft drinks consumed in the United States are colas). Notice too, how this brand is confronted with a situation of special-usage positioning. For instance, it was originally thought of as a hangover cure, and it is still viewed as a special-occasion beverage, for an occasion other than a cola time.[43] Other classic positioning examples following this strategy include Avis and Hertz (an implicit approach in which Avis seldom mentions Hertz) and in the computer field between IBM and Digital Equipment Corporation.

Corporations as well as products may be positioned, and can, in fact, serve to strongly reinforce the chosen product position. For instance, Neiman Marcus has positioned itself at the opposite end of the retailing spectrum from K mart. When companies fail to clearly position themselves, product sales may likely suffer from confusion in the consumer's mind. Perhaps the best illustration of this situation is the case of Goodyear and Goodrich tire companies. B. F. Goodrich faces a situation in which their name is similar to that of a larger company (Goodyear) in the same industry. Attempts by Goodrich to position themselves as "the other guys" and "the ones without a blimp" have not found great success with the tire-buying public. In this case, a name change might produce a better position than the current approach which calls attention to the confusion with its competitor Goodyear.[44]

Another competitive positioning situation which may arise for the marketer of a new product is to dissociate older or typical products in an established category from the new product. In this case, the marketer may seek to distance the innovation from other perhaps similar products so that consumers more clearly recognize the uniqueness and superiority of the new item. Sometimes, seeming disadvantages may be turned into advantages for new products when the right position is determined. For example:

> L'Oreal, a major European hair-care producer, faced the problem of establishing credibility of its name among U.S. women and making its company a dynamic factor in the U.S. hair-color market, which was dominated by Clairol. Research showed that hair-color users were not vulnerable to brand switching because a woman chooses a particular shade and fears she will not obtain that same tint if she switches brands. In addition, because hair color offers a cosmetic benefit, it cannot be positioned solely on a nonemotional basis. L'Oreal decided to position Preference, the highest-priced product within its color line, as "the most expensive hair color in the world." Consumers were to interpret this position to mean superior ingredients and a quality product. In addition, the ad copy line "because I'm worth it," appealed to self-esteem. This positioning resulted in dramatic market-share gains and moved L'Oreal into the number 2 position in the marketplace.[45]

Repositioning Old Products

Usually, products already have a position and a target segment, since they are presently in the market. In this situation (assuming some weakness exists in the product's positioning), the marketer must decide on a strategy for change. One decision is whether to attempt repositioning via focus on change in actual physical product characteristics or via other means such as promotional methods to emphasize product features previously given little attention. A second alternative to actual product changes is the development or reorientation of product images or symbols

FIGURE 5-8

Advertisement for a product positioned on different usage situations. (Courtesy of Sony.)

in order to change consumers' perceptions. A potential problem of relying on actual product changes for repositioning is that consumers will not notice the degree of change or understand its significance to them. Therefore, emphasis is often placed on developing marketing communications to alert consumers of actual product changes or to reorient their perceptions of the existing product.

CHAPTER 5

149

MARKET SEGMENTATION: ADDITIONAL DIMENSIONS

The Sony Walkman

Look around. It's happening everywhere.

More and more people every day are listening to music in a revolutionary way.

The Walkman is a completely portable stereo tape machine that plays music with such power and fidelity, you won't believe you're listening to a cassette player that's just a little bigger than the cassette itself. Because the sound is much closer to that of a huge home stereo system.

You listen through tiny featherweight headphones. And there's even a jack for a second set of headphones, in case you're in the mood to share your music with someone else.

So come into your local Sony dealer and find out what the revolution is all about. After all, the Walkman is from the people who have been revolutionizing an industry for years.

SONY
THE ONE AND ONLY

Several strategies could be utilized for either approach. A modification in the product or its marketing mix may lead to changing segments, adding segments, or broadening segments. Consider the following examples:

Women's Fragrances A recent study of women's perfumes and colognes illustrates the changing nature of brand positions in the marketplace. As new profitable positions become recognized, marketers add brands and may reorient advertising emphasis to appeal on these bases.[46] Figure 5-9 illustrates market-segment sizes and changes in product positioning during the period

FIGURE 5-9

Women's fragrances: positioning by category. (*Source:* Glenn Lebowitz, "'Liberated Woman' Replaces 'Sex' As Emphasis for Fragrance Ads," *Product Marketing,* October 1979, p. 10. Reprinted by permission of *Product Marketing* and Grayson Associates, Inc.)

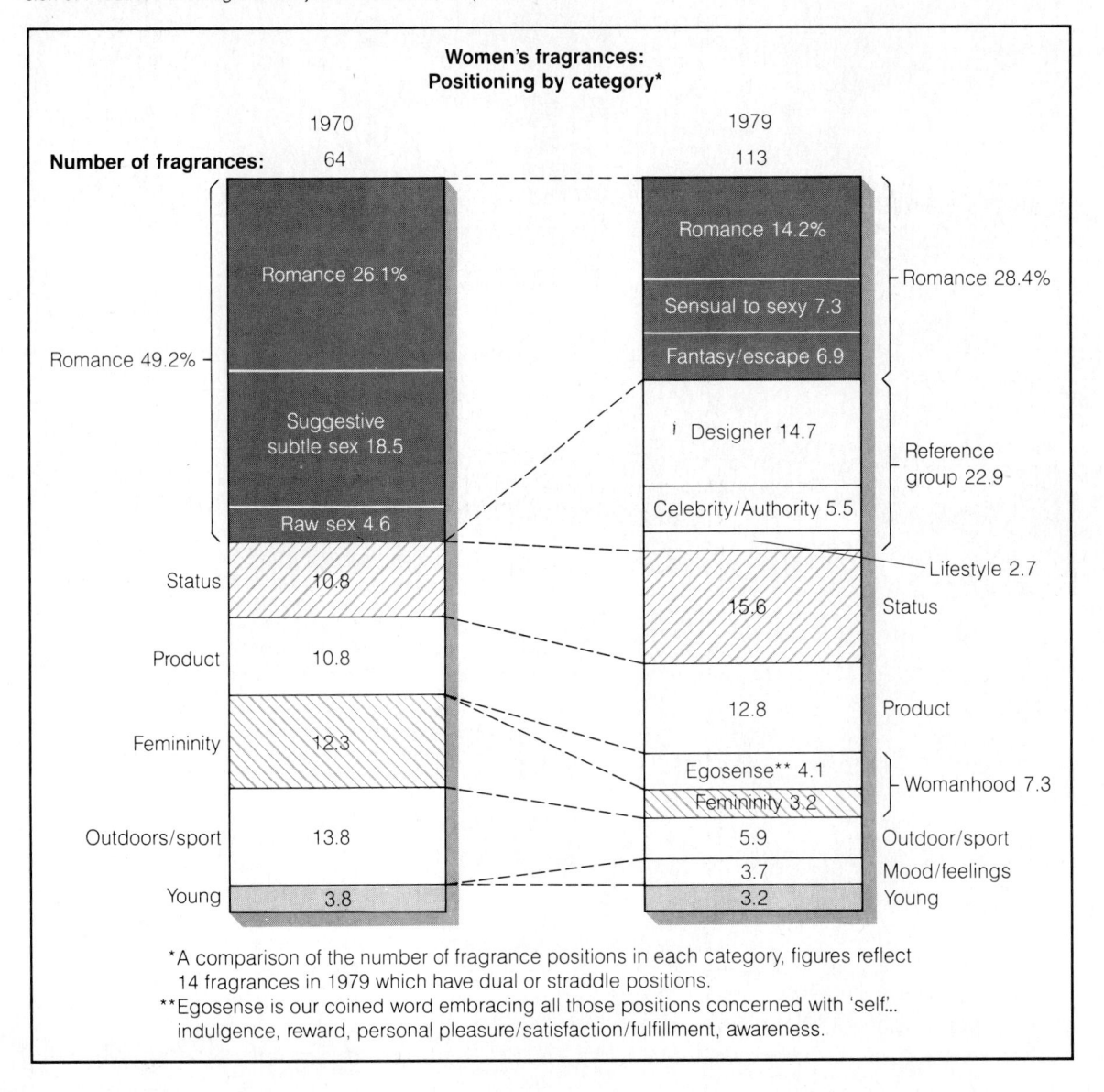

Women's fragrances: Positioning by category*

Category (1970)	1970	1979	Category (1979)
Number of fragrances:	64	113	
Romance 49.2%	Romance 26.1%	Romance 14.2%	Romance 28.4%
	Suggestive subtle sex 18.5	Sensual to sexy 7.3	
		Fantasy/escape 6.9	
	Raw sex 4.6	Designer 14.7	Reference group 22.9
		Celebrity/Authority 5.5	
			Lifestyle 2.7
Status	10.8	15.6	Status
Product	10.8	12.8	Product
Femininity	12.3	Egosense** 4.1	Womanhood 7.3
		Femininity 3.2	
Outdoors/sport	13.8	5.9	Outdoor/sport
		3.7	Mood/feelings
Young	3.8	3.2	Young

*A comparison of the number of fragrance positions in each category, figures reflect 14 fragrances in 1979 which have dual or straddle positions.

**Egosense is our coined word embracing all those positions concerned with 'self'... indulgence, reward, personal pleasure/satisfaction/fulfillment, awareness.

1970–1979. Fragrance marketers are careful to position new brands to appeal to particular age and psychographic groups before millions of dollars become invested.[47]

Boots Corporate repositioning occurs when a company changes its image. For decades, Abington Shoe Co. made inexpensive footwear for department stores and other retailers to sell under their own private labels. Faced with a foreign-import onslaught of footwear, the company needed a new niche. Recognizing that college students were buying work boots, the company decided to produce a top-of-the-line boot to take advantage of the collegiate fad and the boom in hiking and backpacking. It transformed itself into Timberland, and began to manufacture a premium boot under its own label. It then developed an entirely new marketing mix including attractive advertising in the *New Yorker* and *Playboy* featuring an outdoorsy, not a workplace image, and it gained distribution in the kinds of stores where such readers shop (such as Saks Fifth Avenue and Bloomingdale's).[48]

Although marketers must sometimes resort to repositioning attempts, this is a difficult challenge. Once consumer perceptions and attitudes about a brand or company become ingrained over time, they become hard to change.

Positioning Analysis

The marketer may use several techniques for determining the appropriate positioning for a brand. Whether the brand is new or old, focus groups and depth interviews may be helpful in providing insights from consumers. In addition, survey and experimental research approaches such as those discussed in Chapter 3 may provide useful positioning data. Lifestyle information and a technique known as perceptual mapping can also be helpful in positioning decisions.

Lifestyle Positioning Consumer AIOs can be used in designing a marketing strategy for potential markets. This approach is illustrated by positioning for the volunteer army. Table 5-8 compares the attitudes and values of young men who favor an army career and those who do not, and provides insight into how the army might best be positioned through promotion. The data indicate dramatic differences between the two groups, and suggest that it may be a mistake to position the army as a continuous party in which discipline is relaxed and nobody is required to stand in line, clean his room, follow orders, or shoot a gun. Young men who agree that the army is a good career appear to be unusually patriotic and conservative, and are willing to accept hard work, discipline, and direction.[49] Figure 5-10 illustrates the creative response to such findings.

Perceptual Mapping The above discussion suggests that consumers' perceptions of products are developed in a complex way and are not easily determined by the marketer. However, a rather new technique known as perceptual mapping holds promise in exploring consumers' product perceptions. Since products can be perceived on many dimensions (such as quality, price, and strength) the tech-

TABLE 5-8
ATTITUDES TOWARD THE ARMY

	Army Is Good Career, % Agree	Army Is Not Good Career, % Agree
More Patriotic		
We often display the American flag on national holidays	60	33
American made is best made	66	49
More Chauvinistic		
A woman's place is in the home	77	64
Men are smarter than women	71	48
Today blacks get more opportunities than they deserve	43	29
Communism is the greatest peril in the world today	65	52
More Religious		
I go to church regularly	40	22
If Americans were more religious this would be a better country	68	52
More Active in the Community		
I am influential in my neighborhood	39	23
I like to work on community projects	43	26
I work for the Boy Scouts or other service organization on a fairly regular basis	26	4
Less Interested in a Swinging Social Life		
I like to think I am a bit of a swinger	45	63
I like parties where there is lots of music and talk	65	77
There are day people and there are night people; I am a day person	75	61
I would rather spend a quiet evening at home than go out to a party	66	52
Discipline and Work Oriented		
Today most people don't have enough discipline	88	75
Young people have too many privileges today	49	34
I work more than 45 hours a week	71	57
Less Interested in Politics		
I am interested in politics	48	63
I consider myself a member of the silent majority	71	54
Admittedly Old-Fashioned		
I have old-fashioned tastes and habits	77	61
Antiques add a nice touch to any home	79	60
Uncertain about Capacity to Cope with Modern Life		
Everything is changing too fast today	72	53
If I had my life to live over, I would sure do things differently	71	58
Strongly Attracted by Hunting and Guns		
I like to go hunting	82	69
There should be a gun in every home	83	41

Source: Reprinted from William D. Wells, "Life Style and Psychographics: Definitions, Uses and Problems," in William D. Wells (ed.), *Life Style and Psychographics,* American Marketing Association, Chicago, 1974, pp. 323–324.

nique is *multidimensional* in nature. That is, it allows for the influence of more than one stimulus characteristic on product perceptions. Typically, consumers fill out measuring scales to indicate their perceptions of the many characteristics or similarities of competing brands. Computer programs analyze the resulting data to determine those product characteristics or combination of characteristics which are most important to consumers in distinguishing between competing brands. Results of this analysis can be plotted in terms of perceptual "maps," which display how consumers perceive the brands, and their differences, on a coordinate system.

Figure 5-11 presents a two-dimensional map for consumers' actual perceptions of beers. The most important general characteristics to consumers' evaluations here were found to be lightness versus heaviness and prestige price versus popular price. The points labeled with brand names and letters indicate how consumers located actual brands in the perceptual space. Notice that in the prestige price range Schlitz and Budweiser are both perceived to be somewhat heavy compared to the relative lightness of Miller. On the other hand, Hamms occupies a central position in terms of heaviness.

The study also asked consumers to indicate their perception of their ideal beer. The numbered circles show how they tend to cluster togehter in their

FIGURE 5-10

Lifestyle advertisement positioning the Army. (*Source:* U.S. Army.)

responses. The size of the circles indicate the proportion of consumers in each cluster. It can be seen that the largest segments of the market are being shared by the brands just mentioned.

These data provide insight to the marketer in terms of segmentation and brand positioning strategies. For example, one strategy might be to introduce a new, relatively light-tasting, popularly priced beer to capture clusters 3, 5, and 8. Promotional efforts would have to be consistent with such a strategy. Alternatively, producers of Brand D may wish to consider product and/or promotional changes to move their brand more centrally into cluster 4. Thus, a variety of strategy decisions can be aided by measurement and evaluation of such consumer perceptions.[50]

THE FUTURE OF SEGMENTATION AND POSITIONING

The various bases for segmenting markets discussed in this and the previous chapter have underscored the need to understand consumers. Each segmentation approach has merit, and although not all have exhibited ability to predict consumers' purchasing habits, they do enable marketers to understand better their target markets. When combinations of approaches are used in aiming at the total marketing problem, segmentation research can be very meaningful.[51] With enhanced understanding comes the ability to develop more tailored marketing programs.

The great deal of attention and interest generated by the concept of market segmentation is sure to become even more significant in the future. Three environmental factors are expected to lead to this growth. First, the advance of the consumerism movement will foster market segmentation, since critics have pointed to segments they believe are neglected in our present system. The result of pressures such as these is to cause managers to become more attentive to previously unrecognized consumer needs.

A second factor encouraging market segmentation is intensified competition. With the increasingly competitive markets (both domestic and worldwide) of the

FIGURE 5-11

A two-dimensional perceptual map of beer brands. (*Source:* Richard M. Johnson, "Market Segmentation: A Strategic Management Tool," *Journal of Marketing Research*, **8:**16, February 1971, published by the American Marketing Association.)

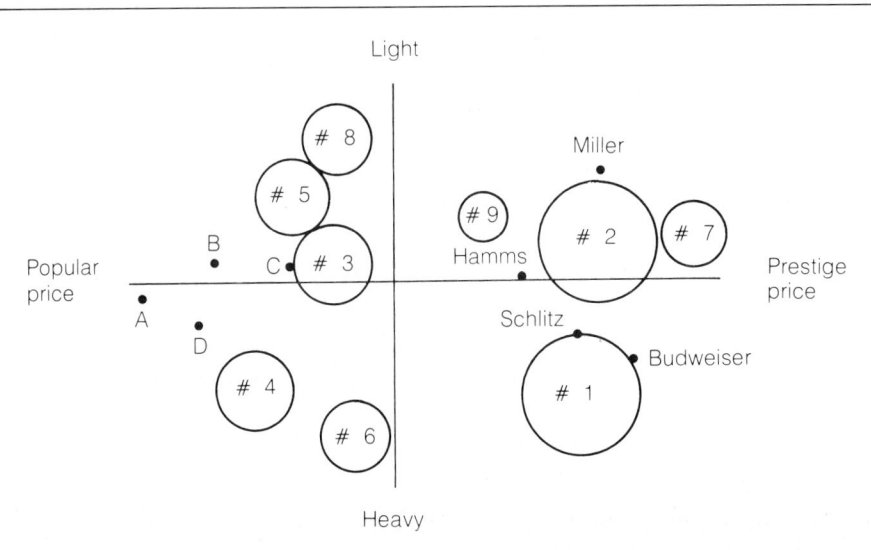

future, business people will seek untapped segments in order to gain an advantage over rivals.

The third factor stimulating market segmentation is the growing awareness of nonbusiness applications of the technique. It will be increasingly utilized for marketing in nontraditional areas such as politics, religion, and public issues.[52]

SUMMARY

In this chapter, some newer approaches to market segmentation were presented. Traditional approaches, however, are still incorporated in these techniques because marketers must have demographic, geographic, and socioeconomic information about any segments chosen if they are to market effectively to them.

The thrust of this chapter has been to suggest techniques that may provide a richer portrait of potential customers, either through usage, benefit, or lifestyle segmentation. This and the previous chapter should be viewed as a unit so that the reader does not form the impression that the approaches suggested are mutually exclusive. All of the techniques suggested as well as others not discussed overlap and are complementary. Therefore, choices have to be made regarding the best combination of methods to employ for each product or service.

The close interrelationship between market segmentation and product positioning was also discussed. Several approaches to product and company positioning were discussed along with analytical methods for making such decisions.

Finally, from these two chapters on market segmentation a clearer understanding should have been gained about the *who* of consumer behavior—that consumers are people of widely varying characteristics. Appreciation of this fact and an understanding of the ways in which clusters of consumers with more homogeneous characteristics may be carved out of the heterogeneous marketplace should put the reader on a firmer foundation for further exploration into the factors that influence consumer behavior.

DISCUSSION TOPICS

1 What is the significance to the marketer of the heavy user?

2 Suggest a marketing strategy to convert nonusers of the following goods and services into users:
   a cancer detection checkups for women aged 40–50
   b bus mass transit and carpools for getting to work
   c unit price information in a supermarket
   d a symphony series
   e paper towels
   f home permanents

3 What are the primary benefits that might be sought by consumers of the following products?
   a hair coloring   **c** barbecue grill   **e** bread
   b mouthwash   **d** compact car

4 How is lifestyle segmentation useful to developing promotion campaigns?

5 For the following goods and services suggest an appropriate segmentation strategy. How would you determine the size and behavioral attributes of the segments? What marketing strategy might be appropriate?
  a a dinner-theater in a medium-sized city
  b a church on campus
  c your university
  d sailboats
  e coffee
  f *Cosmopolitan* magazine

6 Attempt to determine how each of the following products is positioned:
  a Apple II home computer
  b Radio Shack color computer
  c Kodak films
  d Wrangler jeans
  e Calvin Klein jeans
  f Sony radios and TVs
  g General Electric radios and TVs

NOTES

[1] "Why Youth Needs a New Definition," *Business Week,* December 12, 1970, p. 35.
[2] William Lazer, "Life Style Concepts and Marketing," in Stephen Greyser (ed.), *Toward Scientific Marketing,* American Marketing Association, Chicago, 1963, p. 130.
[3] Harper W. Boyd, Jr., and Sidney J. Levy, *Promotion: A Behavioral View,* Prentice-Hall, Englewood Cliffs, N.J., 1967, p. 38.
[4] "A Whiff of Immortality," *Forbes,* September 15, 1975, p. 36.
[5] Fred D. Reynolds and William R. Darden, "An Operational Construction of Life Style," in M. Venkatesan (ed.), *Proceedings of the Annual Conference of the Association for Consumer Research,* 1972, p. 482.
[6] Alvin C. Burns and Mary Carolyn Harrison, "A Test of the Reliability of Psychographics," *Journal of Marketing Research,* 16: 32–38, February 1979.
[7] Joseph T. Plummer, "The Concept and Application of Life Style Segmentation," *Journal of Marketing,* 38:33, January 1974.
[8] Reprinted from Joseph T. Plummer, "Life Style and Advertising: Case Studies," in Fred Allvine (ed.), *AMA Proceedings 1971 Conference,* American Marketing Association, Chicago, 1971, p. 291.
[9] William D. Wells and Douglas J. Tigert, "Activities, Interests and Opinions," *Journal of Advertising Research,* 11:31, August 1971.
[10] Plummer, "Life Style and Advertising," p. 291.
[11] Plummer, "The Concept and Application of Life Style," pp. 35–36.
[12] This section is based on Sunil Mehrotra and William D. Wells, "Psychographics and Buyer Behavior: Theory and Recent Empirical Findings," in Arch G. Woodside, Jagdish N. Sheth, and Peter D. Bennett (eds.), *Consumer and Industrial Buying Behavior,* Elsevier North-Holland, New York, 1977, pp. 49–65; and William D. Wells, "Psychographics: A Critical Review," *Journal of Marketing Research,* 12:196–213, May 1975.
[13] Peter W. Bernstein, "Psychographics Is Still an Issue on Madison Avenue," *Fortune,* 97:78–80, January 16, 1978.
[14] Mehrotra and Wells, "Psychographics and Buyer Behavior," p. 53.
[15] Mehrotra and Wells, "Psychographics and Buyer Behavior," p. 53.
[16] Mehrotra and Wells, "Psychographics and Buyer Behavior," p. 56.
[17] Mehrotra and Wells, "Psychographics and Buyer Behavior," p. 57.
[18] Wells, "Psychographics," p. 199.
[19] "How Colgate Brand Manager Applied Psychos to Market and Media for Irish Spring," *Media Decisions,* December 1976, pp. 70–71, 104, 106.
[20] Plummer, "Life Style and Advertising," pp. 292, 294.
[21] Reprinted from Plummer, "Life Style and Advertising," p. 292, published by the American Marketing Association.
[22] Jacques Neher, "What Went Wrong," *Advertising Age,* April 13, 1981, pp. 61–64; and "Lost at Sea," *Advertising Age,* April 20, 1981, pp. 49–52.
[23] Plummer, "The Concept and Application of Life Style," pp. 36–37.
[24] William D. Wells, "Psychographics: A Critical Review," *Journal of Marketing Research,* 12:209, May 1975.
[25] "Ad Creatives Need Relevant, Honest Attitudinal Data from Researchers," *Marketing News,* May 15, 1981, p. 3.
[26] Kenneth E. Miller and Kent L. Granzin, "Simultaneous Loyalty and Benefit Segmentation of Retail Store Customers," *Journal of Retailing,* 55: 47–60, Spring 1979.
[27] Robert C. Blattberg, Thomas Buesing, and Subrata K. Sen, "Segmentation Strategies for New National Brands," *Journal of Marketing,* 44:59–67, Fall 1980.

[28]"Quaker Oats Life Cereal (A)," Harvard Business School Case M-220R, p. 26.

[29]Craig Reiss, "Brand Report 63: Soaps and Detergents," *Marketing and Media Decisions,* April 1981, p. 170.

[30]Julie Salamon, "Some Banks Try Luring Customers Angry With Credit-Card Fees," *The Wall Street Journal,* February 4, 1981, p. 25.

[31]Bernice Finkleman, "Ads Should Reinforce Current Users, Not Necessarily Convert Nonusers of Products," *Marketing News,* January 15, 1974, p. 1.

[32]Russell I. Haley, "Benefit Segmentation: A Decision-Oriented Research Tool," *Journal of Marketing,* **32**:31, July 1968.

[33]Mark Moriarity and M. Venkatesan, "Concept Evaluation and Market Segmentation," *Journal of Marketing,* **42**: 82–86, July 1978.

[34]Roger J. Calantone and Alan G. Sawyer, "The Stability of Benefit Segments," *Journal of Marketing Research,* **15**:402, August, 1978.

[35]Daniel Yankelovich, "New Criteria for Market Segmentation," *Harvard Business Review,* **42**:83–90, March–April 1964.

[36]Shirley Young, Leland Ott, and Barbara Feigin, "Some Practical Consideration in Market Segmentation," *Journal of Marketing Research,* **15**:405, August 1978.

[37]Robert S. Wheeler, "Marketing Tales with a Moral," *Product Marketing,* April 1977, p. 42.

[38]Vithala R. Rao and Frederick W. Winter, "An Application of the Multivariate Profit Model to Market Segmentation and Product Design," *Journal of Marketing Research,* **15**: 361–368, August 1978; and Allan D. Shocker and V. Srinivasan, "Multiattribute Approaches for Product Concept Evaluation and Generation: A Critical Review," *Journal of Marketing Research,* **16**: 159–180, May 1979.

[39]E. E. Norris, "Your Surefire Clue to Ad Success: Seek Out the Consumer's Problem," *Advertising Age,* March 17, 1975, pp. 43–44.

[40]Much of this section is from Yoram Wind, "Going to Market: New Twists for Some Old Tricks," *The Wharton Magazine,* vol. 4 no. 3, 1980.

[41]Laurel Leff, "As Competition in Radio Grows, Stations Tailor Programs for Specific Audience," *The Wall Street Journal,* November 18, 1980, p. 48.

[42]"GE Restyles Ad Focus for Hair Dryers," *Advertising Age,* July 14, 1980, p. 4.

[43]"7-Up's New Lifestyle," *Media Decisions,* March 1979, p. 75.

[44]Jack Trout and Al Ries, "The Positioning Era: A View Ten Years Later," *Advertising Age,* July 16, 1979, p. 40.

[45]Virginia Miles, "Research Is Key in Changing Your Brand Strategy," *Advertising Age,* July 12, 1976, p. 39.

[46]Glenn Lebowitz, "'Liberated Woman' Replaces 'Sex' as Emphasis for Fragrance Ads," *Product Marketing,* October 1979, p. 10.

[47]Fred Gardner, "Fragrance Marketers Sniff Out Opportunity," *Marketing and Media Decisions,* March 1981, pp. 66–69.

[48]Johnnie L. Roberts, "Boot Maker Transforms Image and Turns a Handsome Profit," *The Wall Street Journal,* August 24, 1981, p. 17.

[49]William D. Wells, "Life Style and Psychographics: Definitions, Uses and Problems," in William D. Wells (ed.), *Life Style and Psychographics,* American Marketing Association, Chicago, 1974, pp. 322–325.

[50]Dennis H. Gensch, "Image-Measurement Segmentation," *Journal of Marketing Research,* **15**: 384–394, August 1978.

[51]Nariman K. Dhalla and Winston H. Mahatoo, "Expanding the Scope of Segmentation Research," *Journal of Marketing,* **40**: 34–41, April 1976.

[52]James F. Engel, Henry Fiorillo, and Murray A. Cayley (eds.), *Market Segmentation: Concepts and Applications,* Holt, New York, 1972, pp. 459–465.

CASES FOR PART TWO

CASE 2-1
THE HAMILTON POWER TOOLS CORPORATION (A)[1]

On July 13, 1978, Mr. Campagna, the marketing manager for Hamilton Tools, was anxiously awaiting his meeting with the marketing research firm. He felt the findings from the marketing research would change Hamilton Tools from a sales-oriented company to a firm that would adopt the consumer-oriented philosophy of the marketing concept.

For more than 30 years, Hamilton Power Tools had been marketing industrial products by catering to the construction and industrial tool markets. Their construction product lines included tools such as power trowels, concrete vibrators, generators, and power-actuated tools. Their industrial lines were primarily pneumatic tools: drills, screwdrivers, etc. One of their products, the gasoline-powered chain saw, was somewhat different from traditional construction and industrial tools. The chain saw line had been added in 1949, when John Hamilton, Sr., had had the opportunity to acquire a small chain saw manufacturer. Mr. Hamilton believed that construction workers would have a need for gasoline-powered chain saws. He had acquired the business in order to diversify the company into other markets.

During the 1970s, the chain saw market was changing rapidly, and Hamilton Tool executives began to realize they needed some expert advice. Mr. Campagna was excited because the company had previously been engaged solely in industrial marketing activities. He felt a major change in Hamilton's corporate direction was on the horizon.

Mr. Campagna had been in the chain saw business for fifteen years. Reports from trade publications, statistics from the chain saw manufacturers association, and personal experience had led him to believe that the state of the chain saw industry in the last few years was composed of roughly the following markets: professionals (lumberjacks), farmers, institutions, and casual users (home or estate owners with many trees on their lots). Several years ago, the marketing executive had included a short questionnaire on the warranty cards that purchasers returned after buying a Hamilton chain saw. On the basis of the warranty card "survey," the fastest growth in the chain saw market was in the homeowner or casual-user market segment. This market consisted of the "weekend woodcutter," who once or twice a year used a chain saw to cut firewood or to prune trees in the back yard.

In March of 1978, when chain saw sales began to slow down because of the seasonal nature of the business, Mr. Campagna and Ray Johnson, the chain saw sales manager, had a meeting with John Hamilton, Sr. Although Mr. Hamilton believed they had been doing well enough in chain saw sales over the past decade, Mr. Campagna and Mr. Johnson were able to persuade the aging executive that some consumer research was necessary. After talking with several marketing research firms, Hamilton Tools hired Consumer Metrics of Chicago to perform two research projects.

Everyone arrived early for the meeting. Dale Conway, vice-president of the research corporation, and Frank Baggins, a young research assistant, were to make the presentation for Consumer Metrics.

Mr. Conway began the presentation. He said, "As you gentlemen know, the nonprofessional user has been a growing factor in the chain saw market. This is the weekend woodcutter or the casual user, who once or a few times a year uses a chain saw to cut firewood or prune trees in the back yard. Beginning in March of this year, we conducted two research projects. The first was a survey of chain saw consumers, and the second was a Thematic Apperception Test (TAT). Today, Frank will give th results of the survey."

Frank stood up, thanked Mr. Conway, and began his presentation.

The West Coast is one of the faster growing markets for Hamilton chain saws. The number of retail outlets and servicing distributors in this area is in line with Hamilton marketing strategies. From a distribution standpoint, it is an excellent market. Therefore, we felt it would be best to sample California men who purchased Hamilton chain saws in 1977 and 1978. Warranty cards that listed the purchasers during those years were used as a sampling frame. Cards that gave only institutional names and no individuals' names were omitted, as the purpose of the study was to learn about the behavior of the ultimate chain saw consumer

---
[1] Written and copyrighted © 1978 by William G. Zikmund, Oklahoma State University. All names are fictitious to assure confidentiality.

rather than about the use of chain saws in private or public institutions. Of the 463 questionnaires mailed, 201 (43.4 percent) were returned and 18 (3.9 percent) were not delivered.

The slides that Mr. Baggins showed are reproduced in Tables 1–15.

CONSUMER PROFILE

In Table 1, the breakdown of age of Hamilton chain saw purchasers, we find that almost all purchasers of Hamilton chain saws are 25 years or older. The median age of a Hamilton chain saw owner is 50.

More than two-thirds of the respondents had combined family incomes above $18,000 per year, and 57 percent were above $20,000 per year. Table 2 shows the actual family income dispersion of the California chain saw owner.

Almost 70 percent of the respondents had graduated from high school, and 41 percent had attended college. Table 3 shows the educational dispersion of chain saw customers.

Of all the people owning Hamilton chain saws in the California market, only 5.5 percent use a chain saw professionally. Twenty percent use chain saws on their farms, and 3 percent rent chain saws at their place of business. More than 70 percent of the respondents to the survey can be classified as casual users,[2] as seen in Table 4.

Significant categories among the casual-user segment of the California market were

1. Handicrafts and skilled workers (16.5 percent)
2. Professional and technical workers (12.0 percent)
3. Operative workers and laborers (9.5 percent)

Almost as significant were

4. Managerial, official, and proprietary (including rental) personnel (12 percent)
5. Government workers (9 percent)
6. Retired persons (10 percent)

As Table 5 shows, the quality of Hamilton chain saws is considered to be good or excellent by more than 85 percent of the respondents. Slightly more than

---

[2]Institutions, such as universities, municipalities, etc., were not sampled. However, this segment is estimated at less than 5 percent of the market.

TABLE 1 AGE OF HAMILTON CHAIN SAW OWNERS

Age Group	Total No.	Total %	1978 No.	1978 %	1977 No.	1977 %
Under 25	4	2.0	1	1.0	3	3.1
25–34	26	13.0	16	15.4	10	10.4
35–44	48	24.0	24	23.0	24	25.0
45–54	65	32.5	37	35.6	28	29.2
55–64	38	19.0	18	17.3	20	20.8
65 and over	18	9.0	7	6.7	11	11.4
No answer	1	0.5	1	1.0	—	—
Base	200	100.0	104	100.0	96	100.0

TABLE 2 INCOME OF HAMILTON CHAIN SAW OWNERS

Income	Total No.	Total %	1978 No.	1978 %	1977 No.	1977 %
Under 15M	7	3.5	3	2.9	4	4.2
15M–17,999	35	17.5	17	16.4	18	18.8
18M–19,999	34	17.0	21	20.2	13	13.5
20M–24,999	64	32.0	33	31.7	31	32.3
25M–over	54	27.0	28	26.9	26	27.0
No answer	6	3.0	2	1.9	4	4.2
Base	200	100.0	104	100.0	96	100.0

TABLE 3
EDUCATION OF HAMILTON CHAIN SAW OWNERS

Education	Total No.	Total %	1978 No.	1978 %	1977 No.	1977 %
Attended grade school	8	4.0	4	3.8	4	4.2
Graduated grade school	26	13.0	12	11.5	14	14.6
Attended high school	28	14.0	14	13.5	14	14.6
Graduated high school	51	25.5	27	26.0	24	25.0
Attended college	44	22.0	21	20.2	23	24.0
Graduated college	42	21.0	25	24.0	17	17.6
No answer	1	0.5	1	1.0	—	—
Base	200	100.0	104	100.0	96	100.0

TABLE 4
OCCUPATIONS OF HAMILTON CHAIN SAW OWNERS

Occupation	Total No.	Total %	1978 No.	1978 %	1977 No.	1977 %
Professional, technical	24	12.0	11	10.6	13	13.5
Managerial, official, proprietary	24	12.0	17	16.3	7	7.3
Clerical/sales	8	4.0	6	5.7	2	2.1
Handicrafts, skilled	33	16.5	19	18.3	14	14.6
Operative and labor	19	9.5	14	13.5	5	5.2
Government	18	9.0	9	8.7	9	9.4
Farmer or rancher	40	20.0	16	15.4	24	25.0
Retired	20	10.0	7	6.7	13	13.5
Student	2	1.0	—	—	2	2.1
Tree surgeon/professional cutter	11	5.5	4	3.8	7	7.3
No answer	1	0.5	1	1.0	—	—
Base	200	100.0	104	100.0	96	100.0

TABLE 5
OPINION OF OWNERS OF QUALITY OF HAMILTON CHAIN SAWS

Quality	No.	%
Excellent	81	40.5
Good	90	45.0
Fair	15	7.5
Poor	7	3.5
No answer	7	3.5
Base	200	100.0

TABLE 6
RETAIL OUTLETS WHERE HAMILTON CHAIN SAWS ARE PURCHASED

Outlet	No.	%
Chain saw specialty	70	35.0
Equipment/tools	41	20.5
Hardware	19	9.5
Department	16	8.0
Farm	14	7.0
Sports	10	5.0
Catalog	8	4.0
Marine	2	1.0
Other	15	7.5
No answer	5	2.5
Base	200	100.0

one-third of the respondents have had their chain saws repaired, and 75 percent of those people were satisfied with the repair work.

RETAIL ACTIVITY

Table 6 shows Hamilton receives 35 percent of its retail sales from chain saw specialty stores, 20.5 percent from equipment or tool stores, and 9.5 percent from hardware stores. Only 7.0 percent of the respondents mentioned purchasing their chain saws from farm stores and only 5.0 percent from sports stores.

Tables 7 and 8 show the number of times Hamilton chain saw purchasers visited a chain saw dealer and the number of different chain saw dealers they visited before purchasing their first chain saw. More than 60 percent of the respondents visited two or more *different* chain saw dealers before purchasing a Hamilton chain saw. Two, three, four, or more trips to chain saw dealers were the general rule for potential buyers.

TABLE 7
NUMBER OF TIMES VISITED CHAIN SAW DEALER

Times Visited	No.	%
0	7	3.5
1	53	26.5
2	40	20.0
3	39	19.5
4	16	8.0
5	7	3.5
6 or more	25	12.5
No answer	13	6.5
Base	200	100.0

TABLE 8
NUMBER OF DIFFERENT CHAIN SAW DEALERS VISITED

Number of Dealers	No.	%
0	9	4.5
1	50	25.0
2	51	25.5
3	47	23.5
4 or more	28	14.0
No answer	15	7.5
Base	200	100.0

TABLE 9
TIME RESPONDENTS HAD BEEN THINKING ABOUT CHAIN SAW PURCHASE

Length of Time	No.	%
Less than 1 week	7	3.5
1 week to 1 month	25	12.5
Over 1 to 3 months	24	12.0
Over 3 to 6 months	37	18.5
Over 6 months to 1 year	35	17.5
Over 1 year	33	16.5
Owned chain saw previously	20	10.0
Don't know/No answer	14	7.0
Part of inventory	2	1.0
Not long	3	1.5
Base	200	100.0

TABLE 10
RESPONDENTS' RATINGS OF FAMILIARITY WITH CHAIN SAWS

Response	No.	%
Completely familiar	64	32.0
Somewhat familiar	88	44.0
Unfamiliar	39	19.5
No answer/Don't know	9	4.5
Base	200	100.0

TABLE 11
RESPONDENTS HAD SPECIFIC BRAND IN MIND ON FIRST VISIT TO CHAIN SAW DEALER

Response	No.	%
Yes	129	64.5
No	67	33.5
No answer	4	2.0
Base	200	100.0

BUYING BEHAVIOR ·

More than one-half of all the respondents thought for three months or more about purchasing a chain saw (Table 9).

Table 10 shows that only 32 percent of respondents rating their familiarity with chain saws said they were completely familiar with them when they first visited a dealer. "Somewhat familiar" (44 percent) was the most common response, and 19.5 percent stated they were unfamiliar with chain saws when they first visited a dealer. Therefore, it can be concluded that at least 63.5 percent of potential chain saw purchasers could use more knowledge about (familiarity with) chain saws.

Almost two-thirds of respondents had a specific brand or brands of chain saw in mind when they first visited a dealer. Only 20 percent of all respondents had planned to buy Hamilton (Tables 11 and 12).

An important finding from this question is that all these people purchased Hamilton chain saws even though more than 50 percent had another brand name in mind before they first visited a chain saw dealer. Although we have no measurement of name brand preference, we can conclude that it is possible to sway some people who have preconceived purchasing plans. The other side of the coin is that 30 percent of the people planned to purchase a Hamilton and actually did. However, perhaps even more significant, we do not know how many people who had planned to purchase other leading brands actually did purchase one of these competitive saws.

The amount of influence a chain saw dealer's recommendation had on the purchasing decision of the consumer is given in Table 13.

We can see that in 45 percent of the cases the dealer had considerable influence on the purchasing decision. In at least 16 percent more cases, the dealer exerted some influence. Thus, the dealer can be an important part of the marketing of chain saws. But we see that there are other influencing factors involved, as 26.5 percent of the respondents mentioned that the dealer had no influence on their decision, 16 percent said only some influence, and 6.5 percent said the dealer hardly influenced their decision.

What happened when the respondents first visited a chain saw dealer? Table 14 shows the activities respondents stated happened. When analyzing the information, it appears significant to look at what did *not* happen at the dealer level. More than one-third of all respondents did not *talk* to a dealer the *first* time they visited. Only 21.5 percent saw the chain saw demon-

TABLE 12
BRAND OF CHAIN SAW PLANNED TO PURCHASE

Brand	No.	%
Homelite	59	45.7
Hamilton	41	31.8
McCulloch	41	31.8
Stihl	2	1.5
Pioneer	1	0.8
Other	5	3.9
Base	129	*

*Multiple answers possible; base exceeds 100 percent.

TABLE 13
DEALER INFLUENCE

Amount of Influence	No.	%
Great	54	27.0
Quite a bit	36	18.0
Some	32	16.0
Hardly any	13	6.5
None	53	26.5
No answer	12	6.0
Base	200	100.0

TABLE 14
ACTIVITIES ON FIRST VISIT TO CHAIN SAW DEALER

Activity That Took Place	No.	%
Talked to salesperson or owner about chain saws	123	61.5
Looked at chain saws	116	58.0
Learned the price of the chain saws	114	57.0
Picked up information about chain saws	71	35.5
Learned proper model of saw for own needs	57	28.5
Watched chain saw demonstrated	43	21.5
Rented or borrowed a chain saw	11	5.5
No answer	13	6.5
Base	200	*

*Multiple mentions; base exceeds 100 percent.

TABLE 15
HOW PURCHASER LEARNED STORE CARRIED CHAIN SAWS

Response	No.	%
Previous visit	101	50.5
Friend/relative recommended	18	9.0
Magazine/newspaper advertising	14	7.0
Yellow pages	12	6.0
Radio/TV	6	3.0
Outside store identification/Driving by	6	3.0
Other	24	12.0
No answer	19	9.5
Base	200	100.0

strated, and only 28.5 percent learned the proper model of chain saw for their needs. In most cases, it looks as if the first visit was a *passive* buying visit to a chain saw dealer. The responses indicate that most potential customers talked to a salesperson rather than looked at chain saws. Thus, with some nonstocking dealers a customer would have to go to another store to see a chain saw.

Finally, Table 15 shows how Hamilton purchasers first learned of the stores where they purchased their chain saw.

Questions

1 Why would a company such as Hamilton wait so long before conducting consumer research?

2 Evaluate the sampling frame used by Consumer Metrics.

3 Develop a marketing plan based upon the information provided in the case.

4 What further information would be needed before a complete plan could be submitted to Hamilton's management?

CASE 2-2
REVEL PRODUCTS, INC.

Jim Robinson, Revel Products' brand manager for Spring Fresh fabric softener, is assessing the results of a comparative study between his brand and several other competitors. Spring Fresh is a relatively new product—a fabric softener sheet to be used in the dryer, as opposed to liquid fabric softeners which are used in the washing machine.

Although several brands were reported in use by consumers in this study, the research specifically concentrated on the two leading brands—Spring Fresh (dryer sheets) and Soft Touch (a liquid softener added to the wash). The goal of the research project was to identify the most important attributes perceived by consumers for fabric softeners and to compare the leading brands along these attribute dimensions. In addition, it was hoped that through a statistical technique known as cluster analysis, the research might suggest whether all consumers perceive these attributes in the same way, or whether groups of consumers perceive fabric softeners in a different fashion. In terms of its use here, cluster analysis segments consumers into groups so that people within a group are homogeneous in terms of their perception toward the category, while people across groups are heterogeneous in terms of their perceptions.

Tables 1, 2, and 3 comprise the data summary output provided to Robinson from the study of 700 washer and dryer owners who use fabric softeners either in their washer or dryer. Table 1 presents the perceptions consumers have of the importance of thirteen fabric softener product attributes, as well as their evaluation of the performance of the two leading brands—Spring Fresh and Soft Touch—along these dimensions.

TABLE 1 PRODUCT AND BRAND PERCEPTIONS

	Overall Product Attribute Importance Rating	Spring Fresh Performance Rating	Soft Touch Performance Rating
No clinging	3.67	4.07	3.81
No wrinkling	3.51	3.73	3.77
Softening	3.30	3.85	4.15
Comfort	3.30	3.71	3.84
Absorbency	3.27	3.52	3.77
Convenience of use	3.16	4.43	3.37
Inexpensive	3.04	2.78	2.84
Penetrates	2.86	3.42	3.90
Pleasant odor	2.91	3.81	3.84
Pleasant to use	2.89	4.24	3.66
Easy to iron	2.83	3.48	3.61
Wear and clean longer	2.66	2.93	3.19
Whitens	2.66	2.52	3.30
Grand mean	3.08	3.55	3.60

TABLE 2
BENEFIT SEGMENTS

	Overall Product Attribute Importance Rating	Group 1 30%*	Group 2 14%	Group 3 22%	Group 4 18%	Group 5 16%
		Importance Ratings by Segment				
No clinging	3.67	3.88	3.37	3.75	3.70	3.38
No wrinkling	3.51	3.85	3.19	3.64	3.61	2.87
Softening	3.30	3.80	3.39	3.29	2.78	2.90
Comfort	3.30	3.79	3.03	3.16	3.48	2.59
Absorbency	3.27	3.72	3.21	3.03	3.52	2.50
Convenience of use	3.16	3.72	2.13	3.42	3.40	2.39
Inexpensive	3.04	3.48	2.63	3.49	2.86	2.17
Penetrates	2.86	3.54	3.29	2.20	3.15	1.80
Pleasant odor	2.91	3.60	2.65	2.90	2.76	2.01
Pleasant to use	2.89	3.58	2.36	2.72	3.24	1.87
Easy to iron	2.83	3.37	2.78	3.00	2.44	2.06
Wear and clean longer	2.66	3.24	2.69	2.72	2.29	1.87
Whitens	2.66	3.42	3.06	2.96	1.64	1.63
Average	3.08	3.61	2.91	3.10	2.99	2.31

*Percent of sample surveyed.

TABLE 3
PURCHASE AND DEMOGRAPHIC DATA

		Total	Group 1 30%*	Group 2 14%	Group 3 22%	Group 4 18%	Group 5 16%
Purchase in last 4 weeks:							
	Spring Fresh (sheet)	47%	40%	43%	53%	52%	51%
	Soft Touch (liquid)	22	25	29	18	20	16
	FabSoft (sheet)	10	11	4	10	11	11
	Rainy Day (liquid)	5	7	7	3	2	2
	Gentle Puff (liquid)	3	5	2	4	2	2
	No-Cling (liquid)	7	6	8	6	9	9
	Final Cycle (liquid)	6	6	7	6	4	9
Age:							
	Under 35	33%	30%	37%	33%	39%	27%
	35–50	34	32	33	42	26	37
	51 and over	33	38	30	25	35	36
Income:							
	High	37%	30%	33%	40%	41%	48%
	Medium	47	50	47	46	44	43
	Low	16	20	20	14	15	9
Education:							
	High	44%	40%	40%	50%	47%	46%
	Average	35	34	34	35	35	39
	Low	20	26	26	15	18	15

TABLE 3 (Continued)

	Total	Group 1 30%	Group 2 14%	Group 3 22%	Group 4 18%	Group 5 16%
Family size: Five or more	25%	23%	27%	34%	18%	20%
Loads dried past 7 days: Mean number	6.8	6.9	7.0	7.0	6.5	6.3

*Percent of sample surveyed.

Because the approach in Table 1 assumes that consumers use the same reference frame, benefit segmentation analysis was performed to determine if all consumers view fabric softeners in the same fashion. Table 2 presents results of the cluster analysis in which consumer benefit segments and also their perceived importance ratings for each attribute were identified. The percentage of the sample respondents accounted for by each cluster is also shown.

Table 3 reports the sample's fabric softener purchase and consumption behavior as well as important demographic characteristics.

Jim is eager to digest this data and determine how Spring Fresh should be positioned based on this research. The brand has been appealing to consumers in its ads primarily on the basis of softness and convenience, with the assumption that all segments were very interested in these two attributes. Less emphasis had been given to cling-free clothes as a reason for purchasing Spring Fresh.

Questions

1 How would you describe each of the consumer groups identified in the research from a demographic and benefit standpoint?

2 In which benefit segments may Spring Fresh have a potential advantage over Soft Touch?

3 What conclusions can be derived from this research which may be of help to Spring Fresh advertising strategy?

4 What additional research should be conducted?

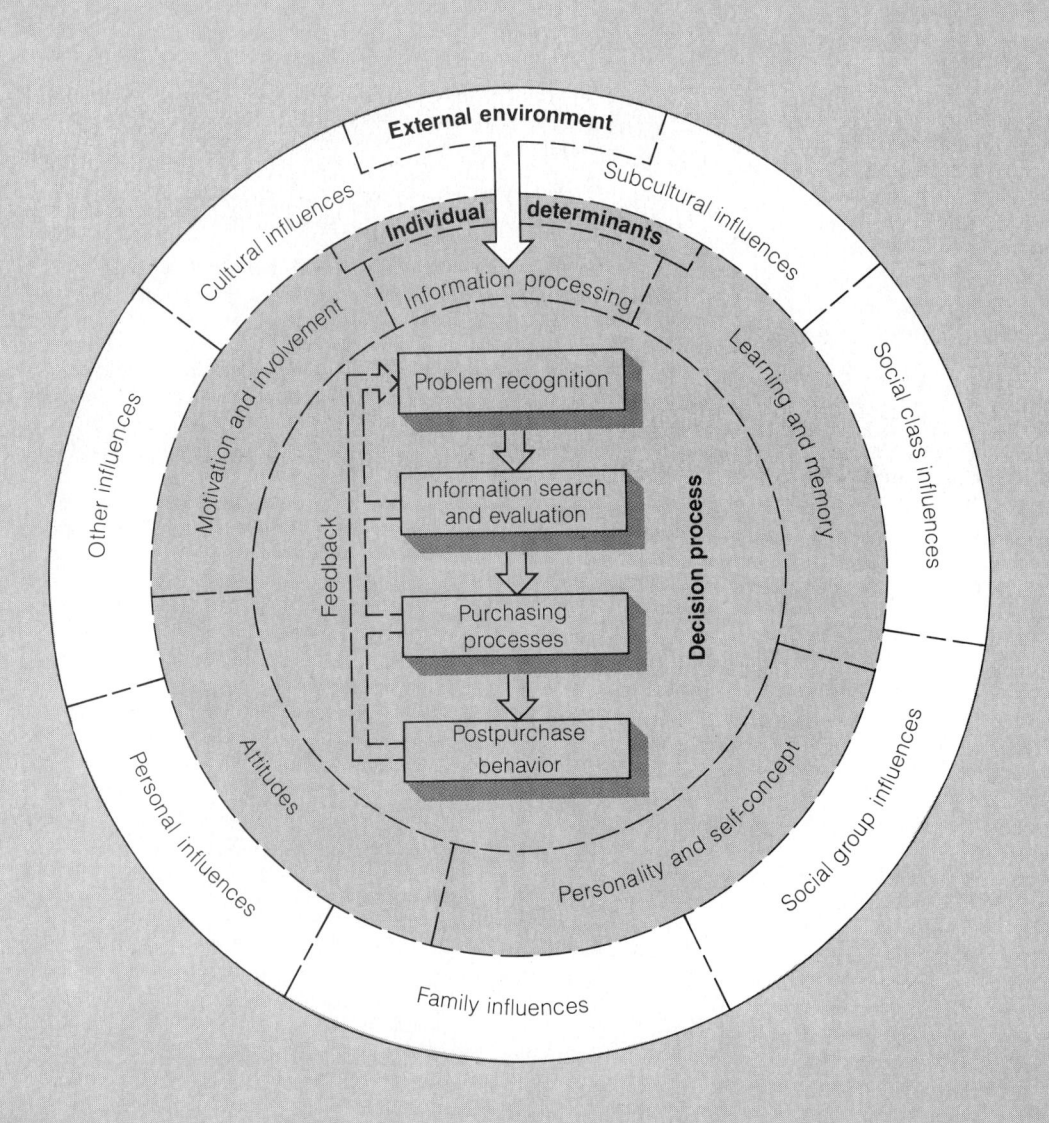

PART THREE
ENVIRONMENTAL INFLUENCES ON CONSUMER BEHAVIOR

6 Culture
7 Subcultures
8 Social Class
9 Social Groups
10 Family
11 Personal Influence and Diffision of Innovations
Cases for Part Three

CHAPTER 6
CULTURE

We begin our study of the environmental elements impinging upon consumers by first looking at a very broad, basic, and enduring factor—the pervasive influence of culture. Consider the following examples of culture's relevance to the marketer:

> Despite figures suggesting that the use of girdles should have been expanding, Playtex executives found in the 1960s that sales were thinning at an alarming rate. Having risen to its dominant position in the industry on the strength of its marketing acumen, Playtex tried pouring more money into its advertising efforts. It established a program in which girdles would be displayed in multiple locations in grocery stores in hopes of attracting more consumer attention. The company even added more loops, belts, and zippers to already formidable products in case women felt the items were not providing enough support. None of these measures helped, however. Research by a consulting firm showed that the main cause of the problem was the new set of social values emerging, not a direct marketing shortcoming. New attitudes toward naturalness and sexuality were beginning to emerge. Feminist books were stirring reexamination of the role of women, especially among suburban women who were prime targets for girdle marketers. The new value system that would eventually reject the traditional American views of self-denial and discomfort was beginning to influence customers who were facing use of the uncomfortable and constraining girdles. The consultants suggested that Playtex shift away from zippers, heavy hardware, and the concept of constraining support and move to the "control underwear" ideal of women's undergarments. When this strategy was implemented the sales slide was reversed.[1]

> Kimberly Clark helped to reorient American consumers to the permissiveness of disposability and waste by introducing Kleenex. Up until that time people were expected to use and launder cloth handkerchiefs, and the thought of such a disposable product was abhorrent to those who had been so strongly influenced by the Protestant ethic which forbade wastefulness. Such a pioneering effort during the 1920s was thought by many to be doomed to failure. Yet today cultural patterns have changed and the disposable business is booming. Disposable paper products are now sold as bath mats, tablecloths, diapers, and work uniforms among a host of other items. However, a counteracting cultural environment of greater ecological concern may, in the future, have a strong negative influence on the use of many disposable products.[2]

A leading U.S. golf ball manufacturer targeted Japan as an important new market because of the expanding popularity of golf in that nation. Although golf balls had been generally packaged in sets of three, six, or twelve for domestic consumption, special packaging in sets of four was developed for the Japenese export market. The company's sales were well below anticipated volume. Research eventually pinpointed the packaging in fours as a primary factor for lagging sales. Four is the number of death in Japan.[3]

Each of these examples illustrates the significance of cultural understanding to the marketer. In this chapter we shall be investigating the role and usefulness of cultural analysis in developing marketing strategies. After defining and characterizing culture, the basic cultural values of American consumers shall be outlined. This will be followed by an examination of cultural change and its effect on consumer behavior. Finally, cross-cultural consumer behavior and its implications for international marketing will be discussed.

CULTURE DEFINED

It is difficult to present only one definition of culture and expect it to portray the richness of the field and its relevance to understanding consumers. However, the following two are representative:

That complex whole that includes knowledge, belief, art, morals, law, custom, and any other capabilities and habits acquired by man as a member of society[4]

The distinctive way of life of a group of people, their complete design for living[5]

Therefore, culture is everything that is socially learned and shared by the members of a society. Culture consists of material and nonmaterial components. Nonmaterial culture includes the words people use; the ideas, customs, and beliefs they share; and the habits they pursue. Material culture consists of all the physical substances that have been changed and used by people, such as tools, automobiles, roads, and farms. In a marketing and consumer behavior context, artifacts of the material culture would include all the products and services which are produced and consumed; marketing institutions such as Safeway supermarkets, K mart discount houses, and 7-11 convenience stores; and advertisements. Nonmaterial culture would include the way in which consumers shop in supermarkets, our desire for newer and better produts, and our responses to the word "sale."

The influence of culture might be better understood by looking at Figure 6-1, which reveals the hierarchy of influence of environmental variables to be discussed in this section. Culture is seen to be the broadest determinant while personal influence is viewed as the most immediate influence on the individual.

The significance of culture in understanding human behavior (of which consumer behavior is a subpart) is that it extends our understanding of the extent to which people are more than just chemistry, physiology, or a set of biological drives and instincts.[6] The implication is that although all customers may be biologically similar, their views of the world, what they value, and how they act differ according to their cultural backgrounds.

CULTURAL RELEVANCE TO MARKETING DECISIONS

It has long been recognized that culture influences consumers. For example, Duesenberry observed in 1949 that all of the activities in which people engage are culturally determined, and that nearly all purchases of goods are made either to provide physical comfort or to implement the activities that make up the life of a culture.[7] Thus, an understanding of culture enables the marketer to interpret the reaction of consumers to alternative marketing strategies. Sometimes guidance from *cultural anthropologists* (those social scientists who study man and his culture) is sought in order to gain a better understanding of the market.

Anthropologists are able to assist the marketer in understanding a number of cultural facets of behavior, such as the following:

National character, or the differences that distinguish one national group from another. That is, the obvious as well as the more subtle cultural differences that distinguish Americans, Swedes, Germans, and Brazilians

Differences in *subcultures* such as blacks, Jews, and Puerto Ricans

FIGURE 6-1

The hierarchy of environmental influences on consumers.

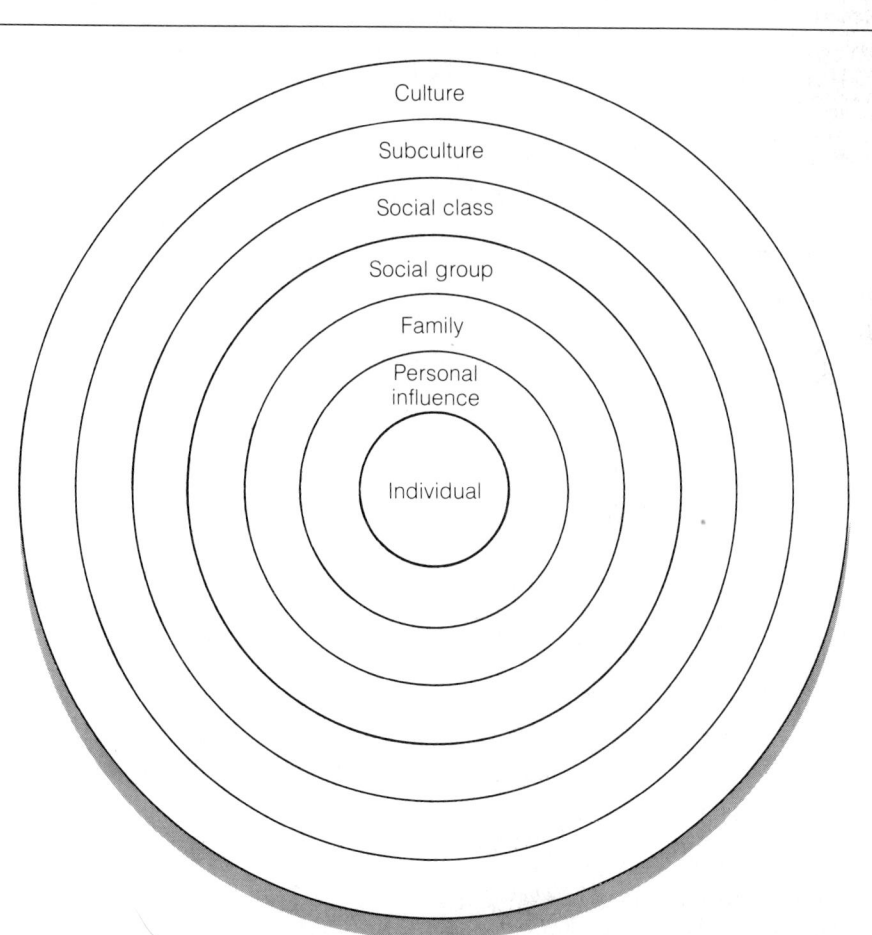

The *silent language* of gesture, posture, food and drink preferences, and other nonverbal clues to behavior

The significance of *symbols* in a society

Rites of passage, or the central points in a person's life at which he may ritually be helped to go from one status to another, such as birth, puberty, or marriage

Taboos or prohibitions in a culture relating to various things such as the use of a given color, phrase, or symbol[8]

The following case history demonstrates one way in which anthropological knowledge was successfully used to solve marketing problems:[9]

> A major manufacturer of women's products was uncertain about whether to continue using the *Fleur de Lis* emblem on its package. Anthropological analysis of this symbol indicated that its association with French kings and other cultural connotations made it more masculine than feminine. Hence, it was recommended that this symbol be replaced.

THE CHARACTERISTICS OF CULTURE

Although the definitions of culture presented earlier are excellent, they seek to characterize culture in only a few words. It is evident that such a concept is difficult to convey clearly in any definition. As one writer notes, "It's like putting your hand in a cloud."[10] This section, therefore, will expand on these definitions by discussing the significant characteristics or features of culture. Many characteristics of culture may be cited to describe its nature, but most social scientists agree on the following features.

Culture Is Man-made

Culture does not simply "exist" somewhere waiting to be discovered. People invent their culture. This invention consists of three interdependent systems or elements: (1) an *ideological system* or mental component that consists of the ideas, beliefs, values, and ways of reasoning that human beings learn to accept in defining what is desirable and undesirable; (2) a *technological system* that consists of the skills, crafts, and arts that enable humans to produce material goods derived from the natural environment; and (3) an *organizational system* (such as the family system and social class) that makes it possible for humans to coordinate effectively their behavior with the actions of others.[11]

Culture Is Learned

Culture is not innate or instinctive, but is learned early in life and charged with a good deal of emotion. The great strength of this cultural stamp handed down from one generation to another is such that at an early age children are firmly imbued with their culture's ways of acting, thinking, and feeling. This obviously has important implications for the behavior of consumers, because these preconditions are molded by our culture from birth.

Culture Is Prescriptive

Culture involves ideal standards or patterns of behavior so that members of society have a common understanding of the right and proper way to think, feel, and act in any given situation. Ideal patterns of behavior, thought, and feeling which groups share are termed *norms*. When actual behavior deviates from the ideal patterns or norms of society, *sanctions* are frequently taken. That is, certain types of pressures are brought to bear on deviant individuals so that they will conform their behavior to what society expects.

Culture Is Socially Shared
Culture is a group phenomenon, shared by human beings living in organized societies and kept relatively uniform by social pressure. The group that is involved in this sharing may range from a whole society to a smaller unit such as a family.

Cultures Are Similar but Different
All cultures exhibit certain similarities. For example, each of the following elements is found in all societies: athletic sports, bodily adornment, calendar, cooking, courtship, dancing, education, family, gestures, government, housing, language, law, music, religious ritual, and numerous other items. There is, however, great variation from society to society in the nature of each of these elements, which may result in important consumer behavior differences around the world.

Culture Is Gratifying and Persistent
Culture satisfies basic biological as well as learned needs. It consists of habits that will be strengthened and reinforced as long as they are gratified. Because of this gratification, cultural elements are handed down from generation to generation. Thus, people are comfortable doing things in the customary way.

Our thorough inculcation of culture causes it to persist even when we are exposed to new cultures. No matter where we go or what we do, we cannot escape our cultural heritage. Its persistence means that, although not impossible, change is often quite difficult because resistance to it may be strong.

Culture Is Adaptive
In spite of our resistance to change, cultures are gradually and continuously changing. Some societies are quite static with a very slow rate of change, while others are more dynamic, with very rapid changes taking place.

Culture Is Organized and Integrated
A culture "hangs together," that is, parts fit together. Although every culture has some inconsistent elements, it tends to form a consistent and integrated whole.

CULTURAL VALUES

Cultural values are important to the organized and integrated nature of culture. A *cultural value* can be defined in a sociological perspective as "a widely held belief or sentiment that some activities, relationships, feelings, or goals are important to the community's identity or well-being."[12] In a psychological vein, Rokeach defines values as centrally held and enduring beliefs which guide actions and judgments across specific situations and beyond immediate goals to more ultimate end-states of existence. Values, therefore, produce inclinations to respond to specific stimuli in standard ways.[13] That is, a specific behavior is expected to either help or hinder the attainment of some value or group of values. Consumers, then, are motivated to engage in behaviors designed to enhance the achievement of certain values and to avoid those behaviors which are perceived to hinder the attainment of certain value states.[14]

Chapter 16 will discuss the concept of attitudes and their relationship to consumer behavior. However, because there often is confusion over the concepts of attitude and value it may be useful at this point to clarify these terms. An attitude can be viewed as the individual's positive or negative evaluation of some object, situation, or behavior which predisposes the individual to respond in some manner. Values, on the other hand, transcend specific objects and situations. They deal with modes of conduct (termed *instrumental values*) and end-states of existence (called *terminal values*). That is, an individual who has a "value" has an enduring belief that a particular mode of conduct or end-state of existence is preferable to some other mode of conduct or end-state of existence. Values serve as standards or criteria that tell us how to act, what to want, and what attitudes to hold, and they allow us to judge and compare ourselves with others. Compared to attitudes, which focus directly on specific objects, situations, or actions, values transcend specific circumstances. In addition, values act as standards or yardsticks guiding attitudes, actions, and evaluations of ourselves and others. Whereas individuals may possess thousands of attitudes, they are likely to possess less than a hundred values.[15]

Since values are culturally determined, this means that they are learned from social interaction, largely from our families and friends in settings such as schools and churches. Values strongly influence consumer behavior; even though the specific situation may dictate slightly different actions, overall there is much similarity in consumer behavior within a given culture, such as in tastes, methods of shopping, and so forth.

It is crucial for the marketer to understand society's basic value structure so that strategy decisions do not fly in the face of ingrained cultural patterns. It is much easier to harmonize with the culture than to attempt to change fundamental cultural values.

United States Cultural Values

Each culture has what may be termed *core values*, which are the dominant or basic cultural values that people accept with little question. In America, although values are not always obvious or easy to analyze, there are major patterns that can be identified. This is not to say that "American values" are exclusive to the United States, or that all Americans share them. However, the American value system is appreciably different from some other cultures, and most Americans do subscribe to the cultural pattern described below.

Rokeach has developed a cultural value inventory for ranking the terminal and instrumental values held by Americans. Table 6-1 presents these thirty-six values.

The following discussion of our cultural values may seem somewhat obvious to the reader; but this simply underscores the fact that Americans accept these values as "givens." The values to be discussed represent abstracted dominant themes which are ideal types, and thus may be subject to some exceptions.

Individualism This value is complex and closely interrelated with a number of other facets such as freedom, democracy, nationalism, and patriotism. It is founded on a belief in the dignity, worth, and goodness of the individual. People have freedom; that is, they are independent from outside constraint. However, they are not freed from all social restraints, but are to act as responsible agents. Figure 6-2 illustrates how Chrysler car advertising has used a patriotic theme in appealing to consumers to reject their dependence on OPEC and strive for self-sufficiency.

The stress on individualism has been reinforced by the trend widely referred to during the 1970s as the "Age of Me." The "Me" decade emphasized self-fulfillment, self-actualization, inner motivation, and a focus on self, and it is exemplified by such slogans as "I want to be me," "I did it my way," and "I'm looking out for number one."

Some think that the 1980s will be the "We Decade" in which self-interest will be focused in terms of collective action, societal effort, and security in numbers spurred on by economic conditions of recession and inflation.[16]

Equality Americans believe in the intrinsic equality of man, that is, that each person is an individual (all are equal before God). Everyone has an equal right to

TABLE 6-1 CULTURAL VALUES

Terminal Values (End-States of Existence)	Instrumental Values (Modes of Conduct)
A comfortable life (a prosperous life)	Ambitious (hard-working, aspiring)
An exciting life (a stimulating, active life)	Broadminded (open-minded)
A sense of accomplishment (lasting contribution)	Capable (competent, effective)
A world at peace (free of war and conflict)	Cheerful (lighthearted, joyful)
A world of beauty (beauty of nature and the arts)	Clean (neat, tidy)
Equality (brotherhood, equal opportunity for all)	Courageous (standing up for your beliefs)
Family security (taking care of loved ones)	Forgiving (willing to pardon others)
Freedom (independence, free choice)	Helpful (working for the welfare of others)
Happiness (contentedness)	Honest (sincere, truthful)
Inner harmony (freedom from inner conflict)	Imaginative (daring, creative)
Mature love (sexual and spiritual intimacy)	Independent (self-reliant, self-sufficient)
National security (protection from attack)	Intellectual (intelligent, reflective)
Pleasure (an enjoyable, leisurely life)	Logical (consistent, rational)
Salvation (saved, eternal life)	Loving (affectionate, tender)
Self-respect (self-esteem)	Obedient (dutiful, respectful)
Social recognition (respect, admiration)	Polite (courteous, well-mannered)
True friendship (close companionship)	Responsible (dependable, reliable)
Wisdom (a mature understanding of life)	Self-controlled (restrained, self-disciplined)

Source: Reprinted by permission of Elsevier Publishing Co., Inc., from Milton Rokeach, "The Role of Values in Public Opinion Research," *Public Opinion Quarterly*, **32**:554, Winter 1968–1969. Copyright 1969 by the Trustees of Columbia University.

FIGURE 6-2

Advertisement for K cars. (Courtesy of Chrysler Corporation.)

life, liberty, and the pursuit of happiness, and an equal opportunity for social and economic rewards.

During the 1960s and 1970s there was an increasing push for social and economic equality in America. One of the most profound impacts during this period was women's demand for equality, which has brought about changes in the marriage relationship and the American family. The women's liberation movement represents a value structure that has resulted in greater independence and equality of women. It has been expressed in numerous ways, such as more women with careers outside the home, changing sex roles within the home, and many women opting for lifestyles other than marriage. Virginia Slims cigarettes has successfully related to this equality movement in a series of ads (see Figure 6-3).

One manifestation of the movement toward equality in our culture is the general trend toward unisex clothing. Women have adopted "male styles," wearing pants, boots, and leather jackets, while men have begun wearing "female-styled" clothing in bright colors, of more delicate fabrics, shaped to the body, and with such accessories as necklaces.

Activity Our culture stresses activity, especially work, as a predominant value. This derives largely from the Puritan or Protestant ethic, which stressed that idleness was evil. An individual was expected to work hard, save money, and be thrifty. Thus, work was conceived as a means of religious discipline.

Today Americans believe not only in working hard but also in playing hard. Increased productivity and affluence have resulted in replacing long hours of hard work with longer vacation periods, shorter workweeks, and more paid holidays. This has generated increased leisure time in which activity is still stressed, but it is manifested in numerous leisure pursuits, as evidenced by the boom in participant sports such as tennis and golf. Often the activity is a competitive one, and marketers frequently use such appeals as the basis for ads.

Progress and Achievement Americans believe in progress for society and achievement and success for the individual. We are oriented toward the future rather than the past, and believe in change and forward movement. Personal achievement is stressed as evidenced by the "success story," and our desire to master the physical world. We also prize the characteristics of self-reliance and initiative.

One manifestation of our emphasis on progress in America is the sometimes wasteful use of material possessions and resources. Contemporary America stresses continuous style changes and discarding the still functionally useful product in order to buy what is new. Of course, the marketer benefits from an environment which is so conducive to innovation, in which consumers are eager to have the most up-to-date item.

An indication of our culture's orientation toward achievement from a mar-

FIGURE 6-3

Advertisement for Virginia Slims. (Reprinted by permission of Philip Morris Incorporated.)

keting perspective is the importance of certain symbols in our society. Because achievement often has a materialistic aspect to it, Americans grant to owners of certain products the stamp of having "arrived." For example, a Cadillac or Mercedes tells something about the achievement of its owner, as does a large house in the "right neighborhood," and expensive clothing. These products are symbols to their owners as well as to others, and their meanings are usually unmistakable.[17]

Efficiency and Practicality Americans greatly appreciate technical values and constantly search for better ways of doing things. Our entire economic system is founded on this concept and emphasizes mass production and mass consumption.

Americans are interested in performance features of products such as speed, economy, safety, and durability. This appreciation of the practical as opposed to the intellectual also helps explain why certain advertising messages are very successful. Advertising-effectiveness tests consistently show that using "How to . . ." oriented headlines does better than using a non-problem-solving approach. Similarly, there is a far more widespread market for *Readers' Digest* and *Popular Mechanics* than for *Smithsonian* and *Omni*.

Another example of our culture's value of practicality concerns the orientation toward informality. We have moved away from the formal traditions (long associated with the eastern United States) and have adopted more informal habits in manners, dress, speech, and social relationships. Moreover, the United States has never placed as much emphasis on formality, ceremony, and tradition as has Europe. Consequently, Americans tolerate, in fact welcome, less structure and rigidity and more comfort in the way they work and relax. Certain regions of the country are particularly high on this scale of informality. For example, the celebrated southern California lifestyle of casual dress, informal entertaining, and outdoor living is a prime example.

Mastery Over the Environment Americans do not like to be controlled by their environment, rather, they seek to control it. This not only includes controlling the weather and harnessing the sun and tides as energy sources, but it also extends to areas like genetic engineering. Even the nature of products introduced in America is indicative of this underlying cultural value. For instance, there seems to be a product answer for every chore the consumer might face. During each Christmas season our television sets bring us news of products that knit our clothes; attach our buttons; and spin, chop, slice, and dice our vegetables. All of these items attest to our desire to provide an engineered answer for almost every situation we face.

We also desire to master our own bodies and surrounding environment. Because of this value, we spend tremendous amounts of money on deodorants, shampoos, colognes, and cosmetics in order to improve or hide our true bodily features, while we buy detergents, cleansers, waxes, rug shampoos, room deodorizers, and electric bug killers to conquer the dirt, germs, pests, and odors that surround us.

Another aspect of this value is that we have long viewed the world and its resources as there to use as we saw fit. In so doing, however, we have encountered numerous environmental and diminishing-resource problems. On the positive side, a growing ecological orientation can be seen in the marketplace. Some manufacturers are using recycled materials to produce new items (such as glass and paper products); more biodegradable products are being marketed (such as laundry detergents); and alternatives to harmful aerosol spray products are now being offered (such as pump hair sprays and solid deodorants).

Religious and Moral Orientation According to one Gallup poll, 94 percent of Americans believe in God and 64 percent believe in life after death. In fact, the United States is found to be more religious than any other industrialized country in the world. More than twice as many adult Americans consider religion to be very important to them compared to Western Europeans, for example. Although less than half the public attend church frequently, almost three-quarters consider themselves to be religious. According to one recent study which investigated major aspects of American life—community involvement, political and moral beliefs, personal relationships, and work—the level of religious commitment was found to be the factor that most consistently and dramatically affects the values and behavior of Americans. The report identifies a cohesive and powerful group of Americans, approximately 45 million strong who are "intensely religious." These citizens form the nucleus of a group which may have increasing impact on the social and political institutions of the United States.[18]

Thus, we are a religious people, and our Judeo-Christian heritage has imbued us with a strong moral and ethical quality. Consequently, we tend to view the world in absolute terms and tolerate few gray areas—that is, we judge things in terms of good or bad, right or wrong, ethical or unethical. This value results in a strong evangelistic spirit among Americans. We are rather *ethnocentric,* believing that our culture and way of life is the best and feeling that it is our duty to bring others around to our way of thinking and acting.

One implication of the religious and moral orientation of Americans is our receptivity to the "marketing" of certain religious views and social causes. For example, some very effective marketers of Christianity include Billy Graham and Robert Schuller.

Humanitarianism Americans have a strong sense of personal concern for the rights and welfare of others. We provide aid in mass disasters, have a large philanthropic system, and feel that we should give our money and/or our time to such organizations as the United Fund, Red Cross, CARE, and the Peace Corps. For example, total contributions to charity in 1979 amounted to over $38 billion in the United States, of which religion received the largest share.[19] The operation of religious and other charitable institutions is a huge business and draws good support even in unfavorable economic times.

Youthfulness Young people set much of the tone of our culture and have been a growing force in our society as their proportion has risen. Because Americans want to look and act young, we consume great quantities of those products that hold promise for achieving these ends. For instance, hair colorings for men and women are very much in demand, as are preparations to do away with wrinkles, flab, and spots caused by the aging process. The array of vitamins and other supplements (such as Geritol) is another indication of our youth orientation.

Marketers have played up the theme of youthfulness in numerous product and service promotions with slogans such as "you're as young as you feel" and "for those who think young." An effective twist on this approach, but accomplishing the same result, was Clairol's slogan for Loving Care hair coloring: "You're not getting older. You're getting better."

Underlying the youth theme pervading our culture is the implication of romance. The younger you look, presumably the more attractive you are, especially to the opposite sex. The weakening of sexual prohibitions in our society has led to more playful, thinly disguised appeals to romantic and sexual motives in product promotions. This *creative eroticism* is reflected in many products and promotional slogans. For instance, Love Cosmetics' choice of the product name "Love" suggests that the items are "love potions."

Other evidence of the strong romantic emphasis in our culture is the fact that more than 20 million Americans weekly follow the dozen or more daytime television soap operas. In addition, more than 1200 romantic novels are published each year to be pored over by avid readers.

Materialism The U.S. culture is materialistic, and Americans are the world's most voracious consumers, each year buying millions of color TV sets, washing machines, refrigerators, vacuum cleaners, lawn mowers, radios, and other items. Material progress has made America a land of abundance where more than half of all families own their homes, and two cars per family is the standard. Progress has also brought about urban renewal, universal education, and eradication of many diseases. Thus, there is a very positive aspect of materialism from which progress results.

There is also a negative side to materialism, seen in shoddy merchandise that falls apart soon after purchase, families that are drowning in debt because of their compulsive spending, resource depletion, and pollution.[20]

Related to the core culture value of materialism is the growing trend toward *hedonism,* or devotion to pleasure. We desire maximum pleasurable sensation with minimum effort. Our culture's increasing devotion to hedonism is reflected in the sale of all sorts of products ranging from luxury cars and homes to many foods and such pastimes as electronic video games. In addition, we are more willing to admit the existence of this situation to ourselves and others. For example, L'Oréal hair color ads state, "It costs a little more, but I'm worth it." This and many other ads stress how good the feeling is that comes from using the product.

Social Interaction and Conformity These values seem in contrast to our emphasis on individualism, but some amount of conformity is necessary for a smoothly functioning society. Americans seem to be especially sensitive to group pressure. For example, David Riesman suggests that America can be characterized as a country of *inner-directed* and *other-directed* persons. Inner-directed individuals have their principles firmly instilled by their elders while other-directed persons receive their direction from contemporaries, directly or indirectly, personally or through the mass media. Although the majority of the population of this country would have to be categorized as inner-directed there is a trend in the metropolitan areas of America toward other-directedness.[21]

The trend of other-directedness suggests that people are seeking satisfaction of some need through greater social involvement with each other. Much of the advertising we are exposed to incorporates this theme. Promotions for products as diverse as motorcycles ("You meet the nicest people on a Honda"), clothing, recreation equipment, cigarettes, and beverages of all kinds incorporate the theme of how beneficial these products are in achieving pleasurable social interaction.

Do Values Influence Consumer Behavior?

Intuitively we can see that culture is a strong force in the consumer's milieu affecting his or her choice behavior. Unfortunately, little research has been conducted assessing the usefulness of cultural values in understanding or predicting consumer behavior.

Some recent studies, however, have found that commonly held cultural values do shape consumption choices to a certain extent.[22] One approach to the study of cultural values as they influence consumer behavior has been the use of the Rokeach value survey presented in Table 6-1 in which respondents rank order the values or respond to an agree-disagree scale for each item. For example, a study incorporating this value survey examined the ownership of generic categories of automobiles (such as full-size, intermediate, compact, and subcompact-size cars) and concluded that culture is an underlying determinant of the type of car purchased.[23] Another study found that car owners' values can also be used to differentiate among owners of small, domestic cars, owners of small, foreign cars, and owners of large, domestic cars.[24]

In addition, an investigation of homemakers' purchases of household appliances has used terminal and instrumental value lists to discover an important relationship between purchase and values. Women were interviewed who planned to make a purchase of one or more of eight major household appliances. Terminal values were found to be related much more strongly than instrumental values to the product-class level of choice (for example, when deciding among clothes washers such as full-size automatics, "mini" automatics, or compact portables). At the brand choice decision level (such as deciding between Maytag and General Electric), instrumental values were found to be related, while terminal values were not related at all. Thus, terminal values would seem to guide choice among product classes, while instrumental values would seem to guide choice among brands.[25] This concept is diagramed in Figure 6-4. As we can see, each set of values is thought to influence choice criteria (product or brand)—that is, the standards used to judge various alternatives. The choice criteria are, in turn, seen as having an influence on the consumer's formation of attitudes toward products or brands. These research findings are useful for directing the positioning of the brand so that advertising may communicate to the prospective buyers how the marketer's offering is superior to its competition.[26]

Studies such as these indicate that understanding personal values of consumers can facilitate market-segmentation decisions as well as those relating to product and promotion planning. For example, one study indicated that segmentation on the basis of personal values was much more advantageous than on the basis of demographics. The study, involving a national chain of family restaurants and its leading competitor, found that brand preference was not differentiated with respect to demographic characteristics of consumers who ate at both chains and had a stated preference for one or the other. However, market segments based on value orientations of these fast-food restaurant customers did reveal differences that predisposed consumers' brand preferences. This kind of information is useful in designing effective advertising campaigns and developing products that incorporate salient product attributes, thereby enhancing the competitive posture of the brand.[27] However, more research is needed on the subject of values as they relate to purchasing behavior. There is still much disagreement on how widely and intensely held values must be among consumers. A greater understanding is also needed on the origins and consequences of values. In addition, more research is necessary to understand cultural value influences on consumer behavior across a broader range of products than has so far been investigated.[28]

Several companies are pursuing such a goal of broadening the application of consumer values to users of a wide range of products. For example, SRI International combines value and lifestyle (termed VALS) information with available demographic data.[29] The purpose of VALS is to create a general psychographic framework that can be used to understand consumers of a variety of products, from deodorants to television sets.

By using this information, SRI has isolated and labeled nine types of consumers, each type so distinctive in its behavior and emotional makeup that it is held to constitute a specific market segment. The three major categories and nine subcategories are identified in Table 6-2.

Based on information gathered by SRI on dozens of products, the VALS program appears to have much usefulness for understanding the purchase habits for each category of consumer. For example, experientials and societally-conscious individuals tend to buy foreign cars, while belongers tend to buy American cars. Media habits also differ among the groups. For instance, in print media, tabloids appeal to sustainers; business magazines are popular with achievers; sports magazines are frequently bought by I-am-me's; and literary magazines are preferred by experientials and societally conscious people. Marketing strategies of client firms

FIGURE 6-4

The nature of cultural value influence in purchase decisions.

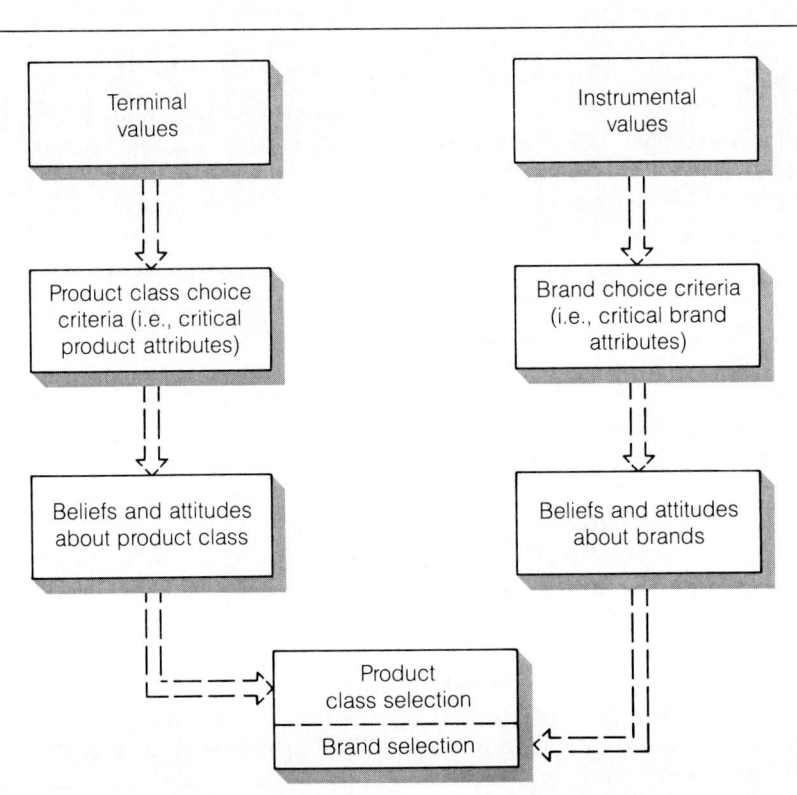

TABLE 6-2
CONSUMER VALUE CATEGORIES

1 Need-driven (12 percent of adult population)—"Money restricted"; struggling just to buy basics. Buy more out of need than choice or whim. Sometimes splurge on luxury items.
   a Survivors (5 percent)—The most disadvantaged; old, poor, depressed, and far-removed from the cultural mainstream.
   b Sustainers (7 percent)—Relatively young, angry, and crafty, struggling on the edge of poverty, and willing to do anything to get ahead.

2 Outer-directed (71 percent)—Middle America. Conduct their lives so that others will think well of them. Buy on the basis of what others will think. Purchase is dominated by outer rather than inner measures.
   a Belongers (38 percent)—Traditional, conservative, conventional, nostalgic, sentimental, puritanical, and unexperimental. Buy to fit in, not stand out. Conforming and traditional in spending. Prime drive is to belong.
   b Emulators (10 percent)—Trying to make it big. Highly visible lifestyle. Ambitious, upwardly mobile, status conscious, and competitive. Distrustful and angry. Little faith they will get a fair shake from the Establishment. Imitate buying patterns of their models, the Achievers.
   c Achievers (23 percent)—Driven, oriented to success. Leaders in business, politics, professions. Characterized by efficiency, fame, status, the good life, comfort, materialistic values. Pragmatic believers in rugged individualism and the traditional American system, and have formed the core of America's leadership elite for the last 100 years. Spend on the good things of life, and dominate top-of-the-line luxury markets.

3 Inner-directed (17 percent)—Idealistic and conservation-oriented. Value the artistic and spiritual. Many are well-educated and form avant garde markets. Buy to meet their own inner wants and pleasures, rather than to respond to norms of others. Only group expected to grow in the 1980s.
   a I-am-me's (2 percent)—A small group, fiercely individualistic, flamboyant, young, zippy, exhibitionistic, narcissistic, dramatic, impulsive, and inventive. Many fads originate here.
   b Experientials (7 percent)—Concerned with inner growth and naturalism. Seek direct experience, intense involvement, a rich inner life. Mature variety of I-am-me's. Important to various here-and-now markets such as outdoor sports, creative home pursuits, arts and crafts, etc.
   c Societally conscious (5 percent)—Acutely aware of social issues. Live in a socially responsible way. Stress simplicity, frugality, conservation, ecological soundness, consumerism. Lean toward items made via appropriate technology. Fastest growing segment.
   d Integrated (3 percent)—Highly developed psychologically. Live in accord with what is fitting, self-fulfilling, releasing, and balanced. Tolerant, assured, self-actualizing. Often have world perspective. Practical dreamers. Evolve from either an inner- or other-directed set of values and represent a synthesis of both power and sensitivity.

Source: "Information on Values and Lifestyles Needed to Identify Buying Patterns," *Marketing News* October 5, 1979, pp. 1, 4, 7; and Niles Howard, "A New Way to View Consumers," *Dun's Review,* August 1981, pp. 42–46.

have been influenced by such research. For example, Merrill Lynch & Co., Inc., changed the thrust of its "Bullish on America" advertising campaign after finding that its prime customers were "achievers," while its bull-herd had greatest appeal to "belongers." Merrill Lynch kept the bull, but deftly shifted the focus by showing a single animal, with the headline "A Breed Apart."[30]

CULTURAL CHANGE AND COUNTERCULTURES

The core values just discussed are not fixed or static but instead are dynamic elements of our culture which may change over time. Cultural change may come about slowly in an evolutionary manner, or it may change rapidly, which tends to place more stress on the system. The marketer needs to understand that cultures do change and to appreciate the implications which this may have for consumer behavior.

Changing Cultural Values in the United States

American values are undergoing some major changes. Opinion research has shown that during the 1960s and 1970s some fundamental and widely shared cultural views had changed in the United States. Only 20 percent of the public now clings to traditional values of hard work, family loyalty, and sacrifice.

Approximately 17 percent of the population cites self-fulfillment as its principal life goal. But the majority (63 percent) embraces some traditional values and also espouses views that would have been considered heretical only a generation ago.[31] Thus, the marketer faces a situation in which new value trends coexist with long-standing values still deeply rooted in the country. This pluralism is one of the characteristics of our emerging society.[32]

Philip Kotler suggests that, generally, the following changes are taking place in American cultural values:[33]

From	To
Self-reliance	Government reliance
"Hard-work"	The "easy life"
Religious convictions	Secular convictions
Husband-dominated home	Wife-dominated home
Parent-centered household	Child-centered household
Respect for individual	Dislike of individual difference
Postponed gratification	Immediate gratification
Saving	Spending
Sexual chastity	Sexual freedom
Parental values	Peer-group values
Independence	Security

The values listed above may be characteristic of intergenerational differences, but differences can also be found between various groups of the same age. For example, noncollege youths appear to be about five years behind the college population in adoption of new social values and moral outlooks.[34] In addition to the insights offered by Kotler, surveys by the Yankelovich organization have uncovered several major current social trends in the United States today. These are presented in Table 6-3.

General Implications of Cultural Change for the Marketer

Changes in norms such as those evidenced in Table 6-3 signal a new American value pattern emerging. Its impact will be felt in many ways by marketers. Just a few such areas are cited here.

First, the search for a new work ethic will mean that leisure activities will occupy a more important place in people's lives. Thus, new opportunities will continue to open up in travel, entertainment, sports, leisure-oriented products, and also in the education and information industries.

Related to the work/leisure situation is the fact that time is becoming a more precious commodity and those items that save time are becoming greatly valued

TABLE 6-3

FIVE MAJOR SOCIAL TRENDS AND THEIR IMPLICATIONS FOR CONSUMER BEHAVIOR

1   **Psychology of Affluence Trends**

The first group are traceable to the effects of "psychology of affluence." That is, they manifest themselves among consumers who feel sufficiently free from economic insecurity to seek the fulfillment of other needs.

Trend toward physical self-enhancement, spending more time, effort, and money on improving one's physical appearance; the things people do to enhance their looks.

Trend toward personalization, expressing one's individuality through products, possessions and new lifestyles. The need to be "a little bit different" from other people.

Trend toward physical health and well-being, the level of concern with one's health, diet, and what people do to take better care of themselves.

Trend toward new forms of materialism, the new status symbols and extent of de-emphasis on money and material possessions.

Trend toward personal creativity, the growing conviction that being "creative" is not confined to the artist. Each man can be creative in his own way, as expressed through a wide variety of activities, hobbies, and new uses of leisure time.

Trend toward meaningful work, the spread of the demand for work that is challenging and meaningful over and above how well it pays.

2   **Antifunctionalism Trends**

A second group of trends underscores a major new force in American life—the quest for excitement, sensation, stimulation, and meaning to counteract the practical and mundane routines of everyday life. There is a reaction among certain groups in the population against the drabness of modern life, giving rise to a many-faceted hunger that reaches beyond the practical.

Trend toward the "new romanticism," the desire to restore romance, mystery and adventure to modern life.

Trend toward novelty and change, the search for constant change, novelty, new experience, reaction against sameness and habit.

Trend toward adding beauty to one's daily surroundings, the stress on beauty in the home and the things people do and buy to achieve it.

Trend toward sensuousness, placing greater emphasis on a total sensory experience—touching, feeling, smelling, and psychedelic phenomena. A moving away from the purely linear, logical and visual.

Trend toward mysticism, the search for new modes of spiritual experience and beliefs, as typified by the growing interest in astrology.

Trend toward introspection, an enhanced need for self-understanding and life experiences in contrast to automatic conformity to external pressures and expectations.

3   **Reaction against Complexity Trends**

A third and important group of trends cluster around the theme of reaction against the complexity of modern life. We find more and more people changing their habits and lifestyles in reaction to crowded conditions, complicated products, unresponsive institutions, restrictive regulations, and information overloads.

Trend toward life simplification, the turning away from complicated products, services, and ways of life.

Trend toward return to nature, rejection of the artificial, the "chemical," the man-made improvements on nature; the adoption of more "natural" ways of dressing, eating and living.

Trend toward increased ethnicity, finding new satisfactions and identifications in foods, dress, customs, and lifestyles of various ethnic groups such as Black, Italian, Irish, Polish, Jewish, German.

Trend toward increased community involvement, increasing affiliation with local, community, and neighborhood activities. Greater involvement in local groups.

Trend toward greater reliance on technology versus tradition, distrust of tradition and reputation that is based on age and experience, due to the swift tempo of change. Greater confidence in science and technology.

Trend away from bigness, the departure from the belief that "big" necessarily means "good," beginning to manifest itself with respect to "big" brands, "big" stores.

TABLE 6-3
(Continued)

4 Trends that Move Away from Puritan Values

The fourth group of trends measure the penetration of certain values at the expense of the traditional and puritanical values

Trend toward pleasure for its own sake, putting pleasure before duty; changing life-styles and what that means for product usage and communication.

Trend toward blurring of the sexes, moving away from traditional distinctions between men and women and the role each should play in marriage, work, and other walks of life.

Trend toward living in the present, straying from traditional beliefs in planning, saving, and living for the future.

Trend toward more liberal sexual attitudes, the relaxation of sexual prohibitions and the devaluation of "virtue" in the traditional sense, among women.

Trend toward acceptance of stimulants and drugs, greater acceptance of artificial agents (legal and illegal) for mood change, stimulation, and relaxation as opposed to the view that these should be accomplished by strength of character alone.

Trend toward relaxation of self-improvement standards, the inclination to stop working as hard at self-improvement; letting yourself be whatever you are.

Trend toward individual religions, rejection of institutionalized religions and the substitution of more personalized forms of religious experience, characterized by the emergence of numerous small and more intimate religious sects and cults.

5 Trends Related to Child-Centeredness

Children born into the child-centered homes of the 40s and 50s are now in their twenties and teens. Although the consequences of this orientation are difficult to isolate, research indicates that a few important personality characteristics and values associated with them can be identified. These provide the source for the final group of trends—trends which have a direct impact on marketing as well as on other facets of modern life.

Trend toward greater tolerance of chaos and disorder, less need for schedules, routines, plans, regular shopping and purchasing; tolerance of less order and cleanliness in the home; less regular eating and entertaining patterns.

Trend toward challenge to authority, less automatic acceptance of the authority and "correctness" of public figures, institutions, and established brands.

Trend toward rejection of hypocrisy, less acceptance of sham, exaggeration, indirection, and misleading language.

Trend toward female careerism, belief that homemaking is not sufficient as the sole source of fulfillment and that more challenging and productive work for the woman is needed.

Trend toward familism, renewed faith in the belief that the essential life satisfactions stem from activities centering on the immediate family unit rather than on "outside" sources such as work and community affairs.

Source: Reprinted from *The Marketing News,* **4**:7, May 1971, and **4**:8, first of June 1971, published by the American Marketing Association.

---

by consumers. Time-saving goods and services include convenience foods, microwave ovens, disposable diapers, fast-drying paints, fast-food restaurants, supermarket deli operations, professional lawn and household care services, and special airline and rental car procedures to eliminate waiting.

Another factor connected to the work/leisure situation is the role of inflation and the home. Inflation has caused people to evolve a new economic logic, and the home is increasingly being seen as an investment. Consequently, there is more of a focus on obtaining items for the home and spending time in the home, which helps to spur the do-it-yourself market and sales of home technology items such as videocassette recorders and computers.

Second, as people shift their notions about individual rights and responsibilities and increasingly expect that they are entitled (regardless of their ability to pay) to such things as adequate retirement income, comprehensive health care, decent housing, and college educations, consumerism may be expected to expand. This entitlement psychology will lead to an escalation in people's insistence on having their "rights" to safe, proven, nonpolluting products and packaging. More informative and truthful labeling and advertising may also be expected.

Third, the trend toward self-fulfillment and self-realization, with its emphasis on inner- rather than other-directed satisfactions, means that consumers will want to live life to the fullest. There is an unprecedented degree of interest in spending time, money, and effort on maximizing looks and feelings of vigor, vitality, and well-being. Studies have shown that 80 percent of consumers are concerned with "being good to myself" and "improving myself."[35] Consequently, marketing opportunities abound for new products and services aimed at self-fulfillment and improvement. The success of books such as *Looking Out for Number One, How to Be Your Own Best Friend,* and *Pulling Your Own Strings* testifies to this movement, as does the fact that the adult sector is the fastest-growing portion of the education market. Opportunities ranging from hobbies (to satisfy personal creativity needs) to weight watching and whirlpool baths (to satisfy health and personal care needs) should remain strong. The broad-based growth in the elite market will foster an increased interest in elegance, sales of certain kinds of high-end products that people associate with the very wealthy, an interest in more home decorating, and generally more concern with status among the "haves" who desire to flaunt it.

Fourth, the new morality of the market reflects changing attitudes toward sex. Implications of this trend range from acceptance of "anatomically correct" dolls in the toy industry to ads with sexually explicit and frank appeals.

Fifth, the back-to-nature or "simple is better" trend has been influential in the rejection of the artificial and the acceptance of the natural. This has found expression in many product areas including apparel (natural fabrics), toiletries (natural makeup and herbal fragrance shampoos), pharmaceuticals (stressing simple ingredients with no harmful side effects), food (natural ingredients, health foods, and home preserving), and housing (earth tones and indoor plants).[36]

Specific Implications for Marketing Decisions

As cultural changes mold a new American consumer, they have significant implications for marketing strategy, including product-planning, distribution, advertising, and market-segmentation decisions.

Product Planning Assessing consumers' present and emerging value orientations can help the marketer identify new product opportunities and achieve better product positioning among consumer segments.[37] For example, as values such as "pleasure," "an exciting life," "a comfortable life," and "self-respect" increase in importance, the marketer may find a need for having products with brand names, colors, and designs that enhance these important values. Consider a furniture manufacturer who might link these changing values with a growing demand for furniture style and design that incorporate bright colors, bold designs, unique materials of construction, and unusual comfort features.

Value segments containing many consumers suggest that products can be positioned by designing them with attributes which are related to the global values distinguishing that particular market segment. For example, a segment of consumers who regard the values "imaginative," "an exciting life," and "independent" as important might be defined as that group which is concerned with individuality and self-expression. The group might be a reliable segment for marketers of products which are partially finished (such as furniture, pottery, and homes) and products which can be tailored to the individual needs of consumers through the use of accessories, styling, chemical formulation, and so on. Marketers of homes, automobiles, clothing, cosmetics, and fast foods have successfully used this approach.[38]

Therefore, contemporary marketing offerings require periodic audits of product and service lines to determine how well they satisfy the complex needs and wants of changing consumers.

Distribution Channels Changing consumer-value systems may lead to different shopping patterns and new outlets may be necessary to reach consumers.

For instance, the "ego-involved," self-gratification values of the marketplace offer many retailing challenges and opportunities.[39]

- Macy's Cellar in New York has been redesigned to provide an exciting, sensuous environment for merchandise oriented to a very specific, younger Manhattan lifestyle segment.

- A new store in downtown Toronto offers individual shops, boutiques, and little "nooks" with special appeal to very individual tastes; ethnic restaurants; natural foods; designer labels; and even competitive specialty stores geared to new lifestyles.

For time-pressured consumers, retailers may offer in-home catalog shopping or toll-free telephone ordering of merchandise. Stores may use discounts and special offers to shift nonemployed consumers to off-peak hours in order to expedite shopping by the most time-impoverished consumers. Even drive-in churches and funeral parlors exist for those who don't have time to get out of their cars.

Promotion New approaches in copy and artwork are called for in communicating memorably and persuasively with changing consumers. The following suggests a number of ways that advertising is moving to appeal to the values of this new society:

1 Defiance of social taboos. For example, Johnson & Johnson advertises condoms in women's magazines and urges that women suggest use of them to the male.

2 More informative copy. Some good examples here are ads for Sears furniture, Simmons studio beds, automobiles, and microwave ovens.

3 More true-to-life vignettes for television commercials. American Express travelers checks feature this approach.

4 Greater use of so-called damaging admissions such as featuring Avis as "No. 2."

5 More advertising that names and debates competitors. For example, Tylenol and Datril have slugged it out, as have Coke and Pepsi.

6 Increasing genuine appeals to the young generation. Dr. Pepper and McDonald's are good illustrations of this.

7 More advertising segmented toward the higher-educated, higher-income groups. No-fault insurance and advertisements for nutritious cereals are examples.

8 More advertising that frankly acknowledges mounting public cynicism about advertising. For example, a Whirlpool ad featuring its toll-free "Cool-Line" (a customer complaint system) admits that a number of those who read the ad will not believe it, so it challenges them to dial the number.

9 Greater stress on ecology. Exxon and Arm & Hammer are two diverse examples of this approach.

10 More advertising that realistically, not paternalistically, acknowledges women's changing role in our society. New York Life Insurance now aims some of its messages at working women.

11 Increasing recognition of the public's advertising resentments, particularly among higher-income, higher-educated consumers. More sophisticated humor and a lighter touch are evident in such ads as those by Benson & Hedges, Alka-Seltzer, and New England Mutual Life Insurance Company.

12 More advertising that breaks with tradition. Charlie perfume is a classic example here.[40]

Market Segmentation Knowledge of consumer value orientations provides a measurable set of variables, related to needs, which gives the marketer insight beyond merely demographic and psychographic dimensions. The growing diversity of individual tastes, coupled with a hedonistic philosophy and increasing incomes are contributing to ever greater segmentation of the market. Thus, understanding such value shifts in American society could be useful in predicting changing consumption patterns for products. Also, the marketer might be able to identify large market segments on the basis of value profiles and then develop programs that would enhance those values important to each consumer segment. For example, when one group views a product in terms of status and another views it in a more functional way, then different promotional messages are likely to be needed for each group as well as, perhaps, tailored products.

It will be necessary for marketers to assess the changes in size and composition of value segments in the marketplace and to understand the implications of these shifts for company activities. Here, marketing research will be useful for conducting broad-based longitudinal studies to identify changes in value orientations. Such research may be helpful to uncover smaller blocs of consumers within the overall U.S. culture who emphasize significantly different cultural values than the dominant cultural patterns. Such groups are often referred to as *countercultures*. For example, a relatively small but important group which is expected to grow dramatically in the future and is significant because of its very different value pattern is the *voluntary simplicity* (VS) segment. During the 1960s and 1970s, marketers generally dismissed these people as "hippies" or "out-of-touch eccentrics" and were uninterested in reaching them. However, many of these people have evolved into a group comprising approximately 3 percent of the current adult population of the United States. It is estimated that by the year 2000 more than 25 percent of the population will lead lives of partial to complete voluntary simplicity.[41]

There are different value premises, social characteristics, and consumer-behavior patterns between the simplifiers and nonsimplifiers. For example, nonsimplifiers prefer

- Bigger products—"Big is beautiful"
- A greater number of products—"The more the merrier"
- Luxury products—"If it looks good, it is good"
- Me-centered products
- Bigger outlets, such as department stores and shopping centers
- Traditional outlets
- TV and mass-media promotion

However, simplifiers prefer

- Smaller products—"Small is beautiful"
- Fewer products—"Less is better"
- Simple, more functional products
- Quality products
- Products that promote interest and involvement
- Do-it-yourself products
- Smaller, personal stores
- Innovative outlets, such as flea markets and street vendors
- Co-op buying
- Print and radio, *informative* promotion[42]

The growth and development of the VS segment will likely result in significant market-strategy changes. Table 6-4 presents a guide to marketers interested in attracting such buyers.

Tracking Cultural Change

The many studies cited above suggest that attitudes prevailing during one period can change dramatically several years later. Thus, markets must be under continuous surveillance in order to detect the formation of new cultural values.

Several information services are available to monitor the changing cultural pattern of values, attitudes, and lifestyles. More than seventy major companies have supported the research by SRI International in the area of values and lifestyles described above. SRI also publishes a report that identifies society's newest trends so that corporations will have insight into the sort of economic and social conditions in which they will have to do business in the future.[43] Perhaps the best-known research service tracking social changes, however, is that of Yankelovich, Skelly, and White, Inc., the Madison Avenue public opinion and research company. While working for approximately 110 sponsoring companies, Yankelovich produces

TABLE 6-4
A GUIDE TO MARKETING TO VOLUNTARY SIMPLICITY CONSUMERS

Product
Change product concept to appeal to the VS consumer
Make your product simple
Make your product better
Make your product more functional
Strip frills from your product
Make your product more efficient
Make your product personally involving to the consumer
Introduce a do-it-yourself version of the product
Make your product environmentally responsible (e.g., recyclable materials, packages, containers)
Introduce products that help consumers conserve
Use simple packaging
Introduce innovative, energy-conserving products

Price
Do not overprice your product to skim the market; simplifiers hate waste
Price strategically and competitively
Do not be afraid of high prices as long as they represent value; simplifiers tend to use life cycle costing
Do not use price-lining as a means to attract VS consumers
Externalize some of your cost, e.g., unfinished furniture, unassembled products, simple or no packaging

Promotion
Reallocate your promotion budget
Stress value
Stress simplicity, functionalism, and quality
Induce product trial
Use more involving media, especially print and radio
Use more specialized media, e.g. professional magazines, newsletters, etc.
Use more informative, soft sell promotion messages
Use simpler advertising layout and less gloss and hype
Do not rely on traditional personal selling and WOM advertising
Dress down your sales force
Increase product knowledge of salesperson

Channel
Redesign and simplify your channel
Use smaller outlets
Use smaller, more localized warehouses
Increase direct-selling and mail-order activities
Externalize some of your distribution cost and reduce your price (e.g., sell through factory outlets)

Source: Avraham Shama, "Coping with Stagflation: Voluntary Simplicity," *Journal of Marketing,* **45:**129, Summer 1981, published by the American Marketing Association.

"Monitor" which annually tabulates the responses of 2500 people surveyed nationwide about, for example, how important they think it is to plan in advance and how much they enjoy doing things at the spur of the moment. Another service, "Corporate Priorities," examines how the public and a cross section of the leadership community feel toward thirty widely discussed public issues such as pollution control, truth in advertising, and business regulation. The goal of these research services is to provide useful data on broad social trends and changes in values that affect demand for these companies' products and services. Such a need is increasingly recognized by business people.[44]

Assessing cultural change still remains a difficult task, however, and marketers are likely to continue to face problems when attempting to understand, appreciate, and reflect changing cultural values. First, these changes are elusive and hard to define, and their practical effects are frequently indirect. Second, the marketer may tend to ascribe fundamental cultural changes simply to the "generation gap" and incorrectly assume that they are only fads which will quickly disappear. Finally, because change often generates complexity, marketers may resist changing cultural values rather than trying to take advantage of them.[45]

CROSS-CULTURAL UNDERSTANDING OF CONSUMER BEHAVIOR

More and more companies have adopted a global outlook in which the world becomes their market. For example, numerous major corporations such as Coca-Cola, Hoover, IBM, Pfizer, and Gillette receive over half of their earnings from foreign operations, while many others also have significant international markets. Such situations require the marketer's appreciation of cultural differences that exist among international markets and their influence on consumer behavior. In this section some of the marketing implications of these cultural subtleties will be discussed. Unfortunately, there have been rather few published cross-cultural studies of consumer behavior that the marketer may use in making strategy decisions. There have been some important recent examples of research in this area, however.[46]

Need for Cross-Cultural Understanding

When American managers venture abroad they experience what anthropologists call *culture shock,* that is, a series of jolts when encountering the wide variety of customs, value systems, attitudes, and work habits, thus reducing their effectiveness in foreign commercial environments.[47] Therefore, it is crucial to effective operations that the manager be well schooled in the host culture. A lack of understanding of the host culture will lead the manager to think and act as he would in his home culture. Such a *self-reference criterion,* that is, the unconscious reference to one's own cultural values—has been termed the root cause of most international business problems abroad. The goal should be to eliminate this cultural myopia.[48]

The marketer needs a frame of reference with which to understand and evaluate the range of cultural values which may be encountered. A useful conceptualization of the possible range of variations in values found in different cultures has been offered by Kluckhohn. Table 6-5 presents a classification of value orientations which might be encountered by the international marketer. In this model, five model orientations are suggested which are thought to be common to all human groups. These relate to human nature, relationship of man to nature, sense of time, activity, and social relationships. The marketer's task then becomes one of seeking to understand what type of value system predominates in any culture, and relating effectively to that system through marketing activities. Thus, the international marketer would benefit from an attempt to assess and classify the culture of a potential foreign market in terms of the nature of that country's value orientations in order to effectively operate within that system.

When marketing products internationally, a thorough understanding of cultural practices is useful in determining whether a single strategy can be effective in different national environments, or whether several strategies must be adopted, with each geared to the distinctive cultural setting. An interesting example of the role of cultural differences as it affects social marketing concerns the development of blood-donor programs. Cultural differences in the role and significance of this gift require that different marketing approaches be taken in different countries.

> Certain societies influenced by tribal customs feel that blood is an inviolable property which, if taken away, weakens the body for life. Consequently, there is widespread ignorance and fear of blood donations with the result that recruitment of donors outside of "forced" institutional settings is largely unsuccessful. In contrast, educational programs in many industrial societies have reduced fears and anxieties of potential donors by positioning blood donations within the system of social exchanges as a means of redistributing scarce resources in society. In the United Kingdom, for example, the sense of duty is strong, and blood donorship is therefore viewed as a moral obligation to the community. Thus, an almost entirely voluntary donor system exists with no promise of remuneration or future return in kind. In the United States, where the sense of duty to community is not as strong, the appeal has been made on the basis of personal and family interests, with a guarantee of regular blood supply for future family blood needs or financial payments to volunteer donors.[49]

Differences in these blood-donorship programs illustrate the close links between attitudes toward giving blood and a society's value system. Therefore, marketers of such social programs must appreciate these complex forces in order to plan effective strategies.

TABLE 6-5 VARIATIONS IN VALUE SYSTEMS

Orientation	Range		
Human nature	Evil (changeable or unchangeable): Most people are basically evil and can't be trusted.	Mixture of good and evil (changeable or unchangeable): There are evil and good people in the world.	Good (changeable or unchangeable): Most people are basically good and can be trusted.
Man-nature relationship	Subjugation-to-nature: Life is largely controlled by outside forces.	Harmony-with-nature: Live in harmony with nature.	Mastery-over-nature: Man should challenge and control nature.
Time-sense	Past-oriented (tradition bound): Man should learn from and emulate the glorious past.	Present-oriented (situational): Make the most of the present moment. Live for today.	Future-oriented (goal-oriented): Plan for the future in order to make it better than the past.
Activity	Being: The spontaneous expression of impulses and desires. Stress on who you are.	Being-in-becoming: Emphasizes self-realization, development of all aspects of the self as an integrated whole.	Doing: Stressing action and accomplishment.
Social relations	Lineal (authoritarian): Lines of authority are clearly established with dominant-subordinate relationships clearly defined and respected.	Collateral (group-oriented): Man is an individual as well as a group member participating in collective decisions.	Individualistic: Man is autonomous and should have equal rights and control over his own destiny.

Source: Adapted from Florence R. Kluckhohn, "Dominant and Variant Value Orientations," in Clude Kluckhohn and Henry A. Murray (eds.), *Personality in Nature, Society, and Culture,* 2d ed., New York, Alfred A. Knopf, 1953, p. 346.

Decision Areas for the International Marketer

The outline presented in Table 6-6 is suggested for use by the international marketer in conducting cultural analysis. It should also be noted that this outline is perhaps as helpful a framework to the domestic marketer as to the international marketer.

Gaining a better understanding of the host culture is made difficult, however, by problems confronting consumer research abroad. Researchers in underdeveloped foreign markets encounter numerous difficulties in obtaining satisfactory consumer interviews because of a mistrust of strangers asking questions. Moreover, certain subjects may be taboo and thus are not to be discussed, especially with strangers. In a number of countries even the subject of consumption habits is considered inappropriate.[50] In such an environment, it is clear that the marketer will have a difficult time piecing together information on which to base the company's strategies. In the remaining pages, several marketing-decision areas will be discussed to reveal some of the cultural barriers that may be present.

Product Considerations Each country has a different mix of consumption. Therefore, the types of products that are saleable in each culture varies. For example, household appliance ownership data for several neighboring Western European nations shows quite differing consumption patterns, even though these countries are at similar levels of economic development. Such a pattern of consumer behavior can be attributed more to cultural differences than to economic differences.

TABLE 6-6
ELEMENTS OF CONSUMER BEHAVIOR ANALYSIS IN A CROSS-CULTURAL SETTING

1 Determine underlying values and their rate of change within the relevant market: What values are generally held strongly within the general market and the intended market segment? What is the rate and direction of value changes taking place within the relevant culture?

2 Evaluate the product concept as it relates to this culture: Is this product concept one that harmonizes with current and evolving values? If there are value conflicts with ownership of this product, can the product be changed to fit these values? How can the product be effectively identified with positive values? What needs does this product satisfy for members of the culture? Are these needs important? How are competitive products and brands currently satisfying these needs?

3 Determine characteristic purchase decision-making patterns: How do consumers make decisions for this product? Which family members are involved in purchase decision making and use of this product? What role does each member typically play in the process? What purchase criteria and sources of information do consumers use in making buying decisions for this product? What is the cultural attitude toward acceptance of innovations? What cultural values might be congruent with or conflict with purchase and use of this product?

4 Determine appropriate promotion methods: What means of communication exist for advertising to consumers? How is advertising perceived among those in the culture? Must different languages be used to reach various cultural groups? What are the most relevant appeals for this product among the culture? What taboos (such as words, themes, colors, or pictures) exist which may impinge on our sales or advertising strategy? What is the role of the salesman in this culture?

5 Determine appropriate distribution channels: What are the characteristic distribution channels for this product? Are capable institutions available for handling this product? Might new channel opportunities exist which would be readily accepted by consumers? What is the nature of the shopping process for this product?

A product being considered for marketing in a foreign country should be assessed for its "fit" with that country's value system. There are numerous examples in the history of international business of products that succeeded here yet sputtered abroad because they failed to take account of differences between American and other countries' value systems. The following examples are representative:

> Holiday Inns' strategy basically assumed that people are the same all over the world. Consequently, its franchises covered Europe with hotels just like those in America—with chrome, coffee shops, and hamburgers. Unfortunately, there weren't enough traveling Americans to fill them, and the locals were unimpressed with features of the boxy concrete inns. As a result, the company lost millions of dollars. Now, Holiday Inns have begun to ethnicize to look as if they fit in with other hotels in the country where they are located, or at least as if they are ambiguously "European."[51]

> Kentucky Fried Chicken (KFC) had a goal of 100 stores when it opened in Sao Paulo, Brazil in 1973. It struggled along, lost money, and now operates only two stores selling food under the name of "Sanders," since Kentucky Fried Chicken is a tongue twister for most Brazilians. KFC's error may have been lack of knowledge of local eating habits. The local variety of charcoal-broiled chicken, which is sold on practically every street corner, is a lot cheaper than the Colonel's recipe, and favored in taste by many Brazilians. In addition, the stores have been selling Mexican tacos and enchiladas which are virtually unknown in Brazil.[52]

Even such seemingly simple elements as package and product color have played havoc with many international marketers. Consider the following cultural caveats regarding colors:

> An American cleansing-product manufacturer operating in Hong Kong worked up a commercial that showed people tossing hats around in jest with a green hat landing on a male model's head. It was pointed out to the advertiser that among Chinese, a green hat signifies that the man was the husband of an unfaithful wife. As a result, the commercial was dropped. The Singer Co., maker of sewing machines, proposed an outdoor advertising campaign in Hong Kong using bright Prussian blue. Singer's local distributor quickly pointed out that blue of that particular shade is known as the death color. The campaign was halted.[53]

Promotion Considerations Promotion represents another area of marketing strategy that must be culturally tempered. Promotion failures have occurred abroad because of lack of understanding of the foreign culture. Some marketers, for example, have committed fatal bloopers in their zeal simply to export intact their product's brand name or advertising themes to a foreign market or to attempt direct translation of such words, as the following examples illustrate:

"Body by Fisher" became "Corpse by Fisher" in Flemish.

Colgate-Palmolive's "Cue" toothpaste is a pornographic word in French.

Enco means "stalled car" in Japanese—a good reason for changing to Exxon, which is meaningless in any language.

Entire promotion campaigns may even fail due to cultural barriers encountered. The following examples illustrate what may happen when the marketer is unable to overcome the self-reference criterion.[54]

> A U.S. bank advertisement showing a squirrel hoarding nuts was transplanted to a Latin American country. Unfortunately, in this particular country there were no squirrels like the one pictured. Therefore, the public interpreted it as a rat stealing—definitely not a favorable image for the bank.

> Avon Products, Inc. had to reshape its personal selling program for Hong Kong. In the United States, the Avon saleswoman was accustomed to being greeted at the door by the woman of the house and led into the living room where she could sell over a cup of coffee. In Hong Kong, however, it was likely to be a servant peering through a metal gate who met the visitor and announced that the mistress of the household wasn't home. Because of this difference, Avon began recruiting special saleswomen for Hong Kong. They tended to be well-to-do housewives or women at a certain professional level, such as travel consultants or executive secretaries, who were thought to be able to sell to their acquaintances or gain access to women in their neighborhoods who would invite them to stop by.

Channel Considerations Failure to understand the foreign culture when making channel decisions often causes problems, as the following cases indicate:

> Kimberly-Clark in France distributed Kotex through the *pharmacie,* a form of drug store limited to dispensing medicines and related items. The company wanted to add supermarket-type outlets for Kotex, as in the United States. When supermarkets began to handle the product, the *pharmaciens* grew angry over the competition. As a result, they put *all* Kimberly-Clark products under the counter and refused to display them.[55]

> The cultural influence on retailing may be seen in the development of supermarkets in the United Kingdom. Although supermarkets in Britain have substantially increased their share of food sales, the stores are rather small by U.S. standards. Because British housewives lack cars and shop on foot in the neighborhood, each store attracts customers from a relatively small area. In addition, the British housewife is not yet completely attuned to all aspects of typical supermarket shopping. She likes the modern convenience of the supermarket, but she still expects the social relationships which are traditional among small shopkeepers and their customers. In order to maintain this formalized daily shopping and social relationship, many have scheduled their purchases so that they may buy fats and oils on Monday, flour and sugar on Tuesday, and so on. Therefore, executives of U.S. food manufacturers doing business in the United Kingdom must realize that British culture assigns a role to supermarkets that differs from their role in the United States. Successful channel management must take that role into account through the marketing strategies used.[56]

SUMMARY

In this chapter we examined one of the most basic influencing factors in the behavior of consumers—their cultural heritage. We described the nature of culture, its functions, and its components. The core U.S. cultural values were presented and the changing orientation of these values was discussed. This shift in values may have great marketing significance, especially as it presents untapped market opportunities.

The chapter also presented examples of foreign cultural differences in order to warn the potential international marketer against an American self-reference criterion that could prove to be disastrous for decision making abroad.

It can be seen, therefore, that the concept of culture offers many general and specific insights into the behavior of consumers. This, then, is a starting point for the marketer who wishes to better understand his market. It is imperative for the marketer to appreciate cultural nuances governing the relevant marketplace, whether it be in the United States or abroad.

DISCUSSION TOPICS

1 Define culture. What are the most important characteristics of culture that describe its nature?

2 Why is the study of culture important to the marketer?

3 What is the function of culture?

4 What are the core cultural values held by members of the American culture?

5 How have core cultural values changed in the United States over the past generation? What shifts do you expect in these core values over your own generation? What effects are likely on consumer behavior and marketing?

6 Cite examples of marketing practices that either conform to or actively take advantage of core cultural values.

7 Name three products that are presently culturally unacceptable. What marketing strategies would you use to overcome their cultural resistance?

8 Why is an understanding of the foreign cultural environment especially important to the international marketer?

9 Locate two articles on marketing failures by companies operating in a foreign market. Could an improved cultural understanding have prevented these failures? How?

10 Select a specific product and foreign market and perform the cross-cultural analysis outlined in Table 6-6.

NOTES

[1] B. G. Yovovich, "Finding the Answers," *Advertising Age,* July 20, 1981, p. 41.
[2] Ronald D. Michman, "Culture as a Marketing Tool," *Marquette Business Review,* Winter 1975, p. 179.
[3] "Adapting Export Packaging to Cultural Differences," *Business America,* December 3, 1979, p. 3.
[4] Edward B. Taylor, *Primitive Culture,* Murray, London, 1891, p. 1.
[5] Clyde Kluckhohn, "The Study of Culture," in Daniel Lewer and Harold D. Lasswell (eds.), *The Policy Sciences,* Stanford, Stanford, CA, 1951, p. 86.

[6] R. P. Cuzzort, *Humanity and Modern Sociological Thought,* Holt, New York, 1969, p. 356.
[7] James S. Duesenberry, *Income, Saving and the Theory of Consumer Behavior,* Harvard, Cambridge, MA, 1949, p. 19.
[8] Charles Winick, "Anthropology's Contributions to Marketing," *Journal of Marketing,* 25:55–56, July 1961.
[9] Winick, "Anthropology's Contributions," p. 57.
[10] "Corporate Culture," *Business Week,* October 27, 1980, p. 149.
[11] Richard T. LaPiere, *Sociology,* McGraw-Hill, New York, 1946.
[12] Leonard Broom and Philip Selznick, *Sociology, A Text with Adapted Readings,* 4th ed., Harper & Row, New York, 1968, p. 54.
[13] Milton J. Rokeach, *Beliefs, Attitudes, and Values,* Jossey Bass, San Francisco, 1968, p. 161.
[14] Jonathan Gutman and Donald E. Vinson, "Value Structures and Consumer Behavior," in William L. Wilkie (ed.), *Advances in Consumer Research: Volume 6,* Association for Consumer Research, Ann Arbor, MI, 1979, pp. 335–336.
[15] Milton J. Rokeach, "The Role of Values in Public Opinion Research," *Public Opinion Quarterly,* 32:550–551, Winter 1969–1970.
[16] Daniel Yankelovich, *New Rules: Searching for Self-Fulfillment in a World Turned Upside Down,* Random House, New York, 1981.
[17] For examples of the symbols we buy, see Sidney J. Levy, "Symbols for Sale," *Harvard Business Review,* 37:117–124, July-August 1959.
[18] *The Connecticut Mutual Life Report on American Values in the 80s: The Impact of Belief,* Connecticut Mutual, Hartford, CT, 1981, pp. 6–7, 17.
[19] "Why Charities Tighten Their Belts," *U.S. News & World Report,* February 26, 1979, p. 76.
[20] Myles Callum, "Materialism: A Threat to Family Life?" *Better Homes and Gardens,* November 1973, p. 4.
[21] David Riesman, Nathan Glazer, and Reuel Denney, *The Lonely Crowd,* abr. ed., Yale, New Haven, 1961.
[22] See, for example, Walter A. Henry, "Cultural Values Do Correlate with Consumer Behavior," *Journal of Marketing Research,* 13:121–127, May 1976; Joseph F. Hair, Jr. and Rolph E. Anderson, "Culture, Acculturation, and Consumer Behavior," in Helmut Becker and Boris Becker (eds.), *Combined Proceedings,* American Marketing Association, Chicago, 1972, pp. 423–428; and Roy A. Herberger and Dodds I. Buchanan, "The Impact of Concern for Ecological Factors on Consumer Attitudes and Buying Behavior," in Fred C. Allvine (ed.) *Combined Proceedings,* American Marketing Association, Chicago, 1971, pp. 644–646; Donald E. Vinson, Jerome E. Scott, and Lawrence M. Lamont, "The Role of Personal Values in Marketing and Consumer Behavior," *Journal of Marketing,* 41:44–50, April 1977; and Kent L. Granzin and Kenneth D. Bahn, "Do Values Have General Applicability to Retail Market Segmentation?" in Robert H. Ross, Frederick B. Kraft, and Charles H. Davis (eds.), *1981 Southwestern Marketing Proceedings,* The Southwestern Marketing Association, Wichita, KA, 1981, pp. 146–149.
[23] Henry, "Cultural Values," pp. 121–127.
[24] Glenn S. Omura, "Cultural Values as an Aid in Understanding Domestic Versus Foreign Ownership," in John H. Summey and Ronald D. Taylor (eds.), *Evolving Marketing Thought for 1980,* Southern Marketing Association, Carbondale, IL, 1980, pp. 141–144.
[25] Alfred S. Boote, "Psychographics: Mind Over Matter," *American Demographics,* April 1980,
[26] Alfred S. Boote, "An Exploratory Investigation of the Roles of Needs and Personal Values in the Theory of Buyer Behavior," unpublished doctoral dissertation, Columbia University, 1975.
[27] Alfred S. Boote, "Market Segmentation by Personal Values and Salient Product Attributes," *Journal of Advertising Research,* 21:29–35, February 1981.
[28] Francesco M. Nicosia and Robert N. Mayer, "Toward a Sociology of Consumption," *Journal of Consumer Research,* 3:65–75, September 1976.
[29] Niles Howard, "A New Way to View Customers," *Dun's Review,* August 1981, pp. 42–46.
[30] Howard, "A New Way," p. 46.
[31] Daniel Yankelovich, "New Rules in American Life: Search for Self-Fulfillment in a World Turned Upside Down," *Psychology Today,* April 1981, p. 60.
[32] "Smith Outlines Eight Trends to Watch," *Advertising Age,* August 24, 1981, p. 22.
[33] Philip Kotler, *Marketing Management: Analysis, Planning, and Control,* 3d ed., Prentice-Hall, Englewood Cliffs, NJ, 1976, p. 43.
[34] "Changing Attitudes of Youth on Sex, Patriotism and Work," *U.S. News & World Report,* June 3, 1974, pp. 66–67.
[35] Roger D. Blackwell, "Successful Retailers of 80s Will Cater to Specific Lifestyle Segments," *Marketing News,* March 7, 1980, p. 3.
[36] "Urgent: Greater Sensitivity to Social Change," *Grey Matter,* 1976.
[37] "Analyze Lifestyle Trends to Predict Future Product/Market Opportunities," *Marketing News,* July 10, 1981, p. 8.
[38] Vinson, Scott, and Lamont, "The Role of Personal Values," p. 49.
[39] Blackwell, "Successful Retailers," p. 3.
[40] E. B. Weiss, "Creative Advertising Moves Toward the New Society," *Advertising Age,* 4:27–28, July 2, 1973.

[41] "Give Them the Simple Life," *Marketing and Media Decisions,* January 1980, p. 75, 127.
[42] Avraham Shama, "Coping with Stagflation: Voluntary Simplicity," *Journal of Marketing,* 45:128, Summer 1981.
[43] "A Dip Into a Think Tank," *Time,* November 30, 1981, p. 65.
[44] "Information on Values and Lifestyles Needed to Identify Buying Patterns," *Marketing News,* October 5, 1979, p. 1.
[45] Lee Adler, "Cashing-In on the Cop-Out: Cultural Change and Marketing Potential," *Business Horizons,* February 1970, pp. 21–27.
[46] See, for example, Hans B. Thorelli, Helmut Becker, and Jack Engledow, *The Information Seekers,* Ballinger, Cambridge, MA, 1975; Jagdish N. Sheth and S. Prakash Sethi, "Theory of Cross-Cultural Buyer Behavior," *Faculty Working Papers,* University of Illinois, May 31, 1973; Robert T. Green and Eric Langeard, "A Cross-National Comparison of Consumer Habits and Innovation Characteristics," *Journal of Marketing,* 39:34–41, July 1975; and Susan P. Douglas, "Cross-Cultural Comparisons: The Myth of the Stereotype," Marketing Science Institute, Cambridge, MA, 1975.
[47] Lawrence, Stessin, "Incidents of Culture Shock Among American Businessmen Overseas," *Pittsburgh Business Review,* November-December 1971, p. 1.
[48] James A. Lee, "Cultural Analysis in Overseas Operations," *Harvard Business Review,* 44:106, March-April 1966.
[49] Susan Douglas and Bernard Dubois, "Looking at the Cultural Environment for International Marketing Opportunities," *Columbia Journal of World Business,* Winter 1977, pp. 104–105.
[50] Harper W. Boyd, Ronald Frank, William Massy, and Mostafa Zoheir, "On the Use of Marketing Research in the Emerging Economies," *Journal of Marketing Research,* 1:23, November 1964.
[51] "An Idea That Didn't Travel Well," *Forbes,* February 15, 1976, pp. 26–27.
[52] Jose R. Penteado, Jr., "U.S. Fast-Foods Move Slowly," *Advertising Age,* May 25, 1981, p. S-8.
[53] Nicole Seligman, "Be Sure Not to Wear a Green Hat if You Visit Hong Kong," *The Wall Street Journal,* May 10, 1979, p. 1.
[54] Seligman, "Be Sure," p. 41.
[55] Vern Terpstra, *International Marketing,* 2d ed., The Dryden Press, Hinsdale, IL, 1978, p. 364.
[56] Jac Goldstucker, "The Influence of Culture on Channels of Distribution," in Robert L. King (ed.), *Marketing and the New Science of Planning,* American Marketing Association, Chicago, 1968, p. 470.

CHAPTER 7
SUBCULTURES

We learned in the previous chapter that one's cultural heritage has a very basic and lasting influence on his or her consumer behavior. Culture was seen to consist of basic behavioral patterns which exist in a society. However, as we saw from the discussion of countercultures, not all segments of a society have the same cultural patterns. Perhaps, therefore, the market can distinguish more homogeneous subgroups within the heterogeneous national society.

We refer to these groups as *subcultures* because they have values, customs, traditions, and other ways of behaving that are peculiar to a particular group within a culture. This means that there are subcultures of students, professors, professional football players, prison inmates, rock musicians, marketers, and other groups. Moreover, individuals may be members of more than one subculture at the same time. Thus, it is imperative that marketers understand who constitutes the most relevant subculture for their particular product or service. By knowing the characteristics and behavioral patterns of the segment they are trying to reach, they are in a better position to refine the marketing mix required to properly satisfy that target segment.

Although subcultures may be categorized along seemingly infinite dimensions, this chapter will examine only a few of the less-understood, but important, subcultures that exist in the United States. The fact that these groups are among the most easily identifiable subcultures in the United States makes their segmentation feasible. This chapter examines consumer behavior within two broad subculture categories: ethnic and age. A final point must be made before proceeding to a discussion of these subcultures, however. The groups to be discussed in this chapter should not be considered monolithic. That is, in spite of numerous similarities within any subculture, it is not merely one homogeneous market, but instead consists of various subsegments.[1]

Ethnic is the generic term used to describe the approximately 106 groups in America characterized by a distinctive origin. Generally, it refers to the minority groups of a society. Their members are identified as such at birth, and they have a shared tradition and social life. Ethnic identification is based on what a person *is* when he or she is born, and it is largely unchangeable after that.[2]

Consumers may be subdivided into the following three types of ethnic dimensions, only the first two of which will be examined further in this chapter:

1 *Race*—Racial subcultures are made up of people with a common biological heritage involving certain physical distinctions. The two most significant minority races in the United States for the marketer are blacks and Orientals. We will examine only the black market, however.

2 *Nationality*—People with a common national origin constitute another ethnic subculture. The nationality grouping is usually characterized by a distinctive language or accent. The minority market segment to be discussed in this category will be the Hispanics.

3 *Religion*—Religious subcultures are comprised of people with a common and unique system of worship. Two important minority religious segments are Jews and Catholics. However, useful knowledge about the consumer behavior of these groups is presently quite limited and will not be discussed in this chapter.[3]

The ethnic dimensions will now be illustrated by discussing two examples of important U.S. subcultures. Then two subcultures based on age will be discussed to better understand how consumer behavior varies among such groups.

THE BLACK SUBCULTURE

There are four reasons why the black market exists and is important: (1) the people making up this market are identifiable, (2) they have definable purchase patterns, (3) the market is very large, and (4) the market is concentrated in certain locations within the United States. This section will review some unique aspects of black consumer behavior and relevant marketing strategy implications.

Demographic Characteristics

Generally, blacks may be described as disadvantaged compared with whites in terms of education and occupational attainment. They are also more likely than whites to live in the crowded, poorer neighborhoods of large cities.

Size In 1980, the black market amounted to more than 26 million people, or almost 12 percent of the total U.S. market. The market increased 17 percent during the 1970s, and it is projected to comprise 36 million people by the year 2000.

Location Although the percentage of blacks in the total U.S. population has remained rather constant since 1900, their geographic distribution has changed significantly during the last few decades. The percent living in the south has decreased slowly, yet it still accounts for about half of all blacks in the United States and for approximately 20 percent of the region's population (compared with a less-than-10-percent share of the population in the north and west).

Income and Employment Patterns Black buying power in 1980 stood at more than $140 billion. However, while the ratio of black family income to that of whites has increased, black income is still far below that of whites.[4]

The proportion of blacks in each occupational category is beginning to approximate more closely their share of the total labor force. Thus, more members of this group have moved into skilled, better-paying jobs.

Education On this factor, blacks have steadily improved their position. Between 1970 and 1975, the enrollment of blacks in college increased about 80 percent, and the number of black college graduates increased 65 percent. Nevertheless, approximately twice the proportion of whites in each age group have completed one or more years of college as compared with blacks.

Family and Age Patterns One of the most striking patterns of the black family is its tendency toward matrilinealism. Almost 34 percent of all black families are headed by a female, compared to only about 10 percent of white families.

A final characteristic that distinguishes this group is its age distribution. It is considerably younger than the white population—with a median age of 22 compared to 29 for whites.

Psychographic Characteristics

Recent lifestyle and psychographic segmentation research on the black market has led to numerous interesting and useful findings, some of which are presented in Table 7-1. The Leo Burnett advertising agency has concluded that black female lifestyle patterns, particularly in an urban setting, indicate a stronger interest in style and fashion than those of whites.[5] There is also less mobility and less involvement in traditional civic and community organizations, greater reliance on the electronic media, and a stronger sense of alienation than with the average white American. Black women also have a stronger commitment to the importance of work and a clearer career orientation than do white women. Their lifestyle patterns and attitudes generally reveal the importance of money and budgeting and the need to be conservative, smart shoppers. As reflects their generally lower incomes, black women are more value conscious, more expectant of future income gains,

TABLE 7-1
BLACK AND WHITE LIFESTYLE DIFFERENCES

	Percent Agreed White	Percent Agreed Black
Strong Pride toward Home		
I take great pride in my home	73%	77%
I get satisfaction out of cleaning because that is what people notice	29	46
I am a very neat person	50	66
A house should be dusted and polished at least three times a week	23	41
A Desire to Improve It		
I would like to move to a larger house	33	47
I like ultra-modern style furniture	14	34
When buying appliances, it pays to get the best even though it's more expensive	61	73
I like to own the most expensive things	14	25
Attitudes toward Money Management		
Our income is satisfactory	48	27
Our family is too heavily in debt today	15	32
I wish we had more money	46	71
Five years from now our income will be a lot higher	39	48
Grocery shopping for my family means following a strict budget	34	43
I watch the advertisements for sales	66	70
I study the grocery store ads in the newspaper each week	66	74

Source: Leo Burnett Company.

and heavier advertising readers. In spite of this orientation, there appears to be little advertising directed toward the black woman acknowledging her needs and attitudes in this area of price and value.[6]

There also are important differences between middle-class black and middle-class white women in the area of the home. Black women have a stronger self-perception about neatness and traditional home pride. They work hard to keep their home neat and clean, and they have a strong desire to live even better in the future and to make improvements such as installing better fixtures and dependable appliances.

Although lifestyle research has found that there are really more similarities than differences between black and white women, there are still a number of implications from findings such as those cited above. First, since black families are larger than white ones, with more working mothers, this group could be an excellent target for many convenience foods and home appliances. Second, because of the unrealized aspirations among black women, advertisers should be careful not to "overpromise" them. Third, their shopping patterns suggest that advertising to black women could stress price and value. Finally, this group appears to be a promising market for home cleaning and personal hygiene products.

Consumer Behavior and Marketing Implications
The following examples illustrate some of the differences between black consumers and the general market:[7]

> How would you advertise liquor and automobiles to blacks? According to a New York advertising executive, not without carefully understanding men's and women's roles in black families. In white families, wives have become increasingly influential in the selection of liquor brands. However, the black male has remained much more dominant in brand selection than his white counterpart. Thus, effective scotch promotion relies on appealing to black masculinity. Scotch is known as the "black man's martini" whereas gin is perceived as a woman's drink. Failing to understand such perceptions, a major scotch and several bourbon brands have hurt their standing by depicting women in ads to blacks. Similarly, one must be careful about depicting families in car ads aimed at blacks. Among blacks, cars are more an individual, ego-oriented product. Unlike white consumers' idea of a "family car," for black men automobiles are a "man's car" that the family just happens to use.

Now let us examine some specific consumer-behavior findings regarding this market. We shall look at the most important elements and see how they relate to marketing-strategy variables.

Product Purchase Patterns Research studies show that there are important differences between black and white purchasing patterns.[8] For example, with regard to the general spending behavior of blacks versus whites, the following three major findings have emerged:

1 Total consumption expenditures are less than for comparable-income whites; that is, blacks save more out of a given income than do whites.

2 Black consumers spend more for clothing and nonautomobile transportation and less for food, housing, medical care, and automobile transportation than do comparable-income whites.

3 There is no consistent racial difference in expenditures for either recreation and leisure or for home furnishing and equipment at comparable income levels.[9]

There are some rather obvious reasons that account for these consumption differences, as well as some reasons that are more subtle.[10] For example, with regard to owning major home appliances, low ownership appears to be primarily related to low income, substandard housing, and lack of proper utility connections. Another reason behind the different black and white consumption patterns is the blacks' narrower spectrum of choice due to their history of discrimination. That is, blacks have had less selectivity in the purchase of homes, vacations, travel, dining, entertainment, and so on, which has resulted in a greater expenditure per unit on other things that are available to them.[11] Nevertheless, the pattern is changing so that today blacks are spending more for such things as housing, recreation, travel, and education. Effective marketing and public relations campaigns by such companies as American Airlines, PepsiCo, and Greyhound have both influenced and benefited from such changing patterns.[12]

Another factor that may cause these different consumption patterns is thought to be the tendency by minority groups to engage in *compensatory consumption,* that is, an attempt to purchase the material goods that are reflective of their achievement of full status in American society. Results of product-usage research, in fact, support this general pattern and suggest that blacks spend more on socially visible products than do whites of the same income class.

It is important to recognize that minorities may use the same products for different reasons and in different ways than do others in the general market. For example, whites use Tide almost exclusively as a laundry detergent, while blacks may use it as a general purpose cleaner, even for washing floors. Therefore, advertising to different segments might reflect why certain consumers need specific products and how they can use them.

Studies have consistently shown that blacks are prone to buy brands that are nationally advertised, those that have a prestige connotation, and those about which they can feel confident.[13] In fact, as prices increase, the movement of black consumers toward private labels and generics is slower than it is for the general population.[14] It has been found that blacks in some shopping situations remain loyal to some national brands even when prices are raised 45 percent or more.[15]

Black consumers are open to trying new products if those products are appropriately presented as items that can perhaps help them live better, save time, or achieve more status. For example, pop wines were positioned as a new, stylish drink to enjoy when having fun, and they immediately became popular with blacks.

One factor affecting new-product adoption has been found to be the social visibility of the product. Blacks appear to be less-innovative than whites with respect to appliances and food—two nonsocially visible items. They are more innovative than whites, however, with respect to socially visible fashions and clothing.[16] Blacks appear to be trend-setters in fashion, hair styles, shoes, and evening apparel.[17] The understanding that black fashion innovation may have different characteristics than that for whites, however, offers opportunities for developing appropriate marketing strategies to deal with those variations. For instance, black female innovators place greater emphasis on the area of credit/billing policies offered by retailers than do whites. They also possess fewer credit cards, have different media patterns (for example, they are much more likely to prefer rock/jazz radio programming as opposed to white's easy-listening music preferences), and have significantly less participation in formal group memberships and organized social activities than do whites.[18]

Shopping Behavior The black market has also been researched on the basis of its shopping patterns. Here, too, differences have been found between whites and blacks. While much of the research deals with food-purchasing habits, other product shopping patterns have also been investigated.

Table 7-2 presents the results of a study by *Progressive Grocer* on factors influencing store choice. Notice that blacks' assessment of supermarkets generally match those of the population at large. There are several differences, however, that could prove useful to supermarket managers when planning marketing strategy. Although brand loyalty is generally high, store loyalty is not as strong. One study showed that only 59 percent of blacks are always or almost always satisfied with the food stores where they do most of their shopping, compared to 72 percent of whites.[19]

No firm conclusion can yet be drawn about black shopping patterns in non-food stores. However, one study did find that blacks frequented discount stores (as opposed to department stores) more often than did whites (although this finding tends to vanish where upper-income blacks are concerned).[20] A probable reason for this patronage is the emphasis on price by black shoppers. Another reason could be related to the atmosphere of large department stores, which has been found to cause some feelings of insecurity among black shoppers.[21]

Clothing purchases by black women have also been the subject of some research studies. A general pattern appears to be the frequent use of department, discount, and chain stores by black women and of department and specialty stores by white women. Findings seem to differ, though, depending on factors such as age, geographic location, social class, and fashion consciousness.[22]

Promoting to Blacks The lack of fuller understanding of black consumer behavior has probably perplexed marketers most in the area of promotion. For instance, marketers have wondered whether they should promote in a specialized way through specialized media to reach the black market, or whether they should expect to reach it through their general appeal to the broad market of consumers. In addition, concern exists regarding whether advertisements should be all-black in content, or mixed, or all-white. These questions are addressed in this section.

MEDIA PATTERNS The issue of specialized versus general advertising programs cannot be resolved easily, but one can obtain a better understanding of the problem by looking at the alternatives. There are three main avenues that may be taken in a specialized appeal to blacks—radio, magazines, and newspapers aimed specifically at the black market. Television, a fourth approach, has been tried, but only to a limited extent. The big advantage of black media is that blacks know the advertisement is meant for them, while in other media they may not always be sure.

Black media have developed mainly since World War II, and they include

TABLE 7-2

HOW 37 FACTORS AFFECT BLACK SHOPPERS' SUPERMARKET CHOICE

\multicolumn{2}{c}{Importance to Black Shoppers}	Factor	Importance to All Shoppers**
Rank	Index*	Factor	Rank
1	98.0	Cleanliness	1
2	97.8	Good meat department	7
3	97.0	All prices clearly labeled	2
4	96.6	Freshness date marked on products	6
5	95.6	Low prices	3
5	95.6	Good produce department	5
7	95.5	Accurate, pleasant checkout clerks	4
8	93.8	Good dairy department	11
9	93.3	Shelves usually well-stocked	8
10	92.5	Helpful personnel in service departments	12
11	91.1	Convenient store location	10
12	90.5	Good layout for fast, easy shopping	13
13	89.6	Good parking facilities	9
14	89.1	Good frozen foods department	21
15	88.6	Good selection of nationally advertised brands	16
16	87.6	Short wait for checkout	15
17	87.5	Frequent "sales" or "specials"	14
17	87.5	Aisles clear of boxes	19
19	86.8	Good selection of low-priced store-brand items	18
20	86.0	Don't run short of items on "special"	17
20	86.0	Pleasant atmosphere/decor	24
22	85.8	Baggers on duty	20
23	85.1	New items that I see advertised are available	23
24	84.7	Unit pricing on shelves	22
25	83.8	Manager is friendly and helpful	25
26	83.0	Check-cashing service	26
27	73.8	Not usually overcrowded	27
28	73.6	Open late hours	30
29	69.3	Good drugs and toiletries section	33
30	67.0	Good assortment of nonfoods merchandise	29
31	65.8	Carry purchases to car	28
32	60.6	Eye-catching mass displays	34
33	59.6	Has in-store bakery	31
34	57.3	Has delicatessen department	32
35	52.0	Trading stamps or other extras	36
36	39.0	People know my name	35
37	37.5	Sell hot foods to take out or eat in store	37

*In filling out the questionnaire, respondents rated each characteristic on a scale of 1-to-6. Their answers were converted into a 0-to-100% index. This means that the larger the proportion of people who gave a top rating, the closer the score is to the highest possible index figure: 100.0

**Based on a P.G.-H.T.I. survey of a national sample of housewives which included blacks in proportion to their incidence in the population.

Source: Robert F. Dietrich, "When Blacks Choose a Super, Some Departments Matter More," *Progressive Grocer,* August 1975, p. 34. Reprinted with permission.

dozens of magazines, several hundred newspapers and radio stations, and one TV channel. Only a very small amount of all advertising, however, is placed in those media. Of the more than $14 billion spent in advertising each year, barely 1 percent is spent in black media, and slightly more than that is spent in advertising specifically created for the black consumer.[23]

The major black-oriented medium is radio, since research shows that blacks spend more time listening to radio than do whites. Moreover, approximately one-half of all listening done by blacks is to black radio stations.[24] Black magazines are read widely by both black men and women, and have substantially higher readership than general-market magazines. Blacks have a strong attachment to such media because they emphasize their achievements in government, business, sports, and the arts. For example, *Ebony* and *Jet* are the two most widely read magazines among both black men and women.[25]

Although there are numerous black-oriented radio and magazine vehicles, black television programming is less widespread. There have been a few network shows featuring blacks and their lifestyles, with black situation comedies being the most popular. Daytime soap operas, news, and game shows also have high viewership among blacks. There is also an increase in the amount of syndicated television programming being developed for this audience. However, television is primarily a white-oriented medium, and as such, many marketing experts doubt that sole reliance on television can effectively sell this ethnic market. In fact, reliance on black-oriented prime-time network series programming to deliver massive tune-in by blacks may not even be justified. An Arbitron television study provides data indicating that in some markets, more blacks would be reached with commercials on some white-oriented programs than on the top black-oriented shows.[26]

Outdoor advertising should also be mentioned as an attractive vehicle by which blacks can be reached because of their geographic concentration. Alka-Seltzer, for example, has used two versions of the same billboard ad. The words are the same on both, but black models are used in black areas and white models in other areas. Liquor, beer, soft-drink, and cigarette manufacturers are other frequent users of outdoor ethnic advertising.

DEVELOPING EFFECTIVE MESSAGES The use of black and white models in integrated ads for general coverage media has been fairly recent. Since 1963, blacks have begun to appear in magazine and TV advertisements, and most research on integrated advertising has shown that both races react favorably to such ads.[27] In most situations it appears that the marketer may use blacks and whites in advertising with favorable results. "Tokenism" in advertising, however, is not viewed favorably among blacks. Therefore, the marketer must take care to avoid such an impression.

Even advertising themes or appeals may need tailoring to special market segments as the following examples show:

> A&P developed its "Price and Pride" campaign for the general market. However, the company was under a great deal of pressure because of its lack of attention to the black consumer. In tone and approach, Mr. Price and Mr. Pride reaffirmed A&P's negative position as far as the black consumer was concerned. Thus, for the black community, A&P came up with the "We're Going to Make Your Bag Our Bag" campaign. In its first phase, the campaign

told black consumers that A&P heard their dissatisfaction and was going to change. Subsequent advertising featured foods purchased more heavily by blacks and black health and beauty aids. The company chose TV, black radio, and black magazines such as *Ebony* and *Essence* to reach its desired segment.[28]

AT&T Long Lines, capitalizing on the desire of people to keep in touch with friends and relatives, has worked hard to include a variety of ethnic groups in its ads. In addition, specific alterations have been made so that certain ads would appeal more to a black audience. For instance, Ella Fitzgerald and other black artists have been used to sing the "Reach Out" theme, and black print and radio media are also used.[29]

Thus, companies should test different appeals among market segments to find which one works best.

Blacks have a distinctive way of looking at ads. They tend to view advertising as doing two things—selling the product and contributing to the overall process of building the image of black people in general. Thus, the marketer should carefully attempt to accomplish both goals. The use of a black celebrity is one way that companies can mount effective promotion programs. A recent survey found that 49 percent of the blacks surveyed said they would be more likely to purchase a product featuring a black ad representative.[30] Consequently, a number of highly regarded blacks have been used in ad compaigns by major companies. For instance, Bill Cosby advertises Del Monte vegetables and Jell-O Puddings (see Figure 7-1), O. J. Simpson advertises Hertz car rentals, Muhammad Ali appears on some public service advertisements, and Reggie Jackson is featured in Volkswagen Rabbit commercials.

THE HISPANIC SUBCULTURE

Hispanics are the nation's second-largest and fastest-growing minority market. In spite of their potential as a consumer goods market, however, they are not well understood by marketers. This is a segment with which the marketer should be familiar. Moreover, the future impact of this group on the United States and on the marketer is expected to be even greater. In order to bring this market more clearly into focus, the important demographic characteristics of this market will first be presented. This will be followed by a discussion of the most significant consumer behavior and marketing implications.

Demographic Characteristics

The Hispanic market differs radically from other ethnic segments and mainstream America in that it is continually infused with new immigrants from the Spanish-speaking world. The old country is never far away, either symbolically or geographically. This group also clings tenaciously to the Spanish language, the Catholic church, and the family unit, and it generally defies the melting-pot concept. Many Hispanics, although they like the idea of living in America, want to keep their culture and language. For example, almost half consider themselves "Hispanic first, American second." Of the remainder, almost all say "Hispanic and American equally."[31]

Size In 1980, the size of this market was approximately 15 million people. Between 1970 and 1980, this segment increased by 61 percent (partially due to a more complete census count of all Hispanics, including the very large number of illegal Hispanic aliens in the United States). During this period, the Hispanic's proportion of the U.S. population grew from 4.7 to 6.4 percent. At the present rate of growth, this segment will become the country's largest ethnic group by the year 1990 or even sooner.[32] A large portion of this market's growth comes from immigration. More than six in ten Hispanic-American adults were born outside the United States.

The U.S. Hispanic population is largely of Mexican origin (61 percent of the total), with Puerto Ricans (15 percent) and Cubans (7 percent) comprising the other significant categories of origin.

Location The Spanish subculture is largely an urban population segment. For example, in 1980 about 82 percent of all Hispanics lived in metropolitan areas, compared to 67 percent of the non-Hispanic population. Moreover, the Hispanic population is concentrated heavily in comparatively few metropolitan areas such as Los Angeles, New York, and Miami, and in a few states—Texas, New Mexico, Arizona, California, Colorado, New York, Pennsylvania, New Jersey, and Florida.[33]

Income and Employment Patterns The income level of Hispanic families is significantly lower than for families of non-Hispanic origin. The median income

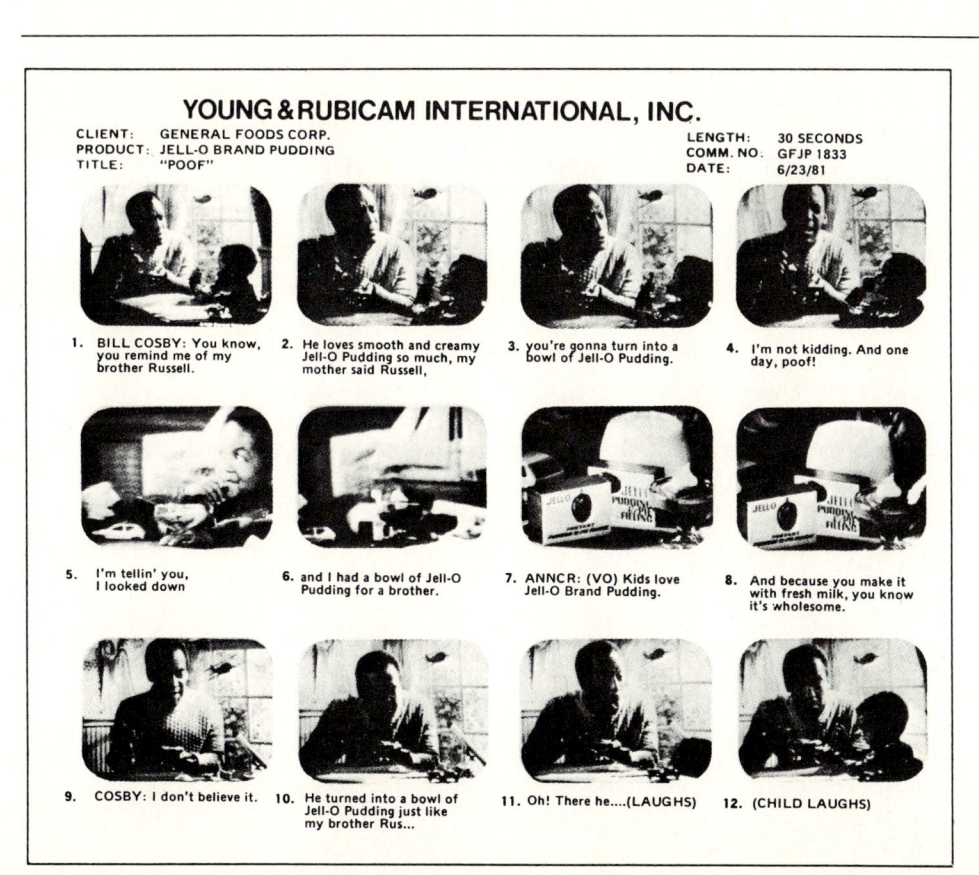

FIGURE 7-1

Advertisement for Jell-O Brand Pudding. (Courtesy of General Foods Corporation.)

YOUNG & RUBICAM INTERNATIONAL, INC.
CLIENT: GENERAL FOODS CORP.
PRODUCT: JELL-O BRAND PUDDING
TITLE: "POOF"
LENGTH: 30 SECONDS
COMM. NO.: GFJP 1833
DATE: 6/23/81

1. BILL COSBY: You know, you remind me of my brother Russell.
2. He loves smooth and creamy Jell-O Pudding so much, my mother said Russell,
3. you're gonna turn into a bowl of Jell-O Pudding.
4. I'm not kidding. And one day, poof!
5. I'm tellin' you, I looked down
6. and I had a bowl of Jell-O Pudding for a brother.
7. ANNCR: (VO) Kids love Jell-O Brand Pudding.
8. And because you make it with fresh milk, you know it's wholesome.
9. COSBY: I don't believe it.
10. He turned into a bowl of Jell-O Pudding just like my brother Rus...
11. Oh! There he....(LAUGHS)
12. (CHILD LAUGHS)

for Hispanic families in 1978 was $12,600, compared to $17,900 for non-Hispanic families. In higher-income brackets this disparity continues with only 13.5 percent of Hispanic families earning more than $25,000, compared to 28.6 percent of the families of non-Hispanic origin.

Occupations of men of Hispanic origin are predominantly blue-collar in nature. Approximately 58 percent of Hispanic men are blue-collar workers, while only 24 percent work at white-collar occupations.

Education Hispanics generally attain a lower level of education than do non-Hispanics. Among people 25 to 29 years of age, approximately 57 percent have completed high school as compared to more than 87 percent of persons of non-Hispanic origin. However, Hispanics believe *saber es poder* (knowledge is power), and younger Hispanics are rapidly closing the education gap.

Family and Age Patterns Hispanic families are, on the average, larger than non-Hispanic families, with the mean number of persons in the Spanish-origin family being 3.85 as compared to 3.28 for non-Spanish-origin families. The family unit also appears to be stronger than does the family unit for non-Hispanics.

The Hispanic market is a much younger market than is the non-Hispanic market. The median age for Hispanics is 22, with approximately 41 percent of the Hispanic market being less than 18 years of age, as compared to 28 percent for the non-Spanish origin population.

Psychographic Characteristics

In spite of the background, migration, and socioeconomic differences among the Hispanic nationality subgroups, there is a great degree of homogeneity in their lifestyle patterns. In comparison with others, some interesting results show up. Table 7-3 presents data comparing the general U.S. population with Hispanics on several lifestyle and product-ownership dimensions.

Consumer Behavior and Marketing Implications

More and more companies are recognizing the importance of the Hispanic-American market. In this section, several of the marketing-mix variables will be examined to understand the major implications of Spanish-American consumer behavior on these decision areas.

Product Purchase Patterns The marketer should be aware that the Hispanic market is highly individualistic in its product and brand preferences, which are often reflective of cultural differences. For some products, particularly food purchases, this market is very significant. Partly because of their larger-than-average families, they spend about 10 percent more per week on food purchases than do other groups. In addition, more Hispanic households visit fast-food restaurants frequently than do non-Hispanic consumers. For example, 20 percent of Hispanic homes visit such outlets more than once per week, versus 9 percent of the non-Hispanic homes.[34] They are also much heavier consumers of beverages such as soft drinks and beer. The Schaefer Brewing Company, for example, estimates Spanish beer consumption to be 1.5 times greater than the national average.

Hispanic Americans are highly brand loyal, trusting well-known, high-quality, and familiar brands. For example, the U.S. Hispanic population is more likely than the U.S. anglo population to stress product quality, to value name or advertised brands, and to be brand loyal, yet, at the same time, to seem receptive to new products.[35] Such strong Hispanic brand loyalty can be a significant resource for a company. For example, a marketing research study within the Los Angeles market shows that Hispanics prefer U.S. autos over imports by a 9 percent margin. Thus, they have a greater likelihood of purchasing U.S. cars than do anglo new-car buy-

TABLE 7-3

HISPANIC LIFE-STYLE AND PRODUCT OWNERSHIP CHARACTERISTICS

Percent Who Agree/Strongly Agree with Statements	Hispanics Total	Puerto Rico	Mexico	Cuba	Other	United States Total
Optimism In Improved Standard of Living						
It is becoming harder to be optimistic that our standard of living in the future is going to be better than it is now	61	67	58	60	66	77
Pleasure from Work						
I don't expect to get much pleasure from my work. Work is just what you do to earn a living	41	46	37	35	52	24
Materialism/Tangibles						
I prefer to spend money on tangible things that I can keep rather than on things that give me temporary enjoyment like a vacation and so on	61	75	55	51	74	48
Live for Today						
I try to have as much fun as I can now and let the future take care of itself	36	29	36	29	41	47
Feelings of Despair						
I often feel there is nothing in this world worth striving for	24	27	22	12	37	16
Interest in Change						
I need to satisfy my hunger for new experiences	62	55	61	65	68	62
Physical Attractiveness						
I need to keep up with the new styles	49	51	42	69	64	46
Physical Fitness						
We are all getting soft; it is more important today than ever to take special measures to maintain our health	86	92	85	79	86	90
Individualism						
People should be free to look, dress, and live the way they want to whether others like it or not						
1. Fits me very well	47	50	42	47	55	43
2. Fits me pretty well	33	24	35	39	33	31
3. All right for others	14	12	17	10	8	17
4. Don't approve at all	6	14	6	4	4	9
Nonconformity						
Many people are puzzled by the changing values of this country. They feel it's difficult to know whether something that is wrong today will still be wrong a year from now. Other people are not at all influenced by changing values; they have their own long-standing personal standards of right and wrong to guide them						
1. Puzzled by changing values	28	45	25	35	30	27
2. Uncertain	25	30	23	37	21	16
3. Guided by personal standards	47	25	52	28	49	57

TABLE 7-3

(Continued)

Percent Who Agree/Strongly Agree with Statements	Hispanics Total	Puerto Rico	Mexico	Cuba	Other	United States Total
Attitude toward Family						
There should be less emphasis on family togetherness and more on the individual						
1. Fits me very well	14	11	10	9	31	13
2. Fits me pretty well	19	20	19	13	23	19
3. All right for others	23	21	23	44	14	24
4. Don't approve at all	44	48	48	34	32	44
Attitude toward Sex Roles						
Being Masculine Means:						
A good provider to his wife and family	55	67	57	58	37	36
Someone you can depend on in times of need	15	10	17	13	12	23
Just a person who happens to have been born a male rather than a female	9	6	9	7	11	18
A leader, not a follower	5	4	3	3	12	10
Sexually attractive to women	3	1		4	12	9
Makes the important decisions for the family	10	9	11	12	7	4
Careers for Women						
Suppose a married woman with children wants to work and is able to handle her home and family while pursuing a career. How do you feel about it?						
Such a woman should definitely be given the opportunity to have a career	48	46	49	56	45	48
Even if she wants to and can work, a woman with children and home responsibilities should only consider part-time work while her children are in school	29	30	29	15	30	35
Unless the extra money is needed, a woman with children should not have an outside job, even is she wants one	23	24	22	26	25	17
Luxury Product Ownership (Percent Who Own):						
Color TV	83	82	83	94	80	83
Stereo equipment	71	81	66	83	73	63
Sewing machine	50	42	54	63	38	57
Tape recorder	47	46	42	62	60	51
TV videogame	11	4	13	20	7	18

Source: Yankelovich, Skelly and White, Inc., *Spanish U.S.A.: A Study of the Hispanic Market in the United States,* The SIN National Television Network, New York, June 1981, pp. 10, 11, 13.

ers. This finding should be of much interest to U.S. car manufacturers, such as Chrysler, in their battles with foreign imports. Despite this favorable Hispanic predisposition toward domestic cars, however, Chrysler has only recently begun to advertise specifically to this group via Spanish-language ads.[36]

The market is also interested in status symbols. Because most Hispanics have come to the United States from poorer countries seeking a better life, they are often interested in purchasing those things that demonstrate that they have "arrived." Bulova watches offer a good example of this attitude:

In 1967, the Bulova image among Hispanics was that of a cheap American product. To counter this attitude, the company began to position itself among this segment as an expensive, but affordable, piece of jewelry. Bulova stressed its use of gold and accentuated the fact that it had an extensive line of 18-karat gold watches—because to Hispanics "14-karat" is synonymous with "gold-plated." By 1979, Bulova enjoyed a 40 percent share of the Hispanic market.[37]

This subculture generally exhibits more new-product openness than do U.S. consumers as a whole. For example, compared with non-Hispanic consumers, a greater percentage of Hispanic shoppers say they seek:

- New foods to eat at home
- New supermarkets and department stores to shop in
- New laundry and household cleaning products to use
- New types of beer, liquor, and cocktails to drink
- New magazines to read
- New TV programs to watch[38]

Because of value differences between Hispanics and mainstream Americans, different product benefits may need to be stressed when selling to the Hispanic segment compared to the non-Hispanic segment. For instance,

New York Telephone Co. wanted to sell Hispanics on the convenience of having one's own telephone at home. Its advertising agency suggested minor adaptation of a general market ad saying, "Hi, Fernando. Hi, Rosa. Keep in touch with friends. Get your own phone." However, it became apparent that no low-income Hispanic man would plunk down a big deposit to buy a phone so his wife could say "Hi" to her friends. Instead a campaign was created by a Hispanic agency calling the telephone "El amigo de la familia a la mano," or "The friend of the family at hand," in which the strong motivation of security was used. The phone could be used by a working mother to call her children at home or by an older person to call the doctor; in emergencies or bad weather the phone would always be at hand. Spanish-speaking operators took orders for over $2 million worth of new phones in 2 years.[39]

Shopping Behavior With regard to store selection, research has shown that many Spanish-speaking housewives feel lost in giant supermarkets where they are surrounded by many unfamiliar products and are inhibited about asking questions. Because such uneasiness exists with regard to large stores, Hispanics do a large amount of their shopping in bodegas, which are small neighborhood stores where only Spanish may be spoken. For example, in New York, bodegas account for 30 percent of the grocery volume among Spanish-speaking residents.

Promoting to Hispanics The Hispanic market, although concentrated geographically and in urban areas, is sometimes difficult to reach because of the language barrier. A 1981 survey found that approximately 90 percent of the adult Hispanic population speak Spanish and 43 percent speak "only enough English to get by."[40] Therefore, in order to effectively reach this market, Spanish-language media frequently must be used.[41] In fact, 70 percent of Hispanics watch, listen to, or read Spanish media every week. Half of them use Spanish media primarily (that is, 50 percent or more of the time). Of the Spanish media, television is used most, followed closely by radio, and print is a distant third.[42]

MEDIA PATTERNS[43]   Television has developed into an important medium for Spanish advertising, with thirteen stations in the United States and four more just across the Mexican border. One study found that 64 percent of Hispanic households in the New York City area were tuned in to a Spanish television station during one weekday evening at prime time.[44] With Hispanic television ownership at approximately the same level as that of the general population, and with the increase in UHF television penetration and the addition of Mexican stations to cable network, the marketer is increasingly able to reach the Hispanic segment by using this medium. Spanish television generally costs much less per thousand viewers reached than does general-market television.

Radio is also an important medium for the Hispanic-American market. There are at least 180 U.S. radio stations that present Spanish-language programming on a full- or part-time basis. Radio ownership in this market is comparable to that for all U.S. households. Moreover, Hispanic-Americans are frequent listeners. A survey of New York Spanish-speaking radio households showed median daily listening of more than 4 hours per day, compared to the average adult listening of 2.5 hours per day for all U.S. radio households. In addition to being frequent listeners, about 60 to 80 percent of Hispanic listeners' time is devoted to Spanish-language programming.[45] Hispanic teens, on the other hand, devote 61 percent of their listening time to contemporary music stations, versus only 14 percent for Spanish stations and almost as much time for black radio stations.[46] Radio is a very effective medium for several reasons: It is inexpensive and flexible; it is accessible when Spanish television may not be on the air (such as mornings); it reaches Hispanics as they engage in day-to-day mobility; and it is often played in the small stores where many Hispanics shop.[47]

Print media, including magazines and newspapers, are also used to reach the Hispanic-American market. These, however, tend to have much less widespread impact than other media because of the lower literacy rates in the Hispanic population. Nevertheless, this medium cannot be overlooked for the wealthier, better-educated Hispanics.

DEVELOPING EFFECTIVE MESSAGES   In order for advertising to the Hispanic-American market to be successful, the communication must fit the people's subculture. Sometimes a general market message may work with Hispanics. For example, the humorous ad shown in Figure 7-2 may be effective without translation into Spanish. However, ads that are authentically Hispanic in setting and language, and highly personal in approach are perceived as most meaningful. Even mass-appeal commercials can be used by substituting a Spanish voice-over, but the marketer should be sure that the video portion is appropriate. Some well-known advertising personalities are effectively used in this market. For instance, the late Colonel Sanders and Frank Perdue have appeared in commercials for their chicken products speaking Spanish.

Numerous language bloopers have been made by firms in advertising to Hispanics. For example, a Spanish-language television commercial for an adhesive bandage recommended for helping *conquitos* on a child's injured knee encountered translation difficulties. Although the word correctly meant "little scratches" to Cubans, to Mexicans it meant "little coconuts"—not exactly what was intended. Several major tobacco companies have advertised low-tar cigarettes with the Spanish word *brea*. Although, *brea* translates literally into "tar," it is the type of tar used on streets. Thus, the companies were actually advertising "low-asphalt" cigarettes.[48]

FIGURE 7-2

Advertisement for Miller Lite Beer. (Courtesy of Miller Brewing Company.)

AMERICA'S BEST KNOWN BEER DRINKERS TALK ABOUT **Lite** BEER...

TITLE: "CARLOS PALOMINO" COMM'L NO.: MOTI 1230

CARLOS: Y'know, one of the best things about coming to America was that I got to try American Beers.

I tried them all.

And the one I like best is Lite Beer from Miller.

It's got a third less calories than their regular beer.

It's less filling.

And it really tastes great.

That is why I tell my friends from Mexico,

"When you come to America, drink Lite Beer.

But,

don't drink the water."

ANNCR: (VO) Lite Beer from Miller. Everything you always wanted in a beer.

And less.

As tailored promotions appear, advertising agencies must keep cultural differences in mind to attain credibility with their Hispanic audiences.[49] The following examples illustrate such an accultured approach:

> Budweiser radio advertising has been subsegmented into four styles of music to correspond with the different ethnic types of Hispanics around the country. The music running in Los Angeles has a mariachi sound that appeals to Mexicans living there; in Texas, a polka Nortena is a familiar sound to Texas Hispanics; in Florida, the Cubans listen to a version of their charanga; and in New York, there is a Puerto Rican salsa. The accent used throughout is broadcast Spanish, a sound with no regional ties.[50]
>
> Advertising for McDonald's in thirty Hispanic markets takes on a twist when you keep in mind the Hispanic family structure. Television and radio commercials for McDonald's were changed so that parents dominated children and the theme song "We do it all for you" was changed to "What matters is you."[51]

A family tie-in can often be appealing because of this group's large family sizes and their high regard for strong family bonds. Figure 7-3 presents a successful family-oriented approach for Johnson & Johnson.

The marketer will have to conduct research to find out what appeals are best for this segment. It may be found that appeals used in the general market are not as successful in the Hispanic segment. For example, Mazola ads don't even mention cholesterol, but stress how good the oil tastes.

In addition to consumer-behavior differences based on ethnic factors, marketers also recognize distinct patterns based on age categories. There are two significant age subcultures with which many marketers should be vitally interested, yet which marketers often fail to fully understand and appreciate. These two groups are the *youth* market and the *older* American market. The characteristics and marketing significance of each of these subcultures will be discussed in this section.

THE YOUTH SUBCULTURE

The youth market is a significant subculture for the marketer. By youth, we are speaking of those between the ages of 14 and 24. The youth market is important to marketers not only because it is lucrative, but also because many consumption patterns held throughout life are formed at this time, and also because of the public policy implications of marketers' activities directed at younger people during their formative years.[52]

Demographic Characteristics

There are many important characteristics of the youth market with which marketers should be familiar. The following is a summary of these factors.

Size In 1980, the youth subculture consisted of approximately 46.5 million persons between the ages of 14 and 24, or 20.5 percent of the population. Although the 18 to 24 age group increased by more than 24 percent between 1970 and 1981, the 14 to 17 category decreased by almost 2 percent during this period. Those under age 14 accounted for an additional 21 percent in 1980. Thus, over 41 percent of the U.S. market is under the age of 25.

Income and Spending   There is no market without income, and the youth segment qualifies on this important dimension. More than 90 percent of men and 75 percent of women 20 to 24 years old receive income during a year. People aged 20 to 24 had an annual income averaging $7,014 per person in 1979, while even

FIGURE 7-3

Advertisement for Johnson's Baby Powder. (Courtesy of Johnson & Johnson.)

JOHNSON'S BABY POWDER

TITLE: "COMPARTA SU BIENESTAR" :30
TITLE: "SHARE THE WELL-BEING" :30

COMM'L. NO.: JJYP 3010
DATE: FEBRUARY 1981

(MUSIC UP)

ANNCR: (VO) Por generaciones...
ANNCR: (VO) For generations...

...las familias han compartido...
...families have shared...

el bienestar del talco Johnson.
the well-being of Johnson's Powder.

SONG: Es un toque que perdura,
SONG: A touch that lasts,

de suavidad
gives softness

y frescura.
and freshness.

El talco Johnson
Johnson's Powder

es carino que haz gozado
is a warm feeling that you have enjoyed

desde nino.
since you were a child.

ANNCR: Johnson's Baby Powder solo de Johnson y Johnson.
ANNCR: Johnson's Baby Powder...only from Johnson & Johnson.

Comparta su bienestar.
Share the well-being.

THE ¡BRAVO! GROUP: HISPANIC MARKETS DIVISION OF YOUNG & RUBICAM INC.

those aged 15 to 19 averaged $2,370. For example, nearly 80 percent of high school seniors held jobs working an average 16 to 20 hours a week.[53]

The most important facet of these incomes is that for some groups, such as for most teens, incomes are almost entirely discretionary; that is, there are few, if any, fixed obligations such as taxes, rent, insurance, or utilities that these youths must meet.

Total spending by the 27.5 million teenagers in the United States in 1980 was estimated at $39.1 billion—a $3 billion growth over 1976.[54] A notable result of the increasing youth income is the increasing tendency of youths to buy more durable and high-priced products, from radios to designer jeans, cosmetics, and footwear. According to the president of a youth-research company, "Products which were considered luxuries a few years ago are deemed necessities by youths and parents alike."[55]

Why do youths have such a strong consumption orientation? According to one researcher, three significant forces have molded their attitudes and consumer behavior. First, the experience of growing up in a period of almost unbroken prosperity has produced a widely shared feeling of economic optimism. A second factor is permissive child rearing, which has been linked by researchers to a reduced capacity for initiative and independence. Third, the new generation has a higher educational level and heavier exposure to the mass media.

These environmental forces have had a significant influence on their consumer-behavior orientations. The result has been that youths tend to be rather optimistic about their future financial situations and levels of living. For example, almost all young people look forward to what has been labeled the "standard package"—the set of durable goods, clothing, food products, and services enjoyed by the majority of Americans.[56] Although they used to be told to save their money, young people in America today are being raised to spend, according to an authority who conducts a yearly youth poll. In 1981, 65 percent of teenagers said thrift was seldom if ever discussed at home or in school, compared with 1956 when 69 percent said thrift was mentioned "a great deal." Similarly, in 1981, 67 percent of teens said their parents were not thrifty, whereas in 1956, 56 percent of the teenagers said their parents were thrifty.[57]

Psychographic Characteristics

The gap between young people and the rest of the population is closing in some areas of attitude and behavior, such as appearance, according to a recent advertising agency report. It finds that today's youths want to look young, healthy, and refreshing, but, unlike their counterparts of the 1960s, they are willing to use artificial means (such as cosmetics, hair coloring, and beauty treatments) to obtain that look.[58] There is more interest in dress among youth today. Even *Rolling Stone* now carries ads for Sasson jeans. Nevertheless, there are some areas in which substantial differences may still be found between youths and older segments, as indicated in Tables 7-4 and 7-5.

Consumer Behavior and Marketing Implications

This section explores the nature of consumer behavior within the youth market of the United States. However, it should be emphasized that many of the findings presented below are for teens. Thus, there may be substantial differences between this group and older youths. The three marketing variables to be discussed are product decisions, shopping patterns, and promotion.

Product Purchase Patterns Marketers are interested in understanding what products will sell well in the youth market. Moreover, it is important to appreciate the influence which youths exert on purchases by others, such as parents. This secondary influence may be more significant to most marketers than is youth's role as primary purchasers of certain items.

How do youths spend their incomes? Both female and male teenagers spend

TABLE 7-4
FEMALE INTERESTS AND OPINIONS (PERCENT AGREEING BY AGE GROUP)

				Age Group			
Statement	Sample Total	Under 25	25–34	35–44	45–54	55–64	65 and Older
Modern—Traditional Ideas							
I have somewhat old-fashioned tastes and habits	84	74	83	83	88	84	89
There is too much emphasis on sex today	82	73	78	82	84	88	91
I like to think I am a bit of a swinger	17	23	19	16	17	17	10
A woman's place is in the home	33	29	23	28	38	40	45
The working world is no place for a woman	9	9	6	6	13	10	16
Young people have too many privileges	75	65	75	76	80	72	81
Religion is an important part of my life	78	66	72	79	86	83	85
My days seem to follow a definite routine—eating meals at the same time each day, etc.	62	57	61	53	57	70	79
Travel and Mobility							
I would like to take a trip around the world	68	75	76	72	65	61	50
I would like to spend a year in London or Paris	37	40	42	41	35	31	27
I would feel lost if I were alone in a foreign country	71	73	69	67	71	72	74
I like to visit places that are totally different from my home	85	86	85	84	87	85	87
We will probably move at least once in the next five years	33	62	46	25	22	23	20
Personal Adornment and Self							
Dressing well is an important part of my life	66	66	63	66	68	67	72
I like to feel attractive to members of the opposite sex	80	86	89	84	75	72	67
I want to look a little different from others	62	63	72	63	59	54	54
I have more stylish clothes than most of my friends	27	31	26	24	25	28	27
View toward Income, Personal Equity, and Spending							
I will probably have more money to spend next year than I have now	59	72	71	65	57	48	30
Five years from now our family income will probably be a lot higher than it is now	63	76	83	77	60	35	21
Our family income is high enough to satisfy nearly all our important desires	65	45	56	64	73	74	80
No matter how fast our income goes up we never seem to get ahead	63	71	72	69	57	55	41
Investing in the stock market is too risky for most families	79	70	79	79	78	80	84
Our family is too heavily in debt today	31	39	44	40	27	14	9
I like to pay cash for everything I buy	71	70	66	70	67	77	78
I pretty much spend for today and let tomorrow bring what it will	22	40	21	25	15	17	17
I would be willing to accept a lower standard of living to conserve energy	49	36	47	46	49	56	64

TABLE 7-4
(*Continued*)

Statement	Sample Total	Under 25	25–34	35–44	45–54	55–64	65 and Older
Staying at Home							
I would rather spend a quiet evening at home than go out to a party	68	57	65	71	70	72	72
I am a homebody	68	54	66	71	72	71	75
I stay home most evenings	79	78	79	75	79	82	84
Children							
Children are the most important thing in a marriage	52	48	44	41	49	63	76
When making important family decisions, consideration of the children should come first	60	71	66	57	57	52	61
Housekeeping and Cooking							
When I see a full ashtray or wastebasket, I want it emptied immediately	68	67	66	70	70	66	73
I am uncomfortable when the house is not completely clean	65	69	69	61	60	64	68
The kind of dirt you can't see is worse than the kind you can see	59	57	55	55	64	60	66
I like to cook	80	78	85	78	77	82	79
Meal preparation should take as little time as possible	53	53	55	53	50	51	56
Optimism, Happiness, Confidence, and Anxiety							
My greatest achievements are still ahead of me	62	84	88	71	53	35	23
I am much happier now than I ever was before	70	67	74	69	71	64	75
I have more self-confidence than most of my friends	63	53	64	66	64	62	65
I dread the future	28	35	24	23	26	31	40
I have trouble getting to sleep	33	38	29	24	28	39	49
I wish I knew how to relax	47	58	44	43	44	50	50
Everything is changing too fast today	64	62	60	59	64	67	78
Personal Influence and Innovation							
I like to be considered a leader	57	53	64	63	58	52	48
My friends and neighbors often come to me for advice about products and brands	44	40	48	48	41	43	39
I often seek out the advice of my friends regarding brands and products	37	41	39	32	35	40	35
I like to buy new and different things	76	75	78	76	76	73	74
I am usually among the first to try new products	43	46	43	39	41	49	43
Media and Advertising							
Television is my primary form of entertainment	44	52	43	42	40	44	49
TV advertising is condescending towards women	71	68	73	73	73	68	64
I consult *Consumer Reports* or similar publications before making a major purchase	53	40	50	55	52	60	59
Advertising insults my intelligence	58	45	57	62	58	62	63
TV commercials place too much emphasis on sex	81	71	78	83	83	86	88

TABLE 7-4
(Continued)

Statement	Sample Total	Under 25	25–34	35–44	45–54	55–64	65 and Older
Information from advertising helps me make better buying decisions	69	65	66	64	71	73	80
I don't believe a company's ad when it claims test results show its product to be better than competitive products	70	59	67	68	76	79	73
Shopping							
Shopping is no fun anymore	43	27	40	45	49	46	52
Before going shopping, I sit down and prepare a complete shopping list	73	73	76	71	67	73	80
I try to stick to well-known brands	55	53	46	48	58	63	74
I find myself checking prices even on small items	80	84	82	81	82	75	75
I like to save and redeem savings stamps	63	64	55	56	63	74	79
I am an impulse buyer	35	44	35	38	29	37	28
I shop a lot for specials	78	85	78	78	76	75	74
Consumption							
When I have a favorite brand I buy it—no matter what else is on sale	54	55	54	51	56	54	53
When I get a free sample of a product, I usually buy that product later	50	66	47	47	46	53	46
A nationally advertised brand is usually a better buy than a generic brand	27	36	22	23	29	34	26
Generally, manufacturers' warranties are not worth the paper they are printed on	40	37	36	40	42	39	47
A well-known brand name is a guarantee of high quality	30	31	23	27	29	33	45
You can usually tell the quality of a product from the quality of its advertising	21	22	15	20	21	28	26
Ralph Nader and others like him do a great deal to protect the American consumer	76	67	78	73	76	79	78

Source: Needham, Harper & Steers Advertising, Inc., *Life Style Survey,* 1983.

most of their money on clothes, records, stereo equipment, entertainment, and travel. Young women spend most on cosmetics, followed by clothes, health and beauty aids, and jewelry. Young men spend the most on dates and autos, followed by sporting goods, cameras, records, stereo equipment, bicycles, athletic shoes, jeans, hobby-type products, musical instruments, and electronic games. The following purchase patterns give an indication of the importance of certain products:[59]

- Teens are said to account for 55 percent of all soft-drink sales and 20 percent of all potato-chip consumption.

- Teenage girls (representing about 12 percent of the total female population) account for 23 percent of all cosmetic expenditures and 22 percent of all women's apparel sales.

- Teenage boys account for 40 percent of all men's slacks and 33 percent of all men's sweater sales.

- 31 percent of people surveyed in the 18-to-29 age bracket took air trips in one year, 33 percent bought cameras, and 36 percent bought ski equipment.

- 90 percent of youths own radios, 86 percent have record players or tape-playback equipment, 86 percent own cameras, and 22 percent own automobiles.

- Consumers between the ages of 21 and 30 drink an average of 5 gallons of wine a year, compared with 2 gallons for older buyers.

- About half of the movie audiences are people between the ages of 16 and 24, while three out of every four movie tickets are purchased by customers under 30.

- About 60 percent of the buyers of phonograph records and tapes in one year were under 25.

- Among college students, 95 percent use a deodorant, 88 percent shampoo their hair three or more times a week, 85 percent of females use a conditioner or creme rinse, and 76 percent of males use after-shave or cologne.

TABLE 7-5 MALE INTERESTS AND OPINIONS (PERCENT AGREEING BY AGE GROUP)

Statement	Sample Total	Under 25	25–34	35–44	45–54	55–64	65 and Older
Modern—Traditional Ideas							
I have somewhat old-fashioned tastes and habits	86	72	83	89	85	91	90
There is too much emphasis on sex today	72	60	64	67	80	82	86
I like to think I am a bit of a swinger	23	35	25	23	16	20	21
A woman's place is in the home	41	37	39	42	39	45	49
The working world is no place for a woman	18	19	18	18	17	16	21
Young people have too many privileges	75	55	73	78	78	82	77
Religion is an important part of my life	64	57	56	65	64	74	75
My days seem to follow a definite routine—eating meals at the same time each day, etc.	63	57	56	58	68	72	77
Travel and Mobility							
I would like to take a trip around the world	69	68	74	76	67	64	49
I would like to spend a year in London or Paris	33	39	32	37	34	27	27
I would feel lost if I were alone in a foreign country	58	60	55	56	57	63	65
I like to visit places that are totally different from my home	78	78	79	76	80	76	79
We will probably move at least once in the next five years	33	69	46	30	20	20	18
Personal Adornment and Self							
Dressing well is an important part of my life	52	52	48	52	59	58	58
I like to feel attractive to members of the opposite sex	78	84	82	77	76	75	68
I want to look a little different from others	48	56	55	48	42	41	46
I have more stylish clothes than most of my friends	23	24	23	22	24	22	24

TABLE 7-5
(Continued)

Statement	Sample Total	Age Group						
		Under 25	25–34	35–44	45–54	55–64	65 and Older
View toward Income, Personal Equity, and Spending							
I will probably have more money to spend next year than I have now	61	71	71	64	63	47	37
Five years from now our family income will probably be a lot higher than it is now	66	79	84	82	62	34	30
Our family income is high enough to satisfy nearly all our important desires	65	37	58	67	67	78	82
No matter how fast our income goes up we never seem to get ahead	66	73	72	73	71	53	46
Investing in the stock market is too risky for most families	78	73	75	76	74	85	86
Our family is too heavily in debt today	31	44	40	36	31	11	11
I like to pay cash for everything I buy	72	78	72	70	67	76	77
I pretty much spend for today and let tomorrow bring what it will	27	38	31	25	26	20	24
I would be willing to accept a lower standard of living to conserve energy	45	37	39	43	48	51	61
Staying at Home							
I would rather spend a quiet evening at home than go out to a party	77	66	80	76	77	82	73
I am a homebody	73	58	69	72	78	80	78
I stay home most evenings	81	74	81	77	81	85	82
Children							
Children are the most important thing in a marriage	57	51	49	54	57	67	72
When making important family decisions, consideration of the children should come first	59	77	65	56	49	59	52
Housekeeping and Cooking							
When I see a full ashtray or wastebasket, I want it emptied immediately	54	47	48	53	52	61	66
I am uncomfortable when the house is not completely clean	49	48	53	51	46	42	56
The kind of dirt you can't see is worse than the kind you can see	63	57	60	62	58	70	73
I like to cook	51	54	58	50	47	44	46
Meal preparation should take as little time as possible	45	38	44	43	45	49	49
Optimism, Happiness, Confidence, and Anxiety							
My greatest achievements are still ahead of me	64	90	91	79	54	26	20
I am much happier now than I ever was before	72	74	72	70	68	75	74
I have more self-confidence than most of my friends	74	76	77	75	80	68	64
I dread the future	24	26	21	19	25	26	36
I have trouble getting to sleep	27	33	23	25	28	26	33
I wish I knew how to relax	44	51	41	42	43	44	49
Everything is changing too fast today	61	62	53	59	62	66	75

TABLE 7-5

(*Continued*)

		Age Group					
Statement	Sample Total	Under 25	25–34	35–44	45–54	55–64	65 and Older
Personal Influence and Innovation							
I like to be considered a leader	70	71	78	73	69	60	59
My friends and neighbors often come to me for advice about products and brands	38	31	40	41	39	36	35
I often seek out the advice of my friends regarding brands and products	37	35	44	37	33	38	26
I like to buy new and different things	63	70	64	60	63	64	63
I am usually among the first to try new products	27	33	23	23	29	27	31
Media and Advertising							
Television is my primary form of entertainment	57	56	56	52	59	60	65
TV advertising is condescending towards women	67	71	66	69	67	66	65
I consult *Consumer Reports* or similar publications before making a major purchase	46	38	46	46	47	43	53
Advertising insults my intelligence	57	39	58	60	58	61	61
TV commercials place too much emphasis on sex	70	56	62	69	75	82	81
Information from advertising helps me make better buying decisions	66	57	61	65	68	75	73
I don't believe a company's ad when it claims test results show its product to be better than competitive products	70	62	66	69	73	76	75
Shopping							
Shopping is no fun anymore	51	39	49	51	55	58	55
Before going shopping, I sit down and prepare a complete shopping list	52	43	51	45	53	60	62
I try to stick to well-known brands	61	54	58	57	61	68	72
I find myself checking prices even on small items	68	69	66	64	66	71	75
I like to save and redeem savings stamps	40	43	30	32	43	46	64
I am an impulse buyer	38	45	44	37	36	34	29
I shop a lot for specials	52	59	49	48	54	54	53
Consumption							
When I have a favorite brand I buy it—no matter what else is on sale	55	54	58	54	55	54	57
When I get a free sample of a product I usually buy that product later	38	44	36	35	37	42	41
A nationally advertised brand is usually a better buy than a generic brand	31	34	35	19	34	31	36
Generally, manufacturers' warranties are not worth the paper they are printed on	45	42	43	45	44	48	45
A well-known brand name is a guarantee of high quality	30	31	28	25	27	34	47
You can usually tell the quality of a product from the quality of its advertising	21	30	22	19	19	16	26
Ralph Nader and others like him do a great deal to protect the American consumer	66	62	64	66	63	68	75

Source: Needham, Harper & Steers Advertising, Inc., *Life Style Survey,* 1983.

As members of a highly consumption-oriented society, teenagers have become increasingly aware of new products and brands. They are natural "triers."

In addition to their direct impact on the marketplace, youths are estimated to influence expenditures of at least another $135 billion. This secondary influence on their parents' product and brand choices is important for a number of items. For example, research studies reveal the following patterns:[60]

- Among teens who own TV sets, 34 percent took part in its selection; for cameras, 43 percent; tape recorders, 42 percent; record players, 29 percent; and typewriters, 42 percent.

- Teens also influence brands chosen by buying the product themselves or specifying the brand. For selected products, the percentages are as follows: mouthwash, 58 percent of girls, 47 percent of boys; toothpaste, 51 percent of girls, 42 percent of boys; shampoo, 75 percent of girls, 72 percent of boys; deodorants, 83 percent of girls, 73 percent of boys; safety razors, 66 percent of girls, 52 percent of boys.

- A study of university students' influence on their families' purchases of television sets and automobiles has found that many students not only provided opinions and information about both products, but also participated in shopping.[61]

With the large growth in the number of working wives, youths are doing more of the food shopping and other shopping for parents. For example, one study of teenage girls found that 78 percent shop for family food, 40 percent "help mother" with product and brand selection, and more than half make specific brand recommendations when asking their mothers to buy snack foods.[62] Another study indicates that teenage girls have prepared an average of 13 meals per week and have spent over $13 billion a year on food, more than one out of every three family food dollars.[63]

Kraft has recognized the importance of teenage grocery shopping, and is advertising with two-page spreads in *Seventeen, Coed,* and *Teen* with the ads emphasizing recipes containing Kraft products. Tied in with the ad campaign is an educational kit on "Food Buymanship" provided to home-economics teachers to distribute to teenagers in school.[64]

Thus, it is clear that this market also occupies an important position in terms of its secondary influence on parents' buying decisions.

Another factor emphasizing the market importance of the youth group is that this is the time when brand loyalties may be formed that could last well into adulthood.[65] For example, a brand-loyalty study prepared by Yankelovich, Skelly and White for *Seventeen* magazine found that a significant percentage of adult women were using the same brand they first chose as teenagers.[66] Translated into total market figures, the findings would mean, for instance, that 6,760,000 women still are using the same brand of mascara and 8,900,000 still are eating the same kind of packaged cheese that they first bought.[67]

During the process of making their buying decision, to what extent are teens influenced by parents, friends, sales clerks, media, or other sources? For many product decisions, friends are the most significant influence. Nevertheless, parents are still an important factor affecting many buying decisions. The important point for the marketer is that although peer pressure is quite strong, family influences are also significant.[68] Thus, the marketer should attempt to keep up with which group predominates at any period in order to properly orient merchandising strategies.

Shopping Behavior Teenagers spend much time engaged in shopping activities. One study learned that more than one-fourth of teenagers questioned spent more than 2 hours shopping on weekends, while another one-fifth spent between 1 and 2 hours.[69] The fact that teens are doing more shopping may result in their spending more money in stores they patronize.

Although the popular belief is that young people buy products impulsively and are less rational than the market as a whole, surveys indicate a different pattern. One study of persons aged 14 to 25 showed that 74 percent of the respondents compare prices and brands before buying.[70] Research on adolescent shopping behavior has produced the following tentative conclusions:[71]

- Adolescents tend to rely more on personal sources for information on products of high socioeconomic and performance risk, and on most media for information on products perceived as low for such risk.

- At the product-evaluation stage of the decision process, price ("sales") and brand name are perceived as the most important evaluative criteria, with a relatively low social influence coming from parents and peers.

- As teenagers mature, they use more sources of consumer information prior to decision making, rely more on friends and less on parents for information and advice in buying, and prefer to purchase products without parental supervision.

In addition, youths often have a great deal of authority in store-selection decisions. For example, one study found that 89 percent of the girls and 80 percent of the boys claimed to have all or most of the say in the choice of a clothing store.[72]

Promoting to Youths A final marketing element that is very important in appealing to youth is promotion. There are many effective media available to reach the youth market—radio, television, direct mail, magazines, and newspapers. However, the marketer should be aware that use of these media varies with family socioeconomic conditions. For instance, teenagers in higher income and higher education families view fewer hours of television than those with lower income and education.[73] Let's examine the media habits of youth and potential promotional strategies that might be successful in appealing to this group.

MEDIA PATTERNS Nearly all teenagers own radios, and they spend considerable time listening to them.[74] Surveys show that 75 percent of teens listen on a daily basis and average almost three hours per day—about one-fifth of their waking hours. In addition, radio reaches more than 90 percent of all teenagers in the course of a week. These listening patterns vary significantly by the time of day, exhibiting heavy nighttime listening, particularly during winter months when apparently the radio is used while studying.

Teen radio-listening preferences are clearly toward contemporary or rock music stations. In addition, almost three-fourths of all teen listening is to stations on the FM dial. They tend to select one or two favorite stations, and they listen to them repeatedly day after day. Consequently, massive teen audiences are available with relatively concentrated station schedules. Hence, radio is probably the fastest, easiest, and most effective way to reach teens.

In contrast to adults, who spend much of their leisure time watching television, teens are relatively light viewers, although virtually all have access to sets.[75] Teens appear to be too busy to spend a lot of time watching television; however, they do have preferred programs, and they may watch these quite regularly. Young teens are significantly heavier viewers than older teens. Television programming that has proved popular with teens includes music-dance shows, movies, sports, situation comedies, and suspense-mystery shows. In 1981, the top network shows among teens were *Happy Days, Chips, Different Strokes, Laverne & Shirley, Dukes of Hazard, M*A*S*H, Love Boat, Enos,* and *Three's Company.*

Print media also are important in promoting to the youth market.[76] Magazines, for example, are viewed by young people as being primary sources of information on a number of different subjects. Newspapers also have heavy youth readership.

Direct mail may also be effective in reaching the youth market. This is one medium that probably will attract more attention than some other alternatives, because youths receive little mail and are likely to be quite receptive to advertising in this form.

> The U.S. Navy reached more than a million high school seniors by direct mail for its enlistment program in 1978, and they achieved a response rate of 2 percent in a market where 1 percent is the norm. A personalized offer of a Navy bumper sticker as a premium was largely responsible for the program's success.[77]

Other effective promotional efforts are utilized by marketers. For example, some companies hire student representatives on many college campuses whose job may include selling or renting merchandise, putting up posters, or distributing advertisements and product samples.

> Many of today's college students are provided with a colorful box labeled "Good Stuff" which is filled with personal-care products that can be sampled. The boxes are distributed to more than 1 million incoming students—mainly freshmen dormitory residents—on 800 campuses across the United States. One of the products that now participates in the program (Oil of Olay) had originally targeted its moisturizing lotion at the 35-plus age female market. However, its inclusion in Good Stuff boxes showed that many of the college women who tried the sample later purchased the product and became regular users. Other research indicates that buying of Good Stuff-distributed brands increased 119 percent on participating campuses.[78]

Some companies reach youth with their own media. For example, Kimberly-Clark uses a publication, *Young Woman,* in which Kotex feminine products is the single advertiser. The magazine is targeted to high school senior women, and is designed to entice more female consumers who are making brand decisions they may stick with over the years. Tie-in promotions or "events marketing" is also increasingly used by marketers to reach the youth group. For example, Expo-

America takes advantage of the spring-break influx of students into such Florida resort towns as Daytona Beach by offering companies such as Anheuser-Busch, McDonald's, and Bristol-Myers the chance to make their pitch to the youth with exhibit-hall presentations, pool-side programs, specially-delivered samples, and dance and fashion shows.

DEVELOPING EFFECTIVE MESSAGES Promotional messages must be carefully designed for today's youth because they are becoming increasingly skeptical about such communications. For example, a recent youth poll found that 24 percent of the respondents said ads directed at them were not believable; 19 percent found them uninformative; 28 percent thought they were silly; and only 7 percent viewed them as sincere. Nevertheless, 87 percent of youths 14 to 25 years old would rather buy advertised than nonadvertised products.[79]

When developing effective sales appeals to the youth market, the advertiser should keep in mind the following rules:[80]

1 Never talk down to youths.
2 Be totally, absolutely, and unswervingly straightforward.
3 Give youths credit for being motivated by rational values.
4 Be as personal as possible.

The successes of certain promotional campaigns aimed at youth indicate several ingredients which marketers should consider incorporating:

- *Sports themes.* Coca-Cola has introduced Mello Yellow, a low-carbonated drink, to sell to young people who like sports. Its commercials feature sports competition, such as auto racing, basketball, and football.
- *A "gimmick."* Pizza Time Theaters in San Jose, California uses a group of computer-controlled stuffed animals that play banjos and sing. Each theater also has pinball, arcade, and video games. Department and specialty stores around the country use music, blinking lights, and space-age displays to lure youths.
- *Celebrities.* Schwinn features Eric Heiden, the champion speed skater at the 1980 Winter Olympics, in its bicycle commercials.
- *Humor.* Many advertisers believe humor has a stronger appeal than factual accounts when advertising to high school and college groups. Examples include Bubble Yum gum and *Time* magazine.

There are two additional factors that should be cited in order to ensure greater success in the youth market. The first is that the youth group is a *perpetually* new market. As consumers move into this market, the advertiser needs to attract them, since every brand is a new brand to someone who has never used it before. This stream of young consumers moves along in age and finally drifts into an older pool of householders. Thus, a marketer must not neglect young consumers who come "on stream" if the company's brand is to have continued success in the older-age market. Two companies utilizing this approach to successfully attract youths are presented below:

American Express has developed a special plan to lure graduating college students as card holders. The usual application requirements are reduced and the program is promoted with a special campaign in college newspapers (see Figure 7-4). The company has even adapted its familiar slogan to reach the youth market. The tag line is "The American Express Card. Don't leave school without it."

Schick has been able to outflank Gillette, the dominant company in the razor-blade market, by consistent and specific efforts to win young shavers. Through various means it offers young men the opportunity to receive Schick razors, either free or at nominal expense. The result has been that Schick has gained a significant presence in this market.[81]

A second point to remember is that companies may be able to utilize youth appeals to a market broader than the traditional age boundary would indicate. Marketers today are defining "youth" more in terms of a state of mind than of a specific

FIGURE 7-4

Advertisement for American Express. (Courtesy of American Express Company.)

age. The result of this is that many companies, ranging from retailers to manufacturers, are broadening their emphasis to include the mature and more affluent customers who "think young."

THE OLDER SUBCULTURE

Although business people have painted a glowing picture of the opportunities in the youth market, the opposite end of the age spectrum has been largely neglected by marketers and frequently by society itself. Many people feel that American marketers have gone overboard in courting the youth market. As one advertising executive explained in *Business Week,* "As I watch television and read magazines and attend movies these days, I sometimes wonder if anybody besides myself is over 30. There seems to be a conscious denial of middle age—and certainly of old age."[82] Another advertising executive observed that marketers have long concentrated only on consumers below the age of 49. He noted that "beyond 49 the world ceases to exist, you fall off the edge."[83]

Why the neglect? One writer explains, "Youth suggests excitement and glamour; the no-longer-young are considered dowdy and uninspiring."[84] Although this situation may be understandable psychologically, it may make poor economic sense, because middle-aged consumers hold considerably more promise for a wide range of consumer goods and services than do the young.

Demographic Characteristics

This section summarizes several important demographic characteristics of older consumers.

Size In 1980, more than 25 million people in the United States were 65 years of age or older, or 11.3 percent of our total population. Each census during this century has found the elderly to make up an increasingly larger share of the total population. In fact, this growth has far outpaced the percentage increase of the population generally, and if present trends continue, those 55 and over could account for 21 percent of the population by the year 2000. Thus, statistics negate a long-held concept that the United States is a nation of young people and is getting younger.

Location The largest group of elderly consumers lives in the central cities of our metropolitan areas. This characteristic differs from the population as a whole, in which suburbanites outnumber residents of central cities.

States with the largest populations also have the largest numbers of senior citizens. For example, New York, California, Pennsylvania, and Illinois account for nearly one-third of the elderly. However, states with the highest proportions of older people are those which have had heavy out-migration by younger people. This is especially true of much of the midwestern farm belt—Iowa, Kansas, Missouri, Nebraska, Oklahoma, and South Dakota.

Many older people who have the means move toward the "gerontopolises" of the Sunbelt when they retire. Florida's elderly, for example, make up 14.6 percent of its population—the highest proportion of any state.

Marital and Family Status A large majority of the elderly are women, most of whom are widowed, and many of whom live by themselves. However, most elderly men are married and live with their wives. Because their children have grown up and moved away, and because many of them are widowed, household size of older prospects is much smaller than for other groups in the population. For example, more than 73 percent of all households in which the head is over 65 consist of only one or two individuals. Contrary to the general impression, very few of the American elderly live in homes for the aged. Only 3 percent of men and 5 percent of women are in such arrangements. The pecentage of men and women living as dependent "other relatives" in family groups may also be lower than commonly believed (7 percent and 17 percent, respectively).

Income The median income for all families in the United States in 1976 was $12,836 but the median family income of persons age 65 and over was only $7,298 for the year. Nearly one in six people age 65 and over lives in poverty, compared with one in ten people under age 65. Although it is true that a sizeable segment of the market is at the poverty-income level, it is also true that a much more significant number of elderly persons live at "comfortable" levels of income.

Even though the incomes of many elderly may be low, these incomes are often able to go farther than those of younger customers because of fewer obligations. For example, there may be no children to educate, clothe, or support; work-related expenses are curtailed; double exemptions are granted on income tax returns; Medicare helps pay for medical expenses; and two-thirds of the aged own their own homes, with 80 percent of these homes being mortgage-free.

Some workers can look forward to perhaps 30 years in retirement, with incomes at approximately the same level as their preretirement, after-taxes income. This market will in the future be one with even more discretionary income and more ways to spend it, because the problem of security will be being taken off the individual's shoulders and placed in the hands of bodies beyond ourselves—such as the government, insurance, pensions, and the like.

Psychographic Characteristics

As seen in Tables 7-4 and 7-5, the segment aged 55 and over has in many cases a different set of activities, interests, and opinions than those of younger groups.

Consumer Behavior and Marketing Implications

The lack of attention by marketers to the senior market shows in the dearth of research findings on this group's behavior as consumers. This section distills some of the most important findings and presents some useful insights for the marketer.

Product Purchase Patterns Significant marketing potential appears to be available to those who provide the proper kinds of products to meet the needs of the senior market. Some have ventured into this market to sell specially designed products more attuned to elderly needs. Not all, however, have succeeded. For instance, H. J. Heinz developed a line of new products called "Senior Foods" because many older consumers seemed to be eating the company's baby food while claiming they were buying it for their grandchildren. However, the new food product failed for reasons which apparently included lack of taste, a patronizing attitude by the company's advertising campaign, and a high retail price.[85]

Some other manufacturers, however, have successfully launched products in this market, or are planning to take advantage of this opportunity. The following examples illustrate the awakening of the "new world" of the older consumer by marketers:

Clothing The great potential of the older market is being recognized in two ways. First, products are being designed with them in mind. Second, they are expected to become more willing to spend money on items now being sold mostly to younger customers. For example, jeans and other casual wear are expected by Levi Strauss to become in the future just as acceptable by men in their fifties and sixties as they are today among people under 25. Responding to this possibility, the company now produces Levis for Men and Bend Over pants for women, new lines of jeans featuring a fuller cut and stretch fabrics to fit the redistributed older physique.

Food Coca-Cola, concerned that the 13 to 24 age group which accounts for such an important part of its soda market (consuming 1.5 times as much per capita as the general public) will shrink by 8 percent in the 1980s, is moving more heavily into wine, orange juice, coffee, and tea—beverages more popular with older consumers. In addition, a new reduced-acid orange juice has been marketed recently. Procter & Gamble is offering High Point, a new decaffinated coffee which is a product older consumers buy much more than regular coffee. Kellogg's markets Special K, Product 19, and Smart Start to provide more vitamins for older consumers (who are the second highest group in consumption of cereal, behind only the under-12 market).

Cosmetics Estee Lauder, Elizabeth Arden, Revlon, Helena Rubenstein, Oil of Olay, and others are now marketing skin-care products which are designed to appeal to older women. Other companies are offering hair care designed to meet the special needs of consumers over 40 or 50. The approach is a delicate one from an industry that has long been based strictly on its youth image. Companies are searching for ways to overcome the age taboo by referring only to "maturing skin" and the like—everything but age.

Older consumers appear to place great importance on manufacturers' brand names. They tend to buy fewer private labels, and appear to demand guarantees and warranties more often than do average consumers.[86] Because many over-65 shoppers are on fixed or low incomes, however, there is a trend toward increased acceptance of private labels and generic items among this shopper group.[87]

There is also an impression that older buyers are generally less-inclined to try new products. One study, however, found that the group aged 65 and over was more-inclined than the middle-aged, 55 to 64 year olds, to say that they buy products for the fun of it or just to try them once. It was also found that there is little self-initiated experimenting; instead, new product and service acceptance often comes as a response to a recommendation by others.[88] This has important promotion implications for the marketer, and it means that messages must be well-planned to take advantage of this word-of-mouth communication.[89] Given the apparent high brand loyalty of this group, it also means that manufacturers and retailers who properly serve those in this group can expect them to be loyal, dependable customers.

Shopping Behavior Most of the research on older citizens' shopping patterns has been conducted in an exploratory manner with limited samples; therefore, the findings must be interpreted with caution. Nevertheless, there are a number of helpful insights.

Business Week provides perspective regarding the shopping patterns of senior citizens by observing that they "tend to be more cautious than younger consumers, more set in their preferences, and shrewder comparison shoppers. They favor larger chain stores and shun small specialty outlets, especially those that gain a name for catering just to the elderly."[90]

Another study found that the primary sources of product information were newspapers and personal observations while shopping. Shopping appeared to be a major part of their lifestyle and provided more of a pleasure than a burden.[91]

Other studies have shown that older consumers shop near their residences since many lack personal transportation. In addition, substantial store loyalty has been exhibited by this group for low-cost items or for products about which the store owner may give advice (such as drugs and medicines). Store loyalty disappears as unit value of an item increases and frequency of purchase decreases (such as when shopping for appliances). Greater store loyalty, however, is exhibited by senior citizens at higher income and age levels.[92]

Some of this country's important retail institutions such as shopping centers and supermarkets have features that make them quite attractive to older shoppers. The general favorable prices and the safe, comfortable atmosphere of these stores contribute to their appeal. At the same time, however, other features of these institutions inhibit older consumers and prevent them from taking advantage of them. First, they are generally located away from older neighborhoods where many aged and most poor live. Moreover, the right merchandise assortment to satisfy the needs of older consumers frequently cannot be found. For these and other reasons, such retail institutions have not adequately met the needs of senior citizens.[93]

Promoting to the Older Market Even developing the right product and getting it to the right place is no guarantee of success among older consumers. It must also be matched with the proper promotion. Marketers who have succeeded in this market have done so largely because of effective promotion.

MEDIA PATTERNS The marketer must select appropriate media for promoting to the senior-citizen market. There are some difficulties, however, when effectively segmenting the senior-citizen market by media. Television programming, for instance, is largely youth-oriented. Nevertheless, viewership by older consumers is above average during certain times of the day. Television viewership for those aged 55 to 64 is heaviest between 7 and 10 A.M. and 5 and 11 P.M., and for those 65 and over it is from 7 A.M. to 7:30 P.M. Thus, daytime and syndicated programming appealing to older adults is the mainstay for the television advertiser. New avenues for reaching older consumers are also opening up. For example, Cineamerica aims to reach 1.5 million homes offering programming for people over age 50 as part of its satellite-linked cable TV package.

Radio is an effective medium to reach older buyers. Formats such as all-news, talk shows, beautiful music, and sports are traditionally strong among those over 55. Nostalgic approaches are also useful with formats such as big-band music and radio drama finding success.

With regard to print media aimed directly at this market, the choices were, until recently, rather limited. Now, however, there are several specialty magazines for older people, in addition to the general audience magazines (such as *Reader's Digest* and *TV Guide* which historically found a large market among this segment). Magazines such as *Prime Time, 50 Plus,* and *Modern Maturity* are useful vehicles for aiming messages at those over 45. In addition, many newspapers around the United States aimed at older consumers allow the marketer to more effectively reach this group. It should also be noted that newspapers may be the most appropriate media if the objective is to have older consumers learn new information. They are frequent users of this medium, and they consider it their most important mass-media source of information. Because their information processing with print media is self-paced, there are liable to be fewer difficulties in learning new information.[94]

DEVELOPING EFFECTIVE MESSAGES   Poor promotion, especially advertising, appears to have contributed to the alienation of older consumers. Much advertising today stereotypes older Americans (often negatively), and thereby insults them. For example, *The Wall Street Journal* states that "Older people in TV ads are recognizable most often by their stereotypes: half-deaf codgers, meddling biddies, grandfatherly authority figures or nostalgic endorsers of products that claim to be just as high-quality as they were in the good old days. Rarely are older people shown just as ordinary consumers."[95] Although those over age 55 comprise approximately 29 percent of U.S. adults, several studies have shown that they account for only about 10 percent of TV-commercial characters, usually those in need of laxatives, denture adhesives, and sleeping pills.

Advertisements which are not sensitive to older consumers may be perceived as offensive. For example, a denture adhesive ad once showed an older couple perched in infant highchairs to indicate that people with loose dentures need easy-to-chew food. More recently, a General Foods ad for Country Time powdered lemonade mix featured a hard-of-hearing grandfather who kept asking his family to repeat the product's name as a device for gaining repetition. However, the ad was perceived very negatively, and because of the protests received, it was quickly withdrawn from broadcast. On the other hand, advertisements such as Clairol's, "You're not getting older, you're getting better," can be very useful in building older consumers' self-esteem.

As indicated previously, older citizens are a prime market and thus promotions should be directed to them in a way commensurate with their value. Many businessmen, however, are reluctant to solicit their trade. A study by the National Council on Aging found that local store managers, even when convinced that elderly consumers represented a sizeable market, refused to direct any advertising or promotion efforts toward the aged for fear it would "hurt their public image" and tend to keep away their most desirable age group—the youth.[96]

On the other hand, promotion should not, as in the Heinz example, blatantly single out senior citizens as the target. Many older consumers do not want to be reminded that they are old, and therefore they react against advertising and marketing programs that separate them from the masses; nor do they want to be treated as kids. An approach which works for many companies is the "trans-generational" strategy or "fence straddling."[97] In this case, ads feature both youngsters and oldsters using and enjoying the product. The key is to use older characters in a matter-of-fact way, not in an unrealistic manner. Advertising for Greyhound, McDonald's, Coca-Cola, AT&T, and Kellogg's (see Figure 7-5) are examples of this strategy. Thus, the marketer must be careful not to alienate any age group. Other marketers catering to the senior market have found success by using well-known senior citizens as spokesmen for their products. For example, Joe Dimaggio, Robert Young, and Lawrence Welk have been very effective in this role.

Another facet of advertising to the older market concerns the way in which messages are presented. It is important to understand that older consumers process information differently from younger buyers because of changes in vision, hearing, and memory, for example. Consequently, marketers should follow certain guidelines when communicating with older buyers. First, ads and packages should not be cluttered with too much visual information. Second, action in commercials should be relevant and not distracting. Humor may also distract and clutter the message. Third, fast-speaking characters and those who don't enunciate clearly should be avoided. Fourth, pictures should be clear, bright, and sharp. Fifth, the language and message should be simple, focusing on one or two selling points. Finally, relate new information to something with which they are already familiar.[98]

The marketer should not, however, automatically run the same ads in specialized media (such as older-oriented magazines) as those run in the general-

FIGURE 7-5

Advertisement for Rice Krispies.® (Reprinted with permission of Kellogg Company.)

audience media. Such unadapted advertising is liable to be largely ineffective with the older group.

Marketers who want to develop successful advertising for this group should consider the following suggestions: (1) include older buyers in focus-group research in order to learn of their motivations and attitudes; (2) hire older copywriters to provide new perspectives on this segment; (3) incorporate older models in advertisements in a genuine and typical way; (4) let the older buyers know the product will appeal to them, but do so subtly.

In summary, the older market represents a powerful economic force that is certain to grow even stronger. Although the youth market has become almost a "religion" to many companies, some are beginning to feel that the senior market is really the "now" generation, because older consumers don't know how long the "now" will last. Thus, there is substantial opportunity in this subculture for the marketer not only to satisfy the goals of his firm, but at the same time to help accomplish some of society's aims as well. However, in order for these goals to be effectively realized, marketers will need to know much more about this neglected segment.

SUMMARY

This chapter has introduced the concept of subcultures, looking particularly at ethnic and age segments in the United States. Ethnic groups were classified according to racial, nationality, or religious bases. Only race and national origin were discussed, however.

The black and Hispanic markets were described as being very large, as being identifiable, and as having important differences in their consumer-behavior patterns from the rest of society. Even within these ethnic subcultures are heterogeneous subgroups which the marketer needs to understand. Each major marketing element was discussed, and consumer-behavior implications were cited. For the marketer, it is important that these significant ethnic groups be approached with carefully planned and executed strategies based on a knowledge of their similarities with and differences from the broader American market.

This chapter also presented two additional subcultures with which marketers need to be more familiar—youths and older citizens. Groups classified by age represent a viable approach to market segmentation, and therefore two of the more important age categories were discussed. Many of the consumer-behavior insights which have been gained through numerous studies of these subcultures were presented. At the same time, however, it is clear from this chapter that much more needs to be learned by marketers in order to really understand such subcultures. Neverthless, a foundation has been laid for more effective marketing.

DISCUSSION TOPICS

1 What is a subculture?

2 Describe some important subcultures that exist in the United States. Why are these important? Are all subcultures equally important to or usable by the marketer?

3 Prepare a report on the current demographic picture of one of the subcultures discussed in this chapter.

4 Look through some black-oriented magazines (such as *Ebony*) and select three advertisements that are similar to those appearing in predominantly white-oriented media except for the models (bring in white ads too). Are there any other differences between the ads, such as language or situation? Explain why or why not.

5 Assume that you are the product manager in charge of marketing for Tide detergent and you are developing an advertising campaign. Use the knowledge you gained in this chapter to put together an effective campaign for the black and Hispanic subcultures.

6 What are the most important considerations in marketing to the Hispanic segment?

7 Why are the youth and senior-citizen markets characterized as "subcultures"?

8 How do the activities, interests, and opinions of youth differ from other age groups? How do those of older citizens differ?

9 Illustrate with food products and automobiles how the marketer might promote to youths in order to take advantage of their secondary influence on family-purchase decisions.

10 Select two product areas that appear to have good potential in the older market but are at present being poorly marketed. Present a plan for more effective marketing in order to take advantage of this opportunity.

11 What improvements can you suggest for the retail environment in order to better meet the needs of today's senior citizens?

NOTES

[1] See "New Survey Reveals Five Lifestyle Segments of Age 18–49 Black Women," *Marketing News,* August 21, 1981, p. 6; "Views from the Inside," *Advertising Age,* April 6, 1981, pp. S-6–S-9; "U.S. Firms Must Act Now to Tap Chicano Market," *Marketing News,* August 22, 1980, pp. 1, 6; Mary C. LaForge, Warren A. French, and Melvin R. Crask, "Segmenting the Elderly Market," in Jerry R. Reeves and James R. Sweigart (eds.), *Proceedings: Volume 1,* 13th Annual Meeting of the American Institute of Decision Sciences, Boston, 1981, pp. 248–250; and Jeffrey G. Towle and Claude R. Martin, Jr., "The Elderly Consumer: One Segment or Many?" in Beverlee B. Anderson (ed.), *Advances in Consumer Research: Volume 3,* Association for Consumer Reaearch, Cincinnati, 1976, p. 467.
[2] Bernard Berelson and Gary Steiner, *Human Behavior: An Inventory of Scientific Findings,* Harcourt, Brace & World, New York, 1964, p. 494.
[3] Jewish consumer behavior is discussed in the following: Elizabeth C. Hirschman, "American Jewish Ethnicity: Its Relationship to Some Selected Aspects of Consumer Behavior," *Journal of Marketing,* 45:102–110, Summer 1981; Dan Lionel, "How to Reach the Jewish Market," *Editor & Publisher,* December 8, 1979, p. 30; Larry A. Rubin, "Jewish Media Problem: Combating Stereotypes," *Advertising Age,* April 16, 1979, p. S-32; and Richard A. Jacobs, "Jewish Media Provide What Others Don't," *Advertising Age,* April 16, 1979, p. S-28.
[4] Herbert Allen, "Product Appeal: No Class Barrier," *Advertising Age,* May 18, 1981, p. S-4.
[5] Leon Morse, "Black Radio Market Study," *Television/Radio Age,* February 28, 1977, pp. A-1–A-31.
[6] "Use Different Ad Tack for Blacks, Meet Urged," *Advertising Age,* February 14, 1977, p. 66; and Kelvin A. Wall, "Trying to Reach Blacks? Beware of Marketing Myopia," *Advertising Age,* May 21, 1979, p. 60.
[7] "Use Different Ad Tack," p. 66 and Wall, "Trying to Reach Blacks?" p. 60.
[8] Simon Bensimon, "Buying Patterns Different," *Advertising Age,* April 7, 1980, pp. S-10, S-24.
[9] Marcus Alexis, "Some Negro-White Differences in Consumption," *American Journal of Economics and Sociology,* 21:11–28, January 1962.

[10] James E. Stafford, Keith K. Cox, and James B. Higginbotham, "Some Consumption Pattern Differences Between Urban Whites and Negroes," *Social Science Quarterly,* 49:629, December 1968.
[11] "Is There Really a Negro Market?" *Marketing Insights,* January 29, 1968, p. 14.
[12] "Marketing Observer," *Business Week,* December 18, 1978, p. 103.
[13] "The Negro Market: 23 Million Consumers Make a $30 Billion Market Segment," *Marketing Insights,* January 29, 1968, p. 11.
[14] Alphonzia Wellington, "Traditional Brand Loyalty," *Advertising Age,* May 18, 1981, p. S-2.
[15] Bernard F. Whalen, "Study Measures Impact of Inflation on Blacks' Product, Brand Choices," *Marketing News,* March 20, 1981, pp. 1, 4.
[16] Donald E. Sexton, Jr., "Black Buyer Behavior," *Journal of Marketing,* 36:38, October 1972; and "Consumer Dynamics in the Supermarket," *Progressive Grocer,* New York, 1969.
[17] Al Harting, "Cultural Differences Offer Rewards," *Advertising Age,* April 7, 1980, p. S-21.
[18] Elizabeth C. Hirschman, "Black Ethnicity and Innovative Communication," *Journal of the Academy of Marketing Science,* 8:100–119, Spring 1980.
[19] Robert F. Dietrich, "Know Your Black Shopper," *Progressive Grocer,* June 1975, p. 46.
[20] Lawrence P. Feldman and Alvin D. Star, "Racial Factors in Shopping Behavior," in Keith K. Cox and Ben M. Enis (eds.), *A New Measure of Responsibility for Marketing,* American Marketing Association, Chicago, 1968, pp. 216–226.
[21] Henry Allen Bullock, "Consumer Motivations in Black and White—Part I," *Harvard Business Review,* May–June 1961, pp. 99–100.
[22] A. Coskun Samli, Enid F. Tozier, and Doris Y. Harps, "Social Class Differentials in the Store Selection Process of Single Black Professional Women," *Journal of the Academy of Marketing Science,* Spring 1980, pp. 138–150.
[23] Keith E. Lockhart, "Missing the Mark on the Black Market," *Broadcasting,* 95:22, September 25, 1978.
[24] Morse, "Black Radio," p. A-24.
[25] Wally Tokarz, "Minority Marketing Looks to the 80s," *Advertising Age,* April 7, 1980, p. S-22.
[26] James P. Forkan, "Arbitron Study Charts Ethnic TV Viewing Habits," *Advertising Age,* October 22, 1979, p. 20.
[27] See Arnold M. Barban and Edward W. Cundiff, "Negro and White Response to Advertising Stimuli," *Journal of Marketing Research,* 1:53–56, November 1964; Arnold M. Barban, "The Dilemma of Integrated Advertising," *Journal of Business,* 42:477–496, October 1969; B. Stuart Tolley and John J. Goett, "Reactions to Blacks in Newspaper Ads," *Journal of Advertising Research,* 11:11–17, April 1971; Lester Guest, "How Negro Models Affect Company Image," *Journal of Advertising Research,* 10:29–34, April 1970; Mary Jane Schlinger and Joseph T. Plummer, "Advertising in Black and White," *Journal of Marketing Research,* 9:149–153, May 1972; William V. Muse, "Product-Related Response to Use of Black Models in Advertising," *Journal of Marketing Research,* 8:107–109, February 1971; and James W. Cagley and Richard N. Cardozo, "White Response to Integrated Advertising," *Journal of Marketing Research,* 10:35–40, April 1970.
[28] Lockhart, "Missing the Mark," p. 22.
[29] Theodore J. Gage, "RSVP: An Invitation to Buy," *Advertising Age,* May 18, 1981, p. S-8.
[30] Leah Rozen, "Black Presenter Makes A Difference: Study," *Advertising Age,* October 13, 1980, p. 20.
[31] Yankelovich, Skelly and White, Inc., *Spanish U.S.A.: A Study of the Hispanic Market in the United States,* The SIN National Spanish Television Network, New York, June 1981, p. 4.
[32] Mark Watanabe, "Hispanic Marketing: A Profile Grows to New Heights," *Advertising Age,* April 6, 1981, p. S-23.
[33] Paul M. Ryscavage and Earl F. Mellor, "The Economic Situation of Spanish Americans," *Monthly Labor Review,* 96:3, April 1973.
[34] Joseph M. Aguayo, "Latinos: Los Que Importan Son Ustedes," *Sales and Marketing Magazine,* July 11, 1977, p. 29.
[35] Yankelovich, Skelly and White, Inc., *Spanish U.S.A.,* p. 12.
[36] "Chrysler Sets Hispanic Test," *Advertising Age,* November 24, 1980, p. 66; and "So They All Speak Spanish," *Media Decisions,* May 1977, pp. 68–71, 117–118.
[37] Luis Diaz-Albertini, "Brand-Loyal Hispanics Need Good Reason for Switching," *Advertising Age,* April 16, 1979, p. S-22, 23.
[38] Yankelovich, Skelly and White, Inc., *Spanish U.S.A.,* p. 13.
[39] Marco Rosales and Sylvia Rosales, "If You Don't Sell Hispanics in Spanish, You Don't Sell," *Advertising Age,* April 16, 1979, p. S-2.
[40] Yankelovich, Skelly and White, Inc., *Spanish U.S.A.,* p. 4.
[41] Karen Rothmyer, "A Spanish Accent is Very 'In' These Days on Madison Avenue," *The Wall Street Journal,* January 24, 1975, p. 1.
[42] Yankelovich, Skelly and White, Inc., *Spanish U.S.A.,* p. 18.
[43] For a discussion of Hispanic media see the following: "Minority Potential Big, But Still Unrealized," *Advertising Age,* April 16, 1979, pp. S-8, 10; Bob Marich, "Broadcast: Los Angeles Espanol," *Advertising Age,* April 6, 1981, pp. S-10–S-14; Jaclyn Fierman, "Meal Foulups Lead to Hunger for Radio," *Advertising Age,* April 6, 1981, pp. S-14–S-15; Steven Reddicliffe, "Print: Magazines Put Accent on Miami," *Advertising*

Age, April 6, 1981, pp. S-16–S-17; Robert Flood, "Outdoor and the Hispanic Market OLE'!" *Marketing & Media Decisions,* May 1981, p. 82; and Yankelovich, Skelly and White, Inc., *Spanish U.S.A.,* pp. 17–23.
[44] Rothmyer, "A Spanish Accent," p. 1.
[45] Richard P. Jones, "Spanish Ethnic Market Second Largest in U.S.," *Marketing Insights,* November 27, 1976, p. 11.
[46] "Latino Media: Available in Any Mood from Conservative to Salsa," *Sales and Marketing Magazine,* July 11, 1977, p. 25.
[47] "So They All Speak Spanish," p. 117.
[48] Wayne E. Green, "Firms Seek to Tighten Links with Hispanics as Buyers and Workers," *The Wall Street Journal,* November 10, 1981, pp. 1, 14.
[49] Aguayo, "Latinos," p. 29.
[50] "Advertising's Missed Opportunity: The Hispanic Market," *Marketing & Media Decisions,* January 1981, p. 134.
[51] "So They All Speak Spanish," p. 117.
[52] George P. Moschis and Gilbert A. Churchill, Jr., "An Analysis of the Adolescent Consumer," *Journal of Marketing,* 43:40, Summer 1979.
[53] "Youth on the Move," *U.S. News & World Report,* December 29, 1980/January 5, 1981, p. 73.
[54] Ben Bodec, "Marketing Paradox: Fewer Teens, More Spending," *Marketing & Media Decisions,* April 1981, p. 77.
[55] "Special Interest Group: Teenagers Continue to Set Spending Records," *The Wall Street Journal,* November 6, 1975, p. 1.
[56] Robert O. Herrmann, "Today's Young Adults as Consumers," *Journal of Consumer Affairs,* 4:23, Summer 1970.
[57] Jane See White, "Study Shows What Teens Do Best—Spend Money," *The Evening Bulletin,* June 12, 1981, p. A-8.
[58] "Youth Market Growing More Conventional," *Advertising Age,* May 16, 1977, p. 84.
[59] Bodec, "Marketing Paradox," p. 78; and "Spending Patterns," *The Wall Street Journal,* February 12, 1981, p. 1; "The U.S. Teen Market," *Sponsor,* 22:25, January 1968; "44 Million Adults—A New Wave of Buyers," *U.S. News & World Report,* January 17, 1972, pp. 16–19; and Rebecca Fannin, "The College Market: Rich, But No Easy Mark," *Marketing & Media Decisions,* August 1981, p. 66.
[60] "The U.S. Teen Market," p. 25.
[61] William P. Perreault, Jr. and Frederick A. Russ, "Student Influence on Family Purchase Decisions," in Fred C. Allvine (ed.), *Combined Proceedings,* American Marketing Association, Chicago, 1971, pp. 386–390.
[62] "The U.S. Teen Market," pp. 25–26.
[63] "Teenage Spenders Rely on Ads in Newspapers," *Editor and Publisher,* January 22, 1966, p. 17.
[64] Bodec, "Marketing Paradox," pp. 78, 116.
[65] George P. Moschis and Roy L. Moore, "A Study of the Acquisition of Desires for Products and Brands," in Kenneth Bernhardt, et. al. (eds.), *The Changing Marketing Environment: New Theories and Applications,* American Marketing Association, Chicago, 1981, pp. 210–204.
[66] "Seventeen Makes a Sales Call," *Madison Avenue,* November 1980, pp. 85–95.
[67] Jaclyn Fierman, "Reaching Teens: Less Emphasis on the Product," *Advertising Age,* April 28, 1980, p. S-24.
[68] See, for example, George P. Moschis and Gilbert A. Churchill, Jr., "Consumer Socialization: A Theoretical and Empirical Analysis," *Journal of Marketing Research,* 15:599–609, November 1978; George P. Moschis and Gilbert A. Churchill, Jr., "Consumer Socialization: A Theoretical and Empirical Analysis," *Journal of Marketing Research,* 6:101–112, September 1979; and Gilbert A. Churchill, Jr. and George P. Moschis, "Television and Interpersonal Influences on Adolescent Consumer Learning," *Journal of Consumer Research,* 6:23–25, June 1979.
[69] Dennis H. Tootelian and H. Nicholas Windeshausen, "The Teen-Age Market: A Comparative Analysis, 1964–1974," *Journal of Retailing,* 52:56–58, Summer 1976.
[70] "Youth Market Growing More Conventional," p. 84.
[71] Moschis and Moore, "Decision Making," pp. 101–112; and Moschis and Churchill, Jr., "Consumer Socialization," pp. 599–609.
[72] Paul E. Smith, "Merchandising for the Teenage Market," *Journal of Retailing,* 37:12, Summer 1960.
[73] George P. Moschis, "Socialization Perspectives and Consumer Behavior," in Ben M. Enis and Kenneth J. Roering (eds.), *Review of Marketing 1981,* American Marketing Association, Chicago, 1981, pp. 48–49.
[74] Edward Papazian, "Teenagers . . . and Broadcast Media," *Media/Scope,* 11:111–115, December 1967; and Wally Tokarz, "Radio Considered Teen Medium," *Advertising Age,* April 28, 1980, pp. S-10, S-15.
[75] Papazian, "Teenagers," pp. 110–111; and Mark Kirkeby, "Youth TV Viewing Habits Vary," *Advertising Age,* April 28, 1980, p. S-6.
[76] "Youth Media Market Diverse," *Advertising Age,* April 28, 1980, p. S-2; and Ellis I. Folke, "Teenagers . . . and Print Media," *Media/Scope,* 11:118, December 1967.

[77]Kate Stoker, "Catching Up with the College Crowd," *Sales and Marketing Management,* October 6, 1980, p. 44.

[78]"Direct Marketing Case Histories," *Advertising Age,* January 21, 1980, p. 30; and "Product Sales Increase After College Students Receive 'Good Stuff' Sample Boxes," *Marketing News,* November 2, 1979, p. 14.

[79]Frank Reysen, "Youth Markets: A Psychedelic Maze," *Media/Scope,* 14:40, February 1970.

[80]George W. Schiele, "How to Reach the Young Consumer," *Harvard Business Review,* 52:85–86, March 1974.

[81]Schiele, "How to Reach the Young Consumer," pp. 83–84.

[82]"The Power of the Aging in the Marketplace," *Business Week,* November 20, 1971, p. 52.

[83]Mark Kirkeby, "The Maturity Market is Coming of Age," *Advertising Age,* August 25, 1980, p. S-11.

[84]Fabian Linden, "The $200 Billion Middle-aged Market," *Conference Board Record,* December 1972, p. 17.

[85]Joyanne E. Block, "The Aged Consumer and the Market Place: A Critical Review," *Marquette Business Review,* 18:78, Summer 1974; James MacDonald, "Rising Market," *The Wall Street Journal,* June 24, 1960, p. 14; and Morse "Old Folks," p. 46.

[86]"Don't Overlook the $200 Billion 55-Plus Market," *Media Decisions,* 12:122, October 1977.

[87]Jo-Ann Zbytniewski, "The Older Shopper: Over 65 and Overlooked?" *Progressive Grocer,* November 1979, pp. 109–111.

[88]*Consumer Interests of the Elderly* (Remarks by Professor John A. Howard, Hearing before the Subcommittee on Consumer Interests of the the Elderly of the Special Committee on Aging, United States Senate, 90th Congress, 1st Session, January 17–18, 1967), Washington, DC: U.S. Government Printing Office, 1967, p. 128.

[89]R. Eugene Klippel and Timothy W. Sweeney, "The Use of Information Sources by the Aged Consumer," *The Gerontologist,* April 1974, pp. 163–66.

[90]"The Power of the Aging in the Marketplace," p. 56.

[91]Joseph Barry Mason and Brooks E. Smith, "An Exploratory Note on the Shopping Behavior of the Low Income Senior Citizen," *The Journal of Consumer Affairs,* 8:204–210, Winter 1974.

[92]A. Coskun Samli, "The Elusive Senior Citizen Market," *Business & Economic Dimensions,* 3:7–16, November 1967; and A. Coskun Samli and Feliksas Palubinskas, "Some Lesser Known Aspects of the Senior Citizen Market—A California Study," *Akron Business and Economic Review,* Winter 1972, pp. 47–55.

[93]John A. Reinecke, "Supermarkets, Shopping Centers and the Senior Shopper," *Marquette Business Review,* 19:106, 1975; and Zarrell V. Lambert, "An Investigation of Older Consumers' Unmet Needs and Wants at the Retail Level," *Journal of Retailing,* 55:35–37, Winter 1979.

[94]Lynn W. Phillips and Brian Sternthall, "Age Differences in Information Processing: A Perspective on the Aged Consumer," *Journal of Marketing Research,* 14:450, November 1977.

[95]Bill Abrams, "Advertisers Start Recognizing Cost of Insulting the Elderly," *The Wall Street Journal,* March 5, 1981, p. 25.

[96]Virginia Knauer, "The Aging Alienated Consumer," in *The Aging Consumer,* "Occasional Papers in Gerontology, No. 8;" Institute of Gerontology, Ann Arbor, MI, p. 20.

[97]"The Power of the Aging in the Marketplace," *Business Week,* November 20, 1971, p. 55.

[98]Abrams, "Advertisers Start," p. 25; Phillips and Sternthall, "Age Differences," p. 450; and "A Biting Analysis on Reaching Elderly," *Advertising Age,* March 15, 1982, pp. 55, 60.

CHAPTER 8
SOCIAL CLASS

In this chapter we shall examine the influence of social class on consumer behavior. In a sense, we may think of social classes or strata as being subcultures, for each class has its distinguishing mode of behavior, or lifestyle. We shall first discuss what is meant by social stratification and how social-class divisions are determined. This will be followed by a discussion of differences in the values of each class and their lifestyle differences. Finally, the nature of consumer behavior within each class will be described as it is determined by these values and lifestyle differences.

THE PROCESS OF SOCIAL STRATIFICATION

As much as we Americans like to think that all people are created equal, we are aware that some are "more equal" than others; that is, there are some people who stand high in the community, while others rank low on the totem pole. We refer to these levels as social strata, or classes. "Social stratification," then, is the general term whereby people in a society are ranked by other members of a society into higher and lower social positions which produces a hierarchy of respect or prestige.[1]

Each society subjectively establishes its set of values. These values are reflected in the ideal types of people in that society. That is, those who more nearly conform to the ideal are accorded more respect and prestige, while those who conform less nearly are ranked lower by the society. In one country, members of the armed services may be accorded the greatest prestige; in another, politicians, educators, or business people may be selected. The particular criteria used, as well as their relative weights, are determined by the values which that society stresses. The concept of social class can be useful to the marketer for understanding consumer behavior and plotting a marketing strategy. In order to use it wisely, however, one must first understand its meaning. The following section elaborates on the nature of social class.

THE NATURE OF SOCIAL CLASS

The term "social class" has been defined as a group consisting of a number of people who have approximately equal positions in a society. These positions may be achieved rather than ascribed, with some opportunity for upward or downward movement to other classes.[2] The following are some basic premises in our study of class and consumer behavior.

No Value Judgments

The term social class is used here in the descriptive, not normative, sense. That is, we are not implying that one class is better than another. We are simply describing the class structure as we know it to be. Some may resent such a discussion or be uncomfortable about it, feeling that it is undemocratic. However, social classes exist and if the marketer is to be successful, their patterns must be understood.

Class and Status

Social class and status are not equivalent concepts although they do have an important relationship. *Status* generally refers to one's rank in the social system as perceived by other members of society. An individual's status, therefore, is a function not only of the social class to which he belongs but also of his personal characteristics. For example, the fact that an individual is a scientist means that he has a high rank in the total social system (as seen in Table 8-1). However, a scientist employed by a prestigious research institute earning $50,000 a year will have

TABLE 8-1 THE RATINGS OF OCCUPATIONS

	White-Collar Groups
350 and up	Very high status occupations—presidents and chairmen of boards; the most highly successful lawyers and physicians
250–349	Successful business and professional people—top managers; owners of substantial but not mammoth businesses; professors at universities and high-prestige colleges; reasonably successful doctors, lawyers, and architects
175–249	Moderately successful people—persons in the less prestigeful professions—managers at lower levels; owners of smaller businesses
130–174	Middle managers; small-business owners (retail only); manufacturers' representatives; wholesale salesmen; and some technicians
115–129	The lowest level of managerial, professional, and kindred workers
95–114	Entry-level clerical and salespeople; managers of quite small, mainly blue-collar enterprises
Under 95	Clerks in low-status retail and wholesale establishments
	Blue-Collar Groups
115 and up	Foremen and craftsmen where the craft requires quite special skills
100–114	Typical craftsmen and skilled manual and service workers
85–99	Ordinary working-class jobs
70–84	Less securely rewarded working-class jobs
55–69	Marginal blue-collar and service jobs
Under 55	Very poor jobs

Source: From *Social Standing in America: New Dimensions of Class* by Richard P. Coleman and Lee Rainwater with Kent A. McClelland. Copyright © 1978 by Basic Books, Inc. By permission of Basic Books, Inc., Publishers, New York.

higher status or rank than a scientist employed by a small firm and earning $25,000, even though both may be members of the same social class. Moreover, an individual's personal contributions to society will help determine his or her status. A scientist who discovers a breakthrough in laser technology, for example, will have higher status than another who has made no such significant contribution.

Although social status and social class are often used interchangeably, they are not equivalent concepts. However, since we are discussing groups of consumers, not individuals, there is little problem in doing so.

Social Class Indicators

Social class is not equivalent to occupation, or income, or any one criterion; however, it may be indicated by or be related to one or more of these measures. It is important for the marketer to realize that some of these variables are more reliable "proxies" (substitutes) than others. As we shall discuss later, income is often misleading as an indicator of social class position. Yet, money, far more than anything else, is what Americans associate with the idea of social class.[3]

On the other hand, occupation generally provides a fairly good clue to one's social class; in fact, some believe it is the best single indicator available because certain occupations are held in higher esteem than others by Americans. Table 8-1 illustrates the hierarchy of prestige accorded to many occupations in the United States. The numerical scores indicate the level of status for the occupational category. Thus, the higher the score, the higher the status is perceived to be. Notice also that both blue- and white-collar groups are included, with some overlap of status between high-blue-collar groups and low-white-collar groups.

Housing is another key social class ingredient, according to most theories. The Johnnie Walker Black Label advertisement in Figure 8-1 illustrates the relationship of housing to that product's consumption image. Most marketers believe "birds of a feather flock together" and thus "You are where you live." Consequently, some researchers cluster U.S. postal zip-code areas together on the basis of key demographic factors. For example, one company characterizes those at the top of the hill as "the blue-blood estates," followed in descending order by "furs and station wagons," and "money and brains," to "blue-chip blues," and "Bunker's neighbors," to "down-home gentry," and "hard scrabble."[4] Such information can be used for market segmentation and strategy decisions. For instance, Colgate-Palmolive used this approach to pick neighborhoods for a drop of 7 million samples of Fresh Start detergent.

Social Class Categorization

Research studies have attempted to stratify social classes in the United States using various measurement approaches. Generally, three methods have been utilized: the subjective method, the reputational method, and the objective method.

The Subjective Method In this approach, individuals are asked to rank themselves in the social class hierarchy. However, because most people are reluctant to categorize themselves as either lower or upper class, the middle class ends up with an unrealistically large share. In a famous survey by *Fortune* magazine, 79.2 percent of the public described themselves as middle-class. Today, file clerks earning as little as $8000 and lawyers making as much as $80,000 think of themselves as middle class, although sometimes with "upper" and "lower" as modifiers.[5]

FIGURE 8-1

Advertisement for Johnnie Walker Black Label. (Created by Smith/Greenland Inc. for Somerset Importers Ltd., importers of Johnnie Walker Black Label Scotch.)

The Reputational Method This approach asks members of a community to rank each other in the status system. Because citizens must know each other in order to rank themselves, this approach is limited to small communities and, therefore, is not able to be widely used by marketers.

The Objective Method Individuals are ranked on the basis of certain objective factors and positioned accordingly in the social-status hierarchy. Probably the best-known study using such an approach has been done by W. Lloyd Warner and his associates.[6] Warner developed an Index of Status Characteristics (ISC) based on the following socioeconomic indicators:

1 Occupation—ranging from professionals and proprietors of large businesses to unskilled workers (weighted by a factor of 4).

2 Source of income—ranging from inherited wealth to public relief and nonrespectable income (weighting of 3).

3 House type—houses ranging from excellent to very poor (weighting of 3).

4 Dwelling area—ranging from very high: Gold Coast, North Shore, and so on; to very low: slum (weighting of 2).

An individual is classified into one of seven categories for each of the above four factors. The classification is then multiplied by the weight and summed across the four factors to obtain the ISC score. This total score is then used to indicate in which social class the individual belongs. Warner discerned a six-class system of stratification, based upon research conducted in several small communities. He categorized the six classes as follows: upper-upper, lower-upper, upper-middle, lower-middle, upper-lower, and lower-lower.

In other approaches, Carman used a large sample to isolate five social class categories on the basis of occupation, education, and home value,[7] while Coleman and Rainwater classified individuals into five social classes on the basis of having respondents evaluate certain profiles given them.[8] Coleman and Rainwater observed that income is of overwhelming importance as to how Americans think about social standing, followed far behind by occupation and then schooling.[9]

Table 8-2 presents the approximate percentage of responses for each class determined by three representative research studies, using different methods.

In spite of the many approaches used to measure and categorize social classes, there are a number of problems with the concept. An analysis of the major research done on this topic has found important shortcomings.[10] The following are a few of the problem areas associated with the social-class measurement system that is currently used by marketers.[11]

1 The ranking of social class is based upon an average of the person's position on several status dimensions; thus it ignores the inconsistencies which arise from an individual ranking high on one dimension (such as income) but low on another (such as education).

2 A person's social class is stable, and thus it ignores the effects of mobility.

TABLE 8-2 SOCIAL CLASS PLACEMENT

	Percentage Distribution		
	Warner	Carman	Coleman and Rainwater
Upper-upper class	1.44%		
Upper class		0.38%	2.20%
Lower-upper class	1.56		
Upper-middle class	10.22	10.82	20.30
Middle class			32.80
Lower-middle class	28.12	30.82	
Working class			36.70
Upper-lower class	32.60	49.96	
Lower class			8.00
Lower-lower class	25.22	8.02	
Other responses	0.84		
	100.00%	100.00%	100.00%

Source: W. L. Warner, Marchia Meeker, and Kenneth Eells, *Social Class in America,* Science Research Associates, Chicago, 1949, p. 14; James M. Carman, *The Application of Social Class in Market Segmentation,* University of California Graduate School of Business Administration, Institute of Business and Economic Research, Berkeley, California, 1965, p. 53; and Richard P. Coleman and Lee Rainwater, *Social Standing in America: New Dimensions of Class,* Basic Books, Inc., New York, 1978, p. 29.

3. An individual identifies with the social class in which she or he is categorized; thus it ignores reference-group effects from other classes.

4. The social class of an entire family can be measured by examining the characteristics of the adult male wage earner; thus it ignores the characteristics of other family members, particularly the employment and education of the adult female in the family.[12]

Resolution of these and other problems would make the concept of social class a more useful one for marketers.[13]

Although the size of different classes may vary depending on the classification method used and may shift over time, it is nevertheless quite important to realize that the bulk of the market for most products exists in the broad middle- and lower-class groups. The upper class is made up of only about 2 to 4 percent of the population; because of its wealth, it is of the utmost importance for the marketing of certain luxury items. However, this group is too small in number to provide the focal point for most marketers. On the other hand, at the lower end of the class spectrum—the lower-lower class—one generally finds a market that, even though sizable, does not have sufficient income for many products. Therefore, most consumer-goods marketers concentrate their major attention on the remaining groups of middle and upper-lower classes.

Symbols of Social Standing

People buy products for what they mean as well as what they can do. That is, products and services are seen to have personal and social meanings in addition to their purely functional purpose. This idea was expressed long ago by Thorstein Veblen who suggested that there is a tendency by some members of each social class to engage in *conspicuous consumption* while others spend more conservatively.[14] By conspicuous consumption Veblen referred to consumers purchasing things that they do not really need so that others can see what they have done. The things consumers buy become "symbols," telling others who they are and what their social class or status is. Consider the wristwatch market:

> There are actually two watch markets in the United States. One is for people who merely want to tell time, the other is for people who want to tell the world something about themselves—who desire, in effect, to wear their bank books on their wrists. Thus, the status symbol long important in Europe is starting to catch on here—the Swiss wristwatch that at $15,000 or more, costs more than an automobile. Such Swiss brands as Vacheron Constantin, Patek Philippe, Audemars Piguet, and Piaget are mostly handmade in very limited editions and are at the apex of the luxury watch pyramid.[15]

Perhaps the most conspicuous site of conspicuous consumption in America is along Rodeo Drive in Beverly Hills, California. For example,

> Bijan, one of the most exclusive men's shops on the Drive, offers $24,000 topcoats, $1200 suits, $300 per ounce perfume, $450 shoes, $300 shirts, and $65 ties. The front door is locked, and shopping is by appointment only in order to keep the "untasty" away! Customers must earn $100,000 a month, and included among the store's client roster are four kings, fifteen princes, and seventeen princesses.[16]

In a complex society in which financial wealth dictates status, one's possessions become a substitute indicator of the individual's worth, value, wealth, and so forth. Possessions, therefore, take the place of income as an indicator of status, since we aren't likely to know how much others are paid. Consequently, there may be members of a society at each social-class level who seek to achieve a certain higher status by virtue of their possessions. It should be noted, however, that others at the same level may be content to save more and spend much less extravagantly.

Marketers have always catered to consumers who were looking for something to give them an edge, whether real or imagined, over their peers. The key to status symbols is their scarcity and social desirability. As such, they are marks of distinction, setting their owners apart from others.

> The Sperry Top-Sider boat moccasin has been transformed into such a product. Originally designed to help sailors stay upright on slippery decks, they now appear on people's feet even away from sailboats—at ski resorts, high schools, and Dallas shopping malls. In fact, one company producing a similar version finds that only 15 percent of its customers ever go on a boat. Why the success? The shoe imparts just the right air of preppiness and wealth. The look is WASPish "old money."[17]

At one time, class differences in status and its symbols were an accepted fact of life in clothing, housing and furnishings, food, drink, speech, and even religious affiliation. Today, however, views of status symbols are changing.[18] Rapid advances in technology and communications have spread the desire for and availability of these material pleasures among all social classes. And as Americans have become more affluent, even those with moderate incomes are able to own their own homes, color televisions, boats, and all sorts of home appliances, and to take exotic vacations. Consequently, if "perfectly ordinary" people can display expensive cars and fancy appliances, then these things obviously have lost much of their effectiveness as status symbols.

A recent fashion phenomenon is the designer label and status emblem on everything from shirts, dresses, sweaters, underwear, and socks to luggage, cologne, and automobiles. Products marketed by LaCoste (Izod), Gucci, Pierre Cardin, Gloria Vanderbilt, Calvin Klein, Ralph Lauren, Halston, and Oleg Cassini, among others, exact high prices, yet they find ready buyers. The mass marketing of these items results in less-than-clear distinctions between the social classes. Thus, people today cannot be sure of who is dramatizing what sort of status with what sort of symbol. According to one writer, "Order Gucci loafers and you only risk winding up shod the same as the boy who delivers them. A Cadillac today signifies nothing about the owner except that he might well pull in at the next Burger King."[19]

Such a situation usually results in new symbols being adopted by higher social classes. In addition, many Americans have lost interest in status showing off. Others have picked unconventional symbols to reflect values other than social rank. For instance, some professional and artistic Americans have downplayed the traditional symbols of economic standing.

In addition, many of the status symbols of today have not filtered down from the upper class to the middle and working classes, but instead have percolated up from the bottom. Recent styles such as blue jeans are indicative of this. Another confusing element is that traditional status symbols are available today even to those who are not wealthy. For instance, art and sculpture can be rented; inexpensive opera and ballet offerings are available; and tennis, skiing, and sailing can be pursued on a low budget.

Thus, traditional status symbols are no longer the clear indicator of social class they once were and marketers must understand these trends in order to take advantage of consumers' changing values. It should also be noted that what is "in" in one region of the United States may be "out" in another. Consequently, status symbols can vary geographically, as Table 8-3 illustrates.

SOCIAL CLASS LIFESTYLES

The significance of social stratification for the marketer is that there are differences in values, attitudes, and behavior of each of the classes. These differences provide a basis on which to segment markets and obtain an enhanced understanding of the behavior of consumers. Some of the major findings from research on general social class differences are summarized in this section which discusses class variations and lifestyle differences. As we describe the lifestyles of each of the major social class groups, the terminology adopted by most marketers will be used, which

TABLE 8-3
REGIONAL GUIDE TO AMERICAN TASTE

New York	Chicago	Los Angeles	Atlanta
In	*In*	*In*	*In*
Mustaches	Croissants, tacos	Owning property	Money-market funds
Wine spritzers	1950s music	Cowboy bars, music, clothes	Exercise at lunchtime
Western bars	Levi's jeans		Racquetball, roller-skating
Wind surfing	Telephones in cars	Pay TV, home computers	Sushi, tofu (raw fish, soybean curd)
Jungle motif in clothes	Antiques	Traditional weddings	South American vacations
Jogging to work	Calligraphy	Nancy Reagan red	
Lightweight earphone radio-tape units	Wine bars	College business courses	1950s and 1960s parties
	Cards, electronic games	Fad-diet books	Women with master's degrees in business
Fish and fowl	Exotic plants	Escapist movies	
Cosmetic surgery for men	Buying through catalogs	Antismoking clinics	Peach as a decorating color
Living alone and liking it		Wash-and-wear hairstyles	International banking TV-game systems
	Out		
Out	Bagels, pizza	*Out*	*Out*
Long hair, beards	Country-and-Western music	Buying records	Gold and silver investments
Tap water		Golf, tennis	
Singles bars	Designer jeans	Gas-guzzling cars	Tanning salons
Courses in education	Vanity license plates, CB radios	Discos	Skateboards
Skintight clothes		Self-realization seminars	Red meat, heavy sauces
Heavy drinking	High-tech décor		
Electronic calculators	Jogging	Philosophy courses	Smoking
	Salad bars	Expensive vacations	Acid-rock music
Red meat, frozen produce	Backgammon, Scrabble	Raucous rock music	Cocktail dresses
Bright colors in home décor	Pets	Jogging	Synthetic fabrics
	Shopping	Skateboards	Selling real estate
Primal-scream therapy			Liberals

includes the categories of upper-upper, lower-upper, upper-middle, lower-middle, upper-lower, and lower-lower class. At times the term "working class" will be used, which is roughly synonymous with the upper-lower class.

As the following classes are discussed it should be kept in mind that we are not implying that all members of the same class have homogeneous behavior. As Coleman observes, "there is a considerable variation in the way individual members of a class realize these class goals and express these values."[20] Moreover, it is impossible to point to a clear line of demarcation where one class changes to another. There is some blurring and overlapping of the social strata. Nevertheless, we will attempt to make some major distinctions between the six-class system, as developed by Warner.[21]

Upper-Upper Class

This is the "Social Register" class composed of old, locally prominent families—the aristocracy of birth and wealth with at least three generations in the community and class. It is the smallest class group, international in residence, friendships, and relationships. Its members have occupations as large merchants, financiers, and in the higher professions. Their reference group is the British upper class. They are oriented toward living graciously, upholding the family reputation, reflecting the excellence of one's breeding, and displaying a sense of community responsibility.

TABLE 8-3
(Continued)

Detroit	Houston	San Francisco	Washington
In	*In*	*In*	*In*
Using coupons	Marriage	Sky diving	Rich people
How-to manuals	Caviar	Tenor Luciano	Maturity
Blazers for men	Elegant parties	Pavarotti	Adolfo, Chanel suits
Long weekends	Plastic surgery	Wardrobe	Alligator handbags
Szechwan cooking	Wine spritzers	consultants	Entertaining at home
Small luxury cars	Salmon as a	Freshly made pasta	Body-building
Romance	decorating color	Beverly Hills diet	equipment
Aerobic dancing	"Preppy" look	Izod shirts	Small convertibles
Metallic look in	Formal, traditional	Home burglar alarms	Kir, champagne with
women's clothes	weddings	Separate vacations	peaches
Mexican vacations in	Dolly Parton diet	Patriotism	Soap operas
Cancún, Cozumel	Republicans	Babies	Moisture creams
Out	*Out*	*Out*	*Out*
Idealism	Living together	$5\frac{1}{4}$ percent savings	Poor people
Books on politics	Quiche	accounts	"Preppy" look
Reversible vests	Huge cocktail parties	Quiche	Long hair
Heavy drinking	Ultrasuede	Gold chains for men	Oil in salad
Steakhouses	Wild, frizzy hairstyles	Chauffeur-driven	dressings
Wild colors on cars	Oversauced food	limousines	Cowboy belts
Sleeping around	Big cars	Disco dancing	Big transistor radios
Westerns	Cancún, Cozumel	Slit skirts	Scotch, Bloody Marys
Thin belts	vacations	Indoor soccer	Democrats
Jamaica, Haiti	Scarsdale diet	Living together	Workaholics
	Cocaine	Kiss-and-tell	In-out lists
		biographies	
		Houseplants	

Source: Reprinted from *U.S. News & World Report,* September 21, 1981, pp. 62–63. Copyright 1981, U.S. News & World Report, Inc.

Lower-Upper Class

This is the nouveau riche, or "newly rich" class, composed of those who have recently arrived at their wealth and are not quite accepted by the upper-uppers. They are the "executive elite," founders of large businesses, and wealthy doctors and lawyers. They have the highest incomes of all the classes and their goals are a blend of the upper-uppers' pursuit of gracious living and the upper-middle success drive.

Many of the nation's millionaires fit this category. In 1979, an estimated 520,000 Americans, or about one in every 424 citizens, had a net worth of $1 million or more. Historically, the greatest proportion of millionaires had inherited wealth (upper-uppers). In recent years, that proportion has sharply diminished. Many of the new millionaires come from the ranks of entrepreneurs, especially those who have founded technological businesses, skilled professionals in fields such as neurosurgery and the law, top corporate executives, and professional entertainers and sports stars.[22]

Upper-Middle Class

This class consists of moderately successful professional men and women, such as doctors, lawyers, and professors; owners of medium-sized businesses; and "organization men" at the managerial level. It also includes younger men and women who are expected to reach those occupational-status levels within a few years. Most members are college-educated, hence, this group is sometimes referred to as "the brains and eyes" of our society.

The motivations of this group are toward achieving success in their careers, reaching a higher income level, and achieving social advancement for themselves and their children. They strive to cultivate charm and polish, and handle a broad range of civic and/or cultural interests. They play bridge, and Scrabble; go to plays, museums, symphonies, and art galleries; and are members of golf clubs, yacht clubs, and college clubs. Their possessions are usually new and their reference group is the upper class.

Lower-Middle Class

This class is at the top of the "common man" or "average man" level. It is composed of nonmanagerial workers, small business owners, and highly paid blue-collars. These lower echelon white-collar workers and small businessmen are at the bottom of the white-collar status ladder while their blue-collar counterparts are at the top of theirs.

The key motivations for this group are "respectability" and "striving." Men and women want to be judged respectable in their personal behavior by their fellow citizens; that is, they desire to live in well-maintained homes which are neatly furnished and located in neighborhoods that are on the right side of the tracks. They strive to do a good job at their work. Home is their focus and much time and effort is spent in it, especially keeping it clean and tidy.

Upper-Lower Class

These are "poor but honest" folks who are also referred to as the "ordinary working class." The largest of all classes, it is composed of skilled and semiskilled workers and small tradesmen. Contrary to what may be expected, many of these class members make very good money; they simply don't use it to become "respectable" the way the lower-middle class does. Upper-lowers are oriented toward living well and enjoying life from day to day rather than saving for the future or being concerned about what the middle classes think of them. They want to be modern, to keep up with the times rather than the Joneses.

The working-class family's world view is one of great anxiety. They value the present, the known, and the personal, while avoiding the competitive, the impersonal, and the uncertain. They indulge rather than invest. They are preoccupied with stable human relationships in their everyday lives. Moreover, because they see themselves as being quite restricted in their ability to rise in social status, those with whom they identify are largely chosen from their own class. The working-class woman tends to be part of a tightly-knit social group composed primarily of female kin. Thus, more than in any other class, the working-class family generally looks horizontally for its norms and standards rather than up to the next class. Here are some additional characteristics of the women in this group:[23]

- Although the necessity of working has expanded the social horizons of many working-class women, the traditional female jobs which most of them hold are not intrinsically rewarding.

- These expanded horizons are reflected in the decreasing propensity of working-class women to define family responsibilities, especially child care, as the central focus of their lives.

- Wives' employment is often viewed as threatening by the working-class husband whose ability to provide for the family is often the major source of his sense of self-worth.

- Working-class husbands and wives tend to adhere to traditional household roles and to engage in sex-segregated leisure activities, even if wives work.

- While feelings of lack of self-worth and competency in dealing with the world outside the home have decreased among working-class women, they have decreased more slowly than have the same feelings among middle-class women. The result is an increasing disparity in feelings of self-worth and self-confidence between the two social-class groupings.

- Working-class women are more likely than their middle-class counterparts to feel that their adult life is better than their childhood. Since part of the perceived improvement is due to acquisition of desired material goods, working-class women are more positive toward business in general and specific products, and toward the media in general and advertising in particular, than are middle-class women.

In lumping people of this class together with lower-middles, the resulting group has been termed "the muscles and hands" of our society, and is characterized as enjoying canasta, rummy, poker, TV, movies, and bowling. The men belong to unions, lodges, and fraternal orders.

Lower-Lower Class

This group consists mostly of unskilled workers, unassimilated ethnics, and those who are sporadically employed. Many are on welfare, and they live in the deteriorated sections of town. Many are categorized as the "American underclass" whose environment is often a "junk heap of rotting housing, broken furniture, crummy food, alcohol and drugs."[24] Their outlook is apathetic and fatalistic, and their behavior generally and as consumers is toward "getting their kicks wherever they can." They have a bad reputation among higher classes who view them as lazy, shiftless, against work, and immoral.

THE ROLE OF SOCIAL CLASS IN SEGMENTING MARKETS

It is evident that the concept of social class should help us to understand better the behavior of the various market segments. However, the marketing practitioner wants to know if segmentation on the basis of social class is an advantageous approach.

Social-class segmentation involves two basic issues.[25] First, opinions differ concerning which procedures are best for identifying social classes. This issue is beyond the scope of our discussion. However, it should simply be noted here that there are various approaches to social class measurement, with each one offering certain advantages and disadvantages. A second and more fundamental problem is whether even to use social class (which is, in effect, a composite index consisting of several variables) in segmenting markets, or to use a single proxy variable such as income (for which data more readily exist). Thus, the basic question here is, Which approach better explains consumer behavior?

Social Class and Income Related to Lifestyle Patterns

While addressing this issue, it may be useful to examine the results of a study that correlated more than 200 lifestyle items with both social class and income. Although none of the correlations was as high as might be desired in order to clearly support the contention that lifestyle is the "essence" of social class, those correlations obtained for social class were generally higher than those obtained for income. The most meaningful lifestyle statements and their correlation coefficients for social class (r_{SC}) and income (r_I) are presented in Table 8-4. Two conclusions from this study should be cited:[26]

1 Many lifestyle items show significant correlations with the index of social class, indicating definite but small differences among the social classes in terms of lifestyles.

TABLE 8-4 CORRELATIONS OF LIFESTYLE ITEMS WITH SOCIAL CLASS AND INCOME

Item	r_{SC}	r_I
I enjoy going to concerts	.26	.11
I enjoy going through an art gallery	.25	.18
I attend a bridge club regularly	.24	.18
I am usually an active member of more than one service organization	.24	.16
I like ballet	.24	.14
I think I'm a pretty nice-looking person	.23	.12
I am a homebody	−.22	−.13
I feel I can do things as well or better than most people	.21	.11
My children are the most important thing in my life	−.19	−.08
I think I have less self-confidence than most people	−.18	−.07
I often take an active part in some local civic issue	.17	.09
I am usually the center of attention in a group	.15	.08

Source: James H. Myers and Jonathan Gutman, "Life-Style: The Essence of Social Class," in William D. Wells (ed.), *Lifestyle and Psychographics,* American Marketing Association, Chicago, 1974, pp. 250–251.

2 Some items show a much greater correlation with social class than with income, suggesting that social class is a better predictor of consumers' living patterns than is income.

Those items that were more related to social class than to income seemed to comprise two "clusters": one representing "cultural" activities; the other representing a group of social-interaction items. Cultural activities (such as concerts, ballet, and bridge games) are available to people of almost any income level. The fact that some people choose to engage in them and others do not is one of the things that makes social class a meaningful concept. Social interaction items (such as confidence, outgoingness, or good looks) may result from higher-class people feeling a sense of belonging and recognition from having a secure place higher up in the social structure. However, upper-social-class people also seem to have less interest in the home in general, and in children in particular, than do upper-income/lower-class individuals.

How may the marketer use such information?[27] General lifestyle items that correlate well with product usage might well explain characteristics of the markets' activity, interest, and opinion to the seller. Such findings could give the marketer some direction for product, promotion, channel, and pricing decisions. A preferred approach, however, would be to design a lifestyle study especially for the particular firm or its product line. These two approaches are illustrated in Table 8-5. In this case, AT&T investigated the style and color preferences for telephones among different social classes. Based only on Table 8-5A, it might appear that the upper and upper-middle classes would be the only groups at which to aim for new styles and colors of phones since they tend to have a greater preference for style, are more likely to have modern, colored appliances, are willing to experiment, and enjoy the better things in life and are willing to pay for them. Yet, by incorporating product-specific items into the analysis (Table 8-5B), the lower-middle class is found to be a surprisingly good prospect group. They place the greatest emphasis on telephones of different patterns, designs, and colors. Thus, had AT&T assumed that only the upper and upper-middle classes were prime prospects for new style telephones (based on Table 8-5A), the important lower-middle class segment would have been overlooked.[28]

Social Class and Income Related to Consumer Behavior Patterns

The previous section assessed the relationship of social class and income to lifestyle and patterns and consumers' interests as a basis of segmenting markets. A fundamental question not specifically addressed above, however, is whether social class or income is more closely associated with specific consumer activity, particularly with product purchase patterns.

Those who believe that social class is much better than income for market segmentation claim that income categories are quite often irrelevant in analyzing markets and explaining consumers' shopping habits, store preferences, and media usage. An example of the superiority of social class to income is the following case of three families, all earning approximately the same amount per year (that is, $25,000), but belonging to different social classes with radical differences in their spending patterns.[29]

An *upper-middle class* family headed, perhaps, by a young lawyer or a college professor is likely to spend a relatively large share of its income on housing in a prestige neighborhood, on expensive furniture, clothing from quality stores, and on cultural amusements or club memberships.

A *lower-middle class* family headed, let's say, by an insurance salesman or a successful grocery store owner probably has a better house, but in not as fancy a neighborhood; as full a wardrobe, although not as expensive; more furniture, but none by name designers; and a much bigger savings account.

A *working-class* family headed, perhaps, by a welder or cross-country truck driver, is likely to have less house and less neighborhood than the others; however it will have a larger, newer car, more expensive kitchen appliances, and a larger TV set in the living room. This family will spend less on clothing and furniture, but more on food and sports.

TABLE 8-5

PSYCHOGRAPHIC PROFILE OF CUSTOMER'S SOCIOECONOMIC STATUS

A. General Profile

Style/Color Statements	Lower-Class Agreement (%)	Lower-Middle-Class Agreement (%)	Upper-Middle-Class Agreement (%)	Upper-Class Agreement (%)
I am generally willing to try even the most radical fashion at least once	32	25	42	37
When I must choose between the two, I usually dress for fashion not for comfort	9	15	24	29
Our home is furnished for comfort, not style	96	87	79	79
I have more modern appliances in my home than most people	17	23	41	48
I prefer colored appliances	57	73	87	92
I enjoy the better things in life and am willing to pay for them	36	70	70	82

B. Product-Specific Profile

Style/Color Statements	Lower-Class Agreement (%)	Lower-Middle-Class Agreement (%)	Upper-Middle-Class Agreement (%)	Upper-Class Agreement (%)
Phones should come in patterns and designs as well as colors	60	80	63	58
A telephone should improve the decorative style of a room	47	82	73	77
Telephones should be modern in design	58	85	83	89
A home should have a variety of telephone styles	8	46	39	51
You can keep all those special phones. All I want is a phone that works	83	67	68	56
The style of a telephone is unimportant to me	86	54	58	51

Source: A. Marvin Roscoe, Jr., Arthur LeClaire, Jr., and Leon G. Shiffman, "Theory and Management Applications of Demographics in Buyer Behavior," in Arch G. Woodside, Jagdish N. Sheth, and Peter D. Bennett (eds.), *Consumer and Industrial Buying Behavior,* North-Holland, New York, 1977, pp. 74–75.

Nevertheless, most of the research that has been conducted has found income to be more useful than social class for segmenting markets. One study showed that for a number of low-priced consumer packaged goods, both income and social class were found to correlate with buying behavior. However, product usage generally proved to be more closely related to income than to social class.[30] A follow-up study included certain durable-goods items plus a few services and confirmed the earlier one by showing income to be superior to social class in segmenting the market for nearly all items.[31] Thus, some products appear to be classless in their appeal. For example, in the hot southwest, income, not social class, largely determines whether a family buys air conditioning. If the family can afford it, it purchases it. Based upon such findings, it would appear that social class, although useful as a concept, has often not been as successful as other approaches in segmenting markets.

Much of the earlier research, however, based its findings on *use* or *nonuse* of a product or service rather than on *how often* that product or service was used. Since there are many products or services that a broad spectrum of consumers would buy or use at least once, one research study examined the role of *frequency of use* in selecting the superior segmentation bases among income, social class, age, and stage in family life cycle for various entertainment activities. This research showed that income and stage in the life cycle were more highly related to *use* of all the entertainment activities than were age and social class. However, all four variables—especially social class—showed strong associations with the *frequency of use* of these entertainment activities.[32] More research is needed on a broad variety of products before a generalization of this finding is made.

Several explanations have been suggested for the apparent lackluster performance of social class as a basis for market segmentation.[33] One factor is the recent and dramatic changes which have taken place in our society's economic, social, and cultural climate and which have diminished the differences in consumer behavior between the classes.

Another explanation for the poor showing of social class is that researchers have failed to account for the diversity within classes. That is, individuals, although in the same social class, may show considerable discrepancy in their ratings on the variables comprising it. For example, some may have high education with low income or vice versa, yet be members of the same social class. This inconsistency in strata variables known as *status incongruency* or *low status crystallization,* presents difficulties not only in ranking individuals but also in understanding their behavior.

The diversity within social classes is particularly evident with income level variations. For example, it has been suggested that there are *overprivileged* and *underprivileged* members within each class; that is, those whose incomes are above average for their class, and those with incomes below the average for that class.[34] For example, an upper-class family earning less than $100,000 a year is "underprivileged" by the standards of its level. That family can't own a mansion and a second home and obtain private schooling. It has to sacrifice. Upper-half middle-American overprivileged starts at $25,000, working-class overprivileged at $18,000, and underprivileged at below $16,500 (in 1979) according to one researcher.[35]

This concept is believed to explain the purchase of certain consumer durables. For example, the dominant market for high-price domestic cars is said to be the overprivileged buyers from each social class rather than high-income Americans as a group. On the other hand, small cars were bought initially by the underprivileged segments of each class. Thus, a struggling young lawyer, as an underprivileged member of the upper-middle class, may purchase a Toyota as a temporary transportation solution until her income rises, then buy a new Buick when she gets to be overprivileged. Similarly, costly household appliances and recreational activities tend to have been consumed by the overprivileged members of each class. Color television sets, for instance, were first bought primarily by this segment.

Based on a recent, thorough research study, the following tentative generalizations are possible regarding when social class, income, or their combination is superior as a segmentation variable:[36]

1 Social class is superior to income for areas of consumer behavior that do not involve high-dollar expenditures, but do reflect underlying lifestyle, value, or homemaker role differences. Relevant products in this situation might include instant, frozen, and canned convenience foods and beverages; snack foods; and imported and domestic wines, for example. Social class is also superior for both method and place of purchase of highly visible, symbolic, and expensive living-room furniture.

2 Income is generally superior for products which require substantial expenditures, and which may no longer serve as symbols of status within a class or as status symbols to the upper-lower class (such as, major kitchen and laundry appliances).

3 The combination of social class and income is generally superior for product classes that are highly visible, serve as symbols of social class or status within class, and require either moderate or substantial expenditure (such as clothing and makeup, automobiles, and television sets).

Before attempting to use social class to segment markets, the marketer should remember three guidelines:

1 Social class may not always be a relevant consideration; that is, segmentation by other criteria, such as age and sex, is frequently more appropriate.

2 Benefits from social class segmentation for undifferentiated products may be less than the costs incurred to achieve such segmentation.

3 Social class segmentation is frequently most effective when used in conjunction with such additional variables as life-cycle stage and ethnic group.[37]

However, even for cases in which social class may have only limited application, it does provide the marketer with helpful insights—some of which may be specifically used in developing marketing strategies, and others of which at least offer an improved general understanding of consumer behavior.[38]

In the remaining section of this chapter, we will present some of the research findings on the relationship of social class, consumer behavior, and the development of marketing mixes.

SOCIAL CLASS AND CONSUMER BEHAVIOR

This section examines the most significant findings concerning various classes' behavior with regard to the products they buy, the places they shop, and the promotions and prices they respond to.

For many products the groups of interest to the marketer are the middle and working classes—by far the largest segment of the market. Because of this, the bulk of our attention in this section will be focused on these two categories in order to provide a more complete understanding of these groups. Where possible, special emphasis will be given to the working class because of the marketer's inherent difficulty in understanding this market, which springs from the fact that most marketing managers are members of the middle or upper classes. These are the groups that form the basis of their *self-reference criterion;* that is, they tend to assume that everyone else is like themselves in values, attitudes, tastes, lifestyle, and so forth. Such a premise is very likely to result in marketing strategy failure.

Products and Services Consumed

Product choice and usage differ among the social classes. There are items that are bought mainly by the upper classes, such as bonds and exotic vacations, and others that are purchased mainly by lower classes, such as roller derby tickets and cheap wine. Not only are there between-class purchasing differences but also within-class variations. As mentioned previously, each class level has its conspicuous consumers and its more conservative buyers—that is, its overprivileged and its underprivileged members. However, most products are purchased by all consumers so it becomes difficult to distinguish class differences in purchasing patterns. For example, all people purchase food, clothing, and shelter items. The differences come into view when we examine not just generic categories, but types of products and particular brands, and frequency of purchase. Before discussing each class specifically, some general product/service differences among the classes will be noted.

Clothing purchases vary by class, with upper- and middle-class consumers being much more interested in fashion and style than in comfort. They are more likely to read fashion magazines, go to fashion shows, observe what others wear, and discuss fashions with other people.[39]

Home furnishings and appliances are another area where orientations differ because of social class. Furniture style has greater symbolic value to the upper-middle and upper classes. They will seek furniture that is stylish and in keeping with some specific personal or family esthetic. They are also likely to depart from the norm because they have great confidence in their taste and because their desire to set themselves apart from lower-class symbols outweighs any fear they may have of being criticized for their taste. This group would have a greater affinity for modern and traditional furniture and sterling silver, for example. They also are more likely to buy modern and colored appliances. Lower-middles have some anxiety over selecting furniture that is "right," (that is, respectable, neat, or pretty). They would probably refuse to hang an original Picasso on their walls even if it were received as a gift. Not only would they dislike the painting, but would also fear the reaction of their friends. This group tends toward formica-covered dinette sets, silverplated tableware in a fancy design, and highly conventional furniture. Lower classes are likely to emphasize sturdiness, comfort, and maintenance in their furniture.[40]

Choice of *transportation vehicles* is also influenced by class. For example, more than half of the people in the upper class have a foreign car, but only a third of those in the upper-middle-class, 20 percent of those in the lower middle class, 7 percent of those in the working class, and only 5 percent of those in the lower class buy foreign imports.[41] Many working-class people say outright, "I won't buy an import." They tend to prefer high-price domestic cars plus RVs and trucks. Trucks have become a "macho symbol" and are moving upward from working class to middle class, but the upper-middle class shuns them. RVs are abhorred by upper-class Americans. They prefer high-price foreign and domestic cars, and fancy sports cars in that order. Lower-middle-class taste runs to high-price domestic autos and station wagons.

Travel, recreation, and *leisure activities* also have class patterns. Frequent or wide-ranging travel and expensive recreation are some of the most vivid symbols of higher social status.[42] Not only where one goes, but how one gets there is related to social class. For example, airlines are basically a form of travel for middle-class people. Waiting rooms, plane interiors, food, drinks, and even stewardess behavior are directly aimed at the upper middle-class. Lower-class people perceive that air travel is not for them and as a consequence, only a very small proportion of air travelers are from these lower classes. Instead, they are more likely to go by bus, train, or car. Even though the airlines have attempted "no frills" service, lower middles have probably been the major beneficiaries of this strategy.

With regard to recreation and leisure activities, class patterns are also evident.[43] Major league baseball, for example, is patronized mostly by upper-lower class fans, while college football attendance is practically all middle class, and predominantly upper-middle. Similarly, bridge, tennis, and ice skating have traditionally been upper-class while television, bingo, boxing, and bowling are lower-class activities.[44]

Working-class men are also much more likely to pursue outdoor "masculine" activities such as hunting, camping, and fishing than are middle-class men. Guns and fishing equipment are aimed primarily at this market by manufacturers. Similarly, upper-lower class men have been the primary target for camping vans. Members of this group also tend to combine their vactations with their sporting interests and are likely to go on hunting or fishing trips as vacations without their wives, and often spend an evening "out with the boys." Such separate vacations and nights out are rare for the middle-class man, whose wife would quickly become suspicious of his strange behavior.[45]

Attendance at culturally-oriented activities also differs by social class. For instance, preference for attending operas, plays, ballet, symphonies, lectures, and museums is greatest for upper-class members, with lower levels of preference reported for middle and lower classes. Attendance at rock concerts is significantly higher for members of the middle class, while attendance at historical landmarks is greater among the upper class.[46]

Finally, there are important differences between the classes regarding their *savings/spending* habits and *financial services* orientation. It has been found that the higher the individual's class position, the more likely he is to express some saving aspiration, particularly investment savings. Spending orientations also differ. For example, lower-class people tend to mention only material artifacts that they would like to purchase while higher-class people tend to mention spending on experiences, such as vacations, recreation, self-education, and hobbies.[47] A last example of money-handling differences shows up in their orientations toward sources for borrowing money and in credit card usage. While middle-class people tend to mention banks or insurance policies as sources of funds, lower-class people might cite personal loan companies, credit unions, and friends.[48]

Charge-card companies have aimed at different target markets based on social-class differences. Fee cards, such as American Express, aim at the upscale segment with higher incomes and professional or managerial jobs, while bank charge cards aim at the mass market.

> Recognizing social class differentials within the financial marketplace, some banks have increased their segmentation marketing strategy. In its basic application, this involves finding out who the richest and biggest customers are, showering them with favors, freebies, and other inducements to open or increase their accounts, and if necessary, raising rates and fees to the less-affluent to pay for it all. For example, a Houston bank turned itself into a "boutique-type bank," servicing high-income, high-net-worth individuals. Although it lost over a third of its customers in the two-year process, deposits doubled to $87 million.[49]

Although our understanding and appreciation of social class differences and similarities in product choice and usage is limited, we can make some rather general statements regarding the product and service orientations of the classes.

Upper-Upper Class The consumption patterns of upper-uppers are quite different from those of other classes. Although expense is frequently no object, they do not purchase in order to impress others. Therefore, they may be content to wear 20-year-old sportcoats and drive 10-year-old cars. They tend to be conservative in their consumption, buying relatively few goods, and use more services than goods. One reason for their low consumption of goods is that many of their belongings are passed on from generation to generation.

Lower-Upper Class The consumer behavior of lower-uppers may be characterized as oriented strongly toward conspicuous consumption. Their purchase decisions are geared toward demonstrating wealth and status through such items as expensive cars, large estates, expensive jewelry, and so forth. This group is the prime target for outlandish gifts offered by Texas retailers Neiman-Marcus and Sakowitz. For instance, if you are willing to spend enough, you may obtain a 50-year lease for his-and-her burglar-proof vaults hidden in the Utah mountains, or you can really be "somebody" with a $50,000 filmed documentary of your life.[50]

While the upper class may be a significant market for many high-priced luxuries, for most new-product introductions this group can be largely ignored. However, they may be used effectively as reference groups in advertising to those below them and sometimes their use of certain products will "trickle down" to the other social class groups. This approach has been used by France's Perrier mineral water and Lenox china and crystal.[51]

The upper classes are effectively used in advertising for Lenox. The ads (see Figure 8-2) show beautiful women in elegant surroundings, which is a very image-conscious and upscale approach. The china is prominent, but not at the center of attention. The aim is to convey the idea that Lenox is the sign of a hostess with excellent taste. The company is selling dreams. If the potential Lenox buyer can't have the model's sophistication or beauty, at least they can have her Lenox.[52]

Upper-Middle Class This group purchases a far greater number of products than any other class. Because they are successful, their purchase decisions reflect strong social implications. Through their consumption they want to project an image of success and achievement. Their purchases emulate higher strata and are a display of their success, not only for their peers but for others lower on the social scale. Because they purchase higher-quality products and attempt to display good taste they are frequently termed the "quality market."

Because this group is so important as a market, many businesses are broadening their appeal to include upper-middles. Country clubs, for example, long considered to be plush, snobby, and oriented mainly to the upper class, have changed their image. Today many of them appear to have a more democratic image and a growing middle-class orientation where members tend to be younger, more informal, and where women and minorities are increasingly included.

The high education level of this group strongly influences the kinds of expenditures they make. As cited earlier their desired consumption pattern is heavily "experience" centered, that is, spending where one is left typically with memories rather than tangible assets.

FIGURE 8-2

Advertisement for Lenox china and crystal. (Courtesy of Lenox, Inc.)

Lower-Middle Class Social acceptability is an important guideline in the consumption activity of this group also. They are more interested in a product's giving them social acceptance than the luxuriousness or functionality of the item. Products, especially home furnishings, are bought on the basis of what is "pretty" and stylish and will suit the housewife and win praise from her friends and neighbors. Product choices are made along safe and conservative lines rather than on the basis of original and imaginative thoughts.

Upper-Lower Class Rainwater reports that there are five basic goals that activate the consumer behavior of the working-class housewife:

1 The search for social, economic, and physical security
2 The drive for a "common man" level of recognition and respectability
3 The desire for support and affection from the people important to her
4 The effort to escape a heavy burden of household labors
5 The urge to decorate, to "pretty up," her world[53]

Their world tends to be more limited in both direct and vicarious experiences, which is reflected in their consumption patterns. Expenditures are concentrated into fewer categories of goods and services. They are more concerned with immediate gratification than are middle-class families, but avoid spending their money in ways that are considered "out-of-place." Their spending is centered more on the interior-exterior interest of their house than on the size and location of the house itself. Since their upward social mobility is quite limited, they are not concerned about socially elite addresses. Instead, their housing tastes are very practical and utilitarian with "decent," "clean," "new," and "safe" characterizing their outlook. An example of this orientation, in spite of an income that would allow other alternatives, is illustrated by Michigan's first million-dollar lottery winner, who collects $50,000 a year for the next 20 years. Although he retired from his manual labor job, he did not move his family from their one-bedroom bungalow. Instead he installed aluminum siding, central air conditioning, storm windows, a sun porch, double-oven gas stove, color television, and finished his basement recreation room with dark green paneling and indirect lighting.[54]

Although working-class consumer behavior resembles middle-class behavior in hard goods spending, the expenditures by upper-lowers for services lags behind. It is also lower than their own expenditures for durables. Some of the reasons suggested for the lack of service-oriented consumption among the working class in comparison with the middle class are: (1) they tend to be do-it-yourselfers; (2) their expenditures for children's education are much smaller; (3) they are more likely to spend their vacation at home or visting relatives, saving on motel and transportation costs; (4) they do not frequent expensive restaurants, but tend to consume their meals away from home with relatives, or at a franchised drive-in.[55] Thus, the tremendous boom in the service sector of our economy is largely a middle-class phenomenon.

Lower-Lower Class Contrary to what might be expected, some members of this group may represent an attractive segment for manufacturers of food products or other frequently purchased items, and certain durables. For example, one study found that such families are consumers of many major consumer durables, frequently the new, more expensive models.[56] Another researcher found that the prevailing market value of the lower-class family's car, television set, and basic appliances average almost 20 percent higher than the average value of similar possessions for upper-lowers, despite a median income which was one-third lower than the working class group.[57] Their behavior can be described as "compensatory consumption." The lower-lower class family's pessimistic outlook on life causes them to spend for immediate gratification. Thus, through their purchasing they try to emulate the "good life."

This group's purchasing patterns also reveal a tendency to buy on impulse with little planning. Low educational level appears to be a primary cause of this.

Shopping Behavior

Shopping behavior also varies by social class. For example, a very close relation between store choice and social class membership has been found, indicating that it is wrong to assume that all consumers want to shop at glamorous, high-status stores. Instead, people realistically match their values and expectations with a store's status and don't shop in stores where they feel out of place.

Thus, no matter what the store, each shopper generally has some idea of the social-status ranking of that store and will tend not to patronize those where they feel they do not "fit," in a social class sense.[58] The result is that the same products and brands may be purchased in different outlets by members of different social classes.[59] Therefore, an important function of retail advertising is to allow the shopper to make social class identification of stores. This is done from the tone and physical character of the advertising.

One research study of the shopping behavior of a group of urban women has provided a number of valuable insights into the influence of social class on the shopping process:

Most women enjoy shopping regardless of their social class; however, reasons for enjoyment differ. All classes enjoy the recreational and social aspects of shopping, as well as being exposed to new things, bargain hunting, and comparing merchandise. However, lower classes found acquiring new clothes or household items more enjoyable, while upper-middles and above specified a pleasant store atmosphere, display, and excitement more frequently.

Middle- and upper-class women shopped more frequently than those in the lower class.

The higher a woman's social class the more she considered it important to shop quickly.

Middle and working classes had a greater tendency to browse without buying anything.

The lower the social status, the greater the proportion of downtown shopping.

A greater percentage of lower-class women favored discount stores than did women in the middle or upper classes. The attraction to high-fashion stores was directly related to social class. Broad-appeal stores were more attractive to the middle class.[60]

Let us examine more closely the nature of social class variations in shopping patterns in order to better understand marketing-strategy decisions.

Upper and Upper-Middle Classes Women of this group organize shopping more purposefully and efficiently than those of lower status. They tend to be more knowledgeable about what they want, where and when to shop for it; their shopping is both selective and wide-ranging. Middle- and upper-class consumers are more likely to search for information prior to purchase. They are more likely to read brochures, newspapers, and test reports before buying appliances.[61]

There is also an emphasis by this group on the store environment. Stores must be clean, orderly, and reflect good taste. Moreover, they must be staffed with clerks who are not only well-versed in their particular product line, but also well aware of their customers' status. This attitude indicates a leaning toward urban and suburban specialty stores and away from larger, more general outlets. For example, wives from this group have been characterized as usually buying most of their public appearance clothes at specialty shops or in specialty departments of the town's best department stores.[62]

Is there a paradox between consumer status and discount-house patronage among this group? Actually, the extent of patronage depends on the nature of the product sought. This group apparently has few qualms about buying appliances in discount houses because they feel they cannot "go wrong" with nationally advertised brand names. A furniture purchase, however, is another matter, and the same consumer is likely to go to a status store which can act as an "authority" on tasteful home furnishings.

Lower-Middle Class Women of this class "work" more at their shopping. They exhibit more anxiety, particularly when purchasing nonfoods, which they feel can be a demanding and tedious process filled with uncertainty. They are value-conscious and try to seek out the best buy for the money. Such an orientation would indicate a strong tendency to patronize discount houses.

Upper-Lower Class Because of this group's strong concern with personal relationships, there is a tendency to shop along known, local friendship lines. This attitude also explains their loyalty to certain stores in which they feel at home. Martineau describe situations in which lower-status women who shopped in high-status department stores felt clerks and higher-class customers in the store "punished" them in various subtle ways. One woman expressed her feeling that in a higher-status store "the clerks treat you like a crumb." Another related how she had vainly tried to be waited on, finally to be told, "We thought you were a clerk."[63]

The shopping behavior of this group has been described as a pattern of routine standardized purchasing, usually of national brands, having infrequent impulsive or unplanned purchases. The factors contributing to this behavior are thought to be their limited perspective, short time horizons, and frustrations.[64]

The lower classes buy with less prepurchase deliberation than middle and upper classes. They are much more likely to use in-store information sources, such as displays and salespeople.[65]

The routinized nature of their shopping suggests for the marketer an emphasis on enticing point-of-purchase displays and easy availability of items. It is clear that this group is a prime target for discount houses, and in fact it has been a potent force in the development of suburban discount retailing.[66]

Lower-Lower Class This group is one that buys largely on impulse. This tendency results in the necessity to rely heavily on credit, since money that might have been spent for big-ticket items has been drained off in impulse buying of small things. At the same time, however, these people can be poor credit risks because of their low-income status. This often forces them into a pattern of dealing with local merchants who offer tailor-made (yet sometimes quite exorbitant) credit terms.

Promotional Response Patterns

Important class differences exist with regard to promotional response. The social classes have differing media choice and usage patterns. For example, readers of *National Geographic* and *The New Yorker* are typically of a higher class than the readers of *Police Gazette*, *True Confessions,* and *The Star*. Even magazines in the same topic area may be aimed at different social classes as target audiences. An example of this is the kind of readers attracted by *Hustler* and *Playboy*. The social classes also have different perceptions and responses to advertising and other promotional messages which are significant in the development of proper marketing strategies. The basis of advertising differences directed at the various classes should be founded on the differing communication skills and interests of these groups. For example, sophisticated and clever advertising such as that appearing in *The New Yorker* and *Esquire* is almost meaningless to lower-class people who don't understand the subtle humor, and are baffled by the bizarre art. This certainly does not imply that they lack intelligence or wit, but merely that their communication skills or experiences have been oriented in a different way. Thus, their symbol systems are different, and they have a quite different approach to humor.[67]

Beer producers segment markets by social class, with different brands and advertising aimed at each group. For instance, Miller and Lowenbrau, produced by the same company, appeal to different social classes. Miller with its "Miller time" theme presents a strong working class, masculine image by featuring people in various tough, physical jobs, whereas Lowenbrau appeals on the basis of more-refined sociability by featuring upscale groups with the theme "Here's to good friends."

The marketer must also cautiously select key advertising words because of their different perceptions among the classes which could cause problems. Consider, for example, potential class reactions to an advertisement for a soap product used to wash baby clothes. In a motivation study of soaps and detergents it was learned that middle-class women associated the words "darling," "sweet," or "mother" with the word "baby," while lower-class women, reacted with such terms as "pain in the neck," "more work," or "a darling but a bother."[68]

In addition, certain voice and speech patterns may be more influential than others for specific consumer segments. Thus, speakers with "upper-class" voices and speech patterns can appear more credible to higher classes than "low-status" sounding speakers.[69] This supports such spokesperson choices as John Gielgud for Paul Masson wines, Alexander Scourby for Zenith, John Houseman for Smith Barney, and Laurence Olivier for Polaroid.

Consequently, marketers must understand their market thoroughly and communicate meaningfully to it within the range of their skills. The media patterns of each class are described below as well as some possible promotional appeals.

Upper Class The upper class tends to buy more newspapers, read more of the newspaper, see more magazines, and watch less television than other classes. They also listen to FM radio.

Upper-Middle Class The media choices of this group tend toward FM radio, particularly classical music stations, magazines such as *Time, Fortune, Vogue, The New Yorker, Consumer Reports,* and *House & Garden,* and newspapers. The upper-middle class does not fully embrace television, worrying about its effect on their children. Nevertheless, they do watch significant amounts, with their programming tastes tending toward current events and drama. Because of later dinner hours and bedtimes, they have a high exposure to late-night television shows, such as the "Tonight Show."

This group and the upper class represent challenging targets to the marketer in developing promotion appeals. They tend to be more critical of advertising, are suspicious of its emotional appeals, and question its claims. They usually display an attitude of sophisticated superiority to it. This is not to say, however, that they are unresponsive to advertising. They can be attracted by approaches that are different, individualistic, witty, sophisticated, stylish, that appeal to good judgment and discriminating taste, and that offer the kinds of objects and symbols that are significant to their status and self-expression goals.

Lower-Middle Class This group tends to read morning newspapers, and middle-class magazines such as *Reader's Digest, Sports Illustrated, Esquire, Good Housekeeping,* and *Ladies' Home Journal* and watches a good deal of television. This group, as well as the upper-lower class, takes a rather straightforward, literal-minded, and pragmatic approach to advertising. Effective promotion appeals are those portraying the home and relating use of the product to success as a housewife and mother. Labor-saving products such as instant foods, for example, are best promoted in a way that also satisfies conscientiousness.

Although attracted by discount coupons, this group is careful in the use of them. They want to be sure that the incentive is worth the effort, that they are being sensible in their use of them.

Upper-Lower Class The media choices of this group tend toward AM radio, heavy television viewing, especially soap operas, game shows, situation comedies, variety shows, and late movies, magazines such as *True Story,* and afternoon and tabloid newspapers. For example *The Star, The National Enquirer,* and *Midnight Globe* sell 11-million copies a week, primarily to women who are over age 46, in blue-collar households, high school graduates, of slightly lower income than average, and with larger-than-average households. Psychographically, such readers believe miracle cures are fascinating; politicians are dishonest; Laetril should be legalized; UFOs are real; and abortions should be outlawed.[70]

A study made by Social Research, Inc. of the women in this group found that some interesting changes are taking place, which could have relevance to the marketer's promotional strategy:

Although they are no longer captives of husband, children, and home and have a new desire for independence, they resent efforts to "put down" the role of wife, mother, and homemaker.

Most have new interests in their communities and jobs. They want products that will free them from housework or contribute to their comfort or gratification.[71]

Given these attitudes, the following conclusions have been advanced for advertising strategy directed at this market:

They are quite receptive to advertising that has a strong visual character, showing activity, energy, on-going work and life, and solutions to practical problems in everyday situations and social relationships.

Advertising should convey an image of the gratifying world in which products fit functionally into the drive for a stable and secure life.

It should communicate a feeling of confidence and safety about the product and its operation.

The advertising setting is important. It should make the item seem desirable—that is, the item should be portrayed as part of the average woman's living and consuming, an expected item in the good life. It could also serve to educate the woman as to how she might use the product and how she might relate it to her own situation.

Advertising should reassure the woman that the product is within her reach socially, psychologically, and economically.

Advertising that emphasizes easing the housewife's burdens should at the same time communicate a sense of her continuing importance to the family and offer fruitful ways to use her idle time to gain more love from them.

Advertising (especially in color) that communicates a "prettied-up" atmosphere gains a good reception.[72]

This class is also the most receptive group to sales promotion offers. They are eager to take advantage of many of the offers that come their way, to cut costs or get something extra.

Lower-Lower Class The media habits of this group are similar to those of the upper-lowers except that they have even lower readership of magazines and newspapers. They are more audio (AM radio)- and video (television)-oriented. Both groups have early dinner hours and thus have heavier exposure to early-evening television than higher social classes. This group comprises a large segment of the heavy television viewers, who tend to be under 30, high school dropouts, removed from the job market, with personal income below the poverty level.[73]

Promotion directed to this class is constrained to their lower education and intelligence levels and the difficulty they have in thinking abstractly. For these reasons it is suggested that simple, concrete appeals be used, with greater visual stimulation, such as the use of color and heavy reliance on symbols.

Price-Related Behavior

Research on these variables is extremely limited and most of what exists relates to the poor. Lower-class consumers are more poorly informed about price and product alternatives.[74] They are also more likely to buy products on sale or priced lower.[75] Regarding price perceptions among the middle and working classes, a shopping simulation showed that working-class housewives have a greater reliance on the general belief that there is a price/quality association; that is, the higher the price of a product the higher the quality. They perceive that they have an inability to discriminate between products and are therefore forced to fall back on a general belief in order to handle this problem of which product to buy. Although the better-educated housewives in both classes had stronger beliefs that price and quality are related, they preferred lower-priced product alternatives. They apparently felt capable of judging the product alternatives on their own merits rather than having to rely on general beliefs in price/quality to make a decision.[76]

Research on commercial-bank credit-card holders has uncovered social-class variations in card use patterns. For example, members of the lower class tend to use their cards for installment purchases and seek out stores that honor their cards, while upper classes use them for convenience and do not seek stores accepting the card.[77]

ARE CLASS DIFFERENCES DISAPPEARING?

The marketer is vitally interested in changes occuring in the social-class system. If this construct is indeed becoming less important as a means of identifying markets, then it will be less effective as a segmenting variable. Unfortunately, the issue addressed in this section cannot be answered unequivocally. There is some evidence supporting both views. That is, social class seems to continue as a permanent fixture in America. Nevertheless, there is some blurring of class boundaries. Our country is becoming less of a rigid and fixed-by-birth system.

Evidence for the decreasing importance of social class comes from the study by Coleman and Rainwater who found that more than two-thirds of their respondents—including nearly 90 percent of those under thirty years of age—viewed social class as becoming less important in America than it used to be. Social mobility has increased as many barriers have fallen. The end of job discrimination by race and minority is one contributing factor. Decline in prejudice related to ancestry and religion is another element. Educational opportunity is much broader today so that all classes have access to higher education to become doctors, lawyers, and so forth. In addition, the changing income distribution and changes in the comparative standing of occupational groups have resulted in less disparity between white- and blue-collar workers.[78] These are some of the factors involved in the decline of the social-class system.

Others suggest that the mass media have had a leveling influence on the values and lifestyle aspirations of all people. As a result, it is argued, differences in product preferences among social classes may have disappeared.[79] Research on this topic, however, has not supported this contention.[80]

It has also been claimed that the development of mass merchandising and the sale of mass-produced consumer goods means that most people buy the same brands in the same stores. The thousands of McDonald's, Sears, and Goodyear stores offer consumers standardized quality and sameness. Thus, the market seems to have become more massified; that is, the broad middle class seems to typify the nation's lifestyle.

In spite of these signs, other evidence points to continued differentiation between the classes. For example, survey research such as that done by the Gallup organization indicates that responses are linked to class, and that class differences do still exist.[81] In addition, there is other evidence that occupational and educational differences are still strong between the classes as well as are differences in lifestyle patterns.[82] Thus, the marketer should be cognizant of a broadened middle-class pattern in the marketplace. Nevertheless, the social-class system is still a factor with which to be reckoned in segmenting markets, developing marketing programs, and understanding consumer behavior.

SUMMARY

This chapter has discussed the major implications of social class for consumer behavior. We defined the concept of social class, and discussed the process of stratification, including the bases on which it may be carried out and the way it may be studied, emphasizing Warner's pioneering and enduring work. It was pointed out that different social classes have different values, attitudes, and behavior. Numerous examples of these differences were cited, especially with regard to the characteristic lifestyles of each class.

We learned that social-class segmentation, while offering potential, is fraught with difficulties, and limitations in its current stage of evolution. Nevertheless, we described much of what is presently known about reactions to products, promotions, shopping, and prices among the different social classes.

A final subject of discussion was the apparently diminishing social-class system. However, class was seen to be still strong, with some important differences existing among segments. From this chapter, we should now have a better understanding of how and why consumer behavior differs among social classes.

DISCUSSION TOPICS

1 What is meant by the term social stratification?

2 Discuss the use of social class as a market-segmentation approach.

3 Select one of the social class categories and prepare a report on its lifestyle.

4 How might a marketer have a problem with his "self-reference criterion" when making marketing decisions involving social class ramifications?

5 Find at least two manufacturer's ads for the same generic product (such as, clothing) that you think are aimed at different social classes. Explain the differences in the ads.

6 Find three newspaper advertisements by local retailers that you think reach the different social classes. Explain the differences in the ads.

7 Classify the major department stores in your area according to your estimation of the social class of their customers. How do the marketing features of these stores differ?

8 What social class would you choose for initial marketing efforts if you were to introduce video-recording machines for television owners? Suggest a marketing strategy.

9 Discuss the relationship of social class and consumption.

10 Are social class differences diminishing? Prepare a report supporting your position.

NOTES

[1] Bernard Berelson and Gary Steiner, *Human Behavior: An Inventory of Scientific Findings,* Harcourt, Brace & World, New York, 1964, p. 453.
[2] David Dressler and Donald Carns, *Sociology: The Study of Human Interaction,* 2d ed., Knopf, New York, 1973, p. 370.
[3] Richard P. Coleman and Lee Rainwater, *Social Standing in America: New Dimensions of Class,* Basic Books, Inc., New York, 1978, p. 29.
[4] Christy Marshall, "Prizm Adds ZIP to Consumer Research," *Advertising Age,* November 10, 1980, p. 22.
[5] Robert C. Yeager, "Caught in the Middle—I," *Across the Board,* November 1980, p. 24.
[6] W. Lloyd Warner, Marchia Meeker, and Kenneth Eells, *Social Class in America,* Science Research Associates, Chicago, 1949, pp. 11-15.
[7] James M. Carman, *The Application of Social Class in Market Segmentation,* University of California Graduate School of Business Administration, Institute of Business and Economic Research, Berkeley, CA, 1965.
[8] Coleman and Rainwater, *Social Standing,* pp. 219-220.
[9] Coleman and Rainwater, *Social Standing,* p. 124.
[10] Luis V. Dominguez and Albert L. Page, "Use and Misuse of Social Stratification in Consumer Behavior Research," *Journal of Business Research,* 9:151-173, 1981.
[11] Gerald Zaltman and Melanie Wallendorf, *Consumer Behavior: Basic Findings and Management Implications,* John Wiley & Sons, New York, 1979, pp. 86-87.
[12] Marie R. Haug, "Social Class Measurement and Women's Occupational Roles," *Social Forces,* 52:86-93, 1973.
[13] See Terence A. Shimp and J. Thomas Yokum, "Extensions of the Basic Social Class Model Employed in Consumer Research," in Kent B. Monroe (ed), *Advances in Consumer Research: Volume 8,* Association for Consumer Research, Ann Arbor, MI, 1981, pp. 702-707; and Dominguez and Page, "Use and Misuse," for suggestions to overcome some of these problems.
[14] Thorstein Veblen, *The Theory of the Leisure Class,* Macmillan, New York, 1899.
[15] Lawrence Minard, "The More it Costs, the Better it Sells," *Forbes,* December, 22, 1980, pp. 59-62.
[16] John Barbour, "Rodeo Drive Values Soar," *Associated Press,* October 19, 1980; and Hal Landcaster, "Trendy Men's Store Finds Locking Door is a Key to its Success," *The Wall Street Journal,* January 22, 1981, pp. 1, 18.
[17] William M. Bulkeley, "A Shoe That Helps You Walk on Water is a Big Hit on Shore," *The Wall Street Journal,* April 1, 1981, p. 1.
[18] "Flaunting Wealth: It's Back in Style," *U.S. News & World Report,* September 21, 1981, pp. 61-64; and "An Authority Tells Why Status Symbols Keep Changing," *U.S. News & World Report,* February 14, 1977, pp. 41-42.
[19] Frank Trippett, "Hard Times for the Status-Minded," *Time,* December 21, 1981, p. 90.
[20] Richard P. Coleman, "The Significance of Social Stratification in Selling," in Martin L. Bell (ed.), *Marketing: A Maturing Discipline,* American Marketing Association, Chicago, Winter 1960, p. 175.
[21] This section is drawn from Coleman, "The Significance of Social Stratification," pp. 171-184; Warner, Meeker, and Eells, *Social Class,* pp. 11-21; Margaret C. Pirie, "Marketing and Social Classes: An Anthropologist's View," *Management Review,* 49:45-48, September 1960; Kim B. Rotzoll, "The Effect of Social Stratification on Market Behavior," *Journal of Advertising Research,* 7:22-27, March 1967; Ronald E. Frank, William F. Massy, and Yorman Wind, *Market Segmentation,* Prentice-Hall, Englewood Cliffs, NJ, 1972, pp. 44-48; and James M. Patterson, "Marketing and the Working-Class Family," in Arthur B. Shostak and William Gomberg (eds.), *Blue-Collar World,* Prentice-Hall, Englewood Cliffs, NJ, 1964, p. 78.
[22] "The Ranks of the Rich Get Richer," *Time,* July 9, 1979, p. 54.
[23] Mary Lou Roberts, "Women's Changing Roles—A Consumer Behavior Perspective," in Kent B. Monroe (ed.), *Advances in Consumer Research: Volume 8,* Association for Consumer Research, Ann Arbor, MI, 1981, p. 594.
[24] "The American Underclass," *Time,* August 19, 1977, p. 14.
[25] Frank, Massy, and Wind, *Market Segmentation,* p. 45.
[26] James H. Myers and Jonathan Gutman, "Life-Style: The Essence of Social Class," in William D. Wells (ed.), *Life Style and Psychographics,* American Marketing Association, Chicago, 1974, p. 252.
[27] This section is adapted from Myers and Gutman, "Life Style," pp. 253-254.
[28] A. Marvin Roscoe, Jr., Arthur LeClaire, Jr., and Leon G. Shiffman, "Theory and Management Applications of Demographics in Buyer Behavior," in Arch G. Woodside, Jagdish N. Sheth, and Peter D. Bennett (eds.), *Consumer and Industrial Buying Behavior,* North-Holland, New York, 1977, pp. 67-76.

[29] Coleman, "The Significance of Social Stratification," pp. 176–177.
[30] James H. Myers, Roger R. Stanton, and Arne F. Haug, "Correlates of Buying Behavior: Social Class vs. Income," *Journal of Marketing*, 35:8–15, October 1971.
[31] James H. Myers and John F. Mount, "More on Social Class vs. Income as Correlates of Buying Behavior," *Journal of Marketing*, 37:71–73, April 1973.
[32] Robert D. Hisrich and Michael P. Peters, "Selecting the Superior Segmentation Correlate," *Journal of Marketing*, 38:60–63, July 1974.
[33] Frank, Massy, and Wind, *Market Segmentation*, p. 49.
[34] Coleman, "The Significance of Social Stratification," pp. 179–182.
[35] "Researcher Breaks Society Into Privilege Levels," *Advertising Age*, June 11, 1979, p. 20.
[36] Charles M. Shaninger, "Social Class Versus Income Revisited: An Empirical Investigation," *Journal of Marketing Research*, 18:206–207, May 1981.
[37] Thomas S. Robertson, *Consumer Behavior*, Scott, Foresman, Glenview, IL, 1970, p. 129.
[38] Roscoe, et al., "Theory," p. 75.
[39] Stuart U. Rich and Subhash C. Jain, "Social Class and Life Cycle as Predictors of Shopping Behavior," *Journal of Marketing Research*, 5:41–49, February 1968.
[40] William T. Tucker, *The Social Context of Economic Behavior*, Holt, New York, 1964, pp. 42–43.
[41] "Researcher," p. 20.
[42] Coleman and Rainwater, *Social Standing*, p. 83.
[43] Robert B. Settle, Pamela L. Alreck, and Michael A. Belch, "Social Class Determinants of Leisure Activity," in William L. Wilkie (ed.), *Advances in Consumer Research: Volume 6*, Association for Consumer Research, Ann Arbor, MI, 1979, pp. 139–145.
[44] D. W. Bishop and M. Ikeda, "Status and Role Factors in the Leisure Behavior of Different Occupations," *Sociology and Social Research*, 54:190–208, January 1970.
[45] James H. Myers and William H. Reynolds, *Consumer Behavior and Marketing Management*, Houghton Mifflin, Boston, 1967, p. 214.
[46] John E. Robbins and Stephanie S. Robbins, "Segmentation for 'Fine Arts' Marketing: Is King Tut Classless as Well as Ageless?" in Neil Beckwith, et al. (eds.), *1979 Educators' Conference Proceedings*, American Marketing Association, Chicago, 1979, pp. 479–484.
[47] Pierre Martineau, "Social Classes and Spending Behavior," *Journal of Marketing*, 23:128–129, October 1958.
[48] Pierre D. Martineau, "Social Class and Its Very Close Relationship to the Individual's Buying Behavior," in Martin L. Bell (ed.), *Marketing: A Maturing Discipline*, p. 191.
[49] Julie Salamon, "More Banks Target Services for Rich, Subsidized with Charges on Others," *The Wall Street Journal*, October 13, 1980, p. 19.
[50] Christy Marshall, "Sakowitz's Bizarre Gifts Rival Neiman's Catalog," *Advertising Age*, Novemeber 6, 1978, p. 36.
[51] "Perrier in Six-Packs," *Time*, May 16, 1977, p. 69; and Bernice Finkleman, "Perrier Pours Into U.S. Market, Spurs Water Bottler Battle," *Marketing News*, September, 7, 1979, pp. 1, 9.
[52] "Lenox's Spending Spree in Print," *Marketing & Media Decisions*, August 1981, p. 75.
[53] Lee Rainwater, Richard P. Coleman, and Gerald Handel, *Workingman's Wife*, Oceana Publications, Inc., New York, 1959, p. 205.
[54] William Mitchell, "First Lottery Millionaire Settles into Easy Living," *Detroit Free Press*, July 8, 1973, p. 3a.
[55] Gerald Handel and Lee Rainwater, "Persistance and Change in Working-Class Life Style," in Shostak and Gomberg (eds.), *Blue-Collar World*, p. 41.
[56] David Caplovitz, *The Poor Pay More*, Free Press, New York, 1963.
[57] Patterson, "Marketing and the Working-Class," p. 79.
[58] Martineau, "Social Class and Spending Behavior," pp. 126–127.
[59] Sidney J. Levy, "Social Class and Consumer Behavior," in Joseph W. Newman (ed.), *On Knowing the Consumer*, Wiley, New York, 1966, p. 153.
[60] Rich and Jain, "Social Class and Life Cycles," pp. 41–49.
[61] Gordon R. Foxall, "Social Factors in Consumer Choice," *Journal of Consumer Research*, 2:60–64, June 1975.
[62] Coleman, "The Significance of Social Stratification," p. 177.
[63] Martineau, "Social Classes," p. 121.
[64] Frank, Massy, and Wind, *Market Segmentation*, p. 47.
[65] Foxall, "Social Factors," p. 62.
[66] David J. Rachman and Marion Levine, "Blue Collar Workers Shape Suburban Markets," *Journal of Retailing*, 42:5–13, Winter 1966–1967.
[67] Martineau, "Social Classes," p. 127.
[68] Pierre Martineau, *Motivation in Advertising*, McGraw-Hill, New York, 1957, p. 166.
[69] L. S. Harms, "Listener Judgments of Status Cues in Speech," *Quarterly Journal of Speech*, 47:164–168, April 1961.
[70] "The Supermarket Tabloids," *Media Decisions*, May 1979, pp. 69, 98.

[71] "Blue Collar Wives Seek Convenience: MacFadden," *Advertising Age,* October 8, 1973.
[72] Rainwater, Coleman and Handel, *Workingman's Wife,* pp. 207–216.
[73] Marilyn Jackson-Beeck and Jeff Sobal, "The Social World of Heavy Television Viewers," *Journal of Broadcasting,* 24:5–11, Winter, 1980.
[74] Andrew Gabor and S. W. J. Granger, "Price Sensitivity of the Consumer," *Journal of Advertising Research,* 4:40–44, December 1964; and Caplovitz, *The Poor Pay More.*
[75] Frederick E. Webster, Jr., "The Deal-Prone Consumer," *Journal of Marketing Research,* 1:32–35, August 1964.
[76] Joseph N. Fry and Frederick H. Siller, "A Comparison of Housewife Decision Making in Two Social Classes," *Journal of Marketing Research,* 7:333–337, August 1970.
[77] H. Lee Mathews and John W. Slocum, Jr., "Social Class and Commercial Bank Credit Card Usage," *Journal of Marketing,* 33:71–78, January 1969.
[78] Coleman and Rainwater, *Social Standing,* pp. 294–296.
[79] J. C. Bieda and H. H. Kassarjian, "An Overview of Market Segmentation," in Bernard A. Morin (ed.), *Marketing in a Changing World,* American Marketing Association, Chicago, 1969, pp. 249–253.
[80] J. Michael Munson and W. Austin Spivey, "Product and Brand User Stereotypes Among Social Classes," in Kent B. Monroe (ed.), *Advances in Consumer Research: Volume 8,* Association for Consumer Research, Ann Arbor, Michigan, 1981, pp. 696–701.
[81] Norval D. Glenn, "Massification vs. Differentiation: Some Trend Data From National Surveys," *Social Forces,* 46, December 1967.
[82] Coleman and Rainwater, *Social Standing.*

CHAPTER 9
SOCIAL GROUPS

We are continuing to narrow our discussion of the environmental variables that influence consumer behavior. In this chapter, we discuss ways in which groups impinge on consumer decision making. This is an important ingredient in the marketer's understanding of consumer behavior.

Our first task will be to define several group concepts essential to our discussion. Next, the major characteristics of groups and group types will be examined. Finally, we shall discuss reference groups and their special relevance for the marketer in understanding consumer behavior.

WHAT IS A GROUP?

Not every collection of individuals is a group, as the term is used by sociologists. Actually, we can distinguish three different collections of people: aggregations, categories, and groups. An *aggregation* is any number of people who are in close proximity to one another at a given time. A *category* is any number of people who have some particular attributes in common. A *group* consists of people who have a sense of relatedness as a result of interaction with each other.[1]

To illustrate these concepts consider four people sitting on a bench at a university. They are an "aggregation" since they are in close proximity. They may be a "category" if they share some attribute such as being majors in the College of Business Administration. They may also be a "group" if they have a shared sense of relatedness through interaction, that is, if they are all friends, or classmates in a consumer behavior course, for example.

Although our emphasis in this chapter is on groups, this does not mean that the marketer is not interested in aggregations and categories. These collections are frequently the focus for developing marketing strategies. For example, market segmentation typically does not involve social groups but instead uses categories, since the people are not all interacting with one another.

CLASSIFICATION OF GROUPS

Groups may be classified according to a number of dimensions, including function, degree of personal involvement, and degree of organization.

Content or Function

Most of us view the content of groups in terms of their function. For example, we categorize them along such lines as students, factory workers, church members, and so on. Actually, these are subtypes of the major kinds of groups that we encounter in a complex society, which could generally be categorized along such lines as family, ethnic, age, sex, political, religious, residential, occupational, educational, and so forth.[2]

Degree of Personal Involvement

By using this criterion, we can identify two different types of groups: primary and secondary. The hallmark of a *primary group* is that interpersonal relationships take place usually on a face-to-face basis with great frequency, and on an intimate level.[3] These groups have shared norms and interlocking roles. Families, work groups, and even recreational groups (if individuals have some depth of personal involvement) are examples of such groups.

Secondary groups are those in which the relationship among members is relatively impersonal and formalized. This amounts to a residual category that includes all groups that are not primary, such as political parties, fraternities, unions, occasional sports groups, and the American Marketing Association. Although such groups are secondary, the interpersonal relationships that occur may nevertheless be face-to-face. The distinction lies in the lack of intimacy of personal involvement.

Degree of Organization

Groups range from those that are relatively unorganized to highly structured forms. We usually simplify this continuum into two types: formal and informal. *Formal* groups are those with a definite structure (for example, they may have a president, vice president, secretary, and treasurer). They are likely to be secondary groups designed to accomplish specific goals, whether economic, social, political, or altruistic. The United Way, the Miss America Pageant, and the local Republican party are examples. *Informal* groups are typically primary groups, characterized by a relatively loose structure, a lack of clearly defined goals or objectives, unstructured interaction, and unwritten rules. Because of the extent of their influence on individuals' values and activities, informal groups are probably of greater importance to us in seeking to understand consumer behavior.

It should be evident from this discussion that the term "group" is multifaceted and that groups have important influences on individuals, including their activities as consumers. Primary informal groups have the greatest degree of impact on consumers and are therefore most important to marketers. From such groups, consumers develop their product-consumption, shopping, and media patterns. Consequently, these groups are generally most influential on consumers' buying behavior. As a result, advertisers normally present their products within a primary group setting such as among friends (Coca-Cola, Pizza Hut), family (Pillsbury, Johnson's Baby Powder, Cheer detergent), or work groups (Dial soap, Haggar suits).

Secondary informal groups probably are the next most influential to consumers and, therefore, are sometimes used in advertising efforts. For example, a new type of golf club, racquetball racket, or snow ski may be featured in the appropriate friendly, competitive, but professional-looking surroundings in which the product and user may be shown excelling and being rewarded with admiration. Or, in the case of other sponsors, the product itself may be the reward (such as Michelob Light beer for the winners of a racquetball match). Primary and secondary formal groups are much less widely used by marketers because they have far less direct, intimate influence on consumer behavior. In specialized situations, however, certain marketers may find them useful. For example, travel or insurance agents may develop specific offerings for members of an organization, such as state employees, or university alumni.

GROUP PROPERTIES

In order to better understand the nature of groups, we need to examine several other important concepts, including status, norms, role, socialization, and power, and their significance for consumer behavior.

Status

Status refers to the achieved or ascribed position of an individual in a group or in society, and it consists of the rights and duties associated with that position. In the last chapter, we referred to status in a prestige sense; however, this is only one of several different ways in which statuses may be classified. Status also may refer to some grouping on the basis of age or sex, family, occupation, and friendship or common interest.[4]

As we have seen in Chapter 8, products or brands are often purchased for status reasons, because they are symbols to others of one's wealth and "superiority." Such items, whether they be clothes, cars, sports equipment, homes, appliances, or furniture, are frequently badges of our position in society. However, it must be remembered that such symbols are not always what they seem. Reverse snobbery may operate in which small foreign cars are higher status than large domestic ones, or casual clothing such as jeans are more symbolic than more formal, expensive clothing. Thus, the marketer must keep current with an understanding of status trends.

Norms

Norms are the rules and standards of conduct by which group members are expected to abide. For informal groups, norms are generally unwritten but are, nevertheless, usually quite well understood. For example, as a salesperson for a large business machines company, you might be expected to live in a certain area of town, drive a certain type of car (perhaps a mid-size Oldsmobile), and dress conservatively (e.g., in a navy-blue suit and striped tie). Behavior deviation outside these latitudes might result in slower advancement in the organization. Thus, as employees or consumers, we often readily know what we can and cannot wear, drive, say, eat, and so on, in order to be well-accepted within the relevant group.

Role

This term is used to designate all of the behavior patterns associated with a particular status. Role is the dynamic aspect of status and includes the attitudes, values, and behavior ascribed by the society to persons occupying this status. The social structure partially prescribes what sort of role behavior is acceptable and thus what is expected. For instance, an upper-class husband who is a successful physician may feel that in his position he is expected to drive an expensive car, live in an exclusive neighborhood, dress in fashionable clothes, attend country club activities, and give generously to charities. Conversely, a lower-class husband who is an assembly-line worker may feel comfortable in a role in which he drives a pickup truck, lives in a bungalow, wears jeans and boots, and fishes, hunts, and drinks beer with his friends.

Essentially, role theory recognizes that an individual carries out life by playing different roles. This concept was expressed in a poetic way by Shakespeare in the following well-known passage:

*All the world's a stage,
And all the men and women merely players.
They have their exits and their entrances;
And one man in his time plays many parts.
His acts being seven ages.*[5]

This means that each consumer enacts many roles, which may change over time, even during the course of a day. For example, a woman may have the role of wife, mother, employee, family financial officer, lover, Sunday School teacher, and many others. Her behavior in each of these roles will differ as she keeps "switching hats," depending on her role at each moment.

Carrying the concept of playing a role further, Goffman suggests that the individual must not only learn his lines (the group's special language) but he needs a costume (the group's accepted dress), props (the group's equipment or accoutrements), a set (where the group interacts), and a team or cast of players (the group members).[6]

Roles in groups (just as those in a play) are learned, but not every individual learns a given role in the same way.[7] Society allows some variation in role performance, but if too much latitude is taken, sanctions of some sort will be imposed. Thus, other people expect us to behave in a certain way, and will reward conformity and punish nonconformity to those expectations.

Roles have a strong, pervasive influence on our activities as consumers. For example, other people have expectations regarding the products we buy to meet the needs of our roles. Just a few of the many consumption decisions directly affected include the places we shop, the clothes we wear, the cars we drive, the houses in which we live, and the recreational activities we engage in. Marketers, therefore, help individuals play their roles by providing the right costumes and props to be used in gaining acceptance by some group. Again, it's the symbols of products that provide so much of the satisfaction that accrues from a product.

Because of the many roles we try to fulfill, whether at different times or simultaneously, we may develop *role conflict* which means that two or more of our roles are incompatible with each other. The strain may often be evidenced in the behavior of consumers. For example, a working wife may feel that the demands on her time may be more easily met by fixing her family quick and easy meals, particularly by using frozen TV dinners. However, in her role as a loving wife and the family's gourmet cook, such product usage may be abhorrent. Thus, some resolution of this conflict will be necessary. A creative advertiser may suggest a solution through purchasing the company's TV dinners because, although easily prepared, when served on her regular china, seasoned to taste, and garnished attractively, they resemble a gourmet meal.

Socialization

Socialization refers to the process by which a new member learns the system of values, norms, and expected behavior patterns of the group being entered. When a new student arrives on a college campus, she or he soon learns from fellow students what is expected in the way of dress, eating patterns, class attendance, extracurricular activities, and so on. Residents new to a neighborhood soon learn what patterns are expected in the group concerning home maintenance, lawns and landscaping, interior decoration, entertaining, and so on. Thus, individuals are continually engaging in the process of socialization (although it is more intense at an early age) as new groups are encountered which have an impact on their lives. Consumer socialization, therefore, is the process by which individuals acquire skills, knowledge, and attitudes relevant to their effective functioning as consumers in the marketplace.[8] This is particularly relevant to young people, although it has usefulness in other situations, too, as was indicated above.

Power

Groups have power to influence their members' behavior. Various sources of social power may be operative in different social group situations, however: reward power, coercive power, legitimate power, expert power, and referent power.[9] Marketers also seek to use these forms of power to influence consumers.

Reward Power This is based on the perception one has of another's ability to reward him. The strength of reward power increases with the size of the rewards which an individual perceives another can administer. Rewards might include either tangible items such as money or gifts, or intangible things such as recognition, praise, or other nonmaterial satisfaction.

Social groups often have a great deal of reward power which they may dispense to their members. This "carrot" approach can often result in the desired behavior being exhibited by members. For example, Amway Products, which uses direct-selling methods for its line of household products, makes effective use of reward power in motivating its sales force, by holding large sales rallies where young salespeople, usually middle-class couples, watch a 20-minute color film that features family scenes of successful Amway couples enjoying the fruits of their labors—swimming pools and motor homes.[10]

Marketers also use reward power in order to influence consumers. Of course, they are able to reward consumers directly by providing high-quality products and services. By making such things available, consumers, in turn, express their satisfaction by repurchasing from the company. Reward power is operating directly in this case.

In other situations marketers promise (implicitly, at least) the rewards of group acceptance, such as love, through use of a product. For example, some brands of beer (such as Lowenbrau and Old Milwaukee) and liquor attempt to show how group acceptance takes place through purchase and consumption of their product.[11] The Johnny Walker ad in Figure 9-1 illustrates another approach in the direct use of reward association for the product. Similarly, Prell Shampoo ads show the rewards of product use as friends and coworkers notice how nice your hair smells. In other instances retailers employ cliques and clubs to make use of reward power. Clothing shops attempt to influence dress styles by telling customers what is "in"—that is, what their group or friends will accept in terms of dress. Also, photography retailers frequently sponsor camera clubs partly to be able to employ group power to influence product purchases.

Coercive Power This is the power to influence behavior through the use of punishment or the withholding of rewards. Punishment, for our purpose, does not refer to the physical kind, but the more subtle, psychological sanctions. For example, students may readily conform to the dress code of some group on campus such as a sorority or fraternity and purchase the accepted clothing of this group in order not to be ridiculed by it.

Marketers are also able to use coercive power effectively in certain situations. Inducing fear is one approach that may be taken by advertisers of some items such as life insurance, mouthwash, reducing aids, dishwashing detergents, cat litter, and deodorants. Coercion occurs through showing the unfortunate consequences that could befall a consumer who fails to own or use such products. For example, the embarrassment of having loose dentures is brought to our attention by Poligrip and other denture adhesive manufacturers. Similarly, the group ridicule which comes from having "b.o." is humorously but effectively illustrated in a Dial soap ad in which several car-pool members all ride in the rear seat of a car while the driver, alone in the front seat, gets the message that she needs to use Dial.

Tupperware and other products sold in social group situations also make

FIGURE 9-1

Advertisement for Johnnie Walker Black Label. (Created by Smith/Greenland Inc. for Somerset Importers Ltd., importers of Johnnie Walker Black Label Scotch.)

effective use of group coercive power. For example, in the case of Tupperware a dealer holds an informal party in a friend's or acquaintance's home to which a group of her friends or neighbors are invited. After a few ice-breaking games are run by the dealer, the group is served coffee and dessert while the dealer demonstrates various Tupperware items and takes orders. The hostess has an opportunity to win a significant prize if enough orders are placed and if two guests agree to host parties in their homes. Thus, group pressure may be strong because some attendees at these sales parties tend to feel that if others are buying something they do not want to be embarrassed by not also making a purchase. They may feel that such an action would let the hostess and her friends down.[12]

Legitimate Power This power stems from members' perception that the group has a legitimate right to influence them. We speak of such behaviors with expressions like "should," "ought to," and so on. Many of these feelings have been internalized from parents, teachers, and religious institutions. Thus, there is some sort of code or standard that the individual accepts, and by virtue of which the group can assert its power.

One small group in which legitimate power can be seen to operate is the family. Each member has a set of roles to carry out which is legitimized by the other members. Thus, the father is expected to perform certain functions while the mother is expected to perform others. There are also functions that are performed jointly by the spouses. Much of the purchasing responsibilities which fall to each of the family members are those that society has inculcated into its members, based on these role patterns.

Marketers are also able to utilize legitimate power in many situations by appealing to consumers' internalized values. That is, appeals are often made on the basis of what one "ought to" or "should" do. Appeals from charitable organizations (such as the United Way and Red Cross) exert legitimate power, as do those for patriotic and nationalistic causes such as "Buy American" or "See America First."

Expert Power This influence results from the expertise of the individual or group. Consumers regularly accept influence from those they perceive to have superior experiences, knowledge, or skill. For instance, we may accept the recommendation of another person for a purchase we are about to make if we view that person as more knowledgeable than ourselves. Salespeople make effective use of this approach with their own product expertise.

Many advertisements rely on an expert's opinion about the product. For instance, Schlitz has used the company's president, who is a master brewer, to promote the product's taste in comparison with other brands; Jimmy Connors promotes Wilson tennis equipment; and A. J. Foyt advertises Goodyear tires. Manufacturers may even "create" experts when no one else seems suitable. For example, General Motors' Mr. Goodwrench, General Mills' Betty Crocker, and A&P's Ann Page are all fictitious, but effective endorsers.

Information power may often be related to expert power, yet it differs in that it is independent of the influencing agent (that is, the expert). This power stems from the "logic," "reasoning," or importance of the communication provided by the influencing agent. The content of the communication alone leads to changes in beliefs, attitudes, and behavior. In most situations, it is difficult to distinguish expert and information power. In fact, it has been suggested that informational influence may follow only after some degree of expert power is perceived by the individual being influenced.[13]

Ads which use information power may explain why the product is good, often citing available evidence such as price, quality of ingredients, performance specifications, and so forth.

Referent Power This influence flows from the feeling of identification an individual has with the group. As a consequence of this feeling of oneness or desire for such an identity, the individual will have a desire to become a member or gain a closer association with the group. The individual's identification with the group can be established or maintained if he or she behaves, believes, or perceives as the group does. The stronger this identification with the group, the greater its referent power. In this chapter and Chapter 11 we will look more closely at the use of referent power.

Advertisers often use referent power in promotions by encouraging consumers to be like or do the same thing as the individual advertising the brand. For instance, with many status-oriented products consumers are encouraged (either subtly or not so subtly) to obtain a similar status to that of the recommender by purchasing the item advertised. Colognes, clothing, automobiles, and stereo equipment often use such an approach. Use of celebrities is especially popular in these situations, whereby consumers may aspire to have hair like Farah Fawcett or skin like Cheryl Tiegs. In other approaches, marketers may use slice-of-life commercials or testimonials from "ordinary" consumers to show that other people experience the same problems and have found satisfaction with the recommended brand. Therefore, the individual advertised to may readily identify with that situation and be highly receptive to the brand. Products such as Oil of Olay, Extra Strength Anacin, Crest gel toothpaste, and Allstate insurance have been promoted with such an approach.

REFERENCE GROUPS

Having discussed some important group concepts necessary for our interests, let us further examine the topic of reference-group influence.

Types of Reference Groups

Reference groups are those an individual uses (that is, refers to) in determining his judgments, beliefs, and behavior. These may be of a number of types, as explained by the following classification system.[14]

Membership versus Nonmembership *Membership* groups are those to which the individual belongs. Membership in some groups is automatic by virtue of the consumer's age, sex, education, and marital status. Before acting, a consumer might consider whether purchase or use of a product would be consistent with one's role as a member of one of these groups. For example, an elderly woman would probably have serious reservations about purchasing extremely wild-looking clothing designed for the young, because such a product would not fit her expected role as a senior citizen.

Nonmembership groups are those to which the individual does not presently belong. Many of these groups are likely to be *anticipatory* or *aspirational* in nature, that is, those to which the individual aspires to belong. Such aspirational groups can have a profound influence on nonmembers because of their strong desire to join the group. This pattern of behavior is evident among upwardly mobile consumers who aspire to join higher-status clubs and social groups.

Positive versus Negative Reference groups can also be classified as to whether they attract or repel the individual. For instance, a *positive* reference group for the upwardly mobile consumer may be the "country club crowd" in that city. There are *negative* groups, however, that a person attempts to avoid being identified with. For example, an individual who is trying to succeed as a new management trainee may attempt through her speech, dress, and mannerisms to disassociate herself from her lower-social-class background in order to have a greater chance of success in her job.

Thus, reference groups can function in important ways for the consumer. They may affect aspiration levels and may also influence the kinds of behavior consumers enact. That is, they may strongly affect store and product choices as well as basic value systems. Reference groups, therefore, are powerful forces influencing members to conform to the group's beliefs, values, norms, and behavior patterns.

Reasons for Accepting Reference-Group Influence

Earlier, we examined the sources of power that groups, including reference groups, may appeal to in affecting consumers. In this section, the reasons why reference-group influence is accepted are discussed. Generally, consumers accept reference-group influence because of the perceived benefits in doing so. It has been suggested that the nature of social interactions between individuals will be determined by the individual's perception of the *profit of the interaction.* An interaction situation may result in *rewards* (such as friendship, information, satisfaction, and so on) but will also exact *costs* (lost time, money expended, alternative people and activities sacrificed). The difference between these rewards and costs, that is, the net profit from the social exchange, will attempt to be maximized by individuals. Thus, individuals will choose their groups and interact with members based upon their perception of the net profit of that exchange, rather than rewards or costs alone.[15]

At a more specific level, consumers may be seen to accept reference-group influence because of their role in providing informational, utilitarian, and value-expressive benefits.[16] Table 9-1 presents a series of statements that typify these three types of reference-group influence situations.

Informational Benefits One reason reference-group influence is accepted (or internalized) is that the consumer perceives that his knowledge of his environment and/or his ability to cope with some aspect of it (such as buying a product) is enhanced. Consumers most readily accept those information sources that are thought to be most credible. A consumer using an informational reference group may (1) actively search for information from opinion leaders or some group with the appropriate expertise or (2) come to some conclusion through observing the behavior of other people. Therefore, actual physical interaction with the group is not necessary in this type of information search.

In this situation, then, the marketer may be able to appeal to consumers through the use of advertising testimonials from experts or even "men in the street," or by encouraging consumers to find out more about the brand from friends, neighbors, or work associates. This personal source of information is often more influential than commercial sources such as advertising and salespeople in purchasing, as studies of food, small appliances, and other products indicate. One of the key linkages in this process is the credibility of the influencer. A consumer contemplating a major appliance purchase will rely on friends, salespersons, or even product-rating magazines if the information obtained is perceived as credible. Thus, consumers accept such expertise because of its informational benefits.

Utilitarian Benefit This reason refers to pressure on the individual to conform to the preferences or expectations of another individual or group. In a product-purchasing situation, the consumer will comply if (1) she believes that her behavior is visible or known to others, (2) she perceives that the others control significant sanctions (rewards or punishments), and (3) she is motivated to realize the reward or avoid the punishment.

Visibility is very important in order for this normative influence to operate. As will be shown later in this chapter, in situations in which the product is visible or the effects from its use or nonuse are visible, reference groups are able to exert

TABLE 9-1 TYPICAL REFERENCE-GROUP INFLUENCES ON BRAND DECISIONS

Informational Influence
1 The individual seeks information about various brands of the product from an association of professionals or independent group of experts.
2 The individual seeks information from those who work with the product as a profession.
3 The individual seeks brand-related knowledge and experience (such as how Brand A's performance compares to Brand B's) from those friends, neighbors, relatives, or work associates who have reliable information about the brands.
4 The brand which the individual selects is influenced by observing a seal of approval of an independent testing agency (such as Good Housekeeping).
5 The individual's observation of what experts do influences his choice of a brand (such as observing the type of car which police drive or the brand of TV which repairmen buy).

Utilitarian Influence
1 To satisfy the expectations of fellow work associates, the individual's decision to purchase a particular brand is influenced by their preferences.
2 The individual's decision to purchase a particular brand is influenced by the preferences of people with whom he has social interaction.
3 The individual's decision to purchase a particular brand is influenced by the preferences of family members.
4 The desire to satisfy the expectations which others have of him has an impact on the individual's brand choice.

Value-Expressive Influence
1 The individual feels that the purchase or use of a particular brand will enhance the image which others have of him.
2 The individual feels that those who purchase or use a particular brand possess the characteristics which he would like to have.
3 The individual sometimes feels that it would be nice to be like the type of person which advertisements show using a particular brand.
4 The individual feels that the people who purchase a particular brand are admired or respected by others.
5 The individual feels that the purchase of a particular brand helps him show others what he is, or would like to be (an athlete, successful businessman, good mother, etc.).

Source: C. Whan Park and V. Parker Lessig, "Students and Housewives: Differences in Susceptibility to Reference Group Influence," *Journal of Consumer Research,* **4:**105, September 1977.

strong normative influence. Thus, products such as clothing and furniture are highly visible to others, and therefore are quite susceptible to normative group influence. Even for items which are not themselves visible to others when in use (e.g., antiperspirant deodorants), normative influence is still likely to be strong, because the effects of nonuse will be rather evident (e.g., body odor and a stained dress or shirt underarm area). Consequently, fear of group reaction will influence the product's use.

Thus, an individual accepts influence from the group because she hopes to attain certain specific rewards or avoid certain punishments controlled by the group. In effect, the individual learns to say or do the expected thing in certain situations, not because she necessarily likes it, but because it is instrumental in producing a satisfying social effect.

Value-Expressive Benefits This relates to an individual's motive to enhance or support his self-concept by associating himself with positive reference groups and/ or disassociating himself from negative referents.

In order for the individual to accomplish this, a comparison must be made between beliefs, attitudes, and behavior of the group and those of the individual. Individuals have a need to compare themselves with others on various attributes in order to judge the consequences of their behavior when physical evidence is not available.[17] The motivation for social comparison, then, may lead the individual to choose reference groups or a reference individual to make such comparisons. This "co-oriented" peer is an individual whose outlook and values are similar to one's own and, therefore, functions as a frame of reference in evaluating one's behavior.

Value-expressive reference-group influence is characterized by two different processes. First, an individual may utilize reference groups to express himself or bolster his ego. Second, an individual may simply like the group, and therefore accept its influence. Thus, an individual adopts behavior derived from the group as a way of establishing or maintaining the desired relationship to the group and the self-image provided by this relationship. The individual may say what the group members say, do what they do, and believe what they believe in order to foster the relationship and the satisfying self-image it provides.

RESEARCH ON REFERENCE-GROUP INFLUENCE

So far we have merely hinted that reference group influence can be quite strong. What research support do we have for this judgment? Several studies confirming this fact are described in this section.

One experiment showing that a group may induce strong pressure on an individual to conform involved groups of seven to nine college students brought together and instructed to judge the lengths of lines drawn on cards. All group members but one—the naive subject—were instructed to give an incorrect response. The naive subject gave his answer after most of the group had answered. He thus found his judgment in opposition to that of the rest of the group. The result of the experiments with 123 naive subjects tested on 12 critical judgments was that 37 percent of the total number of judgments conformed to the incorrect answers of the remainder of the group acting in unison.[18]

Other experiments have been conducted with similar goals but with a different technique. Rather than allowing group members to have face-to-face oral communication with the group as in the situation above, individuals in these experiments were somewhat removed from each other, communicated only indirectly, and were to some degree anonymous. The kind of yielding that occurred and its psychological significance were determined to be the same under both experimental approaches. However, the former situation imposed more powerful group pressure on the individual, resulting in a greater average amount of conformity.[19]

Another experiment provided an indication of the strength of the group norms in forcing conformity. Subjects were brought into a dark room and asked to judge the distance and direction of movement of a small point of light. Although the light was actually stationary, it appeared to move because of the autokinetic effect, that is, an illusion of movement due to small tremors in the eye. Group members arrived at a consensus that tended to be maintained when individual members were asked to give their judgments after the group had dispersed.[20]

Another researcher studied the influence of group pressure on consumer decision making and the effects of choice restriction by group pressure in the consumer decision making process. Student subjects were instructed to evaluate and choose the best suit among three identical men's suits. Three group members (all confederates of the researcher) were instructed to select suit "B" which then put pressure on the naive subject, who was questioned last to agree with the group or to differ in his judgment and thus resist the group influence. It was found that individuals tended to conform to the group norm. The implication is that consumers accept information provided by their peer groups on the quality of a product, of a style, and so forth, which is difficult to evaluate objectively.

In addition, the study sought to determine the extent to which individuals might be controlled in a buying situation. The study's confederate subjects were instructed to give responses which indicated that they were "good guys" merely going along with the group consensus. The implication was that the naive subjects should also go along with the group. They were thus in a position of having to respond to an obvious effort at group pressure. It was found that any attempt to restrict independent choice behavior in the consumer decision-making process may be resisted under certain conditions. We see the occurrence of this in the marketplace when an individual conforms to the group norm by keeping a new product or adopting a new style, but maintains his or her independence by purchasing a different color or brand. This situation is shown as *reactance,* whereby the individual is motivated to resist further reduction in his or her set of free behaviors and to avoid compliance with the inducing agent, in this case his or her reference group. It is possible, therefore, that too obvious an attempt to force compliance with a group may have the opposite effect on consumers and thus they may strike out in an independent direction to avoid going along with the group.[21]

In order for psychological reactance to occur, then, two elements must be present.[22] First, a consumer must expect a measure of freedom to act in a given situation. Second, some threat must arise that infringes upon that freedom. Sources of such threats may range from social influence attempts by other people, to impersonal barriers to action (such as product unavailability), or they may even be self-imposed, simply because the individual, by entering into the process of a decision, arrives at a point beyond which there will be an unwanted reduction in freedom.[23] Here we are concerned with the role of reference groups as mediators of reactance processes. Studies have found, for example, that one's immediate group can suppress manifestations of reactance. When there is expected to be no future interaction between the individual and the group, the individual will tend to act contrary to the pressure (creating a boomerang effect). However, when future interaction is anticipated, subjects tend to conform to the group pressure; that is, the salient group apparently holds the reactance response in check.[24]

Reference groups may also influence shopping/purchasing patterns. A study of in-store shopping behavior indicated that multiple shopping parties made many more changes in shopping plans than did single shoppers. Compared to single shoppers, less than half as many parties of three or more persons purchased as many items as planned. However, group influence worked both ways; compared with single shoppers, larger proportions of parties of three or more bought both more and less than planned.[25]

Another experiment was conducted to determine whether small, informal groups influence the formation of brand loyalty. In this study, consumers from pre-existing reference groups selected a loaf of bread from four identical loaves marked with different letters representing fictitious brands. Based on the individual's choices, it was concluded that informal groups had definite influence on their members toward conformity behavior with respect to brands of bread preferred. Moreover, the extent and degree of brand loyalty within a group was closely related to the behavior of the informal leader.[26] A replication of this experiment, however, produced findings which were contrary. Evidence that group influence was not established was used to support the argument that products low in visibility, complexity, and perceived risk, and high in testability are not likely to be susceptible to personal influence.[27]

The research approaches described above generally suggest that the responses of others establish a norm to which subjects comply. A recent study, however, suggests that such normative effects may have been too readily inferred from observations of unanimous or consensus behavior among group members. In effect, people may use the product evaluation of others as a source of information about products; that is, they infer from such evaluations that the product is, indeed, a better product. Such a situation probably occurs regularly in shopping activities and in social groups.[28] Thus, rather than having a situation whereby the basis for group agreement is normative, it may be that members go along with the group because, as a result of observing the group's reaction, they perceive the product differently.

A final research area has been the influence of group discussion versus lecture or one-way communication when changing consumer attitudes and behavior. In one experiment, an attempt was made to change homemakers' meat consumption habits; half of the groups involved heard a lecture on the subject, while the other groups engaged in discussions. Although each group received the same information, results indicated that more women in the discussion groups used the recommended meats than did individuals in the lecture groups. Thus, group interaction was found to be a strong influence in promoting changed attitudes and behavior in various types of groups, even among those whose members were initially strangers.[29]

The types of groups involved in most of these experiments were made up of subjects who either did not know each other initially or were only slightly acquainted. Imagine how much more significant and strong the potential influence, then, from a group with which the individual strongly identifies or uses as a referent, such as family, close friends, or colleagues.

The Variability of Reference-Group Influence

We have seen that reference groups can be very potent influences on behavior in general, and that they may also be very influential on consumer behavior. For example, before making a decision about purchasing a product, consumers often consider what a particular group would do in this situation, or what they would think of the consumer for purchasing the product. This commonsense notion, however, has been difficult to apply meaningfully in specific marketing situations. The basic problem is one of determining which kinds of groups are likely to be referred to by which kinds of individuals under which kinds of situations in making which decision, and of measuring the extent of this influence. Nevertheless, a start has been made in understanding this process. This section discusses some of what we now know about the variability of reference-group influence on consumers.

Reference Group Influence Varies Among Products Charles Glock[30] first studied the influence of reference groups on the purchase of a number of consumer goods and found that the "conspicuousness" of a product is a strong determinant of its susceptibility to reference-group influence. Conspicuousness may be of two forms, however. First, the item must be exclusive in some way. If virtually everyone owns it, it is not conspicuous in this first sense, even though it may be highly visible. Operationally, we may think of this as the distinction between luxuries (having a degree of exclusivity) and necessities (possessed by virtually everyone). Second, the item must be seen or identified by others. Thus, where an item is consumed has great relevance. In this situation, a distinction may be made between publicly consumed products (which are seen by others) and privately consumed items (not seen by others). Reference groups may influence either the purchase of a product or the choice of a particular brand, or both.

Because of several defects in Glock's work, as well as its age, other consumer researchers have investigated the role of reference-group influence on product and brand choice for several product categories. One of these studies is summarized in Figure 9-2. It combines the concepts of public-private consumption and luxury-necessity items which, when applied to product and brand decisions, offers the following set of eight relationships:[31]

1 *Publicly consumed luxury*—A product consumed in public view and not commonly owned or used (e.g., golf clubs). In this case, whether or not the product is owned and also what brand is purchased is likely to be influenced by others. Relationships with reference group influence:

    a Because it is a luxury, influence for the *product* should be *strong*.
    b Because it will be seen by others, influence for the *brand* of the product should be *strong*.

2 *Privately consumed luxury*—A product consumed out of public view and not commonly owned or used (e.g., a trash compactor). In many cases, the brand is not conspicuous or socially important and is a matter of individual choice, but ownership of the product does convey a message about the owner. Relationships with reference group influence:

    a Because it is a luxury, influence for the *product* should be *strong*.
    b Because it will not be seen by others, influence for the *brand* of the product should be *weak*.

FIGURE 9-2

Combining public-private and luxury-necessity dimensions with product and brand purchase decisions. (*Source:* William O. Bearden and Michael J. Etzel, "Reference Group Influence on Product and Brand Purchase Decisions," *Journal of Consumer Research,* **9:**185, September 1982. Reprinted by permission.)

	Public	
Product / Brand	Weak reference group influence (−)	Strong reference group influence (+)
Strong reference group influence (+) (Necessity)	*Public necessities* Influence: Weak product and strong brand Examples: Wristwatch, automobile, man's suit	*Public luxuries* Influence: Strong product and brand Examples: Golf clubs, snow skis, sailboat (Luxury)
Weak reference group influence (−)	*Private necessities* Influence: Weak product and brand Examples: Mattress, floor lamp, refrigerator	*Private luxuries* Influence: Strong product and weak brand Examples: TV game, trash compactor, icemaker

Private

3 *Publicly consumed necessity*—A product consumed in public view that virtually everyone owns (e.g., a wristwatch). This group is made up of products that essentially all people or a large proportion of people use, although they differ as to what type of brand to use.

Relationships with reference group influence:

    a Because it is a necessity, influence for the *product* should be *weak.*

    b Because it will be seen by others, influence for the *brand* of the product should be *strong.*

4 *Privately consumed necessity*—A product consumed out of public view that virtually everyone owns (such as a mattress). Purchasing behavior is largely governed by product attributes rather than by the influences of others. In this group, neither products nor brands tend to be socially conspicuous, and they are owned by nearly all consumers.

Relationships to reference group influence:

    a Because it is a necessity, influence for the *product* should be *weak.*

    b Because it will not be seen by others, influence for the *brand* of the product should be *weak.*

More refinement is needed for understanding such reference influence, however. Research indicates, for example, that consumers perceive their own personal preferences to strongly outweigh reference groups in arriving at their product and brand decisions. Table 9-2 presents evidence of the extent of reference-group influence for several product categories. It is clear that the perceived influence of reference groups is substantially underestimated by the consumer. The consumer views herself as largely independent of the implicit social pressures exerted on her product and brand selection by reference groups. For major durables or "family products," the greatest group influence comes from the family. Other reference groups are more influential in the case of products linked to social visibility or social status.

The marketer should also be aware that some shifting of product perceptions may occur over time. For example, a product may shift from a category in which reference-group influence is weak to another in which it is strong, especially through the use of heavy promotional efforts designed to create a favorable image and make a product or brand socially conspicuous. Of course, products may also slip in their degree of reference-group influence as they near saturation levels of

TABLE 9-2
REFERENCE GROUP INFLUENCE

	Referent on Product Usage				Referent on Brand Choice			
Product	Family	Friends	Work Associates	Personal Preference	Family	Friends	Work Associates	Personal Preference
Air conditioner	38.7%	29.7%	17.9%	51.4%	40.0%	32.9%	20.5%	52.7%
Beer	11.0	26.9	8.3	74.7	7.6	29.0	6.2	79.5
Canned peaches	36.2	3.4	.7	72.6	35.6	4.1	1.4	73.8
Cars	43.2	28.3	17.2	82.2	44.5	31.0	18.6	82.9
Cigarettes	5.5	9.0	7.6	75.3	3.4	11.0	6.2	80.8
Clothing	27.4	34.5	17.2	80.8	27.2	35.2	11.0	86.3
Drugs	31.7	17.9	6.8	67.1	33.8	19.3	6.9	72.6
Furniture	50.7	13.1	6.2	81.5	45.9	22.1	9.0	78.8
Instant coffee	35.6	15.2	5.5	67.6	34.9	15.9	4.8	70.3
Laundry soap	37.7	9.0	2.8	86.2	40.4	9.7	2.1	68.3
Magazines	24.7	19.3	11.7	85.6	30.1	26.2	13.8	87.7
Radio	30.3	26.2	6.9	80.1	23.4	7.6	1.4	76.6
Refrigerators	45.2	24.8	16.6	52.7	41.4	30.1	13.0	61.0
Soap	29.5	13.1	4.8	80.1	34.9	7.6	1.4	76.6
Toilet soap	32.2	4.8	0	72.4	32.2	2.8	0	74.5
TV (color)	44.5	26.2	12.4	69.9	46.2	35.6	15.1	71.2

	Overall Perceived Group Influence	
Influence Agent	Perceived Group Influence	Most Important Choice Criterion
Product usage:		
Family	33.2%	24.7%
Friends	18.8	6.2
Work associates	8.9	.7
Personal preference		68.4
		100.0%
Brand choice:		
Family	32.6%	22.6%
Friends	21.4	14.4
Work associates	8.7	0
Personal preference		63.0
		100.0%

Source: William G. Lundstrum, William G. Zikmund, and Donald Sciglimpaglia, "Reference Group Influence on Product and Brand Choice: Update of a Classic Study," in Robert S. Franz, Robert M. Hopkins, and Alfred G. Toma (eds.), *Proceedings: Southern Marketing Association 1979 Conference*, Southern Marketing Association, Lafayette, LA, 1979, p. 264.

ownership. Thus, attention to changing perceptions over a product's life cycle is important.

How may the kind of information presented in Figure 9-2 and Table 9-2 be used when making marketing decisions? The following advertising strategies may be adopted depending on the degree of reference-group influence found for the product or brand:

1 Where neither product nor brand appear to be associated strongly with reference-group influence, advertising should emphasize the product's attributes, intrinsic qualities, price, and advantage over competing products.

2 Where reference-group influence is operative, the advertiser should stress the kinds of people who buy the product, reinforcing and broadening where possible the existing stereotypes of users. The strategy of the advertiser should involve learning what the stereotypes are and what specific reference groups enter into the picture, so that appeals can be "tailored" to each main group reached by the different media employed.[32]

It should be noted, however, that not all studies find strong reference-group influence by product type. Although marketers assume intuitively that products perceived to be higher in social conspicuousness and social motives for purchase (e.g., cologne and alcoholic beverages) will be rated higher on group influence than nonsocial products (e.g., headache remedies and pocket calculators), one research study has found minimal differences in group influence on product choice between these product types.[33] Thus, reference influence may sometimes be weaker than commonly expected.

Reference Group Influence Varies Among Groups Reference-group influence has been shown to vary according to characteristics of the group or its type. For example, comparison of reference-group influence scores for students and homemakers across twenty products showed that there are significant differences between the groups in terms of the influence of reference groups on brand selection and that students are generally more susceptible to reference-group influence. Why? Perhaps differences in needs or motivations among the groups result in different responses to reference-group influence. First, the lower age of students perhaps results in their having less familiarity with products and less product information and in their facing greater purchase risk than homemakers. Second, social surroundings and daily activity differences exist between the groups. Students have more frequent social contacts, more interaction within groups (e.g., sororities, fraternities, and dormitory residents) which impose more rules and norms, and more visible behavior subject to group pressure than do homemakers. Third, hedonism may be stronger among students than among homemakers, so that they are more highly ego-involved in their purchases.[34] Thus, we see that different groups exhibit different reference influences. Let's briefly examine a few of these group factors that seem to influence conformity.

First, conformity may be related to *group cohesiveness,* as some of the previous experiments indicated. In addition, a study of brand-choice behavior found group cohesiveness and brand similarities to be positively related.[35] However, not all researchers have found group cohesiveness to be associated with group influence. At least two studies have found no such relationship.[36] Conformity also appears to be related to group size. One set of experiments showed that increasing the number of confederates up to three increased the pressure toward conformity on the naive subject, but beyond this number, the influence was found to be no greater.

Proximity to group members can influence conformity. For example, a study of elderly consumer social-interaction patterns found that more than 80 percent of the exchange of information and advice about a new product occurred between persons living on the same floor.[37] This and other studies have indicated that influencers and influencees live close to each other.

The *individual's relationship* to the group is another factor that determines its influence on conformity. His or her social integration (i.e., the level of acceptance by other group members) and his or her group role are factors that generally are positively related to the degree of group influence on the individual.[38] However, social comparison processes are at work even in socially distant reference groups.[39]

Similarity to the group's characteristics, outlooks, and values is also important. For example, consumers are more likely to seek product information, to trust this information, and to choose the same products as do friends who have similar attributes. This suggests that a new product can be diffused fastest when the market possesses similar value orientations about similar types of products, because the likelihood of interpersonal communication and influence is greatest.[40]

Although similarity is likely to be important, one research study indicates that the single most important element of referent selection for fifteen products commonly purchased by undergraduate males is *stage presence*.[41] The persuasive charisma resulting from this attribute may be very relevant in certain marketing situations. For instance, the marketer may often want to choose a model or potential referent having this attribute when promoting through advertising or personal selling. James Garner and Mariette Hartley as the spokespersons for Polaroid appear to fulfill this criterion. For example, Garner has been rated as the top advertising spokesperson and as the most liked celebrity advertiser.

Reference-Group Influence Varies Among Individuals The strength of reference-group influence not only varies among products and group type, but also among different consumers. That is, some individuals are more susceptible to reference-group influence than others. What individual characteristics seem to be associated with a consumer's susceptibility to reference-group influence? It appears that both demographic and psychological factors are relevant.

First, *personality* factors are important. Conformity has been found to vary by personality type and is positively related to the following personality traits: low intelligence, extroversion, ethnocentrism, weak ego, poor leadership, authoritarianism, need for affiliation, being a firstborn or only child, and feelings of personal inferiority or inadequacy.[42]

The type of *social character* of consumers may also affect reference-group influence. An important consumer typology related to this is Riesman's inner-directed and other-directed individual.[43] This theory describes inner-directed individuals as those who turn to their own inner standards and values to guide their behavior. Early in childhood they are taught by parents, the church, and other cultural institutions to accept and internalize these standards and to use them as a frame of reference for future behavior. These internalized values are relatively durable and change little over the individual's lifetime.

Other-directed individuals depend on others around them for direction and guidance. They have been taught to look to other people for correct standards of behavior and to be sensitive to the values and attitudes of their respected reference groups and associates. An analogy which distinguishes these two social character groups is to think of inner-directeds as being equipped with a gyrocompass, while other-directeds are guided by radar.

A second set of factors relating to reference-group susceptibility is the consumer's *demographic* attributes. For example, differences in reference-group influence have been found between males and females, married couples and singles, younger and older people, and between different nationalities.[44]

Type of Reference-Group Influence Varies A study of reference-group influence on brand decisions of students and housewives investigated the relevance of three types of reference-group influence (informational, utilitarian, and value-expressive) to a consumer's selection of a brand or model.[45] The consumer was assumed to have already decided to buy the product, but was undecided on the brand or model.

The study showed, for example, that among students, ratings of informational influences were most important for half of the products studied, followed by utilitarian influences, with value-expressive influences least important for the products studied. Those products most likely to be subject to informational influence generally were items with greater technological complexity (e.g., color TVs). Those products most subject to utilitarian and value-expressive influences were products that were important means of conforming to group norms or obtaining group identification and support through self-expression (e.g., automobiles and clothing). This study, therefore, indicates that for these subjects and products, informational benefits appear to outweigh the role of utilitarian and value-expressive benefits from the group.

Often, therefore, consumers buy products that others in their groups buy, not to establish some self-fulfilling role relationship to others, nor to obtain reward or avoid some punishment from the group, but simply to acquire what they perceive as a good product. In a similar way, an individual in a shopping situation may use the reactions of other shoppers as a basis for inferring the value of products that she or he is unable to assess completely from direct observation.[46]

Other research studies support the idea that groups may be used by consumers more for the information they provide than for the reward and identification they offer.[47] The consequence of such findings for the marketer may be that more information-oriented advertising can be utilized with groups or referent individuals. In particular, the use of "typical consumers" in advertising to impart information to influencees seems to be in order. Current industry practice emphasizing "hidden" camera interviews with consumers appears to support this.

Reference-Group Influence is Situational Several of the research studies cited previously related the variability of reference-group influence to a behavioral situation. That is, reference-group influence was seen to be related in some cases to the type of product, the item's social visibility, and so forth. Several other research studies also indicate that the nature of the consumer situation has an important impact on the nature of reference influence.[48] For example, investigation of group influence on brand usage of inexpensive grocery items, on patronage among various retail stores, and on utilization of certain services (e.g., a plumber or a physician) has shown that the areas of retail-store patronage and service utilization are perhaps more susceptible to group influence than is brand usage of group products. Apparently, too, the amount of pressure exerted by a group in one behavioral context is not necessarily likely to be exerted in another context. That is, conformity influence appears to be a situation-specific phenomenon.[49]

Marketers should, therefore, carefully assess the extent to which reference-group influence exists for their product, what type of influence appears to be more pervasive, and how customer segments may differ in their responsiveness to such influences. The situational nature of such influence also needs to be understood. From such knowledge, more effective marketing strategies may be developed incorporating referent power.

Identifying Reference Groups

We see, then, that reference groups are highly relevant and potent influences in consumer decision making. But how do we identify the specific individual, group, or groups who are most relevant to the consumer's behavior? Unfortunately, at this stage we are unable to answer this question definitively; we simply are not sure which reference groups will be most important in a given buying decision. Thus, when a young woman goes to the store to buy a new outfit, the ultimate choice may reflect her sorority, her family, her church group, her boyfriend and his friends, or any other group. It is very difficult for the marketer to know which reference group generally dominates.

We can attempt to get some idea of those whom a consumer uses as referents in decision making by using one or more of the following approaches.[50]

1 Asking respondents directly about the groups that may be influencing their opinions or actions in a given situation.

2 Using associative-projective techniques (see Chapter 3) designed to elicit responses from people in such a way that they are not aware that they are committing themselves personally to any specific point of view or attitude. In this technique, the respondent would be asked to react to a reference-group situation indirectly through being asked her opinion of *someone else* behaving in a certain way.

3 Using the sociometric technique, which traces personal relationships by detailed questioning of an entire group of people who are in significant association with each other. Such questions as the following are asked of these people: With whom do they associate? Whom do they like and respect? To whom do they look for advice on specific subjects? To what extent do people turn to them for advice on given subjects?

4 Seeking to identify reference-group influence through observation of the act of buying and social interaction which takes place.

SUMMARY

This chapter has described social-group influences which impinge on the consumer. We first defined the term "group" and distinguished small groups from other collections of individuals. We next described various types of groups classified along a number of dimensions. This was followed by a discussion of group properties including norms, role, status, power and socialization, and the nature of social interaction which is the way in which consumers are influenced by their groups.

Reference groups were examined in detail because these are of great significance for the marketer. We defined many types of reference groups, discussed their functions, and described the nature of their influence on individuals. We elaborated on the marketing implications of reference groups by discussing factors related to their level of influence and by citing their relevance in consumer decision making. Finally, we discussed ways the marketer may go about identifying the consumer's relevant reference groups.

DISCUSSION TOPICS

1. What is meant by the term "group"? What are some types of groups?

2. On what bases may groups be classified?

3. Distinguish between the following types of groups:
    a Primary versus secondary   c Social group versus aggregation
    b Formal versus informal

4. Discuss the basic properties of a group. How do these properties relate to consumer behavior?

5. What is a reference group? Name two reference groups that are important to you. In what way do they influence your consumer behavior?

6. What groups do you belong to that you feel are not influential on you and your behavior as a consumer?

7. What techniques are used by the marketer in identifying reference groups?

8. Suggest a product not listed in Figure 9-2 over which reference groups would exert a strong or weak influence with regard to the purchase of the product and brand or type. Explain.

9. For the following purchase decisions, which of the consumer's reference groups would appear to be most important?
    a Formal evening gown   c A new home
    b Selection of a physician   d A basketball and warm-up suit

10. What factors appear to influence reference-group influence?

11. Bring in ads illustrating the marketer's use of each type of group power influence.

NOTES

[1] David Dressler and Donald Carns, *Sociology: The Study of Human Interaction,* Knopf, New York, 1973, p. 259.
[2] Robert Bierstedt, *The Social Order,* 2d ed., McGraw-Hill, New York, 1963, p. 302.
[3] Charles H. Cooley, *Social Organization,* Scribners, New York, 1909, p. 23.
[4] Ralph Linton, *The Cultural Background of Personality,* Appleton Century Crofts, New York, 1945.
[5] William Shakespeare, *As You Like It,* act 2, scene 7, lines 140–143.

[6]Erving Goffman, *The Presentation of Self in Everyday Life,* University of Edinburgh Social Sciences Research Centre, London, 1958.
[7]David Krech, Richard S. Crutchfield and Egerton L. Ballachey, *Individual in Society,* McGraw-Hill, New York, 1962, p. 313.
[8]Scott Ward, "Consumer Socialization," *Journal of Consumer Research,* 1:1–14, September 1974.
[9]John R. P. French and Bertram Raven, "The Bases of Social Power," in D. Cartwright (ed.), *Studies in Social Power,* Institute of Social Research, Ann Arbor, MI, 1959, pp. 150–167.
[10]"Soft Soap and Hard Sell," *Forbes,* September 15, 1975, pp. 72, 78.
[11]Scott B. MacKenzie and Judy L. Zaichkowsky, "An Analysis of Alcohol Advertising Using French and Raven's Theory of Social Influence," in Kent B. Monroe (ed.), *Advances in Consumer Research: Volume 8,* Association for Consumer Research, Ann Arbor, MI, 1981, pp. 708–712.
[12]Ellen Graham, "'Tupperware Parties' Create a New Breed of Super-Saleswoman," *The Wall Street Journal,* May 21, 1971, pp. 1, 18; and Flavia Krone and Denise Smart, "An Exploratory Study Profiling the Party-Plan Shopper," in Robert H. Ross, Frederick B. Kraft, and Charles H. Davis (eds.), *1981 Proceedings, Southwestern Marketing Association,* Wichita State University, 1981, pp. 200–203.
[13]John L. Swasy, "Measuring the Bases of Social Power," in William L. Wilkie (ed.), *Advances in Consumer Research: Volume 6,* Association for Consumer Research, Ann Arbor, MI, 1979, p. 341.
[14]Francis S. Bourne, "Group Influence in Marketing and Public Relations," in Rensis Likert and Samuel Hayes, Jr., (eds.), *Some Applications of Behavioral Research,* UNESCO, Paris, 1957, pp. 208–209; and Tamotsu Shibutani, "Reference Groups as Perspectives," *American Journal of Sociology,* 60:562–569, May 1955.
[15]George Homans, *Social Behavior: Its Elementary Forms,* Harcourt, Brace & World, New York, 1961; and Michael J. Ryan and E. H. Bonfield, "The Fisbein Extended Model and Consumer Behavior," *Journal of Consumer Research,* 2:118–136, September 1975.
[16]C. Whan Park and V. Parker Lessig, "Students and Housewives: Differences in Susceptibility to Reference Group Influence," *Journal of Consumer Research,* 4:102–110, September 1977; Herbert C. Kelman, "Processes of Opinion Change," *Public Opinion Quarterly,* 25:57–78, 1961; and M. Deutsch and H. B. Gerard, "A Study of Normative and Informational Social Influences Upon Individual Judgment," *Journal of Abnormal and Social Psychology,* 51:624–636, 1955.
[17]Leon Festinger, "A Theory of Social Comparison Processes," *Human Relations,* 7:117–140, May 1954.
[18]Soloman E. Asch, "Studies of Independence and Submission to Group Pressure: A Minority of One Against a Unanimous Majority," *Psychological Monographs,* 70:1956.
[19]Krech, Crutchfield, and Ballachey, *Individual in Society,* p. 511.
[20]Muzafer Sherif, *The Psychology of Social Norms,* Harper, New York, 1936, pp. 89–107.
[21]M. Venkatesan, "Experimental Study of Consumer Behavior, Conformity and Independence," *Journal of Marketing Research,* 3:384–387, November 1966.
[22]For a review of reactance theory and its application to consumer behavior including a discussion of defects of the Venkatesan research see Mona A. Clee and Robert A. Wicklund, "Consumer Behavior and Psychological Reactance," *Journal of Consumer Research,* 6:389–405, March 1980.
[23]Clee and Wicklund, "Consumer Behavior," pp. 396–397.
[24]Clee and Wicklund, "Consumer Behavior," pp. 389–405.
[25]Donald H. Granbois, "Improving the Study of Customer In-Store Behavior," *Journal of Marketing,* 32:30, October 1968.
[26]James E. Stafford, "Effects of Group Influence on Consumer Behavior," *Journal of Marketing Research,* 3 :68–75, February 1966.
[27]Jeffery D. Ford and Elwood A. Ellis, "A Reexamination of Group Influence on Member Brand Preferences," *Journal of Marketing Research,* 17:125–132, February 1980.
[28]Robert E. Burnkrant and Alain Cousineau, "Informational and Normative Social Influence in Buyer Behavior," *Journal of Consumer Research,* 2:206–215, December 1975.
[29]Kurt Lewin, "Group Decision and Social Change," in Harold Proshansky and Bernard Seidenberg (eds.), *Basic Studies in Social Psychology,* Holt, New York, 1965, pp. 423–436.
[30]Glock's research results were written by Francis S. Bourne in "Group Influence."
[31]William O. Bearden and Michael J. Etzel, "Reference Group Influence on Product and Brand Purchase Decisions," *Journal of Consumer Research,* 9:184–185, September 1982.
[32]Bourne, "Group Influence," pp. 221–222.
[33]Richard C. Becherer, Fred W. Morgan, Jr., and Lawrence M. Richard, "Person-Situation Interaction Within a Consumer Behavior Context," *Journal of Psychology,* 102:235–242, July 1979.
[34]Park and Lessig, "Students and Housewives," pp. 103–104.
[35]Robert E. Witt, "Informal Social Group Influence on Consumer Behavior," *Journal of Marketing Research,* 6:473–476, November 1969.
[36]John H. Murphy and William H. Cunningham, "Correlates of the Extent of Informal Friendship-Group Influence on Consumer Behavior," in Subhash C. Jain (ed.), *Research Frontiers in Marketing: Dialogues and Directions,* American Marketing Association, Chicago, 1978, pp. 130–133; and Ford and Ellis, "A Reexamination," pp. 125–132.
[37]Leon G. Schiffman, "Social Interaction Patterns of the Elderly Consumer," in Boris W. Becker and Hel-

mut Becker (eds.), *Combined Proceedings of the American Marketing Association,* American Marketing Association, Chicago, 1972, p. 451.

[38] Thomas S. Robertson, *Consumer Behavior,* Scott, Foresman, Glenview, IL, 1970, p. 74.

[39] Benton A. Cocanougher and Grady D. Bruce, "Socially Distant Reference Groups and Consumer Aspirations," *Journal of Marketing Research,* **8**:379–381, August 1971.

[40] George Moschis, "Social Comparison and Informal Group Influence," *Journal of Marketing Research,* **13**:237–244, August 1976.

[41] W. Thomas Anderson, Jr., Linda L. Golden and Joel Saegert, "Reactional Analysis of Referent Selection in Product Decisions," in Subhash C. Jain (ed.), *Research Frontiers in Marketing: Dialogues and Directives,* American Marketing Association, Chicago, 1978, pp. 134–138.

[42] Lyman O. Ostlund, "Role Theory and Group Dynamics," in Scott Ward and Thomas S. Robertson (eds.), *Consumer Behavior: Theoretical Sources,* Prentice-Hall, Englewood Cliffs, NJ, 1973, p. 245.

[43] Harold H. Kassarjian, "Riesman Revisited," *Journal of Marketing,* **29**:54–56, April 1965; and Richard W. Mizerski and Robert B. Settle, "The Influence of Social Character on Preference for Social Versus Objective Information in Advertising," *Journal of Marketing Research,* **16**:552–558, November 1979.

[44] Donald W. Hendon, "A New and Empirical Look at the Influence of Reference Groups on Generic Product Category and Brand Choice: Evidence From Two Nations," in *Proceedings of the Academy of International Business: Asia-Pacific Dimensions of International Business,* College of Business Administration, University of Hawaii, Honolulu, 1979, p. 757; and Robert T. Green, Joel G. Saegert, and Robert J. Hoover, "Conformity in Consumer Behavior: A Cross-National Replication," in Neil Beckwith, et al. (eds.), *1979 Educator's Conference Proceedings,* American Marketing Association, Chicago, 1979, pp. 192–194.

[45] Park and Lessig, "Students and Housewives."

[46] Burnkrant and Cousineau, "Informational and Normative Social Influence," p. 214.

[47] Fleming Hansen, "Primary Group Influence and Consumer Conformity," in Philip R. McDonald (ed.), *Marketing Involvement in Society and the Economy,* American Marketing Association, Chicago, 1969, pp. 300–305; and Moschis, "Social Comparison."

[48] Bobby J. Calder and Robert E. Burnkrant, "Interpersonal Influence on Consumer Behavior: An Attribution Theory Approach," *Journal of Consumer Research,* 4:29, 37, June 1977; and James H. Leigh and Claude R. Martin, Jr., "A Review of Situational Influence Paradigms and Research," in Ben M. Enis and Kenneth J. Roering (eds.), *Review of Marketing 1981,* American Marketing Association, Chicago, 1981, p. 68.

[49] Murphy and Cunningham, "Correlates."

[50] Bourne, "Group Influence," pp. 230–233.

CHAPTER 10
FAMILY

This chapter examines the family as one of the strongest, most immediate, and most pervasive environmental influences on our behavior as buyers. Consumers' attitudes toward spending and saving and even the brands and products purchased have been molded, often quite indelibly, by their families. Thus, marketers need to understand the nature of the family's influence on its members and the way in which purchase decisions are made by members so that they may effectively program their marketing mix.

The thrust of this chapter will first be to review several terms important in understanding this subject. Second, we shall describe the basic functions of the family. Next, we shall examine the family life-cycle concept and assess its meaning for the marketer. Family organization and decision-making roles will then be discussed, also incorporating marketing implications and examples. Finally, the changing nature of the family, especially here in America, will be discussed along with implications for marketers who face this changing scene.

FAMILIES AND HOUSEHOLDS

It is important to understand the difference between various terms that are frequently encountered when discussing the concept of family. First, we should distinguish between the terms "family" and "household," since market statistics may be gathered on either of these bases. A *household* includes the related family members and all the unrelated persons who occupy a housing unit (whether house, apartment, group of rooms, or other). The term "family," however, is more limited and refers to a group of two or more persons related by blood, marriage, or adoption and residing together in a household. In 1980 there were approximately 80 million households and 58 million families.

Table 10-1 presents data comparing households and husband-wife families on several bases to better understand the distinction.

It should be noted that marketers are interested not only in the concept of families but also of households, since both may form the basis or framework of much consumer decision making and buying behavior. The marketer will use the concept that seems most relevant for segmenting markets. For instance, manufacturers of refrigerators, dishwashers, ranges, and other kitchen appliances would probably find households to be the most relevant dimension in estimating market size since purchase and replacement of these appliances would depend more on household formation than family formation. On the other hand, sellers of children's clothing and toys would probably be more interested in data on families.

SIGNIFICANCE OF THE FAMILY IN CONSUMER BEHAVIOR

In Chapter 9 we examined the topic of social groups in order to understand their relevance to individuals and how marketers could use this knowledge. Now we turn to the family not just as a type of small group, but one that is often predominant in its influence over consumer behavior. The family is both a *primary* group (characterized by intimate, face-to-face interaction) and a *reference* group (with members referring to certain family values, norms, and standards in their behavior). These two factors, however, are not the sole reasons accounting for the

TABLE 10-1
HOUSEHOLDS IN PROFILE

	Total Households	Husband-Wife Families	All Other Households
Total (millions)	79.7	48.2	31.5
Percent	100.0%	100.0%	100.0%
Age of Head			
Under 25	8.2%	6.1%	11.6%
25–34	22.1	23.4	20.0
35–44	17.1	19.8	12.5
45–54	16.6	19.3	12.1
55–64	16.0	17.1	14.3
65 and over	20.0	14.3	29.5
Size of Household			
1 Person	22.0%	0.0%	58.3%
2 Persons	30.7	36.0	21.9
3 Persons	17.2	21.4	10.2
4 Persons	15.7	22.2	5.0
5 Persons or more	14.4	20.4	4.6
Children Under 18			
None	58.7%	46.6%	78.5%
1 Child	15.7	19.5	9.4
2 Children	14.6	19.6	6.5
3 Children	6.9	9.2	3.1
4 Children or more	4.1	5.1	2.5
Income by Income Class*			
Under $10,000	6.3%	2.5%	17.5%
$10,000–14,999	7.2	5.5	14.5
$15,000–19,999	9.8	7.5	17.0
$20,000–24,999	12.2	11.5	13.0
$25,000–34,999	22.8	25.0	18.0
$35,000–49,999	21.6	24.0	10.5
$50,000 and over	20.0	24.0	9.5
Place of Residence			
Central cities	30.2%	24.2%	40.0%
Suburbs	37.4	40.8	31.9
Non-metro area	32.4	35.0	28.1

*Percentages denote the proportion of total personal income flowing to each earning bracket for each household type.
Note: Total households and income distribution are for 1980. All other characteristics are for 1978.
Sources: U.S. Department of Commerce; The Conference Board. Reprinted in Fabian Linden, "The Nuclear Family is Splitting," *Across the Board,* July 1980, p. 55.

strength of the family's influence. Rather it is, first, the fact that the bonds within the family are likely to be much more powerful than those in other small groups. Second, contrary to most other groups to which the consumer belongs, the family functions directly in the role of ultimate consumption. Thus, the family operates as an economic unit, earning and spending money. In doing this, family members must establish individual and collective consumption priorities, decide on products and brands that fulfill their needs, and also decide where these items are to be bought, and how they are to be used in furthering family members' goals.

FAMILY LIFE CYCLE

The concept of family life cycle has proven very valuable for the marketer, especially for segmentation activities. This section will describe the concept and discuss its application to consumer behavior and marketing strategy.

Traditional Life-Cycle Stages

The term "life cycle" refers to the progression of stages through which individuals and families proceed over time. In the United States, the following stages are typical of the family life-cycle progression:

1 The Bachelor Stage: young, single people

2 Newly Married Couples: young, no children

3 Full Nest I: young married couples with youngest child under 6

4 Full Nest II: young married couples with youngest child 6 or over

5 Full Nest III: older married couples with dependent children

6 Empty Nest I: older married couples with no children living with them and household head in labor force

7 Empty Nest II: older married couples with no children living with them and household head retired

8 Solitary Survivor I: older single people in labor force

9 Solitary Survivor II: older retired single people

With the life-cycle concept the marketer is able to better appreciate how the family's needs, outlooks, product purchases, and financial resources vary over time. The major family life-cycle stages are further described below.[1]

Bachelor Stage   At this stage of the life cycle, earnings are relatively low because the individual is often just beginning a career. In spite of a low income, there are also few financial burdens which must be assumed; consequently, discretionary income is quite high. This group is generally recreation-oriented and high on fashion-opinion leadership. As a result, purchase patterns consist of vacations, cars, clothing, and various other products and services needed for the mating game. In addition, the establishment of their own residences away from their family usually requires the purchase of some basic furniture and kitchen equipment.

Newly Married Couples This group is generally better off financially than when they were single because both spouses are likely to be working. They are also healthier financially than they will be in the next stage, which brings added demands on their resources. But for now this family has the highest purchase rate and the highest average purchase of durable goods, especially furniture and appliances. They also spend heavily on cars, clothing, and vacations.

Full Nest I When the first child is born most wives have traditionally stopped working, which causes a reduction in family income. At the same time, new demands are added to the family's purchasing requirements. For example, the increased family size may necessitate more space, so the family moves into a new home and purchases items necessary to fill their new environment. Furniture for the baby's room and other furnishings are bought, as well as such appliances as a washer, dryer, and television set. In addition, many child-related expenses are now added, including baby food, baby medicines, doctor's visits, and toys of all sorts. The parents are quite interested in new products and are susceptible to things they see advertised; however, they also grow more dissatisfied with their financial position and the amount of money capable of being saved.

Full Nest II In this stage, the family's financial position has improved with the husband's advancement and perhaps, too, the wife's return to work. Families in this stage are still new-product-oriented, but tend to be less influenced by advertising because they have more buying experience. Products heavily purchased during this time include many foods (especially in larger packages and multiple-unit deals), cleaning materials, bicycles, and musical instruments and lessons.

Full Nest III During this stage, the family's income continues to advance, more wives return to work, and even the children may be employed. Although they are more resistant to advertising, this type of family has a high average expenditure for durable goods, primarily because of their need to replace older items. They purchase new, more tasteful furniture, luxury appliances, boats, and automobiles. They also do more traveling, and spend more on dental bills and magazines.

Empty Nest I At this stage, the family is most satisfied with its financial position and savings accumulation. Home ownership is at a peak, and major expenditures are necessary for home improvement. Although the couple is not interested in new products, they do show an interest in travel, recreation, and self-education. This spending pattern emphasizes gifts and contributions, vacations, and luxuries.

Empty Nest II During this stage the couple's income is drastically cut. They stay at home more and spend more for medical appliances, medical care, and products that aid their health, sleep, and digestion.

Solitary Survivors If these individuals are still active in the labor force, their income is likely to continue to be good. However, the home is likely to be sold, and more money will be spent for vacations, recreation, and health-oriented items. Those who are retired will suffer a drastic cut in income, but will continue to have the same medical and product needs as other retired groups. During this stage, individuals also have a special need for attention, affection, and security.

A Modernized Family Life Cycle

During recent years, many changes in the family have occurred, particularly in smaller family size, postponement of marriage, and rising divorce rates. Thus, another conception of the life cycle has been offered which includes the stages of divorced and middle-aged married without children. This modernized version is shown in Figure 10-1. It helps to visualize the possible variety of different family life-cycle stages by presenting a diagram of the flow. Both the traditional and modernized conceptualizations are shown in this figure.

Relationship between Life Cycle and Consumer Behavior

Although nine distinct stages were suggested above, there is no unanimity among research studies as to the most appropriate categorization of life cycle. For example, the dividing line for terms such as "young" and "older" might be 40 years of age in one study and 45 in another, which makes it difficult to compare results among various research studies. In spite of these definitional difficulties there is, nevertheless, widespread agreement on the relationship between life cycle and consumer behavior. For example, a study conducted for the Kroehler Manufacturing Company points out that family furniture purchase orientations vary according to life-cycle stage in the following way:

1 The young family places relatively greater emphasis on sensibility and practicality than style and beauty in the majority of its furniture purchases.

2 At later periods of furniture purchase, attractiveness and reflection of good taste become relatively more important.

3 Individual pieces of furniture are typically seen as appropriate to some particular age or stage in the life cycle.[2]

Further evidence is provided by a cross-national research study, in which the sizes and compositions of household expenditures were found to be systematically related to the stage of the family life cycle.[3] Such findings are relevant to marketing managers when developing forecasts, for example. Demand for different product and service categories may be estimated from knowledge of the relationship between demand and stage in life cycle and the predicted number of households in the various stages. A number of other studies have related shopping behavior to life-cycle stage.[4]

Life Cycle versus Age in Segmenting Markets

The reader may wonder whether the life-cycle concept offers a richer explanation of consumer behavior than a single variable such as age. You will recall that we raised a similar question earlier when considering the merits of social class versus income in segmenting markets. The evidence heavily favors the use of life cycle as a way of segmenting markets.[5] One in-depth study on this subject found that for most items investigated life cycle was more sensitive to product consumption than was age.[6] It should be noted, however, that for several categories of products and services the reverse was true. One category for which this was the case was products tied to age-related physical difficulties (e.g., medical appliances and other medical-care items). Age was also more sensitive for products and services classified mainly as luxuries, and for a diverse catchall category.

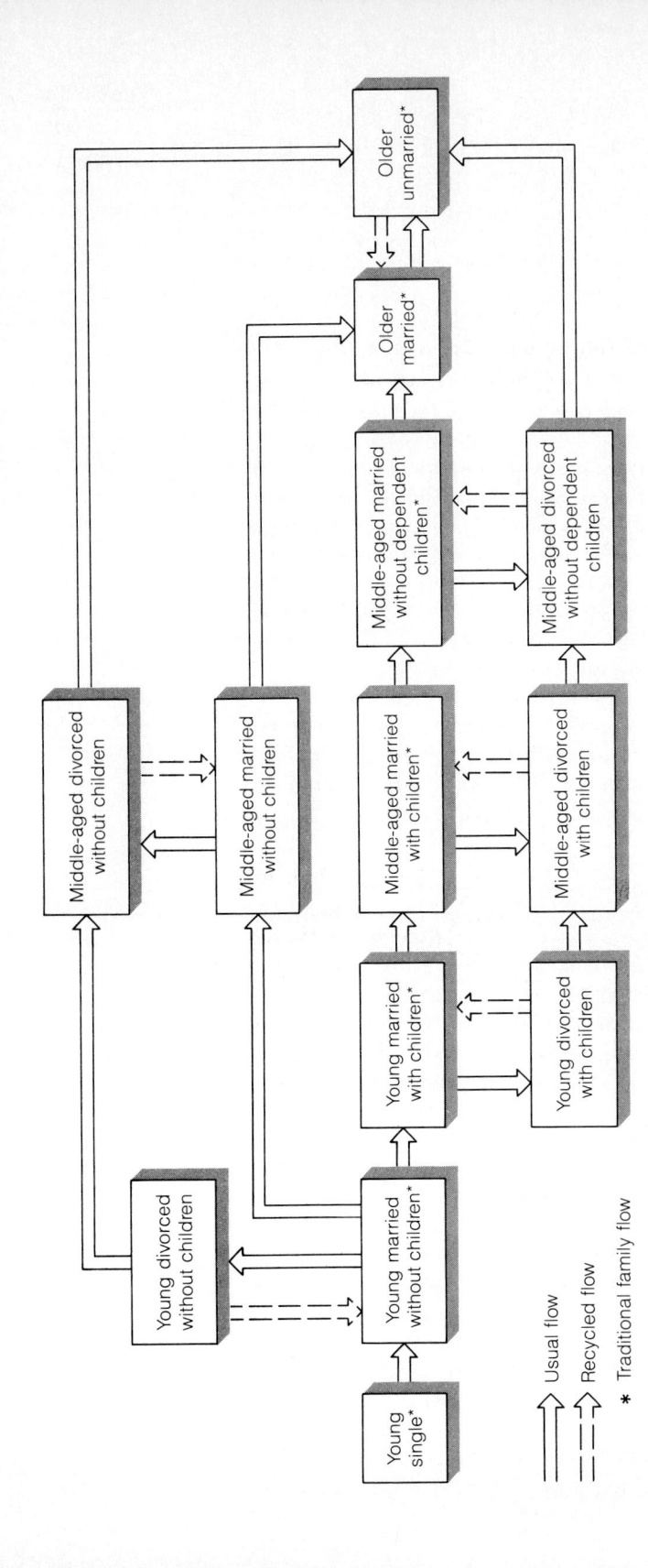

FIGURE 10-1

Family life-cycle flows. (*Source*: Patrick E. Murphy and William A. Staples, "A Modernized Family Life Cycle," *Journal of Consumer Research*, **6**:17, June 1979.)

For most products, however, life-cycle analysis allows the marketer to achieve a richer understanding of the market. A summary overview of life-cycle stages for all family members and their consumer behavior is presented in Table 10-2.

FAMILY PURCHASING DECISIONS

This section probes more deeply into the nature of the decision-making process within the family and its implications for consumer behavior and marketing. Family purchasing decisions will be examined from four perspectives: (1) role structure, (2) power structure, (3) stage in the decision-making process, and (4) family-specific characteristics. It is very important that the marketer understand who influences whom and how in the family buying process so that the proper marketing strategy may be developed.

Role Structure

In our earlier discussion of the concept of roles, we described how society is structured of roles that are occupied (or played) by its members. So, too, does the family have its own structure, with each member playing his or her role.[7] Although several theories have been used to describe the structure of marital roles in decision making, from the standpoint of those interested in consumer behavior, the following role categorizations appear to be perhaps the most helpful.

Instrumental and Expressive Roles Generally, in traditional families among societies throughout the world the husband is more likely to provide material support and primary leadership authority within the family, and the wife is more likely to provide affection and moral support. This distinction relates to what are known as instrumental and expressive needs of all small groups (including the family); that is, the need for leadership and fulfillment of the task on the one hand, and the need for morale and cohesion on the other.[8]

This differentiation of roles is known to result from small group interaction. Leaders are produced who specialize in either *instrumental* functions (known as functional or task leaders) or *expressive* functions (social leaders). The former concern themselves with the basic purpose or goal of the group, while the latter attempt to reduce tension and give emotional support to members in order to maintain intragroup cohesion.[9] Within the family, the instrumental role has typically been played by the father and the expressive role by the mother. That is, men tend to be task-oriented leaders, while women lead in social-emotional behavior. The result of this is that in purchasing decisions husbands tend to concern themselves with functional product attributes and to exert more influence in deciding whether to buy and in closing the sale. The wife concerns herself more with aesthetic product attributes and with suggesting the purchase.[10]

Although the general role pattern cited above has been historically true, these roles are undergoing some degree of change today, particularly as more women enter the labor force. Much more will be said on changing roles in a later section of this chapter. For now it should merely be noted that wives may be just as likely to perform certain instrumental roles as their husbands.[11]

Internal and External Roles Another differentiation of roles occurs in the family with regard to the husband's primary concern with matters *external* to the family and the wife's concern largely with *internal* matters.

TABLE 10-2
CONSUMER ELEMENTS BY CONSUMER LIFE-CYCLE STAGE

Consumer Element	Childhood	Adolescence	Early Singlehood	Mature Single	Newly Married Couples (Young, No Children)
Consumer characteristics	All needs provided by parents Little or no understanding of marketplace Marketplace limited to that of parents Limited cognitive ability Limited and unorganized product knowledge	Basic needs provided by parents Luxuries increasingly provided through part-time work Tastes and preferences evolving Susceptible to peer pressure to conform Limited product knowledge Limited understanding of marketplace Marketplace not solely limited to that of parents	Values and priorities unclear.'. experimentation in life style and associated consumption Highly mobile Few financial burdens Few assets Recreation oriented Fashion opinion leaders Marketplace not limited by parents or legal restrictions due to age Wide product knowledge but little depth	Expectations of financial support by near relatives possible Discretionary income typically high Full marketplace accessible Wide product knowledge in depth likely Independent decision making	Resolution of lifestyle and values concerning consumption Lack of financial planning Financial condition better now than for near future High purchase of durables Wide product knowledge
Typical products and services	Toys Clothes Sweet treats Games Comic books	Records Bicycles Some personal care products Toys Clothes Sporting goods	First car Basic home furnishings Home electronic equipment Vacations Sport equipment Education Personal care products First use of credit Groceries	Tasteful home furnishings Appliances Travel Hobby related purchases Better restaurants Savings for retirement House/ condominium	Home equipment Durable furniture Cars Vacations Insurance
Marketplace concepts and knowledge	Money Store Needs; wants Decision Private property Price Ownership Purchase transaction Products Advertising Consumer Salesman or clerk	Money management Consumer information Price/quality relationship Economic competition Rationality Saving Earning Product assortment Comparison shopping Brands Labels Store types Impulse buying Consumer rights	Sales tax Income tax Budget Inflation Costs of business operation Deceptive practices Credit Interest on savings Contract terminology Owning vs. renting Marginal utility Consumer protection laws Unit pricing; open dating Universal product code	Financial planning Impact of inflation on budget and savings Tax shelters Investments Warranties Opportunity costs Electronic funds transfer	Warranties Opportunity costs Insurance as risk sharing Saving as delayed consumption Net worth Insurance terms Child rearing costs

	Full Nest				Empty Nest			
I	II	III	IV	I	II			
Youngest Child Under Six	Youngest Child Six or Older	Older Married Couples with Dependent Children	Single Parenthood	Older Married Couples; No Children at Home Head in Labor Force	Older Married Couples; No Children at Home Head Retired	Older Solitary Survivor, in Labor Force	Solitary Survivor, Retired
Home purchase of primary concern Low liquid assets Conversion to one income likely Most susceptible to advertising and new products Dissatisfied with financial condition Change in lifestyle due to children Expansion of family influences on purchasing	Change in family risk patterns and concern for security Needs still expanding faster than income Consumption time scheduling difficult Some wives working Less susceptible to advertising Larger unit purchases	Aging parents Recycling of products to younger siblings while protecting individual needs Heavy replacement of durables More wives working Hard to influence with advertising Wide product knowledge in depth likely Some children get jobs	Administration of consumption difficult Product knowledge of spouse lost Dissatisfaction with dual parental role	Pre-retirement planning Home ownership at peak Typically in best financial position Not interested in new products Financial assistance to children	Drastic drop in income Want to keep home Product knowledge becoming obsolete	Income still good but likely to sell home Independent decisions now required due to absence of spouse	Drastic drop in income Independent decisions now required due to absence of spouse
First house Day care Community services more important— schools, hospitals Baby food Toys Fast food Energy use high Bikes Baby furniture	Assortment increases due to expressed preferences Rapid usage of clothing Larger house or remodeling Larger size packages Music lessons and instruments Fast food	Food expense at peak Dental services New furniture Coats Magazines Non-necessary appliances Boats Recreational vehicles College expenses	Home security devices Buyable recreation for children Housekeeping services Day care Education for reentry to job market	Travel Recreation Contributions Self education Vacations Home improvements Savings for retirement Home security devices Hobby related purchases	Medical care and products which aid sleep, health, digestion Leisure time equipment not formerly owned due to time constraints Household services for aging Vacation home Restaurants	Household services Restaurants Similar to mature singlehood except for gifts to grown children Hobby related purchases	Mass transportation Same product needs as other retired
Regularized sales Estate planning same as mature singlehood Economic impact of children Wills Real estate taxes	Combination of previous cells	Funeral costs (for parents) Tax shelters Combination of previous cells Updating of product knowledge to keep up with teenager wants	Community services Combination of previous cells Must acquire complementary market knowledge of spouse	Updating of product knowledge usually necessary	Community resources Medicare Medicaid Social security	Community resources Must acquire complementary knowledge of spouse	Community resources Medicare Medicaid Social security Nursing homes

TABLE 10-2
(*Continued*)

Consumer Element	Childhood	Adolescence	Early Singlehood	Mature Single	Newly Married Couples (Young, No Children)
Marketplace skills	Choosing from many alternatives Transactional sequence Ordering of wants	Simple consumer information gathering Simple price/quality analysis Simple comparison shopping Currency system mastered Simple decision making process Weights and measures conversion Safe usage of products	Simple problem solving Priority setting Using consumer reference material Simple complaint resolution Dealing with discrimination Complex consumer information gathering Dealing with sales people Complex comparison shopping Tax schedule completion Simple budgeting Credit management Computational skills Balancing a checkbook	Complex problem solving Complex price/quality analysis Complex complaint resolution Complex decision making Complex budgeting for life goals Investing Energy audit of home	Choosing health care professionals Record keeping Saving Tax forms Complex decision making-joint Complex budgeting-joint Price negotiation Do-it-yourself skills
Typical marketplace problems	Underdeveloped cognitive defenses to commercials Wanting everything Inability to articulate questions or get usable explanations from parents or teachers	Identifying significant product differences Weak understanding of value of money Weak understanding of own tastes and preferences Shoplifting temptations Illicit markets (drugs, etc.)	Mail order frauds Determining most economical place to shop Tenant/landlord disputes Lack of experience in dealing with sellers Choosing first apartment Simple bargaining (cars, etc.) High mobility results in unfamiliarity with local marketplace Lack of credit rating-insurance terminology	Renting or buying shelter Complex bargaining Gifting as a regular activity Support in times of illness	Lack of savings habits Impulse buying Mail order fraud Mobility Insurance planning Bait and switch seller tactics Assembly and operation of products
Level of resources (time, income human energy)	Money limited by parents Consumption time unlimited Shopping energy limited by attention span only	Some product experience Some discretionary income (allowance, gifts, part time jobs) Consumption time nearly unlimited Shopping energy at high level	Income rising Consumption time plentiful Shopping energy high	High disposable income likely Time for administration of consumption limited since single person has dual role Shopping energy decreasing	Time beginning to emerge as constraint Income good due to dual contribution Shopping energy high

Source: Ronald W. Stampfl, "The Consumer Life Cycle," *Journal of Consumer Affairs*, **12:**214–215, Winter 1978.

		Full Nest		Empty Nest			
I Youngest Child Under Six	II Youngest Child Six or Older	III Older Married Couples with Dependent Children	IV Single Parenthood	I Older Married Couples; No Children at Home Head in Labor Force	II Older Married Couples; No Children at Home Head Retired	Older Solitary Survivor, in Labor Force	Solitary Survivor, Retired
Consumer education of children, i.e., teaching skills Investing Choosing for others Complex budgeting for life goals Complex decision making Complex problem solving Complex complaint resolution Complex price/quality analysis Home buying	Nutritional efficiency in food buying Tax law usage Complex decision making Energy audit of home	Planning for children moving out Probate Executor of will Tax planning Home redecoration Aiding children in college choice	Must acquire complementary skills of spouse	Disposal of excess possessions Consolidation of assets	Management of paperwork in transfer payments and insurance Interaction with social security system	Must acquire complementary skills of spouse	Managing food preparation and diet Must acquire complementary skills of spouse Interaction with social security system
Choosing first house Overcommitted on credit Mobility still a problem Lack of understanding financial implications of having children Finding repair services Computer billing errors	Choosing "mature" house Unexpected expenses make budgeting difficult Purchase quantity and sizes hard to predict Home maintenance	Financing college for children Clothing costs Automotive insurance for teenage dependents Transportation for all family members	Support in times of illness Legal aid in cases of divorce, financial settlement Change in credit rating possible	Home too large Rescaling of all purchases Gifting as a regular activity	Obsolescence of marketplace skills and knowledge Home improvement schemes Lack of willingness to accept publicly provided goods and services if needed	Obtaining household services Support in times of illness Reading labels may be difficult	Exploitation of loneliness by in-house sellers Indecisiveness Support in time of illness Self-medication Quasi-professional products such as hearing aids Lack of mobility
Time constraint evident Income rising for household head but family income may decrease if spouse not employed Shopping often considered "a hassle" and energy low	Time constraint evident Income likely to be stable unless wife returns to work Shopping energy stabilized	Time needed for administration of consumption at maximum Leisure time limited Income stable Shopping routine and energy low	Substantial drop in income possible Time most constrained Shopping energy devoted to necessities	Discretionary income higher due to children's departure Leisure time suddenly high Shopping energy may increase	Leisure time excessive Income often limited Shopping energy low	Similar to mature singlehood except that income level of widow long absent from labor force is typically much lower than for widower	Leisure time excessive Income often limited Shopping energy low

The interaction of the two basic types of roles discussed above is presented in Figure 10-2. This matrix indicates that when expressive-external and instrumental-internal roles are involved in a purchase decision, both husband and wife will be involved; that is, joint decision making will be the case. For product decisions involving expressive-internal and instrumental-external roles, wives and husbands, respectively, will be more heavily involved. We shall elaborate on the nature of each spouse's decision-making input to purchasing processes for various products in a later section of this chapter.

Purchase Process Roles There are several ways of viewing family member roles as they relate to the purchase decision and consumption process. In this context, there are six roles that may be performed by various family members.

First, one or another family member may be the *initiator* (i.e., the individual who recognizes the problem or need for the item). In this role, the suggestion may be made by the wife, for example, that the household needs a food processor in order to more easily prepare meals. A second role is that of *influencer,* which is the person who informs or persuades others in a purchase situation. He may also be thought of as an *opinion leader* in that he exerts personal influence on other family members with regard to a particular purchase situation.

A third and related role is that of *information gatherer* in which one or more individuals will secure information related to the possible purchase. This information may pertain to products or places of shopping. Often, the individual most knowledgeable in the product category will gather information. For example, a husband may well gather information about a possible lawn tractor purchase while the wife may gather information about new financial services offered by a local bank.

The role of *decision maker* involves having authority to make the buying decision. The individual who makes this decision might be the same as the influencer or information gatherer, although not necessarily so. For instance, the wife may make the decision to purchase a microwave oven as well as the decision on which brand to buy, after having gathered information about various models available. Often the decision is a joint or shared one in which more than one family member participates.

The *purchaser* role involves the act of purchase by one of the family members. In other words, the individual who buys the item in the store or, perhaps, places a telephone order for merchandise is acting in the role of purchasing agent for the family. The decider and purchaser need not necessarily be the same individual. For example, a teenage son or daughter may merely execute his or her

FIGURE 10-2

Role interaction. (*Source:* Adapted from James H. Myers and William H. Reynolds, *Consumer Behavior and Marketing Management,* Houghton Mifflin Co., Boston, 1967, p. 245.)

	External	Internal
Expressive	Both	Wife
Instrumental	Husband	Both

parents' supermarket shopping list. In this situation (in which brands, sizes, etc. are specified), the youth is only a purchaser, not a decision maker. At other times, however, the purchaser may occupy a very strategic role in the brand decision. One study, for instance, found that nearly one-third of beer drinkers delegated the brand decision to the purchaser (usually the wife) and that the purchaser was aware of the consumer's preferences nine out of ten times.[12]

Sometimes, the purchaser may be referred to as the *gatekeeper,* that is, a family member who is able to control the flow of products into the family. In other words, the purchase may be consummated or blocked by this individual. The role of gatekeeper is well-illustrated in a study of children's purchase influence on parents. In this research, children were found to suggest which cereal brands their mothers should purchase when shopping. The mothers, however, were in the gatekeeper position, frequently disagreeing with their children as to what cereal should be purchased, and hence controlling the flow of this product into the family.[13]

Users are those who consume the product or service. A user may be the same person who performs each of the other roles, or it may be another person. The latter situation is often possible, for instance, in the case of a child for whom products such as clothing, toys, and so forth, are purchased.

For the marketer, it is important to distinguish each family member's role in order to develop an optimum marketing strategy. Assumptions made about such roles should be checked through consumer research so that the marketer is certain that the correct mix is aimed at the right individual. Knowledge of who generally performs which purchase and consumption process role within the family unit will aid in product planning and development, providing promotion messages, determining distribution decisions, and so forth. More will be said about this topic in the following section.

Power Structure

This factor has to do with which family member is dominant or considered to be the family's head. A family may be *patriarchal,* in which case the father is considered to be the dominant member. In a *matriarchal* family, the woman plays the dominant role and makes most of the decisions, while in the *equalitarian* family, the husband and wife share in decision making somewhat equally. Although the American family is still generally patriarchal and our society is male-dominated, egalitarianism is a continuously emerging pattern.

The United States is also moving increasingly toward a child-centered family in which children have a strong influence on their parents' consumption decisions. For example, parents often yield to their children's television-viewing preferences (such as watching "Sesame Street" rather than an afternoon movie), recreation or entertainment requests (a vacation to Disney World rather than Europe), and product choices (Frosted Flakes rather than Special K).

Purchase Influence Pattern   Research on power relationships in the family has taken several directions. One approach to understanding the marital power structure in consumer decision making categorizes the possibilities for dominance in the following way: (1) *autonomic,* in which an equal number of decisions is made by each spouse, (2) *husband dominant,* (3) *wife dominant,* and (4) *syncratic,* in which most decisions are made by both husband and wife.[14]

A study using this concept measured the relative influence of Belgian husbands and wives in purchase decisions for twenty-five representative products.[15] Figure 10-3 positions these decisions according to the four marital decision-making categories of autonomic, husband dominant, wife dominant, and syncratic. Each decision is positioned in this figure according to two axes. The vertical axis is a scale of the relative influence between husband and wife. Decisions can range along a continuum from 1 (if respondents report husband specialization) to 3 (if respondents report wife specialization). The horizontal axis is a scale of the extent of role specialization as measured by the percentage of families reporting that a decision is made jointly. Syncratic decisions, therefore, are those in which more

FIGURE 10-3

Marital roles in twenty-five decisions. (*Source:* Harry L. Davis and Benny P. Rigaux, "Perception of Marital Roles in Decision Processes," *Journal of Consumer Research,* **1**:54, June 1974.)

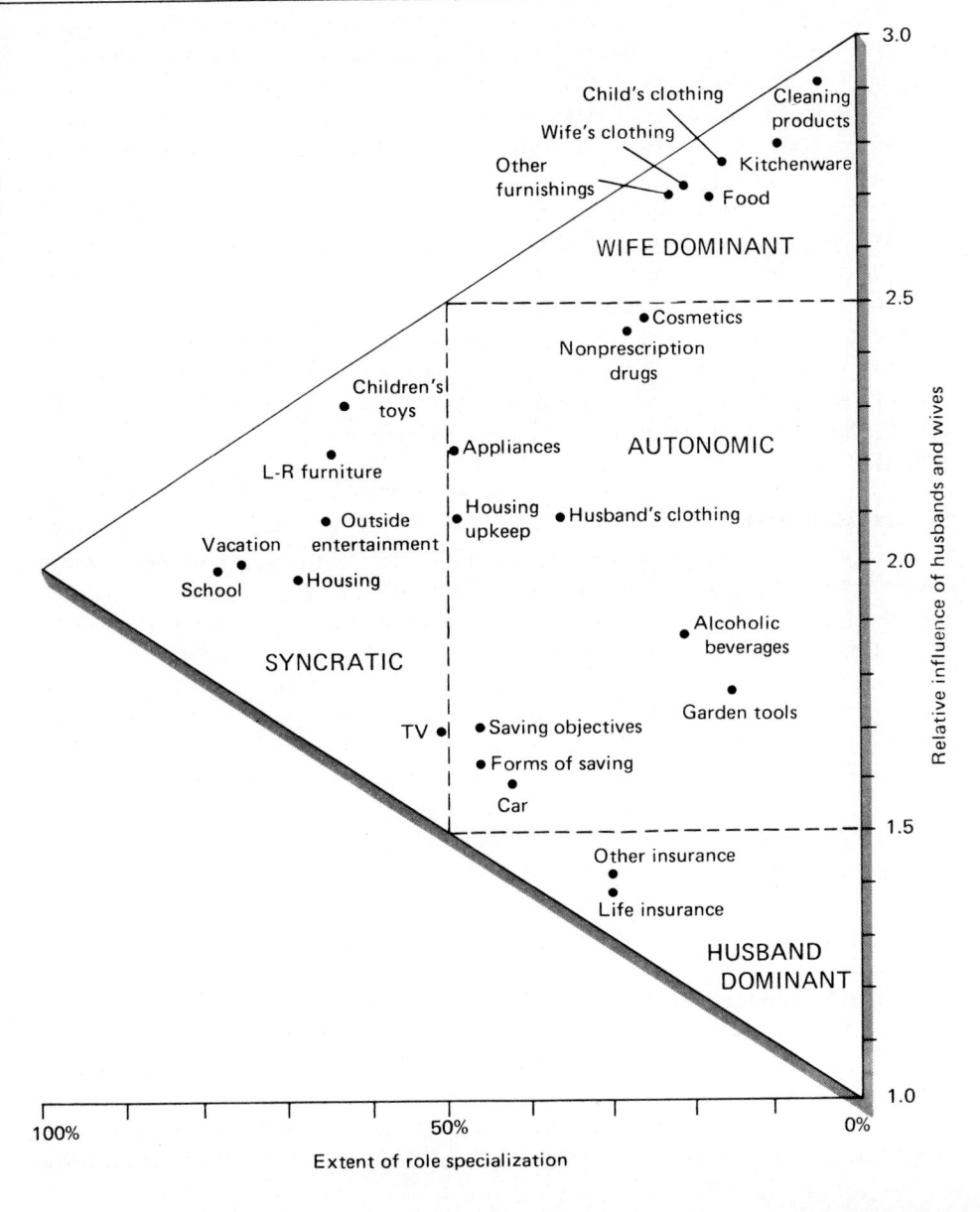

than half the respondents reported that the decision was joint, while in the autonomic case, less than half the respondents indicated the decision was joint, but there was no consensus among respondents as to whether the decision was dominated by husband or wife. Thus, autonomic decisions, as well as husband and wife dominant decisions, represent role specialization. In reading the figure, it may be seen that the relative influence score for household cleaning products is approximately 2.9, with only 6 percent of the families deciding jointly on this item's purchase. Thus, the wife dominates this purchase decision. Similarly, the relative influence score for vacations is approximately 2.0, with 78 percent of families deciding jointly (a syncratic role structure).

A similar study of U.S. couples' perceptions of marital roles in consumer decision processes found that the Belgian results were generally supported.[16]

These and other studies have found that marital role specialization in the consumer decision-making process varies significantly across product categories.[17] Results of these studies lead to the conclusion that joint decision making is most likely to occur for purchases that represent significant economic outlays; whereas routine expenditures for items viewed as necessities will probably be delegated to one of the spouses.

Table 10-3 presents selected data from a thorough analysis of husband-wife relative purchase influence covering 108 different products and services ranging from packaged products to durable goods and services.[18] The study was conducted among both husbands and wives and measured purchase patterns and direct and indirect influences. For all products, measures were made of influence on both the decision to buy the product, and on the decision to select the particular brand purchased. Spousal influence was defined as "a state of mind recalled by the purchaser which affected a specific recent purchase," and was categorized for packaged products as direct (that is, consciously recalled) and indirect (that is, consideration given to satisfaction of the wants and preferences of each spouse by the purchaser). For durables, however, no important distinction was made between direct and indirect influence, since the purchase is discussed and deliberately decided on, thus satisfying both spouses' wants and preferences. Information was also gathered on relative influence on two aspects of prepurchase activity: initiation of the purchase and information gathering prior to the purchase decision.

Family Decision-Making Strategies to Resolve Conflict[19]   Family purchase decisions are often characterized by conflict over differences between the parties on several factors concerning the decision. For example, family members often have different views of who should make the purchase decision; how that decision should be made (e.g., how much information should be gathered); and who should implement the decision. Thus, the family purchasing decision process is not always characterized by stability and easy agreement. Instead, conflict is quite likely, with families engaging in bargaining, compromising, and coercing in order to arrive at a joint decision.

Several strategies for resolving such conflicts may be adopted. These are illustrated in Table 10-4. In this view of family decision-making patterns, members may either agree or disagree about the goals or desired outcomes of a decision. If agreement on such matters exists, *consensus* is said to occur. For example, family members may agree that a winter vacation to Disney World should be taken. On the other hand, *accommodation* may be necessary because of disagreement over goals and outcomes. Thus, such a conflict situation will require accommodation or compromises by one or more family members. It should be recognized that family buying decisions are not totally consensual or accommodating. Yet, we will simplify it to this level in order to describe the various options.

In the *role structure strategy,* the need for family discussion may be reduced or eliminated by having one or perhaps two people responsible for the decision. Frequently, a *specialist* develops who assumes or is delegated the primary responsibility for decision making in a particular product or service decision area. This expertise comes to be accepted by other family members.

In the *budget strategy,* the decision responsibility is controlled by a set of rules that have been decided upon and established by the family. Thus, the *controller* in the family becomes an impersonal budget determined by family members. Once the size and allocation of the budget is set, say, for a new car, decisions are then made only on the basis of the various models available for that price.

TABLE 10-3

WHO MAKES THE BUYING DECISIONS?

Relative Purchase Influence: Husbands and Wives

Percentage of Influence

| | Purchased by | | Direct Influence | | | | Indirect Influence | | | |
| | | | Product | | Brand | | Product | | Brand | |
	W	H	W	H	W	H	W	H	W	H
Cereals:										
Cold (unsweetened)	84	16	74	26	71	29	65	35	67	33
Hot	84	16	67	33	67	33	63	37	59	41
Packaged lunch meat	73	27	60	40	64	36	65	35	68	32
Peanut butter	81	19	70	30	74	26	65	35	68	32
Scotch whiskey	35	65	18	82	18	82	22	78	23	77
Bar soap	85	15	65	35	64	36	60	40	61	39
Headache remedies	67	33	67	33	67	33	64	36	65	35
Cat food (dry)	66	34	75	25	81	19	80	20	80	20
Dog food (dry)	76	24	60	40	59	41	60	40	61	39
Fast-food chain hamburgers	68	32	55	45	55	45	53	47	52	48
Catsup	75	25	68	32	68	32	60	40	62	38
Coffee:										
Freeze-dried	68	32	57	43	62	38	56	44	59	41
Regular ground	74	26	65	35	65	35	58	42	60	40
Mouthwash	72	28	56	44	56	44	52	48	53	47

Share of Influence

| | Purchase Decision Influence | | | | Initiation | | | | Information Gathering | | | |
| | Product | | Brand | | Product | | Brand | | Product | | Brand | |
	W	H	W	H	W	H	W	H	W	H	W	H
Vacuum cleaner	60	40	60	40	80	20	69	31	66	34	65	35
Electric blender	59	41	53	47	67	33	50	50	53	47	52	48
Broadloom carpet	60	40	59	41	82	18	74	26	72	28	69	31
Automobiles	38	62	33	67	22	78	21	79	18	82	18	82

Source: "Purchase Influence Measures of Husband/Wife Influence on Buying Decisions," Haley, Overholser & Associates, Inc., New Canaan, Conn., January 1975 "Buying Study Called Good Support Data," *Advertising Age,* March 17, 1975, p. 52. Percentages reflect relative purchase activity, direct and indirect influence of husbands and wives in the sample. For durables and services, percentages reflect relative activity in purchase decision, initiation of idea to purchase and the gathering of information.

A *problem-solving strategy* is likely when agreement exists about which goals are desirable. Various modes of decision making are possible in this situation. First, an *expert* from within or outside the family may be relied on to help determine the best alternative. Second, family discussion may evoke a *better solution* than that originally suggested by any one family member. Third, a *multiple purchase* may be decided upon that resolves or avoids conflict. For example, a husband and wife may decide to purchase two $6500 subcompact cars instead of one $13,000 family sedan as a way of minimizing conflict over use of a single car.

Persuasion strategies involve attempts to force someone to make a decision that she or he would not otherwise make. For example, generally the spouse who has authority for a decision gets the credit or blame for that decision's outcome. The other spouse, freed from this responsibility, may try to dominate by becoming an *irresponsible critic* who freely criticizes and offers ideas without having to worry about how realistic they are. If the other spouse's decision was right, the critic has lost nothing; if it was wrong, the critic can say "I told you so." The other spouse may increasingly concede decision areas to the critic to avoid this situation.

Intuition is a second strategy in which one spouse learns to identify the moods in which the other spouse is most susceptible to new ideas or persuasion, as well as types of appeals that are most effective with that spouse. A third persuasive strategy is to take another family member along when shopping for a product. *Shopping together,* therefore, can secure a decision commitment that may be difficult to reverse later. Fourth, *coercion* is an extreme form of persuasion which secures unwilling agreement through threats. Finally, *coalitions* may be formed within the family in order to force other members to go along. These latter two persuasive approaches—coercion and coalitions—have been described as the least desirable forms of conflict resolution, because they imply not only disagreement between family members over buying goals, but also over fundamental attitudes and lifestyles. Such fundamental conflicts are more difficult to resolve.[20]

Bargaining represents an alternative approach to resolving disagreements about family goals in purchasing situations. In contrast to persuasion, which rep-

TABLE 10-4 ALTERNATIVE DECISION-MAKING STRATEGIES

Goals	Strategy	Ways of Implementing
"Consensus" (Family members agree about goals)	Role structure	"The Specialist"
	Budgets	"The Controller"
	Problem solving	"The Expert" "The Better Solution" "The Multiple Purchase"
"Accommodation" (Family members disagree about goals)	Persuasion	"The Irresponsible Critic" "Feminine Intuition" "Shopping Together" "Coercion" "Coalitions"
	Bargaining	"The Next Purchase" "The Impulse Purchase" "The Procrastinator"

Source: Harry L. Davis, "Decision Making Within the Household," *Journal of Consumer Research,* **2:**255, March 1976. Reprinted with permission from the *Journal of Consumer Research.*

resents more short-run efforts to win a specific decision, bargaining leads to willing agreement and involves longer-term considerations. Family members must engage in mutual give and take. This approach can occur in several ways. First, certain family members may have their way in a current purchase as long as others get their choice in the *next purchase*. For instance, the wife may buy new clothes now, if the husband will later be able to purchase a new boat. In a second approach, a family member may make an *impulse purchase* and then bargain. For example, the husband may bring a newly purchased boat home and then try to convince his wife that she will love it. Finally, *procrastinating* can continue the bargaining process after a selection has been made. By delaying the purchase, new information may develop or the situation may be changed so that a new choice is made.

Different decision-making strategies are likely for different situations. That is, depending on the family members, the product, the stage in the decision process, and so forth, the strategies selected will vary.

Changing Roles and Family Purchase Decisions Changing role patterns of husbands and wives are having numerous effects.[21] Previous marriage patterns meant that there were generally no decisions to be made regarding the wife's chief life interest and sphere, nor the husband's. She concentrated on domestic activities, and he concentrated on occupational efforts. Today, however, sex-role shifts toward egalitarianism mean that there is less inevitability of such a pattern, and many new and critical decisions must be made. Increasing numbers of younger and better-educated men and women are bargaining with each other about their chief life interests. And this is occurring not only among those soon-to-be or newly married, but also among couples married for some time. There are virtually no nonnegotiable issues among such modern marriages. For example, where to live (near his work or hers), how many children to have and when, who will perform child care and domestic chores, how to spend *their* incomes, and so forth.

In addition to the number of issues to be decided, there is also the matter of how this is negotiated. Women who have more traditional roles in marriage tend to negotiate with their husbands and try to persuade them to compromise on the basis of *collective* interest—what is best for the family group, for their marital relationship, for the children. A woman who has adopted modern roles tends to negotiate more in terms of her own *individualistic* interests—what is best for her. Such a strategy seems to result in achieving more equitable compromises in terms of reaching her goals.

Although purchase influence may change over a period of time as the American family structure adapts, it is difficult to judge whether, and if so, how far purchase-influence roles have shifted.[22]

Stage in the Family Purchase-Decision Process

The marketer is interested not only in the physical act of purchasing a product or brand, but also in the stages leading up to that decision. The research study on family participation and influence in purchasing behavior described above and presented in Table 10-3 also found that roles and influence vary throughout the buyer decision-making process. Such knowledge can be of great help in formulating product, promotion, channel, and pricing strategies. As shown in Table 10-3, for most of the products wives are involved more heavily in the initiation, information seeking, and purchasing stages than are husbands. At all stages, however, there is a greater tendency for husbands to participate in the decision process when the product is high-priced and technically or mechanically complex.

Other studies have examined products not included in the study cited above, with similar findings. Their data support the contention that the extent of husband-wife involvement varies considerably from product to product throughout the decision-making process.[23]

Figure 10-4A and 10-4B graphically illustrate the changes in marital roles occuring among a sample of U.S. husbands and wives as decision making proceeds from phase 1 (problem recognition) to phase 2 (search for information), and from phase 2 to phase 3 (final decision).

Family-Specific Characteristics

There are a number of additional variables that have been found to influence the nature of purchasing decisions made within the family. The influencing factors to be discussed below include culture, subculture, social class, reference groups and social interaction, stage in life cycle, mobility, geographical location, and children.

Culture The roles of husbands and wives may differ dramatically from culture to culture, which may result in numerous differences in consumer decision making. The basic family systems encountered by the marketer around the world fall into three general patterns illustrated as follows: (1) in Moslem cultures, the wife is generally in a subordinate and secluded role, with few rights and little control over the affairs of the family; (2) in the Latin American culture, the wife is freer but is still definitely a junior member of the partnership, with the husband having the final authority in all but minor matters; and (3) in European and North-American cultures the basic patern is equality.[24] This latter region, for instance, evidences substantial similarity with regard to husband-wife involvement for a number of household activities.[25]

Subculture In addition to cultural variations from one country to another, there are also subcultural or ethnic variations in consumer behavior within a country's heterogeneous population. For example, in the United States joint decision making is most pronounced among white families, with husband dominance strongest among Japanese-Americans, and wife dominance strongest among black families.[26]

Social Class Several studies on the relationship of socioeconomic class and joint participation in purchase decision making have indicated that a curvilinear relationship exists. That is, autonomy in decision making is most likely at upper and lower social classes, while joint decision making is most common among the middle class.

Reference Groups and Social Interaction Although no research has been conducted on the role of reference groups in family purchase decisions, it is thought that such relationships are influential. Some authors indicate that the greater the extent to which spouses have social ties or connections with relatives or friends, the less the amount of joint or shared decisions. This is because some decisions may be made in consultation with friends or relatives rather than only with one's spouse.[27]

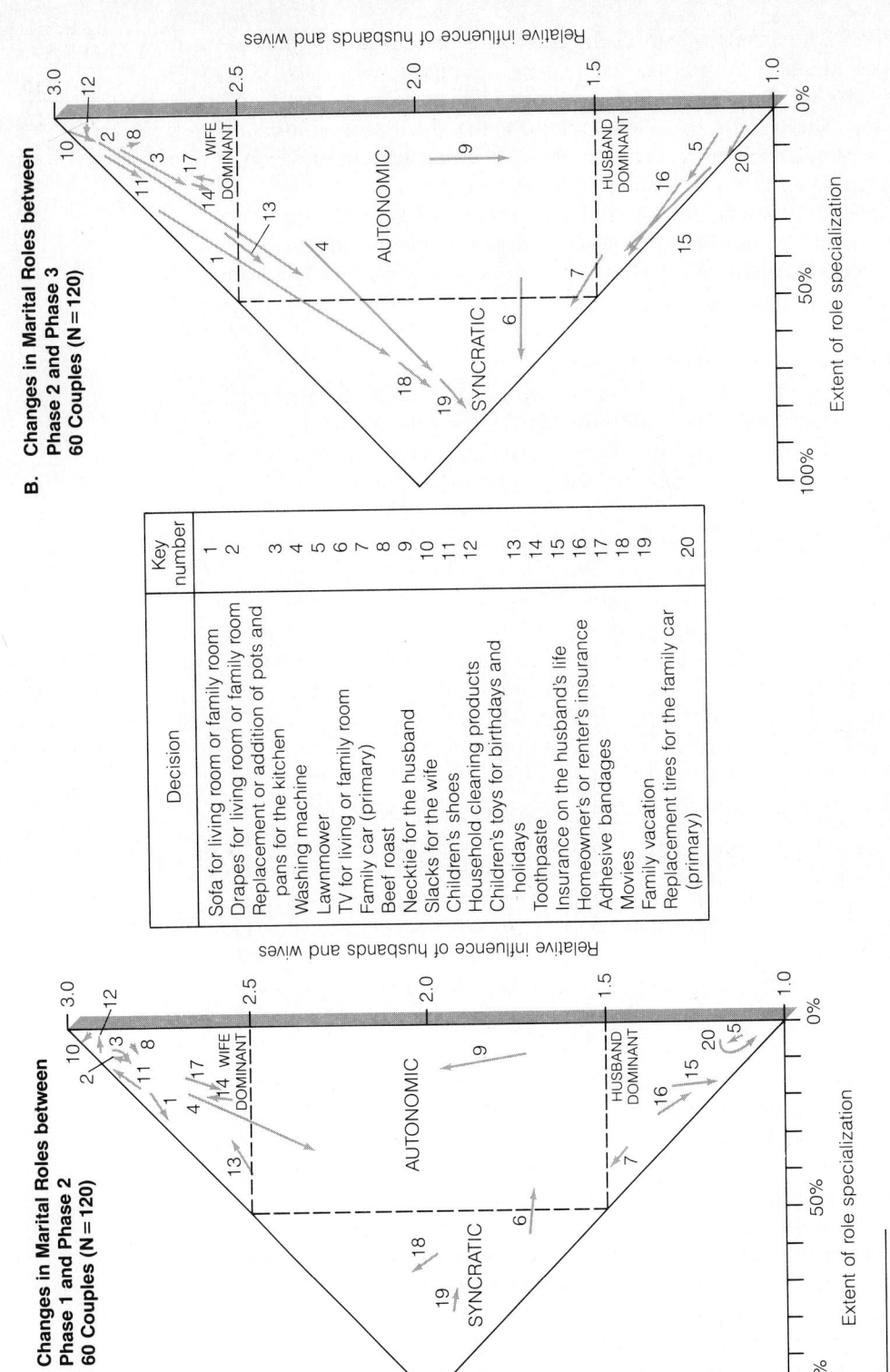

A. Changes in Marital Roles between Phase 1 and Phase 2
60 Couples (N = 120)

B. Changes in Marital Roles between Phase 2 and Phase 3
60 Couples (N = 120)

Decision	Key number
Sofa for living room or family room	1
Drapes for living room or family room	2
Replacement or addition of pots and pans for the kitchen	3
Washing machine	4
Lawnmower	5
TV for living or family room	6
Family car (primary)	7
Beef roast	8
Necktie for the husband	9
Slacks for the wife	10
Children's shoes	11
Household cleaning products	12
Children's toys for birthdays and holidays	13
Toothpaste	14
Insurance on the husband's life	15
Homeowner's or renter's insurance	16
Adhesive bandages	17
Movies	18
Family vacation	19
Replacement tires for the family car (primary)	20

FIGURE 10-4

Marital role changes in the decision process for twenty products. (*Source:* E. H. Bonfield, "Perception of Marital Roles in Decision Processes: Replication and Extension" in H. Keith Hunt (ed.), *Advances in Consumer Research: Volume 5*, Association for Consumer Research, Ann Arbor, MI, 1978, pp. 302, 303, 305.

Stage in Life Cycle   The nature of family decision making changes over the life cycle. For example, wives with pre-school-age children have considerably less independent responsibility for economic decisions than other wives. In addition, families in early stages of the life cycle show a very high frequency of joint decisions.[28] However, evidence indicates that joint decision making declines over the life cycle. This tendency has been explained in terms of an increased efficiency or competence that people develop over a period of time in making purchasing decisions that are acceptable to their spouses. Such competence eliminates the need for extensive interaction.[29]

Mobility   Mobility, both social as well as geographic, tends to increase the extent of intrafamily communication and the degree of joint decision making. One researcher attributes this to the fact that movement away from stable primary groups such as family and close friends "throws spouses upon each other."[30]

Geographical Location   Limited research on the influence of place of residence on family decision making indicates that rural families have a higher frequency of joint decisions than urban families. Also, the wife occupies a less influential role in rural families.[31]

Children   Based on a study of purchase decision processes by families as opposed to couples without children, husbands tended to dominate decision making more in families, while joint decision making was more prevalent among couples. Also, greater variability in the relative influence of husbands and wives across different elements of the decision process was found in family decision-making units.[32]

Marketing Implications of Family Purchasing Decisions

It should be clear by now that the marketer's strategy is influenced at almost every turn by the nature of family role and decision-making patterns. Whether the marketer is concerned with product, promotion, channel, or pricing decisions, family household purchase patterns must be well understood. Consider the following implications for promotion strategy.

The development of advertising and personal selling messages is strongly impacted by family roles and decision-making patterns. For instance, the evaluative criteria by which a family will decide which brand of major appliance to purchase must be understood in developing the sales message. However, these criteria may vary among husbands and wives. For those decisions in which one spouse (e.g., the wife) dominates, then messages may be developed with that segment in mind. However, where joint decision making prevails, the marketer may need to develop separate messages attuned to each party's buying criteria.

Similarly, differences in use of media among family members may necessitate using various message channels in order to reach influential or dominant family members. Reaching the purchaser may require one communication medium, while reaching the user may require another. For example, wives often are the purchasers of their husband's clothing. Consequently, a men's clothing manufacturer may use one campaign to reach men through male-dominated media and another campaign to reach women through female-oriented media to encourage their purchase of the brand. Appealing to both segments with specific media and appeals that are appropriate for each would be ideal, but this assumes a rather large budget.

A similar strategy is often called for when advertising products for which children are significantly involved in the purchase decision. For example, because children directly influence the choice of which fast-food establishment to patronize, Burger King, McDonald's, and other chains find it necessary to appeal to children as well as to their parents. As a result, ads often feature people of all ages, with particular emphasis on families. Toy companies, likewise, often aim their ads at children as well as at parents.

The next section will examine ways in which changes are occurring among families in our culture, and how these changes may be expected to affect the marketer.

THE CHANGING AMERICAN FAMILY

It should come as no surprise to the reader that families in America and other parts of the world are changing. It is important to understand what the major changes are and what these shifting patterns mean for marketers in the 1980s. This section provides some insight into these issues.

Perhaps the most important change occurring today is the shifting view of the roles of marriage partners. Over the last several years, the number favoring shared roles in marriage (in which both work, share homemaking, and child raising) has surpassed those favoring a traditional marriage (in which the husband is the breadwinner and the wife is homemaker) by a ratio of 48 percent to 43 percent. However, the small remaining number favoring alternative living arrangements (such as unmarried couples) reinforces the basic and continuing strength of Americans' belief in the nuclear family system.[33] In addition, it should also be noted that the American norm is still a family including children. More than 94 percent of women are in favor of having at least one child. The real shift has come, however, in attitudes toward the ideal number of children to have, which has decreased over the past 20 years.[34]

Let us examine more closely changing female and male roles, particularly as they exist within the family structure today. In addition, we will discuss some marketing implications of these changes.

Changing Female Roles

One of the most significant areas of change to occur in the American family concerns the role of the wife. More than either the husband or children, the role of the wife has undergone the greatest transformation in the past few decades. More and more women are opting for a shared role situation rather than the traditional approach in marriage. To a large extent, what this means is that the wife has accepted a job outside the home in addition to her job within the home. But fewer than one-third of the men surveyed in a national study approve of the changes in the role of women in American society.[35] Married men were concerned about how these changes may affect their personal comfort and well-being. The biggest drawback to these men is that they have to spend more time on household chores they don't like.

These changing female role patterns will be examined in this section in terms of two dimensions, both of which may be fruitful from a segmentation standpoint. First, it is useful to view women in terms of their traditionalist/feminist orientation. Second, wives may also be categorized along a working dimension which may be partially reflective of their traditional/feminist orientation. Each of these concepts may be helpful in achieving a better understanding of how family patterns are changing today. First, let us look at the traditionalist/feminist lifestyle orientation.

Traditionalists and Feminists   There are significant variations today between women on their lifestyle and demographic characteristics.[36] One study evaluated the attributes of women who were characterized as having either a traditional or a modern feminine lifestyle. Some significant differences between the segments appeared as shown in Table 10-5. From this and other research, it appears that, compared to other groups, feminists tend to be younger and better-educated with a greater sense of independence in terms of how they perceive themselves within the household. They are more liberal in their attitudes toward life, events, and business; have more cosmopolitan interests; are financially optimistic; are very interested in personal appearance; are opposed to sex stereotyping; are more accepting of risk behavior and physically demanding leisure activities; and are more self-confident. Feminists also perceive that role portrayals in ads depict women as sexual objects and do not reflect the market changes that are taking place.

Although the modern role segment has been growing, the marketer should also remember that there is still a sizable group of American men and women who prefer traditional roles in marriage (43 percent, according to a recent survey). Studies indicate that most nonworking mothers are happy with their choice to remain at home with their children, and even exhibit signs of a superiority complex. Compared to their wage-earning counterparts, they more often describe themselves as family-oriented, faithful to their husbands, fun-loving, sexy, and romantic.[37] Consequently, appealing to this group on the basis of its own value system may be very rewarding to many companies. Yet, many advertisements that glorify working women risk turning off millions of full-time homemakers. One-third of the homemakers in one national study said working women are emphasized too much in TV commercials.[38] Thus, advertisers must look beyond the employment dimension and address the many other facets of today's woman.

Even these traditional women are changing in some of the ways they view their lives, and they are adopting different strategies. One of the basic lifestyle changes has been the way full-time homemakers blend family responsibilities with outside activities. What is different about this is that they feel it is legitimate, even essential, that they spend time outside the home and family. Thus, for many housewives, "family" is no longer the central focus or concern in life.[39]

Because of these changing perspectives, they are also changing housework strategies (as are women with jobs outside the house). They are trying to spend this reduced time differently, and they have modified their standards and adopted pragmatic approaches for dealing with their at-home roles.[40]

Another dimension on which the female market may be segmented is working versus nonworking women. The next section will discuss certain important facets of the working-wife segment.

TABLE 10-5

LIFESTYLE PROFILE OF THE TRADITIONAL AND MODERN WOMAN

Statement	Percent Agreeing[a] Traditional	Modern
Traditional Roles: Home & Work		
A woman's place is in the home	68%	30%
The working world is no place for a woman	28	9
I am a homebody	77	62
Traditional Roles: Family Relations		
Men are smarter than women	29%	18%
The father should be the boss in the house	81	59
A wife's first obligation is to her husband, not her children	74	67
Children are the most important thing in a marriage	60	45
Young people have too many privileges	80	72
When children are ill in bed, parents should drop everything else to see to their comfort	82	69
When making important family decisions, consideration of the children should come first	58	52
Orientation toward Housekeeping Activities		
Our home is furnished for comfort, not style	92%	88%
The kind of dirt you can't see is worse than the kind you can see	79	74
I like to save and redeem saving stamps	78	72
My days seem to follow a definite routine—eating meals at the same time each day, etc.	70	62
Meal preparation should take as little time as possible	37	44
I never eat breakfast	30	35
I always bake from scratch	44	37
I went out to breakfast instead of having it at home at least once last year	46	57
I cooked outdoors at least once during the past year	81	65
Satisfaction with Life		
I wish I could leave my present life and do something entirely different	22%	30%
My greatest achievements are still ahead of me	56	70
Physical Attractiveness		
I like to feel attractive to members of the opposite sex	79%	89%
I want to look a little different from others	66	72
All men should be clean shaven every day	76	67
There are day people and night people; I am a day person	72	67
I like to think I am a bit of a swinger	18	39
A drink or two at the end of a day is a perfect way to unwind	18	23
Had a cocktail or drink before dinner at least once last year	56	69
Had wine with dinner at least once during the past year	53	64
Travel Proneness		
I would feel lost if I were alone in a foreign country	75%	64%
I would like to take a trip around the world	59	74
I would like to spend a year in London or Paris	25	39

Working Wives Historically, women have been viewed by marketers in the roles of wife, mother, and homemaker. Roles outside the family, such as career women and professional workers, were given little or no attention. Yet, these latter

TABLE 10-5
(Continued)

Statement	Percent Agreeing	
	Traditional	Modern
Mobility		
We will probably move at least once in the next five years	32%	41%
Attitudes toward Transportation		
I have often thought of buying a subcompact car	42%	50%
I like sports cars	30	47
Financial Outlook		
Five years from now our family income will probably be a lot higher than it is now	60%	70%
Women don't need more than a minimum amount of life insurance	42	32
I am considering buying life insurance	13	22
Attitudes toward American Business		
Americans should always try to buy American products	78%	68%
I admire a successful businessman more than I admire a successful artist or writer	33	25
Views toward Events and Situations		
Everything is changing too fast today	69%	62%
There is too much emphasis on sex today	90	81
I am in favor of very strict enforcement of all laws	94	89
Police should use whatever force is necessary to maintain law and order	76	62
Communism is the greatest peril in the world today	71	55
The U.S. would be better off if there were no hippies	64	46
I think the Women's Liberation movement is a good thing	41	61
Activity Patterns		
I have somewhat old fashioned tastes and habits	91%	81%
I went to the movies at least once in the past year	68	79
I like science fiction	37	53
I visited an art gallery or museum at least once last year	45	52
I gave a speech at least once during the past year	23	30
I attended school at least once during the past year	22	32
I attended church at least once during the past year	89	82
Went to a pop concert at least once last year	7	18
I did a crossword puzzle at least once last year	73	78
I played cards at least once during the past year	80	86
I went swimming at least once last year	57	67
I went bowling at least once last year	30	39
I went skiing at least once during the past year	4	7

Source: Reprinted from Fred D. Reynolds, Melvin R. Crash, and William D. Wells, "The Modern Feminine Life Style," *Journal of Marketing,* **41**:42–43, July 1977, published by the American Marketing Association.
[a]$P \leq .05$

roles are assuming considerable importance today, particularly due to the women's movement in the United States. The predictions are that women will continue to go to work at an unprecedented rate, increasing from approximately 48 percent of all women in 1980 to 51 percent by 1990.[41] The greatest increase in the participation rates of wives has generally been among mothers of children under 3. Figure 10-5 presents a summary of working-wife characteristics.

A woman works outside the home for one or more of the following reasons:

1 To add to the family's economic security

2 To join the mainstream of worldly endeavor

3 To get acquainted with people who are achievers and sharpen her own talents and skills

4 To escape the dullness of housework

5 To prepare for the time when she might again be single or the children may be grown.[42]

Thus, there are both socioeconomic and social-psychological reasons for wives working. Moreover, these determinants or reasons are different for those in higher-income families versus those in lower-income families. It is important to know the reasons wives work, because it may help in understanding their consumer-behavior patterns.[43]

Working women have come to be recognized as prime consumer targets, and marketers are developing strategies to appeal to them as the following examples indicate:

> Travelers Corp. now encourages its agents to sell permanent life insurance policies to young affluent couples as "lifestyle insurance" to "guarantee the maintenance of the large house, the ski vacations, and the cases of Bordeaux" to which some two-income households have become accustomed.[44]

> Holiday Inns, Inc., now includes women in ads to attract the female traveling executive. Management knew by observation that the market existed. To understand its size and what would appeal to the woman executive, Holiday Inns began a $100,000 survey of travelers and their reasons for traveling. The company estimates that women executives now represent at least one out of five guests.[45]

An important consideration for the marketer is whether working women behave as consumers in the same way as do their nonworking counterparts. In general, the answer is that there are some important distinctions between the two groups. For example, working women's media behavior differs from that of nonworking women. They watch less television (particularly daytime) and read more magazines. Working women also spend somewhat more time listening to radio and reading newspapers.[46]

Research results also show that working women respond differently to advertising and that their responses reflect their interests, lifestyle, and usage patterns. For example, products and product categories with higher advertising recognition scores by working women include cigarettes, major appliances, personal hygiene products and hair products, passenger cars, pet supplies, and surprisingly, soaps, cleansers, and polishes.[47] Working versus nonworking women also exhibit some

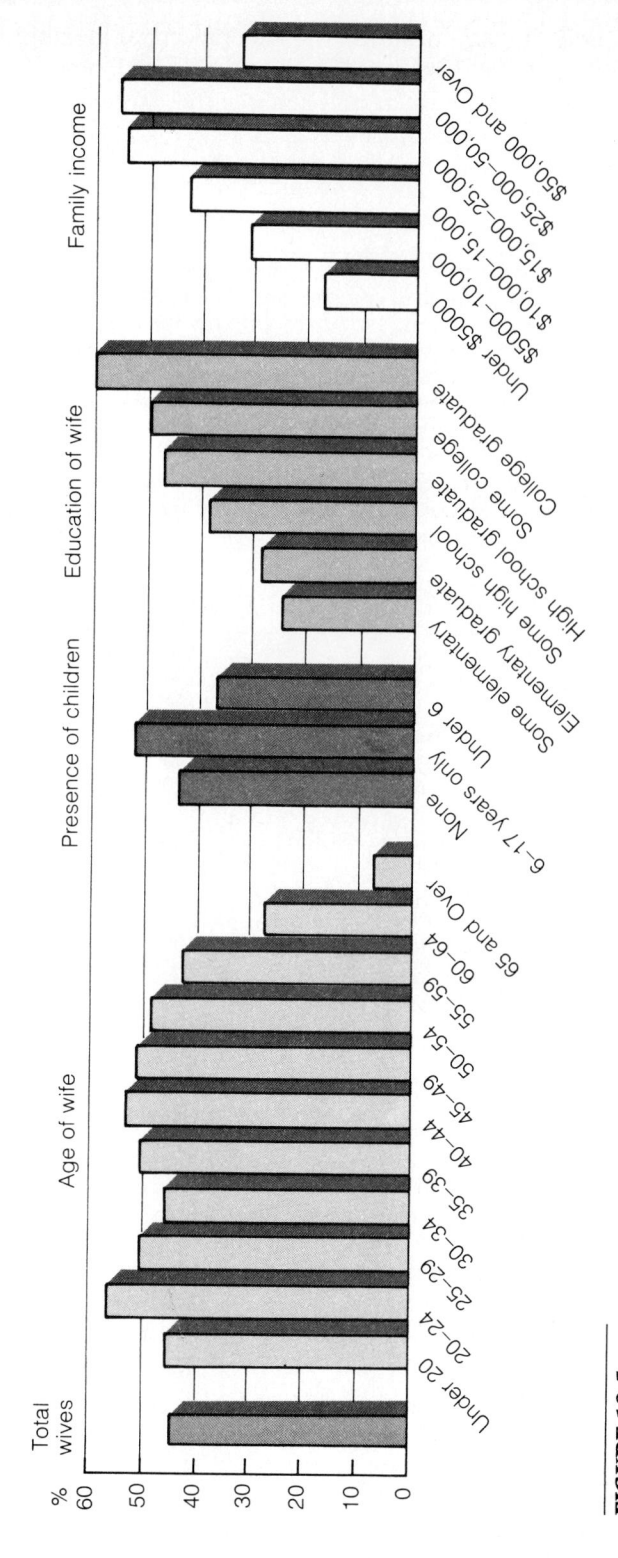

FIGURE 10-5

The working wife: proportion of wives working by selected characteristics, 1975. (*Source:* U.S. Department of Labor and Commerce, The Conference Board, in Fabian Linden, "Woman, Worker," *Across the Board*, March 1977, p. 26.)

differences in product usage patterns. The data presented in Table 10-6 are representative of some of these differences. It should be noted, however, that for some durable goods and other products and services the existence of a working wife does not appear to be a determinant of whether the goods and services are purchased or of how much is spent, according to one recent study. Thus, once the fact

TABLE 10-6
PRODUCT USAGE INDEX: WORKING VERSUS NONWORKING WOMEN

Here's a handy extract for marketers and others from Simmons 1975 study indexing products and services used by working women compared to nonemployed homemakers.

As might be expected, working housewives are not the best market for baby foods or hot cereals, but they do have greater clout as consumers of prepared foods, pet foods, diet sodas, panty hose, cigarettes, gasoline.

Employed women also spend more for bed linens and the like and attend more Tupperware parties (where they buy the brand), probably because it gives them an opportunity to mix with their neighbors at times when they are not away at work.

This cross section also reveals a greater tendency of employed women to buy/use discretionary goods and services, but they also have higher indices in some areas that are not discretionary (cold/allergy remedies, for example).

Product Category	All Women	Employed	Not Employed
Drank beer in the past month	100	115	89
Drank any alcoholic beverages in past month	100	116	89
Drank any wine in past month	100	123	83
Bought panty hose in past month	100	120	86
Own electric hair dryer	100	117	88
Bought gasoline in past three months	100	122	85
Took color snapshots in past year	100	116	89
Bought 33 rpm records in past six months	100	125	82
Bought sterling silver flatware past year	100	124	83
Used analgesic in past month	100	104	97
Used cold/allergy remedy in past month	100	116	88
Used indigestion remedy in past month	100	97	103
Used laxatives in past month	100	85	110
Bought securities in past two years	100	126	82
Regularly smoke cigarettes	100	114	90
Went bowling in past year	100	125	82
Played tennis in past year	100	134	77
Used any eye makeup in past month	100	123	84
Used any face powder in past month	100	102	99
Took domestic air trip in past year	100	120	85
Bought travelers checks in past year	100	126	81
Baby food	100	79	116
Instant powdered breakfast	100	113	91
Hot cereal	100	90	107
Barbecue sauce	100	112	92
Snack or dip cheese	100	118	89
Corn snacks	100	114	90
Frozen main courses	100	115	92
Pizza mix or prepared pizza	100	113	91
Diet cola drinks	100	114	91
Canned dog food	100	112	91
Canned cat food	100	123	84
Avg. wkly. food market expenditures $41+	100	104	97
Spent $15+ for bed sheets past year	100	112	91
Attended Tupperware party in past year	100	115	90

Source: Simmons 1975, in "Buying Habits of the Working Woman," *Media Decisions,* March 1976, p. 69.

that the wife's earnings raise family income is taken into account, families with working wives do not spend any more or less frequently or heavily on some items than do families without working wives.[48] It might also be expected that while employed wives, who report greater time pressures than nonemployed wives, should more intensively use strategies to economize on time (e.g., purchase of microwave ovens), we find that income and life cycle stage are more salient determinants of time use than is employment status.[49]

MARKETING AND ADVERTISING IMPLICATIONS OF CHANGING WOMEN'S ROLES   Mountains of statistical data could be cited regarding the changing role of women. However, what are some of the fundamental marketing implications suggested by these trends? The following list includes some of the more important ones:

Working women can justify economic expenditures for, and psychologically accept, expensive appliances and household equipment, such as microwave ovens and prepared foods, which may even reduce the wives' roles in important household tasks.

Working wives are often unable to shop during regular retailing hours. They might prefer that sales be held in the evening.

Some shopping may be done by wives' surrogates—daughters and sons. Shopping also becomes more of a shared husband and wife activity, or even a family venture. Saturdays, Sundays, and evenings become very important shopping times.

The distinction between men's and women's work in the home has blurred and a sense of shared household duties prevails. Appliances that formerly had an image of being a female appliance, such as a vacuum cleaner, tend to take on a unisex image.

Working women place a premium on a youthful appearance and on the "maintenance of self." Advancement in business is often associated with being young.

Working wives tend more to become equal decision makers in the home. This change is particularly noticeable among lower social classes where wives were very subordinated.

The availability of household services beyond the usual morning and afternoon household hours, e.g., repair services during weekends, will become increasingly important.

Price for some products may become less important than convenience, availability, service, and time savings.[50]

One area of marketing that is likely to be strongly influenced by women's changing roles is advertising. As one writer observes, "If advertising to the new woman is to persuade, it must treat women as intelligent adults who will respond to a reasonable and believable presentation of the product's case."[51] Many have been critical about the treatment of women in advertisements, particularly their limited role portrayal.[52] Role portrayal of females in television commercials, for instance, was found in the early 1970s to be quite different from their actual roles in the population. By the mid-1970s, research indicated considerable improvement in role portrayals of women.[53] However, by 1980 other research indicated that sexual stereotyping in television commercials had continued and even increased in some instances.[54] A study of magazine advertising over a twenty-year period revealed that although the percentage of women portrayed in working positions had not increased significantly since 1958, the kinds of roles they were associated with had been upgraded.[55]

Regarding the way in which women should be portrayed in advertisements, several suggestions have been offered:[56]

1   Ads for health and beauty products should appeal to a woman's sense of well being *for her own sake*—not to enhance her status as a sex object.

2   Whether a woman works or not, she should be shown as competent and creative in using products which help her to perform the tasks she perceives her roles and lifestyle necessitate.

3   If the target market is men, portraying women as decorative or alluring is appropriate. If the target market is traditional women or both women and men, portraying the women as equal partners or participants is appropriate. If the target market is contemporary women, portraying the women as successful or dominant is appropriate.

4   Show women as congenial and supportive of one another in a setting appropriate to the lifestyle of the target market.

5   Traditional women will attribute higher credibility to an authoritative male figure. This is especially true in product categories such as major appliances or those products which represent new technological developments. Contemporary women will prefer a female figure who has the necessary level of technical expertise. In promoting nontechnical products, including home and personal care products, all women will find a female with whose lifestyle they can identify to be the most credible.

Although these ideas have not been fully tested to determine their validity, they do offer the marketer some reasonable guidance in this area.

As advertisers seek to appeal to the changing woman, particularly the woman who works, some are breaking away from the stereotypes by showing dual roles, role switching, and role blending.[57] The use of *dual roles* portrays women in roles that are in addition to a more traditional role in the house, such as a wife/manager or mother/professional. For example, in a campaign aimed at getting female passengers to fly on Boeing aircraft, Boeing shows a businesswoman poring over paper work on a night flight with the caption, "A woman's work is never done."[58]

The pressures of the various roles that many women play today have brought about advertisements pitched along dual role lines such as the TV jingle for Enjoli, "the 8-hour perfume for the 24-hour woman," which suggests:

> *I can put the wash on the line, feed the kids,*
> *Get dressed, pass out the kisses,*
> *And get to work by 5 of 9,*
> *'Cause I'm a wo-man.*

With *role switching*, purchase or use of the product is portrayed by persons of the sex opposite that of the traditional stereotype. For example, a recent "give-me-the-Campbell's-life" commercial showed a husband home from work dancing around the kitchen fixing soup and sandwiches just in time for his working wife to arrive home from the office. Similarly, KitchenAid also features a nontraditional approach involving husbands as shown in Figure 10-6.

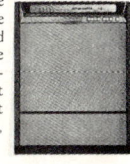

Role blending obscures the role stereotype of purchaser or user by showing scenes in which no sex dominates. For example, car manufacturers often show a man and woman (or even the entire family) engaged in decision-making activity. In addition, food manufacturers sometimes show a man and woman shopping in the supermarket.

Market Segments   Although we have been treating working and nonworking women as different homogeneous groups, it should be recognized that there are also variations within each group. In other words, segmentation of both markets reveals some important differences in orientations among the subsegments.

Recent large samples of U.S. adult females have identified two types of homemakers and two types of working wives. These four groups have been described as: (1) the working woman who thinks her work is a career; (2) the working woman who says it's just a job; (3) the homemaker who plans to work; and (4) the stay-at-home homemaker.[59] The most important characteristics of each group are shown in Table 10-7.

FIGURE 10-6

Advertisement for KitchenAid. (Courtesy of Hobart Corporation.)

TABLE 10-7
SEGMENTS OF WORKING WIVES AND HOMEMAKERS

Career Working Woman	Working Woman Who Feels "It's Just a Job"
Is future (vs. present) oriented in terms of both her personal and her work life	Views her work as dull
Is relatively highly educated	Believes that woman's place is really "in the home"
Virtually 20 percent of the segment is nonwhite	Has the lowest income of all four segments
Is youngest of the four in terms of age	Is the second highest in terms of percentage of single women
Has the largest income of the four segments	Spends the least time in shopping for household articles
Has the largest number of single females of all four segments (Note that this includes divorced, widowed, and separated women)	
Tends not to live in a single-family dwelling	
Most actively involved in shopping for clothes and household articles	
Has the highest frequency of return rates for unsatisfactory products	
Has the strongest positive self-image	
Sees self as broad-minded, dominating, frank, efficient, independent, self-assured, and very amicable	

Plan-to-Work Homemaker	Stay-at-Home Homemaker
Is interested in acquiring tangible products which additional income could provide	High homemaker role orientation
Is extroverted and visits others as well as entertains in her own home	High agreement with traditional attire (white gloves)
Tends to reside in rural vs. urban locations	Lowest educational attainment
Tends to be younger in age	Most live in rural residences
Highest percentage of married women are in this segment	Oldest of all segments
Tends to have a larger household size	Ranks second in terms of incomes over $15,000
Actively involved in shopping for household articles	Most are married
High usage of newspaper ads and sales announcements used in shopping for specials	Largest percentage of households larger than four
Highest usage of a budget in grocery shopping	Largest percentage of single-family dwellings
Tends to be tense, stubborn, and feels awkward	Least inclined to shop for clothes
Describes herself as creative and affectionate	Tends to utilize ads and sale announcements for shopping
	Thinks of herself as kind, refined, and reserved
	Much below the norm in feeling brave, stubborn, dominating, or egocentric

Source: Dan H. Robertson, Danny H. Bellenger, and Barnett A. Greenberg, "Helping Marketers Understand the Female Markets," in Robert S. Franz, Robert M. Hopkins, and Alfred G. Toma (eds.), *Proceedings: Southern Marketing Association 1979 Conference,* Southern Marketing Association, Lafayette, LA, 1979, pp. 319–320; and Rena Bartos, "What Every Marketer Should Know About Women," *Harvard Business Review,* May–June 1978, p. 81.

To summarize a few of the consumer behavior differences among these groups, the plan-to-work segment appears to be the most active and sophisticated in terms of shopping behavior. They are more actively involved in shopping, and devote more skill and attention to it than other groups. The career segment is most concerned with shopping for clothes, and is not oriented toward budgeting or shopping for specials. The stay-at-home group appears to be the most economy-minded of the segments. The least sophisticated and involved in shopping behavior is the just-a-job group.

Additionally, it appears that career women shop at specialty stores more than do either women who view their work as just a job or homemakers. Career and working women tend to shop more in the evenings and on weekends than do homemakers. These three groups also seem to use substantially different criteria for selecting retail stores in which to shop.[60]

Other research has found that career women and women who view their work as just a job display greater usage of print media (i.e., newspapers and magazines), whereas homemakers rely more heavily on television (but not radio).[61]

Descriptions of market characteristics such as those above enable the marketer to tailor distribution approaches, promotional appeals, and product characteristics to one of the segments, based on knowledge of their behavioral and attitude characteristics.

Changing Male Roles

> *I'm really knocked out. I have to take care of three children, prepare the food for them, do their laundry, bring them to school, pick them up. At the same time, of course, I have to make a living and try to hold on to my job.*[62]

This quote does not seem too unusual until we push aside our stereotypes and realize that it comes, not from a woman, but from a 38-year-old divorced man. Such is the nature of changing roles for men in American society. A growing number of men in the 1980s will become single, "mother/father" combinations. Yet, this is only one facet of the nature of these role shifts.

Additional insight into changing men's roles comes from recent studies of the married male segment. An important finding is that large numbers of married men are assuming a wide variety of nontraditional family roles. For example, during a given two-week period:[63]

- 32 percent do the main food shopping
- 80 percent take care of the children (in households with children under age 12)
- 47 percent help cook a family meal
- 33 percent cook an entire meal for the family
- 39 percent vacuum the house
- 29 percent do the laundry
- 74 percent take out the garbage
- 53 percent wash the dishes
- 28 percent clean the bathroom

Not only are men increasingly pushing the shopping carts, but they are exhibiting shopping behavior that differs from that of women. For instance, when husbands do the grocery shopping they may well choose a brand different from the one the wife would have picked.[64]

Segmenting Husbands   Thus, there is an important segment of husbands who help a great deal around the house. This group is only one of the categories of married men, however. For instance, one study divides husbands into the following five segments:[65]

1   New Breed Husbands, representing 32 percent of all married men, willingly share with their wives household chores such as cooking, cleaning, and grocery shopping. They are usually under age 40, and are mostly white-collar workers and well-educated. Their wives work full-time, and they probably have young children.

2   Classics, representing 25 percent, believe women shouldn't work unless it's an economic necessity. They'll share responsibilities, but insist on having the final word.

3   Retired, 16 percent of the total. Typically over age 40, they are less involved in decision making and remote from their families.

4   Bachelor Husband, 15 percent of all married men, is usually under age 30 and a "bachelor at heart." He normally doesn't make decisions with his wife or ask for her advice, and he is less inclined to feel that the family comes first.

5   Strugglers, 12 percent of total, think of themselves as ship captains. They demand that their wives keep the house clean, and they want the final say. Strugglers are usually in lower-income brackets and are middle-aged.

Although the modern role segment represents only one of the married male markets, the size of this group, combined with those who appear to be moving in that direction, offers some interesting possibilities for the marketer.

Marketing Implications   There are a number of implications that flow from the finding that a significant group of married men are much less traditional in their roles. First, increased male use of once traditionally female household products will mean that male users' product needs will have to be increasingly considered, more product testing among men will have to occur, and packaging will have to project an image compatible with men's use. Second, advertising for household products will portray men more often in domestic activities, with the potential for interesting and memorable situations. In fact, people are much more likely to remember commercials that show new roles for men and women than those that perpetuate stereotypes.[66] However, exaggerated and unreal presentations of men or women, whether traditional or progressive in style, cause significant consumer irritation.[67] Advertising of household products to men in a way that does not alienate them may be done by portraying the houseworking husband as a no-nonsense person knocking off a job because it has to be done. The pleasure comes from the accomplishment or completion, not in the esthetic fulfillment. Also, advertisers should be careful not to portray husbands as just helping out their wives. Such an approach might alienate women who expect the sharing of household tasks as a right and obligation, not as a favor on the part of their mates.[68]

Product advantages significant to men will also become part of the advertising message for household products. Thus, ads must reassure men that the product meets their criteria of advantages and carries the appropriate brand image, while simultaneously supporting female selection of the brand. In addition, nontraditional advertising media for household products will be more widely used.[69]

Growth of the Singles Market

One of the important market developments to occur in the last decade has been the tremendous rise of *singles*, especially among the young, which is a segment growing over five times as fast as the nation as a whole, according to the U.S. Census Bureau. Several interesting facts on this market indicate that among those 18 and over almost 40 million, or about 30 percent, of the adult population are singles. This market includes nearly 23 million who never married, almost 12 million widows and widowers, and over 5 million divorced people. Nearly 60 percent of the singles group consists of females, and almost half of this segment are under age 30.[70] It is estimated that this market accounted for $150 billion, or one out of eight dollars, of total consumer spending for goods and services in 1979.[71] This growing segment of the American market has not been ignored by marketers. New product and service opportunities have opened up in a wide range of categories geared to this market. For example, consider the following:

> *Building and Home Furnishing* The smaller household of the future—both families and singles—means more apartments and condominiums and fewer homes. More furniture will be suitable for apartments. Practicality rather than status and prestige will be stressed. Mobility of furniture will be important, giving added emphasis to new design and styles, such as modular arrangements.
>
> *Autos* Smaller cars are the big seller here, but with emphasis on sporty styling and plenty of pleasure-oriented options, such as stereo. For example, Porsche estimated that in a recent year about half of their autos were bought by singles.
>
> *Foods* More single and dual-serving packages, cans, plastic bags, and so on will be marketed, with convenience and disposability rather than economy the prime benefits.
>
> *Appliances* General Electric Co. expects 21 million new households in the 1980s, and it gleefully notes that each will need three to six major appliances plus one or more television sets. Magic Chef Inc. is stressing production of microwave ovens partly because of the numbers of single and divorced people who are setting up houses.[72]

Yet, despite all the interest and efforts of marketers, there has been sparse information about the size, characteristics, and spending patterns of the singles market. Table 10-8 presents age and income characteristics of this segment, and Table 10-9 provides insight into how this group spends. Notice, however, that these data are based on persons aged 20–34 who are living alone or as couples without children. While the couples are no longer "single," their lifestyle, obligations, and spending preferences are still quite different from those of the average family.

TABLE 10-8

THE "SINGLES" HOUSEHOLD MARKET (By Age and Income Class—1978*)

	House- holds (000,000)	Under $4,000	$4,000– 7,000	$7,000– 10,000	$10,000– 15,000	$15,000– 20,000	$20,000– 25,000	Over $25,000	Average Income ($)
All U.S. households	76.0	12.3	12.7	11.7	18.0	15.6	11.5	18.2	16,100
Total "singles"	10.7	11.3	12.6	15.9	24.3	16.2	10.1	9.6	13,437
Head under 25	4.1	18.1	18.6	18.6	23.1	13.2	6.0	2.4	10,097
Head 25–34	6.6	7.1	8.7	14.2	25.1	18.0	12.7	14.2	15,533
One-person households	4.3	15.8	18.3	21.1	27.3	11.5	3.1	2.9	10,016
Head under 25	1.6	25.9	26.4	23.4	18.7	4.3	.7	.6	7,184
Head 25–34	2.7	9.7	13.4	19.8	32.4	15.8	4.6	4.3	11,708
Two-person households	6.4	8.3	8.7	12.4	22.3	19.3	14.8	14.2	15,728
Head under 25	2.5	13.1	13.7	15.5	25.9	18.9	9.4	3.5	11,952
Head 25–34	3.9	5.2	5.5	10.4	20.0	19.5	18.3	21.1	18,175

*Data are based on households as of 1978 income for previous year.
Source: Fabian Linden, "Singular Spending Patterns," *Across the Board*, June 1979, p. 26.

TABLE 10-9

HOW "SINGLES" SPEND THEIR MONEY (Total Expenditures Each Group Equals 100 percent)

	Total U.S. Households	Singles Total	One-Person Household Under 25	One-Person Household 25–34	Two-Person Household Under 25	Two-Person Household 25–34	Singles' Expenditures as Percent of Total U.S.
Total U.S. expenditures	100.0%	12.4	1.2	2.7	2.9	5.6	12.4%
Distribution expenditure	100.0%	100.0%	100.0%	100.0%	100.0%	100.0%	
Food	21.3	14.4	11.8	15.0	13.9	14.8	8.4
At home	16.4	8.2	5.7	6.8	8.3	9.2	6.1
Away from home	4.6	5.8	5.4	7.7	5.2	5.4	15.5
Alcoholic beverages	.9	1.5	2.0	2.8	.9	1.1	20.0
Tobacco products	1.6	1.5	1.7	1.7	1.4	1.5	11.9
Housing	30.2	34.7	35.2	34.4	34.3	34.9	14.2
Shelter	16.5	22.8	26.4	25.0	22.4	21.3	17.2
Rented dwellings	7.2	19.0	25.9	23.4	20.2	15.1	33.0
Owned dwellings	9.0	3.7	.4	1.5	2.1	6.1	5.0
Fuel and utilities	5.1	3.0	2.3	2.4	3.1	3.3	7.2
Housing expenses	3.8	3.4	2.7	3.1	3.1	3.7	11.0
House furnishings & equipment	4.8	5.6	3.8	4.0	5.6	6.6	14.1
Clothing	8.1	8.6	7.3	8.5	8.2	9.2	13.1
Male	2.7	2.8	2.5	3.0	2.5	2.8	12.6
Female	3.9	3.9	2.7	3.2	3.9	4.4	12.4
Clothing care, etc.	1.5	2.0	2.2	2.3	1.8	1.9	16.0
Transportation	19.8	22.5	28.1	20.5	25.4	20.7	14.0
Vehicle purchases & finance charges	9.8	12.2	16.4	10.9	14.4	10.9	15.4
Vehicle operations	9.3	9.4	10.8	8.7	10.3	9.1	12.6

TABLE 10-9
(Continued)

	Total U.S. Households	Singles Total	Singles One-Person Household Under 25	Singles One-Person Household 25–34	Singles Two-Person Household Under 25	Singles Two-Person Household 25–34	Singles' Expenditures as Percent of Total U.S.
Health & personal care	7.3	4.5	3.1	4.0	4.1	5.2	7.7
Recreation	8.0	9.8	9.0	10.3	9.2	10.0	15.2
Vacation trips	3.1	3.4	2.4	3.8	2.6	3.8	13.3
Other*	4.9	6.4	6.6	6.5	6.6	6.2	16.2
All other	2.8	2.5	1.8	2.8	2.6	2.6	11.2

*Includes owned vacation homes, television, boats, aircraft, wheeled goods and other.
Note: Distribution of expenditures based on United States Department of Labor Consumer Survey, 1972–73. Subitems do not always add up to the major category total because of minor items not shown separately.
Source: Fabian Linden, "Singular Spending Patterns," Across the Board, July 1979, p. 32.

SUMMARY

This chapter has described the influence of the family on consumer behavior. First, the terms "family" and "household" were defined. Next, we described several types of families and the purposes of the family. The concept of family life cycle was examined in some detail. This progression of stages through which individuals and families proceed over time was found to be a primary determinant of the family's purchasing behavior. In addition, it was suggested that life cycle offers a richer explanation of consumer behavior than single variables such as age.

The nature of family purchasing decisions was discussed next from four vantage points: (1) role structure and the influence of each family member based on his or her role in the family, (2) power relationships within the family and their ability to explain the dominance of particular family members in various purchase decisions, (3) the purchase decision and the varying roles and influences of particular family members at each stage in the process, and (4) additional variables that are family-specific and have an influence on purchase decisions.

The final section of this chapter discussed the family system especially the changing role of women and men and suggested some of the effects on marketing activities likely to result.

DISCUSSION TOPICS

1   Distinguish between families and households. In what ways is each important to the marketer in analyzing consumer behavior?

2   Discuss the significance of the family in consumer behavior.

3   Describe the traditional and more modern family life-cycle stages. What influence does life cycle have on consumer behavior?

4   How would marketers of the following items use the life-cycle concept in their strategies?
    a mutual funds **b** pianos **c** motor homes **d** camping equipment

5 Describe the meaning of the following family roles. What is their significance in terms of consumer behavior and marketing strategy?
   a instrumental and expressive
   b internal and external
   c purchase process roles

6 Referring to Figure 10-4 showing United States family decision-making power structures, how could a marketer use this information in developing marketing strategies (especially advertising and personal selling activities) for the following products?
   a living room furniture
   c kitchenware
   b life insurance
   d automobile

7 Describe how family-specific characteristics influence the nature of purchasing decisions within the family.

8 Who is the gatekeeper in your family or household for the following product/brand decisions? The opinion leader?
   a furniture b foods c clothing d financial services e toys

9 Write a report on one of the following subjects indicating specifically what some of the effects on consumer behavior and marketing might be:
   a changing family values
   b changing role of women
   c women in advertisements
   d divorce and alternative "family" arrangements

10 Discuss the role of children in family decision making.

NOTES

[1]This summary of life-cycle stages has been adapted from the following sources: William D. Wells and George Gubar, "Life Cycle Concept in Marketing Research," *Journal of Marketing Research,* **3**:355–363, November 1966; S. G. Barton, "The Life Cycle and Buying Patterns," in Lincoln H. Clark (ed.), *Consumer Behavior,* **2**:53–57, New York University Press, New York, 1955; John B. Lansing and James N. Morgan, "Consumer Finances Over the Life Cycle," in Clark (ed.), *Consumer Behavior,* pp. 36–51; and John B. Lansing and Leslie Kish, "Family Life Cycle as an Independent Variable," *American Sociological Review,* **22**:512–519, October 1957.
[2]Social Research, Inc., "Furniture Buying and Life Stages," in Martin H. Grossack (ed.), *Understanding Consumer Behavior,* Christopher Publishing House, Boston, 1964, pp. 288–290.
[3]Johan Arndt, "Family Life Cycle as a Determinant of Size and Composition of Household Expenditures," in William L. Wilkie (ed.), *Advances in Consumer Research: Volume 6,* Association for Consumer Research, Ann Arbor, MI, 1979, pp. 128–132.
[4]Stuart U. Rich and Subhash C. Jain, "Social Class and Life Cycle as Predictors of Shopping Behavior," *Journal of Marketing Research,* **5**:41–49, February 1968; Ben M. Enis and Keith K. Cox, "Demographic Analysis of Store Patronage Patterns: Uses and Pitfalls," in Robert L. King (ed.), *Marketing and the New Science of Planning,* American Marketing Association, Chicago, 1968, pp. 366–370; and Barton, "The Life Cycle."
[5]George P. Moschis, "Socialization Perspectives and Consumer Behavior," in Ben M. Enis and Kenneth J. Roering (eds.), *Review of Marketing, 1981,* American Marketing Association, Chicago, 198, p. 49.
[6]National Industrial Conference Board, *Expenditure Patterns of the American Family,* Life, New York, 1965.
[7]P. G. Herbst, "The Measurement of Family Relationships," *Human Relations,* **5**:3–35, February 1952.
[8]Bernard Berelson and Gary Steiner, *Human Behavior: An Inventory of Scientific Findings,* Harcourt, Brace & World, New York, 1964, p. 314.
[9]R. F. Bales, "In Conference," *Harvard Business Review,* **32**:44–50, March-April 1954.
[10]William F. Kenkel, "Husband-Wife Interaction in Decision-Making and Decision Choices," *The Journal of Social Psychology,* **54**:260, 1961.
[11]Robert Ferber and Lucy Chao Lee, "Husband-Wife Influence in Family Purchasing Behavior," *Journal of Consumer Research,* **1**:43–50, June 1974.
[12]John S. Coulson, "Buying Decisions Within the Family and the Consumer Brand Relationship," in Joseph W. Newman (ed.), *On Knowing the Consumer,* John Wiley & Sons, Inc., New York, 1967, p. 60.
[13]Lewis A. Berey and Richard Pollay, "The Influencing Role of the Child in Family Decision-Making," *Journal of Marketing Research,* **5**:72, February 1968.

[14] P. G. Herbst, "Conceptual Framework for Studying the Family," in O. A. Oeser and S. B. Hammond (eds.), *Social Structure and Personality in a City*, Routledge, London, 1954.

[15] Harry L. Davis and Benny P. Rigaux, "Perceptions of Marital Roles in Decision Processes," *The Journal of Consumer Research*, 1:51–62, June 1974.

[16] E. H. Bonfield, "Perception of Marital Roles in Decision Processes: Replication and Extension," in H. Keith Hunt (ed.), *Advances in Consumer Research: Volume 5*, Association for Consumer Research, Ann Arbor, MI, 1978, pp. 300–307.

[17] See for example, Arch G. Woodside, "Dominance and Conflict in Family Purchasing Decisions," in M. Venkatesan (ed.), *Proceedings of the Third Annual Conference*, Association for Consumer Research, Chicago, 1972, pp. 650–659; and Elizabeth H. Wolgast, "Do Husbands or Wives Make the Purchasing Decisions?" *Journal of Marketing*, 22:151–158, October 1958.

[18] Haley, Overholser & Associates, Inc., *Purchase Influence*, New Canaan, CT, January 1975.

[19] This section is based on Harry L. Davis, "Decision Making Within the Household," *Journal of Consumer Research*, 2:254–256, March 1976; and Michael A. Belch, George E. Belch, and Donald Sciglimpaglia, "Conflict in Family Decision Making: An Exploratory Investigation," in Jerry C. Olson (ed.), *Advances in Consumer Research: Volume 7*, Association for Consumer Research, Ann Arbor, MI, 1980, pp. 475–479.

[20] Jagdish N. Sheth, "A Theory of Family Buying Decisions," in Jagdish N. Sheth (ed.), *Models of Buyer Behavior*, Harper & Row, New York, 1974, p. 33.

[21] John Scanzoni, "Changing Sex Roles and Emerging Directions in Family Decision Making," *Journal of Consumer Research*, 4:185–188, December 1977.

[22] Isabella C. M. Cunningham and Robert T. Green, "Purchasing Roles in the U.S. Family, 1955 and 1973," *Journal of Marketing*, 38:64, October 1974; "Marketing Observer," *Business Week*, September 28, 1974, p. 18; and Haley, Overholser & Associates, Inc., *Purchase Influence*.

[23] See for example, Arch G. Woodside and John F. Willenborg, "Husband and Wife Interactions and Marketing Decisions," *Southern Journal of Business*, 7:55, May 1972; and "A Pilot Study of the Roles of Husbands and Wives in Purchasing Decisions," conducted for *Life* magazine by L. Jaffe Associates, Inc., 1965.

[24] John Fayerweather, *International Marketing*, 2d ed., Prentice-Hall, Englewood Cliffs, NJ, 1970, p. 25.

[25] Susan P. Douglas, "A Cross-National Exploration of Husband-Wife Involvement in Selected Household Activities," in William L. Wilkie (ed.), *Advances in Consumer Research: Volume 6*, Association for Consumer Research, Ann Arbor, MI, 1979, pp. 364–371.

[26] Douglas J. Dalrymple, Thomas S. Robertson, and Michael Y. Yoshino, "Consumption Behavior Across Ethnic Categories," *California Management Review*, 14:64–70, Fall 1971.

[27] James F. Engel, David T. Kollat, and Roger D. Blackwell, *Consumer Behavior*, 2d ed., Holt, New York, 1973, pp. 199–200; and Komarovsky, "Class Differences," p. 258.

[28] Wolgast, "Do Husbands or Wives Make the Purchasing Decisions?" p. 154.

[29] Donald H. Granbois, "The Role of Communication in the Family Decision-Making Process," in Stephen A. Greyser (ed.), *Toward Scientific Marketing*, American Marketing Association, Chicago, 1963, pp. 44–57.

[30] Mira Komarovsky, "Class Differences in Family Decision-Making on Expenditures," in Nelson Foote (ed.), *Household Decision-Making*, New York University Press, New York, 1961, pp. 255–265.

[31] Wolgast, "Do Husbands or Wives Make the Purchasing Decisions?" p. 154.

[32] Pierre Filiatrault and J. R. Brent Ritchie, "Joint Purchasing Decisions: A Comparison of Influence Structure in Family and Couple Decision-Making Units," *Journal of Consumer Research*, 7:131–140, September 1980.

[33] "Poll Shows Shared Roles in Marriage are Gaining," *Providence Sunday Journal*, November 27, 1977, p. A-20.

[34] "Sex . . . Marriage . . . Divorce—What Women Think Today," *U.S. News & World Report*, October 21, 1974, p. 107.

[35] "Males Don't Like New Woman: DDB," *Advertising Age*, October 20, 1980, p. 60.

[36] Alladi Venkatesh, "Changing Roles of Women—A Life-Style Analysis," *Journal of Consumer Research*, 7:189–197, September 1980.

[37] "Ads Glorifying Career 'Superwomen' Can Alienate Full-time Housewives," *Marketing News*, May 1, 1981, pp. 1–2.

[38] "Ads Glorifying Career 'Superwomen.'"

[39] "Research Profiles Pragmatic, Unliberated Woman Segment; Suggests Marketing Appeals," *Marketing News*, May 15, 1981, pp. 1, 7.

[40] "Research Profiles," pp. 1, 7.

[41] Rena Bartos, "The Moving Target: The Impact of Women's Employment on Consumer Behavior," *Journal of Marketing*, 41:31, July 1977.

[42] "The Working Woman," *Media Decisions*, February 1976, pp. 53–54.

[43] Jeanne L. Hafstrom and Marilyn M. Dunsing, "Socioeconomic and Social-Psychological Influences on Reasons Wives Work," *Journal of Consumer Research*, 5:169–175, December 1978.

[44] Cynthia Saltzman, "Troubled Life-Insurance Companies Try Mass-Marketing Tactics to Increase Sales," *The Wall Street Journal*, December 19, 1980, p. 40.

[45]"Female Executives Become a Target for Ads," *Business Week,* August 22, 1977, p. 66.
[46]"The Working Woman," p. 54.
[47]"Marketers Told How to Reach Working Women," *Editor & Publisher,* June 9, 1979, p. 48.
[48]Myra H. Strober and Charles B. Weinberg, "Working Wives and Major Family Expenditures," *Journal of Consumer Research,* 4:141–147, December 1977.
[49]Myra H. Strober and Charles B. Weinberg, "Strategies Used by Working and Nonworking Wives to Reduce Time Pressures," *Journal of Consumer Research,* 6:338–348, March 1980.
[50]Reprinted from William Lazer and John E. Smallwood, "The Changing Demographics of Women," *Journal of Marketing,* 41:21–22, July, 1977, published by the American Marketing Association.
[51]E. B. Weiss, "New Life Styles of 1975–1980 Will Throw Switch on Admen," *Advertising Age,* September 18, 1972, p. 62.
[52]See for example Michael B. Mazis and Marily Beuttenmuller, "Attitudes Toward Women's Liberation and Perception of Advertisements," in M. Venkatesan (ed.), *Proceedings of the Third Annual Conference,* Association for Consumer Research, Chicago, 1972, p. 428; Alice E. Courtney and Sarah W. Lockeretz, "A Woman's Place: An Analysis of the Roles Portrayed by Women in Magazine Advertisements," *Journal of Marketing Research,* 8:95, February 1971; and Louis C. Wagner and Janis B. Banos, "A Woman's Place: A Follow-up Analysis of the Roles Portrayed by Women in Magazine Advertisements," *Journal of Marketing Research,* 10:213–214, May 1973.
[53]Kenneth C. Schneider and Sharon B. Schneider, "Trends in Sex Roles in Television Commercials," *Journal of Marketing,* 43:79–84, Summer 1979.
[54]Michael F. d'Amico and John W. Hummel, "Sex Role Portrayals in Television Commercials: 1971, 1976, 1980," in John H. Summey and Ronald D. Taylor (eds.), *Evolving Marketing Thought for 1980,* Southern Marketing Association, Carbondale, IL, 1980, pp. 396–399.
[55]Marc G. Weinberger, Susan M. Petroshius, and Stuart A. Westin, "Twenty Years of Women in Magazine Advertising: An Update," in Neil Beckwith, et al. (eds.), *1979 Educator's Conference Proceedings,* American Marketing Association, Chicago, 1979, pp. 373–377.
[56]Mary Lou Roberts and Perri B. Koggan, "How Should Women Be Portrayed in Advertisements?—A Call for Research," in William L. Wilkie (ed.), *Advances in Consumer Research: Volume 6,* Association for Consumer Research, Ann Arbor, MI, 1979, pp. 66–72.
[57]William J. Lundstrom and Donald Sciglimpaglia, "Sex Role Portrayals in Advertising," *Journal of Marketing,* 41:78, July 1977.
[58]Ellen Graham, "Advertisers Take Aim at a Neglected Market: The Working Woman," *The Wall Street Journal,* July 5, 1977, pp. 1, 5.
[59]Dan H. Robertson, Danny N. Bellenger, and Barnett A. Greenberg, "Helping Marketers Understand the Female Markets," in Robert S. Franz, Robert M. Hopkins, and Alfred G. Toma (eds.), *Proceedings: Southern Marketing Association 1979 Conference,* Southern Marketing Association, Lafayette, LA, 1979, pp. 317–320; and Rena Bartos, "What Every Marketer Should Know About Women," *Harvard Business Review,* May–June 1978, p. 81.
[60]Elizabeth C. Hirschman, "Women's Self-Ascribed Occupational Status and Retail Patronage," in Kent B. Monroe (ed.), *Advances in Consumer Research: Volume 8,* Association for Consumer Research, Ann Arbor, MI, 1981, pp. 648–654.
[61]Elizabeth C. Hirschman, "Women's Role Perceptions and Usage of Information Sources," in Robert S. Franz, Robert M. Hopkins, and Alfred G. Toma (eds.), *Proceedings: Southern Marketing Association 1979 Conference,* Southern Marketing Association, Lafayette, LA, 1979, pp. 313–316.
[62]Ernest Dichter, "New Roles and Interests for Men in the 1980s," *Marketing Communications,* in SCAN, July 1980, p. 21.
[63]Benton & Bowles, *American Consensus: Men's Changing Role in the Family of the '80s,* Benton & Bowles, Inc., New York, September 1980, pp. 2–3.
[64]Jo-Ann Zbytniewski, "The Men Who Man the Shopping Carts," *Progressive Grocer,* May 1979, p. 44; and Jo-Ann Zbytniewski, "Consumer Watch," *Progressive Grocer,* March 1980, p. 37.
[65]"New Research Identifies Five Subsegments of Married Men," *Marketing News,* November 14, 1980, p. 7.
[66]Cyndy Scheibe, "Sex Roles in TV Commercials," *Journal of Marketing Research,* 19:23–27, February 1979.
[67]Thomas W. Whipple and Alice E. Courtney, "How to Portray Women in TV Commercials," *Journal of Advertising Research,* 20:53–59, April 1980.
[68]"Males Don't Like New Woman: DDB."
[69]Benton & Bowles, *American Consensus: Men's Changing Role;* and Gay Sands Miller, "Change of Pitch: More Food Advertisers Woo the Male Shopper as He Shares the Load," *The Wall Street Journal,* August 26, 1980, pp. 1, 21.
[70]"Rise of the 'Singles'—40 Million Free Spenders," *U.S. News & World Report,* October 7, 1974, pp. 54–56.
[71]Fabian Linden, "Singular Spending Patterns," *Across the Board,* July 1979, p. 31.
[72]"Household Growth Could Spurt in '80s, But Much Hinges on Lifestyle Changes," *The Wall Street Journal,* July 1, 1980, p. 23.

CHAPTER 11

PERSONAL INFLUENCE AND DIFFUSION OF INNOVATIONS

This chapter further investigates the way in which individuals influence each other's behavior as consumers. Two examples are offered to show not only the significance, but also the positive and negative side of such influence:

> Vermont Castings, Inc., a maker of wood and coal-burning cast-iron stoves, generates affectionate word-of-mouth advertising. Owners of Vermont Castings' Defiant, Vigilant, and Resolute stoves boast about how many friends they have converted to them. When the company asked owners whether they would be willing to show curious strangers how their stoves worked, 3000 owners volunteered. The company's showroom has a bulletin board covered with testimonial letters and proud customers' snapshots of installed stoves. On one August weekend 10,000 people showed up at an owners' outing in a central Vermont town of 4500 to take plant tours and listen to lectures on wood and coal burning, insulation, and stove safety.[1]

> Word-of-mouth can have a very negative impact if consumers have a question or complaint that is ignored or unsatisfactorily resolved by the marketer. For instance, although less than 3 percent of a sample of communications received by Coca-Cola from consumers in a recent year were complaints, customers who complained and weren't satisfied with the response typically told nine or ten friends or associates about their experience, and in 12 percent of the cases, they told more than twenty people. In addition, 30 percent said they stopped buying Coca-Cola products, while another 45 percent said they would buy less in the future.[2]

We shall first describe the nature of influence, and then discuss its significance as evidenced by word-of-mouth communication among individuals. Next, models of the flow of communication will be examined to better understand how personal influence occurs. Then we shall discuss the nature and significance of opinion leadership in marketing, and the characteristics of leaders as well as followers. The concept of personal influence is strongly embodied in the process of adoption and diffusion of innovations; thus this topic will also be examined to understand better its significance to the marketer. Finally, we shall see how the marketer can use the concept of influence to his or her advantage by incorporating opinion leadership as a cornerstone of promotional programs.

NATURE AND SIGNIFICANCE OF PERSONAL INFLUENCE

Personal influence is best described as the effect or change in a person's attitudes or behavior as a result of communication with others. It can occur in a number of ways. The following distinctions can be made to indicate the multidimensional nature of this communication phenomenon:

1 Communication leading to influence may be *source initiated* (by the influencer) or *recipient initiated* (by the influencee).

2 Communication may result in *one-way* or *two-way* influence. That is, the individual may influence while being influenced.

3 Communication resulting in influence may be *verbal* or *visual*.[3]

Personal influence is frequently used synonymously with the term "word-of-mouth" advertising or communication, even though the above classification indicates that they are not the same. Since word-of-mouth is oral communication, it is actually a subset of personal influence; however, we shall use the terms synonymously in this chapter.

Promotional activities conducted by the marketer are not the only or necessarily the most important influences on purchasing behavior. There is evidence that favorable word-of-mouth communication can actually have more influence than the huge sums spent on advertising. Consequently, many companies advertise little and depend, instead, on word-of-mouth promotion. As the president of Loehmann's, one of the country's most successful retailers of women's clothing, explains, "There's nothing like a woman's mouth."[4] Of course, this dictum should be broadened to include men as well. Here are some examples of word-of-mouth advertising's impact:

> In-depth interviews on buyer motivations by Ernest Dichter's organization frequently found that friends, experts, or relatives told the individual about the product—and that is why the product was purchased. At times, the influence of "recommenders" ran as high as 80 percent.[5]
>
> A study of durable goods purchases found that word-of-mouth was the major information source, with over 50 percent of the sample turning to friends for advice.[6]
>
> Among male and female students at a large southern university, nearly 50 percent discussed clothing brands, styles, retail outlets, and prices with their friends.[7]
>
> Word-of-mouth advertising is very important in the motion-picture industry. For example, much of the success of *Star Wars,* has been attributed to the fact that word-of-mouth advertising "hit like lightning."[8]

The marketer frequently tries to create a "synthetic" word-of-mouth program by using celebrities in advertising campaigns. These spokespeople enter our homes via the media and speak to us as if it were a one-to-one conversation. This simulated personal influence may nevertheless be very effective. There are two excellent illustrations of the way in which celebrities may affect our behavior as consumers:

> When Clark Gable took off his shirt in a 1934 movie *It Happened One Night*, he revealed a bare chest. As a result, undershirt sales are said to have dropped 75 percent that year.[9]

> Johnny Carson once suggested in his "Tonight Show" monologue that there was an acute shortage of toilet paper in the United States. (His source was a Wisconsin congressman who had actually been referring only to the cheaper federal government issue of toilet paper.) As a result, people dashed to their supermarkets to stock up; within one week, there actually was a shortage of the better toilet paper.[10]

It is clear that personal influence—whether actual or synthetic—can be quite convincing. The marketer is vitally interested in this process because a product's success appears dependent on it. It is very important, therefore, that mostly favorable, not unfavorable, communications take place. As one study of the spread of a new food product in a married students' housing complex showed, exposure to favorable word-of-mouth communication increased the probability of purchase, while exposure to unfavorable comments decreased the probability.[11]

Why is word-of-mouth communication so strong? There seem to be three main reasons for its dominant position in relation to impersonal media:

1 Consumers view word-of-mouth as reliable and trustworthy information which can help people to make better buying decisions.

2 In contrast to the mass media, personal contacts can provide social support and give a stamp of approval to a purchase.

3 The information provided is often backed up by social group pressure to force compliance with recommendations.[12]

In order to understand better the way in which personal influence and word-of-mouth advertising occur, several models of the communication process will be presented.

MODELS OF COMMUNICATION AND INFLUENCE FLOW

Personal influence is necessarily dependent upon the process of communication. The marketer may view the situation in several ways: as a one-step process; as a two-step flow of communication; or as a multiple-step model of interaction. Let's examine these various interpretations of the way in which influence results from communication.

One-Step Model
For years, marketers operated under the assumptions contained in the one-step or one-way model of communication. In this model, portrayed in Figure 11-1, com-

munication is represented as a one-way process flowing from the marketer to consumers. Notice that this model of communication assumes the marketer is directing the appeal to *each* consumer expecting that the consumer will: (1) notice the advertisement, (2) be informed, persuaded, or reminded by it, and (3) buy the product or service.[13]

This model has been criticized, however, for its oversimplification. First of all, few messages actually reach consumers, and those that do are not likely to elicit a response directly. Product sales are influenced by many other marketing and extraneous variables in addition to the promotional communication.

Because of these drawbacks, communications researchers turned to a more sophisticated explanation of the influence process—one that recognized the influence not only of impersonal channels (such as radio, television, and magazines), but also personal channels of communication and influence. This was the development of the two-step flow theory of communication.

Two-Step Flow Model

The process of communication and influence has been found not to be an exclusively direct flow as had been originally supposed. Instead, it appears that influence occurs in a two-step flow, moving first from the mass media directly to influentials or *opinion leaders* who then through interpersonal networks pass on what they have seen or heard to their associates. The two-step model is illustrated in Figure 11-2.

The two-step model represents an improvement over the one-step scheme because it recognizes the influence of interpersonal contact. However, it also has certain limitations. Among the biggest problems are: (1) it suggests that an absolute leader exists for each informal group, when actually all group members have some amount of opinion leadership; (2) information is assumed to flow only from the mass media to opinion leaders who disseminate it to followers—actually followers are also in touch with mass media, but perhaps not to the same degree as leaders; and (3) it is not always *influence* that is transmitted interpersonally, but in some cases simply information, which may be relatively free of influence.[14]

Thus, the two-step communication model has merit, but it implies a passive audience and active, information-seeking opinion leaders. Because of these limi-

FIGURE 11-1

One-step model of communication.

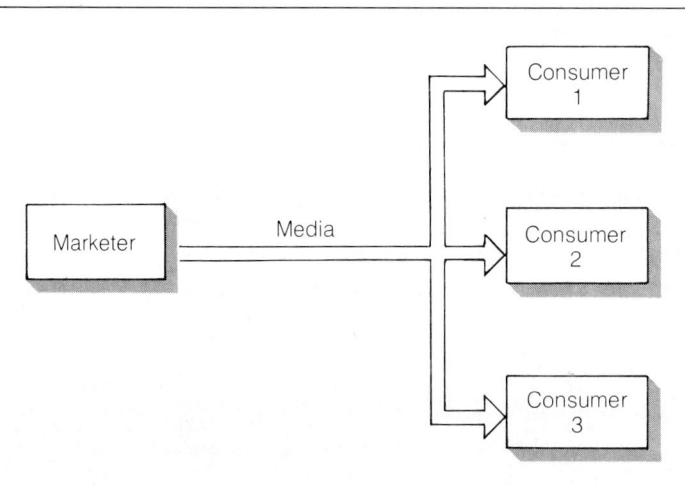

FIGURE 11-2
Two-step model of communication.

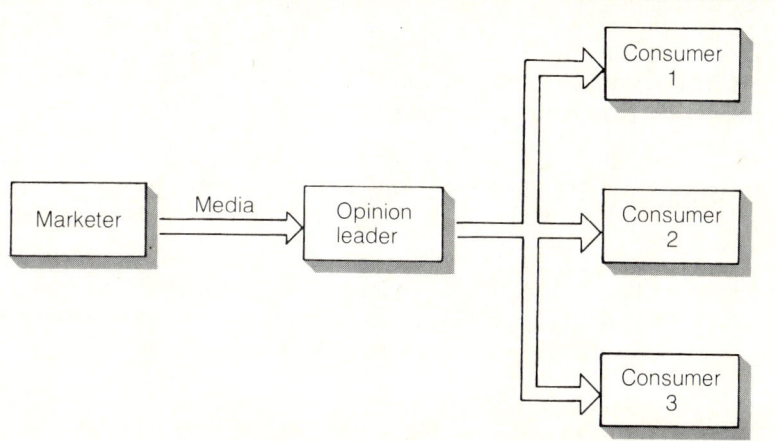

tations, many communications researchers now suggest a multistep interaction model as a more accurate representation of personal influence.

Multistep Models

Researchers have shown that audiences are not simply passive receivers of communication. Instead, they have been found in several studies to be active seekers of information. Many audience members act as transmitters and receivers of information. It has, furthermore, been suggested that the flow of communication may take place through three or more stages. Figure 11-3 presents a model of this process.

Consider the following examples of the different directions that a verbal flow of communication and personal influence may take between a source and a receiver:

1 Source-initiated, one-way influence (this is most typical of the two-step flow model): "Jim told me how good his B.F. Goodrich radials are, so I decided to buy a set."

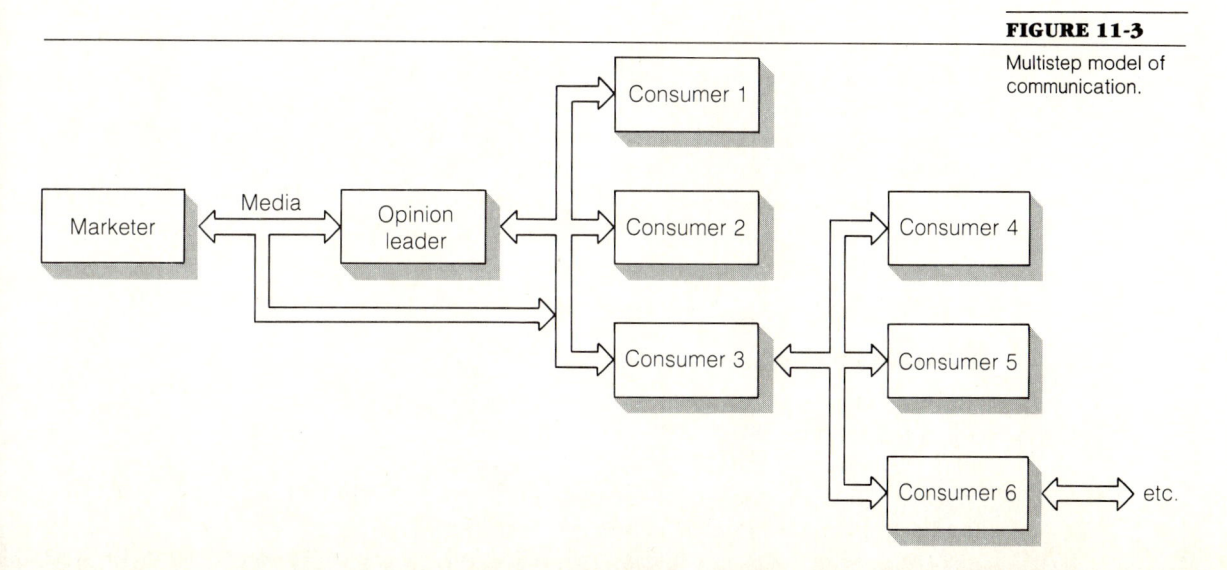

FIGURE 11-3
Multistep model of communication.

2 Receiver-initiated, one-way influence: "I asked Jim what kind of tire he recommends."

3 Source-initiated, two-way influence: "I showed Susan our new Jenn-Air range. She really wants to buy one when her old stove gives out. Her interest made me feel better about our range's higher price."

4 Receiver-initiated, two-way influence: "I asked Carol what she knew about electric ranges. We had an interesting discussion of the features of different brands."

Of course, we could add additional levels to the flow and a visual mode of communication as well. The point is that obviously the communication process and flow of influence is much more involved than previously imagined. In the next section, we will more closely examine the nature of personal influence as effected through opinion leadership.

OPINION LEADERSHIP IN MARKETING

Opinion leaders were defined in Chapter 10 as those people who are able, in a given situation, to exert personal influence. They are the ones to whom others look for advice and information. Now, let us describe these people more specifically.

The term "opinion leader" is perhaps unfortunate because it tends to connote people of high status who make major decisions for the rest of us. In the marketing context, such a designation is unfortunate because it erroneously suggests an absolute leader whom others seek to follow. In effect, opinion leadership is a relative concept, and the opinion leader may not be much more influential than his followers.[15]

Nevertheless, opinion leaders can informally and subtly affect the behavior of others toward products, either positively or negatively. If they like a product or service, they can help to assure its success; if they do not like it, they can contribute to its failure. It all depends on the verbal and/or visual communication that flows between them and others whom they influence.

For communication of marketing information through two- or multistep flow models, opinion leadership is important and is found at all levels in society. That is, consumers tend to be influenced by those who are members of the same groups, people very much like themselves. Thus, every status level and every group will have opinion leaders, with the flow of influence being generally horizontal within them. However, the fact that opinion leaders are found in all strata of society does not necessarily mean that they are equally effective or important to the marketer at each social level. In fact, personal influence appears to be more operative and to have greater importance and effectiveness at higher-income and status levels.[16] These, then, are the levels which the marketer is often more concerned about reaching.

Who Are Opinion Leaders?

Because personal influence of opinion leaders is quite significant, marketers are obviously interested in trying to reach such influentials. To do so, however, requires that they first be identified and segmented. Perhaps they may then be reached with promotional messages, and participate in additional communication and influence with their fellow group members.

Characteristics Numerous studies have been conducted attempting to identify opinion leader characteristics. The research is not conclusive, but we have some understanding of the opinion leader's profile:

1 Opinion leaders have approximately the same social class position as nonleaders, although they may have higher social status within the class.[17] This does not mean that personal influence does not flow across different class lines, but it is likely to be infrequent and of a visual nature rather than verbal.

2 Opinion leaders have greater exposure to mass media that are relevant to their area of interest.[18] For example, opinion leaders for women's fashions could be expected to have higher exposure to such magazines as *Vogue* and *Glamour*. Similarly, automobile opinion leaders might be expected to read *Motor Trend* or *Hot Rod*. Exposure to relevant mass media provides them with information useful in enhancing their leadership potential.

3 Opinion leaders have greater interest and knowledge of the area of influence than do nonleaders. This finding is closely related to their greater media exposure. Of course, knowledge is not a prerequisite for opinion leader influence. Undoubtedly, much influence takes place by those who are ignorant of the topic of conversation.

4 Opinion leaders are more gregarious than nonleaders. This finding is logical, given that they must interact with those whom they influence. Thus, opinion leaders are generally more sociable or companionable.

5 Opinion leaders have more innovativeness than do nonleaders. This does not mean, however, that they are *innovators* (the first people to purchase a new item). In fact, innovators and opinion leaders have been found to have differing characteristics and life styles in several studies. In the fashion market, for instance, the innovator is seen as an adventurer who is the earliest visual communicator of the newest styles aimed at the mass of fashion consumers.[19] The opinion leader, however, may be characterized more as an "editor" of fashions, who defines and endorses appropriate standards.

6 Opinion leaders are also more familiar with and loyal to group standards and values than are nonleaders. This refers to the fact that opinion leaders are vested with leadership authority by group members, and in order to maintain this position, the individual has to reflect underlying norms and values for that area of consumption leadership. The clothing influential, for instance, cannot be too far ahead of or behind fashion, but must reflect the current norms in clothing.

Are There "General" Opinion Leaders? The question of whether generalized opinion leaders exist for a wide variety of products as opposed to specialized opinion leaders for each product has been the subject of much debate. Although research is often conflicting, it appears that there is *moderate* opinion leadership overlap across product categories; that is, general opinion leaders do appear to exist to some extent. One of the keys to this question seems to be the interest patterns of opinion leaders, with highest overlap existing among product categories involving similar interests.[20]

The existence of generalized opinion leaders, or more precisely, opinion leadership overlap, does not mean, however, that such individuals are opinion leaders for *all* product categories. One study of seven product-interest areas, for example, found that only about 3 percent of the respondents were opinion leaders for at least five of the items.[21]

Opinion Leadership Is Situational   In the absence of a standardized, clear-cut opinion leader profile applying across all products, and where influencers and influencees seem to be so much alike, how is the opinion leader distinguished from those who follow? It has been suggested that influence is related to the following factors:

1   *The personification of certain values* (who one is). Thus, individuals who closely represent or personify group values are likely to be opinion leaders. For example, if some particular clothing style is valued by the group, the individual most closely representing this is likely to be influential.

2   *Competence* (what one knows). An individual who is very knowledgeable about some topic valued by the group will probably be influential.

3   *Strategic social location* (whom one knows inside and outside the group). For example, an individual who is available and active in the interpersonal communication process in her sorority will have a better chance for a leadership position.[22]

Thus, influence takes place because opinion leaders personify group norms, exhibit competence, and are accessible with active communication among others.

Because such leadership is situational and does not have a consistent pattern of characteristics across products, marketers might investigate the three characteristics cited above with regard to those who consume particular goods or services. In this way, they may uncover specific patterns which could then guide marketing strategies.

Why Opinion Leaders Attempt to Influence Others

Consumers, generally, do not speak about products or services unless they expect to derive some kind of satisfaction from the activity. We can categorize four reasons why opinion leaders engage in word-of-mouth communication about products or services:

1   *Product-involvement*—Use of a product or service may create a tension that may need to be reduced by way of talk, recommendation, and enthusiasm to provide relief. For example, consumers often are fascinated by new items and feel they must tell someone about how good a product they've found.

2   *Self-involvement*—In this case, the emphasis is more on ways the influencer can gratify certain emotional needs. Product talk can achieve such goals as the following:

Gaining attention—people can have something to say in a conversation by talking about products rather than people or ideas.

Showing connoisseurship—talk about certain products can show one is "in the know," and has good judgment.

Feeling like a pioneer—the speaker likes to identify with the newness and uniqueness of products and their pioneering manufacturers.

Having inside information—the speaker is able to show how much more he or she knows about the product and its manufacturer than the listener (and thus how clever the speaker is).

Suggesting status—talking about products with social status may elevate the speaker to the level of its users.

Spreading the gospel—the speaker may be able to convert the listener to using the product.

Seeking confirmation—the more followers accept his or her advice about the product, the more assured the speaker feels about his or her own decision.

Asserting superiority—recommending products to listeners can help the speaker gain leadership and test the extent to which others will follow.

3 *Other-involvement*—In this case, product talk fills the need to "give" something to the listener, to share one's happiness with the influencee, or to express care, love, or friendship.

4 *Message-involvement*—Talking may also be stimulated by great interest in the messages used to present the product. For example, advertising that is highly original and entertaining may be the topic of conversation, especially since most of us feel we are experts on effective advertising and can thus speak as critics.[23]

Why Followers Accept Personal Influence

The marketer would certainly want to know the situational attributes under which opinion leadership will most likely occur so that he or she could actively cultivate the process. There are numerous product, individual, and group characteristics that can be expected to influence the acceptance of opinion leadership by followers. Only a few of these will be cited here.[24]

Product characteristics are important in judging the significance of personal influence. For example, when products are highly visible or conspicuous (such as clothing as opposed to laundry detergents) they are more susceptible to personal influence. Products that can be tried or tested and compared against objective criteria are less susceptible to personal influence than those that cannot be tried. Product complexity may also give rise to the occurrence of personal influence, as would a product that is high on the amount of risk which consumers perceive to be associated with its purchase.

Use of these four factors to evaluate products helps the marketer to determine when opinion leadership is apt to be strong. For example, most food products would be subject to rather little opinion leadership while small appliances would be subject to much more personal influence. More will be said about these product characteristics under the topic of diffusion.

Individual consumer characteristics and group influences are also important in determining the extent to which opinion leadership will be operative. For example, individuals who are other-directed look to other people for behavioral guidance, in contrast to those who are inner-directed and rely on their own value systems for direction. Also, individuals who face new life experiences (such as newlyweds or retirees) may be very receptive to information and consequently be quite susceptible to personal influence. In addition, those who aspire to membership in particular groups are receptive to personal influence and may emulate the behavior of group members. A final factor to be mentioned that affects acceptance of opinion leadership is the individual's personality. For example, some individuals are more persuasible than others.

ADOPTION AND DIFFUSION OF INNOVATIONS

The adoption and innovation diffusion processes will be discussed in this section to illustrate the way in which communication and interpersonal influence work with new products.

What Is an Innovation?

New-product innovation is an essential element of the dynamic American economy. As new and better products are discovered, they are launched in the marketplace and their fate is determined by votes of consumers through their purchase or rejection.

The term "new" however, is not at all clear in its relation to products and services. Several criteria may be used to assess the newness of products. One concerns the *extent of difference from existing products.* For example, some feel that a new product must be quite different from existing products (although this definition is obviously difficult to measure). The Federal Trade Commission (FTC) is representative of this view as it suggests that a product may properly be called new only if it is either entirely new or has been changed in a functionally significant and substantial respect.[25] Package changes or other modifications that are functionally insignificant or insubstantial do not qualify.

A second way new products may be classified is by the *length of time on the market.* The FTC, for example, advises that the word "new" be limited to 6 months from when the product enters regular distribution after test marketing.[26]

A third way in which new products may be categorized is according to the *sales penetration level.* Marketers frequently refer to products as innovations if they have achieved less than 10 percent of the market potential in a given geographic location.[27]

Fourth, products may be categorized as new depending on *consumer perception of the items.* For example, one source defines an innovation as "any idea, practice, or material artifact perceived to be new by the relevant adopting unit."[28] Although this approach is typical of that taken by many researchers, it too, presents a number of operational difficulties.

In an attempt to overcome the weaknesses in the above approaches, (especially the dichotomy of products being either new, or not new), a continuum or range of newness has been suggested based on the product's effect on established consumption patterns. Under this conception three categories of innovation are classified as described below:

1 *Continuous innovations* have the least disrupting influence on established consumption patterns. Product alteration is involved, rather than the establishment of a totally new product. Examples of products that are representative of this situation are fluoride toothpaste, new-model automobile changeovers, and menthol cigarettes.

2 *Dynamically continuous innovations* have more disrupting effects than continuous innovations, although they do not generally alter established patterns. It may involve the creation of new products or the alteration of existing items. Examples of this would include electric toothbrushes, electric autos, wall-size television screens, and videotelephones.

3 *Discontinuous innovations* involve the establishment of a new product with new behavior patterns. Examples of this situation would include television, computers, and automobiles.[29]

The Adoption Process

Before we examine how products spread among population groups, we need to look at the process as it relates to individuals. The acceptance and continued use of a product or brand by an individual is referred to as "adoption." Figure 11-4 presents a simplified diagram of the adoption process. This model consists of the following stages:

1 *Awareness* At this stage the potential adopter finds out about the existence of a product, but has very little information and no well-formed attitudes about it.

FIGURE 11-4

The adoption decision process. (*Source:* Adapted from Thomas S. Robertson, *Innovative Behavior and Communication,* copyright © 1971 by Holt, Rinehart and Winston, New York, p. 75. Reprinted by permission of Holt, Rinehart and Winston, CBS College Publishing.)

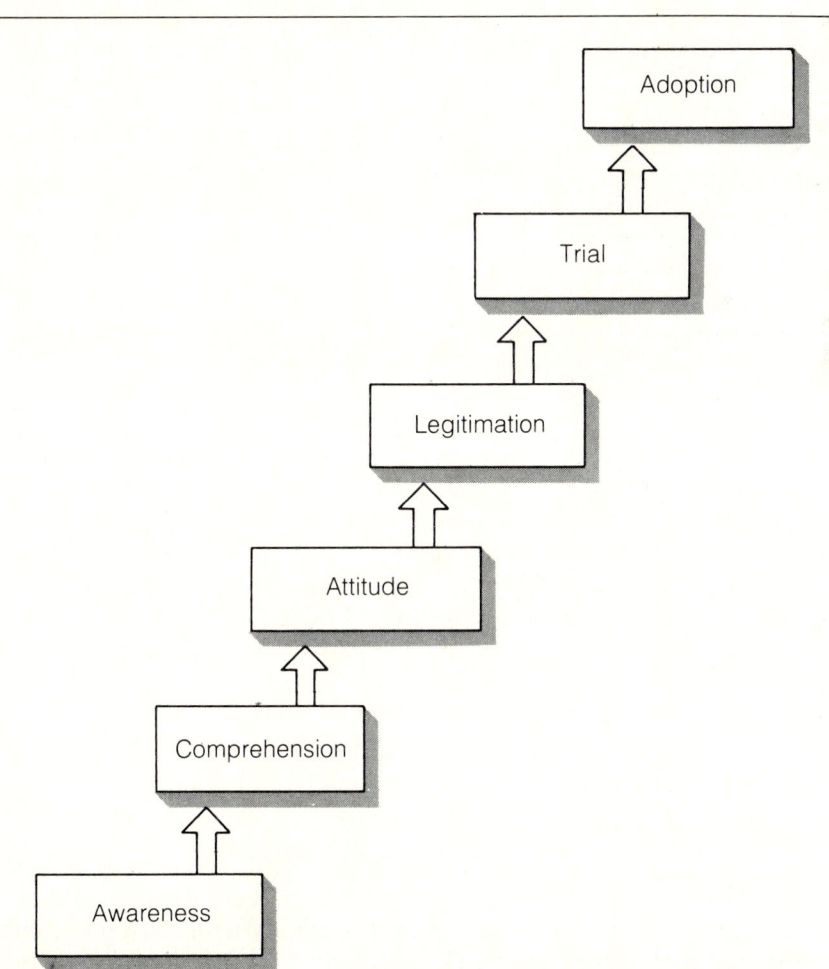

2 *Comprehension* This stage represents the consumer's knowledge and understanding of what the product is and can do.

3 *Attitude* Here, the consumer develops favorable or unfavorable behavioral predispositions toward the product. Termination of the adoption process is likely at this stage if attitudes are not favorable toward the product.

4 *Legitimation* Here, the consumer becomes convinced that the product should be adopted. This stage is predicated upon favorable attitudes toward the innovation, and the consumer may use information already gathered as well as additional information in order to reach a decision.

5 *Trial* If possible, the consumer tests or tries the product to determine its utility. Trial may take place cognitively, that is, whereby the individual vicariously uses the product in a hypothetical situation; or it may be actually used in a limited or total way, depending on the innovation's nature.

6 *Adoption* At this stage, the consumer determines whether or not to use the product in a full-scale way. Continued purchase and/or use of the item fulfills the adoption process.[30]

Thus, adoption is seen to be a sequence of events through which individual consumers pass over a period of time. Some consumers pass through these stages early in a product's life while others may be much later. In addition, the process describes consumers who are actively involved in thinking about and considering a product.

The significance of the adoption process to the marketer is twofold. First, not all consumers pass through the adoption process with the same speed—some move swiftly, while others proceed more slowly. Second, the marketer's communication forms vary in their effectiveness over the different stages in the adoption process. These points can be important in assisting the marketer to develop an effective promotional program. It has been found, for example, that for early stages of the adoption process, the mass media appear to be most effective in creating awareness; thus, the marketer would design awareness- and interest-generating messages to be transmitted by such impersonal sources. At later stages in the adoption process, however, personal sources of information appear to become more important; so the marketer would desire to have effective personal selling and word-of-mouth communications at these points. This indicates then, that as consumers move through the adoption process, the amount of mass-media advertising might be decreased while the amount of personal selling is increased.

The adoption process may not be completed by the individual, which means that the innovation will not be adopted. Several factors that may lead to an incomplete adoption process are listed in Table 11-1. The marketer should take care to see that the marketing problems leading to consumer failure to complete the adoption process are minimized.

The Diffusion Process

In this section, we shall discuss the nature of the process by which innovations spread. The marketer is vitally interested in this because it determines the success or failure of any new product brought to market. The marketer usually desires to secure the largest amount of adoption within the shortest period of time. Whether

TABLE 11-1 POTENTIAL CAUSES OF INCOMPLETED ADOPTION PROCESS

Acceptance Process Stage	Marketing Organization Causes of Incompleted Processes	Consumer Causes of Incompleted Processes
Adoption	Failure to develop new products and improve old products	Replaced by another innovation
Trial	Behavioral response not specified in communications	Alternative equally as good
	Poor distribution system	Innovation not available
Legitimation	Poor source effect of communications	Peer-group pressure against adoption
		Laws regulating use of innovation
Attitude	Communication not persuasive	Complacency
		Suspended judgment
Comprehension	Communication difficult to understand	Selective retention
Awareness	Poorly used or too little communication	Selective exposure
		Selective perception

Source: Gerald Zaltman and Ronald Stiff, "Theories of Diffusion" in Scott Ward and Thomas S. Robertson, eds., Consumer Behavior: Theoretical Sources, © 1973, p. 451. Reprinted by permission of Prentice-Hall, Inc., Englewood Cliffs, N.J.

such an accelerated strategy is chosen (as is the case for most continuous innovations), or one that moves more slowly (as might be taken with discontinuous innovations), the marketer needs to understand the diffusion process so that he can properly manage the spread of the new product or service.[31] Although there are many limitations and weaknesses in much of the diffusion research that has been conducted by scholars, it has helped us understand the communication process for innovations and the social structure within which this occurs.[32]

We should first distinguish the concept of diffusion from that of adoption. As we saw earlier, the adoption process is an *individual* phenomenon relating to the sequence of stages through which an individual passes from first hearing about a product to finally adopting it. The diffusion process, however, refers to a *group* phenomenon, indicating how an innovation spreads among consumers. The diffusion process, of course, necessarily involves the adoption process of many individuals over time.

Perhaps the best marketing-oriented definition of the diffusion process is "the adoption of new products and services over time by consumers within social systems as encouraged by marketing activities."[33] This definition recognizes the various components of the process which are important in the spread of an innovation.

How does diffusion occur? Analysis of fashion life cycles and diffusion provides some insights into the process. Several theories of fashion diffusion have been suggested.[34] First, the theory of upper-class fashion leadership postulates that fashions are initially adopted by the upper class and are then imitated by each succeeding lower class until they have "trickled-down" to the lowest class. The fashion industry has long emphasized elite-oriented fashion, and lesser fashion designers and producers frequently copy the designs of their more-famous counterparts. A second theory proposes that mass production combined with mass communications make new styles and information about new styles available simultaneously to all socioeconomic classes. Fashion diffusion, therefore, has the potential to start at essentially the same time within each class. This mass-market view is sometimes referred to as the horizontal flow or "trickle-across" theory. A third and newer theory of fashion diffusion recognizes that many new fashions have been initiated by subcultural groups such as youths, blue-collar workers, and ethnic minorities such as Indians and blacks. These innovations may range from new ideas (e.g., mini skirts), to customary artifacts of a culture or subculture, to styles resurrected from the past, or even homemade inventions (e.g., tie-died products pioneered by youth which appeared in the 1960s). Whether a fashion is new or customary, the unique subculture style becomes admired and diffuses into the mass population where it is selectively assimilated into the dominant culture. The fourth and most general theory of leadership suggests that nearly all creative or innovative individuals can become leaders of fashion trends if their innovative choices are reasonably in line with the social climate and lifestyles of the times. In this view, fashion leadership is not confined to the upper class, but can emerge by a process in which collective tastes are formed by many people. Styles that most closely represent existing trends in consumers' tastes will slowly gain acceptance as the preferred fashion. Prestigious innovators who select this fashion will help to better define the public's tastes toward what should be the appropriate fashion and to legitimize their choices.

There is evidence to support each of these theories of fashion diffusion. Thus, it is difficult to specify a complete theory of the fashion life cycle. However, an outline of the general principles involved in a theory of consumer behavior geared toward fashions has been offered by one researcher. The following factors are encompassed in that outline:

• New styles enter the beginnings of life cycles from centers of prestige and creativity, including both creative entrepreneurs and fashion conscious consumers.

• Alternative new styles gain public exposure through a cooperative interplay between creative entrepreneurs and fashion conscious consumers who display new alternatives in their social networks and give them social visibility.

• Any new style is most likely to receive substantial acceptance when two conditions are met: initial adoption is by a discernible proportion of fashion conscious consumers, and the new style is consistent with the evolving trend in historical continuity for that class of styles.

• Fashions will diffuse within social networks composed of people having similar social class, prestige, lifestyles, needs, and values. Fashions diffuse across classes and social networks as a result of marketing strategy (communication and pricing), massed availability in all types of retail stores, and social appropriateness to lifestyles in the social networks. These collective forces of the mass market are more powerful than processes of upper-class leadership and social competition between classes for symbols.

- When acceptance of a fashion is substantial, perhaps in one-fourth to one-half of a target market, two forces will jointly determine mass acceptance: the pressures of social conformity, and the likelihood that mass marketing will increasingly feature the style exclusively or provide only minimal range of choice centering on that style.

- Decline and termination begin when two events coincide: social saturation (overuse) of a style is evident and consumers' boredom with the style is apparent, and creative entrepreneurs and fashion conscious consumers begin active experimentation with new ideals of taste that are perceptually different from the established but overused style.

The fashion-conscious or fashion-change-agent sector of the population can be important to the spread of a new fashion. This group is a large and broadly fashion-oriented market segment. Many of the people in the population are interested in or oriented toward fashion monitoring, if not necessarily changing their wardrobes. For example, data consistently show that as much as half the female population and 25 percent of the male population have an active fashion consciousness. This group enjoys monitoring fashion magazines, fashion trends, and new style offerings, and is broadly innovative and communicative.

For a new style to obtain mass endorsement, fashion change agents are important. This group, working across geographical regions and within personal social networks, is significant in the acceptance or rejection of a fashion object.[36]

Now, let's look more closely at the general process of diffusion and what it means for the marketer.

Categories of Adopters Because we know that people will not all adopt an innovation at the same time, we might classify consumers on the basis of time of adoption. In so doing, we will also discover that those who adopt new products at approximately the same time have similar characteristics. Armed with such knowledge, the marketer may thus be able to segment a market by adopter type, and aim strategies, in turn, at each group over time. Five adopter categories have been identified: innovator, early adopter, early majority, late majority, and laggard. Each of these groups' characteristics is summarized below.[37] The percentages that follow represent the proportion of all who adopt an innovation, which may be only a small proportion of the total market.

Innovators (2.5 percent of a market) are the first to adopt new products. They are quite venturesome and are eager to try new ideas. They have more risk capital (both material and social) and can afford to take calculated risks. Innovators are well educated, come from well-established families, and are cosmopolitan, having friends outside the community. Their sources of information also transcend the local community, incorporating other innovators and impersonal and scientific sources. They may belong to state, regional, or national organizations, and are respected for their success by local community members.

Robertson has distilled twenty-one studies of new product diffusion and developed a profile of the innovative consumer. Because the studies span various product categories, sampling populations, research methodologies, and definitions of innovation, the picture they provide of the consumer innovator must be viewed with caution. Nevertheless, Table 11-2 summarizes these characteristics.

Early adopters (13.5 percent of a market) are the second group to adopt an innovation. This group is more socially integrated locally than are innovators, and it has the greatest degree of opinion leadership in most social systems. They are likely to hold positions of leadership within the community and are respected as good sources of information and advice about the innovation. For this reason, they are very important in speeding the diffusion process. They watch the innovators and adopt when the innovation appears successful. They are just ahead of the average individual in innovativeness, so they are able to serve as role-models for others in the market.

Early adopters have less risk capital than do innovators. They are younger than later adopters, higher in social status, and above average in education. Early adopters subscribe to more magazines than later adopters (yet not as many as innovators). They also have been found to have the greatest contact with salespeople.

How important are innovators and early adopters in the success of new products? Quite significant, as General Electric has found in studies of its appliances. One study of a new cordless electric clothes brush, for example, obtained data from warranty cards for the new product and through personal interviews with early buyers. GE found that these early buyers directly influenced other consumers by talking about the product and by having it in their homes.[38]

Moreover, when the early adopters begin buying something new, retailers see the product moving and are likely to advertise it more heavily and feature it prominently in stores. This can enhance the retailer's image as an innovative store by handling "hot" new products.

TABLE 11-2
A PROFILE OF THE CONSUMER INNOVATOR

Findings for the Innovator vs. Noninnovator
Demographic factors
Higher income levels
Often younger
Better educated
Higher occupational status
Social interaction factors
Greater participation in friendship and organizational groups
An opinion leader
Socially mobile
Favorably disposed to innovation
Attitudinal and perceptual factors
More venturesome and perceives less risk in buying new products
Perceives himself as an innovator
Has favorable attitudes toward new products
Communication behavior
Reads more print media
Consumption patterns
Higher usage rate for the innovative product category
Marked willingness to buy new products

Source: Thomas Robertson, *Innovative Behavior and Communications*, Holt, New York, 1971, pp. 100–110.

The *early majority* (34 percent of a market) is the next group to adopt an innovation, and is the most deliberate of all adopter categories. Those in the early majority may consider an innovation for some time before adopting; thus, their adoption period is longer than that of the two previous groups. They adopt an innovation just before the average member of a social system, which puts them in a crucial position to legitimize the new idea for others.

Those in the early majority are slightly above average in age and education, and social and economic status. Although they belong to formal organizations, they are likely to be active members rather than leaders. They rely more heavily on informal sources of information than do earlier adopters. The early majority subscribe to fewer magazines and journals than do previous adopters, but they have considerable contact with salespeople. They are frequently the neighbors and friends of early adopters.

The *late majority* (34 percent of a market) adopts an innovation just after the average consumer in the market place. This group can be described as "skeptical" about new ideas, and may yield only because of economic necessity or increasing social pressures. Those in the late majority are above average in age and below average in education, social status, and income. They belong to few formal organizations and exhibit little opinion leadership with communication patterns oriented primarily toward other late majority members in their neighborhood. There is little use of the mass media (e.g., fewer magazines are taken) but heavy reliance on informal sources of information and influence.

Laggards (16 percent of a market) are the last group to adopt an innovation. They are tradition-bound, with decisions based on what has been done in the past. Laggards are suspicious of innovations and perhaps of those who offer them. The length of the adoption process for this group is quite long; when adoption finally comes, a new innovation has likely superseded the previous innovation.

Laggards have the least education, the lowest social status and income, and are the oldest of any adopter category. They are the most local in orientation, which tends to be their immediate neighborhood, and they communicate mostly with other laggards, who are their main sources of information. Laggards possess almost no opinion leadership, have little participation in formal organizations, and subscribe to few magazines.

Although these categories and descriptions may vary for different products, they do provide the marketer with a helpful framework for managing an innovation's diffusion. One of the most important facets of the work in this regard will be to develop a sound promotional strategy. Clearly, adopter characteristics differ greatly among categories, and this requires that the marketer tailor promotions to appeal to each group over time. Table 11-3 illustrates the kinds of promotional approaches that appear to be most effective for each adopter category.

Factors Influencing the Rate of Diffusion The rate of an innovation's diffusion could range from several weeks to several decades, depending upon consumers' acceptance of the item which, in turn, is determined by how the innovation is perceived by consumers. There appears to have been, over time, a general increase in the rate of adoption of innovations.[39] Thus, a rapidly shortening product life cycle appears to be occurring. This trend has importance to marketers, public policy makers, and consumer researchers because it may represent a significant change in consumption patterns. For example, more and more rapid adoption rates may preclude involved decision processes, so that other purchase approaches may be increasing, such as conformity, imitation, and recommendation. Even the meaningfulness of adopter category distinctions may lose their usefulness as these cycles are decreased.

The marketer, too, is generally interested in understanding how an innovation may be spread more rapidly among a relevant market. There are six product characteristics that seem to influence the rate and extent of adoption of an innovation: (1) relative advantage, (2) compatibility, (3) complexity, (4) trialability, (5) observability, and (6) cost. These characteristics are described below.[40]

Relative advantage is the degree to which an innovation is perceived as superior to preceding products or those with which it will compete. This might be reflected in longer life, easier maintenance, or other measures. Products that have a strong relative advantage will be adopted more rapidly.

Compatibility is the degree to which an innovation is consistent with existing consumer values and past experiences of adopters. Acceptance will be retarded for new products that are not compatible with consumers' norms.

TABLE 11-3 HOW PROMOTION VARIES BY STAGE IN THE DIFFUSION PROCESS

Adopter Category	Promotional Approach
Innovator	Technical or scientific information about the innovation made available in special-interest or professional media and at trade meetings.
	Appeals should stress the excitement of trying something completely new and revolutionary.
	Salespeople should concentrate on people who are relatively young and who have high social status, incomes, and education.
Early adopters	Advertisements should emphasize the prestige of owning the item.
	Testimonials by respected people may be particularly effective.
Early majority	Appeals should concentrate on materials designed for this group's evaluation stage in the adoption process.
	Salespeople should stress that others, especially the relevant opinion leaders, have adopted the innovation.
	Make use of peer social pressure with the "house party" sales technique.
Late majority	Advertising appeals should overcome skepticism by making liberal use of such reassuring terms as: "Guaranteed by Good Housekeeping," "Produced by the makers of . . . ," or "Tested and approved by the . . . Laboratory."
	Salespeople are important and should concentrate on consumers whose income and social status are below average.
	Proper product demonstration is a must when this group is at the trial stage.
Laggards	Best to ignore them, in most instances

Source: Adapted from Gerald Zaltman, *Marketing: Contributions from the Behavioral Sciences,* pp. 51-53 © 1965 by Harcourt Brace Jovanovich, Inc., and reprinted with their permission.

Complexity refers to how difficult the innovation is to understand and use. Diffusion will tend to be slowed for more complex items.

Trialability (or divisibility) is the extent to which an innovation may be tried on a limited basis. Where an item cannot be sampled on a small, less-expensive scale, diffusion is retarded.

Observability (or communicability) refers to the conspicuousness of the innovation. New products that are highly visible in social situations are those that will be communicated most readily to other adopters.

Cost refers to the magnitude of the financial resources required to obtain and operate this innovation. Innovations high in cost would be expected to diffuse more slowly. However, one study indicates that cost does not appear to be significantly correlated with rate of adoption.[41]

The marketing implications of these characteristics are readily apparent. First of all, an innovation should exhibit some clear-cut advantages. In addition, products might be designed so that they could be evaluated on a limited basis (for example, small trial sizes of a new toothpaste). With some products, however, such as automobiles and air conditioners, trial is more difficult. Nevertheless, auto test drives (or in some cases even extended car loans) and free home trials for appliances have been offered. Products should also be designed with minimum complexity and maximum compatibility (these also may make up part of the product's relative advantage). These features should then be stressed in promotional messages to potential adopters. If complexity and noncompatibility are inherent in the innovation, promotion should seek to overcome these limitations (for example, by stressing warranties or product-servicing facilities).

Are There Generalized Innovators? It was concluded earlier that there is a moderate amount of opinion leadership overlap across product categories, with the greatest extent involving related product areas. A similar conclusion can be made with regard to innovators. There is no "superinnovator" who plays this part across a host of products. However, within a product category and perhaps between related product categories some innovative overlap can be expected to occur.[42]

MARKETING IMPLICATIONS OF PERSONAL INFLUENCE

In this section, we shall suggest various marketing strategies that effectively use the process of personal influence. Two cautions are in order, however. First, it should be remembered that opinion leadership is not equally active for all products—some products are very prone to personal influence, while others are not. Second, it may be difficult and expensive to control the process of personal influence.

Kotler and Zaltman suggest that the marketer will want to address several questions when targeting prospects for a new product: (1) the target market's innovative and early adoption propensities, (2) its heavy volume potential, (3) its susceptibility to influence, and (4) the cost of reaching this group. This will require a systematic procedure utilizing information from concept testing, product testing, test marketing, and so forth.[43] If the marketer finds that personal influence is potentially strong for the product, then he may desire to guide the process. There are several strategies which might be adopted: (1) identifying and using opinion leaders directly, (2) creating opinion leaders, (3) simulating opinion leaders, (4) stimulating opinion leadership, and (5) stifling opinion leadership.

Identifying and Using Opinion Leaders Directly

There are two major difficulties in pursuing this strategy. First of all, locating opinion leaders who are influential over a particular product is most complicated. Characteristics of opinion leaders, which were discussed earlier in this chapter, make it clear that they are not easy to isolate. Moreover, for the consumer-goods marketer the task is likely to be hard because of the large number of consumers. In order to identify them, the marketer would need to conduct difficult and expensive research on his own product. Second, there is evidence that in some cases opinion leaders may not be reached by certain advertising media any more effectively than the average consumer in a market.[44] Thus, direct appeal to personal influence may not always be the most effective approach.

If the direct approach is decided upon, however, the first step is to identify opinion leaders. There are several ways in which this may be done. One set of techniques involves measuring the degree of opinion leadership among consumers. Figure 11-5 presents a questionnaire that has been effectively used to ascertain the degree of consumers' opinion leadership through survey research. In this instance, individuals would evaluate themselves on this characteristic.

Another approach to measuring opinion leadership involves the *sociometric* technique, which consists of asking group members to whom they go for advice and information about an idea. Finally, *key informants* in a group may be asked to designate the opinion leaders.

One of the best ways to identify those who may be influential for a company's product is to examine purchase records. For instance, many products today use a warranty card return system as in the General Electric clothes brush example cited earlier. With this approach, the marketer could identify specific individuals who are early adopters of the product and the characteristics of these buyers. Of course, one disadvantage of relying exclusively on this approach is that not all buyers return these cards.

Study of past purchases may indicate which consumers are most likely to adopt new products. For example, by knowing that the most likely adopter of new telephone-system services, such as the videophone, would occur among those who had previously bought such equipment as pushbutton phones, extension phones, and color phones, the telephone company might assess available records to determine the households in the service area which would have the greatest likelihood of adopting the new equipment.

It is also significant to realize that early product triers also tend to be heavy users.[45] Thus, the marketer of a new product might engage in a two-step consumer identification program. First, heavy users of products within the same category as the to-be-introduced item should be characterized in terms of relevant background and behavioral variables, so that a marketing program can be developed which appeals to these persons. Second, once the product is introduced, description of the earliest triers should be obtained quickly so that the marketer may develop inducements for consumers with similar backgrounds.

Names and addresses of potential opinion leaders might be gathered not only from purchase records, but also from sponsorship of consumer contests, use of reader-service cards in magazines, and similar activities. To illustrate, Campbell Soup Company received over 94,000 entries in a recent "Creative Cooking Contest" in which original recipes were submitted. Once names of potential opinion leaders have been secured, the marketer is in a position to utilize their influence effectively. For example, he can promote directly to them. They may be reached through direct-mail advertising, if the cost is not prohibitive. They can also be provided with inside information about new products so that they are in a strategic position to pass along this information to others.

One approach that may work well is to obtain mailing lists containing names of people who have a high level of interest in a particular product category. In other words, identify the "enthusiast" for this product. These people are quite likely to be heavy readers of magazines relating to the product. For instance, consider the automobile buff and the VCR enthusiast.

FIGURE 11-5

Opinion leadership scale. (*Source:* Charles W. King and John O. Summers, "Overlap of Opinion Leadership Across Consumer Product Categories," *Journal of Marketing,* **7:**45, February 1970, published by the American Marketing Association.)

1. In general, do you like to talk about _____ with your friends?

    Yes _____   No _____

2. Would you say *you give very little information, an average amount of information,* or *a great deal of information* about _____ to your friends?

    You give very little information .... _____
    You give an average amount of information .... _____
    You give a great deal of information .... _____

3. During the *past six months*, have *you told anyone* about some _____?

    Yes _____   No _____

4. Compared with your circle of friends, are you *less likely, about as likely,* or *more likely* to be asked for advice about _____?

    Less likely to be asked .... _____
    About as likely to be asked .... _____
    More likely to be asked .... _____

5. If you and your friends were to discuss _____, what part would you be most likely to play? Would you *mainly listen* to your friends' ideas or would *you try to convince them* of your ideas?

    You mainly listen to your friends' ideas .... _____
    You try to convince them of your ideas .... _____

6. Which of these happens more often? Do *you tell your* friends about some _____, or do *they tell you* about some _____?

    You tell them about _____ _____
    They tell you about some _____ _____

7. Do you have the feeling that you are generally regarded by your friends and neighbors as a good source of advice about _____?

    Yes _____   No _____

Readers of the automotive enthusiast press—such as *Road & Track, Car and Driver,* and *Motor Trend*—tend to be the "hardcore car buffs," according to an executive at Chevrolet's advertising agency. "They're the guys who live, breathe, and sleep cars." These media reach the core driver group which really enjoys cars, and they are also read with a certain sense of intensity by the car buff. Manufacturers attempt to establish credibility with this segment, particularly if the new product is dramatically different. Therefore, the enthusiast press is a very important part of any car advertising campaign. One of the basics of automotive advertising is keeping the person who's informed, informed. They consider themselves automotive experts, and people call on them for advice. For instance, 39 percent of *Road & Track's* readers are asked about cars one or more times a week, and one of every two readers is considering the purchase of a new car in the upcoming year. Thus, even if the enthusiast isn't a potential buyer for a new car immediately, he can talk it up and spread information around via word-of-mouth. Therefore, it is good to have your name and message before them because of this amplifying effect in which buffs have an influence beyond their own purchases.[46]

A survey of *Video* readers indicates that a similar pattern holds true in the video product category. Many of the new technology enthusiasts have a tendency to be willing to spend some of their money to experiment with practically every video-related item that comes along, from videocassette recorders, to electronic games, to home earth stations. For instance, among the readers surveyed,

- 78 percent own a VCR
- 28 percent own two or more VCRs
- 34 percent plan to purchase a second VCR within a year
- 2 percent own an earth station
- 9 percent plan to buy an earth station
- 46 percent own an electronic game played on their home screen
- 9 percent plan to buy an electronic game within a year

Thus, if an individual owns a VCR, a related video product may be next in his or her purchase pattern. Consequently, marketers of such items would be able to reach an important segment of this market through subscriber mailing lists or media aimed at this group.[47]

Purchasing habits might also be closely monitored so that trends and adoption patterns among opinion leaders are readily spotted. For example, Hollywood Vassarette has used this approach to predict fashion trends for women's intimate apparel.[48]

This group could also be provided with free samples (if it were an inexpensive product), discounts off the price of new products, or loan of the item (in the case of expensive durables). At one time, Chrysler Corporation offered one of its luxury automobile models for a trial period to professionals such as doctors and lawyers. Also Lincoln Continental dealers in one city recruited a select group of opinion leaders to drive the car at a premiere showing of the new model.[49]

Another approach that has been successfully used is to have opinion leaders model or sell the product. For example, many clothing stores have established "fashion advisory boards" on which high school or college opinion leaders are placed. These fashion leaders may act as retail salespeople for the store or simply model the store's newest fashions for customers. These fashion board members may also appear in store advertising, which should generate additional opinion leadership, especially among the youth market.

Creating Opinion Leaders

When opinion leaders cannot be easily identified or used, it may be possible to "create" them. Such an approach is frequently attempted by aluminum siding and swimming pool manufacturers. Companies will typically select homeowners (especially those with central locations in their neighborhoods) and induce them to buy the product at a very low price if they will then demonstrate the product to others. The homeowner opinion leader is, in effect, being created by the company.

Another successful use of this technique was reported in the introduction of a new pop record. The task was to transform an unknown song recorded by an unknown singer into a hit. The initial step was to seek out social leaders among the relevant buying public—high school students. Names of class presidents, class secretaries, sports captains, and cheerleaders selected from geographically diverse high schools were obtained. Although these were social leaders, prior to the project these students would not likely have been classified as opinion leaders for records because of their low ownership of this item. Next, the students were contacted by mail and invited to join a select panel to assist a manufacturer in evaluating new records. They were to receive free records and were encouraged to discuss their choices with friends.

This inexpensive experiment provided very successful results. Several records reached the top ten charts in the trial cities, while failing to make the top ten selections in any other cities. Thus, without contacting any radio stations or record stores, records were pulled through the channels of distribution and made into hits.[50]

A number of companies have attempted to create opinion leadership by getting the product into the hands of people who have a great deal of public contact or exposure. Ford Motor Company has successfully utilized this approach. For example, when the Mustang was introduced, college newspaper editors, disc jockeys, and airline stewardesses were loaned Mustangs, largely on the presumption that they were influentials with regard to automobiles. Again, when the Pinto was launched, Ford placed the new car with numerous marketing professors and their classes across the country for the purpose of research projects to be conducted for Ford. This also tended to foster opinion leadership.

Numerous other examples could be cited, as indicated by the following:

> During one year's model introduction, Chrysler Corporation attempted to generate word-of-mouth advertising by rewarding 5000 cabdrivers in sixty-seven cities $5 if they asked "mystery" riders whether they had seen the new Plymouth.[51]

> Some restaurants and bars provide cabdrivers and bellhops with meals and drinks at cost if they refer travelers to their establishments.[52]

Earl "Madman" Muntz, the TV tycoon, once hired 400 disc jockeys around the country to plug Muntz television sets.[53]

Adidas pays pro tennis players to wear its tennis shoes, and even outfits entire teams in other professional sports for free.[54]

Jewelry companies often select influential fraternity/sorority representatives to sell the companies' wares to members.

Party-plan selling systems such as Tupperware and Mary Kay Cosmetics rely on opinion leader influence (usually exhibited by the neighbor hosting the party) for much of their effectiveness.

Simulating Opinion Leadership

In this approach, personal influence is simulated by various means, especially advertising. Advertisers frequently simulate opinion leadership by approximating the position of the disinterested and noncommercial speaker who would engage in word-of-mouth communication. By taking such a position, the need for personal influence may be replaced to a certain extent by advertising.

There are several ways in which the marketer can simulate opinion leadership. One approach is that taken by many detergents, foods, laxatives, and other products in which a person (the simulated opinion leader) tells another person about the virtues of the sponsored item. Visual communication also is frequently used in commercials simulating opinion leadership, whereby one shopper watches to see what another shopper (the opinion leader) purchases, and then is seen to buy the same item based on this visual recommendation. Commercials of the sort in which a friend recommends the product to another often use nonprofessionals to enhance the believability and a script which is written in authentic consumer language based on focus-group research.

Often, the advertiser simulates personal influence by using a *testimonial* approach in which the user of the product conveys a favorable experience or opinion about the item. One testimonial approach uses typical people in a seemingly unsolicited recommendation for the product. Commercials featuring man-on-the-street recommendations, hidden camera interviews, and similar techniques may serve to influence viewers through a simulation of opinion leadership. Other testimonials often feature a famous actor or athlete as the endorser, as illustrated in Figure 11-6. For instance, estimates are that from one-third to three-fifths of prime-time television commercials use celebrity endorsements.[55] In total, however, celebrity usage accounts for less than 10 percent of all commercials aired in both program and station breaks.[56]

What effectiveness do celebrity endorsers have? Celebrities will be most effective when there is a close match of personalities with products and advertising copy. A review of hundreds of celebrity commercials over a 12-year period indicates that only 41 percent obtained above-average scores in either brand awareness or attitude shift tests, and only 19 percent were above-average in both categories.[57] It appears that women, athletes, and veteran actors scored best, while younger dramatic actors, comedians, and nonentertainment personalities scored poorly. Thus, the effectiveness varies depending on the situation. For instance, a laboratory experiment of print advertising indicated that for the products of costume jewelry, vacuum cleaners, and cookies the best endorsers were celebrities, experts, and typical consumers, respectively. Furthermore, these particular product-endorser combinations resulted in better overall attitude toward the product, greater intent to purchase the advertised product, and more credibility for the endorser. However, regardless of the type of product, the celebrity endorser was most effective in sustaining brand-name recall and recall of the advertisement.[58] Thus, if the advertiser most desires brand-name and advertisement recall, then a celebrity endorser is appropriate. If, on the other hand, believability of the endorsement, overall attitude toward the advertised product, and initial intent to purchase the advertised product are desired, celebrities may be best when the product purchase involves psychological or social risk. When the product involves financial, performance, and/or physical risk, the advertiser might utilize an expert endorser. For products with little inherent risk, a typical-consumer endorser should be chosen.

Marketers who use celebrities in their advertising must be careful to follow certain regulations. Federal Trade Commission (FTC) guidelines require, for instance, that celebrity or expert endorsers must actually use the product if the advertisements represent that they do, and that the copy must represent the endorser's honest view of the product, with product claims substantiated.[59]

Sometimes a company will use a celebrity look-alike in order to achieve the

FIGURE 11-6

Advertisement for Paul Masson wines. (Courtesy of Paul Masson Vineyards.)

intended effect. At least one company specializes in providing look-alikes for famous people such as U.S. Presidents, movie stars, and so forth. For example, a recent Sony television commercial for its videotape recorder used an Albert Einstein look-alike discussing the "relative" merits of the machine. Such a technique may be very effective at generating word-of-mouth influence.

Because of the potential problems of using celebrities (e.g., cost, death, scandal, etc.), companies often create characters to star in their ads, with some achieving highly effective results.[60] Maytag's Old Lonely, Charmin's Mr. Whipple, Palmolive's Madge the Manicurist, Folger's Mrs. Olson, and even animated characters such as Pillsbury's Doughboy and Kellogg's Tony the Tiger provide instant identification for the companies' products and set them apart from the competition. Maytag's Old Lonely commercials regularly score twice as high as other appliance commercials in consumer awareness surveys. Mr. Whipple, often cited in surveys as one of the most obnoxious characters in TV ads, nevertheless, has made Charmin the top-selling toilet paper. Sometimes, it may be better to be noticed and disliked than not to be noticed at all.[61]

The success of the testimonial approach depends on several things, therefore. First, the customer must believe that the speaker is talking to the interviewer spontaneously and disinterestedly (that is, the speaker is not simply being paid to say it). Second, the speaker needs a believable relationship to the product. Third, the language which is used must sound authentic. In any event, it has been claimed that the use of a testimonial can increase advertising recall by 18 percent, while a celebrity's testimonial will boost it 75 percent.[62]

A final approach to simulating opinion leadership is to use a company's chief executive as the spokesperson for the product or service. Examples abound in the media of this practice. Consider the following recent "stars:" Frank Borman (Eastern Airlines), Lee Iacocca (Chrysler), Frank Perdue (Perdue Farms Chicken), Victor Kiam (Remington Products), Jimmy Dean (Jimmy Dean Meat Co.), and Frank Sellinger (Schlitz). Until recently, about the only heads of companies appearing on TV were local entrepreneurs slotted into late-night shows to push their furniture or appliance stores, or car dealerships. However, more major companies are featuring bosses as pitchmen because the public tends to believe them. They can also be good motivators of the sales force, distributors, and employees around the country. Although credibility can be a major plus, the drawback is that the public may also perceive the company to be in bad financial or other shape. The ads may be seen as spreading unfavorable personal influence, because many corporations put their chief executives on the air when they are fighting an image problem. As the famous advertiser David Ogilvy advised, "Only in the gravest cases should you show the clients' faces."[63]

Stimulating Opinion Leadership

This strategy is designed to get people to talk about the product and thereby exert personal influence. One way this may be encouraged is by using a *teaser* promotional campaign. Such a technique provides only enough information about the new item to pique the customer's curiosity.

A second advertising strategy is to develop such highly entertaining or emotional campaigns that consumers engage in discussions about the product and its advertising. The "Mean Joe Greene" commercial for Coca-Cola was an outstanding success in this regard. Volkswagen and Benson & Hedges have also been very successful in such an approach. Some advertisers are even successful in having their slogans become adopted as part of the everyday language, such as Alka-Seltzer's "I can't believe I ate the whole thing," Avis's "We try harder," Bic's "Flick your Bic," and Miller's "It's Miller Time."

Other advertising strategies encourage consumers to talk about the product. For example, Firestone's ads prompt the reader to "Ask a friend about Firestone." Minolta camera advertisements use the same approach. These and similar techniques attempt to instigate personal influence through having users disseminate product information and potential users request product information. Obviously, the marketer would desire only favorable word-of-mouth communications to be imparted about the product. This suggests that a monitoring system is needed to find out what present and potential customers are saying about the product and to help in the formulation of advertising strategies designed to react to word-of-mouth communication.

Two novel approaches which help the product to be talked about are those taken by Hiram Walker's "C.C." and Philip Morris' "Merit."

> People like treasure hunts, even if the prize is only a case of liquor. That helps to account for the long-running (more than 14 years) success of Hiram Walker Inc.'s hide-a-case pitch for Canadian Club whiskey. Twenty-two cases have been stashed so far, in places ranging from Mount Kilimanjaro, Loch Ness, and the North Pole, to Death Valley, the Superstition Mountains, and Manhattan. Hiram Walker advertises in full-page and double-page spreads in about 30 magazines when a "hide" is made. The ads show the liquor being stashed, detail the clues, and sometimes chronicle the adventures of the finders.[64]

> Philip Morris has found a clever way to get its Merit cigarette brand to be talked about. It is sponsoring "The Merit Report," a public-opinion survey in which the findings of the polls or topics ranging from abortion, energy, and military preparedness are expected to be quoted on radio and TV news shows and in newspapers and magazines. The goal is to achieve greater publicity and recognition for Merit cigarettes.[65]

A related novel way to stimulate personal influence is to incorporate other activities around the product. This approach has worked very successfully for Wham-O Manufacturing Co., for example, which has built a sport around the Frisbee in order to keep sales of the toy at a high level.

> Athletes from across the country compete in the Rose Bowl in Pasadena, California in a world championship meet, vying for titles in various Frisbee throwing events. Wham-O has developed this into an organized sport, offering tavel expenses for players, prize money, and opportunities for some winners to work for the company. It publishes a Frisbee magazine, and is helping schools teach Frisbee in physical education classes. The Frisbee might have gone the way of all fads, except that Wham-O found new uses for it, such as Frisbee games patterned after golf, tennis, and soccer.[66]

A final strategy is for the marketer to use in-store demonstrations and displays at favorable locations (such as in airport terminals) to secure consumer contact with the product. Similarly, sweepstakes are an excellent way to build interest and get customers talking about products or services. All of these approaches may be able to stimulate opinion leadership.

Stifling Opinion Leadership

There may be times when the marketer desires to stifle personal influence, rather than encourage it. Generally negative personal influence may be the result of rumor, a poor product, or misunderstandings among consumers.

One condition under which unfavorable personal influence should be retarded exists when a damaging rumor surfaces about the company or its product. Rumors abound in our society; they are part of people's fascination with the grotesque. For example, the following unfounded business rumors have circulated among the public recently:[67]

- McDonald's adds worms to hamburger meat.
- R. J. Reynolds Tobacco owns marijuana fields in Mexico.
- False teeth dissolve if left overnight in a glass of Coca-Cola.
- General Foods' Pop Rocks Crackling Candy makes your stomach explode.
- Wearing Jockey shorts makes men sterile.
- Procter & Gamble, whose century-old trademark is a man in the moon, is owned by the Rev. Sun Myung Moon's Unification Church. Others have claimed that the trademark is satanical.

Often such rumors run to the macabre, as illustrated in the case of K mart and Bubble Yum bubble gum.

> Recently, as the story goes, a woman shopper at a Detroit K mart store tried on a coat. When she put her arm through the sleeve she felt a stinging sensation, like a pin prick. She ignored it and went home, whereupon her arm began to swell so badly that she was rushed to the hospital, and her arm was amputated. The cause was said to be that a poisonous snake had laid its eggs in a carton of Taiwan-made coats; they hatched inside the coat the woman tried on, and one of the baby snakes bit her. This rumor became the talk of Detroit although no one could produce a victim.[68]

> Bubble Yum, produced by Life Savers, Inc., was the hottest product to hit the chewing gum industry since sugarless gum. Suddenly rumors swept among kids from Los Angeles to New York that the gum caused cancer and/or had spider eggs in it. While sales plummeted, the company hired private detectives to investigate the origins of the rumor and placed full-page ads in thirty newspapers stating, "Someone Is Telling Your Kids Very Bad Lies about a Very Good Gum."[69]

In unfortunate cases such as these, the marketer must take immediate action to stop negative word-of-mouth communication, and must build up a positive image. However, the traditional theoretical and intuitive strategy of directly refuting a rumor appears to be rather ineffective. Instead, information-processing strategies that attempt to influence the way a rumor is stored and retrieved by consumers produce much more favorable results.[70]

When the product is obviously inferior, a campaign to slow personal influence may also be used. For instance, the marketing strategy for a bad movie typically calls for mass advertising, and getting into and out of town quickly before negative word-of-mouth has a chance to spread. A new practice of opening movies in as many as 1000 theaters at once allows the money to roll in before the bad word gets out.[71] An example of the contrasting case is shown by several recent popular movies which involved tasteful ad campaigns, a limited-release pattern permitting good word-of-mouth communication to grow, then saturation bookings timed to coincide with expected Academy Award nominations.[72]

A final factor to be mentioned requiring slowing of personal influence is the result of consumer misunderstandings which could lead to poor word-of-mouth if not corrected. For example, consumers may be operating the product incorrectly, leading to malfunctions. Perhaps the item needs to be redesigned or instruction manuals rewritten to make them clearer. When the product is radically new, such problems are very likely to exist. In these cases demonstrations may be called for in stores and more explicit commercials showing the product in use. Once again the necessity of a system to monitor personal influence and word-of-mouth communication—both good and bad—is underscored.

SUMMARY

In this chapter, we have examined the concept of personal influence and its role in gaining acceptance of innovations. First, we described the way in which personal influence operates and found it to be a significant factor in new product adoption. We next discussed three models of communication and influence flow—the one-step, two-step, and multistep processes—and found the latter conceptualization to have greater validity.

The process of opinion leadership in marketing was discussed by describing the characteristics of those who are marketing opinion leaders and citing the nature of the process. We determined that moderate marketing-opinion leadership overlap exists; that opinion leadership is situational; and that influencers as well as influencees have strong motivations to engage in word-of-mouth communication.

The adoption and diffusion processes were described and their significance for the marketer cited. The adoption process was seen to be an individual phenomenon—the stages through which an individual passes over a period of time in adopting a product. The innovation diffusion process, on the other hand, is a group phenomenon—it describes the categories of adopters who accept an innovation over a period of time. Both processes were related directly to the marketer through promotion strategy implications.

Finally, several marketing strategies were suggested to utilize the process of personal influence. The marketer may desire to identify and use opinion leaders directly, create opinion leaders, simulate opinion leadership, stimulate opinion leadership, and/or stifle opinion leadership.

DISCUSSION TOPICS

1 Describe the nature of personal influence. Why is it important to the marketer?

2 Describe the three models of communication discussed in the text. Which appears to be the most complete model of communication and influence?

3 Who are marketing opinion leaders? How do they differ from those they influence?

4 Think of a product or service about which you communicated by word-of-mouth recently. Were you the influencer or influencee? Which of the reasons for opinion leadership discussed in the text apply to this communication situation?

5 Locate several examples of new products (you might look in *Advertising Age, Business Week,* etc.). How would you classify each of these innovations in terms of their "newness"?

6 Pick one of the products discovered from question 5 and describe how you would market the item.

7 How might promotion differ as consumers move through the adoption process?

8 Describe the adopter categories.

9 Categorize your friends according to their position among the adopter categories. Which tend to be innovators, opinion leaders, laggards?

10 Suggest a plan for using the process of personal influence in the following marketing situations:
- **a** a campus clothing store
- **b** a new food product
- **c** a new, sophisticated stereophonic receiver
- **d** a new sports car
- **e** a new novel

NOTES

[1] William L. Bulkeley, "Woodstove Maker Has Hot Love Affair with Its Customers," *The Wall Street Journal,* September 9, 1981, pp. 1, 19.

[2] "Marketing," *The Wall Street Journal,* October 22, 1981, p. 29.

[3] Thomas S. Robertson, *Innovative Behavior and Communication,* Holt, New York, 1971, p. 170.

[4] Deborah Sue Yeager, "Markdown Mecca," *The Wall Street Journal,* July 6, 1976, p. 1.

[5] Ernest Dichter, "How Word-of-Mouth Advertising Works," *Harvard Business Review,* 44:147, November–December 1966.

[6] George Katona and Eva Mueller, "A Study of Purchasing Decisions," in Lincoln H. Clark (ed.), *Consumer Behavior: The Dynamics of Consumer Reaction,* New York University Press, New York, 1955, pp. 30–87.

[7] John R. Kerr and Bruce Weale, "Collegiate Clothing Purchasing Patterns and Fashion Adoption Behavior," *Southern Journal of Business,* 5:126–133, July 1970.

[8] "Desperation in Hollywood: Actor Jack Lemmon's View," *U.S. News & World Report,* August 22, 1977, p. 44.

[9] Dale M. Elsner, "The Story in Brief is Men's Underwear, and It's Full of Holes," *The Wall Street Journal,* June 3, 1975, p. 1.

[10] Ralph Schoenstein, "It Was Just a Joke, Folks," *TV Guide,* May 8, 1974, pp. 6–7.

[11] Johan Arndt, "Role of Product-Related Conversations in the Diffusion of a New Product," *Journal of Marketing Research,* 4:291–295, August 1967.

[12] Johan Arndt, *Word of Mouth Advertising: Review of the Literature,* Advertising Research Foundation, New York, 1967, p. 25.

[13] James H. Myers and William H. Reynolds, *Consumer Behavior and Marketing Management,* Houghton Mifflin, Boston, 1967, pp. 302–303.

[14] Robertson, *Innovative Behavior,* pp. 126–127.

[15] Robertson, *Innovative Behavior,* p. 175.

[16] Myers and Reynolds, *Consumer Behavior,* p. 306.

[17] Everett M. Rogers, *Diffusion of Innovations,* Free Press, New York, 1962, p. 241.

[18] John O. Summers, "The Identity of Women's Clothing Fashion Opinion Leaders," *Journal of Marketing Research,* 7:178–185, May 1970; and Fred D. Reynolds and William R. Darden, "Mutually Adaptive Effects of Interpersonal Communication," *Journal of Marketing Research,* 8:449–454, November 1971.

[19] Charles W. King, "Fashion Adoption: A Rebuttal to the Trickle Down Theory," in Stephen A. Greyser (ed.), *Toward Scientific Marketing,* American Marketing Association, Chicago, 1964, pp. 108–125.
[20] Charles W. King and John O. Summers, "Overlap of Opinion Leadership Across Consumer Product Categories," *Journal of Marketing Research,* 7:43–50, February 1970.
[21] David B. Montgomery and Alvin J. Silk, "Patterns of Overlap in Opinion Leadership and Interest for Selected Categories of Purchasing Activity," in Philip R. McDonald (ed.), *Marketing Involvement in Society and the Economy,* American Marketing Association, Chicago, 1969, pp. 377–386.
[22] Elihu Katz, "The Two-Step Flow of Communication: An Up-to-Date Report on an Hypothesis," *Public Opinion Quarterly,* 21:73, Spring 1957.
[23] Dichter, "How Word-of-Mouth Advertising Works," pp. 148–152.
[24] Robertson, *Innovative Behavior,* pp. 191–209.
[25] Federal Trade Commission, "Permissible Period of Time During Which New Product May Be Described as New," *Advisory Opinion Digest,* no. 120, p. 1, April 15, 1967.
[26] Federal Trade Commission, "Permissible Period."
[27] William Lazer and William E. Bell, "The Communications Process and Innovation," *Journal of Advertising Research,* 6:4, September 1966.
[28] Gerald Zaltman and Ronald Stiff, "Theories of Diffusion," in Scott Ward and Thomas S. Robertson (eds.), *Consumer Behavior: Theoretical Sources,* Prentice-Hall, Englewood Cliffs, NJ, 1972, p. 426.
[29] Thomas S. Robertson, "The Process of Innovation and the Diffusion of Innovation," *Journal of Marketing,* 31:15–16, January 1967.
[30] Robertson, *Innovative Behavior,* pp. 76–77.
[31] Peter C. Wilton and Edgar A. Pessemier, "Forecasting the Ultimate Acceptance of an Innovation: The Effects of Information," *Journal of Consumer Research,* 8:162–171, September, 1981.
[32] Everett M. Rogers, "New Product Adoption and Diffusion," *Journal of Consumer Research,* 2:290–301, March 1976; and Vijay Mahajan and Eitam Muller, "Innovation Diffusion and New Product Growth Models in Marketing," *Journal of Marketing,* 43:55–68, Fall 1979.
[33] Robertson, *Innovative Behavior,* p. 32.
[34] George B. Sproles, "Analyzing Fashion Life Cycles—Principles and Perspectives," *Journal of Marketing,* 45:116–124, Fall 1981.
[35] Sproles, "Analyzing Fashion," pp. 121–122.
[36] Charles W. King and Lawrence J. Ring, "The Dynamics of Style and Taste Adoption and Diffusion: Contributions from Fashion Theory," in Jerry C. Olson (ed.), *Advances in Consumer Research: Volume 7,* Association for Consumer Research, Ann Arbor, MI, 1980, pp. 13–16.
[37] See Rogers, *Diffusion of Innovations,* pp. 168–171; *The Adoption of New Products: Process and Influence,* Foundation for Research on Human Behavior, Ann Arbor, MI, 1959, pp. 1–8; and Gerald Zaltman, *Marketing: Contributions from the Behavioral Sciences,* Harcourt, Brace & World, New York, 1965, pp. 45–51.
[38] "Early Adopters' an Aid in New Product Success, GE Finds," *Marketing Insights,* April 24, 1967, p. 14.
[39] Richard W. Olshavsky, "Time and the Rate of Adoption of Innovations," *Journal of Consumer Research,* 6:425–428, March 1980.
[40] Everett M. Rogers and F. Floyd Shoemaker, *Communication of Innovations,* Free Press, New York, 1971, pp. 137–157; and Gerald Zaltman and Melanie Wallendorf, *Consumer Behavior: Basic Findings and Management Implications,* John Wiley & Sons, New York, 1979, p. 470.
[41] Olshavsky, "Time and Rate of Adoption."
[42] Thomas S. Robertson and James H. Myers, "Personality Correlates of Opinion Leadership and Innovative Buying Behavior," *Journal of Marketing Research,* 6:164–168, May 1969; Robertson, *Innovative Behavior,* pp. 110–112; and James W. Taylor, "A Striking Characteristic of Innovators," *Journal of Marketing Research,* 14:104–107, February 1977.
[43] Philip Kotler and Gerald Zaltman, "Targeting Prospects for a New Product," *Journal of Advertising Research,* 16:7–18, February 1976.
[44] Douglas J. Tigert and Stephen J. Arnold, *Profiling Self-Designated Opinion Leaders and Self-Designated Innovators Through Life Style Research,* University of Toronto School of Business, Toronto, June 1971, pp. 28–29.
[45] Fred W. Morgan, Jr., "Are Early Triers Heavy Users?" *Journal of Business,* 52:429–434, 1979.
[46] Stuart Elliot, "How to Reach the Automobile Buff," *Advertising Age,* June 22, 1981, pp. S-16–S-18.
[47] Maurine Christopher, "VCR Owners Fair Game for Other New Items," *Advertising Age,* August 24, 1981, p. 56.
[48] James F. Engel, David T. Kollat, and Roger D. Blackwell, *Consumer Behavior,* 2d ed., Holt, New York, 1973, p. 429.
[49] Myers and Reynolds, *Consumer Behavior,* p. 309.
[50] Joseph R. Mancuso, "Why Not Create Opinion Leaders for New Product Introductions?" *Journal of Marketing,* 33:20–25, July 1969.
[51] *The Wall Street Journal,* September 27, 1962, p. 5.
[52] Engel, Kollat, and Blackwell, *Consumer Behavior,* p. 430.
[53] "Would You Buy a Car from this Man?" *The Providence Sunday Journal,* December 21, 1975, p. F-10.

[54] Frederick C. Klein, "Foot Race: Sneaker Makers are Set to Pursue the Athletes at Summer Olympics," *The Wall Street Journal,* April 23, 1976, p. 20.

[55] John C. Mowen, Stephen W. Brown, and Meg Schulman, "Theoretical and Empirical Extensions of Endorser Effectiveness," in Neil Beckwith, et al. (eds.), *1979 Educators' Conference Proceedings,* American Marketing Association, Chicago, 1979, pp. 258–262; Jack Kaikati, "The Current Boom in Celebrity Advertising," in John H. Summey and Ronald D. Taylor (eds.), *Evolving Marketing Thought for 1980,* Southern Marketing Association, Carbondale, IL, 1980, pp. 68–70; and Arthur J. Bragg, "Celebrities in Selling," *Sales and Marketing Management,* February 4, 1980, pp. 30–36.

[56] James P. Forkan, "Product Matchup Key to Effective Star Presenters," *Advertising Age,* October 6, 1980, p. 42.

[57] Forkan, "Product Matchup."

[58] Hershey H. Friedman and Linda Friedman, "Endorser Effectiveness by Product Type," *Journal of Advertising Research,* 19:63–71, October 1979.

[59] Dorothy Cohen, "FTC Issues Guidelines on Endorsements, Testimonials," *Marketing News,* March 21, 1980, p. 3.

[60] Bourne Morris, "Will a Personality Sell a Product Better? Pros and Cons," *Advertising Age,* February 5, 1975, pp. 43–44; and Bill Abrams, "When Ads Feature Celebrities, Advertisers Cross Their Fingers," *The Wall Street Journal,* December 4, 1980, p. 25.

[61] Lawrence Ingrassia, "As Mr. Whipple Shows, Ad Stars Can Bring Long-Term Sales Gain," *The Wall Street Journal,* February 12, 1981, p. 27.

[62] "Ads Should Focus on Products, Not Themselves," *Marketing News,* August 12, 1977.

[63] Ann M. Morrison, "The Boss as Pitchman," *Fortune,* August 25, 1980, pp. 66–73.

[64] Cotten Timberlake, "How Hidden Cases of Booze Keep Hiram Walker Happy," *The Wall Street Journal,* July 23, 1981, p. 25.

[65] Janet Guyon, "To Tout Merit, Philip Morris Creates News," *The Wall Street Journal,* August 21, 1981, p. 19.

[66] Bruce Koon, "How to Keep Sales of a Toy Up: Build a Sport Around It," *The Wall Street Journal,* August 17, 1979, pp. 1, 29.

[67] Jim Montgomery, "Rumor-Plagued Firms Use Various Strategies to Keep Damage Low," *The Wall Street Journal,* February 6, 1979, pp. 1, 22; and Michael Waldholz, "Of Gingerbread Men With Pigtails, Rumor Problems at Entenmann's," *The Wall Street Journal,* October 1, 1980, p. 31.

[68] Charles W. Stevens, "K mart Has a Little Trouble Killing Those Phantom Snakes from Asia," *The Wall Street Journal,* October 20, 1981, p. 25.

[69] John E. Cooney, "Bubble Gum Maker Wants to Know How the Rumors Started," *The Wall Street Journal,* March 24, 1977, p. 1.

[70] Alice M. Tybout, Bobby J. Calder, and Brian Sternthal, "Using Information Processing Theory to Design Marketing Strategies," *Journal of Marketing Research,* 18:73–79, February 1981.

[71] "Hollywood's Hottest Summer," *Time,* August 21, 1978, p. 39.

[72] "Kubrick's Grandest Gamble," *Time,* December 15, 1975, p. 72.

CASES FOR PART THREE

CASE 3-1
THE DISPOSABLE SHAVER[1]

The year 1903 marked the introduction of the first safety razor by an ambitious inventor named King C. Gillette. Since that time, men have become accustomed to continual and extensively advertised advances in shaving technology from The Gillette Company, which spends over $20 million a year on shaving research and development. Probably no company in the United States has so thoroughly dominated its consumer market for so long as has Gillette. Because Gillette controls more than 60 percent of the approximately $700-million razor-blade market, major competitors must remain content to mainly manufacture knock-off versions of and refill blades for Gillette razors.

Gillette's extensive research program uses the latest scientific instruments and a staff of 200 to explore the frontiers of metallurgical technology and biochemical research. Researchers rigorously scrutinize the processes of beard growth and shaving by daily recording the results of a 10,000-man panel of shavers. Five hundred of these men shave in Gillette's plant under carefully controlled and monitored conditions, including two-way mirrors and videotape observation means. Sometimes, shaved whiskers are collected, weighed, and measured, with the results being computer-analyzed. Thus, Gillette knows information such as how many hairs are in the average man's beard, how fast they grow, and how much hair is removed by shaving.

Such research has led to many advances in shaving systems, just at the time when competitors have become adjusted to the older system. For example, in 1971 Gillette introduced Trac II, a razor system that featured two parallel blades mounted in a cartridge $\frac{60}{1,000}$ of an inch apart. The idea had arisen from a phenomenon called hysteresis, discovered by the R&D people, in which the whisker is pulled slightly out of the follicle when cut by a razor. If one blade is followed closely by a tandem blade, a second, closer slice can be taken off the whisker before it can retract, thus leading to a cleaner shave.

In 1977, Gillette introduced another shaving advance with Atra, a twin-blade cartridge razor that swivels in order to follow facial contours more closely. Compared to Trac II blades, which are in contact with the face an average of 77 percent of the time, Atra has an increased facial-contact time of 89 percent. The $4.95 Atra razor weighs a solid $1\frac{1}{2}$ ounces, and is available in a luxurious, beautifully tooled aluminum handle, with refill blades selling for 36 cents each. It is also available in gift versions, such as a gold-plated model with a rosewood handle ($12.95), and a model with a sterling silver handle designed by Reed & Barton to resemble that of an antique table knife ($29.95).

A new entrant to the shaving-instrument field is Bic Corporation, the U.S. subsidiary of the Paris-based Société Bic. In the early 1960s, Bic had entered the U.S. market with disposable pens to compete with Gillette's Paper Mate. In its first advertisement for the Bic pen, the company strapped one of its throwaway pens to the foot of a Hungarian ice skater, who ground figures into the ice with the tip and then stuck the pen into a flame. The pen still wrote. Follow-up ads showed pens shot from a rifle through a board; others were mounted on jackhammers used to pulverize concrete blocks. These pens still wrote, too. Bic's strategy was to convince American consumers that something dirt cheap and designed to be thrown away was worth buying. The strategy worked beautifully.

Gillette executives at first considered Bic as little more than a pesky nuisance, and they complacently viewed Bic's 19-cent throwaway pen as no match for their 98-cent best-selling Paper Mate writing instrument. However, Bic sales soon outstripped those of Paper Mate.

Ten years later, Bic challenged Gillette in the disposable cigarette-lighter business and won handily over the Cricket brand. However, because pens and lighters had together never accounted for more than 15 percent of sales or pretax profits, Gillette never felt unduly threatened by Bic. The razor business is another matter, though, accounting for 30 percent of Gillette's sales, 70 percent of its pretax profit, and most of the company's pride, in a $1-billion-plus worldwide razor and blade market.

In 1975, Bic introduced a single-bladed disposa-

---

[1] Adapted from Chris Welles, "The War of the Razors," *Esquire,* **93**:28–30, February 1980; Linda Snyder Hayes, "Gillette Takes the Wraps Off," *Fortune,* February 25, 1980, pp. 148–150; "What Did We Ever Do Without Them?" *Ft. Wayne Journal Gazette,* January 13, 1983, pp. 1D–2D; Marianne Wilson, "Disposables Get Bigger Slice of Blade Market," *American Druggist,* February 1983, pp. 70–76; and John J. O'Connor, "Gillette Slashes at Bic," *Advertising Age,* April 5, 1982, pp. 2, 70.

ble shaver in Europe, and the company moved it into Canada in 1976. Gillette, anticipating that the United States would be the next target for Bic, brought out its own twin-bladed disposable shaver called Good News! and rushed it to supermarket and drugstore counters where it sold for 25 cents. Later, Bic introduced its shaver to the U.S. market and priced it at $19\frac{3}{4}$ cents. Since 1976, Bic has managed to obtain a 16 percent share of the razor market. Disposables account for 30 to 40 percent of the total wet-shave market, up from 15 percent in 1978. Bic enjoys an almost 50 percent share of that market.

In contrast to Gillette, Bic does not regularly explore the fringes of shaving technology. It also does not possess the sophisticated equipment or the shaver panel collecting the kind of information gathered by Gillette. Bic does not seem to care how many hairs are in the average man's beard or how fast they grow.

Bic's $\frac{1}{4}$-ounce shaver is small, made of white plastic with only one blade mounted on a short, hollow handle. As in the case of the Good News!, when the blade wears out, the whole thing is thrown away. The shaver does not come in fancy handles or gift versions.

Over the years, Gillette and Bic have both pursued disposability, but along different tracks. Gillette has sought to give its blades, and particularly its handles, an aura of superior performance, class, and cachet. As new technological developments were made, a strong jump could be made in price and profit margin. Gillette promoted new captive "systems" or blade-handle combinations, and made most of its profits on blades, not the handles (just as Polaroid and Kodak make theirs on film, not cameras). If buyers could be persuaded to trade up to new, more-expensive handles (e.g., Atra), then new, more-expensive blades, which could fit only that handle, would also have to be bought. Gillette never bothered with the low-price end of the market, instead believing that because shaving was serious business and facial appearance was a matter of importance, most men would be willing

FIGURE 1

UMPIRE: Mr. McEnroe, that's a very close shave.

McENROE: You must be joking. That ball was in!

UMPIRE: No, Mr. McEnroe, your shave. It's very close.
McENROE: Of course. I shave with Bic.

UMPIRE: You earn millions and shave with a 20 cent Bic.

McENROE: Look, why pay more for fancy handles and tricky tops when I get lots of close shaves with Bic.

UMPIRE: Advantage, McEnroe.
McENROE: He's right, I don't have to shave with a 20 cent Bic...but I do.

(SFX UNDER)
McENROE: Look, why pay more for fancy handles and tricky tops when I get lots of close shaves with Bic.

UMPIRE: Advantage McEnroe.

to pay a little more money to get the "best" shave from Gillette.

In contrast, Bic products have succeeded through the process of commoditization, in which certain expensive, high-status objects, such as watches and cigarette lighters, have devolved into inexpensive, nonstatus, basically disposable items. Commoditization is caused by (1) shifts in consumer tastes, in which different eras accord a different level of class to a product; (2) mass-production techniques, in which an item is turned out for very low cost, with a reduction in its status and allure; and (3) consumers' growing resistance to the proliferation of new brands, flavors, and other varieties of consumer goods. Although some consumers have in the past been willing to pay high prices for cosmetic differentiation, they have now become more price and value-conscious, and are reluctant to pay more for individualized frills. Bic's philosophy caters to this view, because it removes the glamour and non-functional frills from the product and reduces it to a commodity having only basic utility and simplicity. It stresses high value for a low price.

The advertising of the Bic Shaver has been a process of educating consumers. The first job was to explain what a disposable shaver was and to show that an inexpensive plastic disposable could tackle the toughest beards with no difference between the close shave of a Bic and any other more-expensive and elaborate shaving system. One of the company's recent advertisements features tennis pro John McEnroe whose message is one of lifestyle and economics. He can afford to shave with anything—but he shaves with a 20-cent Bic. (See Figure 1).

The battle between Bic and Gillette, therefore, is over more than razors. It is a contest over one of the most enduring male rituals of American life. The morning ritual of face shaving is one of the few remaining exclusively male prerogatives, daily affirming one's masculinity. The first shave is a rite of passage into manhood, often celebrated by the gift of a gleaming new razor (or the handing down of a venerable old one) and a demonstration of its use by the father. Some interesting findings surrounding this activity have been discovered:

- A survey reported that although men complain about the nuisance of shaving, 97 percent would not want to use a cream, were one to be developed, that would permanently remove their facial hair.

- Another study indicated that beard production is actually stimulated by the prospect of sexual relations.

Most men still want their razor to reflect a masculine look, heft, and feel, as well as to act as an item of personal identification in which the razor represents an extension of the self and a status symbol. Yet, there are millions of other men who are now shaving with small, asexual, nondescript pieces of plastic, costing 25 cents or less, in an act that would seem to relegate the ritual to a trivial daily task.

Men have not been the only target of disposables, however. Bic's Lady Shaver and Gillette's Daisy compete with American Safety Razor Products' Flicker. Wilkinson and Schick do not market any disposables positioned specifically at women; instead, both companies refer to their products as "neuters" that can be used by both sexes.

Questions

1 What cultural values are involved in this situation?

2 In your opinion, what is the long-run outlook for such disposable products based on the limits or benefits of the cultural environment?

CASE 3-2
TWIN CITIES BOTTLING COMPANY

Twin Cities Bottling Company is assessing the results of a recent promotional program aimed at increasing sales of its soft drink in the market area which it serves. The company bottles the second leading cola in its market territory, and had hoped to move the brand (with a 30 percent share before the promotional program) into the lead in the Twin Cities. Its major competitor had maintained a steady 40 percent share for a number of years.

The southern city served by Twin Cities has a population of approximately 250,000 in its market area, of which approximately 25 percent are black. The bottler has never achieved a strong franchise among blacks and had hoped to gain considerably in its market appeal to this segment during the promotion.

The primary thrust of the campaign was through cents-off coupons contained in newspapers (particularly suburban editions) and direct-mail pieces, worth varying amounts (depending on bottle size) toward the purchase of the cola. Emphasis was placed on promoting the 2-liter-size plastic bottle of the cola, particularly within supermarkets, with large point-of-purchase displays featuring the picture of one of the attractive female stars on *Dallas* and stressing the cola's reduced price. Twin Cities Bottling had particularly targeted the area's newest and largest supermarkets for special emphasis since these accounted for the biggest volume of the cola's store sales. The bottler also ran an increased number of spot TV ads during a local station's early evening news show. These 10-second spots reinforced the sales promotion effort being run by the bottler by featuring a local announcer who encouraged consumers to be on the lookout for their coupons.

After the campaign had run for two months, Twin Cities Bottling management reviewed the success of the program. Although the promotion had been able to shift the bottler's overall market share up to 35 percent during the period, it had not appreciably increased its share among black consumers. This was a disturbing surprise to management, who assumed that all consumers would have responded to the promotion rather equally.

Twin Cities Bottling would like to gain a higher share among the lucrative black segment in any future promotions, but it is not sure what, if anything, it might do differently next time.

Questions

1 What marketing issues are raised in this case?

2 Advise Twin Cities Bottling Company management on future promotional activities.

CASE 3-3
PERRIER[1]

The people in the television commercials look elegant, sophisticated, and rich. In one scene, an attractive woman emerges dripping from a pool. (Could this be Monte Carlo? Santa Barbara?) Her dialogue: "It's refreshing, it's natural, and it doesn't have one single calorie." In another scene, a couple is participating in a terrace buffet. (Could it be Scarsdale? Shaker Heights?) Dialogue: (She) "It goes with good food." (He) "It's what I drink instead of a cocktail." In a third scene, a couple has completed a tennis game. (Could this be Palm Springs? Palm Beach?) Their dialogue: (She) "It quenches my thirst completely." (He) "The carbonation's natural."

With such advertising, Perrier, the French carbonated mineral water, has sought to place itself on a social scale somewhere between the Vanderbilts and European royalty. More Americans have suddenly been convinced that water, although it costs practically nothing from the tap, is not nearly so good as that which costs 26 cents a glass.

Until recently, water in America had no such pretension. Although Europeans continue to visit native spas and drink the water from their famous springs, rich and famous Americans had long stopped flocking to such places as Hot Springs in Arkansas, and Poland Spring in Maine to "take the waters."

In the meantime, a few American spas continued to bottle and sell their water, but in a low-key manner. Only a few trendy consumers scoured out-of-the-way gourmet shops to buy one of the handful of high-priced imports. Most bottled-water businesses consisted of local bottling companies delivering "bulk water"— water in five-gallon jugs that rested on rented water coolers in homes and offices. The trade was lucrative where a commercial market existed or where water tasted bad or was scarce, but the $200-million market for bottled water paled in comparison to the billions of dollars spent each year on liquor, beer, and soft drinks.

In 1978, Perrier stunned the beverage industry with a new marketing strategy that turned a previously obscure brand into the hottest-selling drink since Miller's Lite beer. Spurred by flat sales for Perrier in Western Europe, normally the strongest market for the beverage, it was decided that the U.S. market would be assaulted. Although Perrier had been distributed in the United States since the turn of the century, only 3.5 million bottles had been sold in 1976, amounting to only 0.8 percent of worldwide sales of the beverage, and an almost infinitesimal share of the U.S. soft-drink market. It was purchased in specialty food outlets or fine restaurants by consumers who prized either its perceived healthful properties or its "snob appeal." The brand at that time was sold in just a few major metropolitan areas and had markups of 35 to 40 percent in retail outlets.

This situation changed dramatically after an aggressive, carefully planned marketing program was implemented, so that 200-million bottles of Perrier were sold in 1979 in the United States. Research had shown that the product had potential if the company could improve its distribution system and lower the price (a 23-ounce bottle of Perrier retailed for $1 or more at the time). The plan involved a switch from store-door delivery to centralized distribution through soft-drink bottlers

---

[1] Adapted from "Perrier: The Astonishing Success of an Appeal to Affluent Adults," *Business Week,* January 22, 1979, pp. 64–65; "Perrier: Putting More Sparkle Into Sales," *Sales and Marketing Management,* January 1979, pp. 16–17; "The Selling of H$_2$O," *Consumer Reports,* September 1980, pp. 531–538; and Pamela Sherrid, "Encore?" *Forbes,* December 20, 1982, pp. 119–121.

and beer wholesalers, because they made more calls per week per store, could merchandise, and could set up displays.

The company replaced three-quarters of its distributors, and they began shifting Perrier into supermarkets and convenience stores and out of gourmet shops which had accounted for 60 percent of sales. Supermarkets now account for 70 percent of Perrier's distribution (up from 10 percent before the change), and gourmet shops now account for only 5 percent. The change in distribution enabled the retail price to be reduced to approximately 69 cents.

Perrier was displayed in the soft-drink section of supermarkets, rather than in the gourmet department. However, a secondary display placing Perrier in racks or case stacks elsewhere in the store was critical to sales success. The initial and important promotion of Perrier included in-store tastings, cents-off coupons, and trade allowances. The company also introduced 11-ounce and 6.5-ounce bottles and multipacks to encourage home consumption. In fact, although Perrier may be the "in" drink to order in restaurants and cocktail lounges, fully 80 to 85 percent of sales are for home consumption.

Perrier also expanded carefully to new geographic markets. The company used detailed demographic data as well as sales figures of imported beers, wines, and health foods in selecting twenty-six affluent markets considered to be favorably predisposed to the product's fashionable appeal. After expanding into additional metropolitan areas, Perrier became available to more than two-thirds of the U.S. market.

Perrier advertising has taken advantage of people's desire to appear glamorous, sophisticated, and rich, based on the premise that Americans tend to drink something with an image. Print ads were placed in high-fashion women's magazines, and television ads were narrated by Orson Welles.

Timing may have been one of the most-important factors in the product's success. Perrier was able to take advantage of consumers' rising concern with diet and health and their sudden demand for a drink with neither sugar nor controversial artificial sweeteners. Most bottled-water products use words such as "natural," "no calories," and "health" on their labels. Along with this development was a trend occurring in the beverage industry in which consumers shifted to "lighter" drinks—wine, light beer, and diet soft drinks. No beverage can claim to be lighter than water. It has no calories, no saccharin, no caffeine, and no alcohol. It is the ultimate in lightness. If consumers can be taught to think of bottled water as an alternative—not to tap water, but to soft drinks, beer, or wine—then the 26 cents per glass for the product may not seem so expensive to them after all.

This was the strategy chosen by Perrier—not to secure a large share of the bottled-water market, but to achieve a small share of the beverage market. This latter market represents a much larger volume and thus greater potential for payoff.

Questions

1 To what extent are social-class factors important in influencing the purchase of Perrier and other imported bottled waters?

2 To which social class(es) is Perrier appealing?

CASE 3-4
SELLING SEDUCTIVE LINGERIE[1]

"This," says saleswoman Tiffany James, holding up a peach-colored wisp of diaphanous material, "is a nightie with a supersheer look."

"This next one," she continues, holding up another short and tiny garment in bold red, "is a baby doll with maribou trim at the bust. It's very cute and it's machine washable."

Toward the end of the demonstration, she holds up what looks like two minute triangles of black lace. "These," she says, "are crotchless panties, ladies. And if you're really innovative, you'll get two and wear one as a bra."

Gasp, giggle, shriek. The twenty-five women crowded into the suburban living room are transfixed. It is a scene repeated nearly every night of the week in the color-coordinated, vinyl-wallpapered living rooms of suburbia.

There is, of course, nothing new about the product—clothes of "a seductive nature." They have been sold through the mail for years. What is new and interesting is that these clothes, once snickered about in the same locker room breath as "kinky sex" and cheesecake, have been brought out of their plain brown wrappers to a new market—the solid suburban middle class. To some suburban women, Tiffany James's lingerie par-

---
[1]Adapted from Manli Ho, "Peddling Naughty Lingerie . . . In Suburban Livingrooms," *Boston Globe,* March 2, 1976.

ties have become as popular as Tupperware and cut crystal punch bowls.

Before the show begins, the guests all take a "sensuality test" to break the ice. There are about twenty questions on the test such as "If you've ever read *'The Sensuous Woman,'* give yourself 10 points." A lingerie prize goes to the winner.

Then, it's the moment of truth. "You're welcome to try anything on," James tells them. Although ten of the guests are middle-aged, another fifteen of them are younger—in their twenties and early thirties—slimmer, and much bolder. There is a brief moment of hesitation and looking around. Then a small group of women rushes into the upstairs bathroom with an armful of negligees and closes the door. Others shut themselves in the empty bedrooms. Only the teen-age daughter of the hostess and her friends are unabashed enough to parade the lingerie in front of the living room crowd. Others will only show theirs to one or two close friends.

By the end of the evening, some of the group will have tried on the items. Others, perhaps less bold, will not, but Tiffany James will have sold $300 worth of her supersheer, baby doll, lacy, satiny, backless, frontless, sideless, sexy, and very naughty lingerie.

Questions

1. How would you explain the success of this party selling approach?

2. What market groups would you seek to appeal to in this situation? Why?

3. In what ways are the various types of group power exhibited in this situation?

CASE 3-5
LINDBECK LABORATORIES, FOOD PRODUCTS DIVISION[1]

In 1974, Lindbeck Laboratories entered the market for a cholesterol-free egg substitute with the introduction of its Yolkers. Standard Brands, Inc. and Miles Laboratories had pioneered this product market several years before with their Fleishmann's Egg Beaters and Morning Star Farm's Scramblers.

Because of Fleishmann's strong name identification with low cholesterol (margarine as well as egg substitute) and also the present limited size of the cholesterol-sensitive market, Lindbeck Laboratories was very interested in the possibility of widening the market for Yolkers to include more families from the middle and blue collar class, the majority of which presently did not use egg substitutes.

BACKGROUND OF THE EGG SUBSTITUTE MARKET

During the middle and late 1960s a number of studies reporting a link between high cholesterol diets and the incidence of heart attack were published. Both doctors and nutritionists began publicizing the need for consumers to cut back on foods rich in cholesterol such as bacon, eggs, and a number of dairy products.

This concern over diet opened up a new market for cholesterol-free substitutes that was especially noticeable in the breakfast food group.

Lindbeck Laboratories began product development of a cholesterol-free egg substitute in 1973 and in the fall of 1974 rushed its initial formulation of Yolkers to the market. Initial sales were disappointing and work was begun on an improved version of the product which more closely resembled the look and taste of real scrambled eggs.

After extensive re-engineering and product preference testing, the new version of Yolkers was improved to the point where it was equally preferred to real scrambled eggs in consumer blind taste tests.

This improved version of Yolkers was placed on the market in the summer of 1975. Although sales levels increased somewhat, they still lagged behind projections. The 1975 Yolkers sales fell just short of $10 million a year. While egg sales were temporarily impacted during this period, by 1976, egg sales had returned to nearly their 1972 level. Sales figures for the five-year period beginning in 1972 are shown in Table 1.

With the introduction of Yolkers in 1975, the sales of competitors began gradually falling off until mid-1976 when the market share of the new entrant appeared to be stabilizing at its present market share of 15 percent.

TABLE 1

ANNUAL SALES VOLUME (In Millions)	Year	Egg Substitutes	Eggs
	1972	55.3	1112.3
	1973	77.8	988.4
	1974	89.6	990.7
	1975	110.2	1050.6
	1976	110.4	1109.0

---

[1] Adapted from the original case by Paul S. Hugstad appearing in M. Wayne Delozier (ed.), *Consumer Behavior Dynamics: A Casebook,* Columbus, OH, Merrill, 1977. Used with permission of the author and Charles E. Merrill Publishing Company.

THE PRODUCTS

Yolkers and other egg substitute products were made basically of the same formulation. Their major ingredients included egg white (82 percent), liquid corn oil (10 percent), and nonfat dry milk (7 percent). These ingredients were frozen and packaged in individual cartons of four to eight fluid ounces each, and bundled together with an outer cardboard wrapper. Yolkers came in three, four-ounce cartons, bound together with a foil wrapper.

Instructions on the Yolkers package stated that each four-ounce carton was equivalent to two large eggs. The Yolkers package of three 4-ounce cartons sold for 75¢ with most other brands being competitively priced.

Instructions called for the product to be moved from the freezer to the refrigerator for defrosting twelve hours before use, or to be run under hot water for quicker defrosting. Once defrosted, the cartons needed to be used within seven days and could not be refrozen. Cooking Yolkers was done in the same manner as preparing scrambled eggs.

Egg substitutes were being distributed through the frozen foods section of most grocery stores, displayed alongside other breakfast substitutes such as frozen waffles and bacon substitute.

Yolkers recently had begun a store coupon promotion offering a 10¢ reduction on the next purchase of Yolkers in an attempt to induce brand switching.

Market Analysis of Family Purchases

Lindbeck Laboratories had been subscribing to National Grocers panel data since the introduction of Yolkers in September 1974. Analysis of over twelve periods of brand purchase data revealed no significant differences in the type of purchasers of various brands of egg substitutes, but did show purchasers of egg substitutes to have definite demographic characteristics. Table 2 presents a summary breakdown of National Grocers purchase profile data representing the preceding six months time period.

Interviews with repeat purchasers confirmed expectations that Yolkers were being purchased as a

TABLE 2
PROFILE OF THE YOLKERS BUYER

	Yolkers Purchase Data (In packages/month)
Age of wife:	
18–21	.14
22–27	1.89
28–34	.23
35–45	1.93
46–55	2.34
56 and over	.21
Educational level (wife):	
Less than high school	.10
High school	.89
College graduate	1.30
Post graduate	2.02
Family income:	
0–$8,000	.13
$8,000–$14,000	.28
$14,000–$20,000	.72
$20,000–$35,000	1.83
$35,000 and over	2.31

	Yolkers Purchase Data (In packages/month)
Family size:	
2	1.49
3–4	1.12
5–6	.31
7 or more	.08
Occupation of head of household:	
Professional	2.11
Managerial	2.33
Clerical and sales	1.09
Skilled	.26
Semiskilled and laborer	.22
Unskilled	.08

TABLE 3

ANALYSIS OF EGG SUBSTITUTE USER BUYING MOTIVES

	Primary Buying Motive			
	Ease of Preparation	Taste	Low Cholesterol	Other*
Age of wife:				
18–21	18%	56%	4%	30%
22–27	53	32	12	25
28–34	8	6	4	5
35–45	6	2	40	5
46–55	5	0	38	5
55 and over	10	4	2	30
	100%	100%	100%	100%
Wife's education level:				
Less than high school	0	20%	5%	5%
High school graduate	10	60	10	40
College graduate	50	15	55	40
Post graduate	40	5	30	15
	100%	100%	100%	100%
Family size:				
2	90%	50%	20%	70
3–4	10	35	70	20
5–6	0	10	10	5
7 or more	0	5	0	5
	100%	100%	100%	100%
Total family income:				
0–$8,000	5%	0%	0%	5%
$8,000–$14,000	5	10	15	15
$14,000–$20,000	10	25	30	20
$20,000–$35,000	45	50	45	20
$35,000 and over	35	15	10	40
	100%	100%	100%	100%

*Included such things as easily stored, new, and innovative.

health food primarily by wives with husbands under doctors' orders to restrict cholesterol intake.

Younger couples who were using egg substitutes commented that they had both become aware of the need to prevent cholesterol build-up before they became older, but when asked, commented that they saw no need to so restrict their children's diet. Several of these couples also mentioned the convenience aspect of preparing Yolkers but complained that they sometimes forgot to defrost them in advance.

Most of the couples interviewed were satisfied with the taste of the product although several husbands mentioned that the artificial taste still was noticeable. When asked if they still ate eggs sometimes, the frequent reply was "only on special occasions, when baking, or with the kids."

Tables 3 and 4, respectively, present a summary of the motives and roles of various family types who are users of egg substitutes.

Proposed Change in Market Orientation

Presently, Lindbeck Laboratories was dissatisfied with its restricted market position and was discussing ways of breaking out of its follower role in the egg substitute market. It was noted that presently few lower-middle class and blue collar families were using the product, and since these families also tended to be larger than those from the upper-middle class, a concerted effort should be made to make the product more appealing to them.

Plans were being formulated to re-orient their efforts away from the already saturated market toward

TABLE 4
FAMILY ROLES IN BUYING EGG SUBSTITUTES
(Husband (H), Wife (W), Children (C))

	Purchaser(s)	Major Purchase Influencer(s)	Major User(s)
Age of wife:			
18–21	H or W	H,W	H
22–27	H or W	H,W	H,W,C
28–34	W	W	H,W,C
35–45	W	H,C	H
46–55	W	H,C	H
55 and over	H or W	H,W	H,W
Wife's education level:			
Less than high school	W	H,C	H
High school graduate	W	C	H
College graduate	W	H	H,W,C
Postgraduate	H or W	W	H,W,C
Family size:			
2	H,W	H	H,W
3–4	H,W	C	H,W,C
5–6	W	H	H
7 or more	W	H	H
Total family income:			
0–$8,000	W	W	H
$8,000–$14,000	W	C	H,W
$14,000–$20,000	W	W	H
$20,000–$35,000	H or W	H	H,W,C
$35,000 and over	H or W	H	H,W,C

this new family market which comprised 70 percent of the total breakfast food products market. The key to the development of this new market was an understanding of how the family buying process operated for different types of families. The feasibility of effectively reaching this new market was questioned by some members of management.

A second important decision revolved around which family member(s) a new or revised strategy should be aimed. While there was general agreement that the mother was the most obvious target, the purchase influence pattern was seen as potentially different depending upon the social class and stage of the family life cycle of the families concerned.

The strength of various buying motives also was felt to differ depending upon a family's social class background.

Before proceeding further with a reformulation of the Yolkers marketing strategy, it was felt that the roles of various family members in purchasing a product such as Yolkers must be more clearly delineated for both lower-middle class and blue collar families.

Questions

1 Characterize the family purchase-decision process for Yolkers. How might the role of the husband, wife, and children change depending upon their social class background?

2 What are some of the barriers to reaching the traditional "28–45-year-old housewife" market?

3 Should the stage in the family's life cycle be considered in developing a marketing strategy for breakfast food substitutes? If so, how?

4 Suggest a marketing strategy to more successfully penetrate the lower-middle class and blue collar market for breakfast food substitutes. What will be key to the success of such a program?

CASE 3-6
LITTON INDUSTRIES[1]

In the fall of 1976, Litton's Microwave Cooking Products Division was involved in reviewing and modifying its entire marketing program for expanding sales of microwave ovens in its consumer markets. Because of recent dramatic increases in industry sales of microwave ovens, steepening competition from both domestic and foreign competitors, and the evolution of microwave technology to improve cooking performance, it was felt that a thorough rethinking of the most effective marketing strategy to capture new and developing market segments was needed.

EXISTING PRODUCT LINE COMPETITION

Litton's early entry and aggressive marketing program had gained them a leading 33 percent share of the consumer market. In the last three years, in spite of intense competition from General Electric, Sharp, Amana, Panasonic and Magic Chef, Litton's market share had increased while Amana and several Japanese brands had lost market share. The increased product guarantee of some brands to typically include two years on parts and service and five years on the magnetron (the most important oven part), compared with Litton's one year guarantee on parts and labor and two years on the magnetron, was believed to be partly responsible for a current stabilizing of some competitors' sales.

In addition to strong consumer competition, Litton also experienced competition from Sears, Montgomery Ward, and other large retailers selling microwave ovens under private brands. Competition in these markets was characterized by strong price competition.

Technology had recently led to major feature improvements in microwave ovens, with most brands currently offering a variety of options to their basic product. The most common of these options were variable cooking control, a defrost cycle, and a browning unit. With these feature improvements, it was estimated that 80 percent of a family's normal cooking could now be done with a microwave oven.

Litton's early technological advantages had been responsible for the above options. Amana Refrigeration, Inc. had recently begun to fight back with heavy promotion of its "Touchmatic Radarange" which used a digital "mini-computer" to program defrost and cooking time on a touch-sensitive front panel.

However, Litton had pre-empted this competition with the introduction of its new Model 418 with "varitemp" automatic food temperature control that used a heat probe placed inside the food to automatically stop the cooking cycle when the desired inner food temperature was achieved. Both the Model 418 and the Radarange were perceived as significant advances over previous microwave models.

Along with these feature improvements, prices of microwave ovens had broadened substantially over recent years to include lower and higher priced models. The prices of current models ranged from $250 for a stripped-down version to $500 to $600 for the deluxe models. Most of Litton and Amana sales were near the high end of the price continuum, with the Radarange currently being the most expensive model on the market.

HISTORICAL BACKGROUND OF MICROWAVE OVENS

The microwave oven is based on a relatively new technology using radar principles developed during World War II and is still in the early stages of its life cycle. Although microwave cooking was first introduced in 1954, many consumers still do not understand the principles involved or the cooking techniques for most satisfactory results.

Microwaves are a form of radiant energy, and like other common forms (radio waves, visible light, and infrared heat) they have longer nonionizing wave lengths. Microwaves bounce or deflect off metal surfaces and heat by penetrating nonmetallic surfaces where the energy is absorbed by water molecules and converted to heat. The air and nonmetallic cooking utensils transmit this energy without producing heat, and the metal sides of the oven reflect microwaves, so the oven's walls remain cool outside and in during the cooking operation. Microwave cooking takes approximately one-fourth of the time of conventional cooking.

Early models were generally expensive and troublesome appliances. As recently as 1973 the product was not recommended by *Consumer Reports*.[2] At that time there was a substantial amount of discussion and research in process to determine if microwaves could affect the central nervous system, heart, or liver, cause

---

[1] Adapted from the original case by Paul S. Hugstad appearing in M. Wayne Delozier (ed.), *Consumer Behavior Dynamics: A Casebook*, Columbus, OH, Merrill, 1977. Used with permission of the author and Charles E. Merrill Publishing Company.

[2] "Microwave Ovens—Not Recommended," *Consumer Reports*, April 1973, p. 221.

changes in body protein and enzymes, or cause possible genetic damage. Low-level microwave radiation also was believed to interfere with the functioning of cardiac pacemaker implants.

More recently, qualified scientific institutions have issued statements to remove many doubts covering the safety of microwave ovens.[3] The product also has been certified by the Bureau of Radiological Health (BRH) and Underwriters Laboratories (UL) with certification labels given models that pass the safety tests. However, an updated *Consumer Reports* article still cautioned against possible unknown radiation effects.[4]

BENEFITS OF MICROWAVE COOKING

Because the cooking is fast (for instance, a baked potato can be cooked in 4 to 5 minutes), moisture and flavor are retained and there is less food shrinkage. It also is believed that nutrients are not lost through microwave cooking, and many foods retain their eye appeal.

Since regular serving dishes or paper can be used to prepare food, cleanup time and washing of pots and pans is reduced, and the oven has no "baked on" grease, so it is easy to clean. Soil can be wiped up immediately with a damp cloth or soapy sponge, and grease spatters from browning can be wiped away with a baking soda solution. Both the oven and the kitchen stay cool while cooking is in progress.

Cooked dishes can be reheated in minutes, and leftovers retain their "just-cooked" flavor, since there is little dehydration. Dishes can also be quickly prepared for latecomers or unexpected guests.

Two important disadvantages to microwave cooking include the lack of a browning unit in the portable models and the smaller portable model's oven cavity size (it will not accommodate such items as a large roast). Therefore, the portable microwave oven is suggested as an accessory to a conventional oven and is not recommended for purchase as the sole source of cooking.

MARKETING

Market Development

In January 1971, industry estimates showed about 120,000 microwave ovens in use in the U.S. By the end of 1971 that figure had doubled. Market penetration through the end of 1975 in the consumer market is summarized in Table 1.

---

[3]"Handbook Buying Issue for 1975," *Consumer Research Magazine*, p. 174.
[4]"Is Microwave Leakage Hazardous?" *Consumer Reports*, June 1976, pp. 319–321.

TABLE 1
U.S. MICROWAVE OVEN SALES (in Units)

Year	Annual	Cumulative
1971	120,000	240,000
1972	290,000	530,000
1973	460,000	990,000
1974	725,000	1,715,000
1975	1,000,000	2,715,000
1976	1,400,000*	4,115,000

*Microwave industry forecast

The 1 million microwaves sold in 1975 represent roughly 40 percent of the total number in use at that time, but a market penetration of only 3.8 percent of total U.S. households. The 1976 industry projections represent a growth rate of more than 40 percent.

Microwave ovens were seen as still being in the early growth stage of their life cycle with large numbers of adopter groups just beginning to enter the market.

Market Research

Demographic analysis of present microwave owners, developed from registration questionnaires (see Appendix), produced a profile of the "innovator" segment which is summarized in Table 2 (see next page).

A separately commissioned in-depth study of over 300 California homemakers who owned microwave ovens revealed that the benefits of microwave cooking were perceived as follows by the respondents:

	Major Benefit*	Minor Benefit
Quick meal preparation	80%	10%
Energy savings	60	15
Convenient clean-up	50	15
Moister foods	25	5
Left-over warming convenience	50	10

*Total equals more than 100% due to multiple answers.

The same study also uncovered the following respondent dissatisfactions with microwave cooking.

	Mildly Dissatisfied	Strongly Dissatisfied
Taste of food prepared	30%	15%
Aesthetic appeal of food prepared	30	30
Capacity of microwave oven	30	15
Potential radiation hazard	45	5
High purchase price	35	10

TABLE 2

A PROFILE OF THE "INNOVATOR" FOR MICROWAVE OVENS (1972–1975)

Married	Yes 90%	No 10%		
Both spouses working	Yes 53%	No 47%		
Number of children	0 30%	1–3 60%	4–6 8%	7 or more 2%
Residence type	Homeowner 80%	Renter 20%		
Husband's age	Under 25 10%	25–55 70%	Over 55 20%	
Wife's age	30%	60%	10%	
Family income level	Under $20,000 50%	$20,000–$30,000 30%	$30,000 and Over 20%	
Education level	High school 40%	College 40%	Postgraduate 15%	Other 5%
Microwave purchase location	Appliance store 55%	Department store 15%	Furniture store 10%	Other 20%

Developing New Market Segments

Litton's prime interest presently is to capitalize on the accelerating acceptance of microwave use among U.S. households. It is felt that new segments of the market are ready to be developed and that the existing marketing strategy of courting "innovators" needs to be modified. Current research supports this contention, predicting that industry market penetration will increase to 15 million microwave units by 1980 and 36 million units by 1985.

Corporate discussions currently are under way to determine whether it is desirable to continue the policy of selective distribution through major appliance outlets, in light of the changing nature of competition and forecasted market. Questions also are being raised concerning the proper role and target of the advertising campaign being prepared for 1977. It is felt that important changes in existing marketing programs may be needed to effectively reach these developing market segments.

Questions

1 What major barriers may have slowed the initial adoption of microwave ovens by consumers? Do any of these barriers remain? If so, how could they be removed?

2 Develop a buyer profile of the next potential market segment, "the early adopters." How would this profile change for the early majority? For the late majority?

3 Suggest a marketing program which could be modified over time to effectively reach these new market segments as the diffusion of microwave ovens accelerates.

APPENDIX: QUESTIONNAIRE

MICROWAVE REGISTRATION

MODEL NO. MW- _____   SERIAL NO. _____

PLEASE REGISTER YOUR MICROWAVE BY SENDING IN THIS PREPAID POSTCARD.

IT IS NECESSARY FOR YOU TO REGISTER YOUR MICROWAVE OVEN. MANUFACTURERS ARE REQUIRED TO KEEP THESE RECORDS. PLEASE FILL IN THE INFORMATION REQUESTED BELOW, AND MAIL WITHIN TEN DAYS.

YOUR NAME   YOUR DEALER

ADDRESS   CITY-STATE

CITY, STATE AND ZIP   DATE OF PURCHASE

1. Are You Married? _____Yes _____No
2. If Married, Do Both Husband and Wife Work Outside the Home? _____Yes _____No
3. How Many Children Do You Have Living at Home? _____None _____1–3 _____4–6 _____7 or More
4. Where Do You Live? _____Home _____Apartment
5. Husband's Age? _____Under 25 _____25–35 _____36–45 _____Over 45
6. Wife's Age _____Under 25 _____25–35 _____36–45 _____Over 45
7. Family Income Level: _____$10,000 or Under _____$10,000–$20,000 _____$20,000–$30,000 _____Over $30,000
8. Your Education Status _____High School _____4-Year College _____Postgraduate _____Other
9. Where Was Your Oven Purchased? _____Appliance Store _____Department Store _____Furniture Store _____Other
10. What Brand Conventional Range Do You Own? _____

External environment

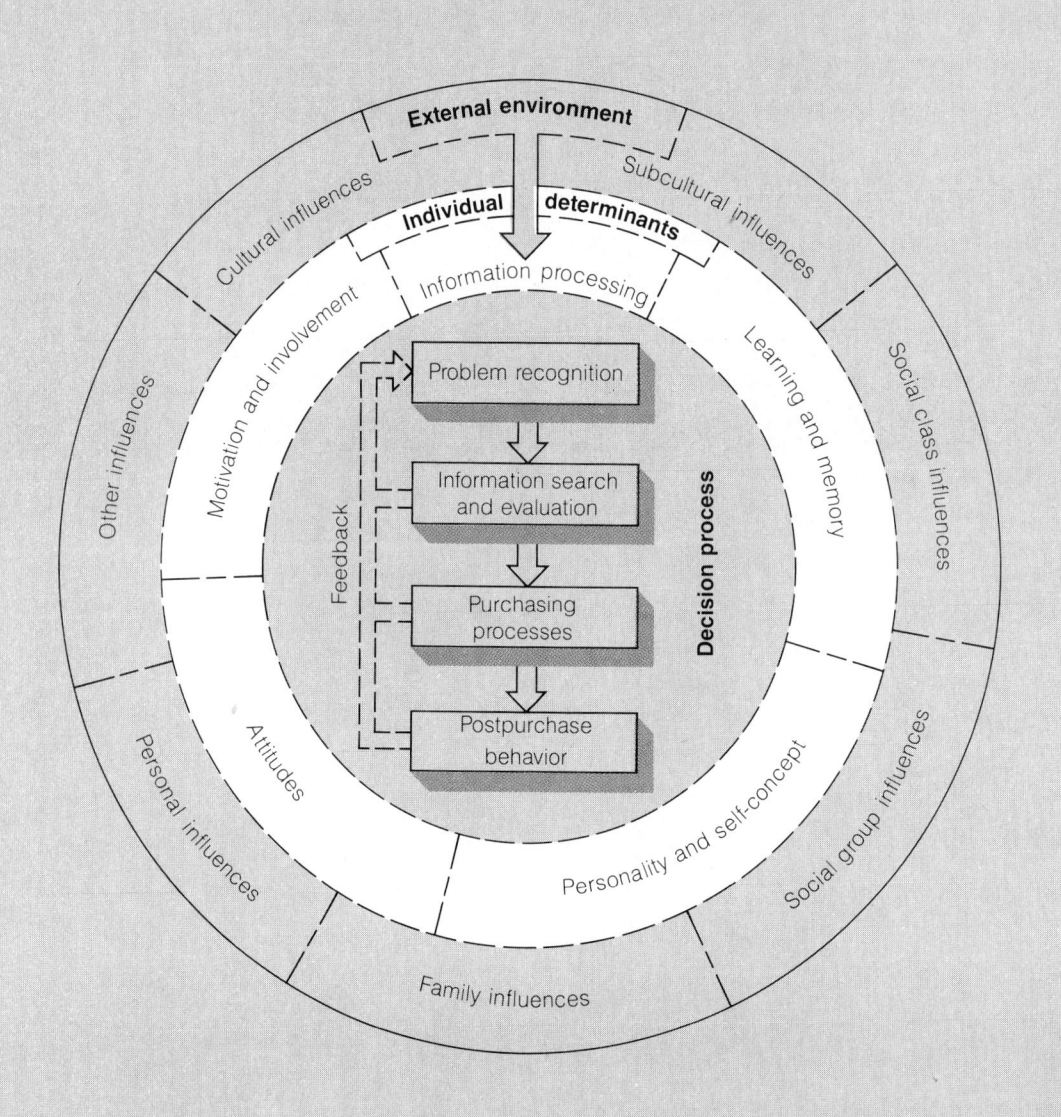

Individual determinants

Decision process

- Problem recognition
- Information search and evaluation
- Purchasing processes
- Postpurchase behavior

Feedback

Cultural influences • Subcultural influences • Social class influences • Social group influences • Family influences • Personal influences • Other influences

Information processing • Learning and memory • Personality and self-concept • Attitudes • Motivation and involvement

PART FOUR
INDIVIDUAL DETERMINANTS OF CONSUMER BEHAVIOR

12 Motivation and Involvement
13 Information Processing
14 Learning and Memory
15 Personality and Self-Concept
16 Attitudes
17 Changing Attitudes
18 Cases for Part Four

CHAPTER 12
MOTIVATION AND INVOLVEMENT

Anyone interested in consumers will soon become concerned with what activates and directs their behavior. This is more than a subject of idle curiosity for marketing managers since many of their decisions are based on knowledge or assumptions about the general forces influencing consumers. Issues faced by management of the Amtrak passenger line connecting Los Angeles to San Diego serve as an illustration.

> Daily, the San Diegan makes several runs between Los Angeles and San Diego providing riders with beautiful Pacific Coast vistas while also connecting with major tourist attractions such as Disneyland. It is one of the most heavily used short-haul passenger trains in the United States.[1] Why do people in a state so heavily dependent on automobiles want to use this train? Is it viewed as being more economical or safe than commuting by car? Is a desire for convenience the underlying factor? If so, what form does this convenience take—avoiding heavy traffic, ease of access to the central city, being able to read or work while traveling, or other reasons? Perhaps the major attraction is the breathtaking scenery, or is it seen as a way to conserve energy? Various market segments such as tourists and residents may be influenced by different factors or combinations of motivations. However, knowledge of these reasons is very important for Amtrak managers who must design appropriate services and promotional programs to maintain and increase future ridership.

It would be surprising if any one variable could fully explain what initiates and guides consumers' actions. Nevertheless, the concept of motivation plays an essential role in any such understanding. This chapter begins by defining motives, indicating their importance and influence, and discussing some methods of classifying them. Attention then turns to what arouses motives and what factors influence how they are structured together. Next, several particular aspects of motivational influences are discussed. Finally, methods of measuring motives and the often controversial subject of motivational research are reviewed.

THE NATURE AND ROLE OF MOTIVES

A number of writers have drawn distinctions between motives and other related concepts such as needs, wants, and drives.[2] For our purposes, these distinctions are not very helpful and will be avoided. We will view a *motive* as an inner state that mobilizes bodily energy and directs it in selective fashion toward goals usually located in the external environment. This definition implies that motives involve two major components:

1 A mechanism to arouse bodily energy.
2 A force that provides direction to that bodily energy.

The arousal component activates general tension or restlessness but does not provide direction for release of this energy. It could be compared to the random thrashing about that newborn babies often show. The directive aspect of motives focuses such aroused energy toward some goal in the individual's environment. Thus, when our hunger is aroused, we are usually directed toward particular foods.

It is useful to note that various concepts have been offered to explain how motives exert their directional influences on consumers. Earlier views held that inborn instincts beyond the control of individuals provided the direction for their behavior. Later it was stressed that basic needs (hunger, thirst, etc.) impelled people toward action. This view also held that behavior instrumental in satisfying a need would become associated with it and have a higher likelihood of occurring in future situations involving the same need arousal.

Many behavioral scientists have found these views of motivation lacking because they imply that people are impelled by various forces and have very little conscious control over the direction of their own actions. For this reason, a *cognitive* orientation has gained in popularity.[3] It emphasizes the role of mental processes such as planning, evaluation, and goal selection in directing behavior. This suggests that consumers have a very active role in selecting their goals, evaluating the relative usefulness of products in terms of these goals, and consciously orchestrating their behavior in terms of these products.

Role of Motives

As has already been noted, the role of motives is to arouse and direct the behavior of consumers. The arousal component activates bodily energy so that it can be used for mental and physical activity. In their directive role, motives have several important functions for guiding behavior.[4] These are discussed below.

Defining Basic Striving Motives influence consumers to develop and identify their basic strivings. Included among basic strivings are very general goals such as safety, affiliation, achievement, or other desired states which consumers seek to achieve. They serve to guide behavior in a general way across a wide variety of decisions and activities.

Identifying Goal Objects Although there are exceptions, people often view products or services as a means by which they can achieve their motives.[5] In fact, consumers often go one step further and think of products as their actual goals, without realizing that they really represent ways of satisfying motives.

This motivational push that influences consumers to identify products as goal objects is of great interest to marketers, particularly since it appears that it can be influenced. Certainly, the features designed into a product can affect the degree to which consumers may accept it as a goal or means for achieving some goal. Much effort is also spent on developing promotions that persuade consumers to consider products as objects useful for achieving some motive. For example, the advertisement in Figure 12-1 effectively suggests that use of the product will lead to certain motive satisfactions.

Influencing Choice Criteria   Motives also guide consumers in developing criteria for evaluating products. Thus, for a car buyer strongly influenced by the convenience motive, features such as electronic speed control and easy-servicing requirements would become more-important choice criteria than styling or mileage.

It appears that marketers are also capable of influencing consumers' choice criteria. In some cases, this occurs because consumers are not consciously aware of their own motives. For example, a salesperson for air conditioners may remark that one model is more efficient than others, thereby making the consumer realize that operating economy is important to his choice. In other cases, people are aware of their motives but unsure of the specific criteria to use in their product evaluations. In this case, the marketer can inform consumers of the importance of particular criteria and how well her product meets these criteria. Figure 12-2 shows one such example.

Other Influences   At a more fundamental level, motives affect the individual determinants of perception, learning, personality, attitudes, and how people process information. This also results in directional influences on behavior. For example, motives influence information processing, which in turn regulates how we interpret and respond to our environment. These influences are discussed in greater detail in the remaining chapters of this section.

CLASSIFYING MOTIVES

Since the early 1900s many thousands of motive concepts have been suggested to account for the great diversity of human behavior.[6] The need to group so many suggestions into a more-manageable set of general categories soon became apparent. A variety of classification schemes ranging from the simplified to the complex has been proposed.

Simplified Schemes

A number of classification methods are simplified so that they group motives on the basis of one unique characteristic of interest. Several of particular relevance to understanding consumers are highlighted as follows.

Physiological versus Psychogenic   One scheme categorizes motives according to their underlying sources. *Physiological* motives are oriented toward directly satisfying biological needs of the individual, such as hunger, thirst, and pain-avoidance. Conversely, *psychogenic* motives focus on the satisfaction of psychological desires. Examples include the seeking of achievement, affiliation, or status. It is interesting to note that consumers often can satisfy physiological needs at the same time they are satisfying psychogenic motives. For example, sharing a favorite drink with friends after a touch football game satisfies affiliation needs as well as one's thirst.

FIGURE 12-1

Example of motive directional influence. (Reproduced by permission of Shulton, Inc.)

FIGURE 12-2

Example of advertisement informing consumers of specific choice criteria. (Reprinted by permission of SCM Corp.)

Although general agreement exists about the number and nature of physiological motives, there is less consensus about their psychogenic counterparts. However, a common characteristic of such psychological motives is that they are learned. This learning can occur throughout life, but the childhood socialization process probably accounts for a majority of these acquired motives. The nature of this learning will be explored in Chapter 14.

Learned or *secondary motives* exert a very important influence on people. In fact, many argue that in economically advanced societies, psychogenic motives dominate over physiological ones in affecting consumers' goals and acquisition of products to attain or express these goals. This is a significant consideration to marketers involved in the design of products and advertising appeals.

Primary versus Selective Motives may also be classified according to how they influence buying decisions. A *primary* influence involves initiating buying behavior and directing it toward certain generic product categories such as televisions or health spas. Conversely, *selective* influences guide choices between stores or brands and models within a generic product class. As noted earlier, this can occur through development of choice criteria that serve as standards for evaluating brands.

Motivational concepts are certainly useful for understanding consumer behavior at both the primary and selective level. However, some suggest that the generalized nature of their influence makes them more useful for understanding consumer choices among generic product classes.[7] Preference and attitude concepts discussed in Chapter 16 may be more appropriate for understanding final choices between brands.

Conscious versus Unconscious Motives also differ in the degree to which they reach consumers' awareness. Conscious motives are those of which consumers are quite aware, whereas a motive is said to be unconscious when the consumer is not aware of being influenced by it.

It has been suggested that people are not conscious of some motives because they don't want to confront the true reason for their purchase. To illustrate, purchases of expensive clothes are frequently justified in terms of the clothes' "fit" or durability rather than the status they are expected to display. In other cases, consumers may simply not be aware of the true motives behind many of their purchases. For example, we really don't understand why we prefer certain colors over others.

Positive versus Negative Motives can exert either positive or negative influences on consumers. Positive influences attract consumers toward desired goals, while negative ones direct them away from undesirable consequences. Positive attractions exert the predominant influence, but a few very important cases of negative forces do exist. One example of a negative force is fear, which can play an important role in some purchases such as toothpaste for decay prevention and insurance to protect loved ones.

A Comprehensive Scheme

Although the aforementioned distinctions provide useful perspective they are limited because only one characteristic serves as the basis of classification. Recently, a more comprehensive method using four bipolar motive tendencies has been suggested by McGuire.[8] As shown in Figure 12-3, the relevant distinctions are cognitive/affective (mental deliberation versus emotional reactions), preservation/growth (maintenance of equilibrium versus self-development), active/passive (self-initiated action versus reactive tendencies) and internal/external (achieve-

FIGURE 12-3
A comprehensive classification of major motive influences. (*Source:* Adapted from William J. McGuire "Some Internal Psychological Factors Influencing Consumer Choice," *Journal of Consumer Research,* **2:**302–319, March 1976.)

		Active		Passive	
		Internal	External	Internal	External
Cognitive	Preservation	1. Consistency	2. Attribution	3. Categorization	4. Objectification
	Growth	5. Autonomy	6. Exploration	7. Matching	8. Utilitarian
Affective	Preservation	9. Tension-reduction	10. Expressive	11. Ego-defensive	12. Reinforcement
	Growth	13. Assertion	14. Affiliation	15. Identification	16. Modeling

ment of new internal states versus new relationships with the environment). These four means of classification are not intended to be mutually exclusive. In fact, when used together they provide an interesting basis for appreciating sixteen major motivational influences on consumer behavior. Each is briefly characterized below.

Consistency   This striving focuses on the need to maintain a coherent and organized view of the world. Beliefs or information that seem to be inconsistent with other known "facts" create tension and a need to understand the situation. An excellent illustration is when a consumer learns that cereals he considered to be very nutritious are not high in protein, vitamin content, and other food value. Such a situation is often disruptive and motivates attempts to find "explanations" for this inconsistency.

Attribution   This term refers to the motivation to understand causes for events occurring in one's environment. The attribution motive influences consumers to ask and seek answers to the following types of questions.

"Is my better gas mileage due to that new synthetic oil I used?"

"Do I buy a lot of expensive things because I want other people to hold me in high esteem?"

"Why is that salesperson trying to persuade me to buy a Sony rather than a Sylvania?"

As these three questions suggest, consumers' attributions are focused in three major directions:

1   Object perception—inferences as to whether certain events (e.g., less weeds in lawn) are caused by specific objects (products, brands, etc.) rather than by some chance occurrence.

2   Self perception—people attempting to understand their own attitudes, motives, etc. by inferring them from the behavior they see themselves engaged in.

3   Person perception—inferences about the reasons for the actions of others (friends, salespeople, celebrities who endorse products, etc.).

The meaning consumers derive from information in their environment can be strongly influenced by their inferred reasons for observed events. This has fostered considerable interest in the attribution process, especially with relevance to its effects on how consumers react to promotional messages and product information developed by marketers.[9]

Categorization   Consumers usually find it necessary to sort complex information into a more organized and easily handled set of categories. Being able to deal with a smaller set of categories simplifies the task of deriving meaning from the many experiences obtained from the real world. For example, clothing is frequently sorted into formal, casual and "hang-around" categories. Many products are also thought of as being either expensive, reasonable, or cheap.

Objectification Emphasis here is on the tendency to use "objective" external information instead of internal reflection to draw conclusions about one's values, attitudes, and so on. This tendency, which is similar to attribution but more passive in nature, would lead to situations in which the number of trips taken and clothes purchased might be used by the consumer as measures of the degree to which he actually enjoys travel and clothes.

Autonomy This motive influences consumers to seek personal growth and individuality through self-actualization and development of a distinct identity. Such strivings are the basis for numerous marketing efforts. For example, a wide variety of popular books and programs (*The Complete Scarsdale Medical Diet Book, I'm O.K.—You're O.K.,* Transcendental Meditation, EST, etc.) are offered to consumers interested in self-development. Numerous other products including clothing, cigarettes, and cologne are promoted as alternatives available to consumers for enhancing or expressing their individuality.

Exploration Consumers usually expend considerable effort to simplify their complex environment. However, in at least some situations they actually seem to seek higher levels of stimulation. This motive has been suggested as one reason for impulse purchasing and brand-switching behavior.[10] We will examine such motivated behavior in more detail shortly.

Matching Many consumers are motivated to develop mental images of ideal situations and then regularly compare (match) their perceptions of existing situations to these ideal mental images. Such comparisons provide feedback as to whether actions are improving progress toward goals. Interestingly, a strong matching motive implies that internal standards, rather than the characteristics of other brands, serve as the criteria for judging products. Of course, the process consumers use to develop such ideals is of significant interest to marketers.

Utilitarian Consumers influenced by this motive view the external environment as a valuable resource for information and skills relevant to solving life's problems. One could expect consumers in such a situation to enjoy shopping and to spend considerable time processing information from advertisements and other sources about products and how they can be used to enrich one's life.

Tension Reduction This concept views consumers as possessing needs which generate tension if they are not being satisfied. Tension is viewed as an undesirable experience to be avoided or minimized. Although it is useful for understanding many consumer actions, this viewpoint is now seen as an incomplete perspective on consumers. As has already been mentioned, exploration motives have been offered to explain why consumers may actually seek stimulation in some instances.

Self-Expression The need to project aspects of one's identity appears to be very important to many consumers. Products easily seen by others (high social visibility) can present excellent vehicles for such self-expression. Examples include clothing, personal care items, and products consumed in social settings. Realizing this, marketers of such items often invest considerable sums of time and money in developing unique images or symbolic meanings for their brands. Examples are the highly liberated-looking women used in Virginia Slims advertisements and the handsome eye-patched man used in Hathaway shirt promotions. Of course, the hope is that consumers identifying with such images will use the brand to project their identity, as the advertisement for the Triumph TR7 shows in Figure 12-4.

Ego Defensive Most people feel that various life situations can arise which will be threatening to their egos. These situations generate social embarrassment, challenges to feelings of self-worth, or other forms of psychological harm. The need to defend against such threats is therefore quite common. A wide variety of products are available to assist consumers in this regard. Promotions for these offerings frequently draw attention to potentially damaging circumstances and how the advertised brand is useful in defending against such harm. This is illustrated by advertisements for many personal-care items which focus on body odor, dandruff, slipping dentures, and other socially sensitive problems.

Reinforcement Consumers influenced by reinforcement have a strong tendency to act in ways that have previously resulted in rewarding situations. Also, experiences which have been associated with rewards in the past can themselves

FIGURE 12-4

Example of advertisement projecting a product image. (Courtesy of Jaguar Rover Triumph, Inc.)

PART FOUR

392

INDIVIDUAL DETERMINANTS OF CONSUMER BEHAVIOR

begin to influence behavior. As noted earlier in the chapter, these secondary or learned motives can have very important effects on the behavior of consumers.

Assertion This group of influences stimulates competition, power, and success aspirations of consumers. The focus is different than a striving for self-actualization because it is more oriented toward achievement and surpassing other people. This emphasizes products in terms of how they help one to succeed, or how they communicate to others that success has been achieved. Some marketers of sporting equipment, furniture, and automobiles have been able to effectively appeal to this motive. An example is presented in Figure 12-5.

Affiliation Consumers having affiliation motives seek acceptance, affection, and warm personal contact with others. Figure 12-6 presents only one of many instances where AT&T has linked use of its products and services to the affiliation motive.

FIGURE 12-5
Example of an appeal to the assertion motive category. (Courtesy of Yamaha Motor Corp., U.S.A.)

BEAT THY

Identification One source of consumer satisfaction is the development of new identities and roles which enhance a person's self-concept. Acting these roles out in social settings allows one to express her values and develop feelings of worth and importance. Advertisements can represent a useful source of information about such new roles. They also suggest a means of expressing these roles to others. More will be said about this topic in Chapter 15.

Modeling Consumers frequently tend to identify and empathize with others. This can lead to behavior which imitates certain individuals. Such a modeling tendency is often capitalized on in advertisements through the use of celebrities and others with high potential for identification. It also appears to be an important ingredient in reference-group influence and opinion leadership as discussed in Chapters 9 and 11.

The description and classification of motives provide useful perspectives for understanding consumers. However, it must be remembered that motives have only a general influence on behavior. Their exact effect is modified by environmental conditions and the consumer's existing states, such as his attitudes and

FIGURE 12-6

Example of an appeal to the affiliation category of motives. (Courtesy of AT&T Long Lines.)

knowledge. Consequently, although we may know that a given motive *can* activate and guide behavior toward a particular direction, this does not necessarily enable us to predict that it *will* do so. Also, any given behavior, such as the purchase of a particular product, can be influenced by many motives. This means that by merely observing consumers' actions we are often not in a good position to specify the motives that are influencing them. These comments demonstrate the need for marketers to understand more about the structuring and operational characteristics of motives, such as how they are aroused, what influences their strength, and why they persist over time. It is to these and similar issues that we now turn.

MOTIVE AROUSAL

The arousal concept concerns what energizes consumers. Remember from our earlier discussion that although arousal activates bodily energy, it provides little, if any, direction to behavior.

Triggering Arousal

A variety of mechanisms can trigger the arousal of motives and energize consumers. The following may work alone or in combination to activate behavior.[11]

Physiological Conditions One source of arousal acts to satisfy our biological needs for food, water, and other life-sustaining necessities. Depriving such a bodily need generates an uncomfortable state of tension. When this tension is sufficiently strong, arousal occurs to provide energy necessary to satisfy the need. The consumer's previous experience and present situation will strongly influence the directions any heightened activity will take.

Cognitive Activity Humans engage in considerable cognitive activity (thinking and reasoning) even when the objects of their thoughts are not physically present. This thinking, considered by some to be daydreaming or fantasy, can also act as a motive trigger. One way this occurs is when consumers deliberate about unsatisfied wants. For example, thinking about one's lack of physical activity can arouse energy to remedy the situation.

Situational Conditions The particular situation confronting consumers may also trigger arousal. This can occur when the situation draws attention to an existing physiological condition, as when noticing an advertisement for Lipton iced tea suddenly makes you aware of being thirsty. Here, the need for liquids may have been present, but not yet strong enough to trigger arousal. Seeing the advertisement draws attention to the condition and leads to activity.

Situational conditions can also work alone to generate motive arousal. This appears to occur when circumstances draw consumers' attention to the disparity between their present state and something viewed as a better condition. For example, a car owner may see an advertisement stressing how a new type of spark plug will result in considerable fuel economy. Such a message might, by itself, be responsible for triggering the aroused state.

Stimulus Properties A number of behavioral scientists have noted that certain properties of external stimuli themselves also seem to have the power to generate arousal.[12] These *collative properties* include the characteristics of novelty, surprisingness, ambiguity, and uncertainty. Stimuli possessing a sufficient amount of these properties have the potential of drawing attention to themselves by arousing an individual's curiosity or desire for exploration. As such, they represent a special type of situational condition.

Stimuli with arousal potential are important for marketers because they can be used to attract and focus consumers' attention. This represents an opportunity to present information, facilitate consumers' processing of that information, and increase involvement and interest in the product. Therefore, a great deal of effort is devoted to incorporating stimuli with arousal potential into promotions and packaging. An important aspect of this effort is to choose stimuli that will also draw sufficient attention to the marketer's message or product as well as to themselves.[13]

Optimal Stimulation and Arousal

Historically, consumers have been viewed mainly as tension avoiders. Similar to the operation described for physiological triggers, events creating tension were seen as generating arousal which initiated tension reduction activity. From this, it might be tempting to conclude that since external variables can also generate tension, consumers might *consistently* seek to minimize such environmental stimulation. However, at best, this conclusion only describes certain activity patterns. Casual observation and research evidence both suggest that in many situations consumers do not act to minimize external sources of stimulation. Sudden purchases of different brands "just for a change," window shopping activity, and the trial of many new products have been cited as examples. Another is the great interest many consumers show in various intriguing products such as Rubik's Cube.[14]

We do not presently know a great deal about the exact causes underlying such behavior. However, several theories suggest the existence of a motivation to seek variety or novelty, or to explore stimuli that are seemingly inconsistent with expectations.[15] This was noted in McGuire's motive classification scheme reviewed earlier. One element common to most of these explanations is that consumers' *optimum* stimulation level is at a moderate (not minimum) magnitude. Therefore, depending on conditions, consumers may seek increases or reductions in their external stimulation.

The theory proposed by Streufert and Driver serves to explain such behavior.[16] In this scheme, the stimulation a consumer derives from the environment is determined by the amount of incongruity or disparity existing between his stored knowledge of the environment and the information that he actually receives from it. For example, a large disparity between what the consumer "knows" about a brand and the experiences he actually has while using it would generate considerable stimulation. However, if the consumer's beliefs and knowledge are confirmed through use of the brand, little stimulation is likely to occur.

Based on past experiences, each consumer is seen as adapting to and expecting certain average levels of incongruity or stimulation from his environment.[17] This level, called the *general incongruity adaptation level* (GIAL), becomes the optimum amount of stimulation derived from the environment. Therefore, more or less than the optimum amount will be uncomfortable and is likely to motivate behavior designed to return to the optimum. The type of behavior that will be

FIGURE 12-7
Diagram based on Streufert and Driver's theory of the relationship between optimum stimulation and affect.

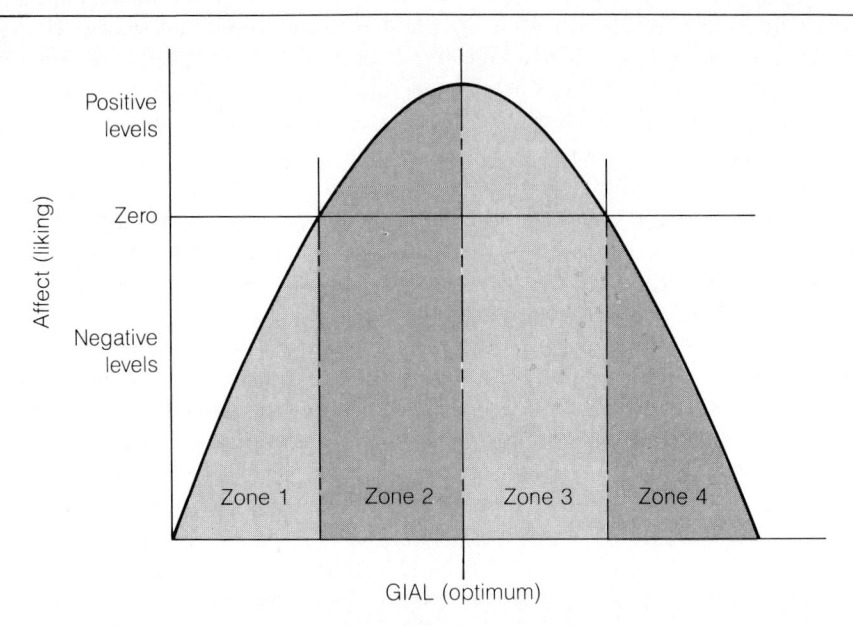

engaged in is influenced by the magnitude and direction of the difference between present levels of environmental stimulation and the GIAL.

These relationships are shown in Figure 12-7. The degree of incongruity or stimulation generated by differences between stored knowledge of the environment and actual experiences is represented on the x axis. The amount of affect (degree of liking) of the stimulation is represented on the y axis. This ranges from negative levels through zero, which is represented by the horizontal line, to positive levels. The parabolic-shaped curve shows the relationship between levels of stimulation and the degree of liking or affect that the consumer will exhibit. Note that the optimum level of stimulation (GIAL), shown on the x axis, corresponds to the greatest degree of consumer satisfaction. Also, note that this value is somewhat *above* the zero point on the x axis, showing that the optimum amount of environmental stimulation is at a moderate level.

Figure 12-7 also shows that very low and very high levels of stimulation produce negative affects, while moderate deviations from the GIAL produce positive affects. In fact there are four ranges or zones of stimulation values that a given stimulus might generate for a consumer. If the stimulus falls into zone 1 the resulting stimulation will be very low, generating the negative affect of considerable boredom. A rather active search for completely new, more stimulating experiences is to be expected in this situation. This behavior is quite descriptive of a consumer who has become extremely familiar with and actually bored by a brand that she has purchased repetitively for a considerable period of time.

In zone 2 stimulation is still below optimum, but not enough to generate negative affects. Consequently, new stimulus experiences will not be sought. Instead, the consumer will be passively receptive to new stimulus situations and will probably devote some effort to exploring existing stimuli in greater depth. Both of these activities are taken to yield moderate increases in stimulation. Consumers facing zone 2 levels of stimulation include those that are only slightly bored by their existing brands. As such, they may be susceptible to negative information about these brands coming from other consumers or producers of competitive brands.

Zone 3 levels of stimulation are slightly above optimum but still within levels that the consumer perceives favorably. Therefore, the motivation to seek new sources of stimulation is not high. Passive reception of other stimuli and examination in greater depth of existing stimuli are likely to occur. In both cases, the goal is to reduce stimulation levels. Consumers who have purchased a new product or brand and then learn that it is a little too different, novel, or complex are likely to experience zone 3 levels of stimulation.

In the fourth zone, present levels of stimulation are so high above optimum that they are quite uncomfortable to the consumer, and they yield negative affects. Additional stimulation certainly will not be sought. In fact the consumer will be motivated to escape from the uncomfortable state and actively seek other more familiar stimuli that will bring him closer to optimum. People in this situation are frequently seen as avoiding unfamiliar or novel brands and preferring known, standard brands. They are also susceptible to advertisements that make brands appear less novel.

To summarize, the theory suggests that the types of information a consumer will seek and be receptive to are a function of the present level of stimulation being received from the environment. If stimulation levels are below optimum, the consumer will be disposed to increase them, and if levels are above optimum, action will be directed toward reducing the stimulation. The nature of the actions will depend on the particular stimulation zone the consumer is facing.

Effects of Arousal

We have already seen that several mechanisms can trigger arousal to release energy for consumers' actions. Factors influencing the extent and direction of aroused behavior will be discussed shortly. What is important to note here is that the intensity of arousal acts to regulate the amount of effort consumers will devote to a particular motivating situation. This can take a variety of forms. One aspect is the degree to which attention mechanisms are sensitized to receive information from the environment. Higher amounts of arousal result in greater attention to stimuli that may have been previously ignored. This increases the chances that the consumer will become aware of information useful in dealing with the motivational situation.

The process just described is quite passive in nature, because the consumer's increased attention is only focused on stimuli that happen to be available. Another effect of arousal can expand the consumer's available information by energizing an active search process. This can involve asking questions of salespeople, reading *Consumer Reports,* or making a point to have a conversation with a friend. Of course, the exact nature of information desired and methods used to obtain it will be strongly influenced by the situation and the consumer's existing behavior patterns. However, active search processes generally include the purposeful seeking of information as well as an increased awareness of stimuli.

Arousal also influences the cognitive activity (thinking and evaluating) devoted to decision making about alternative goods and services. This involves regulating the effort allocated to interpreting potentially informative stimuli such as the EER rating for an air conditioner. It also involves allocating effort to reviewing stored knowledge about brands by using decision rules to evaluate and choose among purchase alternatives. Each of these activities can be accomplished with a great deal of deliberation or with hardly any conscious effort. Aroused energy is an important factor in influencing the extent of such decision making.

MOTIVE STRUCTURING

Motives do not act on consumers in an arbitrary manner. They fit together in a unified pattern. This suggests the existence of a priority scheme or structuring mechanism. The structuring of motives also provides a central theme or organization for the consistency of influence over time.

Motive Hierarchy

The concept of a hierarchy underlies many schemes offered to explain the structuring of motive influences. The most influential motive is seen as enjoying the most dominant position in the hierarchy, the second most influential holds the second most dominant position, and so on through the entire list. To be useful, however, the hierarchy concept must also help explain what factors influence the relative ordering of motives.

Maslow's Hierarchy Perhaps the most widely known hierarchy was proposed by A. H. Maslow. His scheme classified motives into five groupings and suggested the degree to which each would influence behavior.[18] Although this theory certainly is relevant to the topic of motive classification discussed earlier, its treatment has been reserved until now because of its importance to the structuring concept.

Maslow proposed that motives could be classified into five basic categories: physiological, safety, belongingness and love, esteem, and self-actualization. As depicted in Figure 12-8, he also suggested that these groupings are arranged in ascending order with physiological motives occupying the first position on the hierarchy and self-actualization occupying the last step. The degree to which each motive category is essential to existence and survival was seen to define its *prepotency* or initial importance. The first ordering of motives is then determined by their relative prepotency. The most prepotent motives (physiological) would have the greatest influence on behavior until they are adequately satisfied. At that point the next most prepotent motive—safety—would begin to dominate behavior. We would expect this to influence various purchase behaviors, such as concern with auto safety bumpers, burglar alarms, nonskid soles on sneakers, and other similar features or products. If the consumer is capable of adequately satisfying each succeeding motive category, self-actualization will finally tend to dominate behavior.

FIGURE 12-8
Diagram of Maslow's motive hierarchy depicting the relative predominance of motives and the number and variety of wants recognized for each motive. (*Source:* David Krech, Richard S. Crutchfield, and Egerton L. Ballachey, *Individual in Society*, McGraw-Hill, New York, 1962, p. 77.)

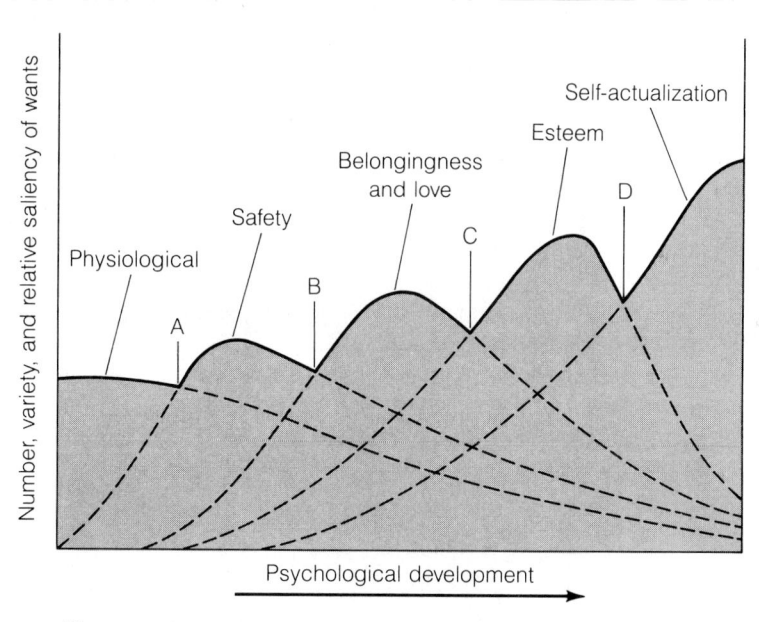

Key:
Physiological: motives which seek basic body requirements including water, food, and oxygen

Safety: motives for security, protection, and stability in one's life

Belongingness and love: those motives oriented toward affection and affiliation with others

Esteem: motives oriented toward achievement, prestige, status, and self-confidence

Self-actualization: those motives relating to self-fulfillment and maximizing one's potential

The pattern of succeeding motive influence is depicted in Figure 12-8. Points A through D define the places where higher level motives will begin to assume dominance over more prepotent, but adequately satisfied motives.

It is also important to note that even after being passed on the hierarchy, a motive can assume temporary dominance over behavior. This will occur as a result of *deprivation*—the extent to which the motive is not being adequately satisfied. The degree to which deprivation can affect the structuring of motives and assume temporary dominance over consumers' actions is easily appreciated if you recall the last time you were extremely hungry.

Maslow also argued that as individuals progress from being dominated by physiological motives toward self-actualization, they grow psychologically and come to develop more wants and to seek a greater variety of ways to satisfy particular motives. Thus, in our economy, consumers dominated by the "higher" motives of esteem or self-actualization will be expected to show interest in a greater variety of products and services than consumers dominated by "lower" order motives. Of course, this focus on goods and services does not necessarily hold for individuals or peoples from other cultures with less materialistic tendencies.

Although Maslow's scheme is useful for a general understanding of motives, it has limited use in attempting to predict specific behavior.[19] Of particular concern is that consumers are continually influenced by motives that they apparently passed on the hierarchy. For example, even in our economy, safety (second on the hierarchy) still appears to motivate many consumer decisions. Some suggest that the theory accounts for this because even though the focus is on dominant motives, the hierarchy still allows for the influence of other motives not in a dominant position. This is said to explain fluctuating behavior under conditions of a stable hierarchy. However, the mechanism regulating this process has not been well defined.

Hierarchy Dynamics Difficulties in explaining changing behavior patterns using a relatively stable motive hierarchy have led some to suggest a goal hierarchy to help bridge the gap between motives and behavior.[20] Motives can then be viewed as exerting a relatively stable influence on goals. Opportunities, constraints, and changing conditions in the consumer's environment may be seen as a dynamic influence. The interaction of these two forces can then lead to changes in goal importance and flexible behavior patterns.

Aspiration levels also help to explain how dynamic consumer goals can occur under the influence of relatively stable motives. A level of aspiration may be thought of as a goal that can be influenced by a number of factors to change either up or down over time. Therefore, as consumers approach achievement of a goal, they can still be influenced by the same motive structure to strive for even higher levels of achievement. Similar to Alice in Wonderland, the goal moves upward so that we run faster and faster to reach it. For example, hunger can easily be satisfied by very basic foodstuffs such as beans and milk, but most American consumers set their sights "higher" for foods such as Big Macs and pizzas. Influences on consumers' levels of aspirations include

1 Achievement—Success yields rising aspiration levels, while failure tends to result in a decline in such goals.

2 Reality orientation—Usually aspirations are set to reflect the individual's assessment of what levels of achievement are within reach.

3 Group influences—Consumers' aspirations are influenced by individuals in membership and reference groups. In addition to pressures to "keep up with the Joneses," this provides consumers with reference points as to what levels of achievement exist for various activities and interests.[21]

These characteristics of aspiration levels demonstrate that wants are insatiable and that consumers' attempts to achieve them through purchases in the marketplace have led to a very advanced economic system in the United States. However, some suggest that it also has created serious resource shortages, a degradation of our environment, and various other problems.[22]

A further influence on motive and goal structuring is learning. As indicated earlier under the discussion of classifying motives, consumers can acquire (learn) new motives from dealing with their environment. Much of this occurs during the childhood socialization process. The acquisition of these *secondary* motives results in restructuring the hierarchy. This occurs because secondary motives are often quite strong and therefore can significantly influence behaviors. Consider, for example, how the learned needs for social approval so strongly influences purchase decisions from personal-care products to automobiles.

Motive Combinations

It is convenient to discuss motives separately, as if they influence consumers independently and one at a time. Actually, they often interact, leading to a combined influence or to situations in which they conflict and exert opposing influences on behavior.[23]

Motive Linking Because motives can differ in how specific they are, it is possible for a linking to occur at various levels of generality. For example, safety may actually be made up of more specific motives, including those relating to security and protection. Therefore, achievement of a specific motive can be a means of approaching a more general motive which is viewed as the goal.[24] This is referred to as the means-end linking of motives. A linking that might exist to influence purchase of a door lock is depicted in Figure 12-9. Here, we see that safety has

FIGURE 12-9
A means-end linking for a door-lock purchase. (*Source:* John A. Howard and Jagdish N. Sheth, *The Theory of Buyer Behavior,* Wiley, New York, 1969, p. 107.)

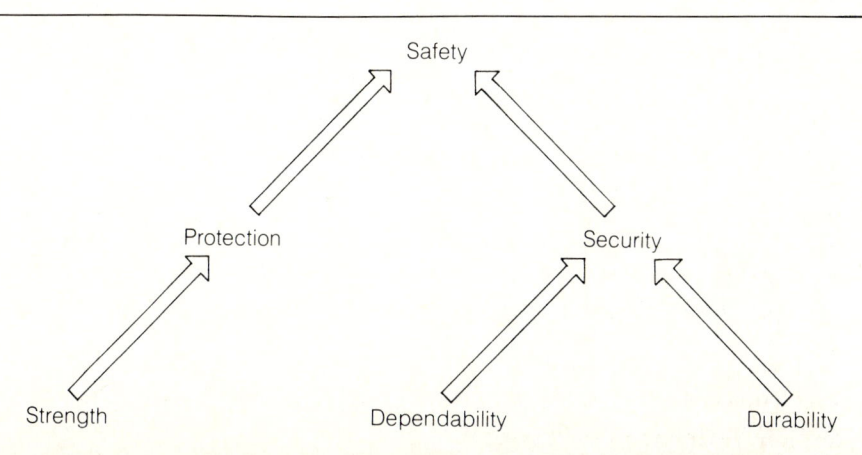

been linked to the more specific motives of protection and security. In turn, these have been linked to strength, dependability, and durability properties of the product. All of these factors can exert a combined influence on the consumer.

Motive Bundling A given product can satisfy various motives at the same approximate level of specific influence. This results in the bundling or combining of influences on consumers' decisions. To illustrate, for an automobile purchase, a desire for transportation can bundle with motives for achievement, social recognition, safety, and economy.

Motive bundling and linking allow development of product and promotional strategies to increase or sustain consumers' interest over a period of time. For example, the diminishing supplies and increasing prices of gasoline resulted in changing both automobiles and their promotions to emphasize fuel economy. Also, Sears has promoted their radial tires at various times as appealing to the economy motive (long-lasting), safety motive (superior handling), and again later in terms of economy (better mileage).

Motive Conflict Motives can also conflict with each other to affect how consumers interact with the marketplace. A major contributor to the topic of motive conflict is Kurt Lewin.[25] He viewed motives as influencing the attracting or repelling forces of goals in the individual's environment. The degree to which a product or service satisfies a motive will therefore determine its attracting (positive) force, and how adverse it is to a motive will influence its repelling (negative) force.

In Lewin's view, conflict is most likely when motives are of approximately equal strength. Three principal cases are possible: approach-approach, avoidance-avoidance, and approach-avoidance conflict. Actually, these terms refer to psychological tendencies for attraction or repulsion, not necessarily actual physical movement.

APPROACH-APPROACH CONFLICT This is a situation in which conflict exists between two desirable alternatives, such as when a consumer must decide how to allocate purchasing dollars between a tennis racket and an electronic calculator (see Figure 12-10). These situations can lead to a period of temporary indecision and vacillation between alternatives. Permanent indecision is rare, however, because approach-approach conflict is said to be unstable. This occurs because the pull toward a positive goal increases as one approaches it, and declines as one moves away. Therefore, a slight tendency to accept one alternative can lead to resolving the conflict quickly. Such resolution can occur through exposure to information useful in evaluating the alternatives. Promotional literature and salespeople's comments play a crucial role in this process.

Resolution of approach-approach conflict can also occur through reassessment of goals that might lead to a decision that achieving one goal is more important than the other. Again, comments of salespeople can be quite influential. Of course, a third resolution involves attempts to achieve modified versions of both goals. In our example, this could occur through purchase of less-expensive models of a calculator and tennis racket.

AVOIDANCE-AVOIDANCE CONFLICT This situation occurs when consumers face choices between two alternatives, both of which are perceived as being negative in nature. For example, when the television set with which a family has been perfectly happy becomes seriously "ill," the alternatives may be a hefty repair bill or the large expense of a replacement set (see Figure 12-10). Such situations are characterized as being stable because consumers tend to vacillate between undesirable alternatives. This occurs because approaching a negative alternative leads to a stronger repulsion by it. Such situations often lead to considerable search for information (window shopping, reading ads, and making inquiries) but often stop short of a purchase commitment.

APPROACH-AVOIDANCE CONFLICT Situations in which consumers are in conflict between a positive and negative alternative make up this category. Such situations often occur when making decisions on a single product in which both positive and negative aspects are involved in the purchase. For example, (see Figure 12-10), to acquire an attractive product such as a car, consumers must part with a sizeable amount of scarce purchasing dollars. These types of cash outflows can generate considerale amounts of purchase avoidance, as demonstrated by the frequent auto sales slumps that occur.

Approach-avoidance conflict also tends to be stable, because both attracting and repelling forces increase as the goal object is approached; but the repelling force increases more sharply. This results in the consumer being attracted by goal

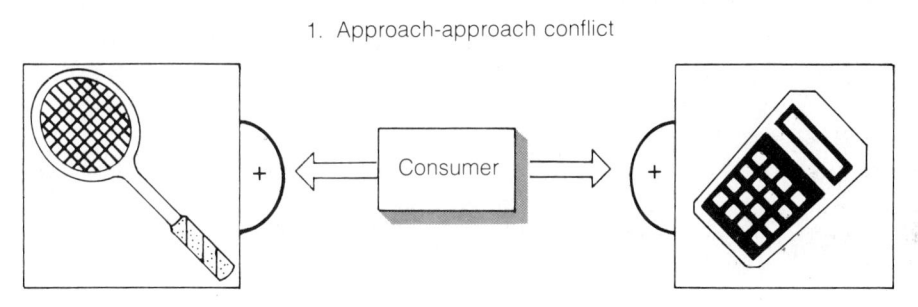

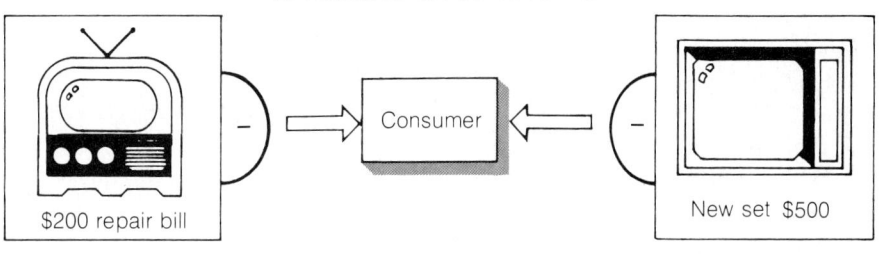

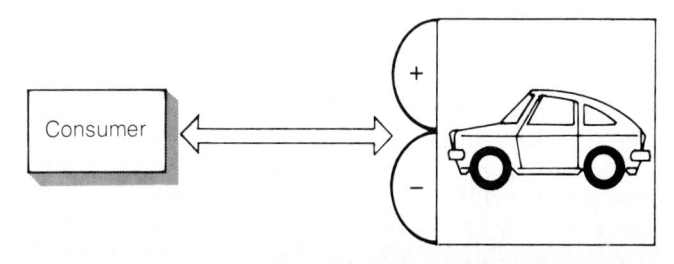

FIGURE 12-10

A typology of motive conflict situations. (*Source:* Kurt Lewin, *A Dynamic Theory of Personality,* McGraw-Hill, New York, 1935.)

objects but experiencing increasing resistance to them as they are approached. Marketers have recognized this problem, and they have developed means to reduce the avoidance aspect of such conflicts. Banks offer loans in which you "borrow in June and start paying in September" and major airlines offer "Fly Now, Pay Later" programs. The availability of credit cards and financing arrangements also contribute to the ease of making large expenditures.

Approach-avoidance conflict also happens in more subtle ways such as when consumers must choose between alternative brands of a given product in which, compared to one another, each brand has both positive and negative features. As a case in point, choosing a Ford over a Chevrolet because of its styling also means sacrificing the traditionally higher trade-in value of Chevrolets. When faced with such important choices, consumers frequently exhibit considerable conflict and indecision. Consequently, salespeople have developed closing techniques to encourage customers to make a decision. The following is just a sampling of such methods.

Advantage/disadvantage close—Negative and positive features of each alternative are summarized to assist the customer in determining which alternative appears to be the better choice.

Critical feature close—Stress is placed on one or a few "critical" features of one brand that the other does not possess.

Critical time close—In cases in which one brand is in short supply, or in which a special sale is about to end, emphasizing the immediacy of the decision can convince a consumer to purchase.

Self-Concept

Although a consumer's motive structure exhibits some flexibility over time, there remains a central theme or organization to the structure. One factor influencing this organization is the individual's self-concept. That is, consumers possess a certain image of themselves, and this self-concept exerts an organizing influence on their motives.

One important effect of this influence on motives is reflected in the types of goods purchased, since consumers appear to prefer some products and brands that are consistent with their self-concepts. Thus, we would expect to see individuals who view themselves as successful businesspersons drive cars, own homes, join clubs, and interact with social groups that reflect this self-image. These points will be more fully discussed in Chapter 15. However, the topic of self-concept is introduced here because of its relationship to consumer involvement.

INVOLVEMENT

Consider a consumer facing two different buying situations. The first involves purchasing a new pair of running shoes. Because this consumer runs an average of 50 miles per week, she is really "into" the sport and quite interested in her footwear. Recent talks with another runner resulted in consideration of a change in brands. This led to a careful reading of many advertisements in several issues of *Runners World* magazine. She also closely studied the special issue that rated all major shoe brands according to a variety of criteria. Based on detailed evaluation of her own running characteristics and the magazine's ratings of shoes, she decided that the more expensive model of New Balance shoes was her best choice. Discussion of this decision with fellow runners and salespeople at a sports store confirmed the choice and led to a purchase. The decision-making process took two weeks.

In the second situation, this same consumer decided it was time to restain the deck of her house. Although she had seen numerous television commercials for Cuprinol stains, they had not captured her interest or attention. Consequently, the brand was not on her mind during the trip to a local hardware store. Upon finding three different brands on display, she began looking at the labels and recognized the Cuprinol name. She was not aware of any previous exposure to this brand, but since a glance revealed no drastic price differences she purchased three gallons of Cuprinol in a redwood color. The entire process occupied only a portion of one Saturday afternoon and involved little effort.

These two buying situations differ considerably in terms of the energy devoted to purchase decisions. Unfortunately, many marketers assume that typically, consumers are actively involved to the extent described in the first example. Although this view may be appropriate for many situations, it appears lacking for a wide variety of other cases that more resemble our second example—consumers having little concern about their consumption activities and adopting a rather detached, reactive stance to stimuli that reach their awareness.

Herbert Krugman proposed the concept of *involvement* to characterize differences in the intensity of interest with which consumers approach their dealings with the marketplace.[26] A major concern is how the level of involvement affects attention given to advertisements, and how it influences the extent to which consumers will actively evaluate or passively accept the information contained in these communications. Special focus is also on low-involvement situations, because they appear to evoke different mental processes than those generated under conditions of high involvement. For example, under low involvement the consumer may learn product information even when not attempting to do so, and his brand attitudes may actually not be a very strong influence on his purchase decisions.

Recently, consumer researchers have become quite interested in the topic of consumer involvement. As one might expect for a relatively new concept, full agreement has not yet been reached regarding its nature.[27] Some definitions emphasize the degree to which the consumer makes personal connections between a product and herself. Others focus on changes in arousal levels or on how involvement affects consumers' processing of information contained in marketing communications. However, most definitions acknowledge that involvement

1 Is related to the consumer's values and self-concept which influence the degree of personal importance ascribed to a product

2 Can vary across individuals and different situations

3 Is related to some form of arousal

Based on a review of these and other characteristics, Mitchell has suggested that involvement has the critical properties of 1) intensity—degree of arousal, and 2) directional influence.[28] Therefore, although involvement as characterized above may not be identical to motivation, the two concepts appear closely related in important aspects.

Dimensions of Involvement

The concept of involvement is multifaceted in that it appears to have a number of important dimensions. The following paragraphs describe several of these dimensions to encourage a fuller appreciation of this potentially important influence on consumers.

Involvement Levels Typically, involvement has been viewed in terms of two broad categories—high and low. More recently, some have suggested that three levels may exist to influence how consumers act with regard to product and brand information in their environment.[29] An important contribution of these schemes is their implication for an understanding of how consumers process information. However, for our purpose here it is sufficient only to draw distinctions between high and low involvement levels.

A highly involved consumer is one who is very interested in differences between particular brands of a product and is willing to invest considerable energy in deliberations about it. Similar to the example about purchasing running shoes, this interest often generates a sizeable amount of active search for information, as well as increased attention to relevant brand advertisements. In addition, highly involved consumers, rather than just passively accepting information, tend to critically evaluate the negative and positive implications of received information. Attitudes are formed about specific brands from the beliefs that consumers develop from such critical evaluations.

When consumers operate under low-involvement conditions they are passive receivers of information who engage in virtually no active information search about alternative brands. Also, advertisements or other information actually reaching attention will only be processed at a very superficial level, receiving little meaningful evaluation. Very low levels of brand awareness and comprehension will be the result. Further, consumers do not appear to develop distinct attitudes about brands from such information.

Influencing Conditions A second involvement dimension deals with the conditions influencing its nature or intensity.[30] One condition appears to be the consumer himself. That is, due to different values, experiences, or self-concepts, individuals differ in the extent to which they become involved with a given product or service. In fact, some consumers actually have such a low concern for material things that they are generally uninterested in purchasing products or services. However, even among the vast majority of other consumers, the amount of involvement expressed for any specific product, such as a pair of running shoes, will differ considerably depending on how the product relates to the individual's values, self-concept, and so on.

Situational influences represent another condition affecting involvement levels. One set of situational influences are product characteristics, such as cost or the degree of product complexity. For example, although a consumer may not be particularly interested in automobiles, their high cost can motivate considerable decision-making effort in order to insure that the "best" alternative is acquired for the money.

The actions or expected actions of other people important to the consumer are another type of situational influence on involvement. Here, products with normally low interest levels can take on considerable significance because the consumer expects other important individuals to view him differently, depending on their reactions to the product and his use of it. As a case in point, consider how many consumers tend to invest more effort in choosing wines, meats, and other food items when special friends or "the boss" has been invited to dinner.

It should be noted that many influences on involvement levels may be regulated by the amount of risk (economic loss, social embarrassment, etc.) that the consumer perceives in a purchase situation. The subject of perceived risk will be discussed in another chapter.

Response Characteristics The response dimension characterizes how a consumer behaves under different involvement conditions. That is, it describes the mental and physical actions or reactions the consumer engages in. Therefore, the response dimension is really a function of the type of involvement generated by personal and situational influences.

Some response characteristics have already been mentioned in our earlier discussion of involvement levels. However, it is useful to provide a fuller view of their nature here. Generally, we can view the response dimension as including different patterns of information search and acquisition, the mental processing of information to evaluate products and make decisions about them, and past decision behavior.[31]

As has already been noted, high involvement generates rather intense efforts on the part of the consumer for attending to and actively searching out sources of product and brand information. Conversely, low involvement appears to result in a passive consumer who engages in little if any active search for information. Exposure to products occurs mainly through advertisements and other information which the consumer happens to confront as a result of engaging in other activities (watching TV, etc.). Also, because of this lack of interest, little attention is devoted to these sources. Consequently, only modest amounts of information may be acquired about a specific brand even after many exposures to advertisements for it.

After acquiring information, consumers process it to determine its meaning. The steps undertaken in this information-processing stage have been viewed in terms of a *hierarchy of effects* because they appear to describe the mental processes that lead to a purchase. A variety of hierarchies have been proposed under one common assumption—the consumer is highly involved. More recently, a different hierarchy of effects has been proposed for low-involvement conditions.[32] The essence of each hierarchy that is relevant to our present discussion is presented in Figure 12-11.

FIGURE 12-11
Hierarchy of effects under high- and low-involvement conditions.

High involvement hierarchy
Cognition
⇓
Attitude
⇓
Behavior

Low involvement hierarchy
Cognition
⇓
Behavior
⇓
Attitude

Cognition in the high-involvement hierarchy refers to the knowledge and beliefs about brands that consumers derive from evaluating information. Active search and attention to information fosters learning about advertisements and other product information. In addition, the consumer engages in considerable thinking about this information to determine its consistency with his existing brand knowledge and beliefs. Critical evaluation and rejection of information inconsistent with existing beliefs are likely to occur. This can happen through the consumer's use of arguments to counter information or advertising claims ("the price is low, but I'll bet the service is bad") and through attempts to discredit the source of the information. Alternatively, consistent information is likely to generate strong supportive arguments. The result is a new or modified set of beliefs about alternative brands.

As the second stage in the high-involvement hierarchy suggests, evaluation of beliefs in a positive and negative sense leads the consumer to form attitudes about the brands and their relative desirability. Resulting behavior is believed to be strongly influenced by the attitudes that the consumer holds.

Cognition in the low-involvement hierarchy differs considerably from its counterpart under conditions of high involvement. Attention levels are low because the consumer has little desire to process information for the purpose of evaluating brands. Despite exposure to many advertisements, knowledge about brands is also very low. In fact, the consumer may not even be consciously aware of the brand name. Consequently, beliefs about brands are not well founded and will not be strong enough to support the formation of brand attitudes.

Another consequence may occur after numerous exposures to advertisements about a particular brand. The brand name can become sufficiently familiar to the consumer so that she recognizes it when shopping for the product. Because the consumer has no strong attitude about any of the specific brands, this familiarity may be a sufficient reason for purchase of the brand. Therefore, as the second stage in the low-involvement hierarchy shows, purchase behavior occurs before strong brand attitudes have developed. After the consumer purchases and experiences the product through direct use, it is likely that she will develop some attitudes about it. However, these attitudes may never become very strong because of the low importance of the product to the consumer.

Marketing Implications

Two essential conclusions emerge from the above review:

1 For numerous products, many consumers are quite uninterested in learning about alternative brands and their characteristics.

2 Consumers may make many purchase decisions without first developing clear brand attitudes or even having much knowledge about alternative brands.

Given that involvement can vary across consumers and situations, these conclusions have a number of marketing strategy implications.[33] A primary consideration is to determine whether any strategy should account for different levels of involvement. If only a small proportion of the market operates on a low-involvement condition for the brand in question, it may not be economical to consider changing strategies. However, if sizeable portions of the potential market might relate to the company's offerings at either level of involvement, then some manner of coping with these different levels would seem highly desirable. One strategy might be to differentiate marketing communications for each condition. For example, high-involvement messages would entail longer advertisements and considerable amounts of more-complex information. In addition, because of its higher involvement demands, print media may be the more appropriate choice for advertising insertions.[34] For the low-involvement advertisements, short visually-oriented messages with little information content could be frequently repeated to foster brand awareness. Many of these might be placed on television because of its lower demands for viewer concentration and the potential for frequent advertising insertions.

A second involvement-related strategy would be an attempt to move low-involvement consumers to higher levels.[35] Of course, the specific situation will determine the feasibility of this alternative. If conditions appear favorable, various methods may be considered. These could include creating controversy (the Pepsi challenge, live taste tests for Schlitz beer, etc.), linking the product to a highly involving issue (air fresheners related to the problem of social disgrace), or changing the product to add features which might increase involvement levels, like the producers of VitaGum did when they added vitamins to chewing gum.

A third strategy option is also possible—segmenting consumers into high- and low-involvement groups and tailoring marketing programs for each.[36] An example might be writing pens. Low-involvement consumers could be catered to with inexpensive models that are rather nondescript and disposable. Frequent television commercials could remind mass audiences of the brand name. Conversely, those concerned with conveying an image with their pen might be willing to spend more than $30 and even as much as $9000.[37] These instruments would have distinctive materials, styling, and craftsmanship. Promotions detailing many product features might be placed in exclusive magazines such as the *New Yorker* or *Smithsonian* to attract high-income readers.

This section has introduced the involvement concept, suggested its general potential for influencing the behavior of consumers, and indicated its implications for marketing strategy. We will build on this introduction in subsequent chapters to show the relevance of involvement to the variables under discussion.

MOTIVATION RESEARCH

We have noted that many consumers are unaware of the motives influencing their purchase behavior. That is, some motives may not reach the consumer's consciousness, and others may be repressed because to deal with them may be uncomfortable. This presents difficulty to the marketer who needs to understand consumers in order to design the most effective mix of marketing offerings. Any direct attempts to determine such motives, say by interviewing consumers, may only yield "surface" explanations or rationalizations that hide true strivings.

The concept of motivation research has been offered as a means of identifying consumers' true, underlying purchase motives. An introduction to this field and its methods was made in Chapter 3, and it would be useful to refer back to it at this point. Briefly stated, the methods involve disguised and indirect techniques in an attempt to probe consumers' inner motives without arousing defense mechanisms which can generate misleading results.

In practice, motivation research has yielded provocative and sometimes strange conclusions. For example, earlier findings included

Many men don't like to fly because they fear that if the plane crashes they will be blamed by their family for not being killed in a decent fashion, such as in a car crash.

When she is baking, a woman is unconsciously and symbolically reenacting the process of giving birth.

Men who use suspenders have an unresolved castration complex.[38]

The novelty of these interpretations is at least partially explained by the central role of fantasy, unconscious antisocial strivings, and sex in Freudian psychology which has apparently strongly influenced conclusions drawn from many motivation-research studies. There have also been a number of other criticisms leveled at motivation researchers.[39] First, sample sizes are frequently small because of the costly nature of depth interviewing. This has created problems with regard to making conclusions about the entire population of consumers. Second, motivation-research studies have generated inconsistent findings, and this leaves the marketer in a quandary as to what action should be taken. Further, some findings are difficult for the marketer to capitalize on. For example, of what practical use is it to know (assuming it is true) that suspender wearers have a castration complex? Finally, and perhaps most importantly, motivation researchers have been criticized for improperly employing research techniques borrowed from psychologists. In psychology, these techniques are used in conjunction with knowledge of a patient's history and normal standards of behavior to serve as references. The lack of such standards in marketing make it difficult to determine whether many motivation-research findings are truly representative of most consumers.

Despite its potential limitations, motivation research has been a valuable research tool in a number of situations. For example, in a now-classic study, Haire discovered evidence suggesting that initial resistance to Nescafé instant coffee may have been due to more than just its taste characteristics. Projective methods revealed that women believed users of the instant product were lazy and not particularly good wives. Thus, it was argued, they would not be quick to adopt it themselves.[40] Other studies have provided data for marketing decisions of major industrial giants such as Alcoa, Colgate-Palmolive, General Mills, and Chrysler Corporation. Therefore, it appears that when properly conducted motivation-research studies are employed with other information, they can provide valuable information about consumers.

SUMMARY

This chapter introduced the first of several individual determinants of consumer behavior. Motives were defined as inner states that mobilize and direct bodily energy toward goals located in the environment. After several schemes for classifying motives were reviewed, the concept of arousal was treated. Here, we learned that the major ways motives can be triggered are through physiological conditions, situational conditions, and cognitive activity. Although the concept of tension is central to motive arousal, we learned that the primary goal of consumers is not always to reduce environmental stimulation. Rather, the optimal level of stimulation appears to be above zero. This implies that, depending on present conditions, consumers may seek to decrease or *increase* stimulation levels. Perhaps this is due to a curiosity motive.

The concepts of motive hierarchies and levels of aspiration were seen to be central to an understanding of motive structuring. However, a practical view of such structuring must consider that motives interact to combine their influence or conflict with each other.

Discussion next turned to the highly related concept of consumer involvement. After involvement was characterized, attention focused on its levels, factors that influence it, and how consumers respond differently under conditions of low and high involvement. A low-involvement hierarchy of effects was seen to be different in important ways from the typical high-involvement hierarchy. Implications of these issues for marketing strategies were discussed.

Finally, the topic of motivation research was briefly reviewed. It appears that after an early flush of popularity, perhaps associated with overzealous application, the discipline has matured to a point in which its valid contributions can be usefully combined with other methods to explore consumers' motives.

DISCUSSION TOPICS

1 What is motive? Indicate the various roles motives play in influencing behavior.

2 Find three examples of advertisements that appeal to psychogenic motives. Be prepared to discuss the appropriateness of the association between the product and the motive.

3 Discuss the problems unconscious motives pose for implementing the marketing concept.

4 What general factors can trigger motive arousal? Cite at least two examples of each type.

5 It has been argued that at times consumers actually seem to increase levels of environmental stimulation as well as strive to reduce them. Review this argument, and suggest situations, as well as marketing strategies that could relate to such situations.

6 Briefly review Maslow's motive hierarchy and the concept of prepotency. Cite at least three products that might appeal to an individual at each state of the hierarchy. Can you suggest any product for which a marketer might be able to appeal to at least three of the stages at the same time?

7 Of what interest is the concept of "levels of aspiration" to the marketer? What relevance does this concept have to the problem of energy shortage and depletion of resources?

8 Review the concepts of motive linking and motive bundling. Show how they can apply to the purchase of a jogging suit.

9 Define each of the major types of motive conflict and cite a personal experience that fits each of these situations. Be sure to indicate the specifics involved, including any relevant products, the duration of the conflict, and how it was resolved.

10. Construct two high-involvement and two low-involvement consumer scenarios, and suggest marketing strategies to accommodate them.

NOTES

[1] See Roy J. Harris Jr., "Amtrak's Los Angeles—San Diego Rail Line Lures Commuters Where the Car is King," *The Wall Street Journal*, March 5, 1981, p. 27.

[2] See Joe Kent Kerby, *Consumer Behavior: Conceptual Foundations*, Dun-Donnelley, New York, 1975; Johan Arndt, "How Broad Should the Marketing Concept Be?" *Journal of Marketing*, 42: 101–103, January 1978; and Gerald Zaltman and Melanie Wallendorf, *Consumer Behavior: Basic Findings and Management Implications*, Wiley, New York, 1979.

[3] See Abraham K. Korman, *The Psychology of Motivation*, Prentice-Hall, Englewood Cliffs, NJ, 1974.

[4] Portions of this section follow the discussion in John Howard and Hagdish Sheth, *The Theory of Buyer Behavior*, Wiley, New York, 1969, pp. 105–118.

[5] One exception is the case of anxiety in which consumers suffer from a lack of direction to their arousal.

[6] See G. W. Allport and H. S. Odbert, "Trait-Names: A Psychological Study," *Psychological Monographs*, 47(1), 1936.

[7] W. Fred van Raaij and Kassaye Wandwossen, "Motivation-Need Theories and Consumer Behavior," in Keith Hunt (ed.), *Advances in Consumer Research: Volume 5*, Association for Consumer Research, Ann Arbor, MI, 1978, pp. 590–595.

[8] See William J. McGuire, "Some Internal Psychological Factors Influencing Consumer Choice," *Journal of Consumer Research*, 2:302–319, March 1976; and William J. McGuire, Psychological Motives and Communication Gratification," in J. G. Blumer and E. Katz (eds.), *The Uses of Mass Communications: Perspectives on Gratifications Research*, Sage Publications, Inc., Beverly Hills, CA, pp. 167–196.

[9] See Richard W. Mizerski, Linda L. Golden, and Jerome B. Kernan, "The Attribution Process in Consumer Decision-Making," *Journal of Consumer Research*, 6:123–140, September 1979; Richard Mizerski, "Causal Complexity: A Measure of Consumer Causal Attribution," *Journal of Marketing Research*, 15:220–228, May 1978; Robert E. Smith and Shelby D. Hunt, "Attributional Processes and Effects in Promotional Situations," *Journal of Consumer Research*, 5:149–158, December 1978; Robert Settle and Linda L. Golden, "Attribution Theory and Advertiser Credibility," *Journal of Marketing Research*, 11:181–185, May 1974; and Robert A. Hansen and Carol A. Scott, "Comments on Attribution Theory and Advertiser Credibility," *Journal of Marketing Research*, 13:193–197, May 1976.

[10] See Howard and Sheth, *The Theory of Buyer Behavior*, pp. 27–28 and 163–164.

[11] Some of this section follows David Krech, Richard S. Crutchfield, and Egerton L. Ballachey, *Individual in Society*, McGraw-Hill, New York, 1962, pp. 84–87.

[12] See, for example, D. E. Berlyne, *Conflict, Arousal and Curiosity*, McGraw-Hill, New York, 1960; Werner Kroeber-Riel, "Activation Research: Psychobiological Approaches in Consumer Research," *Journal of Consumer Research*, 5:240–250, March 1979; and P. S. Raju and M. Venkatesan, "Exploratory Behavior in the Consumer Context: A State of the Art Review," in Jerry C. Olson (ed.), *Advances in Consumer Research: Volume 7*, Ann Arbor, MI: Association for Consumer Research, 1979, pp. 258–263.

[13] For factors to consider in this decision see Werner Kroeber-Riel, "Activation Research" and Kathy A. Lutz and Richard J. Lutz, "The Effects of Interactive Imagery on Learning: Application to Advertising," University of California, Los Angeles Center for Marketing Studies, Paper No. 40, March 1976.

[14] Based on Gail Bronson, "Turn for the Worse: 'Simple' Little Puzzle Drives Millions Mad, *"The Wall Street Journal*, March 5, 1981, pp. 1, 20; Jane Carmichael, "Figure This One Out," *Forbes*, April 27, 1981, p. 34; and "Hot-Selling Hungarian Horror," *Time*, March 23, 1981, p. 83.

[15] See M. Venkatesan, "Cognitive Consistency and Novelty Seeking" in Scott Ward and Thomas S. Robertson(eds.), *Consumer Behavior: Theoretical Sources*, Prentice-Hall: Englewood Cliffs, NJ, 1973, pp. 354–384; and P. S. Raju, "Theories of Exploratory Behavior: Review and Consumer Research Implications," in Jagdish N. Sheth (ed.,), *Research in Marketing, Volume 4*, JAI Press, Greenwich, CT, 1981, pp. 223–249.

[16] S. Streufert and M. J. Driver, "The General Incongruity Adaptation Level (GIAL)," Technical Report 32, Dorsey Press, Homewood, IL, 1971.

[17] This discussion follows Raju, "Theories of Exploratory Behavior"; and P. S. Raju and M. Venkatesan, "Exploratory Behavior in the Consumer Context: A State of the Art Review," in Jerry C. Olson (ed.), *Advances in Consumer Research: Volume 7*, Association for Consumer Research, Ann Arbor, MI, 1980, pp. 258–263.

[18] A. H. Maslow, "A Theory of Human Motivation," *Psychological Review*, 50:370–396, 1943.

[19] See Frederick Herzberg, "Retrospective Comment," in Howard A. Thompson (ed.), *The Great Writings in Marketing*, Commerce, Plymouth, MI, 1976, pp. 180–181; and W. Fred van Raaij and Kassaye Wandwossen, "Motivation-Need Theories and Consumer Behavior," in Keith H. Hunt (ed.), *Advances in Con-*

sumer Research: Volume 5, Association for Consumer Research, Ann Arbor, MI, 1978, pp. 590–595 for critiques of Maslow's contributions.

[20] As an example, see James R. Bettman, *An Information Processing Theory of Consumer Choice,* Addison-Wesley, Reading, MA, 1979.

[21] George Katona, *The Powerful Consumer,* McGraw-Hill, New York, 1960, p. 130.

[22] See John Kenneth Galbraith, *The Affluent Society,* Houghton Mifflin, Boston, 1958.

[23] Some of this section follows Howard and Sheth, *The Theory of Buyer Behavior,* pp. 105–118.

[24] See Bettman, *Information Processing,* pp. 19–22, for an illustration.

[25] Kurt Lewin, *A Dynamic Theory of Personality,* McGraw-Hill, New York, 1935.

[26] H. E. Krugman, "The Impact of Television Advertising: Learning Without Involvement," *Public Opinion Quarterly,* **29**:349–356, Fall 1965.

[27] Anthony G. Greenwald, Clark Leavitt, and Carl Obermiller, "What is Low Consumer Involvement?" in Gerald J. Gorn and Marvin E. Goldberg (eds.), *Proceedings, Division 23 Program of the 88th Annual Convention,* American Psychological Association, Montreal, 1980, pp. 65–74.

[28] Andrew A. Mitchell, "Involvement: A Potentially Important Mediator of Consumer Behavior," in William L. Wilkie (ed.), *Advances in Consumer Research: Volume 6,* Association for Consumer Research, Ann Arbor, MI, 1979, pp. 191–196.

[29] See Andrew Mitchell, "The Dimensions of Advertising Involvement," in Kent B. Monroe (ed.), *Advances in Consumer Research: Volume 8,* Association for Consumer Research, Ann Arbor, MI, 1981, pp. 25–30; and Greenwald, Leavitt, and Obermiller, "What is Low Involvement?" for two different views of the three-level scheme.

[30] See Harold H. Kassarjian, "Low Involvement: A Second Look," in Kent B. Monroe (ed.), *Advances in Consumer Research: Volume 8,* Association for Consumer Research, Ann Arbor, MI, 1981, pp. 31–34; and Michael J. Houston and Michael L. Rothschild, "Conceptual and Methodological Perspectives on Involvement," in Subhash C. Jain (ed.), *Research Frontiers in Marketing: Dialogues and Directions,* American Marketing Association, Chicago, 1978, pp. 184–187, on which much of this section is based.

[31] Houston and Rothschild, "Perspectives on Involvement."

[32] See Michael L. Ray, "Marketing Communication and the Hierarchy-of-Effects," in Peter Clark (ed.), *New Models for Mass Communication Research,* Sage Publication, Inc., Beverly Hills, 1973, pp. 147–176; and Krugman, "Television Advertising: Learning Without Involvement," pp. 349–356.

[33] See Michael L. Rothschild, "Advertising Strategies for High and Low Involvement Situations," in John C. Maloney and Bernard Silverman (eds.), *Attitude Research Plays for High Stakes,* American Marketing Association, Chicago, 1979, pp. 74–93; Tyzoon T. Tyebjee, "Refinement of the Involvement Concept: An Advertising Planning Point of View," in John C. Maloney and Bernard Silverman (eds.), *Attitude Research Plays for High Stakes,* American Marketing Association, Chicago, 1979, pp. 94–111; Richard Vaughn, "How Advertising Works: A Planning Model," *Journal of Advertising Research,* **20**:27–33, October 1980; and Greenwald, Leavitt, and Obermiller, "What Is Low Involvement?"

[34] Herbert E. Krugman, "The Measure of Advertising Involvement," *Public Opinion Quarterly,* **30**:583–596, Winter 1966.

[35] Rothschild, "Advertising Strategies for Involvement."

[36] See Tyzoon T. Tyebjee, "Refinement of the Involvement Concept," pp. 107–108.

[37] Mitchell C. Lynch, "How're Ya Fixed for Fountain Pens?" *The Wall Street Journal,* June 12, 1981, p. 23.

[38] See Ernest Dichter, *Handbook of Consumer Motivations,* McGraw-Hill, New York, 1964, for these and other interesting motivation research findings.

[39] See N. D. Rothwell, "Motivational Research Reinstated," *Journal of Marketing,* **19**:150–154, October 1955.

[40] Mason Haire, "Projective Techniques in Marketing Research," *Journal of Marketing,* **14**:649–656, April, 1950.

CHAPTER 13
INFORMATION PROCESSING

The way consumers deal with stimuli they confront can strongly influence their thoughts and purchase patterns regarding products and services. Consider the following situations involving how consumers process the information in their environment.

> An aerosol disinfectant used to treat minor scrapes and skin irritations was modified by its producer to reduce its stinging properties. However, in a short time the original formulation was reinstated. It appeared that many consumers believed that the spray could not be a strong, effective disinfectant if it did not sting the user.

> Recently, some recorded commercials have been "time compressed"—i.e., the small segments of blank space within and between words are electronically removed. One benefit is the ability to insert more advertising message into the commercial. However, listeners also appear to like the faster paced messages better than their normal counterparts. In addition, brand names mentioned in time-compressed advertisements seem to be recalled up to 40 percent better than under normal conditions.

As these examples illustrate, it is important for the marketer to understand how consumers acquire and handle the information available from stimuli in their environment. This chapter introduces the nature and role of information processing. It begins with a brief overview of the concept. Major aspects of information acquisition, selective attention to stimuli, and the task of deriving meaning from these stimuli are then discussed in greater depth. The application of these concepts to a number of actual marketing decision problems is then reviewed. Additional information-processing topics are also treated later in the learning and attitude chapters as well as in Part Five of the text.

OVERVIEW

It is often helpful to view consumers as problem solvers who use information in an attempt to satisfy their consumption goals. From this perspective, *consumer information processing* may be thought of as the acquisition of stimulus inputs, the manipulation of these inputs to derive meaning from them, and the use of this information to think about products or services. More specifically, five of the major ways in which consumers use information derived from their environment are

1. To understand and evaluate products and services
2. To attempt to justify previous product choices
3. To resolve the conflict between buying or postponing purchases
4. To satisfy a need for being informed about products and services in the marketplace
5. To serve as a reminder to purchase products that must be regularly replenished (soap, beverages, etc.)[1]

It is important to realize that, as its definition implies, information processing is not the end result of an activity, but the actual process itself that consumers engage in when dealing with their environment. Figure 13-1 shows the basic components of information processing and will serve as a framework for our overview.

It should be noted that this model is more descriptive of processing activities that consumers engage in under conditions of high involvement, particularly with regard to stimulus acquisition activities. Processing under conditions of low involvement was briefly described in the previous chapter. That discussion can be used as a guide to draw material from this chapter that is relevant to the low-involvement condition. Future sections will also address this topic. However, because a great deal is not yet known about low-involvement processing, our treatment of it will be brief.

The basic components shown in Figure 13-1 can be arranged into four group-

FIGURE 13-1
An information-processing framework.

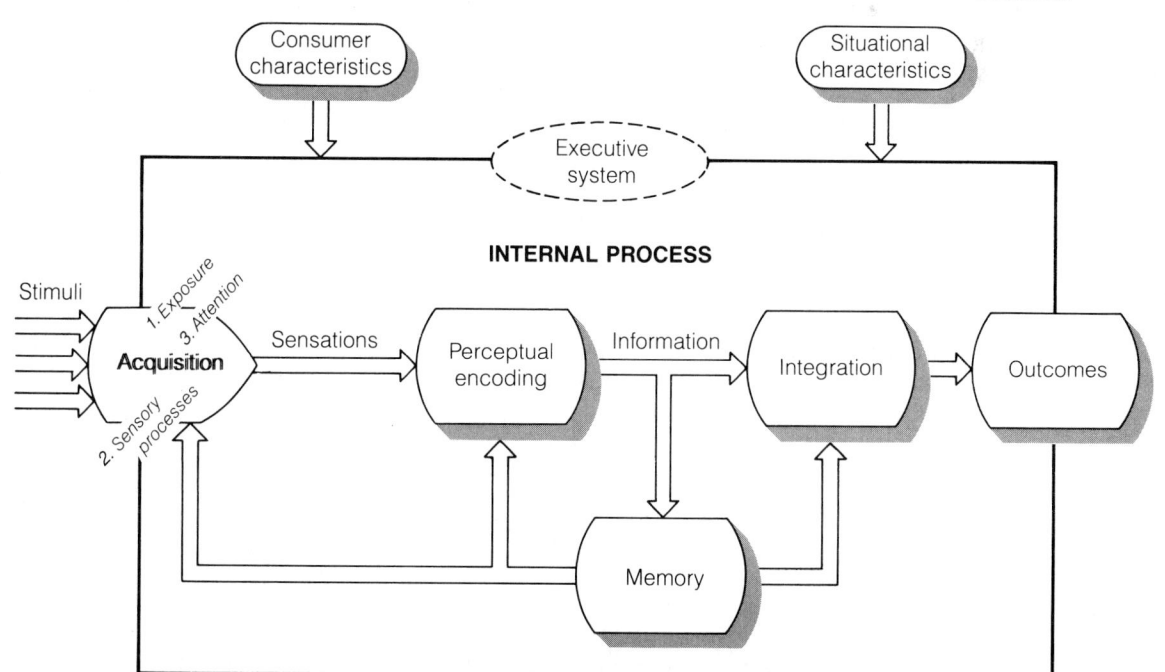

ings: (1) stimuli which serve as the raw material to be processed, (2) the stages of processing activities which are linked by arrows and are mainly internal to the consumer, (3) situational and consumer characteristics which can influence the nature of these processing activities, and (4) an executive system which guides the process by regulating the type and intensity of processing activities engaged in at any time. Each of these is briefly characterized below.

Stimuli may be thought of as units of energy such as light and sounds which can excite our sensory receptors. We have receptors for internally produced stimuli such as hunger pangs, as well as receptors for the commonly known five senses of taste, touch, smell, vision, and hearing. Typically, a given stimulus does not exist in isolation but is part of a larger stimulus situation which comprises many individual stimuli.

The *acquisition process* enables consumers to confront certain stimuli in their environment and begin to process them. *Exposure,* which is part of the acquisition process, occurs in a wide variety of ways, but two major categories exist: active search and passive reception. In active search, the consumer's executive system serves as a guide to seek out specific types of stimuli, such as the nutritional content per serving in a can of soup. As Figure 13-1 shows, this information may already exist in memory, or it can be part of the external environment. The way in which the search process is conducted will be influenced by the consumer's motives, and it is mainly within conscious control. Conversely, in passive reception, consumers confront stimuli in the process of living their daily lives. Exposure to many advertisements, news reports on various products, and information acquired as a by-product of normal shopping activities are all examples of the passive reception mode of stimulus acquisition.

The exposure process, through both active search and passive reception, is capable of acquiring an almost infinite number of stimuli. Because the consumer has limited capacity to process this amount of data, two major mechanisms reduce the number of stimuli to manageable proportions. First, sensory receptors have limited sensitivity, which means that our *sensory processes* produce sensations for only a specific range of stimulus values. Second, we selectively devote *attention* to only a small proportion of the resulting sensations, and we literally ignore the rest. Therefore, with certain exceptions to be discussed later, stimuli that are capable of producing sensations and then attracting the consumer's attention are the main focus of further processing efforts.

Sensations may be thought of as electrical impulses with no innate meaning that are produced by our receptors. A *perceptual encoding* process involves several activities that allow the consumer to interpret these raw inputs. The process can be thought of as constructing mental symbols to represent sensations in order to derive meaning from them. Various symbols such as words or mental images can serve as representations. Of course, characteristics of the stimulus itself will strongly influence how it will be represented. As Figure 13-1 shows, however, another major influence is the information already stored in memory. That is, the meaning we derive from stimuli is greatly affected by our previous experiences. It is for this reason that the perceptual encoding process is said to develop personal meaning called *information* from raw stimulus inputs. Thus, consumers act on their own interpretation of the world, as opposed to what actually may exist.

As Figure 13-1 shows, information generated by perceptual encoding can be stored in *memory* for future use, and it can also be directly transferred to the *integration* stage of processing. Here, the consumer combines and arranges various informational inputs to reach conclusions about the environment. For example, information on the package size, number of servings, price, and brand name of several supermarket products could be arranged in various ways to be meaningful in the consumer's mind. Information available from memory, as well as material obtained directly from the environment, represent inputs to this integration process.

A major goal of information processing is to effectively deal with the environment. Therefore, *outcomes* of information-processing activities are likely to affect evaluation and attitudes. Information that has been integrated involves *attitudes* when the consumer's beliefs or feelings about a particular object (brand, product, purchasing action, etc.) are developed or changed. These attitudes can be held by the consumer to influence later actions toward the object. For example, if the consumer's attitudes toward purchasing Haggar slacks are positively influenced by an advertisement, this is likely to increase the probability of a later purchase.

A second outcome can occur more directly. Information can be processed for the purpose of product *evaluation,* choice, and immediate purchase. Here, the consumer, rather than forming attitudes to influence later decisions, makes a brand choice as the information is processed.

In some cases, the consumer may not think the evaluation or choice task has high importance. This usually results in a brief process of review. Here, various rules of thumb (select the lowest-priced alternative, etc.) may be employed to minimize choice effort. However, when the evaluation and choice situation is perceived to be quite important, considerable effort is likely to be devoted to the process.

Information processing is strongly influenced by *consumer characteristics.* For example, previous attitudes can affect how the consumer will evaluate a particular brand, and the evaluation process can in turn result in attitude change or development of new brand attitudes. Other consumer characteristics exerting a major influence on information processing are the consumer's motives, personality attributes, and learning. *Situational characteristics* can also play a role. For example, the consumer's environment is sometimes overloaded with potential information, and some selection of stimuli for processing must be made. At other times, the environment may actually generate such little stimulation that the consumer begins looking for more. This can result in a window-shopping trip or other activity that provides more stimuli. Of course, it can also result in new learning about products and the formation of additional criteria for choosing among alternative brands.

Information-processing activities do not act independently of each other. Rather, each activity needs to be coordinated with others so that intelligible meaning can be derived from stimuli. Also, because consumers are often engaging in goal-directed behavior, certain types of information can take on much greater importance than others. The *executive system* is the mechanism that coordinates various information-processing activities. It also serves as a command center that directs attention and other processing energies toward those stimuli that are potentially more relevant to the consumer's goals. A further function of the executive system is to develop ways for efficiently dealing with stimuli. Therefore, this system should be viewed as the command center for information processing. Its role is to coordinate and direct processing efforts in a way that will assist the consumer in reaching goals and dealing with the environment.

The vast majority of information-processing activities are internal to the consumer and therefore are unobservable. Two notable exceptions are portions of the stimulus-acquisition process (the number of stores shopped, salespeople consulted, etc.) and certain overt responses (brands purchased, etc.). Figure 13-1 recognizes these overt activities by showing that stimulus acquisition and outcomes are not completely encompassed within the internal framework (lines of the box). Although such overt actions can be directly observed, the majority of information-processing activities must be studied by determining their influence on other variables and measures.

The preceding paragraphs presented a brief overview of the major activities involved in information processing. The chapter now turns to a more-detailed review of two of these components—acquisition and perceptual encoding. Subsequent chapters will treat other activities in greater depth.

INFORMATION ACQUISITION

The term *information acquisition* describes the set of activities or means by which consumers are exposed to various environmental stimuli and begin to process them. As mentioned in the overview, exposure occurs in two major ways: when consumers are motivated to actively seek information, and when they passively receive these stimuli that are confronted in daily activities. We will discuss aspects of the active search process first.

Active Search

Consumers often actively seek and selectively acquire information that has potential usefulness for achieving their consumption goals. The first stage in this process appears to be *internal search,* because of the relative ease with which it can be accomplished compared to external search. Internal search involves scanning memory for stored information that is relevant to the purchase situation under consideration. This available information has been previously acquired from passive reception experiences as well as through active external searches.[2] Consequently, it can include information derived from advertising claims, personal experiences, product test reports, previous solutions to similar purchase problems, and interactions with other consumers.

Internal search will tend to be rather deliberate and comprehensive when the consumer views a situation as important, when the purchase decision is a difficult one, and when the amount of information in memory is considerable or complex. In other cases, such as during the regular replenishment of one's usual brand of bath soap, the memory scan may be so automatic that it never even reaches conscious awareness.

In what actually appears to be the majority of cases, information acquired from an internal memory scan is sufficient for the consumer's needs. Consequently, a decision will be made without seeking any external information. For the remaining situations, the consumer is not satisfied with his existing knowledge and becomes sufficiently motivated to engage in external search. Although external search is treated in some depth in Part Five of the text, a short review of this important topic is provided here.

Influences on Amount of External Search The amount of external search that consumers engage in varies considerably across individuals and different purchase situations. Although a number of explanations have been offered for this variability, the cost/benefit view appears to be the most popular one.[3] This explanation holds that external search will be undertaken and will continue as long as the consumer perceives the benefits of search to be greater than the costs involved. Included among the potential benefits of external search are: (1) a more comfortable feeling about making an "informed" purchase, (2) an increase in the actual chances of making a choice that leads to greater satisfaction, (3) the positive feelings derived from being generally knowledgeable about products and services, and (4) the pleasure that can result from engaging in shopping activities. Potential costs of external search include the commitment of time, foregoing other pleasant activities, and the frustrations or tensions involved, as well as any actual monetary expenditures (fuel, parking fees, etc.).[4] It is important to appreciate that the costs and benefits involved are those that are perceived by the consumer, even if they do not correspond perfectly with reality.

Many factors can influence the amount of external search, either by directly affecting the consumer's cost/benefit perceptions or by indirectly acting as constraints on the process. Although Chapter 19 treats these factors in some detail, it is useful to mention here several categories that have been suggested by others.[5]

MARKET CONDITIONS   Characteristics of the marketplace can have a significant effect on external search behavior. Availability of information, the number of alternatives to consider, and the location of outlets are among the influencing factors. In addition, many market conditions lead consumers to attach importance to the purchase situation or to perceive differences between available alternatives. This appears to foster greater external-search activity. To illustrate, among the conclusions drawn from various studies are that external search is greater when

- prices are higher[6] and price differences between brands are greater[7]
- style and appearance are perceived to be quite important[8]
- it is suspected that substantial differences may exist between product alternatives[9]

SITUATIONAL FACTORS   A number of factors unique to the specific situation can also influence external search. For example, search may be reduced when

- the urgency of a need or the amount of available time exert pressure on the purchase decision[10]
- store conditions are perceived as being crowded[11]
- special opportunities arise to purchase at an especially attractive price[12]

BUYING STRATEGIES   Consumers often adopt various strategies which reduce the amount of external search. For example, patterns of brand and store loyalty can develop through purchase experience over time. Also, evidence suggests that when the purchase decision is complex or when the available information is difficult to process, consumers tend to adopt simple choice rules (e.g., "pick the middle-priced one") and significantly curtail their external search.[13]

INDIVIDUAL FACTORS   Of course, many of the consumer's own characteristics influence the degree of external-search activity. The following generalizations illustrate the variety of relevant findings:

1 Greater market experience with a product is associated with a lower degree of external search.[14]

2 Open-mindedness and self-confidence of consumers have been found to be positively related to greater search activity.[15]

3 The more risk the consumer perceives in a purchase situation, the greater will be the tendency to engage in external search.[16]

4 Socioeconomic characteristics have been related to search. For example, higher educational levels and income have been associated with greater search, while a reduction in activity is related to increasing age.[17]

5 Some evidence suggests that consumers differ in their ability to process information, and if their processing limits are reached, the effect may be to decrease the extent of external search.[18]

6 As mentioned in Chapter 12, higher levels of consumer involvement with a product appear to be associated with a greater degree of external search.

7 Chapter 12 also suggested that consumers appear to require an optimum level of stimulation from their environment. When stimulation is sufficiently below this level, external search for novel and exciting stimuli is likely. Conversely, when stimulation is much greater than optimum, external search will tend to be toward less-novel stimuli. This will help the consumer return to the optimum stimulation level.[19] Notice that this process may be occurring quite independently of any specific purchase problem the consumer may be facing at the time.

Types and Sources of Information A great variety of information of potential interest to consumers exist in the external environment. Three general categories are (1) information about the existence and availability of various product and service offerings, (2) information useful in forming evaluative criteria—the standards which are employed to evaluate alternatives, and (3) information on the properties and characteristics of alternatives. In general, it appears that the type of information sought depends upon what the consumer already knows. For example, when the consumer has little knowledge about available offerings, search effort tends to focus on learning about the existence of alternatives and forming appropriate evaluative criteria. When she feels sufficiently informed in these areas, search is likely to be redirected toward learning more about the characteristics of available offerings in order to evaluate them.[20]

In addition to the direct experience of using products themselves, consumers gain information from three major areas: (1) marketer-dominated sources, (2) consumer sources, and (3) neutral sources. Information in marketer-dominated channels stems from salespeople, packaging, and other sources under the control of the marketer. Consumer sources include all those interpersonal communications not under the control of the marketer. Neutral sources include a portion of the mass media, government reports, and publications from independent product-testing agencies. These groups are not under the direct control of the marketer.

It appears that although marketer-dominated sources may be extensively used in the early stages of product awareness and initial interest, personal sources enjoy the most use in latter stages of the decision process.[21] The perceived trustworthiness of personal sources is usually cited as a reason for this finding.

Amount of External Search Activity Many studies have examined the amount of external search that consumers actually undertake. The majority of these have used only one measure of total search activity.[22] However, when viewed together they paint a rather consistent and somewhat surprising picture of consumers' external-search behavior. The following are representative of the general findings:

1 Research suggests that consumers typically consult few information sources (friends, articles, advertisements, etc.) before making a purchase. For example, one study showed that, prior to purchase, 15 percent of major appliance and car buyers consulted no information sources, while 30 percent consulted only one, and 26 percent consulted two.[23]

2 In terms of outlets visited, various studies suggest that approximately 40 to 60 percent of shoppers visit only one store before making a purchase. This appears to hold across both durable and nondurable goods.[24]

3 Evidence regarding number of alternatives buyers consider again suggests limited search. For example, one study reported that 41 percent of refrigerator shoppers considered only one brand, while those considering only one brand of washing machine and vacuum cleaner were 61 percent and 71 percent, respectively.[25]

4 Shoppers also appear to acquire limited amounts of information about the brands actually under consideration. To illustrate, one study found that of the 560 items of readily available information to consider when choosing among sixteen brands of cereal, the median number of items reviewed was only seven.[26]

Because they are only based on single measures of behavior, each of the above findings provides an incomplete picture of consumers' external search activity. However, taken together these results strongly suggest that the majority of consumers actually engage in quite limited amounts of external search. Also, other studies have used composite indexes of search by combining several measures together.[27] These studies confirm that many, perhaps even a majority of consumers engage in little external search for information. Additional evidence suggests that consumers can be categorized according to their general tendency to engage in external search. For example, a recent investigation identified three different groups among car buyers: low searchers, high searchers, and selective searchers.[28] The latter group used intensively only certain sources of information (e.g., media, friends, etc.) and tended to ignore others.[29] Finally, a number of findings suggest that those who typically engage in considerable external-search activity—the so-called information seekers—are identified by a higher demographic profile (higher educational levels, income, occupational standing, etc.) than are low searchers.[30]

Passive Reception

The preceding section has focused on active search which consumers use when deliberately seeking information relevant to a consumption goal or special interest. As mentioned earlier, the passive reception process is another means of information acquisition. In this mode, consumers confront and acquire information in the process of living their daily lives. For example, when watching a TV program, casually talking to a friend, or searching for literature about house paints, one could be exposed to information about aluminum house siding. This information might be stored away for a future time when the need to address the issue of house siding arises. As this situation demonstrates, passive reception occurs when consumers acquire information that they are not presently seeking. Instead of having a plan of search, the individual responds to environmental stimuli to which she is exposed.

Although virtually any type of stimulus may be passively acquired, substantial amounts of certain types of information are likely to be received in this manner.[31] For example, consumers frequently become aware that various products exist without actively seeking such knowledge. A significant amount of learning about product attributes and their advantages can also be acquired passively. In addition, it is likely that consumers obtain at least some of their knowledge about the quality of products through conversations with friends or other passive means.

The way in which passive reception occurs has important practical implications, because how consumers live their daily lives selectively influences their exposure to advertisements and other sources of consumption-related information. For this reason, marketers spend considerable time and effort on studies of consumers' selective media habits (magazine readership, TV programs watched, etc.) and activity patterns (shopping habits, etc.) that lead to exposure opportunities. Attempts are then made to predict exposure patterns on the basis of such measures as consumers' tastes, interests, and lifestyles. Success in this process yields effective decisions on the type of media to use and their appropriate scheduling for marketing communications. In addition, knowledge of consumers' tastes and interests can assist the marketer in discovering what types of message appeals will attract consumers' attention.

Sensation

The exposure mechanisms of active search and passive reception produce many more stimuli than the consumer is capable of processing. Two of the gatekeeping mechanisms that reduce this "blooming confusion" to more manageable proportions involve consumers' physiological limitations: awareness thresholds and differential thresholds.

Awareness Thresholds   Any given stimulus may be either too small or weak to notice, or so great that it also escapes awareness. Consumers' zones of stimulus awareness can therefore be identified by defining two thresholds:

Absolute Threshold—The minimum value of a stimulus capable of being consciously noticed

Terminal Threshold—The maximum value of a stimulus capable of being consciously noticed

To illustrate, the average person's absolute and terminal thresholds for sound pitch are about 20 and 20,000 cycles per second, respectively. Those familar with audio equipment will notice that this is the exact range stereo manufacturers concentrate on when designing their equipment.

The threshold concept implies that we can determine precise values which mark the boundaries of stimulus awareness. This is actually misleading, since these limits for any given stimulus differ among individuals and even for the same individual over a period of time. Therefore, thresholds must be viewed as being somewhat variable, and are usually defined by the stimulus value that goes undetected 50 percent of the time.

MARKETING RELEVANCE OF ABSOLUTE THRESHOLDS   Consumers' absolute thresholds are often of more interest to marketers than terminal thresholds because of their greater relevance to product designs. For example, the average individual's ability to detect that a light source is flashing is about 60 flashes per second for very bright lights, and considerably less for dimmer sources. Knowledge of this absolute threshold has enormous practical application to product designs as illustrated below:

- Common household light bulbs pulsate at 60 cycles per second but appear to have a constant intensity.
- Home movie systems projecting less-intense light onto a screen show 18 frames of film per second without appearing to flicker.
- Television sets produce an apparent full-screen image by rapidly scanning the entire screen with a narrow beam of light.

In another application, consider the following characteristics of absolute taste thresholds:

- Absolute taste thresholds are high (not sensitive) at a very early age, and sensitivity increases as the individual matures.
- For some substances, people differ considerably in their taste sensitivities, while for others little variability exists.

One area in which consumers' relative lack of taste sensitivity at an early age has been of concern is in the baby-food industry. Here, many producers have deemed it necessary to achieve rather higher flavor standards for their products even though infants' abilities to detect these flavors are quite crude or nonexistent. This occurs because it has been found that parents, with their developed taste sensitivity, sample baby foods in an effort to purchase what they think their babies might enjoy eating.

The finding that adults differ significantly in their taste sensitivities is also important in areas such as the beer industry in which experts have segmented the consuming public into three distinct groupings: (1) discriminating individuals mainly concerned with the taste of beer, (2) discriminating individuals influenced by price and other variables, and (3) nondiscriminating consumers.[32] Marketing strategies directed at such segments could differ significantly.

Differential Thresholds   Many sellers have made changes in their offerings only to find that they went unnoticed in the marketplace. This suggests that consumers also have limited sensitivity for noticing differences between different stimulus values. The *differential threshold* defines this sensitivity as the smallest detectable difference between two values of the same stimulus. For example, a soft-drink producer interested in whether consumers can detect a difference in sweetness between two different sugar concentrations of a drink would need to examine consumers' differential threshold for sweetness.

To measure the differential threshold for a stimulus, one commonly changes its intensity in very small amounts, as in a hearing test. The consumer's threshold exists when he first notices that the stimulus has changed. The difference between this value and the starting value is often referred to as the *just noticeable difference (jnd)*.

WEBER'S LAW   As in the case of absolute thresholds, consumers also differ in their ability to detect differences between stimulus values, and this sensitivity varies with conditions. However, numerous studies have revealed a general relationship known as *Weber's Law* which states that the stimulus change needed to reach the differential threshold (produce a just noticeable difference) is a constant *proportion* of the starting stimulus value. Weber's Law can be expressed as:

$$\frac{\Delta s}{S} = K$$

where S = the initial stimulus value

Δs = the smallest change in the stimulus capable of being detected—the jnd

K = the constant of proportionality

Expressing the equation as $\Delta s = K \cdot S$ suggests that if we know the values of K and S, we could predict how large a change in the stimulus is necessary before consumers detect the change. To illustrate, assume that through testing we found that 1 ounce ($\Delta s = 1$) had to be added to a 10-ounce package ($S = 10$) before consumers detected a change in its weight. This would yield a constant of proportionality of $K = \frac{1}{10} = 0.1$, allowing us to predict that:

- Consumers will not detect a change in the weight of a 50-ounce box of detergent unless at least 5 ounces are added to or removed from it.

- Consumers will be able to detect a 3-pound addition to a 20-pound portable television.

Two points should be noted with regard to Weber's Law: (1) there are different constants of proportionality for different stimuli such as weight, color, and size, and (2) the law is not universal in its applicability because individuals differ and because it does not predict well near absolute or terminal thresholds. However, refinements have been made to the basic law and it appears to hold fairly well over the majority of stimulus range.

APPLYING WEBER'S LAW   Marketers can apply Weber's Law to predicting how consumers will respond to differences between marketing variables or changes in these variables.[33] Sometimes the goal is to have consumers detect differences, and in other cases it is to have differences escape their attention. For example, because the cost of candy ingredients fluctuates widely there is a constant search for more stably priced substitutes. According to one report, this led to the discovery by Peter Paul, Inc., that tasters could not distinguish between one type of chocolate made with vegetable oil and another made with traditional cocoa butter.[34] However, a second firm found that most consumers could detect a difference between a chocolate substitute and the real thing.

A second way to hold prices constant in times of changing costs is to change the size or amount of the product slightly. For example, during a 23-year period the Hershey Foods Corporation changed the price of its basic milk chocolate bar only three times, but varied its weight fourteen times.[35] It should be noted that many of these changes escaping consumers' awareness were weight *increases* allowed by declining costs. Similar changes (increases as well as decreases) have occurred in numerous packages and products, including newspapers, bathroom tissues, and soft drinks.

Another application of Weber's Law lies in the battleground of brand competition. Here producers of major brands such as A. T. Cross pens and Green Giant canned vegetables seek to distinguish their products as quite different from those of private competitors. However some competing firms seek to produce similar products using less costly ingredients that might escape consumers' notice, thereby obtaining a differential price advantage. Also, packages of some privately labeled grocery products bear a striking resemblance to those of major brands.[36] Presumably, this discourages shoppers from detecting any noticeable differences existing between the brands. Figure 13-2 presents examples of this situation.

Pricing decisions may also make use of Weber's Law. For example, many merchants have noted that price reductions of at least 15 percent are usually needed to attract consumers to sales. This experience is supported by experimental evidence suggesting that consumers do possess awareness thresholds for price changes.[37]

Attention

A research study conducted several years ago suggested that the average American adult is aware of seeing less than 100 major media advertisements per day.[38] However, the daily advertising exposure rate for a typical consumer has been estimated to range as high as 3000 or more. This suggests that although exposure and sensory processes both selectively filter stimuli for information processing, additional points of selectivity must also exist. One such filtering mechanism is *attention,* which can be viewed as the allocation of processing capacity to stimuli. That is, attention regulates the amount of additional processing that a stimulus will receive. Generally, the more processing capacity that is devoted to a stimulus, the greater will be the consumer's awareness and comprehension of it.

Voluntary and Involuntary Attention Consumers allocate their attention on both a voluntary and involuntary basis.[39] For voluntary attention, stimuli are deliberately focused on because of their relevance to the task at hand. Careful review of the manufacturer's specifications on a microwave oven that one is about to purchase is an example. The consumer's motives, knowledge, and expectations about what information will be found serve to guide this selective attention.

Conversely, involuntary attention occurs when the consumer confronts novel or unexpected stimuli that seem interesting or distinctive in some way, even though they may be unrelated to the current goal or activity at hand. Funny, "catchy," or otherwise unusual advertisements often fall into this category. Also, many other stimuli consumers confront in living their daily lives are handled by the involuntary attention process. In fact, most of the stimuli that consumers process reach awareness via involuntary attention.

FIGURE 13-2

Examples of package similarity. (*Source:* Candace E. Trunzo, "Checkout-Counter Lookalikes." Reprinted from the May 1976 issue of *Money* magazine, pp. 71–72, by special permission; © 1976, Time Inc. All rights reserved.)

Checkout-Count

Some supermarket and drugstore house brands are becoming masters of disguise.

Cheaper than national-brand products and often comparable or even identical in quality, the house brands of supermarkets and other big retailers have long appealed to the thrifty. Now, as these photographs suggest, some house-brand distributors also seem to be seeking the business of the merely careless.

Chains around the country have begun to feature private-label packages that look remarkably like proven name brands. Sometimes the similarity goes beyond the box. By definition, all petroleum jellies have to be much the same. And labels divulge that Safeway's Town House hominy, for example, has the same ingredients as the regional Burbank brand. On the other hand, Grand Union adds preservatives to its potato chips (69¢ for ten ounces in the New York market where *Money* bought them), while its owlish counterpart (79¢ for eight ounces) doesn't.

A few companies have gone to the courts to stop the lookalikes. Bristol-Myers, which makes Excedrin, has sued to force Dart Drug, a Washington-area discount chain, to change the package and name of Dart's Extracin. Others are unhappy. "We do not want anyone to have the opportunity to confuse or dupe the consumer," says a spokesman for Chesebrough-Pond's, maker of Vaseline.

The chain stores, however, contend that any lookalikes are only in the eye of the beholder. Says John Prinster, a Safeway vice president, "We are very careful not to copy; we don't want to confuse the consumer." A Grand Union spokesman asserts that "even if the consumer bought the wrong thing, he would get more for less." Well, not necessarily. An A&P clerk in Manhattan mistakenly charged one recent shopper the 55¢ Wonder bread price for a similar-looking 43¢ loaf of A&P's own Jane Parker. —*Candace E. Trunzo*

Both types of attention play a useful role for the consumer. Voluntary attention facilitates progress toward immediate goals by concentrating processing capacity on the most task-related stimuli and filtering out others. On the other hand, involuntary attention allows the consumer to be generally knowledgeable about the environment by keeping him or her in touch with stimuli that are potentially relevant to a variety of his or her interests.

Characteristics of Attention We have already noted that the consumer's attention is selectively allocated to only certain stimuli. Before turning to factors influencing this process, three characteristics of attention having important implications for marketers should be mentioned.[40] First, consumers can only attend to a limited number of items at any one time. This limit appears to be from five to seven "chunks" of information, in which a chunk is an organized grouping of data or informational inputs. An example would be how telephone numbers are arranged into three major chunks to facilitate their retention—area code, prefix, suffix. This five- to seven-chunk capacity shows that consumers' span of attention can be quite limited.

Second, many stimuli require attention to be processed, while others that are very familiar to the consumer do not.[41] Because the span of attention is limited, those stimuli requiring attention cannot all be processed at the same time. The consumer must allocate this limited resource to them in some type of sequence or order; while one is being processed, others cannot be attended to. One example is when we are at a party and a friend is talking to us at the same time that we are trying to overhear what is being said by the people next to us. Chances are that we will miss at least some portions of both conversations. Another case in point is when we are unable to both read something and listen to a radio message at the same time. Conversely, stimuli not requiring attention can be received simultaneously from several channels and will be automatically transferred to the next stage of processing. To illustrate, when exposed to a television advertisement for Amtrak trains, consumers might be able to visually process physical attributes of the train (color, shape, and size of the interior, etc.) and how much people seem to enjoy the ride at the same time as they are listening to the tune which accompanies the visual presentation.

A third characteristic is that attention can be allocated to stimuli on a rapid basis. One set of studies found that processing occurred at the rate of twenty-six items per second.[42] This speed tends to compensate for consumers' limited span of attention.

Marketers should give serious consideration to these attention characteristics because they can significantly influence the effectiveness of various efforts to communicate with consumers. Of course, another area of concern is the many factors, both within and outside the marketer's control, that influence how consumers allocate their attention among stimuli. These influences mainly affect involuntary attention, and they can be categorized into stimulus and individual factors.

Selective Attention—Stimulus Factors Certain characteristics of stimuli themselves attract attention. Generally, these include emotion-arousing properties (colors, pleasant phrases, etc.), physically intense values (loud noises, bright colors, etc.), and novel or surprising characteristics.[43] More specifically, the following are mentioned because of their particular importance to promotional campaigns.

COLOR   Historically, color advertisements have been found to attract more attention than those presented in black and white. However, the higher cost of using color may result in capturing less attention per advertising dollar spent.[44] Also, because the attraction power of color may be a result of its novelty, common use of it in any medium such as television may reduce its attention-attracting power unless more intense or unusual hues are employed.[45]

NOVELTY AND CONTRAST   Stimuli that stand out against their background attract attention. Novel stimuli achieve this through unique images, shapes, sounds, and colors. Figure 13-3 contains an excellent illustration. Novelty can also be achieved through messages that seem at odds with commonly held beliefs. Figure 13-4 presents such an example.

Contrast also attracts attention through its distinctiveness. Reversals (white printing on black background) in print media and changes in volume levels (louder or softer) for television or radio advertisements are examples of contrast effects used to capture attention.

SIZE AND POSITION   In print media, attention increases with the size of an advertisement but appears to grow in proportion to the square root of the ad's area. Thus, to double its attention-attracting power, the size of an advertisement would have to be quadrupled.

Position also is an important influence as the following findings illustrate. First, in terms of layout, ads with vertical splits (pictures on one side and copy on the other) and haphazard arrangements of pictures appear to discourage at least some readers.[46] Second, in terms of placement on a page, position does not seem to have an effect unless many ads share the page, in which case the upper right-hand corner appears advantageous.[47] Third, there appears to be an attention advantage for magazine ads placed in the first ten pages or next to related editorial matter, but due to high page traffic, position with a newspaper is not as critical.[48]

FIGURE 13-3

Example of novelty used to attract attention. (Courtesy of Head Strong I.)

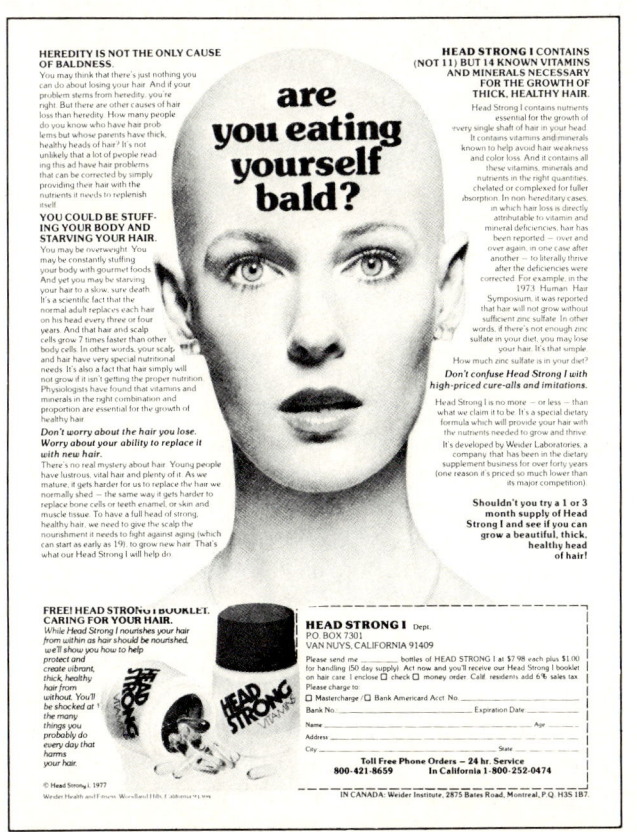

FIGURE 13-4

Example of achieving novelty through a message that is at odds with commonly held beliefs. (Courtesy of the Potato Board.)

HUMOR Ed White, a rugged-looking lineman for the San Diego Chargers professional football team, has been seen on millions of American television sets singing, in nursery rhyme fashion, "Before I put on my cleaties, I get the eaties for my Wheaties." General Mills developed this ad in an attempt to use humor for attracting consumers' attention to a product with declining sales. In fact, estimates are that between 15 and 42 percent of television and radio advertising employs some form of humor, usually designed to attract attention.[49]

Although there appears to be fairly widespread acceptance among practitioners that humor can attract attention, there has not been a great deal of research conducted in an advertising context to test this belief.[50] Based on the evidence that is available, a tenative conclusion appears to be that humorous messages in advertising can generally attract audience attention. However, it also appears that the effectiveness of humor depends on the characteristics of audience members. For example, the attention attracted by humorous messages appears to vary depending on the sex and racial background of audience members.[51]

A wide variety of other stimulus factors have been employed to attract consumers' attention. These include "scratch and sniff" strips in printed promotions, inflatable sections of billboards, and signs with moving parts. Because a detailed treatment of each is beyond the scope of this chapter, we now turn to individual factors influencing attention.

Selective Attention—Individual Factors In addition to stimulus characteristics, individual attributes of consumers themselves also influence whether a given stimulus will receive attention. Some of these individual factors are discussed below.

ATTENTION SPAN We have already noted that consumers' attention span, as measured by the number of items processed at any time, is quite limited. An important implication of this for advertisers is to "keep the message simple." The time that stimuli can hold the consumer's attention also appears to be rather short—perhaps only a matter of seconds. Therefore, attention must be repeatedly captured, even for something as brief as a 15-second spot commercial on television. This is one reason advertisers use a variety of stimulus factors to not only capture, but also to hold consumers' interest.[52]

ADAPTATION Prolonged exposure to constant levels of stimulation results in consumers not noticing the stimuli. This gradual adjustment to stimuli is called *adaptation*. For example, an air-conditioned building first appears quite cool to us, but a short time later we adapt to the temperature and become less aware of it. Similarly, consumers adapt to various marketing stimuli such as price levels and advertising messages. This helps to explain why marketers search for fresh advertising approaches and try to offer new and improved products.

PERCEPTUAL VIGILANCE AND DEFENSE The concept of *perceptual vigilance* explains consumer's heightened sensitivity to stimuli that are capable of satisfying motives. This suggests that consumers will pay increased attention to marketing stimuli relevant to an aroused motive. Based on this concept, it has been suggested that less expensive, small- or medium-sized print advertisements may be more economically effective than large ones for reaching the attention of motivated consumers.[53]

Individuals are also capable of *perceptual defense,* that is, decreasing their awareness of threatening stimuli. For example, one study found that only 32 percent of a sample of smokers consistently read articles relating smoking to lung disease, while 60 percent of a group of nonsmokers read the articles.[54] Apparently, smokers feel threatened by such information, and their perceptual defense mechanisms allow them to ignore it.

The topic of perceptual defense has relevance in advertising, particularly to the use of fear appeals to promote products such as burglar alarms and smoke detectors. Of course, the danger of fear appeals is that they may be so threatening to consumers that they lead to perceptual defenses against the entire message. For example, an advertisement showing burned children to draw viewers' attention to the need for home fire alarms would probably fail because consumers want to avoid thinking of such a tragedy.

Our discussion of the acquisition process has focused on three major sub-components: (1) exposure—the means by which consumers come in contact with stimuli, (2) sensation—the means by which only certain stimulus values produce messages for further processing, and (3) attention—the means by which processing capacity is allocated to stimulus sensations. Focus turns now to how consumers derive meaning from these raw sensory inputs.

PERCEPTUAL ENCODING

Because sensations generated by stimuli are only a series of electrical impulses, they must be transformed into a type of language that is understandable to the consumer. This is accomplished by *perceptual encoding,* which is the process of assigning mental symbols to sensations.[55] These symbols can be words, numbers, pictorial images, or other representations that consumers use to interpret or assign meaning to their sensations. They are also used to remember stimuli and do any subsequent thinking about them.

Much of the encoding process is automatic and not within the consumer's conscious control. That is, the individual typically does not make deliberate decisions as to what type of symbols will be used to represent sensations. Nevertheless, the process is highly individualistic, and a given stimulus is unlikely to be represented in exactly the same way by different consumers. A major reason for this is that each person's previous experiences, as stored in memory, strongly influence the symbolism used. The way different people view a Ford van illustrates this rather well. A contractor may consider it as a piece of construction equipment, someone living in a rural area might think of it as an all-purpose family vehicle, and a young adventurer may consider it as a mobile home. As we might expect, each individual's reactions toward the vehicle will be influenced by the different mental symbols they use to represent it. The important point here is that perceptual encoding is a symbol-assigning process that each individual uses to derive personal meaning from stimulus experiences. Any actions or subsequent thoughts will be based on interpretations derived from stimuli rather than on the actual stimuli themselves.

Stages in the Encoding Process

Two major activities involved in encoding appear to be feature analysis and a synthesis stage.[56] In *feature analysis,* the consumer identifies main stimulus features and assesses how they are organized. In the *synthesis stage,* organized stimulus elements are combined with other information available in the environment and in memory to develop an interpretation of the stimulus. Our previous example of how consumers reacted to the Ford van illustrates these stages. First, each person assessed the basic size, shape, color, and other prominent features of the van. These characteristics were then organized into a unified whole and appreciated as a type of motorized vehicle rather than as separate components of glass, steel, rubber, and so on. However, even in the unlikely event that all three consumers developed the same unified whole during the feature analysis stage, each would interpret it differently depending on her or his individual experience. In fact, it can be said that there are three major influences on the synthesis stage: (1) stimulus features, (2) contextual influences, and (3) memory factors.[57]

We have already mentioned that major aspects of the stimulus will influence the interpretation process. To this must be added the stimulus context. That is, the stimulus being focused on in any particular situation is surrounded by a wide variety of other stimuli which form a context for interpreting the focal stimulus. For example, a cake prominently displayed along with exotic-looking treats at a specialty bakery shop is likely to be perceived differently than if it were placed in a plain display box on a regular supermarket shelf. Marketers are well aware of this influence and frequently use it to promote and position their offerings. The use of highly active and dynamic dancers in Dr. Pepper commercials or the crisp snow-covered scenes in VelaMint promotions are cases in point.

The consumer's experiences stored in memory will also strongly influence how a stimulus is represented. The more closely that major features of a stimulus resemble situations stored in memory, the greater the likelihood that it will be represented in the same way as these experiences. In fact, a major influence on interpretation is derived from *expectations* the consumer has as a result of previous experiences. If other elements remain constant, strong expectations are likely to reduce the consumer's attention to actual stimulus features. Meaning will then be assigned to the stimulus on the basis of its expected characteristics, rather than on the basis of what exists in reality.[58] This has the potential advantage of efficiency, because the consumer can respond to very similar stimuli in much the same way and not expend effort treating each one as a unique case. However, there also is a potential problem of incorrect interpretation as demonstrated by the following message:

<pre>
       △
      /│\
     / │ \
    /PARIS\
   / IN THE \
  / THE SPRING\
 /─────────────\
</pre>

Many readers do not notice that the message involves repetition of a word. Consumers who mistakenly purchase one of the look-alikes in Figure 13-2 or who realize their favorite brand has been "new and improved" only after bringing it home are other examples of such problems. Conversely, when a stimulus is quite novel and has features considerably different than expected, more attention will be allocated to it, and greater effort will be given to its interpretation.

Earlier, it was mentioned that the attention mechanism regulated the amount of processing a stimulus receives. Current though is that this effort can be devoted to increasing the spread of processing, or increasing the depth of processing.[59] Increased *spread of processing* occurs when effort is devoted to further elaboration of the stimulus at the same depth of meaning. Consumers do this when generally reviewing additional physical features (shape, size, etc.) of a stimulus. This would be exhibited by a consumer casually examining a radio, touching its tuning controls, and turning it in different directions to "take in" its basic features. Although many aspects of the product are noted, very little is done in terms of considering the meaning of these features. The term *depth of processing* refers to the degree of effort the consumer expends in developing meaning from stimuli. If little effort is expended, a great deal of meaning will not be derived. However, at deeper levels of processing the stimulus is represented with symbols that are more meaningful to the consumer. For example, reading the ingredients listed on a type of snack-food package could lead the consumer to the relatively shallow interpretation "it's mainly sugar" or to the deeper level "it's a fattening and unhealthy food." Here, we can see that the deeper level of processing results in a more personally relevant representation and interpretation of the stimulus. We will return to this depth-of-processing concept in the next chapter when we consider its relevance to learning and memory.

Influences On Encoding

A wide variety of factors influence the encoding process. Although some were briefly mentioned above, it is useful to give more-detailed treatment to several major influences. The first group of influencing factors is more relevant to feature-analysis activities, while the second group has its primary influence on the synthesis stage.

Factors Influencing Feature Analysis Much of feature analysis involves mentally arranging sensations into a coherent pattern which is often called a *gestalt* (pronounced guh-shtalf). In fact, this process has been the prime interest of gestalt psychologists, and much of this section is based on their work. Although visual examples are primarily used here, many of the principles can also be applied to other stimuli.

FIGURE-GROUND This is one of the most basic and automatic organizational processes perceivers impose on their world. Two properties of this innate perceptual tendency are: (1) the figure appears to stand out as being in front of the more-distant background, and (2) the figure is perceived to have form and to be more substantial than the ground. An example of the way in which the figure-ground process operates is shown in Figure 13-5. Most individuals organize this stimulus

FIGURE 13-5

Example demonstrating figure-ground perception.

situation as a white goblet (figure) on a black ground rather than as two faces (figure) with a white ground separating them.

Print advertisements frequently employ figure-ground techniques to assist readers in organizing symbols and other material that the marketer deems most important.

PROXIMITY   In this organization process, items close to each other in time or space tend to be perceived as being related, while separated items are viewed as being different. The uses of proximity in promotions are many. Mentholated cigarettes are shown in beautiful green, springlike settings or against a deep blue sky to suggest freshness. Soft drinks and fast foods are usually shown being enjoyed in active, fun-oriented settings, and sporty cars are frequently pictured at race-tracks or in other competitive situations. Also, in comparative advertising, the promoted brand is usually shown in the good company of other respected brands and separated from supposedly inferior alternatives.

SIMILARITY   Assuming that no other influence is present, items that are perceived as being similar to one another will tend to be grouped together. This, in turn, can influence the pattern one perceives in a conglomeration of items.

The principle of similarity has been used in various ways to influence consumers' perceptions. For example, some auto manufacturers have attempted to develop certain style similarities between their products and the BMW in the hope that consumers will conclude that the cars are also similar in other important respects. This must have led to concern at BMW, because they responded with advertising messages stressing that their car is a standard that other auto makers have tried to copy but have done so unsuccessfully, since similar looks do not necessarily mean similar cars.

APPARENT MOTION   Sometimes we organize our perceptions so as to produce the appearance of motion. For example, the rapid presentation of still pictures, each slightly different than the other, leads to the perception of motion. Use of the apparent motion technique in advertising no longer seems very dramatic, but it represents one of the most insightful and extensive applications of perception in marketing.

CLOSURE   Frequently, consumers organize incomplete stimuli by perceiving them as complete figures. In other words, a figure such as an opened circle, would tend to be filled in by the individual to result in perception of a whole.

Research suggest that under certain conditions this tendency toward closure can be an effective advertising device, because it motivates consumers to mentally complete the message.[60] This can focus attention and facilitate learning and retention. In fact, the closure concept has been employed by leading producers of consumer products. For example, the Kellogg Company showed its name on the far right-hand side of one billboard ad with the last "g" missing.[61] Also, Salem cigarettes were first advertised heavily in television employing the often quoted jingle: "You can take Salem out of the country but— You can't take the country out of Salem." The verse was repeated several times with a bell ringing between the two halves of the message. Finally, only the first half of the jingle was sung, ending with the bell and leaving the listener compelled to complete the message. Figure

13-6 shows another use of the closure concept to facilitate retention of an important message.

It should be mentioned that not all incomplete advertising messages appear to be remembered better than completed ones. Further investigation of closure is needed to determine both the nature and effectiveness of its role in advertising.

Factors Influencing Synthesis Stage Many additional factors influence how consumers develop meaning from stimuli that have undergone feature analysis.

FIGURE 13-6
Example of a promotional use of the closure concept. (Courtesy of the Advertising Council, Inc.)

The major effect of these influences is to predispose the individual toward interpreting stimuli in a certin way. Five major categories of influences are learning, personality, motivation, attitude, and adaptation levels.

LEARNING   Learning influences consumers to categorize stimuli by developing their abilities to identify stimulus attributes used in discrimination and leveling. In *discrimination,* consumers learn those attributes useful in distinguishing between items in order to categorize them differently. For example, we learn to distinguish fresh from stale bread, and traditional from contemporary furniture. Of course, there is no guarantee that all consumers will learn valid methods of discrimination. It depends on their prior experiences, as in the case where consumers rejected a new, quiet food mixer because they incorrectly perceived it as having less power than older, noisier models.[62] This was perhaps a result of their experience with powerful and noisy appliances in the past.

Learning also influences perceptual *leveling* whereby similar but not identical stimuli are classified into the same perceptual category and therefore generate the same response. For example, when instant coffee was first introduced, many families made clear distinctions between it and perk or drip coffee. However, over time, leveling has taken place to the extent that when coffee is now offered, no distinction is usually made as to its type.

Marketers are interested in these learning influences because they want to provide consumers with information, product cues, and promotional symbolism designed to influence how their product is categorized. In terms of product cues, consider the case in which a major producer of chickens for the Northeast feeds his poultry marigold petals and corn so that they develop the yellow skin that consumers of the region have learned to associate with succulent chicken.[63] The strategy of *positioning* as discussed in Chapter 5 can also influence consumers' interpretation process by manipulating symbols, slogans, and other variables. The goal is to establish a unique perceptual category for the brand in consumers' minds. Examples are promotions that categorize Canadian-brewed Molson Ale as an "imported" ale and Honda motorcycles as transportation for typical people instead of for cycle-gang members.

Learning also influences categorization through the development of *perceptual constancies* which are very stable perceptions of objects across a variety of situations in which they are encountered. For example, consumers realize the actual size of a pen is constant even though it appears much smaller when further away. Perceptual constancies simplify our world, because we do not have to make new judgments every time we encounter these familiar objects in different contexts. In addition, they can serve as standards to judge other, less familiar stimuli. Thus, pens, billfolds, and other familiar objects are often used in advertisements as a frame of reference to judge the size of the product being promoted.

PERSONALITY AND MOTIVATION   Consumers' personality characteristics also influence the meaning they derive from stimuli. For example, one study found that individuals who find it difficult to tolerate uncertain situations tend to be influenced by seals of approval, such as those of Good Housekeeping or Underwriters Laboratory, to a greater degree than do other consumers.[64] In addition, other research suggests that people can be categorized as having risk-avoiding or risk-seeking personalities, and these differences can lead to divergent perceptions of products and marketing communications.

The meaning individuals derive from stimuli is also influenced by their motivational state. This has been demonstrated in one study in which hungry subjects "saw" more food-related items in ambiguously shaped stimuli than did subjects who were not hungry. Such findings help explain why certain products may be highly valued by some groups of consumers, and deemed rather useless by others.

ATTITUDES   For our present purpose, consumers' attitudes may be thought of as predispositions to understand and respond to objects and events in consistent ways. That is, attitudes act as frames of reference which affect consumers' tendencies to interpret stimuli from the environment. These references are influenced by the consumers' values and beliefs that have developed from previous processing experiences.

The greater the consistency of a given stimulus with currently held attitudes, the more likely will the consumer be to interpret it in a way consistent with these attitudes. For example, if a consumer having negative attitudes toward Mazdas sees one stalled on the roadside, she is more likely to interpret the situation as evidence of an inferior product rather than as an isolated problem with a quality car. However, a neighbor's high praise during an 8-year period for his Mazda will be very difficult for this consumer to interpret in the same light.

Because attitudes predispose consumers to interpret stimuli in consistent ways, they often lead to efficient processing. That is, many stimuli can be quickly interpreted without a great deal of processing effort being allocated to them. In addition, it must also be realized that the resulting meaning the consumer derives from these stimuli is very strongly influenced by his predispositions as well as by characteristics of the stimuli themselves. Chapters 16 and 17 will discuss these issues in greater depth.

ADAPTATION LEVEL   Our discussion of selective attention noted that consumers tend to adapt to rather constant stimulus levels. This process leads to the formation of *adaptation levels,* which are standards of reference used to judge new stimulus situations. To demonstrate, assume that two individuals must judge the heaviness of this textbook. Prior to the test, however, one is required to sort envelopes and the other is assigned to moving office furniture. It seems reasonable that, due to their different standards of reference, the mail sorter will judge the text to be heavier than would the furniture mover. In fact, results of many experiments have verified this expectation.[65] They have also demonstrated that adaptation levels can be influenced to *move* by exposing the individual to different stimulus values. This means that the standard of reference for judging stimuli is a sliding scale which can change over time.

The concept of an adaptation level serving as a sliding frame of reference suggests that consumers adapt to levels of service, products, and other marketing variables, and these become standards by which new situations are judged. As a case in point, food-flavor experts have long recognized that consumers have adapted to the taste of packaged foods to such an extent that they now serve as taste standards. This led one food-flavor chemist to remark: "We've moved away from the utilization of fresh flavor—it isn't familiar anymore." In another case, consider the U.S. energy problem and its effect on gasoline prices. In the early 1970s, when gas prices averaged between 30 and 40 cents a gallon, a price of 50 cents would have been judged extremely expensive. However, after we have adapted to gradually increasing gasoline, prices, 50 cents would now be judged as a great bargain![66]

A basic conclusion of the above discussion is that perceptions are *subjective*. Consumers derive meaning from stimuli only by interpreting them in relation to the present situation, their experiences, and their physical and psychological states. This presents both problems and opportunities to the marketing manager. Problems are encountered because it cannot be assumed that consumers will perceive products and other marketing variables in the same way that the marketer does. Opportunities arise from determining how consumers perceive these variables and using this insight to design more competitive offerings.

Information Load

Earlier in the chapter, it was shown that the environment produces many more stimuli than consumers are capable of dealing with. Awareness thresholds, attention, and other mechanisms were mentioned as means consumers have for reducing the number of stimuli to more manageable proportions. Of course, at any time there is no guarantee the consumer will be able to handle all stimuli that succeed in passing through these filtering mechanisms. An interesting point related to this issue has been raised by Jacoby and his coworkers. Their contention, based upon research they have conducted, is that another threshold exists—an upper limit on the amount of information that consumers can effectively deal with in their decision-making process.[67]

Consumers' "information load" can be defined here in terms of the number of brands and/or the number of attributes per brand that are available for processing. The position of these researchers, then, is that a consumer's exposure to an amount of information that exceeds his threshold point will generate conditions of information *overload*. Further, when he is experiencing information overload, the consumer will make poorer decisions (ones that can benefit him less) than he would have made under conditions of less information. This may occur despite the possibility that the consumer will feel more confident with decisions based on large amounts of information. Of course, the implication here is that an overload condition not only involves attention and other information-acquisition mechanisms, but it also may influence perceptual encoding, integration, and evaluation processes.

The research and data that led Jacoby and his colleagues to their conclusions has been the subject of considerable reanalysis, criticism, and debate.[68] Because of this, we are not in a position to positively conclude that information overload can occur. However, recent additional evidence lends support to the contention.[69] We will again raise this issue in Part Five when consumers' decision processes are considered in greater depth.

MARKETING IMPLICATIONS

To this point, the information-processing activities involved in acquiring and interpreting stimulus experiences have been discussed. Soon to be treated in as much depth are memory factors, the information integration stage, and evaluation and choice activities. These processing components will be discussed in subsequent chapters along with related material. At this point, however, it is useful to review briefly some marketing applications of the material already examined.

Product Factors

The relevance of information processing to consumers' product evaluations has already been mentioned in this chapter. We would expect that product evaluations are at least in part based on consumers' attempts to *directly* evaluate physical product attributes, often called *intrinsic cues,* such as size, shape, and grade of ingredients. However, evidence suggests that, for many goods, buyers can have difficulty in distinguishing between different offerings on the basis of such direct product attributes. For example, some studies reveal that smokers have little success in identifying brands of similar types of cigarettes in "blind" taste testing (a blind test is one in which identifying marks on the brands are concealed by the researcher).[70] Other research suggests that beers must differ significantly for consumers to detect differences between them.[71] And finally, for soft drinks, it appears that a sizeable portion of consumers have difficulty in identifying brands of cola when brand names are unavailable.[72] For example, one study found that subjects could discriminate between Pepsi-Cola and Coca-Cola in blind taste tests, but they had difficulty distinguishing each of them from Royal Crown Cola.[73] In 1976, such evidence led to a serious promotional war when Pepsi attempted to gain market share from Coke by using an advertising focus stressing taste differences between the brands. The strategy was to show large numbers of cola drinkers, many with Coke as their favorite brand, actually preferring Pepsi over Coke in blind taste tests called the "Pepsi Challenge." Early advertising responses from Coca-Cola just encouraged consumers to stick to the "real thing." However, since the Pepsi challenge had considerable success, Coke responded more strongly, and hostilities broke out between the two soft-drink giants. Coke aggressively criticized and ridiculed Pepsi's testing methods, and the advertising debate that ensued became quite intense—so much so that some believe the promotional war, which has not completely subsided, left damaging effects on brand images in the soft-drink industry.[74] Despite such dangers, the apparent success of Pepsi, as measured by sales increases, has led other companies to attempt similar strategies. For example, Schlitz ran live taste tests of their beer against competing brands during halftime on televised pro-football playoff games. Burger King has also advertised results of taste tests in which its hamburgers "won" over McDonald's offering. Furthermore, Taylor has advertised how its wines have been judged by wine tasters as superior to competing brands such as Almaden and Gallo. It is interesting that this latter case began to stir strong negative reactions from Taylor's competitors because the company is owned by Coca-Cola—the company that responded so negatively to the Pepsi Challenge.

A very important issue raised by the above discussion is whether consumers' differential thresholds are typically sensitive enough to discriminate between brands. If differences between some brands go undetected in taste tests in which consumers attempt to "tune in" their discriminatory powers, perhaps even larger differences escape notice in everyday consumption activity. Furthermore, even experts can be unable to detect important but subtle product differences, as a wine scandal in France demonstrated. Testimony about the scandal revealed that use of chemicals to change the wine's taste apparently fooled even expert wine tasters as well as consumers.[75]

For other nonfood products, consumers may be capable of using intrinsic cues to discriminate between brands, but not be able to determine whether these differences are important in predicting which brand will provide greater satisfaction. For example, how many would be capable of identifying the "best" grade of carpeting without expert help? Given these problems, it is not surprising to find that product perceptions are often influenced by other factors. That is, in order to form impressions of products, consumers process additional stimuli that are not actual physical characteristics of the product itself. These features, often called *extrinsic cues,* could be packaging characteristics, advertising messages, statements of friends, and many other pieces of information from a wide variety of sources.[76] To illustrate, studies have shown that adding a faint, not consciously noticeable perfume scent to women's hosiery can lead consumers to strongly prefer them over identical but unscented alternatives.[77] Another finding is that bread wrapped in cellophane was judged by conumers to be fresher than identical bread wrapped in waxed paper.[78] Figure 13-7 shows how an advertisement might be designed to address both specific product features and general image characteristics in an attempt to influence consumers' brand perceptions. As we have noted in Chapter 5, this is a major goal of positioning.

Some evidence suggests that consumers' product perceptions are more likely to be influenced by extrinsic cues when the product is complex in nature.[79] Generally, however, little is known about how consumers select such cues to form interpretations, or what the conditions are which influence this process. What is known suggests four propositions that are worthy of consideration:

1 Certain extrinsic cues are more likely than others to be selected for use in judging products. The selection will be influenced by the consumer's experience as well as the type of cues available.

2 The way in which extrinsic cues are encoded can strongly influence consumers' product evaluations. For example, the cellophane wrapping on a food item could be encoded as "packaging," but it also could be encoded as "freshly kept food," "protected food," or something similar. Each is likely to have a different influence on product perception.

3 Certain extrinsic cues may not be encodable in a meaningful way by the consumer. These would then have little if any subsequent effect on how the product is interpreted. The listing of certain packaged-food ingredients such as *sodium ascorbate, calcium propionate,* and *propyl gallate* might fit this description.

4 Available extrinsic cues may lead the consumer to develop additional *inferential beliefs* or interpretations of the product. An inferential belief is one formed without a direct basis in the existing stimulus situation. For example, an advertisement that only mentions the whitening ability of a laundry detergent might also lead some consumers to interpret the brand as having clothes-softening properties. This could occur because ads for other brands claim to have both properties, and consumers have associated the two in their minds. However, since the present advertisement makes no softening claim, such interpretations are based on inference and do not have a basis in the stimulus situation.[80]

We now turn to a special example of cue utilization in the discussion of how consumers process the information content of price. That is, the question of interest here is what meaning do consumers derive from the price variable?

FIGURE 13-7

Example of reference to both extrinsic and intrinsic product cues to influence product perceptions. (Courtesy of the Dannon Company, Inc.).

Dannon Yogurt may not help you live as long as Soviet Georgians. But it couldn't hurt.

Bagrat Topagua, age 89.

His mother.

There are two curious things about the people of Soviet Georgia. A large part of their diet is yogurt. And a large number of them live to be well over 100.

Of course, many factors affect longevity, and we are not saying Dannon Yogurt will help you live longer. But we will say that all-natural Dannon is high in nutrients, low in fat, reasonable in calories. And quite satisfying at lunch or as a snack.

Another thing about Dannon. It contains active yogurt cultures (many pre-mixed or Swiss style brands don't). They make yogurt one of the easiest foods to digest and have been credited with other healthful benefits.

Which is why we've been advising this: If you don't always eat right, Dannon Yogurt is the right thing to eat.

By the way, Bagrat Topagua thought Dannon was "dzelian kargia." Which means he loved it.

Dannon Milk Products, 22-11 38th Ave. Long Island City, N.Y. 11101.

Price Considerations

Traditional microeconomic theory as reviewed in Chapter 2 has apparently influenced many marketers to assume that consumers use price only as an indicator of product cost. Consumers' use of price in this way will generate the classic down-sloping demand curve as portrayed in Figure 13-8a. Here, lower prices result in greater quantities of the product being demanded. However, considerable evidence suggests that the meaning consumers derive from the price variable is much more complex in nature.[81]

Psychological Pricing Much discussion of how consumers encode price information has focused on the concept of "psychological pricing"; this suggests that there is greater consumer demand at certain prices and that this demand decreases at prices above *and below* these points. Such a situation is described by the ratchet-type demand curve in Figure 13-8b. Prices p_1, p_2, and p_3, respectively, are seen to generate a greater quantity demanded than other prices in their immediate range.

One aspect of psychological pricing is the frequently observed retail practice of odd-pricing. Here, it is said that prices ending in an odd number (such as 5, 7, or 9) or just under the round number (such as 96 or 98) generate higher demand than related round-numbered prices. However, this argument is usually based on retailers' experiences and has not yet been confirmed by rigorous testing.

Price and Product Quality Another important price-perception topic is what has become known as the price-quality proposition which holds that consumers tend to use price as an indicator of the quality or satisfaction potential of a product. The use of price as an extrinsic product cue in this way is not unreasonable when consumers lack confidence or ability to directly judge product attributes. For example, previous purchase experiences may lead to an awareness that higher quality products tend to cost more. Adages such as "You get what you pay for" and messages such as the one in Figure 13-9 also act to reinforce this association. Given the uncertainty arising from attempts to directly evaluate today's technically complex products, consumers may rely on these previous experiences to conclude that higher-priced products are of higher quality. This, in turn, suggests that consumers may suspect the quality of some products that bear very low prices.

Based on the above argument, we can see how price may actually hold a dual informational role for consumers—as an indicator of product cost and as an indicator of product quality. Therefore, consumers' demand for a product will depend on the relative degree to which they use price as a measure of cost and quality. This can be shown by the unusually shaped demand curve in Figure 13-8c. The upper portion of the curve has a rather traditional shape reflecting consumers' use of price primarily as a measure of cost: lower prices generate greater quantity demanded. However, when the use of price as an indicator of product quality begins to dominate consumers' purchase decisions, lower prices can actually lead to a drop in quantity demanded. This situation is reflected in the backward-bending portion of the demand curve in Figure 13-8c.

FIGURE 13-8

Potential shapes of the demand curve for a product under conditions of different consumer perceptions of the price variable.

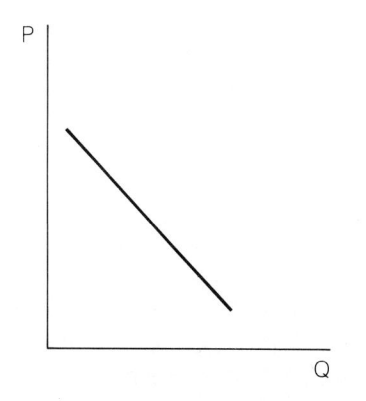

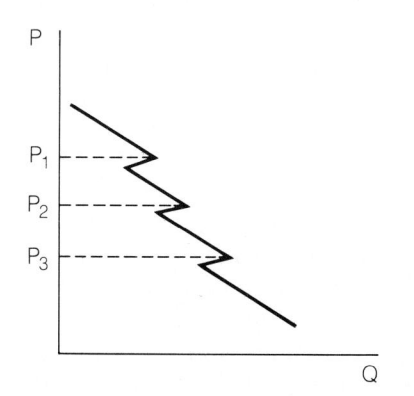

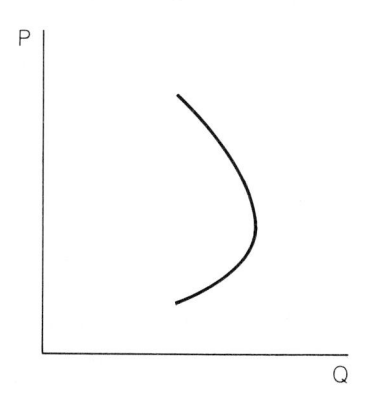

(a) (b) (c)

FIGURE 13-9

Example of an advertising message reinforcing price-quality perceptions. (Courtesy of Jean Patou, Inc.)

> JOY
>
> The costliest perfume in the world...
>
> JEAN PATOU
> PARIS

Given such an important implication, a number of researchers have sought to determine the extent to which consumers might actually use price as an indicator of product quality. To do this, experimental situations were developed in which only the price of a product was allowed to change across various testing situations. These studies found that respondents tended to prefer the higher-priced alternative, expecially when brands were expected to differ considerably in terms of quality. Further studies determined that the price-quality relationship varied across products, and it was highest when consumers faced risky situations and when their confidence in directly judging the quality of products was low.[82]

More recent investigations have researched a variety of products and perhaps more realistic shopping situations. These findings are more complex in nature since they suggest that price is not always the most important influence on quality perception, especially when brand names are known and experience with the product is great.[83] Further, the importance of price in influencing perceptions may depend on the specific product-quality aspects being evaluated.[84] Therefore, overall product perceptions are probably the result of a combination of information derived from price, other extrinsic cues, and judgments of intrinsic product characteristics.[85]

Several other conclusions have been derived from additional studies of how consumers react to the price variable. Monroe and Petroshius have included the following in their recent review of this reasearch:

1 Consumers appear to use price as an indicatior of product quality as well as an indicator of purchase cost.

2 Consumers also tend to develop reference prices as standards for judging prices that they confront in the marketplace.

3 Reference prices are not constant, but are modified by market experiences. Therefore, the consumer's exposure to prices somewhat higher than her reference price is likely to result in an upward adjustment of the reference price. The opposite is likely for exposure to prices somewhat below the reference price.

4 Buyers appear to develop a range of acceptable prices around the standard or reference price. Prices outside the range (above, or *below*) are likely to be judged as inappropriate for the product in question and may result in a decreased willingness to purchase.

5 Certain factors (e.g., brand name, store image) can mitigate the strength of the perceived price-quality relationship and actually overshadow it for some products.

6 When prices are perceived as similar for various alternatives, then price is unlikely to be influential in choices between these alternatives.[86]

Company and Store Image

Astute marketers have long realized that, in addition to brand image, their company's image can strongly influence consumers' behavior toward their enterprise and its products. A company's image is the perception consumers have of its character as a result of their experiences with it and their knowledge of and beliefs about it.

Importance of an Image A strong and clear company image can increase consumers' confidence in its products and their predisposition to purchase them. This is demonstrated by results of a study in which a sample of women were 14 percent more likely to try a new product offered from Heinz than from a large but unspecified food company.[87] Such evidence has encouraged many firms to change their name or company logo in an effort to refine their image. In addition, as companies diversify, merge, or acquire new operations, it often appears appropriate to rename the organization to reflect its new dimensions or make a break with its old identity. Thus, United Aircraft became United Technologies, California Packing became Del Monte, Ligget & Myers was changed to the Liggett Group, and Mobil Oil Corporation is now called Mobil Corporation. Such changes can be quite expensive—

it has been reported that in the early 1970s Humble Oil spent more than $100 million to change its name to Exxon![88]

Because the way in which consumers perceive a company can influence their reactions to its offerings, managers are very concerned with their firm's image, even when a name change is not being considered. For example, the negative way in which businesspeople can be portrayed in various entertainment shows is thought by many executives to create a general image problem for business. After a study by the Media Institute concluded that businesspeople are usually portrayed in a negative light on TV shows, some companies took the initiative to counteract this perceived problem by running communications designed to bring these biases, and their potential danger, to the attention of the public.[89]

Consumers' patronage of a particular retail store can also be significantly influenced by their perception of its image or "personality."[90] Store image may be defined as "the way in which the store is defined in the shopper's mind, partly by its functional qualities and partly by an aura of psychological attributes."[91] This implies that perception of store image is derived not only from so-called functional attributes of price, convenience, and selection of merchandise, but also from the influence of variables such as architecture, interior design, colors, and advertising. Therefore, consumers can develop images of stores regardless of whether retailers consciously attempt to project a specific image. For this reason, it can be very important for retailers to measure their image as consumers perceive it. If consumers' choice criteria for stores can also be identified, the retailer can then determine how the store is evaluated on those factors that are most important in influencing patronage. Strategies for modifying the store image where appropriate can then be considered.

Measuring Store Images Although a variety of methods (including perceptual mapping) exist to measure store images, one frequently used is the semantic differential profile that was described in Chapter 3. First, a list of important tangible and intangible store image attributes are identified. Then, for these attributes, a sample of consumers can indicate their perceptions of the store on semantic scales. This can also be done for competing stores in the same study. Average or median responses can then be calculated to yield an *image profile* for each store. Figure 13-10 serves as an illustration by portraying image profiles actually found for two competing department stores in the Los Angeles area.

These profiles indicate that store A is perceived more favorably than store B, although not by a great degree. Store A appears to have a rather high-price image but, compared to store B, consumers still perceive it as providing good value for the money. Ratings on attractiveness and neatness also reveal a potential problem to which managers of store B may wish to address their attention.

It should not be concluded from the above discussion that measurement of store image reveals only positive/negative image information. For example, one store may be perceived as progressive and another as conservative, neither of which is necessarily a good or bad trait. Research has also revealed some other interesting findings, particularly the fact that stores do have distinguishable images or personalities. Also, different stores appear to attract specific socioeconomic segments, and consumers in different social classes, stages of family life cycle, or other market segments are likely to perceive a given store differently.[92] All of these findings suggest that stores may be more successful in appealing to specific target segments as opposed to the mass market.

Advertising Issues

Applications of information processing to advertising have been cited throughout the chapter. However, two other areas that draw considerable attention are the use of sex in advertising and the controversy over subliminal advertising.

Sex in Advertising The use of sexually attractive models and sexually suggestive themes in advertising has a long history. It is therefore surprising that little is generally known about specific consumer reactions to these methods of promoting products. Because the recent promotional trend has been toward a dramatic increase in the use of more explicit sexual themes and pictures, the need for research in this area is even greater.[93] Of course, it should be kept in mind that the findings of such research may only pertain to the culture in which the investigation was conducted.

The small number of investigations that have been generally published suggest that, in at least some circumstances, the use of sexual themes or nudity in promotions may have significant limitations. For example, some studies indicate that a majority of the public say that they believe that too much use is made of sexual appeals in advertising.[94] Further, because feminists and older individuals appear to hold this belief to a greater degree than do others, an advertiser's use of

FIGURE 13-10

Semantic differential profiles of two competing department stores. (*Source:* Burton H. Marcus, "Image Variation and the Multi-Unit Retail Establishment," *Journal of Retailing*, **48**:39, Summer 1972. Adapted with permission of the *Journal of Retailing*, New York University.)

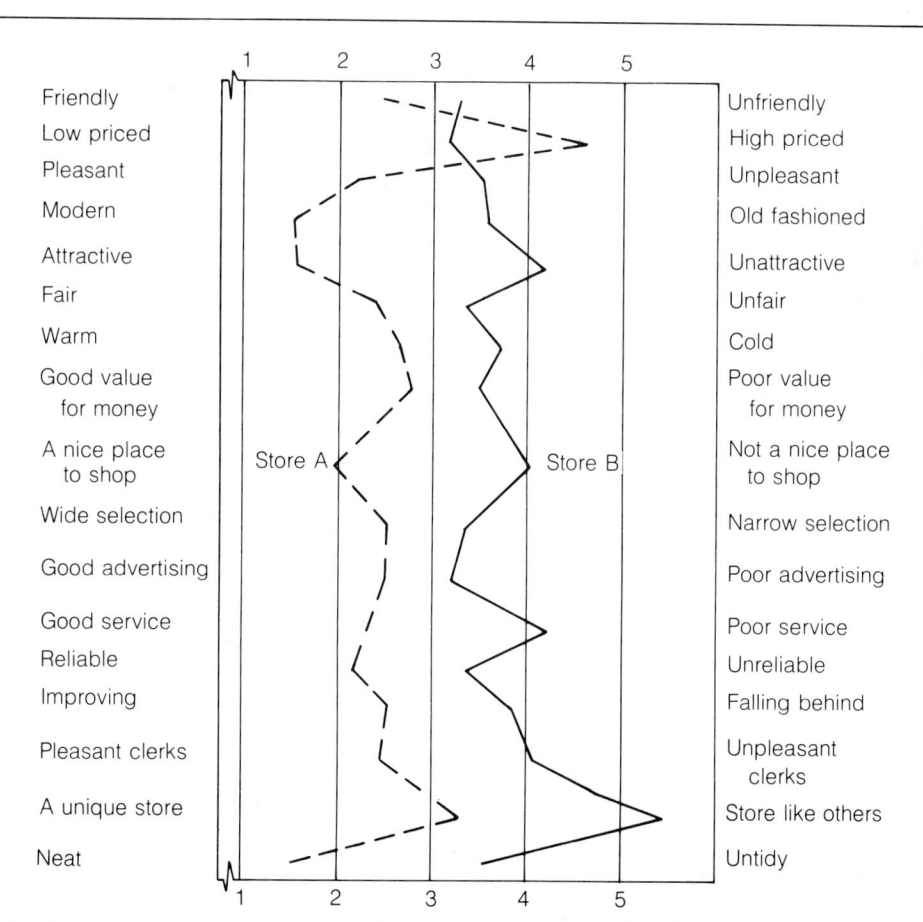

sexual themes could generate negative reactions from substantial portions of the market.

One purpose for incorporating sexual themes or pictorial material into advertisements is to attract consumers' attention to the ad. However, evidence suggests that use of such material may not always have an easily predictable or desired effect. This is demonstrated by one study that found nonsexual and sexual-romantic themes to have a greater influence on consumers' attention than did nudity.[95] Also, an actual print advertisement for an office copier received much greater reader response when the bikini-clad model standing beside it was removed.[96] One explanation is that the model that was employed to attract attention actually drew attention *away* from the advertising message.

Of course, attracting attention is only one purpose of advertising. Consumers must also remember the brand name and advertising message in a favorable manner. It is interesting to note that studies have found that although consumers' recognition or recall of an advertisement may increase through the use of sexual illustrations, at best, no positive influence could be detected for the brand being advertised.[97] Other research indicates that even the higher recognition of advertisements may be confined mainly to the visual material and not to the verbal content of the ad.[98]

A further concern is how the use of sexual content influences consumers' perceptions of the advertisement and advertised brand. Here again, evidence does not consistently favor the use of sexual content in ads. For example, Peterson and Kerin found that ads employing female nudity were perceived by consumers as being less appealing than ads without nude models. Also, the products advertised using nude models were actually perceived as being of lower quality.[99] However, results of this and other studies suggest that several other factors can influence how consumers will react to products advertised using sexual content. First, and quite predictably, consumers' predispositions toward sexual themes appear to be an important determinant of their reaction to ads containing such material. Second, reactions to nudity seem to be negative when a member of the same sex is used as the nude model.[100] Third, the use of sexual themes may be perceived as acceptable for certain products such as those that are designed to increase one's allurement (perfume, aftershave, body oil, etc.).[101] Furthermore, the people present in the viewing situation may also influence how consumers react to a given sexual theme.[102] Apparently, this occurs because the presence of certain people presents an uncomfortable situation for the viewer.

Although these studies are not great in number, they and other studies on the use of sex in advertising generally suggest that the decision to use sexual themes is not a simple, straightforward one. The product to be advertised, the situations involved, and the predispositions (attitudes toward sexual themes and sexual exploitation) of various market segments are all important considerations when making such a decision. This points to the need for a sound evaluation of advertising content and market characteristics before employing sexual themes to promote any specific product.

Subliminal Advertising The technique called subliminal advertising has sparked considerable controversy in promotional and scientific fields. You may recall from earlier discussions that the absolute threshold identifies the minimum value of a stimulus capable of being consciously noticed. Because this is also referred to as a *limen,* the term "sub*liminal* perception" actually means perception of stimuli that are below the level needed to reach conscious awareness. Potentially, this could be achieved in at least three major ways: 1) presenting visual stimuli for a very brief duration, 2) presenting auditory messages through accelerated speech at low volume levels, and 3) imbedding or hiding images or words in pictorial material.[103] The purported benefit of using such techniques in advertising is that a subliminal message will not be strong enough to arouse consumers' selective attention and defense mechanisms, but it will have enough strength to influence them at an unconscious level.

The first widely known test of subliminal advertising was conducted by Vicary during the 1950s.[104] During movie theater tests more than 45,000 unsuspecting viewers were presented with filmed messages every 5 seconds at speeds said to be $\frac{1}{3000}$ of a second in duration. The two messages employed were "Eat Popcorn" and "Drink Coca-Cola." By comparing sales receipts during the test period to those from a previous period, it was reported that popcorn sales increased 58 percent and Coca-Cola sales rose 18 percent.

These results quickly generated considerable concern regarding unethical uses of subliminal methods. However, closer examination of Vicary's research raised questions as to its validity. As one review stated, "There were no reports . . . of even the most rudimentary scientific precautions, such as adequate controls, provisions for replication, etc."[105] The lack of information on these provisions does not generate much confidence in the validity of the results.

Other efforts to subliminally influence audiences have not been able to document the positive effects reported by Vicary.[106] Nevertheless, a number of actual applications of subliminal messages in print and audio media have been reported. These range from attempts to deter shoplifting and influence purchases, to efforts at reducing radio audience stress and increasing the motivation of employees.[107] Popular books on the subject have also charged that effective subliminal images are embedded in many print advertisements, and that messages are also subliminally incorporated into movies and pop music.[108] Unfortunately, because careful steps have not been taken to measure the influence of these messages on the intended audience, their effects have not been well documented.

More carefully controlled experiments suggest that although subliminal messages may be capable of arousing basic drives such as thirst and hunger, evidence of their influence on attitudes or specific motives directing consumers toward particular brands has not been strong.[109] However, Saegert has reviewed studies from the field of psychology which suggest that subliminal messages might possibly be capable of influencing consumers' specific but unconsciously held desires.[110]

In conclusion, some evidence suggests that under certain conditions subliminal perception may occur. However, considerable technical problems result when attempting to capitalize on this perceptual process by developing subliminal advertising messages in a commercial setting. First, the speed of the message must be determined. This may be especially difficult when one considers that the absolute thresholds of various consumers may differ by a considerable amount. Second, the message itself must be brief and simple, since anything more than a few words would probably be too complex to comprehend. Furthermore, we have seen how consumers' motives, personality, and other individual determinants influence selective perception of stimuli above the absolute threshold. There is no guarantee that these factors would not operate on subliminal stimuli. Thus, the subliminal message, "Drink Coke" could be distorted into "Stink Coke" or some other meaning not highly desired by the marketer.

Furthermore, because subliminal messages may arouse only basic drives, they may initiate behavior that is not always beneficial to the advertiser. Thus, a subliminal message for Pepsi may increase a consumer's thirst enough for a trip to the refrigerator for a glass of Dr. Pepper or another liquid refreshment that is on hand. Also, if such messages can actually appeal to consumers' unconscious motives, the problems of identifying and dealing with such motives appear to be quite large. Therefore, it seems safe to conclude that at present, subliminal advertising does not hold the threat of turning consumers into automatons who are at the mercy of marketers. In fact, minimal evidence regarding its effectiveness, technical difficulties associated with its use, and unknown consequences of employing it gives little reason for advertisers to wholeheartedly embrace subliminal advertising.[111]

SUMMARY

This chapter has examined the topic of information processing and its role in influencing consumer behavior. First, an overview of major concepts identified the important processes of information acquisition, perceptual encoding, memory, integration, evaluation, and choice. The importance of the executive system in directing these activities, as well as the influences provided by consumer and situational characteristics, were also reviewed.

Several of these topics were then treated in greater depth. Discussion first focused on information acquisition. Here, active search for and passive reception of stimuli were shown to be the two major activities for acquiring information. Active search involves scanning both internal (memory) and external sources. Internal search was said to provide sufficient information to the consumer in most situations, but external search will be used where presently held information is inadequate.

The nature and intensity of external search were then examined. A primary conclusion from the evidence reviewed is that consumers do not appear to engage in a great deal of external-search activity. Passive reception of information was briefly treated next. Attention then turned to the acquisition topic of how consumers develop sensations from stimuli. Here, the nature and marketing implications of consumers' awareness and differential thresholds were discussed.

The selective nature of consumers' attention to stimuli was then treated. Various stimulus properties, as well as characteristics of the consumer himself, were shown to have a great potential impact on attention.

Perceptual encoding was the next major topic. Encoding involves assessing how the main features of a stimulus are organized (feature analysis) and then combining this information with other available information to interpret the stimulus. A wide variety of stimulus and individual factors can influence this perceptual encoding process. A number of them were reviewed, and marketing examples were provided for many.

The focus of the chapter then switched to considering additional marketing implications of the information-processing material that had been presented. Subsequent chapters will treat the remaining processing topics in some depth and show how they relate to the subject matter of each chapter.

The first marketing implication discussed dealt with consumers' perceptions of products and some of the factors influencing these perceptions. Consumers' difficulty in judging products directly was noted, and their use of extrinsic product cues (packaging, etc.) as a source of product information was suggested. Certain pricing issues were the next topic of discussion. Psychological pricing and the price-quality association that consumers may develop were the two topics reviewed. The influence of these issues on the shape of the demand curve was noted.

The effect of company and store attributes on consumers' perception of the "personality" of these enterprises was also discussed. Methods to measure such perceptions were briefly reviewed.

Finally, two rather controversial advertising issues were discussed. It seems that with regard to sex in advertising, as well as with the technique of subliminal advertising, additional work must be done to define the proper (if any) use of the techniques. Current research suggests that using either of these methods may not yield predictable or desirable results. Because of this, their application to any specific marketing problems should involve careful consideration.

DISCUSSION TOPICS

1 What is information processing? Distinguish between the various activities that comprise the information-processing function.

2 It is often said that the information-acquisition activity is selective in nature. In what ways is this so? What implications does this have for understanding consumer behavior?

3 Select a product that typically retails for more than $100. Interview at least two salespeople of this product to determine their estimate of the typical degree of consumers' external search activity for it. Use as many of the external search measures that are mentioned in the chapter as are feasible. To what degree do you find that your results are consistent with those reported in the chapter?

4 Review that portion of the chapter dealing with consumers' attention processes and then select several advertisements from various media (print, TV, etc.). Describe these advertisements and evaluate them in terms of their potential for attracting consumers' attention. If possible, include examples of the advertisements.

5 It has been established that the tips of the fingers are eight times more sensitive to the touch than are legs, and eighty-three times as sensitive as regions of the foot. Discuss any implications this has for designing products such as men's and women's hosiery or pants.

6 The resemblance of certain private-brand packaging to the packaging of nationally known brands has been so close at times that they have been described as lookalikes. Visit a supermarket and bring back two packaged products to demonstrate this. Also, while you are there, make an effort to determine the prevalence of this phenomenon. In what ways might it influence the behavior of consumers?

7 Assume that consumers have heightened awareness of the following prices for various models in a product line: $11.70, $15.21, and $19.77. Using Weber's Law, predict the next highest price in the line which would generate heightened awareness.

8 Bring to class two print advertisements which use each of the following techniques for influencing perceptual encoding. Be prepared to assess how effectively the techniques have been employed.

a similarity   **b** figure-ground   **c** proximity

9 Write up a procedure that you would employ for conducting a taste test to determine (1) if your fellow students can discriminate between three brands of cola, and (2) if they have a preference for any particular cola based on taste alone. Indicate the variables that might influence the results and how you would design an experiment to minimize their influence.

10 Choose any two restaurants or pubs that are frequented by students at your school. Measure their image profiles by designing a number of semantic differential items and administering them to a random sample of your fellow students. What conclusions can you draw from your data?

11 Find several examples of magazine advertisements that employ sexual themes or illustrations to capture readers' attention or influence perceptual encoding. How appropriate do the methods appear to be for the target market involved? How effectively do the devices appear to accomplish their apparent goals? Can you foresee any possible problems the advertiser might encounter as a result of using the methods?

NOTES

[1] Jagdish N. Sheth, "How Consumers Use Information," Faculty working Paper No. 530, College of Commerce and Business Administration, University of Illinois at Urbana-Champaign, 1978, pp. 14–18.

[2] See Howard Beales, et al., "Consumer Search and Public Policy," *Journal of Consumer Research*, **8**: 11–22, June 1981, for a more comprehensive discussion of this issue and its implications for public policy.

[3] See George Katona, *The Powerful Consumer,* McGraw-Hill, New York, 1960; Louis P. Bucklin, "Testing Propensities to Shop," *Journal of Marketing,* 30:22–27, January 1966; and Allen Newell and Herbert Simon, *Human Problem Solving,* Prentice-Hall, Englewood Cliffs, NJ, 1972, for alternative perspectives.

[4] See Wesley C. Bender, "Consumer Purchase Costs—Do Retailers Recognize Them?" *Journal of Retailing,* 40: 1–8, 52, Spring 1964; Hans B. Thorelli, Helmut Becker, and Jack Engledow, *The Information Seekers,* Ballinger, Cambridge, MA, 1975, p. 16.

[5] See Joseph W. Newman, "Consumer External Search: Amount and Determinants," in Arch G. Woodside, Jagdish N. Sheth, and Peter D. Bennett (eds.), *Consumer and Industrial Buying Behavior,* North-Holland, New York, pp. 86–92; and James R. Bettman, *An Information Processing Theory of Consumer Choice,* Addison-Wesley, Reading, MA, 1979 pp. 123–131, upon which much of this discussion is based.

[6] Joseph Newman and Richard Staelin, "Prepurchase Information Seeking for New Cars and Major Household Appliances," *Journal of Marketing Research,* 9: 249–257, August 1972.

[7] Louis P. Bucklin, "Consumer Search, Role Enactment and Market Efficiency," *Journal of Business,* 42: 416-38, 1969.

[8] John D. Claxton, Joseph N. Fry, and Bernard Portis, "A Taxonomy of Prepurchase Information Gathering Patterns," *Journal of Consumer Research,* 1:35–42, December 1974.

[9] Claxton, Fry, and Portis, "A Taxonomy."

[10] Findings have not been uniform on this issue. For two recent studies showing differing results see William L. Moore and Donald R. Lehmann, "Individual Differences in Search Behavior For a Nondurable," *Journal of Consumer Research,* 7: 296–307, December 1980; and Geoffrey C. Kiel and Roger A. Layton, "Dimensions of Consumer Information Seeking Behavior," *Journal of Marketing Research,* **18**: 233–239, May 1981. Possible explanations for divergent findings include the use of different research products and whether the urgency stems from a felt need or an environmental pressure.

[11] G. D. Harrell and M. D. Hutt, "Crowding in Retail Stores," *MSU Business Topics,* **24**: 31–39, Winter 1976.

[12] George Katona and Eva Mueller, "A Study of Purchasing Decisions," in Lincoln H. Clark (ed.), *Consumer Behavior: The Dynamics of Consumer Reaction,* New York University Press, New York, 1955.

[13] Edward J. Russo, "The Value of Unit Price Information," *Journal of Marketing Research,* **14**: 193–201, May 1977.

[14] Moore and Lehmann, "Individual Differences in Search Behavior"; Udell, "Prepurchase Behavior of Buyers"; and Newman and Staelin, "Prepurchase Information Seeking." See also Kiel and Layton, "Dimensions of Consumer Information Seeking Behavior," for results suggesting that specific experience may exert only a selective influence on search behavior.

[15] William B. Locander and Peter W. Hermann, "The Effect of Self-confidence and Anxiety on Information Seeking in Consumer Risk Reduction," *Journal of Marketing Research,* **16**: 268–274, May 1979; and Paul Green, "Consumer Use of Information," in Joseph W. Newman (ed.), *On Knowing the Consumer,* Wiley, New York, 1966, pp. 67–80. For a recent contradictory finding see Kiel and Layton, "ND Dimensions of Consumer Information Seeking Behavior."

[16] See Noel Capon and Marian Burke, "Individual, Product Class, and Task-Related Factors in Consumer Information Processing," *Journal of Consumer Research,* **7**: 314–326, December 1980; Green, "Consumers' Use of Information"; and Ted R. Roselius, "Consumer Rankings of Risk Reduction Methods," *Journal of Marketing,* **35**: 56–61, January 1971.

[17] See Thorelli, Becker, and Engledow, *The Information Seekers;* Capon and Burke, "Individual, Product Class, and Task-Related Factors in Information Processing"; Donald J. Hempel, "Search Behavior and Information Utilization in the Home Buying Process," in P. McDonald (ed.), *Marketing Involvement in Society and the Economy,* American Marketing Association, Chicago, 1969; and Newman and Staelin, "Prepurchase Information Seeking." See also Kiel and Layton, "Dimensions of Consumer Information Seeking Behavior" for both supporting and divergent findings.

[18] See Jacob Jacoby, Donald Speller, and Carol Kohn Berning. "Brand Choice Behavior As a Function of Information Load: Replication and Extension," *Journal of Consumer Research,* **1**: 33–42, June 1974; John T. Lanyetta and Vera T. Kanareff, "Information Cost, Amount of Payoff and Level of Aspiration as Determinants of Information Seeking in Decision Making," *Behavioral Science,* **7**: 459–473, 1962; and J. Edward Russo, "More Information is Better: A Reevaluation of Jacoby, Speller and Kohn," *Journal of Consumer Research,* **1**: 68–72, December 1974, for information related to this topic.

[19] See P. S. Raju, "Theories of Exploratory Behavior: Review and Consumer Research Implications," in Jagdish N. Sheth (ed.), *Research in Marketing: Volume 4,* JAI Press, Greenwich, CT, 1981, pp. 223–249.

[20] See John A. Howard and Jagdish N. Sheth, *The Theory of Buyer Behavior,* Wiley, New York, 1969, pp. 26–27, 46–47.

[21] See Everett M. Rogers, *Diffusion of Innovations,* Free Press, New York, 1962; and Carol Kohn Berning and Jacob Jacoby, "Patterns of Information Acquisition in New Product Purchases," *Journal of Consumer Research,* **1**: 18–22, September 1974.

[22] For an excellent and more extensive review of this subject see Newman, "Consumer External Search," upon which much of this section is based.

[23] Newman and Staelin, "Prepurchase Information Seeking."

[24] Newman, "Consumer External Search."

[25] William P. Dommermuth, "The Shopping Matrix and Marketing Strategy," *Journal of Marketing Research,* **2**: 130, May 1965.

[26] Jacob Jacoby, et al., "Prepurchase Informaion Acquisition: Description of a Process Methodology, Research Paradigm and Pilot Investigation," in Beverlee B. Anderson (ed.), *Advances in Consumer Research: Volume 3,* Association for Consumer Research, Ann Arbor, MI, 1976, pp. 306–314.

[27] Katona and Mueller, "A Study of Purchase Decisions"; Newman and Staelin, "Prepurchase Information Seeking"; Claxton, Fry, and Portis, "A Taxonomy of Prepurchase Information Gathering Patterns"; and Kiel and Layton, "Dimensions of Consumer Information Seeking Behavior."

[28] Kiel and Layton, "Dimensions of Consumer Information Seeking Behavior."

[29] See Robert A. Westbrook and Claes Fornell, "Patterns of Information Source Usage Among Durable Goods Buyers," *Journal of Marketing Research,* **16**: 303–312, August 1979, for a typology of selective search based on different research evidence.

[30] See Westbrook and Fornell, "Patterns of Information Source Usage"; Katona and Mueller, "A Study of Purchase Decisions"; Newman and Staelin, "Prepurchase Information Seeking"; Hans B. Thorelli, "Concentrations of Information Power Among Consumers," *Journal of Marketing Research,* **8**: 427–432, November 1971; Thorelli, Becker, and Engledow, *The Information Seekers;* and Kiel and Layton, "Dimensions of Consumer Information Seeking Behavior," for representative findings.

[31] See Beals, et al., "Consumer Search and Public Policy," p. 13.

[32] "Does Taste Make Waste?," *Forbes,* June 1, 1974, p. 24.

[33] Some of the following discussion follows Richard Lee Miller, "Dr. Weber and the Consumer,"*Journal of Marketing,* **26**: 57–61, January 1962; and Steuart Henderson Britt, "How Weber's Law Can Be Applied to Marketing," *Business Horizons,* **18**: 21–29, February 1975.

[34] L. Paul Gilden, "Sampling Candy Bar Economics," *The New Englander,* **22**: 32, January 1976.
[35] "Hidden Costs," *The Wall Street Journal,* February 15, 1977, p. 1.
[36] See "Checkout Counter Look-alikes," *Money,* May 1976, pp. 71–72.
[37] Joseph Uhl, "Consumer Perception of Retail Food Price Changes," paper presented at First Annual Meeting of the Association for Consumer Research, 1970.
[38] Raymond Bauer and Stephen Greyser, *Advertising in America: The Consumer's View,* Havard University, Cambridge, MA, 1968, p. 178.
[39] Daniel Kahneman, *Attention and Effort,* Prentice-Hall, Englewood Cliffs, NJ, 1973, p. 4.
[40] Much of this section follows the discussion in Andrew A. Mitchell, "An Information Processing View of Consumer Behavior," in Subhash C. Jain (ed.), *Research Frontiers in Marketing: Dialogues and Directions,* American Marketing Association, Chicago, 1978, pp. 189–190.
[41] Walter Schneider and Richard M. Sheffrin, "Controlled and Automatic Human Information Processing: I. Detecton, Search and Attention," *Psychological Review,* **84**: 1–66, 1977.
[42] S. Sternberg, "High Speed Scanning in Human Memory," *Science,* **153**: 652–654, 1966.
[43] See Geraldine Fennell, "Attention Engagement," in James H. Leigh and Claude R. Martin Jr. (eds.), *Current Issues and Research in Advertising,* University of Michigan, Ann Arbor, MI, 1979, pp. 17–33, for a much fuller discussion of these factors.
[44] J. W. Rosenberg, "How Does Color, Size, Affect Ad Readership," *Industrial Marketing,* **41**: 54–57, May 1956.
[45] Rafael Valiente, "Mechanical Correlates of Ad Recognition," *Journal of Advertising Research,* **13**: 13–18, June 1973.
[46] Stephen Baker, *Visual Persuasion,* McGraw-Hill, New York, 1961.
[47] "Position in Newspaper Advertising: 1," *Media/Scope,* February 1963, p. 57. This finding is contrary to much previous research; see Melvin S. Hattwick, *How to Use Psychology for Better Advertising,* Prentice-Hall, Englewood Cliffs, NJ: 1950, pp. 145–150.
[48] See Hattwick, *Psychology for Better Advertising,* p. 155; and "Position in Newspaper Advertising: 1," p. 57.
[49] See Pat Kelly and Paul J. Soloman, "Humor in Television Advertising," *Journal of Advertising,* **4**: 33–35, Summer 1975; Peter Lubalin, "Humor in Radio," ANNY, November 4, 1977, p. 22; and Dorothy Markiewicz, "Effects of Humor on Persuasion," *Sociometry,* **37**: 407–422, 1974.
[50] See Markiewicz, "Effects of Humor on Persuasion," and Brian Sternthal and Samuel Craig, "Humor in Advertising," *Journal of Marketing,* **37**: 12–18, October 1973.
[51] See Sternthal and Craig, "Humor in Advertising"; and Thomas J. Madden and Marc G. Weinberger, "The Effects of Humor on Attention in Magazine Advertising," Working Paper 81-19, School of Business Administration, University of Massachusetts, Amherst, MA, 1981.
[52] Allan Greenberg and Charles Suttoni, "Television Commercial Wear-out," *Journal of Advertising Research,* **13**: 47–54, October 1973.
[53] See Alvin J. Silk and Frank P. Geiger, "Advertisement Size and the Relationship between Product Usage and Advertising Exposure," *Journal of Marketing Research,* **9**: 22–26, February 1972, which credits this hypothesis to Leo Bogart.
[54] Charles F. Cannell and James C. MacDonald, "The Impact of Health News on Attitudes and Behavior," *Journalism Quarterly,* **33**: 315–323, July-September 1956.
[55] Jerry C. Olson, "Encoding Processes: Levels of Processing and Existing Knowledge Structures," in Jerry C. Olson (ed.), *Advances in Consumer Research: Volume 8,* Association for Consumer Research, Ann Arbor, MI, 1980, p. 154.
[56] See Bettman, *An Information Processing Theory,* pp. 79–82, and Peter H. Lindsay and Donald A. Norman, *Human Information Processing,* Academic Press, New York, 1972, pp. 115–147.
[57] Bettman, *An Information Processing Theory,* p. 79.
[58] Lindsay and Norman, *Human Information Processing,* pp. 131–133.
[59] Jerry C. Olson, "Theories of Information Encoding and Storage: Implications for Consumer Research," in Andrew A. Mitchell (ed.), *The Effect of Information on Consumer and Market Behavior,* American Marketing Association, Chicago, 1978, p. 52.
[60] Norman Heller, "An Application of Psychological Learning Theory to Adverising," *Journal of Marketing,* **20**: 248–254, January 1956; and Dev Pathak, Gene Burton, and Ron Zigli, "The Memory Impact of Incomplete Advertising Slogans," in Henry Nash and Donald Robin (eds.), *Proceedings of the Southern Marketing Association Conference,* 1977, pp. 269–272.
[61] James H. Myers and William H. Reynolds, *Consumer Behavior and Marketing Management,* Houghton Mifflin, Boston, 1967, p. 21.
[62] Robert Froman, "You Get What You Want," in J. H. Westing (ed.), *Readings in Marketing,* Prentice-Hall, Englewood Cliffs, NJ, 1953, p. 231.
[63] William Copulsky and Katherin Marton, "Sensory Cues, You've Got to Put Them Together," *Product Marketing,* January 1977, pp. 31–34.
[64] Thomas L. Parkinson, "The Use of Seals of Approval in Consumer Decision-Making as a Function of Cognitive Needs and Style," in Mary Jane Schlinger (ed.), *Advances in Consumer Research: Volume 2,* Association For Consumer Research, Chicago, 1975, pp. 133–140.

[65] Harry Helson, *Adaptation-Level Theory: An Experimental and Systematic Approach to Behavior*, Harper & Row, New York, 1964.

[66] See Albert J. Della Bitta and Kent B. Monroe, "The Influence of Adaptation Levels on Subjective Price Perceptions," in Scott Ward and Peter Wright (eds.), *Advances in Consumer Research: Volume 1*, Association for Consumer Research, Urbana, IL, 1973, pp. 359–369; and Anthony N. Doob, et al., "Effect of Initial Selling Price on Subsequent Sales," *Journal of Personality and Social Psychology*, 11: 345–350, April 1969.

[67] See Jacob Jacoby, Donald E. Speller, and Carol A. Kohn, "Brand Choice Behavior as a Function of Information Load," *Journal of Marketing Research*, 11: 63–69, February 1974; Jacob Jacoby, Donald E. Speller, and Carol A. Kohn, "Brand Choice Behavior as a Function of Information Load: Replication and Extension," *Journal of Consumer Research*, 1:33–42, June 1974; and Jacob Jacoby, Donald E. Speller, and Carol A. K. Berning, "Constructive Criticism and Programmatic Research, Reply to Russo," *Journal of Consumer Research*, 2: 154–156, September 1975. See also Debra L. Scammon, "Information Load and Consumers," *Journal of Consumer Research*, 4: 148–155, December 1977, for additional relevant evidence.

[68] See Edward J. Russo, "More Information Is Better: A Re-evaluation of Jacoby, Speller and Kohn," *Journal of Consumer Research*, 1: 68–72, December 1974; John O. Summers, "Less Information is Better?," *Journal of Marketing Research*, 11: 467–468, November 1974; William L. Wilkie, "Analysis of Effects of Information Load," *Journal of Marketing Research*, 11: 462–466, November 1974; and Naresh K. Malhotra, Arun K. Jain, and Stephen W. Lagakos, "The Information Overload Controversy: An Alternative Viewpoint," *Journal of Marketing*, 46: 27–37, Spring 1982.

[69] Naresh K. Malhotra, "Information Load and Consumer Decision Making," *Journal of Consumer Research*, 8: 419–430, March 1982.

[70] R. W. Husband and J. Godfrey, "An Experimental Study of Cigarette Identification," *Journal of Applied Psychology*, 18: 220–251, April 1934; and C. K. Ramond, L. N. Rachal, and M. R. Marks, "Brand Discrimination among Cigarette Smokers," *Journal of Applied Psychology*, 34: 282–284, August 1950.

[71] Ralph I. Allison and Kenneth P. Uhl, "Influences of Beer Brand Identification on Taste Perception," *Journal of Marketing Research*, 1: 36–39, August 1964; and Jacob Jacoby, Jerry C. Olson, and Rafael A. Haddock, "Price, Brand Name, and Product Composition Characteristics as Determinants of Perceived Quality," *Journal of Applied Psychology*, 55: 570–579, December 1971.

[72] See Sam Lane, James Zychowski, and Kenneth Lelli, "Cola and Diet Cola Identification and Level of Cola Consumption," *Journal of Applied Psychology*, 60: 278–279, 1975; F. J. Thumin, "Identification of Cola Beverages," *Journal of Applied Psychology*, 46: 358–360, October 1962; and Thomas J. Stanley, "Cola Preferences: Disguised Taste vs. Brand Evaluations," in Keith Hunt (ed.), *Advances in Consumer Research: Volume 5*, Association for Consumer Research, Ann Arbor, MI, 1978, pp. 19–21.

[73] F. J. Thumin, "Identification of Cola Beverages," *Journal of Applied Psychology*, 46: 358–360, October 1962.

[74] See "Coke-Pepsi Slugfest," *Time*, July 26, 1976 pp. 64–65; "The Cola War," *Newsweek*, August 30, 1976, p. 67; "One Sip Not a Taste Test, Coke Tells New Yorkers," *Advertising Age*, August 16, 1976, p. 6; and Peter W. Bernstein, "Coke Strikes Back," *Fortune*, June 1, 1981, pp. 30–36.

[75] Nan Robertson, "Experts at French Wine Trial Explode Some Vintage Myths," *The New York Times*, November 1, 1974, pp. 1+.

[76] See Donald F. Cox, "The Sorting Rule Model of the Consumer Product Evaluation Process," in Donald F. Cox (ed.), *Risk Taking and Information Handling in Consumer Behavior*, Harvard Business School, Cambridge, MA, 1967, pp. 324–369; Jerry C. Olson and Jacob Jacoby, "Cue Utilization in the Quality Perception Process," in M. Venkatesan (ed.), *Proceedings, 3rd Annual Conference of the Association for Consumer Research*, Association for Consumer Research, College Park, MD, 1972, pp. 167–179; Jerry C. Olson, "Inferential Belief Formation in the Cue Utilization Process," in H. Keith Hunt (ed.), *Advances in Consumer Research: Volume 5*, Association for Consumer Research, Ann Arbor, MI, 1978, pp. 706–713; Robert E. Burnkrant, "Cue Utilization in Product Perception," in H. Keith Hunt, (ed.), *Advances in Consumer Research: Volume 5*, Association for Consumer Research, Ann Arbor, MI, 1978, pp. 724–729; and John Wheatley and John S. Y. Chiu, "The Influence of Intrinsic and Extrinsic Cues on Product Quality Evaluations of Experts and Non Experts," in Neil Beckwith, et al. (eds.), *1979 Educators' Conference Proceedings*, American Marketing Association, 1979, pp. 205–209. See also, Allison and Uhl, "Influence of Beer Brand Identification on Taste Perception," for an excellent example of how marketing efforts can influence brand perceptions.

[77] D. A. Laird, "How The Consumer Estimates Quality by Subconscious Sensory Impressions," *Journal of Applied Psychology*, 16: 241–246, June 1932; and *Women's Wear Daily*, January 28, 1961, p. 15.

[78] Robert L. Brown, "Wrapper Influence on the Perception of Freshness in Bread," *Journal of Applied Psychology*, 42: 257–260, August 1958.

[79] Burnkrant, "Cue Utilization in Product Perception."

[80] See Olson, "Inferential Belief Formation," for a discussion of this topic.

[81] For excellent reviews of this evidence see Kent B. Monroe, "Buyers' Subjective Perceptions of Price," *Journal of Marketing Research*, 10: 70–80, February 1973; Jerry C. Olson, "Price as an Informational Cue: Effects on Product Evaluations," in Arch G. Woodside, Jagdish N. Sheth, and Peter D. Bennett (eds.),

PART FOUR

456

INDIVIDUAL
DETERMINANTS OF
CONSUMER
BEHAVIOR

Consumer and Industrial Buyer Behavior, North-Holland, New York, 1977, pp. 267–286; and Kent B. Monroe and Susan M. Petroshius, "Buyers' Perceptions of Price: An Update of the Evidence," in Harold H. Kassarjian and Thomas S. Robertson (eds.), *Perspectives in Consumer Behavior,* 3d ed., Scott, Foresman, 1981, pp. 43–55, upon which much of this section is based.

[82] See Benson Shapiro, "Price as a Communicator of Quality: An Experiment," unpublished doctoral dissertation, Havard University, 1970; and Zarrel Lambert, "Price and Choice Behavior," *Journal of Marketing Research,* 9: 35–40, February 1972.

[83] See, for example, Robert A. Peterson, "Consumer Perceptions As A Function of Product, Color, Price, and Nutrition Labeling," in William D. Perreault, Jr. (ed.), *Advances in Consumer Research: Volume 4,* Association for Consumer Research, Atlanta, 1977, pp. 61–63.

[84] Michael Etgar and Naresh K. Malhotra, "Determinants of Price Dependency: Personal and Perceptual Factors," *Journal of Consumer Research,* 8: 217–222, September 1981.

[85] Jacoby, Olson, and Haddock, "Price and Product Composition Characteristics."

[86] Monroe and Petroshius, "Buyers' Perceptions of Price."

[87] National Probability Sample in Great Britain, Market and Opinion Research International Cooperative Image Study, Spring 1970, reported by Robert Worcester, "Corporate Image Research," in Robert Worcester (ed.), *Consumer Market Research Handbook,* McGraw-Hill, London, 1972, p. 508.

[88] "Humble Exxon in; Esso Out," *National Petroleum News,* June 1972.

[89] "Crooks, Conmen and Clowns: Businessmen in TV Entertainment," The Media Institute, Washington, D.C., 1981.

[90] See, for example, Ponpun Nickel and Albert I. Wertheimer, "Factors Affecting Consumers' Images and Choices of Drugstores," *Journal of Retailing,* 55: 71–78, Summer 1979; B. Rosenbloom, *Retail Marketing,* Random House, New York, 1981; and James M. Kenderdine and Jack J. Kasulis, "The Relationship Between Changes in Perceptions of Store Attributes and Changes in Consumer Patronage Behavior," in Robert F. Lusch and William R. Darden (eds.), *Retail Patronage Theory: 1981 Workshop Proceedings,* Center for Economic and Management Research, University of Oklahoma, Norman, OK, 1981, pp. 100–105.

[91] Pierre Martineau, "The Personality of the Retail Store," *Harvard Business Review,* 36: 47–55, January-February 1958.

[92] See William Lazer and Robert G. Wyckham, "Perceptual Segmentation of Department Store Marketing," *Journal of Retailing,* 45: 3–14, Summer 1969; and William D. Haueisen, "Market Positioning: A New Segmentation Approach," in Robert F. Lusch and William R. Darden (eds.), *Retail Patronage Theory: 1981 Workshop Proceedings,* Center for Economic and Management Research, University of Oklahoma, Norman, OK, 1981, pp. 86–92.

[93] See, for example, Gail Bronson, "King Leer: Sexual Pitches in Ads Become More Explicit and More Pervasive," *The Wall Street Journal,* December 18, 1980, pp. 1, 14; and Christopher Rowley, "Sex in Advertising," *Scan,* 29: 12–15, April 1981.

[94] See, for example, Gordon L. Wise, Alan L. King, and J. Paul Merenski, " Reactions to Sexy Ads Vary With Age," *Journal of Advertising Research,* 14: 11–16, August 1974; and Deborah K. Johnson and Kay Satow, "Consumers' Reactions to Sex in TV Commericals," in Keith H. Hunt (ed.), *Advances in Consumer Research: Volume 5,* Association for Consumer Research, Ann Arbor, MI, 1978, pp. 411–414.

[95] Bruce John Morrison and Richard C. Sherman, "Who Responds to Sex in Advertising?" *Journal of Advertising Research,* 12: 15–19, April 1972.

[96] Baker, *Visual Persuasion.*

[97] See Robert Chestnut, Charles LaChance, and Amy Lubitz, "The Decorative Female Model: Sexual Stimuli and the Recognition of Advertisements," *Journal of Advertising,* 6: 11–14, Fall 1977; Major Stedman, "How Sexy Illustrations Affect Brand Recall," *Journal of Advertising Research,* 9: 15–19, March 1969; and Raymond L. Horton, "The Effects of Nudity, Suggestiveness, and Attractiveness on Product Class and Brand Name Recall," in Vinay Kothari (ed.), *Developments in Marketing Science: Volume 5,* Academy of Marketing Science, Nacogdoches, TX, 1982, pp. 456–459.

[98] Leonard N. Reid and Lawrence C. Soley, "Another Look at the 'Decorative' Female Model: The Recognition of Visual and Verbal Ad Components," in James H. Leigh and Claude R. Martin, Jr. (eds.), *Current Issues and Research in Advertising—1981,* Graduate School of Business Administration, Division of Research, University of Michigan, Ann Arbor, MI 1981, pp. 123–133.

[99] Robert A. Peterson and Roger A. Kerin, "The Female Role in Advertisements: Some Experimental Evidence," *Journal of Marketing,* 41: 59–63, October 1977.

[100] See Donald Sciglimpaglia, Michael A. Belch, and Richard F. Cain, Jr., "Demographic and Cognitive Factors Influencing Viewers Evaluations of 'Sexy' Advertisements," in William Wilkie (ed.), *Advances in Consumer Research: Volume 6,* Association for Consumer Research, Ann Arbor, MI, 1979, pp. 62–65; and Michael A. Belch, et al., Psychophysiological and Cognitive Responses to Sex in Advertising," in Andrew Mitchell (ed.), *Advances in Consumer Research: Volume 9,* Association for Consumer Research, Ann Arbor, MI, 1982, pp. 424–427.

[101] Sciglimpaglia, Belch, and Cain, "Demographic Factors Influencing Evaluations of 'Sexy' Advertisements"; and Deborah K. Johnson and Kay Satow, "Consumers' Reactions to Sex in TV Commercials," in

Keith H. Hunt (ed.), *Advances in Consumer Research: Volume 5,* Association for Consumer Research, Ann Arbor, MI, 1978, pp. 411–414.

[102] Sciglimpaglia, Belch, and Cahn, "Demographic Factors," and Johnson and Satow, "Consumers' Reactions."

[103] Timothy E. Moore, "Subliminal Advertising: What You See Is What You Get," *Journal of Marketing,* 46: 38–47, Spring 1982.

[104] See H. Brean, "What Hidden Sell is All About," *Life,* March 31, 1958, pp. 104–114.

[105] James V. McConnell, Richard L. Cutter, and Elton B. McNeil, "Subliminal Stimulation: An Overview," *American Psychologist,* 13: 230, May 1958.

[106] See M. Mannes, "Ain't Nobody Here but Us Commercials," *Reporter,* October 17, 1957, pp. 35–37; and "Subliminal Ad Okay if it Sells: FCC Peers into Subliminal Picture on TV," *Advertising Age,* 28, 1957.

[107] See, for example, "Secret Voices," *Time,* September 10, 1979, p. 71; Neil Maxwell, "Words Whispered to Subconscious Supposedly Deter Thefts, Fainting," *The Wall Street Journal,* November 25, 1980, p. 25; and Fred Danzig, "Relaxed Radio Soothes—But Subliminally," *Advertising Age,* September 15, 1980, p. 34.

[108] See Wilson Bryan Key, *Subliminal Seduction,* Prentice-Hall, Englewood Cliffs, NJ, 1973; Wilson Bryan Key, *Media Sexploitation,* Prentice-Hall, Englewood Cliffs, NJ, 1976, and Wilson Bryan Key, *The Clam-plate Orgy,* Prentice-Hall, Englewood Cliffs, NJ, 1980.

[109] See Del Hawkins, "The Effects of Subliminal Stimulation on Drive Level and Brand Preference," *Journal of Marketing Research,* 7: 322–326, August 1970, and John G. Caccavale, Thomas C. Wanty III, and Julie A. Edell, "Subliminal Implants in Advertisements: An Experiment," in Andrew Mitchell (ed.), *Advances in Consumer Research: Volume 9,* Association for Consumer Research, Ann Arbor, MI, 1982, pp. 418–423.

[110] Joel Saegert, "Another Look at Subliminal Perception," *Journal of Advertising Research,* 19: 55–57, February 1979.

[111] See Moore, "Subliminal Advertising."

CHAPTER 14
LEARNING AND MEMORY

Consider for a moment the following actual situations that are part of consumers' everyday lives.

Exciting popular music often is used as a background for commercials. Frequently the intent is that this music will also encourage consumers to perceive the advertised brand as exciting and interesting.

Advertisements for Wisk liquid detergent have shown people suffering the social embarassment of "ring around the collar." Later in the same ad, these people are seen having a happy time, in part because Wisk was used to solve their washing problem.

For many years, Shell Oil has effectively used a very specific symbol to facilitate consumers' recognition and memory of the company's name—a scallop shell.

What all of these situations have in common is that they involve aspects of consumers' learning or memory activities. One benefit of the learning mechanism is that consumers are able to adapt to a changing environment. Consequently, knowledge of learning principles can be useful in understanding how consumers' wants and motives are acquired and how their tastes are developed. Also, appreciation of learning and memory processes can aid our understanding of how frequently to repeat advertising messages; how visual symbols, songs, and other techniques can facilitate consumers' learning and memory regarding products and promotions; and how consumers develop habitual purchase patterns for some goods.

This chapter begins by defining learning and describing what it is that we learn. Second, major elements of the learning process are reviewed. Next, several ways by which consumers can learn are described and characterized, followed by a number of additional learning topics particularly useful for understanding the behavior of consumers. Finally, consumers' memory and the process of forgetting are addressed.

CHARACTERIZING LEARNING

Before going further, it is useful to adopt a definition of learning. Several introductory comments concerning the nature of learned material will also provide a beneficial foundation.

Learning Defined

Very simply, learning can be viewed as a relatively permanent change in behavior occurring as a result of experience. The implications of this definition are fairly subtle and, therefore, require some explanation.

First, as before, the term behavior is used to refer to nonobservable cognitive activity as well as overt actions. Therefore, it is very possible for learning to occur without any change in observable behavior. Changes in consumers' attitudes resulting from exposure to new information about a brand demonstrate this point. Second, learning results in relatively permanent changes in behavior. This excludes changes brought about by fatigue or other short-lived influences such as drug-induced behavior. Third, since our definition of learning stresses experience, we must exclude the effects of physical damage to the body or brain and of natural human growth. It is interesting to note, however, that much of our early learning experiences are controlled by the degree of physical development needed to make practice of an activity possible.

Types of Learned Behavior

Nearly every type of behavior we exhibit as humans has been learned. The following paragraphs provide some specific examples.

Physical Behavior Generally, we learn many physical behavior patterns useful in responding to a variety of situations faced in everyday life. For example, all healthy humans learn to walk, talk, and interact with others. As consumers, we also learn methods of responding to various purchase situations. These may take the forms of learning to act dissatisfied when hearing the first price quote on a car, or learning to read closely the fine print in purchase contracts.

Children may also learn certain physical activity through the process termed *modeling* in which they mimic the behavior of their parents or other individuals. One aspect of controversy relating to this is the concern that children who are exposed to television programs showing considerable violence or other undesirable behavior will be prone to similar behavior in their later life.[1] This suggests the important influence of learned physical behavior.

Symbolic Learning and Problem Solving People learn symbolic meanings that enable highly efficient communication through the development of languages. Symbols also allow marketers to communicate with consumers through such vehicles as brand names (Kodak and Sony), slogans ("Coke is it"), and signs (McDonald's Golden Arches). As mentioned previously, the marketer intends for these symbols to connote positive images of the company to consumers in addition to keeping the firm's name familiar to them.

One can also engage in problem-solving learning by employing the processes of *thinking* and *insight*. Thinking involves the mental manipulation of symbols representing the real world to form various combinations of meaning. This often leads to insight, which is a new understanding of relationships involved in the problem. As we have noted, many consumer efforts can be viewed as problem-solving behavior. For example, consumers are constantly engaged in deliberating about how satisfaction of their various wants and needs can be improved by acquiring new or different products or services. Thinking and problem-solving behavior, therefore, enable consumers to evaluate mentally a wide variety of products without having to purchase them.

Affective Learning Humans learn to value certain elements of their environment and dislike others. This means that consumers learn many of their wants, goals, and motives as well as what products satisfy these needs. Learning also influences consumers' development of favorable/unfavorable attitudes toward a company and its products. These attitudes will affect the tendency to purchase various brands.

As we discovered in earlier chapters, consumers' interactions within a social system can have a significant influence on their learning of tastes. This is quite obvious for products such as scotch and tobacco, in which it is said that one has to "acquire a taste" for the product. However, the same process is at work regarding the vast majority of foods, clothes, and other goods. The process that influences such learning includes sanctions and social pressure by group or family members.

The discussion of what we learn could easily fill the remaining pages of this chapter. It is more appropriate, however, that we now direct our attention toward the principal elements of learning and other issues of importance to the understanding of this process.

Principal Elements of Learning

As will be demonstrated shortly, consumers learn in several basic ways. However, four elements seem to be fundamental to the vast majority of situations: motive, cue, response, and reinforcement.[2] The exact nature and strength of these components influence what will be learned, how well it will be learned, and the rate at which learning will occur.

Motives As noted in Chapter 12, motives arouse individuals, thereby increasing their readiness to respond. This arousal function is essential, since it activates the energy needed to engage in learning activity. In addition, any success at achieving the motivating goal, or avoiding some unpleasant situation, tends to reduce arousal. Because this is reinforcing, such activity will have a greater tendency to occur again in similar situations. Thus, marketers strive to have their brand or its name available when relevant consumer motives are aroused because it is expected that consumers will learn a connection between the product and motive. For this reason, we see advertisements for Prestone antifreeze shortly before winter and Coppertone suntan lotion during the summer.

Chapter 12 also suggested that consumers can learn *secondary motives* which are psychological in nature. These secondary motives are acquired through the consumer's association of psychological feelings with the satisfaction of certain physical needs. For example, a baby can develop a motive for affiliation with others when he is regularly fed and pampered in the presence of other people. Conversely, *primary* motives are not learned and are based only on the satisfaction of various physical needs such as hunger and thirst. Actually, secondary motives (such as strivings for money, social approval, and achievement) influence considerably more consumer behavior than do primary motives.

Cues   Cues may be viewed as weak stimuli not strong enough to arouse consumers, but capable of providing *direction* to motivated activity. That is, they influence the manner in which consumers respond to motives. The shopping environment is packed with cues such as promotions and product colors which consumers can use to choose between various response options in a learning situation. For example, when we are hungry we are guided by certain cues such as restaurant signs and the aroma of food cooking, because we have learned that these stimuli are associated with food preparation and consumption.

It is interesting to note that consumers frequently learn such strong bonds between certain cues and products that they are highly reluctant to purchase when these cues are absent. For this reason, sellers make sure that the appropriate cues are present in their products. For example, many prepared foods have artificial coloring added to stimulate purchase. An orange coloring is frequently added to whole oranges because consumers have learned to expect oranges to have such coloring. In yet another case, Heinz ketchup still continues to be packaged in a narrow-neck, hard-to-pour bottle because the producer realizes that consumers have learned to associate the slow-moving thickness of the product with quality.[3]

Response   A response may be viewed as a mental or physical activity the consumer makes in reaction to a stimulus situation. Responses appropriate to a particular situation are learned over time through experience in facing that situation. As we have noted, the occurrence of a response is not always observable. Therefore, it must again be emphasized that our inability to observe responses does not necessarily mean that learning is not taking place.

Chapter 12 introduced the concept of a motive hierarchy, and a similar situation exists for responses. Before learning occurs, our innate characteristics order responses to a stimulus from the most likely to least likely response. Thus, a hungry baby is more likely to cry or exhibit sucking behavior than other responses. Over time, learning will modify the response hierarchy so that other responses have a greater chance of occurring. In this way, consumers are able to adapt to changing environmental conditions which confront them.

Reinforcement   Perhaps the most widely acceptable view of *reinforcement* is anything that follows a response and increases the tendency for the response to reoccur in a similar situation.[4] Because reinforced behavior tends to be repeated, consumers can learn to develop successful means of responding to their needs or changing conditions.

One important type of reinforcement is achieved through reducing motive arousal. This occurs through removing a *negative reinforcer* (something that generates discomfort and is avoided) or receiving a *positive reinforcer* (something that generates pleasure and is sought). In either case, reducing motive arousal is reinforcing to the consumer. For example, drinking Seven-Up on a hot day or purchasing a Norelco smoke detector to lessen the dangers of a home fire can both reduce motive arousal for the consumer.

In still other situations, punishment through mental or physical discomfort is applied as a negative reinforcer. Such circumstances can result in learning to avoid something or to discontinue some behavior pattern. All of these situations demonstrate that reinforcement is a general term that involves more than just receiving or giving rewards.

It should be noted here that a number of learning experiments have not involved the introduction of positive or negative reinforcers.[5] In many cases, it appears that just the accomplishment of a learning task is by itself a reinforcing experience. Thus, consumers may learn about products merely by mentally evaluating their relevance to solving consumption problems. Window-shopping activity and informal discussions with friends or salespeople may be aspects of such learning behavior.

Another point to consider is that our behavior can be reinforced so subtly that we may not even be aware that it has occurred.[6] Simple social gestures such as a nod, smile, or frown are often deceptively powerful in their influence. This type of behavior can be observed in certain television commercials featuring a lead character that speaks directly to viewers while one or more other characters are seen engaged in some activity behind this spokesperson. Close observation of these background players will sometimes reveal that they nod approval or use other body language to support important points the lead character is making. This suggests that consumers can be encouraged to develop attitudes and patterns of behavior toward brands without becoming aware that such changes are occurring.

CLASSIFYING LEARNING

Various theories have been developed to explain different aspects of learning.[7] These theories, however, can be grouped into several major categories for the focus of our present discussion. As Figure 14-1 depicts, the first major division is between the connectionist and cognitive schools of thought. While *cognitive* inter-

FIGURE 14-1
A classification of learning theories.

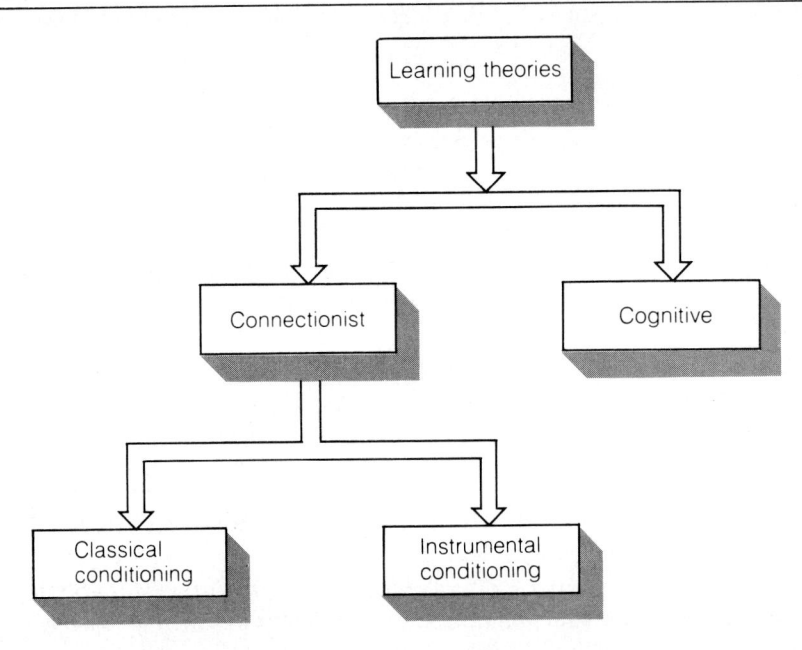

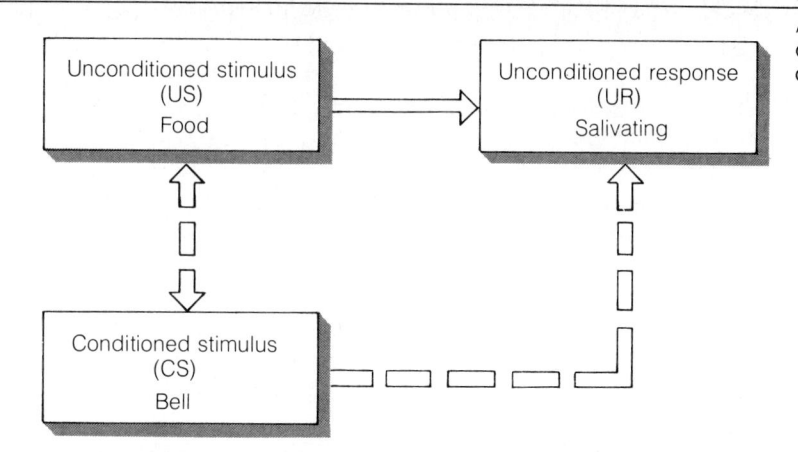

FIGURE 14-2
A representation of classical conditioning.

```
[Unconditioned stimulus (US) Food] ──────▶ [Unconditioned response (UR) Salivating]
         ⇧                                              ⇧
         ⇩                                              ┊
[Conditioned stimulus (CS) Bell] ─ ─ ─ ─ ─ ─ ─ ─ ─ ─ ─ ┘
```

pretations place emphasis on the discovery of patterns and insight, *connectionists* argue that humans learn connections between stimuli and responses. The connectionist school can be further subdivided on the basis of the type of conditioning employed. Each of these subdivisions will be discussed in turn.

Learning Connections

Some learning theorists maintain that learning involves the development of *connections* between a stimulus and some response to it. That is, the association of a response and a stimulus is the connection that is learned.

A portion of this group minimizes the importance of reinforcement to learning, while others stress its crucial role. We shall sidestep this debate by adopting the reinforcement viewpoint because of its attractiveness in explaining consumers' learning behavior.[8] Reinforcement is employed in conjunction with two fundamentally different methods of learning connections: classical and instrumental conditioning.

Classical Conditioning   Essentially, classical conditioning (sometimes called respondent conditioning) pairs one stimulus with another that already elicits a given response. Over repeated trials, the new stimulus will also begin to elicit the same or very similar response.

To appreciate the process involved, it is useful to review the experiment conducted by Pavlov, who pioneered study of classical conditioning.[9] Pavlov reasoned that because food already caused his dog to salivate, it might be possible to link a previously neutral stimulus to the food so that it too would be able to make the dog salivate. This would demonstrate that the dog had learned to associate the neutral stimulus with the food. Pavlov used a bell as the neutral stimulus. His experiment is diagramed in Figure 14-2.

The term "unconditioned stimulus" is used for the food because conditioning is not required for it to cause the dog to salivate. This built-in stimulus-response connection is represented by the solid arrow. Because the salivating response also does not require learning, it is termed the "unconditioned response." The bell is referred to as the "conditioned stimulus," because conditioning is required to learn a connection between it and the food. Pavlov accomplished this by ringing the bell every time he presented the dog with food. After a significant number of conditioning trials, the dog learned a connection between the bell and the food. In fact, the association was strong enough for the bell alone to then become capable of causing the dog to salivate. The dotted arrow connecting the bell and the food symbolizes the learned connection between these stimuli, and the second dotted line indicates that the bell can now cause the dog to salivate.

In this situation, a natural reflex of salivating to food was employed as the unconditioned stimulus. It is important to note, however, that classical conditioning does not require use of reflexive stimuli, and the dog could now be conditioned to a new stimulus by using the bell as the unconditioned stimulus. Learning new associations between stimuli in this manner is termed "second order conditioning." Because evidence suggests that humans are capable of even further levels of conditioning, this concept is more generally referred to as higher-order conditioning.[10]

Higher-order conditioning can be useful for understanding how consumers acquire secondary motives. Here, goals that once had no motivating abilities can become associated with reinforcing stimuli and take on motivating properties themselves. For example, the achievement motive may be acquired by a child because rewarding praise was given to him or her for accomplishing certain tasks. Later, this achievement motive can influence the purchase of various products to assist in accomplishing tasks.

Instrumental Conditioning The method of instrumental conditioning (also called operant conditioning) also involves developing connections between stimuli and responses, but the process involved differs from classical conditioning in several important respects. Although classical conditioning relies on an already established stimulus-response connection, instrumental conditioning requires the learner to discover an appropriate or "correct" response—one that will be reinforced.

The principles of this type of learning can best be illustrated by employing the same "box" that B. F. Skinner made famous with his pioneering work in the area.[11] Assume that we place a pigeon into a box. On one wall is a button which when pressed will deliver food to the pigeon. In this case, the button is the conditioned stimulus. When placed in the box, the pigeon can respond in a variety of ways shown as R_1 through R_n in Figure 14-3. Eventually, it will push button R_3, receive the food, and eat it with great enjoyment. Here, the food, which represents a positive reinforcer, is the unconditioned stimulus.

Most likely, the pigeon will not immediately associate pushing the button with receiving the food. Other responses will occur, but only a push of the button will lead to reinforcement. Therefore, over a number of reinforced trials the pigeon will learn a connection between the stimulus (button) and response (pushing). This can lead to very rapid repetition of the process—perhaps until the bird becomes ill from consuming too much food—which, as we know, also leads to learning.

Distinctions Between Conditioning Methods A number of distinctions can be made between classical (respondent) and instrumental (operant) conditioning.

FIGURE 14-3

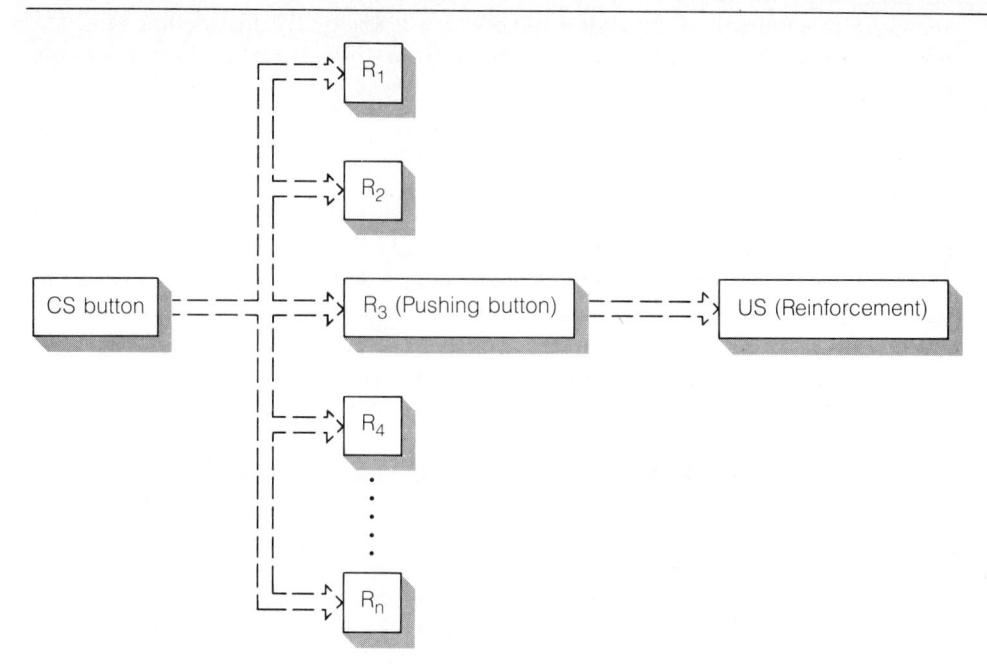

A representation of instrumental conditioning.

Three of the most important ones are summarized in Table 14-1. Note that while classical conditioning is dependent on an already established connection, instrumental conditioning requires the learner to discover the appropriate response. For this reason, instrumental conditioning involves the learner at a more conscious and purposeful level than does classical conditioning.

A second distinction between these two methods concerns the outcome of the learning situation. In classical conditioning, the outcome is not dependent on the learner's actions, but with instrumental conditioning a particular response can change the learner's situation or environment. The response then is actually *instrumental* in producing reinforcement or making something happen in the environment, hence the name for this type of conditioning.

Because of the above differences, each conditioning method is suited to explaining different types of learning. Learning to adapt and control one's environment is better explained by instrumental conditioning because it requires that the learner discover the response that leads to reinforcement. Alternatively, classical

TABLE 14-1

IMPORTANT DISTINCTIONS BETWEEN CLASSICAL AND INSTRUMENTAL CONDITIONING

Classical (Respondent) Conditioning	Instrumental (Operant) Conditioning
1. Involves an already established response to another stimulus.	No previous stimulus-response connection necessary. Learner must discover appropriate response.
2. The outcome is not dependent on learner's actions.	The outcome is dependent on learner's actions.
3. Influences development and changes in opinions, tastes, and goals.	Influences changes in goal-directed behavior.

Source: Based on David Krech, et al., *Psychology: A Basic Course,* Knopf, New York, 1976, pp. 50–61.

conditioning is often more useful in explaining how consumers learn brand names and acquire or change their opinion, tastes, and goals. That is, the material to be learned in such cases is associated with stimuli that already elicit favorable or unfavorable experiences.

Cognitive Interpretations

Instead of viewing learning as the development of connections between stimuli and responses, cognitive theorists stress the importance of perception, problem-solving, and insight. This viewpoint contends that much learning occurs not as a result of trial-and-error or practice but through discovering meaningful patterns which enable us to solve problems. These meaningful patterns are termed "gestalts," and cognitive theories of learning rely heavily on the process of insight to explain the development of gestalts.

Wolfgang Kohler's work with apes provides an interesting example to understand better this view of learning.[12] In one experiment, a chimpanzee was placed in a cage with a box, and bananas were hung from the top of the cage beyond reach, even if the ape jumped. After failing to reach the food, the problem was solved when suddenly the chimp placed the box under the bananas and jumped from it to reach the food. This suggested that the ape's learning was not a result of trial-and-error, but a consequence of deliberation and sudden insight into a problem solution. This feeling of insight is familiar to all of us when we suddenly "see" the solution to a problem situation (the "ah ha" effect).

Although the chimp in Kohler's experiment was able to get rewarded by reaching the bananas, the reward is not so apparent in many cognitive learning situations. For example, no observable reward is present when the student solves a difficult problem in statistics. However, the concept of *closure* is viewed as having important reinforcing properties in the cognitive viewpoint. As long as an individual has not solved a problem, a state of incompleteness produces tension to motivate continued search for a solution. Problem solution results in closure, which reduces the motivating tension and is reinforcing.

Applying Alternative Learning Concepts to Consumer Behavior

We should not be dismayed by alternative explanations of how consumers learn. In fact, it is useful to have these alternatives, since the nature of what consumers learn probably influences the method they use to learn it.

As we have noted, cognitive interpretations stress problem-solving behavior and the learner's active understanding of situations confronting her. It is not "blind" or rote behavior, as the learning of connections can be. This view is therefore most useful in understanding how consumers learn which stores, methods of shopping, or products will best meet their needs. For example, it can take the form of learning about the uses and benefits of products new to the market, especially if they represent significant innovations. It can also explain how consumers learn about existing products for which they have developed a recent interest or need.[13] In either case, the learning that is involved is purposeful and goal directed, requiring conscious problem-solving involvement on the part of the consumer.

Connectionists' theories of learning are appropriate to understanding a variety of other aspects of consumer behavior. As has already been noted, classical conditioning is useful for explaining how consumers acquire tastes and motives. Advertisers also employ the concept by showing their brands in pleasant, exciting, or otherwise emotionally positive surroundings. For example, home computers are shown being enjoyed in interesting settings, Salem cigarettes are depicted against lush green forests, and fast-food products are often shown being consumed in fun-filled social gatherings. Here, the concept of classical conditioning applies to the advertiser's plan for repeated association of a brand with the positive surroundings, which will lead to consumers developing a preference toward the brand. Figure 14-4, which parallels Figure 14-2, suggests how this would occur using a happy situation as the unconditioned stimulus. The setting (a family gathering, etc.) is selected because it already elicits pleasant feelings from consumers—the unconditioned response. Repeated association of the brand with this setting, such as picturing its use during a family gathering, will enable the brand itself to generate similar pleasant feelings. This should increase consumers' preferences for it. Figure 14-5 shows an advertisement that is consistent with the above explanation. Another example is the use of sports announcers in advertisements. Because their voices are strongly linked with the excitement of sporting events, it is expected that a brand they promote will, over repeated exposures, also be able to generate exciting feelings. In yet another application, research suggests that the degree to which a consumer likes the background music in an advertisement may directly affect his preference toward the brand being advertised.[14]

Certain types of habitual behavior are also explained through classical or respondent conditioning. For example, many consumers automatically purchase particular brands such as Scotch tape and Bayer aspirin because they have developed strong associations between the brand name and the generic product. This is often an advantage accruing to marketers who first develop a product that dominates the market. In still other cases, consumers habitually purchase particular brands such as Campbell's soups merely because their parents did. Here, such a strong association has been made between a particular brand and an activity or a need that little consideration may be given to its actual suitability.

Instrumental or operant conditioning is useful for understanding consumer learning where conscious choices resulting in positive or negative reinforcement are made. The obvious case is consumers' purchase and evaluation of products. Favorable experiences will result in positive reinforcement of the particular choice. Of course, learning to avoid certain products due to negative reinforcement from bad experiences with them is also possible. This is strong justification for the marketer's stress on satisfying the customer.

FIGURE 14-4

A representation of how classical conditioning can be used to develop pleasant feelings toward an advertised brand.

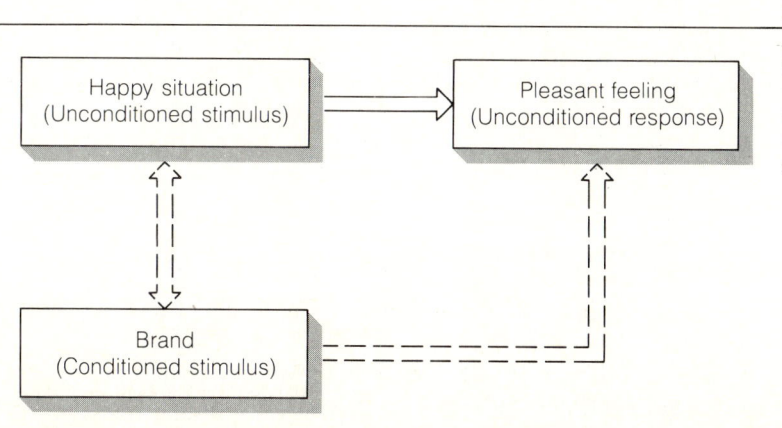

FIGURE 14-5

An advertising example of the use of classical conditioning. (Courtesy of Hershey Foods Company.)

Remember your first Hershey Bar?

You probably got it from your mother, who probably got her first from her mother. And every one of you experienced the same great taste of Hershey's Milk Chocolate. Or Milk Chocolate with Almonds. Now isn't that a nice thing to pass on to your children?

Hershey. The Great American Chocolate Bar.

Advertisements depicting satisfied buyers can also result in consumers learning a connection between a brand and favorable experiences. Other types of promotional efforts, including cash rebates, free product samples, trial periods, or low introductory prices, also make use of instrumental conditioning. The goal in these cases is to structure a situation so that consumers are given rewards as a consequence of having performed an activity that is desired by the marketer.

Many other applications of both cognitive and connectionist learning could be cited. However, we now turn our attention to other useful concepts of consumer learning.

ADDITIONAL CONSUMER LEARNING TOPICS

A number of other aspects of learning have importance for those interested in the behavior of consumers. Although the following topics by no means exhaust the list of useful concepts, they are representative of the potential applications of learning to understanding consumers.

The Behavior Modification Perspective

The emphasis in a behavior modification perspective (BMP) of learning is on a set of intervention techniques designed to influence the behavior of individuals. That is, focus is placed on how environmental events (stimuli, reinforcements, etc.) can be modified to bring about changes in the way people act. In fact, a segment of BMP advocates, containing those who are referred to as behavioralists, completely discards the role of internal psychological processes (needs, attitudes, etc.) and the concept of learning when studying behavioral changes in people. Behavioralists argue that it is sufficient to just consider changes in behavior and the environmental events that appear capable of influencing such behavior, rather than also attempting to *explain* what internal forces within the individual relate these two events together. A less radical view, which is adopted here, proposes retaining explanations of internal processes and blending them with consideration of environmental influences.[15] Therefore, we will view the BMP as having a distinct focus but sharing certain principles such as conditioning and reinforcement with theories of learning that also incorporate internal psychological processes to explain behavior.

Several areas of environmental influence can be considered as within the BMP domain: classical (respondent) conditioning, instrumental (operant) conditioning, modeling, and ecological design. Both classical and instrumental conditioning have already been discussed. The examples given for classical conditioning were sufficient to demonstrate how environmental variables could be used to influence consumers' behavior. Although examples were also provided for instrumental conditioning, it is useful to discuss three additional topics in this area (reinforcement schedules, shaping, and discrimination) to show how they can be used to influence behavior change.

Reinforcement Schedules It is not necessary to reinforce every "correct" response in order for learning to occur. Different reinforcement schedules, however, lead to different patterns of learning. *Continuous reinforcement* schedules, which reward every "correct" response, yield rapid changes in behavior. Conversely, *partial reinforcement* schedules yield a slower rate, but also result in learning that is more permanent in nature. This may at least partially explain why consumers' negative attitudes toward brands are usually very difficult to reverse. That is, negative attitudes can be acquired through partial reinforcement because a few unsatisfactory experiences with a brand can occur over a period of time. This can result in consumers being highly resistant to positive information about the brand, especially if the marketer is the source of such information.

In a different vein, partial-reinforcement schedules can also represent an economical alternative for marketers. Because many marketing forms of reinforcement (advertisements, sales, etc.) can cost considerable sums of money, finding a way to cause changes in consumers' behavior without having to reward every learning experience represents an attractive opportunity.

Shaping The term "shaping" refers to influencing a large change in behavior over time by reinforcing successively closer approximations to that behavior. The thinking behind the idea of shaping is described by an ancient proverb: "a journey of a thousand miles is started with but a single step." That is, although it might be very difficult to achieve a rather large or complex change in consumers' behavior in one step, a series of smaller changes leading to the same end-point may be much less difficult.

An example of shaping would be to offer consumers special prizes to visit a retail store over several weeks and, while they are there, encouraging them to purchase items by using discounts, special sales, or rebates. The behavior of traveling to the store is rewarded, and purchasing at the store is also reinforced. In this way, it is expected that consumers will adopt the behavior of regularly shopping at the store after the special reinforcements are withdrawn. Many similar examples of shaping exist in the selling and consumer-behavior area.

Discrimination Learning to discriminate between various objects or events is important for consumers, because it helps them adapt to their environment. Discrimination is learned over time when the same response to two similar but noticeably different stimuli leads to different consequences (reinforcement). Stimuli which the consumer can use to distinguish between various items in their environment are often termed *discriminative stimuli.*

Consumers make frequent use of discrimination learning. New or different brands as well as different models within the same producer's line must be distinguished, even though they might differ by only a few features. Products that provide rewarding service must also be distinguished from those that are relatively inferior. Of course, a great deal of marketing effort encourages such discrimination learning. Here, the goal is to reinforce consumers' attention to the uniqueness of a brand. In fact, brand names, logos, and trademarks are quite useful discriminative stimuli, but unique colors, shapes, and packages also have utility. In another quite different and interesting case, patrons of a small retail shop were personally telephoned and thanked for shopping at the store. Reaction to this distinctive reinforcement was quite favorable—sales increased 27 percent during the test period.[16] This attests to the impact of reinforcement in consumers' discrimination learning.

Modeling The term modeling refers to learning which occurs as a result of the individual observing both the behavior of others and the consequences of that behavior. This can lead to (1) the learning of new behavior, (2) a change or strengthening of existing behavioral tendencies, or (3) the facilitation of previously learned responses. The potential for modeling in the marketing discipline is considerable, because demonstrations, advertisements, and other promotional means can be used to develop the appropriate modeling scenarios. In fact, the technique is actually employed quite extensively for some of today's most successful products.[17] The usual procedure is to produce a TV advertisement that depicts one or more individuals engaging in certain behavior and receiving a reinforcement. The reinforcement can be in the form of social approval or embarrassment, or in the form of direct product benefits or dissatisfactions. Examples include James Garner receiving perfect pictures from his Polaroid Sun camera, consumers suffering problems because they had a transmission repaired by someone other than AAMCO, and people eliminating the social embarrassment caused by slipping dentures after they started using Poligrip.

Ecological Design The concept of ecological design involves a deliberate attempt to use aspects of physical surroundings to achieve changes in behavior.

Building and landscape architects have made extensive use of ecological principles for the purpose of directing traffic patterns, focusing office workflow, and achieving crowd control. However, similar principles have also been used in the field of marketing. Consider the efforts made to design nightclubs and discos as exciting environments, as well as the placement of displays and demonstrations in central areas of shopping malls to attract shoppers' attention and influence their purchase behavior. Perhaps more obvious examples would include the physical layout of supermarkets to encourage high shopper exposure to a wide variety of merchandise, and the use of racks at checkout counters to display a variety of convenience or so-called "impulse" items to the waiting customer. The potential of ecological design for affecting the behavior of consumers is considerable. We can expect other advances in this field, especially those directed at the use of design to influence consumers' moods, perceptions, and attitudes.

The above comments have provided only a brief review of the BMP which grew out of work by B. F. Skinner and other behaviorally oriented psychologists. A few examples were given of its application to the field of marketing. Table 14-2 presents an excellent summary of additional areas of application and methods for their achievement.

It should be mentioned that the BMP has not enjoyed a high level of awareness and appreciation among those interested in marketing or the behavior of consumers. Despite this, many of the practical marketing tactics that have been developed without knowledge of the field appear to be quite consistent with it. As the perspective achieves wider exposure and additional effort is devoted to exploring its marketing applications, additional insights should lead to the development of more effective tactics. In addition, when combined with more internally oriented viewpoints, the perspective could prove quite beneficial in describing how the purchase-consumption process works.[18]

TABLE 14-2 SOME ILLUSTRATIVE APPLICATIONS OF THE BEHAVIOR MODIFICATION PERSPECTIVE IN MARKETING

I. Some Applications of Respondent Conditioning Principles

A. Conditioning Responses to New Stimuli

Unconditioned or Previously Conditioned Stimulus	Conditioned Stimulus	Examples
Exciting event	A product or theme song	Gillette theme song followed by sports event
Patriotic events or music	A product or person	Patriotic music as background in political commercial

B. Use of Familiar Stimuli to Elicit Responses

Conditioned Stimulus	Conditioned Response(s)	Examples
Familiar music	Relaxation, excitement, "good will"	Christmas music in retail store
Familiar social cues	Excitement, attention, anxiety	Sirens sounding or telephones ringing in commercials

TABLE 14-2
(Continued)

II. Some Applications of Operant Conditioning Principles	
A. Rewards for Desired Behavior (Continuous Schedules)	
Desired Behavior	Reward Given Following Behavior
Product purchase	Trading stamps, cash bonus or rebate, prizes, coupons
B. Rewards for Desired Behavior (Partial Schedules)	
Desired Behavior	Reward Given (Sometimes)
Product purchase	Prize for every second, or third, etc. purchase
	Prize to a fraction of people who purchase

C. Shaping

Approximation of Desired Response	Consequence Following Approximation	Final Response Desired
Opening a charge account	Prizes, etc., for opening account	Expenditure of funds
Trip to point-of-purchase location	Loss leaders, entertainment, or event at the shopping center	Purchase of products
Product trial	Free product and/or some bonus for using	Purchase of product

D. Discriminative Stimuli

Desired Behavior	Reward Signal	Examples
Entry into store	Store signs	50% off sale
	Store logos	K mart's big red "K"
Brand purchase	Distinctive brandmarks	Levi tag

III. Some Applications of Modeling Principles	
Modeling Employed	Desired Response
Instructor, expert, salesperson using product (in ads or at point-of-purchase)	Use of product in technically competent way
Models in ads asking questions at point-of-purchase	Ask questions at point-of-purchase which highlight product advantages
Models in ads receiving positive reinforcement for product purchase or use	Increase product purchase and use
Models in ads receiving no reinforcement or receiving punishment for performing undesired behaviors	Extinction or decrease undesired behaviors

Stimulus Generalization

When a given response to a stimulus has been learned, it will tend to be elicited not only by the original stimulus involved in the learning situation but also by stimuli that are similar to it. This process, called *stimulus generalization,* appears to occur *automatically* unless stopped by discrimination learning.[19] Stimulus gen-

TABLE 14-2
(Continued)

IV. Some Applications of Ecological Modification Principles			
Environmental Design	Specific Example	Intermediate Behavior	Final Desired Behavior
Store layout	End of escalator, end-aisle, other displays	Bring customer into visual contact with product	Product purchase
In-store mobility	In-store product directories, information booths	Bring consumer into visual contact with product	Product purchase
Noises, odors, lights	Flashing lights in store window	Bring consumer into visual or other sensory contact with store or product	Product purchase

Source: Adapted from Walter R. Nord and J. Paul Peter, "A Behavior Modification Perspective on Marketing," *Journal of Marketing,* **44:**42–43, Spring 1980, published by the American Marketing Association.

eralization simplifies the consumer's life, because it means that learning a unique response to every stimulus is not necessary. One response can be used for similar stimuli unless there is some important reason to learn to discriminate between them.

The *gradient of generalization* relates the degree of similarity between two stimuli to the likelihood that both will generate the same response. It has been found that the greater the resemblance between a given stimulus and another that already causes a response, the greater the chance that it will also generate the same response.[20] Conversely, the more dissimilar two stimuli are, the smaller the likelihood of stimulus generalization occurring. As noted in Chapter 13, some producers of private brands make use of the gradient concept by packaging products to closely resemble national brands in appearance. In other cases, firms "ride the coattails" of success of pioneering companies by offering highly similar products. The sudden appearance of various caffeine-free soft drinks and sugarless gums are cases in point.

The generalization gradient also helps us understand the marketing approach of introducing "new" products that often bear a considerable resemblance to their predecessors. This encourages consumers to generalize learned attitudes and preferences from the old product to the new model. The *family brand* strategy employs similar methods. Here, the family brand name is prominently associated with the new product, as in the case of a General Motors car, a Wilson football, or a Panasonic radio. The intention is that consumers' favorable perceptions and attitudes about the family name will be generalized to the new product. Of course, the danger of such a strategy is that unfavorable experiences on the part of consumers with one product in the family line may lead to generalizing poor impressions toward the entire group of products.

Rate and Degree of Learning

In general, learning of all but the simplest tasks appears to follow a rather common pattern which has become known as a *learning curve.* A typical curve is displayed in Figure 14-6 where the amount learned is measured on the y axis and the number of practice trials is shown on the x axis. The characteristic shape of this curve demonstrates that the rate of learning is quite rapid during initial stages. However, in later stages, as the amount learned accumulates, the *rate* of additional learning per trial decreases. This demonstrates the highly effective nature of practice in early stages of learning and its diminishing effect in later trials. It also demonstrates that even though the rate of learning is high initially, many practice trials are needed to ensure a large amount of total learning.

It is important to note that repetition of an advertisement appears to lead to a learning curve similar to the one in Figure 14-6.[21] In these cases, the number of times the advertising message is repeated is measured along the x axis and the extent of consumers' learning of the message is measured along the y axis. Of course, marketers must determine whether this general pattern actually fits their particular products and situations.[22] For example, it may not describe learning in some low-involvement situations in which fewer repetitions might be necessary for storing simple facts, such as brand names, away in memory.[23] For cases in which the curve is appropriate, there are several implications regarding the use of advertising to encourage consumer learning. First, as the curve demonstrates, a marketer must be willing to repeat an advertising message a significant number of times. This is also why a brand name may be repeated several times in just one advertisement. Second, the curve demonstrates that after repeating messages many times, the marketer is paying for small increases in consumer learning. Further, evidence suggests that advertising messages are subject to *wearout* and manipulation by audience members. That is, as the number of message repetitions increases, boredom can result, inattention can increase, and audience members may switch from rehearsing the message to generating and attending to their own less-positive thoughts about the message.[24] This type of evidence might tempt the marketer to

FIGURE 14-6

Graph of a typical learning curve.

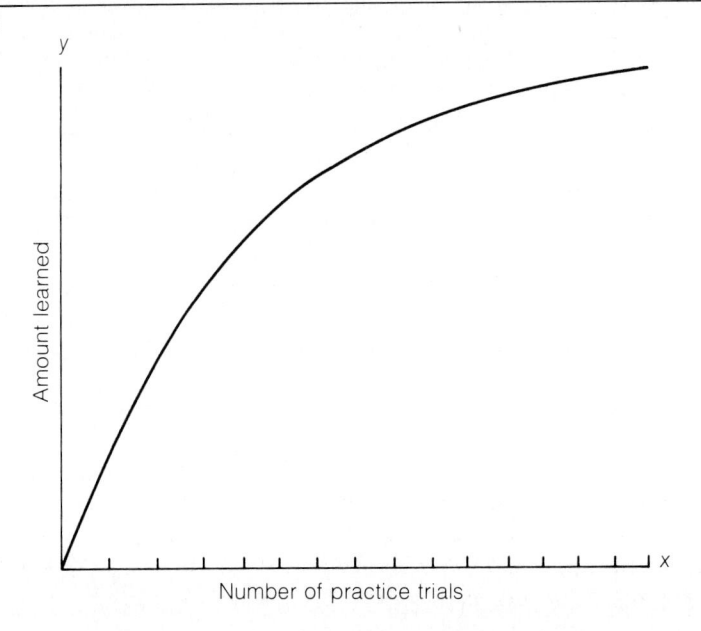

stop advertising after time. However, as will be demonstrated shortly, if a message is not repeated, consumers tend to forget most of it quite rapidly. This indicates the need to repeat advertisements merely to *maintain* consumers' level of learning. One strategy that might reduce wearout and other negative consequences of repetition is to repeat the basic content of an advertising message while periodically changing the method of doing so, to maintain consumers interests. An additional advantage of such variety is that it could encourage consumers to engage in deeper processing of the basic message in order to facilitate learning and memory.[25] It actually may also encourage positive feelings toward the brand.[26] Means of accompanying such a strategy include using different spokespeople, employing various beginnings and endings to the ads, and adopting different themes, scenarios, or backgrounds for the message. Close attention to advertisements on television will reveal that such techniques are actually being employed.

Although the above general patterns of consumer learning appear to exist, a number of variables influence the rate and strength of the process. Two of these factors are briefly reviewed below.

Learning Ability Individuals differ considerably in their abilities to learn, and intelligence is a primary factor influencing this ability. Intelligence appears to be normally distributed within the population with some consumers being much higher than average and others being considerably below average. Highly intelligent consumers are capable of learning more quickly and are often interested in learning different types of information about products than consumers of lower intelligence. In addition, they tend to be more critical of unsubstantiated advertising claims and often have different readership habits than do other consumers. For example, readers of *National Geographic, Scientific American,* and *Saturday Review* tend to have higher intelligence levels than readers of many other magazines. Such differences in learning abilities require marketers to consider carefully intelligence levels of their target market before designing the content of promotional messages.

Practice Schedules If only the time actually spent at a learning task is considered, periods of practice separated by rest intervals achieve much more efficient learning in many situations than do learning periods with no rest. The term *distributed practice* refers to learning sessions with rest periods, while learning without rest periods is known as *massed practice.* Aside from its obvious relevance to students' study habits, practice schedules have implications regarding the proper scheduling of advertising messages over time. Given that distributed practice is an effective learning technique, the marketer is interested in the optimum time interval to plan between advertising repetitions in order to generate the greatest amount of consumer learning. This has sparked a considerable amount of research in the advertising field.[27]

Extinction

We can "unlearn" material or behavior that has been previously learned. This unlearning process is termed "extinction" and occurs when, over time, a learned response is made to a stimulus but reinforcement does not occur. The greater the number of nonreinforced trials, the less likely the response is to occur; but complete extinction is rare. Also, *spontaneous recovery*—the sudden reappearance of an extinguished response—reduces the chance of complete extinction. Resistance to extinction also increases when:

Impelling motives are strong

The number of previously reinforced trials are large

The amount of reward during learning is large

Reward is delayed during the learning process

A partial reinforcement schedule is used in the learning process

Resistance to extinction at least partially explains why consumers are slow to change many tastes, shopping patterns, and consumption habits. For example, many find it difficult to reduce or eliminate sweets, coffee, or smoking. Similarly, others who have developed strong brand or store loyalties over time resist making changes, even if their regular brands or stores are not currently providing the rewards they once did. This poses a great challenge to marketers attempting to draw patronage away from competition.

Forgetting

It is important to distinguish extinction from the process of forgetting. *Extinction* will occur when a previously learned response continues to be made but is no longer reinforced. *Forgetting* can be defined as the loss of retained material due to nonuse or interference from some other learning task. As can be implied from this definition, *retention* is the amount of previously learned material that is remembered.[28]

The process of forgetting, and how it can be minimized, has been of more concern to marketers than has extinction. This is so not only because it is a more significant problem, but also because marketers can influence the process by repeating advertising messages to encourage consumers' retention. To determine the extent of their success, various measures of advertising retention are employed. The two most commonly used methods are:

Recall—the consumer tells an interviewer the advertisement she remembers seeing recently. She may not be prompted at all (unaided recall), or may be given some guidance (aided recall), such as the product category involved.

Recognition—the consumer is presented with an advertisement or series of advertisements and is asked to indicate which ones he has seen recently.

Both methods of measuring retention are used frequently, but as shown in Figure 14-7 the level of retention as measured by recognition is typically greater than indicated by the recall method. Of course, the most appropriate technique will depend on promotional goals and the specific situation, such as the type of product involved. However, the marketing manager must be aware of which technique is being employed to evaluate properly the success of the promotional effort.

Note from Figure 14-7 that regardless of the measure of retention used, the fastest rate of forgetting occurs soon after learning has occurred. As the time since the last learning trial increases, forgetting continues, but its rate slows considerably. This was dramatically demonstrated in one marketing experiment in which

FIGURE 14-7

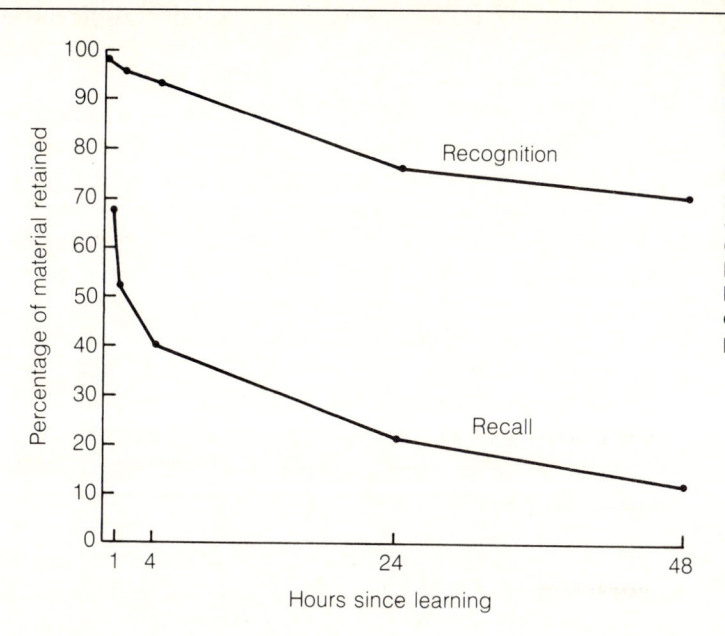

Graph showing loss of retention as measured by recognition and recall methods. (*Source:* C. W. Luh, "The Conditions of Retention," *Psychological Monographs,* **31:**1–87, 1922. Copyright © 1922 by the American Psychological Association. Reprinted by permission.)

the percentage of people who could remember a specific advertisement dropped by 50 percent only 4 weeks after the last repetition.[29]

This characteristic shape of retention curves demonstrates the marketer's concern for repeating advertisements to combat the forgetting process. However, designing effective methods to minimize forgetting requires some understanding of human memory. We now turn our attention to this topic.

MEMORY

As everyone's experience has demonstrated, material that consumers have "learned" is not always readily retrievable by them. Some information, such as popular brand names or the location of merchandise in a supermarket, is easily "remembered." Other information appears to end up lost, or at least it does not appear to be readily obtainable. This section of the chapter focuses on the structure and operation of consumers' memory. The discussion picks up where we left off in the information-processing chapter. Here we are concerned with the storage and retrieval of information after it has been acquired and has undergone initial processing.

Memory processes are of considerable importance to the understanding of consumers. Basically, this is so because consumers act on the basis of their *cognitions*—i.e., their knowledge or beliefs about the world. These cognitions are stored in memory and, as we saw in Chapter 13, they influence how incoming stimuli are interpreted. They also form the basis for attitudes and behavioral intentions which are the subject of the next two chapters. On a more concrete level of illustration, consider the goal of marketers who strive to have consumers retain their brand name or information about it. The challenge is great when one realizes that approximately 23,000 different brands are advertised on a national or regional scale in the United States alone.[30] In a very real sense, each of these brands, as well as many local ones, vie for a prominent place in consumers' memory.

Characteristics of Memory Systems

Several positions have been taken regarding the structure of memory and its operation.[31] One, termed the *multiple store* approach, views memory as being composed of three distinct storage registers (sensory, short-term, long-term) which differ in capacity, storage duration, and functioning. A second perspective which has been quite popular is that there is only one memory and distinct storage registers do not exist in a physical sense. Different storage registers appear to exist because different *levels of processing* are involved. That is, stimuli can receive shallow processing, such as an analysis of basic sensations, as well as deeper processing, such as when people interpret incoming information and relate it to existing knowledge. Different levels of processing exist because humans have limited processing capacity to allocate across a variety of incoming stimuli. Also, information receiving deep levels of processing will enjoy a more complex and longer-lasting memory, while shallow processing is likely to result in only temporary storage.

A third conception of memory, called the *activation model,* also makes use of the single-memory-store concept. However, in this view humans are seen as having only a limited ability to activate their memory. The result is that at any time only a portion of memory can be activated to deal with incoming information. Consequently, the remaining portions are not available for processing. Also, activation is only temporary, which means that the portion of memory that is dealing with incoming information will not stay active unless effort is expended to maintain it.

It has been argued that although these three models of memory are distinct in terms of their emphasis, they are not necessarily incompatible.[32] For example, one could view short-term memory in the multiple-store model as that part of memory which is being *activated* and performing a certain function at a given *level* of processing. Other points of commonality can also be found. Therefore, for purposes of exposition we shall discuss memory in terms of the three-component model. We must be careful to note, however, that each component should *not* be viewed as a physically separate entity, but as a distinct process or *functioning* of memory which has certain unique characteristics. The diagram in Figure 14-8 showing the three components of sensory memory, short-term memory, and long-term memory will facilitate our discussion.

Sensory Memory   As Figure 14-8 shows, information is first received by sensory memory. Input is in the form of sensations that have been produced by the sensory receptors. Memory registers exist for sensations being produced through the visual, auditory, and other sense organs. The capacity of these registers is very large—capable of storing all that the sensory receptors transmit. They also appear to faithfully represent this information in a form that closely resembles the actual stimuli. A good illustration of the nature of these representations is the after-image we "see" in our "mind's eye" immediately after observing an object and closing our eyes. This example also illustrates the duration of sensory memory. Information is stored for only a fraction of a second and will be lost through decay (fading away) unless sufficient attention is allocated to it so that it can be analyzed and transferred to short-term memory for further processing. This initial information analysis is conducted in terms of physical characteristics—size, color, shape, etc.—which is the process of feature analysis described in Chapter 13.

Short-term Memory To a large extent, short-term memory can be viewed as the workspace for information processing. That is, it is a portion of memory activated to temporarily store and process information in order to interpret it and comprehend its meaning. This is accomplished by combining incoming information with other information (past experiences, knowledge, etc.) stored in long-term memory.

Although the duration of this memory register is considerably longer than sensory memory, it still is quite brief, lasting less than one minute. In addition, the capacity of short-term memory is quite limited. Approximately seven items or groupings of items are all that can be sorted at any one time.[33]

Material residing in short-term memory does not bear a one-to-one correspondence with the real world. Instead, the process of *coding* is used to organize information into a more easily handled and remembered format. The primary method of this coding is termed *chunking*, which can be defined as the method of assembling information into a type of organized unit having a more understandable or familiar form to the individual. For example, consider how the numbers 62895091963 could be more easily utilized if they were grouped into the following configurations: 628-9509 1963. In both cases, the information represents a telephone number and the date that it was obtained, but when the information is chunked, as in the second presentation, it is much easier to deal with it.

Brand names as well as symbols, trademarks, and other representations also can serve as chunks to organize material. Thus, the word Campbell or the Bell Telephone symbol are able to bring forth a large number of informational items or thoughts the consumer may have about those companies. Also, when we realize that a chunk can be among the approximately seven items a person can simultaneously hold in short-term memory, it can be appreciated that the capacity of seven items or chunks is not as limited as one might initially suspect.

It appears that to employ the chunking process an individual must be prepared to receive the incoming information. For example, a radio advertisement involving a telephone number should alert consumers that a number will be mentioned so that they will be prepared to chunk it into an exchange plus a four-digit number. Without such preparation, the material may be forgotten before chunking can be used. In addition, the telephone number should be announced in chunked form to facilitate memory.

As Figure 14-8 demonstrates, rehearsal is required to maintain information in short-term memory or to transfer it to long-term memory. If rehearsal does not

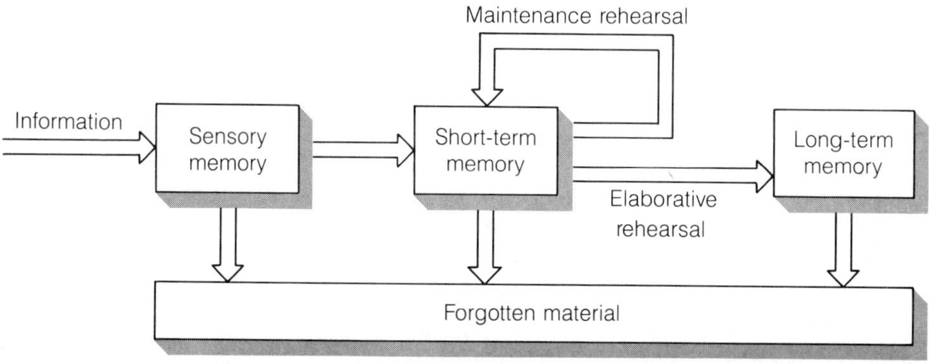

FIGURE 14-8

A representation of memory systems.

occur, the information will be forgotten through the process of decay. However, it appears that the type of rehearsal involved differs depending on whether the goal is to retain material in short-term memory for additional processing or to transfer it to long-term memory. The process of *maintenance rehearsal* involves the continual repeating of information so that it can be held in short-term memory.[34] For example, after hearing a new brand name of interest, the consumer might keep on repeating it silently until she could write it down. The type of rehearsal used to transfer information to long-term memory is frequently called *elaborative rehearsal*, because it appears to involve relating the new information to prior experiences and knowledge in order to derive meaning from it. This is considered to involve "deeper" levels of processing than mere repetition of the information.

Long-term Memory This memory system can be thought of as the relatively permanent storehouse for information that has undergone sufficient processing. Material can be maintained in long-term memory for as little as a few minutes to as long as many years. In addition, this system has the capacity to store an almost unlimited amount of information.

A predominant key to coding material for storage in long-term memory is *meaningfulness*—the personal understanding an individual can derive from the information. That is, through elaborative rehearsal the individual uses his existing knowledge to interpret incoming information and code it in a way that is consistent with his existing cognitive structure (knowledge base). The degree of success in accomplishing this will affect how well the new information can be retained and made available for future use.[35]

Some people claim that we never really forget anything that has been transferred to long-term memory.[36] Instead, they argue, what is forgotten is the key which tells us where the material is located in our memory. Of course, such a position is difficult to prove or disprove. We therefore will side-step this issue by expanding the term "forgetting" to refer to a general inability to access material that has been stored in long-term memory. Given this, we can now state that material, instead of just decaying over time, appears to be forgotten from long-term memory as a result of other learning *interfering* with retention of the material. The interference concept holds that material can be forgotten in two basic ways. In *retroactive inhibition*, new learning interferes with material already in long-term memory, and the material in memory is forgotten. This could occur, for example, when studying concepts in this chapter results in forgetting material studied in the chapter on information processing. In *proactive inhibition*, material already in memory interferes with the remembering of new material. In either case, the greater the similarity between two sets of different material, the more they will interfere with each other.

The above paragraphs presented an overview of the sensory memory, short-term memory, and long-term memory systems. Their duration, capacity, type of coding, and major forgetting mechanisms were noted. These characteristics are also summarized in Table 14-3. At this point, it is useful to explore long-term memory in somewhat greater depth. Our attention is focused on this system because of its central role in interpreting new stimulus situations and its functioning as a storehouse for what consumers know about their world.

CONTENT OF LONG-TERM MEMORY Because long-term memory is a depository for the wide variety of material that a person can learn, it stands to reason

TABLE 14-3

SUMMARY OF MEMORY SYSTEMS CHARACTERISTICS

Memory System	Duration	Capacity	Type of Coding	Major Forgetting Mechanism
Sensory memory	Fraction of a second	All that perceptual sensors can deliver	Quite direct representation of reality	Decay
Short-term memory	Less than one minute	Approximately seven items	Indirect—chunking	Decay
Long-term memory	Up to many years	Almost unlimited	Indirect—clustering via meaningfulness	Interference

Source: Adapted from David Krech et al., *Psychology: A Basic Course,* Knopf, New York, p. 83. Copyright © Alfred A. Knopf, Inc.

that different ways should exist for storing or coding this information. Evidence suggests that this is the case.[37] As indicated in the previous section, one heavily used method of coding involves semantic concepts and the associations between them. By *semantic concepts* we mean one's general abstracted knowledge about facts, objects and their attributes, and other aspects of the world. Therefore, the individual does not perform semantic coding by directly representing an object in memory. Instead, it is stored in a generalized form which has meaning for the individual. Because of this, each of us may store an object in a different way. For example, some people might conceptualize an Atari computer as a powerful method of performing business or household tasks, while others might conceptualize it primarily as a home-entertainment device. Still others might think of it as a learning tool for their children. In each case, the same object will be represented in memory differently, and each representation is likely to be associated with emotions and other already-existing memory concepts that are similar to it.

Other material coded into memory includes chronological representations of events that have occurred in the past. That is, we often store information about happenings by coding them as a sequence of events that occur in a certain time order. The notion of scripts appears to be one example of such coding.[38] A *script* is a representation in memory of a series of actions occurring in some particular type of past situation. What seems to be important is that a well-defined script tends to influence the consumer's expectations about what actions will occur at a future time when a similar situation occurs. As a result, it tends to guide behavior. Therefore, we can see that the name "script" was chosen because the representation in memory resembles an outline of actions that actors follow in a play or movie. An example might be the script that guides behavior when purchasing a new pair of slacks—find an appropriate size, choose a color, make a comparison to other available brands with similar prices and quality, select a brand, try on two different sizes to select the best fit, and so forth.

Scripts are believed to be useful to consumers because they can be activated automatically when the consumer confronts a familiar situation, and because they guide behavior without requiring much thought or deliberation from the consumer.[39] This relatively automatic behavior also has a number of implications for marketing strategy. For example, it suggests that for many products consumers may not be highly conscious of some of their purchasing patterns. Also, these patterns may be resistant to influence attempts because they are so well established in long-term memory.

A third method of coding information into long-term memory appears to be visual in nature. That is, people appear to use mental images to represent certain information, especially when something tangible such as a physical object is involved.[40] To demonstrate this, we only have to try to remember what is hung on a given kitchen wall in our home. Most people will accomplish this by recalling a "mental picture" of the wall and its contents. It has been shown that using such mental images to store information often leads to a very strong long-term memory for the material.[41]

The strong memory potential for visually coded information has important implications for those who design packaging, company logos, and promotional messages. However, evidence suggests that more is involved than just the old conclusion that "a picture is worth a thousand words." This is so because certain types of verbal stimuli which are not associated with any visual presentations also appear capable of influencing consumers to develop distinct mental images.[42] In addition, some methods of designing pictures, graphics, and similar presentations appear more effective than others for facilitating consumers' visual memory. For example, research has shown that interactive images are more effective for influencing consumers to remember brand names than are normal visual presentations.[43] In this context, an *interactive image* is one that actually becomes part of the brand name or visually integrates the brand name with the product or service being provided. Figure 14-9 presents examples of such interactive images for two hypothetical retail firms. In order to use interactive imagery to its full potential, marketers will have to carefully design their visual presentations.

There is also evidence that other formats are used for coding information into long-term memory—including auditory (coding by sounds), taste, and olfactory (coding by smells) methods of representation.[44] These various methods do not appear to be completely independent. Instead, they interact to influence the retention and retrieval of information.

It has been suggested that the various methods of long-term memory coding can be grouped into three general categories which interact with each other: episodic memory, procedural memory, and semantic memory.[45] In *episodic memory*, a record of events in one's personal life are stored according to the time order in

FIGURE 14-9

Examples of using interactive imagery in advertising.

Ron's Tire Service

Mercury Lawnmowing Service

which they occurred. Facts are stored independent of each other and more in terms of how and when they occurred, rather than in terms of the meaning they have. Therefore, retrieval of such information requires that we "play back the tape" from a starting point. For example, when asked how much liquid we had to drink today, most of us would probably try to remember by tracing our steps from when we got up in the morning. Statements reflecting episodic memory include: "I bought that sweater during the fall," "*Barney Miller* reruns are on Channel 12 right before dinner," and "That store always has a sale right after Valentine's day."

Our *procedural memory* holds knowledge about skills and methods for dealing with facts, concepts, and episodes. Therefore, it is a memory for knowing *how* to perform certain functions or tasks, and it plays an important role in problem-solving behavior. Statements reflecting procedural memory include: "When buying a car, always offer the seller less than the stated price," "A new coat of paint adheres better if the old coat is lightly sanded first," and "Always check unit prices before buying packaged food products."

Our *semantic memory* contains general knowledge we have about the world—facts and concepts, as well as objects and their attributes. It seems that this knowledge is not linked to the means or the time period in which it was obtained. For example, most of us have stored information about Kellogg's Corn Flakes, but we usually cannot remember when or how we acquired this information. Because of this, retrieval of material from semantic memory can be direct without the need to "replay" a sequence of events as in episodic memory. Another important characteristic of semantic memory is that it is *associational* in nature. That is, new information is related to existing stored knowledge so that associations are formed between elements and they develop into a type of meaningful cognitive structure. Statements reflecting semantic memory include: "Stereo systems can be expensive," "Cassette players produce better sound than 8-track systems," and "Craig car stereos have a good reputation." How such knowledge can be associated in a memory structure is addressed next.

STRUCTURE OF SEMANTIC MEMORY   It is currently believed that memory is organized into numerous groupings or packets of information. Various types of packets have been suggested by researchers.[46] However, one of the most frequently mentioned schemes is the associative network model of semantic memory. We have already described aspects of this model, but it is useful to look at it a little more closely.

The network model depicts semantic memory as an interconnected system of "nodes" representing the concepts being stored. Figure 14-10 shows how that portion of a consumer's memory for a Craig car stereo system might be represented using the model. The first thing to note is that a hierarchical structure is involved. That is, the general category of stereos is shown at the top of the figure, and car stereos installed after a car is purchased (retrofit) are seen as only one type of system. Next, we see that the Craig system is one of several types of retrofit brands of which the consumer is aware. Finally, the consumer's knowledge of various characteristics of the Craig system are shown.

We can also see from the figure that each concept in semantic memory is integrated into an organized structure involving one or more other concepts. This is shown by the connecting lines which also represent the strength of the indicated relationship—the darker the line the stronger the association between concepts.

FIGURE 14-10

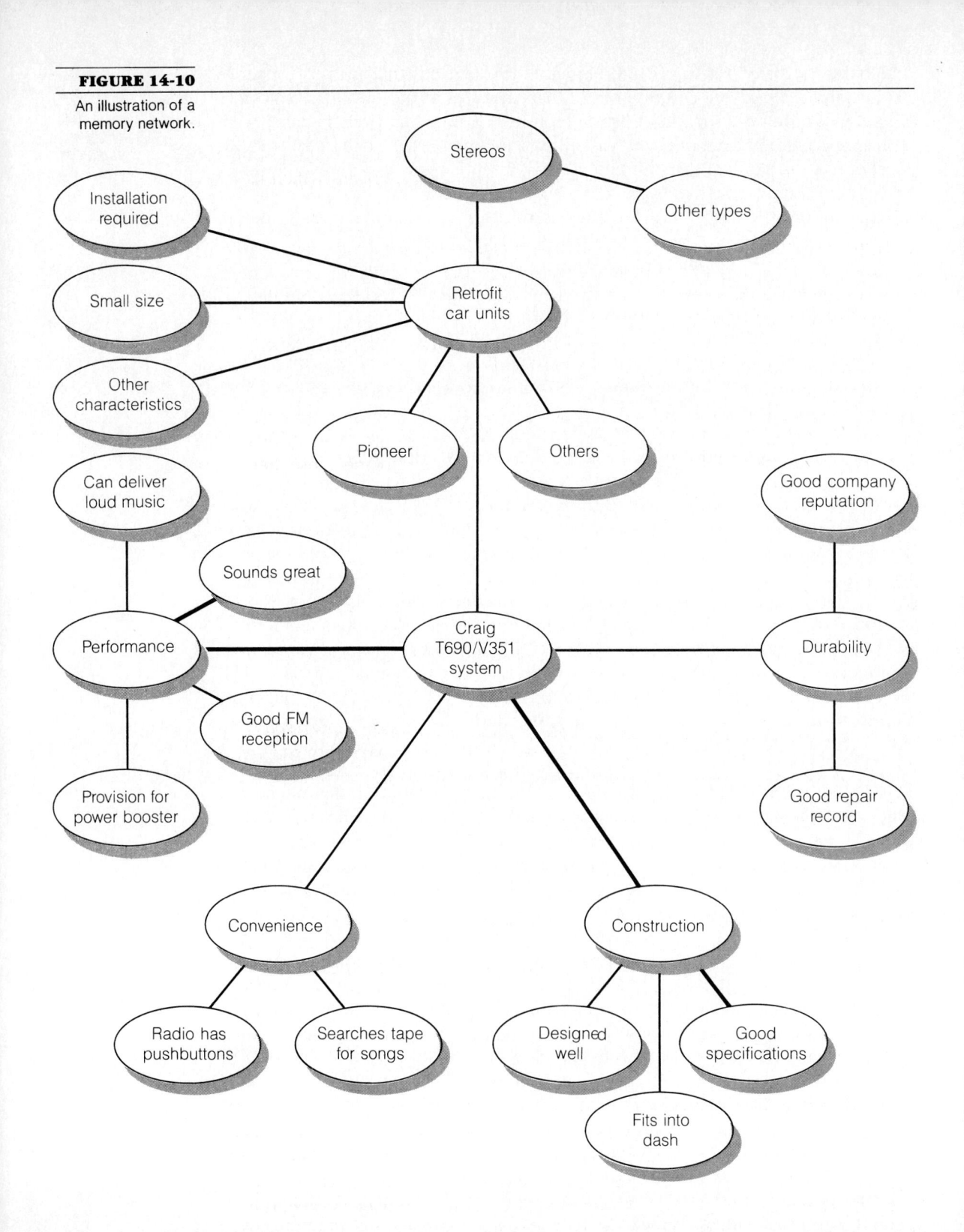

An illustration of a memory network.

Specifically, the lines show that the consumer has remembered the Craig system as one type of auto retrofit stereo system. She also has associated performance, durability, construction, and convenience concepts with the Craig system. The performance concept is most strongly linked to the Craig, followed by the construction concept. Each of the concepts also has particular characteristics which have made enough of an impression on the consumer to be remembered.

It should be clear that semantic memory is viewed as a highly organized structure of knowledge and beliefs. Progressive marketers have shown interest in this conclusion, because it implies that an awareness of consumers' memory structures is useful in predicting how they will interpret and respond to new inputs such as product information and promotions. However, as discussed below, evidence has been accumulating recently which adds additional importance to the need to understand consumers' cognitive structures.

Surprisingly, it is possible for semantic memory to contain more than what was received from the environment. That is, associations between concepts in memory are not part of the environment, but are actively *formed* by consumers when they attempt to interpret and store incoming information. One consequence of this is that consumers can develop beliefs about a specific product without ever receiving information directly relevant to that belief.[47] As an example, assume that our consumer examined several Craig models and found that all of these units had good FM reception. It is then quite possible that when introduced to a new Craig unit, this consumer might just infer that it also has good reception, even if she never directly evaluates the new model. Because of the way in which they are formed, such beliefs are termed *inferential beliefs*.

Another closely allied process also occurs while consumers are rehearsing new material and attempting to interpret it for storage in long-term memory. This involves what has become known as *cognitive response*—positive or negative thoughts generated by the consumer as a result of being exposed to information.[48] When information is in the form of advertising messages, the major forms of cognitive response are generated thoughts that support the message, refute or diminish the message, or degrade the source of the message so that its impact can be minimized. We will examine this in greater detail when dealing with consumers' attitudes. What is important to understand here is that these self-generated thoughts can also be stored in long-term memory along with the information that generated them. This means that they also become part of long-term memory and can be retrieved to influence the interpretation of future information. For example, while a consumer is watching a TV commercial for a brand of home computer, she or he might think "Basically, they just look like fancy game machines to me." If this concept is associated with home computers in long-term memory, it could be retrieved at some future date to have a strong influence on the interpretation of additional messages about home computers. How this could occur is the subject of the next section.

Retrieval of Information

Retrieval is the process of accessing information in long-term memory and bringing it into consciousness. The retrieved data may then be combined with other material available in short-term memory, elaborated on, and formed into a coherent package of meaningful information. Therefore, retrieval may be viewed as the means of transferring information from long-term memory into the activated workspace of short-term memory so that it can be processed further.

Several factors are important influences on the process of retrieval. One is the extent of original learning—the more thoroughly material is learned, the easier it should be to retrieve. As we have seen, the thoroughness of learning is a function of the degree of elaborative processing used to fit material into a cognitive structure, as well as the amount of rehearsal involved. A second factor influencing retrieval appears to be the goals involved in the original learning situation. For example, evidence suggests that consumers have better recall for information when their original purpose is to commit it to memory rather than to use it to choose between various brands.[49] A third major influence on retrieval is the context of the situation. Context is important because it contains cues providing guidance as to which portion of long-term memory should be accessed. For example, assume that we hear the word "ring" mentioned. It is quite possible that this word is stored in several parts of our cognitive structure to represent (1) something a telephone does, (2) a dirt line on a shirt collar, (3) something worn on a finger, or (4) a layer of scum in the bathtub. The context in which the word is used will strongly influence what aspects of memory will be retrieved.

Because concepts in long-term memory are associated or linked with other concepts, retrieval typically involves bringing an interrelated packet of information to consciousness. Usually an environmental event will trigger a search of long-term memory, and elements of the context will influence which node or nodes will be activated. Other concepts that are strongly linked to the activated nodes are themselves likely to be activated. However, concepts that are weakly linked or not linked at all are unlikely to be activated. The result is that when a situation initiates a search of long-term memory, activated concepts as well as material they are linked to are likely to be retrieved and reach conscious attention. These interrelated informational items may then be combined with other material in short-term memory and be modified or expanded upon for use in a variety of ways.

An example can help to explain the interrelationships involved. Assume that while shopping in a department store a customer asks some salesperson about a particular Zenith color television set. He is told that the set is a 19-inch table model of all solid-state design. The salesperson also mentions that the set is mostly hand crafted and it has an excellent warranty. As shown in Figure 14-11, this information represents environmental input into the initial stage of short-term memory. The term "initial" is being used here to indicate the status of memory stores at the start of some event.

As we know, information can only be maintained if it is rehearsed. The arrow from initial short-term memory to expanded short-term memory represents maintenance of a portion of the information through rehearsal. Specifically, information about the size of the set and its warranty have been maintained, while the remaining items have been lost from memory.

Based on previous experience, the consumer has retained certain beliefs and knowledge about Zenith television sets. The figure shows that this material is stored in initial long-term memory along with other information that is not relevant to the situation. The dotted line entering this part of the figure indicates that information from the salesperson has activated long-term memory. The solid line leading from this part to expanded short-term memory shows that activation has resulted in three items of information being transferred from long-term memory to the consumer's conscious attention.

The salesperson's comments are also shown by a dotted line as activating the consumer's inferential and cognitive responses. Thus, even though the salesperson never really stated it, the consumer has inferred that the 19-inch measurement actually represents screen size as measured on the diagonal. We also see that the salesperson's comments have stimulated the consumer to generate a supportive cognitive response—the set is well made. The line leading from initial long-term memory to these conclusions suggests that they are at least partially influenced by what resides in memory as well as by what transpires in the situation at hand. The inference and cognitive response are then transferred to expanded short-term memory to be combined with other material.

We can now see that short-term memory is "where it all comes together." To use a cooking analogy, a pinch of this is added to a measure of that and a dash of something else. Elaborative rehearsal develops a meaningful pattern from material received from the environment, from inferences and cognitive responses, and from the retrieval of information in long-term memory. As shown in Figure 14-11, the result is that long-term memory now holds an expanded and coherent packet of information about the Zenith television set. This is available for immediate use, such as deciding on a purchase, and it is also available in long-term memory for future reference.

FIGURE 14-11

A representation of retrieval and the interrelationship between memory elements.

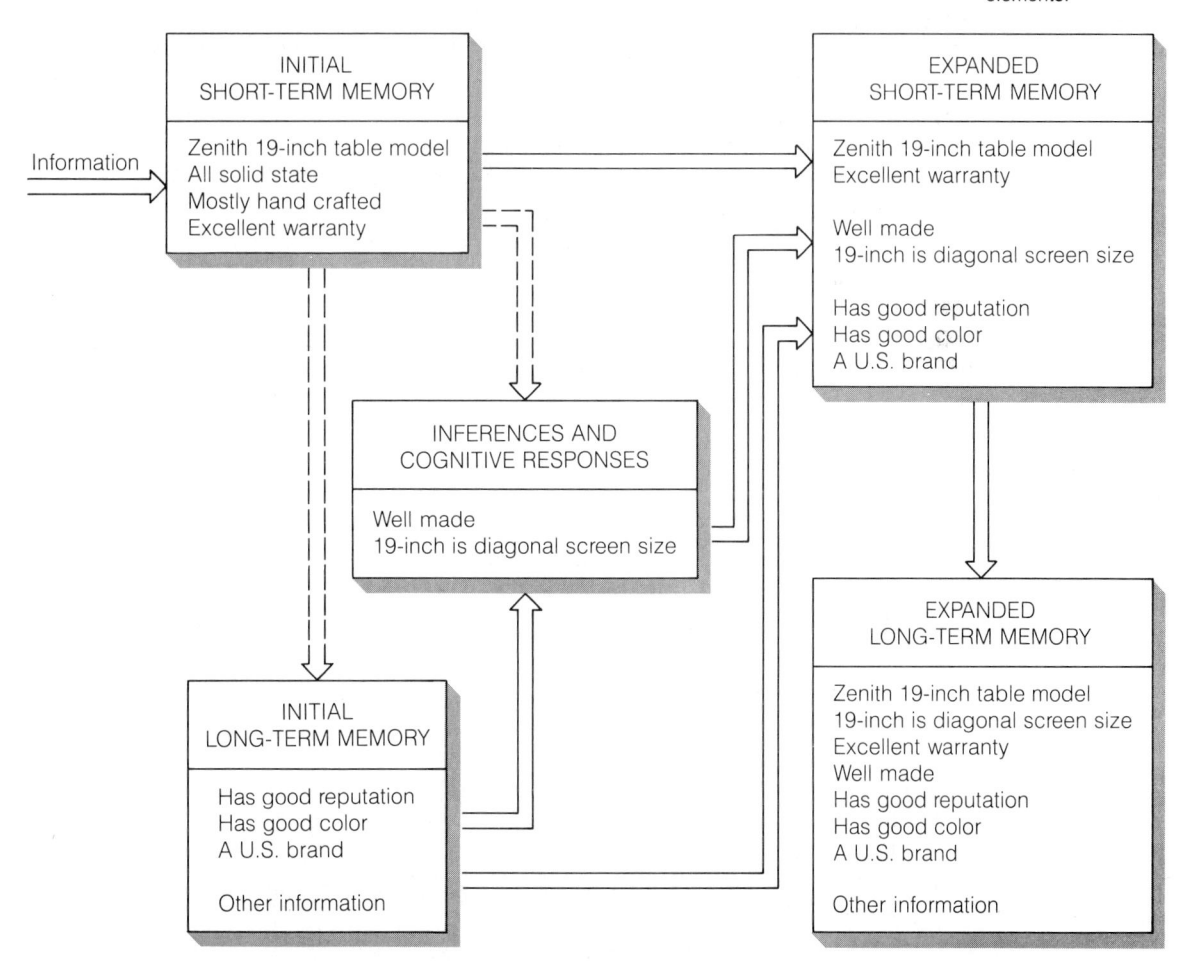

Advertising Applications

Numerous memory concepts have significant implications for the field of advertising. The following conclusions represent only a sampling of the useful guidelines that are available. While some are drawn directly from our previous discussion, others represent extensions of that material.[50] Of course, in all cases these conclusions are generalizations which will not apply in every specific case.

1 *Advertising messages with unique aspects have a greater potential for being remembered*—This occurs because material with unusual aspects is least affected by the interference process of forgetting. This is one factor that motivates advertisers to seek novel approaches and themes for their messages.

2 *The order in which material is presented seems to influence how well it will be retained, with the middle portion being most easily forgotten*—This apparently occurs because the beginning and ending of messages stand out the most and interfere with remembering material in-between (retroactive and proactive inhibition). The implication is that the most important parts of advertising messages should be placed at the beginning or end, or both. Conversely, some direct-mail advertisers bury the price of their merchandise in the middle of a long letter so as to minimize its negative impact on a purchase decision.

3 *Messages that encourage immediate rehearsal of material stimulate its retention*—Maintenance rehearsal maintains material in short-term memory. Elaborative rehearsal will encourage the transfer of material to long-term memory. This is why some radio and television advertisers encourage listeners to repeat a telephone number or address several times, and also attempt to develop some meaningful pattern to the numbers.

4 *The amount of information that can be transferred to long-term memory is a function of the time available for processing*—When recall of a message will be required, approximately 5 to 10 seconds is required to transfer one chunk of information to long-term memory through memorization. The amount of information that an advertiser presents should therefore be tailored to the amount of time available for processing and the way the information can be packaged.[51]

5 *More information can be processed and retained if it is chunked*—Because the capacity of short-term memory is approximately seven items, chunking can be viewed as a way to efficiently package a greater amount of information. This suggests that advertisers should attempt to find appropriate methods of chunking information for consumers so that they can deliver a greater amount of message content in the limited time or space at their disposal.

6 *Memory is cue-dependent, and presentation of relevant cues will stimulate recall*—Apparently, certain cues present during the learning context become associated with the material in memory. Their presentation at a later date facilitates recall of the learned material. This process can be very effectively employed by designing packages and point-of-purchase displays to contain the same cues used in advertisements for the product. For example, a picture of a snow-capped mountain reminds some consumers of Busch beer, James Garner reminds others of Polaroid, and just the word "blimp" reminds others of Goodyear.

7 *Material retained in long-term memory can be quite different than the information presented in a learning situation*—This is so because some information will be lost from short-term memory, the consumer may generate inferences and cognitive responses, and material will also be drawn from long-term memory. It is important for advertisers to understand these activities and their potential in any specific situation for influencing the meaning that consumers derive from promotional messages.

8 *Material that is meaningful to the individual is learned more quickly and therefore has a greater chance of being retained than nonmeaningful material*—Apparently, meaningful material actively involves the individual's mental capacities, and this leads to its greater retention. Therefore, the strong recommendation that has been made for some time is to design advertisements that stimulate consumers' mental involvement, thereby making messages meaningful to them. However, the marketer should develop the specific meaning desired for the message rather than relying on chance for consumers to determine what meaning they will derive from it themselves. Some methods of accomplishing this are listed below. Of course, the specific situation will dictate the degree to which they are appropriate.

    a *Visual material*—Information presented as visual content is frequently more memorable than verbal content. This suggests that, where possible, advertisers find ways to "say it with pictures" rather than conveying information with advertising copy.[52]

    b *Interactive imagery*—Use of pictures, symbols, and other visual devices that depict how two concepts or properties relate to each other can be a highly effective aid to consumers' memory. Such imagery can be used to link a specific brand to particular needs or to a general product group. A spendid example is using the image of the sun kissing an orange for the Sunkist brand of oranges.

    c *Showing mistakes*—During demonstration of mechanical skills, performance, or decision making, it is often useful to show how things should *not* be done, as well as how they should be done. The Midas muffler commercial that depicts a car owner's trauma when attempting to get his muffler replaced at service stations is such an example. An additional technique, which also heightens involvement, is to simulate situations as if the viewer were actually experiencing them.

    d *Incomplete messages*—Leaving some messages open-ended so that consumers must become involved to complete them has been found to increase retention.[53] This may be quite overtly done by simply not completing the entire message, as in the advertisement for preventing forest fires cited in the last chapter, or it may be more subtly accomplished by having the announcer ask a question or pose a decision problem for the viewer to answer.

    e *Mnemonic techniques*—The art of mnemonics (ne-mon'-ics) involves the development of a pattern for a series of seemingly unrelated facts so that they can be more easily remembered. Therefore, any technique that allows consumers to "see" some pattern for associating otherwise meaningless facts will usually be helpful. When possible, you should provide word associations for telephone numbers. For example, some cities have reserved the telephone number HELP (4357) for their emergency hotlines. A number of private firms have employed a similar technique. In other cases, a melodic pattern can be employed. The singing jingle Sheraton hotels devised to promote consumers' memory of their toll-free reservation number (800-325-3535) is a good illustration. In a similar fashion, a narrative or song can sometimes be devised to promote retention of other information. An excellent example is the jingle using the lyrics of "Two all-beef patties, special sauce, lettuce, cheese, pickles, onions on a sesame-seed bun." The proportion of Americans that remember these product characteristics for the Big Mac hamburger is probably astounding.

Again, it should be stressed that the above list of general guidelines regarding consumers' memory is not by any means exhaustive. In addition, the specific situation must be considered before employing any of them. However, the list is illustrative of the potential benefits of applying such concepts to the design of marketing communications.

SUMMARY

This chapter has dealt with two of the fundamental methods by which consumers are able to adapt to their environment. The influence of the learning and memory processes were seen to be pervasive, affecting factors from consumers' basic likes and dislikes to typical methods of shopping. After some introductory comments, attention turned to principal learning elements—motives, cues, responses, and reinforcements. Next, some of the basic methods by which consumers learn were introduced. Distinctions between cognitive and connectionist schools of thought were highlighted, and the usefulness of each of these concepts to understanding consumer learning were addressed. Cognitive theories appear best-suited for understanding problem-solving behavior, while classical conditioning is useful for explaining rote, unconscious learning. Instrumental conditioning falls between these extremes.

Attention then turned to some additional learning topics including behavior modification, generalization and discrimination, the rate and degree of learning, and factors influencing these variables. The last major section dealt with consumers' memory systems. It appears most useful to view memory as being comprised of three sets of component processes: sensory memory, short-term memory, and long-term memory. The nature of these memory components and their interrelationships were discussed. Finally, a number of useful guidelines for advertisers were drawn from a sampling of the memory concepts that have potential applicability.

DISCUSSION TOPICS

1 What is learning? Briefly indicate its importance to understanding consumer behavior.

2 What method of learning (classical conditioning, instrumental conditioning, or cognitive) seems best able to explain each of the following:
    a smoking cigarettes

b purchasing an air conditioner primarily for reducing the humidity in a hot, humid room

c writing Scotch tape on a shopping list instead of cellophane tape

3 What are stimulus generalization and discrimination learning, and how are they important to the marketer?

4 Draw a learning curve, and discuss its implications for repeating a given advertising message to consumers.

5 Add a typical retention curve to the end of the learning curve drawn for question 4. Discuss the implications of these curves for advertisers.

6 Design examples of how a marketer could employ the following behavior modification elements:
a Shaping   **b** Modeling   **c** Classical conditioning

7 Suggest some circumstances in which an advertiser might be more interested in using the recall method for measuring retention rather than the recognition method. Do the same for the recognition method as opposed to the recall method.

8 Officials of the federal government have decided that the United States will "go metric." They are now concerned with how to promote learning of the metric system among the citizenry. Suggest methods and programs to assist in accomplishing this goal.

9 Compare and contrast the sensory memory, short-term memory, and long-term memory systems. Indicate the relevance of each to advertising strategies.

10 Cite some suggestions you would give to advertisers who were concerned with consumers remembering the following:

a To start a rotary lawn mower safely, one should make sure that (1) the deflector chute or grass bag is attached, (2) no objects or debris are next to the mower, (3) the left foot is placed on the mower, and (4) the right foot is placed well back.

b Choose a brand name for earth-moving equipment which contractors will remember and associate with their need for such equipment.

c Have consumers learn how to pronounce the airline name Alitalia so that they will not be reluctant to ask for it on their trips to Europe.

11 Choose a brand name for a particular product. Develop your semantic network (as in Figure 14-10) for this brand. Be sure to include where the specific brand fits into a hierarchical structure of the product class and where it fits into the set of alternative brands.

NOTES

[1] See "From Bugs to Batman, Children's TV Shows Produce Adult Anxiety," *The Wall Street Journal*, October 19, 1976, p. 1, for one of a series of articles reviewing the effects of this and other issues concerning the influence of television.

[2] Much of this section is based on John Dollard and Neal Miller, *Personality and Psychotherapy*, McGraw-Hill, New York, 1950, pp. 25–47.

[3] See William Copulsky and Katherin Marton, "Sensory Cues, You've Got to Put Them Together," *Product Marketing*, January 1977, pp. 31–34.

[4] Winfred F. Hill, *Learning: A Survey of Psychological Interpretations,* Chandler, San Francisco, 1963, p. 225.

[5] Hill, *Learning,* pp. 100–112.

[6] Leonard Krasner, "Studies of the Conditioning of Verbal Behavior," *Psychological Bulletin,* **55**:148–170, 1958.

[7] See Ernest R. Hilgard and Gordon H. Bower, *Theories of Learning,* 3rd ed., Appleton-Century-Crofts, New York, 1966, for a comprehensive review of these theories.

[8] The two schools of thought are referred to as the reinforcement and contiguity advocates. See Hill, *Learning,* pp. 31–89, for a review of their differences and many similarities.

[9] Ivan Pavlov, *Conditioned Reflexes. An Investigation of the Psychological Activity of the Cerebral Cortex,* edited and translated by G. V. Anrep, Oxford University Press, London, 1927.

[10] Clark L. Hull, *Principles of Behavior,* Appleton-Century-Crofts, New York, 1943, p. 94.

[11] B. F. Skinner, *The Behavior of Organisms: An Experimental Analysis,* Appleton-Century-Crofts, New York, 1938.

[12] Wolfgang Kohler, *The Mentality of Apes,* Harcourt, Brace & World, New York, 1925.

[13] See Alan R. Andreasen and Peter G. Durkson, "Market Learning of New Residents," *Journal of Marketing Research,* **5**:166–176, May 1968.

[14] See Gerald J. Gorn, "The Effects of Music In Advertising On Choice Behavior: A Classical Conditioning Approach," *Journal of Marketing,* 46:94–101, Winter 1982.

[15] See Walter R. Nord and J. Paul Peter, "A Behavior Modification Perspective on Marketing," *Journal of Marketing,* 44:36–47, Spring 1980; Michael L. Rothschild and William C. Gaidis, "Behavioral Learning Theory: Its Relevance to Marketing and Promotions," *Journal of Marketing,* 45:70–78, Spring 1981; and J. Paul Peter and Walter R. Nord, "A Clarification and Extension of Operant Conditioning Principles in Marketing," *Journal of Marketing,* 46:102–107, Summer 1982, upon which much of this discussion is based.

[16] J. Ronald Carey, et al., "A Test of Positive Reinforcement of Customers," *Journal of Marketing,* 40:98–100, October 1976.

[17] See Rom J. Markin and Chem L. Narayana, "Behavior Control: Are Consumers Beyond Freedom and Dignity?" in Beverlee B. Anderson (ed.), *Advances in Consumer Research: Volume 3,* Association for Consumer Research, Ann Arbor, MI, 1976, p. 225.

[18] Nord and Peter, "A Behavior Modification Perspective."

[19] Bernard Berelson and Gary A. Steiner, *Human Behavior: An Inventory of Scientific Findings.* Harcourt, Brace & World, New York, 1964, pp. 138–139.

[20] C. I. Hovland, "The Generalization of Conditioned Responses: I," *Journal of General Psychology,* 17:125–148, 1937.

[21] See Hubert A. Zielske, "The Remembering and Forgetting of Advertising," *Journal of Marketing,* 23:239–243, January 1959; and Julian L. Simon and Johan Arndt, "The Shape of the Advertising Response Function," *Journal of Advertising Research,* 20:11–28, August 1980.

[22] Michael L. Ray, Alan G. Sawyer, and Edward C. Strong, "Frequency Effects Revisited," *Journal of Advertising Research,* 11:14–20, February 1971.

[23] See Herbert Krugman, "What Makes Advertising Effective?" *Harvard Business Review,* **53**:96–103, March-April 1975; and Howard Kamin, "Advertising Reach and Frequency," *Journal of Advertising Research,* 18:21–25, February 1978.

[24] See Bobby Calder and Brian Sternthal, "Television Commercial Wearout: An Information Processing Perspective," *Journal of Marketing Research,* 17:173–186, May 1980; and George E. Belch, "The Effects of Television Commercial Repetition on Cognitive Response and Message Acceptance," *Journal of Consumer Research,* 9:56–65, June 1982.

[25] See Joel Saegert and Robert Young, "Comparison of Effects of Repetition and Levels of Processing in Memory for Advertisements," in Andrew Mitchell (ed.), *Advances in Consumer Research: Volume 9,* Association for Consumer Research, Ann Arbor, MI, 1982, pp. 431–434.

[26] See Alan G. Sawyer, "Repetition and Affect: Recent Empirical and Theoretical Developments," in Arch Woodside, Jagdish Sheth, and Peter Bennett (eds.), *Consumer and Industrial Buyer Behavior,* North-Holland, New York, 1977, pp. 229–242; and Belch, "Effects of Television Commercial Repetition."

[27] See Edward C. Strong, "The Use of Field Experimental Observations in Estimating Advertising Recall," *Journal of Marketing Research,* 11:369–378, November 1974, for one such investigation.

[28] Howard H. Kendler, *Basic Psychology: Brief Version,* W. A. Benjamin, Menlo Park, CA, 1977, p. 448.

[29] Zielske, "Forgetting of Advertising."

[30] Leo Bogart and Charles Lehman, "What Makes A Brand Name Familiar?" *Journal of Marketing Research,* 10:17, February 1973.

[31] See James Bettman, *An Information Processing Theory of Consumer Choice,* Addison-Wesley, Reading, MA, 1979, pp. 139–143.

[32] Bettman, *An Information Processing Theory.*

[33] See George A. Miller, "The Magical Number Seven, Plus or Minus Two: Some Limits on Our Capacity for Processing Information," *Psychological Review,* 63:81–97, 1956.

[34] Peter H. Lindsay and Donald A. Norman, *Human Information Processing: An Introduction to Psychology,* 2d ed. Academic Press, New York, 1977, p. 319.

[35] See Joel Saegert, "A Demonstration of Levels-of-Processing Theory in Memory for Advertisements," in William L. Wilkie (ed.), *Advances in Consumer Research: Volume 6,* Association for Consumer Research, Ann Arbor, MI, pp. 82–84; Leonard N. Reid and Lawrence C. Soley, "Levels-of-Processing in Memory and the Recall and Recognition of Television Commercials," in James H. Leigh and Claude R. Martin, Jr. (eds.), *Current Issues and Research in Advertising, 1980,* The University of Michigan, Ann Arbor, MI, 1980, pp. 135–145; and Joel Saegert, "Comparison of Effects of Repetition and Levels of Processing in Memory for Advertisements," in Andrew Mitchell (ed.), *Advances in Consumer Research: Volume 9,* Association for Consumer Research, Ann Arbor, MI, 1982, pp. 431–434.

[36] See Allan G. Reynolds and Paul W. Flagg, *Cognitive Psychology,* Winthrop Publishers, Cambridge, MA, 1977, pp. 144–147.

[37] Reynolds and Flagg, *Cognitive Psychology,* pp. 139–144, 163–170.

[38] See R. P. Abelson, "Psychological Status of the Script Concept," *American Psychologist,* 36:715–729, 1981.

[39] See Lorne Bozinoff, "A Script Theoretic Approach of Information Processing: An Energy Conservation Application," in Andrew Mitchell (ed.), *Advances in Consumer Research: Volume 9,* Association for Consumer Research, Ann Arbor, MI, 1982, pp. 481–486, for an elaboration and some examples.

[40] Different methods of storing information do not necessarily require different storage registers. Rather, material processed in different ways (visual, verbal, etc.) may just be represented in different ways in long-term memory. See, for example, Zenon W. Pylyshyn, "What the Mind's Eye Tells the Mind's Brain: A Critique of Mental Imagery," *Psychological Bulletin,* 80:1–24, July 1973; and John R. Anderson and Gordon H. Bower, *Human Associative Memory,* Winston, Washington, DC, 1973.

[41] See Allan Paivio, *Imagery and Verbal Processing,* Holt, Rinehart and Winston, New York, 1971.

[42] See, for example, Kathy A. Lutz and Richard J. Lutz, "Imagery-Eliciting Strategies: Review and Implications of Research," in H. Keith Hunt (ed.), *Advances in Consumer Research: Volume 5,* Association for Consumer Research, Ann Arbor, MI, 1978, pp. 611–620; Larry Percy, "Psycholinguistic Guidelines for Advertising Copy," in Andrew Mitchell (ed.), *Advances in Consumer Research: Volume 9,* Association for Consumer Research, Ann Arbor, MI, 1982, pp. 107–111; and Morris B. Holbrook and William L. Moore, "Feature Interactions in Consumer Judgments of Verbal Versus Pictorial Presentations, *Journal of Consumer Research,* 8:103–111, June 1981.

[43] Kathy A. Lutz and Richard J. Lutz, "Effects of Interactive Imagery on Learning: Applications to Advertising," *Journal of Applied Psychology,* 62:493–498, 1977.

[44] See Reynolds and Flagg, *Cognitive Psychology,* pp. 163–170.

[45] Lyle E. Bourne Jr., Roger L. Dominowski, and Elizabeth F. Loftus, *Cognitive Processes,* Prentice-Hall, Englewood Cliffs, NJ, 1979, pp. 10–11.

[46] See Andrew A. Mitchell, "Models of Memory: Implications for Measuring Knowledge Structures," in Andrew A. Mitchell (ed.), *Advances in Consumer Research: Volume 9,* Association for Consumer Research, Ann Arbor, MI, 1982, pp. 45–51.

[47] See Jerry C. Olson, "Inferential Belief Formation in the Cue Utilization Process," in H. Keith Hunt (ed.), *Advances in Consumer Research: Volume 5,* Association for Consumer Research, Ann Arbor, MI, 1978, pp. 706–713; and Philip A. Dover, "Inferential Belief Formation: An Overlooked Concept in Consumer Behavior Research," in Andrew Mitchell (ed.), *Advances in Consumer Research: Volume 9,* Association for Consumer Research, Ann Arbor, MI, 1982, pp. 187–189.

[48] Peter L. Wright, "The Cognitive Processes Mediating Acceptance of Advertising," *Journal of Marketing Research,* 10:53–62, February 1973.

[49] See Gabriel Biehal and Dipanker Chakravarti, "Information-Presentation Format and Learning Goals as Determinants of Consumers' Memory Retrieval and Choice Processes," *Journal of Consumer Research,* 8:431–441, March 1982.

[50] For additional guidelines see Steuart Henderson Britt, "How Advertising Can Use Psychology's Rules of Learning," *Printer's Ink,* 252:74+, September 1955; and Steuart Henderson Britt, "Applying Learning Principles to Marketing," *MSU Business Topics,* 23:5–12, Spring 1975.

[51] James R. Bettman, "Memory Factors in Consumer Choice: A Review," *Journal of Marketing,* 43:37–53, Spring 1979.

[52] See John R. Rossiter, "Visual Imagery: Applications to Advertising," in Andrew Mitchell (ed.), *Advances in Consumer Research: Volume 9,* Association for Consumer Research, Ann Arbor, MI, 1982, pp. 101–106.

[53] See, for example, James T. Heimbach and Jacob Jacoby, "The Zeigarnik Effect in Advertising," in M. Venkatesan (ed.), *Proceedings of the Third Annual Conference,* Association for Consumer Research, College Park, MD, 1972, pp. 746–757.

CHAPTER 15
PERSONALITY AND SELF-CONCEPT

"Did you see the new Mazda sports coupe that Dave just bought? It really fits him and his 'life in the fast lane' to a tee."

"I could have predicted that Mike would throw such a great party. He usually knows what people like, and he goes out of his way to help them get it."

"Jane's promotion comes as no surprise to me. She is career oriented, a hard worker, and gets along well with people. Why, her clothes even seem to say that she is on the way to the top."

These statements, and many more like them, reflect a belief that most people seem to share—the behavior of an individual is organized into a coherent pattern. That is, although a person's behavior changes to deal with many different circumstances, there is a tendency for him or her to behave in a consistent way through these various situations. This view emphasizes the *totality* of a person's makeup rather than specific actions that he or she will take in any particular instance.

Personality and self-concept are two psychological notions that have been used by those studying consumer behavior to account for the organized totality of the consumer's makeup. Our purpose in studying these variables is to determine their usefulness in understanding consumers' basic orientations and their brand and store preferences, media usage patterns, susceptibility to persuasion, and other facets of consumer behavior. The hope is that knowledge of consumers' personalities and self-concepts will allow us to appreciate the underlying consistency or pattern reflected in their product choices and other behavior.

This chapter begins with a fuller characterization of the term personality and a short description of some methods used to measure it. Next, several of the many theories that have been offered to explain the concept are reviewed briefly. One concept that has seen extensive marketing application is then assessed in terms of its usefulness in predicting and understanding consumer behavior. After relating personality theory to psychographics and its consumer-behavior relevance, attention then turns to the topic of consumers' self-concept. Finally, the importance of self-concept to understanding the motivations and behavior of consumers is addressed.

PERSONALITY THEORIES AND APPLICATIONS

The study of personality and its relationship to human behavior can be traced back to the earliest writings of the Europeans, Greeks, Chinese, and Egyptians. Also, people have always made judgments about the personalities of others in terms of the degree to which they are aggressive, adventuresome, sociable, charismatic, and so on. Despite this long history of interest, and even though most of us believe that we have an intuitive grasp of what constitutes personality, behavioral scientists have been unable to agree on a precise definition of the concept. However, it has been noted that there are three major aspects of similarity among the various definitions:

1 They focus on unique characteristics that account for differences between individuals rather than on how people are alike.

2 They stress the consistency of an individual's *dispositions* rather than changes in his or her actual behavior across different situations.

3 Each definition includes a behavioral tendency to reflect how an individual's personality will tend to influence his or her actions and reactions to environmental situations.[1]

Most theories of personality also stress how it is integrative in nature, encompassing various processes that interact with each other. That is, among other factors, personality is usually considered to include the interactions of an individual's moods, values, attitudes, motives, and habitual methods of responding to situations.

Within this general framework, a number of methods for measuring personality have evolved, as have a variety of alternative theories of the exact nature of the concept. We will first look briefly at the general methods of measurement, and then we will provide a short review of several major personality theories.

Measuring Personality

It should be clear from the above discussion that personality is not a concept that has a single characteristic. Instead, it is multidimensional in nature, with many interacting elements. Therefore, measurement methods have to account in some way for this variety, rather than focusing solely on only one aspect of the complex whole. Four general approaches to measurement that have had popularity and can accommodate the multidimensional nature of personality are rating methods, situational tests, projective techniques, and inventory schemes.

Rating Methods Typically, the rating method involves one or more evaluators assessing predetermined personality characteristics of a subject on a number of standardized rating scales. In some cases, the basis of the evaluation is a somewhat informal interview with the subject. In other cases, observation of the subject's behavior is used in place of an interview. This observation may be accomplished in a setting designed for the purpose, or it may take place in a portion of the subject's everyday environment. Of course, the type of scale employed for evaluation (5 point versus 6 point, definitions of each category provided versus no definitions provided, etc.), the personality characteristics chosen for study, and the skills of evaluators can all have an influence on final results.

Situational Tests With this technique, a situation is devised that closely resembles a typical real-life situation. Usually, several people are allowed to interact with each other in a group setting. A topic or scenario is provided to them as a focus of discussion, and the behaviors of the subjects are observed and measured. This may take the form of tabulating the frequency of occurrence for specific activities (aggression, submissiveness, etc.) or rating the intensity of certain behaviors on standard scales. A special form of situation technique is the stress test which places an individual in a pressure-type situation; his methods of acting in the situation are assessed to reveal aspects of his personality.

Projective Techniques The objective behind development of most projective methods is to uncover the basic organization of an individual's personality as well as his underlying conflicts and motives. Typically, the individual is presented with a vague visual image and is asked to explain it or relate any meaning it has to him. The assumption is that because the stimulus itself is vague, the individual is actually projecting his own interpretations onto it, and in the process he reveals aspects of his own personality. One popular type of projective technique is called the *Rorschach test* which consists of ten inkblots similar to the one shown in Figure 15-1, but varying in color, shape, and shading. Another frequently used projective technique is the *Thematic Apperception Test* (TAT) which typically involves presentation of twenty pictures showing different vague situations. The subject is asked to develop a story that is based on each picture. The stories are assessed by a trained evaluator for basic interpretations the individual appears to relate about the pictures and, therefore, about himself.

FIGURE 15-1

Example of a Rorschach-type inkblot.

Inventory Schemes A potential limitation of rating methods, situational tests, and projective techniques is subjective scoring. That is, the measurement of an individual's personality is largely dependent upon the evaluator's subjective interpretation of the information obtained. In addition, these methods require a considerable amount of time and effort to set up, administer, and evaluate. The personality inventory is designed to minimize these potential problems by exposing subjects to a large number of standardized questions with prespecified answer options from which they can select. Usually, the inventory is in written form, and a subject responds to the instrument much in the same way as he would to an "objective" test. For example, one popular inventory, the Minnesota Multiphasic Personality Inventory (MMPI), consists of 550 statements such as "I like to try new things." If the subject feels a statement describes her, she will mark the "true" answer option. "False" and "cannot say" options are also available.

The same personality characteristics are addressed through a variety of different statements contained in such inventories. This minimizes the danger of a subject being able to manipulate the results of her or his testing, and enables one to assess personality aspects from different perspectives. As a consequence, the number of items included in the inventory is much larger than the number of personality dimensions being measured. For example, the MMPI's 550 statements assesses ten personality characteristics.

Scoring of personality inventories is standardized and based on norms which have been established from previous testings of large numbers of individuals. Because of their ease of administration and the availability of standardized scoring, the inventory method has been the most popular approach to personality measurement in the field of consumer behavior. Inventories that have been commonly employed by consumer-behavior researchers include the Edwards Personal Preference Schedule, Gordon Personal Profile, and the California Personality Inventory. We now turn our attention to several of the major concepts of personality that have enjoyed considerable popularity.[2]

Some Major Personality Theories

It certainly is not possible in the scope of this text to review all major concepts of personality. It should also be appreciated that to fully characterize even a few of the major theories would require a great deal of space. Therefore, the following paragraphs are offered as brief "thumb-nail" sketches of only some of the important aspects of several major personality theories.

Psychoanalytic Personality Theory Freud, the father of psychoanalytic theory, proposed that every individual's personality is the product of a struggle among three interacting forces—the id, the ego, and the superego. According to Freud, the *id* is the source of strong inborn drives and urges such as aggression and sex. The id operates on what is called the *pleasure principle;* that is, it acts to avoid tension and seek immediate pleasure. However, it tends to operate at a very subjective and unconscious level and is not fully capable of dealing with objective reality. Also, many of its impulses are not acceptable to the values of organized society. For example, when an individual is hot and thirsty his id would urge him to grab something cold to drink. There would be no concern about how the drink was acquired or whether it belonged to someone else.

The *ego* comes into being because of the limitations of the id in dealing with the real world. Through learning and experience, it develops the individual's capabilities of realistic thinking and ability to deal appropriately with his environment. It operates on what is called the *reality principle,* which is capable of postponing the release of tension until that time when it will be effectively directed at coping with the external environment. To illustrate, although the hungry individual's id would encourage him to just take food away from his friend, the ego might reason that asking for the food may take longer but may also result in getting a greater portion. Because it serves in this way as the organized focal point for effective action in the environment, the ego is said to be the executive of the personality.

The *superego* is the third component of personality. It constitutes the moral part of the individual's psychic structure through internalizing the values of society. It represents the ideal by defining what is right and good, and influences the individual to strive for perfection. Therefore, it acts to control basic strivings of the id which could disrupt the social system, and influences the ego to strive for socially approved goals rather than purely realistic ones. As an example, people often compliment their friends on their taste in selecting new clothes or other products. The ego might influence such behavior, because it is instrumental in maintaining a friendship. However, the superego would also have an influence, because the activity is something that our society has accepted as proper and good behavior. This may be happening while the id is actually fostering feelings of jealousy. However, because these feelings will not be very effective for dealing with the environment, the ego will act to suppress them.

According to Freud, the individual's total personality develops and is defined by the relationships among the id, ego, and superego. The ego serves to administer the interaction between moral standards of the superego and the often socially unacceptable desires and attempted expressions of the id. This usually results in realistic compromises between very basic strivings and accepted behavior. Many of these compromises are said to be accomplished at the unconscious level. In fact, Freudian psychology argues that a vast portion of our behavior is unconsciously motivated or affected by subconscious factors—ones that only occasionally reach the individual's conscious level of awareness. Therefore, to fully understand the causes of behavior and the interactions of personality, one must appreciate what factors are influencing the consumer at unconscious and subconscious levels.

Although the ego is capable of resolving many of the conflicts that arise between the three personality components, on some occasions no resolution is achieved, and the individual is placed under considerable tension. It is usually at this time that defense mechanisms are enacted to deal with the tension. *Defense mechanisms* can be thought of as unconsciously determined techniques for avoiding or escaping from high levels of tension brought about by unresolved conflict between components of the personality.

Many defense mechanisms have been characterized, but only a few will be described here to give an impression of their general nature. One very basic form is called *repression.* Basically this mechanism allows the individual to forget aspects of the conflicting situation so that the conflict is no longer apparent. For example, a consumer might be in conflict about going to sporting events that are violent but also entertaining. If the ego cannot reach some sort of compromise, it is possible that the consumer may diminish and forget the violent aspects of these sports. In this way, he has avoided the conflict and can continue to watch the events.

Projection is the term used to describe the defense mechanism, in which feelings generated by the individual's id or superego are ascribed by her to another person or group. In this way, she escapes the tension generated from realizing that the feelings are her own. For example, a person's disdain for how others are constantly purchasing various products and displaying them for others to see may actually be a mask for her own desire to engage in the same behavior.

In *identification,* the individual unconsciously imitates the behavior of another person whom he believes has successfully handled the conflict with which he is currently dealing. And finally, the last defense mechanism to be mentioned here is *reaction formation,* in which unconscious feelings held toward others are consciously expressed as opposites. For example, a consumer with hostile feelings toward a friend might actually purchase many gifts for this person.

APPLICATIONS OF PSYCHOANALYTIC THEORY Marketers have sometimes used Freudian psychoanalytic theory as a basis for attempts at influencing consumers. One such application is the appeal to fantasy, which plays an important role in the operation of the pleasure principle of the id. Fantasy has been used in promotions for perfume (Chanel No. 5), home video games (Coleco), men's cologne (Old Spice), and jeans (Levi's). In addition, Maidenform has employed a series of fantasy advertisements in which women are shown in various interesting situations and roles dressed in a Maidenform bra and very little else.

In another area of application, Freudian proponents suggest that various appeals can assist in resolving the conflict which can develop between the id, ego, and superego in some purchase situations. Appeals directed to the id, but disguised by a veiled appeal to the superego, are said to result in a situation that can be satisfactorily resolved by the ego. In this way, the ego directs behavior that is also acceptable to the id and superego. The idea has been translated into advertising themes such as those found in early Miss Clairol hair color commercials. Here, advertisements show a lovely woman with the announcer asking, "Does she or doesn't she?"—a clearly sexual theme appealing to the id. The camera next focuses in on the woman's left hand which is obviously bearing a wedding band. This is said to satisfy the moral concerns that would be raised by the superego. The ego then reasons that sex is socially acceptable behavior under conditions of marriage, and therefore the sexual innuendo of the ad is acceptable. In advertising, this approach is sometimes referred to as the *triple appeal,* because the id is sexually stimulated and allowed to engage in fantasy while the moral requirements of the superego are placated. The ego arbitrates the acceptability of these two forms of expression among both the id and superego. A similar situation occurs in more recent ads for the Playtex Free Spirit bra. Here, a young woman, shown above the waist wearing only a bra, is pictured in the intimate company of a young man. However, rings that appear to be wedding bands are prominently displayed on the left hand of both models to satisfy moral concerns of the superego.

Marketers have made many other uses of sexual and aggressive symbols that appeal to the id while avoiding those that are directly offensive to the superego. For example, many people have argued that the shape of containers for various personal-care products (e.g., Macho cologne for men) are clearly phallic. Also, the bottles for Jóvan men's and women's cologne have quite discernible male and female shapes.

Although most people believe that Freudian applications to marketing are restricted to sex, we have already shown that there are many themes which are not. Wish fulfillment, fantasy, aggression, and escape from life's pressures are Freudian themes upon which some appeals are based. For example, a suburban real estate company might advertise to city dwellers with the theme, "Escape to country living." Also, sporting events are often promoted by showing aggression or violent scenes. Previews for racing events and boxing matches as well as the "agony of defeat" befalling a ski jumper in the introduction to *The Wide World of Sports* are excellent illustrations. In other cases, promotions for Bermuda, Las Vegas, the Bahamas, and other vacation resorts frequently employ themes stressing escape, freedom, and a chance to "let it all hang out." Figure 15-2 presents yet another example of a fantasy appeal.

Finally, an understanding of the operation of defense mechanisms can assist the marketer in developing marketing and promotional strategies. For example, knowledge that a group of consumers have repressed aspects of a conflicting situation would alert the marketer that such topics should probably not be addressed in a promotional message. Because the topics have been repressed, consumers

FIGURE 15-2

Example of a fantasy appeal. (Courtesy of the Mercury Outboard Division of the Brunswick Company.)

would not be aware of the issues. Consequently, a promotion raising such issues would have little meaning to these consumers. In a similar vein, knowing that a group of consumers have employed the defense mechanism of identification can also be of considerable potential benefit. For example, many men and women experience conflict arising from hostile feelings they hold toward their spouses, for whom they believe they should have strong affection. A well-known celebrity who has had marital problems and has publicly reconciled with his or her spouse could therefore be a source of strong identification for these people. Use of such a person to promote and endorse various products could be even more effective than the use of other spokespeople.

Social Theories Even though they were not in total agreement on an alternative, Alfred Adler, Erich Fromm, Karen Horney, and Harry Stack Sullivan were among the first to reject Freud's id-based theory of personality. Instead, they reasoned that the individual develops a personality through numerous attempts to deal with others in a social setting. These social theorists, sometimes collectively called the neo-Freudian school, view individuals as striving to overcome feelings of inferiority, and searching for ways to obtain love, security, and brotherhood. Their argument minimized the role of id-based instincts that Freud emphasized. Instead, they stressed that childhood experiences in relating to others produce feelings of inferiority, insecurity, and lack of love. These feelings motivate individuals to perfect themselves and also to develop methods to cope with anxieties produced by such feelings of inferiority.

The first major consumer-behavior study using a neo-Freudian approach was conducted by Cohen, and it was based on the theoretical scheme of Karen Horney.[3] Horney identified ten major needs which are acquired as a consequence of individuals attempting to find solutions to their problems in developing a personality and dealing with others in a social environment. These ten needs were then classified into three major orientations which describe general strategies for relating to others:

1 Compliant Orientation—those who move toward people and stress the need for love, approval, and affection. These individuals tend to exhibit large amounts of empathy and humility, and are unselfish.

2 Aggressive Orientation—those who move against people and stress the need for power, strength, and the ability to manipulate others.

3 Detached Orientation—those who move away from people. These individuals stress the need for independence, freedom, and self reliance in their dealings with others. An important consideration is that no strong emotional ties develop between themselves and others.

Cohen developed a CAD (Compliant, Aggressive, Detached) instrument to measure people's interpersonal orientations within a consumer context. Results of the study indicated that different products and brands were used by individuals having different personality types. For example, Cohen found that "compliant" types prefer known brand names and use more mouthwash and toilet soaps; "aggressive" types prefer to use razors instead of electric shavers, use more cologne and after-shave lotions, and purchase Old Spice and Van Heusen shirts;

and "detached" types appear to have the least awareness of brands. Although such findings are interesting, social personality theories have found little application in the consumer-behavior area. Additional research is necessary to generate a wider base of findings from which to develop marketing strategies.

Stimulus-Response Theories Stimulus-response theories of personality are grounded on contributions from notable learning theorists such as Pavlov, Skinner, and Hull. Although there are differences among these theorists there is agreement that personality results from habitual responses to specific and generalized cues. Theorists believe that complex behavior patterns, attitudes, and so on, are learned from stimulus-response situations that are continually reinforced, either positively or negatively. The personality, therefore, is created and changed by reinforcement of these stimulus-response associations. However, because of the lack of measuring instruments to study these propositions critically, few if any consumer-behavior studies have been conducted relating stimulus-response concepts of personality to purchase behavior.

Trait and Factor Theories The most popular personality concepts used to explain the behavior of consumers have been trait and factor theories. The concept of a *trait* is based upon three assumptions or propositions: (1) individuals possess relatively stable behavioral tendencies, (2) people differ in the degree to which they possess these tendencies, and (3) when identified and measured, these relative differences between individuals are useful in characterizing their personalities. Therefore, we see that traits are general and are relatively stable personality characteristics which influence tendencies to behave.

Factor theories are based on the quantitative technique of *factor analysis* which explores the interrelationship between various personality measures across a large number of individuals. Basically, the underlying logic is that if responses to certain personality-inventory items are correlated across many different testing situations, then these responses are probably each related to some underlying personality characteristic or trait. If the measures are highly correlated with each other, they probably tend to measure the same dimension of the trait, and if their correlation is lower, they probably reflect somewhat different aspects of the same trait. Therefore, a factor can be viewed as a general-level variable that is based on a combination of test items and is used to identify personality traits.

Various traits or factors are identified when subgroups of measures form. That is, factors emerge when certain measures show higher levels of correlation within themselves but quite low degrees of correlation across other subgroups of items. The task of the researcher is to use factor analysis to assist in identifying these interrelated groups of variables. The actual number of factors that will be identified depends on how well the variables in various subgroups correlate among themselves. Once factors are identified, each one can be quantified with a factor score—a weighted combination of the measures that have correlated together to identify the factor.

A second task is to label or describe the factors that have been identified. This is accomplished by interpreting the factor loadings—correlations between the original measures and the factor score that is based on these measures. For example, consider a factor score that had strong loadings (correlations) with the personality measures of despondency, moodiness, and pessimism. The researcher might use this information to label the factor as "depression." It is important to note that even though the naming of factors is guided by reference to the factor loadings, a considerable amount of subjective interpretation is still involved in this process.

After doing years of careful research, some theorists have proposed that most personalities can actually be described by a small number of factors. In essence, this view is that factor analysis of the results of many test situations has identified core personality traits.[4] Therefore, results of an individual's testing using a personality inventory enables the researcher to compare the individual's raw score and factor scores to the results of other subjects. This assists in the interpretation of the individual's personality.

APPLICATIONS OF TRAIT AND FACTOR THEORIES   In terms of their use in studying consumers, the advantage of trait and factor theories is that they are based on a number of readily available and standardized personality inventories and evaluative techniques. Using these techniques, a large number of researchers have tried to find a relationship between personality and the behavior of consumers. These attempts have met with various degrees of success. Several representative studies are reviewed below to give the reader some appreciation of the nature of research in this area.

Koponen, using the Edwards Personal Preference Schedule (EPPS), collected data from almost 9000 consumer panel participants.[5] His results indicate a positive relationship between cigarette smoking and the traits of sex dominance, aggression, and achievement needs among males. He also found personality differences among smokers of filter and nonfilter cigarettes, and between readers' preferences for certain magazines. However, in a later reanalysis of Koponen's data, Brody and Cunningham found that personality traits accounted for only a small number of the differences among these groups.[6]

Another study using the Gordon Personal Profile found associations between certain personality traits and use of alcoholic beverages, automobiles, chewing gum, mouthwash, and other products.[7] Unfortunately, in this as in many other studies, the associations were not very strong.

In what has now become a classic study, Evans employed the EPPS to determine if personality differences could be found between Ford and Chevrolet owners. His findings were that measurable personality differences were of little value in predicting whether a consumer would own a Ford or a Chevrolet.[8] Many studies have reexamined this research, and the basic conclusion appears to be that personality traits are not very helpful in predicting consumers' brand choice for automobiles. However, some evidence indicates that they may be useful in predicting preferences for the type of automobile (sedan versus convertible, for instance).[9]

Other more recent studies have attempted to relate personality differences to innovativeness and to other consumer characteristics. As in previous cases, these studies have met with varying degrees of success.[10]

After reviewing more than 200 personality studies that have been conducted in consumer research, Kassarjian concluded that the results can be described by a single word, "equivocal."[11] Although a few studies indicate a strong relationship between personality and aspects of consumer behavior, some studies indicate no relationship, and the vast majority of studies suggest that if a relationship does exist, it is so weak that it is of little practical value to the marketer. Yet, experts still contend that personality is a critical variable in influencing consumers' purchasing processes. They argue that the lackluster performance of previous studies is due to inappropriate research methods and an inadequate understanding of the role of personality in influencing consumers. Some of these criticisms are reviewed below to provide guidelines for evaluating future personality studies:

1 Personality tests have frequently been inappropriately employed in consumer studies. Often, a standard test designed by psychologists to detect general personality traits, or to use in clinical studies for understanding abnormal behavior, is used to predict consumers' product or brand purchases. Because the test was not designed for such predictions, it is not surprising to find a low success rate in this type of use. Future efforts should employ tests that are designed for the specific needs of a consumer investigation.[12]

2 Personality tests have not always been carefully administered when used in consumer studies. Also, in a number of consumer investigations, standardized inventories have been arbitrarily shortened or modified.[13] Because such changes can seriously alter the validity and usefulness of a test, future modifications should be validated prior to their actual use.[14]

3 Many studies have searched for a relationship between personality and specific aspects of consumer behavior (brand choice, brand loyalty over time, amount of product use, etc.). In many cases, the analysis was performed without much prior thought regarding why or how one should expect personality to relate to such behavior.[15] In fact, as mentioned earlier, personality usually interacts with a variety of other variables to influence general tendencies to behave. Specific actions will be strongly affected by the particular consumer situation as well as this general influence.[16] Therefore, it is more likely that personality would show stronger relationships with broad strategies and procedures that people adopt to deal with various consumer situations. Recent studies investigating such relationships between personality and general patterns of information acquisition and brand choice have tended to support these expectations.[17]

4 A sizeable number of consumer studies have focused on specific personality traits (tolerance for ambiguity, rigidity, self-actualization, need for affiliation, etc.) and their relationship to certain types of behavior. This has led some to lose sight of the importance of the whole personality for understanding consumer behavior. It must be remembered that each trait is only a partial component of the entire personality. Therefore, because traits can interact to result in a personality that is different from the sum of its parts, individuals are best understood through appreciation of the entire personality structure. Future investigations should be more strongly influenced by this perspective.[18]

One review of the status of personality investigations concludes that because of the above limitations, it is actually surprising that many previous studies were able to find *any* relationship between personality and consumer behavior.[19] Future research must be more carefully designed and must employ more relevant tests of consumers' personalities. One development in this regard is the use of the personality concept as part of a larger research "package" to understand consumers. This reorientation has resulted in the psychographic profiling of consumers.

PSYCHOGRAPHICS

Some studies demonstrating the nature and use of psychographics for understanding consumers were reviewed in Chapter 5. Major areas of application included segmentation research, developing profiles of target markets, exploring the potential for new products, and devising promotional strategies. A return to Chapter 5 at this point to briefly review the methods and applications of psychographics is recommended.

The reader may have noticed a strong resemblance between the nature and form of psychographic test items and those used in personality inventories. Review of the material in Chapter 5 may also have revealed that some psychographic items appear to address aspects of consumer motivation. Actually, these resemblances are not the result of coincidence. In fact, the field of psychographics is said to have originated from a merger of the areas of personality assessment and motivation research.[20] The merger yielded potential benefits in overcoming two limitations that had been noted about personality inventories and motivation research: (1) psychographics promise to be less abstract and more directly related to consumer situations than standardized personality testing, and (2) psychographic tests allow more efficient and apparently objective measurement of consumers' desires than the long interview methods of motivation research. Also, psychographics yields quantitative results which can be easily submitted to statistical analysis. This is not true of the long narratives produced by motivational research interviews.

A variety of applications for psychographics were also mentioned in Chapter 5. Notable among these were the uses in developing advertising strategy and copy. For example, Tigert has demonstrated that, based on extensive research, psychographic profiles of media users can be more important to advertisers' selection of media than can traditionally used demographic variables. He successfully argues that lifestyles of product and brand users cut across demographic and socioeconomic segments. Media selection should therefore be based upon the appeal directed toward the selected target audience and its lifestyle.[21]

Psychographic studies have also benefited other consumer-related decisions including the design of marketing channels. Getting the goods and services consumers want to the best place for a profit is a goal of distribution systems. However, with changing lifestyles affecting channels of distribution, psychographics can provide useful data for channel designs. For example, because women are increasingly desirous of employment, they have less free time for shopping, and they therefore demand more convenience in their purchase activity. It has been suggested that many purchase decisions will become more routine for reasons of efficiency. Therefore, strong advertising programs designed to build a brand's reputation can assist in moving certain sales transactions away from stores and toward more automatic order systems that can be used in the home.[22]

Psychographic data also has been shown to be useful to industrial designers in creating product designs to satisfy consumer wants. For instance, one study involving industrial design compared the usefulness of demographics versus psychographic data to the styling of a clock radio. A class of industrial design students was given a paragraph describing either the demographic characteristics or the psychographic characteristics of a given market and asked to create the radio's design based solely on the paragraph of information given them. Interviewers returned to the subjects from whom they had originally obtained the demographic and psychographic data and asked them to state their preferences for each of the radio designs. They found that the radios designed from psychographic data were preferred to those designed from demographic data.[23]

As these and the previous examples in Chapter 5 illustrate, psychographic information can be useful in a variety of ways, including market segmentation, creation of advertising strategy and copy, media selection, and product design.

PERSONALITY AND MARKETING: A SUMMARY

Personality research in general, and those studies related to consumer behavior in particular, have evolved through various stages and in several directions. The application of personality measurements to studying consumer behavior has produced many contradictory findings and often disappointing relationships. Ironically, of all the personality concepts available, the one that has probably enjoyed the greatest popularity and use among business practitioners is psychoanalytic theory, especially as used in one of the most highly subjective and least scientific areas—motivation research.

Of the remaining personality viewpoints, trait theory has been used in research on consumers more than has any other concept. As noted previously, however, its ability to predict or explain consumer behavior has often met with lackluster success. Some new and promising directions regarding the use of personality in understanding general consumer strategies or behavior patterns were mentioned. In addition, personality concepts have made significant contributions to the area of psychographics. Instead of being used alone, personality traits are combined with information on activities interests, opinions, demographics, and other measures to *profile,* not predict, consumers and their behavior.[24] Therefore, psychographics has emerged in the last decade as an approach to developing composite "pictures" of consumer types and to "humanizing" the data that are collected from consumers. In the next section we look at another theory which takes a total view of consumers and attempts to relate it to their behavior.

SELF-CONCEPT

Self-concept (or self-image) has become a popular approach in recent years to investigating possible relationships between how individuals perceive themselves and what behavior they exhibit as consumers. An advantage of studying consumer behavior using the theory of self-concept is that consumers provide descriptions of themselves, as opposed to having descriptions made by outside observers. That is, each consumer describes his or her own view of himself or herself, which is in contrast to personality tests that fit consumer responses into predetermined categories or traits. This distinction is important, because the way in which a consumer perceives himself or herself might differ substantially from the way in which the researcher sees or categorizes that same consumer.

As defined by Newcombe, *self-concept* is "the individual as perceived by that individual in a socially determined frame of reference."[25] More simply, the self-concept may be thought of as the person's perception of himself. This self-perception is not confined just to the physical being, but includes such characteristics as strength, honesty, good-humor, sophistication, justice, guilt, and others.[26] In short, it refers to the totality of an individual's thoughts and feelings about himself.[27]

Although the self-concept is highly complex, it is well-organized and works in a consistent way. To the outside observer, a person may appear irrational and inconsistent in her behavior, but the individual taking such action is behaving in the only way she knows, given her frame of reference. When this individual's point of view is known, it usually becomes clear that she is not acting in an inconsistent way. For example, we may think a consumer is irrational to patronize a store that charges higher prices than does its competition for identical products. However, the consumer may show this loyalty because of the good service or because the salespeople make her feel important. Therefore, when viewed through her eyes, the slightly higher cost for her store loyalty may be well worth the money.

How the Self-Concept Develops

Behaviorists have formed various theories of how people develop their self-concepts. Social interaction provides the basis for most of these theories. Four particular views of self-concept development are presented below.

Self-Appraisal Some theorists believe that a person fashions a self-concept by labeling his own dominant behavior patterns according to what is socially acceptable and unacceptable behavior. For example, certain behaviors are classified as "social," and others are labeled as "antisocial." By observing his own behavior, a person might begin to develop an awareness that his behavior falls into the general category "antisocial." With repeated confirmation of this label, a portion of the person's self-concept emerges, playing a dominant role in how he views himself.

Reflected Appraisal A second theory of self-concept development is termed reflected appraisal or the "looking-glass self." Basically, this theory holds that appraisals a person receives from others mold self-concept. The extent of this influence depends upon characteristics of the appraiser and his or her appraisal. Specifically, greater impact on the development of a person's self-concept is said to occur when (1) the appraiser is perceived as a highly credible source, (2) the appraiser takes a very personal interest in the person being appraised, (3) the appraisal is very discrepant with the person's self-concept at the moment, (4) the number of confirmations of a given appraisal is high, (5) the appraisals coming from a variety of sources are consistent, and (6) appraisals are supportive of the person's own beliefs about himself or herself. Appraisals from "significant others" such as parents, close friends, trusted colleagues, and other persons the individual strongly admires influence self-concept development.

Social Comparison The reflected appraisal theory gives a rather depressing picture of self-concept development, because it emphasizes that people are passive and merely reflect the appraisals of others. The social comparison theory, however, states that people's self-concepts depend on how they see themselves in relation to others. Thorstein Veblen, the major proponent of this theory, was curious as to why people so strongly desired to acquire more goods and services than were necessary to meet their physical needs. The absolute amount of products, property, and services was not as important, he felt, as the *relative* amount accumulated; that is, in comparison with others. "The end sought by accumulation is to rank high in comparison with the rest of the community.... So long as the comparison is distinctly unfavorable to himself, the normal, average individual will live in chronic dissatisfaction."[28]

This theory has much more direct bearing upon the development of marketing strategies than have the theories discussed so far. In particular, this view of how people perceive themselves is dependent upon their perception of their relative status as compared to social class, reference groups, and other groups important to them. By determining which groups a person compares himself or herself to in the consumption of products and services, marketers can develop messages that communicate the group referent's use of particular products and brands. Purchases would then be seen by the person as a means to increase relative position in the group.

Festinger improved upon the social comparison theory by arguing that people need to affirm continuously that their beliefs and attitudes are correct and that they compare their beliefs and attitudes with others to determine the validity of their own.[29] If, for example, a person is asked whether she is conservative, romantic, or sociable, the answer will depend to a large extent on how the person perceives himself in comparison with others.

Biased Scanning The last theory we shall discuss is concerned with motivation and biased scanning. In essence, this theory views self-concept development in terms of identity aspirations and biased scanning of the environment for information to confirm how well the person is meeting his or her aspirations. It suggests that a person who aspires (is motivated) to be a good lawyer, for example, will seek out information that helps to confirm this aspiration and filter out information that contradicts it. Thus, perceptual scanning is biased toward seeing ourselves as we would like to be (that is, it is biased toward self-gratification).

As we can see, these theories of self-concept development take somewhat different views of how people see themselves. In reality, probably all of the theories are working to some extent. Our self-concepts are very likely shaped to varying degrees according to how we perceive ourselves relative to others, our levels of aspirations and biased selection of information about ourselves, the labeling of ourselves according to how we perceive society categorizes us, and the reflected appraisals of significant others.[30]

Consistency of the Self

Although theories vary on the development of a self-concept, psychologists agree that a person's conception of self displays a high degree of consistency, particularly in the short run. This relatively fixed structure of self is due to two conditions. First, as with many systems, self has an inertial tendency, that is, it tends to resist change. Second, after the self has become established, change becomes less likely because of selective perception of environmental information. That is, the self tends to interpret concepts in terms of the self.[31] Thus, ideas formed from a new experience are easily absorbed into the existing organization of self when the experience is perceived as consistent with the existing structure. In contrast, ideas perceived as inconsistent with the present structure are either rejected or altered to fit into the self, since they pose a threat to the individual. As Lecky states, there is a continuous "compulsion to unify and harmonize the system of ideas by which we live."[32]

Self-Concept and Consumer Behavior

Consumers' self-perceptions can have a strong influence on their behavior in the marketplace. For example, the way an individual perceives various products could be affected by the image he has of himself. In fact, preferences might actually develop for certain brands because the consumer perceives them as reflecting his own self-image. Certain other brands may be desired because the consumer views them as projecting an image that he presently does not possess but aspires to have. Because of these and other possible influences, consumer researchers and marketers have developed a strong interest in self-concept theory. The following sections address some main concerns of those who have studied self-concept and its influence on consumer behavior.

Alternative Views of the Self Up to this point, self-concept has been discussed as if total agreement existed regarding its exact nature. Actually, as implied in our discussion of self-development, this is not the case. Especially in the field of consumer behavior, a wide variety of philosophies regarding the self have emerged. These viewpoints can be generally divided into two groups: single- and multiple-component theories.[33] Those using a single-component perspective have focused on the *actual self*—the perception of oneself as one believes she actually is.[34]

Other researchers subscribe to multiple-component perspectives which argue that a full understanding of the self is best obtained by using schemes that account for two or more components or dimensions. The simplest multiple-component model proposes that the self is two-dimensional, having an ideal as well as an actual component. The *ideal self* may be defined as the perception of oneself as one would ideally like to be.[35] Other multiple-component advocates have suggested additional aspects which would extend views of the self into three or more dimensions. Among several viewpoints, these newer perspectives include the *social self*—the perception of oneself as one believes others actually perceive him to be; the *ideal social self*—the perception of one's image as he would like others to have of him; and the *expressive self*—the ideal self or the social self, depending on situational and social factors.[36] Figure 15-3 graphically portrays these components of the self.

While this wide variety of perspectives on self-concept has led to a degree of confusion in the field, some researchers have recently argued that the various definitions should be viewed as complements to each other rather than as competing viewpoints to choose among. One recent argument along this line is that the self has a variety of dimensions (actual, ideal, social, etc.), and the consumer's goals, as well as the situation she confronts at any particular time, will determine which aspect of the self will influence her behavior.[37] For example, the ideal self may be the predominant influence on an individual when she is purchasing sweaters, while the actual self may exert a strong influence when she is purchasing an automobile.

Major Areas of Investigation In a comprehensive review of the self-concept area, Sirgy identified five major types of research investigations relating consumer behavior to self-concept:

1   Attempts to determine if specific types of self-concepts are related to socioeconomic or psychological factors such as social stratification and personality type.

2   Studies of whether the behavior of consumers is related to the degree of congruity between their self-concepts and their perception of product and brand images.

FIGURE 15-3

Various viewpoints of self-concept.

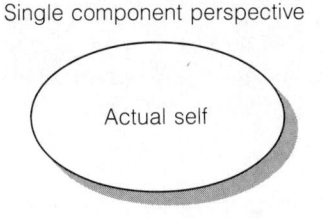

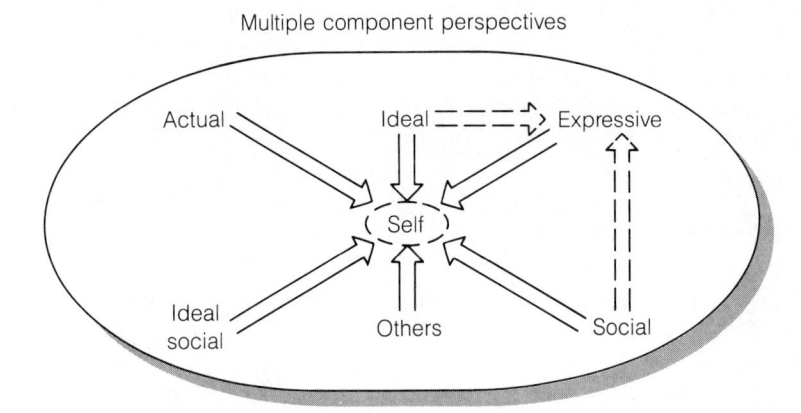

Single component perspective

Actual self

Multiple component perspectives

Actual — Ideal ╌╌> Expressive
Ideal social — Others — Social
→ Self ←

3 Investigations of the degree to which consumers' behavior is consistent with their perceptions of themselves (e.g., do consumers who perceive themselves as innovative tend to act as innovators in their purchasing patterns?).

4 Studies relating to the possibility that consumers attribute their self-images to products that have similar images, or to products that they regularly purchase—"I purchase this product, so it must be like me."

5 Research focused on whether product images that are consistent with the consumer's self-concept influence his self-perceptions—"this product resembles me in a number of ways, so I probably am like it in many other ways."

These five areas of investigation have generated a wide variety of interesting and informative findings which are reviewed by Sirgy.[38] Although a comprehensive treatment of each area is beyond the scope of this chapter, we turn our attention to one major focus of investigation as described in item two above—how the behavior of consumers is related to the degree of congruity between their self-concepts and their perception of products and brands.

Consumer Behavior and Self-Concept/Product Image Congruence As we have noted in previous chapters, consumers appear to hold images of various products, and these images can be viewed as symbols that communicate meaning about those who purchase them. Therefore, an area of considerable practical interest is the degree to which a consumer might actually prefer certain products or brands because she perceives their images as consistent with her view of herself, what she would like to be, or some other aspect of self-concept. An explanation of this behavior, proposed by Grubb and Grathwohl,[39] and modified by others, can be summarized as follows:

1. Consumers form their self-concepts through psychological development and social interaction. Because the individual's self-concept has value to him, he will act to define, protect, and further it.

2. Products and brands are perceived by consumers as having images or symbolic meaning.

3. Because of their symbolic role, selective possession, display, and use of these good-symbols assist an individual in defining and enhancing his self-concept for himself and for others.

4. Therefore, the behavior of individuals will be motivated toward furthering and enhancing their self-concept through the consumption of goods as symbols.

5. The brands that will be preferred are those that the consumer perceives as having images which are most consistent with his self-concept.

Figure 15-4 shows this process whereby the consumer's preferred brands are identified through a matching between her self-image and her perception of various brand images. Congruity theory proposes that the greater the brand/self-image congruence, the more a brand will be preferred. It should again be noted that congruity can exist along a number of self-concept dimensions. For example, the consumer may not perceive a strong match between the brand's image and her actual self-concept, but she may perceive a close match with her ideal self. The theory would still predict that the consumer can have a strong preference for this brand because of the degree of congruity existing between the brand image and

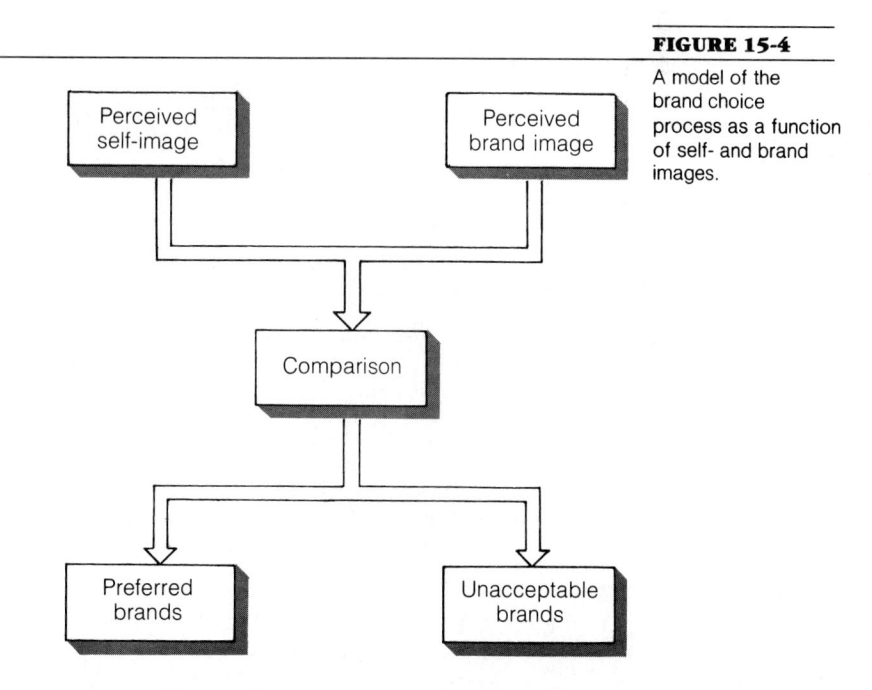

FIGURE 15-4

A model of the brand choice process as a function of self- and brand images.

what she aspires to become. This appears to be a motivating force behind the design of advertisements such as the one shown in Figure 15-5. Here, we see that the brand is effectively linked to a handsome model whom many males might aspire to look like.

MEASUREMENT ISSUES   It is not difficult to envision that if self-concept theory has validity it could be very useful in such areas as product design, positioning of product images, and predicting consumers' behavior toward various brands. To achieve its potential, however, adequate measures of the relevant variables are required. As one might suspect, various measurement methods have been developed. In the following discussion of measurement, we will continue to focus on the issue of congruity between self-concept and perceived product images.

One rather direct approach to measuring the degree of congruity between consumers' self-concepts and their perception of product images employs Q-sort methods. Here the consumer is asked to sort various brands into a number of categories with labels describing the degree of correspondence with an aspect of the self. Categories ranging from "most like me" to "least like me," or from "most like what I would like to be" to "least like what I would like to be," are two alternatives for determining the degree of congruity with the actual or ideal self, respectively. A potential limitation of this method is that it assumes consumers are highly con-

FIGURE 15-5

Example of advertisement useful in appealing to ideal self-image. (Courtesy of the Arrow Company.)

scious of their self-images and the images they hold of various brands. This may not always be the case. In addition, although the method provides measures of congruity, it may not reveal much information about what consumers actually perceive their self-concepts to be. Therefore, it provides little guidance to the marketer interested in developing strategies that appeal to consumers' self-images.

Another popular strategy that overcomes some of the above problems is the use of the same measurement technique for assessing consumers' self-concepts as well as their perception of various brand images. A frequently chosen technique is the semantic differential that was first described in Chapter 3. Recall that the semantic differential typically consists of seven-point scales, with bipolar adjectives or antonym phrases (happy-sad, reserved-outgoing, etc.) labeling the two scale endpoints. To employ this technique, the researcher must first identify the most important personality/image attributes to measure and then develop semantic scales for these attributes. Consumers are next asked to reveal the dimension of their self-concept under investigation (real, ideal, etc.) by marking the scales in order to most appropriately describe themselves. A second set of scales are used to measure the same consumers' perceptions of brand images. If numbers are assigned to each response option on the semantic scales, it is then possible to determine the numerical distance between consumers' self-perceptions and their brand images. This numerical distance is used to represent the degree of congruence that exists for each brand.

To use a specific example, assume the goal is to measure the degree of congruence between womens' actual self-concepts and three different brands of perfume. Assume further that five personality/image components are thought to influence perfume purchases, and seven-point semantic scales are developed for each component. Numbers 1 through 7 are then assigned to the reponse options. Each consumer in the study would next indicate on the scales her image of each brand and her own self-image.

Adjectives used to describe scale endpoints, and one woman's numerical evaluation of herself and three brands, are shown in Table 15-1. One method of determining "how close" the woman perceives each brand image to her own self-image is the general distance formula found in solid geometry.[40] Here, it is referred to as the D measure and is represented as

$$D_{Kj} = \sqrt{\sum_{i=1}^{n}(S_{ij} - P_{ij})^2}$$

where D_{Kj} = the overall linear discrepancy between the jth consumer's self-image and her perception of the image of the Kth brand.

i = the specific image components used to assess both brand and self-image.

S_{ij} = the jth consumer's self-perception on the ith image component.

P_{ij} = the jth consumer's brand perception on the ith image component.

TABLE 15-1

A WOMAN'S NUMERICAL RATINGS FOR SELF-IMAGE AND THREE BRANDS OF PERFUME

	Concepts			
Scales	Self-Image	Brand A	Brand B	Brand C
Sexy-reserved	2	7	1	3
Unadorned-sophisticated	1	2	2	6
Innocent-flirty	6	1	7	4
Sensitive-insensitive	2	4	1	3
Daring-cautious	2	6	1	4

The various D measures can be calculated to represent the degree of congruity between a consumer's self-image and her image of each brand. For example, calculations for the distance between self-image and the image of Brand B for the woman described in Table 15-1 would be:

$$D_{Bj} = \sqrt{(2-1)^2 + (1-2)^2 + (6-7)^2 + (2-1)^2 + (2-1)^2}$$

$$D_{Bj} = \sqrt{1+1+1+1+1}$$

$$D_{Bj} = \sqrt{5}$$

$$D_{Bj} = 2.2$$

Similar calculations for the discrepancy between self-image and the image of Brands A and C would yield measures of $D_{Aj} = 8.4$ and $D_{Cj} = 5.9$ respectively. Our prediction would then be that the woman would prefer Brand B, because her image of it best matches (has lowest discrepancy with) her own self-image. Developing these D measures across many consumers could enable prediction of general market behavior.

RESEARCH EVIDENCE   More than thirty research efforts have examined the possible relationship between brand/self-image congruity and various aspects of consumer behavior. Sirgy has conducted an excellent review of the majority of these studies.[41] Although the research has produced a number of inconsistencies and areas of confusion, several generalizations can still be made:

1 Many findings support the argument that consumers prefer, intend to purchase, or actually use brands with images they see as being congruent with their actual self-concept. To illustrate, in one of the earliest studies, Birdwell found that a sample of car owners had self-perceptions more closely matching their image of their own car than that of eight other brands.[42]

2 A number of studies have also found that consumers are more likely to prefer, intend to purchase, or use brands with images that they see as being congruent with their ideal self-concept.

3 The relationship between consumers' brand/social self-image congruity and their brand preferences, purchase intentions, or loyalties has not been strongly supported by research evidence. However, the relationship with brand/ideal social self-image congruity has been moderately supported.

4 A moderate amount of evidence also supports the argument that consumers perceiving themselves as feminine (or masculine) more frequently use products that they perceive as having feminine (or masculine) images.

5 Whether or not a product is conspicuous (i.e., displayed or consumed in social settings) has not been found to generally influence the relationship between brand/self-image congruence and brand preference or choice. However, some research has suggested that product conspicuousness may influence the brand preferences of upper social classes.

6 Some evidence suggests that several other variables may affect the relationship between brand/self-image congruence and various aspects of consumers' behavior toward brands. Included are the type of decision (routine versus nonroutine), personality type, and the degree to which a product has an image that is strongly stereotyped with a particular type of user—as Calvin Klein jeans, Brut cologne, or Mercedes Benz automobiles might be.

Marketing Applications It has been noted that several limitations of the self-concept notion can impede its usefulness in marketing applications. In addition to problems of measurement common to many concepts, there is also lack of a clear-cut agreement on what is specifically meant by the "self." Different interpretations of the concept can create uncertainty regarding its use in understanding consumers. Further, the self-image concept stresses consumers' self-awareness at the conscious level and tends to minimize the importance of subconscious or unconscious levels of influence. As we have noted in Chapter 12 and earlier in this chapter, such deeper mainsprings of behavior can have an important influence on consumers' behavior.

In spite of these potential limitations, self-image is a powerful concept which has many implications and applications in the field of consumer behavior. The concept has been used in market segmentation, advertising, packaging, personal selling, product development, and retailing.

Some people have suggested that companies can segment markets into more homogeneous sets of self-image profiles. These self-descriptions could then serve as "blueprints" useful to marketers in designing total marketing programs. It is argued that decisions based on markets segmented by consumer self-images operationalize the marketing concept by viewing the consumer from the consumer's point of view.[43]

The self-image concept is quite heavily used in a variety of aspects of promotion. This is clearly demonstrated in the area of clothing. For example, certain types of men's suits are shown being worn by distinguished, conservative-looking models, often with a touch of gray in their hair. Such suits are usually seen on bankers and businessmen who have achieved considerable success. Other suits, frequently those with continental styling, are shown being worn by younger men with longer hair, who appear much more contemporary. The setting for these advertisements frequently involves active, informal social settings where the model often is shown without a tie. Salespeople will often emphasize such self-image messages by telling customers they know that items are either consistent or not consistent with their self-images ("that suit is just not you").

In another promotional area, notice the differences between advertisements showing women using Dial and Camay bath soaps. Women using Dial are depicted as having very active days with a great deal of excitement and exercise. They are shown using Dial in invigorating, refreshing showers, and they generally seem to live life with gusto. Conversely, women who use Camay tend to be portrayed as considerably more feminine in nature. They seem to embrace the product for the delicate way in which it will treat their skin and the softness that it will yield. As opposed to taking refreshing showers they appear to desire the sensual experience of long, warm, relaxing baths. It is interesting to note how packaging of each product appears to support such distinctions in the image of each product.

In Chapter 13, we noted the importance for retailers to know the image of their store as perceived by customers. It should again be emphasized here that consumer segments with various self-images will probably exist within the trading area of any given store. It is quite possible that the store's image may not be consistent with some consumers' self-images. Therefore, it is essential for the retailer to determine the market segment to which the store is appealing.[44] Decisions must then be made on the appropriate target segments. This could entail adjustments of the store's image in order to coincide better with the self-images of target patrons.

Analysis of consumers' self-images and their images of brands can also aid marketers in developing products. New brands can be created based on consumer self-image profiles for which there are no "matching" brand images existing. Product categories having particular promise in this area include those that generate high ego involvement and have high social visibility among the upper social classes. Examples include home furnishings, clothing, and automobiles, as opposed to such products as fingernail clippers and light bulbs. Therefore, measurement of consumers' product-image perceptions would involve more than just the assessment of product attributes as described in the perceptual mapping example in Chapter 5. Consumers' perceptions of nonphysical image components and the degree of their correspondence to self-image perceptions must also be assessed.

One final comment regarding the self-image concept is important to mention. Studies have suggested that self-image can be an important predictor of consumers' brand preferences. However, brand preferences are not necessarily translated directly into purchases. Constraining factors such as price and other individual or environmental influences can modify these brand preferences before they are acted upon.

SUMMARY

This chapter reviewed two broad concepts that attempt to take rather complete views of consumers. The concept of personality suggests that individuals possess quite stable and enduring properties which influence them to respond in certain characteristic ways. After discussing some measurement issues, several major concepts of personality, including psychoanalytic, social, and stimulus-response theories, were reviewed. However, the greatest amount of study regarding the relevance of personality to consumer behavior has involved trait and factor theories. After reviewing a number of the relevant studies in this area, it appears that even though research evidence has not offered a great deal of confirming support, experts believe that personality plays a significant role in influencing consumers.

After briefly discussing the relevance of trait-related psychographic studies to several marketing-decision areas, attention next turned to the topic of consumers' self-concept. A discussion of the development of self-concepts and their consistency over a period of time led to consideration of representative self-concept studies in the field of consumer behavior. The evidence relating self-images to product and brand images certainly seemed worthy of further study. In addition, the chapter concluded by demonstrating the practical relevance of consumers' self-concepts to a variety of marketing decision areas including product designs, promotions, and market-segmentation strategies.

DISCUSSION TOPICS

1 Distinguish between the id, ego, and superego in the Freudian personality scheme. Suggest the basic influence each might exert on a purchase decision.

2 Of what relevance is the personality concept to understanding consumer behavior?

3 Describe the major characteristics of trait theories of personality, indicating their major advantages and disadvantages. Review their usefulness in explaining consumer behavior.

4 Find at least three examples of promotions that appear to be using Freudian concepts. Be specific in describing which concepts are involved and how you think they are being used.

5 Cite at least two product examples in which it would appear that an understanding of consumers' psychographic profiles would be useful in describing their reaction to the products involved.

6 What are the significant limitations of the self-concept in explaining consumer behavior?

7 Of what usefulness is it for a marketing manager to know that the self tends to be consistent?

8 Why is it important for the marketer to understand the distinction between consumers' self-image and ideal self-image?

9 Choose two brands within the same product category that appear to be projecting different images. Characterize each image being projected by comparing and contrasting them. What methods or techniques are being used to project these images?

NOTES

[1] Gerald Zaltman and Melanie Wallendorf, *Consumer Behavior: Basic Findings and Management Implications,* Wiley, New York, 1979, p. 357.
[2] Some of the following discussion follows Harold H. Kassarjian, "Personality and Consumer Behavior: A Review," *Journal of Marketing Research,* **8**: 409–418, November, 1971.
[3] Joel B. Cohen, "An Interpersonal Orientation to the Study of Consumer Behavior," *Journal of Marketing Research,* **4**: 270–278, August, 1967. Also see Joel B. Cohen, "Toward an Interpersonal Theory of Consumer Behavior," *California Management Review,* **10**: 73–80, Spring 1968.
[4] Seymour Epstein, "Traits Are Alive and Well," in David Magnusson and Norman Endler (eds.), *Personality at the Crossroads: Current Issues in Interactional Psychology,* Lawrence Eribaum Associates, Hillsdale, NJ, 1977, pp. 83–98; and David Krech, et al., *Psychology: A Basic Course,* Knopf, New York, 1976, pp. 322–323.
[5] Arthur Koponen, "Personality Characteristics of Purchasers," *Journal of Advertising Research,* **1**:6–12, September 1960.
[6] Robert Brody and Scott Cunningham, "Personality Variables and the Consumer Decision Process," *Journal of Marketing Research,* **5**:50–57, February 1968.

[7] William T. Tucker and John Painter, "Personality and Product Use," *Journal of Applied Psychology,* 45:325–329, October 1961.

[8] Franklin B. Evans, "Psychological and Objective Factors in the Prediction of Brand Choice," *Journal of Business,* 32:340–369, October 1959.

[9] See Alan S. Marcus, "Obtaining Group Measures from Personality Test Scores: Auto Brand Choice Predicted from the Edwards Personal Preference Schedule," *Psychological Reports,* 17:523–531, October 1965; Gary A. Steiner, "Notes on Franklin B. Evans 'Psychological and Objective Factors in the Prediction of Brand Choice,'" *Journal of Business,* 34:57–60, January 1961; Charles Winick, "The Relationship Among Personality Needs, Objective Factors, and Brand Choice: A Re-examination," *Journal of Business,* 34:61–66, January 1961; and Ralph Westfall, "Psychological Factors in Predicting Product Choice," *Journal of Marketing,* 26:34–40, April 1962.

[10] See, Charles M. Schaninger and Donald Sciglimpaglia, "The Influence of Cognitive Personality Traits and Demographics on Consumer Acquisition," *Journal of Consumer Research,* 8:208–216, September 1981; Raymond L. Horton, "Some Relationships Between Personality and Consumer Decision Making," *Journal of Marketing Research,* 16:233–246, May 1979; Thomas S. Robertson, *Innovation and the Consumer,* Holt, New York, 1971; and Louis E. Boone, "The Search for the Consumer Innovator," *Journal of Business,* 43:135–140, April 1979, for representative findings.

[11] See Kassarjian, "Personality and Consumer Behavior," and Harold H. Kassarjian and Mary Jane Sheffet, "Personality and Consumer Behavior: One More Time," in Edward M. Mazze (ed.), *1975 Combined Proceedings,* American Marketing Association, Chicago, 1975, pp. 197–201.

[12] See William D. Wells, "General Personality Tests and Consumer Behavior," in Joseph W. Newman (ed.), *On Knowing the Consumer,* Wiley, New York, 1966, pp. 187–189; and Kathryn E. A. Villani and Yoram Wind, "On the Usage of 'Modified' Personality Trait Measures in Consumer Research," *Journal of Consumer Research,* 2:223–228, December 1975.

[13] Ibid.

[14] See George Brooker, "Representativeness of Shortened Personality Measures," *Journal of Consumer Research,* 5:143–144, September 1978; and Kathryn E. A. Villani and Yoram Wind, "On the Usage of 'Modified' Personality Trait Measures in Consumer Research," *Journal of Consumer Research,* 2:223–228, December 1975.

[15] Kassarjian, "Personality and Consumer Behavior," p. 416.

[16] See Robert A. Peterson, "Moderating the Personality-Product Usage Relationship," in Ronald C. Curhan (ed.), *1974 Combined Proceedings,* American Marketing Association, Chicago, 1975, pp. 109–112.

[17] See Shaninger and Sciglimpaglia, "Personality and Information Acquisition," and Horton, "Personality and Consumer Decision Making."

[18] See Stewart Bither and Ira Dolich, "Personality as a Determinant Factor in Store Choice," in M. Venkatesan (ed.), *Proceedings of the Third Annual Conference,* Association for Consumer Research, College Park, MD, 1972, pp. 9–19; Robert A. Peterson and Louis K. Sharpe, "Personality Structure and Cigarette Smoking," in Barnett A. Greenberg (ed.), *Proceedings: Southern Marketing Association 1974 Conference,* Southern Marketing Association, 1975, pp. 295–297; and Larry Percy, "A Look at Personality Profiles and the Personality-Attitude-Behavior Link in Predicting Consumer Behavior," in Beverlee B. Anderson (ed.), *Advances in Consumer Research: Volume 3,* Association for Consumer Research, Ann Arbor, MI, 1976, pp. 119–224.

[19] Kassarjian and Sheffet, "Personality and Consumer Behavior."

[20] Sunil Mehrotra and William D. Wells, "Psychographics and Buyer Behavior: Theory and Recent Empirical Findings," in Arch G. Woodside, Jagdish N. Sheth, and Peter D. Bennett (eds.), *Consumer and Industrial Buying Behavior,* Elsevier North-Holland, New York, 1977, pp. 49–65.

[21] Douglas J. Tigert, "Life Style Analysis as a Basis for Media Selection," in William D. Wells (ed.), *Life Style and Psychographics,* American Marketing Association, Chicago, 1974, pp. 173–201.

[22] Calvin Hadock, "Use of Psychographics in Analysis of Channels of Distribution," in Wells (ed.), *Life Style and Psychographics,* pp. 215–216.

[23] Robert W. Frye and Gary D. Klein, "Psychographics and Industrial Design," in Wells (ed.), *Life Style and Psychographics,* pp. 225–232.

[24] William D. Wells, "Personality as a Determinant of Buyer Behavior: What's Wrong? What Can Be Done About It?" in David Sparks (ed.), *Broadening the Concept of Marketing,* American Marketing Association, Chicago, 1970, p. 20.

[25] Theodore M. Newcombe, *Social Psychology,* Holt, New York, 1950, p. 328.

[26] Donald Snygg and Arthur W. Combs, *Individual Behavior,* Harper, New York, 1949, p. 57; and William James, *Psychology,* Henry Holt and Company, New York, 1892, p. 176.

[27] Morris Rosenberg, *Conceiving the Self,* Basic Books, New York, 1979, p. 7.

[28] Thorstein Veblen, *The Theory of the Leisure Class,* Mentor Books, New York, 1958, p. 42; a reprint from Thorstein Veblen, *The Theory of the Leisure Class,* Macmillan, New York, 1899.

[29] Leon A. Festinger, "A Theory of Social Comparison," *Human Relations,* 14:48–64, 1954.

[30] For additional views on principles influencing the development of the self, see Rosenberg, *Conceiving the Self,* pp. 62–77.

[31] Snygg and Combs, *Individual Behavior,* p. 57.

[32] Prescott Lecky, "The Theory of Self Consistency," in Chad Gordon and Kenneth J. Gergen (eds.), *The Self in Social Interaction,* Wiley, New York, 1968, p. 297.

[33] M. Joseph Sirgy, "Self-Concept in Consumer Behavior: A Critical Review," *Journal of Consumer Research,* 9:287–300, December 1982.

[34] See, for example, Edward L. Grubb and Gregg Hupp, "Perception of Self, Generalized Stereotypes, and Brand Selection," *Journal of Marketing Research,* **5**:58–63, February 1968; G. Hughes and P. Noert, "A Computer Controlled Experiment in Consumer Behavior," *Journal of Business,* 43:354–372, 1970; and Edward L. Grubb and Bruce L. Stern, "Self-Concept and Significant Others," *Journal of Marketing Research,* **8**:382–385, August 1971.

[35] See Curtis B. Hann and Edward W. Cundiff, "Self Actualization and Product Perception," *Journal of Marketing Research,* 6:470–472, November 1969; George E. Belch and E. Laird Landon, Jr., "Discriminant Validity of a Product Anchored Self-Concept Measure," *Jounal of Marketing Research,* 14:252–256, May 1977; and George E. Belch, "Belief Systems and the Differential Role of the Self-Concept," in Keith H. Hunt (ed.), *Advances in Consumer Research: Volume 5,* Association for Consumer Research, Ann Arbor, MI, 1978, pp. 320–325, for examples.

[36] See, for example, M. Joseph Sirgy, "Self-Concept in Relation to Product Preference and Purchase Intention," in V. V. Bellur (ed.), *Developments in Marketing Science: Volume 3,* Marquette, MI, Academy of Marketing Science, 1980; G. David Hughs and Jose L. Guerrero, "Automobile Self-Congruity Models Reexamined," *Journal of Marketing Research,* **8**:125–127, February 1971; and J. Michael Munsen and W. Austin Spivey, "Assessing Self-Concept," in Jerry C. Olson (ed.), *Advances in Consumer Research: Volume 7,* Association for Consumer Research, Ann Arbor, MI, 1980, pp. 598–603.

[37] Carolyn Turner Schenk and Rebecca H. Holman, "A Sociological Approach to Brand Choice: The Concept of Situational Self Image," in Jerry C. Olson (ed.), *Advances in Consumer Research: Volume 7,* Association for Consumer Research, Ann Arbor, MI, 1980, pp. 610–614.

[38] Sirgy, "Self-Concept in Consumer Behavior."

[39] Edward L. Grubb and Harrison L. Grathwohl, "Consumer Self Concept, Symbolism and Market Behavior: A Theoretical Approach," *Journal of Marketing,* 31:25–26, October 1967.

[40] For a review of alternative models of self/brand image congruity and their predictions of product preference and purchase intention, see M. Joseph Sirgy and Jeffrey E. Danes, "Self-Image/Product-Image Congruence Models: Testing Selected Models," in Andrew Mitchell (ed.), *Advances in Consumer Research: Volume 9,* Association for Consumer Research, Ann Arbor, MI, 1982, pp. 556–561.

[41] The following list of generalizations follows closely the review, in Sirgy, "Self Concept and Consumer Behavior."

[42] A. Evans Birdwell, "Influence of Image Congruence on Consumer Choice," in George South (ed.), *Reflections on Progress in Marketing,* American Marketing Association, Chicago, 1965, pp. 290–303.

[43] Wayne DeLozier and Rollie Tillman, "Self Image Concepts—Can They Be Used to Design Marketing Programs?" *The Southern Journal of Business,* 7:11, November 1972.

[44] For two endeavors of this nature, see Joseph Barry Mason and Morris L. Mayer, "The Problem of the Self-Concept in Store Image Studies," *Journal of Marketing,* **34**:67–69, April 1970; and Ira J. Dolich and Ned Shilling, "A Critical Evaluation of 'The Problem of Self-Concept in Store Image Studies,'" *Journal of Marketing,* **35**:71–73, January 1971.

CHAPTER 16
ATTITUDES

The topic of attitudes has been one of the most important subjects of study in the field of consumer behavior. Widespread investigations of attitudes among academicians and practicing marketers supports this statement. Attitude research forms the basis for developing new products, repositioning existing products, creating advertising campaigns, and predicting brand preferences as well as general purchase behavior. Understanding how attitudes are developed and how they influence consumers is a vital ingredient to the success of any marketing program.

Material presented in Chapters 12 and 13 provide useful perspective for our discussion in this chapter. Recall from Chapter 12 that the role of attitudes differs depending on the level of consumer involvement in a purchase situation. It was argued that in low-involvement situations attitudes toward a brand are formed *after* a purchase has been made—when the brand is being evaluated through actual use. However, in high-involvement situations consumers are seen as forming attitudes about brands and then making a purchase decision based on these attitudes. This means that in high-involvement cases, attitudes are formed on the basis of product evaluations that are made *prior* to purchase. Therefore, they represent one outcome of the information-processing activities that are shown in Figure 13-1.

The high-involvement perspective is most relevant to our discussion of attitudes in this chapter. That is, the sequence of steps an involved consumer takes can be thought of as (1) processing information, (2) forming attitudes, and then (3) making choices in the marketplace that are guided by these attitudes.

In this chapter, we explore how attitudes are formed and organized. The functions of attitudes in our daily lives and their relationship to purchase behavior are then discussed. Additionally, we describe several well-known attitude models and theories which help us to measure and predict consumer behavior. These principles form a foundation for Chapter 17, which treats attitude change and the role of marketing communications in influencing consumers.

DEFINITIONS OF ATTITUDE

Social psychologists, unfortunately, do not agree on the precise definition of an attitude. In fact, there are more than 100 different definitions of the concept.[1] However, four definitions are more commonly accepted than others. One conception is that an attitude is how positive or negative, favorable or unfavorable, or pro or con a person feels toward an object.[2] This definition views attitude as a feeling or an evaluative reaction to objects.

A second definition represents the thoughts of Allport, who views attitudes as "learned predispositions to respond to an object or class of objects in a consistently favorable or unfavorable way."[3] This definition is slightly more complicated than the first, because it incorporates the notion of a readiness to respond toward an object.

A third definition of attitude popularized by cognitively oriented social psychologists is: "an enduring organization of motivational, emotional, perceptual, and cognitive process with respect to some aspect of the individual's world."[4] This views attitudes as being made up of three components: (1) the *cognitive* or knowledge component, (2) the *affective* or emotional component, and (3) the *conative* or behavioral-tendency component.

More recently, theorists have given more attention to a new definition of attitude which has generated much research and has been useful in predicting behavior. This definition explicitly treats attitudes as being multidimensional in nature, as opposed to the unidimensional emphasis taken by earlier definitions. Here, a person's overall attitude toward an object is seen to be a function of (1) the strength of each of a number of beliefs the person holds about various aspects of the object, and (2) the evaluation he gives to each belief as it relates to the object.[5] A *belief* is the probability a person attaches to a given piece of knowledge being true.

This last definition has considerable appeal, because it has been shown that consumers perceive a product (object) as having many attributes, and they form beliefs about each of these attributes. For example, a consumer may believe strongly that Listerine mouthwash kills germs, helps prevent colds, gives people clean, refreshing breath, and prevents sore throats. If this consumer evaluates all four of these attributes as favorable qualities, then according to the definition he would have a strongly favorable overall attitude toward the brand. On the other hand, a second consumer might believe just as strongly as the first consumer that Listerine possesses all four of these traits; however, she may not evaluate all attributes as favorably as the first consumer. Therefore, her overall attitude toward the brand would be less favorable. This idea will be discussed in more detail later in the chapter.

It has been important to provide all four attitude definitions, because the majority of attitude studies have been based upon them. In fact, results of this research serve as the basis of this and the next chapter.

CHARACTERISTICS OF ATTITUDES

Attitudes have several important characteristics or properties, namely, they (1) have an object, (2) have direction, intensity, and degree, (3) have structure, and (4) are learned.

Attitudes Have An Object

By definition, attitudes must have an object. That is, they must have a focal point. The object can be an abstract concept, such as "consumerism," or it can be a tangible item, such as a motorcycle. The object can be a physical thing, such as a product, or it can be an action, such as purchasing a product. In addition, the object can be either one item, such as a person, or a collection of items, such as a social group; it also can be either specific (Pontiac Firebird) or general (General Motors, Inc.).

Attitudes Have Direction, Degree, and Intensity

An attitude expresses how a person feels toward an object. It expresses (1) direction—the person is either favorable or unfavorable, or for or against the object; (2) degree—how much the person either likes or dislikes the object; and (3) intensity—the level of sureness or confidence of expression about the object, or how strongly a person feels about his or her conviction. Although degree and intensity might seem the same and are actually related, they are not synonymous. For example, a person may feel that an Ariens riding mower is very unreliable. This indicates that his attitude is negative and the *degree* of negative feeling is quite extensive. However, the individual may have very little *conviction* or feeling of sureness (intensity in attitude) that he is right. Thus, his attitude could be more easily changed in a favorable direction than a person who feels a strong conviction that Ariens mowers are very unreliable.

The direction, degree, and intensity of a person's attitude toward a product has been said to provide marketers with an estimate of his or her readiness to act toward, that is, purchase the product. However, a marketer must also understand how *important* the consumer's attitude is vis-à-vis other attitudes, and the situational constraints, such as ability to pay, that might inhibit the consumer from making a purchase decision.

Attitudes Have Structure

As explained below, attitudes display organization, which means that they have internal consistency and possess interattitudinal centrality. They also tend to be stable, to have varying degrees of salience, and to be generalizable.

The structure of human attitudes may be viewed as a complex Tinker Toy set erected in a type of circular pattern. At the center of this structure are the individual's important values and self-concept. Attitudes close to the hub of this system are said to have a high degree of *centrality*. Other attitudes located farther out in the structure possess less centrality.

Attitudes do not stand in isolation. They are associated (tied in) with each other to form a complex whole. This implies that a certain degree of *consistency* must exist between them. That is, because they are related, there must be some amount of "fit" between them, or conflict will result. Also, because more central attitudes are related to a larger number of other attitudes, they must exhibit a greater degree of consistency than more peripheral attitudes do.

Because attitudes cluster into a structure, they tend to show *stability* over time. The length of time may not be infinite, but it is far from being temporary. Also, because attitudes are learned, they tend to become stronger, or at least more resistant to change, the longer they are held.[6] Thus, newly formed attitudes are easier to change and less stable than older ones of equal strength.

Attitudes tend to be *generalizable*. That is, a person's attitude toward a specific object tends to generalize toward a class of objects. Thus, a consumer who purchases a Porsche which develops mechanical difficulties may believe that all Porsches and Volkswagen products, and possibly all German-made products, are poorly constructed. Consumers tend to generalize in such a manner in order to simplify their decision making.

Among all of the attiudes in a person's attitudinal structure, some are more important or salient to her than others. For example, a U.S. consumer might feel that "buying American" is more important than saving energy. Therefore, she might purchase an American car that consumes more gasoline than a comparable foreign car that uses less. Also, the "buy American" attitude can be closely tied to attitudes of creating American jobs, keeping money at home, and the like which thereby support the "buy American" attitude and increase its salience.

Attitudes are Learned

Just as a golf swing, a tennis stroke, and tastes are learned, so are attitudes. They develop from our personal experiences with reality, as well as from information from friends, salespeople, and news media. They are also derived from both direct and indirect experiences in life. Thus, it is important to recognize that learning precedes attitude formation and change, and that principles of learning discussed in Chapter 14 can aid marketers in developing and changing consumer attitudes.

FUNCTIONS OF ATTITUDES

Attitudes serve four major functions for the individual: (1) the adjustment function, (2) the ego-defensive function, (3) the value-expressive function, and (4) the knowledge function.[7] Ultimately, these functions serve people's need to protect and enhance the image they hold of themselves. In more general terms, these functions are the motivational bases which shape and reinforce positive attitudes toward goal objects perceived as need-satisfying, and/or negative attitudes toward other objects perceived as punishing or threatening. These situations are diagramed in Figure 16-1. The functions themselves can help us to understand why people hold the attitudes they do toward psychological objects.

The Adjustment Function

The adjustment function directs people toward pleasurable or rewarding objects and away from unpleasant, undesirable ones. It serves the utilitarian concept of maximizing reward and minimizing punishment. Thus, the attitudes of consumers depend to a large degree on their perceptions of what is need satisfying and what is punishing. Because consumers perceive products, services, and stores as providing need-satisfying or unsatisfying experiences, we should expect their attitudes toward these objects to vary in relation to the experiences that have occurred.

The Ego-Defensive Function

Attitudes formed to protect the ego or self-image from threats help fulfill the ego-defensive function. Actually, many outward expressions of such attitudes reflect the opposite of what the person perceives himself to be. For example, a consumer who has made a poor purchase decision or a poor investment may staunchly defend the decision as being correct at the time or, as being the result of poor advice from another person. Such ego-defensive attitudes help us to protect our self-image, and often we are unaware of them.

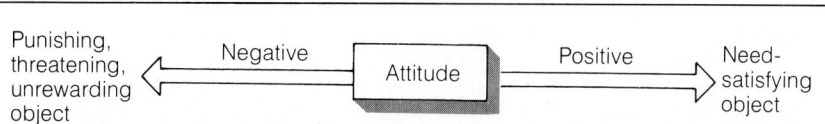

FIGURE 16-1

Attitude development and function based on perceived need satisfaction or harm avoidance.

Punishing, threatening, unrewarding object ← Negative — Attitude — Positive → Need-satisfying object

The Value-Expressive Function

Whereas ego-defensive attitudes are formed to protect a person's self-image, value-expressive attitudes enable the expression of the person's centrally held values. Therefore, consumers adopt certain attitudes in an effort to translate their values into something more tangible and easily expressed. Thus, a conservative person might develop an unfavorable attitude toward bright clothing and instead be attracted toward dark, pin-striped suits.

Marketers should develop an understanding of what values consumers wish to express about themselves, and they should design products and promotional campaigns to allow these self-expressions. Not all products lend themselves to this form of market segmentation, however. Those with the greatest potential for "value expressive" segmentation are ones with high social visibility. Cross pens, Saks Fifth Avenue clothes, Mercedes automobiles, and Bang & Olufsen stero systems are examples.

The Knowledge Function

Human beings have a need for a structured and orderly world, and therefore they seek consistency, stability, definition, and understanding. Out of this need develops attitudes toward acquiring knowledge. In addition, the need to know tends to be specific. Therefore, an individual who does not play golf or wish to learn it is unlikely to seek knowledge or an understanding of the game. Out of the need to know comes attitudes about what we believe we need or do not need to understand.

SOURCES OF ATTITUDE DEVELOPMENT

The preceding section not only discussed the functions of attitudes, but also provided us with an initial understanding of how and why attitudes develop. All attitudes ultimately develop from human needs and the values people place upon objects that satisfy those perceived needs. This section discusses sources that make us aware of needs, their importance to us, and how our attitudes develop toward objects that satisfy needs.

Personal Experience

People come into contact with objects in their everyday environment. Some are familiar, while others are new. We evaluate the new and reevaluate the old, and this evaluation process assists in developing attitudes toward objects. For example, consider a gourmet cook who has searched two months for a new food processor only to have it break down 3 months after purchase. Through direct experience, she will then reevaluate her earlier attitude toward the processor.

Our direct experiences with sales representatives, products, services, and stores help to create and shape our attitudes toward those market objects. However, several factors influence how we will evaluate such direct contacts:

Needs—Because people's needs differ and also vary over time, they can develop different attitudes toward the same object at different points in their life.

Selective perception—We have seen that people operate on their personal interpretation of reality. Therefore, the way people interpret information about products, stores, and so on, affects their attitudes toward them.

Personality—Personality is another factor influencing how people process their direct experiences with objects. How aggressive-passive, introverted-extroverted, and so on, that people are will affect the attitudes they form.

Group Associations

All people are influenced to one degree or another by other members in the groups to which they belong. Attitudes are one target for this influence. For example, our attitudes toward products, ethics, warfare, and a multitude of other subjects are influenced strongly by groups that we value and with which we do or wish to associate. Several groups, including family, work and social groups, and cultural and subcultural groups, are quite important in affecting a person's attitude development:

Family—The family is perhaps the most influential group in shaping a person's attitudes. Parents orient a child's early thinking and this influence on attitudes is often so strong that it carries over to adult life.

Peer Groups—The norms, standards, and influence attempts of important groups in the consumer's work and social life make a strong impact on a wide variety of the person's attitudes.

Culture and subculture—Cultural and subcultural inheritances are a result of the socialization process. This legacy results in a sense of identification about who we are, and it strongly affects attitudes about a variety of objects in our environment.

Influential Others

A consumer's attitude can be formed and changed through personal contact with influential persons such as respected friends, relatives, and experts. Opinion leaders are examples of people who are respected by their followers and who may strongly influence the attitudes and puchase behavior of followers.

To capitalize on this type of influence, advertisers often use actors and actresses who look similar to or act similar to their intended audiences. People tend to like others who are similar to themselves, because they believe that they share the same problems, form the same judgments, and use the same criteria for evaluating products.[8] Another application which advertisers use to influence audience attitudes is the so-called slice of life commercial. These ads show "typical" people confronting "typical" problems and finding solutions in the use of the advertised brand. Examples include ads for Head and Shoulders shampoo (to solve dandruff problems), Crest toothpaste (to fight cavities), and Midas mufflers.

Although sales representatives are sometimes viewed with a certain amount of suspicion, they can also positively influence consumers' attitudes when they express opinions similar to the consumer's viewpoint. A second condition for effective influence, however, usually is that the salesperson is also perceived by the customer as having some degree of expertise regarding the product.[9]

A pictorial summary of what we have learned so far is depicted in Figure 16-2. The model is a simple representation of the concepts that have been discussed in the previous sections. It shows that several sources provide consumers with information and influence about products, services, retail stores, and other objects. The individual selectively receives and distorts the information according to her individual needs, values, and personality, and according to how well the information "fits" with currently held beliefs and attitudes. This processed infor-

FIGURE 16-2

A simple model of the interrelationships of attitude and other psychological processes.

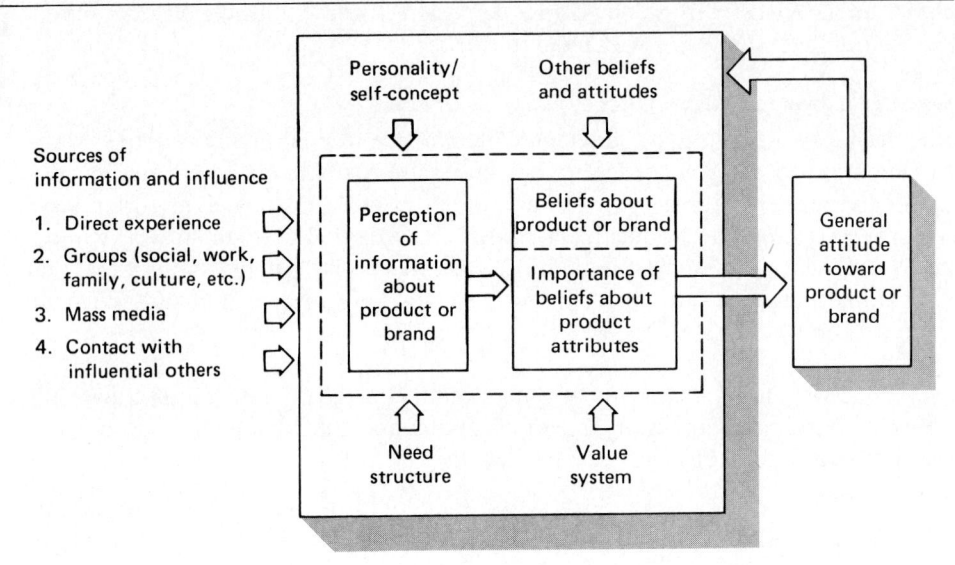

Sources of information and influence

1. Direct experience
2. Groups (social, work, family, culture, etc.)
3. Mass media
4. Contact with influential others

Personality/self-concept → Perception of information about product or brand

Other beliefs and attitudes → Beliefs about product or brand → Importance of beliefs about product attributes → General attitude toward product or brand

↑ Need structure   ↑ Value system

mation initiates either development, change, or confirmation in the consumer's beliefs about the product and the importance of each of the product's attributes to her and her current needs. Out of this process is synthesized a general attitude toward a product. Admittedly, this model is an oversimplification. However, it reflects current understanding of attitudes, and presents a concise picture of the psychological and external elements involved in the process of forming attitudes toward products. Also, it should be pointed out that the process is dynamic; it continues to change over time.

ATTITUDE THEORIES AND MODELS

This section describes several attitude theories and models.[10] Although at first glance some may appear to be somewhat complicated, their essence is usually quite simple and useful in understanding the role of attitudes in consumer behavior.

Attitude theories primarily are concerned with how attitudes develop and change. Three of the more popular viewpoints are founded on the general principle that *the human mind strives to maintain harmony or consistency among currently perceived attitudes.* If the mind perceives an inconsistency within its attitude structure, mental tension develops to return the structure to a consistent state. The three classical theories based upon the consistency principle are congruity, balance, and cognitive dissonance. Newer multiattribute attitude theories are discussed after a consideration of these traditional views.

Congruity Theory

A basic understanding of the congruity model can be gained through consideration of the following examples. Assume that a consumer holds attitudes toward entertainer Bob Hope (positive attitude of scale value +2) and Texaco (negative attitude of scale value −2), as illustrated in Figure 16-3. Also assume that the consumer sees Bob Hope in a television advertisement in which he makes positive statements about Texaco. Given this situation, the consumer will have inconsistent attitudes: "Bob, whom I like, said something nice about Texaco, which I don't like." In this case, the consumer is in a state of *incongruity*. This condition produces uncomfortable tension which must ultimately resolve the incongruous state. The congruity model would predict that a person in this situation would reduce his favorable attitude toward Bob Hope and decrease his unfavorable attitude toward Texaco, as shown in part (*b*) of Figure 16-3. The model would predict a movement of two units of each concept toward each other (the center in this case), because the consumer perceives both objects as being of equal strength but in opposite directions of the neutral point of zero.

Most of the time, the resulting equilibrium point is not determined so simply. Figure 16-4 presents another situation of a consumer's perceived attitudes toward Bob Hope and Texaco. Note that the scale distance between the two concepts is four units as before. However, resolution is not the midpoint between the two concepts (+1), as we might expect. Instead, the model would predict that resolution would occur at +2, reducing the consumer's perceived attitude of Bob Hope by only one scale unit and increasing his attitude toward Texaco by three scale units.

Although the mathematics used to predict the resolution point will not be presented here, the greater shift for Texaco than for Bob Hope is intuitively understandable.[11] Strong attitudes are more difficult to change than are weak or moderate ones. Thus, the consumer's stronger positive attitude toward Bob Hope exerts greater pull on his weaker negative attitude toward Texaco. This idea suggests that when consumers develop a strong dislike toward a brand, company efforts to improve consumer attitudes will require a tremendous marketing effort, which may not be worth the cost. The company may be better off in many cases either to (1) drop the brand and reintroduce it under another name, if promotional positioning has been the problem, or (2) introduce a new reformulated brand, if product quality, design, or formulation has been the problem. Conversely, if the consumer holds an extremely positive attitude toward the brand, considerable unfavorable

FIGURE 16-3

A simple example of resolving incongruity.

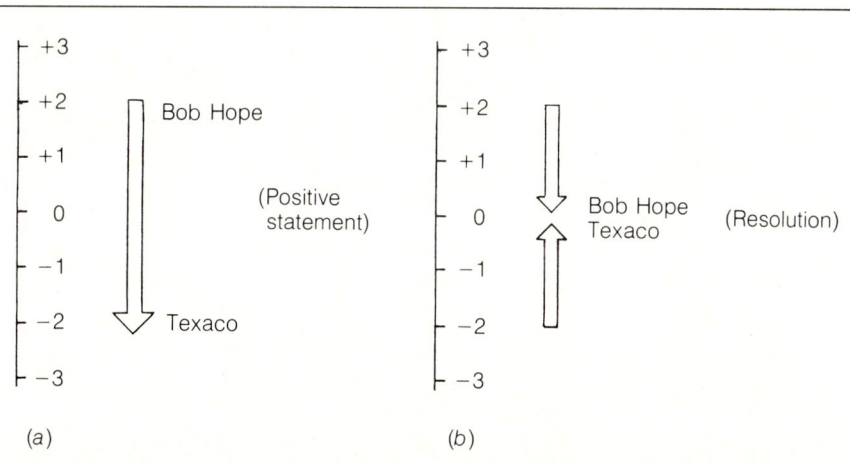

FIGURE 16-4

A more complex example of the resolution of incongruity.

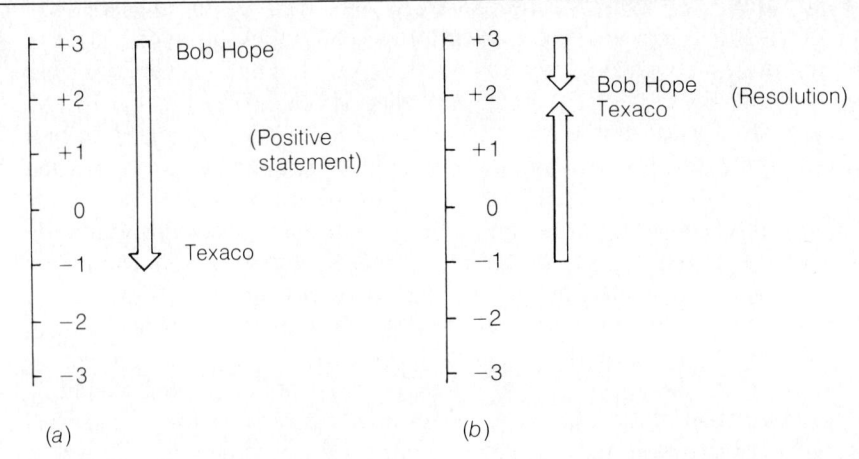

(a) Bob Hope +3 (Positive statement) → Texaco −1

(b) Bob Hope Texaco +2 (Resolution)

experiences and word-of-mouth influence would be required to deteriorate the attitude significantly.

It should be noted that although the model predicts resolution at a value of +2 in Figure 16-4, there are qualifications. First, if the consumer perceives the information he had heard to be totally unbelievable, he can reject it, and no attitude change will occur. In this instance, the information would be totally discounted. Second, if the consumer experiences only some disbelief instead of total disbelief, his attitudes will change only slightly.[12] This qualification for disbelief adds further strength to the marketing examples previously mentioned. Specifically, consumers who hold extremely negative attitudes toward a brand will not only be difficult to change, but will ignore or discount information to the contrary.

The congruity principle is used frequently in marketing.[13] Advertisers often use hired celebrities to endorse brands, services, organizations, and causes. Athletes speak against drug use among young people, movie actresses endorse various kinds of beauty aids, and race-car drivers promote brands of tires, spark plugs, and other automobile accessories. Of course, the intent is to have consumers who hold positive attitudes toward a source (the person making such favorable statements about an object) to develop a positive value association between the source and the object.

Balance Theory

Several balance models have been developed, all of which are based upon the pioneering work of Fritz Heider.[14] According to balance theory, a person perceives her or his environment in terms of *triads*. That is, a person views herself or himself as being involved in a triangular relationship in which all three elements (persons, ideas, and things) have either positive (liking, favorable) or negative (disliking, unfavorable) relationships with each other. This relationship is termed *sentiment*.

Unlike the congruity model, there are no numerical values used to express the degree of unity between elements. Instead, the model is described as *unbalanced* if the multiplicative relationships among the three elements is negative, and *balanced* if the multiplicative relationship is positive. To illustrate, consider the consumer situation expressed as three statements: (1) "I like large luxurious cars," (2) "I don't like energy-wasting products," (3) "I believe large, luxurious cars waste energy." This situation is described by the triad shown in Figure 16-5. Notice that the structure is not in balance, because there is a positive relationship on two sides of the triad and a negative relationship on the third side, and this results in a negative multiplicative product.

Because the relationship presented in the example is unbalanced, it will produce tension for the consumer. It may be possibe for her to "live with" the tension and do nothing to resolve it. However, if sufficient tension exists, it is likely that attitude change will occur regarding at least one element in the triad in order to restore balance to the system. These attempts at resolution can result in the consumer (1) disliking large, luxurious cars, (2) believing that large, luxurious cars are not really energy-wasting products, or (3) liking energy-wasting products (they create jobs and provide psychological satisfaction, for example). As we can see, rationalization can help to change our perceptions of relationships and thus our attitudes.

Cognitive Dissonance

The theory of cognitive dissonance was developed in 1957 by Leon Festinger.[15] Festinger describes cognitive dissonance as a psychological state which results when a person perceives that two cognitions (thoughts), both of which he believes to be true, do not "fit" together; that is, they seem inconsistent. The resulting dissonance produces tension, which serves to motivate the individual to bring harmony to inconsistent elements and thereby reduce psychological tension.

Dissonance can arise in three basic ways. First, any *logical inconsistency* can create dissonance. For example, "all candy is sweet; my candy is sour." Second, dissonance can be created when a person experiences an *inconsistency either between his attitude and his behavior or between two of his behaviors.* For example, Michael actively compliments Nike running shoes on many occasions and then purchases a pair of Adidas running shoes. This is an example of an inconsistency between two behaviors. On the other hand, a discrepancy between an attitude and behavior would exist when David strongly dislikes gambling but bets on the outcome of football games. Third, dissonance can occur when a strongly held

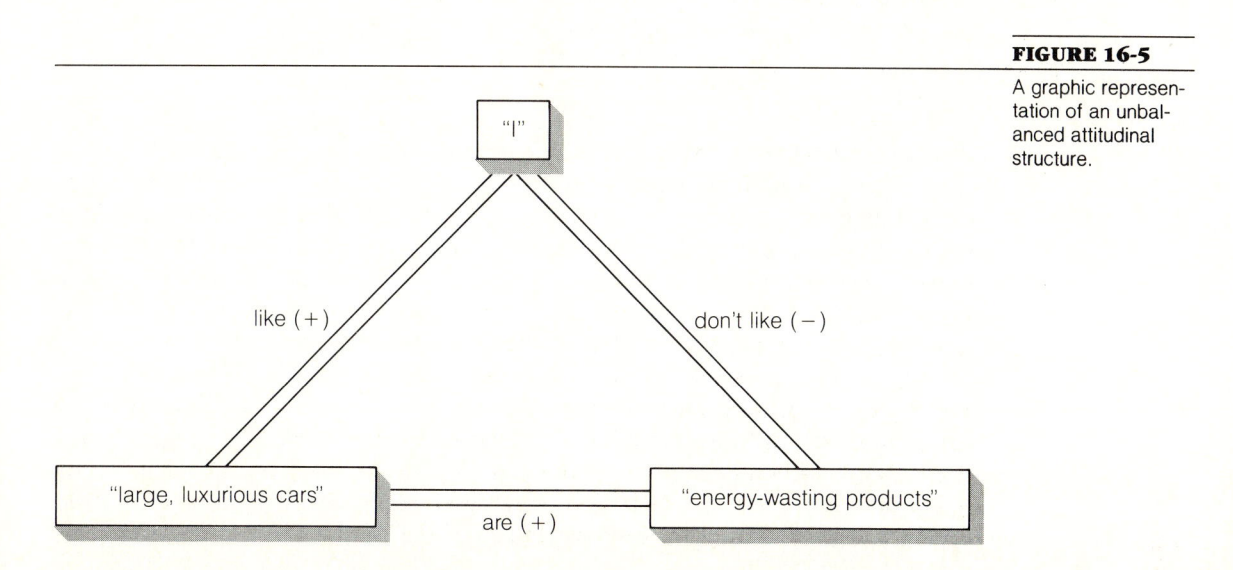

FIGURE 16-5

A graphic representation of an unbalanced attitudinal structure.

expectation is disconfirmed. To illustrate, Margaret expects to find significant savings at a sidewalk sale, but finds only unstylish and damaged merchandise.

In all three cases, it is necessary for a person to perceive the inconsistency; otherwise, no dissonance will occur. Some people are very capable of holding an attitude that contradicts their behavior without perceiving the contradiction. Therefore, they suffer no dissonance.

Regardless of its source, cognitive dissonance arises *after* a decision has been made. The decision, in effect, *commits* the person to certain positions or attitudes, when prior to that time that person was capable of adjusting her attitudes or behavior to avoid dissonance.

A person experiencing cognitive dissonance has three major ways to reduce it. They are, (1) rationalization, (2) seeking additional information that is supportive of or consistent with his behavior, and (3) either eliminating or altering some of the dissonant elements, which can be accomplished by either forgetting or suppressing dissonant elements, or by changing his attitude so that it is no longer dissonant with another attitude or behavior. Each of these strategies may be used alone or in combination.

To illustrate these methods, consider Diane who has purchased a Nikon 35-mm, single-lens reflex camera outfit for $560 after seriously considering other brands such as Pentax, Canon, and Minolta in the same general price range. Besides the investment of $560, she also has invested much thought and searching time and a considerable amount of ego in the purchase decision. Therefore, the amount at stake in this purchase is considerable. After evaluating the pros and cons of each brand of camera, she has selected the Nikon. Subsequent to the purchase, Diane found that her camera was hard to focus and the lenses were difficult to change. Furthermore, the strap broke on the carrying case. She now begins to doubt the wisdom of her purchase. A tension arises from her two beliefs that (1) Nikons are well-constructed, precision cameras and (2) "my Nikon is difficult to focus for clear pictures, takes too much time and effort to change lenses, and the strap on the carrying case has broken."

Diane can reduce the tension arising from these two cognitions by *rationalizing* that any fine camera can have its faults and that the retailer probably treated the carrying case with abuse which caused the eventual strap break. Or she might *seek information* which reinforces her belief that Nikon cameras are among the very best in the world, thereby amplifying the strong points of the camera, such as rapid film advancement, nice styling, and a solid shutter click indicating durability. Finally, a third option is to *change her opinion* toward Nikon cameras: "They are not good cameras. I should have purchased a Canon."

This example illustrates a very common type of marketing related phenomenon—*postpurchase dissonance*. Postpurchase dissonance occurs when a person makes a decision to buy one brand from among several alternative brands within a product category. The dissonance becomes particularly strong when the consumer makes a large commitment in the purchase. Such commitment refers not only to the amount of money, but also to the investment of time, effort, and ego as was illustrated in the previous example. Therefore, a purchase decision involving choice among brands of chewing gum at a supermarket check-out counter is unlikely to produce much perceptible dissonance. Goods requiring the consumer to commit much of himself or his money, however, are likely to generate considerable postpurchase dissonance. In general, therefore, durable and luxury goods are more likely to produce dissonance than are convenience goods, because they usually require larger consumer investment in time, ego, and money.

During purchase decisions, dissonance can result when the consumer recognizes that alternative brands have both positive and negative characteristics. Therefore, after making a decision, the consumer realizes that he has acquired some *relatively* undersirable traits of the selected brand while foregoing some relatively desirable traits of the alternative brands. At this point, the consumer may even rate the unchosen alternatives higher than the brand purchased. In the consumer's mind, positive attributes of unchosen brands and negative characteristics of the chosen brand are emphasized. This period of postpurchase process is called the *regret* phase, and it usually is very brief. The next phase is termed the *dissonance reduction period*. In this stage, the consumer is very likely to evaluate the chosen brand more positively than at the time of purchase, and he may evaluate the unselected brands less positively.

Multiattribute Models

In recent years, the adequacy of earlier attitude theories and models has come under question. An important criticism has been the lack of attention to the complexity and interactions of attitude components. In fact, early work employed only one-component definitions of attitude by focusing exclusively on a person's overall feelings or evaluative reactions toward objects. Later theories expanded on this view by stressing that attitudes have three major components: (1) the *cognitive* component which accounts for the individual's perceptions and knowledge about an object, (2) the *affective* component which describes the individual's feelings or emotional reactions (like/dislike) toward the object, and (3) the *conative* component which encompasses a tendency to act in certain ways toward the object. Unfortunately, although the importance of the three component view of attitudes was widely recognized, many marketers continued to employ measures that only focused on the affective component for determining an individual's overall evaluation of an object. As a consequence, it was difficult to determine the basis of a person's overall attitude and how it might be possible to influence this attitude to change.[16] Of course, as we might expect, the basis or reasons for holding an attitude, and the factors which might influence it to change over time are two considerations of high importance for the design of marketing strategies. Therefore, attitude measures that continued to focus only on the affective component were of limited usefulness to marketers.

Rosenberg and Fishbein pioneered new models of attitudes which have overcome many of the shortcomings of previous theories.[17] Because marketers and consumer behaviorists have given more attention to the Fishbein model, it will be reviewed here as an example of multiattribute attitude models.[18]

Fishbein's Attitude Model Fishbein's position is that people form attitudes toward objects on the basis of their *beliefs* (perceptions and knowledge) about these objects. Beliefs are in turn acquired by processing information which is obtained from direct experiences with objects and from communications about them received from other sources. Therefore, to adequately understand consumers' attitudes we must determine the beliefs that form the basis of these attitudes. Notice how this view is consistent with the flow of high-involvement consumer activities that has been presented in this text: information processing leads to cognitions or beliefs about products which in turn, lead to attitudes that are involved in the evaluation of products.

Because any object such as a product has numerous attributes (size, features, shape, etc.), an individual will process information and form beliefs about many of these individual attributes. Positive or negative feelings are also formed on the basis of the beliefs held about these attributes. Therefore, Fishbein's model is constructed so that a person's overall attitude toward some object is derived from his beliefs and feelings about various attributes of the object. This is why we refer to it as a *multiattribute* attitude model.

Fishbein's attitude model can be expressed in equation form as

$$A_o = \sum_{i=1}^{n} b_i e_i$$

where A_o = the person's overall attitude toward the object

b_i = the strength of the belief that the object is related to attribute i (such as the strength of the belief that Wrangler jeans are durable)

e_i = the person's evaluation or intensity of feelings (liking or disliking) toward attribute i

n = the number of relevant beliefs

We can see that the model explicitly incorporates the cognitive (belief) and affective (evaluation) components of attitudes. It also accounts for the strength or intensity of these elements. The conative component, to be discussed in more depth shortly, is related to these two components.

The model states that to determine a person's overall attitude toward some object, it is first necessary to determine those beliefs that have the most influence on her attitude. These most relevant beliefs, called *salient* beliefs, frequently do not exceed nine in number.[19] The overall attitude toward an object can then be obtained by multiplying the belief score by the evaluation score for each attribute and then summing across all relevant beliefs to obtain the value A_o.

An example will reinforce our understanding of the model. Assume that we want to determine a consumer's overall attitude toward a certain brand of wristwatch and that through questioning we have been able to identify five beliefs that appear to be salient for this consumer. The strength of each belief can be measured on a bipolar scale such as the following:

The wristwatch is high in price

likely ___ ___ ___ ___ ___ ___ ___ unlikely
(+3) (+2) (+1) (0) (−1) (−2) (−3)

By responding to this scale, the consumer is indicating the degree to which she believes that the wristwatch possesses the attribute in question—in this case, a high price. If we were attempting to assess the attitudes of more than one consumer, we could question a sample of them and then select as salient beliefs those that are most frequently mentioned. The entire group of consumers would then be asked to respond to these salient beliefs, as indicated above.

After obtaining belief scores, the consumer would be asked to indicate her evaluation of each product attribute for which a salient belief exists. This is frequently accomplished on the following type of scale:

A high price for the wristwatch is:

good _____ _____ _____ _____ _____ _____ _____ bad
    extremely moderately slightly neither/nor slightly moderately extremely
    (+3)   (+2)   (+1)   (0)   (−1)   (−2)   (−3)

Be careful to note that these evaluation scores measure the consumer's feelings about each attribute itself (high price, accurate time, etc.). They do *not* measure how much the consumer is pleased or displeased that the product in question possesses the attribute.

Table 16-1 presents hypothetical results of these data collection efforts. As the model requires, each of the consumer's belief scores are now multiplied by their respective evaluation scores to obtain the last column of the table. Adding all of the products in this column reveals that the consumer's overall attitude toward the brand stands at +5. This represents a slightly positive attitude toward the brand when compared to a maximum attainable attitude score of +45. The consumer's attitude toward other wristwatch brands could also be calculated and compared to this brand. For the additional brands, it would only be necessary to obtain new belief scores because as mentioned, the evaluation score measures feelings toward general product attributes and therefore does not vary across brands.

It is important to note how differences in belief scores and evaluation scores can influence the consumer's overall attitude toward the product. For example, note in Table 16-1 that the first two salient beliefs both have the same evaluation score of +2. However, because the consumer is more confident that this brand of wristwatch keeps good time (+3) than she is that it has a waterproof case (+2), the time accuracy attribute contributes more to her attitude toward the brand. Conversely, notice that the first and fourth salient beliefs both have the same belief strength, but they differ considerably in terms of evaluation scores (+2 versus −2), yielding *offsetting* contributions to the consumer's overall attitude. This points out an important characteristic of this type of attitude model—in addition to being multiattribute in nature, it is also a *compensatory* model. This means that the product of belief and evaluation scores on one brand attribute can be offset or *compensated* for by products derived from one or more other attributes. The impli-

TABLE 16-1 EXAMPLE OF CALCULATING A CONSUMER'S ATTITUDE TOWARD A BRAND OF WRISTWATCH

Salient Beliefs	Belief Strength (b_i)	Evaluation Score (e_i)	Product ($b_i e_i$)
Keeps accurate time	+3	+2	+6
Has waterproof case	+2	+2	+4
Has day/date calendar	+1	+3	+3
Is high in price	+3	−2	−6
Has digital display	+2	−1	−2

$$\text{Overall attitude score } (A_o) = \sum_{i=1}^{5} b_i e_i = +5$$

cation is that a poor response of the consumer to one feature of a brand does not necessarily cancel this brand out in her eyes.

These last comments demonstrate an important potential of multiattribute models. As Wilkie and Pessemier have stated:

The potential advantage of multi-attribute models over the simpler "over-all affect" approach (unidimensional model) is in gaining understanding of attitudinal structure. *Diagnosis* **of brand strengths and weaknesses on relevant product attributes can then be used to suggest specific changes in a brand and its marketing support.**[20]

That is, information regarding consumers' beliefs and evaluations generated by a multiattribute model provides important knowledge relevant to marketing strategy. The information can be used to suggest changes in brand attributes, modifications of promotional messages to better acquaint consumers with existing brand attributes, and the identification of new market opportunities. More will be said about these strategies in the next chapter.

MODEL LIMITATIONS   Many marketers were quick to capitalize on the potential of Fishbein's model and similar multiattribute models for predicting the behavior of consumers. Consequently, numerous studies were undertaken to establish the strength of this attitude-behavior linkage. Unfortunately, these studies did not yield a consistently positive relationship. Several reasons have been offered for these lackluster results:

1 Consumption situations can vary, and this will influence the strength of the attitude-behavior relationship.[21] In fact, evidence suggests that consumers' attitudes toward a given brand can actually vary depending on the situation.[22]

2 Time usually elapses between when consumers form attitudes and when they are ready to act on these attitudes. During that time, many variables, both expected and unexpected, can intervene to also influence behavior. For example, an unexpected need for a new family car could quickly postpone or cancel plans to purchase a home video recorder.

3 A distinction must be made between attitudes toward objects and attitudes toward behaving in a certain way toward these objects. For example, many consumers could have a favorable attitude toward Ferrari automobiles, but, because of their cost, few would realistically have a favorable attitude toward purchasing one. The consumer's attitudes toward some type of behavior are influenced by his evaluation of the perceived consequences (positive and negative) of taking such action. Therefore, these attitudes are more relevant for predicting consumers' actions than are attitudes toward the objects themselves.

4 Consumers are often influenced by their *perceptions* of what others will think of their actions. Therefore, even though a consumer may have a favorable attitude toward making some purchase, he may refrain from doing so because of his perception that others who are important to him may not approve of the action. This influence is referred to as a *subjective norm*.

These considerations convinced attitude theorists that it is inappropriate to expect attitude-toward-object models to successfully predict behavior. New modeling efforts were necessary to account for the additional complexity introduced by such factors. Fishbein responded with the behavioral intentions model.[23]

Fishbein's Behavioral Intentions Model The new model offered by Fishbein, and contributed to by Ajzen, can be presented in diagram form as shown in Figure 16-6. Here, we see that a person's behavior is a function of his intention to behave in a certain manner and other intervening factors. This means that intention to behave cannot be expected to be a perfect predictor of behavior.

Two factors are seen to influence the person's intention to act in a certain manner: (1) his attitude toward acting in that manner and (2) subjective norms which we said are the individual's perceptions of how others who are important to him will react to such behavior. The relative influence of each of these factors will determine the exact nature of the person's behavioral intentions. The figure also shows that attitudes toward behavior are determined by beliefs and evaluations that the consumer holds about the consequences of behavior. Subjective norms are determined by the consumer's beliefs about reactions of others regarding his intended behavior, and his motivations to comply with their standards for behavior.

Fishbein expressed these relationships in equation form as

$$B \approx BI = w_1(A_B) + w_2(SN)$$

where B = the person's actual behavior, which is approximately equal to BI

BI = his intention to behave in a specific manner

A_B = his attitude toward performing that behavior

SN = the subjective norm regarding this behavior, and

w_1 and w_2 = weights representing the relative influence of A_B and SN respectively on the behavioral intention

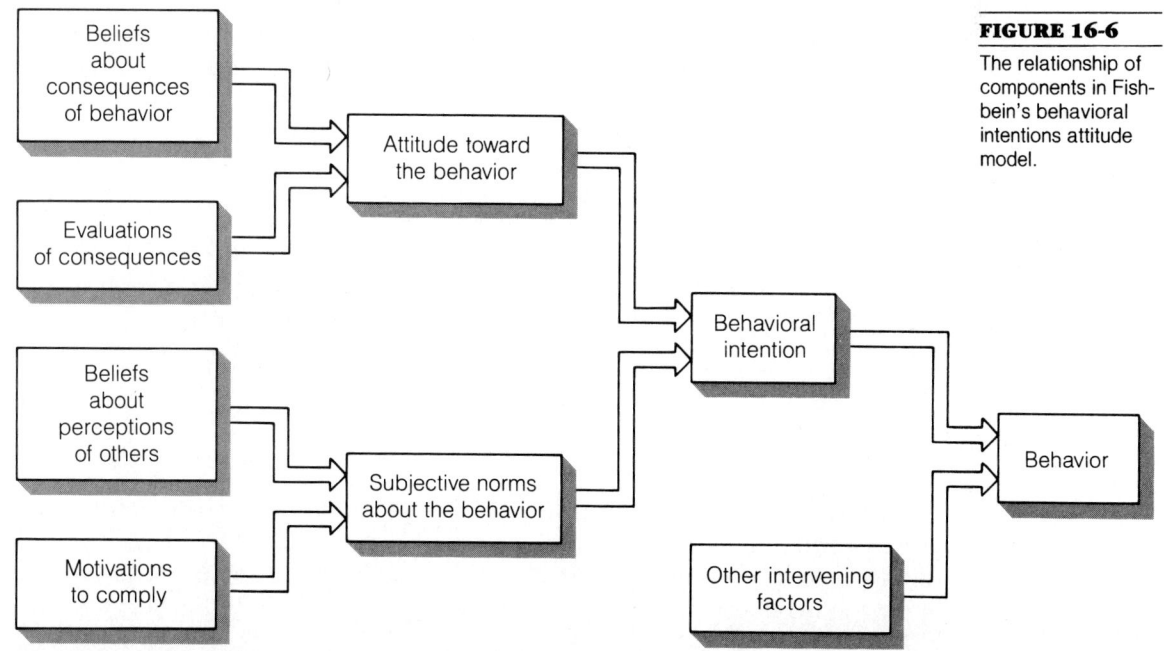

FIGURE 16-6

The relationship of components in Fishbein's behavioral intentions attitude model.

As the model shows, to predict behavior one must determine the individual's attitude toward the specific behavior in question (A_B), and his subjective norm (SN) regarding that behavior. Each of these would then be weighted by w_1 and w_2 respectively (which add up to 1.0) to reflect their relative importance in influencing the behavioral intention. Such weights would be derived by regression analysis from a preliminary study. The weighted components would then be combined to yield a measure of behavioral intention to be used for prediction. We can see, therefore, that use of the model requires determination of its two components—A_B and SN. Each of these is discussed, in turn, below.

The individual's attitude toward performing the specific behavior (A_B) is expressed as

$$A_B = \sum_{i=1}^{n} b_i e_i$$

where A_B = the individual's overall attitude toward performing the specific behavior

b_i = the person's belief that performing that behavior results in consequence i

e_i = the person's evaluation of consequence i

n = the number of relevant behavioral beliefs

It will be noticed that the form of this component is identical to the model for attitude toward objects that was discussed earlier. As was stated before, relevant beliefs must be determined and then these beliefs and the accompanying evaluations must be measured on scales. The important change here is that beliefs and evaluations are about certain *actions* and the consequences of these actions, rather than about attributes of an object.

The subjective norm component of the behavioral intentions model can be expressed as follows:

$$SN = \sum_{i=1}^{k} b_i m_i$$

where SN = the individual's subjective norm regarding the specific behavior in question

b_i = his normative belief that reference group or person i thinks he should or should not perform the behavior

m_i = his motivation to comply with the thoughts of referent i

k = the number of relevant referents.

An example will provide more meaning to these formulas. Assume that a consumer is considering the purchase of a chartered vacation package for a 2-week period during the first half of July. To simplify the situation, also assume that she is only interested in choosing between two vacation packages—one to England and one to Japan. The consumer's behavioral intention toward these alternatives will be a function of her attitude toward purchasing each and of the subjective norms she holds about each purchase. These components are each examined in turn below.

As our formula for A_B shows, to determine the consumer's attitude toward purchasing either vacation package we must first identify the salient beliefs she holds toward the consequences of a purchase. Often these can be obtained through a questioning process. However, if the attitudes of a large number of consumers needed to be measured, questioning a sample of them would identify the most frequently held salient beliefs. In either case, once consumers' salient beliefs regarding the consequences of actions have been identified, we would need to measure their belief strengths and their evaluations of these consequences. The difference between the scales that would measure these variables and the ones used for Fishbein's earlier attitude model is that now focus is on the *consequences* of purchase *behavior* rather than on the attributes of the object.

Table 16-2 presents results that we could have been obtained from our consumer. The first column identifies six salient beliefs this consumer holds about the consequences of purchasing the two chartered vacation packages. Notice that the statements refer to a specific time interval for the actions. The second and third columns represent the degree to which the consumer believes these consequences describe the England trip and Japan trip, respectively. The third column represents the consumer's evaluation of the consequences described in column 1. Notice that these evaluations would be the same for the various trips, because they reflect feelings about consequences and not feelings about the extent to which such consequences would result from particular trips.

TABLE 16-2 EXAMPLE OF CALCULATING A CONSUMER'S ATTITUDE TOWARD PURCHASING DIFFERENT VACATION PACKAGES

Salient Beliefs about Consequences	Belief Strengths (b_i) England Trip	Belief Strengths (b_i) Japan Trip	Evaluation Score (e_i)	Product ($b_i e_i$) England Trip	Product ($b_i e_i$) Japan Trip
Taking the England/Japan vacation package in July will:					
• increase my social contacts	+2	+2	+3	+6	+6
• provide a restful vacation	+2	+1	+1	+2	+1
• improve my mental attitude	+1	+3	+2	+2	+6
• be expensive	+2	+3	−2	−4	−6
• make me a more interesting person	+1	+3	+2	+2	+6
• involve difficult language skills	−2	+2	−3	+6	−6

$$\text{Overall attitude toward purchase } A_B = \sum_{i=1}^{6} b_i e_i = \quad +14 \quad +7$$

The last two columns present the product of belief and evaluation scores for each trip; the sum of these columns shows that the consumer holds a more favorable attitude toward taking the England trip (+14) than she does the Japan trip (+7).

Now, in order to determine the consumer's subjective norm for purchasing either vacation package, we must first identify the groups and individuals who have the most influence on her regarding the behavior in question. These are called the *salient referents*. Often, this information can be obtained through a questioning process. Assume for our purposes that there are three individuals who are salient referents for this consumer: her brother, a special friend, and her boss.

We next must identify the consumer's beliefs about thoughts or reactions of these people regarding her purchase of each of the vacation trips. Her motivation to comply with these thoughts must also be measured. This information could be obtained from the following types of measurement scales:

My brother thinks that I

should ____ ____ ____ ____ ____ ____ ____ should not
       (+3) (+2) (+1) (0) (−1) (−2) (−3)

take the charter trip to England in July

How much do you want to do what your brother thinks that you should do?

	Not at all	(0)
____	Slightly	(+1)
____	Moderately	(+2)
____	Strongly	(+3)

Table 16-3 summarizes results of our data collection regarding the subjective norm component in much the same way as previous tables have done. It is useful to notice how the consumer's motivation to comply weights the perceptions of salient referent opinions. For example, she believes that both her special friend and her boss hold the same opinions about the Japan trip, but because she is more motivated to comply with her friend's opinion, it carries more weight in influencing her subjective norm. Overall, we see from a summation of the last columns that the subjective norm considerably favors the Japan trip (+11) over the England trip (+1).

TABLE 16-3

EXAMPLE OF CALCULATING A CONSUMER'S SUBJECTIVE NORM TOWARD PURCHASING DIFFERENT VACATION PACKAGES

| | Normative Belief Strength (b_i) || Motivation to Comply (m_i) | Product ($b_i m_i$) ||
Salient Referents	England Trip	Japan Trip		England Trip	Japan Trip
Brother	+2	+1	+1	+2	+1
Special Friend	−1	+2	+3	−3	+6
Boss	+1	+2	+2	+2	+4

$$\text{Subjective Norm } SN = \sum_{i=1}^{3} b_i m_i = \;+1 \quad\quad +11$$

The last ingredients needed to determine our consumer's behavioral intentions are weights that reflect the relative importance of her attitude toward behavior and her subjective norm. Recall that these weights would have to come from regression analysis of a preliminary study. Assume that such an investigation generated weights of .4 and .6 for the attitude and subjective norm components respectively. We now can substitute these weights and information from Tables 16-2 and 16-3 into the equation that was presented earlier and repeated below:

$$BI = w_1(A_B) + w_2(SN)$$

For the England trip we find that $BI = .4(14) + .6(1) = 6.2$ and for the Japan trip $BI = .4(7) + .6(11) = 9.4$. We see that, in this case, even though the consumer's attitude strongly favors the England trip, her subjective norm strongly favors the Japan trip. Because the subjective norm carries more weight in her decision making on this issue (.6 versus .4), the prediction is that she intends to purchase the Japan trip. However, recall from our earlier discussion and Figure 16-6 that because of other influencing factors the consumer's behavioral intentions will only be an approximation of her actual behavior.

MODEL EVALUATION A number of issues and limitations of the Fishbein behavioral intention model still need to be resolved.[24] Nevertheless, evidence accumulating from tests of the model has been quite encouraging.[25] Our ability to predict the behavior of consumers has improved when compared to the earlier attitude-toward-object model. However, what appears to be just as important are the implications this model has for marketers in terms of factors influencing consumers' intentions to behave. These attitudinal and subjective norm components can enable diagnosis of reasons for behavior, and also suggest alternative marketing strategies for effecting changes in consumers' attitudes and intentions to behave. These practical implications will have much of our attention in the next chapter.

SUMMARY

This chapter introduced the concept of attitudes, described their basic characteristics, and reviewed their basic functions. Various sources of attitude development also served as a focus for discussion.

Several theories and models of attitudes were depicted next. Specifically, the congruity, balance, and cognitive dissonance views were treated. Although these viewpoints provide significant insight, recent attention has turned to multiattribute attitude models. The attraction of these newer models lies in their explicit recognition that attitudes have more than one dimension. This focuses attention on the factors that contribute to overall attitudes (product attributes, consequences of actions, etc.) and how they are evaluated by the consumer. The practical implications for marketing strategies that result from understanding these factors were addressed.

Models offered by Fishbein were discussed in some detail as representatives of these multiattribute attitude concepts. His earlier model of attitude toward objects was seen as an important contribution to thinking in the area. Its limitations in predicting consumer behavior were also discussed. This model has given way to a newer conceptualization of behavioral intentions, in which consumers' intentions to behave in a specific way are seen to be a function of their attitudes toward that behavior and their subjective norms. Discussion in this chapter serves as a foundation for the next chapter which treats attitude change and the role of various types of marketing communications in this process.

DISCUSSION TOPICS

1 A variety of definitions of attitude exist. What appears to be the emphasis of the more recent definitions?

2 What are the major characteristics of attitudes? Assume an attitude regarding a specific product and use this as an example to demonstrate each characteristic.

3 What are the functions of an attitude? Can you cite specific personal experiences that demonstrate each of these functions?

4 What are the sources of attitude development? Can you foresee how these sources might conflict with one another in their influence on developing attitudes? If so, cite an example to demonstrate your point.

5 Review the attitude theories of congruity, balance, and cognitive dissonance. Highlight their major characteristics.

6 Some advertisements make highly exaggerated claims for a brand which probably cannot be fulfilled. Using your knowledge of cognitive dissonance, assess the wisdom of this technique.

7 Distinguish between the Fishbein attitude model and earlier attitude theories. What implications does this have for predicting consumer behavior?

8 It has been argued that the consequences of action referred to in Fishbein's behavioral intentions model can be linked to the concepts of consumers' perceived benefits and benefit segmentation. Discuss this argument.

9 Think of a product, or action toward a product, about which you hold an attitude. Did you use a compensatory method in formulating this attitude? If so, explain how. If not, explain why you think this is the case.

10 Choose a brand about which a friend has formed some attitudes. Using the methods discussed in this chapter, determine your friend's intention to purchase this brand in the next two weeks. Be prepared to discuss each step of your project and its implications.

NOTES

[1] Martin Fishbein, "The Relationship between Beliefs, Attitudes, and Behavior," in Shel Feldman (ed.), *Cognitive Consistency,* Academic, New York, 1966, pp. 199–223.
[2] The term "object" is used here to include abstract concepts such as enjoyment, as well as physical things.
[3] Gordon W. Allport, "Attitudes," in C. A. Murchison (ed.), *A Handbook of Social Psychology,* Clark University Press, Worcester, Ma, 1935, pp. 798–844.
[4] D. Krech and R. Crutchfield, *Theory and Problems in Social Psychology,* McGraw-Hill, New York, 1948.
[5] Martin Fishbein, "A Behavior Theory Approach to the Relations between Beliefs about an Object and the Attitude Toward the Object," in Martin Fishbein (ed.), *Readings in Attitude Theory and Measurement,* Wiley, New York, 1967, p. 394.
[6] T. M. Newcomb, R. H. Turner, and P. E. Converse, *Social Psychology,* Holt, New York, 1965, p. 115.

[7] Daniel Katz, "The Functional Approach to the Study of Attitudes," *Public Opinion Quarterly,* 24:163–204, 1960.

[8] M. Wayne DeLozier, *The Marketing Communications Process,* McGraw-Hill, New York, 1976, p. 81.

[9] Arch G. Woodside and J. William Davenport, "The Effect of Salesman Similarity and Expertise on Consumer Purchasing Behavior," *Journal of Marketing Research,* 11:198–202, May 1974.

[10] This section is based largely upon the works of Charles E. Osgood, George J. Suci, and Percy H. Tannenbaum, *The Measurement of Meaning,* University of Illinois Press, Urbana, IL, 1957; Milton J. Rosenberg, et al., *Attitude Organization and Change,* Yale, New Haven, CT, 1960; Leon A. Festinger, *A Theory of Cognitive Dissonance,* Stanford, Stanford, CA, 1957; Roger Brown, *Social Psychology,* Free Press, New York, 1965; and Martin Fishbein and Icek Ajzen, *Belief, Attitude, Intention and Behavior,* Addison-Wesley, Reading, MA, 1975.

[11] For a thorough treatment of the mathematics involved in predicting the resolution of such cases, see Osgood, Suci, and Tannenbaum, *Measurement of Meaning,* pp. 199–207.

[12] See Jonathan L. Freedman, Jr., Merrill Carlsmith, and David O. Sears, *Social Psychology,* Prentice-Hall, Englewood Cliffs, NJ, 1970, p. 263; and Charles E. Osgood and Percy H. Tannenbaum, "The Principle of Congruity in the Prediction of Attitude Change," *Psychological Review,* 62:42–55, 1955.

[13] Some of the ideas in this section are attributable to Brown, *Social Psychology,* pp. 566–670.

[14] Fritz Heider, "Attitudes and Cognitive Organizations," *Journal of Psychology,* 21:107–112, January 1946.

[15] See Festinger, *Cognitive Dissonance.*

[16] See Fishbein and Ajzen, *Belief, Attitude, Intention and Behavior,* pp. 11–13; and Icek Ajzen and Martin Fishbein, *Understanding Attitudes and Predicting Social Behavior,* Prentice-Hall, Englewood Cliffs, NJ, 1980, pp. 18–20.

[17] See Milton J. Rosenberg, "Cognitive Structure and Attitudinal Affect," *Journal of Abnormal and Social Psychology,* 53:367–372, November 1956; Martin Fishbein, "An Investigation of the Relationship between Beliefs about an Object and the Attitudes toward That Object," *Human Relations,* 16:233–240, 1963; and Martin Fishbein, "Attitude and the Prediction of Behavior," in Martin Fishbein (ed.), *Readings in Attitude Theory and Measurement,* Wiley, New York, 1967, pp. 477–492.

[18] Some examples are Arch G. Woodside and James D. Clokey, "Multi-Attribute/Multi-Brand Models," *Journal of Advertising Research,* 14:33–40, October, 1974; Frank M. Bass and W. Wayne Talarzyk, "An Attitude Model for the Study of Brand Preference," *Journal of Marketing Research,* 9:93–96, February 1972; Michael B. Mazis, Olli T. Ahtola, and R. Eugene Klippel, "A Comparison of Four Multi-Attribute Models in the Prediction of Consumer Attitudes," *Journal of Consumer Research,* 2:38–52, June 1975; and James R. Bettman, Noel Capon, Richard J. Lutz, "Multi-attribute Measurement Models and Multi-attribute Theory: A Test of Construct Validity," *Journal of Consumer Research,* 1:1–14, March 1975.

[19] Ajzen and Fishbein, *Understanding Attitudes and Predicting Social Behavior,* p. 63.

[20] William L. Wilkie and Edgar A. Pessemier, "Issues in Marketing's Use of Multi-attribute Attitude Models," *Journal of Marketing Research,* 10:428, November 1973.

[21] See William O. Bearden and Arch G. Woodside, "Interactions of Consumption Situations and Brand Attitudes," *Journal of Applied Psychology,* 61:764–769, 1976.

[22] See Kenneth E. Miller and James L. Ginter, "An Investigation of Situational Variation in Brand Choice Behavior and Attitude," *Journal of Marketing Research,* 16:111–123, February 1979.

[23] See Martin Fishbein, "Attitude and the Prediction of Behavior"; and Ajzen and Fishbein, *Understanding Attitudes and Predicting Social Behavior.*

[24] See, for example, Paul R. Warshaw, "Predicting Purchase and Other Behaviors from Generally and Contextually Specific Intentions," *Journal of Marketing Research,* 17:26–33, February 1980; and Michael J. Ryan and E. H. Bonfield, "Fishbein's Intentions Model: A Test of External and Pragmatic Validity," *Journal of Marketing,* 44:82–95, Spring 1980.

[25] See, for example, Richard L. Oliver and Philip K. Berger, "A Path Analysis of Preventive Health Care Decision Models," *Journal of Consumer Research,* 6:113–122, September 1979; and Ryan and Bonfield, "Fishbein's Intentions Model."

CHAPTER 17
CHANGING ATTITUDES

In the following example, consider the situation faced by Spiegel—the large catalog retailer that focuses on clothing and related needs of women.[1]

Social changes had resulted in more than 50 percent of American women joining the labor force and, as a consequence, significantly changing their lifestyles and product desires. In order to meet the needs of this new market, Spiegel had made a number of changes, including modifications in their product lines. An advertising campaign was also deemed necessary to announce these modifications, to change attitudes regarding nonstore shopping, and to encourage women's intentions to purchase from their Speigel catalog. This campaign stressed the new image—an upscale, "fashion oriented" nonstore retailer with merchandise which could be obtained through stay-at-home, leisurely, and convenient catalog shopping. Although market response was positive, research revealed that the target audiences' attitudes toward shopping at Spiegel had not changed sufficiently in the directions intended. Therefore, a dramatically new campaign was designed to emphasize very chic fashions, style, and quality merchandise represented by well-known and prestigious brand names. At the same time, the previous theme of leisurely stay-at-home buying was scrapped, because evidence suggested that high fashion and quality brands were attributes more important to attitudes and buying intentions of the target market than was convenience.

The situation faced by Speigel involves considerations commonly faced by many marketers who are attempting to change consumer attitudes through use of persuasive messages. Consideration must be given to various characteristics of the audience that will receive communications, the type of spokespeople or other sources to use in these communications, and the content of messages that will be delivered. In addition, care must be taken to understand the nature of situations surrounding consumer decisions to purchase the advertised product or service.

As we have just suggested, the persuasive communication process appears capable of influencing attitude change among consumers. It should also be kept in mind, however, that many of the methods for influencing attitude change that will be discussed in this chapter are also useful for encouraging the development of new attitudes—as in the case of consumers' attitude formation for new products. The reader should also note that the degree of success in changing consumers' attitudes depends on how strongly existing attitudes are held. Those that are strongly entrenched are difficult to change, while neutral and weakly held attitudes are much easier to influence.

The chapter begins by discussing strategies for changing consumers' attitudes and reviewing the general nature of the communication process used to accomplish these strategies. Several major components of such communications are discussed next in terms of their influence on attitude change. First, various communication sources and their potential effects are addressed. Different properties of the message itself are then treated. Finally, characteristics of the intended audience which affect their receptivity to persuasive communications are examined.

STRATEGIES FOR CHANGING ATTITUDES AND INTENTIONS

Some strategies for influencing changes in consumers' attitudes toward certain behaviors have already been identified. Other strategies exist, however, that accomplish changes in behavioral intentions without directly affecting attitudes. Because Fishbein's behavioral intentions model links these concepts so closely together, the various change strategies are discussed collectively below. Although many factors can influence the marketer's choice among these alternatives, one fundamental consideration should be the degree of involvement that consumers are experiencing with the product.

Low-Involvement Strategies

In Chapter 12, we noted that under low-involvement conditions consumers are not likely to make brand choices on the basis of well-formed attitudes. In essence, their interest is too low for evaluating product attributes and forming beliefs about various brands. Given this, it is unproductive for the marketer to develop communications designed to modify prepurchase attitudes. The options that remain stress capitalizing on a means to transform the situation into one characterized by high involvement. For example, remember that the low-involvement hierarchy of effects model (review Figure 12-11) indicates that consumers may form attitudes on the basis of *postpurchase* brand evaluations. This highlights the importance for marketers of delivering quality products that will receive positive evaluations during use, which will result in favorable consumer attitudes. If such postpurchase attitudes are sufficiently formed, they will guide subsequent purchases. The marketer would then be able to employ attitude-change strategies developed for high-involvement situations.

A second attitude-change strategy option for low-involvement situations entails encouraging consumers to increase their prepurchase involvement levels. Success here would allow use of high-involvement attitude-change methods to influence brand choices. How can this increase in prepurchase involvement be accomplished? Assael has complied a list of options suggested by various researchers.[2]

1 *Link the product to an involving issue.* Because issues are often more involving than are products, this linkage could increase involvement regarding the product. Linking a breakfast cereal to problems of deficient performance among schoolchildren who have not had a wholesome breakfast would be one example.

2. *Link the product to a presently involving personal situation.* On some occasions, a message can be targeted to audiences at the time they are engaged in an activity related to the product. At this time, their interest could be sufficiently high to qualify as high-involvement. An example might be radio advertisements for a suntan lotion during midday hours of summer weekends.

3. *Develop high-involvement advertisements.* Because consumers' involvement in a product is low, it does not necessarily mean that they cannot become involved in advertisements for the product. The use of humor, dramatic events, or other methods can create an involving advertisement to which the product could then be linked. Examples might include the active dance scenes of Dr. Pepper television commercials and other television ads showing the humorous woes of businesspeople who failed to use Federal Express service.

4. *Change the importance of product benefits.* This option is quite difficult to pursue, because it attempts a frontal attack on consumers' perceptions of product benefits. To illustrate, if consumers could be convinced that the fiber content in dried cereal is very important to their health, they might become involved in their choice of cereal. The brands that possess this attribute are then likely to be the recipient of favorable consumer attitudes.

5. *Reveal or introduce important product characteristics.* New attributes can be associated with a product, and consumers can also be made aware that some favorable attributes have been product characteristics for a long time. These have the potential for increasing involvement levels. The absence of caffeine and sugar in a number of soft drinks certainly appears to capture the interest of many consumers because of their implications regarding the health and appearance of the body. Fortification of milk and other foods with vitamins represents another example.

In all of these cases, the attempt has been to increase involvement levels among consumers to the point where they will form attitudes prior to purchase and use these attitudes to influence their purchase decisions. We now turn to strategies designed for conditions in which these prepurchase attitudes are likely to be formed.

High-Involvement Strategies

Potentially, a variety of strategies are available for changing consumer attitudes under high-involvement conditions. Before implementing such strategies, however, the marketer must be clear on whether the attempt is to change consumer attitudes about the brand, or whether it is to change attitudes about behaving toward the brand. As we found in the last chapter, consumer attitudes about behaving toward a brand are more closely related to their intentions to purchase. Therefore, we will focus on attitudes toward behavior in the following discussion.

Figure 17-1, which closely parallels portions of Figure 16-6, suggests a variety of potential strategies for influencing change in consumers' attitudes toward behavior.[3] Employing the same reasoning as Fishbein used to develop his model, we can argue that behavioral change is a function of changes in behavioral intentions and other intervening factors. Changes in behavioral intentions are related to changes in attitudes toward the behavior and changes in subjective norms about the behavior. Each of these, in turn, are functions of their components. These relationships suggest the following potential strategies:

1 *Change existing beliefs about the consequences of behavior.* Consumers often hold incomplete or incorrect beliefs about the consequences of purchasing and using particular brands. Modification of those beliefs that will positively influence attitudes can increase intentions to purchase. How can this be accomplished? One way is for advertisements to focus on *brand benefits.* Here, the message would be that purchase of the brand will yield certain beneficial results (consequences) for the consumer. As an example, consider the following message: "Users of Top Flight Golf balls get up to 14 more yards per drive than users of other brands." Of course, a second option is for advertisements to suggest that few negative consequences will result from purchasing the brand. Stress on a low price is one such method.

2 *Change consumers' evaluation of the consequences of a particular action.* In many cases, consumers may believe that using a brand will lead to certain consequences, but these consequences are not evaluated very positively. Measures taken to increase evaluations of the consequences can have positive results. For example, an advertisement for Listerine mouthwash has stressed that its strong taste is associated with effectiveness in killing germs and giving fresh breath—"It tastes strong because it is strong." Potential results are more positive evaluations of the strong taste and enhancement of attitudes toward the brand.

3 *Introduce new belief/evaluation combinations.* In some cases, marketers can add or delete product attributes and generate positive consequences for the consumer. In other cases, the presence or absence of existing product attributes can be stressed in terms of their favorable consequences for the consumer. The former

FIGURE 17-1

A diagram relating some strategy options for attitude change in high-involvement conditions. (*Source:* Martin Fishbein and Icek Ajzen, *Belief, Attitude and Behavior: An Introduction to Theory and Research*, Addison-Wesley, Reading, MA, 1975, p. 407.)

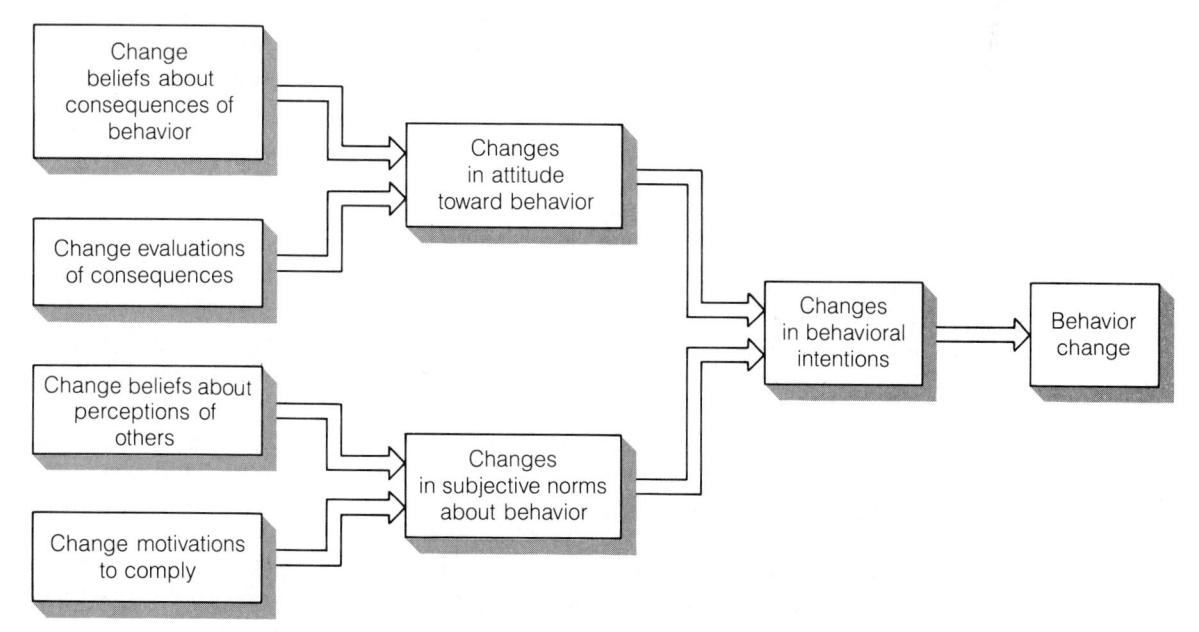

case is exemplified by the addition of Floristat to Crest toothpaste. This ingredient was advertised as being more effective in preventing tooth decay than its previous fluoride compound known as Flouristan. An example of the latter strategy was used by Canada Dry when in 1982 it announced that its ginger ale does not have caffeine and it never did. This was important information to consumers who wanted to minimize their caffeine intake.

4 *Change existing normative beliefs.* In some situations, consumers may hold favorable attitudes toward certain behaviors but be reluctant to take action because of an unfavorable reaction on the subjective norm component. Such a situation would occur when the consumer holds a belief that others who are important to her will not react favorably to the actions in question. This can be an important consideration with regard to the purchase of certain clothing items and other socially visible products. Although it may be difficult, the possibility exists that changes in such beliefs can be achieved. For example, promotions may simulate group settings in which people with whom the consumer might identify express favorable reactions to purchasing the advertised brand. Given sufficient realism, such advertisements may weaken the consumer's beliefs that people important to her will have negative reactions to purchase of the brand.

5 *Change motivations to comply with subjective norms.* A second strategy to modify the subjective norm component of behavioral intentions is to alter consumers' motivations to comply with the influences of people important to them. One way this can be accomplished is to diminish or increase the perceived importance or status of these influential others for at least the decision in question. For example, advertisements for a particular brand might stress the importance of being an individual and not always heeding the opinions of friends or important others.

6 *Introduce new normative components.* Subjective norms can also be influenced by the addition of new normative components which will be strong in their influence on the consumer. This can occur through the introduction of additional salient referents to the subjective norm component of the behavioral intentions equation. Promotions showing how family members, friends, and so on, react to certain purchase decisions, and why these reactions might be important to the consumer, are possibilities.

The above review suggests that a variety of potential strategies exist for influencing attitude change among consumers in high-involvement situations. Selection of one or more strategies will be affected by the competitive environment, consumers' existing conditions, knowledge and beliefs, characteristics of the product, and related factors. A few comments are useful on several of these issues.

Experience has shown marketers that it is much easier to change the intensity of attitudes than it is to change their direction. For example, if consumers have negative attitudes toward a brand, it would be a difficult task to transform these attitudes into positive ones. Efforts may be successful in reducing the intensity of negative attitudes, but the payoff involved in such endeavors would be questionable. In such cases, the frequent recommendation is to "go with the flow," which could mean withdrawing the brand or redesigning or reformulating it and introducing it to consumers under another name so that it will be given a fighting chance in the marketplace. For brands that receive generally favorable consumer acceptance, the strategy is typically to identify and concentrate on those components that yield the most positive change in attitudes for a given amount of investment in promotion.

Related to the above paragraph is the point that weakly held attitudes are easier to change than ones that are strongly held. Attitude strength has a variety of sources. One is the strength of the consumer's beliefs. The more confident a consumer is about his or her brand beliefs, the more difficult they are to change. For example, two consumers may believe that Michelin tires will yield only moderate levels of tread wear. However, the strength of one's beliefs may be much greater than the other. It would be more difficult to convince the consumer with strong beliefs that Michelins give excellent tread wear. Strong beliefs are formed through personal experience and from information about products that is clear and readily available for a period of time. Weaker beliefs tend to exist under opposite conditions.

A second influence on attitude strength is the degree of involvement a consumer has with the product in question. Greater involvement reflects more personal relevance of the product to the consumer. Consequently, an involved consumer is likely to hold stronger beliefs about the brands in question. Additional evidence suggests that more-involved consumers will be less willing to accept statements that diverge from beliefs held about a brand.[4] The degree of divergence that will be accepted is referred to as the consumer's *latitude of acceptance*. Conversely, statements that the consumer does not accept will fall into his *latitude of rejection*. The implication of this is that highly involved consumers are likely to hold strong beliefs about a brand and accept only those advertising claims that deviate very little from these beliefs. On the other hand, consumers who are not highly involved will have wider latitudes of acceptance, and their attitudes can be changed by more-discrepant advertising claims. As a consequence, more advertising dollars will probably have to be expended to gradually change the brand beliefs of highly involved consumers, while more rapid change with fewer resources may be possible for less-involved consumers.

A final point to mention here is that typically it appears to be easier to change consumers beliefs than to change their evaluations of the consequences of certain actions. This is probably so because evaluations are based on the consumer's need structure, which is more enduring and central to his values and self-concept than are beliefs about purchasing a particular brand.

Discussion in the previous paragraphs has focused on strategies for making absolute changes in consumers' attitudes toward the marketer's brand. Of course, in most situations consumers face competing brands and perceive them relative to each other. Therefore, a potential strategy not yet mentioned would be for the marketer to increase her brand's *relative* attitude standing by encouraging consumers to develop more negative attitudes toward competing brands. This would require communications that directly attack competing brands, initiate or encourage damaging rumors about these brands, or utilize similar measures. Generally speaking, there has been very little of this type of behavior in the marketplace. In addition to the ethical issues that speak against it, such efforts are likely to result in damaging counterattacks from competitors. The ensuing battle would probably hurt all those involved. Therefore, we will not discuss such strategies further.

THE COMMUNICATION PROCESS

The primary means available to marketers for influencing attitude change is the design and implementation of persuasive communications. Properly designed communications can be effective in persuading consumers to modify their beliefs, evaluations, and subjective norms. In order to design and effectively use persuasive messages, an appreciation of the general nature of the communication process is needed. A simplified model of this process is shown in Figure 17-2 and described below.

The sender initiates a communication message. This individual or group has as an objective the transmission of an intended message to one or more individuals acting as receivers. In marketing, the sender usually represents a company or its brand, and the intended message is usually conceived of as a mechanism to change consumers' attitudes toward the brand or toward purchasing it.

An intended message is the meaning a sender wishes to convey to receivers. In order to deliver this intended meaning, however, the message must be suitably formed for transmission in the channel selected for its delivery. That is, the intended message must be *encoded* into symbols making up the actual message which represent thoughts of the sender. These symbols are usually words, but often they involve pictures and actions of the sender.

The sent (actual) message is transmitted over a channel of communication. In marketing, the potential channel alternatives are varied, ranging from radio to in-store displays and personal messages. Therefore, considerable deliberation must be taken to select the channel with characteristics most appropriate to the message involved.

FIGURE 17-2
A simplified model of the communication process.

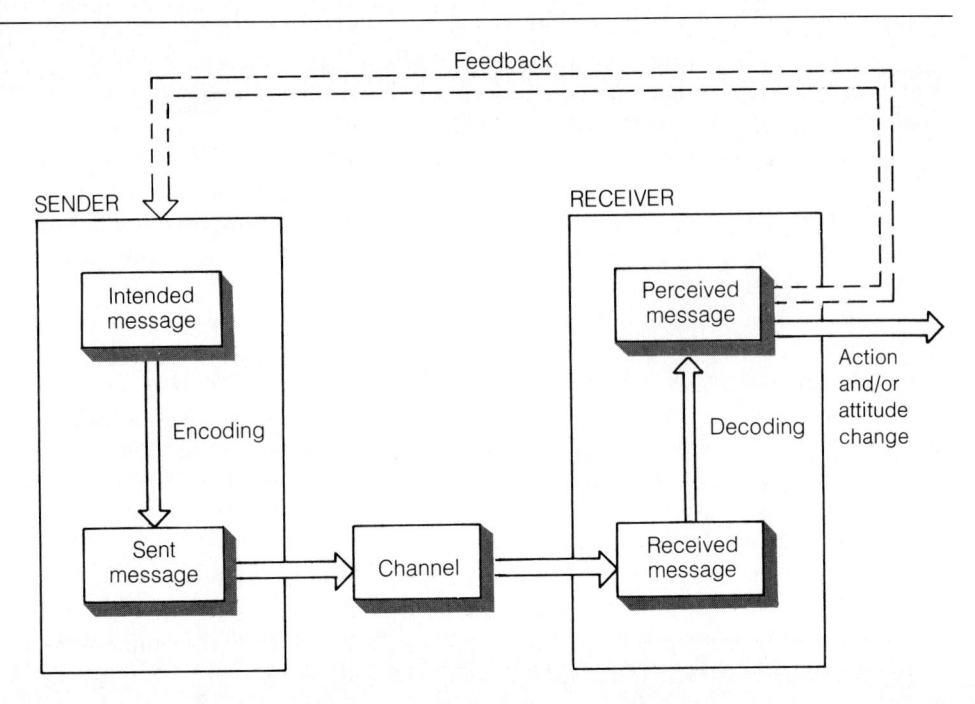

The sent message is acquired by one or more receivers. However, received messages are rarely identical to sent messages. Characteristics of the channel of transmission are one set of factors accounting for this difference. For example, it is very difficult to accurately reproduce product colors and textures on television or in newspapers. Consequently, the received message can differ significantly from the sent message.

The received message is transformed into a perceived message through the receiver's information-processing activities. That is, the message is *decoded*—received symbols are transformed back into meaning or thoughts by the receiver. As we have seen, an individual's experiences, as well as the context in which she perceives the message, will influence any meaning she derives from it. Attitude change and/or actions will then be based on this perceived message.

The feedback loop in Figure 17-2 recognizes that the communication process involves a two-way flow. That is, individuals or groups are both receivers and senders of messages, and they interact with each other. Therefore, feedback can be viewed as the initiation of another communication in which the receiver can now be construed as a message sender. This feedback process enables the original sender to monitor how well her intended meaning was conveyed and received. In many marketing situations, communications are transmitted via mass media to widely distributed consumers; therefore, accurate feedback information is very rare and difficult to obtain.

The concept of *noise* is frequently used to refer to a type of disruption in the communication process. We have seen that a variety of noise sources exist. The sender may have difficulty with formulating an intended message, and further problems can occur while attempting to encode a message for transmission. The channel of communication itself is also capable of interfering with a message. The receiver may also introduce noise through the decoding process. Of course, the feedback loop may contribute additional noise. Therefore, each state of the communication process is susceptible to message distortion.

In order to appreciate the persuasive communication process, it is necessary to understand three general kinds of factors that operate to influence beliefs, attitudes, and behavior. They are source, message, and receiver factors.[5] These three sets of factors interact to produce intended and unintended communication effects. For simplicity, each set of factors is next examined one at a time. However, the reader should continually bear in mind that these factors are interactive.

SOURCE FACTORS

What characteristics do certain individuals, companies or groups possess that facilitate their effectiveness in changing views and attitudes of others? This section discusses major characteristics of persuasive communication sources. The major types of marketing communication sources are reviewed first, and factors influencing their persuasiveness are discussed next.

Marketing Communication Sources

In a marketing context, several sources can be employed in an attempt to reach consumers with persuasive communications. These can be used alone or in combination to produce a combined source effect on consumers. Five prominent marketing sources are briefly described below.

The Company Consumers perceive companies as sources of information, and some are seen as highly credible but others are viewed with suspicion. Most consumers feel that Procter & Gamble, for example, is a trustworthy company, because P&G has built an excellent reputation by developing good products and spending considerable sums of money on advertising and consumer research. Because of its highly credible image, P&G can have more success than some other firms in introducing new brands to the market.

Companies develop source credibility in a variety of ways, among which are: (1) producing dependable, need-satisfying products, (2) developing sound advertising and public relations programs, (3) providing reliable warranties and guarantees, (4) using friendly and helpful sales representatives, (5) providing dependable delivery, and (6) acting in a socially responsible manner. Building a good company reputation takes time, but it pays handsome dividends, especially in the form of consumer loyalty.

Sales Representatives Because of their face-to-face contacts with current and prospective customers, sales representatives are viewed by consumers as information sources. Also, salespeople who are viewed as knowledgeable (expert) and trustworthy often are more persuasive than those not so highly regarded.[6] In addition, evidence suggests that consumers are more receptive to salespeople from highly credible companies such as the Prudential Insurance Company and Colgate-Palmolive than from unknown or low-credibility companies.[7] Thus, sales representatives from a well-known company can have an advantage over those from less well-known or less-respected companies.

The Media Consumers use the media extensively for product information. Although media are actually channel links between companies and consumers (receivers), people view them as sources; thus, it is important to understand their effects on persuading consumers to purchase products. *Good Housekeeping* and *Parents' Magazine* are examples of media that consumers perceive as credible sources of product information. Because of their product-screening processes and "seals of approval," they have built reputations as expert and trustworthy sources upon which consumers can rely.

Specialized print media also are very persuasive sources of information. Examples are *The Wall Street Journal, Popular Photography, Golf Digest,* and *Consumer Reports.* Consumers perceive these media as expert and trustworthy sources for product information. They can create positive halo effects for products mentioned in them and can therefore increase the persuasive impact of the advertiser's message.

Hired Promoters Companies typically employ individuals as representatives in advertising. In fact, on-camera spokespeople appear in a significant portion of television advertising. Effective hired promoters are ones who have established reputations for themselves, often in occupations unrelated to the advertised product. For example, Bob Hope over the years has established himself as an honest, sincere, and likable person. He has tremendous credibility among many consumers, particularly since people perceive that he has virtually nothing to gain financially from his commercial recommendations.

Frequently, people unknown to audiences are used in testimonial advertisements. This approach often takes the form of "candid" conversations with people on the street or in supermarket. The purpose of using such unknowns in unrehearsed, unsolicited conversations is to improve credibility by showing people who have no intention of manipulating the audience and therefore nothing to gain by their endorsement of a particular brand. Such a technique has been the basis of the Pepsi Challenge, "live" taste tests conducted for Schlitz beer, and advertisements for Excedrin. The issue of source credibility will be addressed in greater depth shortly.

Retailers At the local level, retailers often act as sources for marketing communications. A department store that has a good local reputation can more easily sell unknown brands than less-reputable stores. Also, specialty shops are successful in selling unknown brands because of their perceived expertise in the product line, such as cameras and stereo equipment. Thus, a manufacturer who produces brands with low consumer awareness can benefit from using specialty outlets if he can convince the retailers to carry his line.

Combined Source Effects Although we have described each of the above marketing sources separately, in reality there are combined source effects that interact to produce a persuasive impact on consumers. Therefore, producers must carefully select hired promoters, media, and retailers to deliver persuasive brand messages. One bad selection can cancel the positive effects of other message sources used. All source components must be reviewed from a system's point of view to gain maximum effectiveness.

Influences on Source Effectiveness

A variety of factors can influence the persuasiveness of those who transmit marketing communications. Among many factors influencing the ability of a source to change attitudes are his credibility, his similarity to audience members, and his attitudes toward himself, the message, and audience members. This section reviews these major influences.

Credibility and Its Effects Perhaps the most investigated source factor in persuasion is credibility (believability). A long-held conclusion from numerous research studies has been that highly credible sources achieve greater attitude change in consumers than those having less credibility. One important aspect of this finding is that credibility rests in the eyes of receivers. That is, receivers must *perceive* a source as credible, regardless of whether or not he *actually* is honest, trustworthy, and so on.

This general finding about the effectiveness of highly credible sources for generating attitude change reflects common sense to many of us. However, recent evidence suggests that the impact of source credibility is complex, depending on a number of specific conditions. Some of these are addressed below. In this discussion, we are assuming that conditions of high involvement exist, so that consumers are actively attending to the communications being sent.

INFLUENCE OF RECEIVER'S OPINION The initial opinion of audience members appears to be one important influence on the impact of source credibility. Specifically, when receivers already hold opinions that are opposite to those presented in a message, a highly credible source is likely to generate more attitude change than sources of lower credibility. However, when audience opinions already favor positions to be presented in a message, then highly credible sources have not been found more effective in generating attitude change than sources of lower credibility. In fact, some research even suggests that sources of lower credibility will actually be *more* effective in generating attitude change.[8]

To appreciate why these statements may have validity, we must understand that communications can generate cognitive responses among consumers. Recall from the section on memory in Chapter 14 that *cognitive response* refers to thoughts a consumer will retrieve from long-term memory upon exposure to a communication such as an advertising message. Those responses most relevant to our discussion here are (1) counterarguments—thoughts stored in long-term memory that are used to contradict aspects of the message being received, and (2) support arguments—thoughts stored in long-term memory that are used to support aspects of the received message. Counterarguments are generated by receivers when messages oppose their initial opinions, and support arguments are developed for messages consistent with initial positions. One interesting finding is that highly credible sources appear to have such significant believability that they tend to block cognitive responses.[9] This means that when receivers are initially opposed to information in a message, highly credible sources will tend to block counterarguments. The message is therefore likely to be accepted without much modification, yielding a considerable change in attitudes. However, the same message received from sources having lower credibility will be critically reviewed. This will generate counterarguments, tending to neutralize points made in the message. Therefore, the amount of attitude change will be less than what a highly credible source could achieve.

What happens when receivers' initial opinions or beliefs are consistent with the content of a message? The message transmitted from a highly credible source will again be accepted without much critical examination. However, because it is consistent with the receiver's existing position, a large amount of attitude change is unlikely. Conversely, as before, the same message received from a less-credible source will be critically reviewed and will generate cognitive responses. Because the cognitive responses will now be in the form of support arguments, the resulting attitude change can be greater than that achieved by the highly credible source.

Important practical implications can be drawn from this analysis. First, marketers may usually want to avoid developing communications that oppose consumers' opinions because of their requirements for a highly credible source. Since the task of achieving very high credibility in a marketing context is quite difficult, often expensive, and sometimes impossible, an alternative to carefully consider is using communications consistent with consumers' positions. However, when fighting rumors, bad publicity, and various other forms of unwarranted consumer beliefs, the design of such opposing communications may be necessary. In these cases, it would be quite important to carefully identify and use sources that will have high credibility for the specific situation at hand.

MESSAGE DISCREPANCY CONDITIONS   A topic closely related to the above discussion is message discrepancy. Highly discrepant messages do not oppose receivers' initial opinions, but are quite deviant from their beliefs. Marketers encounter such situations when they wish to demonstrate extraordinary products such as Super Glue or to make claims about their offerings that differ considerably from current beliefs in the target market. Similar to the situation of negative initial opinions, very credible sources are most effective in achieving attitude change for highly discrepant messages. As before, the explanation appears to be that high credibility minimizes cognitive responses, which are likely to be counterarguments in cases of high discrepancy.[10] For messages of little discrepancy, counter-arguments are less likely, while support arguments will be more prevalent. Therefore, under such conditions less-credible sources can be effective in achieving attitude change.

What are the strategy implications of these findings? If the marketer can achieve a high credibility standing in the target market, discrepant promotional claims can be employed to yield considerable attitude change. However, as we have noted, very high levels of credibility are often difficult to achieve. In such cases, the suggestion has been to design only mildly discrepant messages.

EFFECTIVENESS OF LOW CREDIBILITY Are there situations in which highly credible sources can actually inhibit attitude change in an audience? Research suggests that this may be the case. In fact, we have already mentioned one such situation—when audience members hold initial opinions that are in agreement with points to be made in the message. A second situation appears to be when the marketer wishes to change consumers' behavior directly and have this lead to later attitude change.[11] Such a case could occur when free brand samples or trials are offered to encourage development of favorable attitudes.

In other situations, high credibility may be most effective in changing attitudes, but using a less-credible source is more feasible. Here, a potential strategy is to improve the amount of attitude change that can be achieved with a low-credibility source. One method to accomplish this is to develop a situation in which the source will argue against her own self-interest. By doing so, the communicator appears to establish credibility, because it becomes obvious to an audience that she has nothing to gain by arguing for someone else's position. For example, in one advertisement the spokesperson states that he is not getting "one red cent" for endorsing the advertised product.

A low-credibility source also can increase his persuasiveness if he is identified *after,* rather than *before* presenting his message. The reason is that an audience will attend to the message if they do not know he is a low-credibility source. Otherwise, they will selectively ignore the presentation if they strongly suspect his credibility.

Care must be taken in using these strategies. Their implementation can be difficult and can cause problems for other aspects of the message. Therefore, it probably would be wise to consider other options before embracing such strategies.

THE SLEEPER EFFECT The above review suggests that under certain circumstances highly credible communicators can influence significant attitude change. However, a very valid question is whether we can expect this change in attitudes to be long-lasting. Research evidence suggests that the initial effect can dissipate rather rapidly, which is not completely surprising given our understanding of the learning curve. However, a startling finding of early research was that an audience exposed initially to a low-credibility source develops opinions *more* closely in line with the source as time passes.[12] This result became known as the "sleeper effect." Consideration of both findings would lead one to predict that as time passes, opinion change achieved by high- and low-credibility sources would tend toward equality. Figure 17-3 graphically illustrates this conclusion, which drew the attention of astute marketers interested in long-run attitude change.

The explanation offered for these findings is that receivers tend to forget message sources more rapidly than they forget message content. Thus, as the "enhancing" and "depressing" effects of high- and low-credibility sources dissipate, what will tend to remain is message content, which is the same in both cases.

Unfortunately, additional research has not shown consistent support for the sleeper effect.[13] This means that we cannot unquestioningly accept that small amounts of initial attitude change achieved by using a low-credibility source will increase over time. A further finding adds one more piece to the puzzle—if original sources are reinstated (allowed to reintroduce their position), the effect is to restore audience opinion levels to nearly the points they were right after initial message exposure.[14] In effect, reintroduction of a source tends to yield the same effect as when it was initially used. Figure 17-4 graphically summarizes these points. Note how the dashed lines duplicate the situation shown in Figure 17-3. Therefore, the assumption being used here is that other things being held constant, (1) the sleeper effect is valid, and (2) a decline in attitude change will occur over time for the highly credible source. The new solid lines in this figure now indicate that reinstatement of each source tends to hold attitude change levels near their original conditions. If one were to assume that the sleeper effect was not valid, the dashed and solid lines for the low-credibility source would coincide and run horizontally.

The evidence presented above and summarized in Figure 17-4 tends to favor

FIGURE 17-3

An illustration of attitude change convergence predicted by early research evidence on source credibility effects over time.

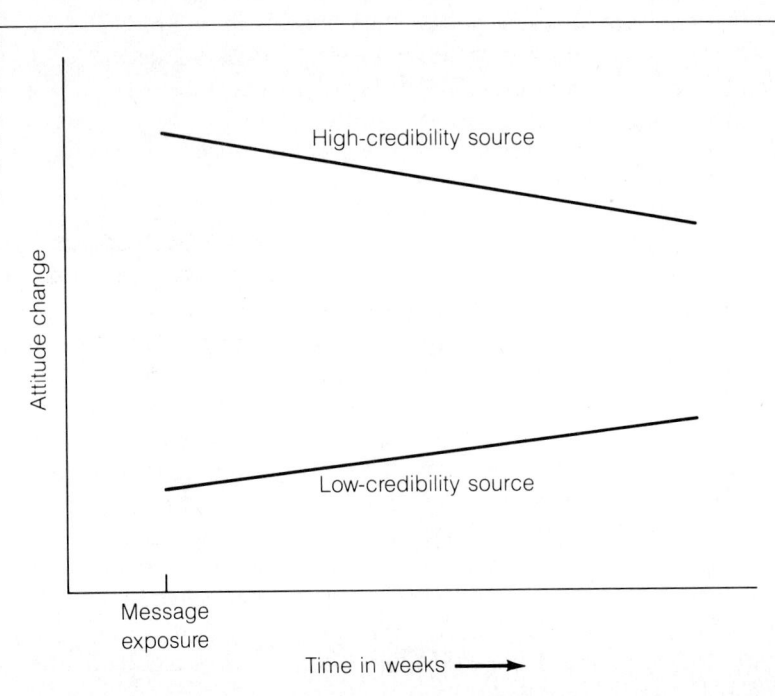

FIGURE 17-4

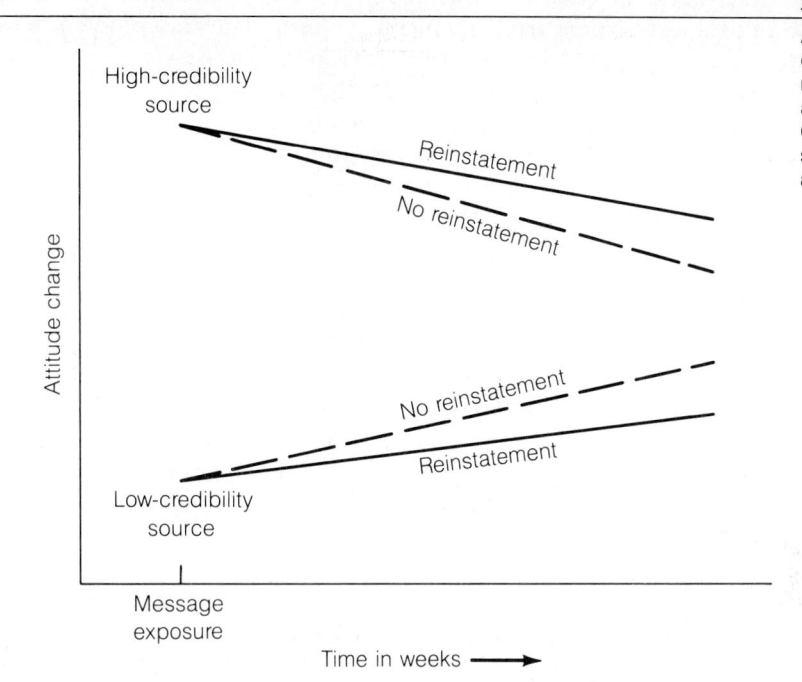

An illustration of the effects of reinstatement on long-run attitude change. Conditions of a sleeper effect are assumed.

use of a high-credibility source when situations discussed in the previous sections warrant. Typical marketing applications, such as advertising repetition, could easily involve source reinstatement which would act to maintain initially favorable attitude change levels achieved with a highly credible source. Therefore, whether or not a sleeper effect does exist would only influence the *degree* to which a highly credible source would generate more long-run attitude change than one of low credibility. Combined conditions favoring a low-credibility source would be (1) the existence of a valid sleeper effect, (2) a relatively large expense involved in identifying and using a highly credible source and, (3) as suggested in Figure 17-4, a strategy that does not involve source reinstatement.

BASES OF CREDIBILITY   Our conclusion is that in a number of circumstances, using a highly credible communicator can benefit the persuasiveness of marketing messages. Practically speaking, therefore, many marketers may wish to identify sources that have high credibility in communicating to an audience about a particular brand. But what factors influence the credibility of a source in the eyes of an audience? Five major bases are (1) trustworthiness, (2) expertise, (3) status or prestige, (4) likeability, and (5) an assortment of physical traits. Each of these is discussed below.

A source will be perceived as more credible if her audience views her as honest or trustworthy, and this is related to the degree she is perceived as having an *intention to manipulate*. If the audience believes that the communicator, no matter how generally honest, has something to gain personally by her message, then her persuasive attempts will lose effectiveness.

This idea suggests one reason why advertising and personal selling is generally less effective than the advice of a trusted friend for changing consumer attitudes. Advertisers have attempted to overcome this problem to some extent by using "candid interviews" with consumers who were not aware that they were giving testimony to a company's brand. Other similar approaches have been used by advertisers to reduce their perceived "intention to manipulate," such as disguised brand tests. This technique has been used for Ivory Snow, Pepsi, Schlitz, Anacin, and Mercury automobiles. Another way to reduce the communicator's perceived attempt to manipulate is through the "overhead conversation." An example would be commercials showing actor Robert Young reducing his friends' tension levels by getting them to try Sanka coffee. A simulation of the method in a humorous light is also the basis of promotions for the E. F. Hutton brokerage firm. The general notion in all of these methods is that a communicator can be successful in increasing his credibility by being perceived as having no intention to manipulate the audience for personal gain.

Another basis of source credibility is perceived expertise. That is, when an audience views a communicator as having higher qualifications than others to speak on a topic, he will be more persuasive than a person viewed as less qualified. In marketing, experts in a field related to a company's product often are used to promote its brands. However, the wisdom of once using Joe Namath to advertise Hanes pantyhose certainly must be questioned on expertise grounds.

A communicator whom an audience perceives as high in status or prestige is often more credible than one perceived as low in these attributes. As we have learned, society "confers" status and prestige upon individuals according to the roles they occupy. For example, a physician is generally regarded as having higher status and prestige than a nurse, and a scientist usually has more prestige than an engineer. Marketers often attempt to obtain as endorsers of their products individuals who have obtained high status. Examples include using former President Gerald Ford to endorse the Boy Scouts and former astronaut Frank Borman as a spokesman for Eastern Airlines. It should be noted that although the concepts of prestige and expertise overlap, they are not synonymous.[15]

Finally, the physical characteristics and other features of communicators can influence their credibility. For example, age, sex, color, dress, likeability, and voice inflections, as well as general attractiveness can affect source credibility.[16] Regarding age, older people tend to be influential on younger people in many cultures. The tendency for youth to accept their elders' advice and influence might be due largely to the younger generation's perception of their elders' experience in life, thus viewing them as more "expert."

Other cues for assessing the expertise of a communicator are voice qualities, accent, dress, and mannerisms. An announcer who speaks with an authoritative voice, dresses "like a millionaire," and uses confident nonverbal cues[17] can be very persuasive and influential on his audience's attitudes in a "money-making opportunity," for example.[18] Amway distributors have used this approach in television advertising.

This discussion has focused on the influence of source credibility in achieving attitude change. Two other groups of source factors that can also be important are briefly reviewed in the following sections.

Attitudes of Communicator A communicator is more persuasive when she has a positive attitude toward herself, her message, and her receiver.[19] Within a marketing context, a sales representative who has a positive attitude toward herself is one who has self-confidence. Her self-confidence is perceived by the prospective buyer and can influence the decision to buy.

Sales representatives are trained to show a positive attitude toward their product and sales presentation (their message). That is, they are trained to *believe* in the product they are selling and what they say about it. Thus, many sales training programs are designed to develop representatives' confidence in their company and the products they sell.

The marketer must demonstrate respect and admiration toward his prospective buyers to be successful. Consumers quickly realize when they are being "talked down to," and in such cases they will quickly react negatively to the presentation and brand involved.

Similarity with Audience Another finding regarding communication sources is that people are persuaded more by a communicator they perceive to be similar to themselves.[20] That is, people seem to be influenced by others who are like themselves. Similarity can be perceived in a variety of ways, such as personality, race, interests, self-image, and group affiliations. This has led marketers to use so-called slice-of-life advertisements in many cases. For example, ads for Maxwell House coffee, Calgon dishwasher detergent, and Crest toothpaste, as well as many other brands, attempt to show "typical" people finding satisfaction with their products.

MESSAGE FACTORS

It is important to understand what components make up a persuasive message. This section discusses three sets of message factors: (1) message structure, (2) message appeal, and (3) message code.

Message Structure

Message structure refers to how the elements of a message are organized. Three structures that have been extensively studied are message sidedness, order of presentation, and conclusion drawing.

Message Sidedness A message can be either one-sided or two-sided. A *one-sided message* is one in which only the strengths of the communicator's position are described. That is, a spokesperson uses a one-sided message when describing only the good points of his company's products and does not mention their weaknesses, or the good features of competing products. For example, advertisements for Chevrolet automobiles only talk about their advantages, and they don't mention any of their possible weaknesses or possible advantages of Fords. A *two-sided message*, on the other hand, presents the strengths of the communicator's position as in the one-sided message, but it also either admits to weaknesses in the communicator's position or to some strengths in the opposite position. In a marketing context, the typical method of implementing the two-sided approach would be for the spokesperson to mention one or two weaknesses in her company's products or to admit to one or two strong features of competitor's products. Cases include the Avis Rent-A-Car campaign, "We're not number one, but we try harder," and Listerine ads which suggest that the product does not have the greatest taste, but it is very effective. Another example of a two-sided message is presented in Figure 17-5, a direct-mail advertisement sent by Publishers Clearinghouse.

Two questions arise regarding message sidedness. First, why would anyone

FIGURE 17-5

An example of a two-sided message. (Courtesy of Publishers Clearing House.)

want to admit to weaknesses in his or her own product or mention the strengths of competing products? Second, which approach is more effective? The answer to the first question lies in discussion of the second. Either approach can be more effective than the other depending upon conditions under which the message is presented. The relevant conditions are (1) the audience's initial opinion on the issue, (2) their exposure to subsequent counterarguments, and (3) the audience's educational level.[21]

In the first condition, a one-sided argument appears to be more effective when the audience is already in agreement with the communicator's position, and a two-sided message is more effective when the audience initially disagrees with the communicator's position. The one-sided message is more effective for an audience in agreement because it reinforces what they already believe. A two-sided message under this condition would serve only to place doubt in their minds. However, the use of a one-sided message for an audience *not* in initial agreement with the communicator's stance tends to be less effective than a two-sided message, because the audience will perceptually resist a view counter to its own. In this case, a two-sided message is more effective, because the audience tends to view the communicator as more objective and honest (credible) since he admits to the merits of their position. The approach allows a communicator to get through the audience's perceptual filters, to present his views, and thereby to increase the likelihood of gaining some measure of attitude change.

A second condition that may influence the relative effectiveness of one-sided and two-sided messages is the kind of information that receivers will be exposed to at a later date. If an audience is likely to receive counterarguments in the future, such as when competitors make counteradvertising claims, some theorists would suggest using two-sided messages. This suggestion is derived from what has become known as *innoculation* or *immunization* theory. In essence, the position is that just as people are innoculated with vaccines (weakened disease cultures) to increase their resistance to diseases, exposure of an audience to weak forms of counterarguments will tend to immunize them from more strongly stated opposing arguments that they will confront at a later time. Therefore, by using this technique, salespeople could take the "wind out of their competitors' sails" (and sales) by presenting buyers with two-sided messages. Although we cannot yet say for sure that innoculation theory is completely valid, research evidence tends to support it as a justification for using two-sided messages.[22]

A third condition for determining whether to use a one-sided or two-sided message is the educational level of an audience. A two-sided message appears to be more persuasive on better-educated audiences, whereas a one-sided message is more effective in changing the opinions of less well-educated audiences. Because better-educated people generally are more capable of seeing both sides of an argument anyway, a communicator should either admit the strengths of opposing views or weaknesses in his own position. In this way, the communicator is established as being more objective and credible in the minds of his audience. Less-educated people are not as capable of seeing another side of an issue and therefore are more likely to accept the argument they hear. To present both sides might confuse them, and they would find it difficult to know which side to accept.

Evidence of the effectiveness of one- and two-sided messages in an advertising context has been studied by Faison, who asked half of those in a 500-subject sample group to listen to one-sided radio commercials for an automobile, gas range, and floor wax. Each commercial was "conventional" in the sense that it presented only positive product features. The second half of those in the sample group was presented two-sided commercials comparable to the one-sided messages, except that some negative features were included. Among Faison's findings were the following:

1 Two-sided advertisements were more effective on higher-educated subjects, whereas one-sided advertisements were more effective on less-educated subjects.

2 Two-sided messages were more effective on subjects who used competing brands, whereas one-sided commercials were more effective on subjects using the brand featured in the commercial. In this case, a subject who used the advertised brand is similar to one who has initial agreement with the communicator. A subject who used the competing brand is similar to one who does not have initial agreement with the communicator.

3 The commercials' effectiveness in changing opinions appears to be influenced by characteristics of the product being promoted. For example, greater attitude change was created for the low-cost floor wax than the high-priced automobile.

This finding can be explained in terms of the amount of commitment (or investment) a person has made in the product in terms of money, search time, and effort. With greater commitment involved, consumers hold more tightly to their purchase decision.

4 After 4 to 6 weeks, subjects showed no diminishing effects in their attitudes toward the advertised brands. In fact, subjects exposed to the two-sided advertisements actually showed an increase in attitude toward the advertised brand.[23]

Perhaps unfortunately, many companies have generally rejected the idea of their spokespeople ever admitting to either a competitor's product's strengths or to their own product's weaknesses. However, in a number of situations this could be a very viable approach. First, where it is possible to segment consumers into loyal and nonloyal groups, it may be useful to direct one-sided messages toward loyal customers and two-sided ads toward the nonloyal group.[24] Of course, this strategy requires that each group is capable of being isolated enough so that they are not inadvertently exposed to both messages. For personal selling, salespeople may also find it to their advantage to use a two-sided sales pitch, either by admitting to minor weaknesses in their companies' brands or by mentioning one or two strengths of competitors' brands. Such a tactic may create a resistance in prospects' minds toward competitors' sales claims. Additionally, in an industrial selling situation, sales representatives usually are confronted by well-educated purchasing agents, consulting engineers, and others of similar education. In these cases, a two-sided sales pitch should prove more effective than a one-sided message. However, for door-to-door salespeople in a low-income (and therefore very likely poorly educated) neighborhood, a one-sided argument should be more effective.

Message Order What is the best order in which to present persuasive arguments in an advertising message? Should the most important parts to the communicator be presented at the beginning, middle, or end? If a two-sided message is used, should the marketer use a pro-con or con-pro order? For a series of advertisements in a medium such as television, does the first or last ad have an advantage in influ-

FIGURE 17-6
Three orders of message presentation.

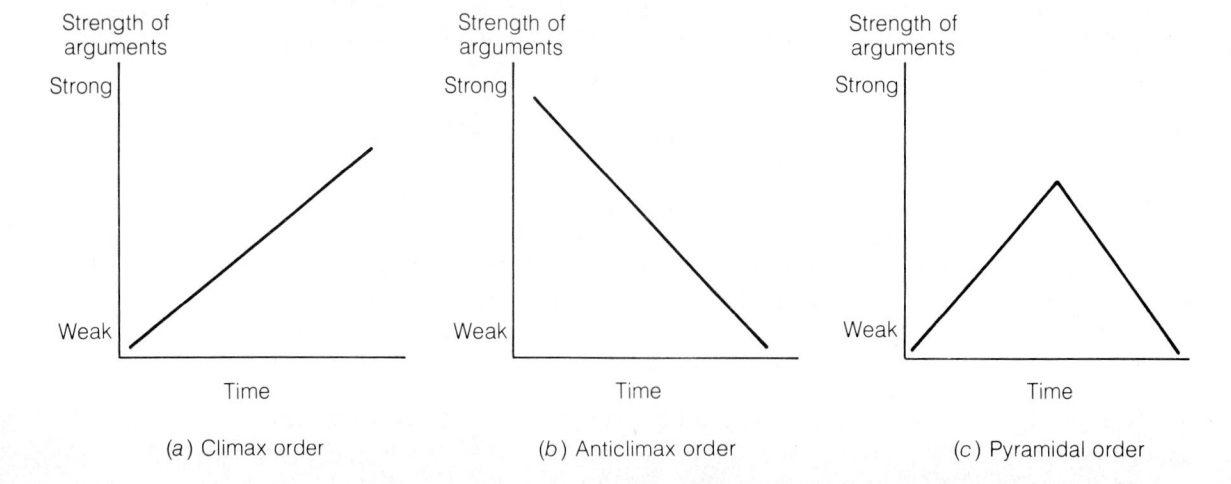

(a) Climax order

(b) Anticlimax order

(c) Pyramidal order

encing attitude change? This section briefly addresses these questions and reviews some of the evidence relevant to them.

CLIMAX VERSUS ANTICLIMAX ORDER   To address the first of our questions above, it is necessary to define a few terms. A *climax order* refers to ordering message elements whereby the strongest arguments are presented at the end of a message. An *anticlimax order* refers to the presentation of the most important points at the beginning of a message. When the most important materials are presented in the middle of a message, it is referred to as a *pyramidal order.* Figure 17-6 graphically describes these three alternatives.

Based on research findings, the following tentative guidelines can be offered regarding the ordering of messages:

1 An anticlimax order tends to be most effective for an audience having a low level of interest in the subject being presented.

2 A climax order tends to be most effective for an audience having a high level of interest in the subject being presented.

3 The pyramidal order is the least effective order of presentation.

The first two generalizations can be explained in terms of audience interest. Where interest is low, the stronger, more interesting points in a message have the greater potential for gaining audience attention, and therefore they should be placed first (anticlimax order). In this way, a communicator is better able to get her message across and thus effect change in the audience. However, with this approach the communicator also must be careful of avoiding an audience "let down" when the weaker points in a message follow.

When audience interest in the subject is high, there is no need to present the stronger points first, because the message will be attended to out of interest. Therefore, the climax order should be used, because points made at the end of the message exceed expectations created by the points initally presented.[25]

The lesson marketers must learn from these statements is that for low-interest products an anticlimax order appears effective. In addition, in some cases each method can perhaps be strengthened by presenting the important points at *both* the beginning and end of the message—in the form of an introduction and summary of important points. However, very little if any justification exists for a pyramidal order.

RECENCY AND PRIMACY EFFECTS   Two additional questions were raised above. When presenting a two-sided message, should the points favorable to the advertiser's brand be presented first or second? If many competing messages are involved, as they are in magazines and during commercial breaks on television, does the first or last communication tend to have the advantage? Both of these issues involve the subject of primacy and recency effects. When the material presented first produces the greater opinion or attitude change, a *primacy effect* has occurred. When material presented last produces the greater change, then a *recency effect* has been observed.

Research into the question of which presentation of order is more effective when using a two-sided message has not been very conclusive. It appears that sometimes a primacy and sometimes a recency effect is observed. The reasons for these contradictory findings is not at all clear. Therefore, we will not even offer tentative guidelines on this subject.

The evidence on whether it would be better for a promotional message to appear first or last in a series of messages is also not clear. However, many advertisers who favor evidence suggesting a primacy effect are willing to pay a premium for early placement in a magazine or during a commercial break. Others act the same way regarding placement at the end of a series of advertisements. Unfortunately, at the present time each set of advocates can point to research evidence supporting their position. More investigation of the factors accounting for such contradictory findings is certainly needed.

Drawing a Conclusion Is it better to draw a conclusion for your audience at the end of a message or let them draw their own conclusion? Although the answer to this question is dependent upon several conditions, the most useful generalization is that communicators appear to be more effective in changing opinions of an audience if they draw a conclusion for them.[26]

Investigations of this question have shown that a conclusion must often be drawn to achieve attitude change among less-intelligent audience members. If this is not done, they may draw either the wrong conclusions or no conclusions and therefore the intended opinion change will not occur. For audiences of higher intelligence, it usually makes no difference whether a conclusion is drawn, because they have the ability to reach the "correct" conclusion.[27] Therefore, to be safe, it is better generally to draw a conclusion at the end of a message, regardless of the educational level of the audience.

Repetition In Chapter 14, we saw that repetition of persuasive messages can be beneficial in encouraging rehearsal, transferring information to long-term memory, and forestalling forgetting. Other benefits were also suggested. That is, some research evidence indicates that increased repetition of an advertising message can, by itself, encourage consumers to develop positive feelings toward the brand.[28] This suggests that consumers' attitudes can be changed in a positive direction through frequent advertising exposures. Conditions which appear to produce such an effect are (1) when the audience initially favors the message position, and (2) when a soft-sell (as opposed to a hard-sell) is employed.

Even under the conditions just cited, marketers should not expect continuous positive attitude change from increased repetitions of a communication. At some point, message *wearout* occurs. Here, the positive effects of repetition diminish as repetition occurs because of audience boredom, inattention, and increased cognitive response activity that is less positive in content than the message.[29] The conclusion from these studies is that moderate levels of advertising repetition over time appear to positively influence attitudes as well as rehearsal and memory. The effects of wearout can probably be forestalled by employing a series of messages having a central theme with unique components to provide different information and some novelty to maintain audience interest.

Message Appeals

The above review summarized some major conclusions regarding the structuring of messages to achieve maximum attitude change. We now turn our attention to message appeals and how they can be used to enhance the persuasiveness of messages. Message appeals are requests for audiences to respond in ways that are desired by the communicator. Several kinds of appeals used by marketers are discussed in this section.

Fear Appeals In some situations, it seems reasonable for marketers to consider using fear in their attempts to persuade consumers. That is, fear of physical danger, social disapproval, or other consequences seem potentially useful in influencing consumers' attitudes and/or behavior toward the advertised brand. In fact, fear appeals have been employed to promote the use of a wide range of goods from toothpaste to life insurance. Figure 17-7 presents an example of an advertisement capable of evoking fear among at least some readers.

The earliest fear research by Janis and Feshbach appeared to suggest that as the intensity of a fear appeal increases, its effectiveness in persuading audiences will decrease.[30] One explanation is that strong fear-evoking components of a message cause consumers to set up perceptual defenses, and in so doing they also reject the rest of the message. The result of these and other early findings was that

FIGURE 17-7

Example of a fear-evoking advertisement. (Courtesy of the American Express Company.)

most advertisers become highly reluctant to use fear appeals for promoting their products or services.

Several years after these initial studies were reported, other investigations began to uncover results that appeared to contradict earlier findings.[31] That is, the more-recent studies suggested that higher fear appeals could actually motivate *more* attitude change than could mild fear appeals. However, after a lengthy review of the research, Ray and Wilkie noted that the studies may actually not contradict each other. They argued that various investigators had probably found difficulty in controlling the amount of fear content in their messages, and this led to the apparently contradictory, but actually consistent findings.[32] The result of this argument can be summarized as follows: low fear appeals generate little motivation for attitude change; high fear appeals also yield little attitude change, because they activate *defense mechanisms* against feared aspects which also screen out other parts of the message. Moderate fear appeals, which provide sufficient motivation but which do not activate perceptual defenses, appear most effective in generating attitude change.

More recently, others have argued that it is probably inappropriate to draw general conclusions about any given level of fear, because numerous factors may influence how audiences will respond to the appeal. For example, factors that appear to influence the persuasiveness of fear appeals include (1) source credibility, (2) audience characteristics, (3) the type of fear appeal used, and (4) the context of message presentation.[33] Generally, the following conclusions appear warranted:

1 Highly credible sources are more effective in employing fear to change attitudes, because their credibility tends to block counterarguments consumers use to protect themselves from fear-evoking messages.

2 Characteristics of an audience can influence the degree to which they are persuaded by fear appeals. Receivers who are high in self-esteem, are effective in coping with tension, and do not perceive themselves as particularly vulnerable to the feared consequences appear to be more persuaded by high fear appeals than receivers who do not have these characteristics. This suggests that marketers must investigate their target audience in order to determine whether a high fear appeal is warranted. For example, people who perceive themselves as having very risky occupations might not be receptive to high fear appeals for occupational related disability insurance. More moderate fear appeals can be employed for such target groups.

3 Some evidence suggests that fear appeals are more effective when they focus audience attention on the specific danger or threat and practical steps that may be taken to avoid any undesirable consequences. Messages that dwell on the unpleasant circumstances, without suggesting practical ways to avoid them, will tend to be less persuasive.

4 Certain conditions in the environment (humor, etc.) which can distract audience attention away from a strong fear appeal can increase message persuasiveness. Some evidence also suggests that fear of social disapproval may be more effective in influencing actual behavior change than will an appeal based on fear of physical harm.

Certain promotional messages appear to be using some of these more-recent findings regarding fear appeals. In many cases, the technique often appears to involve a means that makes it easier for the audience to deal with the fear-arousing message. This may include making light of the object involved, presenting it in a humorous way, or using an indirect technique such as making some third party bear the brunt of the feared consequences. An example of a message using both humor and the third-party technique is shown in Figure 17-8.

FIGURE 17-8

Example of using humor and a third-party technique to reduce negative effects of a fear-evoking message. (Courtesy of New England Mutual Life Insurance Company.)

Distraction Some studies and actual promotional experiences have suggested that pleasant forms of distraction can often work to increase the effectiveness of persuasive appeals in encouraging attitude change.[34] Sales representatives often practice this principle when they take clients out to dinner. Advertisers can also use such pleasant forms of distraction as music or background activity.

The explanation for the effectiveness of distraction on attitude change has been that it retards counterargumentation. That is, distraction tends to make the receiver loose his train of thought or forget to argue against the message. This, according to the explanation would result in greater message acceptance.

Studies have shown conflicting evidence on the distraction concept.[35] Also, in some cases distraction may actually reduce receivers' attention to the message. Therefore, evidence is still not clear regarding the effectivenss of this method of increasing attitude change and the conditions that influence it.

Participation As was discussed earlier in the text, active participation is a means of gaining attention to and enhancing the learning of a message. Similarly, participation can increase the effectiveness of a persuasive appeal.[36] Marketers have learned the value of giving product samples to prospective customers, encouraging

FIGURE 17-9

Example of using humor to focus audience attention on product attributes expected to be instrumental in attitude formation or change. (Courtesy of the American Tourister Company.)

trial use of their products, and providing coupons for trial purchase. In addition, they often develop television advertisements that place the viewer in the position of vicariously "trying" a product by using well-developed camera angles and other production techniques that make one feel a part of the commercial.

Humor As noted in Chapter 13, estimates are that between 15 and 42 percent of radio and television advertising employs humorous appeals. Print media also contain many similar messages. To a considerable extent, much of this humor is designed to attract audience attention. However, in other cases the intent is to moderate the perceived threat of fear appeals or to assist message persuasiveness in some manner.

Some advertisers, such as Volkswagen and Alka Seltzer, have developed extensive compaigns based on humor, while others never give it serious consideration, arguing that amusing circumstances are not universal in appeal, they wear out quickly, and they consume too much valuable advertising time or space. Daily experience and research evidence seems to support the contention that humor is not universal in its appeal. For example, studies investigating reactions to three basic types of humor (hostile, sexual, and nonsensical) find that females and males differ in their perception as to what is amusing.[37]

Certainly, universal agreement does not exist on the benefits of this message factor. However, in reviewing the relevant research, Sternthal and Craig included the following conclusions:[38]

1 Humorous messages can attract attention, but they may also have a detrimental effect on message comprehension. (In an advertising context, one can sometimes counter this potential problem by focusing humor on product attributes that are expected to be instrumental in influencing attitudes. Figure 17-9 provides an illustration.)

2 Humorous appeals appear to increase the credibility of a source and may also increase audience liking for the source, as well as create a positive mood toward it.

3 Although humorous appeals appear to be persuasive, they do not seem to be more persuasive than serious appeals.

These and other findings indicate that more needs to be generally known about the effectiveness of humor and conditions which affect its ability to influence attitude change.

Emotional Versus Rational Appeals Should marketers use emotional or rational appeals in promoting their products? As the reader might guess, experts are also divided on this question. Neither approach has been shown to be generally superior to the other. This seems understandable, because the effectiveness of appeals is likely to be a function of the underlying motives consumers have for considering the product.

When emotional appeals appear to be appropriate, the following points have been offered as guidance for constructing the appeal:

1 Use emotionally charged language, especially words that have a high personal meaning to the target consumers.

2 If the brand or message is unfamiliar to the audience, associate it with well-known ideas.

3 Associate the brand or message with visual or nonverbal stimuli that arouse emotions. (The advertisement for Johnson's Baby Shampoo in Figure 17-10 provides an excellent example of this technique.)

4 The communication should be accompanied by nonverbal cues, such as hand motions, which support the verbal message.[39]

Message Codes

The way in which marketers assemble and use message codes can have an impact on the persuasiveness of their messages. Three broad classes are verbal codes, nonverbal codes, and paralinguistic message codes.

Verbal Code The verbal code is a system of word symbols that are combined according to a set of rules, as in the English language. Although a variety of alter-

FIGURE 17-10

Example of associating an advertised brand with visual stimuli that are capable of arousing emotions. (Reproduced with permission of Johnson & Johnson Baby Products Company, 1982.)

natives exist for devising verbal code structures, advertisers tend to use modifier words, such as adjectives and adverbs, to elicit favorable emotions within a consumer. For example, the same factual information is conveyed by using either of the following advertising messages, but one conveys the facts with words higher in emotion.

1 The new plastic product resembling leather will soon be available to shoe manufacturers.

2 The fabulous new plastic product which out-leathers leather will soon replace all other products used in the manufacture of superior quality shoes.[40]

The advertiser is likely to use the second statement, because it expresses the same idea but with more highly charged modifiers.

Nonverbal Code Nonverbal codes are extremely important in persuasive communication, and they have not been given the attention they deserve in published research.[41] For example, a communicator's facial expressions, gestures, posture, and dress can affect how a receiver responds to a message.

Sales representatives have found the study of nonverbal communications extremely helpful in better understanding prospective customers and in meeting sales resistance. Astute representatives can tell when a client is bored, receptive, doubtful, critical, interested, and so forth by observing nonverbal cues such as crossed legs, body lean, hand gestures, and mannerisms. Advertisers also are aware of the importance of nonverbal communications in television and print advertisements, particularly ones that use models.

Paralinguistic Code The paralinguistic code is one which lies between the verbal and nonverbal code. It primarily involves two components—voice qualities and vocalizations.[42]

Voice qualities refer to such speech characteristics as rhythm pattern, pitch of voice, and precision of articulation. They can communicate urgency, boredom, sarcasm, and other feelings. *Vocalizations*, on the other hand, are sounds such as yawns, sighs, and various voice intensities which reflect certain emotions.

Advertisers are very careful to select models whose tonal qualities match the product message. For example, when facial soaps, body creams, and shampoos that are soft and gentle are being promoted the model's voice tends to be quite soothing. However, advertisements for pick-up trucks, tools, and some heavy-duty cleansers typically employ low, powerful-sounding voices.

RECEIVER FACTORS

To be a persuasive communicator and an effective marketer, it is important to adopt a "know your audience" position. In our discussion throughout this chapter, we have already focused on a number of receiver factors that affect the persuasiveness of communications. For example, we have noted that the effectiveness of fear and humor appeals depends on characteristics of audience members. This section briefly deals with two remaining general receiver characteristics that deserve mention. These are the receiver's personality traits and belief types.

Personality Traits

Behavioral research has shed light on the relationship between personality traits and persuasibility. Among these traits are self-esteem, rich imagery, and intelligence.

Self-Esteem Self-esteem refers to a person's feelings of adequacy and self-worth. In general, research has suggested that people who have low self-esteem tend to be more persuasible than those with high self-esteem.[43] This generalization appears to be particularly true in situations in which people are motivated by social approval. Researchers believe that people who feel inadequate are more persuasible because they lack confidence in their judgments and therefore tend to rely upon the opinions of others. On the other hand, people with feelings of high self-worth have confidence in their abilities to make good judgments without accepting the opinions of others.

In a marketing study concerning the persuasibility of women subjects in a personal selling situation, it was found that women with medium self-esteem showed the greatest opinion change, while women at the high and low ends of the self-esteem spectrum were low in their susceptibility to the persuasive sales pitch. The researchers suggested that women with low self-esteem acted in an ego-defensive manner, such as to say "I don't need help in making up my mind," while those with high self-esteem behaved as had subjects in previous experiments.[44] The apparent contradiction of these findings to previous research may be due to the broader range of self-esteem of subjects in this sample. Also, differences in experimental settings may have influenced the results. Earlier studies used social approval to motivate subjects to change opinions, whereas this study and other later studies involved subjects in problem-solving situations.[45]

Rich Imagery People who are high in rich imagery, or live out much of their lives through dream worlds and fantasy, are more persuasible than those who are not high in rich imagery. Recall from an earlier example in Chapter 5 how Schlitz learned that one significant trait of the frequent beer drinker is that he is high in rich imagery. With this information, the company developed its advertising theme, "You only go around once in life," which stressed a number of situations that audience members could fantasize about.

Intelligence People of both high and low intelligence are susceptible to persuasion, depending upon the message approach a communicator uses. Two general principles which emerge from behavioral research on audience intelligence are the following:

1 Persons with high intellectual ability will tend—mainly because of their ability to draw valid inferences—to be more influenced than those with low intelligence when exposed to persuasive communications that rely primarily on impressive logical arguments.

2 Persons with high intelligence will tend—mainly because of their superior critical ability—to be less influenced than those with low intelligence by unsupported generalities or false, illogical, irrelevant arguments.[46]

A person's intellectual capacity is made up of three interacting components: (1) learning ability, which is the mental capacity to acquire and recall information; (2) critical ability, which is the ability to assess the rationality of information and to accept or reject it on a logical basis; and (3) ability to draw inferences, which refers to the ability to interpret information and to use facts to make sound implications. In the first principle stated above, the relationship between intelligence and persuasibility is based upon a person's ability to draw correct inferences; in the second principle, the relationship is based upon a person's critical ability.

In marketing, audiences can be segmented according to levels of intelligence, often by inference rather than through data collection. Physicians, engineers, business leaders, and other similar occupations generally are made up of people with high intellectual ability. Specialized media are available to advertise products that are pertinent to their fields and to them personally.

Belief Types

As indicated in Chapter 16 and in the introduction of this chapter, a receiver's existing attitude and belief structure can be an opportunity for, or an obstruction to, persuasive marketing communications.[47] The direction of attitudes and the strength of beliefs are two factors that were mentioned as particularly important. Three basic belief types influence the commitment that the consumer will have regarding his knowledge. Of course, these in turn will influence the difficulty in changing attitudes. *Central beliefs* form the core of a person's cognitive structure. Because they are deeply rooted to so many other beliefs, they are quite resistant to change. This was suggested in our discussion of memory structure in Chapter 14. *Derived beliefs* are an outgrowth of central beliefs. For example, "Retailers should be free to charge whatever prices they feel are appropriate" is a belief derived from a central belief about freedom. As the name implies, *central-free beliefs* exist separate and apart from other beliefs in the consumer's cognitive structure. "I believe that Al's market is the best in town" is an example.

In order of difficulty, central beliefs are the hardest to change, derived beliefs are the next most difficult, and central-free beliefs the easist to change. Marketers should avoid attacking central beliefs and instead should see them as opportunities. That is, messages that are aligned with central beliefs are readily acceptable, because they reinforce already strongly held attitudes. Similarly, beliefs derived from more central ones may be used as a basis for an advertising theme. In this way, the beliefs are not attacked, but instead are used as a means of enhancing the value of the advertised brand. The lesson to be learned is that a consumer's psychological barriers should be avoided and turned into opportunities.

SUMMARY

This chapter focused on the important marketing goal of attitude change. First, Fishbein's model of attitude served as a basis for suggesting strategies for changing attitudes. Next, a simple model of the communication process was presented. Then, the many factors influencing attitudes via communications were categorized into source, message, and receiver factors.

The category of source factors concerns properties or characteristics of message senders. In marketing, these include salespersons, companies, hired promoters, media, and other marketing sources of product and brand information. A number of characteristics of sources including credibility and similarity to the audience were discussed. It was noted that, particularly with regard to the sleeper effect of source credibility, the influence of these variables on attitude change can be complex.

Attention then turned to message factors, including message structure, order of presentation, appeals, codes, and the drawing of conclusions for an audience. Again, although general guidelines could be offered, the influence of the particular situation was stressed.

Of course, significant aspects of the situation include characteristics of the audience itself. This became the next topic of interest. Here, the audience characterisitcs of personality (including self-esteem, imagery, and intelligence) as well as belief types were addressed. Strategies to handle situations arising from these characteristics were suggested.

DISCUSSION TOPICS

1   Who are the major marketing communicators of a firm?

2   What major factors assist a source in being perceived as credible? Cite specific advertising examples of the use of each factor.

3   What is the so-called sleeper effect, and if it were shown to exist what implications would there be for the communicator?

4   What recommendations would you make to a communicator regarding the following aspects of message structure: (1) message sidedness, (2) order of presentation, and (3) message code?

5   What suggestions would you offer regarding drawing a conclusion in a marketing communication? Watch a number of TV advertisements and try to determine the extent to which these suggestions are being followed.

6   What conclusions can you offer regarding the effective use of message appeals? Can you point out any specific advertisements that might not be following these conclusions?

7   Under what conditions might a highly credible source detract from the persuasiveness of a message?

8   If you were going to present a speech to United States business leaders on "The Declining Quality of America's Goods and Services," what guidelines could you employ from this chapter?

9   Design a specific advertisement for an actual product using material you have learned from this chapter.

10   Suggest the characteristics of some fear appeals that might be used for the following: (1) the American Heart Association attempting to get people to regularly check their blood pressure, (2) Goodrich steel-belted radial tires, (3) Prudential disability insurance, and a (4) Sears burglar alarm system for the home.

NOTES

[1] "Advertisers Attack Tough Marketing Problems," *Advertising Age*, December 22, 1980, pp. 28–29.
[2] Henry Assael, *Consumer Behavior and Markting Action*, Kent, Belmont, CA, 1981, p. 91.
[3] Richard J. Lutz, "Changing Brand Attitudes Through Modification of Cognitive Structure," *Journal of Consumer Research*, 1:49, March 1975, has discussed some of these strategies.
[4] See John L. Lastovicka and David M. Gardner, "Components of Involvement," in John C. Maloney and Bernard Silverman (eds.), *Attitude Research Plays For High Stakes*, American Marketing Association, Chicago, 1979, pp. 53–73; and C. W. Sherif, M. Sherif, and R. E. Nebergall, *Attitude and Attitude Change: The Social Judgment Involvement Approach*, Yale University Press, New Haven, CT, 1965.
[5] One might validly suggest that channel factors should be included in this list. However, for purposes of this chapter, these effects are included within the source, because consumers frequently view a medium as a source of information and influence.
[6] Arch G. Woodside and J. William Davenport, "The Effect of Salesman Similarity and Expertise on Consumer Purchasing Behavior," *Journal of Marketing Research*, 11:198–202, May 1974.
[7] Theodore Levitt, "Communications and Industrial Selling," *Journal of Marketing*, 31:15–21, April 1967.
[8] See, for example, Brian Sternthal, Ruby Dholakia, and Clark Leavitt, "The Persuasive Effects of Source Credibility: Tests of Cognitive Response," *Journal of Consumer Research*, 4:252–260, 1978; D. Bock and T. Saine, "The Impact of Source Credibility, Attitude Valence, and Task Sensitization on Trait Error in Speech Evaluation," *Speech Monographs*, 37:342–358, 1975; and Robert R. Harmon and Kenneth A. Coney, "The Persuasive Effects of Source Credibility in Buy and Lease Situations," *Journal of Marketing Research*, 14:255–260, May 1982.
[9] See Sternthal, Dholakia, and Leavitt, "The Persuasive Effects of Source Credibility."
[10] See Brian Sternthal, Lynn Phillips, and Ruby Dholakia, "The Persuasive Effect of Source Credibility: A Situational Analysis," *Public Opinion Quarterly*, 42:285–314, 1978; and Daniel R. Toy, "Monitoring Communication Effects: A Cognitive Structure/Cognitive Response Approach," *Journal of Consumer Research*, 9:66–76, June 1982.
[11] See Ruby Dholakia and Brian Sternthal, "Highly Credible Sources: Persuasive Facilitators or Persuasive Liabilities?" *Journal of Consumer Research*, 3:223–232, March 1977.
[12] See Carl Hovland and Walter Weiss, "The Influence of Source Credibility on Communication Effectiveness," *Public Opinion Quarterly*, 15:635–650, 1951–1952; Herbert Kelman and Carl Hovland, "'Reinstatement' of the Communicator in Delayed Measurement of Opinion Change," *Journal of Abnormal and Social Psychology*, 48:327–335, 1953; and Carl Hovland, Arthur A. Lunsdaine, and Fred D. Sheffield, *Experiments on Mass Communications*, Princeton University Press, Princeton, NJ, 1949, pp. 188–189.
[13] See, for example, N. Capon and J. Hulbert, "The Sleeper Effect: An Awakening," *Public Opinion Quarterly*, 37:333–358, 1973; and C. Gruder, et al., "Empirical Tests of the Absolute Sleeper Effect Predicted from the Discounting Cue Hypothesis," *Journal of Personality and Social Psychology*, 36:1061–1074, 1978.
[14] Kelman and Hovland, "Reinstatement of the Communicator."
[15] For a more complete discussion, see E. P. Bettinghaus, *Persuasive Communication*, 2d ed., Holt, New York, 1973, p. 10.
[16] See, for example, E. Aronson and B. Golden, "The Effect of Relevant and Irrelevant Aspects of Communicator Credibility on Opinion Change," *Journal of Personality*, 30:135–146, 1962; also see Peter Bennett and Harold Kassarjian, *Consumer Behavior*, Prentice-Hall, Englewood Cliffs, NJ, 1972, p. 89.
[17] For elaboration on the importance of nonverbal cues, see G. I. Nierenberg and H. H. Calero, *How to Read a Person like a Book*, Hawthorne, New York, 1971.
[18] See, for example, Paul Friggens, "Pyramid Selling—No. 1 Consumer Fraud," *Reader's Digest*, March 1974, pp. 79–83.
[19] David K. Berlo, *The Process of Communications*, Holt, San Francisco, 1960, pp. 45–48.
[20] M. Karlins and H. I. Abelson, *Persuasion*, 2d ed., Springer, New York, 1970, p. 128.
[21] See C. Hovland, A. Lumsdaine, and F. Sheffield, *Experiments in Mass Communication, Volume 3*, Princeton University Press, Princeton, NJ, 1948; also see Linda Golden and Mark Alpert, "The Relative Effectiveness of One-Sided and Two-Sided Communication for Mass Transit Advertising," in H. Keith Hunt (ed.), *Advances in Consumer Research: Volume 5*, Association for Consumer Research, Ann Arbor, MI, 1978, pp. 12–18.
[22] See Stewart W. Bither, "Resistance of Persuasion: Innoculation and Distraction," in Arch Woodside, Jagdish Sheth, and Peter Bennett (eds.), *Consumer and Industrial Buying Behavior*, North Holland, New York, pp. 243–250; and Michael Etgar and Stephen A. Goodwin, "One-Sided versus Two-Sided Comparative Message Appeals for New Brand Introductions," *Journal of Consumer Research*, 8:460–465, March 1982.
[23] E. W. J. Faison, "Effectiveness of One-Sided and Two-Sided Mass Communications in Advertising," *Public Opinion Quarterly*, 25:468–469, 1961.
[24] M. Wayne Delozier, *The Marketing Communications Process*, McGraw-Hill, New York, 1976, p. 95.
[25] C. I. Hovland, I. L. Janis, and H. H. Kelley, *Communication and Persuasion*, Yale, New Haven, CT, 1953, p. 119.

[26] Hovland, Janis, and Kelley, *Communication and Persuasion,* pp. 103–105.

[27] D. L. Thistlethwaite, H. de Haan, and J. Kamenetzky, "The Effects of 'Directive' and 'Nondirective' Communication Procedures on Attitudes," *Journal of Abnormal and Social Psychology,* 51:107–113, 1955.

[28] See Alan G. Sawyer, "Repetition and Affect: Recent Empirical and Theoretical Developments," in Arch Woodside, Jagdish Sheth, and Peter Bennett (eds.), *Consumer and Industrial Buyer Behavior,* North-Holland, New York, 1977, pp. 229–242; and George E. Belch, "The Effects of Television Commercial Repetition on Cognitive Response and Message Acceptance," *Journal of Consumer Research,* 9:56–65, June 1982.

[29] See Bobby Calder and Brian Sternthal, "Television Advertising Wearout: An Information Processing View," *Journal of Marketing Research,* 17:173–186, May 1980.

[30] I. Janis and S. Feshbach, "Effects of Fear Arousing Communications," *Journal of Abnormal and Social Psychology,* 48:78–92, 1953.

[31] See L. Berkowitz and D. R. Cottingham, "The Interest Value and Relevance of Fear-Arousing Communication," *Journal of Abnormal and Social Psychology,* 60:37–43, 1960; A. S. DeWolf and C. N. Governale, "Fear and Attitude Change," *Journal of Abnormal and Social Psychology,* 69:119–123, 1964; H. Leventhal, R. P. Singer, and S. Jones, "Effects of Fear and Specificity of Recommendation upon Attitudes and Behavior," *Journal of Personality and Social Psychology,* 2:20–29, 1965; and C. A. Insko, A. Arkoff, and V. M. Insko, "Effects of High and Low Fear-Arousing Communications upon Opinions toward Smoking," *Journal of Experimental Social Psychology,* 1:254–266, August 1965.

[32] Michael L. Ray and William L. Wilkie, "Fear: The Potential of an Appeal Neglected by Marketing," *Journal of Marketing,* 34:54–62, January 1970.

[33] See Brian Sternthal and C. Samuel Craig, "Fear Appeals: Revisited and Revised," *Journal of Consumer Research,* 1:22–34, December 1974; John J. Burnett and Robert E. Wilkes, "Fear Appeals to Segments Only," *Journal of Advertising Research,* 20:21–24, October 1980; and John J. Burnett and Richard L. Oliver, "Fear Appeal Effects in the Field: A Segmentation Approach," *Journal of Marketing Research,* 16:181–190, May 1979.

[34] M. Karlins and H. I. Abelson, *Persuasion,* 2d ed., Springer, New York, 1970, p. 15.

[35] See Stewart W. Bither, "Effects of Distraction and Commitment on the Persuasiveness of Television Advertising," *Journal of Marketing Research,* 9:1–5, February 1972; and David Gardner, "The Distraction Hypothesis in Marketing," *Journal of Advertising Research,* 10:25–31, December 1970.

[36] See Hovland, Janis, and Kelley, *Communication and Persuasion,* pp. 228–237; also see W. Watts, "Relative Persistance of Opinion Change Induced by Active Compared to Passive Participation," *Journal of Personality and Social Psychology,* 5:4–15, 1967.

[37] See Thomas W. Whipple and Alice E. Courtney, "How Men and Women Judge Humor: Advertising Guidelines for Action and Research," in James H. Leigh and Claude R. Martin Jr. (eds.), *Current Issues and Research in Advertising,* University of Michigan, Ann Arbor, MI, 1981.

[38] Brian Sternthal and C. Samuel Craig, "Humor in Advertising," *Journal of Marketing,* 37:12–18, October 1973.

[39] E. P. Bettinghaus, *Persuasive Communication,* 2d ed., Holt, New York, 1973, pp. 160–161.

[40] Bettinghaus, *Persuasive Communication,* pp. 121–122, in reference to G. L. Trager, "Paralanguage: A First Approximation," *Studies in Linguistics,* 13:1–12, 1958; also see Larry Percy, "Psycholinguistic Guidelines for Advertising Copy," in Andrew Mitchell (ed.), *Advances in Consumer Research: Volume 9,* Association for Consumer Research, Ann Arbor, MI, 1982, pp. 107–111, for some practical guidelines for using verbal codes.

[41] For a recent exception, see Patrick L. Schul and Charles W. Lamb, Jr., "Recoding Nonverbal and Vocal Communications: A Laboratory Study," *Journal of the Academy of Marketing Science,* 10:154–164, Spring 1982.

[42] Bettinghaus, Persuasive Communication, pp. 121–122, in reference to G. L. Tragar, "Paralanguage: A First Approximation," *Studies in Linguistics,* 13:1–12, 1958.

[43] See I. L. Janis, "Personality Correlates of Susceptibility to Persuasion," *Journal of Personality,* 22:504–518, 1954; F. J. Divesta and J. C. Merivan, "The Effects of Need-Oriented Communications on Attitude Change," *Journal of Abnormal and Social Psychology,* 60:80–85, 1960; and I. L. Janis and C. I. Hovland (eds.), *Personality and Persuasibility,* Yale, New Haven, CT, 1959, pp. 55–68.

[44] D. F. Cox and R. A. Bauer, "Self Confidence and Persuasibility in Women," *Public Opinion Quarterly,* 28:453–466, Fall 1964.

[45] R. A. Bauer, "Games People and Audiences Play," paper presented at seminar on Communications in Contemporary Society, University of Texas, March 17, 1967.

[46] Hovland, Janis, and Kelley, *Communication and Persuasion,* p. 183.

[47] This discussion is based in part upon Bettinghaus, *Persuasive Communication,* pp. 59–61.

CASES FOR PART FOUR

CASE 4-1
DOODLE, DAZZLE, AND SPARKLE[1]

A California dentist tries to amuse his young patients by dressing up in a red cape with blue tights and calling himself "Plaque Invader." Actually, he uses a total of twelve different costumes in his practice. This same dentist drives to work in a white Volkswagen that has a top formed in the shape of a molar. The vehicle is called a "Plaquemobile." For adults, a hot tub and choice wines are available while waiting for an appointment, or after a visit. In addition, chances to win record albums, free dinners, and turkeys are given away.

Is this a professional that has gone off the deep end, or is he an entrepreneur with particularly good insight into consumers? A little information on the dental-care industry provides some perspective. For decades, dentists have been in the tooth repair business while being almost evangelistic in promoting good oral hygiene to reduce the risk of additional cavities and other dental problems. At the same time, dental schools have been training a growing number of professionals to repair teeth that have fallen victim to decay. Nevertheless, until the 1970s, demand for dental services in the United States continued to significantly exceed the supply of dentists. However, during the 1970s the number of active dentists increased 21 percent to about 124,000 while the population increased only 8.8 percent. The consequence has been that average patient loads per dentist have declined perceptively. This is especially noticeable in California where the number of dentists per 1000 persons is higher than in any other state.

Factors other than changing demographics have also contributed to declines in the demand for dental chairs. Better oral-hygiene practices promoted by dentists actually have reduced the need for corrective dentistry. Also, fluoridation of drinking water for about one-half of the nation's population has had a similar effect. One study showed that a child who drinks fluoridated water from infancy to 14 years of age develops 60 percent fewer cavities than others who drink unfluoridated water. More efficient dentistry has also had a dramatic impact. High-speed, diamond tipped drills and other advances have reduced the duration of appointments for some procedures by two-thirds or more.

Of course, there also is a negative side to these statistics and trends. In many areas of the country, dentists are becoming concerned about declines in revenues as a result of fewer and shorter patient visits. Some critics, who have referred to the profession as "Drill, Fill, Bill, and Coupe DeVille" have not shown a great deal of sympathy. But dentists, and the associations that represent them, are quite concerned.

Because of this, one portion of the marketplace has become the focus of considerable attention—those people who do not visit a dentist on a regular basis. Surprisingly, about one-half of the U.S. population falls into this category. Therefore, there is considerable potential demand for dentistry services among these residents. Some dentists, like the one described earlier, have focused on novelty, humor, and extras to lure potential customers. Others have constructed elaborate offices with wood paneling and stained glass windows. Still others have offered unique features such as a disco called the "waiting room" for those that come early for their appointments. In addition, a dentist in California actually offers special tattoo work on new caps. He features the slogan "Get Drilled at Ernie's" on T-shirts and other displays.

The American Dental Association has also become involved by sponsoring a variety of promotional messages on behalf of member dentists. In contrast to previous messages that educated the public on proper dental hygiene, current focus is on encouraging people to visit their dentist. One theme has been referred to as Dazzle because its basic message is "Dazzle. When your teeth have it, you have it. So go get some at your dentist's." An offshot of this is the "Sparkle" theme as shown in Figure 1. Another recent message is referred to as Doodle because it focuses on the consequences of tooth decay and warns: "Don't doodle around with your teeth. Call your dentist today."

Still other dentists have concluded that the high cost of dental work serves as a deterrent to regular office visits. One response has been dental care centers installed in department stores and in shopping malls.

---

[1] This case is based on information appearing in "Drilling for New Business," Time, December 1, 1980, p. 110; "Retail Dentistry," Newsweek, November 27, 1978, p. 63; Elizabeth Bailey, "The Department Store Dentist," Forbes, March 19, 1979, pp. 112–114; and Darolyn Lendio, "Dentists Ponder Case of the Missing Patients as Appointments Lag," The Wall Street Journal, October 10, 1980, pp. 1, 14.

FIGURE 1

Example of advertisement focusing on the concept of sparkle. (Courtesy of the American Dental Association).

> # SPARKLE:
>
> ### Get it for her at the dentist regularly.
>
> It's a look. It's a feeling. Mostly it's an attitude, one kids will keep for the rest of their lives: the self-assurance that comes with strong, beautiful teeth. Advances like fluoride toothpaste mean a lot, but not without an early program of regular dental visits. So start them out young, yes, even before they're three. A checkup takes just a few minutes of your time. And it costs less than what it takes to keep a child in shoes for a year.
> Sparkle. It's a quality you've admired in others. It's something you can give your kids for a lifetime.
>
> **The American Dental Association**

Because of the high volume of business, these centers are often capable of offering a fee structure that is 20 to 40 percent below regular dental rates. In addition, an added bonus of such centers is convenience, because they are usually open 10 to 12 hours, Monday through Saturday, and 6 hours on Sunday.

Still others point to evidence suggesting that cost ranks seventh out of eleven "barriers" to regular dental visits. Fear and concern about pain are the major factors to deal with according to this group. However, little has been done to address this issue. Some progress has been made to make dentists' offices look less imposing through changes in decor. Also, some claim that locating offices in more typical surroundings, such as at a shopping mall, and placing chairs out in an open area have resulted in reduced patient anxiety. The use of nitrous oxide to relax patients and the availability of more effective pain killers have also been communicated to the public in low-key ways to help dispel anxiety. However, to date, the magic key has not yet been found to encourage the majority of the public to make regular dental appointments.

Questions

1   Suggest motivating influences that might be involved in the decision to visit a dentist. How would you categorize these and how do they relate to one another?

2   In what ways might the motives that actually influence use of a dentist be determined?

3 What appeals can you find in the case that have been used to encourage people to visit a dentist? How do these appeals match up with your answer to Question 1?

4 How are consumers' attitudes potentially relevant to visits to a dental office?

5 Can you suggest any approaches dentists or their associations might take to encourage more people to make regular dental visits?

CASE 4-2
STANTON CHEMICAL COMPANY[1]

Stanton Chemical Company produces Clo-White, a liquid laundry bleach, and distributes it on a regional basis. The company was founded in 1950 by its current president, Robert M. Stanton. From a modest beginning, the company has grown in size until it now has annual sales of over $6 million out of an estimated total industry sales in 1975 of $130 million. Stanton Chemical has its headquarters in a large southern city and operates several mixing and bottling plants in the Southeast.

The manufacture of bleach is simple, since it is merely sodium hypochlorite and water mixed together in a solution. All of the bleaches on the market contain 5.25 percent sodium hypochlorite and 94.75 percent inert ingredients (water), but bleach produced in this manner is subject to an "aging" problem. When first produced, laundry bleach has no odor and is at its highest potency level. However, once it has been on the shelf for a length of time (5 to 8 days), the solution begins to break down chemically. The chlorine in the mixture is given off as a gas; hence, the strong smell that certain bleaches exhibit. When a bleach breaks down in this manner, it loses some of its potential for whitening and stain removal, but smells "stronger" to the consumer.

Stanton has developed the capability to deliver its bleach quicker and more consistently than any of its competitors by locating mixing and bottling plants close to its markets. This quick, efficient delivery results in Clo-White's being able to outperform competing bleaches in stain removal power and whitening ability.

Despite the availability of detergents with bleach additives, homemakers still look to the chlorine-based laundry bleach as the means to remove stains and whiten clothes. Independent research studies suggest that the woman's attitude toward domestic activities and the degree of family orientation are primary determinants in brand selection. Women who possess a strong domestic orientation are more likely to perceive real or imagined differences in the quality of various bleaches, while women who possess weaker orientations will tend to rate all brands equal in quality and will prefer to shop for the lowest priced brands.

CURRENT PROBLEM

Top management has expressed concern over the ability of Snowy-White, a regional competitor, to outsell Clo-White, particularly since price and promotional expenditures for both products are approximately equal. To find a remedy for the situation, Mr. Pearl, vice president of marketing, recommended that research be conducted to determine what consumers actually thought of Clo-White compared with other brands and, if possible, some reasons for the particular brand image.

A sample of 1000 homemakers was selected at random from several large southern cities where Clo-White enjoyed a large market share. They were asked to rank pairs of leading regional brands in terms of their perceived similarity then to rank the brands according to their own individual preferences. Finally, respondents were asked to give reasons why they ranked the bleaches in that particular order. The data were analyzed by a multidimensional routine and are displayed as a perceptual map in Figure 1. The labeled axes represent the two main dimensions on which brands of bleach appear to have been evaluated. Consumers' perception of the ideal bleach is also indicated. Some of the typical comments from the respondents were:

"All the bleaches are the same. I just buy the cheapest one."

"There's not much difference in price, so I usually buy the stronger bleach. It gets my clothes cleaner and that's what I want."

"Well, you can take the cap off this one (Snowy-White), and smell the bleach."

"The other brands just don't have that kind of smell. I always buy the stronger bleach to get my clothes cleaner."

---

[1] Adapted from the original case by Daniel L. Sherrell appearing in M. Wayne DeLozier (ed.), *Consumer Behavior Dynamics: A Casebook*, Merrill, Columbus, Oh., 1977. Used with permission of the author and Charles E. Merrill Publishing Company.

FIGURE 1
Relative brand-image position.

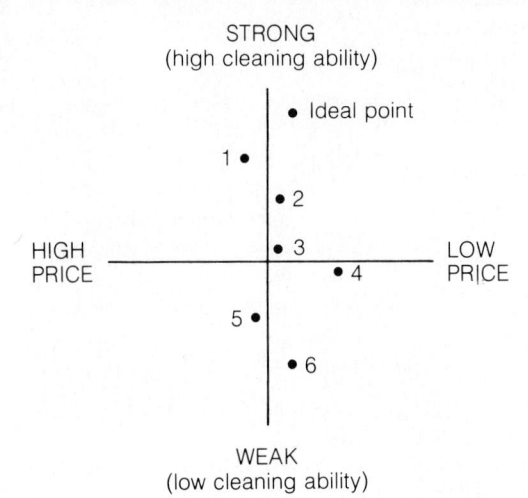

```
                    STRONG
              (high cleaning ability)
                      |
                      |    • Ideal point
                   1• |
                      |  • 2
                      |  • 3
    HIGH  ────────────┼────────────  LOW
    PRICE             |     • 4       PRICE
                      |
                   5• |
                      |  • 6
                      |
                    WEAK
              (low cleaning ability)
```

Composite brand ranking:

1 Snowy-White   4 Dixie Day
2 Blue Sky   5 Miracle-White
3 Clo-White   6 Quality

Pearl feels that what most consumers want is the strongest bleach on the market and that they are willing to pay at least the competitive price for it. Thus, he feels that Stanton should mount an advertising campaign that "educates" the consumer about the superiority of Clo-White over its competitors. "Tell them the research results and tell them that smell doesn't make any difference. We must maintain our quality."

Mr. Lawrence, brand manager for Clo-White, feels that the research results indicate the importance consumers attach to smell as an indicator of strength. "Telling them that Clo-White is the strongest bleach won't convince them once they take the cap off and smell it. They just won't believe that kind of advertising." He believes that Stanton must allow its bleach to "age" to develop a stronger smell. "Most consumers go by the smell. Let's give them what they want." Lawrence's plan is to introduce "Clo-White Plus" and advertise it as a new and stronger bleach. "Shoot, we won't be lying to them; it will have a stronger smell and that's what they want. Gentlemen, we're dealing with consumer perceptions. How do you think Snowy-White got ahead of us?"

Questions

1 What other alternatives might Stanton Chemical consider?

2 What would be the short- versus long-run effects of each strategy?

3 How important is olfactory perception in the consumer's evaluation of bleach and other similar products? How easy (difficult) would it be for a company to "educate" consumers about product characteristics that are contradictory to their own perceptions of the product?

4 Is Mr. Lawrence's suggestion unethical, or is he right in giving consumers what they "want"?

CASE 4-3
SEARS, ROEBUCK AND CO.[1]

HISTORICAL PERSPECTIVE

In 1886, Richard Warren Sears entered the mail-order business with the founding of the R. W. Sears Company in Minneapolis. The following year, Sears moved his business to Chicago and Alvan C. Roebuck was hired as the Company's watchmaker. In 1893, the firm became Sears, Roebuck and Co., an organization destined to become the largest retailer of general merchandise in the United States.

The company's first mail-order catalog, distributed in 1888, featured only watches and jewelry, but by 1895 its 532-page catalog offered a wide variety of products. Because Sears purchased goods in large

---
[1]The original version of this case was developed by the authors and Davina Velleneuve. Reprinted by permission.

quantities, often directly from the manufacturer, it was able to offer them at lower prices than could local merchants and storekeepers. In addition, because it was a mail-order retailer, Sears could satisfy needs of consumers in remote rural locations rather than have them travel great distances to shop at various retail stores. Because of this, Sears developed a reputation as a retailer of many basic goods to the rural population of our country.

Through the assistance of Julius Rosenwald and Aaron E. Nusbaum, who joined Sears in 1895, the company was organized to handle mail orders more economically and efficiently. However, it was not until 1925 that Sears opened its first retail store, largely due to the influence of General Robert E. Wood, who joined the company in 1924. Wood, known as the father of Sears' retail expansion, identified the trend toward urbanization in the United States. American cities began growing and Sears' largely rural customers were abandoning the farm for the factory. And with the advent of the automobile, customers were no longer limited to shopping by catalog. Unless Sears opened stores of its own, Wood reasoned, the company would end up serving only a small fraction of the total American buying public. By 1929, more than 300 Sears retail stores were in operation, and in 1931 retail sales topped mail-order sales for the first time. Because of this growth, Sears was able to contract with manufacturers to produce distinct products which were sold under Sears' own brand names.

In response to many customers' need for low-cost automobile insurance, Allstate Insurance Co. was developed in 1931 as a wholly-owned Sears subsidiary. Although Allstate initially operated only a mail-order business, by 1933 sales locations were placed directly in Sears stores.

Even though World War II did call a halt to Sears' retail expansion, the company correctly projected the economic climate which immediately followed the war. In contrast to its competitors, Sears anticipated major growth and expanded rapidly by adding new stores. Sales accelerated from $1.9 billion in 1948 to $2.9 billion in 1954, while competitors such as Montgomery Ward experienced a significant decline in sales.

AN ERA OF ERRORS

Sears won the hearts of America with its emphasis on high quality and low-priced merchandise, backed up with reliable service. The company had an especially strong base in its mail-order business and in the hardware departments of its retail stores. Throughout the company's history, slogans such as "Shop at Sears and Save" and "Satisfaction Guaranteed or Your Money Back" were also used to instill an image of quality merchandise at low cost in the consumer's mind. These positioning strategies resulted in the attraction of a middle-class clientele for Sears.

During the late 1960s, however, the retailing environment began to change rapidly. Sears found itself caught in the middle of the spectrum between emerging forms of retailing—discounters and specialty shops. While these retailers began establishing outlets in new suburban malls, Sears's stores built years earlier often looked shabby by comparison. Sears awoke to find that it was losing more and more of its traditional middle-class customers to the new forms of competition.

In an effort to regain lost market share, Sears began to compete directly with the specialty shops. In 1967, based on a forecast of increasing affluence among American families, the company changed its long-standing strategy and began to position itself to attract more-affluent shoppers. That is, Sears moved "uptown" by upgrading its product lines and adding merchandise at the higher end of the price ladder. Stylish and expensive items, like Musk Oil After Shave and Johnny Miller's men's sportswear, were emphasized to help build a fashion-apparel image.

There were negative results from these moves. It appears that existing upper-income consumers were not attracted by the switch to new higher fashion (and higher cost) items since they continued to shop at their traditional retail shops. Even worse, traditional middle-class customers, who had historically turned to Sears because of its functional and lower-priced product offerings, began to purchase such items at discount stores, such as K mart.

Consequently, while Sears' share of the market remained relatively stable during most of the 1970s, K mart took advantage of Sears' trade-up and grew from 1972 sales of $3.8 billion to $8.4 billion in 1976. At the same time, J. C. Penney strengthened its software image and began attracting Sears's traditional apparel customers.

Most analysts agree that Sears accurately forecasted changing American lifestyles, with two-income households generating more discretionary income. A strategy to move toward an upgraded product line was therefore not in error according to many industry sources. It is Sears' implementation of this strategy which has been criticized. Says retail analyst Stanley H. Iverson of Duff and Phelphs, Inc., "They just moved too fast and too far with the program. When you have that broad 80 percent of the market in the middle, you have to move very, very gradually."[2] Other observers have been more critical. Says an executive of a major discounter, "What they didn't realize was those families would use that discretionary income in other stores and in products with some ego value."[3]

Sears apparently realized its error: "We will never be the store where a young lady will want to buy a cocktail dress for a date with her best guy," admitted Garland K. Ingraham, vice president of retail sales.[4] In an effort to correct its mistake, the company again began competing with discount stores. In 1977, an extensive, price-cutting campaign was launched. Sears spent $518 million advertising lengthy and frequent sales, an increase from $419 million in 1976. To encourage store managers into such efforts, a bonus system based strictly on volume was developed.

The intent of the campaign was, through drastic price cuts, to attract shoppers who would then buy additional items carrying normal markups. However, Sears' shoppers seemed to have walked directly to the sales counters and then straight to the cash registers.

A popular view was that Sears had succeeded only in attracting customers back to shop for bargains. While sales increased to $17.2 billion, retail profits fell 13 percent for the year (additional financial data are provided in Table 1). Meanwhile, Penney's retail net rose by almost 28 percent, K mart's by 13.1 percent, and Montgomery Ward's by 17.4 percent.

Despite Sears' strategic errors, the company remained the largest merchandiser in the United States. By 1977, however, the company's long-standing reputation as "The Store Where Middle America Shops" had deteriorated. "What does Sears really stand for?" asks one industry analyst when referring to how consumers have responded to Sears' moves.

To correct errors of the past, the company adopted a back-to-basics strategy. It returned to offering more middle-of-the-road goods, geared toward function rather than fashion. That is, Sears attempted to target straight back toward the middle-class homeowner. In addition, major policy decisions were centralized at the Sears Tower in Chicago, and the pricing and presentation of goods in stores became more standardized. Edward R. Telling, then president of Sears, hoped to boost profitability by cashing in on the retailer's traditional strengths—product, service, and value.

Edward A. Brennan, president and chief operating officer for retailing since April 1980, agrees with recent policy changes, but thinks the company's appeal is more widespread. "I think sometimes people try to put us into a neat little package and tie a bow around us. You can't say Sears is appealing to just this customer, period. We should have goods the customer wants, rather than only an assortment of merchandise that fits Chicago's requirements. If the customer wants fashion, we should have fashion."[5]

Brennan, believing that advertising and store displays are a vital route to sharpening the company's merchandising approach, turned this responsibility over to Robert E. Wood II, vice president of advertising and sales. Wood believed the company's focus was wrong for the times. "We are not quite as up-to-date as we ought to be, particularly in our stores' looks. We're considered the store of the middle-class, the middle aged, and not so much for the young. We need a more-contemporary appeal."[6]

In February 1981, Sears launched its first corporate image campaign since the early 1960s with the theme "You Can Count On Sears." This was supplemented by highlighting Sears' customer service, credit

TABLE 1

FINANCIAL PERFORMANCE DATA (IN MILLIONS OF DOLLARS)

Year	Sales	Pretax Income
1965	6390.0	586.40
1966	6804.9	592.82
1967	7330.1	664.40
1968	8198.0	779.06
1969	8863.0	838.35
1970	9562.2	829.40
1971	10006.1	949.97
1972	10991.0	1030.16
1973	12306.2	1113.40
1974	13101.2	815.59
1975	13639.9	915.09
1976	14950.2	1076.06
1977	17224.0	1194.00
1978	17946.3	1264.02
1979	17514.3	1028.98
1980	25194.9	697.80

Source: Industrial Compustat® II

---

[2]"Can Sears Come Back?" *Dun's Review*, February 1979, p. 70.
[3]"Sears' Strategic About-Face," *Business Week*, January 8, 1979, p. 81.
[4]Ibid, p. 81.
[5]Steve Weiner, "Sears' New Merchandising Chief Aims to Unify Field Operations With Policy," *The Wall Street Journal*, March 17, 1980, p. 10.
[6]Steve Weiner, "New Sears Retail Plan Sets Precise Goals for Sales, Costs, Profits at Every Store," *The Wall Street Journal*, December 3, 1980, p. 31.

availability, and money-back guarantee. Says Wood of Sears' prior slogan, "Where America Shops For Value," "We haven't found it registers very high in telling what Sears is all about."[7] The new campaign communicates attributes of shopping at Sears and attempts to portray the company as a more contemporary retailer.

As part of the company's attempt to obtain a more contemporary appeal, while at the same time adopting a back-to-basics strategy, more than 100 separate "challenge lines" were introduced in 1981. These are defined as "goods which are right for the time," which management feels will be extremely successful if backed by extra advertising, stocking, display, and promotion. Also, although the company has never been successful with celebrity labels, Sears recently introduced a new line of women's apparel—Cheryl Tiegs sportswear, endorsed by the famous model. Wood described the Tiegs line as "contemporary, uncluttered stuff with some flair." He also noted that the clothes have "pizzazz," at a price that fits well with the entire company. The company also broke with a long tradition when it recently agreed with Levi Strauss & Company to sell Levi's in Sears stores.

THE NEW SEARS

In addition to changes in its merchandising approach, Sears also began a diversification strategy beyond its retailing and Allstate activities. On January 22, 1981, it announced the opening of experimental business machine stores in stores in Dallas, Chicago, and Boston. Sales at the experimental stores exceeded expectations and forty-five more were opened in 1982. Brennan said that Sears plans to have 200 open by the end of 1984.

The business centers stock personal computers, copiers, word processors, calculators, and other products made by such leading producers as IBM, Hewlett-Packard, and Exxon. Besides entering a new area of business, Sears also broke its long-standing one-roof merchandising policy by keeping the business centers physically separate from its department stores. A Sears executive stated that the market for office equipment is sufficiently different from Sears' traditional customers and therefore separate locations would be more conducive to their needs. However, the Sears name is still used on these distinct outlets.

Perhaps the most shocking news has been Sears' recent acquisition of Coldwell Banker & Co., the country's largest real estate brokerage concern, and Dean Witter Reynolds Organization, the fifth largest stock brokerage firm. These mark the boldest acquisitions in the company's 97-year history. Sears has announced that it intends to become the "largest consumer-oriented financial services firm in the United States." It is hoping to duplicate the success it achieved with Allstate, which is second only to State Farm Insurance Company in property-casualty insurance. To do this, the Financial Services Group was established in 1981. By August 1982, Sears opened the first branches of its Financial Network, a kind of financial supermarket located within Sears retail stores where shoppers can obtain stocks, bonds, insurance, loans, and IRAs (Individual Retirement Accounts). If successful, the company plans to expand the Financial Network to all of its retail stores.

Although some bankers are doubtful that many people will want to buy their "stocks and socks" under the same roof, Sears officials believe that the company's trusted name will bring customers. A recent Roper Organization poll found Sears to be "viewed most favorably" by customers who rated it against a wide range of U.S. corporations.[8] Sears is also relying heavily on its in-house credit-card customers. Although 25 million U.S. households actively use Sears credit cards, fully 48 million or 57 percent of all households hold one. That compares with 53 percent for Visa cards, 39 percent for the J. C. Penney card, 27 percent for Montgomery Ward, and 11 percent for American Express.[9] The Financial Services Group is also considering adding a large array of additional financial services, such as automatic teller machines to be located in retail stores.

But adding financial services does not fully address the company's ongoing problems in merchandise retailing. Sears executives say that the new focus on financial services will, in no way, deemphasize traditional retailing activities. But how the giant is going to integrate the two huge and seemingly disparate businesses is anybody's guess. "The two businesses require very different skills," says Finn M. W. Caspersen, chairman of Beneficial Corporation. "I would tend to give Sears management the benefit of the doubt, but it is my belief that retailing and full-scale financial services are going be be very difficult to combine," he

---

[7] Ibid., p. 31.

[8] "The New Sears," *Business Week*, November 16, 1981, p. 140.
[9] Ibid, p. 143.

adds.[10] Phillip Purcell, vice president of corporate planning, is more optimistic. "There's no reason why someone shouldn't go into a Sears store and buy a shirt and coat, and then maybe some stock. I don't consider that any more outrageous than the first idea like that that came up, that someone might buy a coat and tie, then buy auto insurance. [Do you have] any idea how preposterous Allstate sounded in 1934?"[11]

Questions

1 What problem or problems did Sears seem to confront starting in the later 1960s? Can you indentify any factors leading to the problem(s)?

2 How might management obtain information to help identify the specific nature of Sears' problem(s)?

3 What aspects of Sears' recent strategies might relate to the problem(s) you have identified?

4 Are there any strategies or actions that you might suggest to Sears' management?

CASE 4-4
EASY LIFE, INC.[1]

Michael Evans, a marketing manager in the kitchen products division for Easy Life, a leading small household appliance manufacturer, regularly attends conferences where the latest research evidence on consumer behavior is discussed. Consequently, Mike's awareness of different methods for studying how consumers process information is quite high. He believes that investigations of consumer information-processing yield insights into how consumers make purchase decisions. These insights can have an important impact on the design of advertisements and other aspects of Easy Life's marketing strategy.

One method of learning about how consumers process information is sometimes called the *thought protocol method*. This technique basically requires that consumers "think aloud" as they engage in some task, such as choosing which of several brands they will purchase. Typically, a brand-choice situation is set up by displaying several competing brands as they might appear in a retail store. The consumer is asked to make a purchase decision and speak out loud the thoughts that he or she has during the decision process. These verbalized thoughts are recorded and then converted into a typed transcript for further analysis. Although many subjects do not verbalize a high proportion of their thoughts initially, they soon become at ease with the process and the number of thoughts that are mentioned increases considerably.

After analyzing written protocols with his staff, Mike has concluded that they provide useful insights into, among other things, the images consumers have of various brands, how consumers process the information presented with a product, and what features of a product elicit positive responses among consumers. Of course, considerable effort is required to analyze just a small number of consumers' thought protocols. For this reason, large samples of consumers cannot be studied using this method. Consequently, any insights gained must be examined further to determine how representative they are of a wider group of consumers.

Another method of investigating how consumers process information is *eye movement analysis*. Use of this method requires that a consumer view a stimulus display (a product, an advertisement, etc.) while the movement of his or her eyes is being recorded by a very sophisticated piece of equipment. The result of this process can be a picture of the stimulus display that the consumer was viewing with a series of dots, numbered consecutively, superimposed on the picture. The dots show exactly where the consumer's eyes fixated on the display, and the numbers show the sequence in which each fixation occurred. A limitation of this method is that it typically requires the consumer to remain motionless during the stimulus presentation so that equipment can track eye movements. However, valuable information can be gained about which aspects of the stimulus presentations (product feature, advertising element, etc.) attract viewer attention and when they do so. For example, Mike learned that when viewing a display of the company's food mixer and its accessories, very few consumers looked at the special paddles used to knead bread dough.

At a recent conference Mike was intrigued by a rather novel suggestion. The author of one paper was proposing that by combining the methods of thought protocols and eye movement analysis one could learn more about how consumers decide among alternative brands than when either method is used alone. In this

---

[10] Ibid, p. 141.
[11] "Sears Finds Broadening Its Image Takes Time, Presses Staff to Adjust," *The Wall Street Journal*, October 31, p. 20.
[1] This case is based on Raymond J. Smead, James B. Wilcox, and Robert E. Wilkes, "An Illustration and Evaluation of a Joint Process Tracing Methodology: Eye Movement and Protocols," in Jerry C. Olson (ed.), *Advances in Consumer Research: Volume 7*, Ann Arbor, MI: Association for Consumer Research, 1980, pp. 507–512. Figures 1 and 2 from this source are reproduced here with permission of the Association for Consumer Research.

approach, thought protocols are used in traditional fashion but eye movement analysis is used at a more macro-level to show which of several alternative brands the consumer is looking at. The combined method was referred to as *joint process tracing* (JPT) by the researcher.

One of the professed benefits of the JPT method for studying brand-choice situations is that it allows a rather natural simulation of in-store choice environments. An experimental situation might be set up as follows. A moderator would accompany an experimental subject into the testing room where a shelf several feet in front of a wall containing a mirror displays several alternative brands of a given product. A microphone in the room would be connected to a tape recorder using a two-track (stereo) sound system. Anything said by either person would be recorded on one track of the tape. The moderator would instruct the subject regarding the choice situation and encourage the subject to say out loud all thoughts he or she has as the brands are reviewed.

A second researcher is seated behind the mirror wall and is able to see the subject through the mirror. This researcher's task is to speak into a second microphone and indicate the brand name the subject is viewing during each second of the experiment. A metronome audibly clicks off each second of time to assist the researcher in accomplishing this task. Therefore brand names are recorded on the second track of the stereo tape. The result of this data collection effort is one tape which has recorded which brand is being viewed and the verbalized thoughts of the subject that are occurring while the brand is being viewed. The recorded information is then transformed into a typed transcript called a "protocol-graph."

Figures 1 and 2 contain portions of protocol-graphs from two subjects who participated in an experiment involving six different brands of coffee makers.

Each brand was coded as indicated below:

Code	Brand
1	Proctor Silex
2	Sunbeam
3	Mr. Coffee
4	Sears
5	Norelco
6	General Electric

Certain conventions are used in producing protocol-graphs. Typically the leftmost column (see Figure 1) provides a running count of time in seconds. As the figures show, time progresses *down* the page of a graph. Columns 2 through 6 indicate the code number of the brand being observed at the time indicated in column 1. Multiple eye fixations are recorded as a SCAN which may be thought of as the subject's eyes wandering over various points of the display. If a scan lasts longer than one second it is coded as SCAN 2, SCAN 3, and so forth. Also, in Figures 1 and 2, two scans separated by a one second fixation are treated as a single scan. If at any time the subject takes his or her eyes off the brand display, it is recorded as a PAUSE on the protocol-graph. The length of the pause is coded by its duration if it lasts longer than one second (e.g., PAUSE 2 represents a 2-second pause). Finally, the protocol-graph also displays the thought protocol of experimental subjects. These comments, listed in numerical order are positioned at the correct time-position on the graph.

Mike obtained the two protocol-graphs (shown in Figures 1 and 2) from the conference paper. He was reviewing them to learn what insights about consumer

FIGURE 1

	Cols. 23456			Cols. 23456	
1	6		19	PAUSE 3	
2	6		20	1	
3	6		21	1	
4	1		22	1	
5	SCAN 1		23	2	
6	2		24	2	
7	1		25	2	
8	1		26	1	
9	1		27	1	
10	1		28	1	
11	1		29	1	
12	1		30	1	1) this one is 19.99
13	1		31	1	
14	1		32	1	
15	2				

FIGURE 1
(continued)

	Cols. 23456			Cols. 23456	
33	1	2) price is always a consideration of course	93	6	15) which I don't have much of
34	1		94	1	
35	2		95	1	
36	2		96	1	
37	2	3) $26.64, Sunbeam	97	6	
38	2		98	3	
39	2		99	6	
40	2		100	6	
41	2	4) I am acquainted with quality	101	6	16) (Mod.-what are you thinking?)
			102	5	
			103	6	
42	2		104	1	17) well, I'm thinking that probably everything else was equal in quality
43	2				
44	2	5) it's usually pretty good in my experience	105	1	
			106	2	
				SCAN 1	18) I'd rule those two out just on size
45	2				
46	2				
47	2	6) Mr. Coffee, I guess was one of the first ones that went this way	108	5	
			109	5	
			110	5	
48	3		111	6	19) because I have such a limited amount of counter space
49	3				
50	3				
51	3		112	6	
52	3		113	5	
53	4		114	4	
54	4		115	3	
55	4			PAUSE 1	20) if Proctor-Silex was equal in quality
56	4	7) Flav-o-fresh I don't know			
57	4		117	6	
58	4		118	6	
59	4		119	6	
	SCAN 1			PAUSE 1	21) which I have no way of knowing
61	4				
62	2		121	6	
63	4	8) dial-a-brew I would assume would give you more choice	122	5	22) except I have had a Proctor iron which was very good
			123	4	
64	4		124	1	
65	5		125	1	
66	5		126	1	21) its cost is least
67	5		127	1	
68	5		128	4	
69	5		129	5	
70	5	9) strength etc.	130	1	24) as I said, at my house we always look at the price tag
71	5				
72	4		131	1	
73	5	10) than any of these others	132	4	
74	5	11) judging by looks	133		25) sometimes before other things which isn't necessarily good
	PAUSE 1				
76	5				
77	5		134	5	
78	5	12) GE same price approximately	135	6	
			136	6	26) but I think for my purposes
79	4		137	5	
80	6		138	5	
81	6		139	5	
82	6		140	6	27) being as how I really am not making a lot of coffee nowadays
83	6				
84	5				
SCAN 1			141	6	
86	1		142	6	
87	1	13) well, at my house GE	143	6	
88	2		144	6	
89	3		145	5	
90	3			SCAN 1	
91	6		147	3	28) and because of the limited amount of space
92	1	14) and Mr. Coffee would take more room			

FIGURE 1
(continued)

Cols. 23456			Cols. 23456		
148	3		320	4	48) and I ruled out Mr. Coffee
149	5		321	4	
150	5		322	4	
151	5		323	4	
152	5	29) I'd probably rule out GE and Mr. Coffee sizewise	324	4	
			325	5	49) because I'm prejudiced
			326	5	
	PAUSE 1		327	6	
154	5		328	4	50) because of a past experience with a Sears electrical product
155	5				
156	2	30) GE certainly because that is the biggest one			
			329	6	
157	5		330	4	
158	5		331	2	
159	5		332	2	
	PAUSE 2		333	1	
162	6		334	1	
	PAUSE 2		335	2	51) I would probably rule against this one when I see a Sears
165	6				
166	6				
	SCAN 2	31) (Mod.-yes?)	336	5	
169	1		337	4	
170	6	32) well, I was just trying to figure out maybe what all this does	338	4	
			339	4	52) that's prejudiced, I realize it is.
171	6		340	4	
172	5		341	4	53) but we all are that way are we not?
173	5				
174	5		342	4	
175	5		343	4	
176	5		344	4	
177	5	33) that has nothing to do with strength, apparently, or does it?	345	4	
			346	4	
			347	4	
178	5		348	4	
179	5		349	4	
180	5		350	4	
181	5	34) that number of cups or is that the kind of brew	351	4	
			352	4	
182	5		353	4	
183	5		354	4	
184	5		355	4	
185	5		356	4	
186	5		357	5	
187	5		358	5	
188	5		359	5	
189	5		360	5	
190	5		361	5	
191	5			SCAN 1	
192	5		363	5	
193	5		364	2	
194	5		365	2	
195	5		366	2	
196	5		367	2	
197	5		368	2	
198	5		369	2	54) ok, that one tells you to clean it twice a year
199	5				
200	5		370	2	
(BREAK)			371	2	
	PAUSE 3		372	2	
309	3		373	2	55) this one doesn't tell you what to do
310	3				
311	3		374	2	
312	3		375	2	
313	3		376	2	
314	1		377	2	
315	2		378	2	56) yes, maybe it does.
	PAUSE 2		379	5	
318	4	47) I ruled out GE	380	5	
319	4		381	5	

FIGURE 1 (continued)

Cols. 23456			Cols. 23456	
382	5	57) clean according to instructions	443	1
383	5	58) ok, so somewhere its got to tell you.	444	1
			445	1
			446	1
384	5		447	1
385	5		448	1
386	2		449	2
387	2		450	2
388	2		451	2
389	2		452	2
390	2		453	2	70) well, let's see, Sunbeam
391	2	59) stainless steel	454	2
392	2		455	2
393	2		456	2	71) yeah, that's the kind of mixer I've got
394	2	60) well that's maybe nicer		
395	2		457	2
396	2		458	2
397	2		459	2
398	2	61) oh you might say it's more permanent etc. than plastic	460	2
			461	2
			462	2
399	2		463	2
400	2		464	2
401	2		465	2
402	2		466	2
403	2		467	2
404	2	62) which may or may not be true under the circumstances but	468	2
			469	2	72) it's worked for 30 years
			470	2	73) it's worked beautifully
405	2		471	2
406	2		472	2
407	2		473	2
	PAUSE 1		474	3	74) so if their other products are as good as that
409	2	63) it does have warm		
410	2		475	3
411	2	64) now let's see about	476	4
412	2		477	5	75) well there again I might be prejudiced because of good experience with a Sunbeam
413	2			
414	2			
415	2			
416	2			
417	2		PAUSE 1	
418	2	65) this is just on and on I guess	479	2
			480	2
419	2		481	2
420	2		482	2
421	2		483	1
	PAUSE 2	66) this one has a different switch to brew than warm, looks like	484	1	76) $26, that one's $28
			485	1
			486	2
424	5		487	2
425	5		488	2
426	5		489	2
427	5		490	2	77) I wish I had a little more information on both of them
428	5			
429	5			
430	5		491	2
431	5		492	2
432	5		PAUSE 4		78) but since I don't
433	5		497	5
434	5		498	5
435	2		499	2
436	2		500	5
437	2	67) no it doesn't have a different switch	501	2	79) say that probably today I would buy the Sunbeam
			502	2
438	2		503	2
439	2	68) it just has a different light	504	2
440	2		505	2
441	2		506	2
442	2	69) that one comes on when it's done probably		

FIGURE 2

	Cols. 23456				Cols. 23456		
11	4	1)	the first thing that would come into my mind	62	3		
12	3			63	4	21)	so I'll just go with the best I can find
13	4	2)	if I were buying a coffee maker	SCAN 4		22)	also this is kind of funny
	SCAN 1	3)	is that I already have a Mr. Coffee	PAUSE 2		23)	the higher prices seem to me to be good
	PAUSE 3	4)	and I consider that the brand name in coffee makers	70	3		
				71	3		
				72	3		
18	3			73	3	24)	and the fact that you think well
19	3			74	3		
20	3	5)	the problem is that the heating element seems to go bad on the	75	3	25)	I'm paying for more quality
21	3				SCAN 1		
22	2			77	1	26)	so sometimes I tend to rule out the lowest priced thing
23	3						
	PAUSE 1			78	1		
25	3			79	3		
26	3	6)	I've talked to friends		SCAN 1	27)	I think, well, that couldn't be as good as the highest priced
	PAUSE 1	6)	whose element has gone out totally				
28	3			81	6		
29	3			82	6		
30	3	8)	mine doesn't keep my coffee very hot anymore	83	3		
				84	1	28)	but now that I've had a Mr. Coffee
31	3						
32	3	9)	so I've gone back to using instant coffee	85	1	29)	I think I would start down here with Proctor-Silex
				86	1		
33	3						
	PAUSE 1						
35	4	10)	this doesn't look like Mr. Coffee though:	87	1		
					PAUSE 1		
36	4			89	1		
37	3	11)	so probably if I were going to start all over	90	1		
				91	1	30)	and readily consider them all
38	3						
39	3			92	1		
40	3	12)	I would look at another Mr. Coffee:	93	1		
				94	1		
41	3	13)	and I would ask a salesperson	95	1		
				96	1		
42	3			97	1		
43	SCAN 1	14)	if they had improved the heating element	98	1		
				99	1		
44	3			100	1		
45	3	15)	and if they don't have problems with them any more	101	2		
				102	3		
				103	3	31)	Okay, because I have a basis of comparison
46	3						
47	3			104	3		
48	3			105	3	32)	I'll probably keep going back to Mr. Coffee
49	3	16)	mine was an older model				
50	3			106	3		
51	3			107	3		
52	3			108	3		
53	3	17)	so that wouldn't keep me from considering it	109	3	33)	it looks to me like they've improved
54	3			110	3		
55	3			111	3		
56	3			112	3	34)	their pot looks different
57	4	18)	but I think I wouldn't be so prejudiced	SCAN 1		35)	another problem we've had
				114	3		
58	3						
59	3			115	3	36)	is that you always spill your coffee as you pour it
	SCAN 1	19)	as I was the first time around				
				116	3		
61	3	20)	I thought well Mr. Coffee invented these machines	117	3	37)	maybe its the lip design that causes that

FIGURE 2 (continued)

	Cols. 23456				Cols. 23456			
118	3			390	1		103)	something else that happened to my Mr. Coffee pot is
119	3							
120	3		38) but it is very embarrassing for guests	391	1			
121	3			392	1		104)	that the handle got loose and you have to get out a knife
122	1		39) because they always wind up drinking their coffee over the counter					
123	1			393	1			
124	1			394	3			
125	1			395	3			
126	1			396	3		105)	because I didn't have a screwdriver to tighten it up
127	1							
128	1		40) this pot looks very different and it feels very heavy	397	3			
				398	3			
129	1			399	3			
130	1			400	3			
131	1		41) so I would probably be impressed with the Proctor-Silex	401	3			
				402	3			
				403	3			
132	1			404	1			
133	1			405	1			
134	1			406	1			
135	1			407	1			
136	1				SCAN 4			
137	1			412	1		106)	(Mod.-what are you thinking?)
138	1							
139	1			413	3			
140	1			414	3			
141	1			415	1		107)	well, I'm thinking that everything is so relative
142	1							
143	1				SCAN 1			
144	1			417	4		108)	that there is no perfect truth
145	1		42) the whole machine on the Mr. Coffee always felt a bit flimsy		PAUSE 3			
				421	6		109)	and even though I didn't like the GE
146	1			422	6			
147	1			423	5			
148	1		43) evidently it doesn't take a lot of mechanism in it	424	5		110)	I would probably consider that
					PAUSE 3		111)	I thought it was gimmicky
149	3							
150	3			428	6		112)	that it had extra painted things on it
151	3							
152	3			429	6			
153	3		44) the Proctor-Silex doesn't wiggle on its base like my old Mr. Coffee	430	6		113)	that it didn't need
154	3			431	6		114)	but it has an overall good look
155	3			432	6		115)	it looks neater than the others
156	3							
157	3			433	6			
158	3			434	6			
(BREAK)				435	3			
377	6		98) okay, after looking at all three	436	6			
				437	1		116)	okay, I'm thinking if I were going to buy one right now
378	6							
	SCAN 1			438	1			
380	6		99) I think I would go back to the first two	439	1			
381	6			440	1		117)	having the experience I had with Mr. Coffee
382	6							
383	2			441	1			
384	1		100) I don't know	442	3			
385	1		101) I like the heavy feel of the pot	443	3		118)	and knowing it wasn't the great thing I thought it was going to do
386	1							
387	1		102) on the Proctor-Silex					
388	1							
389	1			444	3			

FIGURE 2 (continued)

Cols. 23456			Cols. 23456		
445	3		451	3	
446	1			SCAN 1	
447	3		453	1	119) I'd probably spend the least and buy the Proctor-Silex
	PAUSE 2				
450	3				

decision making they might yield. He also wondered in what way this new JPT method might represent an improvement over singular methods of studying consumer decision making.

Questions

1 What insights about consumer decision making can be gained from this investigation into how consumers behave?

2 Does there seem to be any evidence to indicate that the joint process method produces more insights into consumer information-processing than either method taken alone?

3 If the experimental findings were generally representative of consumers' reactions to coffee makers, would there be any marketing implications for producers of the product?

CASE 4-5
PURITEEN COSMETICS, INC.[1]

Puriteen, a cosmetics company based in Atlanta, recently acquired a faltering perfume and cologne company located in Orangedale, Florida (a suburb of Jacksonville). The small producer, Henri's, was started by Henri and Marie Depuy in 1972, but local and area business was not enough to keep alive the dreams of the married couple to develop their own perfume and cologne business.

BACKGROUND ON HENRI'S

Henri and Marie came to the United States in 1965 from Grasse, France, the world's chief center of perfume manufacture. Having become naturalized U.S. citizens, the well-educated Depuys decided to sink their life savings, if necessary, into their new business venture. Both had worked in a Grasse perfume company and had gained the necessary technology and skills to manufacture perfume.

The Depuys began in their garage producing two fragrances, "Henri's" and "Marie," named after themselves. Henri's was a special formulation handed down from generation to generation through the Depuy family in France. (Such practices are quite common among the French.)

However, after struggling for four years producing and selling the two fragrances, the Depuys realized the coming demise of their business and decided to seek a buyer for their family-heirloom formula.

Raymond L. "Pete" Dozier, vice president of marketing at Puriteen, learned of the Depuys' situation through a friend, Mitchell R. Morris, while in Jacksonville on a business trip. Morris, a district sales manager for Puriteen, had bought a bottle of Henri's for his wife Jil and was recently made aware of the Depuys' situation. Jil and Mitch were impressed with the fragrance of Henri's and were saddened that the Depuys were planning to sell their business.

Speaking with Dozier, Morris learned of Puriteen's interest to expand into the perfume and cologne business to complement its cosmetic lines. During the conversation, Morris told Dozier of the Depuys' business and strongly urged Dozier to discuss a business deal with Henri.

After six weeks of negotiations with the Depuys, the Puriteen Company agreed to pay Henri and Marie a 10 percent royalty on the net sales of the two perfumes and to hire the Depuys to supervise the manufacture of the perfumes. The success of the negotiations for the Depuys was largely due to Marie's idea of sending a bottle of each fragrance to the wives of Puriteen's top management.

BACKGROUND ON PURITEEN

Puriteen was founded in 1946 by William D. "Son" Grimsley and Raymond L. "Pete" Dozier. Son and Pete met in the Navy during World War II and found that they had a mutual interest in developing a business at the war's end. Son, who had earned a B.S. degree in chem-

---

[1]This case was written by M. Wayne De Lozier. Permission to reprint granted by the author.

PART FOUR

istry at Georgia Tech, took his first job in a cosmetics firm before the war. During his three years with the cosmetics company, Son advanced to assistant director of research before volunteering for military service.

Pete received a degree in economics at a well known northeastern university and after graduation spent four years in the sales division of a regional pharmaceutical company.

Before the war's end, Son had received legal notice that his Aunt Jeanette had died and left him $26,000 in cash, seventy-five acres of land near Covington, Georgia, and forty hogs, ten horses, and twenty-five milk-producing cows. His inheritance provided the major portion of capital for starting up a business, and in 1946 Son and Pete created Puriteen.

Son took on the responsibilities of production and development of several cosmetic lines, while Pete handled sales and finance.

By year-end 1975, Puriteen had become a leader in cosmetics in the Southeast with $125 million in sales. Distribution of Puriteen products stretched from Virginia south to Florida and west to the Mississippi River.

THE NEW PRODUCT

In mid-1975, Puriteen's top management had decided to expand their lines by entering the perfume and cologne market. Long-range plans were to enter the shaving cream and deodorant markets as well. Dozier had defined their business as a personal care business and believed that these and other products were essential to long-term growth.

In February 1976, Puriteen acquired Henri's, and Dozier began to consider plans for marketing the two newly acquired perfumes.

Henri's and Marie perfumes were fresh, new fragrances to the market, Both rated very high in consumer smell preference tests and certainly had tremendous potential. However, Dozier knew from his experiences and those of other companies that the success of such products depended upon the creation of an appealing image for the brand.

The Generic Product

Perfume is a fragrant substance which has been used since prehistoric times. The essence of many fragrances comes from the oils in the petals of fresh flowers, such as the rose, carnation, and orange blossom. However, fragrances are not limited to the petal, but can come from the leaves of lavendar, peppermint, and geranium. Also, the oils of cinnamon and balsam are derived from bark, while the oils of cedar come from its wood. The fragrance of ginger and sassafras comes from roots, whereas that of orange, lemon, and nutmeg comes from fruits and seeds. Thus, there are many sources from which to derive fragrances for perfume.

Certain materials must be added to the perfume fragrances to prevent evaporation by a process called *fixation*. Ambergris, musk, and castor are fixatives which are often used in the production of perfumes.

Artificial perfumes have been created at a lower cost through the use of synthetics and semisynthetics. They generally are classified under the categories of aldehydes, esters, and ethers, and are rapidly growing in use.

Henri's and Marie are produced with natural ingredients and are therefore more expensive to produce and higher priced than many of the more popular brands of perfume on the U.S. market.

ENTERING THE PERFUME MARKET

Pete Dozier had recently taken several evening courses in marketing at Georgia State in Atlanta to keep track of the current developments in marketing. One of the courses he took was Consumer Behavior. He became very interested in the notion of developing brands which were based upon consumer self concepts.

In March of 1976, Dozier decided to use his understanding of self theory to develop a marketing program for Henri's. By June, he had developed a semantic differential to measure the self and ideal-self images of female consumers and the images they held for three unfamiliar perfume brands (the brand names were fictitious).

The tests were conducted in New Orleans, Tallahassee, Atlanta, Raleigh, and Memphis. Four hundred ninety-six personal interviews were conducted (approximately 100 interviews per city). Subjects were given a semantic differential scale on which to describe their self and ideal-self concepts, and their perceptions of each of three perfume advertisements presented them. Each perfume advertisement was a videotaped version of a proposed Henri's advertisement. However, fictional names were used in each case. The order of presentations of the ads and self concepts were randomized. Subjects were asked at the end of the session to select which of the brands they preferred. They were offered the brand they selected as a prize if their numbers were selected at a later drawing.

The advertised "brands" were given three different themes. One used a sensual theme, the second a romantic theme, and the third a prestigious, regal theme. The following is a partial reproduction of each theme:

Nakū. "Nakū—the naked scent. Unadorned, primitive, sensuous Nakū. Nakū is for the woman who has a mind of her own; for the woman who goes her own free and feminine way. It's for the woman who understands that perfume is feminine power! Nakū—the naked scent. It is the essential you!" (Sensual theme)

Rumāns. "Fragrance admittedly triggers emotions, but science doesn't know why. The whole wide world of scents is full of mysteries. However, Rumāns has captured the one scent that can make your world come alive with excitement and romance.

"Rumāns is a word of endearment, full of affection. Like dew sparkling, brooks babbling, stars smiling, lovers meeting, Rumāns goes about its business of making its wearer feel spirited, airy, romantic.

"Wear Rumāns day and night. Because love comes without warning!" (Romantic theme)

El Primo. "Once she was the *only* woman in the world allowed to wear this perfume. The Queen of

TABLE 1
PERFUME IMAGES

1 Appealing, sexy	Modest, reserved
2 Individualistic, nonconforming	Conservative, traditional
3 Fashionable, vogue	An ordinary, everyday type
4 Natural, unadorned	Ornate, sophisticated
5 Aristocratic, refined, dignified	Plain, ordinary
6 One of the most popular	Socially acceptable
7 Youthful, exciting, vibrant	Content, somewhat inhibited
8 Adventurous	Not adventurous
9 Delicate, sensitive	Somewhat harsh and insensitive
10 Innocent	Flirty
11 Free-spirited	Practical
12 Given to prestige, status	Not given to prestige, status
13 Bold, daring	Shy, restrained
14 Economical, thrifty	Luxurious
15 Choosy, particular	Not too choosy, particular

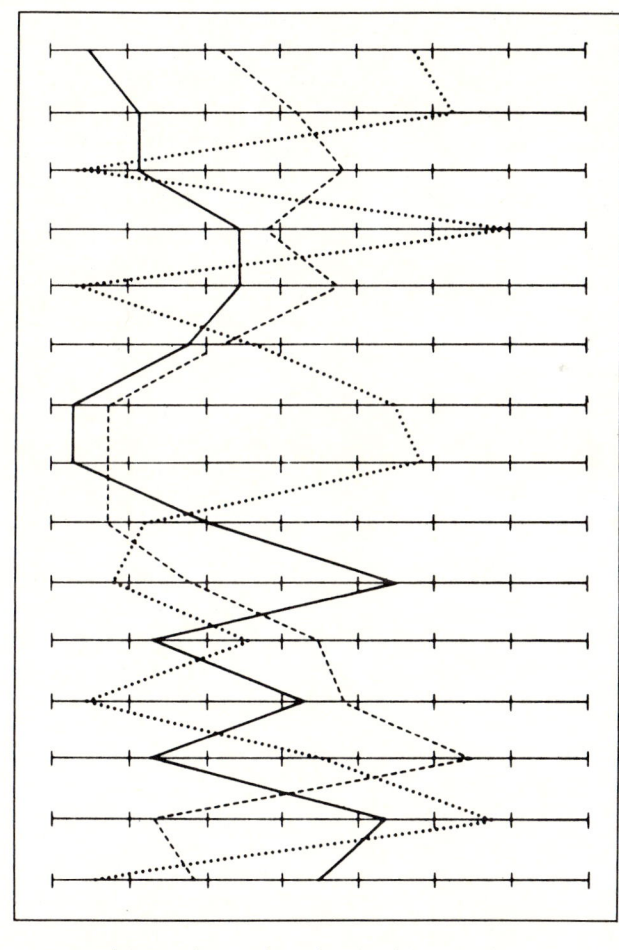

———Subjects who preferred Nakū ($n_1 = 148$)
-----Subjects who preferred Rumāns ($n_2 = 188$)
........Subjects who preferred El Primo ($n_3 = 160$)

TABLE 2
SELF CONCEPTS

1. Appealing, sexy — Modest, reserved
2. Individualistic, nonconforming — Conservative, traditional
3. Fashionable, vogue — An ordinary, everyday type
4. Natural, unadorned — Ornate, sophisticated
5. Aristocratic, refined, dignified — Plain, ordinary
6. One of the most popular — Socially acceptable
7. Youthful, exciting, vibrant — Content, somewhat inhibited
8. Adventurous — Not adventurous
9. Delicate, sensitive — Somewhat harsh and insensitive
10. Innocent — Flirty
11. Free-spirited — Practical
12. Given to prestige, status — Not given to prestige, status
13. Bold, daring — Shy, restrained
14. Economical, thrifty — Luxurious
15. Choosy, particular — Not too choosy, particular

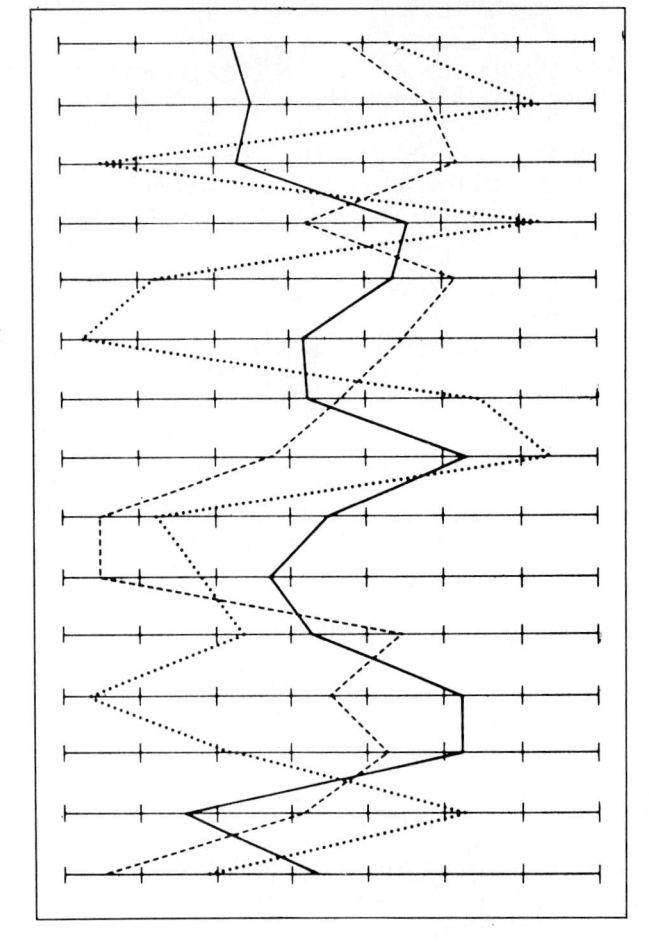

——— Self concepts of those who prefer Nakū (n = 148)
----- Self concepts of those who prefer Rumäns (n = 188)
.... Self concepts of those who prefer El Primo (n = 160)

Navarre commissioned the most famed alchemist in Paris to create a perfume of magical potency and bewitching powers. A perfume so irresistable, it disarmed her competitors. A perfume so feminine, it intensified her legendary appeal, drawing the great and the glorious to her court. This magical perfume was Ei Primo. Unchanged since 1572, it casts its spell for great women today. El Primo, the perfume made for a queen!" (Prestigious, regal theme)

Each script was provided with an appropriate model and picture sequence to match the theme.

The results of the test are presented in Tables 1 through 4.

DEVELOPING THE MARKETING PROGRAM

Dozier feels sure that the quality of the two perfumes is the best on the market. But he also knows that product quality alone does not sell a product. It requires a sound communications program. He feels that matching brand image to consumer self image is a sound approach. He must recommend a plan to the Puriteen board next week.

TABLE 3

IDEAL-SELF CONCEPTS

1. Appealing, sexy		Modest, reserved
2. Individualistic, nonconforming		Conservative, traditional
3. Fashionable, vogue		An ordinary, everyday type
4. Natural, unadorned		Ornate, sophisticated
5. Aristocratic, refined, dignified		Plain, ordinary
6. One of the most popular		Socially acceptable
7. Youthful, exciting, vibrant		Content, somewhat inhibited
8. Adventurous		Not adventurous
9. Delicate, sensitive		Somewhat harsh and insensitive
10. Innocent		Flirty
11. Free-spirited		Practical
12. Given to prestige, status		Not given to prestige, status
13. Bold, daring		Shy, restrained
14. Economical, thrifty		Luxurious
15. Choosy, particular		Not too choosy, particular

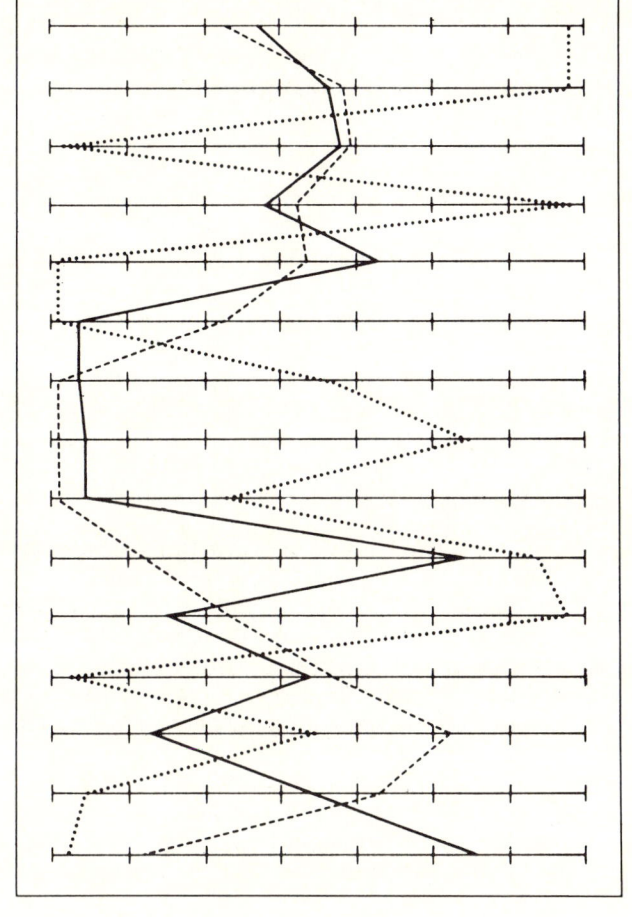

——— Subjects who preferred Nakū ($n_1 = 148$)
----- Subjects who preferred Rumäns ($n_2 = 188$)
.... Subjects who preferred El Primo ($n_3 = 160$)

Questions

1 A portion of self theory holds that individuals try to protect or enhance their self concept, that is, they make decisions which are most consistent with their self or ideal-self images. Given this theory, what marketing plan should Dozier recommend to the Board of Directors of Puriteen?

2 What analyses might you perform on the data?

3 What additional information would you want in developing a program for Puriteen?

4 Evaluate the dimensions used in Dozier's semantic differential. How would you improve it?

5 Which self concept is most useful—self or ideal-self concept—in developing marketing programs? Defend your answer.

6 How does the use of consumer self concept differ from the use of consumer personality traits as a basis for developing brand images? Explain.

TABLE 4

AGES AND FAMILY INCOMES OF SUBJECTS PREFERRING EACH BRAND

Family Income	Nakū				Rumāns				El Primo				Totals
	Age Categories				Age Categories				Age Categories				
	18–25	26–35	36–49	50 and over	18–25	26–35	36–49	50 and over	18–25	26–35	36–49	50 and over	
$6,000–9,999	2	22	2	—	18	12	1	—	3	—	—	1	61
$10,000–14,999	5	30	15	—	33	8	15	1	2	6	2	4	121
$15,000–19,999	3	15	17	4	29	14	14	3	18	6	14	22	159
$20,000 and over	1	27	2	3	15	6	13	6	19	8	19	36	155
Totals	11	94	36	7	95	40	43	10	42	20	35	63	
Grand total		148				188				160			496

CASE 4-6
CERTAIN[1]

Marketing consultants say it rubs Americans the wrong way. However, domestic and European companies are preparing to attack the U.S. market in an attempt to sell "wet toilet paper." Actually, for Procter & Gamble this will be the second attempt. It was unsuccessful in its first test market for Certain moistened bathroom tissue.

One market researcher who worked on the P&G test said, "Price is a limiting factor because it's just not competitive with toilet paper." He also said the product would have more appeal in countries with "less comfortable" toilet paper than the U.S. "The P&G test failed because people said the tissue didn't feel good, and it clogged up the toilet."

With the reincarnation of Certain moistened bathroom tissue, Procter & Gamble Co. is reaching for a broader following than it attracted when the product was tested in its previous form. In contrast to the previous formulation, the Certain now being sold is less greasy and priced at parity with other quality bathroom tissues.

Reformulated "to improve the tactile feel," Certain still is coated with oil-based emollients that are absorbent and will not evaporate. However, it now is said to "feel almost like a tissue with talcum powder." While in its original form it was so heavily covered with lotion some consumers complained it crumbled.

"They have to balance out its efficacy with its gooeyness" observed Leo J. Shapiro, chairman of Leo J. Shapiro & Associates research company. "They made it a little less efficacious but appealing to a broader group of people."

Mr. Shapiro, whose company conducted a consumer survey on Certain in Indiana several years ago, said, "There was a small group of people who really loved it and a large group of people who hated it." Apparently undeterred by "the large group who hated it," P&G is out to win them over. The marketer's research shows there is a significant consumer desire for bathroom tissue that cleanses comfortably, and the Cincinnati company is apparently determined to fill that need.

The problem everywhere is marketing the product. What exactly are anal tissues? Although they are shaped and packaged like common facial tissues or airline refreshment towels, they are soaked with a cleanser and emollients—no perfumes, no alcohol. In P&G's case, Certain came on an actual toilet paper roll, and was marketed as more economical than ordinary dry toilet paper. Ad copy emphasizes "the light touch of lotion in every sheet," positioning Certain as "The first bathroom tissue that goes beyond softness to comfort."

---

[1]This case is based on Jennifer Alter, "P & G Not Giving Up on Moistened Tissue," *Advertising Age*, October 5, 1981, P. 40, and Elizabeth Guider, "Wet Anal Tissues A Tough Sell," *Advertising Age*, February 16, 1981, p. 78. Adapted with permission from the October and February, 1981 issues of *Advertising Age*. Copyright 1981 by Crain Communications, Inc.

While one-ply Certain is priced per roll at the same level as P&G's White Cloud and Charmin, the Certain rolls contain approximately 200 sheets, compared to 300 and 400 for the other brands. However, P&G says, Certain's consistency enables the consumer to use fewer sheets. Additionally, it contends, larger rolls would become unwieldy on standard dispensers.

When Certain entered its first test market it was priced approximately 15 percent above other brands. One month into the test, when Mr. Shapiro conducted his research, 13 percent of those questioned mentioned Certain's high price as a negative. By the time Certain was withdrawn from those markets, P&G says, it was at parity with other brands.

Procter & Gamble is not the only company eyeing the market. Cederoth A. B. of Sweden, which is now selling chemically-treated toilet tissues in 49 countries, plans to introduce the product in the United States and Canada. Despite the obvious difficulties of advertising products to the anal hygiene market, sales are growing at a 25 percent clip worldwide, the company says. In addition, American Can has tested Fresh'n as "cleansing bathroom tissue," and Lehn & Fink has promoted Wet Ones treated tissues to adults. This latter product, however, is a different form from P&G's Certain. Wet Ones Towelettes are packaged in a cylindrical dispenser for home use. A slim rectangular Porta-Pack is also available for use away from home. Advertisements position Wet Ones as a supplement to toilet paper, rather than as a substitute for it. Promotions suggest use of the product after using "bathroom tissue" as a final step in personal cleanliness. It is also suggested that they are ideal for feminine hygiene and for young children who "might not be as careful as they should."

Wet tissues for anal use are highly successful in Europe. In fact, Mr. Shapiro claims "We are the only major western civilization that uses only dry tissues."

Questions

1 Can you suggest reasons or sources for U.S. consumers' apparent resistance to wet anal tissues?

2 How strongly held do you think any negative attitudes are? Why?

3 Can you suggest any positioning or advertising strategies to producers of the product?

4 Is there any additional information about consumers you would like to have before developing marketing strategy for the product?

CASE 4-7
EASTERN STATE UNIVERSITY[1]

Shana Birk, chief admissions officer of Eastern State University, a school with current enrollment of 10,000 full-time students, was reviewing a research report on the college choice process. Her level of interest was particularly high because recent trends suggested rather significant declines in the number of college-age students.

Shana had been the prime mover behind this study because, in her opinion, maintaining enrollment at ESU through the 1980s and 1990s was going to be somewhat of a challenge. She convinced the university's president to fund the study and had approached two professors in the marketing department to serve as principal investigators. These professors suggested that the college choice process is most likely based on fairly careful consideration of how well various educational alternatives match certain choice criteria of prospective students.

The first step was a review of existing literature to determine what could be learned from previous research into the college choice process. Results of this stage were informative but Shana found them limited in at least two respects. First, most previous studies had only surveyed recently enrolled or recently admitted students. Therefore, they did not sample students in the process of making a choice regarding college attendance, or those who had gone to other institutions. Second, research to date had been mainly associational rather than predictive in nature. That is, the studies had focused on discovering what demographic variables and other student characteristics are related to college enrollment, rather than targeting on what variables might *predict* the enrollment choices of prospective students. Shana felt that predictive studies were needed so that groups of students representing the best prospects for ESU could be targeted, contacted, and supplied with appropriate information about the university.

After a discussion of these thoughts, the principal investigators suggested that the Fishbein A-act multiat-

---

[1]This case is based on material appearing in Robert E. Spekman, James W. Harvey, and Paul N. Bloom, "The College Choice Process: Some Empirical Results," in Jerry C. Olson (ed.) *Advances in Consumer Research: Volume 7,* Ann Arbor, MI: Association for Consumer Research, 1980, pp. 700–704. Adapted with permission of the Association for Consumer Research.

tribute attitude model might represent a useful conceptual approach to explaining how prospective students proceed in the decision process regarding college enrollment. Further work led to a study involving 2000 randomly selected junior and senior high school students in the state. In-state students were focused on because they represent the most important pool of potential enrollees.

STUDY DESIGN

The basic approach was to define components of the A-act model, measure respondents on these components, independently measure their overall attitude toward enrollment, and then determine how well the component measures were able to predict the independently measured attitude toward enrollment. However, discussions led to two modifications which made this basic approach even more interesting to Shana. Located in the state was a nationally recognized private university and a state-supported 4-year college. These institutions also competed with ESU for in-state students. Therefore, it was decided that all three institutions should be addressed in the attitude study. In this way, it might be possible to determine whether some attitude components vary in their influence on enrollment attitudes for the different in-state institutions. Second, the research team (Shana and the two principal investigators) reasoned that by including measures of certain respondent characteristics, they might be able to identify different subgroups or segments of the applicant pool. That is, certain attitude components might vary in their influence across these potentially different segments.

As a result, the study design involved collection of a number of pieces of information. First, the dependent variable was defined as attitude toward the act of enrolling at each of the three institutions. This was measured independently on a seven-point scale ranging from "very favorable" to "very unfavorable."

Next, exploratory research with prospective students and previous research suggested seventeen school attributes which might be potentially relevant to attitudes toward enrolling at the institutions. These attributes are shown in the left column of Table 1. As can be seen in the table, the first thirteen belief statements refer to attributes of the college or university in question, while the last four were identified as potentially relevant normative beliefs. Each survey participant was asked to respond to all seventeen beliefs for each of

TABLE 1
ATTRIBUTE DESCRIPTIONS AND FACTOR ANALYSIS RESULTS

Attribute Descriptions	College Environment	Authority Recommendations	Size	Cost	Social Aspects	Friends
1. Quality academics	.71	.13	.08	−.09	.05	.06
2. National reputation	.68	.07	.06	.06	−.05	.01
3. Friendly people	.60	.05	−.02	.04	.29	.22
4. Opportunities for part-time work	.58	.15	.00	.11	.05	−.30
5. Fair treatment of minorities	.57	.14	−.10	−.02	.27	.17
6. Athletic team I could play for	.39	.09	.27	−.06	.13	−.04
7. Recommendations of teachers	.17	.85	−.04	−.03	−.08	.06
8. Recommendations of counselors	.16	.83	.04	−.02	−.00	−.06
9. Recommendations of parents	.29	.56	.33	.11	.04	.12
10. Large classes	−.01	.07	.86	−.01	−.05	−.00
11. Many students	.08	.00	.80	.05	.19	.04
12. Near home	.04	.07	.16	.78	−.12	.01
13. Low cost of education	−.04	−.07	−.13	.74	.15	.05
14. Many parties	.16	−.07	.16	−.10	.70	.01
15. Location near city	.24	.02	.00	.29	.56	.01
16. Old friends from home	.32	−.02	.10	12	−.23	.72
17. Recommendations from friends	−.28	.43	−.08	−.04	.31	.57

the three institutions being studied. Responses were made on seven-point scales (ranging from "very likely to have" to "very unlikely to have") indicating how certain the individual was that the school in question possessed each of the seventeen attributes.

For measurement of the affect component (e_i) relevant to these attributes, respondents were asked to express their feelings along a seven-point scale as to how desirable ("very good" to "very bad") it would be for them if the school they enrolled in had each of the seventeen attributes described in Table 1.

Demographic information collected from respondents included academic potential as measured by current grades and SAT scores, race, geographical location in the state, and current class (junior or senior in high school). In addition, attention focused on how serious each respondent appeared to be regarding the college choice decision. The research team concluded that this level of seriousness resembled the concept of involvement because more-involved prospects were more likely to engage in a more intensive search process. This involvement was quantified by combining, with equal weights, respondents' answers regarding the number of schools applied to, the number of schools visited, the length of the decision process, the degree of care being taken in the decision, how important the respondent felt the decision was, and how certain the respondent was of his or her intended area of study.

The survey generated 583 usable responses, which represented a 29 percent response rate. The split between juniors and seniors was about even. In addition, the racial composition and reported SAT scores closely matched data available from census and educational testing service reports. Other information suggested that although response rates were rather low, no significant bias had been introduced into the study because of the low rate of returns.

ANALYSIS AND RESULTS

The first major data analysis step was to determine the product of belief and evaluation scores ($B_i e_i$). The second step was to use these data to determine whether all seventeen items in Table 1 were independent and important determinants of attitudes toward the enrollment decision, or whether some were highly related and could be combined to define a new, smaller set of composite variables. This was accomplished through use of a technique called factor analysis which is helpful in identifying how a set of measures may group together to form more aggregate variables which are termed factors. Table 1 presents results of this analysis step.

The research team concluded that factor analysis had identified six composite variables or factors. These were identified and named by the researchers (see column headings in Table 1) after consideration of the manner in which the initial measures grouped together to form the composite variables. The degree of correlation between composite variables and the initial measures are shown in each column of Table 1. Also, the underscored correlations in any one column indicate which initial measures were combined to form the composite variables. Thus, we see that $B_i e_i$ scores for the first six attribute items listed in the table all combined to identify the new composite variable (factor) which was named "college environment." Components of the other five factors are also denoted with underscores in the table. As in the case of the first factor, study of the initial measures that were most related to the remaining five composite variables guided the research team in naming those composite variables.

Given that attitudes toward enrollment at three different institutions were being studied, it is reasonable to expect that the composite variables identified for one school might not be the same as those identified for another school. However, this was not the case. The same set of composite variables were identified in the same way for all three institutions. Therefore, Table 1 can be used to characterize results for each school.

Next, the research team explored how important each of the six factors were in predicting attitudes toward enrollment at the three schools. This was accomplished using regression analysis where the six factors were used as predictor variables and the independently measured attitude toward enrollment was used as the dependent variable. Table 2 presents results of this analysis by showing the relative importance-ranking of each predictor variable. Thus, for ESU size was the most important predictor, followed by authority recommendations and cost respectively. However, for the private university the top three predictors were authority recommendations, social, and cost, respectively. A different pattern emerged for the state college. But for each of the three institutions the total predictive ability of the six factors was quite high.

Study of the regression results revealed another interesting finding. For both the state university and the state college, one factor (size and environment, respectively) appeared to play a very important role in predicting attitudes toward enrollment. In fact, these factors (denoted with asterisks in Table 2) clearly dominated all other factors in influencing attitudes

TABLE 2

RELATIVE IMPORTANCE OF SIX COMPOSITE VARIABLES IN INFLUENCING ATTITUDES TOWARD ENROLLMENT

	Environment	Authority Recommendations	Size	Cost	Social	Friends
State university	4	2	1*	3	6	5
Private university	4	1	6	3	2	5
State college	1*	3	6	2	5	4

*Importance rating was considerably higher than other attributes

toward enrolling at the state schools. However, for the private university each factor had about equal predictive ability. These results suggest that a noncompensatory model may be most appropriate for describing the attitude formation process for the state schools, but a compensatory model might be best for the private university.

The last analysis step was to examine results across groups of respondents to determine whether distinct segments of prospective students appeared to exist. Table 3 summarizes the most significant results for the indicated groups. The second column of the table reveals those variables that were most influential in determining attitudes toward enrollment. The word "various" indicates that different attributes dominated, depending on the type of institution. The third column suggests the most likely type of attitude formation process. That is, it indicates (1) whether a given factor dominated prediction of attitudes toward enrollment (indicating a noncompensatory model), (2) whether no variable tended to dominate (indicating a compensatory model), or (3) whether a variable dominated for the state schools but did not dominate for the private university (indicating that the type of model depends on the type of institution being studied). As can be seen from columns 2 and 3, enrollment attitudes of blacks, high-involvement groups, and juniors all seemed to be most influenced by the authority recommendation factor. However, for blacks and high-involvement groups, this factor dominated all enrollment decisions investi-

TABLE 3

SUMMARY OF GROUP DIFFERENCES

Groups	Attributes Most Determinant of A-Act	Most Likely Attitude
Race		
Black	Authority recommendations	Noncompensatory
White	Various	Depends on type of institution
Involvement		
Low	Cost	Compensatory
High	Authority recommendations	Noncompensatory
Grade Point		
Low	Little difference	Depends on type of institution
High	Little difference	Depends on type of institution
Year		
Juniors	Authority recommendations	Depends on type of institution
Seniors	Various	Depends on type of institution

gated, while it only influenced attitudes on the public institutions among juniors. White students and seniors did not appear to be consistently influenced by any one variable, and students with high or low grade-point averages acted in similar ways. In addition, enrollment attitudes of low-involvement prospects were most influenced by the cost factor, but this was not a dominant variable for either the private or public institutions.

Shana was attempting to wade through these results in order to determine what would be an appropriate plan of action. She believed that the results were quite relevant to attracting in-state students to ESU university, but as yet she had not studied them enough to assess their implications.

Questions

1 Summarize the findings of the research conducted for ESU University.

2 Are there any suggestions you might make for improving the study or conducting additional research.

3 If the validity of these research findings were established, what implications might they hold for recruitment of in-state students to ESU University?

External environment

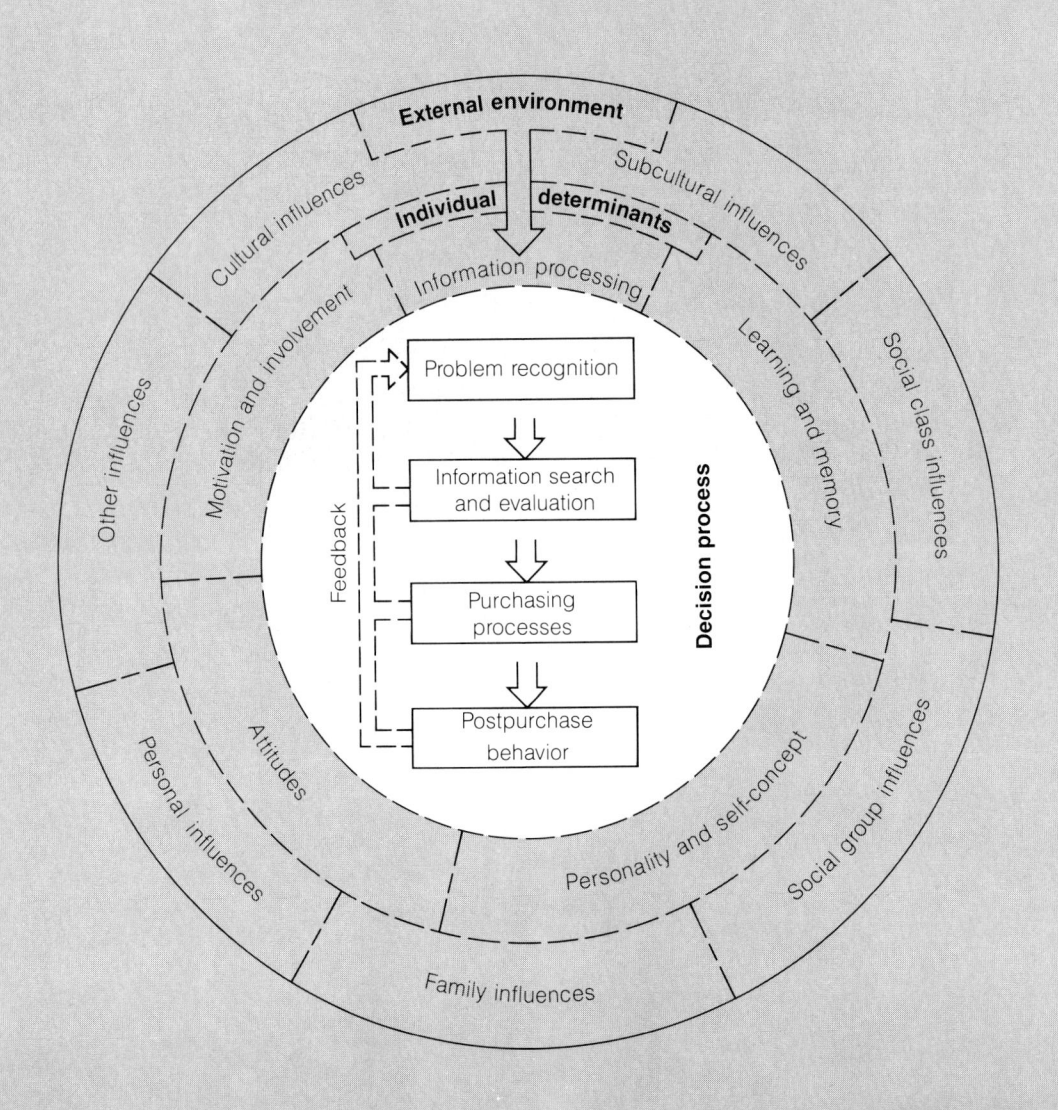

- Cultural influences
- Subcultural influences
- Social class influences
- Social group influences
- Family influences
- Personal influences
- Other influences

Individual determinants

- Information processing
- Learning and memory
- Personality and self-concept
- Attitudes
- Motivation and involvement

Decision process

- Problem recognition
- Information search and evaluation
- Purchasing processes
- Postpurchase behavior

Feedback

PART FIVE
CONSUMER DECISION PROCESSES

18 Problem Recognition
19 Search and Evaluation
20 Purchasing Processes
21 Postpurchase Behavior
   Cases for Part Five

CHAPTER 18
PROBLEM RECOGNITION

In this chapter, we shall examine the types of consumer decisions which are possible and shall see that these may range from very simple to quite complicated processes. Next, the basic model of steps involved in consumer decision making will be highlighted to set the stage for the remainder of this section. The bulk of this chapter will then discuss the nature of problem recognition, its determinants, and implications of this particular consumer decision stage to marketers.

TYPES OF CONSUMER DECISIONS

There are a myriad of decision options possible for the consumer in today's market economy. These options, however, may be distilled into five main types of decisions: (1) what to buy, (2) how much to buy, (3) where to buy, (4) when to buy, and (5) how to buy.

Deciding *what* to buy is one of the consumer's most basic tasks. No buying activity may take place unless this fundamental decision is made. A consumer's product or service decision may encompass not only the generic category of products desired, such as appliances, but more specifically, the narrower range of items, such as kitchen appliances. Consumers must even make decisions on brands, prices, and product features. For example, a homemaker may decide to purchase an Amana Radarange 700-watt microwave oven, Model RR-1000, with electronic digital controls and stainless steel interior, for a price of $599. This is a specific decision as to what will be purchased, and with this particular decision finalized the consumer moves closer to completion of the overall purchase-decision process.

A second basic decision by the consumer relates to *how much* of the item will be purchased. For example, when shopping for groceries the consumer must determine whether three cans of Libby's green beans will be bought or perhaps a greater supply purchased.

Another determination to be reached by the consumer involves *where* the selected product or service will be purchased. This is a very important decision, which interacts thoroughly with the previous decision on what to buy. Two products, although physically the same, are likely to be perceived differently because of other facets associated with them. For example, consider an air conditioner sold with delivery, installation, and in-home servicing guaranteed by a full-service department store compared with the same model priced lower but sold on a no-frill basis in a discount house, with none of the above services. Consumers clearly are likely to perceive these same air conditioners in quite different ways, based on the nature of the prices and services attached.

Consequently, what one purchases is closely related to decisions of where one decides to purchase. Not all sales outlets are alike, and consumers have many options concerning location (such as downtown or suburban stores), services offered (discount or full-service), merchandise lines (full versus narrow), prices (high versus low), and so on. Consumers must decide not only on the general type of store to purchase from but also determine the particular outlet. In fact, buyers may decide not to even visit a store, but to purchase from a catalog instead.

The consumer must also determine *when* to buy. Such a decision is influenced by such factors as urgency of the need and availability of the chosen item. Other elements such as store opening times, periods of sales and clearances, availability of transportation, and freedom of family members to shop all have a bearing on when one purchases.

Finally, the decision of *how* to buy is another complex issue. Many factors influence how the consumer buys. To indicate merely a few of the elements involved, consider some of the alternative strategies consumers use: shop extensively or buy from the first outlet, pay cash or charge it, have it delivered or take it home.

Numerous purchasing patterns occur in the marketplace, with each consumer relying on whatever strategy seems to work well for himself. The problems that consumers must solve, however, could benefit from the cold logic of a computer rather than the "hit or miss" decision approach taken by some consumers. The next section outlines the general purchase-decision process often followed by consumers, particularly for major purchases.

INTRODUCTION TO THE CONSUMER DECISION-PROCESS MODEL

Consumer decision processes vary considerably in their complexity. Most of the decisions consumers are required to make are probably rather simple ones such as the purchase of staple foods (although a disadvantaged consumer might argue persuasively that merely buying food is difficult when one is functionally illiterate). However, consumers also must make decisions that are comparatively complicated, such as when buying durable goods. The range of difficulty of consumer decision processes extends even further to problem solving that may be characterized as being highly complex, such as might well typify the consumer's purchase of a very expensive item like a home.

The examples of consumer decision making cited above may be generalized toward a typical consumer problem-solving model consisting of four basic types of activities in the process of purchasing. The consumer's four steps are: (1) problem recognition, (2) information search and evaluation, (3) purchase decision, and (4) postpurchase behavior. The assumptions underlying this and other decision-process approaches to consumer behavior seem to be the following:[1]

1 Two or more alternatives exist, so that a choice must be made by the consumer.

2 Consumer evaluative criteria facilitate the forecasting of each alternative's consequences for the consumer's goals or objectives.

3   The consumer uses a decision rule or evaluative procedure to determine the chosen alternative.

4   Information obtained from external sources and/or memory is used in the application of the decision rule or evaluative procedure.

However, it has been suggested that for certain purchase situations some consumers do not engage in a prepurchase decision process. For example, they may not have stored information, it may not be retrieved or retrievable, and they may not search externally.[2] Thus, some purchases may occur as a result of approaches other than a decision process. They can occur out of necessity (such as allocation of income within certain categories of expenditures, e.g., food/beverage, housing, and medical care); they can be derived from certain culturally-mandated lifestyles (for example, the "standard package" of goods desired throughout American society, including transportation, personal care, and household appliances and furnishings items); they can be interlocked with other purchases (such as gasoline, repair services, and insurance being interlocked with the purchase of an automobile); they can reflect purchase preferences acquired in early childhood (such as with food preferences and store choices); they can result from conformity to group norms or imitation of others (such as adoption of smoking behavior among teens); they can result from recommendations by personal or nonpersonal sources (such as often occurs in the adoption process); they can be made on the basis of various surrogates (such as price, manufacturer's reputation, or packaging); they can even occur on a more superficial basis (such as selecting a brand on the basis of convenience of the shelf height).[3]

Additional information will be provided in later chapters to indicate that a significant proportion of purchases appear not to be preceded by a decision process of any extensiveness. Nevertheless, the decision sequence discussed in this section represents a useful framework for integrating much of the material from earlier chapters in a pragmatic way for the marketer. In the remainder of this chapter, the first stage in this problem-solving model will be further examined. The other processes will be discussed in detail in the following chapters.

PROBLEM RECOGNITION

Problem recognition results when a consumer recognizes a difference of sufficient magnitude between what is perceived as the desired state of affairs and the actual state of affairs sufficient to arouse and activate the decision process.[4]

This process integrates many of the concepts that have been discussed in previous chapters. For example, consumer information processing and the motivation process are highly relevant here. Consumers must become aware of the problem or need through processing of information arising internally or externally. They then become motivated. Thus, the process of problem recognition means that the consumer becomes aroused and activated to engage in some purposeful purchase-decision activity.

This motivation to resolve a particular problem, however, depends on two factors: the magnitude of the discrepancy between the desired and actual states, and the importance of the problem.[5] For instance, a consumer may desire to own a new front-wheel-drive automobile of the same size and gas mileage consumption as his current one-year-old rear-wheel-drive model. A discrepancy may exist between the consumer's actual and desired state, but it is not likely to be large enough to motivate him to proceed further in the decision process. In addition, the importance of the problem may be such that the consumer may not be motivated toward further decision-process behavior. Assume that the consumer in the previous example had a sufficient difference between desired and existing states of auto ownership. However, the importance of this particular problem may be low compared to other consumption needs the consumer faces, such as food, housing, and clothing. Thus, consumers facing time and/or budget constraints will attempt to solve only the most-significant problems as they perceive them (and not, incidentally, as an objective outsider might view them).

Problem recognition must also result in the problem being sufficiently defined if the consumer is to engage in meaningful behavior aimed at solving it. Sufficient problem definition occurs for the consumer to be able to act on it in many problem-recognition situations. For instance, the consumer who runs out of milk or bread has a clear definition of the problem. Other situations exist, however, in which the consumer may not have a clear definition of the problem, even though problem recognition has occurred. For example, the matter of self-image may lead to such an occurrence, such as when the consumer feels that her expression of a desired image is not quite right and yet she is unable to define exactly what is wrong. In such cases, information search may be engaged in to more clearly identify the problem. These cases of problem recognition and definition may often be complex.[6]

Types of Problem Recognition[7]

Rather than viewing problem recognition as occurring in only one way, it is useful to understand that there may be varying types of problem-recognition processes. One approach has been to develop a classification system of situations based on the factors of immediacy of required solution and whether or not the problem was expected. The resulting matrix of problem types is shown in Table 18-1 consisting of routine, emergency, planning, and evolving situations. Immediacy of problem solution is a relevant factor in determining the decision time horizon; that is, how soon a problem solution is needed will affect the length of decision process and intensity of decision effort. Expectancy of the problem can affect such facets as the sources of information used in the decision process, for example, as well as the number of alternatives considered. It should be remembered, too, that importance of the problem will be a significant factor influencing decisions within each category of problem recognition. Thus, some decisions (in the same category or type

TABLE 18-1
TYPES OF PROBLEM RECOGNITION

Expectancy of Problem	Immediacy of Solution	
	Immediate Solution Required	Immediate Solution Not Required
Occurrence of problem expected	Routine	Planning
Occurrence of problem unexpected	Emergency	Evolving

Source: Del I. Hawkins, Kenneth A. Coney, and Roger J. Best, *Consumer Behavior*, Business Publications, Inc., Dallas, 1980, p. 390.

of problem recognition situation) are more important to us than others and, as a result, we find different decision-process strategies being used.

Routine problems are those in which the differences between actual and desired states is expected to occur and an immediate solution is required. Typically, convenience goods are associated with this type of problem recognition, such as most grocery purchases made by consumers. In these cases, items are ordinarily used up and must soon be replaced.

Planning problems occur when the problem occurrence is expected but an immediate solution is not necessary. For instance, a consumer who expects that his car will only last one additional year may begin to engage in window shopping for autos, to have discussions with friends about various brands, and to pay closer attention to automotive ads.

Emergency problems are those that are unexpected in which immediate solutions are necessary. For instance, a consumer who is involved in an automobile accident and "totals" his car may need a quick solution to his transportation problem. Consequently, the individual may have little time to engage in shopping for the perfect replacement vehicle, but instead may purchase something that is reasonably satisfactory and available for immediate delivery. Notice that in such a case the vehicle may be viewed as a temporary solution, with a trade-in likely in the near future in order to obtain a better car. This now becomes a planning problem. Some retailers cater to customers facing emergency problems. Convenience stores such as 7-Eleven meet the needs of this segment by offering more extended shopping hours.

Evolving situations occur when the problem is unexpected but no immediate solution is required. The fashion-adoption process illustrates this case. Fashion adoption ordinarily occurs over a lengthy period of time for many consumers. Although one may become aware of the new fashion item's existence, there may be no initial desire to own that item. Over time, as the innovation spreads and more consumers buy the item, a discrepancy between the consumer's desired and actual state may develop and increase. At some point, the consumer may purchase the fashion innovation. Thus, the diffusion of an innovation often involves the situation of evolving problems.

Situations Leading to Problem Recognition

There are numerous situations that may cause consumer problem recognition to occur. Although discussion of all of the potential sources is impossible, we can present the most significant reasons and explain briefly how each one might arise.

Depleted or Inadequate Stock of Goods These are probably the most frequent reasons for consumers recognizing problems. In the first situation, the consumer uses up the assortment of goods she has and must repurchase in order to resupply her needs. As long as there still is a basic need for the item, problem recognition should result from its consumption. The most obvious purchasing situations which result from this are caused by consumers running out of groceries, gasoline, health and grooming aids, and other similar convenience goods.

Sometimes the consumer's stock of goods is inadequate for even her everyday needs and may require a purchase. For instance, she may want to install a bracket for a hanging planter but finds that she doesn't have the necessary tools such as a ruler, a drill, and a screwdriver.

Discontentment with the Stock of Goods Frequently, consumers become discontented with products they own, and this leads to problem recognition. For example, men's ties and jacket lapels narrow and widen as fashion cycles progress. Consequently, men may feel their clothing is no longer stylish, and they may desire to update their wardrobes. Even though the old clothes might be perfectly serviceable, they may be an embarrassment to wear. As a result, this problem is resolved by purchasing some of the latest fashions.

The consumer's dissatisfaction with her present assortment of goods can also arise as the result of other decisions. For instance, consider the case of a family that remodels their 20-year-old home. After the work is completed and the house looks new again, then comes the letdown and dissatisfaction of having to move all the family's old hand-me-down furniture into the newly decorated rooms. The result of this problem recognition may be the purchase of new furniture to go with the remodeled house.

Finally, discontentment may lead the consumer simply to search for something new and different, to break out of a rut. Problem recognition in this case is really founded on a desire to do something novel for a change. One research study on new-product adoption has shown, for example, that one-third of those switching to a new brand did so simply because they desired a change, not because they were dissatisfied with their present brand.[8]

Changing Environmental Circumstances Consumers sometimes encounter changes in their environmental circumstances which lead to problem recognition. One of the most significant of these situations is the family's changing characteristics. As we learned in earlier chapters, different life-cycle stages produce needs for different products. Consequently, as the family evolves, new problems are continually being recognized which result in different assortments of goods over time.

Another important force in the consumer's environment which leads to problem recognition is the influence of reference groups. As we identify with different reference groups, their standards are likely to influence our consumption patterns. For example, the code of dress among a college student's fraternity or sorority group may cause that student to recognize a problem with his or her current wardrobe. Several items of new clothing may be purchased so that the person fits in with this reference group.

Changing Financial Circumstances The financial status of the consumer has a very important relationship to problem recognition. The present or anticipated financial picture may trigger problem recognition as the consumer determines what purchases can be afforded. A consumer, for example, who inherits $50,000, or receives a $2000 salary increase, or receives an income tax refund of $800 may begin to consider alternative ways of spending or saving the money which had not been thought of before. The person may substantially alter his or her desired state in a positive direction based on a financial windfall. Problem recognition, in this case, may lead to purchasing a new car, a new boat, a dishwasher, or taking a vacation. If, on the other hand, the consumer expects to lose his or her job and livelihood, then the financial expectations and desired state will be altered in a negative direction.

Marketing Activities The marketer frequently attempts to precipitate problem recognition through promotional efforts aimed at the consumer. With such efforts, the marketer seeks to have the consumer perceive a difference of sufficient magnitude between her desired state (ownership of the product) and her actual state (not owning it) to engage in search, evaluation, and purchasing activity for the marketer's brand.

Although such marketing efforts may have some influence on problem recognition on the part of the consumer, it is ordinarily not an easy process to accomplish. As we learned in the discussion of information processing, consumers have the capability of filtering out any messages in which they are not interested or with which they disagree. Consequently, marketing activity may achieve its greatest effectiveness once consumer problem recognition has already occurred. For instance, large numbers of those who take home movies may be dissatisfied with currently available products utilizing film. As a result, this group may be highly receptive to videotape equipment having appropriate desirable features. The marketer's job, then, is to develop a marketing mix that appeals to these dissatisfied consumers. Decisions regarding product features, prices, distribution, and promotion may then be molded to suit particular desired segments of potential buyers. Thus, with many consumers having already engaged in problem recognition and accepted the merits of videotape, the marketer's promotion activity is much more likely to fall on fertile ground than when he is trying to convince uninterested and unbelieving consumers that there is a better product available.

Results of Problem Recognition

Once the consumer becomes aware of a problem, two basic outcomes are possible. One result is for the consumer, in effect, not to pursue any further problem-solving behavior, which might occur if the difference between the consumer's perceived desired and actual states is not great enough to cause him to act to resolve the difference. For example, assume that a consumer has a six-month-old, 19-inch color television set that works perfectly. One day he visits his neighbor who has just bought a 25-inch model, and sees how much larger the picture is compared to his set. Although our consumer's desired state may be to own a larger screen TV, there is not likely to be a difference of sufficient magnitude between that and his actual state (the 19-inch set) to cause him to purchase one. If, however, his set were to give out, then he might be motivated to purchase the larger model.

Another situation in which problem recognition may not lead to further stages of consumer decision-making occurs when certain environmental elements preclude it. For example, suppose the consumer from our previous illustration has his household belongings (including his TV) destroyed by a fire. In replacing his possessions, one of the first things he wants to buy is a new 25-inch television set, like his neighbor's. However, because his insurance policy does not cover the full replacement value of all his belongings, and other items are of greater urgency, he determines that he can get along well enough for a while without a TV. Thus, in spite of a difference of sufficient magnitude between the consumer's desired state (owning a TV) and actual state (not owning a TV), financial considerations restrict the consumer's ability to proceed further in the decision-making process.

Other constraints may similarly preclude further decision activity by the consumer. Factors such as time constraints, social class values, and differing family desires may all impede the process.

The second type of response that may occur from the problem-recognition process is for the consumer to proceed into further stages of decision-making activity by engaging in information search and evaluation.

Problem Recognition Under Low-Involvement Conditions

Much of what we have discussed so far relates to high-involvement buying decisions. If you refer back to Chapters 12 and 13, you will recall that two purchasing conditions were summarized—high-involvement and low-involvement. High-involvement purchase situations are those which, because of their relevance and significance for the individual, are characterized by more extensive decision-process behavior. The consumer moves through the sequence of stages diagramed at the beginning of Part 5. However, when products have little relevance and importance to consumers, the decision process is quite different.

Problem recognition under low-involvement conditions is thought to be different from that under high-involvement conditions. Rather than being anything dramatic and highly goal-oriented, it is characterized more by point-of-purchase triggering or stimulation of problem recognition based on familiarity with the brand developed through repetitive advertising. Problem recognition, therefore, occurs in this case not as a result of first-time exposure to promotion, but perhaps because of a low level of appeal in which the consumer may develop a mild interest in checking out the product's suitability at some point in the future. If the product is purchased, tried, and then favorably evaluated, it may become a routine purchase because it is consumed and must be replenished from time to time. Most supermarket items fall into the category of low-involvement purchases, and they are bought in this way.

MARKETING IMPLICATIONS OF PROBLEM RECOGNITION

The significance to marketers of the problem-recognition stage of consumer decision making is that the process can be effectively measured and can be used to develop and evaluate marketing strategies.

Measurement of Problem Recognition

Consumer researchers have found that the best way to assess the problem-recognition process is through scaling techniques, which measure purchase intentions. Purchase intentions incorporate the consumer's attitudes toward the product and may be viewed as the mental forerunner of buying behavior. The continuum presented in Table 18-2 indicates attitudes that correspond to the various levels of buyer predisposition and are indicative (where positive) of a situation in which problem recognition has occurred and the consumer has some intention of resolving the problem.

Utilizing Problem-Recognition Information

The marketer may find information on buyer intentions to be useful in the following ways.

Analyzing Purchase-Intention Categories From measurement of the speed, direction, and size of shifts in buying likelihoods for a product over several periods in various market segments, the marketer may discover what trends are taking place as well as the timing and size of their potential impact on sales.[9] For example, consider the kinds of comparisons that may be made based on Table 18-2.[10] From this table, we can see that consumers who use either statement in Category 1 to describe their intentions appear highly predisposed to buy. Consumers who

TABLE 18-2 RANGE OF CONSUMER'S PREDISPOSITIONS

Category	Predisposition	Attitudes
1	Firm and immediate intent to buy a specific brand.	"I am going to buy some right away." "I am going to buy some soon."
2	Positive intention without definite buying plans.	"I am certain I will buy some sometime." "I probably will buy some sometime."
3	Neutrality: Might buy, might not buy.	"I may buy some sometime." "I might buy some sometime, but I doubt it."
4	Inclined not to buy the brand but not definite about it.	"I don't think I'm interested in buying any." "I probably will never buy any."
5	Firm intention not to buy the brand.	"I know I'm not interested in buying any." "If somebody gave me some, I would give it away, just to get rid of it."
6	Never considered buying.	"I have never heard of the brand."

Source: Adapted from William D. Wells, "Measuring Readiness to Buy," Harvard Business Review, **39**:82, July–August 1961.

describe their readiness in terms of statements from Category 2 are favorable disposed, but are without immediate purchasing intentions. Consequently, a low Category 1- to- Category 2 ratio means that there is a large reservoir of goodwill that needs to be converted into a stronger intention to buy. If this ratio increases over a period of time, it suggests that consumers holding favorable disposition toward the brand are increasing their intentions to purchase it. Deficiencies at the point of sale may be a reason for failure to convert predispositions into purchases. Perhaps price reductions or special promotional deals might be called for in such a situation.

Concentrations of respondents in Category 3 may not be unfavorable since these consumers are still psychologically accessible because their intentions are not yet firmly set. Of course, the marketer would want to shift these respondents into higher categories over a period of time. A strong, effective promotion campaign may be called for in this instance.

A concentration of persons in Category 5 is very undesirable. These respondents have strong, preformed negative intentions about the brand and are likely to be extremely difficult to convince to buy. If the marketer suspects that these attitudes could be the result of his promotion campaign, new and different appeals might be tried with this segment. Since laggards (the last adopter category) are likely to be in Categories 4 and 5, such changed appeals will probably be necessary. Personal selling may also be more heavily needed for this group.

Failure to shift respondents out of Category 6 (those who have never heard of the brand) into higher categories probably indicates lack of a sufficient program to establish ready brand recognition. Heavier advertising and free product sampling may be called for in this case in order to increase consumers' knowledge levels.

If the marketer fails to convince consumers that his brand is worth trying, this pattern will show up as a movement of respondents from Category 6 into 5, 4, or 3, rather than into the top two categories. Product or package improvements may be called for in this case. Product improvements are almost certainly in order if the marketer finds a shift into lower categories by those who have already used the brand.

Analyzing Conversion of Purchase Intentions[11] The marketer may also find significant implications for his marketing strategy by investigating the relationships between purchasing intentions and buying behavior. Longitudinal analysis of intentions data allows the marketer to understand the dynamics of marketplace activity. He obtains a clearer picture of which brands are converting predispositions into buying action. This information can help him to determine the point at which marketing success or failure is occurring and isolate the reasons.

In order to conduct this analysis, data on purchase intentions and behavior over a period of time are necessary, such as those contained in Figure 18-1. Assume that there are three national brands in a particular appliance category for which such data have been gathered from interviews conducted 12 months apart. Figure 18-1 indicates that 44 percent of those who stated a definite intention to buy a Brand A appliance actually bought an appliance during this period (we are not concerned at this moment with brand decisions, only generic product decisions).

FIGURE 18-1

Comparison of buying intentions and behavior (12 months between interviews). (*Source*: Adapted from Robert W. Pratt, Jr., "Understanding the Decision Process for Consumer Durable Goods: An Example of the Application of Longitudinal Analysis," in Peter D. Bennett (ed.), *Marketing and Economic Development*, published by the American Marketing Association, Chicago, 1965, p. 249.)

Comparison of buying intentions and behavior
(12 months between interviews)

Of each 100 persons who stated a definite intention to buy a (brand) appliance.

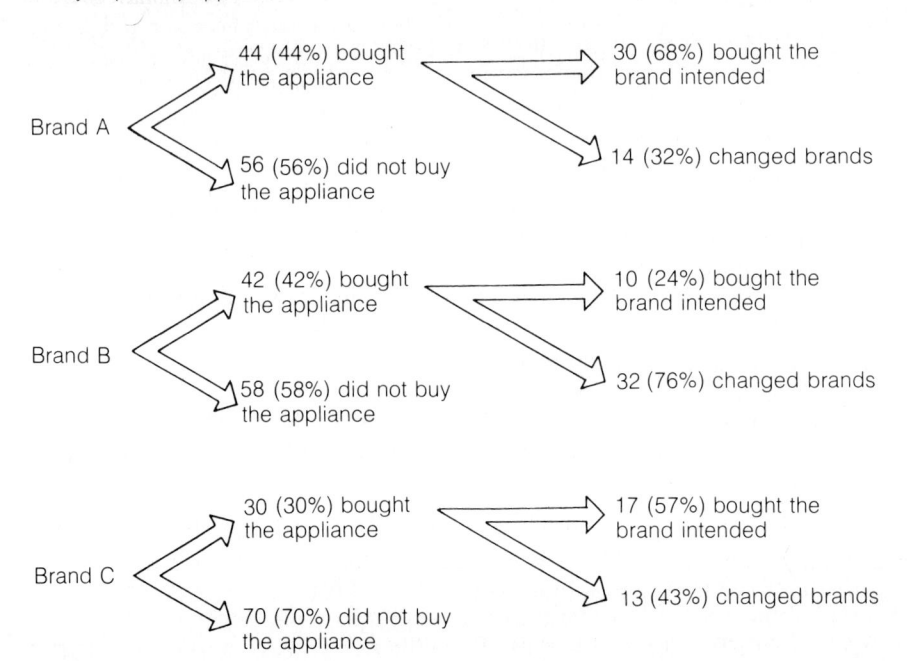

Brand A
- 44 (44%) bought the appliance
  - 30 (68%) bought the brand intended
  - 14 (32%) changed brands
- 56 (56%) did not buy the appliance

Brand B
- 42 (42%) bought the appliance
  - 10 (24%) bought the brand intended
  - 32 (76%) changed brands
- 58 (58%) did not buy the appliance

Brand C
- 30 (30%) bought the appliance
  - 17 (57%) bought the brand intended
  - 13 (43%) changed brands
- 70 (70%) did not buy the appliance

From Figure 18-1 it can be seen, therefore, that Brand A had a higher percentage of intenders making purchases than either Brands B or C.

A second very important aspect of these conversion patterns is the *brand intention-fulfillment rate*. Looking again at Figure 18-1 it may be seen that 68 percent of those who intended to buy Brand A actually did so, while 32 percent bought an alternative brand. According to the brand-fulfillment data in Figure 18-1, Brand A was most successful at converting brand-preference intentions, followed by Brand C and Brand B. Thus, Brand A appears to have the most effective marketing strategy, while Brand C is more effective than Brand B. Based on information such as this, the manager of Brand B might seek to determine the reasons for his brand's disappointing sales by assessing the various elements in its marketing program.

SUMMARY

This chapter has initiated our discussion of consumer decision making. First, various types of consumer decisions were described to indicate the diversity and complexity of consumer purchasing processes. Next, the consumer decision-process model was introduced, and purchasing processes were seen to range from those that are rather simple and highly programmable to those that are extremely complicated. The remainder of this chapter was devoted to examining the first stage of the decision process, problem recognition.

Problem recognition amounts to a condition in which the consumer recognizes a difference of sufficient magnitude between what is perceived as the actual state and what is perceived as the desired state of affairs. Types of problem recognition and situations causing problem recognition were then described. The outcome of problem recognition could be for the consumer to continue into other stages of decision making or to be restrained by environmental circumstances from further purchasing behavior. Problem recognition was also characterized under conditions of high- and low-involvement. The chapter concluded with a discussion of applications of problem-recognition information to marketing analysis.

DISCUSSION TOPICS

1   Why is it important to understand consumer decision making?

2   Describe the types of consumer decisions. Illustrate them with a recent decision of your own.

3   What is problem recognition?

4   Describe from your own recent experience what factors led to problem recognition in at least three different product or service situations (not necessarily purchases). Explain the similarities or differences that exist in these situations.

5   Distinguish between problem recognition under conditions of low-involvement and under conditions of high-involvement. What implications might each of these situations have for promotional plans?

6   How can the marketer use purchase-intentions data?

NOTES

[1] Richard W. Olshavsky and Donald H. Granbois, "Consumer Decision Making—Fact or Fiction?" *Journal of Consumer Research,* 6:93, September 1979.

[2] Harold H. Kassarjian, "Presidential Address, 1977: Anthropomorphism and Parsimony," in H. Keith Hunt (ed.), *Advances in Consumer Research: Volume 5,* Association for Consumer Research, Ann Arbor, MI, 1978, pp. xii–xiv.

[3] Olshavsky and Granbois, "Consumer Decision Making," pp. 93–99 and Roger A. Formisano, Richard W. Olshavsky, and Shelley Tapp, "Choice Strategy in a Difficult Task Environment," *Journal of Consumer Research* 8:474–479, March 1982.

[4] James F. Engel and Roger D. Blackwell, *Consumer Behavior,* 4th ed., Dryden Press, New York, 1982, p. 300.

[5] Del I. Hawkins, Kenneth A. Coney, and Roger J. Best, *Consumer Behavior,* Business Publications, Inc., Dallas, 1980, p. 388.

[6] Hawkins, Coney, and Best, *Consumer Behavior,* p. 389.

[7] This section is based on Hawkins, Coney, and Best, *Consumer Behavior,* pp. 389–393.

[8] Elihu Katz and Paul Lazarsfeld, *Personal Influence,* Free Press, New York, 1955.

[9] C. Joseph Clawson, "How Useful Are 90-Day Purchase Probabilities?" *Journal of Marketing,* 35:43–47, October 1971.

[10] William D. Wells, "Measuring Readiness to Buy," *Harvard Business Review,* 39:81–87, July–August 1961.

[11] This section is drawn from Robert W. Pratt, Jr., "Understanding the Decision Process for Consumer Durable Goods: An Example of the Application of Longitudinal Analysis," in Peter D. Bennett (ed.), *Marketing and Economic Development,* American Marketing Association, Chicago, 1965, pp. 244–260.

CHAPTER 19
SEARCH AND EVALUATION

Once a consumer has recognized the existence of a problem, and assuming there are no constraints preventing further behavior, the next stage in the decision-making process involves a search for and evaluation of information.

In this chapter, we shall first examine what the information-seeking process entails and the many ways it is influenced. Next, the process of evaluation will be discussed. Finally, some marketing implications will be presented to indicate how the marketer may seek to influence consumer search processes.

THE INFORMATION-SEEKING PROCESS

In this section, we shall examine the search process engaged in by consumers and the factors that influence it.

Types of Consumer Search Activities

For our purposes here, *information* may be considered to be knowledge obtained about some fact or circumstance. And in the context in which we are dealing within this chapter, such knowledge is to be used in a consumer-behavior situation.

As discussed in Chapter 13, the term "search" refers to mental as well as physical information-seeking and processing activities which one engages in to facilitate decision making regarding some goal-object in the marketplace.[1] Consequently, search may be undertaken in order to find out about products, prices, stores, and so on, related to the product. Search may be active or passive, internal or external. *Active* search could involve visiting stores to make product and price comparisons, while *passive* search may entail only reading a magazine advertisement with no specific goal in mind or thinking about the features of a desired product.

The processes of internal and external search consist of different activities. These activities are described in detail below.

Internal Search This is the first stage to occur after the consumer experiences problem recognition. It is a mental process of recalling and reviewing information stored in memory that may relate to the purchase situation. For instance, a consumer may recall that a friend made very negative comments about a particular brand of coffee maker (which the consumer is now considering buying) while playing bridge several months ago. Notice that these derogatory comments were stored in the consumer's memory and now have come into play by affecting her attitudes unfavorably toward the brand. Thus, the consumer relies on any attitudes, information, or past experiences that have been stored in memory and can be recalled for application to the problem at hand. The recall may be immediate or may occur slowly, as a conscious effort is made to bring the information to mind. Once recalled, the information may be used in the evaluation process as the consumer seeks to resolve the purchase decision confronting her.

The reliance on internal search may be a very important part of shoppers' strategies. For instance, one study showed that most shoppers rely on experiential information sources in retail shopping trips.[2] That is, they turn inward to their previous shopping experiences for making decisions about where to shop. Only a limited number of people engage in any external information search (whether from family, friends, or advertisements) prior to making a major shopping trip. This situation makes it especially difficult to overcome a negative image or mistaken impression that people in the market may have of a retail store. Once the store has been removed from the consumer's mental set of acceptable alternatives it may be quite difficult to get that consumer to reconsider or reexperience the store.

As described in Chapter 3, the research technique utilized in understanding the consumer's internal-search process is *protocol analysis.* Here, the consumer is asked to think out loud while engaging in a decision process such as shopping. The technique's previously noted limitation of reporting only conscious information processes should be restated at this point also. Nevertheless, it is presently the most useful approach for understanding consumer internal-search activities.[3]

The result or outcome of internal search and alternative evaluation may be that a consumer (1) makes a decision and proceeds to engage in purchase behavior, (2) is constrained by certain environmental variables (such as a determination that his checking account cannot stand the purchase), or (3) determines that insufficient or inadequate information exists in his memory to make a decision now, so that external search is undertaken.

External Search This refers to the process of obtaining information from other sources in addition to that which can be recalled from memory. Some sources from which such information might be obtained are advertisements, friends, salespeople, store displays, and product-testing magazines. Whereas internal search is always passive, external search may be either passive or active.

During external search, the brand alternatives to the buyer's product-choice decision are identified. Although there may be many brands in existence in the product category (which we may call the *total* set of brands), the consumer is not likely to be aware of all of them. Thus, some brands will not be considered by the consumer because of this unawareness. Consequently, the marketer seeks to make consumers aware of the availability of his brand and to supply them with sufficient information to evaluate it and, hopefully, purchase it.

Even among brands of which the consumer is aware, however, are some that he would not consider purchasing for several reasons:

1 He may feel they are beyond his reach.

2 They are not perceived as adequate for his motives.

3   He has insufficient information on which to evaluate them.

4   He has tried and rejected them.

5   He is satisfied with his current brand.

6   He has received negative feedback from advertising or from word-of-mouth communication.[4]

It has been suggested, therefore, that there actually exist three subsets of brands within the awareness set of alternatives: (1) evoked set, (2) inert set, and (3) inept set.[5]

The *evoked set* consists of the few select brands evaluated positively by the consumer for purchase and consumption. The *inert set* consists of those brands that the consumer has failed to perceive any advantage in buying; that is, they are evaluated neither positively nor negatively. Perhaps the consumer has insufficient information on which to evaluate them, or she simply may not perceive them as better than the brands in her evoked set. The *inept set* is made up of brands that have been rejected from purchase consideration by the consumer because of an unpleasant experience or negative feedback from others. Thus, the brands in this set are evaluated negatively by the consumer and will not be considered at all in their present form.

Knowledge of consumers' awareness sets of brands is valuable to marketers because they are interested in moving their items into their evoked set. Only if consumers are aware of the brand and have evaluated it positively will it be purchased. Later in this chapter we will discuss alternatives for moving a brand into consumers' evoked sets.

Now that we have a better understanding of the nature of search activities engaged in by the consumer, it is time to examine some of the factors that influence the process.

Nature of the Search Process

Unless consumers are dealing with a purchase situation in which they have no experience, they will not have to learn the relevant attributes on which to evaluate different products or brands. There are times, however, when a consumer is confronted with an entirely new buying situation. For example, the purchase of a home computer would likely mean that the prospective buyer would have to learn the relevant computer terminology as well as those product features that are most important in order to make a wise purchase. Similarly, an apartment dweller who buys a home may have much to learn about outdoor maintenance-product purchase, and a newlywed couple making its first furniture purchase needs to know what to look for. In situations such as these, consumers are likely to rely more heavily on friends or experts and neutral information sources (such as *Consumer Reports*). Advertising that has a helpful and factual or objective tone may also be favorably received (see Figure 19-1).

The marketer may be interested in knowing how consumers process the information gathered during the search process. There are two approaches: brand processing or attribute processing. In brand processing, the buyer assesses one brand at a time. Thus, the consumer may decide to look at a particular brand, examine several attributes of that brand, then assess several attributes for a second and

FIGURE 19-1

Advertisement for smart furniture buying. (Courtesy of Roitman & Son, Inc.)

third brand, for instance. In attribute processing, the consumer examines a specific attribute and then compares several other brands on that attribute. Then, a second attribute may be selected for comparison, and so on. These two information-processing strategies are referred to as choice by processing brands (CPB) and choice by processing attributes (CPA), respectively.[6]

Generally, a CPB strategy appears to be common, although research also indicates that consumers in early stages of the decision process use a CPA strategy, switching to a brand-processing approach in later stages. Perhaps those with considerable experience or knowledge regarding a product and its purchase can be expected to rely more on a brand-processing approach.[7]

Amount of Information Seeking by Consumers

Consumers appear to engage in a rather limited information search when making purchase decisions. Marketer-supplied information such as that obtained from advertisements or retail stores is not actively used by all consumers. The findings presented in this section (some of which were cited in Chapter 13, but are reviewed here in greater detail) are illustrative of this pattern.

Use of Advertisements Several research studies have indicated that consumer use of advertisements is not very great. Consider the following conclusions:

Only about one shopper in ten checks advertisements before shopping for shoes and personal accessories.[8]

An early study of consumers buying food products found that only 19 percent were able to recall obtaining information from advertisements.[9] However, a more recent study by the FTC showed that almost nine out of ten representative shoppers regularly look at newspaper ads of grocery prices, with 44 percent regularly relying on television advertising and 23 percent on radio advertising.[10]

Of consumers purchasing small electrical appliances, such as radios, hair dryers, toasters, and coffee makers, only 25 percent consulted newspaper advertising, 15 percent read magazine advertising, 14 percent saw television advertising, and 7 percent listened to radio advertising before buying.[11]

It can be seen from this that consumers generally do not appear to be active users of advertising, although this varies by product and among individuals and perhaps by time period.

Information Obtained from Retail Outlets Another source of marketer-supplied information is the retail store. Here, consumers are able to see and assess products, and this facilitates their evaluation process. Two aspects of the usage of store-provided information are relevant here: the number of stores visited and the amount of information secured within stores.

NUMBER OF STORES SHOPPED Table 19-1 presents findings from several research studies in which consumers were asked the number of stores they visited before purchasing the items listed. It is clear from this table that very often consumers do not visit more than one store in order to obtain information before purchasing. It should also be noticed that the number of stores visited differs according to the product. Thus, most consumers appear to have little need for securing information from several different stores during their search process. But what about their in-store information-seeking? Is this also minimal?

AMOUNT OF IN-STORE SEARCH Of course, neither the number of stores visited nor the number of visits per store by consumers may be truly indicative of the amount of information-seeking that takes place within retail stores. Unfortunately, there is relatively little research on consumers' in-store search activities. Thus, marketers have little insight into how much information-seeking really goes on inside retail stores.

One measure of the amount of in-store information search is the number of brands consumers compare in making a purchase decision. One study showed that there was considerable variation by product, with 41 percent of the shoppers evaluating only one brand of refrigerator, with 49 percent for television sets, 61 percent for washing machines, 65 percent for electric irons, and 71 percent for vacuum cleaners. It was also found that only 29 percent compared four or more brands of refrigerators, while 9 percent shopped four or more brands of irons.[12]

Another measure of the amount of in-store information search is the extent to which consumers consider products in other price ranges and seek information on product features. A study of this found that 46 percent of buyers of durable

TABLE 19-1

NUMBER OF STORES CONSUMERS VISIT BEFORE PURCHASE

Product	Don't Know or None	One Store	Two Stores	Three or More Stores
Toys*		87.4	6.1	6.5
Small electrical appliances†	2.0	60.0	16.0	22.0
Refrigerators‡		42.0	16.0	42.0
Living room furniture§	2.4	22.0	13.4	62.1
New cars and major appliances¶		49.0	26.0	23.0

Percentage of Purchases by Number of Stores Visited

Source: *Alderson and Sessions, Inc., "Basic Research Report on Consumer Behavior," in Ronald E. Frank, Alfred A. Kuehn, and William F. Massy, (eds.), *Quantitative Techniques in Marketing Analysis*, Irwin, Homewood, IL, 1962, pp. 129–145.
†Jon G. Udell, "Prepurchase Behavior of Buyers of Small Electrical Appliances," *Journal of Marketing*, **30:**50–52, October 1966.
‡William P. Dommermuth, "The Shopping Matrix and Marketing Strategy," *Journal of Marketing Research*, **2:**128–132, May 1965.
§Bruce LeGrand and Jon G. Udell, "Consumer Behavior in the Market Place—An Empirical Study in the Television and Furniture Fields with Theoretical Implications," *Journal of Retailing*, **40:**32, Fall 1964.
¶Joseph W. Newman and Richard Staelin, "Prepurchase Information Seeking for New Cars and Major Household Appliances," *Journal of Marketing Research*, **9:**249–257, August 1972.

goods did not consider items in other price ranges. The study also measured the extent to which consumers sought information on such product features as quality, performance, style, operating cost, service and guarantees. Omitting price and brand, 27 percent did not consider any features; 34 percent considered one feature; 18 percent considered two features; and 17 percent considered three or more.[13]

These studies have focused on only single measures of external-search activity. However, as mentioned in Chapter 13, studies that have used composite indexes of search activity yield similar findings. In conclusion, therefore, it can be seen that consumers generally do not seek large amounts of information. Clearly, their search process is highly selective. This does not necessarily mean, however, that consumers entering the marketplace are uninformed. The studies referred to do not really address the question of information *quality*, only certain aspects of information *quantity*. It is possible that buyers, although visiting only one store, are able to obtain large amounts of helpful information from that one source. They may examine the product, check prices, practice using the item, talk with the salesperson, read product literature, and study the package.

It is also possible that many consumers begin their external search processes with large amounts of relevant information stored in memory, which therefore requires that little additional data be gathered. Consumers are continuously gathering information from advertising, personal conversations, observation, and so forth. Some of this may later become relevant to a purchase-decision situation.

In any event, more research needs to be done before we have a clear idea of how much search consumers *actually do* or *should do* for purchasing decisions. Later in this chapter, some of the public policy implications of information search and processing activities will be offered.

Factors That Influence the Search Process
There are quite a few variables that determine the amount of search consumers undertake. The following factors are not mutually exclusive, however.

Costs Versus Benefit of Search Activity There are many potential benefits from engaging in search activity. Yet, there are also costs associated with information seeking that may partially counteract the perceived benefits. Hence, consumers may tend to apply the principle of *marginality* in search activities. That is, additional search activity may be engaged in if the the added benefits are perceived to be greater than the additional costs involved. These benefits and costs could take several forms.

One benefit to be derived from search is the possibility of making a "better" purchase decision—at least as the consumer perceives it. Shopping can provide consumers with information on the best product features, warranties, service, and prices, for example. As support for the benefit of shopping, it has been found that consumers are more willing to shop for higher-priced than for less expensive items, since the potential gains to be realized are greater.[14]

Another benefit of search is the sheer pleasure of the shopping experience for many consumers. Most people like to buy new things, and thus shopping and buying become an excellent way to get out of a rut. Many consumers find shopping to be an enjoyable activity, one of the pleasurable parts of their day, and sometimes an escape mechanism from their cares.[15] Thus, search is more likely to be undertaken when viewed as a pleasurable activity.

Search activity is usually not without costs, however.[16] There are several types of costs that may or may not be explicitly recognized by consumers. First, there is the direct cost associated with traveling to various stores and parking. It is questionable whether consumers carefully consider this cost. However, higher costs of travel in the future may increase consideration given to it. At least one study has found that consumers make more comparisons between stores when this requires little expense and effort.[17]

A second cost involves time. Search frequently entails visits to retail stores to gather information. Such shopping excursions often turn into all-day adventures. For example, there is the time involved in traveling between home and the place of shopping, time spent parking, time spent walking from the car to store and back and from store to store, and the time spent selecting and paying for goods in each store.[18] Thus, the use of one's time for search as opposed to a game of tennis or watching television may represent a cost to many consumers. This is particularly true for those who work because they may more readily equate their time with money that might be earned in alternative pursuits. As one study concluded, "Today's shopper must weigh the opportunity cost involved in expending time for prolonged search against the probable benefits to be derived from it. Relative to total income, the time involved may outweigh potential economic benefits."[19] Consequently, if the time pressure or opportunity cost is great to the consumer, extensive search is less likely.

A third searching cost to the consumer is the resultant delay in enjoying ownership of the product. Some consumers may be unwilling to engage in extensive search because this forestalls their satisfaction from using the product. Hence, when delay in making a decision is unattractive, less extensive search will result.

A final cost exacted by external search is its toll on the consumer's psyche.

Although the consumer may look forward to shopping as a pleasurable activity, it sometimes turns out to be a nightmare, as during holiday sales. The shopper may pay a high price in terms of frustration and anger. Thus, the psychological costs involved in search may be high, which will tend to reduce the intensity of the process.

Type of Product The nature of the product has an important influence on the amount of information seeking. Traditionally, marketers have recognized three types of products and shopping patterns.[20] *Convenience goods* are classified as those that the customer usually purchases frequently, immediately, and with a minimum of effort in comparison and buying. *Shopping goods* are those that, in the process of selection and purchase, customers usually compare on such bases as suitability, quality, price, and style. Finally, *specialty goods* are those with unique characteristics and/or brand identifications for which a significant group of buyers are habitually willing to make a special purchasing effort.

The type of product, therefore, can be seen to affect the nature and amount of search undertaken. This factor relates also to our previous discussion of search cost and benefit. The probable gain from comparing price and quality of shopping goods is significant enough to lead to more extensive search activities, whereas such would not be the case for convenience goods.[21] A number of research studies have affirmed that consumers engage in more information seeking when their purchases are more expensive.[22]

Type of Store The amount of information search that is engaged in by consumers may also be strongly related to the type of retail store at which they shop. For instance, a study of audio-equipment buyers who purchased from different types of retailers—from audio-equipment specialty stores (offering intensive choices of major foreign and domestic brands) or from full-line department stores (providing limited lines of audio equipment as part of their major appliance departments)—found that specialty and department store shoppers differed in terms of their information-related predispositions and information-seeking activities. In contrast to department store buyers, those who purchased their audio equipment from a specialty store were found to be more knowledgeable, to possess more related experience, to read more product-oriented special interest magazines, to visit more stores, and to be more likely to examine manufacturers' literature and seek advice from friends and neighbors. In other words, specialty store buyers were more willing to accumulate product-related information from a variety of sources than were department store buyers.[23]

Perceived Risk Risk or uncertainty regarding the most appropriate purchase decision or the consequences of the decision is a third variable influencing the total amount of information gathered by consumers.

It is important to recognize that risk is subjective. That is, the risk involved in a purchase decision is *perceived* by the consumer and may or may not bear a strong relationship to what actually exists. For example, an objective observer may not evaluate the purchase of a canned ham as involving much risk. However, the choice may involve considerable risk in terms of the impression a homemaker wishes to make when she is purchasing the ham for a dinner party she is having for her husband's boss.

SITUATIONS INFLUENCING RISK   There are several situations that influence the consumer's perception of uncertainty or consequences and thus the perception of risk:

1   Uncertainty regarding buying goals. For example, should a new sport jacket be purchased for more formal occasions or for very informal get-togethers?

2   Uncertainty regarding which alternative (such as product, brand, or model) will best match or satisfy the purchase goals. That is, if private transportation to school is desired, what should be purchased: car or motorcycle; Ford, Chevrolet, or Plymouth; two-door or four-door?

3   The consumer can perceive possible undesirable consequences if the purchase is made (or not made) and the result is failure to satisfy buying goals.[24]

If any of these situations are sensed by the consumer, then he or she is said to perceive risk in the situation.

TYPES OF RISK   As one may expect, there are also several kinds of risk that consumers may perceive in a purchase situation.[25]

Financial Risk—The consumer may lose money if the brand doesn't work at all, or costs more than it should to keep it in good shape.

Performance Risk—The brand may not work properly.

Physical Risk—The brand may be or become harmful or injurious to one's health.

Psychological Risk—The brand may not fit in well with the consumer's self-image or self-concept.

Social Risk—The brand may negatively affect the way others think of the consumer.

Time Loss Risk—The brand may fail completely, thus wasting the consumer's time, convenience, and effort getting it adjusted, repaired, or replaced.

Thus, overall risk is a combination of several factors as perceived by consumers when buying a product.

HOW CONSUMERS DEAL WITH RISK   Because most purchase behavior appears to involve at least some risk, consumers may take various steps to handle the problem. In most cases, this results in attempts to reduce risk. Consumers develop various strategies to relieve perceived risk, including the following:

1   Buy the brand whose advertising has endorsements or testimonials from typical consumers, from a celebrity, or from an expert on the product.

2   Buy the brand that the consumer has used before and has found satisfactory.

3   Buy a major, well-known brand, and rely on its reputation.

4   Buy the brand that has been tested and approved by a private testing company.

5   Buy the brand offering a money-back guarantee with the product.

6 Buy the brand that has been tested and approved by a branch of the government.

7 Buy the most expensive and elaborate model of the product.[26]

Thus, as some of the approaches on the above list indicate, consumers may reduce risk through information acquisition aimed at reducing uncertainty. Several consumer research studies have confirmed this process.[27] Information acquisition can also be used to help reduce the perceived consequences of a decision, as can reduction of the amount at stake (for example, purchasing a smaller size), reducing expectations about how perfect the product will be, or minimizing the consequences (such as a cigarette lighter slogan that states, "For 99 cents it's a pretty good lighter").

Learning and Experience The consumer's past experience with a product and the amount and nature of information learned will affect the extent of search.[28] A particular purchase may become routine or habitual when the customer repeats the buying behavior frequently and if the consumption experience has been pleasurable, thus reinforcing the behavior. Because the consumer feels that her previous experience is sufficient, she is likely to perceive less need for additional search activity.

Various research studies have confirmed the role of learning from previous experience as an important variable in consumer search. The amount and appropriateness of information stored by consumers influences their search patterns.

AMOUNT OF INFORMATION The amount of information that has been stored by the consumer will depend on his or her length and breadth of experience. Thus, the occurrence and extensiveness of search activity undertaken by a consumer will be greater to the extent that he or she has a shorter and narrower range of purchase experience with brands in a product category.[29]

APPROPRIATENESS OF INFORMATION Appropriateness of the consumer's stored information depends on several factors. First, satisfaction with past purchases will affect search. If the consumer has achieved great satisfaction in the product's consumption, she is likely to engage in less search when the problem is recognized again.[30] Second, appropriateness is determined by the similarity perceived between problems. If the present consumer problem is seen to be the same as an earlier situation that was satisfactorily resolved, then the consumer is likely to rely on the previous solution (i.e., buy the same brand) and thus engage in less external search.[31]

A third variable affecting the appropriateness of stored information involves changes in the alternatives available on the market. Products come and go from the marketplace, prices change, and retail stores open and close. The extent to which these variables are altered affects the appropriateness of the consumer's stored information such that she is likely to engage in search to up-date her knowledge.[32]

Changes in the mix of market alternatives are very likely to occur with the passage of time. Thus, time between purchases is a final factor affecting information appropriateness. As interpurchase time increases, the consumer is more likely to engage in search activity.[33]

There are several other determinants of information search that have been suggested. The following are indicative of the more important ones and the direction of their influence.

Recognition and Intensity of Need It appears that consumers' product needs are often not well defined before shopping. Because of this, the retail store serves as an important information source in meeting their search needs. As they shop, they gather information and their needs become more clearly defined. Therefore, if consumers have not identified their needs before shopping they will tend to engage in more search.[34]

If a consumer has an urgent need, then the chances are that search activity will be reduced in order to satisfy that need.[35] However, the greater the consumer's intensity of need for a particular product, the more likely she is to engage in extensive search for that product.[36]

Level of Consumer Involvement Information-search activities differ depending on the level of consumer involvement. For example, consumers buying under low-involvement conditions are not very concerned about gathering large amounts of information pertaining to the decision. Why? Because the purchase does not represent an important or risky situation. They do not have a significant stake in the purchase; their egos are not on the line. Hence, there is little motivation to gather information to reduce what little uncertainty or risk may exist.

Personality and Self-Concept Certain personality types appear to be more information-sensitive than others, hence, they engage in greater search activities.[37] It has also been suggested that the extent to which a woman sees herself as being a deliberate searcher, the more extensive her search to obtain any given product.[38]

The various determinants of the extent of information search (some of which were discussed in Chapter 13) are summarized in Table 19-2.

Types of Information Sought

It would be important for the marketer in planning promotional campaigns and merchandising strategies to know what types of information consumers look for in search activities. It has been suggested that consumers need three types of information. First, they need information about the existence or availability of a product or brand before they can purchase it; that is, they must be aware. Second, they need information that will give them reason to become interested in the product (assuming they must be interested in an item before they will consider it for purchase). Third, consumers need information that will help them evaluate a product in terms of its ability to satisfy their needs.[39]

Evaluative information includes information about the product itself, such as cost, characteristics, functions, variations, performance, and so on; about products or brands that compare to it; and about the psychological and social consequences of buying the product. It has been found that the type of product appears to determine to some extent the type of information people seek.[40]

Sources of Information

The consumer has three sources of information in purchase-decision making: (1) marketer-dominated channels of communication, (2) consumer channels, and

TABLE 19-2

DETERMINANTS OF THE EXTENT OF INFORMATION SEARCH

Market environment:
- Number of alternatives
- Complexity of alternatives
- Marketing mix of alternatives
- Stability of alternatives on the market (new alternatives)
- Information availability

Situational variables:
- Time pressure
- Social pressure (family, peer, boss)
- Financial pressure
- Organizational procedures
- Physical and mental condition
- Ease of access to information sources

Potential payoff/product importance:
- Price
- Social visibility
- Perceived risk
- Difference among alternatives
- Number of crucial attributes
- Status of decision-making activity (in the family, organization, society)

Knowledge and experience:
- Stored knowledge
- Usage rate of product
- Previous information
- Previous choices (number and identity)
- Satisfaction

Individual differences:
- Ability
- Training
- Approach to problem solving (compulsiveness, open-mindedness, preplanning, innovativeness)
- Approach to search (enjoyment of shopping, sources of information, etc.)
- Involvement
- Demographics (age, income, education, marital status, household size, social-class, occupation)
- Personality/lifestyle variables (self-confidence, etc.)

Conflict and conflict-resolution strategies

Source: William L. Moore and Donald R. Lehmann, "Individual Differences in Search Behavior for a Nondurable," *Journal of Consumer Research,* **7**:298, December 1980. Reprinted by permission.

(3) neutral sources. Each of these sources offers certain advantages to consumers who might use it.[41]

Marketer-Dominated Sources This source of information is under the direct control of the marketer and includes such means of communication as the product itself, packaging, pricing, advertising, sales promotion, personal selling, displays, and distribution channels.

The advantages favoring consumer use of this source are (1) the information is readily available, (2) it is obtainable with little effort on the consumer's part (i.e., it is low in cost), and (3) it is perceived as competent and technically accurate information. However, consumers may also believe that there are drawbacks to using this source: (1) superficial information may be provided, (2) the information may not be perceived as trustworthy, and (3) all information may not be provided.

Consumer Sources Consumer-oriented channels of communication include all interpersonal sources of information that are not under the direct control of the marketer. These sources are valued for the following reasons: (1) flexibility; that is, the information can be tailored to meet the consumer's needs, (2) trustworthiness, and (3) large amounts of information are available for them. Certain factors hinder the use of this channel by consumers, however. The primary disadvantages are: (1) the information is not always correct, and (2) the information may have to be sought out, which means that it may be high in cost. The nature of this influence process was discussed extensively in Chapter 11.

Neutral Sources Neutral sources include such means as newspaper and magazine articles, government reports, research agencies, and publications by testing groups such as Consumers Union (publisher of *Consumer Reports*). These groups provide product information but are supposedly not directly influenced by either the marketer or consumer. The perceived advantages of using neutral sources are the following: (1) the source is perceived as competent and trustworthy and (2) information is perceived as factual and unbiased.

Utilization of neutral sources (particularly product-testing information) is hindered, however, by the fact that (1) the information may be incomplete (for example, not all brands may be tested and reported on), (2) securing information may be time-consuming or expensive, (3) information may be outdated or incomplete, (4) consumers may need rather highly developed intellectual skills in order to use some of the lengthy and technical product-test information (such as appears in *Consumer Reports*), and (5) consumers may disagree with the emphasis on "rational" performance-related evaluative criteria as opposed to how well the product may satisfy certain social or psychological needs.[42]

Determinants of Information Source Usage Although consumers have access to various sources of information, these sources may have varying degrees of influence.

In terms of exposure, marketer-dominated sources are usually the most important. With regard to the influence criterion, however, consumer and neutral sources are most effective. Which sources consumers choose are determined by the following factors:

1 *Type of information sought.* Consumers usually rely on marketer-dominated sources when searching for information on the availability of alternatives and their attributes. Consumer-dominated sources tend to be relied on more heavily at the evaluation stages of decision making.

2 *Previous experience with product.* If the consumer has had experience with the product, this will affect his reliance on sources of information. For example, if he has previously purchased the item and been satisfied with its use, he is likely to rely simply on the retail store for information rather than on other sources.[43]

3 *Perceived risk.* When perceived risk is high, consumers appear to try to reduce this risk, often through personal sources of information. Consumers have also been found to use neutral sources of information such as seals and certifications (e.g., *Good Housekeeping, Parents' Magazine, Underwriters' Laboratory,* U.S.D.A. Choice) more when there is a high degree of perceived risk.[44]

4 *Type of Product.* Consumer-dominated sources appear to be of great importance for many types of products purchased. For example, in a summary of the information sources for a number of studies on different products it was found that consumer-dominated sources were by far the most important for major appliances. They were also somewhat more important than the next source for new cars, small electrical appliances, new grocery and household items, and clothing. The marketer-dominated retail store was found to be second in overall importance as a source of information. Newspaper ads were also found to be important when style and fashion are important considerations.[45]

THE INFORMATION-EVALUATION PROCESS

As the consumer is engaged in search activity, he or she is also actively engaged in information evaluation. Evaluation involves those activities undertaken by the consumer to carefully appraise, on the basis of certain criteria, alternative solutions to market-related problems. The search process determines what the alternatives are, and in the evaluation process they are compared so that the consumer is ready to make a decision.

Evaluative or Choice Criteria

A consumer evaluates a brand on the basis of a number of choice criteria. These criteria are the standards and specifications the consumer uses in evaluating products and brands. Thus, they are preferred product/brand features that a consumer seeks in a purchase and may be either objective or subjective in nature.[46] For example, a new car buyer may have in mind certain objective characteristics when purchasing, such as mileage and engine characteristics. There may be other criteria which are subjective, however, such as the social-class image projected with the car.

Evaluate criteria may vary from one consumer to another. For example, when purchasing a food processor one buyer may be most concerned about electric motor horsepower, blade revolutions per minute, and safety. Another shopper, however, may use a different set of evaluative criteria, including color and style of the processor, durability, warranty, and versatility: still another shopper may use only price as a criterion.

No matter how many criteria are evaluated by the consumer, they are likely to differ in their importance, usually with one or two criteria being more important than others. Thus, while several evaluative criteria are *salient* to the consumer (i.e., important), some are *determinant* (i.e., they are most important and are also perceived to differ among the alternatives). Some refer to a determinant attribute which meets both of these conditions for a consumer as a *critical* attribute. That is, a critical attribute is the most determinant attribute for that consumer. For instance, in the purchase of running shoes, brand name, quality, price, and comfort may all be important to a buyer, but comfort is likely to have determinance for most runners. Notice that in this case a subjective factor is considered to be most important.

The marketer should be careful in assuming, however, that a certain feature ranked as most important by consumers is actually determinant. For instance, in studies asking consumers to evaluate such automobile attributes as power, comfort, economy, appearance, and safety, consumers often rank safety as first in importance. However, safety is not a determinant attribute to these same consumers, because they do not see various makes of cars as differing widely with respect to safety. Without the knowledge that consumers see small difference among autos with regard to safety, the marketer might naturally conclude that safety *is* a crucial attribute in their purchasing decision, and may therefore stress this feature in promotion efforts. However, these funds might be more effectively used in promoting other attributes that actually determine brand choice. Of course, the marketer would not ignore safety considerations, because then the brand might become perceived as being so unsafe that its share of the market could slip. At that point, safety could achieve determinance until the "unsafe" company brought its product back in line with the others. Thus, determinance should be viewed as a dynamic concept, and marketers must conduct longitudinal research to stay informed of possible shifts in attitudes related to buying behavior.[47]

The number and type of evaluative criteria may vary by product. Consumers generally use few evaluative criteria when purchasing most grocery items. However, when one is purchasing a home, car, or other major durable item, more evaluative criteria would typically be used in the evaluation process. This also means that consumers would tend to use more evaluative criteria for high-involvement products than for low-involvement ones. Generally, however, the number of evaluative criteria used in a consumer decision is six or fewer, although there is some evidence that the number may be as high as nine.[48]

Evaluative criteria may also change over time. As consumers gain new experiences and information, their evaluative criteria may shift. When innovations appear with previously unknown features, consumers may begin to incorporate these features into their evaluative criteria. As they learn from marketers or friends what features they should look for in a particular product purchase, there may be changes in their evaluative criteria. Of course, this has important implications for the marketer who seeks to influence their evaluative criteria favorably toward his brand. As will be mentioned later, however, it is often difficult to change such ingrained decision factors.

Evaluating Alternatives

How do consumers perform the product-evaluation process? Recent research indicates that consumers may use a variety of decision rules in making a brand selection. Consumers often have these decision rules stored in memory and may enact them in a shopping strategy, while at other times they may work them out as they move through the process of evaluating alternatives.[49]

Essentially, there appear to be two basic decision-rule approaches used by consumers in evaluating purchase alternatives: noncompensatory processes and compensatory processes. However, there may be occasions when the consumer does not make full use of either of these approaches stored in memory and instead, takes a constructive approach to the situation by utilizing only fragments or elements of these rules. Such an approach may occur when the consumer has little product experience[50] or when pertinent information is available at the point of purchase.[51] The noncompensatory and compensatory decision-rule formats are discussed below.

Before proceeding, however, assume that the consumer has evaluated four brands of basic electronic calculators along only six dimensions. These evaluative criteria are shown in Table 19-3, along with the consumer's rating of each dimension. Notice also that this shopper has some standards by which these criteria are being evaluated. These are shown as the acceptable levels of performance required on each dimension, that is, as minimum levels of performance which must be met by each brand. Keep in mind that these evaluations are the individual consumer's *perceived* assessments. A truly objective product evaluation might arrive at different results.

Noncompensatory Decision Rules Decision rules are said to be noncompensatory when good performance on one evaluative criterion does not offset or compensate for poor performance on another evaluative criterion of the brand. Several varieties of noncompensatory rules may be used by consumers. The following summary of each type will be illustrated with data from the example provided in Table 19-3.

DISJUNCTIVE RULE This approach is used when the consumer establishes minimum acceptable performance standards which each brand must meet. Any brand will be acceptable if it exceeds the minimum standard on any criterion. The decision rule will then be to select the brand that exceeds the others by the greatest amount on the criterion selected. For example, if the electronic calculator buyer with the evoked set presented in Table 19-3 were to use price as the criterion, the disjunctive decision rule in this case would lead to the choice of the TI 1001, because (1) it is less than $12, and (2) it is the lowest priced alternative in the acceptable group.

CONJUNCTIVE RULE The conjunctive decision rule requires the consumer to establish minimum levels of acceptability on each brand attribute. Thus, for each evaluative criterion of importance to the consumer a cutoff point will be set below which a brand would not be considered further. Table 19-3 shows the minimum levels of acceptability for each evaluative criterion involved in this consumer's pur-

TABLE 19-3
ELECTRONIC CALCULATORS
In Evoked Set

Evaluative Criteria	KMC 3000	Texas Instruments TI 1001	Royal LC-80	Canon LC-20	Acceptable Level
Price	$9.00	$7.00	$13.75	$7.50	Less than $12
Ease of use	Very good	Very good	Fair	Very good	Good
Readability of display	Very good	Fair	Very good	Very good	Good
Warranty	90 Days	1 Year	6 mos. parts, 3 mos. labor	1 year	6 mos.
Functions/features	Fair	Good	Very good	Good	Good
Battery life	Good	Fair	Very good	Very good	Good

chase of an electronic calculator (as determined by the consumer). Based on the conjunctive decision-rule process, every brand but the Canon LC-20 would be discarded from further consideration because each has one or more unacceptable attribute levels. For example, while the KMC 3000 has an acceptable price level and is rated as easy to use, it has a less-attractive warranty and does not offer as complete a range of functions/features as desired by this shopper. Thus, the Canon LC-20 would be the chosen brand if this buyer followed a conjunctive decision-rule process.

LEXICOGRAPHIC RULE   This extension of the disjunctive decision rule allows additional evaluative criteria to be incorporated in the decision if necessary. Thus, if a choice cannot be made by evaluating the most important criterion, other evaluative criteria will be assessed in their order of importance. For instance, assume that the consumer's hierarchy of importance for the evaluative criteria presented in Table 19-3 were as follows: ease of use, functions/features, warranty, price, readability of display, and battery life. Using this decision approach, all brands would be first evaluated on the most important dimension—in this case, ease of use. A tie exists between the KMC 3000, TI 1001, and Canon LC-20, which are all rated as very good. Discarded from any further consideration would be the Royal LC-80 (even though it ranks highest on the next-most-important dimension). The three remaining brands are then assessed on the evaluative criterion of functions/features, and the KMC 3000 would now be dropped from further evaluation. The TI 1001 and the Canon LC-20 are evaluated equally on the next most important dimension, so an additional criterion must be assessed. On the fourth most important attribute, price, the TI 1001 as the lowest-priced brand would be the chosen alternative. Of course, each consumer may have a different hierarchy of importance for these criteria, which would result in other brands being selected by these shoppers.

SEQUENTIAL ELIMINATION RULE   In this decision approach, the consumer has established acceptable performance minimums for each evaluative criterion and then proceeds to evaluate each brand and eliminate any which do not measure up to these minimums. This process is different from the lexicographic approach in that it does not require any specific ordering of attributes. To understand its operation, assume that our calculator shopper evaluated each criterion in the order in which they are shown in Table 19-3. First, price would be considered, and any brand whose price exceeded the acceptable limit would be eliminated. This leaves three remaining brands in consideration (KMC 3000, TI 1001, and Canon LC-20). Next, ease of use is evaluated, and all three brands exceed the minimum, with none being eliminated. Readability of display is assessed next, and the TI 1001 is eliminated because it does not meet the minimum acceptable performance standard. Warranty is the next criterion assessed, and one more model (KMC 3000) is eliminated from consideration. Therefore, the Canon LC-20 would be the brand chosen for purchase using the sequential elimination decision rule.

Comparative advertising strategies are sometimes designed along this approach in an attempt to convince consumers of the wisdom of a course of action. The advertiser may begin by showing all of the brand's competitors and then eliminating them from consideration as certain relevant evaluative criteria are considered. The sponsoring brand is then left as the "obvious" choice from among many competitors.

Compensatory Decision Rule Consumers using a compensatory decision rule will allow perceived favorable ratings or brand evaluative criteria to offset unfavorable evaluations. That is, brand strengths can compensate for brand weaknesses. This approach, therefore, uses more than one evaluative criterion for assessment by consumers. This decision rule should be recognized as similar to the Fishbein multiattribute model discussed in detail in Chapter 16. It evaluates brands individually along all dimensions, or attributes with the overall evaluation being the sum of the weighted ratings along each attribute. The brand obtaining the highest sum would be the brand purchased by the consumer. As an illustration of how this decision rule might operate in the electronic calculator purchase situation, consider the information presented in Table 19-4. This carries the previous information in Table 19-3 one step further by providing a rating of the importance of each evaluative criterion (assigned a weight between 1 and 10) and a quantitative evaluation of how well each brand measures up on these evaluative dimensions (again, assigned a rating between 1 and 10). The evaluation scores are multiplied by the importance weights and summed to provide each brand's total score. The brand scoring highest in terms of total satisfaction contributed would be the alternative selected. In this case, the Canon LC-20 would be purchased.

While it should be emphasized that consumers do not calculate actual scores for brands as shown in Table 19-4, they do: (1) determine the brands to be considered; (2) define their needs and rank them (3) determine the degree to which brands meet their needs; and (4) select the brand that will best meet their most-important needs as they perceive them.[52]

Consensus A growing body of research on decision rules used by consumers indicates that compensatory strategies tend to be utilized under high-involvement conditions when the number of alternatives is small and the evaluative criteria may be large, and by those with greater education.[53] When the consumer is confronted

TABLE 19-4 COMPENSATORY MODEL OF EVALUATION FOR ELECTRONIC CALCULATORS

Evaluative Criteria	Importance Weight (I)	KMC 3000 Evaluation (E)*	I × E	Texas Instruments TI 1001 Evaluation (E)	I × E	Royal LC-80 Evaluation (E)	I × E	Canon LC-20 Evaluation (E)	I × E
Price	9	5	45	10	90	1	9	8	72
Ease of use	10	9	90	9	90	3	30	9	90
Readability of display	7	9	63	3	21	9	63	9	63
Warranty	3	3	9	10	30	6	18	10	30
Functions/features	8	3	24	6	48	9	72	6	48
Battery life	2	6	12	3	6	9	18	9	18
			243		285		210		321

*Assume the following evaluation scoring system:
Very good = 9–10
Good = 6
Fair = 3
Poor = 1

with many alternatives, it appears that a conjunctive decision rule may be used to reduce the alternatives to a manageable number, and then a compensatory strategy may be used to assess the remaining brands for a final decision.

Only the lexicographic and sequential elimination approaches discussed above assume that consumers process information by attribute (CPA), while the remaining alternatives all assumed a processing by brand approach (CPB). The processing approach used by consumers has much to do with marketing strategies. For example, if consumers presently engage in a CPB approach and prefer this manner, then attribute information should continue to be provided in the context of the brand as it is normally now done in promotion and retail displays. However, if consumers prefer to process information by means of a CPA approach, then the attributes themselves might be more prominently featured, such as in retail displays which might group products and brands by salient attributes.[54]

Factors Influencing the Amount of Evaluation

The same factors that were discussed earlier with regard to the extent of search activity will determine the amount of evaluation that occurs. For example, at least to some extent, the following guidelines are true:

1 The more urgent the need, the less evaluation will take place.

2 The more significant the product is to the buyer (e.g., a house, car, boat), the greater the amount of evaluation.

3 The more complex the alternatives, the more evaluation will take place.

Results of Evaluation

The appraisal of information produced during search may have several possible results, depending on the extent to which the buyer reconciles his desired and available alternatives. One outcome is for the consumer to stop searching because he has found an acceptable product which satisfies the recognized problem. At this point, assuming no further constraints, the consumer would purchase the item. A second possibility is for the consumer to discontinue search because no acceptable product has been identified. A third possible outcome is for the consumer to continue searching even though no acceptable alternative has yet been found. At this point, he obviously feels that the benefits of continued search outweigh the costs involved.

Alternative Evaluation in Low-Involvement Situations

The information-evaluation process differs under low-involvement conditions because it mainly occurs after purchase, not before. That is, the consumer has some expectations, but not strong ones, about the product's anticipated performance. Purchase may occur based on name recognition (drilled in through advertising) of the brand in the store. Although the consumer perhaps has been exposed to the brand's name and attributes, no strong belief about the brand has been formed at this stage. Thus, the consumer makes a purchase anticipating that the brand will confirm certain expectations. As use occurs, the consumer evaluates the brand and develops attitudes toward it that may lead to repurchase, if favorable, or to brand switching, if unfavorable. Even though the consumer's attitudes toward the brand may be favorable based on usage of the item, brand switching is still likely to occur because several other brands may be seen to be relatively equal in quality, and any of these brands offering an incentive to purchase (e.g., coupon or price rebate) may get the consumer's nod.

MARKETING IMPLICATIONS

There are a number of marketing implications that flow from this exposition of search and alternative evaluation processes. In this section, we shall examine some of the significant ramifications of this process for the marketer's task.

Researching the Information-Seeking Process

In order for the marketer to influence the process of search and alternative evaluation, he first must have information about it among his market segments. There are several pieces of the information-processing puzzle that he should seek to fill in (assuming that search activity is engaged in by a significant segment of his market). First, he needs to determine what sources of information are actually used by consumers. Next, he must determine each source's influence.

Determining Sources of Information Several useful approaches by which data may be gathered on information-source effectiveness were discussed in Chapter 3. For example, the techniques of verbal protocols, eye movement analysis, information monitoring, observation, and surveys may be usefully applied in this situation. Although these methods are growing in popularity, the following two research activities probably represent the easiest and most widely used approaches to date.

WARRANTY CARDS Where appropriate, many marketers use warranty registration cards to gather data on the information seeking activities of their customers. These questionnaires enable the respondent to check the source of information as well as the place of purchase for a product. However, these cards are often so small, in order to be machine-processed, that the amount of information obtainable on them is rather limited. Thus, such questions as where the consumer shopped (as opposed to purchased) and which information source was the most important are usually left for the company to speculate about. As a result, this type of research approach, although useful, leaves many unanswered questions for the marketer attempting to make distribution or promotion decisions.

IN-DEPTH RESEARCH The marketer may also utilize cross-sectional or longitudinal research approaches to obtain information on consumer search processes. While cross-sectional approaches may be acceptable for products with relatively short decision times, longitudinal studies may be more useful, especially when the decision time for a product is long.

When formulating questionnaires to be used in such studies, it is suggested that the influence of information sources can be obtained by asking several types of questions:[55] (1) *specific influence* questions about the decision process itself (rather than specific sources), such as "How did you learn about this new product?" or "Why did you decide to buy this brand?" (2) questions *assessing overall influence,* such as, "Overall, what was the most important thing in causing you to purchase this product?" and (3) questions about *exposure* to various sources of information, such as checklists like those used on warranty cards.

Determining Source Influence We learned in the previous chapter that analysis of purchase intentions and fulfillment rates over time could help to pinpoint weaknesses in marketing strategy. One of the variables that needs to be assessed to determine its strength or weakness is the influence of information sources on brand-purchase intentions and fulfillment.

Building on the discussion in the last chapter, we can see the type of analysis that might be necessary in order for the marketer to secure greater intention-fulfillment rates. Several steps of analysis are required. First, the marketer should determine the effectiveness of information sources to which consumers of each brand are exposed. This necessitates gathering data for each brand and each information source with regard to whether that source was effective for consumers, and the degree of its effectiveness. Once this information is known, brands can then be compared on the basis of how effective each information source is. It may be found, for example, that one brand's word-of-mouth and television advertising is especially ineffective when compared to other brands.

One typology that has been suggested for comparing various information sources categorizes each one according to the following dimensions:[56]

1 *Decisive effectiveness*—The consumer evaluates this source as having a major or dominant impact on the decision process.

2 *Contributory effectiveness*—The consumer evaluates this source as playing a specific role in the decision process, although it is not among the most important sources.

3 *Ineffective*—This source is rated as having no particular role in the decision process, even though exposure to it did occur.

Several other facets of analysis would be helpful in isolating the problem. For example, analysis of information source effectiveness by type of customer (demographic or psychographic bases) would help to determine which consumers are being effectively or ineffectively influenced. Of course, once the weak link in the information search and evaluation process is known (such as poor word-of-mouth advertising), the reasons for the poor performance must still be determined and corrected.

Influencing the Consumer's Evoked Set

It is also beneficial for the marketer to determine whether his brand is perceived as being in the consumer's evoked, inert, or inept set.[57] The marketer can conduct research among a sample of consumers to determine all the brands they are aware of, the brand names that they do and do not consider buying, as well as the reasons for this. Using this approach, the marketer can learn what percentage are aware of his brand and which awareness set it primarily falls into. From such study, it is likely that the marketer will find that although consumers are aware of many brands in a product category they generally hold only a few brands in their evoked and inept sets. If the marketer determines that a large share of the market is unaware of his brand, this would indicate the need for an intensified advertising campaign. Reasons for a brand's position within consumers' awareness sets may also be learned by assessing information on their evaluative beliefs regarding the brand. This information may help explain why certain brands are in the evoked set while others are in the inept set. For instance, it may be learned that many consumers reject the marketer's brand because of its physical characteristics, or dislike of the brand's advertising, or lack of adequate information with which to evaluate the brand. Thus, the marketer might rectify these problems by modifying the physical features of the brand, changing the ad copy, or utilizing comparative advertising and free samples. As a result of such strategies, a brand currently in consumers' inept set may be able to move into their inert or evoked sets.

Measuring Evaluative Criteria

In order for the marketer to develop a successful marketing mix, there must be an understanding of what criteria are used by consumers in making a purchase decision for this product, as well as how important each criterion is, and how the consumer rates each brand on the various criteria. Each of these topics will be discussed below.

Determining Which Criteria Are Used by Consumers The marketer will first need to determine which evaluative criteria are used by consumers in a purchase decision. This may be accomplished by *directly asking* consumers what factors they consider when they compare alternatives for purchase. It might be done in a survey questionnaire format, or perhaps through a focus group meeting. The greatest drawback to this approach is that it assumes that consumers know why they buy or prefer one product to another, and it assumes that they are willing to provide the requested information. Recall from Chapter 3, however, that consumers may at times be unwilling or unable to accurately answer such questions. For example, they may provide the researcher with "socially acceptable" responses rather than their true feelings. In addition, they may have forgotten what the most-important criterion was in a recent purchase. In order to secure valid data using this approach, the marketer should seek to develop questioning/measuring approaches that very carefully obtain the desired information.

If the marketer believes that consumers cannot or will not directly reveal their evaluative criteria, then an *indirect* approach may be utilized. In this situation, the marketer may for instance, ask the consumer what evaluative criteria she thinks "someone else" would use. This type of questioning allows consumers to acceptably project their own attitudes through another individual.

Still another technique for determining evaluative criteria is *perceptual mapping*. One approach to this involves multidimensional scaling (MDS), in which consumers rate, two at a time, brand alternatives along a scale ranging from similar to dissimilar. The responses are processed by a computer, and a graphic output is produced revealing the extent to which consumers perceive these alternatives to be similar. The axes of such a map are assumed to be the evaluative criteria by which consumers made their judgments of similarity/dissimilarity. That, however, is one of the drawbacks to the approach. Because the marketer must infer the criteria and label these axes based on intuition or additional research conducted, there is great room for subjectivity and mistake in the process. (See Figure 5-12 for an example of a perceptual map.)

Determining the Importance of Criteria Used by Consumers Once the evaluative criteria are known, a second measure that the marketer will find useful is the relative importance consumers place on these criteria. That is, the marketer is seeking to know the salience of each attribute in a purchase decision. A direct method for researching this could involve the use of a *rating scale* method whereby consumers would be asked to evaluate the salience of each criterion on a 6-point scale ranging from perhaps "unimportant" to "important." Another approach would be to use a *semantic differential,* with pairs of adjectives characterizing the criteria, such as "high price" and "low price." A third approach involves what is known as a *constant sum scale,* in which respondents typically allocate 100 points across the evaluative criteria according to their judgment of each one's importance. For example, a buyer of a ceiling fan might make the following allocation according to his perceived importance of each attribute:

Evaluative Criteria	Importance (in points)
Motor quietness	20
Electricity consumption	5
Cubic feet per minute of air moved at high speed	25
Style	30
Price	10
Warranty period	15
	100

For this consumer, style is perceived as being most important, followed by ability to circulate air, quietness of motor, length of warranty, price, and rate of electricity consumption.

Merely asking consumers which attributes are important in choosing a product may not be sufficiently meaningful to allow the focus to be narrowed to attributes which truly determine consumer behavior. Thus, a dual questioning approach may be much more useful. In this approach, consumers are first asked what factors they consider important in a purchasing decision. Next, they are asked how they perceive these factors as differing among the various brands. This approach is illustrated in Tables 19-5 and 19-6, which were developed from a survey of the general public in a major metropolitan area relative to attitudes towards savings-and-loan associations.[58]

These results illustrate that while some items rank high in importance (e.g., safety of money, government reassurance), they are not thought to differ much among the various savings-and-loan associations. Therefore, these attributes are not the most determinant, even though they are rated as being among the most important. Conversely, some elements differ greatly among the various associations (e.g., years in business, parking convenience) but have relatively little influence in determining the choice of a savings-and-loan association. Additionally, some attributes are viewed as being very important, and a large percentage of those responding said that there is a big difference (and a small percentage saying there is no difference) between associations. Thus, such features as interest rates and financial strength may be relatively determinant attributes.

Conjoint analysis is another technique that offers marketers the opportunity to determine the salience of consumers' evaluative criteria. Conjoint measurement starts with the consumer's overall judgments (expressed as preference or likelihood of purchase orderings, or as any other explicit judgmental criterion) about a set of complex alternatives (perhaps expressed as combinations of various potential attributes such as alternative package designs, prices, and brand names), and

TABLE 19-5

IMPORTANCE RATINGS OF SAVINGS AND LOAN CHARACTERISTICS

Benefit or Claim	Average Ratings*
Safety of money	1.4
Interest rate earned	1.6
Government insurance	1.6
Financial strength	2.0
Ease of withdrawing money	2.0
Management ability	2.0
Attitude of personnel	2.1
Speed/efficiency of service	2.2
Compounding frequency	2.2
Branch location convenience	2.3
Time required to earn interest	2.3
Parking convenience	2.4
Years in business	2.5
Other services	3.1
Building/office attractiveness	3.4
Premiums offered	4.0

*1—"extremely important" 3—"fairly important"
2—"very important" 4—"slightly important"

Source: James H. Myers and Mark I. Attitudes: Meaning and Measurement," *Journal of Marketing,* **32:**15, October 1968, published by the American Marketing Association, Chicago.

then proceeds to decompose these original evaluations into separate utility scales by which the original global judgments can be reconstituted. Computation of the utility scales of each attribute, which determines how important each is in consumers' evaluations, is accomplished by various computer programs. Such an approach can provide managers with valuable information about the relative importance of various attributes of a product, as well as the value of various levels of a single attribute.[59]

TABLE 19-6

DIFFERENCE RATING OF SAVINGS AND LOAN CHARACTERISTICS

Benefit or Claim	Big Difference	Small Difference	No Difference	Don't Know
Years in business	52%	31%	10%	6%
Financial strength	40	32	22	6
Parking convenience	37	35	22	6
Safety of money	36	15	47	2
Management ability	35	26	27	12
Government insurance	35	11	51	3
Branch location convenience	34	36	28	2
Attitude of personnel	34	28	33	5
Interest rate earned	33	30	35	2
Speed/efficiency of service	32	28	35	5
Ease of withdrawing money	29	18	48	5
Compounding frequency	28	36	31	5
Time required to earn interest	26	34	33	7
Building/office attractiveness	24	44	30	2
Other services offered	21	34	29	16
Premiums offered	15	36	38	11

Source: James H. Myers and Mark I. Alpert, "Determinant Buying Attitudes: Meaning and Measurement," *Journal of Marketing,* **32:**16, October 1968, published by the American Marketing Association, Chicago.

Determining Consumers' Evaluations of Brand Criteria Performance In this case, the marketer is seeking judgments by consumers relating to performance on various evaluative criteria by the brand. Many of the measurement techniques discussed in Chapter 3 are available for use in this situation. For instance, a sample of respondents, using a semantic differential, might rate the performance of various evaluative criteria found to be important for a particular brand of stereo receiver. A summary of the individual respondents' ratings could then be compiled. Such information allows the marketer to better judge the strengths and weaknesses of a brand on dimensions of importance to consumers.

Influencing Consumers' Evaluation

The marketer may decide to change his brand's image upon finding that his brand suffers from continued existence in consumers' inept or inert sets. If he pursues this change, he has a choice between two main strategies. He may alter the characteristics of dominant cues and/or he may alter the information value of the cues.[60]

Altering Cue Characteristics Changing the characteristics of a dominant cue can have a dramatic effect on the product image. This is particularly important in the many cases where brands are perceived very similarly. The marketer may be able to move his brand from the inert or inept set into the consumer's evoked set by a very minor change in a cue (for example, making an electric food mixer slightly noisier so that it seems more powerful to consumers). A "just noticeable difference" between brands can be accomplished by emphasizing a minor (but easy to evaluate with high confidence) difference in product, price, or package. Moreover, such changes appear to be more effective than claiming a large and nearly unbelievable (that is, difficult to evaluate with confidence) brand difference (such as, "This electric food mixer is powerful enough to churn concrete.").

Altering Information Value Rather than changing characteristics of a cue, the marketer may attempt to change the way consumers evaluate a product. For instance, rather than changing the sound of the mixer in the above example, the marketer could educate consumers to base their evaluation of power on another cue (such as horsepower rating or wattage). Thus, the marketer may seek to increase the degree of association in the mind of the consumer between horsepower rating and actual mixer power. This might be accomplished through advertising and personal selling efforts. At the same time, the marketer may attempt to teach consumers how to be sure that a given horsepower rating was adequate or inadequate for a mixer (so that consumers could confidently evaluate the cue).

It should be carefully noted, however, that the marketer will generally find it difficult to change the evaluative criteria consumers use to assess products. Attempts to educate consumers or convince them of the "error of their ways" in terms of past product evaluation criteria they have used generally fall flat. Such evaluative criteria are so thoroughly embedded in consumers' minds (particularly in high-involvement purchasing conditions) that they are very resistant to conversion. As a result, consumers may selectively screen-out messages seeking to change these criteria, and they may continue to hold their previous views. Obviously, marketers will at times need to educate consumers as to the "proper" evaluative criteria to use in purchasing (see Figure 19-2). However, criteria that fly in the face

FIGURE 19-2

Advertisement for Ross bicycle. (Courtesy of Chain Bike Corporation.)

of consumers' common-sense perceptions will find difficulty in gaining acceptance among large segments of the market.

How Much Information for the Consumer?

It is felt by many in legislative, regulative, and judicial circles that the consumer does not have adequate information on which to base decisions. Critics of current marketing practices claim that much factual information relevant to consumer choice is simply unavailable and that this results in higher prices, "artificial" brand differences, and a stress on frills that represent no real value to consumers. Marketers, on the other hand, rebut these claims by noting that in many of the cases in which product promotions contained numerous facts, there has been little positive effect on sales. In addition, marketers feel that if consumers really wanted and would use more product information, our system of competition would provide it.[61]

In any event, there is growing pressure for businesses to provide more and better quality information so that more rational or better decisions can be made by consumers. A result of this belief has led to a number of consumer information programs.

Unit Pricing Unit pricing means that the retailer not only displays the total price of the item, but also displays the price per relevant unit of the product (such as dollars per pound, fluid ounce, and so forth). The basis for this program arose from consumerists who alleged that consumers could not identify the most-economical item in a product class because of the large variety of brands, package sizes, and quantity sizes (e.g., jumbo, super, giant, large economy size, and so on), and the poor presentation of quantity information on packages. Even educated shoppers sometimes find it difficult to identify the most-economical items.

The results of studies on usage of unit pricing have not been consistent, however. Most have found higher usage among higher socioeconomic categories rather than among the lower-income groups who might appear really to benefit most from them. Research generally indicates a high awareness among consumers of unit pricing, but much variability with regard to claimed usage and effectiveness.[62] There are at least two reasons for such findings. First, even with access to unit price information, consumers may not necessarily buy the most-economical item because of such factors as brand quality differences and the convenience of smaller but more expensive sizes (such as to a single elderly buyer). Second, the method of unit price information presentation varies considerably. Some unit price programs have been very effectively introduced and run, while others meet the letter of the law without really facilitating consumers' usage.

Nutritional Labeling With the growing concern over dietary deficiencies among the American public (particularly among young people) and the increasing demand to know what really goes into the foods we eat, manufacturers have been under pressure to increase their nutritional labeling.[63] Yet, whether consumers are able to understand and thus use such additional information is questionable. It has been shown that some consumers would refer to additional nutritional information and could buy more nutritious products as a result.[64] But just how much information should be provided is not clear. One study showed that consumers preferred labels with moderate levels of nutritional information, compared with those with either the least or the most information.[65]

As with research on unit pricing, most studies on nutrient labeling have found that consumers in lower socioeconomic categories are less likely to use such information.

Open Dating This is the practice whereby dates are printed on packaged food products to inform consumers of their freshness. Consumers appear to desire this information more than unit pricing or nutrient labeling. However, studies conducted on open dating indicate that only a small percentage of consumers are able to interpret the dates. Moreover, the system of dating used in most programs is the one least preferred by consumers.[66]

Truth-In-Lending The effects of federal truth-in-lending legislation (which requires full disclosure of the rate of finance charges and other aspects of a consumer credit transaction) are also unclear. One study showed that although the practice of making such information available apparently improves consumer knowledge of credit rates and charges, it has been found to do little to change credit behavior because of the importance of the retailer in the credit decision. Moreover, it was shown that most consumers (particularly those with lower incomes and education) remained uninformed about interest rates; many did not even understand the concept of interest, nor could they calculate it in dollars. Thus, this study concluded that consumers must not simply be provided with information but should also be taught to understand it and use it.[67]

Are Consumers Overloaded with Information? Many of the foregoing research studies on consumer-information programs indicated that consumers do not heavily use them. What causes this lack of use? Some researchers suggest that the problem may be the result of information overload. That is, there are limits to the amount of information that consumers can process; hence, too much information is dysfunctional for them.[68]

The first systematic study of the information-overload phenomenon was done by Jacoby and his colleagues, in which subjects were asked to make decisions on product brands with varying quantities of information.[69] The researchers concluded that as the amount of information increased, consumers were less able to select the brand best for them; yet, the information had beneficial effects on the consumer's degree of satisfaction, certainty, and confusion regarding his selection. That is, subjects appeared to feel better with more information while actually making worse purchase decisions! This result was taken to mean that an information-overload phenomenon had been identified. Similar results were found in a succeeding study in which information overload was observed to be related to an increase in the number of brands. It was found, however, that increased information per brand resulted in better decisions.[70]

Critics of these two studies raised a number of conceptual and methodological issues.[71] Moreover, reanalysis of the data obtained in these research projects with a more powerful analytical procedure, resulted in the finding that information overload had not occurred in the experiments.[72] However, recent research by Malhotra of a more-complex product-choice situation (house buying), incorporating four different means of information overload, with a more sophisticated analytical methodology, has again led to a finding of information overload.[73] Thus, additional replication is desirable across other decision-making situations in order to understand the nature and extent of the information-overload phenomenon.

How does the consumer cope with information overload? There may be several strategies employed to reduce the amount of information actually used in purchase decision making so as not to be overwhelmed by the great amount available. It has been suggested that consumers base their decisions on the most important three to five product-attribute dimensions rather than on all of the information available.[74] Another suggestion is that consumers organize and integrate the separate information bits into larger information "chunks," as described in the learning chapter. For example, a brand name may serve as the consumer's basic device for summarizing the impressions and comparisons that exist among brand alternatives in the marketplace.[75]

Although few definitive statements can yet be made, the concept of information overload may become an extremely important issue among marketers, consumerists, legislators, regulators, and others who seek to provide even more information to the consumer. The "more information is better" argument, however, may result in American shoppers feeling better but making worse purchase decisions.

For the marketer to provide more information than he now does may also prove to be uneconomical. For instance, industry experience indicates that a 30-second television commercial is economically superior to a 60-second ad both in terms of recall and sales (except in the case of new products). Thus, if the marketer were compelled to run a longer commercial in order to provide more information to the consumer, this would be uneconomical from the brand's own standpoint, although perhaps justifiable from the position of industry's obligation to the consumer. Perhaps it is possible to restructure ads to provide more of the "right kind" of information within the same time limit. In order to resolve this potential problem, more advertising research will be needed.[76]

SUMMARY

This chapter has expanded our discussion of consumer decision processes by examining search and alternative evaluation. First, the meaning of information search was discussed, and it was found that consumers may engage in active or passive, and internal or external search activities.

The information-seeking process was then described. Although consumers do not appear to rely to any great extent on marketer-dominated sources of information, the true extent of search activity is not well known. The amount of information-seeking activity was seen to be determined by a number of factors. The types of information sought as well as the major sources of consumer information were also discussed.

Consumer evaluation was extensively discussed and conceptualized according to various decision rules by which consumers determine which products to buy. Finally, several marketing implications of search and evaluation activities were presented.

DISCUSSION TOPICS

1 Distinguish between active and passive, internal and external search.

2 "Consumers should read more advertisements and visit more retail stores during the information-gathering stage of the decision process." Evaluate this statement.

3 What are the benefits and costs of search activity?

4 What types of risk might consumers perceive in a purchase situation? How might consumers deal with these risks? How could the marketer seek to minimize each type?

5 Read several recent product rating reports contained in *Consumer Reports* and evaluate the rating system used. What other information would you find helpful?

6 Choose a product category and develop a table similar to Table 19-5. Show what decision each evaluation method discussed in the text would yield.

7 Visit a local supermarket and attempt to evaluate five brands of cereal by employing the processing-by-attribute model. What conclusions do you reach?

8 Select a product category and design a warranty registration card that you think would provide insight into the information-search and evaluation process.

9 Visit a supermarket and select one aisle of products to obtain the following information:
  a Number of products
  b Number of brands
  c Number of sizes in each brand

Based on this experience, do you think there is information overload? Why or why not?

NOTES

[1] Robert F. Kelly, "The Search Component of the Consumer Decision Process—A Theoretic Examination," in Robert L. King (ed.), *Marketing and the New Science of Planning,* American Marketing Association, Chicago, 1968, p. 273.

[2] Elizabeth C. Hirschman and Michael K. Mills, "Sources Shoppers Use to Pick Stores," *Journal of Advertising Research,* 20: 47–51, February 1980.

[3] James R. Bettman, "Data Collection and Analysis Approaches For Studying Consumer Information Processing," in William D. Perreault, Jr. (ed.), *Advances in Consumer Research: Volume 4,* Association for Consumer Research, Atlanta, 1977, pp. 342–345.

[4] Chem L. Narayana and Rom J. Markin, "Consumer Behavior and Product Performance: An Alternative Conceptualization," *Journal of Marketing,* 39:2, October 1975.

[5] Narayana and Markin, "Consumer Behavior," p. 2.

[6] James R. Bettman, *An Information Processing Theory of Consumer Choice,* Addison-Wesley, Reading, MA, 1979, pp. 132–133.

[7] James R. Bettman and C. Whan Park, "Effects of Prior Knowledge and Experience and Phase of the Choice Process on Consumer Decision Processes: A Protocol Analysis," *Journal of Consumer Research,* 7:234–248, 1980.

[8] Louis P. Bucklin, "The Informative Role of Advertising," *Journal of Advertising Research,* 5:11–15, 1965.

[9] George Fisk, "Media Influence Reconsidered," *Public Opinion Quarterly,* 23:85, 1959.

[10] "Food Shoppers Shop Newspaper Ads: FTC," *Advertising Age,* September 15, 1980, p. 4.

[11] Jon G. Udell, "Prepurchase Behavior of Buyers of Small Electrical Appliances," *Journal of Marketing,* 30:51, October 1966.

[12] William P. Dommermuth, "The Shopping Matrix and Marketing Strategy," *Journal of Marketing Research,* 2:130, May, 1965.

[13] George Katona and Eva Mueller, "A Study of Purchasing Decisions," in Lincoln H. Clark (ed.), *Consumer Behavior: The Dynamics of Consumer Reaction,* New York University Press, New York, 1955, pp. 30–87.

[14] Louis P. Bucklin, "Testing Propensities to Shop," *Journal of Marketing,* 30:22–27, January 1966.

[15] Ernest Dichter, *Handbook of Consumer Motivations,* McGraw-Hill, New York, 1964, pp. 82–83.

[16] Wesley C. Bender, "Consumer Purchase-Costs—Do Retailers Recognize Them?" *Journal of Retailing,* 40:1–8, 52, Spring 1964.

[17] Bucklin, "Testing Propensities to Shop."

[18] Anthony Downs, "A Theory of Consumer Efficiency," *Journal of Retailing,* 37:7, Spring 1961.

[19] William P. Dommermuth and Edward W. Cundiff, "Shopping Goods, Shopping Centers and Selling Strategies," *Journal of Marketing,* 31:32, October 1967.

[20] Melvin T. Copeland, "Relation of Consumers' Buying Habits to Marketing Methods," *Harvard Business Review,* April 1923.

[21] Richard H. Holton, "The Distinction Between Convenience Goods, Shopping Goods, and Specialty Goods," *Journal of Marketing,* 23:53–56, July 1958.

[22] Dommermuth and Cundiff, "Shopping Goods"; Katona and Meuller, "A Study of Purchasing"; Bucklin, "Testing Propensities to Shop"; and Udell, "Prepurchase Behavior."

[23] Joseph F. Dash, Leon G. Schiffman, and Conrad Berenson, "Information Search and Store Choice," *Journal of Advertising Research,* 16:35–40, June 1976.

[24] Donald F. Cox (ed.), *Risk Taking and Information Handling in Consumer Behavior,* Division of Research, Graduate School of Business, Harvard University, Boston, 1967, pp. 5–6.

[25] The first five risks listed were suggested in Jacob Jacoby and Leon Kaplan, "The Components of Perceived Risk" in M. Venkatesan (ed.), *Proceedings of the Third Annual Conference of the Association for Consumer Research,* Association for Consumer Research, Chicago, 1972, pp. 382–393. The sixth risk was suggested in Ted Roselius, "Consumer Rankings of Risk Reduction Methods," *Journal of Marketing,* 35:56–61, January 1971.

[26] Roselius, "Consumer Rankings," pp. 57–58.
[27] See Dommermuth and Cundiff, "Shopping Goods"; Dommermuth, "The Shopping Matrix"; and Jagdish N. Sheth and M. Venkatesan, "Risk-Reduction Processes in Repetitive Consumer Behavior," *Journal of Marketing Research,* 5:307–310, August 1968.
[28] John A. Howard, *Marketing Management: Analysis and Planning,* rev. ed., Irwin, Homewood, IL, 1963, p. 58.
[29] See for example George Katona, *The Mass Consumption Society,* McGraw-Hill, New York 1964, pp. 289–290; Paul E. Green, Michael Halbert, and J. Sayer Minas, "An Experiment in Information Buying," *Journal of Advertising Research,* 4:17–23, September 1964; and G. David Hughes, Seha M. Tinic, and Philippe A. Naert, "Analyzing Consumer Information Processing," in Philip R. McDonald (ed.), *Marketing Involvement in Society and the Economy,* American Marketing Association, Chicago, 1969, pp. 235–240.
[30] Katona and Mueller, "A Study of Purchasing"; Joseph Newman and Richard Staelin, "Multivariate Analysis of Differences in Buyer Decision Time," *Journal of Marketing Research,* 8:192–198, May 1971; Peter D. Bennett and Robert Mandell, "Prepurchase Information Seeking Behavior of New Car Purchasers—The Learning Hypotehsis," *Journal of Marketing Research,* 6:430–433, November 1969; and John E. Swan, "Experimental Analysis of Predecision Information Seeking," *Journal of Marketing Research,* 6:192–197, May 1969.
[31] Swan, "Experimental Analysis"; Katona, *The Mass Consumption Society;* and Frederick E. May, "Adaptive Behavior in Automobile Brand Choices," *Journal of Marketing Research,* 6:62–65, February 1969.
[32] Geroge Katona, *Psychological Analysis of Economic Behavior,* McGraw-Hill, New York, 1951, pp. 67–68.
[33] Katona, *The Mass Consumption Society,* pp. 289–290.
[34] David T. Kollat, "A Decision-Process Approach to Impulse Purchasing," in Raymond M. Haas (ed.) *Science, Technology and Marketing,* American Marketing Association, Chicago, 1966, pp. 626–639; and Bucklin, "Testing Propensities to Shop."
[35] Katona and Mueller, "A Study of Purchasing."
[36] Kelly, "The Search Component," p. 277.
[37] Paul E. Green, "Consumer Use of Information," in Joseph W. Newman (ed.), *On Knowing the Consumer,* Wiley, New York, 1966, p. 76.
[38] Kelly, "The Search Component," p. 277.
[39] Donald F. Cox, "The Audience as Communicators," in Stephen A. Greyser (ed.), *Toward Scientific Marketing,* American Marketing Association, Chicago, 1963, pp. 58–72.
[40] Bruce LeGrand and Jon G. Udell, "Consumer Behavior in the Market Place," in *Journal of Retailing,* 40:32–40, 47, Fall 1964; Newman and Staelin, "Multivariate Analysis"; and Katona and Mueller, "A Study of Purchasing."
[41] Cox, "The Audience as Communicators."
[42] See Hans B. Thorelli, Helmut Becker, and Jack Engledow, *The Information Seekers,* Ballinger, Cambridge, MA, 1975, p. 19.
[43] Newman and Staelin, "Multivariate Analysis."
[44] Thomas L. Parkinson, "The Influence of Perceived Risk and Self-Confidence on the Use of Neutral Sources of Information in Consumer Decision-Making," in Barnett A. Greenberg (ed.), *Proceedings: Southern Marketing Association 1974 Conference,* pp. 298–301.
[45] Joseph W. Newman and Bradley D. Lockeman, *Consumers' Information-Seeking Processes for Fashion Goods: A Literature Review,* Bureau of Business Research, University of Michigan, Ann Arbor, MI, 1972, p. 88.
[46] John A. Howard, *Consumer Behavior: Application of Theory,* McGraw-Hill, New York, 1977, p. 29.
[47] James H. Myers and Mark I. Alpert, "Determinant Buying Attitudes: Meaning and Measurement," *Journal of Marketing,* 32:14, October 1968.
[48] James F. Engel and Roger D. Blackwell, *Consumer Behavior,* 4th ed., Dryden Press, New York, 1982, p. 418.
[49] Bettman, *An Information Processing Theory of Consumer Choice,* pp. 179–185.
[50] James R. Bettman and Pradeep Kakkar, "Methods for Implementing Consumer Choice in Product Class Experience," in Subhash C. Jain (ed.), *Research Frontiers in Marketing Dialogues and Directions,* American Marketing Association, Chicago, 1978, pp. 198–201; and James R. Bettman and Michael A. Zins, "Constructive Processes in Consumer Choice," *Journal of Consumer Research,* 4:75–85, September 1977.
[51] James R. Bettman and C. Whan Park, "Implications of a Constructive View of Choice for the Analysis of Protocol Data: A Coding Scheme for Elements of Choice Processes," in Jerry C. Olson (ed.), *Advances in Consumer Research: Volume 7,* Association for Consumer Research, Ann Arbor, MI, 1980, pp. 148–153.
[52] Henry Assael, *Consumer Behavior and Marketing Action,* Kent, Boston, 1981, p. 38.
[53] Michael L. Rothschild, "Advertising Strategies for High and Low Involvement Situations," in John C. Maloney and Bernard Silverman (eds.), *Attitude Research Plays for High Stakes* American Marketing Association, Chicago, 1979, pp. 74–93; and Denis A. Lussier and Richard W. Olshavsky, "Task Complexity and Contingent Processing in Brand Choice," *Journal of Consumer Research,* 6:154–165, September 1979.

[54] Engel and Blackwell, *Consumer Behavior*, pp. 423–424.
[55] Engel and Blackwell, *Consumer Behavior*, p. 335.
[56] Engel and Blackwell, *Consumer Behavior*, p. 334.
[57] Narayana and Markin, "Consumer Behavior."
[58] Myers and Albert, "Determinant Buying Attitudes," p. 16.
[59] Paul E. Green and Yoram Wind, "New Way to Measure Consumers' Judgments," *Harvard Business Review*, 53:108–109, July/August 1975.
[60] Donald F. Cox, "The Sorting Rule Model of the Consumer Product Evaluation Process," in Donald F. Cox (ed.), *Risk Taking and Information Handling in Consumer Behavior*, pp. 365–368.
[61] William L. Wilkie, *Public Policy and Product Information: Summary Findings from Consumer Research*, National Science Foundation (RANN), Washington, DC, 1975, p. vii.
[62] See, for example, Kent B. Monroe and Peter J. La Placa, "What Are the Benefits of Unit Pricing?" *Journal of Marketing*, 36:16–32, July 1972; and Monroe Peter Friedman, "Consumer Responses to Unit Pricing, Open Dating, and Nutrient Labelling," in M. Venkatesan (ed.), *Proceedings,* pp. 361–369.
[63] Warren A. French and Hiram C. Barksdale, "Food Labelling Regulations: Efforts toward Full Disclosure," *Journal of Marketing*, 38:14–19, July 1974.
[64] Raymond C. Stokes, "The Consumer Research Institute's Nutrient Labelling Research Program," *Food Drug Cosmetic Law Journal*, 27:263–270, May 1972.
[65] Edward H. Asam and Louis P. Bucklin, "Nutrition Labelling for Canned Foods: A Study of Consumer Response," *Journal of Marketing*, 37:32–37, April 1973.
[66] Friedman, "Consumer Responses."
[67] George S. Day and William K. Brandt, "Consumer Research and the Evaluation of Information Disclosure Requirements: The Case of Truth in Lending," *Journal of Consumer Research*, 1:21–32, June 1974.
[68] G. A. Miller, "The Magical Number Seven, Plus or Minus Two: Some Limits on Our Capacity for Processing Information," *Psychological Review*, 63:81–97, 1956; and Richard N. Cardozo, "Customer Satisfaction: Laboratory Study and Marketing Action," in L. George Smith (ed.) *Reflections on Progress in Marketing,* American Marketing Association, Chicago, 1964, pp. 283–289.
[69] Jacob Jacoby, Donald E. Speller, and Carol A. Kohn, "Brand Choice Behavior as a Function of Information Load," *Journal of Marketing Research*, 11:63–69, February 1974.
[70] Jacob Jacoby, Donald E. Speller, and Carol Kohn Berning, "Brand Choice Behavior as a Function of Information Load—Replication and Extension," *Journal of Consumer Research*, 1:33–42, June 1974.
[71] J. Edward Russo, "More Information Is Better: A Reevaluation of Jacoby, Speller and Kohn," *Journal of Consumer Research*, 1:68–72, December 1974; John O. Summers, "Less Information Is Better?" *Journal of Marketing Research*, 11:467–468, November 1974; and William L. Wilkie, "Analysis of Effects of Information Load," *Journal of Marketing Research*, 11:462–416, November 1974.
[72] Naresh K. Malhotra, Arun K. Jain, and Stephen W. Lagakos, "The Information Overload Controversy: An Alternative Viewpoint," *Journal of Marketing*, 46:27–37, Spring 1982.
[73] Narish K. Malhotra, "Information Load and Consumer Decision Making," *Journal of Consumer Research*, 8:419–430, March 1982.
[74] Fleming Hansen, "Consumer Choice Behavior: An Experimental Approach," *Journal of Marketing Research*, 6:436–443, November 1969; and Jerry Olson and Jacob Jacoby, "Cue Utilization in the Quality Perception Process," in M. Venkatesan (ed.), *Proceedings,* pp. 167–179.
[75] Jacoby, Speller, and Berning, "Brand Choice Behavior."
[76] John A. Howard, "Conceptualizing the Adequacy of Information," in M. Venkatesan (ed.), *Proceedings,* pp. 99–100.

CHAPTER 20
PURCHASING PROCESSES

In this chapter we shall be looking at the actual purchasing process of consumers, seeking to build a better understanding of how consumers make their purchases. Purchasing processes involve not only the purchase decision, but also activities directly associated with the purchase. The purchase-decision stage itself involves selecting a course of action based on the preceding evaluation process. Some of the elements of the purchasing process stage, such as choosing a store, may actually be viewed as part of search and evaluation activities. However, because they are more directly connected with making a purchase, they are best discussed at this point. Thus, we are considering in this chapter the various facets of the consumer purchase environment of which the marketer should be aware in order to attract the chosen segments successfully.

The first topics to be discussed in this chapter will be the motives consumers have for shopping and the matter of consumer store choice. This will be followed by a presentation of research findings regarding both in-store and out-of-store purchasing behavior. Finally, we shall examine some repeat purchasing patterns. Implications of these topics to the marketer will be discussed throughout the chapter.

WHY DO PEOPLE SHOP?

Before discussing the subject of why consumers shop where they do, a more basic question might be asked—Why do people shop? The obvious answer that "they need to purchase something" may not reflect the consumer's actual motivation in each circumstance. It has been suggested that both personal and social motives influence consumer shopping activities. The following list has been suggested from exploratory research by means of individual in-depth interviews with men and women:[1]

Personal Motives

Role Playing: Many activities are learned behaviors, traditionally expected or accepted as part of a certain position or role in society—mother, housewife, husband, or student.

Diversion: Shopping can offer an opportunity for diversion from the routine of daily life and thus represents a form of recreation.

Self-Gratification: Different emotional states or moods may be relevant for explaining why (and when) someone goes shopping. For example, a person may go to a store in search of diversion when he is bored or go in search of social contact when he feels lonely. Thus, the shopping trip is motivated not by the expected utility of consuming, but by the utility of the buying process itself.

Learning About New Trends: Products are intimately entwined in one's daily activities and often serve as symbols reflecting attitudes and lifestyles. An individual learns about trends and movements and the symbols that support them when he visits a store.

Physical Activity: Shopping can provide people with a considerable amount of exercise. Some shoppers apparently welcome the chance to walk in centers and malls.

Sensory Stimulation: Retail institutions provide many potential sensory benefits for shoppers. Customers browse through a store looking at the merchandise and at each other; they enjoy handling the merchandise. Sound can also be important, such as a "noisy" environment or one which is characterized by silence or soft background music. Even scent may be relevant.

Social Motives

Social Experience Outside the Home: Shopping can provide the opportunity for a social experience outside the home (e.g., seeking new acquaintenances or meeting those of the opposite sex). Some shopping trips may result in direct encounters with friends (e.g., neighborhood women at a supermarket); for others the social contact may be more indirect, as exemplified by the pastime of "people watching."

Communication With Others Having a Similar Interest: Stores that offer hobby-related goods serve as a focal point for people with similar interests to interact. People like to talk with others about their interests, and sales personnel are frequently sought to provide special information concerning the activity.

Peer Group Attraction: The patronage of a store sometimes reflects a desire to be with one's peer group or a reference group to which one aspires to belong. Certain stores provide a meeting place where members of a peer group may gather.

Status and Authority: Many shopping experiences provide the opportunity for an individual to command attention and respect. A person can expect to be "waited on" without having to pay for this service, and can attain a feeling of status and power in this limited "master-servant" relationship.

Pleasure of Bargaining: For some shoppers, bargaining is an enjoyable process by which goods can be reduced to a more reasonable price. To the extent that a person perceives himself as a wise shopper, he will seek bargains in fixed-price situations by looking at relative prices between stores (comparison shopping) or relative prices over time (special sales).

Thus, consumers' motives for shopping are a function of many variables, some of which are unrelated to the actual buying of products. Consequently, retailers need to understand the variety of shopping motives that may be present and incorporate this information into retailing strategy.

CHOOSING A STORE

We all like to think of ourselves as intelligent shoppers. But how do consumers actually make store-choice decisions? Basically, the consumer has certain evaluative store criteria established in her mind and compares these with her perception of a store's characteristics. As a result of this process, stores are categorized as either acceptable or unacceptable, and hence will be patronized on that basis. If the resulting shopping experience is favorable, the consumer is reinforced in her learning experience and the matter of store choice will become largely routinized over a period of time.

It is clear from this description that consumers engage in a decision-process approach for store choice as well as for product and brand choices. Thus, much of what we have already said regarding choice processes applies here also. For example, consumers may face complex store-choice decisions, or they may be able to routinize their store decisions. A couple new to an area may face a complex decision process as new store patronage patterns are being developed, particularly for clothing or durables. However, a long-time resident or one facing a convenience-good purchase will probably have the decision process refined to more of a habitual or routinized response.[2]

A summary model of the store-choice process is presented in Figure 20-1.

FIGURE 20-1

Sequence of effects in store choice. (*Source:* Kent B. Monroe and Joseph P. Guiltinan, "A Path-Analytic Exploration of Retail Patronage Influences," *Journal of Consumer Research,* **2**:21, June 1975.)

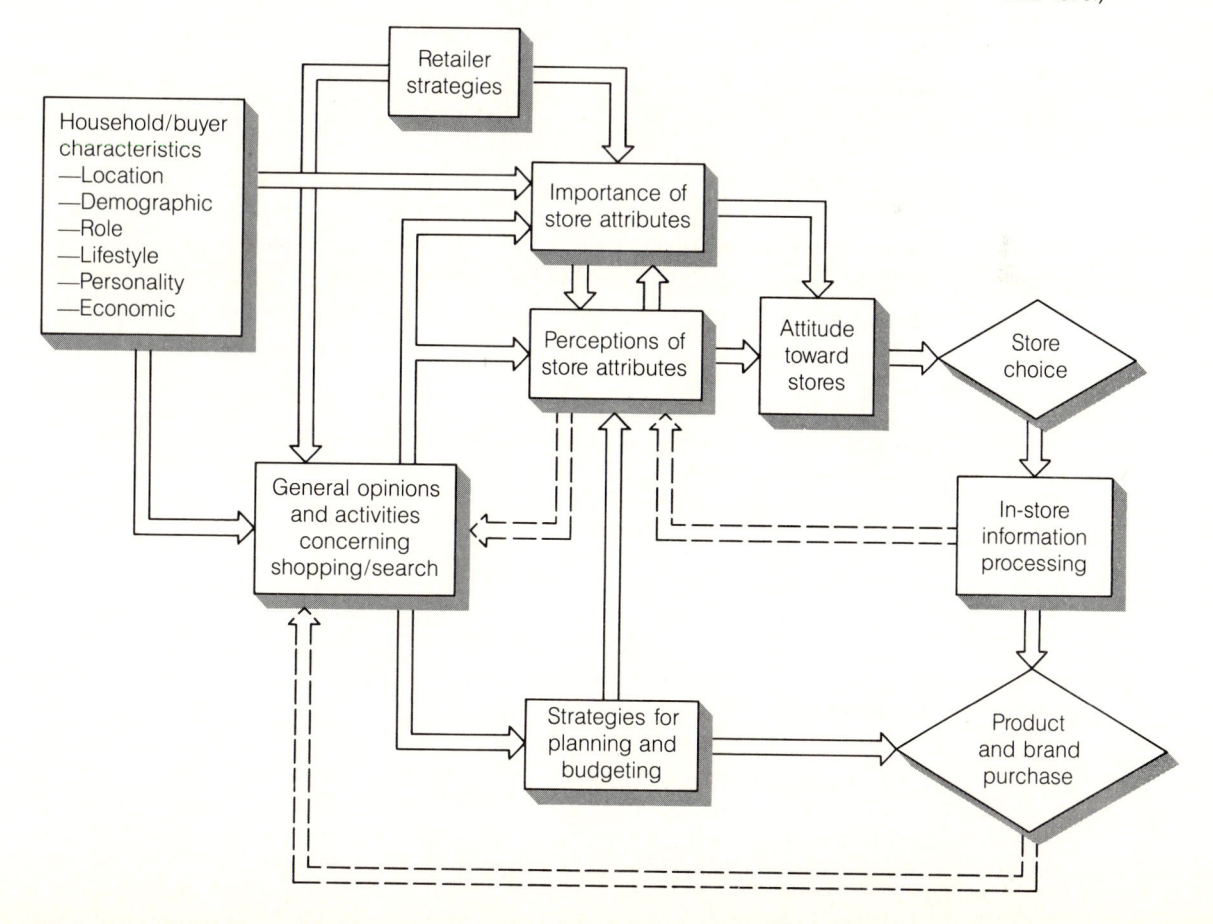

This flowchart depicts the relative directions of influences among variables involved in store-choice behavior. The model indicates that demographic characteristics, lifestyle characteristics, and other buyer characteristics lead to general opinions and activities concerning shopping and search behavior. These consumer characteristics also affect the importance consumers place on store attributes as they evaluate store alternatives and the consumer's store perception or store image. The consumer's store attitudes then influence store choice and ultimately the product and brand-choice decision. Satisfaction with the process will lead through feedback to a reinforcement in the store's image, which will then increase the likelihood of continued patronage, that is, greater store loyalty.[3]

In selecting a store to shop, just as in selecting products and brands within stores, the consumer makes use of certain information sources. One research study which assessed the source shoppers use to pick stores found that previous shopping was more important than advertising. Table 20-1 illustrates, for two cities, the information sources usually used for retail shopping trips. This finding suggests that only a limited number of consumers—generally less than half—engage in active external information search when making retail trips. Thus, most consumers appear to be using a routinized behavior pattern. This may mean that retail advertisers may be restricted in potential effectiveness to less than half of the target population.[4]

Factors Determining Store Choice

There are several important factors that influence consumer store-choice behavior. Although the influence of these elements differs, depending on such variables as the type of product purchased, the type of store (such as discount, department, or other), and the type of consumer, the factors discussed in this section have been found to exert general influence on store choice. They include store location, physical design, assortment, prices, advertising, sales promotion, personnel, and services.

Store Location Location has an obvious impact on store patronage. Generally, the closer consumers are to a store, the greater their likelihood to purchase from that store. The further away consumers are from a store, the greater the number of intervening alternatives, and thus the lower the likelihood to patronize that store. Research on the influence of location on store choice has taken several directions described in the following sections.

TABLE 20-1 INFORMATION SOURCES USUALLY USED FOR RETAIL SHOPPING TRIPS

	City A N	City A %	City B N	City B %
Habit	234	48.2	253	54.3
Newspaper advertisement	188	38.3	179	38.4
Friend or relative	26	5.4	11	2.4
Television commercial	14	2.9	9	1.9
Radio commercial	5	1.0	3	0.6
	471	100.0	465	100.0

Source: Elizabeth C. Hirschman and Michael K. Mills, "Sources Shoppers Use to Pick Stores," *Journal of Advertising Research*, **20**:49, February 1980.

INTERCITY CHOICE Marketers have long been interested in the factors that cause consumers outside metropolitan areas to choose city A rather than city B in which to shop. Reilly and Converse conducted research on the drawing power of urban areas on consumers located near these cities. Believing that population and distance were not the causes of consumer store choice but could be used as good substitute variables for all the factors influencing consumers, Reilly developed a "law of retail gravitation" to explain the strength of one city's attraction on consumers living near it.[5] In effect, this law states that two cities attract retail trade from an intermediate city or town in the vicinity of the breaking point (that is, where 50 percent of the trade is attracted to each city) approximately in direct proportion to their population and in inverse proportion to the square of the distances from these two cities to the intermediate town. Reilly tested this law by computing the breaking point between thirty pairs of cities. The predictions were very close to results of actual field studies in which the breaking point was measured.

In applying the laws of retail gravitation it should be kept in mind that they were meant to apply only to two large cities. In addition, the laws apply only to the division of shopping goods trade, and particularly to fashion goods (often referred to as style or specialty goods), because a large part of convenience and bulk goods is purchased locally.[6] Although the work by Reilly and Converse has helped marketers to conceptualize intermarket behavior, these laws are incomplete as explanations for store-choice behavior because they ignore such factors as income levels, the character of retailing in the two cities, and consumer preferences.

While the above approach has taken a macro orientation to the examination of intermarket patronage, others have taken a micro approach, which rests on the assumption that consumers have different characteristics and therefore have a differential predisposition to forego secondary costs such as time, money, and effort in selecting one trade area over another. Studies have found that consumers frequently shop out-of-area *(outshoppers),* and they can be distinguished from non-outshoppers by certain demographic and psychographic characteristics.[7]

INTRACITY CHOICE As shopping centers developed during the period since 1950, researchers began to investigate their influence on the shopping behavior of consumers. These suburban alternatives to the central downtown shopping district introduced new wrinkles in explaining store choice.

To determine the factors that influence store choice within urban areas, some studies have examined the role of driving time on shopping center preference. Travel times longer than 15 minutes appear to be a barrier to many shopping center patrons.[8] Those who are willing to drive longer times seem to be attracted by the size of the shopping center.[9] Another study indicates, however, that location of the shopping center is not nearly as important as other variables, such as price, value, variety of product and store, store quality and cleanliness, and friendly sales personnel.[10] This result is contrary to the emphasis placed on distance measures in most site location models.

An important aspect of store choice as it pertains to store location is that the consumer's perceived location has been found to be more important in understanding shopping patterns than actual store or shopping area location.[11] Thus, cognitive maps incorporating consumers' cognized shopping distances and travel times are finding increased use among consumer researchers. Consumers have been found to generally overestimate both their actual distance and time.

Other work in the area of shopping center preference has been done by Huff, who developed a model to determine the retail trade area for a shopping center.[12] The model estimates the probability that shoppers in homogeneous geographical segments (such as census tracts or neighborhoods) will visit a particular shopping center for a particular type of product purchase. The two fundamental variables associated with probability of patronage are square feet of floor space in the shopping center and travel time to the center. These variables substitute for population and distance used in Reilly's model.

Although Huff's model achieves a higher level of sophistication than Reilly's, it nevertheless fails to adequately incorporate variables that may influence consumer store preferences.[13] The use of travel time and shopping center size, although important, are not the only factors that influence store choice.[14] Lusch has developed a model of patronage behavior which incorporates key concepts from geography, social psychology, and economics, and it appears to offer a more complete explanation of shopping behavior.[15]

INTERSTORE CHOICE Store location can also be very influential in shopper choice among competing stores, especially through its effect on store image. For example, stores in attractive surroundings are more likely to be patronized than those in unattractive surroundings. The remainder of this section looks at other components of a store's image and the way in which these factors affect store choice.

Store Design and Physical Facilities As we noted in Chapter 13, the design characteristics of a store visibly reflect its image and can dramatically influence patronage.[16] Many consumers appear to "size up" a store based on its outward appearance of architecture and signs and hence are drawn to the store or repelled by it, based on their perception of whether this store looks "right" for them. Interior design continues the image-fostering process. Such design features as store layout, aisle placement and width, carpeting, and architecture, as well as physical facilities in a store, including elevators, lighting, air conditioning, and washrooms, influence store assessment by consumers.[17]

Merchandise This image element has to do with the goods and services offered by a retail outlet. There are five attributes considered to be important here: quality, selection or assortment, styling or fashion, guarantees, and pricing. For example, the product variety and assortment of a store have been found to influence store choice. Consumers prefer stores that offer either a wide variety of product lines, brands, and prices, or substantial depth to their assortment, such as in sizes, colors, and styles, over stores with only medium depth or breadth of assortment.[18]

Of course, manufacturers contribute to the variety available by launching new brands. For instance, research on forty leading packaged-goods product categories found 2696 brand names in existence (excluding private labels), a 9 percent increase in 5 years.[19]

Evidence on the influence of merchandise price on store choice behavior has been mixed. For example, among supermarket shoppers, some studies indicate that price is very important, while others have found it relatively unimportant.[20] The same is true for discount store shoppers.[21] Some department store shoppers have also reported that price is not a very high-priority reason for selecting a particular store.[22] Yet, more recent research for both supermarkets and department stores indicates that prices are an important factor.[23] Thus, perhaps during periods of high inflation or economic recession this variable assumes greater significance to consumers. Nevertheless, it is difficult to draw firm conclusions about the overall significance of price on store-choice behavior.

Advertising and Sales Promotion Within this category, such influences as advertising, sales promotion, displays, trading stamps, and even symbols and colors are considered important. Retail advertising does not have a consistent impact but instead appears to vary in influence, depending on product and store type. Nevertheless, it is certainly true that retail advertising can be important in fulfilling any of its three goals: (1) to inform consumers, such as for a new store opening, (2) to persuade consumers that they should patronize a certain store or buy a particular brand, and (3) to remind customers of the store that they are appreciated. As we also have learned, advertising can be highly influential in cultivating a store image in consumers' minds.

The effect of sales-promotion activities on store choice also appears to be rather inconsistent. One means of sales promotion for stores has been the use of trading stamps which had a history of growth until the early 1960s and then declined.[24] Although some consumers place great importance on stamps, they rarely seem to have enough significance to be a dominant factor in choice.[25] During the 1970s and 1980s the use of sweepstakes has increased greatly among companies, from an estimated 300 in 1975 to 1000 nationally advertised contests in 1981.[26] These are said to appeal to one of the consumer's most basic instincts: greed.

Personnel Employees of a retailer also are very instrumental in influencing the store's image. Consumers generally desire to trade where store personnel, particularly salespeople, are helpful, friendly, and courteous.[27] For example, shopping center preference is strongly influenced by such factors, as demonstrated in one survey of five large metropolitan areas which found salesperson knowledgeability and helpfulness to be an important element in choice for more than 75 percent of those questioned.[28]

If salespeople are not properly selected and well-trained, the results may be devastating for sales. One estimate has it that 70 percent of all consumers who stop patronizing a particular store do so because of employee attitude. In fact, one study found that some salespeople often preferred to purchase in competing stores because they considered their coworkers to be too uncooperative.[29]

Other research indicates that less than one-half of consumers interviewed in a national study believe what a salesperson tells them, and that the situation has worsened over time.[30]

Customer Services Retail stores may offer numerous services in order to attract customers. One scheme classifies services according to those which (1) increase product satisfaction (such as credit, alterations, installation, and shopper information), (2) increase convenience (such as delivery, telephone ordering, and parking), and (3) provide special benefits (such as gift wrapping, product returns, and complaint offices).[31]

The extent of the effect of customer services on store choice is unclear. Generalizations are difficult in view of the conflicting evidence, and appear to vary considerably across products and consumers. Not to be minimized, however, is the importance of post-transaction satisfaction which may relate not only to the merchandise in use, but also to any returns or adjustments that may be necessary. Such a factor is particularly important in store-choice decisions for such high-involvement products as automobiles, major appliances, and furniture. This topic will be discussed in greater detail in the following chapter.

Clientele As we learned earlier, consumers' store choices have much to do with their social-class membership. Consumers will tend to patronize those stores where persons similar to themselves are perceived to be shopping. Thus, an important matching process occurs between the consumer's self-image and the store's image to influence where people shop, with choices being made of stores that possess images which are similar to the images that consumers perceive of themselves.[32]

Store Atmosphere This image attribute has to do with atmosphere, that is, the quality of the store surroundings. Kotler cites the importance of *atmospherics* (which is defined as the conscious designing of buying environments to produce specific emotional effects in buyers, that enhance their purchase probability) in several examples, such as the following:[33]

> Fine furniture retailers provide mock room settings featuring integrated furniture arrangements in order to help the customer in problem solving. Piped-in soothing background music immerses the buyer in a positive feeling toward the store and its furniture.

> Large department stores often operate a bargain basement selling lower-priced lines of merchandise or marked-down items for customers pursuing bargains. The atmosphere is typically stark and functional, with narrow aisles, harsh lighting, and counters loaded with chaotically arranged merchandise which reinforces the bargain image.

Not only are the nonperson atmospheric elements of the retail store important (such as shelf space, in-store point-of-purchase promotion, lighting, noise, aisle design, and square footage), but also important are the atmospherics created by shoppers within the retail store.[34] One of the intended or unintended products of various current merchandising emphasis is retail crowding. This store atmosphere consequence is a result of high-density shopping environments, such as regional malls and super stores, as well as population shifts and concentrated shopping hours for working families. The result of such perceived crowding is to systematically affect shopping behavior and consumer feelings about retail outlets and shopping trips.[35]

Attribute Importance Varies by Store

How important is each of these attributes when customers make store choice decisions? It depends on the store type. Department store shoppers seem to be concerned about the quality of the store's merchandise, the degree of ease of the shopping process, and post-transaction satisfaction. Grocery shoppers are concerned about the store's merchandise mix, ease of the shopping process, and cleanliness of the store.

The Effect of Store Image on Purchasing

Store image is a complex of tangible or functional factors and intangible or psychological factors that a consumer perceives to be present in a store. It is the way in which the store is defined in the consumer's mind.[36] The various determinants of store choice just discussed are intimately related to a store's image and influence its attracting power. Consequently, retailers need to understand what evaluative criteria consumers use in store choice, how important each criterion is, what image consumers have of the retailer's store, and how this image compares to an ideal image and to competitors' images. Berry has suggested the model presented in Figure 20-2 as being useful for retailers making image decisions. Specific programs similar to this reflect the need for store managers to determine the unique market segments they want to attract and then develop a store image useful in influencing patronage by those segments. The need to periodically review desired market segments and the consistency of store image to those segments is also stressed. Such activities should prove useful in satisfying consumer needs and in maintaining the vitality of the organization.

General Shopper Profiles

It has been found that consumers tend to shop at different stores, depending partly on their demographic characteristics and their attitudes toward shopping. One useful approach to establishing a customer typology on this basis was that suggested by Stone who has identified four types of shoppers: (1) economic, (2) personalizing, (3) ethical, and (4) apathetic.[37] Although probably no single consumer is adequately described by any of the models, they do represent composites of actual consumers and their characteristic role orientations.

The *economic consumer* is a close approximation to the classical economist's "economic man." She is quite sensitive to price, quality, and assortment of merchandise. Clerical personnel and the store are viewed merely as instruments of her purchase of goods.

The *personalizing consumer* shops where she is known by name. Strong personal attachments are formed with store personnel, and this personal, often intimate, relationship is crucial to her store-patronage decision.

The *ethical consumer* shops where she feels she "ought" to. That is, she is willing to sacrifice low prices or wide merchandise selection in order to "help the little guy out" or because "the chain store has no heart or soul." She sometimes forms strong attachments with personnel and store owners.

The *apathetic consumer* shops only because she "has" to. Shopping is viewed as an onerous task and one to be completed quickly. Convenient location is her crucial store selection criterion, and since she is not interested in shopping, she minimizes her expenditure of effort in purchasing products.

What is particularly interesting is that each of these consumer types was characterized by a distinctive pattern of social position and community identification. For example, economic consumers were lower-middle-class housewives with little allegiance to the area. Personalizing consumers had lower social status and a positive allegiance to the local area. Ethical consumers were relatively high in social status and long-time residents in the area, while apathetic consumers were char-

FIGURE 20-2

Image-decision program for department stores. (*Source:* Leonard L. Berry, "The Components of Department Store Image: A Theoretical and Empirical Analysis," *Journal of Retailing,* Spring 1969, p. 18. Reproduced by permission of *Journal of Retailing,* New York University.)

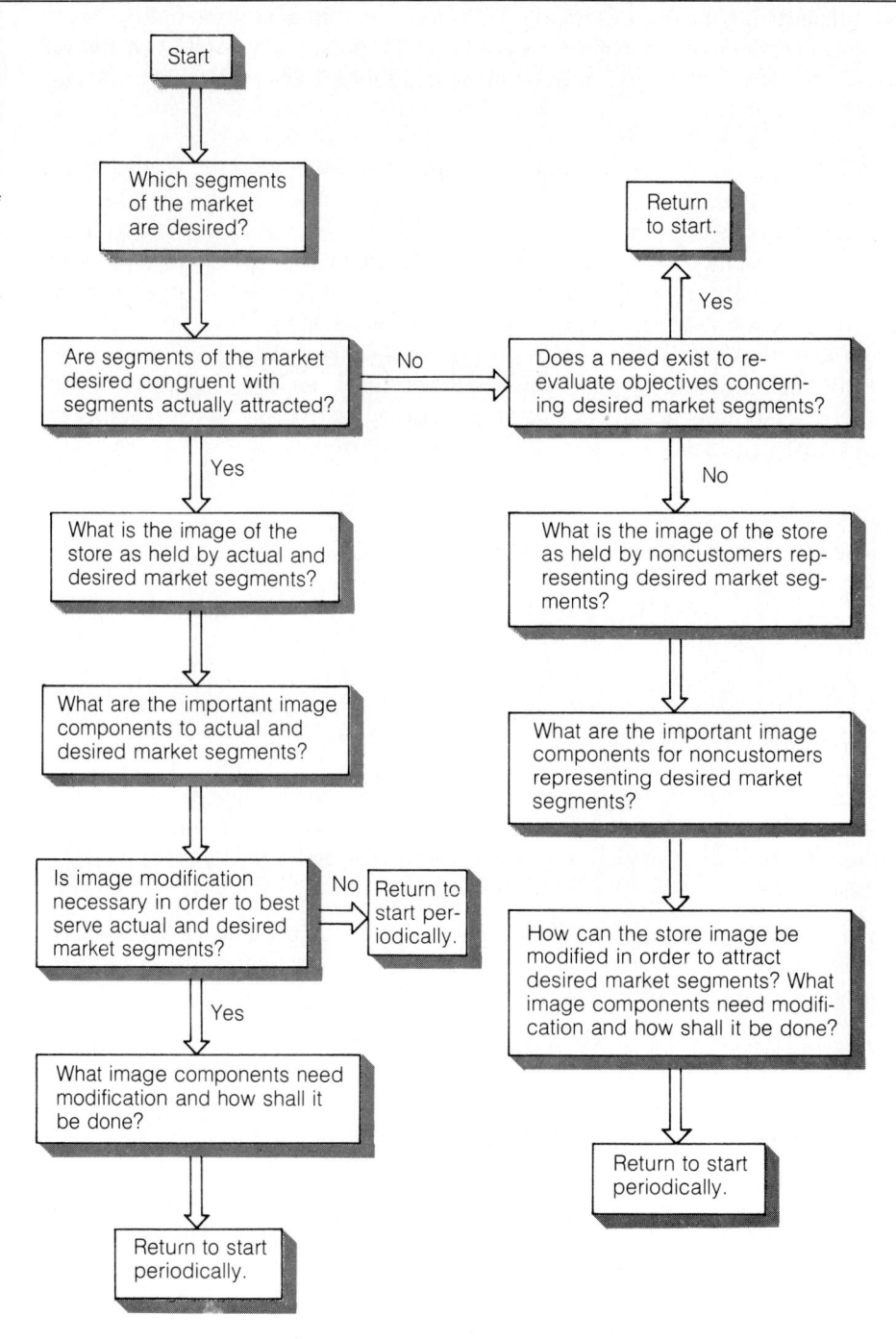

Start

↓

Which segments of the market are desired?

↓

Are segments of the market desired congruent with segments actually attracted? —No→ Does a need exist to reevaluate objectives concerning desired market segments? —Yes→ Return to start.

↓ Yes ↓ No

What is the image of the store as held by actual and desired market segments?

What is the image of the store as held by noncustomers representing desired market segments?

↓ ↓

What are the important image components to actual and desired market segments?

What are the important image components for noncustomers representing desired market segments?

↓ ↓

Is image modification necessary in order to best serve actual and desired market segments? —No→ Return to start periodically.

How can the store image be modified in order to attract desired market segments? What image components need modification and how shall it be done?

↓ Yes ↓

What image components need modification and how shall it be done?

Return to start periodically.

↓

Return to start periodically.

acteristically older women who were also long-time residents. Stone's typology has been supported by more recent empirical research.[38] Other consumer taxonomies have also been developed on the basis of shopping orientations, and research is continuing in this field.[39]

Store-Specific Shopper Profiles

It has been found that consumers tend to shop at different stores, depending on their demographic/socioeconomic and lifestyle attributes. For instance, one study has characterized those who shop most often at either traditional department stores (e.g., Foley's, Abraham & Straus), national chain department stores (e.g., Sears, J. C. Penney), or discount department stores (e.g., K mart) with the following results:[40]

Traditional department store shoppers are described as

- singles, under and over age 35
- older couples with no dependent children
- from higher social classes
- higher in educational attainment
- players of bridge or golf
- innovative in apparel purchases
- placing high importance on store's layout and atmosphere, but less importance on merchandise pricing and the savings at sales

National chain department store customers were found to be described as

- most likely to carry credit cards for this type of store
- attending movies more regularly
- emphasizing merchandise variety and pricing

Discount department store customers can be described as

- families with children over age 6
- lowest in having traditional or national chain department store credit cards
- from the lower social classes
- having low educational attainment
- nonparticipants in social activities such as golf, bridge, or movies
- most concerned with merchandise pricing and sale savings

Shoppers may also be characterized in greater detail by retailers of each store type as a useful way of segmenting the market.[41] For example, the marketer may desire to know more about his store's frequent customers and may be able to develop a portrait of the demographic, psychographic, and media patterns of store shoppers.

Store Loyalty

The term "store loyalty" refers to the consumer's inclination to patronize a given store during a specified period of time. Because consumer patronage results in revenue, store loyalty can be a very important factor influencing the company's profits. Loyal customers will tend to concentrate their purchases in the store and therefore may represent a very profitable market segment if they can be readily identified. Consequently, an important question for the marketer concerns the wisdom and ease of attracting this segment.

First of all, it is known that store loyalty among consumers can be measured in the marketplace. It is also thought that store loyalty may be diminishing. According to a recent study, 41 percent of the housewives in 1954 shopped in one supermarket exclusively. In 1975, however, only 10 percent were that loyal.[42] It should also be mentioned that store loyalty may vary by store type as well as consumer type. For example, some evidence indicates that although store loyalty may be high for supermarkets, little loyalty appears to exist for department stores.

Second, it appears that the financial benefit to the retailer of pursuing the store-loyal consumer may be very significant. With regard to supermarket customers, for example, one writer states that the greatest opportunities lie in attracting the best possible mix of customer loyalties for the traffic that the store will carry. Particularly when many competitors exist, a store's best bet for holding and increasing sales volume is to improve the quality of its customer loyalty mix.[43] In support of this, one research study found that more-loyal consumers allocate much larger proportions of their expenditures to their first choice store than do less-loyal consumers, and that stores with the largest number of loyal customers have the largest market share. Moreover, loyal customers were found to be no more expensive to serve than nonloyal customers.[44]

Several studies have examined the demographic, socioeconomic, and psychographic characteristics of store-loyal shoppers and found that there are patterns of personal characteristics.[45] The generally store-loyal consumer tends to be older, have a lower educational attainment, and a lower family income than the store switcher. Psychographically, she tends not to be a fashion opinion leader, style conscious, venturesome in trying new products, urban-oriented, gregarious, or a credit user. However, she does tend to be time-conscious, and a radio and television user. Thus, the store-loyal's profile is one of a relatively conservative, inactive, time-conscious, home-town oriented person. She expresses a positive attitude toward local shopping conditions but negative attitudes toward shopping in the nearest large city.[46]

Another study finds that highly store-loyal shoppers engage in less comparison search among stores before purchasing, know about the existence of and have visited fewer stores, and concentrate their purchases in a smaller subset of stores than do other consumers.[47]

Store loyalty seems to represent a potentially profitable approach to market segmentation for at least some stores, although research findings have been limited and not altogether consistent. In order to capitalize on store loyalty, the retailer needs to know a significant amount about his loyal customers. However, since loyalty is not a strongly inherent consumer trait and cannot be identified in advance of shopping behavior, the retailer must seek to identify loyal patrons by the frequency of their shopping activity. Interviews could then be held with these patrons to determine the extent of their loyalty to the store, their particular wants and needs, and purchase behavior patterns such as their mass media exposure, store hour preferences, and credit card usage. Store credit card usage, particularly, is often an important dimension of patron behavior and may distinguish heavy shoppers and purchasers from lighter store users. For instance, the average charge customer spends about four times as much at Sears as a cash customer.[48]

Not only should the marketer seek to understand the store loyalty characteristics and patterns of her own customers but also of her competitors' customers. Generally, it is important to learn as much as possible about why these families buy where they do. One element of the research should involve measuring the store's image in relation to the images of competitors. As a result of this kind of research, the marketer will be able to identify specific marketing programs to attract more store-loyal customers.

IN-STORE PURCHASING BEHAVIOR

Once consumers have selected the stores they will patronize, they must then proceed to consummate the purchase. A number of factors influence consumers' behavior within the store environment. In this section, we shall examine some of the important variables affecting consumer shopping activities within stores.

Merchandising Techniques

Merchandising techniques have an important influence on consumer shopping behavior. This is particularly true for low-involvement purchase decisions. For example, it is known that nearly two out of three supermarket purchase decisions are not specifically planned.[49]

Because there is generally little consideration of such purchases until at the point of sale, merchandising techniques affecting the consumer in the store are often of great significance in securing purchase. A number of topics are discussed under the umbrella of merchandising techniques, including store layout, displays, product shelving, pricing strategies, branding, and promotional deals.

Store Layout and Traffic Patterns A store's interior is organized in such a manner as to accomplish the firm's merchandising strategy. Retailers sometimes find, however, that their layout and design approach is failing to achieve company objectives. In such cases, a new store design may be necessary. Two recent examples of such a change are Montgomery Ward & Co. and K mart.

> Ward's had acquired the image of being behind-the-times. The strategy chosen was to change the chain's appearance by adding selling space at little or no cost and engineering store layouts to steer shoppers toward the most profitable merchandise. Such techniques used were: (1) painting interior walls beige and installing neutral-colored carpet so as not to detract from the merchandise; (2) converting long supermarket-style aisles into short aisles in a honeycomb-maze arrangement, so that shoppers could encounter aisle-ends containing eye-catching product displays; and (3) installing more interior walls to help organize products by category and to boost available display space.[50]
>
> K mart's growth through expansion has diminished due to its saturation of stores in all of the top metropolitan areas in the United States. Consequently, the chain is trying for more volume, and more profitable volume per store,

from the cost-conscious consumers attracted to K mart. In order to get K mart customers to spend more, the cavernous buildings of plain design filled with racks, bins, and metal shelves are changing to emphasize the merchandise at least as much as the price signs. Clothing and other goods are now of a higher quality and are being displayed in ways that are intended to stimulate increased impulse buying. In addition, rather than having shoppers being greeted by a popcorn stand as many K marts used to do, shoppers in the new format are met by a jewelry and camera department. Besides cut-rate auto filters and folding lawn chairs, these K marts now handle German wines, designer eyeglass frames, and gourmet cookware.[51]

Much of the research on store layout and its effect on consumers has been done in supermarkets. For example, supermarkets are traditionally organized on the basis of the following principles:

1 Spread major departments and demand items as widely as possible in order to expose more customers to more products.

2 Place service and perishables departments adjacent to work areas to reduce time and effort for servicing them.

3 Place high-margin, high-impulse departments and categories in the flow of traffic before demand products. As a result, impulse purchases are made before planned purchases.[52]

Figure 20-3 presents an example of a contemporary approach to supermarket layout showing traffic pattern data.

Traffic pattern studies are very popular with retailers in order to determine where good or bad sales areas are within the store. Supermarkets especially conduct such research in order to determine optimum layout and placement of goods. Shopper activity is diagrammed on these layouts for both density and main direction of traffic for each aisle and for passing and buying rates within the aisles. From these statistics, it can readily be seen that shoppers shop a store in different ways. There are also differences in the times spent in the store among different patrons. Consequently, depending on the type of shopper and the length of time spent shopping, different expenditures result.[53]

Although use of passing, buying, and passing-buying ratios can be helpful in visualizing *what* consumers did, they fail to explain *why* these patterns exist. Thus, further research would need to be conducted by the retailer to understand why such passing and buying ratios exist and how a change in store layout could alter these patterns.

Additional research might also be conducted to determine consumers' ease in locating items. Because there are indications that shoppers are inaccurate in their perceptions of product location within supermarkets,[54] this could lead to greater use of locational cues to aid their product search.

Displays An effective combination of good store layout and attractive displays can change a humdrum retail environment into one that not only is more exciting but also produces more sales.

Special displays are used in stores in order to attract shopper attention to one

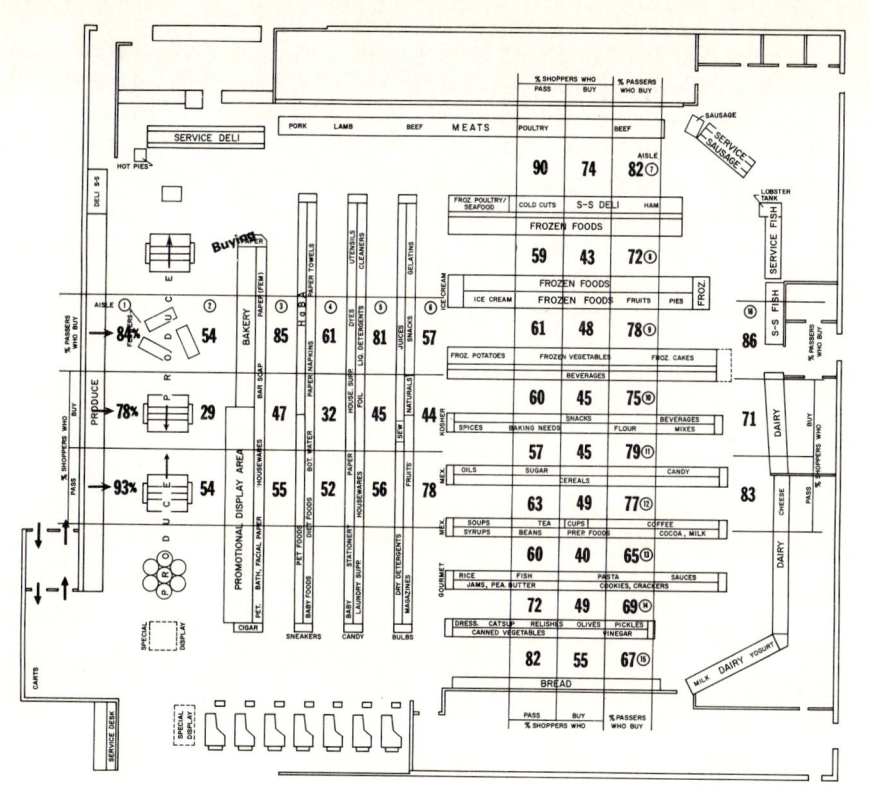

FIGURE 20-3

Contemporary supermarket layout. (*Source:* "Consumer Behavior in the Super Market—Part III," *Progressive Grocer*, January 1976, pp. 70–71. Reprinted with permission.)

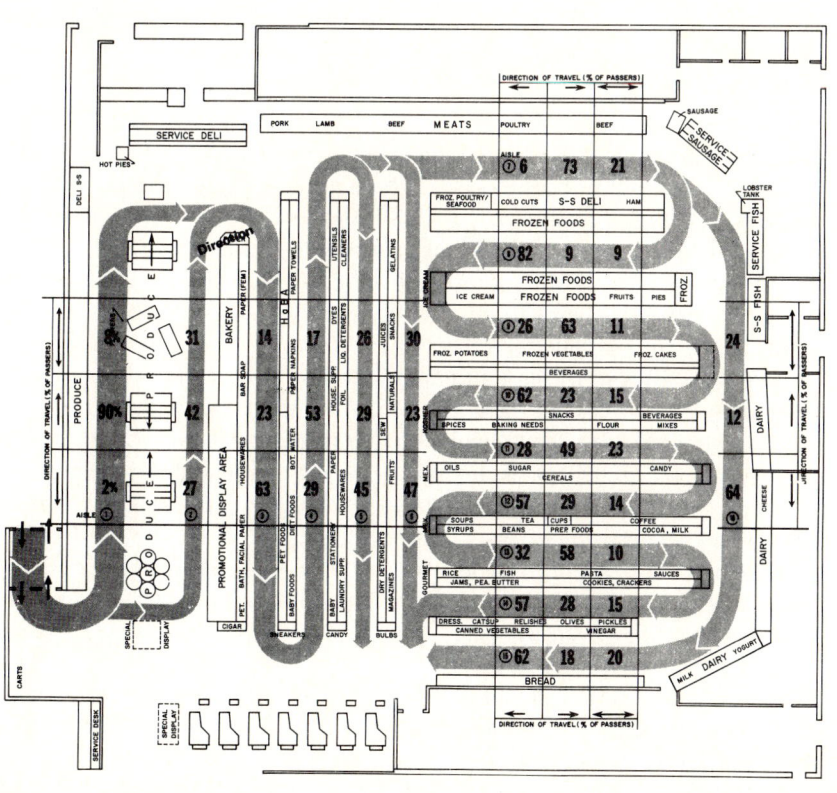

661

or more products. The use of displays and store signs has grown so that in 1976 national advertisers spent well over $2.2 billion for these materials. It is also known that 88 percent of all retail outlets use promotional displays. In a study of chain drug stores, supermarkets, full-line discount stores, and home improvement centers, it was found that drug stores use the most displays (96 percent of stores) and home improvement centers use the least (74 percent). Moreover, 36 percent of store managers say they are now using more promotional displays than they were in 1974.[55]

The bulk of published research conducted on the effectiveness of displays has come from the supermarket and drugstore fields. Numerous examples of the effectiveness of displays in attracting consumer attention could be cited. The following are representative of the findings:

1 Of 2473 supermarket shoppers interviewed, 38 percent had purchased at least one brand or item they had never before bought. The reason cited most frequently (25 percent) for a first-time purchase was that it had been displayed.[56]

2 A study of 5215 customers in supermarkets, variety stores, drugstores, hardware stores, liquor stores, and service stations found that one–third had purchased at least one of the displayed items.[57]

3 Interviews with 2803 shoppers in 16 drugstores spread across the United States discovered that 30 percent of those who decided to try a new brand after entering the store did so because of displays.[58]

4 Studies by the Point-of-Purchase Advertising Institute and Du Pont Co. found higher purchase activity when displays were used in supermarkets. When a newspaper or other ad reinforced an in-store display, purchase incidence jumped even more.[59]

9 K mart discovered a 251 percent sales increase for sports products featured on continuous loop film in point-of-purchase audiovisual displays.[60]

Although displays can have quite positive results, they must be used correctly in order to achieve their potential. A series of studies conducted by *Progressive Grocer* yielded important conclusions regarding various methods employed. Some of these findings are presented in Figure 20-4.

It is clear from these results that displays are effective in increasing sales. A legitimate question by the reader may be whether the display takes sales away from ordinary shelf sales. It has been found that displays do tend to reduce normal shelf sales. However, net sales of display and shelf combined are usually so far above normal that use of displays appears to be strongly substantiated. Moreover, tests show that there is a rapid return to normal shelf sales once the item is removed from display. This would indicate that customers are not simply stocking up on the item but are actually consuming more. Thus, displays have much evidence to support their continued strong usage as a merchandising tool.

Product Shelving Product shelving has an important influence on consumer behavior. Both the height at which products are displayed and the number of rows presented (facings) can influence sales of products. In addition, the use of shelf signs and extenders can affect sales, as seen above.

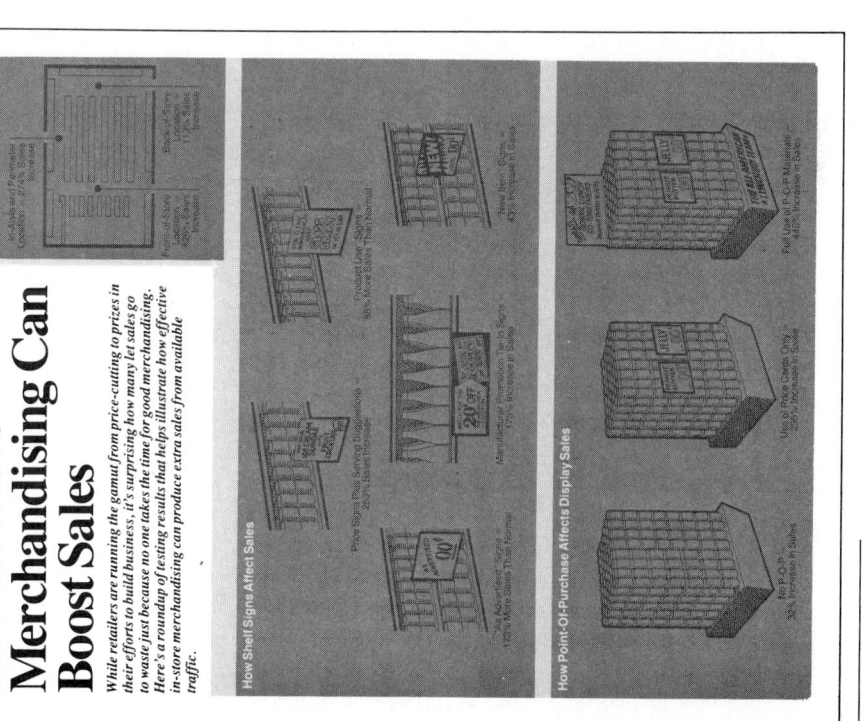

FIGURE 20-4

How in-store merchandising can boost sales. (*Source: The Magic of Merchandising*, January 1981, vol. 60, Part 2.)

SHELF HEIGHT When it is realized that the average shopper selects only 35 of the available 7000 or more grocery products during the average 27-minute shopping trip, it is easy to see why manufacturers clamor for the most visible eye-level shelf position.

Tests conducted by *Progressive Grocer* indicate that the most favorable shelf position is generally at eye level, followed in effectiveness by waist level, and knee or ankle level. It has been calculated from *Progressive Grocer* data that sales from waist-level shelves were only 74 percent as great, and sales from floor-level shelves were only 57 percent as great as sales from equivalent space allocations on eye-level shelves.[61]

Beyond the physical impossibility of stocking all products at eye level, there are also valid arguments for placing products on lower shelves. Actually, the shelf height dictated for an item is a function of its package size, its normal movement, whether or not it is being advertised, and its market target.

SHELF SPACE It is crucial for a product to be given enough shelf space to attract the buyer's attention. In order to help ensure this, the science and industry of packaging has mushroomed. Yet, all of the manufacturer's careful packaging efforts can be counteracted by an insufficient amount of shelf space in the store. Without adequate shelf facings, the item will be lost in the mass of 22,000 other facings lining the average supermarket's shelves.

There have been a number of experiments on *shelf space elasticity,* that is, the ratio of relative changes in unit sales to relative change in shelf space. The result of these experiments is that there is a small positive relationship between shelf space and unit sales. However, the relationship is not uniform among products, or across stores or intrastore locations.[62] *Progressive Grocer's* tests have concluded that products can have too many as well as too few facings, with both situations resulting in wrong use of space.

An adequate number of facings is especially important for new products. Tests show that doubling shelf facings on new items during their first 2 to 3 weeks in stores produced sales increases from 85 percent to 160 percent over stores that stocked the items but did not make any facing adjustments. In addition, fast-moving items tend to react much more dramatically to changes in shelf space than do slow-moving products.

In-Store Information Program Although the factors to be discussed here are not strictly merchandising strategies, they most definitely can have an influence on where consumers shop and which brands they choose. Many shoppers are dissatisfied with their regular supermarket on this score. In fact, a survey among one magazine's readers found that 51 percent of the respondents thought that information in the store to help make buying decisions was inadequate.[63] Figure 20-5 provides a general overview of consumers' familiarity, evaluation of usefulness, and usage of three major consumer-information programs, according to a survey by *Progressive Grocer.*

In spite of the attractiveness of instituting various information programs for consumers in order to help them make more intelligent shopping decisions, there

FIGURE 20-5

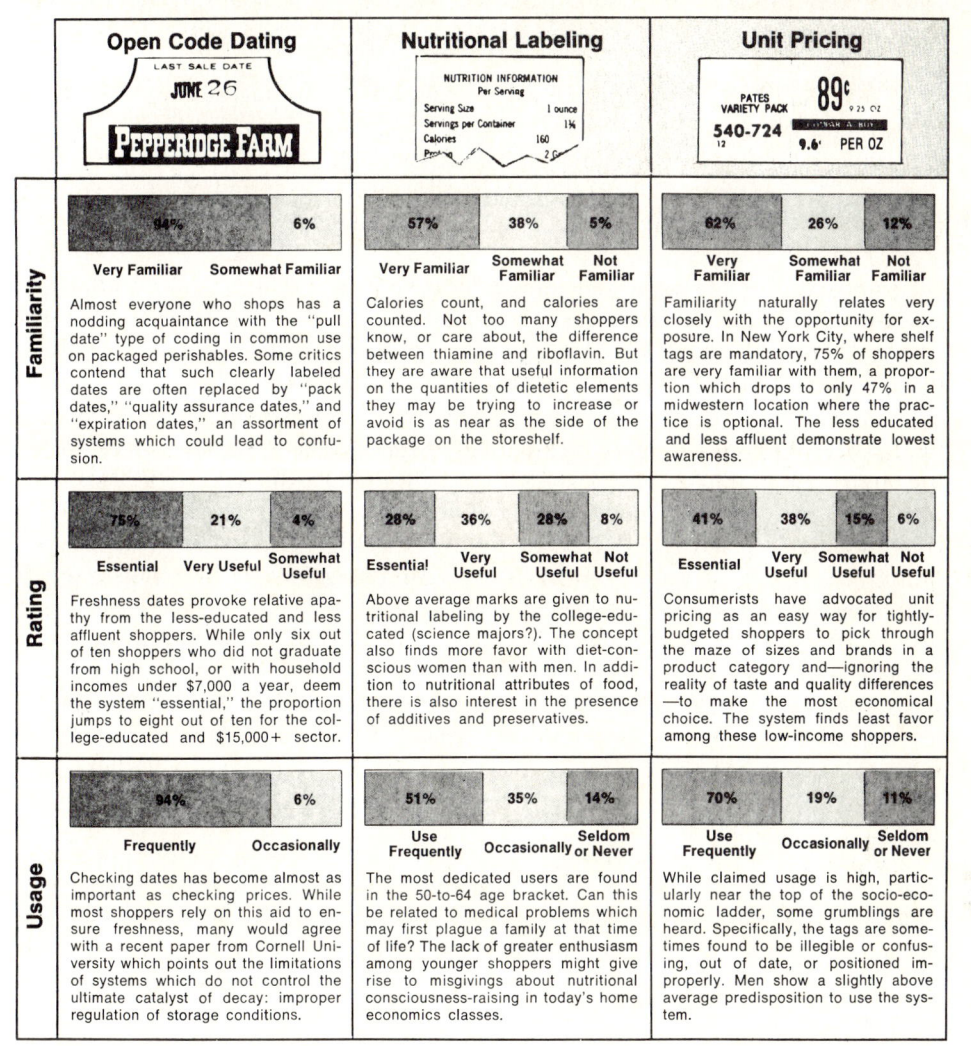

How consumers view information programs. (*Source:* Robert F. Dietrich, "Some Signs of Our Times on the Road to Smarter Shopping," *Progressive Grocer,* November 1976, p. 43. Reprinted with permission.)

Open Code Dating

LAST SALE DATE
JUNE 26
PEPPERIDGE FARM

Familiarity

Very Familiar	Somewhat Familiar
94%	6%

Almost everyone who shops has a nodding acquaintance with the "pull date" type of coding in common use on packaged perishables. Some critics contend that such clearly labeled dates are often replaced by "pack dates," "quality assurance dates," and "expiration dates," an assortment of systems which could lead to confusion.

Rating

Essential	Very Useful	Somewhat Useful
75%	21%	4%

Freshness dates provoke relative apathy from the less-educated and less affluent shoppers. While only six out of ten shoppers who did not graduate from high school, or with household incomes under $7,000 a year, deem the system "essential," the proportion jumps to eight out of ten for the college-educated and $15,000+ sector.

Usage

Frequently	Occasionally
94%	6%

Checking dates has become almost as important as checking prices. While most shoppers rely on this aid to ensure freshness, many would agree with a recent paper from Cornell University which points out the limitations of systems which do not control the ultimate catalyst of decay: improper regulation of storage conditions.

Nutritional Labeling

NUTRITION INFORMATION
Per Serving
Serving Size 1 ounce
Servings per Container 1¼
Calories 160
Protein 2 G

Familiarity

Very Familiar	Somewhat Familiar	Not Familiar
57%	38%	5%

Calories count, and calories are counted. Not too many shoppers know, or care about, the difference between thiamine and riboflavin. But they are aware that useful information on the quantities of dietetic elements they may be trying to increase or avoid is as near as the side of the package on the storeshelf.

Rating

Essential	Very Useful	Somewhat Useful	Not Useful
28%	36%	28%	8%

Above average marks are given to nutritional labeling by the college-educated (science majors?). The concept also finds more favor with diet-conscious women than with men. In addition to nutritional attributes of food, there is also interest in the presence of additives and preservatives.

Usage

Use Frequently	Occasionally	Seldom or Never
51%	35%	14%

The most dedicated users are found in the 50-to-64 age bracket. Can this be related to medical problems which may first plague a family at that time of life? The lack of greater enthusiasm among younger shoppers might give rise to misgivings about nutritional consciousness-raising in today's home economics classes.

Unit Pricing

PATES
VARIETY PACK 89¢ 9.25 OZ
540-724 9.6¢ PER OZ

Familiarity

Very Familiar	Somewhat Familiar	Not Familiar
62%	26%	12%

Familiarity naturally relates very closely with the opportunity for exposure. In New York City, where shelf tags are mandatory, 75% of shoppers are very familiar with them, a proportion which drops to only 47% in a midwestern location where the practice is optional. The less educated and less affluent demonstrate lowest awareness.

Rating

Essential	Very Useful	Somewhat Useful	Not Useful
41%	38%	15%	6%

Consumerists have advocated unit pricing as an easy way for tightly-budgeted shoppers to pick through the maze of sizes and brands in a product category and—ignoring the reality of taste and quality differences—to make the most economical choice. The system finds least favor among these low-income shoppers.

Usage

Use Frequently	Occasionally	Seldom or Never
70%	19%	11%

While claimed usage is high, particularly near the top of the socio-economic ladder, some grumblings are heard. Specifically, the tags are sometimes found to be illegible or confusing, out of date, or positioned improperly. Men show a slightly above average predisposition to use the system.

---

is some question about the effectiveness of such practices. Consequently, more research needs to be conducted on ways to make information programs more beneficial not only to consumers but also as a competitive technique for the retailer.[64]

It seems clear that well-thought-out programs of information carefully provided to the consumer can pay dividends for manufacturers or retailers in attracting consumers. Consumers may well switch to companies that provide more helpful information to them. Whether or not consumers make better decisions because of the increased amount of information is not known since it is difficult to define what a "better decision" is. It would help to answer this question if we knew how much time and money consumers saved because of these programs, how much better their nutritional levels were because of diet changes, and what levels of satisfaction are achieved by users.

Pricing Strategies We have already discussed the microeconomic view of consumer reactions (Chapter 2) and the way in which consumers' perceptual processes influence their evaluation of prices (Chapter 13). There are other elements of pricing which can affect consumers in their shopping activities. This section presents two of those influencing strategies.

PRICE AWARENESS Although consumers have a critical attitude toward the general price level and supermarket prices in particular, they apparently have little specific knowledge about actual product prices. For example, only about one shopper in twelve can name the exact price of even one out of a broad range of common food store items.[65] Because price is one of the most important criteria in food store choice, it is important for most supermarket operators to achieve a low-price image. Yet, at the same time it is obvious that shoppers are not at all clear what constitutes a "good" price for even popular items, much less those that are bought infrequently. Consequently, an appropriate strategy to achieve a low-price image among consumers would be to concentrate price advertising for only the most popular items where consumers would be most cognizant of price differences. This is often accomplished by the use of *loss leaders*—products that are sold slightly above cost to draw traffic into the store and create an impression of low prices. Moreover, as many supermarkets do, the regular or competitor's price could be cited along with the special or store's price in both media advertising and in-store materials.

PROMOTIONAL PRICING This section discusses marketing approaches in which a price incentive for purchase is offered to the consumer. One form of promotional pricing involves multiple-pricing, the technique by which retailers price items in multiple quantities such as 2 for 25 cents, 3 for 49 cents, and so on. The basic idea of multiple-pricing is to offer the customer a lower price on a quantity purchase. However, the technique has long been complained about by some consumerists as a device that confuses customers more than it saves them money, and one that causes them to buy more than they had planned. Nevertheless, 74 percent of supermarket customers usually buy items priced in multiple-units.[66]

In addition to multiple-pricing, other price dealing approaches in which the marketer merely cuts the price of an item, offers a "cents-off" special, or provides some sort of rebate on the product may be useful ways of stimulating sales. One consideration in all such approaches, however, is the effectiveness of the price deal for accomplishing marketing objectives. For example, it appears that price promotions can induce brand switching in favor of the dealt brand. It is not clear, however, that they remain with the brand once the deal is withdrawn (and, hence, the price is raised).[67] Thus, the marketer may not achieve lasting impact with price deals.

Another facet of price promotions concerns whether consumers stock up on the specially-priced item.[68] Such behavior would serve to remove them from the market for such a product for a longer period of time; that is, it may be a way of generating greater brand loyalty if consumers stockpile and then slowly work the product off. It appears that consumers do indeed stockpile the items on price deal situations. This may be occurring not through getting more units per purchase, but through buying early, although results differ by product class.[69]

A final factor concerns the characteristics of the "deal-prone" consumer. Can this buyer be identified and segmented? That is, do certain consumers react more favorably than others to deals? Although research results are inconsistent,[70] recent studies indicate that for certain frequently purchased goods, deal-prone households can be identified, and that the key variables are household resource variables (such as home and car ownership). Buyers with higher incomes, and owners of cars and homes are more deal prone.[71]

COUPONING This is a form of price dealing in which a cents-off coupon is redeemed during purchase, thus reducing the product's price. Couponing has had a sharp, continuing growth over the past few years. In 1980, an estimated 91 billion coupons (400 per capita) were distributed by 1300 companies. The face value of these coupons averaged 18.5 cents, representing a potential consumer savings of $17 billion (or about 5 percent of all food expenditures). However, because only 4–5 percent of coupons are redeemed (with perhaps one in 5 being redeemed improperly—without the product for which it is issued being purchased), and because of the cost of producing, distributing, and redeeming them, the total cost of coupons is greater than the redemption values received by consumers from manufacturers.[72]

Cents-off coupons have been criticized on several bases: (1) they discriminate against low-income and minority consumers and shoppers with high time costs; (2) they slow the check-out process; (3) they force food retailers to stock slow-moving items; (4) they impose costs on the food system by generating demand surges; and (5) they distort consumer choices between advertised and private labels.[73]

In spite of these criticisms, the practice of couponing continues to grow, and more consumers are using them each year. At least four out of five households use them as an integral part of their shopping.[74]

Although coupons are generally claimed to influence consumers to try new products or improve the position of older products, it is hoped they will result in long-term loyalty once trial occurs. However, most coupons have been shown to result in short-term sales gains only,[75] although such gains may be impressive.[76]

Who uses coupons? Coupon usage is greater among middle- and upper-income groups and those with higher educational levels. Such refunds also attract larger and older families. In addition, redemption varies by region, with 81 percent of households in the northeast redeeming them, compared with only 68 percent in the southeast.[77]

Packaging One of the most important point-of-sale influences is the package, including graphics, product information contained on the package, and the physical design of the package. In addition, the package can be extremely instrumental in the success of store displays. Thus, it is a basic ingredient in attracting the shopper's attention while in the store—the marketer's "silent salesman."

Brand Choice—National Versus Private For a number of years now, there has been a "battle" between manufacturers' national brands and distributors' private brands for brand predominance in certain product categories. To the winner go greater product sales and profits. Consequently, it is important, particularly from the marketer's viewpoint, to know whether there are any distinguishing characteristics between private- and national-brand customers which might make possible their effective market segmentation.

POSITION OF PRIVATE BRANDS The competitive position of private brands differs from industry to industry. For example, although they account for less than 10 percent of sales in portable appliances, private brands control more than 50 percent of the market in shoes. In grocery and drug stores, private brands have less than a 30-percent share of the market. As for the number of consumers who purchase private label merchandise, the figures are quite large. Research by A. C. Nielsen found that 80 percent of buyers of grocery products have purchased private brands.[78] Nevertheless, based on the evidence available, no significant swing away from national brands to private brands is expected to occur.[79]

Although it has been shown that consumers view private and national brands differently, it is not clearly known what consumer characteristics differentiate between private- and national-brand users.[80] Thus, more research is needed to determine the extent to which such buyers are different, how they can be reached, and what the best marketing approaches might be.

GENERIC BRANDS Generic or "no-name" brands are a relatively new feature in grocery retailing. Pioneered by the French supermarket chain, Carrefour, these products are easily distinguishable due to their basic and plain packaging characteristics coupled with the attribute of primary emphasis on the contents of the package rather than on brand name. Early introductions were often marketed in stark white packages with bold black content labeling. This approach contrasts with private-label merchandise, which more closely resembles manufacturers' brands in that a brand name is stressed in the primary labeling with secondary emphasis given to content.[81]

The shopper's awareness level has increased toward generics since their introduction. At least three out of four shoppers are aware of them, and 60 percent of those who say generics are available to them are buying them.

Of course, price is an important factor in generics' success. They usually sell for 30 to 40 percent less than major advertised brand prices, and some sell for 20 percent less than supermarket private-label prices. As a result of this price difference, it appears that generics' gains have come more at the expense of name brands' market share than the private-label business.[82]

Who buys generic products? Studies tend to suggest the following general profile:[83]

- larger families
- shoppers with large weekly grocery expenditures
- better-educated customers

- those age 35–44
- those in middle stages of the family life cycle
- less brand-loyal customers, and less one-store oriented
- mildly innovative and venturesome customers
- those who claim to be less-influenced by advertisements

Compared to infrequent purchasers and nonpurchasers, however, high-volume generic buyers are a relatively burdened group, who tend to rent rather than to own their homes, and who are likely to have a young child, a relatively low income, and restricted time for shopping trips, with a preference for discount stores.[84]

Some retailers are dramatically increasing the selling power of generics by creating a "brand" identity and adding color to the package. One study showed that when identical products were packaged in a generic package and a colored package with a "brand" name affiliated with a store, three–fourths of respondents perceived the "brand" to be of superior quality and manufactured by a reputable company.[85] The "brand" was viewed as a cut above generics yet at a better price than private and national labels.

Other In-Store Merchandising Activities The area of in-store merchandising is continually changing as marketers seek to discover new ways of reaching consumers with their promotional messages closest to the point of purchase. As a result, such approaches as the following have been used, with varying degrees of success:

- In-store advertising over loudspeaker systems
- Ad messages placed on shopping carts
- Video advertising messages presented over color TV sets to shoppers waiting in supermarket checkout lines (for an average of $6\frac{1}{2}$ minutes)[86]
- Movie projectors, videocassette and videodisc players, and computerized store displays are also finding increased use in augmenting a salesperson's selling efforts by presenting product information and inducing trial of products.[87]

Personal Selling Effects

We have been primarily discussing in-store purchasing behavior for items that are sold via self-service. However, there are also many product purchase situations in which customers interact with salespeople.

Personal selling in which a salesperson interacts with a consumer is referred to as a "dyad." Such an influence may be very strong, as seen in our earlier discussion of interpersonal influence and social group behavior. From a consumer-behavior viewpoint, however, little is known about what factors make this process a success. Studies of salespeople have generally sought to learn what main characteristics lead to success, and have assumed homogeneity among prospects. Usually, researchers point to a bundle of personality variables as predictors of good sales performance. More recently, however, researchers have begun to view selling as dyadic interaction in terms of not only the characteristics of the salesperson but also the buyer, and how the two parties react to each other.[88]

As this recent research suggests, it appears that rather than focusing merely on the salesperson's traits, the marketer would do well to also consider the customer's traits. Careful research into market-segment characteristics and needs may result in more effective sales management. By hiring salespeople who more closely match desired customers and preparing them better to perform effectively in the dyadic interaction process, the firm may achieve more success in the market.

THE SITUATIONAL NATURE OF CONSUMER DECISIONS

One of the most important factors influencing the choice and purchasing process is the situation surrounding the consumer's decision. Depending on the set of circumstances faced by the consumer in making a purchase, behavior may take any number of directions. Thus, consumer behavior may be said to depend largely on the situation. For instance, the type of car the consumer may purchase for commuting might well differ from the type of car bought for vacationing. The brand of canned ham bought to serve at a dinner party for one's boss may be different from the brand bought for everyday consumption. The type of clothes bought for gardening and landscape work at home are likely to be different from those worn at a neighborhood bridge party.

In these and countless other decisions, consumers may base their purchase acts on the situation attached to those acts. A *situation,* therefore, may be viewed as comprising all of those factors particular to a time and place of observation which do not follow from a knowledge of personal (intraindividual) and stimulus (choice alternative) attributes and which have a demonstrable and systematic effect on current behavior.[89]

Based upon this definition, five groups of situational characteristics may be identified:[90]

1 *Physical surroundings* are the most readily apparent features of a situation, including geographical and institutional location, decor, sounds, aromas, lighting, weather, and visible configurations of merchandise or other materials surrounding the stimulus object.

2 *Social surroundings* include such factors as other persons present, their characteristics, their apparent roles, and interpersonal interactions.

3 *Temporal perspective* is a dimension of situations which may be specified in units ranging from time of day to season of the year. Time may also be measured relative to a past or future event for the situational participant, such as time since the last purchase.

4 *Task Definition* includes an intent or requirement to select, shop for, or obtain information about a general or specific purchase. It may also reflect different buyer and user roles anticipated by the individual. For example, a consumer shopping for a small appliance as a wedding gift for a friend is in a different situation than would be the case in shopping for a small appliance for personal use.

5 *Antecedent states* are momentary moods (such as acute anxiety, pleasantness, hostility, and excitation) or momentary conditions (such as cash on hand, fatigue, and illness) rather than chronic individual traits, and they are immediately antecedent to the current consumer situation.

Patterns have been found among consumer segments in the type of products bought for certain situations, ranging across snack foods, beverages, leisure activities, fast foods, and numerous additional items.[91]

Although the situation is an important influence in the purchase and consumption decision, it may frequently be overriden by product considerations. For example, the degree of brand loyalty a consumer exhibits may be very influential in purchase decisions. A highly brand-loyal consumer will tend to purchase a favorite brand time after time no matter what the variation in the consumption situation. Thus, strong brand loyalty results in weaker situational influence. Another factor tempering situational influence is product involvement. Research indicates that when product involvement is low, the situation tends to determine behavior; however, in high-product-involvement cases, situational factors are not as important.[92]

NONSTORE PURCHASING PROCESSES

Consider the following scenario:

> You check your product file code and see that wristwatches are #W178. You punch #W178 on your home computer, which is hooked up to your color TV set. Then you sit back and spend as much time as you need browsing through a "video catalogue."
> Most of the major watch manufacturers have their products listed in the electronic shop-at-home system. So all you have to do is examine the color photos of their watches and read the detailed specifications and price information on your TV screen.
> Once you've made a selection, you're ready to order. On the computer keyboard you enter the manufacturer's code number, the product code number, your name, address, credit card number, and bank number.
> The next week you open up your mailbox and find a new watch inside, along with a guarantee and receipt. Payment has already been made by electronic funds transfer between your bank and the manufacturer's. Of course, you've already recorded the expenditure on your home computer's personal accounting program.[93]

This illustration may seem farfetched, but it is not, according to those who carefully study the mail order industry. Although the vast bulk of consumer purchasing processes now take place in stores, there is a growing amount of in-home shopping. Marketers usually refer to this approach as *nonstore marketing* or *direct marketing*. It includes ordering via direct response TV, cable TV, catalogues, party and club plans, door-to-door selling, video cassettes, Teletext, direct mail, and other developing electronic technologies.

Significance of Nonstore Buying

According to U.S. census retail trade statistics, in-home buying is increasingly urban and has been growing appreciably faster than total store sales and general merchandise sales for some time. Due to classification and measurement problems of the census, however, there is not a clear picture of the significance of this activity. Estimates of nonstore buying range from 2 to 12 percent of total retail sales.

To illustrate the significance of this purchasing approach consider the following items:

- The average American household receives 40 catalogues a year.[94]

- More than 10,000 U.S. businesses use mail order as a distribution method.

- More than 7 out of 10 Americans made a mail order purchase in a recent year.[95]

- Mail order business is growing 50 to 100 percent faster than regular retail business.[96]

- It is estimated that by 1990, 20 percent of all general merchandise sales will be via mail.[97]

- 6.5 million toll-free "800" number phone calls replying to print and TV direct-response advertisements were made in January 1982.[98]

The seeds of this change toward telecommunication-based merchandising are several:[99]

- An increased emphasis on consumer self-identify, with individuality expressed through goods and services, which leads to a desire to consider more items than a store can display

- A higher proportion of working women who have less time to shop

- Increased leisure-time pursuits of self-development and creative expression which allow less time to shop from store to store

- Greater demand for specialty products and services that are difficult to get in most shopping centers

- Rapid acceptance of new technology such as videotape recorders, home computers, and automated bank-teller machines, which means that more consumers are becoming technologically competent for new merchandising approaches

- Increased popularity of such recent nonstore innovations as pay-by-phone, special-interest mail-order catalogs, and televised direct marketing, resulting in consumers who are becoming psychologically prepared for new shopping forms

However, in spite of these favorable conditions leading to a receptive environment for new video-based marketing approaches, a survey by Benton & Bowles, Inc. indicates that only 10 percent of consumers are very interested in shopping at home via two-way television. The major reasons consumers express in opposition to more active involvment in new video technologies are:[100]

1 They like to see products "in person" before they buy.

2 They "just don't need it."

3 They like to "go out" to shop.

4 They want to relax while watching TV and don't want to push buttons.

5 They feel they might be tempted to buy products they don't really need.

6 They fear that being "hooked up" to a computer would invade their privacy.

Characteristics of Purchasers[101]

There are a number of differences that are notable between in-home shoppers and other shoppers. These differences may be classified according to socioeconomic status, race, wife's employment status, and geographic location. It must be pointed out that, because of methodological differences between studies and the limited amount of research, these results are not conclusive.

1 *"Upscale" Households*—With few exceptions, in-home shoppers are described as above-average in socioeconomic status. These differences increase with in-home shopping intensity, and are especially pronounced among households utilizing several in-home shopping modes.

2 *Racial Patterns*—It appears that black and white households differ little on total in-home shopping expenditures or frequency. However, shopping mode differences do exist. For example, blacks do less mail-order buying than do whites at similar income levels.

3 *Working Wives*—It might be expected that working women restricted in shopping time flexibility, would be especially likely to take advantage of in-home shopping. However, this relationship has not been supported so far. In fact, some studies have found employed women even more willing to shop in stores than women not employed outside the home.

4 *Geographic Location*—There is limited evidence that geographical location within a trading area influences in-home shopping, with those in rural areas utilizing it more than their urban counterparts. Its use seems to be higher where there is greater retail inaccessibility and inadequacy.

In-Home Shopping Motivations

There are several motivational and lifestyle factors which influence in-home buying. The most important ones are discussed in this section.

Convenience Shopping convenience is probably the most important motivator in consumer decisions to shop at home and is the one so often stressed by the industry. High convenience orientation does explain some but not all in-home shopping motivation. For example, phone shoppers seem especially convenience-oriented, while catalog buyers not only want shopping convenience, but also merchandise assortment and uniqueness, competitive prices, and useful descriptive shopping information. Mail order's strength today seems to lie less in its shopping convenience than its ability to offer new, unique, personalized products.

Risk of Buying In spite of the obvious advantages of shopping at home, the high perceived risk that is associated with buying by description partially explains why many consumers are hesitant to use this particular technique. Research on telephone and mail-order shopping supports this hypothesis.

Lifestyle Active in-home buyers are more cosmopolitan, style- and value-conscious, convenience-oriented, and generally are more demanding shoppers than other consumers. They are more flexible in shopping style, visit stores more frequently, and view shopping and shopping risk more positively. Their in-home buying is discretionary, often impulse- or convenience-oriented, and they use a variey of in-home buying methods and sources.

One advertising agency's lifestyle analysis of direct response purchasers found that those characterized as "impulse" buyers and those who found it "difficult to get to the store" were the most attractive.[102] For example, of the fifteen product categories in which direct response sales are significant, the "impulse" shopper ranks above average in nine of them.

Personality characteristics found among in-home shoppers indicate that they tend to be more self-assured, venturesome, and cosmopolitan in outlook and in shopping behavior.

Marketing Implications

The home shopper segment is becoming an increasingly attractive and competitive market. Especially with the growing revolution in technology and the possibilities it brings for in-home marketing is the future of this area sure to be exciting. At present, however, not nearly enough is known about such shoppers.

Many companies not presently active in in-home marketing will have to assess the cost/benefit potential of serving this market. Once a firm makes a positive decision to pursue this group, it is necessary to locate important customer segments. In some cases this may be relatively easy. The frequent catalog buyer, for instance, may be reached by direct mail through the use of zip codes related to geographic areas having the greatest potential, as defined by this segment's demographic profile (such as upscale consumers), or by using mailing lists based on this pattern of discriminating demographic characteristics.[103]

Designing a promotional mix appealing to at-home shoppers is a challenging task. The themes and copy should be consistent with this group's lifestyle, such as emphasizing their venturesome, self-assured, and cosmopolitan orientation. Both in message design and layout, catalogs and circulars offered to this group should be carefully developed so as to be congruent with the images the marketer wants to project. To overcome hesitancy among buyers due to perceived risk associated with at-home shopping, promotional materials should provide buyers with sufficient information about products offered (perhaps including testimonials from satisfied users where appropriate) and safeguard the purchaser by offering easy, guaranteed return privileges.

PURCHASING PATTERNS

The final section of this chapter focuses on two important purchasing patterns. We shall examine (1) the extent to which consumers develop repeat purchasing patterns and (2) the extent to which purchases are unplanned. These subjects will be discussed in the context of brand loyalty and impulse purchasing.

Brand Loyalty

Brand loyalty is a topic of much concern to all marketers. Every company seeks to have a steady group of unwavering customers for its product or service. The significance of brand loyalty is illustrated in the following examples:

In the cereal market, people switch brands as often as ten times a year, and a new brand has only six months to establish itself before losing out to a more popular competitor. Consequently, cereal brands scrap hard for shelf space and advertise loudly to catch consumer attention to be the one in three new brands that survives.[104]

Chrysler estimates that repeat brand purchases among import buyers approach 50 percent, compared with only 15 percent for domestic small cars.[105]

Brand loyalty in big-ticket durable purchases is relatively low (only one out of three repurchases the same brand in a particular product category), although category repurchases comprise two of every three sales in a product category on average.[106]

Thus, brand loyalty is a challenging goal each marketer seeks to attain; yet, the lack of brand loyalty seems to have accelerated during the last decade, because of several factors:

- Sophisticated advertising appeals and heavy media support
- "Parity" of products in form, content, and communication
- Price competition from private and generic labels
- Sales promotion tactics of mass displays, coupons, and price specials that appeal to consumer impulse buying
- General fickleness of consumers in buying behavior

Nature of Brand Loyalty A study of repeat purchase behavior for nine products based on a *Chicago Tribune* purchase panel suggested that there were four brand loyalty patterns, as follows:[107]

1 *Undivided loyalty* is exhibited by families purchasing Brand A in the following sequence: A A A A A A.

2 *Divided loyalty* is exhibited by the family purchasing Brands A and B in the following sequence: A B A B A B.

3 *Unstable loyalty* is shown by the family buying Brands A and B in the following sequence: AAA BBB.

4 *No loyalty* is shown by families buying Brands A, B, C, D, E, and F in the following sequence: A B C D E F.

On the basis of the products studied, it was concluded that the majority of consumers tend to purchase a favorite brand or set of brands.

Although the degree of loyalty varied by product, the percentage of consumers exhibiting some brand loyalty was rather high. Efforts to group products by a type of merchandise classification (for example, foods and nonfoods) showed no relationship to brand loyalty, although a definite relationship was discovered between strength of brands and nature of the loyalty shown. Loyalty appears to be high for well-established products in which little or no changes have occurred, and low where product entries are frequent.

Various other studies have used these and other measures of brand loyalty and have generally concluded that brand loyalty exists and is a relatively widespread phenomenon.[108] Most studies, however, suffer from a lack of comparability because of differing conceptions of brand loyalty. Until consumer-behavior researchers agree on a common definition, there will continue to be difficulty synthesizing results. Some researchers have suggested a useful definition of brand loyalty that recognizes that true brand-loyal consumers should exhibit not only a high degree of repeat purchasing but also a *favorable attitude* toward the purchased brand. Perhaps the most complete definition recognizing this position describes brand loyalty as (1) the biased (i.e., nonrandom) (2) behavioral response (i.e., purchase) (3) expressed over time (4) by a decision-making unit (5) with respect to one or more alternative brands out of a set of such brands, and is (6) a function of psychological (i.e., decision-making, evaluative) processes.[109]

What Factors Explain Brand Loyalty? Numerous studies attempting to explain brand loyalty have been largely inconclusive to this point. The following results appear to be indicated:

1 Some socioeconomic, demographic, and psychological variables are related to brand loyalty (when extended definitions are used) but tend to be product-specific rather than general across products.

2 Loyalty behavior of an informal group leader influences the behavior of other group members.

3 Some consumer characteristics are related to store loyalty, which in turn is related to brand loyalty.

4 Brand loyalty is positively related to perceived risk and market structure variables such as the extensiveness of distribution and market share of the dominant brand, but inversely related to the number of stores shopped.[110]

Effect of Out-of-Stock Conditions A potentially important influence on brand loyalty is the possibility of brand substitution. It has been found that between 19 percent and perhaps as much as 33 percent of shoppers presold by an advertising campaign change their minds and switch to another brand when they get inside the supermarket.[111] An important reason for brand substitution is an out-of-stock (OOS) condition. To appreciate the impact out-of-stock conditions may have on the retailer, consider that for a moderate-sized supermarket these costs have been estimated to run between $13,000 and $15,000 per year.[112]

Although the result of OOS conditions appears to be significant, little research has been done on its effect on brand loyalty. The A. C. Nielsen Company, however, has provided some indication of the extent of brand substitution in the supermarket. A large survey of shoppers found that 25 percent left the store with some portion of their wants unsatisfied because of OOS conditions among desired brands or package sizes. Although 42 percent of the consumers refused to accept a substitute brand, 58 percent were willing to do so. The proportion of consumers refusing to accept a substitute brand varied among products studied, from 23 percent for toilet tissue to 62 percent for toothpaste. Among consumers who failed to find their desired package size, 52 percent bought another size of the same brand, while 30 percent bought another brand, and 18 percent would not accept a substitute.[113]

Thus, customer reactions to OOS conditions may be either short- or long-run in nature, including switching brands, substituting product class, shopping at other stores, postponing purchase, or altering choice behavior for later decisions.[114]

Marketing Implications Several marketing implications flow from our discussion of brand loyalty. The first question, of course, for the marketer attempting to attract more brand-loyal customers is the feasibility of segmenting this group. That is, are these consumers identifiable? As we have just seen from the correlates of brand loyalty, those customers generally do not appear to differ significantly from other customers on most segmentation bases. The marketer may be more successful, however, in discerning unique characteristics of customers loyal to his particular brand or product. The results of such an analysis may provide him with useful insights for developing attractive marketing strategies.

Wind has proposed the matrix, presented in Figure 20-6, incorporating attitudes and behavior by which the marketer may assess the brand's vulnerability. It provides some indication of the magnitude of exposure. In the first two rows, the more the brand is disliked, the greater its vulnerability. In the third row, the greater the brand is liked, the more vulnerable are customers to competitive brands. Of course, the marketer would need to identify the relevant reasons for consumers liking or disliking the brand. With such information, insights may be gained into not only the size of the loyal and vulnerable segments but also the magnitude and nature of customers' vulnerability. Marketing programs may then be developed

FIGURE 20-6

The vulnerability matrix. (*Source:* Adapted from Yoram Wind, "Brand Loyalty and Vulnerability," in Arch G. Woodside, Jagdish N. Sheth, and Peter D. Bennett (eds.), *Consumer and Industrial Buying Behavior,* North-Holland Publishing Company, New York, 1977, p. 314. Reprinted by permission. Copyright © 1977 by Elsevier Science Publishing Company, Inc.)

		Attitude toward this brand		
		"Like" it	"Indifferent" to it and others	"Dislike" it
Purchase pattern with respect to this brand	Buy it regularly	"Loyal" to it 1	Customers of this brand who are vulnerable to competitors 2	3
	Buy it occasionally	Customers of this brand who are vulnerable to competitors 4	5	6
	Do not buy it	Customers of this brand who are vulnerable to competitors 7	8	Unlikely target for this brand 9

aimed at reducing buyers' vulnerability while attracting customers of competing brands.[115]

These various goals of the marketer may necessitate different marketing strategies. For instance, increasing brand loyalty of present customers may necessitate better after-sale service, while attracting new customers to become steady users may require certain inducements such as price discounts. Thus, the varying ranges of brand loyalty that the marketer faces point to different competitive actions. For less highly committed consumers, a catchy advertising message, coupon offer, free sample, point-of-purchase display, or attractive package could cause a switch to the marketer's brand. This is the reason we see so much of these sorts of activities and the resultant brand switching in certain product groups (e.g., foods, soaps, and detergents). The packaged consumer goods field can generally be considered highly dynamic in this regard.

In order to induce brand switching among customers who are more highly loyal, the marketer is likely to require more fundamental changes in consumer perceptions and attitudes. Therefore, significant revisions in product image are often necessary, frequently accomplished through revamped promotional programs.

Advertising decisions are usually geared to the loyalty situation that confronts the brand. It is suggested that if brand loyalty is high, the advertiser has a good case for "investment" expenditures where large amounts are expended over short periods of time to attract new users, because continued purchases after the advertising has been curtailed will "amortize" the advertising investment. Where a low degree of brand loyalty exists in the product class, advertising expenditures should be made at a fairly steady rate on a pay-as-you-go basis, with demonstrated returns in extra sales equal to or greater than the extra advertising costs.[116]

Finally, it is clear that both retailers and manufacturers need to strive to avoid out-of-stock conditions, which might lead not only to reduced sales but also to less store and brand loyalty.

Impulse Purchasing

Impulse buying, or as some marketers prefer to call it—unplanned purchasing—is another consumer purchasing pattern. As the term implies, the purchase was not specifically planned. In this section, we will find that the process is rather widespread and may have significant implications for the marketer.

Nature of Impulse Purchasing It is difficult for marketers to agree on a definition of impulse buying. Stern cites four types of impulse purchases:

1 *Pure Impulse*—a novelty or escape purchase which breaks a normal buying pattern.

2 *Reminder Impulse*—a shopper sees an item and is reminded that the stock at home needs replenishing, or recalls an advertisement or other information about the item and a previous decision to purchase.

3 *Suggestion Impulse*—a shopper having no previous knowledge of a product sees the item for the first time and visualizes a need for it.

4 *Planned Impulse*—a shopper enters the store with the expectation and intention of making some purchases on the basis of price specials, coupons, etc.[117]

Extent of Impulse Buying   There are several studies which have indicated the significant and growing trend toward unplanned purchasing. Here are some of the conclusions on the extent of impulse buying:

More than 33 percent of all purchases in variety and drugstores are unplanned.[118]

One-half of buying decisions in supermarkets are unplanned.[119]

Only 41 percent of grocery shoppers use a shopping list. However, list users are more intensive shoppers and bigger spenders than nonusers.[120]

Thirty-nine percent of all department store shoppers and 62 percent of all discount store shoppers purchased at least one item on an unplanned basis.[121]

These statements are somewhat deceiving in that no distinction is made between the various kinds of impulse purchases possible for consumers. The picture painted is one of consumers running around somewhat out of control making irrational decisions on the spur of the moment in the store. Actually, although most consumers may not use a shopping list, their product and brand purchases are certainly rational (as we have defined it) and most probably fit into the reminder and planned impulse categories rather than the pure and suggestion impulse types.

At the same time, however, it is more important for retailers to realize that there is a large amount of decision making occuring at the point of purchase within the store. Thus, as far as the retail decision maker is concerned, impulse buying can be pragmatically defined as purchasing resulting from a decision to buy after the shopper has entered the store.[122]

Factors Influencing Impulse Purchases   The rather limited amount of research on unplanned purchases indicates that there are several product, marketing, and consumer characteristics which appear to be related to the process. Product characteristics that may influence greater impulse purchasing are those low in price, for which there is a marginal need, having a short product life, small in size or light in weight, and easy to store.

Marketing factors influencing impulse purchasing include mass distribution in self-service outlets with mass advertising and point-of-sale materials, and prominent display position and store location.[123] Few consumer personality, demographic, or socioeconomic characteristics have been shown to be related to the rate of impulse buying. However, the percentage of unplanned supermarket purchases appears to increase with: (1) size of the grocery bills, (2) number of products purchased, (3) major shopping trips, (4) frequency of product purchase, (5) absence of a shopping list, and (6) number of years married.[124] Among department store shoppers, age and race may influence the amount of impulse purchasing.[125]

Marketing Implications   The unplanned nature of much purchasing behavior today places a greater burden on manufacturers and retailers. The extent to which shoppers buy on impulse and without written lists puts a strong emphasis on the various kinds of in-store merchandising and personal selling stimuli which the marketer may use.

Managers of retail outlets need to carefully understand the types and extent of occurrence of impulse purchases in order to better plan store layout, merchandise and display location and allocation, and so on. Manufacturers also could benefit from an improved understanding of impulse purchasing by determining how much in-store product information may be necessary to provide on or with their products.

SUMMARY

This chapter began with an explanation of the nature of shopper motives and of the purchasing process, which was found to involve not only the purchase decision but activities directly associated with the purchase. We then examined the influence of various factors on the consumer's store choice decision. Factors such as location, store design, merchandise assortment, prices, advertising and sales promotion, personnel, and services are all very important influencing variables. Taken together, these and other elements form a store's image to the consumer that is of fundamental importance in store selection decisions. We also profiled various types of shoppers and discussed the significance and implications of store loyalty.

In-store purchasing behavior was described in detail. Merchandising techniques and personal selling efforts were discussed to provide a better understanding of effective techniques which the marketer might utilize.

The situational nature of consumer choice and purchasing decisions was examined. Five situational characteristics surrounding the consumer decision process were described: physical, social, temporal, task, and antecedent elements.

Nonstore consumer purchasing processes were also discussed. This growing market is expected to have much significance for the marketer as we enter the electronic era and a period of diminished driving.

Finally, we examined two often-used purchasing approaches: brand loyalty and impulse purchases. Both of these have important implications to the marketer and several strategies were suggested.

DISCUSSION TOPICS

1 Visit competing discount houses, supermarkets. department stores, or specialty shops in your area and describe the image you have of each store. What factors account for the image differences?

2 For the poorest image store in question 1 design a strategy for upgrading its image.

3 Visit a supermarket and observe the extent to which displays are used and whether they conform to the guidelines suggested in this chapter.

4 Does this supermarket appear to conform to the text's guidelines on multiple-pricing?

5 Bring to class two print advertisements for the same product type illustrating different usage situations. How may the market segments appealed to in these ads differ?

6 Keep a record of your product purchases for a period of time. How brand loyal are you? What factors seem to explain your degree of brand loyalty? How does your pattern and explanation differ from other students in the class?

7 Which of the above purchases were bought on impulse? Categorize them as to price, reminder, suggestion, or planned impulse purchases.

NOTES

[1] Adapted from Edward Tauber, "Why Do People Shop?" *Journal of Marketing,* 36:4–48, October 1972, published by the American Marketing Association.
[2] Kent B. Monroe and Joseph B. Guiltinan, "A Path-Analytic Exploration of Retail Patronage Influences," *Journal of Consumer Research,* 2:19–28, June 1975.
[3] Monroe and Guiltinan, "A Path-Analytic Exploration."
[4] Elizabeth C. Hirschman and Michael K. Mills, "Sources Shoppers Use to Pick Stores," *Journal of Advertising Research,* 20:47–51, February 1980.
[5] William J. Reilly, *Methods for the Study of Retail Relationships,* University of Texas, Bureau of Business Research, Austin, TX, Research Monograph, No. 4, 1929.
[6] Paul D. Converse, "New Laws of Retail Gravitation," *Journal of Marketing,* 14:379–384, October 1949.
[7] See, for example, Robert O. Herrmann and Leland L. Beik, "Shoppers' Movements Outside Their Local Retail Area," *Journal of Marketing,* 23:49–51, October 1968; John R. Thompson, "Characteristics and Behavior of Outshopping Consumers," *Journal of Retailing,* 47:70–80, Spring 1971; and Fred D. Reynolds and William R. Darden, "Intermarket Patronage: A Psychographic Study of Consumer Outshoppers," *Journal of Marketing,* 36:50–54, October 1972.
[8] James A. Brunner and John L. Mason, "The Influence of Driving Time Upon Shopping Center Preference," *Journal of Marketing,* 32:57–61, April 1968.
[9] William E. Cox, Jr. and Ernest F. Cooke, "Other Dimensions Involved in Shopping Center Preference," *Journal of Marketing,* 34:12–17, October 1970.
[10] James W. Gentry and Alvin C. Burns, "How 'Important' Are Evaluative Criteria in Shopping Center Patronage?" *Journal of Retailing,* 53:77, Winter 1977–1978.
[11] David B. Mackay and Richard W. Olshavsky, "Cognitive Maps of Retail Locations: An Investigation of Some Basic Issues," *Journal of Consumer Research,* 2:197–205, December 1975; Robert Mittlestaedt, "Psychophysical and Evaluative Dimensions of Cognized Distance in an Urban Shopping Environment," in Ronald C. Curhan (ed.), *1974 Combined Proceedings,* American Marketing Association, Chicago, pp. 190–193; and Edward M. Mazze, "Determining Shopper Movement by Cognitive Maps," *Journal of Retailing,* 50:14–48, Fall 1974.
[12] David L. Huff, "A Probabilistic Analysis of Consumer Spatial Behavior," in William S. Decker (ed.), *Emerging Concepts in Marketing,* American Marketing Association, Chicago, 1962, pp. 443–461.
[13] For a discussion of problem areas in the Huff model, see David L. Huff and Richard R. Batsell, "Conceptual and Operational Problems with Market Share Models of Consumer Spatial Behavior," in Mary Jane Schlinger (ed.), *Advances in Consumer Research: Volume 2,* Association for Consumer Research, Chicago, 1975, pp. 165–172; Joseph Barry Mason, "Retail Market Area Shape and Structure: Problems and Prospects," in Schlinger (ed.), *Advances;* and Louis P. Bucklin, "The Concept of Mass in Intra-urban Shopping," *Journal of Marketing,* 31:37–42, January–February 1958.
[14] "Why They Shop Some Centers," *Chain Store Age Executive,* May 1978, pp. 31–35.
[15] Robert F. Lusch, "Integration of Economic Geography and Social Psychological Models of Patronage Behavior," in Kent B. Monroe (ed.), *Advances in Consumer Research: Volume 8,* Association for Consumer Research, Ann Arbor, MI, 1981, pp. 644–647.
[16] See Pierre Martineau, "The Personality of the Retail Store," *Harvard Business Review,* 36:47–55, January–February 1958.
[17] Jay D. Lindquist, "Meaning of Image," *Journal of Retailing,* 50:31, Winter 1974–1975.
[18] Wroe Alderson and Robert Sessions, "Basic Research on Consumer Behavior: Report on a Study of Shopping Behavior and Methods for Its Investigation," in Ronald E. Frank, Alfred A. Kuehn, and William F. Massy (eds.), *Quantitative Techniques in Marketing Analysis,* Irwin, Homewood, IL, 1962, pp. 129–145.
[19] Bill Abrams, "Marketing," *The Wall Street Journal,* January 14, 1982, p. 33.
[20] "Consumer Behavior in the Supermarket," *Progressive Grocer,* October 1975, p. 37.
[21] "How Housewives See the Discount Store Today," *Discount Merchandiser,* March 1970, pp. 77–90; and "Why Shoppers Choose Discount Stores vs. Downtown Stores," *Discount Merchandiser,* December 1971, pp. 31–32.
[22] Stuart U. Rich and Bernard D. Portis, "The 'Imageries' of Department Stores," *Journal of Marketing,* 28:10–15, April 1964.
[23] Jo-Ann Zbytniewski, "Consumer Watch," *Progressive Grocer,* June 1980, p. 31; and Gentry and Burns, "How 'Important.'"
[24] "38th Annual Report of the Grocery Industry," *Progressive Grocer,* April 1971, p. 65.
[25] T. Ellsworth, D. Benjamin, and H. Radolf, "Customer Response to Trading Stamps," *Journal of Retailing,* 33:165–169, 206, Winter 1957–1958.

[26] Franklynn Peterson and Judi Kesselman-Turkel, "Catching Customers With Sweepstakes," *Fortune,* February 8, 1982, pp. 84–88.

[27] Rich and Portis, "The 'Imageries'"; and David J. Rachman and Linda J. Kemp, "Profile of the Discount House Customer," *Journal of Retailing,* 39:1–8, Summer 1963.

[28] "Why They Shop Some Centers,"

[29] E. D. Fraser, "Inside Information on Retailers," *Journal of Retailing,* 30:21 ff, Spring 1954.

[30] "7th National Consumer Survey," *Merchandising,* October 1979, p. 18.

[31] C. Glenn Walters, *Consumer Behavior: Theory and Practice,* rev. ed., Irwin, Homewood, IL, 1974, p. 425.

[32] Bruce L. Stern, Ronald F. Bush, and Joseph F. Hair, Jr., "The Self-Image/Store Image Matching Process: An Empirical Test," *Journal of Business,* 50:63–69, January 1977.

[33] Philip Kotler, "Atmospherics as a Marketing Tool," *Journal of Retailing,* 49:50, 56, Winter 1973–1974.

[34] Robert J. Donovan and John R. Rossiter, "Store Atmosphere: An Environmental Psychology Approach," *Journal of Retailing,* 58:34–57, Spring 1982.

[35] Gilbert D. Harrell, Michael D. Hutt, and James C. Anderson, "Path Analysis of Buyer Behavior Under Conditions of Crowding," *Journal of Marketing Research,* 17:45–51, February 1980.

[36] Martineau, "The Personality," p. 47.

[37] Gregory P. Stone, "City Shoppers and Urban Identification: Observations on the Social Psychology of City Life," *American Journal of Sociology,* 60:36–45, 1954.

[38] William R. Darden and Fred D. Reynolds, "Shopping Orientations and Product Usage Rates," *Journal of Marketing Research,* 8:505–508, November 1971; and Louis E. Boone, el al., "'City Shoppers and Urban Identification' Revisited," *Journal of Marketing,* 38:67–69, July 1974.

[39] See, for example, P. Ronald Stephenson and Ronald P. Willett, "Analysis of Consumers' Retail Patronage Strategies," in Philip R. McDonald (ed.), *Marketing Involvement in Society and the Economy,* American Marketing Association, Chicago, 1969, pp. 316–322; William R. Darden and Dub Ashton, "Psychographic Profiles of Patronage Preference Groups," *Journal of Retailing,* 50:99–112, Winter 1974–1975; and George P. Moschis, "Shopping Orientations and Consumer Use of Information," *Journal of Retailing,* 52:61–70, 93, Summer 1976.

[40] Elizabeth C. Hirschman, "Intratype Competition Among Department Stores," *Journal of Retailing,* 55:20–34, Winter 1979.

[41] Melvin R. Crask and Fred D. Reynolds, "An In-depth Profile of the Department Store Shopper," *Journal of Retailing,* 54:23–32, Summer 1978.

[42] Robert F. Dietrich, "Know Thy Consumer: A Quiz That Shows How Well You do," *Progressive Grocer,* March 1975, p. 55.

[43] Ross M. Cunningham, "Customer Loyalty to Store and Brand," *Harvard Business Review,* 39:137, November–December 1961.

[44] Ben M. Enis and Gordon W. Paul, "'Store Loyalty' as a Basis for Market Segmentation," *Journal of Retailing,* 46:42–56, Fall 1970.

[45] Enis and Paul, "'Store Loyalty,'" pp. 51, 53; and Fred D. Reynolds, William R. Darden, and Warren S. Martin, "Developing an Image of the Store-Loyal Customer," *Journal of Retailing,* 50:79, Winter 1974–1975.

[46] Reynolds, Darden, and Martin, "Developing an Image," p. 79.

[47] Arieh Goldman, "The Shopping Style Explanation for Store Loyalty," *Journal of Retailing,* 53:33–46, 94, Winter 1977–1978.

[48] "Protest from an Angry 'Middle American,'" *Fortune,* April 21, 1980, p. 15.

[49] Louis J. Haugh, "Buying-Habits Study Update," *Advertising Age,* June 27, 1977, p. 58.

[50] Dean Rotbart, "Store Designer Raises Profits for Retailers," *The Wall Street Journal,* December 5, 1980, p. 25.

[51] Charles W. Stevens, "K mart Stores Try New Look to Invite More Spending," *The Wall Street Journal,* November 26, 1980, pp. 23, 28; and Charles W. Stevens, "K mart, Beset by Steady Drop in Earnings, Tries to Attract Higher-Income Shoppers," *The Wall Street Journal,* August 10, 1982, p. 29.

[52] "Consumer Behavior in the Super Market—Part III," *Progressive Grocer,* January 1976, p. 68.

[53] "Consumer Behavior in the Super Market—Part I," *Progressive Grocer,* October 1975, p. 40.

[54] Robert Sommer and Susan Aitkens, "Mental Mapping of Two Supermarkets," *Journal of Consumer Research,* 9:211–215, September 1982.

[55] Howard Stumpf, "P-O-P State-of-the-Art Review," *Marketing Communications,* September 1976, pp. 53, 76.

[56] Stumpf, "P-O-P," p. 75.

[57] *Awareness, Decision, Purchase,* Point-of-Purchase Advertising Institute, New York, 1961, p. 14.

[58] *Drugstore Brand Switching and Impulse Buying,* Point-of-Purchase Advertising Institute, New York, 1961, p. 14.

[59] Haugh, "Buying-Habits Study," p. 58.

[60] "POP-AV Displays Boost Retail Sales," *Marketing News,* 2:18, November 27, 1981.

[61] Ronald C. Curhan, "Shelf Space Allocation and Profit Maximization in Mass Retailing," *Journal of Marketing,* 37:56, July 1973.

[62] Curhan, "Shelf Space," p. 56.

[63] Robert F. Dietrich, "New Survey Shows In-Store Information Tops Shoppers' Needs," *Progressive Grocer,* September 1976, p. 33.

[64] Jacob Jacoby, Robert W. Chestnut, and William Silberman, "Consumer Use and Comprehension of Nutrition Information," *Journal of Consumer Research,* 4:119–128, September 1977; J. Edward Russo, "The Value of Unit Price Information," *Journal of Marketing Research,* 14:193–201, May 1977; and J. Edward Russo, Gene Krieser, and Sally Miyashita, "An Effective Display of Unit Price Information," *Journal of Marketing,* 39:11–19, April 1975.

[65] Jo-Ann Zbytniewski, "Shoppers Cry 'Remember the Price'—But Do They Practice What they Screech?" *Progressive Grocer,* 59:119–122, November 1980.

[66] "Multiple-Pricing Makes the Most of the Moment of Purchase," *Progressive Grocer,* March 1964, p. 128; and "How Multiple-Unit Pricing Helps . . . and Hurts," *Progressive Grocer,* June 1971, pp. 52–58.

[67] Robert W. Shoemaker, "An Analysis of Consumer Reactions to Product Promotions," in Neil Beckwith (ed.), *1979 Educator's Conference Proceedings,* American Marketing Association, Chicago, 1979, pp. 244–248; Robert G. Brown, "Sales Response to Promotions and Advertising," *Journal of Advertising Research,* 14:33–39, August 1974; B. C. Cotton and Emerson M. Babb, "Consumer Response to Promotional Deals," *Journal of Marketing,* 42:109–113, July 1978; J. A. Dodson, Alice M. Tybout, and Brian Sternthal, "Impact of Deals and Deal Retraction on Brand Switching," *Journal of Marketing Research,* 15:72–81, February 1978; Anthony N. Doob, J. Merrill Carlsmith, Jonathan L. Freedman, Thomas K. Landayer, and Tom Soleng, Jr., "Effect of Initial Selling Price on Subsequent Sales," *Journal of Personality and Social Psychology,* 11:345–350, no. 4, 1979; and Carol A. Scott, "The Effects of Trial and Incentives on Repeat Purchase Behavior," *Journal of Marketing Research,* 13:263–269, August 1976.

[68] P. S. Raju and Manof Hastak, "Consumer Response to Deals: A Discussion of Theoretical Perspectives," in Jerry Olson (ed.). *Advances in Consumer Research: Volume 7,* Association for Consumer Research, Ann Arbor, MI, 1980, pp. 296–301.

[69] Robert C. Blattberg, Gary D. Eppen, and Joshua Lieberman, "A Theoretical and Empirical Evaluation of Price Deals for Consumer Nondurables," *Journal of Marketing,* 45:116–129, Winter 1981; Shoemaker, "An Analysis of Consumer Reactions;" and Cotton and Babb, "Consumer Response."

[70] William F. Massy and Ronald E. Frank, "Short-Term Price and Dealing Effects in Selected Market Segments," *Journal of Marketing Research,* 2:171–185, May 1965; Frederick E. Webster, Jr., "The 'Deal-Prone' Consumer," *Journal of Marketing Research,* 2:186–189, May 1965; and David B. Montgomery, *Consumer Characteristics and 'Deal' Purchasing,* Marketing Science Institute, Cambridge, MA, 1970.

[71] Robert C. Blattberg, Thomas Buesing, Peter Peacock, and Subrata Sen, "Identifying the Deal Prone Segment," *Journal of Marketing Research,* 15:369–377, August 1978.

[72] J. N. Uhl, "Cents-Off Coupons: Boon or Boondoggle for Consumers?" *The Journal of Consumer Affairs,* 16:162, Summer 1982; and William Nigut, Sr., "Is the Boom in Cents-Off Couponing Going to Burst?" *Advertising Age,* December 15, 1980, p. 41.

[73] Uhl, "Cents-Off Coupons," p. 162.

[74] "Recent Trends in Couponing," *The Nielsen Researcher,* Number 4, 1979, p. 10.

[75] K. C. Blair, "Coupon Design, Delivery Vehicle, Target Market Affect Conversion Rate: Research," *Marketing News,* May 28, 1982, pp. 1–2.

[76] "How Coupon Promotions Can Affect Sales," *The Wall Street Journal,* September 25, 1980, p. 31.

[77] "Recent Trends in Couponing," p. 19; and Louis J. Haugh, "How Coupons Measure Up," *Advertising Age,* June 8, 1981, p. 58.

[78] D. R. McCurry, "Shifts in Supermarket Buying Patterns, 1975," *The Nielsen Researcher,* Number 2, 1975, p. 7.

[79] Joseph C. Cayce, "Are Brand Names Losing Their Luster? A Respected Consumer Watcher Says 'No, But . . .'" *Progressive Grocer,* October 1976, pp. 64–65.

[80] See, for example, John G. Myers, "Determinants of Private Brand Attitude," *Journal of Marketing Research,* 4:73–81, February 1967; Ronald E. Frank and Harper W. Boyd, Jr., "Are Private-Brand-Prone Grocery Customers Really Different?" *Journal of Advertising Research,* 5:27–35, December 1965; and James T. Rothe and Lawrence M. Lamont, "Purchase Behavior and Brand Choice Determinants," *Journal of Retailing,* 49:19–33, Fall 1973.

[81] Jim L. Parks, *Generics in Supermarkets,* A. C. Nielsen Company, Northbrook, IL, 1980, p. 2.

[82] Charles G. Burck, "Plain Labels Challenge the Supermarket Establishment," *Fortune,* March 26, 1979, p. 71.

[83] T. J. Sullivan, "Generic Products in Supermarkets," *The Nielsen Researcher,* Number 3, 1979, p. 3; Roger A. Strang, Brian F. Harris, and Allan L. Hernandez, "Consumer Trial of Generic Products in Supermarkets: An Exploratory Study," in Neil Beckwith (ed.), *1979 Educators' Conference Proceedings,* American Marketing Association, Chicago, 1979, pp. 386–388; and Dub Ashton and Larry Anvik, "Generic Product Purchasers, A Discriminant Analysis," in Robert S. Franz, Robert M. Hopkins, and Alfred G. Toma (eds.), *Proceedings: Southern Marketing Association 1979 Conference,* Southern Marketing Association, Lafayette, LA, 1979, pp. 234–237; and Joseph A. Bellizzi, Harry F. Krueckeberg, John R. Hamilton and Warren S. Martin, "Consumer Perceptions of National, Private, and Generic Brands," *Journal of Retailing,* 57:56–70, Winter 1981.

[84]Kent L. Granzin, "An Investigation of the Market for Generic Products," *Journal of Retailing*, **57**:39–55, Winter 1981.

[85]"The Generic Metamorphosis: Now They're Third-Tier Brands With Names, Colorful Labels," *Marketing News*, April 30, 1982, pp. 1, 7.

[86]Anna Sobczynski, "In-store Ads Nourish Sales," *Advertising Age*, April 27, 1981, pp. S-14–S-18.

[87]Bill Abrams, "Firms Start Using Computers to Take the Place of Salesman," *The Wall Street Journal*, July 15, 1982, p. 31.

[88]Franklin B. Evans, *Dyadic Interaction in Selling: A New Approach*, Graduate School of Business, University of Chicago, Chicago, 1964, p. 25.

[89]Russell W. Belk, "Situational Variables and Consumer Behavior," *Journal of Consumer Research*, **2**:158, December 1975.

[90]Belk, "Situational Variables," p. 149.

[91]For a summary of these research efforts, see James H. Leigh and Claude R. Martin, Jr., "A Review of Situational Influence Paradigms and Research," in Ben M. Enis and Kenneth J. Roering, *Review of Marketing, 1981*, American Marketing Association, Chicago, 1981, pp. 57–74.

[92]Keith Clarke and Russell W. Belk, "The Effects of Product Involvement and Task Definition on Anticipated Consumer Effort," in William L. Wilkie (ed.), *Advances in Consumer Research: Volume 6*, Association for Consumer Research, Ann Arbor, MI, 1979, pp. 313–318.

[93]"Socioeconomic Trends Cause High Growth in Nonstore Marketing Field," *Marketing News*, February 8, 1980, p. 1, published by the American Marketing Association.

[94]"Catalogue Cornucopia," *Time*, November 8, 1982, p. 72.

[95]"Socioeconomic Trends," p. 1.

[96]*The Wall Street Journal*, January 22, 1981, p. 1.

[97]"Catalogue Cornucopia," p. 73.

[98]*Marketing News*, April 16, 1982, p. 2.

[99]Larry J. Rosenberg and Elizabeth C. Hirschman, "Retailing Without Stores," *Harvard Business Review*, **58**:105, July/August 1980.

[100]"Research on New Video Technologies," *Marketing News*, May 29, 1981, p. 1, published by the American Marketing Association.

[101]This section is based largely on Peter L. Gillett, "In-Home Shoppers—An Overview," *Journal of Marketing*, **40**:81–88, October 1976.

[102]*A Look Before We Leap Into the 1980s*, Ogilvy & Mather, Direct Response, Inc., New York, 1979, p. 28.

[103]Fred D. Reynolds, "An Analysis of Catalog Buying Behavior," *Journal of Marketing*, **38**:51, July 1974.

[104]"Food in the A.M." *Time*, March 31, 1980, p. 53.

[105]*The Wall Street Journal*, October 9, 1980, p. 1.

[106]"Big-Ticket Buyers Seek Fulfillment, Not Utility," *Advertising Age*, July 4, 1977, p. 3.

[107]George H. Brown, "Brand Loyalty—Fact or Fiction?" *Advertising Age*, January 26, 1953, p. 75.

[108]See, for example, Ross M. Cunningham, "Brand Loyalty—What, Where, How Much?" *Harvard Business Review*, **34**:116–128, January–February 1956; Lester Guest, "A Study of Brand Loyalty," *Journal of Applied Psychology*, **28**:16–27, 1944; Lester Guest, "Brand Loyalty—Twelve Years Later," *Journal of Applied Psychology*, **39**:405–408, 1955; and Lester Guest, "Brand Loyalty Revisited: A Twenty-Year Report," *Journal of Applied Psychology*, **48**:93–97, 1964.

[109]Jacob Jacoby and Robert W. Chestnut, *Brand Loyalty: Measurement and Management*, Wiley, New York, 1978, pp. 80–81.

[110]James F. Engel and Roger D. Blackwell, *Consumer Behavior*, 4th ed., The Dryden Press, New York, 1982, pp. 577–578.

[111]Gerald O. Caballo and M. Lewis Temares, "Brand Switching at the Point of Purchase," *Journal of Retailing*, **45**:27–36, Fall 1969.

[112]F. H. Graf, "The Logistics of Grocery Products," presented to the National Association of Food Chains, 55th Annual Meeting, A. C. Nielsen Co.

[113]J. O. Peckham, Sr., "The Wheel of Marketing," *The Nielsen Researcher*, 1973, pp. 9–11.

[114]Paul H. Zinszer and Jack A. Lesser, "A Behavioral Model of Customer Response to Stock-Out," in Robert S. Franz, Robert A. Hopkins, and Alfred G. Toma (eds.), *Proceedings: Southern Marketing Association 1979 Conference*, Southern Marketing Association, Lafayette, LA, 1979, pp. 377–378.

[115]Yoram Wind, "Brand Loyalty and Vulnerability," in Arch G. Woodside, Jagdish N. Sheth, and Peter D. Bennett (eds.), *Consumer and Industrial Buying Behavior*, North-Holland, New York, 1977, pp. 313–319.

[116]Brown, "Brand Loyalty," p. 76.

[117]Hawkins Stern, "The Significance of Impulse Buying Today." *Journal of Marketing*, **26**:59–60, April 1962.

[118]Vernon T. Clover, "Relative Importance of Impulse Buying in Retail Stores," *Journal of Marketing*, **15**:66–70, July 1950.

[119]*Consumer Buying Habits Studies*, E. I. Du Pont de Nemours and Co., Wilmington, DL, 1965.

[120]"Consumer Behavior in the Super Market—Part I," p. 44.

[121]V. Kanti Prasad, "Unplanned Buying in Two Retail Settings," *Journal of Retailing*, **51**:3–12, Fall 1975.

[122] Danny N. Bellenger, Dan H. Robertson, and Elizabeth C. Hirschman, "Impulse Buying Varies by Product," *Journal of Advertising Research,* **18**:17, December 1978.
[123] Stern, "The Significance of Impulse," pp. 61–62.
[124] David T. Kollat, "A Decision-Process Approach to Impulse Purchasing," in Raymond M. Haas (ed.), *Science, Technology, and Marketing,* American Marketing Association, Chicago, 1966, pp. 626–639.
[125] Bellenger, Robertson, and Hirschman, "Impulse Buying," pp. 15–18.

CHAPTER 21
POSTPURCHASE BEHAVIOR

Consumer decisions do not end with the act of purchase but continue as the consumer uses the product and evaluates his or her purchase decision. In this chapter we shall examine the nature of consumer postpurchase behavior. We will first discuss the types of behavior that may be exhibited as a result of and related to the purchase. Next, the concept of postpurchase evaluation and the significant implications it holds for marketing strategy will be examined. Finally, the topic of consumer product disposition is discussed along with marketing implications.

BEHAVIOR RELATED TO THE PURCHASE

Once the consumer makes a decision to purchase a product, there can be several types of additional behavior associated with that decision. Three activities are of primary importance: (1) decisions on financing the purchase; (2) decisions on the product's installation and use; and (3) decisions on products or services related to the item purchased.

Decisions on Product Payment

Although many small purchases are made for cash, our society is increasingly run on credit. The consumer's access to numerous credit avenues such as MasterCard, Visa, oil company and department store credit cards, means that for a vast number of purchases, especially expensive durables, a major decision involves the nature of payment to be used in the purchase. Such payment decisions may be very simple, reflexive decisions in which the consumer may instinctively pay cash or reach for her Visa card, for example. Other decisions to use credit may be classified as extended problem solving. For instance, a consumer may shop around for the most favorable credit terms, thus considering numerous alternatives.

Decisions on Product Set-up and Use

All consumers who have purchased consumer durables are familiar with the need to have their product set up or installed. The product must be made ready for the buyer to use, as with a car, for example. Many other durables could be cited which necessitate some set-up in order for them to be properly used. Televisions, stereos, furniture, clothes washers, air conditioners, for example, all must be carefully set up if the consumer is to find satisfaction from their use.

Many other types of products require very little in the way of set-up, however.

Even apparently simple products, though, can be very complicated and frustrating in their set-up processes. For example, many a parent can tell horror stories about simple assembly of products for their children on Christmas Eve which turned out to be all-night exercises.

Of course, another element of product set-up and use concerns instructions given to the buyer for assembly and operation of the item. Products such as autos, calculators, microwave ovens, and so forth may require detailed explanations as to methods of operation. In order to ensure buyer satisfaction, such brochures (even books for some products) must be carefully developed to provide sufficient instructions.

Decisions on Related Products or Services

It often happens that a buyer of one item becomes a candidate for all sorts of options and related products or services. For instance, a 35-mm-camera buyer may become interested in numerous optional lenses, a camera bag, dust brush, filters, a slide projector and trays, photo developing equipment, and even photography lessons. In fact, many retailers have learned that the big profits are often in the optional extras that a consumer purchases, rather than in the original product itself. As a result, for example, many camera retailers sell 35-mm cameras close to cost or as a loss leader in order to draw customers into the store and sell accessories on which the markup runs much higher. Similarly, a camping enthusiast may begin with a tent and buy a wide range of related products such as a stove, lantern, sleeping bag, and backpack.

Marketing Implications

Some very important marketing implications flow from these consumer postpurchase decisions. First of all, marketers clearly must make the arrangement of payment as easy as possible. Retailers have moved to ease the payment decision in numerous ways. For instance, making store checkouts easier facilitates the consumer's payment process. The use of electronic scanners at the point of checkout combined with compatible credit cards should also make the payment decision process easier and quicker. Moreover, retailers generally offer numerous payment alternatives in order to meet consumers' needs.

Banks have also joined the move to facilitate purchase-payment decisions. Not only are numerous bank cards and loan plans available, but even after regular banking hours, electronic funds transfers may be effected in order to obtain the necessary credit or cash with which to pay for purchases. Because consumers from different social classes use bank credit cards for different purposes (upper classes use them for convenience, while lower classes use them as installment credit), it may be helpful to incorporate appeals appropriate for each group in a bank's or retailer's advertising of its credit plans.[1] Certainly retailers and financial institutions need to research their chosen market segments to determine their desired financing alternatives and if possible, to offer and promote these alternatives.

A second set of implications flows from decisions on product set-up and use. As mentioned previously, products such as televisions, ranges, washers, and so forth requiring set-up must be carefully installed and explained to the user. Unless such activities are conscientiously undertaken, consumer dissatisfaction is likely to result, and the consequence of consumer dissatisfaction, as we have seen, is likely to be poor word-of-mouth communications about the product, the retailer, or both.

Thus, manufacturers need to carefully select retailers as members of their distribution team who will provide the kind of quality after-sale installation or warranty service that will enhance the manufacturer's image. The retailer needs to be considerate of such activities for the same reasons—that it can be an important factor in generating a favorable image and repeat customers.

The importance of information on product set-up and use becomes even more critical in today's self-service economy. Consumers are buying many complicated products from self-service discount outlets which may offer very little product knowledge or installation assistance. As a result, they must rely almost exclusively on whatever literature comes with the product. Such a situation provides an added impetus for manufacturers to assess their product literature and make sure it is readable and understandable. The consumer who fails to follow instructions with her microwave oven is likely to blame the manufacturer rather than herself.

Even more fundamental than the provision of information to consumers is the marketer's first understanding how his product is used by the consumer, and how this product fits into the consumer's "consumption system." For example, the marketer needs to know how his product is used by consumers, not only to make improvements in its quality and functions, but also to suggest new uses for it (as done by Jell-O and Arm & Hammer Baking Soda). If marketers were to research more thoroughly the use environment and behavior of their products prior to full-scale launching, we would undoubtedly see fewer failures and products more carefully attuned to consumers' lifestyles.

It is also important for the marketer to understand the user's consumption system, that is, the manner in which the consumer performs the total task of whatever she is trying to accomplish when using the product whether it is washing clothes or cooking a meal.[2] By understanding how this product (let's say a washing machine) fits in with other products (e.g., dryer, iron, and detergents) in terms of consumption behavior, new marketing opportunities may arise.

A third factor for the marketer to consider with regard to postpurchase activities concerns buyers' interests in related products and services. This is another area of potential profit that should be actively cultivated. An example of successful product linking is illustrated by a major oil company which, when replacing a customer's stolen credit card, distributes a flier offering a "pickpocket-proof wallet" for sale.

Because buyers may become interested in related items, they need to be made aware of the potential products that exist. Thus, literature enclosed with a product could present other products in the line. For example, camera manufacturers do an excellent job of presenting their full line of attachments and accessories in this way. Also, appliance manufacturers such as Whirlpool and Hotpoint frequently feature a number of their major appliances in one advertisement, because the buyer who purchases a clothes washer may soon be interested in a matching dryer. It is known, for instance, that there is an underlying common order of acquisition for many durables. Thus, marketers of these as well as nondurable goods might cultivate the potential products that exist by linking products together.[3] Another example of this practice is the packing of Tide detergent and Bounce fabric softener in certain makes of washers and dryers. Buyers of these appliances may be very susceptible to brand switching at this time. Consequently, new customers may be gained through such sampling.

In order to capitalize on the sales potential of related items, many marketers have diversified their operations. Gillette sells razors, shaving cream, hair spray, and deodorants; Starcraft makes boats and motor homes; Coleman produces coolers, tents, trailers, and other camping gear. Thus, the marketer's task is to determine what product mix is most appropriate to the firm. This is largely a function of applying the marketing concept to identify products that may be related in nature and can be effectively marketed.

POSTPURCHASE EVALUATION

In addition to the overt types of behavior that result from purchase, the consumer also engages in an evaluation of the purchase decision. Because the consumer is uncertain of the wisdom of his decision, he rethinks this decision in the post-purchase stage. There are several functions which this stage serves. First, it serves to broaden the consumer's set of experiences stored in memory. Second, it provides a check on how well he is doing as a consumer in selecting products, stores, and so on. Third, the feedback that the consumer receives from this stage helps to make adjustments in future purchasing strategies.[4]

Consumer Satisfaction/Dissatisfaction

Satisfaction is an important element in the evaluation stage. According to Howard and Sheth, *satisfaction* refers to the buyer's state of being adequately rewarded in a buying situation for the sacrifice he has made. *Adequacy* of satisfaction is a result of matching actual past purchase and consumption experience with the expected reward from the brand in terms of its anticipated potential to satisfy the consumer's motives.[5] Figure 21-1 presents a diagram of the process.

The concept of satisfaction is one about which there are presently few agreed-upon definitions or approaches to measurement. Nevertheless, Hunt has summarized the concept in the following statement:

Satisfaction is a kind of stepping away from an experience and evaluating it. . . . One could have a pleasurable experience that caused dissatisfaction because even though pleasurable, it wasn't as pleasurable as it was supposed or expected to be. So satisfaction/dissatisfaction isn't an emotion, it's the evaluation of an emotion.[6]

Consumers form certain expectations prior to the purchase. These expectations may be about (1) the nature and performance of the product or service (that is, the anticipated benefits to be derived directly from the item), (2) the costs and efforts to be expended before obtaining the direct product or service benefits, and (3) the social benefits or costs accruing to the consumer as a result of the purchase (that is, the anticipated impact of the purchase on significant others).[7] Advertising may often be an important factor influencing these expectations, as we shall see later.

Once consumers purchase and use a product, they may then become either satisfied or dissatisfied. Research has uncovered several determinants which appear to influence satisfaction, including demographic variables, personality variables, expectations, and other factors. For example, older consumers tend to have lower expectations and to be more satisfied. Higher education tends to be associated with lower satisfaction. Men tend to be more satisfied than women. The more confidence one has in purchase decision making and the more competence in a given

FIGURE 21-1

Purchase evaluation process.

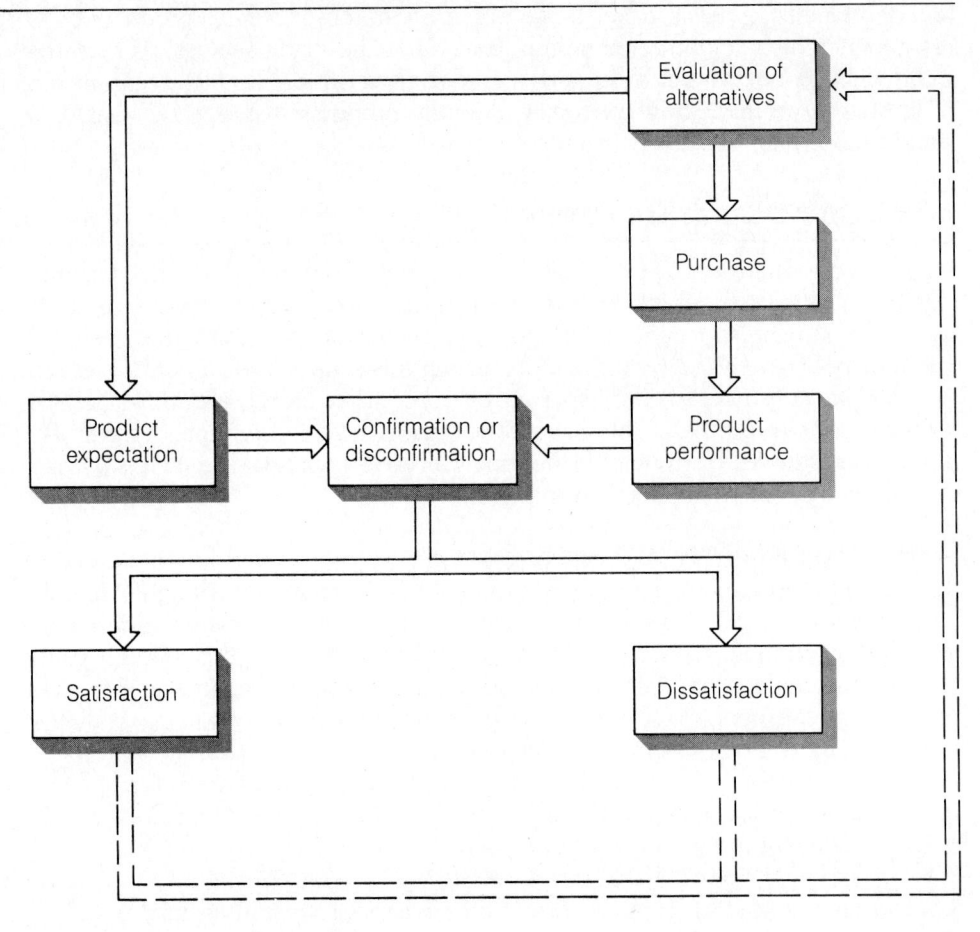

product area, the greater one's satisfaction tends to be. There is also greater satisfaction when relevant others are perceived to be more satisfied.[8] Higher levels of product satisfaction are also indicated by persons who are more satisfied with their lives as a whole, and by persons with more favorable attitudes toward the consumer domain, that is, the market place, business firms, and consumerism.[9]

The interaction between expectations and actual product performance produce either satisfaction or dissatisfaction. However, there does not appear to be merely a direct relationship between the level of expectations and the level of satisfaction. Instead, a modifying variable known as "disconfirmation of expectations" is thought to be a significant mediator of this situation. When a consumer does not get what is expected, the situation is one of disconfirmation. Such disconfirmation can be of two varieties: a *positive* disconfirmation occurs when what is received is better than expected, and a *negative* disconfirmation occurs when things turn out worse than anticipated. Thus, any situation in which the consumer's judgment is proven wrong is a disconfirmation.[10] Consumers' expectations from a product, as well as whether those expectations are met, are strong determinants, then, of satisfaction.

The result of satisfaction to the consumer from the purchase of a product or service is that more-favorable postpurchase attitudes, higher purchase intentions, and brand loyalty are likely to be exhibited. That is, the same behavior is likely to be exhibited in a similar purchasing situation. Thus, as long as positive reinforcement takes place, the consumer will tend to continue to purchase the same brand. It is true, however, that consumers will sometimes not follow these established patterns, but will purchase differently simply for the sake of novelty.[11] On the other hand, if consumers are dissatisfied, they are likely to exhibit less-favorable postpurchase attitudes, lower or nonexistent purchase intentions, brand switching, complaining behavior, and negative word-of-mouth.

Theories of Disconfirmed Expectations

There are several psychological theories that address the issue of disparity between consumer expectations and actual or objective product performance and its effects on product evaluation and customer satisfaction. Five views of the situation in which expectations are disconfirmed are described here: (1) assimilation, (2) contrast, (3) generalized negativity, (4) assimilation-contrast, and (5) opponent-process. These theories are diagramed in Figure 21-2 and Figure 21-3.

Assimilation Theory This view proposes that any discrepancy between expectations and product performance will be minimized or assimilated by the consumer's adjusting her perceptions of the product to be more consistent (less dissonant) with her expectations. With this theory, it would generally be recommended that the promotional mix for a product should substantially lead to expectations above

FIGURE 21-2
Theories of disconfirmation of expectations. (*Source:* Rolph E. Anderson, "Consumer Dissatisfaction: The Effect of Disconfirmed Expectancy on Perceived Product Performance," *Journal of Marketing Research,* **10**:39, February 1973, published by the American Marketing Association.)

Theories of disconfirmation of expectations

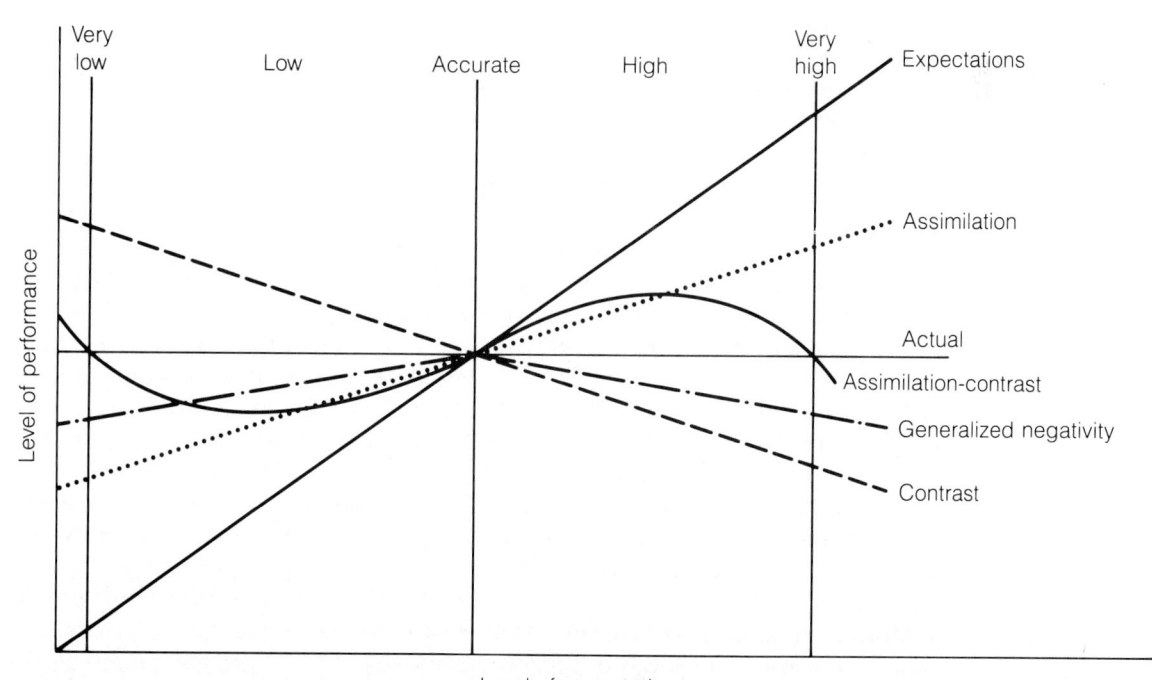

FIGURE 21-3

Operation of opponent-process phenomena as applied to shopper satisfaction and its determinants. (*Source:* Richard L. Oliver, "Measurement and Evaluation of Satisfaction Processes in Retail Setting," *Journal of Retailing,* **57**:31, Fall 1981. Reprinted by permission.)

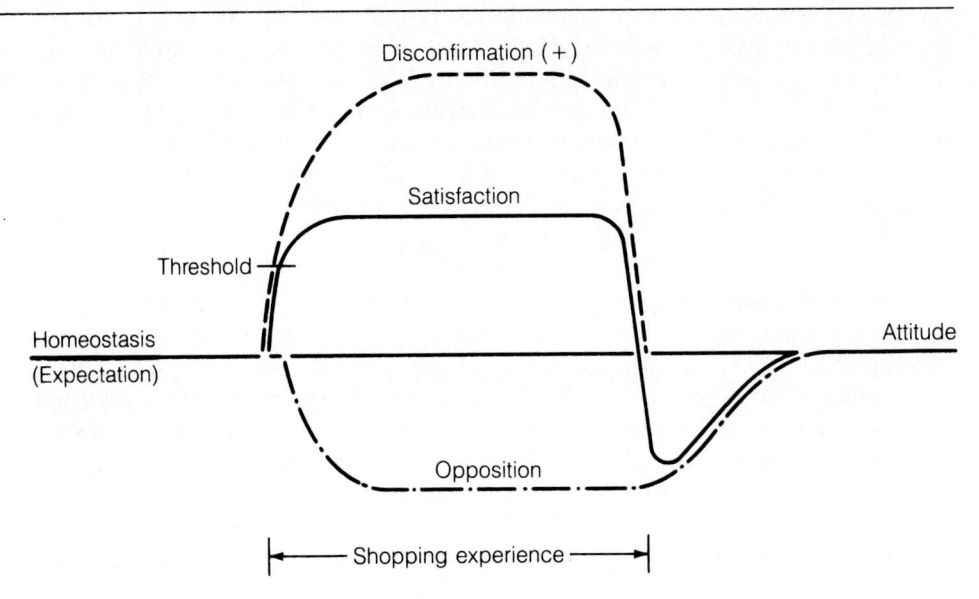

product performance to obtain a higher consumer evaluation or perception of the company's product. This concept is diagramed as a dotted line in Figure 21-2.

Contrast Theory This theory assumes that the consumer will magnify the difference between the actual product performance and its expectations. That is, if the objective performance of the product fails to meet the consumer's expectations, she will evaluate the product less favorably than if she had no prior expectations for it. This theory is the converse of the assimilation theory, and suggests to the marketer that slight understatement of the product's qualities in advertising might lead to greater satisfaction with the product. However, it should not so understate the case that consumers then ignore it and purchase other alternatives. This concept is diagramed as a dashed line in Figure 21-2.

Generalized Negativity Theory This theory suggests that any discrepancy between expectations and reality causes a generally negative state for the consumer. That is, if a consumer expects a particular product performance from a product but a different performance occurs (even if it exceeds the consumer's expectations), he will judge the product to be less pleasant than if he had no previous expectations. Such a case is shown in Figure 21-2 as a line of alternating dots and dashes, indicating that only when expectations and performance coincide is the consumer's evaluation as favorable as the product's objective performance. Implications for the marketer are that promotional claims aimed at target customers should attempt to create expectations that are consistent with actual product performance.

Assimilation-Contrast Theory This theory proposes that consumer perceptions have zones or latitudes of acceptance and rejection. If product performance differs only slightly from the consumer's expectations, she will assimilate the difference and evaluate the product more favorably than its objective performance justifies. However, if the discrepancy between expectations and performance is quite large, a contrast effect is exhibited in which the consumer magnifies the perceived difference. Consumer perceptions in this case take the form of the S-shaped curve shown in Figure 21-2. It suggests to the marketer that promotional messages should be developed that create expectations for the product as high as possible without creating too great a disparity between expectations and performance which would fall into the consumer's latitude of rejection.

Opponent-Process or Opposition Theory[12]   A recent addition to the subject of satisfaction/dissatisfaction has been the concept of opposition or opponent process model. This idea is rooted in the concept of "homeostasis" which, as we saw in Chapter 12, refers to a basic physiological process in which the body adapts to stimuli in such a way that a constant level (e.g., of temperature) is maintained. Homeostasis is accomplished by a process known as *opposition* which counters a disruptive stimulus to bring the body back to equilibrium. Thus, if the level of positive or negative emotional excitement exceeds a certain threshold which may be threatening to that individual's emotional homeostasis, then the body will bring into play the opposition or opponent process, swinging one's emotional state back into balance. The process starts, as shown in Figure 21-3, when a stimulus initiates a primary reaction moving the individual's emotional state away from a neutral position—which may be viewed as the consumer's attitude or expectation toward the product before usage. The primary process is illustrated as a positive or pleasant experience which results in a state of immediate satisfaction, while the opponent process is set off internally by the primary stimulus and causes satisfaction to decay to a new or prior level of attitude (homeostasis). Once the primary stimulus, and the primary reaction with it, is eliminated, however, the opponent process continues causing the body to experience "overshoot" in a direction opposite to that of the original response. Such a phenomenon seems to characterize many of life's common experiences in which we feel "down" after a period of elation, or relieved after removal of a threatening or unpleasant situation.

Frequent repetition of the initial stimulus results in some interesting effects. Although repetition of the primary stimulus may result merely in repetition of the primary response, the opponent process is thought to strengthen and grow more potent and enduring after a series of primary stimulations, as opposed to only one or a few stimulations.

How does the opponent process influence customer satisfaction and dissatisfaction? First, we see that satisfaction states are difficult to maintain. Because of the opponent process, initial feelings of pleasure, joy, or elation in a purchase experience decrease over time to a state of being merely pleased. Thus, if the product is purchased infrequently and consumed over a short period of time, levels of initial excitement are high and the negative aftereffect is moderate. However, with repeated back-to-back purchases of a basically satisfying nature (such as with chewing gum, toothpaste, and detergent), the level of positive satisfaction is lower in magnitude, and the negative aftereffect is much more pronounced and of longer duration because of a strengthened opponent process. Thus, frequently purchased (or used) products may be more susceptible to brand switching than products used infrequently. The customer's felt satisfaction is likely to be lower, resulting in a greater receptivity to alternative brands. In addition, if the customer is induced to try a competitive brand, any positive feeling for the new brand will stand out more strongly because of the neutral or negative afterimage of the previous brand.

Because of this situation, the marketer must continually change the product, its package, and so on, or risk competitive encroachment. An alternative strategy, however, could be to prevent the opponent process by maintaining felt satisfaction below the threshold at which opposition is triggered, perhaps through effective positioning of promotional claims.

Dissatisfaction can be seen as the upside-down version of Figure 21-3 such that the customer's initial feeling is negative and the aftereffect is positive. The goal then becomes one of changing consumer behavior by capitalizing on the positive aftermath of negative experiences.

There are several alternative ways of measuring product/service satisfaction.[13] However, less use is being made today of satisfied-dissatisfied questions in favor of disguised questions sampling such things as disappointment, surprise, excitement, regret, relief, gratification, enjoyment, and need fulfillment.[14]

Postpurchase Dissonance

As we learned in Chapter 16, consumers may become dissonant over a purchase decision. As explained by Festinger, cognitive dissonance occurs as a result of a discrepancy between a consumer's decision and the consumer's prior evaluation. Consider the illustration in Chapter 16 of the Nikon camera buyer who encounters some problems with the brand he has purchased. This is a typical situation leading to postpurchase dissonance. Festinger's theory was derived from two basic principles: (1) dissonance is uncomfortable and will motivate the person to reduce it and (2) dissonant individuals will avoid situations that produce more dissonance. Let us examine this concept more closely to see what factors lead to dissonance, how the consumer deals with the conflict, and what marketing implications are embodied in the concept.

Conditions Leading to Dissonance From a review of research findings on cognitive dissonance, Engel and Blackwell suggest that dissonance is likely to occur under the following conditions:[15]

1 Once a minimum threshold of dissonance tolerance is passed. That is, consumers may tolerate a certain level of inconsistency in their lives until this point is reached.

2 The action is irrevocable. For instance, when the consumer purchases a new car, there is little likelihood that he will be able to reverse his decision and get his money back.

3 Unselected alternatives have desirable features. In our camera example earlier, the Pentax, Canon, and Minolta (brands not selected), all had attractive features.

4 There are several desirable alternatives. Today's car buyer, for example, has an abundance of choices among similar attractive models. In fact, research indicates that those consumers who experience greater difficulty in making purchase decisions, or who consider a wider range of store and brand options, are more likely to experience greater magnitudes of postpurchase dissonance.[16]

5 Available alternatives are quite dissimilar in their qualities (i.e., there is little "cognitive overlap"). For instance, although there are many automobile models, each one may have some unique characteristics.

6 The buyer is committed to his decision because it has psychological significance. A large and important living room furniture purchase is likely to have great psychological significance to the buyer because of its dramatic reflection of one's decorating tastes, philosophy, and life style. Ego involvement will be quite high.

7 There is no pressure applied to the consumer to make the decision. If the consumer is subjected to outside pressure, he will do what he is forced to do without letting his own viewpoint or preference really be challenged.

It is clear that dissonance is likely to be strongest for the purchase of durables, although it can exist for almost every purchase. The factors cited above and others are illustrated in Table 21-1 which presents conditions under which high or low dissonance would be expected.

Dissonance Reduction There are several major ways in which the consumer strives to reduce dissonance. He may (1) change his evaluation of the alternative, (2) seek new information to support his choice, or (3) change his attitudes.

CHANGING PRODUCT EVALUATIONS One of the ways consumers seek to reduce dissonance is to reevaluate product alternatives. This is accomplished by the consumers' enhancing the attributes of the products selected while decreasing the importance of the unselected products' attributes. That is, consumers seek to polarize alternatives in order to reduce their dissonance.[17]

Another approach to reducing dissonance is for the consumer to reevaluate product alternatives to view them as being more alike than was thought at the purchase stage; that is, to establish or imagine that cognitive overlap exists. As a result of viewing the alternatives as essentially the same, it makes little difference which one is chosen; hence, little dissonance would be experienced.

In addition, selective retention may operate to allow the consumer to forget positive features of the unselected alternative and negative features of the chosen product while remembering negative attributes of the unchosen item along with favorable features of the chosen alternative.

SEEKING NEW INFORMATION A second way consumers may reduce dissonance is by seeking additional information in order to confirm the wisdom of their product choice. According to Festinger's theory, dissonant individuals would be expected to actively avoid information that would tend to increase their dissonance and seek information supporting their decision. It seems reasonable to assume that consumers would seek out advertisements for products they have purchased and tend to avoid competing ads. Research on this topic, however, has failed to support this hypothesis. Although it is widely documented that consumers experiencing dissonance do seek additional information, there is no evidence to substantiate either a general preference by consumers for supportive over nonsupportive information or a greater information-seeking/avoidance tendency by high-dissonance consumers. Consumers sometimes seek consonant information to support their choice, sometimes seek discrepant information to refute it, and sometimes merely

TABLE 21-1
DISSONANCE AND BUYING SITUATIONS

Factors Affecting Dissonance	Buying Situation	Conditions with High Dissonance Expectation	Conditions with Low Dissonance Expectation
1. Attractiveness of rejected alternative	A high school graduate decides which of several pictures to order	Three of the proofs have both attractive and desirable features.	One of the proofs clearly is superior to the rest.
2. Negative factors in chosen alternative	A man chooses between two suits of clothing.	The chosen suit has the color the man wanted but not the style.	The chosen suit has both the color and style the man wanted.
3. Number of alternatives	A teacher shops for a tape-recorder.	There are eight recorders from which to choose.	There are only two recorders from which to choose.
4. Cognitive overlap	A housewife shops for a vacuum sweeper.	A salesman offers two similarly priced tank types.	A salesman offers a tank type and an upright cleaner.
5. Importance of cognitions involved	A child buys a present for her sister.	The sister has definite preferences for certain kinds of music.	The sister has no strong tastes for certain records.
6. Positive inducement	Parents decide to buy a photo-enlarger for their son.	The son already has hobby equipment and does not need the enlarger.	The son never has had a true hobby and needs something to keep him occupied.
7. Discrepant or negative action	A man purchases an expensive watch.	The man had never before paid more than $35 for a watch.	Fairly expensive watches had been important gift items in the man's family.
8. Information available	Housewife buys a detergent.	The housewife has no experience with the brand purchased—it is a new variety.	The housewife has read and heard a good deal about the product, and has confidence in the manufacturer.
9. Anticipated dissonance	A small boy buys a model airplane.	The boy anticipates trouble at home because of the cost of the model.	The boy expects no trouble at home relative to the purchase.
10. Familiarity and knowledge	A family buys a floor polisher.	The item was purchased without much thought.	The item was purchased after a careful selection process.

Source: Robert J. Holloway, "An Experiment on Consumer Dissonance," *Journal of Marketing,* **31**:40, January 1967, published by the American Marketing Association.

look for useful information, no matter what the content. It appears to depend on the amount of information gathered before his decision and whether he perceives that he has made a wise choice. Thus, if the consumer gathered much evidence before purchase to support his decision and if he strongly believes he made a wise selection, he will feel free to seek out exposure to discrepant as well as consonant information.[18]

Unfortunately, the research findings in this area have numerous methodological problems; so at present it cannot be concluded that dissonance factors have any effect on the consumer's postpurchase information-seeking behavior.[19] Nevertheless, the fact that individuals do engage in selective exposure to marketing information and may at the same time be dissonant does have some implications for the marketing manager; these will be examined shortly.

CHANGING ATTITUDES   As a result of dissonance, the consumer may change his attitudes to make them consonant with his behavior. For example, when the marketer secures new product trial among target customers who initially have an unfavorable attitude toward the item (let's say they purchased it because of a coupon offer, or were given a free sample), this situation is likely to produce dissonance. That is, unfavorable attitudes toward the product are inconsistent with the behavior of product trial. Motivation to achieve consonance will likely take the form of attitude change because that is easier than renouncing the purchase and returning the product. By reevaluating the product and adopting a positive attitude toward it, attitudes and behavior are now consistent and consonance is achieved.

Marketing Implications   There are several marketing implications that arise from our discussion of cognitive dissonance. Most of these suggestions relate to the promotional variable.

CONFIRMING EXPECTATIONS   When the purchase confirms the consumer's expectations, reinforcement takes place. When expectations are not confirmed, however, cognitive inconsistency develops and the consumer will likely reduce the dissonance by evaluating the product (or store) somewhat negatively. Thus, where a product fails to measure up to the consumer's expectations or guidelines for evaluation, the result may be no initial sale, no repeat sale, or unfavorable word-of-mouth communication.[20]

It is important, therefore, for the product to confirm expectations. Similarly, it is imperative that the marketer not build up expectations unrealistically. Marketers should first design products that will fulfill consumers' expectations insofar as possible. As our scientific progress advances, people come to expect fewer technical deficiencies in products. These expectations may be set unrealistically high, with resultant dissatisfaction when they are not fulfilled, as when the product breaks down for some reason. In order to reduce this occurrence, products should be carefully developed with the consumer in mind. A clear understanding of how the product will be used and how it fits into the consumer's lifestyle is necessary.

Much of the advertising done today may appear to be harmless exaggeration or puffery, but it may actually be contributing unwittingly to less satisfaction on the part of buyers. Promotions that promise more than products can possibly deliver may be destined for problems. As a result, disconfirmed customers can spread unfavorable word-of-mouth communications and refuse to purchase the item again.

How can the advertiser counter this potential problem? One way is to develop promotions that are consistent with what the product can reasonably deliver. A number of recent ad campaigns have adopted this approach. Not only are positive product attributes mentioned, but some of the brand's deficiencies may also be cited. Such two-sided approaches to advertising can be very effective.

Packaging, too, can help present a more-balanced picture of the product's attributes. As examples of how companies are seeking to foster lower expectations more in line with what the product will deliver, consider the case faced by Philip Morris:

> Philip Morris launched Cambridge cigarettes as an ultra-low-tar brand. Cigarettes in the crushproof box variety of the brand, however, were difficult to keep lit and offered so little taste that the company printed a warning on the package that promised an "experience substantially different from other cigarettes you have smoked."[21]

For the marketer interested in conducting consumer analysis, surveys may be undertaken to find out what consumers like and dislike about a product. Ford Motor Company conducts thousands of interviews with its buyers to learn what they like and do not like about their Fords. In addition, consumer expectations should be measured to determine how well the firm's product is meeting these expectations. Both manufacturer and dealer promotion should be assessed to determine if either is promising more than can be delivered.

A large-scale survey focusing on satisfied as well as unsatisfied product users might yield several important types of information:

- areas for improvement of the physical product
- ideas for promotional copy to create favorable attitudes toward the firm's brand
- promotional copy illustrating why our brand is better, based on competitive product failures
- guidelines for developing warranties or other kinds of guarantees[22]

Thus, to prevent cognitive dissonance from arising, marketers would be well advised not to create unrealistic expectations in the minds of consumers.

INDUCING ATTITUDE CHANGE We saw earlier that when attitudes are inconsistent with purchase behavior, they are likely to change. Consequently, the marketer may seek to induce behavior changes in consumers through various means. Promotional tools including free samples and cents-off coupons are frequently used by the marketer to accomplish this. By offering these deals to consumers they may be enticed to try the item and as a result adopt the product or switch brands. However, the size and nature of the inducements should be carefully considered.

There is some evidence that the smaller the incentive, the greater the consumer's dissonance and the greater the attitude change.[23] That is, small inducements force the consumer to confront his purchase behavior without a ready explanation for it, whereas large inducements may allow the consumer to simply rationalize his behavior. Therefore, a coupon worth 25 cents off on an item may produce more attitude change than one for 50 cents off.

In the case of free samples, however, acceptance of the brand may never take place because the consumer could fail to fully expose herself to attitude change from use of the sample. Thus, there may very well be an optimum value range over which promotional techniques produce the desired attitude and behavior change; beyond that point (either too low or too high) they may be relatively ineffective.

REINFORCING BUYERS   Although it has not been proved that one reason consumers engage in postpurchase information-seeking behavior is to reduce dissonance, it may nevertheless be the prudent marketing approach to proceed on this supposition. Such an approach may pay handsome dividends to the company undertaking some promotion aimed at new buyers. It could be especially important in the case of a company launching an innovation.

The marketer may not have to develop special ads aimed at new buyers. Much of his regular advertising may be sufficient to reinforce buyers about their decision. Buyers are likely to be looking for the kind of support stressed in ads featuring the product's major sales features. Toyota's "Oh, what a feeling" campaign, for example, seeks to convey a feeling of satisfaction among Toyota owners (see Figure 21-4). Nevertheless, if a sufficient advertising budget can be mustered, some ads

FIGURE 21-4

Advertisement for Toyota. (Courtesy of Toyota Motor Sales, U.S.A., Inc.)

specifically designed to reduce dissonance among buyers could be developed. Besides, the marketer may find that the kind of advertisement designed to attract customers may not be very effective in reducing dissonance among present buyers. Thus, ads more specifically tailored for new buyers may be necessary. Ford, for instance, has aimed certain advertisements specifically at new buyers for this reason.[24]

There are many illustrations of marketing strategies that appear to be logical approaches to reducing dissonance, in spite of the lack of substantiation in the published literature. For example, the marketer should supply sufficient dealer literature, which could provide new buyers with reinforcement. Moreover, instruction manuals should not only tell how to install and operate the product properly but also seek to convince the buyer of the wisdom of his selection. Information about warranties, guarantees, and where and how to secure service should help reduce postpurchase dissonance. These materials should be packed with the product. In addition, some firms spend huge sums to promote the availability and quality of their aftersales service in order to forestall dissonance (see Figure 21-5).

Manufacturers and retailers may inaugurate correspondence with the new buyer as part of a dissonance-reducing campaign. For instance, auto companies publish magazines that are sent to new car buyers telling them how to gain more enjoyment from their purchase. Retailers have also learned that postpurchase messages to buyers can be beneficial. One study found that individuals receiving post-transaction letters from a retailer reinforcing their purchase decision experienced less dissonance.[25] Another study found that automobile buyers who received favorable postpurchase reinforcement from car salespeople had significantly lower back-out or cancellation rates.[26] Thus, marketers may develop several effective informational programs aimed at reducing cognitive dissonance in buyers.

PRODUCT DISPOSITION

A final topic of interest concerns the disposition of what the consumer has purchased. Most of the consumer-behavior literature has ignored this subject. However, it is important from a public policy perspective as well as from a marketing management orientation to better understand how consumers make disposition decisions for a product.

Disposition Alternatives and Determinants

There are various alternatives for disposing of a product. These are diagramed in Figure 21-6 (p. 704). In addition, the method of disposition may vary considerably across products. For example, while bicycles tend to be given away, this is not true of phonograph records, which are usually thrown away or stored. At present, little is known about the factors that influence the disposition choice made by the consumer. The following categories of factors have been suggested, however:[27]

1 *Psychological characteristics of the decision maker:* personality, attitudes, emotions, perception, learning, creativity, intelligence, social class, level of risk tolerance, peer pressure, social conscience, and so on. Although consumer demographic variables have not proved to be very enlightening in understanding disposition behavior, lifestyle factors have proved to be moderately useful.[28]

2 *Factors intrinsic to the product:* condition, age, size, style, value, color, and power source of the product, technological innovations, adaptability, reliability, durability, initial cost, replacement cost, and so on.[29]

3 *Situational factors extrinsic to the product:* finances, storage space, urgency, fashion changes, circumstances of acquisition (gift versus purchase), functional use, economics (demand and supply), legal considerations (giving to avoid taxes), and so on.

It has been suggested, too, that consumer product disposition is actually a process involving the steps of problem recognition, search and evaluation, disposition decision, and postdisposition outcomes.[30]

Using these reference frames, it is interesting for the marketer to speculate on the various possibilities for consumer product disposition as in the following situation:

> Consider a wristwatch which still runs but is no longer stylish. The consumer is faced with a first level decision: keep it, get rid of it permanently, or get rid of it temporarily. Assume that he decides to keep it because of his thriftiness (psychological characteristic). He could have also decided to keep it because, although it was not stylish, it was still very reliable (product characteristic) or because he had no money for another one (situational factor). At some later time, the old watch is again brought to mind. He may decide to get rid of it permanently this time, because his status needs are no longer met by the watch (psychological characteristics), the band is worn (product characteristic), and/or he has too many old watches in his dresser drawer (situational factor). At the second level, he may decide to give it away to a charitable institution so that he can claim a tax deduction.[31]

Marketing Implications

The implications of the consumer product disposition process reflect on several areas of marketing. There are implications from a public policy perspective as well as from a strategy perspective.

The public policy effects of disposition are many. For example, the effects of disposition choice on the environment include the long-run effects of a throwaway lifestyle, the resources wasted when an item is discarded, and the resource depleted when it is replaced.[32] Thus, a study of the many problems of polluting and littering could be better addressed by considering consumer disposition.[33]

Habits of throwing away and littering might be changed by providing consumers with information about possible product uses or conversions (for example, having an automobile body shop inexpensively spray paint a refrigerator so that it will fit in with new decor). In addition, inappropriate disposition decisions might be discouraged through educational activities designed to change basic attitudes and values. More recycling centers might be established and consumers made aware of the significance of these centers for their own well-being.

Consumer disposition can influence a company's marketing strategy in several dimensions. First, marketers may have to become more involved in facilitating consumers' disposition processes if buyers are not to become discouraged and withdraw from the purchasing process. For instance, old products must often be

FIGURE 21-5

Advertisement for Sears service. (By permission of Sears, Roebuck and Co.)

You can count on Sears service

Few places in the U.S. are beyond the reach of Sears 16,000 service trucks — and even if you move to Ely, Nevada or Blairs Mills, Kentucky, Sears will arrange for your service and honor your warranties.

EVERY YEAR, one American family in five moves to a new home. New address, new phone number, new schools, new friends — but if your appliances came from Sears, the same old reliable service is only a phone call away.

If you want help hooking up Sears appliances you've taken with you, call your new Sears store in advance and let them know when you expect to move in. Sears will do its best to be there that very day.

If you bought a Sears appliance from any Sears store in the U.S., every Sears store and service center in the U.S. will offer you service — and of course you can charge it on your Sears credit card.

If you bought a maintenance agreement from Sears, every Sears store will honor it.

Sears operates 16,000 service trucks, each driven by a Sears-trained technician and stocked with parts for Sears products. Chances are very good that a single service call will have things humming again.

disposed of before new ones can be purchased. This might be due to the need for money with which to make a downpayment on the new item, or it could be a lack of storage space for both the old and new product that dictates its disposal. Second, forecasting sales of new products will have to take into account stocks of used goods which may also be on the market. For example, publishers and authors do not receive any income from college textbooks after the initial sale. The large used-

o follow you when you move

Most of America's eighty million homes are within easy reach of this immense service organization. But if you happen to move beyond its range—for example, to some parts of Nevada or Kentucky or Montana—Sears still takes responsibility for providing service for your Sears appliances.
Sears will arrange for a qualified technician in a town near you to get your appliances back in order. If any Sears warranty or maintenance agreement applies, Sears will pay all charges that come under it.
Sears service is the final link in a chain of activities that goes far beyond simply offering goods for sale.
Sears works closely with hundreds of manufacturers to make sure that Sears products give customers what they want, and perform as they expect.
Beyond that, Sears' own laboratory tests over 10,000 products a year. The laboratory is by no means a rubber stamp. Its suggestions have led to improvements in thousands of the products Sears sells. And backing up everything you buy at Sears is this famous promise:

Satisfaction guaranteed or your money back.

Sears
© Sears, Roebuck and Co. 1981

book market for college texts in which old books are bought and then resold makes sales and income forecasting difficult for books in a publisher's line, and substantially reduces the market for new titles.[34]

Third, the marketer can effectively use information on consumer disposition decisions in developing promotion strategy. For example, the marketer may learn the reason why consumers acquire new products even though their old ones are

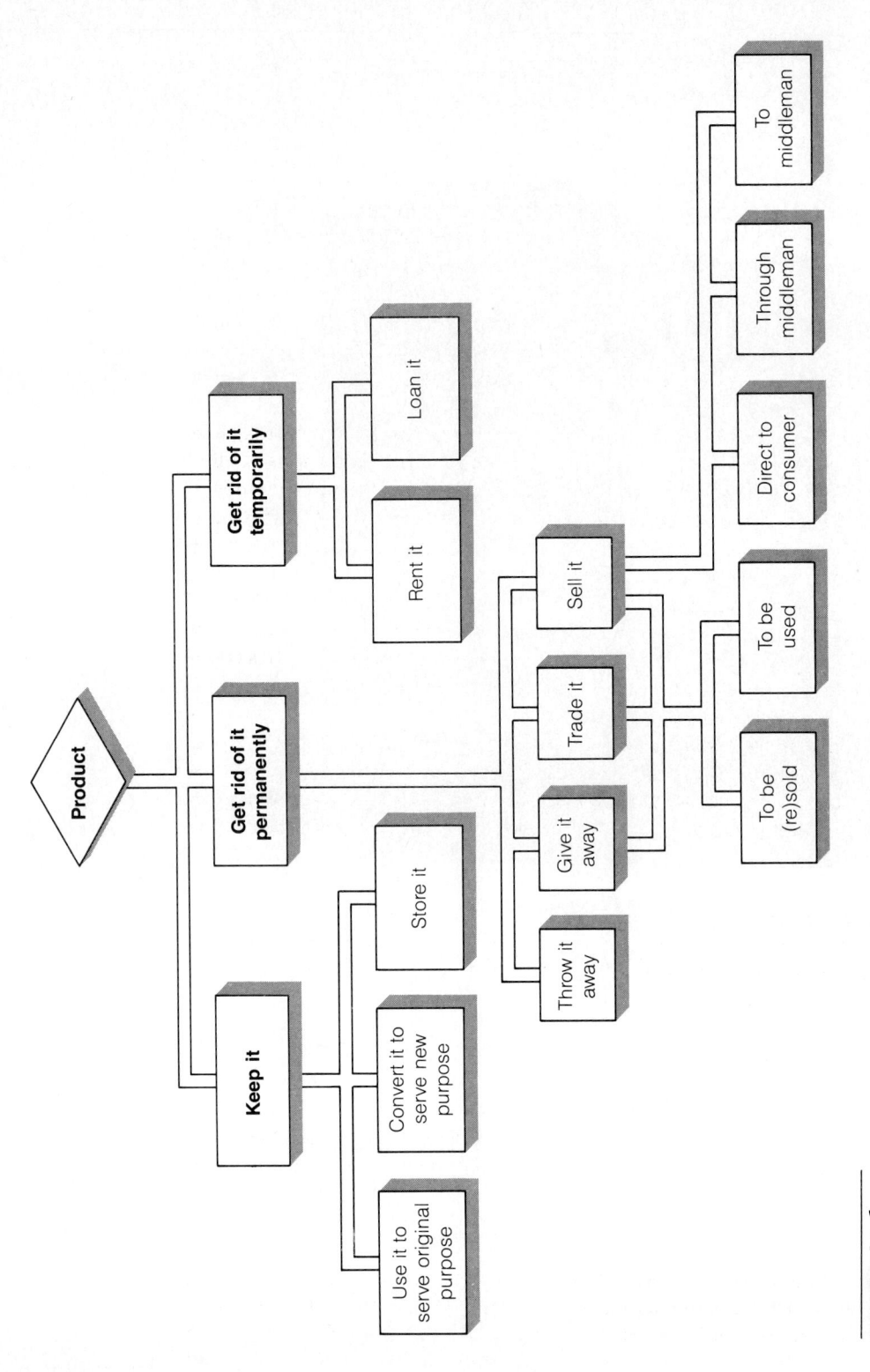

FIGURE 21-6

Product-disposition alternatives. (SOURCE: Jacob Jacoby, Carol K. Berning, and Thomas F. Dietvorst, "What About Disposition?" *Journal of Marketing*, **41**:23, April 1977, published by the American Marketing Association.)

still performing satisfactorily (e.g., the new product has better features or fits better with their perceived self-images). Identification of reasons such as these and their relative incidence by product can provide marketing and advertising managers with information useful for developing promotional strategies.[35]

SUMMARY

This chapter has examined the postpurchase stage of consumer behavior. Postpurchase behavior refers to those behaviors exhibited after the purchase decision. Consumers generally make several types of decisions related to the purchase, including financing, installation, and purchase of other related items.

In the postpurchase evaluation stage, we discussed the concepts of consumer expectations, satisfaction, postpurchase dissonance, and the feedback mechanism. Satisfaction was seen to be an essential ingredient of this stage and one that determines future purchasing behavior.

Postpurchase or cognitive dissonance occurs as a result of a discrepancy between a consumer's decision and his prior evaluation. The conditions leading to dissonance were discussed, as well as ways in which consumers attempt to reduce dissonance. Because of methodological and conceptual limitations of dissonance research studies, definite statements about the applicability of dissonance theory to consumer behavior are difficult to make. Nevertheless, the evidence is substantially in favor of it (except as noted with regard to postpurchase information-seeking behavior). Marketing implications of cognitive dissonance were explored in order to suggest numerous ways in which promotional strategies could be used to offset dissonance and achieve a more favorable evaluation of the marketer's brand.

Product disposition behavior was seen to be an important element of the postpurchase process and yet one that is not well understood. A framework of disposition alternatives was described and several factors influencing it were discussed. Finally, marketing strategy and public policy implications of product disposition were cited.

DISCUSSION TOPICS

1   Why should the marketer be concerned with postpurchase behavior?

2   Discuss the concept of satisfaction/dissatisfaction.

3   What is postpurchase dissonance, and what conditions lead to it?

4   How do consumers reduce cognitive dissonance?

5   Why should the marketer be concerned about consumer expectations in purchasing? What strategy implications are there in connection with expectation confirmation?

6   How can marketers reinforce buyers after the purchase?

7   Select a consumer durable good and survey twenty people to determine their disposition behavior. What is the significance of your findings to marketers of that product and to public policy formulation?

NOTES

[1] H. Lee Mathews and John W. Slocum, Jr., "Social Class and Commercial Bank Credit Card Usage," *Journal of Marketing,* 33:71–78, January 1969.

[2] Harper W. Boyd, Jr., and Sidney J. Levy, "New Dimension in Consumer Analysis," *Harvard Business Review,* 41:129–140, November-December 1963.

[3] Jack Kasulis, Robert F. Lusch, and Edward F. Stafford, Jr., "Consumer Acquisition Patterns for Durable Goods," *Journal of Consumer Research,* 6:47–57, June 1979.

[4] C. Glenn Walters, *Consumer Behavior: Theory and Practice,* rev. ed., Irwin, Homewood, IL, 1974, pp. 559–560.

[5] John A. Howard and Jagdish N. Sheth, *The Theory of Buyer Behavior,* Wiley, New York, 1969, p. 145.

[6] H. Keith Hunt, "CS/D—Overview and Future Research Directions," in H. Keith Hunt (ed.), *Conceptualization and Measurement of Consumer Satisfaction and Dissatisfaction,* Marketing Science Institute, Boston, 1977, pp. 459–460.

[7] Ralph L. Day, "Toward a Process Model of Consumer Satisfaction," in Hunt (ed.), *Conceptualization,* pp. 163–167.

[8] Gerald Linda, "New Research Works on Consumer Satisfaction/Dissatisfaction Model," *Marketing News,* September 21, 1979, p. 8.

[9] Robert A. Westbrook, "Intrapersonal Affective Influences on Consumer Satisfaction with Products," *Journal of Consumer Research,* 7:49–54, June 1980.

[10] Linda, "New Research," p. 8; Richard W. Olshavsky and John A. Miller, "Consumer Expectations, Product Performance, and Perceived Product Quality," *Journal of Marketing Research* 9:19–21, February 1972; Rolph E. Anderson, "Consumer Dissatisfaction: The Effect of Disconfirmed Expectancy on Perceived Product Performance," *Journal of Marketing Research,* 10: 38–94, February, 1973; and Richard L. Oliver, "Effect of Expectation and Disconfirmation on Postexposure Product Evaluations: An Alternative Interpretation," *Journal of Applied Psychology,* 62:480–486, August 1977.

[11] M. Venkatesan, "Cognitive Consistency and Novelty Seeking," in Scott Ward and Thomas S. Robertson (eds.), *Consumer Behavior: Theoretical Sources,* Prentice-Hall, Englewood Cliffs, NJ, 1973, pp. 354–384.

[12] This section is based on Richard L. Oliver, "What is Customer Satisfaction?" *The Wharton Magazine,* Spring 1981, pp. 36–41; Richard L. Oliver, "A Cognitive Model of the Antecedents and Consequences of Satisfaction Decisions," *Journal of Marketing Research,* 17:460–469, November 1980; and Richard L. Oliver, "Measurement and Evaluation of Satisfaction Processes in Retail Settings," *Journal of Retailing,* 57:25–48, Fall 1981.

[13] Robert A. Westbrook, "A Rating Scale for Measuring Product/Service Satisfaction," *Journal of Marketing,* 44:68–72, Fall 1980.

[14] Oliver, "What is Customer Satisfaction?" p. 38.

[15] James F. Engel and Roger D. Blackwell, *Consumer Behavior,* 4th ed., The Dryden Press New York,

[16] Michael B. Menasco and Del I. Hawkins, "A Field Test of the Relationship Between Cognitive Dissonance and State Anxiety," *Journal of Marketing Research,* 15:650–655, November 1978.

[17] See William H. Cummings and M. Venkatesan, "Cognitive Dissonance and Consumer Behavior: A Review of the Evidence," in Mary Jane Schlinger (ed.), *Advances in Consumer Research,* 2d ed., Association for Consumer Research, Chicago, 1975, pp. 21–31; and Leonard A. LoSciuto and Robert Perloff, "Influence of Product Preference on Dissonance Reduction," *Journal of Marketing Research,* 4:286–290, August 1967.

[18] Engel, and Blackwell, *Consumer Behavior,* p. 507.

[19] Cummings and Venkatesan, "Cognitive Dissonance." Also see William H. Cummings and M. Venkatesan, "Cognitive Dissonance and Consumer Behavior: A Review of the Evidence," *Journal of Marketing Research,* 13:303–308, August 1976, for a review of the methodological problems.

[20] Richard N. Cardozo, "An Experimental Study of Customer Effort, Expectation, and Satisfaction," *Journal of Marketing Research,* 2:244–249, August 1965.

[21] John Koten, "After String of Cigarette Hits, Philip Morris Finds Its Ultra-Low-Tar Entry a Poor Draw," *The Wall Street Journal,* August 18, 1980, p. 13.

[22] John E. Swan and Linda Jones Combs, "Product Performance and Consumer Satisfaction: A New Concept," *Journal of Marketing,* 40:33, April 1976.

[23] Thomas S. Robertson, *Consumer Behavior,* Scott, Foresman, Glenview, IL, 1970, p. 58.

[24] George H. Brown, "The Automobile Buying Decision within the Family," in Nelson N. Foote (ed.), *Household Decision-Making,* New York University Press, New York, 1961, pp. 193–199.

[25] Shelby D. Hunt, "Post-Transaction Communications and Dissonance Reduction," *Journal of Marketing,* 34:46–51, July 1970.

[26] James H. Donnelly, Jr. and John M. Ivancevich, "Post-Purchase Reinforcement and Back-Out Behavior," *Journal of Marketing Research,* 7:399–400, August 1970.

[27] Jacob Jacoby, Carol K. Berning, and Thomas F. Dietvorst, "What About Disposition?" *Journal of Marketing,* 41:26, April 1977.

[28] Marian Burke, W. David Conn, and Richard J. Lutz, "Using Psychographic Variables to Investigate Product Disposition Behavior," in Subhash C. Jain (ed.), *Research Frontiers in Marketing: Dialogues and Directions,* American Marketing Association, Chicago, 1976, pp. 321–326.

[29] M. DeBell and R. Dardis, "Extending Product Life: Technology Isn't the Only Issue," in William Wilkie (ed.), *Advances in Consumer Research: Volume 6,* Association for Consumer Research, Ann Arbor, MI, 1979, pp. 381–385.

[30] James W. Hanson, "A Proposed Paradigm for Consumer Product Disposition Processes," *Journal of Consumer Affairs,* 14:49–67, Summer 1980.

[31] Jacoby, Berning, and Dietvorst, "What About Disposition?" pp. 26–27, published by the American Marketing Association.

[32] Burke, Conn, and Lutz, "Using Psychographic Variables," p. 321.

[33] Hanson, "A Proposed Praradigm," pp. 64–65.

[34] Del I. Hawkins, Kenneth A. Coney, and Roger J. Best, *Consumer Behavior: Implications for Marketing Strategy,* Business Publications, Inc., Dallas, 1980, p. 503.

[35] Jacoby, Berning, and Dietvorst, "What About Disposition?" p. 26.

CASES FOR PART FIVE

CASE 5-1
ROGER AND HENRY[1]

In order to better understand how consumers process information and decide to buy specific products and brands, a research study was conducted with two middle-aged beer drinkers. The drinkers (one heavy user and one light user) met individually with an interviewer in the subjects' homes to discuss their beer-related consumer behavior. Questions focused on the specific strategies subjects used in their beer product, brand, purchase, and consumption decisions. Blind taste tests were also held in which the subjects drank four different brands of beer. Finally, the respondents were asked to complete an extensive questionnaire on beliefs, attitudes, intentions, and behaviors toward beer as well as to report on demographics, psychographics, and media-exposure patterns. A summary of the research study follows:

THE CASE OF ROGER

Roger is a friendly, family-oriented, 41-year-old man. He has a B.S. in mechanical engineering and met his wife in college. They have four children, three sons and one daughter, ages 12 to 20.

Roger owns and operates his own automobile body-repair service and employs his 20-year-old son. He owns his own home and has a $25,000 yearly family income.

Roger has five close friends in the neighborhood, and he and his wife usually spend an evening per week with one or more couples. His friends are important to Roger and his wife.

Roger drinks coffee consistently and beer erratically. In the following excerpt, Roger discusses his beverage consumption (R = Roger; I = interviewer):

R I drink what I am told is an uncommonly large amount of coffee—probably twelve to fifteen cups of coffee in a normal day.

I Even on a hot day?

R Even on a hot day. When I go to work, coffee is my beverage, and even in the evening. It can be 90 or 99 degrees outside and I'll still have my coffee.

I Do you ever drink soft drinks or anything like that?

R Not too much.

I Iced tea?

R Iced tea I enjoy on occasions. I do like, of all the soft drinks, I guess I would prefer the sugar-free beverages, such as the Tab variety. But the supersweet things, I don't care for them.

I Are there any occasions in which you might prefer perhaps something like bourbon or Scotch or a mixed drink?

R Yes, I'll drink hard liquor. I think most predominantly my biggest consumption of hard liquor would be almost when I am alone and that is still very limited. Because, to tell the truth, I enjoy it, not the quantity and not like some of my friends—they like what it does to them, the way it makes them feel. I enjoy the flavor. I can probably identify by brand between ten and fifteen different types of whiskeys by a sip. Within the bourbon class, I can probably pick four or five of just the bourbon and give you the brand name of it and so forth for other types like that.

I About how much beer would you say that you drink, let's say in an average day or over a week's time?

R If you're going to divide it into a week's time, I have to say it would depend on the week.

I Say a nice, hot week, where you've had to mow the lawn.

R Okay. It depends on the week because in one week I might not have one single drop of it. The next week I might consume a case. It depends on how I'm feeling and so forth. Another thing, too. This again [beer in glass] is something very nice to look at. Whereas you could pour something out of that quart [liquor] bottle over some ice cubes and it doesn't have anything near equal the appeal to look at. This apparently has something to do with it.

Roger narrowed his beer-consumption occasions to three situations:

---

[1] Adapted from Arch G. Woodside and Robert A. Fleck, Jr., "The Case Approach to Understanding Brand Choice," *Journal of Advertising Research*, vol. 19, no. 2, April 1979, pp. 25–29. Reprinted by permission of Advertising Research Foundation.

1 While watching football games on television during weekends

2 While with friends in the neighborhood on Friday or Saturday evenings

3 During and after mowing the lawn on hot days

The second situation often produces the most single-occasion consumption by Roger: ten to twenty 12-ounce servings.

Purchase Decisions

Roger's household purchases beer informally, and the home frequently contains beer or empty beer bottles and cans, but not both.

I   You said your son very often—sometimes brings in beer. When somebody notices that beer is running low, is there anybody in particular who makes the decision that this is the time to go out and buy beer?

R   No, it's not on the shopping list. If there's beer in the house I'm afraid it's going to be me to bring it in, or my son Rusty on occasion will, if he has some [money] left over. But it's not a thing that is part of a shopping list. I will buy a case or two cases at a crack or sometimes just a six-pack or two, and if I know some friends are coming at a specific time I will try and have at least a case or so on hand. I will check it [beer at home] for them. But it doesn't usually matter to me if I run out and don't have one for this evening.

I   Is there any particular place you might go to buy beer—like at a supermarket or a packaged-goods store or somewhere else?

R   No particular place. Usually it is our local supermarket because [of] its convenience and no other reason. Of course, its convenience and price compared to the quicky store right up the street. . . . If I wanted to go out and buy two or three cases for a party, as you mentioned, I would probably go to my local supermarket, and what was easiest for me to handle of the better-known premium brands of beer, that's what I would get. . . . If I knew I was going to get a rather [!large] quantity of beer, I would have a cart with me through the supermarket. I don't go to a beverage store simply because there's none convenient to my home. And whichever one [beer] is laid out easier for me to get, that's the one I'm going to get—a brand well known to me.

CASE 5-1

Brand Decisions

Roger requires that his brands be well known, on his "premium list," low-priced, and liked by friends if they were "coming over."

I   Okay. Well, could you characterize, or could you give me, the names of two or three of your favorite brands—two of your favorite ones?

R   Well, I think I can say definitely that I buy probably more Blue Ribbon [PBR] and Old Milwaukee than anything else.

I   Okay. Well, let's say that Old Milwaukee and Pabst Blue Ribbon are in this display, and you are getting ready for a party. And Old Milwaukee has a price tag on it of $1.49 a six pack and Pabst Blue Ribbon has $1.89. Would you still end up buying some of both?

R   No, I would buy the cheaper one. The beers are comparable.

I   Okay. Let's say there's only maybe a 10-cent difference between them in the six pack. Would that make a difference?

R   Yes, I would still buy the cheaper one.

I   So, then, price does become a very important. . . .

R   Of course it does.

I   Okay. You mentioned earlier that some of your friends might make a choice if they had one, given that you had a cooler full of beer. What are some of the brands that some of your friends drink? Can you recall any of those?

R   Yes. Ray is partial to Schlitz and/or Old Milwaukee; Grady is definitely a Blue Ribbon fan—that's about all he buys; Rusty is Miller—every time he buys it, he brings home Miller.

I   So, if you were having a party and they were coming over, you would normally expect to be buying three different brands of beer?

R   That's right.

Roger reported that he and his friends do not drink Budweiser, Busch, and import beers.

Roger expressed a preference for saying "I'll believe I'll have a Blue."

R   It just rolls out so smooth, and it's easy to say, and it's easy to think, and perhaps another one of our commercial brainwashings won out, I don't know.

Taste Tests

Roger could not correctly identify six different brands of beer in blind taste tests. We served each beer in a clean 12-ounce glass with the beer poured down the center of the glass from the lip.

Roger could assign specific attributes to different brands when shown the labels following the blind tests. For example, he judged Budweiser as "harsh," Pabst Blue Ribbon as "heavy" but "very drinkable," and Schlitz Light as the "lightest."

Advertising Awareness

Using unaided recall, Roger could recall only one advertising theme—Schlitz Malt Liquor. He reported that he really disliked that "stupid bull ad on television." We unsuccessfully made several other attempts to have Roger relate other commercials or advertisements for brands of beer.

In aided recall tests, Roger could identify the "King of Beers" as Budweiser, but could not correctly identify other advertising themes.

THE CASE OF HENRY

Forty-eight-year-old Henry teaches business at a small college. He has a master's in business administration. Teaching is Henry's second career, following 20 years in the military.

Henry makes $32,000 a year, and he and his 42-year-old wife live in their own house. They have no children.

Henry drinks beer consistently and heavily. He is loyal to Anheuser-Busch beers. Henry drinks fifteen to thirty 12-ounce servings of Michelob, Busweiser, or Busch Bavarian on a typical evening.

Henry designed one room in his home for beer consumption. The game room, 20' by 25', includes a wet bar with a keg of beer on top, Budweiser lamps and wall decorations, bumper pool table, color television set, fireplace, bar stools, and two soft chairs, and a couch. (In the following dialogue, H = Henry and I = interviewer.)

H   I drink mostly Michelob or Budweiser or Busch and, as a result, I really can't compare it too much with any others because I don't drink that much of the others except usually if we go out to dinner at a restaurant and they do have a foreign beer, such as Heineken or Löwenbräu or one of those, I will order it. Just for the simple reason that you don't normally have it in your house because of the cost factor. When you're out for an evening you don't mind paying a premium price.

Purchasing Decisions

Henry purchases beer more formally than Roger. He buys a pony keg of Michelob every 2 to 3 weeks from a local distributor. The keg holds $7\frac{3}{4}$ gallons. Henry buys one or two cases of beer when the keg runs dry and before he has the opportunity to refill the keg. He buys either Busch or Budweiser by the case at the military base. Henry's wife rarely buys beer for him, and she infrequently drinks beer (i.e., one glass or less per week).

Brand Decisions

I   Is there any kind of bitterness [to A-B beer]?

H   Yes, again something with A-B products, a lot of people do not like Bud because of its taste. It is a distinctive taste.

I   When you said a lot of people don't like Bud, I gather you have talked with others who don't like Bud for that reason.

H   Yes. For many years I did not like Budweiser either. And then I was stationed in Alaska once, and at the country club I became very good friends with a district A-B representative—not a distributor, but a representative employed out of St. Louis with A-B and stationed in Alaska. Always at the club he was setting up beers for people. Naturally, knowing that he was a Bud man and being closely associated with him, his wife, and kids, I became a Bud drinker out of respect to the man. I didn't feel I should drink anything else around him. Consequently, I became a great Budweiser fan. Had my tastes converted.

I   Do you often drink other kinds of beer? Other than Anheuser-Busch beers?

H   No.

I   Just at the restaurants?

H   Just on a night out, I do drink beer that I don't normally have in the house.

Henry, unlike Roger, would not purchase brands of beer other than Anheuser-Busch brands for friends coming over for an evening. He explained, "Because I normally don't have any beer except the Michelob because of the draught. And I've never had anybody say they wouldn't like the draught beer. And again, I think part of it is the novelty of drawing your own glass of beer, and secondly, most of the people that come, if you are a beer drinker, you will drink any kind of beer when you're in somebody else's home. At least that's the attitude I take. And again, if they serve me a beer that I don't especially like, I just don't drink much of it."

Taste Tests

Henry correctly identified five out of six brands of beer by name in blind taste tests. He could not identify Schlitz Light. He reported later that he had never tasted Schlitz Light before the study. Schlitz Light had been available one month prior to the study.

Henry provided specific reasons for attributing brand names in the blind tastes. For example:

I With all the beers that you can remember having tasted, which brand do you think this might come closest to?

H Probably Schlitz.

I How are you making that comparison—the basis?

H The taste. It tastes to me a lot, with no bitterness in here, but I have a feeling in my mind if I get one of the Anheuser-Busch beers I'll probably be able to recognize it. I'm not saying I always will, because the temperature makes such a difference, including [the fact that] the same beer served at different temperatures will give you a different taste.

I Why would you say that this is Schlitz, then?

H I would say [it is because of] the sweetness. It's an ingredient that I don't really care for in beer, not that if I visit you at your house and you offer me a Schlitz I won't turn it down.

Advertising Awareness

In aided-recall tests Henry could identify ten out of ten advertising themes correctly by brand. But in prior unaided tests, he could only identify Clydesdale horses with A-B advertising.

CASE 5-1

711

STRUCTURED RESPONSES

Roger's and Henry's responses to the structured questions in the third interview supported their responses in the prior interviews. Roger reported consumption of eleven 12-ounce servings in the past seven days, and Henry reported consumption of ninety-four similar servings for the same time period (sixty servings of Michelob, fourteen servings of Budweiser, and eight servings of Busch Bavarian).

Henry strongly agreed with two of eleven statements on a seven-point scale: I prefer a good-tasting beer; I prefer a beer for people who drink a lot of beer. He disagreed with the following statements: I prefer a beer that is a good value for the price; I prefer a beer that my friends like; I prefer a beer that is on sale a lot.

Roger strongly agreed with three statements: I prefer a good-tasting beer; I prefer a beer that is easy to find in stores; I prefer a high-quality beer. Roger did not disagree with any statements.

Henry strongly agreed to the following three product-specific psychographic statements:

1 One of the great pleasures in life is sitting in front of the TV at night and having several beers.

2 I often drink beer when I feel a bit nervous and edgy.

3 I am drinking more now than I used to.

Henry disagreed with the following: The only time I drink a lot of beer is in the summer. Roger strongly disagreed with all four of these statements.

While Roger rated the consumption of Pabst Blue Ribbon, Old Milwaukee, and Budweiser somewhat to very likely for ten situations and Schlitz unlikely, Henry ranked Budweiser only as very likely for all ten situations. (Only four brands were rated on a seven-point scale, from very unlikely to very likely.)

Questions

1 Diagram, in flowchart fashion, the brand-decision process for both Roger and Henry. State explicitly the decision guidelines each is using at each stage in the process.

2 Discuss the concept of evoked, inert, and inept brand sets as it applies to each buyer.

3 How important is brand loyalty to Roger and Henry?

4 What environmental variables can you identify from this case as significant influences on beer purchasing? How do situational influences play a role in this purchase?

5 Discuss the role of involvement as it relates to Roger and Henry in this product situation.

6 What type of information-processing decision model appears to be used in this case? Based on this case would you agree that consumers always seek to reduce risk?

7 If Roger and Henry were typical of large segments of consumers, what hypotheses might you advance concerning buying behavior based on this case?

CASE 5-2
JOHNSONS BUY A FOOD PROCESSOR[1]

At 4:52 P.M. on Friday, January 19, 1983, Brock and Alisha Johnson bought a food processor. There was no doubt about it. Any observer would agree that the purchase took place at precisely that time. Or did it?

When questioned after the transaction, neither Brock nor Alisha could remember which of them at first noticed or suggested the idea of getting a food processor. They do recall that in the summer of 1981 they attended a dinner party given by a friend who specialized in French and Chinese cooking. The meal was scrumptious, and their friend Brad was very proud of the Cuisinart food processor he had used to make many of the dishes. The item was quite expensive, however, at about $200.

The following summer, Alisha noticed a comparison study of food processors in *Better Homes and Gardens*. Four different brands were compared across a number of dimensions. At about the same time, Brock noticed that *Consumer Reports* also compared a number of brands of food processors. In both instances, the Cuisinart brand came out on top. Brock had even run his own weighting schemes on some of the results, using additive, conjunctive, and disjunctive weightings on the reports of the study to confirm the Cuisinart as the top-rated brand.

---

[1]Copyright © 1979 by Roy D. Adler of Xavier University. Reproduced by permission.

Later that fall, new models of the Cuisinart were introduced and the old standard model went on sale in department stores at $140. The Johnsons searched occasionally for Cuisinarts in discount houses or in "wholesale showroom" catalogs, hoping to find an even lower price for the product. They were simply not offered there.

For Christmas 1982, the Johnsons traveled from Atlanta to the family home in Michigan. While there, the Johnsons received a gift of a Sunbeam Deluxe Mixer from a grandmother. While the mixer was beautiful, Alisha immediately thought how much more versatile a food processor would be. One private sentence to that effect brought immediate agreement from Brock. The box was (discretely) not opened, although many thanks were expressed. The box remained unopened the entire time the Johnsons kept the item.

Back home in Atlanta in January, Alisha again saw the $140 Cuisinart advertised by Rich's, one of the two major full-service department stores in Atlanta. Brock and Alisha visited a branch location on a Saturday afternoon, and saw the item. The salesperson, however, was not knowledgeable of its features and not very helpful in explaining its attributes. The Johnsons left, disappointed.

Two days later, Alisha called the downtown location, where she talked to Mrs. Evans, a seemingly knowledgeable salesperson who claimed to own and love exactly the model that the Johnsons had in mind. Furthermore, Mrs. Evans said that they did carry Sunbeam mixers and would make an exchange of the mixer which had been received as a gift and for which no receipt was available.

On the following Friday morning, Brock put the mixer in his car trunk when he left for work downtown. That afternoon, Alisha and six-month-old Brock, Jr., rode the bus downtown to meet her husband and to make the transaction. After meeting downtown, they drove through heavy, rainy-day traffic to Rich's to meet Mrs. Evans, whom they liked as much in person as they did through telephone contact. After a brief "dry run" demonstration of the use and operation of the attachments for all of the models, the Johnsons confirmed their initial decision to take the $140 basic item. They then asked about exchanging the Sunbeam mixer that they had brought with them "No problem," said Mrs. Evans.

After making a quick phone call, Mrs. Evans returned with bad news. Rich's had not carried that particular model of mixer. This model mixer (i.e., I-73) was a single-color model that is usually carried at discount houses, catalog sales houses, and jewelry stores. The one carried by the better department stores, such as

Rich's, was a two-tone model which allowed a two-tiered pricing structure through two different channels of distributions. Mrs. Evans was sorry she could not make the exchange, but suggested that other stores such as Davison's, Richway Discount, or American Jewelers might carry the item. She even offered to allow the Johnsons to use her phone to verify the availability of the item. The Johnsons did exactly that.

Alisha dialed several of the suggested stores, looking for a retailer who carried both the Cuisinart and the Sunbeam model I-73, but she quickly learned that they were distributed through mutually exclusive distribution channels. The young man who answered the phone at American Jewelers, however, seemed friendly and helpful and Alisha was able to obtain his agreement to take the item as a return if she could get there that afternoon.

American Jewelers was about one-half mile away. Brock volunteered to baby-sit for Brock, Jr., at Rich's while Alisha returned the mixer. She took the downtown shopper bus to American Jewelers with the still unopened mixer box under her arm.

About an hour later, Alisha returned, cold and wet, with a $57 refund. Brock, having run out of ways to entertain a six-month old, was very happy to see her. Together they bought the Cuisinart at 4:52 P.M., and proudly took it home.

Questions

1 Which of the Johnsons decided to buy a food processor? A Cuisinart? Defend your answer.

2 When was the decision to buy made? Discuss.

3 What, in your opinion, was the deciding factor in purchasing the item? The particular brand?

4 Would you consider this purchase process to be careful and deliberate? Was it an inefficient use of time? Is it a good model to follow?

5 Would your answer to question 4 change if you learned that on February 19, 1983, discount stores began to sell the same model Cuisinart for $99.98?

6 You are suddenly granted perfect hindsight and are thrust into the role of Brock or Alisha (your choice) at the 1981 dinner party. How would your subsequent behavior differ from that reported here? (*Note:* The events described in question 5 may or may not happen.)

INDEX

INDEX

Absolute thresholds, 422–423, 448–449
Adaptation, 431
Adaptation level, 438–439
Adler, Alfred, 119
Adopter categories, 349–351
Adoption:
    causes of incompleted process, 347
    definition of, 345
    stages of, 345–346
Adoption process, 345–346
Advertising regulation, 19–20
Advertising wearout, 474–475, 562
Affiliation motives, 392–393
Aggregation, 272
AIOs, 120
Allport, Gordon W., 520
Anticipatory group, 280
Apathetic consumers, 655
Approach-approach conflict, 402–403
Approach-avoidance conflict, 403–404
Arousal, 394–398
Aspirational group, 280
Aspirations, 400
Assael, Henry, 543
Assimilation-contrast theory, 692–693
Assimilation theory, 691–692
Atmospherics, 15, 654
Attention:
    characterized, 425–428
    factors influencing selectivity, 428–432
    span of, 431
Attitude:
    characteristics of, 521–523
    compensatory model of, 533–534
    components of, 521
    definitions of, 520–521
    functions of, 523–524
    and information processing, 438
    multiattribute attitude toward object model, 531–535
    multidimensional nature of, 521, 531–539
    role in behavioral intentions model, 535–539
    role of beliefs, 521, 531–533, 535–537, 545–546, 571

Attitude *(Cont.)*:
    role of subjective norms, 534–536, 538–539
    sources of development, 524–526
    theories and models of, 526–539
Attitude change:
    balance theory of, 528–529
    cognitive dissonance theory of, 529–531
    congruity theory of, 526–528
    and dissonance reduction, 697
    influence of: message factors, 552–553, 557–569
        receiver factors, 569–571
        source factors, 549–557
    role of communication process, 548–549
    strategies of, 543–547
Attitude-measurement scales, 74–75
Attribution, 389
Autonomic decision making, 307
Avoidance-avoidance conflict, 402–403
Awareness thresholds, 422–423
Axiom Market Research Bureau, 136

Balance theory of attitudes, 528–529
Behavior modification (*see* Learning)
Behavioral intentions, 534–539
Behavioral sciences, 8–9
Belief types, 571
Benefit segmentation, 138–144
Benton & Bowles, 672
Berry, Leonard L., 655
Biased scanning, 508
Black box concept, 26
Blacks:
    consumer behavior of, 203–208
    demographic characteristics of, 201–202
    psychographic characteristics of, 202–203
Blackwell, Roger D., 34, 694
Brand loyalty:
    and extinction, 476
    as purchasing pattern, 674–678

717

INDEX

Brand-user segmentation, 134–135
Branding, 668–669
Brody, Robert, 303
Burnett, Leo, 202
Business Week, 233
Buyer-seller interactions, 669–670
Buying motives, 387

California Personality Inventory, 497
Carman, James M., 245
Category, 272
Census Bureau, 329
Chicago Tribune, 136, 675
Choice by processing attributes (CPA), 618
Choice by processing brands (CPB), 618
Choice criteria, 385, 628–629
Chunking (*see* Memory)
Classical conditioning, 463–468, 471
Closing techniques, 404
Closure, 435–436, 466, 489
Coercive power, 277–278
Cognitions, 477
Cognitive activity, and motive arousal, 395
Cognitive dissonance:
  conditions leading to, 694–695
  marketing implications of, 697–700
  reduction of, 695–697
  theory of attitudes, 529–531
Cognitive learning, 359–360, 362, 466–467
Cognitive response:
  defined, 485
  and distraction, 566
  role in memory, 485–487
  and source credibility, 552
Cohen, Joel B., 501
Cohort factors, 91
Coleman, Richard P., 243, 245, 249, 267
Communication process, 243, 245, 249, 264, 548–549
  (*See also* Persuasive communications)
Comparative advertising, 16
Compensatory consumption, 204, 262
Compensatory decision rules, 632
Concentrated marketing, 81
Conditioning, 463–465, 471–472
Confirming expectations, 530, 697–698
Conformity, 282
Congruity theory of attitudes, 526–528

Conjoint analysis, 637
Conscious motives, 388
Consolidated metropolitan statistical area (CMSA), 102
Conspicuous consumption, 246
Constant sum scale, 637
Consumer, characterized, 6–7
Consumer activity, 70
Consumer behavior:
  areas of application, 9–21
  cross-cultural understanding of, 192–196
  decision process of (*see* Consumer decision process)
  defined, 6
  macro perspective of, 10
  micro perspective of, 10
  models of, 31–39
  multidisciplinary nature of, 8–9
  problems in studying, 27–29
  reasons for studying, 9–21
  regional differences in, 97–99
  researching of, 55–77
  roles, 7
  subset of human behavior, 8–9
Consumer decision process:
  characterized, 8
  degrees of complexity, 604–605
  in Engel-Blackwell model, 34–36
  model of, 604–605
  situational nature of, 670–671
Consumer decisions, types of, 603–604
Consumer education, 21
Consumer panel, 63–64
Consumer protection, 19–20
Consumer Reports, 4, 627
Consumer research:
  cognitive, 70–77
  conclusive, 62–63
  cross-sectional, 63
  defined, 55
  demographic, 68–70
  exploratory, 59–62
  longitudinal, 63–64
  methods of data gathering, 64–68
Consumer suggestions, 59–60
Consumers Union, 627
Consumption system, 688
Contrast theory, 692
Convenience goods, 622
Converse, Paul D., 651
Core cultural values, 174–181
Counterargumentation, 552, 566
Countercultures, 189

INDEX

Couponing, 667
Craig, C. Samuel, 567
Creative eroticism, 180
Credibility of communicators:
  bases of, 555–556
  sleeper effect, 553–556
Cross-cultural studies of consumers, 192–196
Cues, 461, 486, 488
  extrinsic, 441
  intrinsic, 440
  role in learning, 461
Cultural anthropology, 171
Cultural values:
  changes in, 184–186
  description of, 173–181
  influence on consumer behavior, 181–183
Culture:
  characteristics of, 172–173
  defined, 170
  relevance of marketing, 171–172
Culture shock, 192
Cunningham, Scott, 503
Customer, 6

Deal-prone consumers, 667
Decision-maker role, 306
Decision process (see Consumer decision process)
Defense mechanisms, 498, 564
Demarketing, 20–21
Demographics, 68
Deprivation, 400
Depth interviews, 73–74
Dichter, Ernest, 336
Differential thresholds, 423–425, 440–441
Diffusion process:
  and categories of adopters, 349–351
  definition of, 345
  for fashions, 348–349
  influence on rate of, 351–353
Direct marketing, 671
Disconfirmation of expectations, 690–694
Discretionary income, 106
Discrimination, 470, 472
Discrimination learning, 437, 470, 472
Displays, 660–662
Disposable personal income, 106
Dissonance (see Cognitive dissonance)

Distraction, 566
Driver, M. J., 396
Dual roles in advertising, 324
Duesenberry, James, 171
Dyads, 669

Early adopters, 350
Early majority, 351
Ecological design, 470–471
Economic consumers, 655
Edwards Personal Preference Schedule (EPPS), 503
Ego, 497–498
Engel, James F., 694
Engel-Blackwell model, 34–39
Equalitarian families, 307
Ethical consumers, 655
Ethnic:
  basis for segmentation, 200–201
  definition of, 200
Ethnocentrism, 179
Evaluative criteria, 36, 385, 628–629, 636–639
Evans, Franklin B., 503
Evoked set, 617, 635–636
Experimental research, 66–67
Expert power, 278–279
Expressive role, 301
External environment, 28–29, 35–36, 40–42
External role, 301
Extinction, 475–476
Eye movement analysis, 76

Faison, E. W. J., 559
Family:
  changes in, 316–329
  definition of, 295
  versus household, 295
  power structure in, 307–312
  purchasing decisions of, 301–316
  role structure in, 301–307
  significance to consumer behavior, 296–297
  as social group, 296
Family life cycle:
  versus age in market segmentation, 299–301
  and relation to consumer behavior, 299

INDEX

Family life cycle (Cont.):
  stages in, 297–299
Family purchasing decisions:
  and family-specific characteristics, 313–315
  influence of changing roles, 312
  and influence patterns, 307–309
  marketing implications of, 315–316
  stages in, 312–313
  and strategies to resolve conflict, 309–312
Fear appeals, 563–565
Feature analysis, 432, 434–436
Federal Trade Commission (FTC), 16, 19, 359, 619
Feminist women, 317
Feshbach, S., 563
Festinger, Leon, 508, 529, 694, 695
Figure-ground effect, 434–435
Fishbein, Martin, 531–532, 535, 544
Focus groups, 60–62
Forgetting, 476–477, 480–481
Formal group, 273
Fortune, 243
Free elicitation, 76
Freud, Sigmund, 497

Gallup poll, 179
Gatekeeper, 307
General incongruity adaptation level (GIAL), 396–398
Generalized negative theory, 692
Generic brands, 668–669
Gerontopolises, 230
Gestalt, 434, 466
Glock, Charles, 285
Goffman, Erving, 275
Gordon Personal Profile, 503
Governmental decision making, relevance of consumer behavior, 18–20
Gradient of generalization, 473
Grathwohl, Harrison, L., 511
Group (see Social groups)
Grubb, Edward L., 511

Habitual behavior, 467
Haire, Mason, 72
Heavy users, significance of, 136
Hedonism, 180

Heider, Fritz, 528
Hierarchy of effects, 407–408
Higher-order conditioning, 464
Hispanics:
  consumer behavior of, 210–216
  demographic characteristics of, 208–210
  psychographic characteristics of, 210–212
Homeostasis, 693
Household, 295
Howard, John A., 689
Huff, David L., 652
Humor:
  and attitude change, 567
  used to attract attention, 430
Hunt, H. Keith, 689
Hypothetical constructs, 26–27

Id, 497–498
Identification, 499
Image:
  of companies and stores, 445
  and semantic profiles, 446–447
Impulse purchasing, 678–680
Index of Status Characteristics (ISC), 244–245
Individual determinants of behavior, 28, 40, 42–43
Industrial buyer, versus ultimate consumer, 7
Inept set of brands, 617
Inert set of brands, 617
Inference process, 26–27
Inferential beliefs, 441, 485–487
Influencer role, 7, 306
Informal group, 273
Information:
  adequacy of, for consumers, 640–643
  definition of, 615
  sources of, 625–628
  types sought by consumers, 625
Information evaluation:
  factors influencing amount, 633
  in low-involvement situations, 633–634
  marketer influence on, 639–640
  nature of, 629–633
  outcomes, 633
  process of, 628–633
Information gatherer role, 306
Information integration, 76
Information overload, 420–421, 439, 642

INDEX

Information processing:
   acquisition stage, 418–432
   active search, 36, 418–421
   and advertising issues, 447–450
   attention factors, 425–432
   characterized, 36–39, 415–418
   and company and store image, 445
   and consumer search, 615–643
   defined, 414–415
   depth of processing, 433–434, 478
   measures of, 75–77
   passive reception, 421–422
   price implications, 442–445
   role of memory (see Memory)
   spread of, 433
   uses of, by consumers, 415
   (See also Perception)
Information programs within stores, 663–664
Information seeking:
   active versus passive, 418, 421, 615
   amount of, 418–421, 618–620
   and consumer involvement, 625
   factors influencing, 621–625
   internal versus external, 418–419, 615–617
   nature of process, 617–618
   researching, 634–635
Information sources:
   consumers as, 420, 627
   determinants of usage, 627–628
   determining influence, 635
   identifying, 634
   marketer-dominated, 420, 618–620, 626–627
   neutral, 420, 627
Informational influence of groups, 280–281
Informational monitoring, 76
Initiator role, 7, 306
Inner-directed personalities, 180, 289
Innoculation theory, 559
Innovation, 344–345
Innovators, 349
Insight, 466
In-store merchandising, 659–669
Instrumental conditioning, 464–468, 472
Instrumental role, 301
Instrumental values, 174
Intelligence:
   and attitude change, 570
   and learning ability, 475
Interactive imagery, 483–484, 489
Internal role, 301

Interurbia, 102
Intervening variables, 25–27
Involvement:
   and attitude change strategies, 543–547
   characterized, 405
   dimensions of, 406–408
   in Engel-Blackwell model, 34–35, 37–38
   examples of influence, 404–405
   and information evaluation, 633–634
   and information seeking, 625
   marketing implications of, 408–409
   and problem recognition, 610

Jacoby, Jacob, 421, 642
Janis, I. L., 563
Just noticeable difference (jnd), 424

Kassarjian, Harold H., 503
Katona, George, 31, 113
Kerin, Roger A., 448
Key informants, 354
Kluckhohn, Florence R., 192
Kohler, Wolfgang, 466
Kollat, David T., 34
Koponen, Arthur, 503
Kotler, Philip, 184, 353, 654
Krugman, Herbert, 405

Laggards, 351
Late majority, 351
Latitude of acceptance, 547
Latitude of rejection, 547
Law of diminishing marginal utility, 33
Learning:
   ability of learners, 475
   and attitudes, 523–526
   behavior modification perspective, 469–472
   definition of, 459
   and information processing, 417, 437, 443
   and personality development, 501
   and practice schedules, 475
   principal elements involved, 460–462
   rate and degree of, 473–475
   and repetition, 473–475, 480, 488

INDEX

Learning *(Cont.)*:
  theories of, 462–468
  types of learned behavior, 459–460
Learning curve, 473–475
Lecky, Prescott, 508
Legitimate power, 278
Lewin, Kurt, 26, 402
Life cycle, of families, 297–299
Lifestyle:
  black versus white, 202–203
  definition of, 119
  and market segmentation, 119–134
  of social classes, 248–252
Likert scale, 74
Limen, 449
  (*See also* Absolute thresholds)
Linden, Fabian, 98
Long-term memory, 479–487
Loss leaders, 665
Loyalty segmentation, 135–136

Macroeconomic models of consumer behavior, 31–32
Mail surveys, 67–68
Malhotra, Naresh K., 642
Marginal utility, 32–33
Market:
  definition of, 88
  demographic characteristics of, 88–94
Market aggregation, 80–81
Market atomization, 81
Market-opportunity analysis, 11–12
Market segmentation:
  approaches: benefit, 138–144
    demographic, 88–94
    geographic, 94–105
    lifestyle and psychographic, 114–115
    socioeconomic, 105–114
    usage, 134–138
  benefits and costs of, 82
  criteria for, 82–84
  definition of, 81
  future of, 154–155
  limitations of demographic approaches, 114–115
  and perceptual mapping, 151–154, 446
  performing, 84–88
  and product positioning, 145
  role of family life cycle in, 299–301
  role of social class in, 252–256

Market segmentation *(Cont.)*:
  and store images, 446–447
Marketing, definition of, 10–11
Marketing concept, 11–16
Marketing mix, 12–16
Martineau, Pierre, 263
Maslow, A. H., 398
Maslow's hierarchy, 398–401
Matriarchal family, 307
McGuire, William J., 388
Megalopolis, 102
Membership group, 279
Memory:
  alternative views of, 478
  chunking process, 479, 488
  coding process, 479–483
  episodic, 482–483
  long-term, 480–487
  procedural, 483
  retrieval of stored information, 485–487
  role of, 477–478, 485–487
  sensory, 478–479, 481
  scripts, 481–482
  semantic, 481, 483–485, 487
  short-term, 479–481
Message appeals, 562–568
Message codes, 568–569
Message order, 560–562
Message sidedness, 557–560
Metropolitan statistical area (MSA), 102
Microeconomic model of consumer behavior, 32–33
Minnesota Multiphasic Personality Inventory (MMPI), 497
Mitchell, Andrew, 405
Mnemonic techniques, 489–490
Modeling behavior, 393–394, 459, 470, 472
Models:
  of consumer behavior, 31–39
  defined and characterized, 29–30
Monroe, Kent B., 445
Motivation:
  arousal of motives, 394–398
  classification schemes, 385–394
  conscious versus unconscious, 388
  directive aspect of, 383
  and drives, needs, and wants, 383
  influence: on choice criteria, 385
    on goal objects, 384
  means-end linking, 401
  optimum stimulation levels, 396–398
  structuring of motives, 398–402

Motivation research, 70–74, 409–410
Motive:
   conflict, 402–404
   defined, 384
   hierarchy of motives, 398
   nature and role of, 383–385
   role in learning, 460
   secondary or learned, 387
Motive bundling, 402
Motive combinations, 401–404
Motive linking, 401–402
Multistep communication model, 339–340

National character, 171
National Council on Aging, 234
Needham, Harper & Steers, 122
Needs, 383
Negative motives, 388
   (See also Motivation, conflict of motives)
Negative reference group, 280
Newcombe, Theodore M., 506
Nielsen, A. C., Co., 64, 668, 676
Noncompensatory decision rules, 630–631
Nonmembership group, 279
Nonprofit marketing, 16–18
Nonstore marketing, 671
Nonstore purchasing:
   characteristics of purchasers, 673
   motivations for, 673–674
   significance of, 671–673
Nonverbal communications, 569
Norms, 173, 274
Nouveau riche, 250
Nutritional labeling, 641

Observational research, 64–66
Older consumers:
   consumer behavior of, 231–236
   demographic characteristics of, 230–231
   psychographic characteristics of, 231
One-step model of communication, 337–338
Open dating, 641
Opinion leaders:
   characteristics of, 341
   creating, 357–358

Opinion leaders (Cont.):
   definition of, 306
   in family purchasing process, 306
   generalized nature of, 341–342
   identifying and using, 354–357
   simulating, 358–360
   situational nature of, 342
   stifling, 362–363
   stimulating, 360–362
   and two-step flow model, 338
Opinion leadership, strategies incorporating, 354–363
Opposition theory, 693–694
Optimal stimulation, 395–398
Other-directed personalities, 180, 289
Out-of-stock conditions, 676–677
Outshopper, 651
Overprivileged classes, 255

Packard, Vance, 103
Paralinguistic codes, 569
Participation, 566–567
Patriarchal family, 307
Pavlov, Ivan, 463
Perceived risk, 622–624
Perceptual constancies, 437
Perceptual defense, 431
Perceptual encoding, 432–439
Perceptual leveling, 437
Perceptual mapping, 151–154, 636
Perceptual vigilance, 431
Permanent-income hypothesis, 31
Personal income, 106
Personal influence:
   and communications models, 337–340
   marketing implications of, 353–363
   nature and significance of, 336–337
   reasons for acceptance of, 343–344
   reasons for exerting, 342–343
Personal interviews, 67
Personality:
   characterized, 494–495
   evaluation of consumer research on, 503–504
   measurement of, 495–497
   theories of, 497–504
Personalizing consumers, 655
Persuasibility, 569–571
Persuasive communications (see Attitude change)
Pessemier, Edgar A., 534
Peterson, Robert A., 448

INDEX

Petroshius, Susan M., 445
Physiological motives, 385–387
Physiological variables, 27–28
Place component of marketing mix, 14–15
Pleasure principle, 497
Point-of-Purchase Advertising Institute, 662
Population:
    changing age mix of, 90–91
    decline in birth rate of, 90
    geographic characteristics of, 94–105
    marketing implications of changes, 91–94
    metropolitan, 98
    mobility of, 103–105
    nonmetropolitan, 103
    regional distribution of, 95–98
    rural to urban shift of, 98
    size and growth of, 88
    socioeconomic characteristics of, 105–114
Positioning, 437
Positive motives, 388
    (See also Motivation, conflict of motives)
Positive reference groups, 280
Postpurchase behavior:
    and attitude formation, 529–531, 533
    marketing implications of, 687–689, 697–705
    as product disposition activity, 700–705
    purchase evaluation stage, 689–700
    related purchasing activities, 686–689
Postpurchase dissonance (see Cognitive dissonance)
Power:
    in family structures, 307–312
    sources of, in social groups, 276–279
Prepotency, 399–401
Price:
    awareness of, 14, 665
    component of marketing mix, 13–14
    and product quality, 443–445
Primary effects, 561–562
Primary data, 63
Primary group, 273, 296
Primary metropolitan statistical area (PMSA), 102
Primary motives, 387–388
Private branding, 473, 668
Proactive inhibition, 480

Problem-inventory analysis, 143
Problem recognition:
    definition of, 605
    and involvement conditions, 610
    marketing implications of, 610–613
    measurement of, 610
    results of, 609
    situations leading to, 36, 607–609
    types of, 606–607
Product, component of marketing mix, 12–13
Product cues, 440–441
Product differentiation, 80
Product disposition, 700–705
Product positioning, 144–154, 437
    analysis, 150–154
    repositioning products, 147–150
    strategies, 145–147
Product-user segmentation, 135
Progressive Grocer, 14, 205, 662, 663
Projection, 499
Projective tests, 72–73, 496
Promotion, component of marketing mix, 15–16
Promotional pricing, 666
Protestant ethic, 177
Protocol analysis, 616
Proximity, 435
Psychoanalytic personality theory, 497–501
Psychogenic motives, 385–387
Psychographics, 120, 505
Psychological pricing, 443
Psychological structure, 28
Purchase influence, family pattern of, 307–309
Purchase intentions, 610–613
Purchaser role, 7, 306–307
Purchasing processes:
    family roles in, 306–307
    in-store behavior, 659–670
    store choice, 649–659
    (See also Shopping behavior)
Puritan ethic, 177
Pyramidal message order, 560–561

Rainwater, Lee, 245, 261, 267
Rating scale, 637
Ray, Michael L., 564
Reactance, 283
Reaction formation, 499
Reality principle, 498

INDEX

Recall, 476
Recency effects, 561–562
Recognition, 476
Reference groups:
    families as, 296
    identifying, 291
    reasons for accepting influence, 280–282
    research on influence process, 282–291
    situational nature of influence, 290–291
    types of, 279–280
    variability of influence, 285–291
Referent power, 279
Referents, 538
Rehearsal, 479–480, 488
    (See also Repetition)
Reilly, William J., 651
Reinforcement, 391–392, 461–465, 469, 472
Relative-income hypothesis, 31
Repetition, 474–477, 479–480, 562
Repression, 498
Response hierarchy, 461
Response variables, 24–27
Retail gravitation law, 651
Retail store (see Store)
Retention, 476–477
Retroactive inhibition, 480
Reward power, 276
Rich imagery, 576
Riesman, David, 180, 289
Risk (see Perceived risk)
Rites of passage, 172
Robertson, Thomas S., 349
Rokeach, Milton J., 173, 174, 181
Role blending in advertising, 325
Role conflict, 275
Role switching in advertising, 324
Roles:
    changes within family, 312, 316–329
    changes in female, 316–327
    changes in male, 327–329
    of consumers, 7
    in social groups, 274–275
Rorschach test, 496
Rosenberg, Milton J., 531
Routine purchase action, 36

Saegert, Joel, 449
Sales closing techniques, 404

Sanctions, 173
Satisfaction/dissatisfaction, 689–691
Search (see Information seeking)
Secondary data, 63
Secondary group, 273
Selective motives, 387–388
Self-concept:
    alternative views of, 509
    and consumer behavior, 508–512
    definition of, 506
    influence on motive structure, 404
    major areas of investigation, 509–512
    marketing applications of, 515–516
    measurement issues, 512–514
    research evidence, 514–515
    theories of development, 507–508
Self-reference criterion, 192, 257
Semantic differential:
    described, 74–75
    and evaluative criteria, 637
    and self-concept measurement, 513–514
    and store image measurement, 446–447
Semantic memory, 481, 483–485, 487
Sensation, 421–425
Sensory memory, 478, 486–487
Sentence-completion, 71–72
Sex in advertising, 447–448
Shaping, 469–470, 472
Shelving of products, 662–663
Sheth, Jagdish N., 689
Shopper profiles, 655–657
Shopping behavior:
    amount of in-store search, 619–620
    and motive conflict, 402–404
    number of stores shopped, 619
    (See also Purchasing processes)
Shopping goods, 622
Shopping motives, 647–648
Short-term memory, 479–480, 485–487
Silent language, 172
Singles market, 329
Sirgy, M. Joseph, 509, 514
Situational conditions:
    and consumer decisions, 670–671
    influencing risk, 623
    leading to problem recognition, 607–609
    and motive arousal, 395
    and opinion leadership, 342

INDEX

Situational conditions *(Cont.)*:
    and reference group influence, 290–291
Skinner, B. F., 464, 471
Sleeper effect, 553–556
Social class:
    and consumer behavior, 257–267
    decline of, 267–268
    definition of, 241
    and income, 252–256
    indicators of, 243
    lifestyles, 248, 252
    measurement of, 243–246
    overprivileged and underprivileged, 255
    relationship to status, 242–243
Social exchange equation, 280
Social groups:
    classification of, 272–274
    conformity in, 282–284
    norms in, 274
    power in, 276–279
    properties of, 274–279
    roles within, 274–275
    status in, 274
Social marketing, 16–18
Social personality theories, 501–502
Social Research, Inc., 265
Social stratification, 241
Socialization, 275–276
Sociometric technique, 354
Source credibility, 551–557
Specialty goods, 622
Spending patterns, 110–113
Spontaneous recovery, 475–476
SRI International, 182, 190
Stagflation, 110
Status:
    characterized, 242
    in groups, 274
    symbols of, 246–248
Status incongruency, 255
Status symbols, 246–248
Stern, Hawkins, 678
Sternthal, Brian, 567
Stimuli, 416, 463–465
Stimulus generalization, 472–473
Stimulus-response personality theories, 502
Stimulus variables, 24–27
Stone, Gregory P., 655
Store:
    image of, 445–447, 652–654
    layout of, 659–660

Store *(Cont.)*:
    loyalty to, 658–659
    merchandising techniques in, 659–669
Store choice:
    attribute importance in, 654
    effect of store image on, 655
    factors determining, 650–654
    and shopper profiles, 655–657
    and store loyalty, 658–659
Story-completion, 72
Streufert, S., 396
Subcultures:
    age, 216–236
    defined, 200
    ethnic, 200–216
Subliminal advertising, 448–450
Sunbelt, 95
Superego, 498
Supernumerary income, 106
Survey research, 67–68
Survey Research Center, 32, 113
Symbolic learning, 459
Symbols, 172
Syncratic decision-making, 307

Taboos, 172
Target-market selection, 12–13
Telephone surveys, 67
Terminal thresholds, 422–423
Terminal values, 174
Test marketing, 66–67
Testimonials, 358, 515–516
Thematic Apperception Tests (TAT), 72–73, 496
Theory, 30
Time compressed advertisements, 414
Traditionalist women, 317
Trait and factor personality theories, 502–504
Transgenerational advertising, 234
Triple appeal, 499
Truth-in-lending, 641–642
Two-sided messages, 557–560
Two-step model of communication, 338–339

Ultimate consumers, 7
Unconscious motives, 388
Underclass, 251
Underprivileged classes, 255

INDEX

Undifferentiated marketing, 80
Unit pricing, 641
Universal product code (UPC), 65
Unobservable variables (see Intervening variables)
Usage segmentation, 134–144
User role, 7, 307
Utilitarian influence of groups, 281–282

Warner, W. Lloyd, 244, 245, 249
Warranty cards, 634
Weber's law, 424–425
Wilkie, William L., 534–564
Wind, Yoram, 677
Word-association tests, 71–72
Word-of-mouth advertising, 336
Working wives, 318–325

VALs, 182
Value-expressive influence of groups, 282
Variable classes, 24–29
Veblen, Thorstein, 246, 507
Verbal protocol, 75
Vicary, James, 449
Vocalizations, 569
Volume segmentation, 136–138
Voluntary simplicity (VS), 189

Yankelovich, Daniel, 184
Yankelovich, Skelly, and White, Inc., 190, 225
Yielding/acceptance, 36
Youth:
   consumer behavior of, 218–230
   demographic characteristics of, 216–218
   psychographic characteristics of, 218–224

Wall Street Journal, The, 234
Wants, 383

Zaltman, Gerald, 353
Zero Population Growth (ZPG), 88